THE
LAWYER'S
ALMANAC
2·0·1·7

The Leading Reference of
Vital Facts and Figures
About the Legal Profession

 Wolters Kluwer

Published by Wolters Kluwer in New York.

Wolters Kluwer Legal & Regulatory U.S. serves customers worldwide with CCH, Aspen Publishers and Kluwer Law International products.

Printed in the United States of America

ISBN 978-1-4548-7128-6
ISSN 0277-9544

1 2 3 4 5 6 7 8 9 0

About Wolters Kluwer Legal & Regulatory U.S.

Wolters Kluwer Legal & Regulatory U.S. delivers expert content and solutions in the areas of law, corporate compliance, health compliance, reimbursement, and legal education. Its practical solutions help customers successfully navigate the demands of a changing environment to drive their daily activities, enhance decision quality and inspire confident outcomes.

Serving customers worldwide, its legal and regulatory portfolio includes products under the Aspen Publishers, CCH Incorporated, Kluwer Law International, ftwilliam. com and MediRegs names. They are regarded as exceptional and trusted resources for general legal and practice-specific knowledge, compliance and risk management, dynamic workflow solutions, and expert commentary.

WOLTERS KLUWER SUPPLEMENT NOTICE

This product is updated on a periodic basis with supplements and/or new editions to reflect important changes in the subject matter.

If you would like information about enrolling this product in the update service, or wish to receive updates billed separately with a 30-day examination review, please contact our Customer Service Department at 1-800-234-1660 or email us at: *customer.service@wolterskluwer.com.* You can also contact us at:

Wolters Kluwer
Distribution Center
7201 McKinney Circle
Frederick, MD 21704

Important Contact Information

- To order any title, go to *www.wklawbusiness.com* or call 1-800-638-8437.
- To reinstate your manual update service, call 1-800-638-8437.
- To contact Customer Service, e-mail *customer.service@wolters kluwer.com*, call 1-800-234-1660, fax 1-800-901-9075, or mail correspondence to: Order Department—Wolters Kluwer, PO Box 990, Frederick, MD 21705.
- To review your account history or pay an invoice online, visit *www.WKLawBusiness.com/payinvoices.*

CONTENTS

PART I
THE LEGAL PROFESSION

CONTENTS

PART II
THE JUDICIARY

CONTENTS

PART III
GOVERNMENT DEPARTMENTS AND AGENCIES

PART IV
COMMONLY USED ABBREVIATIONS

PREFACE

This 2017 edition of *The Lawyer's Almanac* provides vital facts and figures on the courts, government, law schools, lawyers, and their work and organizations. Complete and up-to-date, it is the standard reference guide on the American legal scene and is useful for attorneys, law librarians, judges, law students, journalists, and anyone who needs quick access to information on the legal profession.

This 2017 edition includes sections on legal research sites on the Internet, listings for government agencies, as well as the most up-to-date bar examination statistics, and more.

Included in the *Almanac* is a complete picture of the workload in the nation's courts. The reader can discern which types of cases are being litigated heavily; the nature of the current caseloads; and the manner in which these cases were resolved.

The Lawyer's Almanac reflects the size and density of the legal profession. It includes a detailed listing of the nation's 700 largest law firms, along with their contact information.

The 2017 edition of *The Lawyer's Almanac* includes the complete text of the mandatory continuing legal education (MCLE) requirements for the state jurisdictions that have them, along with contact information for each MCLE state.

In addition, the 2017 edition includes a complete listing of bankruptcy courts and judges, on a state-by-state basis.

The Lawyer's Almanac is divided into four main sections:

(1) The Legal Profession. The legal profession is charted in detail, from a listing of the nation's 700 largest firms to marketing by associates. More than 80 top Internet legal research sites are listed, along with a detailed description of each. The Association of American Law Schools membership list is included, as is a listing of the officers of the American Bar Association, its sections and divisions. Additionally, the contact information, principal officers, and annual meeting dates are listed for all the state bar associations.

(2) The Judiciary. Federal and state benches are catalogued in depth. The names of all federal judges and of chief justices of state supreme courts, the terms and qualifications of judges on lower state courts, specific data on the selection process, and a survey of state court salaries are all included, as are litigation statistics for federal courts.

(3) Government Departments and Agencies. This section provides the names, addresses, phone numbers, and Internet addresses of hundreds of federal departments and agencies, the U.S. Attorneys, state attorneys general, securities commissioners, state mental health departments, and insurance commissioners, in addition to a wealth of useful data on how to locate birth, death, and marriage and divorce records in each of the 50 states.

(4) Commonly Used Abbreviations. This section lists the meanings of many familiar and unfamiliar abbreviations encountered in legal papers and government reports

and documents. It also includes the acronyms for the federal agencies and citation abbreviations for the federal and state courts.

The Lawyer's Almanac is a working tool for those in need of specific information. Yet, as with any good reference work, readers will discover a wealth of previously unrealized sources of essential information.

One last caveat is in order. The information in the Almanac was compiled from a wide array of published sources. While we believe the original work of the compilers and publishers of the data was reliable, we have not verified their research independently. The reader should also be aware that some materials, such as addresses, Internet sites, and telephone numbers, are subject to frequent change. Despite our diligent attempts to draw from the most up-to-date sources available, inevitably some information will become obsolete rather rapidly.

We welcome readers' suggestions about additional information to be included in future editions.

Finally, we wish to thank Rachel Kane for producing the 2017 edition of The Lawyer's Almanac.

Wolters Kluwer
New York
December 2016

PART I
THE LEGAL PROFESSION

A. LAW FIRMS

OF COUNSEL 700	**Table of Contents**

Part I: Analysis

Page 3: According to figures supplied by law firms to the *2016-2017 Of Counsel 700 Annual Survey of the Nation's Largest Law Firms,* the number of attorneys at the top 700 partnerships in the United States has increased from 169,928 last year to 176,347 this year. This spike of 6,419 attorneys translates into a 3.7 percentage increase. Interestingly, but not surprisingly, many of the firms that grew are midsized.

Now the survey's conclusion about the growth hike in the profession differs from what's been happening in recent years, a stabilization and even a shrinkage in the total lawyer headcount. This year's survey might have caught a very interesting, and meaningful, blip in the current trend line toward an overall do-more-with-fewer-lawyers strategy. That blip is explained because the time that many firms reported their numbers coincided with a rush to refill lawyer job slots on as-needed basis. In other words, the survey captured a mini hiring spree amid the over-arching downward hiring trend, something that shouldn't be interpreted as a full-blown counter trend. But it's nonetheless an interesting development.

Page 5: If you don't consider Pittsburgh, maybe you should. For the last 5 to 10 years, the city's been undergoing a renaissance, a very well-planned, strategic renovation that's attracting many tourists to visit and creative, talented people to live and work. Business in many economic sectors is thriving. Consequently, law firms headquartered in the City of Bridges are also doing quite well.

Part II: The List

Page 13: The 700 largest law firms ranked by size.

Part III: Selected Law Firm Profiles

Part IV: International Offices

Page 139: US firms' international offices listed by country.

Part V:Index

Page 169: Alphabetical directory and telephone listing.

OF COUNSEL 700 | The List

The *Of Counsel* 700

Listed below is the Of Counsel 700. Information on lawyer numbers was supplied in most cases by the firms themselves. In some cases, numbers were taken from published sources, primarily the law firms' websites.

Rank 2016/2015	Firm Name	Home Office	Total Number of Lawyers 2016/2015
1/5	Dentons	Chicago, IL	7300/2746
2/2	Norton Rose Fulbright	Houston, TX	3622/3800
3/3	DLA Piper	New York, NY	3527/3329
4/4	Clifford Chance US LLP	New York, NY	3300/3300
5/1	Baker & McKenzie	Chicago, IL	3294/4200
6/6	HoganLovells LLP	Washington, DC	2600/2500
7/7	Jones Day	Washington, DC	2500/2400
8/8	Latham & Watkins	New York, NY	2300/2000
9/8	K&L Gates LLP	Pittsburgh, PA	2000/2000
10/10	Greenberg Traurig, LLP	New York, NY	1991/1868
11/12	White & Case LLP	New York, NY	1990/1860
12/13	Sidley Austin LLP	Chicago, IL	1918/1825
13/14	Reed Smith LLP	Pittsburgh, PA	1880/1712
14/11	Morgan Lewis & Bockius	New York, NY	1876/1862
15/15	Skadden, Arps, Slate, Meagher & Flom LLP and Affiliates	New York, NY	1700/1700
16/16	Kirkland & Ellis	Chicago, IL	1686/1607
17/17	Mayer Brown	Chicago, IL	1583/1583
18/18	Squire Patton Boggs	Cleveland, OH	1550/1350
19/19	Ropes & Gray LLP	New York, NY	1257/1266
20/20	Gibson, Dunn & Crutcher	Los Angeles, CA	1253/1243
21/21	Cleary Gottlieb Steen & Hamilton	New York, NY	1200/1200
21/23	Holland & Knight LLP	New York, NY	1200/1106
23/26	McGuireWoods	Richmond, VA	1120/1099
24/22	Wilmer Cutler Pickering Hale and Dorr	Washington, DC	1112/1113
25/27	Orrick, Herrington & Sutcliffe LLP	San Francisco, CA	1100/1077
25/24	Weil, Gotshal & Manges LLP	New York, NY	1100/1100
27/45	Covington & Burling LLP	Washington, DC	1056/850
28/30	Morrison & Foerster LLP	San Francisco, CA	1025/1000
29/24	McDermott Will & Emery	Chicago, IL	1021/1100
30/32	Lewis Brisbois Bisgaard & Smith	Los Angeles, CA	1000/987

OF COUNSEL 700

Rank 2016/2015	Firm Name	Home Office	Total Number of Lawyers 2016/2015
30/43	Paul, Hastings, Janofsky & Walker LLP	Los Angeles, CA	1000/865
30/31	Perkins Coie	Seattle, WA	1000/992
33/28	Littler	San Francisco, CA	993/1037
34/33	King & Spalding, LLP	Atlanta, GA	974/974
35/34	Seyfarth Shaw LLP	Chicago, IL	970/942
36/29	Bryan Cave LLP	St. Louis, MO	967/1019
37/36	Dechert LLP	New York, NY	965/907
38/43	Simpson Thacher & Bartlett LLP	New York, NY	958/865
39/37	Baker & Hostetler LLP	Cleveland, OH	950/900
40/48	Davis Polk & Wardwell	New York, NY	933/827
41/35	Akin Gump Strauss Hauer & Feld LLP	Washington, DC	924/926
42/45	Cooley LLP	Palo Alto, CA	900/850
42/42	Goodwin Procter LLP	Boston, MA	900/875
44/40	Winston & Strawn LLP	Chicago, IL	891/888
45/45	Shearman & Sterling LLP	New York, NY	850/850
46/37	Foley & Lardner, LLP	Milwaukee, WI	839/900
47/41	Locke Lord LLP	Dallas, TX	823/876
48/50	Wilson, Elser, Moskowitz, Edelman & Dicker LLP	New York, NY	818/785
49/56	Paul, Weiss, Rifkind, Wharton & Garrison LLP	New York, NY	817/741
50/55	Polsinelli	Kansas City, MO	800/747
51/49	Sullivan & Cromwell	New York, NY	797/800
52/58	Ogletree, Deakins, Nash, Smoak & Stewart, P.C.	Atlanta, GA	783/736
53/37	Alston & Bird LLP	Atlanta, GA	782/900
54/53	Duane Morris LLP	Philadelphia, PA	775/757
55/66	Fox Rothschild LLP	Philadelphia, PA	773/662
56/51	Jackson Lewis LLP	White Plains, NY	769/784
57/56	Faegre Baker Daniels	Chicago, IL	750/741
57/68	Sheppard, Mullin, Richter & Hampton	Los Angeles, CA	750/655
59/54	Arnold & Porter LLP	Washington, DC	749/751
60/52	Hunton & Williams	Washington, DC	746/761
61/59	Baker Botts LLP	Houston, TX	725/725
62/70	Gordon & Rees LLP	San Francisco, CA	700/648
62/81	Husch Blackwell LLP	St. Louis, MO	700/590
62/64	Nixon Peabody LLP	New York, NY	700/672
62/60	O'Melveny & Myers LLP	Los Angeles, CA	700/700
62/65	Pillsbury Winthrop Shaw Pittman LLP	New York, NY	700/667
62/60	Proskauer Rose LLP	New York, NY	700/700
68/88	Quarles & Brady LLP	Milwaukee, WI	694/536
69/63	Baker, Donelson, Bearman, Caldwell & Berkowitz, P.C.	Memphis, TN	692/690
70/78	Akerman LLP	Orlando, FL	665/611

Rank 2016/2015	Firm Name	Home Office	Total Number of Lawyers 2016/2015
71/67	Debevoise & Plimpton LLP	New York, NY	660/660
72/76	Milbank, Tweed, Hadley & McCloy	New York, NY	659/623
73/72	Venable LLP	Washington, DC	651/633
74/73	Kilpatrick Townsend & Stockton LLP	Atlanta, GA	650/630
74/60	Quinn Emanuel Urquhart & Sullivan LLP	Los Angeles, CA	650/700
74/69	Willkie Farr & Gallagher	New York, NY	650/650
77/73	Wilson Sonsini Goodrich & Rosati	Palo Alto, CA	647/630
78/71	Katten Muchin Rosenman LLP	Chicago, IL	625/643
79/82	Dinsmore & Shohl LLP	Cincinnati, OH	621/572
79/75	Vinson & Elkins	Houston, TX	621/625
81/77	Cozen O'Connor	Philadelphia, PA	620/620
82/87	Blank Rome LLP	Philadelphia, PA	619/540
83/80	Troutman Sanders LLP	Atlanta, GA	615/600
84/84	Barnes & Thornburg LLP	Indianapolis, IN	600/550
84/79	Drinker Biddle & Reath LLP	Philadelphia, PA	600/605
86/83	Haynes and Boone, LLP	Dallas, TX	587/558
87/84	Womble Carlyle Sandridge & Rice, PLLC	Winston-Salem, NC	550/550
88/92	Davis Wright Tremaine LLP	Seattle, WA	548/524
89/89	Dorsey & Whitney LLP	Minneapolis, MN	547/530
90/90	Ballard Spahr	Philadelphia, PA	528/528
90/90	Buchanan Ingersoll & Rooney	Pittsburgh, PA	528/528
92/105	Hinshaw & Culbertson LLP	Chicago, IL	525/459
93/100	Kutak Rock LLP	Omaha, NE	510/471
94/98	Nelson Mullins Riley & Scarborough	Columbia, SC	505/496
94/94	Shook, Hardy & Bacon	Kansas City, MO	505/505
96/104	Cravath, Swaine & Moore LLP	New York, NY	503/463
96/94	Marshall Dennehey Warner Coleman & Goggin	Philadelphia, PA	503/505
98/101	Bradley Arant Boult & Cummings	Birmingham, AL	500/470
98/106	Jenner & Block LLP	Chicago, IL	500/450
98/96	Steptoe & Johnson LLP	Washington, DC	500/500
101/93	Pepper Hamilton LLP	Philadelphia, PA	498/510
102/86	Mintz Levin Cohn Ferris Glovsky and Popeo	Boston, MA	490/544
103/101	Frost Brown Todd LLC	Cincinnati, OH	489/470
104/99	Crowell & Moring LLP	Washington, DC	487/487
105/118	Fragomen, Del Rey, Bernstein & Loewy	New York, NY	480/391
106/103	Bracewell LLP	Houston, TX	465/465
107/96	Stinson Leonard Street	Kansas City, MO	439/500
108/109	Sutherland Asbill & Brennan LLP	Atlanta, GA	438/419
109/107	Cadwalader, Wickersham & Taft	New York, NY	430/448
110/108	Dykema	Detroit, MI	426/433

Rank 2016/2015	Firm Name	Home Office	Total Number of Lawyers 2016/2015
111/121	Dickinson Wright PLLC	Detroit, MI	421/388
112/111	Arent Fox	Washington, DC	418/418
113/112	Fried, Frank, Harris, Shriver & Jacobson LLP	New York, NY	414/414
114/113	McCarter & English	Newark, NJ	410/410
114/115	Stoel Rives LLP	Portland, OR	410/400
116/109	Snell & Wilmer	Phoenix, AZ	404/419
117/117	Kaye Scholer LLP	New York, NY	400/394
117/114	Taft Stettinius & Hollister LLP	Cincinnati, OH	400/403
119/123	Fenwick & West LLP	Mountain View, CA	396/376
120/122	Jones Walker LLP	New Orleans, LA	380/386
120/126	Thompson Coburn	St. Louis, MO	380/372
122/120	Carlton Fields Jorden Burt	Tampa, FL	375/390
122/129	Vorys, Sater, Seymour and Pease	Columbus, OH	375/363
124/124	Thompson Hine LLP	Cleveland, OH	369/375
125/127	Fish & Richardson	Boston, MA	367/367
126/128	Jackson Walker LLP	Dallas, TX	362/365
127/135	Clark Hill PLC	Detroit, MI	357/344
127/134	Schulte Roth & Zabel LLP	New York, NY	357/347
129/129	Eckert Seamans Cherin & Mellott, LLC	Pittsburgh, PA	353/363
129/133	Finnegan, Henderson, Farabow, Garrett & Dunner	Washington, DC	353/353
131/132	Manatt, Phelps & Phillips	Los Angeles, CA	349/356
132/124	Kramer Levin Naftalis & Frankel LLP	New York, NY	345/375
133/129	Chadbourne & Parke LLP	New York, NY	340/363
133/143	Fisher Phillips	Atlanta, GA	340/300
135/154	Loeb & Loeb LLP	Los Angeles, CA	338/281
136/135	Winstead PC	Dallas, TX	335/344
137/139	Sedgwick, LLP	San Francisco, CA	330/330
138/116	Andrews Kurth LLP	Houston, TX	328/397
138/140	Steptoe & Johnson PLLC	Bridgeport, WV	328/328
140/141	Butler Snow	Ridgeland, MS	327/321
141/137	Hughes Hubbard & Reed LLP	New York, NY	324/343
142/142	Lathrop & Gage LLP	Kansas City, MO	323/317
143/118	Schiff Hardin LLP	Chicago, IL	318/391
144/146	Lowenstein Sandler PC	Roseland, NJ	310/299
145/151	Stroock & Stroock & Lavan LLP	New York, NY	305/289
146/196	Boies Schiller & Flexner	Oakland, CA	300/200
146/143	Epstein Becker & Green P.C.	New York, NY	300/300
146/155	GrayRobinson	Fort Lauderdale, FL	300/280
146/150	Ice Miller LLP	Indianapolis, IN	300/291
146/143	Kelley Drye & Warren LLP	New York, NY	300/300

Rank 2016/2015	Firm Name	Home Office	Total Number of Lawyers 2016/2015
151/149	Adams and Reese LLP	New Orleans, LA	293/293
152/147	Vedder Price	Chicago, IL	292/295
153/153	Moore & Van Allen PLLC	Charlotte, NC	291/282
154/177	Bass, Berry & Sims PLC	Nashville, TN	290/230
154/175	Lewis Roca Rothgerber LLP	Phoenix, AZ	290/233
156/160	Day Pitney LLP	Parsippany, NJ	283/274
157/166	Honigman Miller Schwartz and Cohn LLP	Detroit, MI	282/257
158/161	Knobbe Martens Olson & Bear, LLP	Irvine, CA	281/272
159/162	Curtis, Mallet-Prevost, Colt & Mosle LLP	New York, NY	280/270
160/157	Burr & Forman LLP	Birmingham, AL	279/278
161/155	Miller, Canfield, Paddock and Stone, P.L.C.	Detroit, MI	277/280
162/138	Fredrikson & Byron, P.A.	Minneapolis, MN	276/339
163/158	Barclay Damon	Syracuse, NY	275/275
163/179	McElroy, Deutsch, Mulvaney & Carpenter, LLP	Morristown, NJ	275/228
165/158	Williams & Connolly	Washington, DC	273/275
166/162	Saul Ewing LLP	Philadelphia, PA	270/270
166/165	Shutts & Bowen LLP	Miami, FL	270/258
168/168	Foley Hoag LLP	Boston, MA	267/250
169/164	Phelps Dunbar LLP	New Orleans, LA	266/266
170/179	Bond, Schoeneck & King	Syracuse, NY	264/228
171/147	Thompson & Knight	Dallas, TX	263/295
172/152	Cahill Gordon & Reindel LLP	New York, NY	253/283
173/170	Shumaker, Loop & Kendrick, LLP	Toledo, OH	245/241
174/169	Brown & Rudnick	Boston, MA	242/242
175/178	Brownstein Hyatt Farber Schreck	Denver, CO	236/229
176/174	Balch & Bingham LLP	Birmingham, AL	234/235
177/184	Armstrong Teasdale LLP	St. Louis, MO	233/219
178/175	Gardere Wynne Sewell LLP	Dallas, TX	230/233
178/173	Miles & Stockbridge P.C.	Baltimore, MD	230/238
178/172	Williams Mullen	Richmond, VA	230/239
181/183	Warner Norcross & Judd LLP	Grand Rapids, MI	227/222
182/171	Chapman and Cutler LLP	Chicago, IL	225/240
182/187	Michael Best & Friedrich	Milwaukee, WI	225/215
184/179	Maynard, Cooper & Gale, P.C.	Birmingham, AL	224/228
185/182	Robins Kaplan LLP	Minneapolis, MN	219/226
186/186	Smith Moore Leatherwood LLP	Greensboro, NC	216/218
187/192	Reinhart Boerner Van Deuren s.c.	Milwaukee, WI	215/204
188/189	Harris Beach PLLC	Pittsford, NY	210/210
189/188	Strasburger & Price	Dallas, TX	209/212
190/191	Hodgson Russ	Buffalo, NY	206/207

Rank 2016/2015	Firm Name	Home Office	Total Number of Lawyers 2016/2015
191/209	McGlinchey Stafford	New Orleans, LA	203/187
191/193	Porter Wright Morris & Arthur LLP	Columbus, OH	203/203
193/195	Gibbons	Newark, NJ	202/202
193/216	Hall Render Killian Heath & Lyman P.C.	Indianapolis, IN	202/179
195/205	Goulston & Storrs	Boston, MA	200/192
195/221	Lane Powell	Seattle, WA	200/172
195/204	Nexsen Pruet	Columbia, SC	200/193
195/196	Parker Poe Adams & Bernstein LLP	Charlotte, NC	200/200
195/201	Waller Lansden Dortch & Davis	Nashville, TN	200/198
200/354	Greenspoon Marder, P.A.	Fort Lauderdale, FL	199/100
200/196	Robinson & Cole LLP	Hartford, CT	199/200
202/203	Stites & Harbison, PLLC	Louisville, KY	195/195
203/202	Allen Matkins	Los Angeles, CA	193/197
203/212	Stradley Ronon Stevens & Young, LLP	Philadelphia, PA	193/184
205/196	Patterson Belknap Webb & Tyler	New York, NY	192/200
205/210	Smith, Gambrell & Russell	Atlanta, GA	192/186
207/206	Fennemore Craig	Phoenix, AZ	191/190
208/212	Morrison Mahoney LLP	Boston, MA	190/184
209/217	Sherman & Howard L.L.C.	Denver, CO	189/176
210/189	Bingham Greenebaum Doll LLP	Indianapolis, IN	188/210
210/208	Jackson Kelly PLLC	Charleston, WV	188/188
210/193	Munger, Tolles & Olson	Los Angeles, CA	188/203
213/167	Wiley Rein LLP	Washington, DC	187/255
214/224	Gray Plant Mooty	Minneapolis, MN	186/170
215/210	Phillips Lytle LLP	Buffalo, NY	185/186
216/222	Best Best & Krieger	Riverside, CA	182/171
216/200	Wyatt, Tarrant & Combs, LLP	Louisville, KY	182/199
218/232	Buchalter Nemer	Los Angeles, CA	178/162
218/279	Spencer Fane Britt & Browne LLP	Kansas City, MO	178/136
220/218	Archer & Greiner	Haddonfield, NJ	177/175
220/224	Gunster	West Palm Beach, FL	177/170
220/214	McAfee & Taft, A Professional Corporation	Oklahoma City, OK	177/180
220/222	Roetzel & Andress, A Legal Professional Association	Akron, OH	177/171
224/269	Benesch, Friedlander, Coplan & Aronoff LLP	Cleveland, OH	176/140
225/206	Morris, Manning & Martin, LLP	Atlanta, GA	175/190
226/245	Constangy, Brooks, Smith & Prophete	Atlanta, GA	173/152
227/243	Seward & Kissel LLP	New York, NY	171/153
227/234	Shipman & Goodwin LLP	Hartford, CT	171/160
229/229	Varnum LLP	Grand Rapids, MI	170/165
230/220	Choate, Hall & Stewart LLP	Boston, MA	168/174

Rank 2016/2015	Firm Name	Home Office	Total Number of Lawyers 2016/2015
231/231	Dickie, McCamey & Chilcote	Pittsburgh, PA	167/163
232/243	Lewis, Rice & Fingersh, L.C.	St. Louis, MO	166/153
233/218	Calfee, Halter & Griswold LLP	Cleveland, OH	165/175
233/245	Rivkin Radler LLP	Uniondale, NY	165/152
233/228	Schwabe, Williamson & Wyatt	Portland, OR	165/166
236/237	Broad and Cassel	Orlando, FL	164/158
237/232	Hanson Bridgett	San Francisco, CA	162/162
237/226	Lindquist & Vennum LLP	Minneapolis, MN	162/167
237/226	Sullivan & Worcester	Boston, MA	162/167
240/267	Bressler Amery & Ross	New York, NY	161/141
241/239	Arnall Golden Gregory LLP	Atlanta, GA	160/155
241/238	Whiteford, Taylor & Preston	Baltimore, MD	160/156
241/245	Wicker Smith O'Hara McCoy & Ford P.A.	Coral Gables, FL	160/152
244/239	Miller Nash Graham & Dunn LLP	Portland, OR	159/155
245/256	Hinckley, Allen & Snyder P.C.	Providence, RI	155/147
245/249	Kelly, Hart & Hallman LLP	Fort Worth, TX	155/151
247/253	Rutan & Tucker	Costa Mesa, CA	154/148
248/245	Cohen & Grigsby, P.C.	Pittsburgh, PA	152/152
248/249	Procopio, Cory, Hargreaves & Savitch LLP	San Diego, CA	152/151
250/252	Greensfelder, Hemker & Gale, P.C.	St. Louis, MO	151/149
250/229	Ulmer and Berne LLP	Cleveland, OH	151/165
250/267	von Briesen & Roper, s.c.	Milwaukee, WI	151/141
253/242	Kean Miller LLP	Baton Rouge, LA	150/154
253/259	Stevens & Lee	Reading, PA	150/146
253/266	Stoll, Keenon & Ogden, PLLC	Lexington, KY	150/142
256/234	Bodman PLC	Detroit, MI	148/160
257/256	Becker & Poliakoff, P.A.	Fort Lauderdale, FL	147/147
257/262	Nutter McClennen & Fish LLP	Boston, MA	147/143
259/251	Crowley Fleck PLLP	Billings, MT	146/150
260/285	Pierce Atwood LLP	Portland, ME	145/133
261/269	Adelson, Testan, Brundo & Jimenez	Van Nuys, CA	144/140
261/261	Pryor Cashman LLP	New York, NY	144/144
263/288	Richards, Layton & Finger	Wilmington, DE	143/132
263/214	Schnader Harrison Segal & Lewis LLP	Philadelphia, PA	143/180
265/256	Arnstein & Lehr LLP	Chicago, IL	141/147
266/260	Bricker & Eckler, LLP	Columbus, OH	140/145
266/253	Briggs and Morgan, P.A.	Minneapolis, MN	140/148
266/269	Davis Graham & Stubbs LLP	Denver, CO	140/140
266/262	Herrick, Feinstein LLP	New York, NY	140/143
266/274	Howard & Howard Attorneys PLLC	Royal Oak, MI	140/138

Rank 2016/2015	Firm Name	Home Office	Total Number of Lawyers 2016/2015
271/279	Fitzpatrick, Cella, Harper & Scinto	New York, NY	139/136
272/292	Chiesa Shahinian & Giantomasi PC	West Orange, NJ	138/130
272/262	Cullen and Dykman	Brooklyn, NY	138/143
274/288	Butzel Long	Detroit, MI	137/132
274/273	McDonald Hopkins LLC	Cleveland, OH	137/139
274/276	Neal, Gerber & Eisenberg LLP	Chicago, IL	137/137
274/184	Riker Danzig Scherer Hyland & Perretti LLP	Morristown, NJ	137/219
278/279	Parsons Behle & Latimer, A Professional Law Corporation	Salt Lake City, UT	136/136
278/253	Plunkett Cooney	Detroit, MI	136/148
278/274	Sills Cummis & Gross	Newark, NJ	136/138
278/282	Windels Marx Lane & Mittendorf, LLP	New York, NY	136/135
282/283	Norris, McLaughlin & Marcus	Bridgewater, NJ	135/134
282/285	Wiggin and Dana	New Haven, CT	135/133
284/288	Liskow & Lewis, A Professional Law Corporation	New Orleans, LA	134/132
284/310	Post & Schell	Philadelphia, PA	134/121
284/318	Verrill Dana	Portland, ME	134/115
287/303	Foster Pepper PLLC	Seattle, WA	133/125
288/276	Cox, Castle & Nicholson LLP	Los Angeles, CA	131/137
288/285	Miller & Martin	Chattanooga, TN	131/133
290/298	Crowe & Dunlevy, A Professional Corporation	Oklahoma City, OK	130/127
290/288	McNees Wallace & Nurick LLC	Harrisburg, PA	130/132
290/292	Mitchell Silberberg & Knupp LLP	Los Angeles, CA	130/130
293/294	Harter Secrest & Emery	Rochester, NY	129/129
294/300	Burns & Levinson LLP	Boston, MA	128/126
294/303	Smith, Anderson, Blount, Dorsett, Mitchell & Jernigan, LLP	Raleigh, NC	128/125
296/303	Gray, Reed & McGraw, a Professional Corporation	Houston, TX	127/125
296/309	Hall, Estill, Hardwick, Gable, Golden & Nelson, P.C.	Tulsa, OK	127/122
296/298	Robinson Bradshaw	Charlotte, NC	127/127
299/300	Farella Braun + Martel LLP	San Francisco, CA	126/126
299/283	Freeborn & Peters	Chicago, IL	126/134
299/262	Irell & Manella LLP	Los Angeles, CA	126/143
299/300	Spilman Thomas & Battle, PLLC	Charleston, WV	126/126
303/294	Babst, Calland, Clements and Zomnir, P.C.	Pittsburgh, PA	125/129
304/276	Bowles Rice LLP	Charleston, WV	124/137
304/307	Cole, Schotz, Meisel, Forman & Leonard, P.A.	Hackensack, NJ	124/124
304/316	Winthrop & Weinstine	Minneapolis, MN	124/116
307/330	Dewitt Ross & Stevens	Madison, WI	122/109
308/313	Ryley Carlock & Applewhite	Phoenix, AZ	120/120
309/314	Davis & Gilbert	New York, NY	119/118
309/303	Garvey Schubert Barer	Seattle, WA	119/125

Rank 2016/2015	Firm Name	Home Office	Total Number of Lawyers 2016/2015
311/296	Hahn Loeser & Parks LLP	Cleveland, OH	118/128
311/315	Montgomery, McCracken, Walker & Rhoads, LLP	Philadelphia, PA	118/117
313/320	Chamberlain Hrdlicka White Williams & Aughtry	Houston, TX	117/114
313/316	Stearns Weaver Miller Weissler Alhadaff & Sitterson, P.A.	Miami, FL	117/116
315/339	Jaffe, Raitt, Heuer & Weiss, P.C.	Southfield, MI	116/106
316/269	Connell Foley LLP	Roseland, NJ	115/140
316/334	Haynsworth Sinkler Boyd, P.A.	Columbia, SC	115/108
316/318	Munsch Hardt Kopf & Harr, P.C.	Dallas, TX	115/115
319/324	Harness Dickey	Troy, MI	114/110
319/356	Swift, Currie, McGhee & Hiers, LLP	Atlanta, GA	114/99
321/310	Sirote & Permutt, P.C.	Birmingham, AL	113/121
321/330	Wilentz, Goldman & Spitzer P.A.	Woodbridge, NJ	113/109
323/321	Ober, Kaler, Grimes & Shriver, P.C.	Baltimore, MD	112/112
324/324	Jeffer, Mangels, Butler & Mitchell LLP	Los Angeles, CA	111/110
325/324	Brown & James, P.C.	St. Louis, MO	110/110
325/324	Conner & Winters LLP	Tulsa, OK	110/110
327/336	McConnell Valdes LLC	San Juan, PR	109/107
328/330	Margolis Edelstein	Philadelphia, PA	108/109
328/321	Obermayer Rebmann Maxwell & Hippel LLP	Philadelphia, PA	108/112
328/321	Rawle & Henderson LLP	Philadelphia, PA	108/112
331/324	McNair Law Firm, P.A.	Columbia, SC	107/110
332/339	Cassiday Schade LLP	Chicago, IL	106/106
332/336	Keating Muething & Klekamp PLL (KMK Law)	Cincinnati, OH	106/107
332/342	Merchant & Gould	Minneapolis, MN	106/105
332/345	Murtha Cullina LLP	Hartford, CT	106/104
336/336	Bernstein Shur	Portland, ME	105/107
336/310	Miller & Chevalier Chartered	Washington, DC	105/121
336/342	Ray Quinney & Nebeker P.C.	Salt Lake City, UT	105/105
336/324	Severson & Werson, A Professional Corporation	San Francisco, CA	105/110
336/339	Young Conaway Stargatt & Taylor, LLP	Wilmington, DE	105/106
341/371	Miller Johnson	Grand Rapids, MI	104/95
342/334	Clausen Miller	Chicago, IL	102/108
342/367	Morrison Cohen LLP	New York, NY	102/96
344/350	Musick, Peeler & Garrett LLP	Los Angeles, CA	101/101
345/356	Beveridge & Diamond, P.C.	Washington, DC	100/99
345/354	Burke, Williams & Sorensen, LLP	Los Angeles, CA	100/100
345/360	Halloran & Sage, LLP	Hartford, CT	100/98
345/361	Peckar & Abramson	River Edge, NJ	100/97
349/330	Bose McKinney & Evans LLP	Indianapolis, IN	99/109
349/367	Downey Brand LLP	Sacramento, CA	99/96

Rank 2016/2015	Firm Name	Home Office	Total Number of Lawyers 2016/2015
351/372	Banner & Witcoff, Ltd.	Chicago, IL	98/94
351/379	McLane Graf Raulerson & Middleton, P.A.	Manchester, NH	98/91
351/348	Preti, Flaherty, Beliveau & Pachios LLP	Portland, ME	98/103
354/361	Glaser, Weil, Fink, Jacobs, Howard, Avchen & Shapiro	Los Angeles, CA	97/97
354/361	Kaufman & Canoles, A Professional Corporation	Norfolk, VA	97/97
354/387	Moses & Singer LLP	New York, NY	97/87
354/342	Stark & Stark	Lawrenceville, NJ	97/105
358/350	Archer Norris, A Professional Corporation	Walnut Creek, CA	96/101
358/425	Jones Waldo Holbrook & McDonough PC	Salt Lake City, UT	96/75
360/348	Dilworth Paxson LLP	Philadelphia, PA	95/103
360/398	Drew Eckl & Farnham, LLP	Atlanta, GA	95/84
360/367	Greenbaum, Rowe, Smith, & Davis, LLP	Iselin, NJ	95/96
360/356	Shulman, Rogers, Gandal, Pordy & Ecker, P.A.	Potomac, MD	95/99
364/396	Bilzin Sumberg Baena Price & Axlerod LLP	Miami, FL	94/85
364/350	Oblon, McClelland, Maier & Neustadt, LLP	Alexandria, VA	94/101
364/345	Poyner Spruill LLP	Raleigh, NC	94/104
367/381	Kitch Drutchas Wagner Valitutti & Sherbrook, A Professional Corporation	Detroit, MI	93/90
367/432	Wolf Greenfield & Sacks, PC	Boston, MA	93/72
369/367	Foster Swift Collins & Smith, PC	Lansing, MI	91/96
369/345	Johnson & Bell, Ltd.	Chicago, IL	91/104
369/378	Ward and Smith, P.A.	New Bern, NC	91/92
372/379	GableGotwals	Tulsa, OK	90/91
372/361	Hill Ward Henderson	Tampa, FL	90/97
372/372	Ropers, Majeski, Kohn, & Bentley, P.C.	Redwood City, CA	90/94
375/372	Lowndes, Drosdick, Doster, Kantor & Reed	Orlando, FL	89/94
375/396	Pullman and Comley, LLC	Bridgeport, CT	89/85
377/361	Carter, Ledyard & Milburn LLP	New York, NY	88/97
377/361	Mitchell Williams Selig Gates Woodyard, PLLC	Little Rock, AR	88/97
377/383	Rumberger, Kirk & Caldwell	Orlando, FL	88/89
380/406	Hawkins, Delafield & Wood	New York, NY	87/82
380/391	Olshan, Frome & Wolosky LLP	New York, NY	87/86
382/377	Foulston Siefkin LLP	Wichita, KS	86/93
382/398	Friday, Eldredge & Clark, LLP	Little Rock, AR	86/84
382/391	Greenberg Glusker	Los Angeles, CA	86/86
382/372	Mound, Cotton, Wollan & Greengrass	New York, NY	86/94

Rank 2016/2015	Firm Name	Home Office	Total Number of Lawyers 2016/2015
382/383	Much Shelist, P.C.	Chicago, IL	86/89
382/398	Potter Anderson & Corroon	Wilmington, DE	86/84
382/391	Sughrue Mion, PLLC	Washington, DC	86/86
382/391	Swartz, Campbell & Detweiler	Philadelphia, PA	86/86
382/391	Tucker Arensberg, P.C.	Pittsburgh, PA	86/86
391/386	McCormick, Barstow, Sheppard, Wayte & Carruth LLP	Fresno, CA	85/88
391/381	Porzio, Bromberg & Newman	Morristown, NJ	85/90
391/372	Van Ness Feldman LLP	Washington, DC	85/94
394/415	Groom Law Group, Chartered	Washington, DC	84/78
394/415	Maslon Edelman Borman & Brand	Minneapolis, MN	84/78
394/398	Mendes & Mount, LLP	New York, NY	84/84
394/387	Morris, Nichols, Arsht & Tunnell LLP	Wilmington, DE	84/87
394/387	Tonkon Torp LLP	Portland, OR	84/87
399/409	Murchison & Cumming	Los Angeles, CA	83/80
400/428	Hirschler Fleischer	Richmond, VA	82/74
400/406	Klehr, Harrison, Harvey, Branzburg & Ellers LLP	Philadelphia, PA	82/82
402/398	Anderson Kill & Olick, P.C.	New York, NY	81/84
402/408	Baird Holm LLP	Omaha, NE	81/81
402/409	Bartlit Beck Herman Palenchar & Scott	Chicago, IL	81/80
402/398	Evans & Dixon	St. Louis, MO	81/84
402/356	Krieg Devault LLP	Indianapolis, IN	81/99
402/383	Smith Haughey Rice & Roegge	Grand Rapids, MI	81/89
408/436	Budd Larner, P.C.	Short Hills, NJ	80/71
408/409	Meagher & Geer, PLLP	Minneapolis, MN	80/80
408/350	Tressler LLP	Chicago, IL	80/101
411/413	Davis, Brown, Koehn, Shors & Roberts	Des Moines, IA	79/79
411/398	Morris Polich & Purdy	Los Angeles, CA	79/84
411/415	Trenam Kemker	Tampa, FL	79/78
414/421	Hall & Evans, LLC	Denver, CO	78/76
414/432	Zelle Hofmann Voelbel & Mason LLP	Minneapolis, MN	78/72
416/436	Higgs, Fletcher & Mack LLP	San Diego, CA	77/71
416/445	Larkin Hoffman Daly & Lindgren Ltd.	Minneapolis, MN	77/68
416/462	Parker Hudson Rainer & Dobbs	Atlanta, GA	77/64
419/387	Gallagher & Kennedy, P.A.	Phoenix, AZ	75/87
419/431	Hinman, Howard & Kattell, LLP	Binghamton, NY	75/73
419/398	Kegler, Brown, Hill & Ritter	Columbus, OH	75/84
419/421	Liner LLP	Los Angeles, CA	75/76
419/425	Motley Rice LLC	Mount Pleasant, SC	75/75
424/419	Brouse McDowell	Akron, OH	74/77
424/436	Carmody Torrance Sandak & Hennessey LLP	Waterbury, CT	74/71

Rank 2016/2015	Firm Name	Home Office	Total Number of Lawyers 2016/2015
424/445	Certilman Balin Adler & Hyman, LLP	East Meadow, NY	74/68
424/428	Rubin and Rudman LLP	Boston, MA	74/74
428/415	Carlsmith Ball LLP	Honolulu, HI	73/78
428/425	Keesal, Young & Logan, P.C.	Long Beach, CA	73/75
428/428	Keller and Heckman LLP	Washington, DC	73/74
431/459	Barley Snyder LLP	Lancaster, PA	72/65
431/445	Semmes, Bowen & Semmes, A Professional Corporation	Baltimore, MD	72/68
431/432	Williams Kastner	Seattle, WA	72/72
434/421	Eastman & Smith	Toledo, OH	70/76
435/436	Breazeale, Sachse & Wilson, LLP	Baton Rouge, LA	69/71
435/442	Graves, Dougherty, Hearon & Moody, P.C.	Austin, TX	69/69
435/462	Parr Brown Gee and Loveless, A Professional Corporation	Salt Lake City, UT	69/64
435/409	Rogers Towers	Jacksonville, FL	69/80
439/421	Graydon Head & Ritchey LLP	Cincinnati, OH	68/76
439/445	McGrath, North, Mullin & Kratz, P.C.	Omaha, NE	68/68
439/445	Phillips Nizer LLP	New York, NY	68/68
439/455	Secrest, Wardle, Lynch, Hampton, Truex, and Morley, P.C.	Troy, MI	68/66
443/452	Boardman & Clark LLP	Madison, WI	67/67
443/452	Morris James	Wilmington, DE	67/67
443/485	Updike, Kelly & Spellacy P.C.	Hartford, CT	67/57
443/543	Van Cott Bagley Cornwall & McCarthy	Salt Lake City, UT	67/38
447/462	Buckingham, Doolittle & Burroughs, LLC	Akron, OH	66/64
447/455	Gordon Feinblatt LLC	Baltimore, MD	66/66
447/462	Herzfeld & Rubin, P.C.	New York, NY	66/64
450/440	Caplin & Drysdale, Chartered	Washington, DC	65/70
450/459	Davis & Kuelthau, S.C.	Milwaukee, WI	65/65
450/445	Devine, Millimet & Branch, P.A.	Manchester, NH	65/68
450/483	Haight, Brown & Bonesteel LLP	Los Angeles, CA	65/58
450/442	Hand Arendall LLC	Mobile, AL	65/69
450/452	Jennings, Strouss & Salmon, PLC	Phoenix, AZ	65/67
450/440	Rodey, Dickason, Sloan, Akin & Robb, P.A.	Albuquerque, NM	65/70
457/455	Cades Schutte LLP	Honolulu, HI	64/66
457/462	Parker McCay P.A.	Mt. Laurel, NJ	64/64
457/472	Richards, Watson & Gershon	Los Angeles, CA	64/62
457/472	Willcox & Savage, P.C.	Norfolk, VA	64/62
457/462	Wright, Lindsey & Jennings, LLP	Little Rock, AR	64/64
462/445	Carroll, Burdick & McDonough LLP	San Francisco, CA	63/68
462/432	Naman, Howell, Smith & Lee	Waco, TX	63/72
464/472	Cantey & Hanger, L.L.P.	Fort Worth, TX	62/62
464/459	Cummings & Lockwood LLC	Stamford, CT	62/65

Rank 2016/2015	Firm Name	Home Office	Total Number of Lawyers 2016/2015
464/468	Deutsch, Kerrigan & Stiles, LLP	New Orleans, LA	62/63
464/485	Goodsill Anderson Quinn & Stifel LLP	Honolulu, HI	62/57
464/413	Modrall, Sperling, Roehl, Harris & Sisk, P.A.	Albuquerque, NM	62/79
464/477	Moss & Barnett, P.A.	Minneapolis, MN	62/61
470/477	Chaffe McCall, LLP	New Orleans, LA	61/61
470/479	DeCotiis FitzPatrick & Cole	Teaneck, NJ	61/60
470/472	Hawley Troxell Ennis & Hawley LLP	Boise, ID	61/62
470/485	Stone Pigman Walther Wittmann LLC	New Orleans, LA	61/57
474/442	Leitner, Williams, Dooley & Napolitan, PLLC	Chattanooga, TN	60/69
474/483	Posternak Blankstein & Lund LLP	Boston, MA	60/58
476/481	Lester, Schwab, Katz & Dwyer	New York, NY	59/59
476/468	McGinnis, Lochridge & Kilgore, LLP	Austin, TX	59/63
476/485	Smith, Currie & Hancock	Atlanta, GA	59/57
476/468	Woods Rogers PLC	Roanoke, VA	59/63
480/472	Bowditch & Dewey, LLP	Worcester, MA	58/62
480/492	D'Amato & Lynch	New York, NY	58/55
480/479	Sheehan, Phinney, Bass & Green, Professional Association	Manchester, NH	58/60
483/485	Adler Pollock & Sheehan P.C.	Providence, RI	57/57
483/492	Chambliss Bahner & Stophel	Chattanooga, TN	57/55
483/481	Ladas & Parry LLP	New York, NY	57/59
483/510	Weston Hurd LLP	Cleveland, OH	57/51
487/492	Hancock Estabrook, LLP	Syracuse, NY	56/55
487/308	Kenyon & Kenyon LLP	New York, NY	56/123
487/501	La Follette, Johnson, De Haas, Fesler & Ames	Los Angeles, CA	56/53
490/501	Cline Williams Wright Johnson & Oldfather	Omaha, NE	55/53
491/513	Ervin Cohen & Jessup LLP	Beverly Hills, CA	54/50
491/496	Giordano, Halleran & Ciesla, P.C.	Red Bank, NJ	54/54
491/491	Pircher, Nichols & Meeks	Los Angeles, CA	54/56
491/485	Pretzel & Stouffer, Chartered	Chicago, IL	54/57
491/518	Strauss & Troy, A Legal Professional Association	Cincinnati, OH	54/49
496/496	Bullivant Houser Bailey PC	Portland, OR	53/54
496/496	Meyer, Unkovic & Scott LLP	Pittsburgh, PA	53/54
496/492	Snow, Christensen & Martineau	Salt Lake City, UT	53/55
496/505	Watt, Tieder, Hoffar & Fitzgerald	McLean, VA	53/52
500/496	Emmet, Marvin & Martin, LLP	New York, NY	52/54
500/505	Gallagher Sharp LLP	Cleveland, OH	52/52
500/505	Hollingsworth LLP	Washington, DC	52/52
500/501	Karr Tuttle Campbell	Seattle, WA	52/53
504/510	Lavin, O'Neil, Cedrone & DiSipio	Philadelphia, PA	51/51
504/505	Peabody & Arnold LLP	Boston, MA	51/52

Rank 2016/2015	Firm Name	Home Office	Total Number of Lawyers 2016/2015
504/520	Sullivan, Ward, Asher & Patton, P.C.	Southfield, MI	51/47
507/523	Hunter Maclean Exley & Dunn, P.C.	Savannah, GA	50/46
507/513	Linowes & Blocher LLP	Bethesda, MD	50/50
507/510	Otterbourg PC	New York, NY	50/51
507/455	Sands Anderson Marks & Miller, PC	Richmond, VA	50/66
511/527	Ogden Murphy Wallace, P.L.L.C.	Seattle, WA	49/45
512/513	Carrington, Coleman, Sloman & Blumenthal L.L.P.	Dallas, TX	48/50
512/527	Jaeckle Fleischmann & Mugel, LLP	Buffalo, NY	48/45
514/527	Lashly & Baer, P.C.	St. Louis, MO	46/45
514/527	Miller Starr Regalia	Walnut Creek, CA	46/45
514/534	Wallace, Saunders, Austin, Brown & Enochs, Chartered	Overland Park, KS	46/43
517/527	Jackson & Campbell, P.C.	Washington, DC	45/45
517/520	Reid and Riege, P.C.	Hartford, CT	45/47
519/520	Best & Flanagan LLP	Minneapolis, MN	44/47
519/513	Boehl, Stopher & Graves, LLP	Louisville, KY	44/50
519/513	Borton Petrini, LLP	Bakersfield, CA	44/50
519/468	Fiddler, Gonzalez & Rodriguez, P.S.C.	Hato Rey, PR	44/63
519/544	Robinson & McElwee LLP	Charleston, WV	44/37
524/519	Cowan, Liebowitz & Latman, P.C.	New York, NY	43/48
524/527	Fellers Snider	Oklahoma City, OK	43/45
524/501	Gordon, Thomas, Honeywell, Malanca, Peterson & Daheim, LLP	Tacoma, WA	43/53
524/534	Hahn & Hessen LLP	New York, NY	43/43
524/534	Seltzer Caplan McMahon Vitek, A Law Corporation	San Diego, CA	43/43
529/538	Hill, Farrer & Burrill LLP	Los Angeles, CA	42/41
529/538	Hoge, Fenton, Jones & Appel, Inc.	San Jose, CA	42/41
531/538	Callister, Nebecker & McCoullogh PC	Salt Lake City, UT	41/41
531/523	Gould & Ratner	Chicago, IL	41/46
531/534	Kemp Smith, P.C.	El Paso, TX	41/43
531/496	Kronick, Moskovitz, Tiedemann & Girard	Sacramento, CA	41/54
535/538	Christian & Barton, LLP	Richmond, VA	40/41
536/546	Hinkle, Hensley, Shanor & Martin	Roswell, NM	38/36
536/523	Macfarlane, Ferguson, McMullen	Tampa, FL	38/46
538/527	Milberg LLP	New York, NY	37/45
539/546	Parker, Milliken, Clark, O'Hara & Samuelian, P.C.	Los Angeles, CA	36/36
540/553	Roberts & Holland LLP	New York, NY	35/32
541/542	Berenbaum Weinshienk PC	Denver, CO	34/40
541/553	Mitchell, McNutt, & Sams, P.A.	Tupelo, MS	34/32
541/561	Querrey & Harrow	Chicago, IL	34/31
544/550	Braun Kendrick Finkbeiner	Saginaw, MI	33/33
544/550	Cooper, White & Cooper LLP	San Francisco, CA	33/33

Rank 2016/2015	Firm Name	Home Office	Total Number of Lawyers 2016/2015
544/561	Ruberry Stalmack & Garvey	Chicago, IL	33/31
547/553	Coolidge Wall	Dayton, OH	32/32
547/553	Gilbert, Kelly, Crowley & Jennett	Los Angeles, CA	32/32
547/546	Helsell Fetterman LLP	Seattle, WA	32/36
547/523	Schuyler, Roche & Crisham, P.C.	Chicago, IL	32/46
551/553	Keleher & McLeod, PA	Albuquerque, NM	31/32
551/563	MehaffyWeber, P.C.	Beaumont, TX	31/30
551/563	Miller, Stratvert & Torgerson, P.A.	Albuquerque, NM	31/30
551/567	Sommers, Schwartz, P.C.	Southfield, MI	31/28
555/544	Burnham Brown	Oakland, CA	30/37
555/569	Milling Benson Woodward LLP	New Orleans, LA	30/27
555/565	Waters, McPherson, McNeill, P.C.	Secaucus, NJ	30/29
558/546	Ater Wynne LLP	Portland, OR	29/36
558/553	Pedersen & Houpt, PC	Chicago, IL	29/32
560/567	Carr Maloney PC	Washington, DC	28/28
560/553	Cowles & Thompson, P.C.	Dallas, TX	28/32
562/550	Sutin, Thayer & Browne A Professional Corporation	Albuquerque, NM	26/33
563/575	Lane, Alton & Horst LLC	Columbus, OH	25/23
564/574	Long & Levit LLP	San Francisco, CA	24/24
564/569	Williams Montgomery & John Ltd.	Chicago, IL	24/27
566/569	Crabbe, Brown & James	Columbus, OH	23/27
566/553	McCandlish Holton PC	Richmond, VA	23/32
568/572	King & Ballow	Nashville, TN	22/25
569/565	Christie Sullivan & Young PC	Philadelphia, PA	21/29
570/576	Harrington, Foxx, Dubrow & Canter	Los Angeles, CA	20/21
570/576	Knapp, Petersen & Clarke, A Professional Corporation	Glendale, CA	20/21
572/580	Berger Kahn	Irvine, CA	19/19
572/578	McKenna Storer	Chicago, IL	19/20
574/578	Keevican, Weiss, Bauerle & Hirsch, LLC	Pittsburgh, PA	18/20
574/582	Meyer, Darragh, Buckler, Bebenek & Eck, P.L.L.C.	Pittsburgh, PA	18/18
574/580	Montgomery Barnett, LLP	New Orleans, LA	18/19
577/582	Kramer, Deboer, Endelicato & Keane	Woodland Hills, CA	16/18
577/584	Rosenfeld, Meyer & Susman, LLP	Beverly Hills, CA	16/17
579/572	Bonne, Bridges, Mueller, O'Keefe & Nichols	Los Angeles, CA	13/25
580/586	Climaco, Wilcox, Peca, Tarantino & Garofoli LPA	Cleveland, OH	11/11
581/585	Harvey, Pennington, LTD	Philadelphia, PA	8/14

OF COUNSEL 700

Selected Law Firm Profiles

ALABAMA

Balch & Bingham LLP

1901 Sixth Avenue North
Suite 1500
Birmingham, AL 35203
Phone: 205-251-8100
Fax: 205-226-8798
Email: nchandler@balch.com
Web Site: www.balch.com

2016 Total Lawyers: 234
2015 Total Lawyers: 235

Bradley Arant Boult & Cummings

One Federal Place
1819 Fifth Avenue North
Birmingham, AL 35203-2104
Phone: 205-521-8000
Fax: 205-521-8800
Email: info@bradleyarant.com
Web Site: www.bradleyarant.com

2016 Total Lawyers: 500
2015 Total Lawyers: 470

Burr & Forman LLP

420 North Twentieth Street
Suite 3400
Birmingham, AL 35203
Phone: 205-251-3000
Fax: 205-458-5100
Web Site: www.burr.com

2016 Total Lawyers: 279
2015 Total Lawyers: 278

Hand Arendall LLC

RSA Tower, Suite 30200
11 North Water St
Mobile, AL 36602
Phone: 251-432-5511
Web Site: www.handarendall.com

2016 Total Lawyers: 65
2015 Total Lawyers: 69

2016 Staff
Equity Partners: 51
Associates: 12
Staff Attorneys: 2

Offices: No. Attys.
2001 Park Place N, Ste 1200, Birmingham,
AL 35203: 26
11 N. Water St., Ste 30200, Mobile, AL
36602: 37

Hand Arendall LLC (Continued)
71 N. Section Street, Suite B, Farihope, AL
36532: 4
102 South Jefferson St., Athens, AL 35611: 2

Hiring and Promotion
2015 Associates Hired: 2
2015 First-Year Hires: 1
2016 First-Year Hires (Est.): 1
2015 Equity Partners Named: 0

Leading Practice Areas
(Department Heads)
Personal Injury/Property Damage/Defense
35% (Caine O'Rear)
Business Transaction/Commercial Law 17%
(Brooks Milling)
Civil/Commercial Lit/Defense 12%
(Caine O'Rear)
Real Estate/Commercial 7% (Neil Johnston)
Labor Management Rep. 5%
Securities Law 4% (Preston Bolt)
Admiralty/Marine Defense 4%
(Hodge Alves)

Leading Officials
Roger L. Bates, Managing Partner
James T. Allen, Firm Adminisrator
Katie Hammett Hassell, Recruiting Director
Nicole Weinacht, Marketing Director
Melvin Evans, Technology Director

Other Offices
11 North Water Street
Suite 30200
Mobile, Alabama 36602
Phone: 251-432-5511
Fax: 251-694-6375
R. Preston Bolt, Jr.

Maynard, Cooper & Gale, P.C.

1901 Sixth Avenue N.
2400 Regions Harbert Plaza
Birmingham, AL 35203-2618
Phone: 205-254-1000
Fax: 205-254-1999
Email: macoga@mcglaw.com
Web Site: www.maynardcooper.com

2016 Total Lawyers: 224
2015 Total Lawyers: 228

Sirote & Permutt, P.C.

2311 Highland Avenue, South
Birmingham, AL 35205
Phone: 205-930-5100
Fax: 205-930-5101
Web Site: www.Sirote.com

2016 Total Lawyers: 113
2015 Total Lawyers: 121

ARIZONA

Fennemore Craig

2394 East Camelback Road
Suite 600
Phoenix, AZ 85016-3429
Phone: 602-916-5000
Fax: 602-916-5999
Email: info@fclaw.com
Web Site: www.fennemorecraig.com

2016 Total Lawyers: 191
2015 Total Lawyers: 190

2016 Staff
Equity Partners: 90
Non-Equity Partners: 32
Associates: 37
Of Counsel: 30
Staff Attorneys: 2

Offices: No. Attys.
Phoenix, AZ: 118
Tucson, AZ: 6
Nogales, AZ: 3
Denver, CO: 22
Las Vegas, NV: 25
Reno, NV: 17

Hiring and Promotion
2015 Associates Hired: 10
2015 First-Year Hires: 6
2016 First-Year Hires (Est.): 5
2015 Equity Partners Named: 7
2015 Lateral Equity Partners: 2

ARIZONA

Fennemore Craig (Continued)

Leading Practice Areas
(Department Heads)
Litigation (Douglas C. Northup
602-916-5362)
Real Estate (Joseph Chandler 602-916-5403)
Employment & Labor Relations (John J.
Balitis, Jr. 602-916-5316)
Business & Finance (Susan M. Wissink
602-916-5319)
Bankruptcy, Creditors' Rights and
Restructuring (Cathy L. Reece
602-916-5343)
Estate Planning & Probate (James T. Lee
602-916-5422)
Intellectual Property (Bruce E. Dahl
303-291-3205)
Natural Resources, Energy, Environment, &
Utilities (Patrick J. Black and Robert
Anderson 602-916-5400, 602-916-5455)
Government Affairs (James Wadhams
702-692-8039)
Healthcare Litigation and Regulation (Scott
Finical 602-9165300)

Client Representations
Freeport-McMoRan Copper & Gold
ML Manager LLC - bankruptcy cases
Reno-Tahoe Airport Authority

Leading Officials
Sarah Strunk, Chairman, Board of Directors,
602-916-5327
Stephen Good, Chairman, Management
Committee, 602-916-5395
Kathy Hancock, Executive Director,
602-916-5410
Robert Kramer, Chief Talent Officer,
602-916-5464
Laura Zilmer, Attorney Recruitment
Administrator, 602-916-5272
Whitney Murray, Marketing Director,
602-916-5290
Dean Seiveno, Information Systems Director,
602-916-5802
Alexis Soard, Knowledge Manager,
602-916-5023
Phillip F. Fargotstein, Chief Diversity
Officer, 602-916-5453

Gallagher & Kennedy, P.A.

2575 East Camelback Road
Phoenix, AZ 85016-9225
Phone: 602-530-8000
Fax: 602-530-8500
Email: gk@gknet.com
Web Site: www.gknet.com

2016 Total Lawyers: 75
2015 Total Lawyers: 87

Jennings, Strouss & Salmon, PLC

One East Washington Street, Ste 1900
Phoenix, AZ 85004-2554
Phone: 602-262-5911
Fax: 602-253-3255
Email: info@jsslaw.com
Web Site: www.jsslaw.com

2016 Total Lawyers: 65
2015 Total Lawyers: 67

Lewis Roca Rothgerber LLP

201 East Washington
Suite 1200
Phoenix, AZ 85004
Phone: 602-262-5311
Fax: 602-262-5747
Email: info@LRRLaw.com
Web Site: www.LRRLaw.com

2016 Total Lawyers: 290
2015 Total Lawyers: 233

Ryley Carlock & Applewhite

One North Central Avenue
Suite 1200
Phoenix, AZ 85004
Phone: 602-440-4800
Fax: 602-257-9582
Web Site: www.rcalaw.com

2016 Total Lawyers: 120
2015 Total Lawyers: 120

Snell & Wilmer

One Arizona Center
400 E Van Buren Street
Phoenix, AZ 85004
Phone: 602-382-6000
Fax: 602-382-6070
Web Site: www.swlaw.com

2016 Total Lawyers: 404
2015 Total Lawyers: 419

ARKANSAS

Friday, Eldredge & Clark, LLP

400 W. Capitol, Suite 2000
Little Rock, AR 72201-3493
Phone: 501-376-2011
Fax: 501-376-2147
Email: eiseman@fridayfirm.com
Web Site: fridayfirm.com

2016 Total Lawyers: 86
2015 Total Lawyers: 84

Mitchell Williams Selig Gates Woodyard, PLLC

425 West Capitol Avenue
Suite 1800
Little Rock, AR 72201-3525
Phone: 501-688-8800
Fax: 501-688-8807
Web Site: www.mitchellwilliamslaw.com

2016 Total Lawyers: 88
2015 Total Lawyers: 97

Wright, Lindsey & Jennings, LLP

200 West Capitol Avenue
Suite 2300
Little Rock, AR 72201-3699
Phone: 501-371-0808
Fax: 501-376-9442
Email: info@wlj.com
Web Site: www.wlj.com

2016 Total Lawyers: 64
2015 Total Lawyers: 64

CALIFORNIA

Adelson, Testan, Brundo & Jimenez

5805 Sepulveda Blvd, #800
Van Nuys, CA 91411
Phone: 818-225-5868
Email: vannuys@atblaw.net
Web Site: www.atblaw.net

2016 Total Lawyers: 144
2015 Total Lawyers: 140

Allen Matkins

515 South Figueroa Street
9th floor
Los Angeles, CA 90071-3398
Phone: 949-851-5435
Fax: 949-553-8354
Email: communications@allenmatki
Web Site: www.allenmatkins.com

2016 Total Lawyers: 193
2015 Total Lawyers: 197

2016 Staff
Equity Partners: 88
Non-Equity Partners: 31
Associates: 71
Of Counsel: 3

Offices: No. Attys.
Los Angeles, CA (home office): 57
Orange County, CA: 42
San Diego, CA: 24
San Francisco, CA: 44
Century City, CA: 26

CALIFORNIA

Allen Matkins (Continued)

Hiring and Promotion
2015 Associates Hired: 13
2015 First-Year Hires: 6
Starting Salary for First-Year
Assocs: $160,000
2016 First-Year Hires (Est.): 7
2015 Equity Partners Named: 0

Leading Practice Areas
(Department Heads)
Real Estate 46% (Anton N. Natsis
310-788-2400)
Business Litigation 21% (Robert R. Moore
415-837-1515)
Corporate, Finance, & Tax 16% (Paul
O'Connor 949-851-5404)
Bankruptcy, Receiverships & Special
Creditor Remedies 7% (William Huckins
415-273-7426)
Labor & Employment 5% (Dwight L.
Armstrong 949-851-5424)
Environmental 5% (Sandi Nichols
415-273-7454)

Revenues and Profits
Revenues: $151,600,000
Profits: $80,200,000

Client Representations
Represented AEW Capital Management LP
in its sale of the West Eight Street building
in Seattle to Deutsche Asset Management's
RREEF division for $370 million. (6th
largest RE transaction in Q1)
Represented Kilroy Realty Corp. in its sale of
Santa Fe Summit Phase II in San Diego to
Intuit for $262 million. (9th largest RE
transaction in Q1)
Represented California-American Water
Company ("Cal-Am") as Trial Counsel in a
case involving a $400 million water
desalination project in Monterey County.

Leading Officials
David Osias, Managing Partner,
619-233-1155
Ralph Allen, Chief Operating Officer,
949-553-1313
Brian C. Leck, Lateral Hiring Integration
Partner, 213-622-5555
Lorraine Connally, Director of Recruiting and
Diversity, 213-622-5555
Adam Stock, Chief Marketing and Client
Services Officer, 415-837-1515
Ramona Whitley, Director or Client Services,
619-233-1155
Clark Snyder, Chief Technology Officer,
949-553-1313
Lorraine Connally, Director of Recruiting and
Diversity, 213-622-5555

Allen Matkins (Continued)

Other Offices
Downtown Los Angeles
515 South Figueroa Street
9th Floor
Los Angeles
California
90071-3309
Phone: 213-622-5555
Fax: 213-620-8816
George T. McDonnell, Office
Operating Partner

Orange County
1900 Main Street
5th Floor
Irvine
California
92614-7321
Phone: 949-553-1313
Fax: 949-553-8354
Drew M. Emmel, Office Operating Partner

San Diego
501 West Broadway
15th Floor
San Diego
California
92101-3541
Phone: 619-233-1155
Fax: 619-233-1158
Jeffrey R. Patterson, Office Operating Partner

Century City
1901 Avenue of the Stars
Suite 1800
Los Angeles
California
90067-6019
Phone: 310-788-2400
Fax: 310-788-2410
John M. Tipton, Office Operating Partner

San Francisco
Three Embarcadero Center
12th Floor
San Francisco
California
94111-4074
Phone: 415-837-1515
Fax: 415-837-1516
David D. Cooke, Office Operating Partner

Archer Norris, A Professional Corporation

2033 North Main St, Ste 800
Walnut Creek, CA 94596
Phone: 925-930-6600

2016 Total Lawyers: 96
2015 Total Lawyers: 101

Berger Kahn

2 Park Plaza
Suite 650
Irvine, CA 92614
Phone: 949-474-1880
Fax: 949-474-7265
Email: info@bergerkahn.com
Web Site: www.bergerkahn.com

2016 Total Lawyers: 19
2015 Total Lawyers: 19

Best Best & Krieger

3390 University Avenue, 5th Floor
P.O. Box 1028 92502
Riverside, CA 92501
Phone: 951-686-1450
Fax: 951-686-3083
Email: info@bbklaw.com
Web Site: www.bbklaw.com

2016 Total Lawyers: 182
2015 Total Lawyers: 171

2016 Staff
Equity Partners: 54
Non-Equity Partners: 43
Associates: 47
Of Counsel: 38

Offices: No. Attys.
Riverside, CA: 48
Indian Wells, CA: 6
Ontario, CA: 14
Irvine, CA: 19
San Diego, CA: 30
Sacramento, CA: 29
Walnut Creek, CA: 10
Los Angeles, CA: 20
Washington, D.C.: 6

Hiring and Promotion
2015 Associates Hired: 5
2015 First-Year Hires: 5
Starting Salary for First-Year
Assocs: $100,000
2016 First-Year Hires (Est.): 6
2015 Equity Partners Named: 4
2015 Lateral Equity Partners: 3

Leading Practice Areas
(Department Heads)
Municipal Law 33% (Jeffrey S. Ballinger
909-989-8584)
Business Services 17% (Howard B. Golds
951-686-1450)
Environmental & Natural Resources 16%
(Jeffry F. Ferre 951-686-1450)
Public Finance 8% (John R. Rottschaefer
951-686-1450)
Labor & Employment 7% (Alison D. Alpert
619-525-1300)
Special Districts 6% (Jeffry F. Ferre
951-686-1450)
Eminent Domain 5% (Mark A. Easter
951-686-1450)
Education Law 4% (Tyree K. Dorward
619-525-1300)
Bankruptcy 1% (Howard B. Golds
951-686-1450)
Estate Planning 1% (Howard Golds
951-686-1450)

CALIFORNIA

Best Best & Krieger (Continued)

Leading Officials
Eric L. Garner, Managing Partner,
  213-617-8100
Jamie B. Zamoff, Chief Operating Officer,
  619-525-1300
Danielle G. Sakai, Partner/Recruitment
  Committee Chair, 951-686-1450
Jill N. Willis, Chief Talent Officer,
  213-617-8100
Lisa C. Macias, Marketing Director,
  951-686-1450
Tim W. Haynes, Information Technology
  Director, 951-686-1450
Mark A. Gediman, Information Services
  Director, 951-686-1450
Danielle G. Sakai, Partner/Recruitment
  Committee Chair, 951-686-1450

Boies Schiller & Flexner

1999 Harrison Street
Suite 900
Oakland, CA 94612
Phone: 510-874-1000
Fax: 510-874-1460
Email: www.bsfllp.com

2016 Total Lawyers: 300
2015 Total Lawyers: 200

Bonne, Bridges, Mueller, O'Keefe & Nichols

3699 Wilshire Boulevard
Tenth Floor
Los Angeles, CA 90010
Phone: 213-480-1900
Fax: 213-738-5888
Web Site: www.bonnebridges.com

2016 Total Lawyers: 13
2015 Total Lawyers: 25

Borton Petrini, LLP

5060 California Avenue
Suite 700
Bakersfield, CA 93309
Phone: 661-322-3051
Email: bpbak@bpclaw.com
Web Site: www.bpclaw.com

2016 Total Lawyers: 44
2015 Total Lawyers: 50

Buchalter Nemer

1000 Wilshire Blvd, Ste 1500
Los Angeles, CA 90017-2457
Phone: 213-891-0700
Fax: 213-896-0400
Email: info@buchalter.com
Web Site: www.buchalter.com

2016 Total Lawyers: 178
2015 Total Lawyers: 162

Burke, Williams & Sorensen, LLP

444 S. Flower St.
Suite 2400
Los Angeles, CA 90071
Phone: 213-236-0600
Fax: 213-236-2700
Web Site: www.bwslaw.com

2016 Total Lawyers: 100
2015 Total Lawyers: 100

Burnham Brown

1901 Harrison Street
14th Floor
Oakland, CA 94612
Phone: 510-444-6800
Fax: 510-835-6666
Email: info@burnhambrown.com
Web Site: www.burnhambrown.com

2016 Total Lawyers: 30
2015 Total Lawyers: 37

Leading Officials
Gregory D. Brown, Firm Chair,
  510-444-6800
John J. Verber, Managing Partner,
  510-444-6800
Alice Wiley, Director of Human Resources,
  510-444-6800
Roxanne Jolicoeur, Marketing Manager,
  510-444-6800
Eloisa Mangliemot, IT Director,
  510-444-6800
Ahmina James, Head Librarian,
  510-444-6800
Rohit Sabnis, Attorney, 510-444-6800

Other Offices
Las Vegas
6671 S. Las Vegas Blvd.
210
Las Vegas
CA
89119
Phone: 702-761-6736
Lynn Rivera

Los Angeles
515 Flower Street
36th Floor
Los Angeles
CA
90071
Phone: 213-236-3647
Fax: 877-648-5288
Email: info@burnhambrown.com
Aneiko Hickerson

Burnham Brown (Continued)

Reno
200 S. Virginia Street
8th Floor
Reno
NV
89501
Phone: 775-398-3065
Fax: 877-648-5288
Email: info@burnhambrown.com
Lynn Rivera

Carroll, Burdick & McDonough LLP

44 Montgomery Street
Suite 400
San Francisco, CA 94104
Phone: 415-989-5900
Fax: 415-989-0932
Email: marketing@cbmlaw.com
Web Site: www.cbmlaw.com

2016 Total Lawyers: 63
2015 Total Lawyers: 68

2016 Staff
Equity Partners: 15
Non-Equity Partners: 26
Associates: 18
Of Counsel: 2
Staff Attorneys: 2

Offices: No. Attys.
San Francisco, CA: 41
Los Angeles, CA: 6
Sacramento: 5

Hiring and Promotion
2015 Associates Hired: 2
2015 Equity Partners Named: 0

Leading Practice Areas
(Department Heads)
Insurance Coverage (Gretchen Ramos
  415-989-5900)
Commercial and Business Litigation
  (Matthew Miller, Daniel Wu
  415-989-5900, 213-833-4500)
Appellate (Laurie Hepler, Troy Yoshino
  415-989-5900)
Corporate, Finance and Commercial Law
  (Siegmar Pohl 415-989-5900)
Practice Group Chair Leader (Gretchen
  Ramos 415-989-5900)
Intellectual Property (Matthew Miller, Jorg
  Staudenmayer, Daniel Wu 415-989-5900,
  7031-439-9600, 213-833-4500)
Products Liability (Justs Karlsons
  415-989-5900)

CALIFORNIA

Carroll, Burdick & McDonough LLP (Continued)

Leading Officials
Matthew Kemner, Chairman of the Firm,
415-989-5900
Doris Alexander, Executive Director,
415-989-5900
David Rice, Hiring Partner, 415-989-5900
Mary Holland, Human Resources Director,
415-989-5900
Marcia Delgadillo, Business Development
Manager, 415-989-5900
Joseph Craven, Director of Information
Systems, 415-989-5900
Caren Doyle, Head Librarian, 415-989-5900
Garrett Sanderson III, Partner, 415-989-5900

Cooley LLP

3175 Hanover Street
Palo Alto, CA 94306-2155
Phone: 650-843-5000
Fax: 650-857-0663
Web Site: www.cooley.com

2016 Total Lawyers: 900
2015 Total Lawyers: 850

Cooper, White & Cooper LLP

201 California Street
17th Floor
San Francisco, CA 94111
Phone: 415-433-1900
Fax: 415-433-5530
Web Site: www.cwclaw.com

2016 Total Lawyers: 33
2015 Total Lawyers: 33

Cox, Castle & Nicholson LLP

2049 Century Park East
28th Floor
Los Angeles, CA 90067-3284
Phone: 310-277-4222
Fax: 310-277-7889
Web Site: www.coxcastle.com

2016 Total Lawyers: 131
2015 Total Lawyers: 137

Downey Brand LLP

621 Capitol Mall
18th Floor
Sacramento, CA 95814
Phone: 916-444-1000
Fax: 916-444-2100
Email: downey@downeybrand.com
Web Site: www.downeybrand.com

2016 Total Lawyers: 99
2015 Total Lawyers: 96

Ervin Cohen & Jessup LLP

9401 Wilshire Boulevard
Ninth Floor
Beverly Hills, CA 90212
Phone: 310-273-6333
Fax: 310-859-2325
Email: info@ecjlaw.com
Web Site: www.ecjlaw.com

2016 Total Lawyers: 54
2015 Total Lawyers: 50

2016 Staff
Associates: 7
Of Counsel: 9
Partners 34

Offices: No. Attys.
Beverly Hills, CA: 50

Farella Braun + Martel LLP

235 Montgomery Street, 17th Floor
San Francisco, CA 94104
Phone: 415-954-4400
Fax: 415-954-4480
Web Site: www.fbm.com

2016 Total Lawyers: 126
2015 Total Lawyers: 126

2016 Staff
Associates: 44
Of Counsel: 4
Special Counsel: 2
Partners: 76

Offices: No. Attys.
St. Helena, CA: 3
San Francisco, CA: 123

Leading Officials
Steven Lowenthal, Firm Chairman,
415-954-4405
Judy Todd, Executive Director,
415-954-4477
Tyler Gerking, Hiring Partner, 415-954-4968
Ingrid Hester, Director of Human Resources,
415-954-4923
David Bruns, Director of Client Services,
415-954-4484
Shirley Crow, Chief Information Officer,
415-954-4986
Judy Heier, Head Librarian, 415-954-4714
Priscilla Zaccalini, Diversity Coordinator,
415-954-3547

Fenwick & West LLP

Silicon Valley Center
801 California St.
Mountain View, CA 94041
Phone: 650-988-8500
Email: info@fenwick.com
Web Site: www.fenwick.com

2016 Total Lawyers: 396
2015 Total Lawyers: 376

Fenwick & West LLP (Continued)

2016 Staff
Associates: 206
Of Counsel: 12
Counsel: 5
Senior Counsel: 2
Staff Attorneys: 12
Partners 117

Offices: No. Attys.
Mountain View, CA: 220
San Francisco, CA: 84
Seattle, WA: 34
Williston, VT: 2

Hiring and Promotion
Starting Salary for First-Year
Assocs: $160,000
2015 Equity Partners Named: 9
2015 Lateral Equity Partners: 3

*Leading Practice Areas
(Department Heads)*
Corporate (Alan Smith 206-389-4530)
Intellectual Property (Lawrence Granatelli
650-335-7151)
Litigation (Rodger Cole 650-335-7603)
Tax (David L. Forst 650-335-7254)

Revenues and Profits
Revenues: $363,500,000

Client Representations
Represented King Digital in $5.9B
acquisition by Activision Blizzard
Represented Supercell Oy in $8.6B majority
stake acquisition by Tencent
Represented Symantec in $7.4B sale of
Veritas Technologies to the Carlyle Group

Leading Officials
Richard Dickson, Chair, 650-335-7679
Kathryn J. Fritz, Managing Partner,
415-875-2328
Scott Pine, Chief Operating Officer,
650-428-4404
Cheri Vaillancour, Chief Professional
Development Officer, 650-335-7277
Julieta Stubrin, Director of Attorney Talent
Acquisition, Diversity & Inclusion,
415-875-2464
Robert A. Kahn, Chief Marketing Officer,
650-335-7616
Michael Zwerin, Director of Business
Development, 650-335-7378
Matt Kesner, Chief Information Officer,
650-428-4488
Camille Reynolds, Director of Knowledge
Management , 415-875-2433
Julieta Stubrin, Director of Attorney Talent
Acquisition, Diversity & Inclusion,
415-875-2464

Other Offices
San Francisco, CA
555 California St.
12th Floor
San Francisco
CA
94104
Phone: 415-875-2300

CALIFORNIA

Fenwick & West LLP (Continued)

Mountain View, CA
801 California St.
Mountain View
CA
94041
Phone: 650-988-8500

Gibson, Dunn & Crutcher

333 South Grand Avenue
Los Angeles, CA 90071-3197
Phone: 213-229-7000
Fax: 213-229-7520
Web Site: www.gibsondunn.com

2016 Total Lawyers: 1253
2015 Total Lawyers: 1243

2016 Staff
Equity Partners: 371
Associates: 814
Of Counsel: 67
Senior Attorneys: 1
Partners 368

Offices: No. Attys.
Denver, CO: 36
Dallas, TX: 60
Orange County, CA: 70
Brussels, Belgium: 15
Munich, Germany: 15
Paris, France: 19
London, England: 78
Palo Alto, CA: 49
San Francisco, CA: 85
Washington, D.C.: 204
New York, NY: 322
Los Angeles, CA: 225
Dubai, UAE: 15
Singapore: 13
Beijing, China: 3
Century City, CA: 27
Hong Kong: 15
Sao Paulo, Brazil: 2

Hiring and Promotion
2015 First-Year Hires: 119
Starting Salary for First-Year
   Assocs: $160,000
2016 First-Year Hires (Est.): 0
2015 Equity Partners Named: 22
2015 Lateral Equity Partners: 14

Revenues and Profits
Revenues: $1,535,271,042

Leading Officials
Kenneth M. Doran, Managing Partner
Charles Woodhouse, Executive Director
Steven Sletten, Hiring Committee Chair
Leslie Ripley, Chief Recruiting Officer
Judy Bay, Chief Marketing Officer
Brett Fazio, Chief Information Officer
Dena Hollingsworth, Associate Director
Zakiyyah Salim-Williams, Chief Diversity
   Officer. 212-351-2326

Gibson, Dunn & Crutcher (Continued)

Other Offices
New York
200 Park Avenue
New York
NY
10166-0193
Phone: 212-351-4000
Fax: 212-351-4035
Mark Kirsch, Steven Shoemate, Co-Partners
in Charge

Washington, DC
1051 Connecticut Avenue N.W.
Washington
DC
20036-5306
Phone: 202-955-8500
Fax: 202-467-0539
Daniel Nelson, Andrew Tulumello,
   Co-Partners in Charge

Orange County
3161 Michelson Drive
Irvine
CA
92612-4412
Phone: 949-451-3800
Fax: 949-451-4220
Michael Flynn, Meryl Young, Co-Partners
in Charge

San Francisco
555 Mission Street
Suite 3000
San Francisco
CA
94105-0921
Phone: 415-393-8200
Fax: 415-393-8306
Charles Stevens, Partner in Charge

Los Angeles
333 South Grand Avenue
Los Angeles
CA
90071-3197
Phone: 213-229-7000
Fax: 213-229-7520
Christopher Chorba, Amy Forbes,
   Co-Partners in Charge

London
Telephone House, 2-4 Temple Avenue
London
UK
EC4Y 0HB
Phone: 440-207-0714 ext. 000
James Cox, Jeffrey Trinklein, Co-Partners
in Charge

Dallas
2100 McKinney Avenue
Suite 1100
Dallas
TX
75201-6912
Phone: 214-698-3100
Fax: 214-571-2900
Robert Walters, Partner in Charge

Gilbert, Kelly, Crowley & Jennett

1055 West Seventh St, Ste 2000
Los Angeles, CA 90017
Phone: 213-615-7000
Fax: 213-615-7100
Web Site: www.gilbertkelly.com

2016 Total Lawyers: 32
2015 Total Lawyers: 32

Glaser, Weil, Fink, Jacobs, Howard, Avchen & Shapiro

10250 Contellation Blvd
19th Floor
Los Angeles, CA 90067
Phone: 310-553-3000
Fax: 310-556-2920
Email: info@glaserweil.com
Web Site: www.glaserweil.com

2016 Total Lawyers: 97
2015 Total Lawyers: 97

Gordon & Rees LLP

275 Battery Street
Suite 2000
San Francisco, CA 94111
Phone: 415-986-5900
Fax: 415-986-8054
Web Site: www.gordonrees.com

2016 Total Lawyers: 700
2015 Total Lawyers: 648

Greenberg Glusker

1900 Avenue of the Stars
21st Floor
Los Angeles, CA 90067
Phone: 310-553-3610
Fax: 310-553-0687
Email: info@ggfirm.com
Web Site: www.ggfirm.com

2016 Total Lawyers: 86
2015 Total Lawyers: 86

Haight, Brown & Bonesteel LLP

555 South Flower Street
45th Floor
Los Angeles, CA 90071
Phone: 310-215-7100
Fax: 310-215-7300
Email: contacthbb@hbblaw.com
Web Site: www.hbblaw.com

2016 Total Lawyers: 65
2015 Total Lawyers: 58

CALIFORNIA

Hanson Bridgett

425 Market Street
Floor 26
San Francisco, CA 94105
Phone: 415-777-3200
Fax: 415-541-9366
Email: info@hansonbridgett.com
Web Site: www.hansonbridgett.com

2016 Total Lawyers: 162
2015 Total Lawyers: 162

2016 Staff
Equity Partners: 62
Non-Equity Partners: 33
Associates: 33
Of Counsel: 4
Counsel: 13
Senior Counsel: 15
Contract Attorneys 2

Offices: No. Attys.
San Francisco, CA: 133
Sacramento, CA: 15
Larkspur, CA: 8
Walnut Creek, CA: 6

Hiring and Promotion
2015 Associates Hired: 7
2015 First-Year Hires: 2
2016 First-Year Hires (Est.): 4
2015 Equity Partners Named: 3
2015 Lateral Equity Partners: 1

Leading Practice Areas
(Department Heads)
Construction (Lisa Dal Gallo 415-995-5188)
Health & Long-Term Care (Deidr Schnfeldt 415-995-5050)
Labor & Employment (Jahmal Davis 415-995-5815)
Litigation (Merton Howard 415-995-5033)
Government (Patrick Miyaki 415-995-5048)
Business & Commercial (Jonathan Storper 415-995-5040)
Real Estate (David Longinotti 415-995-5041)
Technology (Robert McFarlane 415-995-5072)
Intellectual Property (Susan O'Neill 415-995-5037)
Employee Benefits (Alison Wright 415-995-5083)

Client Representations
Golden Gate Bridge, Highway &
Transportation District
American Seniors Housing Association
Prologis, Inc.

Hanson Bridgett (Continued)

Leading Officials
Andrew G. Giacomini, Managing Partner, 415-995-5059
James J. Nichols, Chief Operating Officer, 415-995-5198
Jahmal T. Davis, Partner, 415-995-5815
Naomi J. Smith, Director of Attorney Recruiting & Diversity, 415-995-5877
Michelle H. Klopp, Chief Marketing Officer, 415-995-5075
Christopher J. Fryer, Chief Information Officer, 415-995-5850
Open Position
André Campbell, Partner, Diversity Committee Chair, 916-491-3014

Other Offices
San Francisco
425 Market Street
Floor 26
San Francisco
CA
94105
Phone: 415-777-3200
Fax: 415-541-9366
Email: info@hansonbridgett.com
Andrew G. Giacomini

Harrington, Foxx, Dubrow & Canter

1055 West Seventh Steet
29th Floor
Los Angeles, CA 90017
Phone: 213-489-3222
Web Site: www.hfdclaw.com

2016 Total Lawyers: 20
2015 Total Lawyers: 21

Higgs, Fletcher & Mack LLP

401 West A Street
Suite 2600
San Diego, CA 92101-7910
Phone: 619-236-1551
Fax: 619-696-1410
Email: info@higgslaw.com
Web Site: www.higgslaw.com

2016 Total Lawyers: 77
2015 Total Lawyers: 71

Hill, Farrer & Burrill LLP

One California Plaza, 37th Floor
300 South Grand Avenue
Los Angeles, CA 90071-3147
Phone: 213-620-0460
Fax: 213-624-4840
Email: info@hillfarrer.com
Web Site: www.hillfarrer.com

2016 Total Lawyers: 42
2015 Total Lawyers: 41

2016 Staff
Equity Partners: 29
Associates: 5
Of Counsel: 8

Hill, Farrer & Burrill LLP (Continued)

Offices: No. Attys.
Los Angeles, CA: 42

Hiring and Promotion
2015 Associates Hired: 2
2015 First-Year Hires: 1
2016 First-Year Hires (Est.): 0
2015 Equity Partners Named: 0

Leading Practice Areas
(Department Heads)
Litigation (Neil D. Martin 213-620-0460)
Corporate & Business Law (Michael J. DiBiase 213-620-0460)
Tax & Estate Planning (Thomas F. Reed 213-620-0460)
Labor & Employment (James A. Bowles 213-620-0460)
Real Estate Law (Stacey A. Sullivan 213-620-0460)
Condemnation (Kevin H. Brogan 213-620-0460)
Bankruptcy (Daniel J. McCarthy 213-620-0460)
ERISA (Thomas F. Reed 213-620-0460)

Leading Officials
Scott L. Gilmore, Managing Partner, 213-620-0460
Dalia Cleveland, Chief Financial Officer, 213-620-0460
Scott L. Gilmore, Hiring Partner, 213-620-0460
Scott L. Gilmore, Recruiting Director, 213-620-0460
Sara Bittle, Marketing Coordinator, 213-620-0460
Gerry Rubalcaba, IT Manager, 213-620-0460
Monica Justice, Librarian, 213-620-0460

Hoge, Fenton, Jones & Appel, Inc.

60 South Market Street
Suite 1400
San Jose, CA 95113-2396
Phone: 408-287-9501
Fax: 408-287-2583
Web Site: www.hogefenton.com

2016 Total Lawyers: 42
2015 Total Lawyers: 41

Irell & Manella LLP

1800 Avenue of the Stars
Suite 900
Los Angeles, CA 90067
Phone: 310-277-1010
Fax: 310-203-7199
Web Site: www.irell.com

2016 Total Lawyers: 126
2015 Total Lawyers: 143

CALIFORNIA

Jeffer, Mangels, Butler & Mitchell LLP

1900 Avenue of the Stars
7th Floor
Los Angeles, CA 90067
Phone: 310-203-8080
Fax: 310-203-0567
Email: info@jmbm.com
Web Site: www.jmbm.com

2016 Total Lawyers: 111
2015 Total Lawyers: 110

Keesal, Young & Logan, P.C.

400 Oceangate
P.O. Box 1730
Long Beach, CA 90801-1730
Phone: 562-436-2000
Fax: 562-436-7416
Email: marilyn.wills@kyl.com
Web Site: www.kyl.com

2016 Total Lawyers: 73
2015 Total Lawyers: 75

Knapp, Petersen & Clarke, A Professional Corporation

550 North Brand Boulevard
Suite 1500
Glendale, CA 91203
Phone: 818-547-5000
Fax: 818-547-5329
Web Site: kpelegal.wld.com

2016 Total Lawyers: 20
2015 Total Lawyers: 21

Knobbe Martens Olson & Bear, LLP

2040 Main Street
14th Floor
Irvine, CA 92614
Phone: 949-760-0404
Fax: 949-760-9502
Email: info@knobbe.com
Web Site: www.knobbe.com

2016 Total Lawyers: 281
2015 Total Lawyers: 272

2016 Staff
Equity Partners: 152
Associates: 129
Counsel: 2
Staff Attorneys: 11
Patent Counsel 3

Offices: No. Attys.
San Francisco, CA: 13
Washington D.C.: 8
Silicon Valley, CA: 3
Seattle, WA: 16
Los Angeles, CA: 9

Knobbe Martens Olson & Bear,
LLP (Continued)
San Diego, CA: 65
Orange County, CA: 167

Hiring and Promotion
2015 Associates Hired: 34
2015 First-Year Hires: 29
Starting Salary for First-Year
Assocs: $150,000
2016 First-Year Hires (Est.): 24
2015 Equity Partners Named: 2

*Leading Practice Areas
(Department Heads)*
Patent Prosecution 42%
IP Litigation 35%
Other IP Services 17%
Trademark Prosecution 6%

Client Representations
Successful representation of CardiAQ Valve
  Technologies in trade secret
  misappropriation jury trial resulting in $70
  million verdict
Lead IP counsel for Masimo Corp. in many
  significant IP matters
Lead trademark counsel for Broadcom Corp.,
  including in acquisition by Avago
  Technologies

Leading Officials
Steven J. Nataupsky, Managing Partner,
  949-760-0404
Jenny Cox, Director of Administration,
  949-760-0404
Ben Katzenellenbogen, Attorney Recruiting
  Committee Chair, 949-760-0404
Amy Langan, Senior Attorney Recruiting
  Coordinator, 949-760-0404
Krista Hosseinzadeh, Director of Business
  Development, 949-760-0404
Mike Treanor, Director of Information
  Technology, 949-760-0404
Renee Cabaruvias, Information Resource
  Specialist, 949-760-0404
Rabi Narula, Partner, 949-760-0404

Other Offices
Knobbe Martens Orange County
  Headquarters
2040 Main Street
14th Floor
Irvine
CA
92614
Phone: 949-760-0404
Fax: 949-760-9502
Email: info@knobbe.com
Steven J. Nataupsky

Knobbe Martens San Diego Office
12790 El Camino Real
San Diego
California
92130
Phone: 858-707-4000
Fax: 858-707-4001
Email: info@knobbe.com
Ned Israelsen

Kramer, Deboer, Endelicato & Keane

21860 Burbank Blvd
Suite 3
Woodland Hills, CA 91363
Phone: 818-657-0255
Fax: 818-657-0256
Web Site: www.kdeklaw.com

2016 Total Lawyers: 16
2015 Total Lawyers: 18

2016 Staff
Equity Partners: 3
Non-Equity Partners: 6
Associates: 7

Offices: No. Attys.
Indian Wells, CA: 8
Los Angeles: 8

Hiring and Promotion
2015 Associates Hired: 1
2015 First-Year Hires: 1

Client Representations
The Doctors Company
NORCAL
AIG/YORK

Kronick, Moskovitz, Tiedemann & Girard

400 Capitol Mall
27th Floor
Sacramento, CA 95814
Phone: 916-321-4500
Fax: 916-321-4555
Email: info@kmtg.com
Web Site: www.kmtg.com

2016 Total Lawyers: 41
2015 Total Lawyers: 54

La Follette, Johnson, De Haas, Fesler & Ames

865 South Figueroa Street
Suite 3200
Los Angeles, CA 90017-5431
Phone: 213-426-3600
Fax: 213-426-3650
Web Site: www.ljdfa.com

2016 Total Lawyers: 56
2015 Total Lawyers: 53

Lewis Brisbois Bisgaard & Smith

221 North Figueroa St, Ste 1200
Los Angeles, CA 90012
Phone: 213-250-1800
Web Site: www.lbbslaw.com

2016 Total Lawyers: 1000
2015 Total Lawyers: 987

CALIFORNIA

Liner LLP

1100 Glendon Ave, 14th Floor
Los Angeles, CA 90024
Phone: 310-500-3500
Fax: 310-500-3501
Web Site: http://www.linerlaw.com/

2016 Total Lawyers: 75
2015 Total Lawyers: 76

Littler

CA
Web Site: www.littler.com

2016 Total Lawyers: 993
2015 Total Lawyers: 1037

2016 Staff
Equity Partners: 388
Non-Equity Partners: 93
Associates: 512
Littler categorizes Of Counsel attorneys in the Associates category. 512

Offices: No. Attys.
Albuquerque, NM: 1
Anchorage, AK: 1
Atlanta, GA: 36
Birmingham, AL: 5
Boston, MA: 17
Charlotte, NC: 7
Chicago, IL: 35
Cleveland, OH: 29
Columbia, SC: 1
Columbus, OH: 17
Dallas, TX: 38
Denver, CO: 17
Detroit, MI: 7
Fayetteville, AR: 2
Flextime Attorneys, Miami: 54
Fresno, CA: 10
Houston, TX: 29
Indianapolis, IN: 7
Irvine, CA: 22
Kansas City, MO: 8
Las Vegas, NV: 12
Lexington, KY: 4
Long Island, NY: 12
Los Angeles, CA (Downtown): 20
Los Angeles, CA (Century City): 56
Memphis, TN: 10
Mexico City, MX: 18
Miami, FL: 19
Milwaukee, WI: 7
Minneapolis, MN: 33
Monterrey, MX: 8
Morgantown, WV: 5
Nashville, TN: 7
New Haven, CT: 8
New York, NY: 38
Newark, NJ: 24
Orlando, FL: 6
Philadelphia, PA: 29
Phoenix, AZ: 15
Pittsburgh, PA: 15
Portland, ME: 5
Portland, OR: 9
Providence, RI: 3
Reno, NV: 11
Rochester, NY: 8

Littler (Continued)
Sacramento, CA: 8
San Diego, CA: 25
San Francisco, CA: 70
San Jose, CA: 26
Seattle, WA: 12
St. Louis, MO: 13
Tyson's Corner, VA: 8
Walnut Creek, CA: 15
Washington, D.C.: 37
Austin, TX: 4
Valencia, VZ: 7
Caracas, VZ: 12

Hiring and Promotion
2015 Associates Hired: 89
2015 First-Year Hires: 17
Starting Salary for First-Year Assocs: Per
    Littler's policy, we do not disclose salary
    information
2016 First-Year Hires (Est.): 16
2015 Equity Partners Named: 32
2015 Lateral Equity Partners: 7

Leading Practice Areas
(Department Heads)
Labor & Employment 100%

Client Representations
Per Littler's policy, we do not disclose client
    information.

Leading Officials
Lisa (Lee) Schreter, Chairman of the Board,
    404-233-0330
Jeremy Roth and Thomas Bender,
    Co-President and Managing Directors,
    619-232-0441
Robert Domingues, Chief Operating Officer,
    415-433-1940
Jeremy Roth and Thomas Bender, Co-Chair
    National Recruiting Committee,
    619-232-0441
Karen Herz, Sr. Director Attorney Recruiting
    & Development, 415-433-1940
James Durham, Chief Marketing & Business
    Development Officer, 617-378-6000
James Durham, Chief Marketing & Business
    Development Officer, 617-378-6000
Durgesh Sharma, Chief Information Officer,
    206-623-3300
Cynthia Brown, Director, Research Services,
    559-244-7532
Mark Phillis, Co-Chair, Diversity and
    Inclusion Council, 412-201-7636

Other Offices
Los Angeles - Century City
2049 Century Park East
5th Floor
Los Angeles
CA
90067
Phone: 310-553-0308
Fax: 310-553-5583
Email: rblumberg@littler.com
Robert Blumberg

Littler (Continued)
San Francisco, CA
333 Bush Street
34th Floor
San Francisco
CA
94104
Phone: 415-433-1940
Fax: 415-399-8490
Email: mbrewer@littler.com
Michael Brewer

Loeb & Loeb LLP

10100 Santa Monica Boulevard
Suite 2200
Los Angeles, CA 90067
Phone: 310-282-2000
Fax: 310-282-2200
Email: alerts@loeb.com
Web Site: www.loeb.com

2016 Total Lawyers: 338
2015 Total Lawyers: 281

Long & Levit LLP

465 California Street
Suite 500
San Francisco, CA 94104
Phone: 415-397-2222
Fax: 415-397-6392
Web Site: www.longlevit.com

2016 Total Lawyers: 24
2015 Total Lawyers: 24

Manatt, Phelps & Phillips

11355 West Olympic Boulevard
Los Angeles, CA 90064
Phone: 310-312-4000
Fax: 310-312-4224
Web Site: www.manatt.com

2016 Total Lawyers: 349
2015 Total Lawyers: 356

2016 Staff
Equity Partners: 63
Non-Equity Partners: 139
Associates: 103
Counsel: 32
Senior Counsel: 6
Staff Attorneys: 6

Offices: No. Attys.
Los Angeles, CA: 157
New York, NY: 59
Costa Mesa, CA: 33
Palo Alto, CA: 8
Sacramento, CA: 3
San Francisco, CA: 43
Washington, DC: 40
Albany, NY: 6

Hiring and Promotion
2015 Associates Hired: 28
2015 First-Year Hires: 10
2016 First-Year Hires (Est.): 7
2015 Equity Partners Named: 3
2015 Lateral Equity Partners: 1

CALIFORNIA

Manatt, Phelps & Phillips (Continued)

*Leading Practice Areas
(Department Heads)*
Litigation 45% (Matt Kanny 310-312-4000)
Business, Finance & Tax 26% (Gordon Bava
310-312-4000)
Land, Environment & Natural Resources
13% (Craig Moyer 310-312-4000)
Healthcare 8% (William Bernstein
212-790-4500)
Government and Regulatory 5% (George
Kieffer 310-312-4000)
Advertising, Marketing & Media 3% (Linda
Goldstein 212-790-4500)

Revenues and Profits
Revenues: $324,000,000
Profits: $81,600,000

Leading Officials
William T. Quicksilver, Chief Executive and
Managing Partner
Edith Gould, Executive Director
William T. Quicksilver, Recruiting
Committee Chair
Susan Reonegro, National
Recruiting Manager
Jodie Collins, Senior Director of Business
Development & Marketing
Bob Schneider, Director of Technology
Debbie Schwarz, Director of
Information Services
Michelle Cooke, Diversity Committee Chair,
310-312-4208

Other Offices
New York, NY
7 Times Square
New York
NY
10036
Phone: 212-790-4500
Fax: 212-790-4545

McCormick, Barstow, Sheppard, Wayte & Carruth LLP

7647 N. Fresno Street
Fresno, CA 93720
Phone: 559-433-1300
Fax: 559-433-2300
Web Site: www.mccormickbarstow.com

2016 Total Lawyers: 85
2015 Total Lawyers: 88

Miller Starr Regalia

1331 North California Boulevard
Fifth Floor
Walnut Creek, CA 94596
Phone: 925-935-9400
Fax: 925-933-4126
Email: MSR@msrlegal.com
Web Site: www.msrlegal.com

2016 Total Lawyers: 46
2015 Total Lawyers: 45

Mitchell Silberberg & Knupp LLP

11377 West Olympic Boulevard
Los Angeles, CA 90064-1683
Phone: 310-312-2000
Fax: 310-312-3100
Email: info@msk.com
Web Site: www.msk.com

2016 Total Lawyers: 130
2015 Total Lawyers: 130

Morris Polich & Purdy

1055 West Seventh Street
Twenty-Fourth Floor
Los Angeles, CA 90017
Phone: 213-891-9100
Fax: 213-488-1178
Email: gbrandon@mpplaw.com
Web Site: www.mpplaw.com

2016 Total Lawyers: 79
2015 Total Lawyers: 84

2016 Staff
Equity Partners: 24
Non-Equity Partners: 20
Associates: 30
Of Counsel: 5

Offices: No. Attys.
Los Angeles: 47
Las Vegas, NV: 7
San Francisco: 15
San Diego: 10

Hiring and Promotion
2015 Associates Hired: 5
2015 Equity Partners Named: 2

Morris Polich & Purdy (Continued)

*Leading Practice Areas
(Department Heads)*
Civil Litigation (Michael West
213-417-5310)
Life Sciences/Products Liability (Marilyn
Jager 213-417-5112)
Commercial Litigation (Tim Flaherty
415-984-8507)
Employment Law (Beth Kahn 213-417-5131)
Long Term Care & Health Care (Marc Katz
213-417-5114)
Construction & Design (Theodore Levin, P.E.
213-417-5309)
Insurance Coverage (Douglas Wood
415-984-8502)
Appellate Advocacy (Richard Nakamura
213-417-5335)
Professional Liability (Penelope Deihl
213-417-5313)
Environmental Law (Steve Hoch
213-417-5185)

Leading Officials
Donald Ridge, Managing Partner,
213-417-5117
Tammie McQuain, Executive Director,
213-417-2433
Dean Olson, Hiring Partner, 213-417-5132
Neomi Escudero, Attorney Recruiting
Coordinator, 213-417-5154
George Brandon, Partnership Development
Leader, 213-417-5124
Pedro Rios, IT Manager, 213-417-5159

Other Offices
Los Angeles
1055 West Seventh Street
Twenty-Fourth Floor
Los Angeles
CA
90017
Phone: 213-891-9100
Fax: 213-488-1178

Morrison & Foerster LLP

425 Market Street
San Francisco, CA 94105
Phone: 415-268-7000
Fax: 415-268-7522
Email: info@mofo.com
Web Site: www.mofo.com

2016 Total Lawyers: 1025
2015 Total Lawyers: 1000

Munger, Tolles & Olson

355 South Grand Avenue
35th Floor
Los Angeles, CA 90071-1560
Phone: 213-683-9100
Fax: 213-687-3702
Email: info@mto.com
Web Site: www.mto.com

2016 Total Lawyers: 188
2015 Total Lawyers: 203

CALIFORNIA

Murchison & Cumming

801 South Grand Avenue
9th Floor
Los Angeles, CA 90017
Phone: 213-623-7400
Fax: 213-623-6336
Web Site: www.murchisonlaw.com

2016 Total Lawyers: 83
2015 Total Lawyers: 80

Musick, Peeler & Garrett LLP

One Wilshire Boulevard
Suite 2000
Los Angeles, CA 90017
Phone: 213-629-7600
Fax: 213-624-1376
Web Site: www.musickpeeler.com

2016 Total Lawyers: 101
2015 Total Lawyers: 101

O'Melveny & Myers LLP

400 South Hope Street
Los Angeles, CA 90071
Phone: 213-430-6000
Fax: 213-430-6407
Email: omminfo@omm.com
Web Site: www.omm.com

2016 Total Lawyers: 700
2015 Total Lawyers: 700

Orrick, Herrington & Sutcliffe LLP

405 Howard St
San Francisco, CA 94105-2669
Phone: 415-773-5700
Fax: 415-773-5759
Email: pr@orrick.com
Web Site: www.orrick.com

2016 Total Lawyers: 1100
2015 Total Lawyers: 1077

Parker, Milliken, Clark, O'Hara & Samuelian, P.C.

555 South Flower St
30th Floor
Los Angeles, CA 90071
Phone: 213-683-6500
Fax: 213-683-6669
Web Site: www.parkermilliken.com

2016 Total Lawyers: 36
2015 Total Lawyers: 36

Paul, Hastings, Janofsky & Walker LLP

515 South Flower Street
Twenty Fifth Floor
Los Angeles, CA 90071
Phone: 213-683-6000
Fax: 213-627-0704
Email: info@paulhastings.com
Web Site: www.paulhastings.com

2016 Total Lawyers: 1000
2015 Total Lawyers: 865

Pircher, Nichols & Meeks

1925 Century Park East
Suite 1700
Los Angeles, CA 90067
Phone: 310-201-8900
Fax: 310-201-8922
Web Site: www.pircher.com

2016 Total Lawyers: 54
2015 Total Lawyers: 56

Procopio, Cory, Hargreaves & Savitch LLP

525 B Street
Suite 2200
San Diego, CA 92101
Phone: 619-238-1900
Fax: 619-235-0398
Web Site: www.procopio.com

2016 Total Lawyers: 152
2015 Total Lawyers: 151

2016 Staff
Equity Partners: 42
Non-Equity Partners: 24
Associates: 41
Of Counsel: 11
Senior Counsel: 24
Staff Attorneys: 10

Offices: No. Attys.
San Diego, CA: 106
Phoenix, AZ: 1
Del Mar Heights, CA: 35
Silicon Valley, CA: 8
Austin, TX: 2

Hiring and Promotion
2015 Associates Hired: 7
2015 First-Year Hires: 4
2016 First-Year Hires (Est.): unknown
2015 Equity Partners Named: 2

Procopio, Cory, Hargreaves & Savitch
LLP (Continued)

Leading Practice Areas
(Department Heads)
Litigation (S. Todd Neal 619-525-3890)
Corporate/Securities (Dennis J. Doucette
858-720-6322)
Real Estate and Environmental (Michael E.
Lyon 760-496-0782)
Tax (Patrick W. Martin 619-515-3230)
Intellectual Property (Richard E. Campbell
619.515.3289)
Healthcare, Education, and Government
(Gregory C. Moser 619-515-3208)
Labor & Employment (Marie Burke Kenny
619-525-3876)
Construction (Craig A. Ramseyer
619-515-3227)
Business & Technology (John P. Cleary
619-515-3221)
Intellectual Property Litigation (Anthony J.
Dain 619-515-3241)

Leading Officials
Thomas W. Turner, Managing Partner,
619-515-3276
James G. Perkins, Chief Operating Officer,
619-515-3211
Lauren Symington, Director of HR &
Administration, 619-525-3823
Kim Jewell, Director of Marketing and
Marketing Technology, 619-906-5784
Craig Crosby, Director of Information
Services, 619-515-3275
Tiffany O'Neil, Director, Knowledge
Management & Research Services,
619-515-3232
Sandra L. Shippey, Partner, 619-515-3226

Other Offices
525 B Street
Ste 2200
San Diego
CA
92101
Phone: 619-238-1900
Fax: 619-235-0398
Thomas W. Turner, Managing Partner

Quinn Emanuel Urquhart & Sullivan LLP

865 S. Figueroa St, 10th Fl
Los Angeles, CA 90017
Phone: 213-443-3000
Fax: 213-443-3100
Web Site: www.quinnemanuel.com

2016 Total Lawyers: 650
2015 Total Lawyers: 700

CALIFORNIA

Richards, Watson & Gershon

355 South Grand Avenue
40th Floor
Los Angeles, CA 90071
Phone: 213-626-8484
Fax: 213-626-0078
Email: msugg@rwglaw.com
Web Site: www.rwglaw.com

2016 Total Lawyers: 64
2015 Total Lawyers: 62

Ropers, Majeski, Kohn, & Bentley, P.C.

1001 Marshall Street, Suite 500
Redwood City, CA 94063
Phone: 650-364-8200
Fax: 650-780-1701
Web Site: www.rmkb.com

2016 Total Lawyers: 90
2015 Total Lawyers: 94

2016 Staff
Equity Partners: 28
Non-Equity Partners: 23
Associates: 26
Of Counsel: 13

Offices: No. Attys.
Redwood City, CA: 33
San Francisco, CA: 8
Los Angeles, CA: 20
New York, NY: 15
Boston, MA: 1
San Jose, CA: 13
Seattle, WA: 1
Las Vegas, NV: 3
Paris, France: 1

Hiring and Promotion
2015 Associates Hired: 3
Starting Salary for First-Year Assocs: WND
to all
2016 First-Year Hires (Est.): N/A
2015 Equity Partners Named: 0

Leading Practice Areas
(Department Heads)
Miscellaneous Commercial Litigation 26%
Insurance Services 15%
Corporate Transactions 15%
Labor & Employment 13%
Intellectual Property 10%
Professional Liability 5%
Banking Liability 5%
Real Estate 5%
Construction 3%
Product Liability 3%

Client Representations
Wipro Limited
HCL America, Inc.
Maxim Integrated Products, Inc.

Ropers, Majeski, Kohn, & Bentley,
P.C. (Continued)

Leading Officials
Michael J. Ioannou, Chairman, 408-287-6262
Darcy Diaz, Executive Director,
650-780-1695
Michael J. Ioannou, Chairman, 408-287-6262
Darcy Diaz, Executive Director,
650-780-1695
Jill Yamasaki, Director of Business
Development, 650-780-1738
Maks Agamir, Chief Information Officer,
650-780-1657
Enrique Marinez, Esq., Diversity Committee
Chair, 650-364-8200

Rosenfeld, Meyer & Susman, LLP

9601 Wilshire Boulevard
Suite 710
Beverly Hills, CA 90210-5288
Phone: 310-858-7700
Fax: 310-860-2430
Email: rms@rmslaw.com
Web Site: www.rmslaw.com

2016 Total Lawyers: 16
2015 Total Lawyers: 17

Rutan & Tucker

611 Anton Boulevard
Suite 1400
Costa Mesa, CA 92626-1931
Phone: 714-641-5100
Fax: 714-546-9035
Email: ckaiser@rutan.com
Web Site: www.rutan.com

2016 Total Lawyers: 154
2015 Total Lawyers: 148

Sedgwick, LLP

333 Bush Street
30th Floor
San Francisco, CA 94104
Phone: 415-781-7900
Fax: 415-781-2635
Email: email@sdma.com
Web Site: www.sdma.com

2016 Total Lawyers: 330
2015 Total Lawyers: 330

Seltzer Caplan McMahon Vitek, A Law Corporation

750 B Street
2100 Symphony Towers
San Diego, CA 92101
Phone: 619-685-3003
Fax: 619-685-3100
Web Site: www.scmv.com

2016 Total Lawyers: 43
2015 Total Lawyers: 43

Severson & Werson, A Professional Corporation

1 Embarcadero Center
Suite 2600
San Francisco, CA 94111
Phone: 415-398-3344
Web Site: www.severson.com

2016 Total Lawyers: 105
2015 Total Lawyers: 110

Offices: No. Attys.
San Francisco: 87
Irvine, California: 32

Leading Practice Areas
(Department Heads)
Financial Services (Michael Steiner
415-398-3344)
Insurance (Michael Murphy 415-398-3344)
Construction (David Ericksen 415-398-3344)

Leading Officials
Mark D. Lonergan, Chief Executive Officer
Ron Manuel, Chief Operating Officer
Joel Halverson, Hiring Partner
Oleg Berylant, Technology Manager
Sara Dudley, Librarian

Sheppard, Mullin, Richter & Hampton

333 South Hope Street
43rd Floor
Los Angeles, CA 90071
Phone: 213-620-1780
Fax: 213-620-1398
Email: info@sheppardmullin.com
Web Site: www.sheppardmullin.com

2016 Total Lawyers: 750
2015 Total Lawyers: 655

Wilson Sonsini Goodrich & Rosati

650 Page Mill Road
Palo Alto, CA 94304-1050
Phone: 650-493-9300
Fax: 650-493-6811
Email: wsgr@wsgr.com
Web Site: www.wsgr.com

2016 Total Lawyers: 647
2015 Total Lawyers: 630

COLORADO

Berenbaum Weinshienk PC

370 17th Sreet
Suite 4800
Denver, CO 80202
Phone: 303-825-0800
Fax: 303-629-7610
Email: info@bwlegal.com
Web Site: www.bwlegal.com

2016 Total Lawyers: 34
2015 Total Lawyers: 40

Brownstein Hyatt Farber Schreck

410 17th Street
Suite 2200
Denver, CO 80202-4437
Phone: 303-223-1100
Fax: 303-223-1111
Email: info@bhfs.com
Web Site: www.bhfs.com

2016 Total Lawyers: 236
2015 Total Lawyers: 229

Davis Graham & Stubbs LLP

1550 17th Street
Suite 500
Denver, CO 80202
Phone: 303-892-9400
Fax: 303-893-1379
Email: info@dgslaw.com
Web Site: www.dgslaw.com

2016 Total Lawyers: 140
2015 Total Lawyers: 140

2016 Staff
Equity Partners: 68
Associates: 49
Of Counsel: 20
Senior Counsel: 7
Staff Attorneys: 3

Offices: No. Attys.
Denver, CO: 143
Reno, NV: 4

Hiring and Promotion
2015 Associates Hired: 14
2015 First-Year Hires: 5
Starting Salary for First-Year
Assocs: $115,000
2016 First-Year Hires (Est.): 5
2015 Equity Partners Named: 5
2015 Lateral Equity Partners: 3

Leading Practice Areas
(Department Heads)
Finance & Acquisitions 33% (Ronald R.
Levine, II)
Natural Resources 33% (Randall E. Hubbard)
Trial 33% (Chad Williams)

Davis Graham & Stubbs LLP (Continued)

Leading Officials
Chris Richardson, Managing Partner
Debbie Schoonover, Executive Director
Jacki Abraham, Director of
Professional Resources
Jenna Lewis, Director of Marketing &
business Development
Thom Curtis, Chief Information Officer
Andrea Hamilton, Library and Information
Resources Manager
Kenzo Kawanabe, Chair, Diversity
Committee, 303-892-7541

Hall & Evans, LLC

1125 17th Street,
Suite 600
Denver, CO 80202
Phone: 303-628-3300
Fax: 303-628-3368
Email: hallevans@hallevans.com
Web Site: www.hallevans.com

2016 Total Lawyers: 78
2015 Total Lawyers: 76

Sherman & Howard L.L.C.

633 Seventeenth Street
Suite 3000
Denver, CO 80202
Phone: 303-297-2900
Fax: 303-298-0940
Email: info@shermanhoward.com
Web Site: www.shermanhoward.com

2016 Total Lawyers: 189
2015 Total Lawyers: 176

2016 Staff
Equity Partners: 80
Non-Equity Partners: 30
Associates: 40
Of Counsel: 27
Staff Attorneys: 1
Special Attorneys: 6
Contract Attorneys: 5

Offices: No. Attys.
Colorado Springs, CO: 12
Steamboat, CO: 1
Aspen, CO: 5
Denver, CO: 118
Phoenix, AZ: 16
Reno, NV: 5
Scottsdale, AZ: 10
St. Louis, MO: 1
Atlanta, GA: 4

Hiring and Promotion
2015 Associates Hired: 5
2015 First-Year Hires: 1
Starting Salary for First-Year
Assocs: $117,000
2016 First-Year Hires (Est.): 4
2015 Equity Partners Named: 2
2015 Lateral Equity Partners: 6

Sherman & Howard L.L.C. (Continued)

Leading Practice Areas
(Department Heads)
Litigation 35% (Peter Koclanes
303-297-2900)
Business & Real Estate 25% (Jeffrey
Kesselman 303-297-2900)
Employment Law 16% (William Wright
303-297-2900)
Tax & Probate 14% (Bridget Sullivan
303-297-2900)
Public Finance 10% (James Lane
303-297-2900)

Leading Officials
Karen L. Chapman, Chair of the Firm,
303-297-2900
Gregory Densen, Chief Executive,
303-297-2900
Darryl Hair, Chief Operating Officer,
303-297-2900
Christopher R. Mosley, Hiring Partner,
303-297-2900
Lisa Liss, Professional Recruitment &
Development Manager, 303-297-2900
Kimberly Miller, Director of Marketing,
303-297-2900
Jasmine Ocken, Director of IT, 303-297-2900
Margi Heinen, Manager of Library Services,
303-297-2900
Andrew W. Volin, Attorney, 303-297-2900

Other Offices
633 17th Street
Suite 3000
Denver, CO 80202
Phone: 303-297-2900
Fax: 303-298-0940
R. Michael Sanchez

CONNECTICUT

Carmody Torrance Sandak & Hennessey LLP

50 Leavenworth Street,
Waterbury, CT 06702
Phone: 203-573-1200
Fax: 203-575-2600
Email: contactus@carmodylaw.com
Web Site: www.carmodylaw.com

2016 Total Lawyers: 74
2015 Total Lawyers: 71

2016 Staff
Associates: 17
Of Counsel: 3
Counsel: 2
Partners 52

Offices: No. Attys.
New Haven, CT: 28
Waterbury, CT: 27
Stamford, CT: 19

Hiring and Promotion
2016 First-Year Hires (Est.): 0
2015 Equity Partners Named: 0

CONNECTICUT

Carmody Torrance Sandak & Hennessey LLP (Continued)

*Leading Practice Areas
(Department Heads)*
Corporate (Thomas Candrick 203-777-5501)
Energy and Public Utilities (Joseph Dornfried 203-573-1200)
Healthcare (Kristin Connors 203-573-1200)
Intellectual Property (Arthur G. Schaier 203-573-1200)
Labor and Employment (D. Charles Stohler 203-573-1200)
Litigation (David Hardy 203-573-1200)
Medical Malpractice Defense/Products Liability (Trudie R. Hamilton 203-573-1200)
Trust & Estates (David L. Sfara 203-573-1200)
Real Estate (John D. Yarbrough, Jr. 203-573-1200)

Client Representations
MacDermid Corporation
Eversource
Webster Bank

Leading Officials
Ann H. Zucker, Managing Partner, 203-573-1200
Craig Appel, Executive Director, 203-573-1200
Kristin Connors, Hiring Partner, 203-573-1200
Laurie Logan-Priscott, Human Resources Director, 203-573-1200
Renee Gilroy, Marketing Director, 203-573-1200
David Orschel, MIS Director, 203-573-1200
Pat LaPiere, Librarian, 203-573-1200
Laurie Logan-Priscott, Human Resources Director, 203-573-1200

Cummings & Lockwood LLC

Six Landmark Square
Stamford, CT 06901
Phone: 203-327-1700
Fax: 203-351-4534
Email: info@cl-law.com
Web Site: www.cl-law.com

2016 Total Lawyers: 62
2015 Total Lawyers: 65

2016 Staff
Equity Partners: 23
Non-Equity Partners: 23
Associates: 16
Counsel: 2

Offices: No. Attys.
Greenwich, CT: 12
Bonita Springs: 6
Palm Beach Gardens, FL: 2
West Hartford, CT: 5
Stamford, CT: 29
Naples, FL: 10

Cummings & Lockwood LLC (Continued)

Hiring and Promotion
2015 Associates Hired: 7
2015 First-Year Hires: 1
Starting Salary for First-Year Assocs: 110,000 (West Hartford and Florida office), 125,000 (Stamford and Greenwich)
2016 First-Year Hires (Est.): 1
2015 Equity Partners Named: 0

*Leading Practice Areas
(Department Heads)*
Private Clients 80%
Corporate & Finance 13%
Litigation 7%

Revenues and Profits
Revenues: $48,000,000
Profits: $15,977,000

Leading Officials
Jonathan B. Mills, Chairman
Bonnie Artinian, Legal Recruiting Coordinator
Teresa Dutkevitch, Marketing Director

Halloran & Sage, LLP

One Goodwin Square
225 Asylum Street
Hartford, CT 06103
Phone: 860-522-6103
Fax: 860-548-0006
Web Site: www.halloran-sage.com

2016 Total Lawyers: 100
2015 Total Lawyers: 98

Murtha Cullina LLP

CityPlace I
185 Asylum Street, 29th Floor
Hartford, CT 06103-3469
Phone: 860-240-6000
Fax: 860-240-6150
Email: firm@murthalaw.com
Web Site: www.murthalaw.com

2016 Total Lawyers: 106
2015 Total Lawyers: 104

Pullman and Comley, LLC

850 Main Street
P.O. Box 7006
Bridgeport, CT 06601-7006
Phone: 203-330-2000
Fax: 203-576-8888
Email: info@pullcom.com
Web Site: www.pullcom.com

2016 Total Lawyers: 89
2015 Total Lawyers: 85

Reid and Riege, P.C.

One Financial Plaza
21st Floor
Hartford, CT 06103
Phone: 860-278-1150
Fax: 860-240-1002
Email: info@rrlawpc.com
Web Site: www.rrlawpc.com

2016 Total Lawyers: 45
2015 Total Lawyers: 47

2016 Staff
Equity Partners: 30
Non-Equity Partners: 3
Associates: 11
Of Counsel: 1

Offices: No. Attys.
Hartford, CT: 44
New Haven, CT: 1

Hiring and Promotion
2015 Associates Hired: 2
2015 First-Year Hires: 2
2016 First-Year Hires (Est.): 0
2015 Equity Partners Named: 1

Leading Officials
Bruce C. Lyon, Director of Administration, 860-240-1064

Robinson & Cole LLP

280 Trumbull Street
Hartford, CT 06103-3597
Phone: 860-275-8200
Fax: 860-275-8299
Email: btsmith@rc.com
Web Site: www.rc.com

2016 Total Lawyers: 199
2015 Total Lawyers: 200

Shipman & Goodwin LLP

One Constitution Plaza
Hartford, CT 06103-2819
Phone: 860-251-5000
Fax: 860-251-5099
Web Site: www.shipmangoodwin.com

2016 Total Lawyers: 171
2015 Total Lawyers: 160

Updike, Kelly & Spellacy P.C.

100 Pearl Street
17th Floor
Hartford, CT 06123
Phone: 860-548-2600
Fax: 860-548-2680
Email: info@uks.com
Web Site: www.uks.com

2016 Total Lawyers: 67
2015 Total Lawyers: 57

CONNECTICUT

Wiggin and Dana

One Century Tower
265 Church Street
New Haven, CT 06510-1832
Phone: 203-498-4400
Fax: 203-782-2889
Email: info@wiggin.com
Web Site: www.wiggin.com

2016 Total Lawyers: 135
2015 Total Lawyers: 133

DELAWARE

Morris James

500 Delaware Avenue, Suite 1500
P.O. Box 2306
Wilmington, DE 19899-2306
Phone: 302-888-6800
Fax: 302-571-1750
Web Site: www.morrisjames.com

2016 Total Lawyers: 67
2015 Total Lawyers: 67

Morris, Nichols, Arsht & Tunnell LLP

1201 North Market Street, 18th Floor
P.O. Box 1347
Wilmington, DE 19899-1347
Phone: 302-658-9200
Fax: 302-658-3989
Email: contact@mnat.com
Web Site: www.mnat.com

2016 Total Lawyers: 84
2015 Total Lawyers: 87

Potter Anderson & Corroon

1313 North Market Street, P.O. Box 951
Wilmington, DE 19899-0951
Phone: 302-984-6000
Fax: 302-658-1192
Email: info@potteranderson.com
Web Site: www.potteranderson.com

2016 Total Lawyers: 86
2015 Total Lawyers: 84

Richards, Layton & Finger

One Rodney Square
920 North King Street
Wilmington, DE 19801
Phone: 302-651-7700
Fax: 302-651-7701
Email: info@rlf.com
Web Site: www.rlf.com

2016 Total Lawyers: 143
2015 Total Lawyers: 132

Richards, Layton & Finger (Continued)

2016 Staff
Equity Partners: 64
Associates: 66
Senior Attorneys: 3
Counsel: 10

Offices: No. Attys.
920 N King St, One Rodney Square,
Wilmington, DE: 137

Hiring and Promotion
2015 Associates Hired: 19
2015 First-Year Hires: 17
Starting Salary for First-Year
Assocs: $160,000
2016 First-Year Hires (Est.): 21
2015 Equity Partners Named: 2

Leading Officials
Gregory V. Varallo, President, 302-651-7772
Doneene K. Damon, Executive Vice
President, 302-651-7526
Wayne T. Stanford, Chief Operating Officer,
302-651-7686
Paul N. Heath, Hiring Partner, 302-651-7590
Joni Peet, Legal Recruitment Manager,
302-651-7778
Courtney Woolridge, Director of Business
Development & Marketing, 302-651-7652
Allen Hart, Director of Information
Technology, 302-651-7820
Robert L. Guerrero, Head Librarian,
302-651-7775
Marcos A. Ramos, Diversity Committee
Chair, 302-651-7566

Young Conaway Stargatt & Taylor, LLP

100 North King Street
Wilmington, DE 19801
Phone: 302-571-6600
Fax: 302-571-1253
Email: info@ycst.com
Web Site: www.YoungConaway.com

2016 Total Lawyers: 105
2015 Total Lawyers: 106

DISTRICT OF COLUMBIA

Akin Gump Strauss Hauer & Feld LLP

Robert Strauss Building
1333 New Hampshire Avenue
Washington, DC 20036
Phone: 202-887-4000
Fax: 202-887-4288
Email: info@akingump.com
Web Site: www.akingump.com

2016 Total Lawyers: 924
2015 Total Lawyers: 926

Akin Gump Strauss Hauer & Feld
LLP (Continued)

2016 Staff
Equity Partners: 322
Non-Equity Partners: 12
Associates: 275
Senior Attorneys: 21
Counsel: 166
Senior Counsel: 103
Staff Attorneys: 17
Trainee Solicitors 8

Offices: No. Attys.
Washington, DC: 238
Dallas, TX: 95
New York, NY: 207
San Antonio, TX: 18
Houston, TX: 66
Los Angeles, CA: 72
Philadelphia, PA: 20
Moscow, Russia: 26
London, England: 97
San Francisco, CA: 15
Beijing, China: 4
Abu Dhabi, UAE: 11
Geneva, Switzerland: 8
Hong Kong: 20
Singapore: 7
Longview, TX: 1
Fort Worth, TX: 5
Irvine, CA: 8
Dubai, UAE: 2
Frankfurt, Germany: 4

Leading Practice Areas
(Department Heads)
Litigation (Stephen Baldini 212-872-1062)
Corporate (Kerry E. Berchem 212-872-1095)
Labor and Employment (Robert G. Lian Jr.
202-887-4358)
Intellectual Property (Steven M. Zager
713-220-8109)
Policy and Regulation (Don Pongrace (public
law and policy) and Jorge Lopez
(regulatory) 202-887-4466 and
202-431-1305)
Financial Restructuring (Fred S. Hodara and
Daniel H. Golden 212-872-8040 and
212-872-8010)
Tax (Patrick B. Fenn and Stuart E. Leblang
212-872-1040 and 212-872-1017)
Investment Funds (Prakash H. Mehta and
Stephen M. Vine 202-887-4248 and
212-872-1030)
Global Energy and Transactions (Rick
Burdick 202-887-4110)
International Trade (Hal Shapiro
202-887-4053)

Revenues and Profits
Revenues: $930,070,718

Leading Officials
Kim Koopersmith, Chairperson,
212-872-1060
Sally King, Chief Operating Officer,
212-872-1029
David H. Botter, Hiring Partner,
212-872-1055
Aleisha C. Gravit, Chief Marketing Officer,
214-969-4200
Mike Lucas, Chief Information Officer,
202-887-4350
Karol Kepchar, Partner & Chair, Diversity
Committee, 202-887-4104

DISTRICT OF COLUMBIA

Akin Gump Strauss Hauer & Feld
LLP (Continued)

Other Offices
Washington, DC
1333 New Hampshire Avenue. N.W.
Washington
D.C.
20036
Phone: 202-887-4000
Fax: 202-887-4288
Email: washdcinfo@akingump.com
Anthony T. Pierce, Partner in Charge

Dallas
1700 Pacific Avenue
Suite 4100
Dallas
TX
75201
Phone: 214-969-2800
Fax: 214-969-4343
Email: dallasinfo@akingump.com
J. Kenneth Menges, Partner in Charge

New York
One Bryant Park
New York
NY
10036
Phone: 212-872-1000
Fax: 212-872-1002
Email: newyorkinfo@akingump.com
Daniel H. Golden, Partner in Charge

Houston
1111 Louisiana Street
44th Floor
Houston
TX
77002
Phone: 713-220-5800
Fax: 713-236-0822
Email: houstoninfo@akingump.com
Christine LaFollette, Partner in Charge

Los Angeles
2029 Century Park East
Suite 2400
Los Angeles
CA
90067
Phone: 310-229-1000
Fax: 310-229-1001
Email: losangelesinfo@akingump.com
C.N. Franklin Reddick III, Partner in Charge

London
Ten Bishops Square
Eighth Floor
London
UK
E1 6EG
Phone: 207-012-9600
Fax: 207-012-9601
Email: londoninfo@akingump.com
Sebastian Rice, Managing Partner and James
Roome, Senior Partner

Arent Fox

1050 Connecticut Avenue N.W.
Washington, DC 20036-5339
Phone: 202-857-6000
Fax: 202-857-6395
Email: webmaster@arentfox.com
Web Site: www.arentfox.com

2016 Total Lawyers: 418
2015 Total Lawyers: 418

Arnold & Porter LLP

555 12th Street N.W.
Washington, DC 20004
Phone: 202-942-5000
Fax: 202-942-5999
Email: website@aporter.com
Web Site: www.arnoldporter.com

2016 Total Lawyers: 749
2015 Total Lawyers: 751

Beveridge & Diamond, P.C.

1350 I Street N.W.
Suite 700
Washington, DC 20005
Phone: 202-789-6000
Fax: 202-789-6190
Email: contact.bd@bdlaw.com
Web Site: www.bdlaw.com

2016 Total Lawyers: 100
2015 Total Lawyers: 99

2016 Staff
Equity Partners: 62
Associates: 32
Of Counsel: 3
Senior Counsel: 2

Offices: No. Attys.
Washington, DC: 53
Baltimore, MD: 12
New York, NY/Englewood, NJ: 10
San Francisco, CA: 11
Wellesley, MA: 7
Austin, TX: 6

Hiring and Promotion
2015 Associates Hired: 12
2015 First-Year Hires: 4
2016 First-Year Hires (Est.): 3
2015 Equity Partners Named: 7
2015 Lateral Equity Partners: 1

Leading Practice Areas
(Department Heads)
Environmental (Karen M. Hansen
(512)391-8040)
Litigation (James B. Slaughter
(202) 789-6040)
Natural Resources & Project Development
(Fred R. Wagner (202) 789-6041)
Other

Beveridge & Diamond, P.C. (Continued)

Client Representations
Defeated negligence claims against DC
Water. See
www.bdlaw.com/news-1829.html
Secured unanimous ruling in Pennsylvania
Supreme Court shielding biosolids land
application from tort claims. See
www.bdlaw.com/news-1823.html
Secured major Clean Water Act ruling in U.S.
Court of Appeals for 7th Circuit in a citizen
suit against MWRDGC. See
www.bdlaw.com/news-1760.html

Leading Officials
Benjamin F. Wilson, Managing Principal,
202-789-6023
Katherine J. Harris, Chief Operating Officer,
202-789-6160
Peter C. Mayer, Human Resources Director,
202-789-6161
Nathan A. Darling, Chief Business
Development and Marketing Officer,
202-789-6142
Mark E. Stanley, Chief Information Officer,
202-789-6163
Scott N. Larson, Librarian, 202-789-6166
Paula J. Schauwecker, Principal, Diversity &
Inclusion Committee Chair , 212-702-5417

Other Offices
Washington, DC
1350 I Street, N.W.
Suite 700
Washington
DC
20005
Phone: 202-789-6000
Fax: 202-789-6190
Email: bdlaw@bdlaw.com
Benjamin F. Wilson

Caplin & Drysdale, Chartered

One Thomas Circle NW
Suite 1100
Washington, DC 20005
Phone: 202-862-5000
Fax: 202-429-3301
Email: marketing@capdale.com
Web Site: www.caplindrysdale.com

2016 Total Lawyers: 65
2015 Total Lawyers: 70

2016 Staff
Equity Partners: 32
Non-Equity Partners: 4
Associates: 19
Of Counsel: 5
Senior Counsel: 5

Offices: No. Attys.
600 Lexington Avenue, New York, NY
10022: 6
One Thomas Circle, Washington, DC
20005: 59

Caplin & Drysdale, Chartered (Continued)

Hiring and Promotion
2015 Associates Hired: 1
2016 First-Year Hires (Est.): 1
2015 Equity Partners Named: 1
2015 Lateral Equity Partners: 1

Leading Practice Areas
(Department Heads)
Tax 50% (Scott D. Michel 202-862-5030)
Exempt Organizations 10% (Douglas N.
  Varley 202-862-7818)
Political Law 10% (Trevor Potter
  202-862-5092)
Private Client 10% (Beth Shapiro Kaufman
  202-862-5062)
Complex Litigation 5% (Trevor W. Swett
  202-862-5081)
Corporate Law 5% (William M. Klimon
  202-862-5022)
Creditors' Rights 5% (Elihu Inselbuch
  212-379-6040)
Employee Benefits 5% (Joanne C. Youn
  202-862-7855)

Client Representations
It is Caplin & Drysdale's policy to refrain
  from publishing information concerning
  our clients.

Leading Officials
Beth Shapiro Kaufman, President,
  202-862-5062
Beth Shapiro Kaufman, President,
  202-862-5062
John Riggleman, Jr., Firm Administrator,
  202-862-5095
Trevor Swett III, Member, 202-862-5081
Nawel L. Amerg, Recruiting Manager,
  202-862-5010
Sheryl K. Miller, Senior Marketing &
  Business Development Manager,
  202-862-7857
Edward Terry, Information Services
  Manager, 202-862-5053
Nalini Rajguru, Library Manager,
  202-862-5073

Carr Maloney PC

2000 L St NW
Suite 450
Washington, DC 20036
Phone: 202-310-5500
Fax: 202-310-5555
Web Site: www.carrmaloney.com

2016 Total Lawyers: 28
2015 Total Lawyers: 28

Covington & Burling LLP

1201 Pennsylvania Avenue N.W.
Washington, DC 20004-2401
Phone: 202-662-6000
Fax: 202-662-6291
Web Site: www.cov.com

2016 Total Lawyers: 1056
2015 Total Lawyers: 850

Crowell & Moring LLP

1001 Pennsylvania Avenue N.W.
Washington, DC 20004-2595
Phone: 202-624-2500
Fax: 202-628-5116
Email: info@crowell.com
Web Site: www.crowell.com

2016 Total Lawyers: 487
2015 Total Lawyers: 487

Finnegan, Henderson, Farabow, Garrett & Dunner

901 New York Avenue, NW
Washington, DC 20001-4413
Phone: 202-408-4000
Fax: 202-408-4400
Email: info@finnegan.com
Web Site: www.finnegan.com

2016 Total Lawyers: 353
2015 Total Lawyers: 353

Groom Law Group, Chartered

1701 Pennsylvania Avenue, N.W.
Suite 1200
Washington, DC 20006
Phone: 202-857-0620
Fax: 202-659-4503
Email: info@groom.com
Web Site: www.groom.com

2016 Total Lawyers: 84
2015 Total Lawyers: 78

HoganLovells LLP

555 Thirteenth Street, N.W.
Washington, DC 20004
Phone: 202-637-5600
Fax: 202-637-5910
Web Site: www.hoganlovells.com

2016 Total Lawyers: 2600
2015 Total Lawyers: 2500

Hollingsworth LLP

1350 I Street, NW
Washington, DC 20005
Phone: 202-898-5800
Fax: 202-682-1639
Email: info@hollingsworthllp.com
Web Site: www.hollingsworthllp.com

2016 Total Lawyers: 52
2015 Total Lawyers: 52

Hunton & Williams

2200 Pennsylvania Avenue N.W.
Washington, DC 20037
Phone: 202-955-1500
Fax: 202-778-2201
Web Site: www.hunton.com

2016 Total Lawyers: 746
2015 Total Lawyers: 761

2016 Staff
Equity Partners: 315
Associates: 337
Counsel: 94

Offices: No. Attys.
Washington, DC: 138
Richmond, VA: 196
New York, NY: 98
Dallas, TX: 80
Atlanta, GA: 39
McLean, VA: 32
Miami, FL: 30
Los Angeles, CA: 25
Charlotte, NC: 21
Raleigh, NC: 9
Norfolk, VA: 6
San Francisco, CA: 8
Austin, TX: 4
Houston, TX: 2

Hiring and Promotion
2015 Associates Hired: 92
2015 First-Year Hires: 30
Starting Salary for First-Year
  Assocs: $160,000
2016 First-Year Hires (Est.): 32
2015 Equity Partners Named: 17
2015 Lateral Equity Partners: 5

Revenues and Profits
Revenues: $528,000,000

Client Representations
Diageo
Cleco Corporation
General Electric

DISTRICT OF COLUMBIA

Hunton & Williams (Continued)

Leading Officials
F. William Brownell, Chair of Executive
  Committee, 202-955-1555
Walfrido (Wally) J. Martinez, Managing
  Partner, 212-309-1316
Jacob Kerkhoff, Chief Administrative
  Officer, 804-788-8647
Kimberly C. MacLeod, Firmwide Hiring
  Partner, 804-788-8529
Judith H. Itkin, Partner in Charge of Lawyer
  Recruiting and Development,
  212-309-1058
Anne Malloy Tucker, Chief Marketing
  Officer, 202-778-2203
Rich McClain, Chief Information Officer,
  804-788-8461
Frosty Owen, RIS Sr. Services Manager,
  804-788-8272
A. Todd Brown, Partner and Co-Chair,
  Diversity Committee, 704-378-4727

Other Offices
2200 Pennsylvania Avenue N.W.
Washington
DC
20037
Phone: 202-955-1500
Fax: 202-778-2201
David A. Higbee, Managing Partner

200 Park Avenue
New York
NY
10166-0136
Phone: 212-309-1000
Fax: 212-309-1100
Lisa Sotto, Managing Partner

Fountain Place
1445 Ross Avenue
Suite 3700
Dallas
TX
75202
Phone: 214-979-3000
Fax: 214-880-0011
Patrick Mitchell, Managing Partner

Riverfront Plaza, East Tower
951 East Byrd Street
Richmond
VA
23219
Phone: 804-788-8200
Fax: 804-788-8218
John D. O'Neill, Jr., Managing Partner

Jackson & Campbell, P.C.

1120 20th Street, N.W.
South Tower
Washington, DC 20036-3437
Phone: 202-457-1600
Fax: 202-457-1678
Email: marketing@jacksoncampbell
Web Site: www.jackscamp.com

2016 Total Lawyers: 45
2015 Total Lawyers: 45

Jones Day

51 Louisiana Avenue, N.W.
Washington, DC 20001-2113
Phone: 202-879-3939
Fax: 202-626-1700
Email: counsel@jonesday.com
Web Site: www.jonesday.com

2016 Total Lawyers: 2500
2015 Total Lawyers: 2400

2016 Staff
Associates: 1313
Of Counsel: 164
Counsel: 62
Staff Attorneys: 46
Partners 938

Offices: No. Attys.
Cleveland, OH: 225
Washington, DC: 246
London, UK: 175
Dallas, TX: 144
Chicago, IL: 158
Los Angeles, CA: 84
Atlanta, GA: 129
Columbus, OH: 60
Paris, France: 104
Pittsburgh, PA: 68
Frankfurt, Germany: 44
Houston, TX: 46
Hong Kong: 53
San Francisco, CA: 85
Madrid, Spain: 30
Taipei, Taiwan: 35
Brussels, Belgium: 38
Singapore: 25
Irvine, CA: 46
Munich, Germany: 33
Tokyo, Japan: 48
Milan, Italy: 39
Shanghai, China: 21
Beijing, China: 10
San Diego, CA: 43
Sydney, Australia: 49
Palo Alto, CA: 64
New York, NY: 261
Moscow, Russia: 10
Dubai, United Arab Emirates: 11
Mexico City, Mexico: 40
Boston, MA: 33
Riyadh, Saudi Arabia: 2
Alkhobar, Saudi Arabia: 3
Dusseldorf, Germany: 19
Jeddah, Saudi Arabia: 5
Sao Paulo, Brazil: 9
Amsterdam, Netherlands: 18
Miami, FL: 9
Perth, Australia: 1

Hiring and Promotion
2015 Associates Hired: 301
2015 First-Year Hires: 156
Starting Salary for First-Year Assocs:
  $160,000 (Boston, Chicago, Dallas,
  Houston, Irvine, LA, NY, San Diego, San
  Francisco, Silicon Valley, Washington);
  $150,000 (Atlanta) ; $145,000 (Cleveland,
  Columbus, Pittsburgh); $135,000 (Miami)
2016 First-Year Hires (Est.): 128(US)
2015 Equity Partners Named: 84
2015 Lateral Equity Partners: 50

Jones Day (Continued)

Leading Practice Areas
(Department Heads)
Business & Tort Litigation 17% (Daniel E.
  Reidy; John M. Majoras 312-269-4140;
  614-281-3835)
Mergers & Acquisitions 12% (Robert A.
  Profusek; James P. Dougherty
  216-586-3939)
Intellectual Property 9% (Anthony M.
  Insogna; John J. Normile 858-314-1130;
  212-326-3777)
Banking & Finance 6% (Robert J. Graves;
  Brett P. Barragate; Edward Nalbantian
  (London); Alban Caillemer du Ferrage
  (Paris) 312-269-4356; 212-326-3446;
  44-20-7039-5145; 33-1-56-59-38-18)
Global Disputes 6% (Thomas F. Cullen, Jr.
  202-879-3924)
Capital Markets 4% (Christopher M. Kelly;
  Giles P. Elliott (London) 216-586-1238;
  44-20-7039-5229)
Labor & Employment 4% (Lawrence C.
  DiNardo 312-269-4306)
Real Estate 4% (David J. Lowery, Robert C.
  Lee. David A. Roberts (London)
  214-969-3710; 312-269-4173;
  44-20-7039-5286)
Private Equity 4% (Charles W. Hardin Jr.;
  Adam Greaves (London) 216-586-7084;
  44-20-7039-5251)
Antitrust & Competition 4% (David P. Wales
  202-879-5451)

Client Representations
City of Detroit
Texas Keystone
Proctor & Gamble

Leading Officials
Stephen J. Brogan, Managing Partner,
  202-879-3939
Bonnie L. Shute, Firm Director of
  Administration, 202-879-3939
Sharyl A. Reisman, Firm Hiring Partner,
  212-326-3939
Jolie A. Blanchard, Firm Director of
  Recruiting, 202-879-3939
Cherie W. Olland, Firm Director of Business
  Development and Communications,
  216-586-3939
William W. Gregory, Firm Director of
  Technology Support Services,
  216-586-7709
M. Carter DeLorme, Diversity Task Force
  Chair, 202-879-3939

Other Offices
North Point, 901 Lakeside Avenue
Cleveland
OH
44114-1190
Phone: 216-586-3939
Fax: 216-579-0212
Email: counsel@jonesday.com
Christopher M. Kelly, Partner-in-Charge

51 Louisiana Avenue, N.W.
Washington, D.C.
D.C.
20001-2113
Phone: 202-879-3939
Fax: 202-626-1700
Email: counsel@jonesday.com
Gregory M. Shumaker, Partner-in-Charge

DISTRICT OF COLUMBIA

Jones Day (Continued)

2727 North Harwood Street
Dallas
TX
75201-1515
Phone: 752-220-3939
Fax: 214-969-5100
Email: counsel@jonesday.com
Patricia J. Villareal, Partner-in-Charge

77 West Wacker
Chicago,
IL
60601-1692
Phone: 312-782-3939
Fax: 312-782-8585
Email: counsel@jonesday.com
Tina M. Tabacchi, Partner-in-Charge

222 East 41st Street
New York
NY
10017-6702
Phone: 212-326-3939
Fax: 212-755-7306
Email: counsel@jonesday.com
Wesley R. Johnson, Jr., Partner-in-Charge

1420 Peachtree Street, N.E.
Suite 800
Atlanta
GA
30309-3053
Phone: 404-521-3939
Fax: 404-581-8330
Email: counsel@jonesday.com
Lizanne Thomas, Partner-in-Charge

555 South Flower Street
Fiftieth Floor
Los Angeles
CA
90071
Phone: 213-489-3939
Fax: 213-243-2539
Email: counsel@jonesday.com
Christopher Lovrien, Partner-in-Charge

325 John H. McConnell Boulevard
Suite 600
Columbus
OH
43216-5017
Phone: 614-469-3939
Fax: 614-461-4198
Email: counsel@jonesday.com
Elizabeth P. Kessler, Partner-in-Charge

21 Tudor Street
London EC4Y 0DJ
United Kingdom
Phone: 442-070-395 ext. 959
Fax: 442-070-395 ext. 999
Email: london@jonesday.com
John Phillips, Partner-in-Charge

2 rue Saint Floretin
75001 Paris
France
Phone: 331-565-939 ext. 39
Fax: 331-565-939 ext. 38
Email: counsel@jonesday.com
Sophie Hagege, Partner-in-Charge

Jones Day (Continued)

500 Grant Street
Suite 4500
Pittsburgh
PA
15219-2514
Phone: 412-391-3939
Fax: 412-394-7959
Email: counsel@jonesday.com
Laura E. Ellsworth, Partner-in-Charge

555 California Street
26th Floor
San Francisco
CA
94104-1500
Phone: 415-626-3939
Fax: 415-875-5700
Email: counsel@jonesday.com
Aaron Agenbroad, Partner-in-Charge

1755 Embarcadero Road
Palo Alto
CA
94303
Phone: 650-739-3939
Fax: 650-739-3900
Email: counsel@jonesday.com
Greg Lanier

31st Floor, Edinburgh Tower
15 Queen's Road Central, The Landmark
Hong Kong
Phone: 852-252-6689 ext. 5
Fax: 852-286-8587 ext. 1
Email: counsel@jonesday.com
Robert L. Thompson

Keller and Heckman LLP

1001 G Street N.W.
Suite 500 West
Washington, DC 20001
Phone: 202-434-4100
Fax: 202-434-4646
Email: info@khlaw.com
Web Site: www.khlaw.com

2016 Total Lawyers: 73
2015 Total Lawyers: 74

2016 Staff
Equity Partners: 31
Non-Equity Partners: 10
Associates: 26
Counsel: 7

Offices: No. Attys.
Washington, DC: 59
Brussels: 5
San Francisco, CA: 4
Paris: 1
Shanghai: 4

Hiring and Promotion
2015 Associates Hired: 6
2015 First-Year Hires: 3
Starting Salary for First-Year
  Assocs: $127,500
2016 First-Year Hires (Est.): 1
2015 Equity Partners Named: 2

Keller and Heckman LLP (Continued)

Leading Officials
Richard F. Mann, Chair of Management
  Committee
John Barker, Director of Administration
Pamela L. Langhorn, Chair of the
  Recruitment Committee
Sharon D. Drummond, Director of
  Administrative Operations
Caryn Wick, Marketing Manager
Robert E. Mirowicz, Director of
  Information Systems
Abigail E. Ross, Library Manager
Joan Sylvain Baughan, Chair, Diversity
  Committee, 202-434-4100

Other Offices
1001 G Street, NW
Suite 500 West
Washington, DC
20001
Phone: 202-434-4100
Email: info@khlaw.com
Richard F. Mann

Miller & Chevalier Chartered

655 Fifteenth Street N.W.
Suite 900
Washington, DC 20005-5701
Phone: 202-626-5800
Fax: 202-628-5801
Email: inquiries@milchev.com
Web Site: www.millerchevalier.com

2016 Total Lawyers: 105
2015 Total Lawyers: 121

Steptoe & Johnson LLP

1330 Connecticut Avenue NW
Suite 700
Washington, DC 20036-1795
Phone: 202-429-3000
Fax: 202-429-3902
Web Site: www.steptoe.com

2016 Total Lawyers: 500
2015 Total Lawyers: 500

Sughrue Mion, PLLC

2100 Pennsylvania Avenue N.W.
Suite 800
Washington, DC 20037-3202
Phone: 202-293-7060
Fax: 202-293-7860
Email: sughrue@sughrue.com
Web Site: www.sughrue.com

2016 Total Lawyers: 86
2015 Total Lawyers: 86

DISTRICT OF COLUMBIA

Van Ness Feldman LLP

1050 Thomas Jefferson Street, NW
7th Floor
Washington, DC 20007
Phone: 202-298-1800
Fax: 202-338-2416
Email: vnf@vnf.com
Web Site: www.vnf.com

2016 Total Lawyers: 85
2015 Total Lawyers: 94

2016 Staff
Equity Partners: 56
Associates: 27
Of Counsel: 7
Counsel: 1
Senior Counsel: 3

Offices: No. Attys.
Washington, DC: 64
Seattle, WA: 21

Hiring and Promotion
2015 Associates Hired: 3
2016 First-Year Hires (Est.): 2
2015 Equity Partners Named: 0
2015 Lateral Equity Partners: 1

Leading Practice Areas
(Department Heads)
Electric 25% (Doug Smith (202) 298-1902)
Natural Gas 25% (Susan Olenchuk
202-298-1896)
Hydroelectric 10% (Michael Swiger
(202) 298-1891)
Government Relations & Public Policy 10%
(Bob Szabo 202-298-1920)
Real Estate 10% (Jay Derr 206-623-9372)
Environment 8% (Stephen Fotis
(202) 298-1908)
Land & Water 8% (Joe Nelson
202-298-1894)
Climate Change 5% (Kyle Danish
(202) 298-1876)
Transportation 5% (Bob Szabo
(202) 298-1920)
Native American 4% (Ed Gehres
202-298-1878)

Client Representations
Gulf South Pipeline Company
McKesson Corporation
State of Alaska

Leading Officials
Richard Agnew, Chairman, 202-298-1800
Jay Derr, Managing Partner, Seattle,
206-623-9372
Britt Fleming, Recruiting Partner,
202-298-1863
Lisa Pavia, Director of Business and
Professional Development, 202-298-1899
Jorge Sanabria, Technology Manager,
202-298-1872
Susan Pries, Head Librarian, 202-298-1901
David Yaffe, Chair of Diversity Committee,
202-298-1840

Venable LLP

575 7th Street, NW
Washington, DC 20004
Phone: 202-344-4000
Fax: 202-344-8300
Email: info@venable.com
Web Site: www.venable.com

2016 Total Lawyers: 651
2015 Total Lawyers: 633

Wiley Rein LLP

1776 K Street NW
Washington, DC 20006
Phone: 202-719-7000
Fax: 202-719-7049
Web Site: www.wileyrein.com

2016 Total Lawyers: 187
2015 Total Lawyers: 255

Williams & Connolly

The Edward Bennett Williams Building
725 12th Street N.W.
Washington, DC 20005
Phone: 202-434-5000
Fax: 202-434-5029
Web Site: www.wc.com

2016 Total Lawyers: 273
2015 Total Lawyers: 275

Wilmer Cutler Pickering Hale and Dorr

1875 Pennsylvania Avenue, NW
Washington, DC 20006
Phone: 202-663-6000
Fax: 202-663-6363
Email: law@wilmerhale.com
Web Site: www.wilmerhale.com

2016 Total Lawyers: 1112
2015 Total Lawyers: 1113

FLORIDA

Akerman LLP

420 South Orange Ave, Suite 1200
Orlando, FL 32801
Phone: 407-423-4000
Email: contact@akerman.com
Web Site: www.akerman.com

2016 Total Lawyers: 665
2015 Total Lawyers: 611

Becker & Poliakoff, P.A.

1 East Broward Boulevard Suite 1800
Fort Lauderdale, FL 33301
Phone: 954-987-7550
Fax: 954-985-4176
Email: bp@becker-poliakoff.com
Web Site: www.becker-poliakoff.com

2016 Total Lawyers: 147
2015 Total Lawyers: 147

Bilzin Sumberg Baena Price & Axlerod LLP

1450 Brickell Avenue
23rd Floor
Miami, FL 33131
Phone: 305-374-7580
Fax: 305-374-7593
Email: info@bilzin.com
Web Site: www.bilzin.com

2016 Total Lawyers: 94
2015 Total Lawyers: 85

Broad and Cassel

Bank of America Center, Suite 1400
390 North Orange Avenue
Orlando, FL 32801
Phone: 407-839-4200
Fax: 407-425-8377
Email: pgc@broadandcassel.com
Web Site: www.broadandcassel.com

2016 Total Lawyers: 164
2015 Total Lawyers: 158

Carlton Fields Jorden Burt

4221 West Boy Scout Boulevard, Suite 1000
Tampa, FL 33607
Phone: 813-223-7000
Fax: 813-229-4133
Email: info@cfjblaw.com
Web Site: www.carltonfields.com

2016 Total Lawyers: 375
2015 Total Lawyers: 390

Offices: No. Attys.
Tampa, FL (Home): 116
Miami, FL: 119
West Palm Beach, FL: 33
Orlando, FL: 22
Tallahassee, FL: 12
Atlanta, GA: 28
New York, NY: 9
Los Angeles, CA: 7
Hartford, CT: 17
Washington, DC: 27

Carlton Fields Jorden Burt (Continued)

Leading Practice Areas
(Department Heads)
Business Litigation and Trade Regulation 23% (Chris S. Coutroulis 813-223-7000)
Real Estate & Finance 14% (Edgel C. Lester, Jr. 813-223-7000)
Corporate, Securities & Tax 12% (Dennis J. Olle 305-530-0050)
Construction 10% (Luis Prats 813-223-7000)
Products and Toxic Tort Liability 8% (Gregory M. Cesarano and Stephen Krigbaum 305-530-0050)
Appellate Practice and Trial Support 7% (Wendy F. Lumish 305-530-0050)
Government Law and Consulting 6% (Nancy G. Linnan 850-224-1585)
Insurance 4% (Daniel C. Brown and Anthony H. Pelle; 850-224-1585)
Real Property Litigation 4% (Mark A. Brown 813-223-7000)
White Collar Crime & Government Investigations 3% (Kevin J. Napper 813-223-7000)

Client Representations
AIG Claim Services
Wells Fargo Bank
HCA, Inc.

Leading Officials
Benjamine Reid, Chair of Board of Directors, 305-530-0050
Gary L. Sasso, President & CEO, 813-223-7000
Anastasia C. Hiotis, Chief Operating Officer, 813-223-7000
Gwynne A. Young, Firmwide Hiring Chair, 813-223-7000
Shannon Williams, Director of Attorney Recruitment, 813-223-7000
Elizabeth B. Zabak, Director of Marketing and Client Development, 813-223-7000
David Bailey, Director of Information Systems and Library Services, 813-223-7000
Terry Psarras, Manager of Library Services, 813-223-7000
Nancy J. Faggianelli, Chief Diversity Officer, 813-229-4321

Other Offices
Miami, FL
100 S.E. Second Street
Suite 4200
Miami
FL
33131
Phone: 305-530-0050
Fax: 305-530-0055
Email: sbrodie@cfjblaw.com
Steven J. Brodie and Amy Furness, Miami Office Co-Managing Shareholders

Carlton Fields Jorden Burt (Continued)

Atlanta, GA
1201 W. Peachtree Street
Suite 3000
Atlanta
GA
30309
Phone: 404-815-3400
Fax: 404-815-3415
Email: dleonard@cfjblaw.com
David Leonard, Atlanta Office Managing Shareholder

Orlando, FL
450 S. Orange Avenue
Suite 500
Orlando
FL
32801
Phone: 407-849-0300
Fax: 407-648-9099
Email: ccacciabeve@cfjblaw.com
Charles Cacciabeve, Orlando Office Managing Shareholder

Tallahassee, FL
215 S. Monroe Street
Suite 500
Tallahassee
FL
32301
Phone: 850-224-1585
Fax: 850-222-0398
Email: nlinnan@cfjblaw.com
Nancy Linnan, Tallahassee Office Managing Shareholder

Tampa, FL
4221 West Boy Scout Boulevard
Suite 1000
Tampa
FL
33607
Phone: 813-223-7000
Fax: 813-229-4133
Email: ndoliner@cfjblaw.com
Nathaniel Doliner, Tampa Office Managing Shareholder

West Palm Beach, FL
525 Okeechobee Boulevard
Suite 1200
West Palm Beach
FL
33401
Phone: 561-659-7070
Fax: 561-659-7368
Email: thanson@cfjblaw.com
Thomas Hanson, West Palm Beach Office Managing Shareholder

Los Angeles, California
2000 Avenue of the Stars
Suite 530 North Tower
Los Angeles
CA
90067-4707
Phone: 310-843-6300
Fax: 310-843-6301
Email: mneubauer@cfjblaw.com
Mark A. Neubauer, Office Managing Shareholder

Carlton Fields Jorden Burt (Continued)

Hartford, CT
One State Street
Suite 1800
Hartford
CT
06103-3102
Phone: 860-392-5000
Fax: 860-392-5058
Email: acicchetti@cfjblaw.com
Anthony N. Cicchetti, Office Managing Shareholder

New York, NY
405 Lexington Avenue
29th Floor
New York
NY
10174-0002
Phone: 212-785-2577
Fax: 212-785-5203
Email: brosner@cfjblaw.com
Brian Rosner, New York Office Managing Shareholder

Washington, DC
1025 Thoomas Jefferson Street, NW
Suite 400 East
Washington
DC
20007-5208
Phone: 202-965-8100
Fax: 202-965-8104
Email: rgoss@cfjblaw.com
Roland Goss, Washington, DC Office Managing Shareholder

GrayRobinson

401 E Las Olas Blvd, Ste 1850
Fort Lauderdale, FL 33301
Phone: 954-761-8111
Fax: 954-761-8112
Web Site: www.gray-robinson.com

2016 Total Lawyers: 300
2015 Total Lawyers: 280

Greenspoon Marder, P.A.

100 West Cypress Creek Road
Suite 700
Fort Lauderdale, FL 33309
Phone: 954-491-1120
Fax: 954-771-9264
Email: info@gmlaw.com
Web Site: www.gmlaw.com

2016 Total Lawyers: 199
2015 Total Lawyers: 100

FLORIDA

Gunster

777 South Flagler Drive
Suite 500 East
West Palm Beach, FL 33401
Phone: 561-655-1980
Fax: 561-655-5677
Web Site: www.gunster.com

2016 Total Lawyers: 177
2015 Total Lawyers: 170

Hiring and Promotion
2016 First-Year Hires (Est.): 0
2015 Equity Partners Named: 0

Leading Practice Areas
(Department Heads)
Corporate (Bill Hyland 561-655-1980)
Technology & Entrepreneurial Companies
(David Bates 561-655-1980)
Banking & Financial Services (Greg Bader
954-462-2000)
Tax (Jim Davis 954-462-2000)
Immigration (Sarah Tobocman
305-376-6000)
Labor & Employment (Joe Curley, Joe
Santoro 561-655-1980, 561-655-1980)
Business Litigation (Mike Marcil, John
Mariani 954-462-2000, 561-655-1980)
Private Wealth Services (Dan Hanley
561-655-1980)
Real Estate, Land Use (Dan Mackler, Brian
Seymour 954-462-2000)
Environmental (Luna Phillips 954-462-2000)

Leading Officials
George S. LeMieux, Chairman of the Board,
850-521-1980
H. William Perry, Managing Shareholder,
561-655-1980
Stephen McDermott, COO, CFO (Chief
Operating Officer, Chief Financial
Officer), 561-655-1980
Brad Sprayberry, Director of Attorney
Recruiting & Professional Development,
561-655-1980
Jenni Garrison, Director of Marketing and
Corporate Communications, 561-655-1980
Carrie Hanna, CSO, Chief Strategy Officer,
561-655-1980
Grant Sagear, Director of Information
Technology, 561-655-1980
Roxann Waggener, Director of Library
Services, 561-655-1980

Other Offices
777 S. Flagler Drive
Suite 500 East
West Palm Beach, FL 33401
Phone: 561-655-1980
Fax: 561-655-5677
H. William Perry, managing shareholder

Hill Ward Henderson

P.O. Box 2231
Tampa, FL 33601
Phone: 813-221-3900
Fax: 813-221-2900

2016 Total Lawyers: 90
2015 Total Lawyers: 97

Lowndes, Drosdick, Doster, Kantor & Reed

215 North Eola Drive
Orlando, FL 32801
Phone: 407-843-4600
Fax: 407-843-4444
Email: lddk&r@lowndes-law.com
Web Site: www.lowndes-law.com

2016 Total Lawyers: 89
2015 Total Lawyers: 94

2016 Staff
Equity Partners: 62
Associates: 9
Of Counsel: 9
Senior Attorneys: 9

Offices: No. Attys.
Orlando, FL: 71
Melbourne FL: 2
Orlando 2, FL: 14
Mount Dora: 2

Hiring and Promotion
2015 Associates Hired: 3
2015 First-Year Hires: 2
Starting Salary for First-Year Assocs: N/A
2016 First-Year Hires (Est.): 3
2015 Equity Partners Named: 3

Leading Practice Areas
(Department Heads)
Real Estate 32.0% (Aaron J. Gorovitz
407-418-6336)
Litigation 18.0% (Terry C. Young
407-418-6347)
Corporate 18.0% (Peter E. Reinert
407-418-6291)
Wealth Management 8.0% (Julia L. Frey
407-418-6243)
Family & Marital Law 6.0% (Terry C. Young
407-418-6472)
Bankruptcy/Foreclosure/Creditors' Rights
5.0% (Robert F. Higgins, Gary Soles
407-418-6304, 407-418-6331)
Hospitality 5.0% (Richard J. Fildes
407-418-6412)
Tax 2.5% (Matthew R. O'Kane, Joseph
Zitzka 407-418-6255, 407-418-6318)
Construction Law 2.0% (Michael R. Gibbons,
Joseph A. Lane 407-418-6378,
407-418-6343)
Intellectual Property & Technology 1.0%
(Jon Gibbs, Richard Dellinger
407-418-6441, 407-418-6480)
Labor & Employment 1.0% (Rachel D.
Gebaide 407-418-6258)
Immigration & Naturalization 1.0% (Teresa
B. Finer 407-418-6262)
Healthcare 0.5% (James F. Heekin
407-418-6276)

Lowndes, Drosdick, Doster, Kantor &
Reed (Continued)

Client Representations
CNL
ROC | Seniors Housing & Medical Properties
Fund LP
Alan Ginsburg/CED Companies

Leading Officials
William T. Dymond, Jr., Managing Partner,
407-843-4600 ext. 342
Terry Navin, Chief Operating Officer,
407-843-4600 ext. 428
Greg McNeill, Hiring Partner, 407-843-4600
ext. 309
Daniel F. McIntosh, Recruiting Partner,
407-843-4600 ext. 272
Susanne Mandel, Chief Marketing &
Business Development Officer,
407-843-4600 ext. 421
Richard J. Hall, Director of Information
Technology, 407-843-4600 ext. 363
Nora Everlove, Head Librarian,
407-843-4600 ext. 248
Joaquin E. Martinez, Partner; Diversity
Committee Chair, 407-843-4600 ext. 475

Macfarlane, Ferguson, McMullen

201 North Franklin Street
Suite 2000
Tampa, FL 33601
Phone: 813-273-4200
Fax: 813-273-4396
Web Site: www.macfar.com

2016 Total Lawyers: 38
2015 Total Lawyers: 46

Rogers Towers

1301 Riverplace Boulevard
Suite 1500
Jacksonville, FL 32207
Phone: 904-398-3911
Fax: 904-396-0663
Email: rtlaw@rtlaw.com
Web Site: www.rtlaw.com

2016 Total Lawyers: 69
2015 Total Lawyers: 80

2016 Staff
Equity Partners: 39
Non-Equity Partners: 17
Associates: 21
Of Counsel: 3

Offices: No. Attys.
Jacksonville, FL: 73
St. Augustine, FL: 2
Amelia Island, FL: 1
Ponte Vedra Beach, FL: 9
Boca Raton: 3
Ft. Myers: 2
Orlando: 3
Tampa Bay: 1

Rogers Towers (Continued)

Hiring and Promotion
2015 Associates Hired: 5
2015 First-Year Hires: 2
2016 First-Year Hires (Est.): 0
2015 Equity Partners Named: 0

Leading Practice Areas
(Department Heads)
Real Estate (Christine Adams 904-346-5546)
Governmental and Regulatory Law (Wyman
    Duggan 904-346-5502)
Business and Tax (Richard Vermut
    904-346-5573)
Construction (Cheryl L. Worman
    904-346-5554)
Family Law (Sandra J. Mathis 904-346-5732)
Probate, Wills & Trusts (Clay Meux
    904-346-5534)
Intellectual Property (Richard S. Vermut
    904-346-5573)
Labor and Employment (Rene Fix
    904-346-5557)
Eminent Domain (A. Graham Allen
    904-346-5799)
Commercial Litigation (Christopher Hazelip
    904-346-5532)

Leading Officials
Fred Franklin, Jr., Managing Director
Pamela S. Bass, Executive Director
William Scheu, Recruiting Director
Andrew I. Aleman, Esq., Chief
    Strategic Officer
Kevin Rorabaugh, Director of
    Information Systems

Rumberger, Kirk & Caldwell

Lincoln Plaza
300 South Orange Avenue, Suite 1400
Orlando, FL 32801
Phone: 407-872-7300
Fax: 407-841-2133
Web Site: www.rumberger.com

2016 Total Lawyers: 88
2015 Total Lawyers: 89

Shutts & Bowen LLP

201 South Biscayne Boulevard
Suite 1500
Miami, FL 33131
Phone: 305-358-6300
Fax: 305-381-9982
Web Site: www.shutts.com

2016 Total Lawyers: 270
2015 Total Lawyers: 258

Stearns Weaver Miller Weissler Alhadaff & Sitterson, P.A.

150 West Flagler Street
Museum Tower, Suite 2200
Miami, FL 33130
Phone: 305-789-3200
Fax: 305-789-3395
Web Site: www.stearnsweaver.com

2016 Total Lawyers: 117
2015 Total Lawyers: 116

Trenam Kemker

101 East Kennedy Boulevard
Suite 2700
Tampa, FL 33602
Phone: 813-223-7474
Fax: 813-229-6553
Email: trenam@trenam.com
Web Site: trenam.com

2016 Total Lawyers: 79
2015 Total Lawyers: 78

Wicker Smith O'Hara McCoy & Ford P.A.

2800 Ponce de Leon Boulevard
Suite 800
Coral Gables, FL 33134
Phone: 305-448-3939
Fax: 305-441-1745
Web Site: www.wickersmith.com

2016 Total Lawyers: 160
2015 Total Lawyers: 152

Alston & Bird LLP

One Atlantic Center
1201 West Peachtree Street N
Atlanta, GA 30309-3424
Phone: 404-881-7000
Fax: 404-881-7777
Web Site: www.alston.com

2016 Total Lawyers: 782
2015 Total Lawyers: 900

Arnall Golden Gregory LLP

171 17th Street, NW
Suite 2100
Atlanta, GA 30363-1031
Phone: 404-873-8500
Fax: 404-873-8501
Email: info@agg.com
Web Site: www.agg.com

2016 Total Lawyers: 160
2015 Total Lawyers: 155

Constangy, Brooks, Smith & Prophete

230 Peachtree Street, N.W.
Suite 2400
Atlanta, GA 30303-1557
Phone: 404-525-8622
Fax: 404-525-6955
Email: info@constangy.com
Web Site: www.constangy.com

2016 Total Lawyers: 173
2015 Total Lawyers: 152

2016 Staff
Equity Partners: 53
Non-Equity Partners: 48
Associates: 35
Of Counsel: 24
Senior Counsel: 3

Offices: No. Attys.
Atlanta, GA: 28
Asheville, NC: 5
Birmingham, AL: 7
Columbia, SC: 2
Fairfax, VA: 6
Jacksonville, FL: 9
Kansas City, MO: 13
Macon, GA: 11
Nashville, TN: 10
Tampa, FL: 8
Winston-Salem, NC: 13
Austin, TX: 3
Greenville, SC: 1
Boston, MA: 9
Chicago, IL: 1
Los Angeles County, CA: 10
Ventura County, CA: 1
Madison, WI: 7
Dallas, TX: 4
Princeton, NJ: 5
Port St. Lucie, FL: 1
St. Louis, MO: 1
Opelika, AL: 1
West Point, GA: 1
Denver, CO: 5
New York, NY: 4

Hiring and Promotion
2015 Associates Hired: 12
2015 First-Year Hires: 2
2016 First-Year Hires (Est.): 0
2015 Equity Partners Named: 4
2015 Lateral Equity Partners: 2

Leading Practice Areas
(Department Heads)
Employment & Labor 100% (Neil Wasser
    404-525-8622)

Leading Officials
Neil H. Wasser, Chairman of Executive
    Committee, 404-230-6782
James Gillespie, Executive Administrator,
    404-230-6703
Victoria L. Whitaker, Chief Marketing
    Officer, 404-230-6730
Pramesh Naik, Chief Information Officer,
    404-230-6727
Steven Williamson, Head Librarian,
    404-230-6758
Neil Wasser, 404-525-8322

GEORGIA

Drew Eckl & Farnham, LLP

880 West Peachtree Street (30309)
P.O. Box 7600
Atlanta, GA 30357-0624
Phone: 404-885-1400
Fax: 404-876-0992
Web Site: www.deflaw.com

2016 Total Lawyers: 95
2015 Total Lawyers: 84

Fisher Phillips

1075 Peachtree Street, NE
Suite 3500
Atlanta, GA 30309
Phone: 404-231-1400
Fax: 404-240-4249
Email: info@laborlawyers.com
Web Site: www.fisherphillips.com

2016 Total Lawyers: 340
2015 Total Lawyers: 300

2016 Staff
Equity Partners: 119
Non-Equity Partners: 56
Associates: 98
Of Counsel: 49
Senior Counsel: 11
Staff Attorneys: 7

Offices: No. Attys.
Atlanta, GA: 47
Charlotte, NC: 6
Chicago, IL: 11
Columbia, SC: 14
Dallas, TX: 4
Denver, CO: 13
Ft. Lauderdale, FL: 12
Houston, TX: 9
Irvine, CA: 35
Kansas City, MO: 6
Las Vegas, NV: 4
Louisville, KY: 18
Murray Hill, NJ: 12
New Orleans, LA: 9
Orlando, FL: 5
Radnor, PA: 22
Portland, OR: 7
San Diego, CA: 15
San Francisco, CA: 8
Tampa, FL: 7
Baltimore, MD: 1
Boston, MA: 5
Cleveland, OH: 23
Columbus, OH: 7
Gulfport, LA: 2
Los Angeles, CA: 13
Memphis, TN: 7
Phoenix, AZ: 3
Portland, OR: 10
Sacramento, CA: 2
San Antonio, TX: 3
Seattle, WA: 6
Washington, D.C.: 1

Fisher Phillips (Continued)

Hiring and Promotion
2015 Associates Hired: 35
2015 First-Year Hires: 4
2016 First-Year Hires (Est.): 6
2015 Equity Partners Named: 3

Leading Officials
Roger Quillen, Chairman & Managing
Partner, 404-240-4241
Steven Mauro, Chief Operating Officer,
404-240-4282
Raffaele Murdocca, Director of Recruiting &
Professional Development, 404-240-5840
Kevin Sullivan, Chief Marketing Officer,
404-240-4248
James Miskovsky, Director of Information
Technology, 404-240-5844
Scott Snipes, Director of Research &
Knowledge Services, 404-240-4262

Hunter Maclean Exley & Dunn, P.C.

200 East Saint Julian Street
P.O. Box 9848
Savannah, GA 31412
Phone: 912-236-0261
Fax: 912-236-4936
Email: infosavannah@huntermaclea
Web Site: www.huntermaclean.com

2016 Total Lawyers: 50
2015 Total Lawyers: 46

Kilpatrick Townsend & Stockton LLP

1100 Peachtree Street
Suite 2800
Atlanta, GA 30309
Phone: 404-815-6500
Fax: 404-815-6555
Email: ktslegal@kilpatricktownse
Web Site: www.KilpatrickTownsend.com

2016 Total Lawyers: 650
2015 Total Lawyers: 630

Leading Practice Areas
(Department Heads)
Intellectual Property Department (Wab P.
Kadaba 404-815-6500)
Corporate, Finance, and Real Estate
Department (including Banking &
Financial Institutions) (Rex R. Veal
404-815-6500)
Litigation Department (Stephen E. Hudson
404-815-6500)

Kilpatrick Townsend & Stockton LLP (Continued)

Leading Officials
Henry Walker, Chair, 404-815-6500
Susan Spaeth, Managing Firm Partner
Gary Dacey, Chief Operating Officer,
404-815-6500
Kim Dechiara, Associate Director, Attorney
Recruitment & Development,
404-815-6500
Brian Colucci, Chief Marketing Officer,
415-546-0200
Randy Pulley, Director of Business
Development, 919-420-1700
Jamie Usher, Chief Information Officer,
404-815-6500
Lynda Murray-Blair, Diversity Manager,
404-815-6500

King & Spalding, LLP

1180 Peachtree Street NE
Atlanta, GA 30309
Phone: 404-572-4600
Fax: 404-572-5100
Email: king&spalding@kslaw.com
Web Site: www.kslaw.com

2016 Total Lawyers: 974
2015 Total Lawyers: 974

Morris, Manning & Martin, LLP

1600 Atlanta Financial Center
3343 Peachtree Road, NE
Atlanta, GA 30326
Phone: 404-233-7000
Fax: 404-365-9532
Email: jes@mmmlaw.com
Web Site: www.mmmlaw.com

2016 Total Lawyers: 175
2015 Total Lawyers: 190

Ogletree, Deakins, Nash, Smoak & Stewart, P.C.

191 Peachtree Street, N.E.
Suite 4800
Atlanta, GA 30303
Phone: 404-881-1300
Fax: 404-870-1732
Email: clientservices@ogletree
Web Site: www.ogletreedeakins.com

2016 Total Lawyers: 783
2015 Total Lawyers: 736

2016 Staff
Equity Partners: 162
Non-Equity Partners: 219
Associates: 251
Of Counsel: 95
Staff Attorneys: 9

Offices: No. Attys.
Greenville, SC: 38
Atlanta, GA: 36

GEORGIA

Ogletree, Deakins, Nash, Smoak & Stewart, P.C. (Continued)
Birmingham, AL: 14
Charleston, SC: 5
Chicago, IL: 34
Dallas, TX: 24
Houston, TX: 19
Indianapolis, IN: 33
Los Angeles, CA: 42
Nashville, TN: 13
Raleigh, NC: 31
San Antonio, TX: 7
St. Thomas, Virgin Islands: 6
Washington, DC: 31
Columbia, SC: 13
Austin, TX: 9
Miami, FL: 8
Morristown, NJ: 18
Charotte, NC: 11
Kansas City, MO: 16
Phoenix, AZ: 19
Tampa, FL: 19
Torrance, CA: 1
Tucson, AZ: 3
Cleveland, OH: 13
Pittsburgh, PA: 14
Philadelphia, PA: 10
Boston, MA: 17
Denver, CO: 15
Detroit, MI: 14
Jackson, MS: 3
Las Vegas, NV: 9
Memphis, TN: 9
New Orleans, LA: 14
Orange County, CA: 25
San Francisco, CA: 26
St. Louis, MO: 22
Minneapolis, MN: 8
San Diego, CA: 14
London, England: 4
Richmond, VA: 7
Berlin, Germany: 8
New York City: 16
Portland, OR: 18
Milwaukee, WI: 9
Stamford, CT: 5
Mexico City, Mexico: 5

Hiring and Promotion
2015 Associates Hired: 60
2015 Equity Partners Named: 21
2015 Lateral Equity Partners: 15

Revenues and Profits
Revenues: $373,000,000

Client Representations
D.R. Horton, Inc. v. NLRB, No. 12-60031, United States Court of Appeals for the 5th Circuit
Mach Mining, LLC v. EEOC, No. 13-1019, Supreme Court of the United States
Browning-Ferris Industries of California, Inc., d/b/a BFI Newby Island Recyclery, et al. v. Teamsters Local 350

Ogletree, Deakins, Nash, Smoak & Stewart, P.C. (Continued)

Leading Officials
Kim F. Ebert, Managing Shareholder
Jim McGrew, Chief Marketing Officer
Jennifer Bratcher, Director of Business Development and Client Services
Gary Berger, Director of Technology
Marcia Burris, Senior Manager, Firm Library Services
Michelle Wimes, Director of Professional Development and Inclusion

Parker Hudson Rainer & Dobbs

1500 Marquis Two Tower
285 Peachtree Center Ave, NE
Atlanta, GA 30303
Phone: 404-523-5300
Fax: 404-523-8409
Web Site: www.phrd.com

2016 Total Lawyers: 77
2015 Total Lawyers: 64

Smith, Currie & Hancock

2700 Marquis One Tower
245 Peachtree Avenue, N.E.
Atlanta, GA 30303
Phone: 404-521-3800
Fax: 404-688-0671
Web Site: www.smithcurrie.com

2016 Total Lawyers: 59
2015 Total Lawyers: 57

Smith, Gambrell & Russell

1230 Peachtree Street, NE
Promenade, Suite 3100
Atlanta, GA 30309-3592
Phone: 404-815-3500
Fax: 404-815-3509
Email: info@sgrlaw.com
Web Site: www.sgrlaw.com

2016 Total Lawyers: 192
2015 Total Lawyers: 186

Sutherland Asbill & Brennan LLP

999 Peachtree Street, NE
Atlanta, GA 30309
Phone: 404-853-8000
Fax: 404-853-8806
Email: info@sutherland.com
Web Site: www.sutherland.com

2016 Total Lawyers: 438
2015 Total Lawyers: 419

Swift, Currie, McGhee & Hiers, LLP

1355 Peachtree Street NE
Suite 300
Atlanta, GA 30309-3238
Phone: 404-874-8800
Fax: 404-888-6199
Web Site: www.swiftcurrie.com

2016 Total Lawyers: 114
2015 Total Lawyers: 99

Troutman Sanders LLP

600 Peachtree Street, N.E.
Suite 5200
Atlanta, GA 30308
Phone: 404-885-3000
Fax: 404-885-3900
Web Site: www.troutmansanders.com

2016 Total Lawyers: 615
2015 Total Lawyers: 600

HAWAII

Cades Schutte LLP

1000 Bishop Street
Suite 1200
Honolulu, HI 96813-4216
Phone: 808-521-9200
Fax: 808-521-9210
Email: cades@cades.com
Web Site: www.cades.com

2016 Total Lawyers: 64
2015 Total Lawyers: 66

Carlsmith Ball LLP

ASB Tower
1001 Bishop Street, Suite 2200
Honolulu, HI 96813
Phone: 808-523-2500
Fax: 808-523-0842
Email: media@carlsmith.com
Web Site: www.carlsmith.com

2016 Total Lawyers: 73
2015 Total Lawyers: 78

Goodsill Anderson Quinn & Stifel LLP

999 Bishop Street
Suite 1600
Honolulu, HI 96813
Phone: 808-547-5600
Fax: 808-547-5880
Email: info@goodsill.com
Web Site: www.goodsill.com

2016 Total Lawyers: 62
2015 Total Lawyers: 57

IDAHO

Hawley Troxell Ennis & Hawley LLP

877 Main Street
Suite 1000
Boise, ID 83701-1617
Phone: 208-344-6000
Fax: 208-342-3829
Email: info@hawleytroxell.com
Web Site: www.hawleytroxell.com

2016 Total Lawyers: 61
2015 Total Lawyers: 62

ILLINOIS

Arnstein & Lehr LLP

120 South Riverside Plaza
Suite 1200
Chicago, IL 60606-3913
Phone: 312-876-7100
Fax: 312-876-0288
Email: info@arnstein.com
Web Site: www.arnstein.com

2016 Total Lawyers: 141
2015 Total Lawyers: 147

2016 Staff
Equity Partners: 39
Non-Equity Partners: 72
Associates: 22
Of Counsel: 14
Partner Emeritus: 1
General Counsel: 1

Offices: No. Attys.
Chicago, IL: 92
Miami, FL: 31
Milwaukee, WI: 2
Tampa, FL: 5
West Palm Beach, FL: 5
Fort Lauderdale, FL: 12

Hiring and Promotion
2015 Associates Hired: 8
2015 First-Year Hires: 3
2016 First-Year Hires (Est.): 1
2015 Equity Partners Named: 2
2015 Lateral Equity Partners: 6

Leading Practice Areas
(Department Heads)
Litigation 33% (Michael C. Gesas)
Real Estate 26% (Paul Diamond, Joel
   M. Hurwitz)
Corporate Transactions & Counseling 16%
   (Mark F. Miller)
Estate Planning and Probate Administration
   7% (Jay P. Tarshis)
Heathcare 4% (Thomas Conley)
Tax Controversy 3% (Robert E. McKenzie)
Bankruptcy & Creditors' Rights 3% (Barry
   A. Chatz)
Governmental and Municipal Affiars 3%
   (Arthur Janura)

Arnstein & Lehr LLP (Continued)

Leading Officials
Raymond J. Werner, Chairman of the
   Executive Committee, 312-876-7100
Edward O'Connell, Chief Operating Officer,
   312-876-7172
Robert D. Butters, Hiring Partner,
   312-876-7100
Susan Thompsonn, Director of Human
   Resources, 312-876-7100
Jeffrey A. Hild, Director of Marketing,
   312-876-7100
John Emel, Chief Information Officer,
   312-876-7100
Robert T. Cichocki, Chair of the Diversity
   Committee, 312-876-7100

Other Offices
120 South Riverside Plaza
1200
Chicago
Illinois
60606
Phone: 312-876-7100
Fax: 312-876-0288

Baker & McKenzie

300 East Randolph Drive, Suite 43
Chicago, IL 60601
Phone: 312-861-8800
Fax: 312-861-8823
Web Site: www.bakernet.com

2016 Total Lawyers: 3294
2015 Total Lawyers: 4200

Banner & Witcoff, Ltd.

10 South Wacker Drive
Suite 3000
Chicago, IL 60606
Phone: 312-463-5000
Fax: 312-463-5001
Email: info@bannerwitcoff.com
Web Site: www.bannerwitcoff.com

2016 Total Lawyers: 98
2015 Total Lawyers: 94

Bartlit Beck Herman Palenchar & Scott

Courthouse Place
54 West Hubbard St, Ste 300
Chicago, IL 60654
Phone: 312-494-4400
Fax: 312-494-4440

2016 Total Lawyers: 81
2015 Total Lawyers: 80

Cassiday Schade LLP

20 North Wacker Drive
Suite 1000
Chicago, IL 60606
Phone: 312-641-3100
Fax: 312-444-1669
Email: info@cassiday.com
Web Site: www.cassiday.com

2016 Total Lawyers: 106
2015 Total Lawyers: 106

2016 Staff
Associates: 38
Of Counsel: 4
ALL Partners 61

Offices: No. Attys.
Libertyville, IL: 7
Naperville, IL: 5
Rockford, IL: 3
Crown Point, IN: 4
Milwaukee, WI: 2
Chicago: 74
Springfield: 4

Hiring and Promotion
2015 Associates Hired: 6
2015 First-Year Hires: 2
2016 First-Year Hires (Est.): 0

Leading Officials
Joseph A. Giannelli, Managing Partner
John D. Hackett, Managing Partner
Karen L. Peacock, Controller
Anne Junia, Hiring Partner
Jennifer R. Pogvara, Human Resources and
   Personnel Manager
Dan Maguire, Marketing Manager
Robert Biedron, Technology Manager
Daniel Byrne, Administrative
   Services Manager
Kimberly L. Robinson, Partner

Chapman and Cutler LLP

111 West Monroe Street
Chicago, IL 60603
Phone: 312-845-3000
Fax: 312-701-2361
Web Site: www.chapman.com

2016 Total Lawyers: 225
2015 Total Lawyers: 240

2016 Staff
Equity Partners: 96
Non-Equity Partners: 47
Associates: 58
Of Counsel: 2
Counsel: 3
Senior Counsel: 13
Staff Attorneys: 6

Offices: No. Attys.
New York, NY: 22
Chicago, IL: 170
Salt Lake City, UT: 3
San Francisco, CA: 17
Washington, DC: 13

Hiring and Promotion
2015 Associates Hired: 7
2015 First-Year Hires: 5

ILLINOIS

Chapman and Cutler LLP (Continued)

*Leading Practice Areas
(Department Heads)*
Corporate and Securities (Eric F. Fess)
Illinois Public Finance (William E.
  Corbin, Jr.)
Banking and Financial Services (James R.
  Theiss, Jr.)
Corporate Finance (Anthony M. Yager)
Bankruptcy and Restructuring (Franklin H.
  Top, III, Michael Friedman)
Tax (Melanie J. Gnazzo)
Trusts and Estates (David A. Lullo)
National Public and Health & Education
  Finance (Nancy A. Burke, Michael
  J. Mitchell)
Asset Securitization (Walter P. Begley)
Credit Enhancement (R. William Hunter)

Leading Officials
Timothy P. Mohan, Chief Executive Partner,
  312-845-2966
William M. Libit, Chief Operating Partner,
  312-845-2981
Mark T. Verbecken, Executive Director,
  312-845-3440
Aaron J. Efta, Chair, Employment
  Committee, 312-845-3796
Stacey Kielbasa, Director of Professional
  Development, Attorney Recruitment and
  Diversity, 312-845-2997
Nancy Linder, Director of Marketing,
  312-701-2388
David Hambourger, Chief Information
  Officer, 312-845-3737
Sarah Andeen, Knowledge and Research
  Services Manager, 312-845-3749
Walter L. Draney / Juliet H. Huang, Partner,
  312-845-3000

Clausen Miller

10 South LaSalle Street
Chicago, IL 60603-1098
Phone: 312-855-1010
Fax: 312-606-7777
Email: info@clausen.com
Web Site: www.clausen.com

2016 Total Lawyers: 102
2015 Total Lawyers: 108

2016 Staff
Equity Partners: 36
Non-Equity Partners: 40
Associates: 25
Of Counsel: 1

Offices: No. Attys.
Chicago, IL: 60.5
New York, NY: 29
Florham, NJ: 2
Irvine, CA: 10
Michigan City, IN: .5

Hiring and Promotion
2015 Associates Hired: 6
2016 First-Year Hires (Est.): 2
2015 Equity Partners Named: 3

Clausen Miller (Continued)

*Leading Practice Areas
(Department Heads)*
Casualty 45%
Liability Coverage 18%
Property 17%
Subrogation 10%
Appellate 5%
Commercial Litigation 4%
Fidelity 1%

Leading Officials
Dennis Fitzpatrick, President
Vincent McInerney, Director of
  Administration
William Pistorius, Hiring Partner
Colleen Cheraitia, Human
  Resources Manager
Stephanie Lyons, Marketing Coordinator
Scott Timmerman, Technology Manager
Dennis Fitzpatrick, President

Dentons

233 South Wacker Drive
Suite 8000
Chicago, IL 60606-6404
Phone: 312-876-8000
Fax: 312-876-7934
Web Site: www.dentons.com

2016 Total Lawyers: 7300
2015 Total Lawyers: 2746

Faegre Baker Daniels

311 S. Wacker Drive
Suite 4400
Chicago, IL 60606
Phone: 312-212-6500
Fax: 312-212-6501
Email: info@FaegreBD.com
Web Site: www.FaegreBD.com

2016 Total Lawyers: 750
2015 Total Lawyers: 741

2016 Staff
Associates: 287
Partners: 377
Of Counsel / Counsel: 77

Offices: No. Attys.
Minneapolis, MN: 283
Indianapolis, IN: 201
Denver, CO: 67
Fort Wayne, IN: 31
Chicago, IL: 54
Des Moines, IA: 27
London, England: 20
South Bend, IN: 18
Boulder, CO: 17
Shanghai, China: 10
Washington, D.C.: 7
Beijing, China: 1
Silicon Valley, CA: 5

Faegre Baker Daniels (Continued)

*Leading Practice Areas
(Department Heads)*
Labor/Employment (including immigration)
  and Benefits (Scott Wright, Maureen Maly
  612-766-7000, 612-766-8414)
Intellectual Property (Cal Litsey
  650-324-6708)
Corporate (corporate finance, emerging
  business, international) and Tax Advocacy
  (Chris Hofstad, Francina Dlouhy
  612-766-7000, 317-237-0300)
Health Care & FDA (Tom Schroeder
  612-766-7220)
Finance & Restructuring (Mike Stewart
  612-766-7928)
Government Advocacy and Consulting
  (David Zook 202-312-7440)
Wealth Management (David Shannon
  612-766-7000)
Exempt Organizations (Lowell Haines
  317-237-0300)
Insurance (Dick Freijie 317-237-1208)
Litigation (business, product liability and
  environmental, construction and real
  estate) (David Herzog, Joseph Tanner,
  Mark Voigtmann 317-237-0300)

Leading Officials
Andrew G. Humphrey, Managing Partner
Thomas C. Froehle, Jr., Chief
  Operating Partner
Maggie Gloyeske, Director of Lawyer &
  Consultant Recruiting
Melanie S. Green, Chief Client
  Development Officer
Brad Frederiksen, Chief Information &
  Knowledge Management Officer
Constance Matts, Director of
  Information Resources
Kristine L. McKinney, Director of Diversity
  & Inclusion, 612-766-7195

Other Offices
  90 South 7th Street
  2200 Wells Fargo Center
  Minneapolis
  MN
  55402
  Phone: 612-766-7000
  Fax: 612-766-1600
  Steven C. Kennedy, Office Leader

  300 N. Meridian Street
  Suite 2700
  Indianapolis
  IN
  46204
  Phone: 317-237-0300
  Fax: 317-237-1000
  Murray Clark, Office Leader

  1700 Lincoln Street
  3200 Wells Fargo Center
  Denver
  CO
  80203
  Phone: 303-607-3500
  Fax: 303-607-3600
  Heather Perkins, Office Leader

ILLINOIS

Faegre Baker Daniels (Continued)

311 S. Wacker Drive
Suite 4300
Chicago
IL
60606
Phone: 312-212-6500
Fax: 312-212-6501
Rick Michaels, Office Leader

Freeborn & Peters

311 S. Wacker Drive
Suite 3000
Chicago, IL 60606-6677
Phone: 312-360-6000
Fax: 312-360-6520
Email: jmazurek@freebornpeters.c
Web Site: freebornpeters.com

2016 Total Lawyers: 126
2015 Total Lawyers: 134

Gould & Ratner

222 North LaSalle St, Ste 800
Chicago, IL 60601
Phone: 312-236-3003
Fax: 312-236-3241
Email: info@gouldratner.com
Web Site: www.gouldratner.com

2016 Total Lawyers: 41
2015 Total Lawyers: 46

Hinshaw & Culbertson LLP

222 North LaSalle Street
Suite 300
Chicago, IL 60601-1081
Phone: 312-704-3000
Fax: 312-704-3001
Email: info@hinshawlaw.com
Web Site: www.hinshawlaw.com

2016 Total Lawyers: 525
2015 Total Lawyers: 459

2016 Staff
Equity Partners: 116
Non-Equity Partners: 218
Associates: 163
Of Counsel: 19
Senior Counsel: 9

Offices: No. Attys.
Chicago, IL: 157
Rockford, IL: 37
Minneapolis, MN: 22
Miami, FL: 46
Fort Lauderdale, FL: 16
Milwaukee, WI: 13
Belleville, IL: 15
Peoria, IL: 11
San Francisco, CA: 29
Tampa, FL: 14
Springfield, IL: 10
Jacksonville, FL: 8

Hinshaw & Culbertson LLP (Continued)
St. Louis, MO: 5
Schererville, IN: 14
Phoenix, AZ: 7
West - Los Angeles, CA: 27
Edwardsville, IL: 1
Third Avenue - New York, NY: 32
Appleton, WI: 7
Boston, MA: 27
Sacramento, CA: 1
Irvine, CA: 4
Downtown - Los Angeles, CA: 21
London, England: 1

Hiring and Promotion
2015 Associates Hired: 42
2015 First-Year Hires: 8
2016 First-Year Hires (Est.): 5
2015 Equity Partners Named: 5
2015 Lateral Equity Partners: 2

Leading Practice Areas
(Department Heads)
Insurance Services 18% (Ronald L. Kammer
and Scott M. Seaman 305-428-5100 and
312-704-3699)
Commercial Transactions 12% (Dean E.
Parker 312-704-3117)
Business Litigation 11% (Daniel K. Ryan
312-704-3248)
Professional Responsibility, Professional
Liability & Risk Management 11% (John
W. Sheller 310-909-8080)
Consumer Financial Services 9% (Ellen B.
Silverman 612-333-3434)
Health Care 9% (Stephen T. Moore
815-490-4903)
Personal Injury & Property Damage 9% (Dan
L. Boho and Renee J. Mortimer
312-704-3453 and 219-864-4505)
Labor & Employment 8% (Aimee E. Delaney
312-704-3258)
Government 7% (Sergio E. Acosta
312-704-3000)
Product Liability 6% (Daniel W. McGrath
312-343-3482)

Revenues and Profits
Revenues: $227,300,000

Leading Officials
Kevin Joseph Burke, Firm Chairman,
312-704-3488
Robert T. Shannon, Managing Partner,
312-704-3901
Paul R. Boken, Executive Managing Director,
312-704-3208
Mary J. Hess, Hiring Partner, 312-704-3830
Mary Beth Walsh, Attorney Recruitment &
Development Manager, 312-704-3493
John R. Neidecker, Chief Marketing Officer,
312-704-3097
Tracy H. Elmblad, Chief Information Officer,
312-704-3330
Jennifer M. Soria, Library Manager,
312-704-3422
Leslie Richards-Yellen, Chief Diversity and
Inclusion Officer, 312-704-3562

Hinshaw & Culbertson LLP (Continued)

Other Offices
Chicago
222 N. LaSalle Street
Suite 300
Chicago
IL
60601
Phone: 312-704-3000
Fax: 312-704-3001
Email: Info@hinshawlaw.com
Diane E. Webster

Jenner & Block LLP

353 N. Clark St.
Chicago, IL 60654
Phone: 312-222-9350
Fax: 312-527-0484
Web Site: www.jenner.com

2016 Total Lawyers: 500
2015 Total Lawyers: 450

2016 Staff
Equity Partners: 114
Non-Equity Partners: 117
Associates: 204
Of Counsel: 13
Staff Attorneys: 60

Offices: No. Attys.
Chicago, IL: 304
Washington, DC: 101
New York, NY: 70
Los Angeles, CA: 45
London, UK: 9

Hiring and Promotion
2015 Associates Hired: 61
2015 First-Year Hires: 26
Starting Salary for First-Year Assocs:
$160,000 (as of July 1, 2016—$180,000)
2016 First-Year Hires (Est.): 40
2015 Equity Partners Named: 7
2015 Lateral Equity Partners: 1

Revenues and Profits
Revenues: $464,891,012
Profits: $195,644,144

Leading Officials
Anton R. Valukas, Firm Chairman
Terrence J. Truax, Firm Managing Partner
Meredith W. Mendes, Executive Director &
Chief Operating Officer
Charlotte L. Wager , Chief Talent Officer
Alexis M. Reed, Director of Lateral
Partner Recruiting
Suzanne Donnels, Chief Marketing Officer
Amol V. Bargaje, Chief Information Officer
Mitchell D. Klaich, Director of Library &
Information Resources
Jami de Lou, Associate Director of Talent
Development, Diversity & Inclusion

ILLINOIS

Jenner & Block LLP (Continued)

Other Offices
Washington, DC
1099 New York Avenue, NW
Suite 900
Washington
DC
20001-4412
Phone: 202-639-6000
Fax: 202-639-6066
Samuel L. Feder, DC Managing Partner

New York
919 Third Avenue
New York
NY
10022-3908
Phone: 212-891-1600
Fax: 212-891-1699
Susan J. Kohlmann, NY Managing Partner

Johnson & Bell, Ltd.

33 East Monroe Street
Suite 2700
Chicago, IL 60603-5896
Phone: 312-372-0770
Fax: 312-372-9818
Web Site: www.johnsonandbell.com

2016 Total Lawyers: 91
2015 Total Lawyers: 104

Katten Muchin Rosenman LLP

525 West Monroe Street
Chicago, IL 60661-3693
Phone: 312-902-5200
Fax: 312-902-1061
Email: postmaster@kattenlaw.com
Web Site: www.kattenlaw.com

2016 Total Lawyers: 625
2015 Total Lawyers: 643

Kirkland & Ellis

300 North LaSalle Street
Chicago, IL 60654
Phone: 312-862-2000
Fax: 312-862-2200
Email: info@kirkland.com
Web Site: www.kirkland.com

2016 Total Lawyers: 1686
2015 Total Lawyers: 1607

2016 Staff
Associates: 885
Total Partners 801

Offices: No. Attys.
Chicago, IL: 580
New York, NY: 393
Washington, DC: 176
London, England: 145
San Francisco, CA: 103

Kirkland & Ellis (Continued)
Los Angeles, CA: 92
Hong Kong: 73
Houston, TX: 54
Munich, Germany: 37
Palo Alto, CA: 22
Shanghai: 6
Beijing: 5

Hiring and Promotion
2015 Associates Hired: 277
2015 First-Year Hires: 141
Starting Salary for First-Year
   Assocs: $180,000
2016 First-Year Hires (Est.): 158
2015 Lateral Equity Partners: 39

Leading Practice Areas
(Department Heads)
Transactional 45%
Litigation 26%
Intellectual Property 13%
Restructuring/Bankruptcy 6%
Tax 6%
Real Estate 2%
Other 2%

Client Representations
Energy Future Holdings Co.
GM
Vista Equity Partners

Leading Officials
Jeffrey C. Hammes, P.C., Chairman,
   312-862-2000
Brigitte Wooster, Executive Director,
   Firmwide Administrative Services,
   312-447-1962
Elizabeth Deeley and Jason Kanner,
   Co-Chairs, Firmwide Recruiting
   Committee, 312-862-2000
Wendy Cartland, Senior Director of
   Firmwide Human Resources,
   312-862-2037
Maria Black, Senior Director of Business
   Development, 312-862-3493
Dan Nottke, Chief Information Officer,
   312-862-2870
Joan Batchen, Senior Director of Library
   Services, 312-862-2399
Rina Alvarez, Director of Firmwide
   Diversity, 312-862-2918

Other Offices
New York
601 Lexington Avenue
New York
NY
10022
Phone: 212-446-4800
Fax: 212-446-4900

Washington, D.C.
655 Fifteenth Street, N.W.
Washington
DC
20005
Phone: 202-879-5000
Fax: 202-879-5200

Kirkland & Ellis (Continued)

Los Angeles
333 South Hope Street
Los Angeles
CA
90071
Phone: 213-680-8400
Fax: 213-680-8500

Chicago
300 North LaSalle
Chicago
IL
60654
Phone: 312-862-2000
Fax: 312-862-2200

London
30 St Mary Axe
London
England
EC3A 8AF
Phone: 442-074-692 ext. 000
Fax: 442-074-692 ext. 001

San Francisco
555 California Street
San Francisco
CA
94104
Phone: 415-439-1400
Fax: 415-439-1500

Hong Kong
The Landmark, 15 Queen's Road Central
26th Floor, Gloucester Tower
Hong Kong
Phone: 852-376-1 ext. 3300
Fax: 852-376-1 ext. 3301

Houston
600 Travis Street
Suite 3300
Houston
TX
77002
Phone: 713-835-3600
Fax: 713-835-3601

Mayer Brown

71 South Wacker Dr
Chicago, IL 60606-4637
Phone: 312-782-0600
Fax: 312-701-7711
Email: info@mayerbrown.com
Web Site: www.mayerbrown.com

2016 Total Lawyers: 1583
2015 Total Lawyers: 1583

2016 Staff
Equity Partners: 656
Associates: 970
Counsel: 163
Staff Attorneys: 21

Offices: No. Attys.
Bangkok: 4
Beijing: 24
Brussels: 19
Charlotte: 40
Chicago: 414
Hanoi: 4

ILLINOIS

Mayer Brown (Continued)
Ho Chi Minh City: 5
Hong Kong: 215
Houston: 51
London: 242
Los Angeles: 41
Mexico City: 2
New York: 222
Palo Alto: 31
Paris: 82
Rio de Janeiro: 78
Sao Paolo: 82
Singapore: 8
Washington DC: 193

Hiring and Promotion
2015 Associates Hired: 254
2015 First-Year Hires: 106

Revenues and Profits
Revenues: $1,257,000,000
Profits: $445,679,000

Client Representations
TransCanada's $13 billion buyout of
   Columbia Pipeline Group
Wells Fargo's $32 billion acquisition of
   certain GE Capital business units
Spokeo's landmark Supreme Court win in
   standing dispute

Leading Officials
Paul W. Theiss, Chairman, 312-782-7359
Kenneth S. Geller, Managing Partner,
   202-263-3000
Evan Merberg, Chief Operating Officer,
   212-506-2500
Jerry DeBerry, Director of Diversity &
   Inclusion, 212-506-2761

McDermott Will & Emery

227 West Monroe Street
Chicago, IL 60606-5096
Phone: 312-372-2000
Fax: 312-984-7700
Web Site: www.mwe.com

2016 Total Lawyers: 1021
2015 Total Lawyers: 1100

McKenna Storer

33 N. LaSalle Street
Suite 1400
Chicago, IL 60602
Phone: 312-558-3900
Fax: 312-558-8348
Web Site: www.mckenna-law.com

2016 Total Lawyers: 19
2015 Total Lawyers: 20

Much Shelist, P.C.

191 North Wacker Drive
Suite 1800
Chicago, IL 60606-1615
Phone: 312-521-2000
Fax: 312-521-2100
Email: info@muchshelist.com
Web Site: www.muchshelist.com

2016 Total Lawyers: 86
2015 Total Lawyers: 89

2016 Staff
Equity Partners: 19
Non-Equity Partners: 38
Associates: 13
Senior Attorneys: 5
Special Counsel: 7
Retired 4

Offices: No. Attys.
Chicago, IL: 86
Irvine, CA: 4

Hiring and Promotion
2015 Associates Hired: 4
2015 First-Year Hires: 1
Starting Salary for First-Year Assocs: Much
   Shelist does not provide salary
   information.
2016 First-Year Hires (Est.): Unknown
2015 Equity Partners Named: 0

Leading Practice Areas
(Department Heads)
Business & Finance (Michael B.
   Shaw/Katherine Bonk Lewis
   312-521-2610 312.521.2744)
Labor & Employment (Sheryl Jaffee Halpern
   312-521-2637)
Litigation & Dispute Resolution (Edward D.
   Shapiro / Martin J. O'Hara 312-521-2421
   312-521-2725)
Real Estate Law (Harold S. Dembo /
   Courtney E. Mayster 312-521-2684
   312-521-2677)
Creditors' Rights, Insolvency & Bankruptcy
   (Jeffrey M. Schwartz 312.521.2626)
Intellectual Property & Technology (Adam
   K. Sacharoff 312.521.2775)
Construction Law (Scott R. Fradin / Josh M.
   Leavitt 312.521.2610 312.521.2627)
Health Care Law (Robert K. Neiman/Ned
   Milenkovich 312.521.2646 312.521.2482)
Venture Capital & Emerging Growth
   Companies (Gregory D. Grove
   312.521.2798)
Wealth Transfer & Succession Planning
   (Gregg M. Simon / Gregory B. Mann
   312.521.2605 312.521.2461)

Much Shelist, P.C. (Continued)

Leading Officials
David T. Brown, Chairman of the Board,
   Much Shelist, P.C., 331-521-2754
Mitchell S. Roth, Chair, Management
   Committee, 312-521-2477
Mitchell S. Roth, Chair, Lateral Task Force,
   312-521-2477
Jennifer Gallison, Director of Attorney
   Recruitment & Development,
   312-521-2119
Michael C. James, Director of Marketing &
   Business Development, 312-521-2120
Paul Austin, Director of Technical Services,
   312-521-2160
Kendalle Jacobson, Head Librarian,
   312-521-2102

Other Offices
Chicago, IL
191 N. Wacker
Suite 1800
Chicago
IL
60606-1615
Phone: 312-521-2000
Fax: 312-521-2100
Email: info@muchshelist.com

Irvine, CA
2 Park Plaza
1075
Irvine
CA
92614
Phone: 949-385-5353
Fax: 949-385-5355
Email: info@muchshelist.com

Neal, Gerber & Eisenberg LLP

2 North LaSalle Street
Suite 1700
Chicago, IL 60602
Phone: 312-269-8000
Fax: 312-269-1747
Web Site: www.ngelaw.com

2016 Total Lawyers: 137
2015 Total Lawyers: 137

2016 Staff
Equity Partners: 66
Non-Equity Partners: 21
Associates: 22
Of Counsel: 3
Counsel: 4
Senior Counsel: 11
Associate Counsel 9
Contract Attorneys 1

Offices: No. Attys.
Chicago: 137

Hiring and Promotion
2015 Associates Hired: 4
Starting Salary for First-Year
   Assocs: $150,000
2016 First-Year Hires (Est.): 0
2015 Equity Partners Named: 1

ILLINOIS

Neal, Gerber & Eisenberg LLP (Continued)

Leading Officials
Scott J. Fisher, Managing Partner,
312-269-8035
Sonia Menon, Chief Operating Officer,
312-269-8079
Jenny S. Kim, Hiring Committe Chair,
312-269-8000
Maria J. Minor, Director of Professional
Recruitment & Development,
312-269-5226
Holly L. Barocio, Marketing and
Communications Manager, 312-269-8065
Clint M. Kehoe, Director of Information
Technology, 312-269-8482
Diana J. Koppang, Library Manager,
312-269-5219
Jenny S. Kim and Leah A. Schleicher,
Partners & Co-Chairs of Diversity &
Inclusion Committee, 312-269-8000

Pedersen & Houpt, PC

161 North Clark Street
Suite 3100
Chicago, IL 60601-3224
Phone: 312-641-6888
Fax: 312-641-6895
Web Site: www.pedersenhoupt.com

2016 Total Lawyers: 29
2015 Total Lawyers: 32

Pretzel & Stouffer, Chartered

One South Wacker
Suite 2500
Chicago, IL 60606-4673
Phone: 312-346-1973
Fax: 312-346-8242
Web Site: www.pretzel-stouffer.com

2016 Total Lawyers: 54
2015 Total Lawyers: 57

Querrey & Harrow

175 West Jackson Boulevard
Suite 1600
Chicago, IL 60604
Phone: 312-540-7000
Fax: 312-540-0578
Email: info@querrey.com
Web Site: www.querrey.com

2016 Total Lawyers: 34
2015 Total Lawyers: 31

Ruberry Stalmack & Garvey

500 West Madison Street
Citicorp Center, Suite 2300
Chicago, IL 60661-2511
Phone: 312-466-8050
Fax: 312-466-8001
Email: info@rsg-law.com
Web Site: www.rsg-law.com

2016 Total Lawyers: 33
2015 Total Lawyers: 31

Schiff Hardin LLP

233 South Wacker Drive
Suite 6600
Chicago, IL 60606
Phone: 312-258-5500
Fax: 312-258-5600
Web Site: www.schiffhardin.com

2016 Total Lawyers: 318
2015 Total Lawyers: 391

2016 Staff
Equity Partners: 101
Non-Equity Partners: 98
Associates: 101
Of Counsel: 29
Senior Attorneys: 28
Counsel: 23
Staff Attorneys: 8

Offices: No. Attys.
Chicago, IL: 240
Washington, DC: 38
New York, NY: 53
Lake Forest, IL: 11
Atlanta, GA: 14
San Francisco, CA: 38
Ann Arbor, MI: 12

Hiring and Promotion
2015 Associates Hired: 25
2015 First-Year Hires: 9
Starting Salary for First-Year
Assocs: $160,000
2016 First-Year Hires (Est.): 9
2015 Equity Partners Named: 3
2015 Lateral Equity Partners: 3

Schiff Hardin LLP (Continued)

Leading Practice Areas
(Department Heads)
Construction (Kenneth M. Roberts)
Corporate, Securities & Tax including Market
Regulation (Stephen J. Dragich, Robert R.
Pluth Jr.)
Intellectual Property (Stephen M. Hankins)
Product Liability (Robert H. Riley &
Jeffrey Williams)
General Commercial & White Collar
Litigation (Thomas B. Quinn, Patricia
Brown Holmes)
Finance (Scott E. Pickens)
Real Estate (David A. Grossberg)
Labor & Employment/Employee Benefits and
Executive Compensation (Patricia
C. Slovak)
Private Clients, Trusts and Estates (Thomas
W. Abendroth)
Environmental/Energy & Public
Utilities/Climate Control (Gabriel M.
Rodriguez, Sherry Quirk)
Restructuring, Bankruptcy & Creditors'
Rights (Louis T. Delucia)

Revenues and Profits
Revenues: $238,270,438

Leading Officials
Robert H. Riley, Chairman, 312-258-5664
Ronald S. Safer, Managing Partner,
312-258-5765
Joseph A. Vasquez, Jr., Executive Director,
312-258-3950
Lisa A. Brown (law students): Robert H.
Riley (laterals), Hiring Partner,
312-258-5500
Lisa A. Brown, Professional Development
Partner, 312-258-5753
Brad A. Byrum, Interim Director of
Marketing and Communications,
415-901-8748
Garry Eades, Director of Information
Technology, 312-258-4650
Ruth Bridges, Manager of Library &
Research Services, 312-258-4701
Patricia Brown Holmes, Partner; Diversity
Committee Chair, 312-258-5722

Other Offices
New York, New York
666 Fifth Avenue
Suite 1700
New York
New York
10103
Phone: 212-753-5000
Fax: 212-753-5044

Schuyler, Roche & Crisham, P.C.

130 East Randolph Street
One Prudential Plaza, Suite 3800
Chicago, IL 60601
Phone: 312-565-2400
Web Site: www.srzlaw.com

2016 Total Lawyers: 32
2015 Total Lawyers: 46

ILLINOIS

Seyfarth Shaw LLP

131 South Dearborn Street
Suite 2400
Chicago, IL 60603
Phone: 312-460-5000
Fax: 312-460-7000
Email: seyfarthshaw@seyfarth.com
Web Site: www.seyfarth.com

2016 Total Lawyers: 970
2015 Total Lawyers: 942

Sidley Austin LLP

One South Dearborn Street
Chicago, IL 60603
Phone: 312-853-7000
Fax: 312-853-7036
Web Site: www.sidley.com

2016 Total Lawyers: 1918
2015 Total Lawyers: 1825

2016 Staff
Equity Partners: 712
Associates: 924
Counsel: 171
Senior Counsel: 66
Staff Attorneys: 45

Offices: No. Attys.
Chicago, IL: 490
New York, NY: 424
Washington DC: 291
Los Angeles, CA: 140
London, England: 117
Hong Kong: 81
Dallas, TX: 63
San Francisco, CA: 67
Palo Alto, CA: 41
Houston, TX: 41
Brussels, Belgium: 30
Singapore: 28
Geneva, Switzerland: 19
Beijing, China: 14
Tokyo, Japan: 13
Boston, MA: 13
Shanghai, China: 10
Sydney, Australia: 14
Century City: 22

Hiring and Promotion
2015 Associates Hired: 257
2015 First-Year Hires: 112
Starting Salary for First-Year Assocs:
   $180,000 effective July 1, 2016
2016 First-Year Hires (Est.): 129
2015 Equity Partners Named: 59
2015 Lateral Equity Partners: 35

Sidley Austin LLP (Continued)

Leading Practice Areas
(Department Heads)
Bankruptcy and Reorganization
Litigation/Employment/Appellate
Corporate/Securities/M&A/Tax
Financial Services/Insurance/Global Finance
Intellectual Property
International Arbitration/International Trade
Investment Funds, Advisors and Derivatives
Energy
Real Estate
Healthcare

Revenues and Profits
Revenues: $1,867,000,000

Client Representations
Not Provided
Not Provided
Not Provided

Leading Officials
Carter G. Phillips, Chairman of the Executive Committee
Larry A. Barden, Chairman of the Management Committee / Vice Chairman of the Management Committee
Timothy F. Bergen, Executive Director/Administration
Anthony Aiello, Rebecca K. Wood, Kelly L.C. Kriebs, John Kuster, Recruiting of Associates - Co-Chairs
Michael S. Prapuolenis, Chief Human Resources Officer
Barry Solomon, Chief Marketing Officer
Janet Zagorin, Client Services Officer
Vince Marin, Chief Information Officer
Sally L. Olson, Chief Diversity Officer

Other Offices
1501 K Street, NW
Washington
DC
20005
Phone: 202-736-8000
Fax: 202-736-8711
Mark D. Hopson - Managing Partner

555 West Fifth Street
Los Angeles
CA
90013
Phone: 213-896-6000
Fax: 213-896-6600
Dan Clivner & Michael C. Kelley - Managing Partners

787 Seventh Avenue
New York
NY
10019
Phone: 212-839-5300
Fax: 212-839-5599
Michael J. Schmidtberger - Managing Partner

One South Dearborn Street
Chicago
IL
60603
Phone: 312-853-7000
Fax: 312-853-7036
Larry A. Barden - Managing Partner

Sidley Austin LLP (Continued)

Woolgate Exchange
25 Basinghall Street
London, EC2V 5HA
United Kingdom
Phone: 442-073-603 ext. 600
Fax: 442-076-267 ext. 937
Matthew Dening - Managing Partner

39/F Two International Finance Center
8 Finance Street
Central
Hong Kong
Phone: 852-250-978 ext. 88
Fax: 852-250-931 ext. 10
Thomas W. Albrecht & Constance Choy - Managing Partners

555 California Street
Suite 2000
San Francisco
CA
94104
Phone: 415-772-1200
Fax: 415-772-7400
Sharon R. Flanagan - Managing Partner

2001 Ross Avenue
Suite 3600
Dallas
TX
75201
Phone: 214-981-3300
Fax: 214-981-3400
Yvette Ostolaza - Managing Partner

Tressler LLP

233 South Wacker Drive
Willis Tower, 22nd Floor
Chicago, IL 60606
Phone: 312-627-4000
Fax: 312-627-1717
Web Site: www.tresslerllp.com

2016 Total Lawyers: 80
2015 Total Lawyers: 101

Vedder Price

222 North LaSalle Street
Suite 2600
Chicago, IL 60601
Phone: 312-609-7500
Fax: 312-609-5005
Web Site: www.vedderprice.com

2016 Total Lawyers: 292
2015 Total Lawyers: 295

ILLINOIS

Williams Montgomery & John Ltd.

233 South Wacker Dr.
Suite 6100
Chicago, IL 60606-3094
Phone: 312-443-3200
Fax: 312-630-8500
Email: wmjinfo@willmont.com
Web Site: www.willmont.com

2016 Total Lawyers: 24
2015 Total Lawyers: 27

Winston & Strawn LLP

35 West Wacker Drive
Chicago, IL 60601-9703
Phone: 312-558-5600
Fax: 312-558-5700
Email: info@winston.com
Web Site: www.winston.com

2016 Total Lawyers: 891
2015 Total Lawyers: 888

2016 Staff
Equity Partners: 210
Non-Equity Partners: 165
Associates: 428
Of Counsel: 51
Senior Attorneys: 3
Senior Counsel: 1
Staff Attorneys: 33

Offices: No. Attys.
Chicago, IL: 303
New York, NY: 203
Washington, DC: 89
Los Angeles, CA: 64
San Francisco, CA: 52
Paris, France: 30
London, England: 20
Charlotte, NC: 35
Newark, NJ: 3
Moscow, Russia: 4
Hong Kong: 20
Beijing, China: 1
Shanghai, China: 7
Houston, TX: 46
Silicon Valley, CA: 4
Brussels, Belgium: 1
Taipei, Taiwan: 4
Dubai, UAE: 5

Hiring and Promotion
2015 Associates Hired: 42
2015 First-Year Hires: 44
Starting Salary for First-Year
Assocs: $160,000
2016 First-Year Hires (Est.): 54
2015 Equity Partners Named: 9
2015 Lateral Equity Partners: 5

Winston & Strawn LLP (Continued)

*Leading Practice Areas
(Department Heads)*
Litigation 52% (George Lombardi / Steve
D'Amore 312-558-5969 312-558-5934)
Corporate 28% (Dominick DeChiara
212-294-2609)
Labor & Employment 6% (Michael Roche
312-558-7508)
Tax 4% (Amit Kalra 312-558-5736)
Energy Group 3% (Joseph Karp
415-591-1529)
Real Estate 2% (Corey Tessler
212-294-6685)
Environmental 1% (Eleni Kouimelis
312-558-5133)
Employee Benefits 1% (Michael Falk
312-558-7232)
Maritime 1% (Charlie Papavizas
202-282-5732)
Trusts & Estates 0.5% (Bill Doyle
312-558-5898)

Revenues and Profits
Revenues: $818,300,000
Profits: $384,500,000

Client Representations
Ericsson--ITC Section 337 cases
against Apple
Treehouse Foods--2.7 billion dollar
acquisition of ConAgras private
brands operation
Goldman Sachs--antitrust and
multidistrict litigation

Leading Officials
Dan K. Webb & Jeffrey Kessler, Firm
Co-Chairman, 312-558-5856
Thomas P. Fitzgerald, Firmwide Managing
Partner, 312-558-5845
Scot Farrell, Chief Operating Officer,
202-282-5910
William O'Neil & Suzanne Jaffe Bloom,
Co-Chair of Hiring Committee,
312-558-7334
Deborah S. Caldwell, Director of Attorney
Resources & Recruitment, 312-558-5222
Anne M. Heathcock, Managing Director,
Marketing, 312-558-5620
Cynthia M Holbrook, Managing Director,
Global Practice Development,
415-591-6859
David Cunningham, Chief Information
Officer, 713-651-2626
Mark Stull, Chief Administrative Officer,
202-282-5880
Chiymelle Nunn, Diversity Manager,
312-558-6138

Other Offices
New York
200 Park Avenue
New York
NY
10166
Phone: 212-294-6700
Fax: 212-294-4700
Michael Elkin

Winston & Strawn LLP (Continued)

Washington, D.C.
1700 K Street, N.W.
Washington
DC
20006
Phone: 202-282-5000
Fax: 202-282-5100
Thomas Buchanan

Los Angeles
333 S. Grand Avenue
38th Floor
Los Angeles
CA
90071
Phone: 213-615-1700
Fax: 213-615-1750
Eric Sagerman

San Francisco
101 California Street
San Francisco
CA
94111
Phone: 415-591-1000
Fax: 415-591-1400
Joan Fife

INDIANA

Barnes & Thornburg LLP

11 South Meridian Street
Indianapolis, IN 46204
Phone: 317-236-1313
Fax: 317-231-7433
Web Site: www.btlaw.com

2016 Total Lawyers: 600
2015 Total Lawyers: 550

Bingham Greenebaum Doll LLP

2700 Market Tower
10 West Market Street
Indianapolis, IN 46204
Phone: 317-635-8900
Fax: 317-236-9907
Web Site: http://www.bgdlegal.com/

2016 Total Lawyers: 188
2015 Total Lawyers: 210

2016 Staff
Equity Partners: 63
Non-Equity Partners: 41
Associates: 32
Of Counsel: 31
Senior Attorneys: 20
Staff Attorneys: 1

Offices: No. Attys.
Indianapolis, IN: 85
Jasper, IN: 4
Vincennes, IN: 1
Louisville, KY: 71
Lexington, KY: 16
Evansville, IN: 5
Cincinnati, OH: 6

INDIANA

Bingham Greenebaum Doll LLP (Continued)

Hiring and Promotion
2015 Associates Hired: 18
2016 First-Year Hires (Est.): 0

Leading Practice Areas
(Department Heads)
Corporate and Transactional (Keith Bice
317-686-5233)
Economic Development (Matthew Price
317-686-5225)
Estate Planning (John Cummins
502-587-3602)
Labor and Employment (D. Rusty Denton
317-968-5370)
Litigation (John Bush 502-587-3669)
Tax and Finance- (Mark Loyd 502-587-3552)

Client Representations
Osborn/Holt v. Griffin, Case Nos.
2:11-CV-89 and 2:13-CV-32
(consolidated), United States District Court
for the Eastern District of Kentucky. Client
name: Plaintiff Elizabeth ("Betsy")
A. Osborn
Alonso, et al. v. Blue Sky Resort, et al. U.S.
District Court for the Southern District of
Indiana (New Albany Division)(Cause No.
4:15-cv-00016 TWP-TAB). Client name:
Blue Sky/French Lick Resort
BGD served as counsel to Angel's Share
Brands during the acquisition and continue
to represent the company after the deal.
Angel's Envy was recognized with the
"2015 Kentucky Deal of the Year" award.

Leading Officials
W. Tobin McClamroch, Managing Partner,
317-968-5396
James L. Turner, Chief Operating Officer,
317-968-5314
Rick M. Olgine, Chief Financial Officer
Roz Hazzard, Human Resources Director,
317-968-5353
Robyn Radomski, Chief Business
Development and Marketing officer,
317-968-5455
Robyn Radomski, Chief Business
Development and Marketing officer,
317-968-5455
David Otte, Chief Information and
Administrative Officer
Howard Trivers, Library Manager,
317-968-5572
David Tandy

Other Offices
Indianapolis Office
10 West Market Street
2700 Market Tower
Indianapolis
IN
46204
Phone: 317-635-8900
Fax: 317-236-9907
Office Managing Partner: Hans Steck

Bingham Greenebaum Doll LLP (Continued)

Louisville Office
101 South Fifth Street
3500 National City Tower
Louisville
KY
40202
Phone: 502-589-4200
Fax: 502-587-3695
Office Managing Partner: Mark H.
Oppenheimer

Bose McKinney & Evans LLP

111 Monument Circle
Suite 2700
Indianapolis, IN 46204
Phone: 317-684-5000
Fax: 317-684-5173
Email: webmaster@boselaw.com
Web Site: www.boselaw.com

2016 Total Lawyers: 99
2015 Total Lawyers: 109

2016 Staff
Equity Partners: 51
Non-Equity Partners: 24
Associates: 8
Of Counsel: 15
Staff Attorneys: 1

Offices: No. Attys.
Washington, DC: 3
Indianapolis, IN: 93
Fort Wayne, IN: 3

Hiring and Promotion
2015 Associates Hired: 2
2016 First-Year Hires (Est.): 0
2015 Equity Partners Named: 4
2015 Lateral Equity Partners: 1

Leading Practice Areas
(Department Heads)
Litigation / Creditors Rights 27% (Sam
Laurin / James Carlberg)
Business Organization / Securities 21%
(Roberts Inveiss)
Real Estate 10% (Gary Chapman)
Utilities 9% (L. Parvin Price)
Taxation/Trusts & Estates 8% (Donald Meyer
& R.J. McConnell)
Government Relations/Public Finance 7%
(Douglas Brown / Dennis Otten)
Intellectual Property 6% (Michael Bartol)
Employment 6% (David Swider)
Administrative Law / Environmental Law 3%
(Lisa McKinney / David Pippen)
Healthcare / Medical Malpractice 3%
(Mary Feldhake)

Client Representations
City of Fort Wayne, Indiana
Eli Lilly and Company
JPMorgan Chase

Bose McKinney & Evans LLP (Continued)

Leading Officials
Jeffrey R. Gaither, Managing Partner,
317-684-5182
Christine Birch, Chief Financial Officer,
317-684-5164
Bryan Babb, Hiring Partner, 317-684-5172
Vicki Bruce Hansen, Chief Operations
Officer, 317-684-5268
Jennifer Walker, Chief Marketing Officer,
317-684-5214
Jonathan Miller, Chief Information Officer,
317-684-5108
Cheryl Niemeier, Head Librarian,
317-684-5166
Lisa McKinney, Partner, 317-684-5124

Hall Render Killian Heath & Lyman P.C.

One American Square, Suite 2000
P.O. Box 82064
Indianapolis, IN 46282
Phone: 317-633-4884
Fax: 317-633-4878
Web Site: www.hallrender.com

2016 Total Lawyers: 202
2015 Total Lawyers: 179

Ice Miller LLP

One American Square
Suite 2900
Indianapolis, IN 46282-0200
Phone: 317-236-2100
Fax: 317-236-2219
Email: info@icemiller.com
Web Site: www.icemiller.com

2016 Total Lawyers: 300
2015 Total Lawyers: 291

Krieg Devault LLP

One Indiana Square
Suite 2800
Indianapolis, IN 46204-2079
Phone: 317-636-4341
Fax: 317-636-1507

2016 Total Lawyers: 81
2015 Total Lawyers: 99

IOWA

Davis, Brown, Koehn, Shors & Roberts

The Davis Brown Tower
215 10th Street, Suite 1300
Des Moines, IA 50309-3993
Phone: 515-288-2500
Fax: 515-243-0654
Email: info@DavisBrownLaw.com
Web Site: www.DavisBrownLaw.com

2016 Total Lawyers: 79
2015 Total Lawyers: 79

2016 Staff
Equity Partners: 40
Non-Equity Partners: 4
Associates: 24
Of Counsel: 9

Offices: No. Attys.
Davis Brown Tower - Des Moines, IA: 66
Highland Building - West Des Moines, IA: 7
The Ames Office - Ames, IA: 2
The Emmetsburg Office - Emmetsburg, IA: 1

Hiring and Promotion
2015 Associates Hired: 8
2015 First-Year Hires: 2
Starting Salary for First-Year
   Assocs: $90,000
2016 First-Year Hires (Est.): 2
2015 Equity Partners Named: 5

Leading Practice Areas
(Department Heads)
Business 20% (Jason M. Stone)
Real Estate Foreclosures 7% (Gary
   M. Myers)
Intellectual Property 7% (Sean D. Solberg)
Immigration 6% (Lori T. Chesser)
Health 6% (Susan J. Freed)
Real Estate Transactions 6% (Gary
   M. Myers)
Estate Planning/Probate 5% (Thomas
   J. Houser)
Employment and Labor Law Litigation 5%
   (Jo Ellen Whitney)
Communications and Utilities 4% (John
   C. Pietila)
Real Estate Closings 3% (Gary M. Myers)

Revenues and Profits
Revenues: $26,300,000
Profits: $13,500,000

Leading Officials
Gene R. La Suer, President, Board
   of Directors
Andrew G. Elston, Controller
David B. VanSickel, Attorney
Barbara J. Hardy, Professional Resources
Cara L. Seidl, Marketing Director
Brian D. Torresi, Attorney
Ted Kumsher, Information Services
Barbara J. Hardy, Professional Resources
Summer J. Herring, Human
   Resources Director

KANSAS

Foulston Siefkin LLP

1551 North Waterfront Parkway
Suite 100
Wichita, KS 67206
Phone: 316-267-6371
Fax: 316-267-6345
Email: info@foulston.com
Web Site: www.foulston.com

2016 Total Lawyers: 86
2015 Total Lawyers: 93

Wallace, Saunders, Austin, Brown & Enochs, Chartered

10111 West 87th Street
Overland Park, KS 66212
Phone: 913-888-1000
Fax: 913-888-1065
Email: info@wsabe.com
Web Site: www.wsabe.com

2016 Total Lawyers: 46
2015 Total Lawyers: 43

KENTUCKY

Boehl, Stopher & Graves, LLP

Aegon Center, Suite 2300
400 West Market Street
Louisville, KY 40202-3354
Phone: 502-589-5980
Fax: 502-561-9400
Web Site: www.bsg-law.com

2016 Total Lawyers: 44
2015 Total Lawyers: 50

Stites & Harbison, PLLC

400 West Market Street
Suite 1800
Louisville, KY 40202
Phone: 502-587-3400
Fax: 502-587-6391
Web Site: www.stites.com

2016 Total Lawyers: 195
2015 Total Lawyers: 195

Stoll, Keenon & Ogden, PLLC

300 West Vine Street
Suite 2100
Lexington, KY 40507
Phone: 859-231-3000
Web Site: www.skp.com

2016 Total Lawyers: 150
2015 Total Lawyers: 142

Wyatt, Tarrant & Combs, LLP

500 West Jefferson Street, Suite 2800
Louisville, KY 40202
Phone: 502-589-5235
Fax: 502-589-0309
Web Site: www.wyattfirm.com

2016 Total Lawyers: 182
2015 Total Lawyers: 199

Offices: No. Attys.
Louisville, KY: 80
Lexington, KY: 42
Memphis, TN: 36
Nashville, TN: 13
Jackson, MS: 9
New Albany, IN: 2

Leading Practice Areas
(Department Heads)
Litigation (Byron Leet, Robert Craddock)
Corporate & General Business (Bob Heath)
Intellectual Property (Mark Vorder-Bruegge)
Real Property (Leo Camp)
Labor & Employment (Tyson Gorman)
Bankruptcy (Mary Fullington)
Health Care (Tad Myre, Carole Christian)
Tax, Business & Personal Planning
   (Turney Berry)
Financial Institutions & Public Finance
   (Cindy Young)
Natural Resources and Environmental (Brian
   Wells, Karen Greenwell)

Client Representations
International Paper Company
General Electric Company
Smith & Nephew

Leading Officials
J. Mark Burton, Chair of the Executive
   Committee, 859-259-0649
Franklin K. Jelsma, Managing Partner,
   502-562-7285
Michael Mack, Chief Operating Officer,
   502-562-7577
Jefferey Yussman, Hiring Partner,
   502-562-7544
Laura Toon, Professional Personnel
   Coordinator, 502-562-7159
Andrew Payton, Chief Marketing Officer,
   502-562-7160
Emily Feeney, Business Development
   Manager, 502-562-7138
Julie A. Hensley, Chief Information Officer,
   859-288-7657
Diane M. Cox, Director, Library Services,
   502-562-7368
Odell Horton, Chairman of Diversity
   Committee, 901-537-1082

LOUISIANA

Adams and Reese LLP

One Shell Square
701 Poydras Street, Suite 4500
New Orleans, LA 70139
Phone: 504-581-3234
Fax: 504-566-0210
Email: info@arlaw.com
Web Site: www.adamsandreese.com

2016 Total Lawyers: 293
2015 Total Lawyers: 293

2016 Staff
Equity Partners: 126
Non-Equity Partners: 62
Associates: 54
Of Counsel: 13
Counsel: 32
Staff Attorneys: 6

Offices: No. Attys.
Birmingham, AL: 19
Memphis, TN: 13
New Orleans, LA: 81
Nashville (Downtown), TN: 29
Nashville (Music Row), TN: 2
Jackson, MS: 26
Houston, TX: 28
Baton Rouge, LA: 15
Mobile, AL: 18
Washington, DC: 5
Tampa, FL: 20
Sarasota, FL: 7
St. Petersburg, FL: 10
Tallahassee, FL: 2
Jacksonville, FL: 10
Columbia, SC: 17

Hiring and Promotion
2015 Associates Hired: 5
2016 First-Year Hires (Est.): 3
2015 Equity Partners Named: 6

Leading Practice Areas
(Department Heads)
General Litigation 17.71% (John Rogerson III, Lee Reid, Louis Ursini III 904-493-3303, 504-581-3234, 813-402-2880)
Commercial Litigation 17.21% (John Rogerson III, Lee Reid, Louis Ursini III 904-493-3303, 504-581-3234, 813-402-2880)
Legislative and Governmental Affairs 15% (Jeff Brooks 202-737.3234)
Corporate Law 11.38% (W. David Johnson 251-650-0855)
Real Estate 10.11% (David S. Bernstein 727-502-8200)
Copyrights/Patents/Intellectual Property 7% (Raymond R. Ferrera 713-308-0127)
Environmental and Toxic Tort 5.56% (E. Gregg Barrios 504-581-3234)
Labor and Employment 4.41% (Elizabeth A. Roussel 504-585-0445)
Oil, Gas and Energy Resources 4.01% (Jeff Trotter 601-292-0711)
Administrative and Regulatory Law 3.51%

Adams and Reese LLP (Continued)

Leading Officials
William P. McElveen, Jr., Chairman, Executive Committee, 202-737-3234
Guilford F. Thornton, Jr., Managing Partner, 615-259-1492
Paul J Lassalle, Chief Financial Officer, 504-581-3234
Mark R. Beebe, Liason Partner - Recruiting, 504-585-0436
Brittany Dunton, Legal Recruiting Coordinator, 504-585-0462
Ann M. Wallace, Chief Marketing and Business Development Officer, 504-581-3234
David Bender, IT Manager, 615-259-1450
Catherine Filippi, Librarian, 504-581-3234
Jaimme Collins, Diversity Chairwoman, 504-585-0218

Other Offices
Baton Rouge
450 Laurel Street
Suite 1900
Baton Rouge
LA
70801
Phone: 225-336-5200
Fax: 225-336-5200
Email: info@arlaw.com
William D. Shea

Birmingham
1901 6th Avenue North
Suite 3000
Birmingham
AL
35203
Phone: 205-250-5000
Fax: 205-250-5034
Email: info@arlaw.com
David K. Bowsher

Houston
1221 McKinney
Suite 4400
Houston
TX
77010
Phone: 713-652-5151
Fax: 713-652-5152
Email: info@arlaw.com
Raymond R. Ferrera

Jackson
1018 Highland Colony Parkway
Suite 800
Jackson
MS
39157
Phone: 601-353-3234
Fax: 601-355-9708
Email: info@arlaw.com
C. Phillip Buffington, Jr.

Mobile
11 North Water Street
Suite 23200
Mobile
AL
36602
Phone: 251-433-3234
Fax: 251-438-7733
Email: info@arlaw.com
Britton Bonner

Adams and Reese LLP (Continued)

Washington, D.C.
20 F Street NW
Suite 500
Washington
DC
20001
Phone: 202-737-3234
Fax: 202-737-0264
Email: info@arlaw.com
Matt Paxton

Nashville Music Row
901 18th Avenue South
Nashville
TN
37212
Phone: 615-341-0068
Fax: 615-341-0596
Email: info@arlaw.com
Lynn Morrow

Nashville (Downtown)
424 Church Street
Suite 2700
Nashville
TN
37219
Phone: 615-259-1450
Fax: 615-259-1470
Email: info@arlaw.com
Kolin Holladay

Memphis
6075 Poplar Avenue
Suite 700
Memphis
TN
38119
Phone: 901-525-3234
Fax: 901-524-5419
Email: info@arlaw.com
Jay Campbell

New Orleans
701 Poydras St.
Suite 4500
New Orleans
LA
70139
Phone: 504-581-3234
Fax: 504-566-0210
Email: info@arlaw.com
E. Paige Sensenbrenner and Johnny Domiano

Sarasota
1515 Ringling Boulevard
Suite 700
Sarasota
FL
34236
Phone: 941-316-7600
Fax: 941-316-7676
Email: info@arlaw.com
Jason T. Gaskill

St. Petersburg
150 Second Avenue North
Suite 1700
St. Petersburg
FL
33701
Phone: 727-502-8200
Fax: 727-502-8282
Email: info@arlaw.com
Richmond C. Flowers

LOUISIANA

Adams and Reese LLP (Continued)

Tampa
101 East Kennedy Boulevard
Suite 400
Tampa
FL
33602
Phone: 813-402-2880
Fax: 813-402-2887
Email: info@arlaw.com
Deborah H. Oliver

Tallahassee
108 East Jefferson Street
Suite C
Tallahassee
FL
32301
Email: info@arlaw.com

Jacksonville
501 Riverside Avenue
7th Floor
Jacksonville
FL
32202
Phone: 904-355-1700
Fax: 904-355-1797
Email: info@arlaw.com
Leslie A. Wickes

Columbia
1501 Main Street
5th Floor
Columbia
SC
29201
Phone: 803-254-4190
Fax: 803-779-4749
Email: info@arlaw.com
Robert P. Bethea Jr.

Breazeale, Sachse & Wilson, LLP

One American Place
301 Main Street, 23rd Floor
Baton Rouge, LA 70821
Phone: 225-387-4000
Fax: 225-381-8029
Email: info@bswllp.com
Web Site: www.bswllp.com

2016 Total Lawyers: 69
2015 Total Lawyers: 71

Chaffe McCall, LLP

2300 Energy Centre
1100 Poydras Street
New Orleans, LA 70163-2300
Phone: 504-585-7000
Fax: 504-585-7075
Web Site: www.chaffe.com

2016 Total Lawyers: 61
2015 Total Lawyers: 61

Chaffe McCall, LLP (Continued)

2016 Staff
Equity Partners: 23
Non-Equity Partners: 13
Associates: 12
Of Counsel: 3
Senior Attorneys: 5
Senior Counsel: 5

Offices: No. Attys.
Baton Rouge, LA: 4
Houston, TX: 5
New Orleans, LA: 53
Lake Charles, LA: 1

Hiring and Promotion
2015 Associates Hired: 1
2015 First-Year Hires: 1
2016 First-Year Hires (Est.): 1
2015 Equity Partners Named: 0

Leading Practice Areas
(Department Heads)
Litigation 32.21% (Brent A. Talbot)
Admiralty 20.26% (Daniel A. Tadros)
Corporate 16.39% (Walter F. Becker)
Labor 8.18% (Julie D. Livaudais)
Real Estate 5.49% (E. Howell Crosby)
Estate and Trusts 3.43% (G. Wogan Bernard)
Tax Law 3.38% (Keith M. Benit)
Bankruptcy 2.71% (E. Howell Crosby)
Administrative Law 1.05% (Keith M. Benit)
Antitrust Law 0.22% (Robert S. Rooth)

Client Representations
Citgo Petroleum Company
Alamoth, LLC
Watco Companies, Inc.

Leading Officials
E. Howell Crosby, 504-585-7212
Timothy P. Doody, Firm Administrator,
  504-585-7000
Charles D. Marshall, III, Hiring Partner,
  504-585-7000
Chelsea Block, Recruiting Director,
  504-585-7000
Wendy Pineda-Welch, 504-585-7000
James C. Zeller, Manager of Information
  Services, 504-585-7000
Debbie Wynot, Librarian, 504-585-7000

Other Offices
New Orleans Office
1100 Poydras Street
2300 Energy Centre
New Orleans
LA
70163-2300
Phone: 504-585-7000
Fax: 504-585-7075
John Olinde

Deutsch, Kerrigan & Stiles, LLP

755 Magazine Street
New Orleans, LA 70130-3672
Phone: 504-581-5141
Fax: 504-566-1201
Web Site: www.dkslaw.com

2016 Total Lawyers: 62
2015 Total Lawyers: 63

Jones Walker LLP

201 St. Charles Avenue
New Orleans, LA 70170-5100
Phone: 504-582-8000
Fax: 504-582-8583
Email: info@joneswalker.com
Web Site: www.joneswalker.com

2016 Total Lawyers: 380
2015 Total Lawyers: 386

2016 Staff
Associates: 65
Of Counsel: 2
Partners: 227
Special Counsel: 86

Offices: No. Attys.
New Orleans, LA: 149
Baton Rouge, LA: 49
The Woodlands, TX: 5
Washington, DC (Capitol Hill): 12
Lafayette, LA: 17
Miami, FL: 11
Houston, TX: 19
Mobile, AL: 19
Birmingham, AL: 19
Phoenix, Arizona: 2
Jackson, MS: 46
Gulfport, MS: 6
Lafayette (River Ranch), LA: 1
Atlanta, GA: 9
New York, NY: 2
Tallahassee, FL: 3
Cincinnati, OH: 4
Washington, DC (Downtown): 7

Hiring and Promotion
2015 First-Year Hires: 3

Leading Practice Areas
(Department Heads)
Admiralty & Maritime (R. Scott Jenkins
  504-582-8346)
Business & Commercial Litigation (R.
  Patrick Vance 504-582-8194)
Business & Banking (J. Marshall Page, III
  and Ronald A. Snider, Co-Chairs
  504-582-8248; 251-439-7548)
Corporate & Securities (Curtis R. Hearn
  504-582-8308)
Government Relations (John J. Jaskot
  202-203-1014)
Labor & Employment (Sidney F. Lewis, V
  504-582-8352)
Real Estate (Robert W. Scheffy, Jr.
  225-248-2032)
Tax, Trusts & Estates (William M.
  Backstrom, Jr. 504-582-8228)

LOUISIANA

Jones Walker LLP (Continued)

Leading Officials
William H. Hines, Managing Partner,
   504-582-8272
Amy Garrity Scafidel and Kevin O.
   Ainsworth, Hiring & Recruiting
   Committee, Co-Chairs
Julie B. Prechter, Director of Recruiting &
   Legal Professional Development,
   504-582-8406
Kim A. Perret, Chief Marketing Officer,
   504-582-8438
Ruark W. Chick, Chief Information Officer,
   225-248-3508
Tina M. Gambrell, Manager of Library
   Services, 504-582-8589
Richard F. Cortizas, Chair, Diversity
   Committee

Kean Miller LLP

**400 Convention Street,
Suite 700
Baton Rouge, LA 70802
Phone: 225-387-0999
Fax: 225-388-9133
Email: client_services@keanmille
Web Sites:
www.keanmiller.com
www.louisianalawblog.com**

2016 Total Lawyers: 150
2015 Total Lawyers: 154

Liskow & Lewis, A Professional Law Corporation

**701 Poydras Street
Suite 5000
New Orleans, LA 70139-5099
Phone: 504-581-7979
Fax: 504-556-4108
Email: firm@liskow.com
Web Site: www.liskow.com**

2016 Total Lawyers: 134
2015 Total Lawyers: 132

2016 Staff
Equity Partners: 67
Associates: 39
Of Counsel: 28

Offices: No. Attys.
New Orleans, LA: 82
Lafayette, LA: 24
Houston: 28

Hiring and Promotion
2015 Associates Hired: 10
2015 First-Year Hires: 8
2015 Equity Partners Named: 6
2015 Lateral Equity Partners: 1

Liskow & Lewis, A Professional Law Corporation (Continued)

*Leading Practice Areas
(Department Heads)*
Energy & Natural Resources 30% (Richard
   W. Revels, Jr. & Jonathan A. Hunter
   337-232-7424 & 504-556-4131)
Admiralty 23% (David W. Leefe
   504-556-4137)
Environmental Litigation 15% (Jonathan A.
   Hunter 504-556-4131)
Environmental Regulatory 10% (Jonathan A.
   Hunter 504-556-4131)
Corporate (Business Law) 10% (Robert S.
   Angelico 504-556-4112)
Bankruptcy 7% (Philip K. Jones, Jr.
   504-556-4132)
Labor & Employment 5% (Thomas J.
   McGoey 504-299-6101)

Leading Officials
Robert S. Angelico, President & Managing
   Partner, 504-581-7979
Scott Perkins, Executive Director,
   504-581-7979
Paul C. Kitziger, Hiring Partner,
   504-581-7979
Amy Harang, HR/Recruiting Director,
   504-581-7979
Eric Fletcher, Chief Marketing Officer,
   504-581-7979
Joey Guillory, IT Director, 504-581-7979
Katherine Boudreaux, Head Librarian,
   504-581-7979
Tiffany Davis , Chair of Diversity
   Committee, 504-581-7979

Other Offices
701 Poydras St.
Suite 5000
New Orleans, LA 70139
Phone: 504-581-7979
Fax: 504-556-4108
Email: firm@liskow.com
Robert S. Angelico

McGlinchey Stafford

**601 Poydras Street
12th Floor
New Orleans, LA 70130
Phone: 504-586-1200
Fax: 504-596-2800
Email: mcglinchey@mcglinchey.com
Web Site: www.mcglinchey.com**

2016 Total Lawyers: 203
2015 Total Lawyers: 187

Milling Benson Woodward LLP

**909 Poydras Street
Suite 2300
New Orleans, LA 70112-1010
Phone: 504-569-7000
Fax: 504-569-7001
Email: vodems@millinglaw.com
Web Site: www.millinglaw.com**

2016 Total Lawyers: 30
2015 Total Lawyers: 27

2016 Staff
Equity Partners: 9
Non-Equity Partners: 18
Associates: 3

Offices: No. Attys.
New Orleans, LA: 8
Lafayette, LA: 4
Baton Rouge, LA: 5
Mandeville, LA: 10

Hiring and Promotion
2016 First-Year Hires (Est.): 0
2015 Equity Partners Named: 0

*Leading Practice Areas
(Department Heads)*
1. Tax
2. Health Care
3. Oil & Gas

Leading Officials
Robert L. Cabes, Esq., Management
   Committee Chair, 337-232-3929
Richard E. Santora, Chief Operating Officer,
   504-569-7412
Vanessa Odems, Head Librarian

Montgomery Barnett, LLP

**3300 Energy Centre
1100 Poydras Street, Suite 3300
New Orleans, LA 70163
Phone: 504-585-3200
Web Site: www.monb.com**

2016 Total Lawyers: 18
2015 Total Lawyers: 19

Phelps Dunbar LLP

**Canal Place
365 Canal Street, Suite 2000
New Orleans, LA 70130-6534
Phone: 504-566-1311
Fax: 504-568-9130
Email: info@phelps.com
Web Site: www.phelpsdunbar.com**

2016 Total Lawyers: 266
2015 Total Lawyers: 266

2016 Staff
Equity Partners: 127
Associates: 107
Of Counsel: 6
Counsel: 29

Offices: No. Attys.
Jackson, MS: 27

LOUISIANA

Phelps Dunbar LLP (Continued)
Baton Rouge, LA: 49
Tupelo, MS: 10
Houston, TX: 13
Tampa, FL: 45
Gulfport, MS: 6
Mobile, AL: 19
Raleigh, NC: 4
New Orleans, LA: 77
Dallas/Fort Worth, TX: 13

Hiring and Promotion
2015 Associates Hired: 26
2015 First-Year Hires: 6
Starting Salary for First-Year
 Assocs: $100,000
2016 First-Year Hires (Est.): 12
2015 Equity Partners Named: 4
2015 Lateral Equity Partners: 2

Leading Practice Areas
(Department Heads)
Commercial Litigation
 (Commercial/General/Tort/Environmental)
 36% (Lawrence P. Ingram 813-472-7555)
Business (Banking/Corporate/Gaming/Health
 Care/Energy/Public Utilities/Real
 Estate/Securities/Tax) 23% (Jeffrey Moore
 662-842-7907)
Insurance and Reinsurance 18% (Matthew L.
 Litsky 813-472-7558)
Employment Law (Labor and
 Employment/Employee Benefits) 14%
 (Reed L. Russell 813-472-7589)
Admiralty 7% (Brian Wallace 504-584-9204)

Client Representations
UPS
Underwriters at Lloyd's London
Edison Chouest Offshore

Leading Officials
Michael D. Hunt, Chairman, Policy and
 Planning Committee and Managing
 Partner, 225-346-0285
William White, Administrator, 813-472-7550
Rachel Woolridge, Manager of Legal
 Recruiting, 504-584-9373
Lynne Donaghy, Director of Marketing &
 Business Development, 813-472-7550
Chris D. Rigamer, Director of Technology,
 504-566-1311
Jennifer Dabbs, Reference Librarian,
 504-566-1311

Other Offices
Canal Place
 365 Canal Street, Suite 2000
 New Orleans, Louisiana 70130-6534
Phone: 504-566-1311
Fax: 504-568-9130
Email: info@phelps.com
Marshall M. Redmon

Stone Pigman Walther Wittmann LLC

546 Carondelet Street
New Orleans, LA 70130
Phone: 504-581-3200
Fax: 504-581-3361
Email: info@stonepigman.com
Web Site: www.stonepigman.com

2016 Total Lawyers: 61
2015 Total Lawyers: 57

MAINE

Bernstein Shur

100 Middle Street Plaza, West Tower
P.O. Box 9729
Portland, ME 04104
Phone: 207-774-1200
Fax: 207-774-1127
Email: info@bernsteinshur.com
Web Site: www.bernsteinshur.com

2016 Total Lawyers: 105
2015 Total Lawyers: 107

Pierce Atwood LLP

Merrils Wharf
254 Commercial Street
Portland, ME 04101
Phone: 207-791-1100
Fax: 207-791-1350
Email: info@pierceatwood.com
Web Site: www.pierceatwood.com

2016 Total Lawyers: 145
2015 Total Lawyers: 133

Preti, Flaherty, Beliveau & Pachios LLP

One City Center
P.O. Box 9546
Portland, ME 04112-9546
Phone: 207-791-3000
Fax: 207-791-3111
Email: info@preti.com
Web Site: www.preti.com

2016 Total Lawyers: 98
2015 Total Lawyers: 103

2016 Staff
Equity Partners: 40
Non-Equity Partners: 15
Associates: 23
Of Counsel: 22
Senior Counsel: 3

Offices: No. Attys.
Portland, ME: 48
Concord, NH: 18
Augusta, ME: 15
Boston, MA: 15
Salem, MA: 1
Washington, DC: 1

Preti, Flaherty, Beliveau & Pachios
LLP (Continued)

Hiring and Promotion
2015 Associates Hired: 3
2016 First-Year Hires (Est.): 1
2015 Equity Partners Named: 0

Leading Practice Areas
(Department Heads)
Litigation 30% (Dan Rapaport/Tim Bryant
 207-791-3000)
Business Law 24% (Michael Sheehan/Kara
 Sweeney 207-791-3000)
Government Affairs 10% (Dan Walker
 207-623-5300)
Energy & Utilities 9% (Tony Buxton
 207-623-5300)
Intellectual Property 7% (Stanley
 Schurgin/Steve Wilson 617-226-3800)
Environmental 5% (David Van Slyke
 207-791-3000)
Bankruptcy 5% (Gregory Moffett/Anthony
 Manhart 207-791-3000)
Employment 4% (Michael Messerschmidt
 207-791-3000)
Health 3% (John Doyle 207-791-3000)
Workers Compensation 3% (Evan Hansen
 207-791-3000)

Leading Officials
John M. Sullivan, 603-410-1500
Rachel Lawrence, Chief Operating Officer,
 207-791-3000
Jeffrey Talbert, 207-791-3000
Pamela Loring, Director of Human
 Resources, 207-791-3000
Lisa Meyer, Director of Marketing &
 Business Development, 207-791-3000
Darryl Hendricks, IT Director, 207-791-3000
Rita Bouchard, Librarian, 207-791-3000
Rachel Lawrence, COO, 207-791-3000

Verrill Dana

One Portland Square
P.O. Box 586
Portland, ME 04112-0586
Phone: 207-774-4000
Fax: 207-774-7499
Email: info@verrilldana.com
Web Site: www.verrilldana.com

2016 Total Lawyers: 134
2015 Total Lawyers: 115

2016 Staff
Equity Partners: 54
Non-Equity Partners: 12
Associates: 24
Counsel: 34
Senior Counsel: 10

Offices: No. Attys.
Portland, ME: 86
Augusta, ME: 1
Boston, MA: 28
Westport, CT: 18
Providence, RI: 1

MAINE	MARYLAND

Verrill Dana (Continued)

Hiring and Promotion
2015 Associates Hired: 5
2015 First-Year Hires: 3
Starting Salary for First-Year
  Assocs: $77,000
2016 First-Year Hires (Est.): 2-5
2015 Equity Partners Named: 6
2015 Lateral Equity Partners: 1

Leading Practice Areas
(Department Heads)
Litigation 30% (Martha Gaythwaite
  207-253-4650)
Business Law 20% (Christopher Graham
  203-222-3121)
Health Care 13% (Jeffrey Heidt
  617-3092605)
Regulatory and Legislative 11% (William S.
  Harwood 207-253-4702)
Real Estate 10% (Anthony M. Calcagni
  207-253-4516)
Labor and Employment 10% (Douglas P.
  Currier 207-253-4450)
Family Law 9% (Regina Hurley
  617-309-2600)
Construction 8% (Rob Ruesch
  207-253-4610)
Employee Benefits and Executive
  Compensation 7% (Suzanne Meeker
  207-253-4906)
Private Clients and Fiduciary Services 6%
  (Kurt E. Klebe 207-253-4806)

Leading Officials
Robert Ruesch, Chair of Executive Board
Keith C. Jones, Managing Partner
David L. Bois, Chief Operating Officer
Kelly Baetz, Hiring Committee Chair
Michele S. Pattenaude, Director of
  Human Resources
Gretchen A. Johnson, Director of Marketing
James I. Cohen, Business Development
  Committee Chair
Michael L. Sides, Director of Information
  Technology
Anne M. Reiman, Firm Librarian
Michelle S. Pattenaude, Human
  Resources Director

Other Offices
One Portland Square
Portland
ME
04112-0586
Phone: 207-774-4000
Fax: 207-774-7499
Email: info@verrilldana.com
Keith C. Jones

Gordon Feinblatt LLC

233 East Redwood Street
Baltimore, MD 21202
Phone: 410-576-4000
Fax: 410-576-4246
Email: info@gfrlaw.com
Web Site: www.gfrlaw.com

2016 Total Lawyers: 66
2015 Total Lawyers: 66

2016 Staff
Associates: 11
Of Counsel: 3
Senior Attorneys: 45
Counsel: 3
Staff Attorneys: 1

Hiring and Promotion
2015 Associates Hired: 5
2015 First-Year Hires: 2
Starting Salary for First-Year Assocs:
  $115,000, plus clerkship bonus, plus
  discretionary bonuses
2016 First-Year Hires (Est.): 2
2015 Equity Partners Named: 0

Leading Practice Areas
(Department Heads)
Financial Services 18% (Marjorie Corwin
  410-576-4041)
Personal Injury 13% (Robert Katz
  410-576-4287)
Health Care 9% (Barry Rosen 410-576-4224)
Real Estate 9% (Edward J. Levin
  410-576-1900)
General Litigation 6% (Jerry Thrope
  410-576-4295)
Trusts & Estates 6% (Lynn Sassin
  410-576-4151)
Benefits/ERISA 6% (Matthew P. Mellin
  410-576-4047)
Environmental & Energy 6% (Todd Chason
  410-576-4069)
General Business 6% (Elliott Cowan
  410-576-4108)
Intellectual Property/Tech 6% (Ned T.
  Himmelrich 410-576-4171)
General Employment 6% (Robert Kellner
  410-576-4239)
Bankruptcy & Restructuring 3% (Lawrence
  Coppel 410-576-4238)
Government Relations 3% (D. Robert Enten
  410-576-4114)
Tax 3% (Douglas Coats 410-576-4002)

Gordon Feinblatt LLC (Continued)

Leading Officials
Barry Rosen, Chairman and CEO,
  410-576-4224
Michael C. Powell, Managing Member,
  410-576-4175
Jeffrey Hackett, Executive Director,
  410-576-4020
John Morton, Hiring Member, 410-576-4176
Robyn Seabrease, Director of Human
  Resources, 410-576-4286
Pamela Custer, Marketing Director,
  410-576-4156
Donna West, Technology Director,
  410-576-4165
Sara Witman, Director of Library Services,
  410-576-4010
Alicia L. Wilson, Chair, Diversity
  Committee, 410-576-4085

Linowes & Blocher LLP

7200 Wisconsin Ave
Suite 800
Bethesda, MD 20814
Phone: 301-654-0504
Fax: 301-654-2801
Web Site: www.linowes-law.com

2016 Total Lawyers: 50
2015 Total Lawyers: 50

Miles & Stockbridge P.C.

100 Light Street
Baltimore, MD 21202
Phone: 410-727-6464
Fax: 410-385-3700
Web Site: www.milesstockbridge.com

2016 Total Lawyers: 230
2015 Total Lawyers: 238

2016 Staff
Equity Partners: 71
Non-Equity Partners: 59
Associates: 59
Of Counsel: 8
Counsel: 30
Staff Attorneys: 3

Offices: No. Attys.
Baltimore, MD: 148
Frederick, MD: 13
Easton, MD: 5
Tysons Corner, VA: 23
Towson, MD: 6
Rockville, MD: 18
Washington, DC: 17

Hiring and Promotion
2015 Associates Hired: 12
2015 First-Year Hires: 6
Starting Salary for First-Year
  Assocs: $125,000
2016 First-Year Hires (Est.): 6
2015 Equity Partners Named: 6

MARYLAND

Miles & Stockbridge P.C. (Continued)

*Leading Practice Areas
(Department Heads)*
Creditors' Rights & Bankruptcy (Linda V.
Donhauser 410-385-3684)
Labor, Employment, Benefits & Immigration
(Kirsten M. Eriksson 410-385-3583)
Products Liabilty and Mass Torts (Laura A.
Cellucci 410-385-3867)
Real Estate & Construction (Nancy W.
Greene 410-385-3639)
Intellectual Propery & Technology (Michael
A. Messina 703-610-8627)
Banking & Finance (Benjamin D. Horowicz
410-385-3613)
Corporate, Securities & Tax (Christopher R.
Johnson 410-385-3532)
Family Law & Private Clients (Stephen J.
Cullen 202-465-8374)
Government Contracts (Gene R.
Schleppenbach 703-610-8623)
Litigation & Dispute Resolution (E.
Hutchinson Robbins, Jr. 410-385-3408)
Health Care (Peter P. Parvis 410-823-8165)

Leading Officials
John B. Frisch, Chairman/CEO,
410-385-3507
Joseph W. Hovermill, President/COO,
410-385-3433
William G. Psillas, Jr. Director of
Administration, 410-385-3580
Scott R. Wilson, Chairman of Recruitment
Committee, 410-385-3590
Dina Billian , Director of Recruitment &
Professional Development, 410-385-3626
Elizabeth Lockett Byrne, Chief Marketing
Officer, 410-385-3636
Brandon McAfee, Business Development
Manager, 410-385-3633
Kenneth E. Adams, Chief Information
Officer, 410-385-3575
Sara Thomas, Director of Research &
Information Services, 410-385-3671
Michael A. Brown, Principal and Board
Member, 410-385-3439

Other Offices
100 Light Street
Baltimore, MD 21202
Phone: 410-727-6464
Fax: 410-385-3700
Email: www.milesstockbridge.com,
jfrisch@milesstockbridge.com
John B. Frisch Chairman/CEO

Ober, Kaler, Grimes & Shriver, P.C.

**100 Light Street
Baltimore, MD 21202
Phone: 410-685-1120
Fax: 410-547-0699
Email: info@ober.com
Web Site: www.ober.com**

2016 Total Lawyers: 112
2015 Total Lawyers: 112

Ober, Kaler, Grimes & Shriver, P.C. (Continued)

2016 Staff
Equity Partners: 41
Non-Equity Partners: 24
Associates: 20
Counsel: 21
Staff Attorneys: 3

Offices: No. Attys.
Washington, DC: 18
Baltimore, MD: 89
Towson, MD: 1

Hiring and Promotion
2015 Associates Hired: 5
2015 First-Year Hires: 1
2016 First-Year Hires (Est.): 0
2015 Equity Partners Named: 2
2015 Lateral Equity Partners: 2

*Leading Practice Areas
(Department Heads)*
Construction (John F. Morkan, Joseph C.
Kovars 410-347-7355 , 410-347-7343)
Creditors' Rights (F. Thomas Rafferty,
Nikolaus F. Schandlbauer 410-347-7372,
202-326-5016)
Employment & Labor (Jerald J. Oppel
410-347-7338)
Estates & Trusts (Mathew A. Mace, Mary
Baker Edwards 410-347-7690,
410-347-7307)
Health (Catherine A. Martin, Julie E. Kass
410-347-7320, 410-347-7314)
Litigation (James E. Edwards, Jr., E. John
Steren 410-347-7330; 202-326-5017)
Intellectual Property (Royal W. Craig, E.
Scott Johnson 410-347-7303,
410-347-7388)
Finance (Alan J. Mogol, Darlene R. Davis
410-347-7332, 410-347-7306)
Business/Tax (Robert L. Ash, Stuart M.
Schabes, Kenneth B. Abel 202-326-5005,
410-347-7696, 410-347-7394)
Financial Institutions (Frank C. Bonaventure
410-347-7305)

Leading Officials
S. Craig Holden, Chair / CEO, 410-347-7322
Darlene R. Davis, President / COO,
410-347-7306
Ken G. Cook, Executive Director,
410-347-7351
Cynthia Cherry, Chief Human Resources
Officer, 410-230-7139
Vickie J. Gray, Chief Marketing Officer,
410-347-7378
Donald W. Shifflett, Chief Technology
Officer, 410-685-1120
Kumar Jayasuriya, Head Librarian and
Research Services Manager, 410-230-7011
Cynthia Cherry, Chief Human Resources
Officer, 410-230-7139

Semmes, Bowen & Semmes, A Professional Corporation

**25 South Charles St
Suite 1400
Baltimore, MD 21201
Phone: 410-539-5040
Fax: 410-539-5223
Web Site: www.semmes.com**

2016 Total Lawyers: 72
2015 Total Lawyers: 68

Shulman, Rogers, Gandal, Pordy & Ecker, P.A.

**12505 Park Potomac Avenue
6th Floor
Potomac, MD 20854
Phone: 301-230-5200
Fax: 301-230-2891
Email: lawfirm@shulmanrogers.com
Web Site: www.shulmanrogers.com**

2016 Total Lawyers: 95
2015 Total Lawyers: 99

2016 Staff
Equity Partners: 38
Non-Equity Partners: 18
Associates: 29
Of Counsel: 9
Senior Counsel: 1

Offices: No. Attys.
Potomac, MD: 95

Hiring and Promotion
2015 Associates Hired: 5
2015 First-Year Hires: 3
2016 First-Year Hires (Est.): 2
2015 Equity Partners Named: 1

*Leading Practice Areas
(Department Heads)*
Commercial Litigation (Kevin P. Kennedy
301-230-5219)
Contingent Litigation (Martin Levine
301-230-5255)
Corporate (Aaron Ghais/Scott Museles
301-255-0557 301-230-5246)
Real Estate (Douglas K. Hirsch
301-230-5225)
Trust and Estates (Jay M. Eisenberg
301-230-5223)
Telecommunications (Alan S. Tilles
301-231-0930)

Leading Officials
Samuel M. Spiritos, Managing Shareholder,
301-230-5236
Michael J. Bonanno, Director of
Administration, 301-945-9256
Gina De Vittorio, Recruiting Manager,
301-945-9289
Lori A. Swim, Marketing Manager,
301-255-0527
Robert J. Baumgarten, Chief Information
Officer, 301-255-0523
Belinda Cain, Head Librarian, 301-230-5200
Paul Chung, Shareholder, 301-230-5230

MARYLAND

Whiteford, Taylor & Preston

Seven Saint Paul Street
Baltimore, MD 21202
Phone: 410-347-8700
Fax: 410-752-7092
Email: info@wtplaw.com
Web Site: www.wtplaw.com

2016 Total Lawyers: 160
2015 Total Lawyers: 156

MASSACHUSETTS

Bowditch & Dewey, LLP

311 Main Street
P.O. Box 15156
Worcester, MA 01615-0156
Phone: 508-791-3511
Fax: 508-756-7636
Email: info@bowditch.com
Web Site: www.bowditch.com

2016 Total Lawyers: 58
2015 Total Lawyers: 62

2016 Staff
Equity Partners: 19
Non-Equity Partners: 27
Associates: 7
Of Counsel: 7

Offices: No. Attys.
Worcester, MA: 40
Framingham, MA: 14
Boston, MA: 8

Hiring and Promotion
2015 Associates Hired: 6
2016 First-Year Hires (Est.): 2
2015 Equity Partners Named: 0
2015 Lateral Equity Partners: 2

Leading Practice Areas
(Department Heads)
Litigation 29% (Louis M. Ciavarra
508-926-3408)
Business & Finance 24% (Jane V. Hawkes
617-757-6510)
Real Estate & Environmental 22% (Paul
Bauer 617-757-6535)
Estate, Financial & Tax Planning 17% (John
F. Shoro 508-926-3433)
Labor & Employment 8% (David M. Felper
508-926-3452)

Leading Officials
Michael P. Angelini, Firm Chair,
508-926-3400
James D. Hanrahan, Managing Partner,
508-416-2404
Tina Bussone, Executive Director,
508-926-3319
Robert D. Cox, Jr., Hiring Partner,
508-926-3409
Vickie E. Manning, Firm Administrator,
508-926-3312
Jennifer Irvine, Director of Marketing and
Business Development, 508-926-3348
Jason Matthew, Director of IT, 508-926-3300
Leslie Bitman, Librarian, 508-926-3332
AiVi , Nguyen, 508-926-3402

Brown & Rudnick

One Financial Center
Boston, MA 02111
Phone: 617-856-8200
Fax: 617-856-8201
Web Site: www.brownrudnick.com

2016 Total Lawyers: 242
2015 Total Lawyers: 242

Burns & Levinson LLP

125 Summer Street
Boston, MA 02110-1624
Phone: 617-345-3000
Fax: 617-345-3299
Email: clientservices@burnslev.c
Web Site: www.burnslev.com

2016 Total Lawyers: 128
2015 Total Lawyers: 126

2016 Staff
Equity Partners: 47
Non-Equity Partners: 38
Associates: 35
Of Counsel: 8
Counsel: 1

Offices: No. Attys.
Boston, MA: 118
Providence, RI: 9
Andover, MA: 1

Hiring and Promotion
2015 Associates Hired: 14
2015 First-Year Hires: 1
Starting Salary for First-Year Assocs: N/A
2016 First-Year Hires (Est.): 0
2015 Equity Partners Named: 2
2015 Lateral Equity Partners: 2

Leading Practice Areas
(Department Heads)
Corporate 35% (Frank A. Segall, Josef B.
Volman. 617-345-3684; 617-345-3895)
Private Clients 22% (Brian D. Bixby, Clifford
R. Cohen, Robin Lynch Nardone
617-345-3694; 617-345-3000)
Intellectual Property 18% (Bruce Jobse,
Deborah J. Peckham. 617-345-3207;
617-345-3577)
Business Litigation 17% (Paul R. Mastrocola;
Jeffrey R. Martin. 617-345-3336;
617-345-3248)
Real Estate 5% (Anatoly M. Darov, Donald
E. Vaughan. 617-345-3820;
617-345-3237)
Tax 3% (Howard D. Medwed, Harry S. Miller
617.345.3236; 617-345-3352)

Client Representations
N/A
N/A
N/A

Burns & Levinson LLP (Continued)

Leading Officials
David P. Rosenblatt,, Managing Partner,
617-345-3300
Paul R. Morton, Executive Director.
617-345-3583
Mark W. Manning. Hiring Partner,
617-345-3468
Kristen Weller, Director of Marketing,
617-345-3555
Karen Katz, Director of Client Relations and
Development, 617-345-3309
Henry B. Chace, Chief Information Officer,
617-345-3317
Abbi L. Maher, Manager of Library Services,
617-345-3605

Choate, Hall & Stewart LLP

Two International Place
Boston, MA 02110
Phone: 617-248-5000
Fax: 617-248-4000
Email: info@choate.com
Web Site: www.choate.com

2016 Total Lawyers: 168
2015 Total Lawyers: 174

Fish & Richardson

One Marina Park Drive
Boston, MA 02210-1878
Phone: 617-542-5070
Fax: 617-542-8906
Email: info@fr.com
Web Site: www.fr.com

2016 Total Lawyers: 367
2015 Total Lawyers: 367

2016 Staff
Associates: 136
Of Counsel: 24
Staff Attorneys: 6
Principals: 189
Senior Principals: 9
Fellowship Attorney 1

Offices: No. Attys.
Boston, MA: 66
Washington, DC: 58
Dallas, TX: 44
Twin Cities, MN: 37
Silicon Valley, CA: 30
New York, NY: 33
Southern California, CA: 30
Atlanta, GA: 21
Wilmington, DE: 18
Houston, TX: 11
Munich, Germany: 6
Austin, TX: 11

Hiring and Promotion
2015 Associates Hired: 34
2015 First-Year Hires: 24
2015 Equity Partners Named: 16
2015 Lateral Equity Partners: 2

MASSACHUSETTS

Fish & Richardson (Continued)

*Leading Practice Areas
(Department Heads)*
Patent (John F. Hayden 202-626-6416)
Litigation (Kurt L. Glitzenstein
617-521-7042)
Regulatory (Terry G. Mahn 202-626-6421)
Trademark, Copyright, New Media and
Entertainment (Cynthia Johnson Walden
617-956-5928)

Revenues and Profits
Revenues: $394,959,808
Profits: $158,508,153

Client Representations
LG Electronics v. InterDigital
Communications - Won series of
complicated patent litigation cases with
millions of dollars in dispute for LG.
Supreme Court granted cert, vacated Fed
Cir decision.
In the Matter of Certain Sleep-Disordered
Breathing Treatment Systems - won huge
ITC victory for ResMed. Competitor
infringed multiple patents, excluded from
import/sale in US; cease and desist order.
Chicago Bd. Options Exchange v. Int'l
Securities Exchange – Fed. Cir. affirmed
Fish's client, CBOE, did not infringe a
patent the ISE believed to be fundamental.
ISE ordered to pay attorneys' fees.

Leading Officials
Peter J. Devlin, President, 617-542-5070
Richard J. Anderson, Chief Operating
Officer, 612-337-2501
Roger A. Denning, Hiring Partner,
858-678-5070
Kelly M. Mixon, National Director for
Attorney Hiring, 512-472-5070
Kelly K. Largey, Chief Marketing Officer,
617-542-5070
Loretta M. Auer, Chief Information Officer,
617-542-5070
Ahmed J. Davis, Principal, National Chair of
Diversity Initiative, 202-626-6379

Other Offices
Fish & Richardson P.C.
One Marina Park Drive
Boston, MA 02210-1878
Phone: 617-542-5070
Fax: 617-542-8906
Email: info@fr.com
Timothy A. French

Fish & Richardson P.C.
1425 K Street, NW
Suite 1100
Washington, DC 20005
Phone: 202-783-5070
Fax: 202-783-2331
Email: info@fr.com
Terry G. Mahn

Foley Hoag LLP

**Seaport World Trade Center
155 Seaport Boulevard
Boston, MA 02210-2600
Phone: 617-832-1000
Fax: 617-832-7000
Web Site: www.foleyhoag.com**

2016 Total Lawyers: 267
2015 Total Lawyers: 250

Goodwin Procter LLP

**Exchange Place
53 State Street
Boston, MA 02109-2881
Phone: 617-570-1000
Fax: 617-523-1231
Web Site: www.goodwinprocter.com**

2016 Total Lawyers: 900
2015 Total Lawyers: 875

2016 Staff
Equity Partners: 200
Non-Equity Partners: 120
Associates: 432
Of Counsel: 11
Senior Attorneys: 20
Counsel: 71
Senior Counsel: 2
Staff Attorneys: 19

Offices: No. Attys.
New York, NY: 184
Washington, DC: 106
Silicon Valley, CA: 64
Los Angeles, CA: 28
San Francisco, CA: 50
Boston, MA: 412
Hong Kong: 10
London, England: 21

Hiring and Promotion
2015 Associates Hired: 84
2015 First-Year Hires: 59
Starting Salary for First-Year
Assocs: $160,000
2015 Equity Partners Named: 10
2015 Lateral Equity Partners: 5

Goodwin Procter LLP (Continued)

*Leading Practice Areas
(Department Heads)*
Technology Companies 15% (John J. Egan
III, William J. Schnoor, Anthony J.
McCusker 617-570-1000, 650-752-3100)
Real Estate Capital Markets 12% (Gilbert G.
Menna 617-570-1000)
Private Equity 10% (John R. LeClaire,
Andrew J. Weidhaas 617-570-1000,
212-813-8800)
IP Litigation 8% (Douglas J. Kline
617-570-1000)
Securities Litigation and White Collar
Defense 7% (R. Todd Cronan, Richard M.
Strassberg 617-570-1000, 212-813-8800)
Financial Institutions 6% (Robert M.
Kurucza, William P. Mayer 202-346-4000,
617-570-1000)
Speciality Litigation 6% (Joanne M. Gray
212-813-8800)
Business Litigation 5% (Brenda R. Sharton
617-570-1000)
Life Sciences 5% (John J. Egan III, William J.
Schnoor, Mitchell S. Bloom
617-570-1000)
Consumer Financial Services Litigation 3%
(Thomas M. Hefferon 202-346-4000)

Revenues and Profits
Revenues: $785,500,000
Profits: $329,500,000

Client Representations
Teva Pharmaceuticals (client/Supreme Court
Copaxone win; $3.2B acquisition of
Auspex Pharmaceuticals)
Trulia ($3.5B sale to Zillow)
Paramount ($2.3B IPO, largest ever
REIT IPO)

Leading Officials
David M. Hashmall, Chairman,
212-813-8800
Robert S. Insolia, Managing Partner,
212-813-8800
Michael R. Caplan, Chief Operating Officer,
212-813-8800
Jeffrey A. Simes, Hiring Partner,
212-813-8800
Joan E. Tagliareni, Managing Director, Legal
Recruitment, 617-570-1000
Emma van Rooyen, Chief Marketing Officer,
212-813-8800
Emily Thall, Managing Director of Business
Development, 212-813-8800
Lorey Hoffman, Chief Information Officer,
617-570-1000
Anne M. Stemlar, Managing Director,
Research & Knowledge Management,
617-570-1000
Laura Acosta, Manager of Diversity &
Professional Development, 617-570-1000

Other Offices
New York Office
The New York Times Building, 620
Eighth Avenue
New York
NY
10018

MASSACHUSETTS

Goodwin Procter LLP (Continued)

Washington, D.C. Office
901 New York Avenue, N.W.
Washington
DC
20001

Silicon Valley Office
135 Commonwealth Drive
Menlo Park
CA
94025

San Francisco Office
Three Embarcadero Center
24th Floor
San Francisco
CA
94111

Goulston & Storrs

400 Atlantic Avenue
Boston, MA 02110-3333
Phone: 617-482-1776
Fax: 617-574-4112
Email: nneedle@goulstonstorrs.co
Web Site: www.goulstonstorrs.com

2016 Total Lawyers: 200
2015 Total Lawyers: 192

Mintz Levin Cohn Ferris Glovsky and Popeo

One Financial Center
Boston, MA 02111
Phone: 617-542-6000
Fax: 617-542-2241
Web Site: www.mintz.com

2016 Total Lawyers: 490
2015 Total Lawyers: 544

Morrison Mahoney LLP

250 Summer Street
Boston, MA 02210
Phone: 617-439-7500
Fax: 617-439-7590
Email: info@mail.mm-m.com
Web Site: www.mm-m.com

2016 Total Lawyers: 190
2015 Total Lawyers: 184

Nutter McClennen & Fish LLP

155 Seaport Boulevard
Seaport West
Boston, MA 02210-2604
Phone: 617-439-2000
Fax: 617-310-9000
Email: web@nutter.com
Web Site: www.nutter.com

2016 Total Lawyers: 147
2015 Total Lawyers: 143

Peabody & Arnold LLP

600 Atlantic Avenue
Federal Reserve Plaza
Boston, MA 02210
Phone: 617-951-2100
Fax: 617-951-2125
Web Site: www.peabodyarnold.com

2016 Total Lawyers: 51
2015 Total Lawyers: 52

Posternak Blankstein & Lund LLP

Prudential Tower
800 Boylston Street
Boston, MA 02199
Phone: 617-973-6100
Fax: 617-367-2315
Email: pbl@pbl.com
Web Site: www.pbl.com

2016 Total Lawyers: 60
2015 Total Lawyers: 58

Rubin and Rudman LLP

50 Rowes Wharf
Boston, MA 02110
Phone: 617-330-7000
Fax: 617-330-7550
Web Site: www.rubinrudman.com

2016 Total Lawyers: 74
2015 Total Lawyers: 74

2016 Staff
Equity Partners: 39
Non-Equity Partners: 26
Associates: 6
Of Counsel: 1

Offices: No. Attys.
Rowes Wharf, Boston, MA: 66
Yarmouth Port, MA: 4
Washington, DC: 2

Hiring and Promotion
2016 First-Year Hires (Est.): 1
2015 Equity Partners Named: 4
2015 Lateral Equity Partners: 4

Rubin and Rudman LLP (Continued)

Leading Practice Areas
(Department Heads)
Business/Labor 26.1% (Neal Splaine
617-330-7155)
Trust, Estates, Probate 21.50% (Roland Gray
617-330-7169)
Real Estate 19.60% (James Sperling
617-330-7116)
Energy/Tele/Utilities 17.4% (Chris Pollart
617-330-7003)
Litigation 15.4% (John McGiveny
617-330-7007)

Revenues and Profits
Revenues: $32,761,000
Profits: $15,722,000

Leading Officials
John DeTore
Laura Long, 617-330-7085
Patricia Palmer, 617-330-7129
Linda Therault, Rick Snow, 617-330-7121

Sullivan & Worcester

One Post Office Square
Boston, MA 02109
Phone: 617-338-2800
Fax: 617-338-2880
Email: info@sandw.com
Web Site: www.sandw.com

2016 Total Lawyers: 162
2015 Total Lawyers: 167

2016 Staff
Equity Partners: 40
Non-Equity Partners: 48
Associates: 44
Of Counsel: 9
Counsel: 19
Staff Attorneys: 2

Offices: No. Attys.
Washington, DC: 15
Boston: 101
New York: 39
London, England: 7

Hiring and Promotion
2015 Associates Hired: 6
2015 First-Year Hires: 3
Starting Salary for First-Year
Assocs: $145,000
2016 First-Year Hires (Est.): 4
2015 Equity Partners Named: 1

MASSACHUSETTS

Sullivan & Worcester (Continued)

Leading Practice Areas
(Department Heads)
Corporate 28% (Lewis Segall 617-338-2807)
Real Estate 16% (John Balboni, Louis Monti 617-338-2800)
Tax 16% (David Nagle 617-338-2800)
Litigation 12% (Andrew Solomon 212-660-3000)
Investment Management 9% (David Mahaffey 202-775-1207)
Trusts & Estates 7% (Lisa Mingolla 617-338-2800)
Environmental 4% (Jeff Karp 202-370-3921)
Intellectual Property 3% (Kim Herman 617-338-2800)
Trade Finance 3% (Geoff Wynne +44 (0)20 7448 1001)
Bankruptcy & Restructuring 2% (Jeanne Darcey 617-338-2800)

Revenues and Profits
Revenues: $101,427,344
Profits: $44,411,644

Client Representations
Iron Mountain Incorporated
John Hancock Financial Services
American Tower Corporation

Leading Officials
Joel Carpenter, Managing Partner, 617-338-2815
Michael Kiskinis, Chief Operating Officer, 617-338-2408
Jeanne Darcey, Hiring Partner, 617-338-2995
Janet Brussard, Director of Legal Recruiting, 617-338-2806
Leah Schloss, Director of Marketing, 617-338-2448
Aidan Browne, Business Development Partner, 617-338-2996
Nancy Wahl, IT Director, 617-338-2975
Geoffrey Valentine, Director of Library Services, 617-338-2959
Darwin Conner and Ashley Brooks, Co-Leaders of the Diversity Committee, 617-338-2412

Other Offices
One Post Office Square
Boston, MA 02109
Phone: 617-338-2800
Fax: 617-338-2880
Joel R. Carpenter, Managing Partner

Wolf Greenfield & Sacks, PC

600 Atlantic Ave
Boston, MA 02210
Phone: 617-646-8000
Web Site: www.wolfgreenfield.com

2016 Total Lawyers: 93
2015 Total Lawyers: 72

MICHIGAN

Bodman PLC

6th Floor at Ford Field
1901 St. Antoine Street
Detroit, MI 48226
Phone: 313-259-7777
Fax: 313-393-7579
Email: info@bodmanlaw.com
Web Site: www.bodmanlaw.com

2016 Total Lawyers: 148
2015 Total Lawyers: 160

2016 Staff
Equity Partners: 53
Non-Equity Partners: 51
Associates: 37
Of Counsel: 12
Staff Attorneys: 7

Offices: No. Attys.
Detroit, MI: 95
Troy, MI: 37
Ann Arbor, MI: 18
Cheboygan, MI: 4
Dallas, TX: 1

Hiring and Promotion
Starting Salary for First-Year Assocs:
$105,000 (including $5,000 bonus payable upon graduation)

Leading Practice Areas
(Department Heads)
Banking (Robert J. Diehl, Jr. 313-393-7597)
Bankruptcy (Robert J. Diehl Jr. 313-393-7597)
Corporate/M&A (Timothy R. Damschroder 734-930-0230)
Workplace (Maureen Rouse-Ayoub 313-392-1058)
Environmental (Fredrick J. Dindoffer 313-393-7595)
Individual Clients (David P. Larsen 313-393-7575)
Intellectual Property (Alan N. Harris 734-930-0236)
Litigation (Thomas J. Tallerico/Joseph J. Shannon 248-743-6073; 313-393-7549)
Health Care (E. William S. Shipman 313-393-7562)
Real Estate (Nicholas P. Scavone, Jr. 313-393-7580)
Enterprise Procurement (Courtland W. Anderson 248-743-6063)

Client Representations
Comerica Bank
Blue Cross Blue Shield of Michigan
Lear Corporation

Bodman PLC (Continued)

Leading Officials
Ralph E. McDowell, Chairman, 313-393-7592
Christopher J. Dine, Administrative Partner, 313-393-7574
William P. Scarbrough, COO, 313-393-7558
Thomas P. Bruetsch, Hiring Partner, 313-393-7541
Anthony J. Allegrina, Director of Business Development, 313-393-7564
Steve Carey, Information Technology Manager, 313-392-1077
Michael Powell, Librarian, 313-656-2554
Damali A. Sahu / Jaimee L. Witten, Co-Chairs, Diversity Committee, 313-259-7777

Braun Kendrick Finkbeiner

4301 Fashion Square Blvd
Saginaw, MI 48603
Phone: 989-498-2100
Fax: 989-799-4666
Web Site: www.Braunkendrick.com

2016 Total Lawyers: 33
2015 Total Lawyers: 33

2016 Staff
Equity Partners: 13
Non-Equity Partners: 8
Associates: 3
Of Counsel: 3
Staff Attorneys: 1

Hiring and Promotion
2016 First-Year Hires (Est.): 0
2015 Equity Partners Named: 1

Leading Officials
David J. Klippert, Executive Committee Chair, 989-399-0207
Jamie Hecht Nisidis, Hiring Partner, 989-399-0227

Butzel Long

150 West Jefferson
Suite 100
Detroit, MI 48226
Phone: 313-225-7000
Fax: 313-225-7080
Email: melnick@butzel.com
Web Site: www.butzel.com

2016 Total Lawyers: 137
2015 Total Lawyers: 132

MICHIGAN

Clark Hill PLC

500 Woodward Avenue
Suite 3500
Detroit, MI 48226-3435
Phone: 313-965-8300
Fax: 313-965-8252
Email: email@clarkhill.com
Web Site: www.clarkhill.com

2016 Total Lawyers: 357
2015 Total Lawyers: 344

2016 Staff
Equity Partners: 80
Non-Equity Partners: 77
Associates: 63
Of Counsel: 54
Senior Attorneys: 83

Offices: No. Attys.
Detroit, MI: 80
Lansing, MI: 12
Birmingham, MI: 50
Chicago, IL: 62
Grand Rapids, MI: 21
Phoenix, AZ: 21
Washington, D.C.: 20
Pittsburgh, PA: 66
Philadelphia, PA: 18
Wilmington, DE: 1
Morgantown, WV: 1
Princeton, NJ: 5

Leading Practice Areas
(Department Heads)
Construction (Kevin S. Hendrick
313-965-8315)
Corporate (Douglas E. Gilbert 412-394-7771)
Labor & Employment Law (Thomas P. Brady
313-965-8591)
Government & Public Affairs (Charles R.
Spies 202-572-8663)
Education & Municipal Law (John L. Gierak
248-988-5845)
Litigation (Thomas M. Dixon & Jerri A. Ryan
313-965-8587)
Real Estate (Timothy M. Koltun
313-965-8326)
Banking & Finance (Jeffrey J. Conn
412-394-2324)
Personal Legal Services (J. Thomas
MacFarlane & Keith H. West
248-988-5846)
Environment, Energy & Natural Resources
(Kenneth von Schaumburg 202-772-0904)

Revenues and Profits
Revenues: $139,815,000

Clark Hill PLC (Continued)

Leading Officials
John J. Hern, Chief Executive Officer,
313-965-8320
Stephen P. Ormond, Managing Partner of
Detroit Office, 313-965-8228
Philip E. Ross, Chief Operating Officer,
313-965-8590
Kathleen M. Sullivan, Senior Director of
Human Resources, 412-394-2404
Jacki Herzog, Legal Recruitment Manager,
412-394-7721
Donald J. Lee, Chief Marketing Officer,
313-965-8331
Steven L. Ratliff, Chief Information Officer,
313-965-8465
Kathleen A. Gamache, Librarian,
313-965-8277
Linda Watson & Dave Cessante, Members,
248-988-5881

Other Offices
Pittsburgh, PA
301 Grant Street
14th Floor
Pittsburgh
PA
15219
Phone: 412-394-7711
Fax: 412-394-2555
Email: email@clarkhill.com
Jeff Conn

Birmingham, MI
151 S. Old Woodward
Suite 200
Birmingham
MI
48009
Phone: 248-642-9692
Fax: 248-642-2174
Email: email@clarkhill.com
Dan Minkus

Chicago, IL
150 N. Michigan Avenue
2700
Chicago
IL
60601
Phone: 312-985-5900
Fax: 312-985-5999
Email: email@clarkhill.com
Ray Koenig

Dickinson Wright PLLC

500 Woodward Avenue
Suite 4000
Detroit, MI 48226
Phone: 313-223-3500
Fax: 313-223-3598
Email: jgorzalski@dickinsonwrigh
Web Site: www.dickinsonwright.com

2016 Total Lawyers: 421
2015 Total Lawyers: 388

2016 Staff
Equity Partners: 124
Non-Equity Partners: 131
Associates: 118
Of Counsel: 47
Senior Attorneys: 1

Dickinson Wright PLLC (Continued)

Offices: No. Attys.
Detroit, MI: 62
Troy, MI: 80
Lansing, MI: 15
Grand Rapids, MI: 21
Washington, DC: 23
Ann Arbor, MI: 23
Nashville, TN: 31
Phoenix, AZ: 61
Toronto, ON: 45
Las Vegas, NV: 18
Columbus, OH: 22
Saginaw, MI: 5
Lexington, KY: 9
Reno, NV: 6

Hiring and Promotion
2015 Associates Hired: 21
2015 First-Year Hires: 11
Starting Salary for First-Year Assocs:
$100,000 + $5,000 signing bonus
2016 First-Year Hires (Est.): 13
2015 Equity Partners Named: 12
2015 Lateral Equity Partners: 5

Leading Practice Areas
(Department Heads)
Commercial Litigation 23% (D. D. Quick
248-433-7242)
Corporate--Securities 20% (S. C. Crow
614-744-2585)
Intellectual Property 13% (P. E. Rettig
248-433-7533)
Real Estate 12% (H. W. Robins
614-744-2575)
Municipal Finance 5% (W. P. Shield
313-223-3602)
Banking 4% (W. P. Shield 313-223-3602)
Labor & Employment Relations 4% (M. R.
Estes, Jr. 615-620-1737)
Bankruptcy 4% (J. A. Plemmons
313-223-3106)
Construction & Real Estate Litigation 3% (S.
E. Richman 602-285-5017)
Trusts & Estates 3% (C.A. Moore
248-433-7295)

Client Representations
JMorgan Chase Bank, N.A.
Enbridge Energy Company, Inc.
Federal Mogul

Leading Officials
William T. Burgess, CEO, 313-223-3634
John D. Gorzalski, Chief Administrative
Officer, 313-223-3515
Jason P. Klingensmith & Michael C.
Hammer, Chair Recruitment Committee &
Hiring Partner, 313-223-3500
Christine A. Scurto, Director of Legal
Recruiting, 313-223-3150
James J. Stapleton, Chief Marketing Office,
313-223-3081
Michael P. Kolb, Chief Information Officer,
313-223-3608
Mark Heinrich, Head Librarian,
313-223-3572
W. Anthony Jenkins, Harlan W. Robins and
Anna M. Maiuri, Co-Chairpersons,
313-223-3500

MICHIGAN

Dickinson Wright PLLC (Continued)

Other Offices
Troy, MI
2600 West Big Beaver Road
300
Troy
MI
48084
Phone: 248-433-7200
Fax: 248-433-7274
Monica J. Labe

Phoenix, AZ
1850 N. Central Avenue
1400
Phoenix
AZ
85004
Phone: 602-285-5000
Fax: 602-285-5100
Gary L. Birnbaum

Dykema

400 Renaissance Center
Detroit, MI 48243-1668
Phone: 313-568-5439
Fax: 313-568-5440
Email: clueth@dykema.com
Web Site: www.dykema.com

2016 Total Lawyers: 426
2015 Total Lawyers: 433

Foster Swift Collins & Smith, PC

313 South Washington Square
Lansing, MI 48933-2193
Phone: 517-371-8100
Fax: 517-371-8200
Email: info@fosterswift.com
Web Site: www.fosterswift.com

2016 Total Lawyers: 91
2015 Total Lawyers: 96

Harness Dickey

5445 Corporate Drive
Suite 200
Troy, MI 48098
Phone: 248-641-1600
Fax: 248-641-0270
Email: info@hdp.com
Web Site: www.hdp.com

2016 Total Lawyers: 114
2015 Total Lawyers: 110

2016 Staff
Equity Partners: 57
Non-Equity Partners: 12
Associates: 37
Counsel: 4

Offices: No. Attys.
Troy, MI: 58

Harness Dickey (Continued)
St. Louis, MO: 24
Reston, VA: 23
Dallas, TX: 5

Hiring and Promotion
2015 Associates Hired: 6
2015 First-Year Hires: 1
Starting Salary for First-Year Assocs: 0
2016 First-Year Hires (Est.): 2
2015 Equity Partners Named: 8
2015 Lateral Equity Partners: 2

Leading Practice Areas
(Department Heads)
Intellectual Property 100%

Client Representations
Emerson Electric
Seiko Epson Corporation
Marvell Semiconductor, Inc.

Leading Officials
David A. Roback, Chief Operating Officer,
248-641-1600
Lynette J. Barrett, Recruiting Coordinator,
248-641-1600
Alona Gordon, Marketing Manager,
314-726-7500
Jason Russo, Information Services Manager,
248-641-1600
Kris Potter, Head Librarian, 248-641-1600
Lisabeth Coakley, Partner, 248-641-1600

Honigman Miller Schwartz and Cohn LLP

2290 First National Building
660 Woodward Avenue
Detroit, MI 48226-3506
Phone: 313-465-7000
Fax: 313-465-8000
Web Site: www.honigman.com

2016 Total Lawyers: 282
2015 Total Lawyers: 257

2016 Staff
Equity Partners: 143
Non-Equity Partners: 63
Associates: 51
Of Counsel: 13
Senior Counsel: 1
Staff Attorneys: 11

Offices: No. Attys.
Detroit, MI: 150
Lansing, MI: 14
Bloomfield Hills, MI: 55
Ann Arbor, MI: 12
Kalamazoo, MI: 26
Chicago, IL: 23

Hiring and Promotion
2015 Associates Hired: 21

Honigman Miller Schwartz and Cohn LLP (Continued)

Leading Practice Areas
(Department Heads)
Corporate/Securities (Donald J. Kunz
313-465-7454)
Real Estate (Lawrence D. McLaughlin
313-465-7474)
Litigation (J. Michael Huget 734-418-4254)
Intellectual Property (Jonathan P. O'Brien,
Ph.D. 269-337-7704)
Environmental (Richard A Barr
313-465-7308)
Health Care (Linda S. Ross, Ann T.
Hollenbeck 313-465-7526, 313-465-7680)
Insurance/Captives (Julie E. Robertson
313-465-7520)
Tax (James H. Combs 313-465-7588)
Tax Appeals (Stewart L. Mandell
313-465-7420)
Trusts and Estates (Jeffrey W. Barringer
313-465-7310)

Leading Officials
David Foltyn, Chairman & Chief Executive
Officer, 313-465-7380
Robert D. Kubic, Chief Operating Officer,
313-465-7008
Karl A. Hochkammer, 313-465-7582 and
Anessa Owen Kramer, 248-566-8406,
Lateral Hiring Partners
Julie K. Norris, Chief Attorney Development
and Recruitment Officer, 313-465-7022
Stephanie C. Miller, Chief Marketing Officer,
312-701-9360
Craig W. Hardtke, Chief Information Officer,
313-465-7014
Kineret A. Gable, Director of Library
Services, 313-465-7080
Denise J. Lewis, Partner, 313-465-7464

Other Offices
2290 First National Building
660 Woodward Avenue
Detroit
MI
48226-3506
Phone: 313-465-7000
Fax: 313-465-8000

39400 Woodward Avenue
Suite 101
Bloomfield Hills
MI
48304-5151
Phone: 248-566-8300
Fax: 248-566-8315

Howard & Howard Attorneys PLLC

450 West Fourth Street
Royal Oak, MI 48067-2557
Phone: 248-645-1483
Fax: 248-645-1568
Web Site: www.howardandhoward.com

2016 Total Lawyers: 140
2015 Total Lawyers: 138

MICHIGAN

Howard & Howard Attorneys PLLC (Continued)

2016 Staff
Equity Partners: 97
Associates: 27
Of Counsel: 12
Senior Attorneys: 3
Staff Attorneys: 1

Offices: No. Attys.
Royal Oak, MI: 69
Peoria, IL: 13
Las Vegas, NV: 19
Ann Arbor, MI: 5
Chicago, IL: 34

Leading Practice Areas (Department Heads)
Financial Services 50% (Joseph B. Hemker 312-372-4000)
M&A/Business and Corporate 50% (Joseph J. DeVito 248-645-1483)
Financial Services 50% (Scott C. Frost 312-372-4000)
M&A/Business and Corporate 50% (Miriam Leskovar Burkland 312-372-4000)
Environmental (Gary A. Peters 248-645-1483)
Intellectual Property (Sam Haidle 248-645-1483)
Tax (Lee A. Sartori 248-645-1483)
Commercial Litigation (Patrick M. McCarthy 734-222-1483)
Real Estate (Mark A. Davis 248-645-1483)
Labor, Employment and Immigration (Leonard W. Sachs 309-672-1483)
Employee Benefits (Robert B. Johnston 248-645-1483)

Leading Officials
Mark A. Davis, President & CEO, 248-645-1483
Mark A. Davis, President & CEO, 248-645-1483
Cynthia Richards, Director of Marketing, 248-645-1483
Darren Ginter, Director of Information Technology, 248-645-1483
Kimberlee Hersch, Head Librarian, 248-645-1483

Jaffe, Raitt, Heuer & Weiss, P.C.

27777 Franklin Road
Suite 2500
Southfield, MI 48034
Phone: 248-351-3000
Fax: 248-351-3082
Email: rmarsolais@jaffelaw.com
Web Site: www.jaffelaw.com

2016 Total Lawyers: 116
2015 Total Lawyers: 106

2016 Staff
Equity Partners: 66
Non-Equity Partners: 17
Associates: 27
Of Counsel: 6

Jaffe, Raitt, Heuer & Weiss, P.C. (Continued)

Offices: No. Attys.
Southfiled, MI: 108
Ann Arbor, Michigan: 6
Detroit, Michigan: 2

Hiring and Promotion
2015 Associates Hired: 11
2015 First-Year Hires: 3
2016 First-Year Hires (Est.): 4
2015 Equity Partners Named: 4

Leading Practice Areas (Department Heads)
Litigation 25% (David Williams/Mark Kowalsky)
Corporate 20% (Lee Kellert/Chris Moceri)
Real Estate 15% (Mark Rubenfire)
Estate Planning 10% (Aaron Sherbin)
Electronic Payments and Card Processing 10% (Holli Targan)
Intellectual Property 5% (Larry Jordan)
Family Law 5% (Susan Lichterman)
Insolvency & Reorganization 5% (Jay Welford)
Tax 5% (Marko Belej)

Leading Officials
William Sider, Chief Executive Officer
Jeanne Wong, Chief Operating Officer
Pam Sikorski, Recruiting Director
Richard Marsolais, Marketing Director
Maggie Carver, IT Director
Sylvia Arakelian, Head Librarian

Kitch Drutchas Wagner Valitutti & Sherbrook, A Professional Corporation

One Woodward Avenue
Suite 2400
Detroit, MI 48226-5485
Phone: 313-965-7900
Fax: 313-965-7403
Web Site: www.kitch.com

2016 Total Lawyers: 93
2015 Total Lawyers: 90

Miller, Canfield, Paddock and Stone, P.L.C.

150 West Jefferson Avenue
Suite 2500
Detroit, MI 48226
Phone: 313-963-6420
Fax: 313-496-7500
Web Site: www.millercanfield.com

2016 Total Lawyers: 277
2015 Total Lawyers: 280

Miller Johnson

250 Monroe Avenue NW
Suite 800
Grand Rapids, MI 49503-2250
Phone: 616-831-1700
Fax: 616-831-1701
Email: info@millerjohnson.com
Web Site: www.millerjohnson.com

2016 Total Lawyers: 104
2015 Total Lawyers: 95

2016 Staff
Equity Partners: 50
Non-Equity Partners: 13
Associates: 20
Of Counsel: 1
Senior Attorneys: 7
Staff Attorneys: 4

Offices: No. Attys.
Grand Rapids, MI: 83
Kalamazoo, MI: 12

Hiring and Promotion
2015 Associates Hired: 4
2015 First-Year Hires: 2
2016 First-Year Hires (Est.): 2
2015 Equity Partners Named: 7
2015 Lateral Equity Partners: 3

Leading Practice Areas (Department Heads)
Employment/Labor (general) 15% (John F. Koryto 269-226-2979)
Business (general) 15% (Robert D. Wolford 616-831-1726)
Estate Planning & Probate 9% (Lauretta K. Murphy 616-831-1733)
Employee Benefits 7% (Mary V. Bauman 616-831-1704)
Hospital/Medical Reimbursement 7% (Stephen R. Ryan 616-831-1746)
Family Law 5% (Michael B. Quinn 616-831-1755)
Real Estate 3% (Cynthia P. Ortega 269-226-2959)
Employment Litigation 2% (Thomas R. Wurst 616-831-1775)
Immigration 2% (John F. Koryto 269-226-2979)

Client Representations
Spectrum Health
Gordon Food Service
Stryker Corporation

Leading Officials
Craig A. Mutch, Managing Member
Betsy Raymond, COO
Nathan D. Plantinga, Recruitment Committee Chair
Michelle Smith, Director of Recruitment & Development
Lance Hartman, Director of Marketing & Business Development
Isidore Okoro, Director of Information Technology
Jessica Fields, Library Information Services Manager
Jeffrey J. Fraser, Diversity Member

MICHIGAN

Plunkett Cooney

535 Griswold
Suite 2400
Detroit, MI 48226
Phone: 313-965-3900
Fax: 313-983-4350
Email: plunkettinfo@plunkettcoon
Web Site: www.plunkettcooney.com

2016 Total Lawyers: 136
2015 Total Lawyers: 148

Secrest, Wardle, Lynch, Hampton, Truex, and Morley, P.C.

2600 Troy Center Drive
P.O. Box 5025
Troy, MI 48007-5025
Phone: 248-851-9500
Fax: 248-538-1223
Email: info@secrestwardle.com
Web Site: www.secrestwardle.com

2016 Total Lawyers: 68
2015 Total Lawyers: 66

2016 Staff
Equity Partners: 6
Non-Equity Partners: 45
Associates: 14
Of Counsel: 3

Offices: No. Attys.
Lansing, MI: 3
Grand Rapids, MI: 11
Troy, MI: 55

Hiring and Promotion
2015 Associates Hired: 6

Leading Officials
Bruce A. Truex, President
Mark E. Morley and Bruce A. Truex,
   Co-Chairmen of the Executive Committee
Lois Martin, Human Resources Manager
Mark F. Master, Senior
   Partner/Marketing Director
Lois Martin, Human Resources Manager
Mark F. Masters, Senior
   Partner/Marketing Director
Julie Gorney, IT Manager
Kellie C. Joyce, Partner/Librarian

Other Offices
Troy, MI
2600 Troy Center Drive
P. O. Box 5025
Troy
Michigan
48007-5025
Phone: 248-851-9500
Fax: 248-538-1223
Email: info@secrestwardle.com
Mark E. Morley and Bruce A. Truex,
   Executive
   Committee/Co-Managing Partners

Smith Haughey Rice & Roegge

100 Monroe Center NW
Grand Rapids, MI 49503-2251
Phone: 616-774-8000
Fax: 616-774-2461
Email: info@shrr.com
Web Site: www.shrr.com

2016 Total Lawyers: 81
2015 Total Lawyers: 89

2016 Staff
Equity Partners: 34
Non-Equity Partners: 19
Associates: 20
Of Counsel: 16

Offices: No. Attys.
Traverse City, MI: 22
Ann Arbor, MI: 8
Grand Rapids, MI: 55
Muskegon, MI: 4

Hiring and Promotion
2015 Associates Hired: 5
2015 First-Year Hires: 2
2016 First-Year Hires (Est.): 0
2015 Equity Partners Named: 0

Leading Practice Areas
(Department Heads)
Health Law (Brian J. Kilbane 616-458-0296)
Commercial Litigation (Kristen E. Guinn
   616-458-9481)
Medical Malpractice Defense (Christopher R.
   Genther 616-458-0222)
Trusts & Estates (George F. Bearup
   231-929-4878)
Business Law (Eugene A. Franks
   231-724-4334)
Labor & Employment Law (Janis L. Adams
   231-486-4539)
Real Estate Law (Eugene A. Franks
   231-724-4334)
Mediation (William W. Jack 616-458-6243)
Personal Injury Litigation Defense (E.
   Thomas McCarthy, Jr. 616-458-9224)

Client Representations
University of Michigan Health System
Trinity Health
Northwestern Michigan College

Leading Officials
Robert W. Parker, CEO
Lori L. Gibson, COO
Mark A. Gilchrist, Hiring Committee Chair
Shannon Cunningham, Marketing Director
Thomas J. Geyer, Chief Technology Officer
Penelope A. Turner, Information
   Services Director
Thomas W. Aycock, Charissa C. Huang,
   Attorneys, 616-774-8000

Other Offices
Grand Rapids
100 Monroe Center
Grand Rapids
Michigan
49503
Phone: 616-774-8000
Fax: 616-774-2461
Email: info@shrr.com

Sommers, Schwartz, P.C.

2000 Town Center
Suite 900
Southfield, MI 48075-1100
Phone: 248-266-2536
Web Site: www.s4online.com

2016 Total Lawyers: 31
2015 Total Lawyers: 28

Sullivan, Ward, Asher & Patton, P.C.

25800 Northwestern Highway
Suite 1000
Southfield, MI 48075-1000
Phone: 248-746-0700
Fax: 248-746-2760
Email: swappc@swappc.com
Web Site: www.swappc.com

2016 Total Lawyers: 51
2015 Total Lawyers: 47

Varnum LLP

Bridgewater Place
333 Bridge Street NW
Grand Rapids, MI 49501
Phone: 616-336-6000
Fax: 616-336-7000
Email: info@varnumlaw.com
Web Site: www.varnumlaw.com

2016 Total Lawyers: 170
2015 Total Lawyers: 165

Warner Norcross & Judd LLP

900 Fifth Third Center
111 Lyon Street, NW
Grand Rapids, MI 49503-2487
Phone: 616-752-2000
Fax: 616-752-2500
Email: contactwnj@wnj.com
Web Site: www.wnj.com

2016 Total Lawyers: 227
2015 Total Lawyers: 222

2016 Staff
Equity Partners: 100
Non-Equity Partners: 16
Associates: 34
Of Counsel: 44
Senior Counsel: 21
Staff Attorneys: 12

Offices: No. Attys.
Grand Rapids, MI: 149
Southfield, MI: 29
Muskegon, MI: 8
Holland, MI: 5
Lansing, MI: 2
Macomb County, MI: 11
Midland, MI: 6
Kalamazoo, MI: 17

MICHIGAN

Warner Norcross & Judd LLP (Continued)

Hiring and Promotion
2015 Associates Hired: 6
2015 First-Year Hires: 5
Starting Salary for First-Year
  Assocs: $100,000
2016 First-Year Hires (Est.): 6
2015 Equity Partners Named: 3

Leading Practice Areas
(Department Heads)
Business 25% (Charlie Goode 616-752-2176)
Litigation 25% (Michael G. Brady
  248-784-5032)
Technology and Intellectual Property 10%
  (Chad E. Kleinheksel 616-752-2313)
Trusts and Estates 10% (Susan G. Meyers
  616-752-2184)
Environmental 5% (Steven C. Kohl
  248-784-5141)
Real Estate 5% (James J. Rabaut
  616-752-2178)
Employee Benefits 5% (Heidi A. Lyon
  616-752-2496)
Financial Services 5% (Rodney D. Martin
  616-752-2138)
Labor and Employment 5% (Jonathan P. Kok
  616-752-2487)
Restructuring and Insolvency 5% (Stephen B.
  Grow 616-752-2158)

Client Representations
Stryker
Amway
Fifth Third Bank

Leading Officials
Douglas A. Dozeman, Managing Partner,
  616-752-2148
Bruce Clearing Sky Christensen, Executive
  Director, 616-752-2238
Brian J. Masternak, Recruiting Partner,
  616-752-2205
Carin Ojala, Director of Recruiting and
  Development, 616-752-2173
Randall S. Goble, Director of Marketing,
  616-752-2446
Kevin J. Wilson, Director of Client
  Relationships, 616-752-2224
Dale F. de Longpre, Director of Information
  Systems, 616-752-2463
Emma MacGuidwin, Library Manager,
  616-752-2297
Rodney D. Martin, Diversity Partner,
  616-752-2138

MINNESOTA

Best & Flanagan LLP

225 South Sixth Street
Suite 4000
Minneapolis, MN 55402-4331
Phone: 612-339-7121
Fax: 612-339-5897
Email: info@bestlaw.com
Web Site: www.bestlaw.com

2016 Total Lawyers: 44
2015 Total Lawyers: 47

Briggs and Morgan, P.A.

2200 IDS Center
80 South Eighth Street
Minneapolis, MN 55402
Phone: 612-977-8400
Fax: 612-977-8650
Email: briggs@briggs.com
Web Site: www.briggs.com

2016 Total Lawyers: 140
2015 Total Lawyers: 148

Dorsey & Whitney LLP

50 South Sixth St
Suite 1500
Minneapolis, MN 55402-1498
Phone: 612-340-2600
Fax: 612-340-2868
Email: dorsey.whitney.llp@dorsey
Web Site: www.dorsey.com

2016 Total Lawyers: 547
2015 Total Lawyers: 530

2016 Staff
Equity Partners: 271
Associates: 196
Of Counsel: 80

Offices: No. Attys.
Anchorage, AK: 7
Delaware, MD: 3
Denver, CO: 39
Des Moines, IA: 19
Fargo, ND: 2
Minneapolis, MN: 222
Missoula, MT: 7
New York, NY: 61
Palo Alto, CA: 13
Salt Lake City, UT: 34
Seattle, WA: 52
Costa Mesa, CA: 22
Washington, DC: 12
Toronto, Canada: 5
Vancouver, Canada: 2
London, UK: 27
Hong Kong, China: 15
Shanghai, China: 3
Beijing: 2

Hiring and Promotion
2015 Associates Hired: 26
2015 First-Year Hires: 4
2016 First-Year Hires (Est.): 0
2015 Equity Partners Named: 0

Dorsey & Whitney LLP (Continued)

Leading Practice Areas
(Department Heads)
Mergers & Acquisitions (William Jonason
  (612) 492-6111)
Corporate (Robert Rosenbaum
  612-340-5681)
Financing & Restructuring (Thomas Kelly III
  612-492-6029)
Commerical Litigation (Michael Lindsay
  612-340-7819)
Regulatory Affairs (Andrew Brown
  612-340-5612)
Tax, Trust & Estates (William Berens
  612-340-2621)
Public Finance (Leonard Rice 612-343-7971)
Intellectual Property (Thomas Vitt
  612-340-5675)
Health Care (Neal Peterson 612-343-7943)
Benefits & Compensation (Timothy Arends
  612-343-2165)

Revenues and Profits
Revenues: $336,500,000

Leading Officials
Ken Cutler, Managing Partner, 612-340-270
Sandra Edelman, Partner, 212-415-9269
Bryn Vaaler, Partner, 612-343-8216
Pat Courtemanche, Director, Business
  Development, 612-492-5322
Paul Miller, Chief Information Officer,
  612-492-5920
Jan Rivers, Director, Information Resource
  Services, 612-492-5508
Lynnette Slater Crandall, Partner,
  612-343-8288

Other Offices
Dorsey & Whitney Minneapolis
50 South Sixth Street
Suite 1500
Minneapolis
MN
55402
Phone: 612-340-2600
Fax: 612-340-2868
Email: Minneapolis@Dorsey.com
Skip Durocher and Bridget Logstrom Koci

Dorsey & Whitney New York
51 West 52nd Street
New York
NY
10019-6119
Phone: 212-415-9200
Fax: 212-953-7201
Email: NewYork@dorsey.com
Steven Khadavi

Dorsey & Whitney Seattle
701 Fifth Avenue
Columbia Center, Suite 6100
Seattle
WA
98104-7043
Phone: 206-903-8800
Fax: 206-903-8820
Email: Seattle@dorsey.com
Randal R. Jones

OF COUNSEL 700

MINNESOTA

Fredrikson & Byron, P.A.

200 South Sixth Street
Suite 4000
Minneapolis, MN 55402-1425
Phone: 612-492-7000
Fax: 612-492-7077
Email: market@fredlaw.com
Web Site: www.fredlaw.com

2016 Total Lawyers: 276
2015 Total Lawyers: 339

Gray Plant Mooty

80 South Eighth Street
500 IDS Center
Minneapolis, MN 55402-5383
Phone: 612-632-3000
Fax: 612-632-4444
Web Site: www.gpmlaw.com

2016 Total Lawyers: 186
2015 Total Lawyers: 170

2016 Staff
Equity Partners: 110
Associates: 39
Of Counsel: 17
Senior Attorneys: 10
Senior Counsel: 5
Staff Attorneys: 5

Offices: No. Attys.
Minneapolis, MN: 146
St Cloud, MN: 20
Washington, DC: 18
Fargo, ND: 2

Hiring and Promotion
2015 Associates Hired: 17
2015 First-Year Hires: 4
2016 First-Year Hires (Est.): 4
2015 Equity Partners Named: 5

Leading Practice Areas
(Department Heads)
Franchise and Franchise Distribution 17%
(John Fitzgerald, Kirk Reilly, Robert Zisk
612-632-3064)
Corporate Transactions 15% (John Brower,
Mark D. Williamson 612-632-3377)
Litigation 13% (Charles Maier, Brian Dillon,
John Krenn, Rick Kubler 612-632-3242)
Estate and Trusts 13% (Ann Burns
612-632-3402)
General Business & Tax 11% (Jeffrey C.
Anderson, Daniel R. Tenenbaum
612-632-3002)
Employment Law 7% (Carl Crosby Lehmann
612-632-3234)
Real Estate Law 6% (Wade Anderson,
Edward Laubach 612-632-3005)
Health and Non Profit Organizations 6%
(Jennifer Reedstrom Bishop
612-632-3060)
Commercial Financial Services 6% (Phillip
W. Bohl 612-632-3019)
Intellectual Property, Technology & Privacy
5% (Jennifer Debrow 612-632-3357)

Gray Plant Mooty (Continued)

Client Representations
Slumberland
Campbell Soup Company
Anytime Fitness

Leading Officials
Sarah Duniway / Charlie Maier,
Co-Managing Partner, 612-632-3055
Amy Moller, Executive Director,
612-632-3442
Ryan Gerads, Chair, Attorney Personnel
Committee, 320-202-5315
Martha Gentilini, Legal Recruiting Manager,
612-632-3071
Kelly Klopotek, Chief Business Development
Officer, 612-632-3365
Rick Thompson, Chief Information Officer,
612-632-3363
Scott Raver, Manager, Research Services and
Knowledge Management, 612-632-3303
Mike Sullivan Jr, Chair of the Firm Culture &
Diversity Committee, 612-632-3350

Other Offices
80 South Eighth Street
500 IDS Center
Minneapolis, MN 55402-5383
Phone: 612-632-3000
Fax: 612-632-4444

Larkin Hoffman Daly & Lindgren Ltd.

7900 Xerxes Avenue South
Suite 1500
Minneapolis, MN 55431
Phone: 952-835-3800
Fax: 952-896-3333
Email: info@larkinhoffman.com
Web Site: www.larkinhoffman.com

2016 Total Lawyers: 77
2015 Total Lawyers: 68

Lindquist & Vennum LLP

4200 IDS Center
80 South Eighth Street
Minneapolis, MN 55402
Phone: 612-371-3211
Fax: 612-371-3207
Web Site: www.lindquist.com

2016 Total Lawyers: 162
2015 Total Lawyers: 167

2016 Staff
Equity Partners: 97
Non-Equity Partners: 38
Associates: 24
Of Counsel: 8

Offices: No. Attys.
Minneapolis, MN: 141
Denver, CO: 15
Sioux Falls, SD: 11

Lindquist & Vennum LLP (Continued)

Hiring and Promotion
2015 Associates Hired: 6
2015 First-Year Hires: 4
2016 First-Year Hires (Est.): 5
2015 Equity Partners Named: 7
2015 Lateral Equity Partners: 1

Leading Practice Areas
(Department Heads)
Private Equity (Frank B. Bennett
612-371-3931)
Litigation (Eric J. Nystrom 612-371-3503)
Banking (Scott Coleman 612-371-2428)
Bankruptcy (James A. Lodoen
612-371-3234)
Employee Benefits (Nancy Flury Anton
612-371-3934)
Real Estate (LB Guthrie 612-371-3942)
Public Companies (Jonathan B. Levy
612-371-2412)
Trusts & Estates (Marya P. Robben
612-371-3933)
Environment, Natural Resources (Howard
Kenison 303-454-0505)
Health Law (David R. Melloh 612-371-3943)
Mergers & Acquisitions (Robert E. Tunheim
612-371-3915)
Intellectual Property (Garrett M. Weber
612-371-3296)
Securities (Terrence J. Fleming
612-371-3248)

Leading Officials
Dennis M. O'Malley, Managing Partner,
612-371-3273
Mark Dietzen, 612-371-2452
Lisanne Weisz, Director of Recruiting,
612-371-5777
Jill LaMere, Chief Marketing Officer,
612-371-3210
Suzette Allaire, Chief Information Officer,
612-371-2419
Charlie Wilson, Library Manager,
612-752-1087
Richelle Wahl, Partner, 612-371-3979

Maslon Edelman Borman & Brand

3300 Wells Fargo Center
90 South Seventh Street
Minneapolis, MN 55402
Phone: 612-672-8200
Fax: 612-672-8397
Email: email appropriate contact
Web Site: www.maslon.com

2016 Total Lawyers: 84
2015 Total Lawyers: 78

MINNESOTA

Meagher & Geer, PLLP

33 South Sixth Street
Suite 4400
Minneapolis, MN 55402
Phone: 612-338-0661
Fax: 612-338-8384
Web Site: www.meagher.com

2016 Total Lawyers: 80
2015 Total Lawyers: 80

Merchant & Gould

80 South 8th Street
3200 IDS Center
Minneapolis, MN 55402-4131
Phone: 612-332-5300
Fax: 612-332-9081
Email: info@merchantgould.com
Web Site: www.merchantgould.com

2016 Total Lawyers: 106
2015 Total Lawyers: 105

Moss & Barnett, P.A.

150 South Fifth Street
Suite 1200
Minneapolis, MN 55402
Phone: 612-877-5000
Fax: 612-877-5999
Email: contact@lawmoss.com
Web Site: www.LawMoss.com

2016 Total Lawyers: 62
2015 Total Lawyers: 61

2016 Staff
Associates: 13
Staff Attorneys: 9
Shareholders 40

Offices: No. Attys.
Minneapolis, MN: 62

Hiring and Promotion
2015 Associates Hired: 11
2015 First-Year Hires: 4
2016 First-Year Hires (Est.): 0
2015 Equity Partners Named: 2

Leading Practice Areas
(Department Heads)
Corporate (Mitchell H. Cox 612-877-5291)
Communication & Government (Brian T.
   Grogan 612-877-5340)
General Litigation (Curtis D. Smith
   612-877-5285)
Family Law (Susan C. Rhode 612-877-5303)
Real Estate (M. Cecilia Ray 612-877-5289)
Estates & Tax (Dave F. Senger
   612-877-5262)
Bankruptcy
Employment & Labor Law
Miscellaneous
Creditors' Remedies & Bankruptcy (John
   Rossman 612-877-5396)

Moss & Barnett, P.A. (Continued)

Leading Officials
Timothy L. Gustin, Chairman of the Board,
   612-877-5409
Brian T. Grogan, President, 617-877-5340
Thomas J. Shroyer, CEO, 612-877-5281
Thomas J. Shroyer, Hiring Partner,
   612-877-5281
Deborah Weinstock, Marketing Manager,
   612-877-5424
Cheryl Thompson, Technology Director,
   612-877-5441
Andy Malec, Librarian, 612-877-5322

Robins Kaplan LLP

800 LaSalle Avenue
Suite 2800
Minneapolis, MN 55402
Phone: 612-349-8500
Fax: 612-339-4181
Web Site: www.RobinsKaplan.com

2016 Total Lawyers: 219
2015 Total Lawyers: 226

2016 Staff
Associates: 73
Of Counsel: 20
Staff Attorneys: 10
Partners 86
Principal Attorneys 17
Document Review Attorneys 9
Other 4

Offices: No. Attys.
Minneapolis, MN: 141
Los Angeles, CA: 29
Boston, MA: 15
Naples, FL: 3
New York, NY: 27
Mountain View, CA: 5

Hiring and Promotion
2015 Associates Hired: 14
2015 First-Year Hires: 8
Starting Salary for First-Year Assocs:
   $110,000 (Minnneapolis), $125,000
   (Atlanta), $135,000 (Boston), $140,000
   (Los Angeles), $160,000 (New York),
   $160,000 (Mountain View)
2016 First-Year Hires (Est.): 7
2015 Equity Partners Named: 5

Robins Kaplan LLP (Continued)

Leading Practice Areas
(Department Heads)
Antitrust Litigation (K. Craig Wildfang and
   Hollis Salzman 612-349-8554;
   212-980-7405)
Business Litigation (Chris Madel
   612-349-8703)
Insurance Litigation (William N. Erickson
   617-859-1780)
Intellectual Property Litigation (Ronald J.
   Schutz 612-349-8435)
Mass Tort (Tara D. Sutton 612-349-8577)
Personal Injury and Medical Malpractice
   (Peter A. Schmit 612-349-8778)
Entertainment & Media (Mark D. Passin
   310.229.851)
E-Discovery (Michael A. Collyard
   612-349-0975)
Financial Litigation (David Beehler and
   Stacey Slaughter 612-349-0802;
   612-349-8289)
Healthcare Litigation (V. Robert Denham
   404-760-8206)
Government and Internal Investigations (Tim
   Purdon and Brendan Johnson
   612-349-8767; 612-349-8797)

Leading Officials
Martin R. Lueck, Chairman of the Board,
   612-349-8587
Steven A. Schumeister, Managing Partner,
   612-349-8751
Patrick A. Mandile, COO, 612-349-8567
Denise Rahne, Hiring Committee Chair,
   612-349-8433
Martha G. Capper, Recruiting Administrator,
   612-349-0620
Dennis Meyer, Chief Business Development
   and Marketing Officer, 612-349-0108
Kathryn Frickstad and Michael Williams,
   612-349-8500
Jennifer L. Doyle, Library Manager,
   612-349-0940
Matt McFarlane and Kellie Lerner, Principal
   and Co-Chair, Diversity Committee;
   Partner and Co-Chair, Diversity
   Committee, 212-980-7400

Winthrop & Weinstine

Capella Tower, Suite 3500
225 South Sixth Street
Minneapolis, MN 55402
Phone: 612-604-6400
Fax: 612-604-6800
Web Site: www.winthrop.com

2016 Total Lawyers: 124
2015 Total Lawyers: 116

2016 Staff
Equity Partners: 44
Non-Equity Partners: 32
Associates: 37
Of Counsel: 2
Staff Attorneys: 4
Contract Attorneys 5

Offices: No. Attys.
Minneapolis, MN: 124

Winthrop & Weinstine (Continued)

Hiring and Promotion
2015 Associates Hired: 11
2015 First-Year Hires: 4
Starting Salary for First-Year
Assocs: $125,000
2016 First-Year Hires (Est.): 5
2015 Equity Partners Named: 2

*Leading Practice Areas
(Department Heads)*
General/Commercial Litigation 30%
(Matthew McBride 612-604-6426)
General Corporate 20% (Scott J. Dongoske
612-604-6565)
Real Estate/Tax Credits/Environment 20%
(Todd Urness, Thomas Hart 612-604-6657,
612-604-6624)
Banking/Securities/Finance 10% (Edward J.
Drenttel, Phil Colton 612-604-6675,
612-604-6729)
Legislative/Administrative 5% (John A.
Knapp 612-604-6404)
Intellectual Property/IP Litigation 5%
(Stephen R. Baird, Devan Padmanabhan
612-604-6585, 612-604-6748)
Insurance/Insurance Litigation 2% (David M.
Aafedt 612-604-6447)
Employment/Employment Litigation 1%
(Laura Pfeiffer, Mark Pihart
612-604-6685, 612-604-6623)
Products Liability/Personal Injury 1%
(Robert R. Weinstine 612-604-6614)
Probate/Estate 1% (Ryan K. Crayne
612-604-6551)

Leading Officials
Scott J. Dongoske, President, 612-604-6565
Bob Olck, Chief Financial Officer,
612-604-6443
Dean Willer, Recruiting Partner,
612-604-6633
Sandra J. Ricci, Human Resources Director,
612-604-6626
Gretchen Milbrath, Director of Marketing and
Business Development, 612-604-6640
Craig Wilson, Director of Technology,
612-604-6455
Nancy Evans, Director of Research Services,
612-604-6450
Tammera R. Diehm, Shareholder,
612-604-6658

Zelle Hofmann Voelbel & Mason LLP

500 Washington Ave S.
Suite 4000
Minneapolis, MN 55415
Phone: 800-899-5291
Fax: 612-336-9100
Email: info@zelle.com
Web Site: www.zelle.com

2016 Total Lawyers: 78
2015 Total Lawyers: 72

Butler Snow

1020 Highland Colony Parkway
Suite 1400
Ridgeland, MS 39157
Phone: 601-948-5711
Fax: 601-985-4500
Email: info@butlersnow.com
Web Site: www.butlersnow.com

2016 Total Lawyers: 327
2015 Total Lawyers: 321

2016 Staff
Equity Partners: 137
Non-Equity Partners: 54
Associates: 66
Of Counsel: 17
Counsel: 18
Senior Counsel: 35

Offices: No. Attys.
Albuquerque, NM: 1
Atlanta, GA: 6
Baton Rouge, LA: 3
Birmingham, AL: 24
Denver, CO: 13
Gulfport, MS: 10
Ridgeland, MS: 134
London, UK: 4
Macon, GA: 1
Memphis, TN: 53
Montgomery, AL: 3
Nashville, TN: 59
New Orleans, LA: 6
New York, NY: 4
Oxford, MS: 4
Bethlehem, PA: 2
Singapore: 1
Washington, DC: 4

Hiring and Promotion
2015 Associates Hired: 13
2015 First-Year Hires: 7
2016 First-Year Hires (Est.): 4
2015 Equity Partners Named: 4

*Leading Practice Areas
(Department Heads)*
Pharmaceutical, Medical Device and
Healthcare Group (Alyson Bustamante
Jones 601-985-4427)
Commercial Litigation (William R. O'Bryan,
Jr. 615-651-6724)
Business Services (John J. Healy III, Robert
M. Holland 601-985-4577, 615-651-6704)
Finance, Real Estate, & Restructuring (James
E. Bailey III 901-680-7347)
Public Finance, Tax Incentives & Credit
Markets (John England F. England, Thad
W. Varner 601-985-4563, 601-985-4518)
Product Liability, Toxic Tort and
Environmental Group (Michael E.
McWilliams 601-985-4562)
Regulatory and Government Relations
(Tommie S. Cardin 601-985-4570)
Healthcare Regulatory and Transactions
(Charles F. Johnson III 601-985-4528)
General Litigation (Richard M. Dye
601-985-4513)
Labor and Employment (Kara E. Shea
615-651-6712)

Butler Snow (Continued)

Leading Officials
Donald Clark, Jr., Chairman, 601-948-5711
Howard Belknap, Chief Operating Officer,
601-985-4554
Melody McAnally, Recruiting Committee
Chair, 901-680-7322
Nina Fitch, Recruiting Manager,
601-985-4110
Sherry Vance Allen, Chief Marketing and
Communications Officer, 601-985-4103
Jennifer O'Donnell, Senior Business
Development Manager, 678-515-5032
Kevin Rutledge, Chief Technology Officer,
601-985-4126
Barbara Neil, Head Librarian, 601-985-4155
Charles Griffin, Diversity Committee Chair,
601-985-4583

Other Offices
Memphis
6075 Poplar Avenue
Suite 500
Memphis
TN
38119
Phone: 901-680-7200
Fax: 901-680-7201

Nashville
150 3rd Avenue South
Suite 1600
Nashville
TN
37201
Phone: 615-651-6700
Fax: 615-651-6701

Mitchell, McNutt, & Sams, P.A.

105 South Front Street
P.O. Box 7120
Tupelo, MS 38802-7120
Phone: 662-842-3871
Fax: 662-842-8450
Web Site: www.mitchellmcnutt.com

2016 Total Lawyers: 34
2015 Total Lawyers: 32

2016 Staff
Non-Equity Partners: 11
Associates: 2
Of Counsel: 1
Equity Shareholders 20

Offices: No. Attys.
Tupelo, MS: 24
Columbus: 9
Oxford, MS: 2
Corinth, MS: 1

Hiring and Promotion
2015 Associates Hired: 1
2016 First-Year Hires (Est.): 1
2015 Equity Partners Named: 0

MISSISSIPPI

Mitchell, McNutt, & Sams, P.A. (Continued)

Leading Practice Areas
(Department Heads)
Bankruptcy (D. Andrew Phillips
662-234-4845)
Corporate (Albert G. Delgadillo
662-842-3871)
Estate Planning/Tax (Albert G. Delgadillo
662-842-3871)
Labor/Employment (Berkley N. Huskison
662-328-2316)
Litigation (John G. Wheeler 662-842-3871)
Municipalities (Guy Mitchell III
662-842-3871)
Products Liability (William C. Spencer
662-842-3871)
Professional Liability (John G. Wheeler
662-842-3871)
Real Estate (Michael D. Ferris 662-842-3871)
Workers Compensation/Municipalities (John
S. Hill 662-842-3871)

Revenues and Profits
Revenues: $10,500,000

Client Representations
City of Starkville, MS
North MS Health Services
Burlington Northern

Leading Officials
Gary W. Mitchell, III, President
James T. Allen, Executive Director
Lowry Wilson, Technology Manager
Teresa Neaves, Head Librarian

MISSOURI

Armstrong Teasdale LLP

7700 Forsyth Blvd
Suite 1800
St. Louis, MO 63105
Phone: 314-621-5070
Fax: 314-621-5065
Email: at@armstrongteasdale.com
Web Site: www.armstrongteasdale.law

2016 Total Lawyers: 233
2015 Total Lawyers: 219

2016 Staff
Equity Partners: 79
Non-Equity Partners: 51
Associates: 70
Of Counsel: 26
Senior Counsel: 1
Staff Attorneys: 1
Contract Attorneys 2
Independent Contractors 3

Offices: No. Attys.
St. Louis, MO: 164
Kansas City, MO: 22
Jefferson City, MO: 6
Shanghai, China: 4
Las Vegas, NV: 13
Denver, CO: 20

Armstrong Teasdale LLP (Continued)

Hiring and Promotion
2015 Associates Hired: 32
2015 First-Year Hires: 5
Starting Salary for First-Year Assocs:
Associate salaries are not determined by
associates graduating class. We pay
competitive market salaries.
2016 First-Year Hires (Est.): 10
2015 Equity Partners Named: 6
2015 Lateral Equity Partners: 2

Leading Practice Areas
(Department Heads)
Litigation 98% (Matt Reh 314-621-5070)
Intellectual Property 56% (Patrick Rasche
314-621-5070)
Corporate Services 44% (Tessa Trelz
314-621-5070)
Financial & Real Estate Services 31% (Rob
Klahr 314-621-5070)

Revenues and Profits
Revenues: $112,000,000

Client Representations
Ameren
Peabody Energy
St. Luke's Hospital

Leading Officials
John Beulick, Managing Partner,
314-621-5070
Lou Ann Wilcox, Director of Operations,
314-621-5070
Chris LaRose, Hiring Committee Chair,
314-621-5070
Julie Stapf, Director of Human Resources,
314-621-5070
Lisa Hanly, Marketing Manager,
314-621-5070
Katie Davis, Business Development Director
Timothy Pyatt, Information Technology
Manager, 314-621-5070
Carolyn Weber, Research and Library
Services, 314-621-5070
Jovita Foster, Diversity Committee Chair,
314-621-5070

Brown & James, P.C.

800 Market Street
Suite 1100
St. Louis, MO 63101
Phone: 314-421-3400
Fax: 314-421-3128
Email: brownjames@bjpc.com
Web Site: www.brownjames.com

2016 Total Lawyers: 110
2015 Total Lawyers: 110

2016 Staff
Equity Partners: 18
Non-Equity Partners: 25
Associates: 62
Of Counsel: 3
Counsel: 7

Offices: No. Attys.
Kansas City, MO: 8
Belleville, IL: 17

Brown & James, P.C. (Continued)
Springfield, MO: 3
St. Louis, MO: 87

Hiring and Promotion
2015 Associates Hired: 5
2015 First-Year Hires: 13
2016 First-Year Hires (Est.): 12
2015 Equity Partners Named: 3

Leading Practice Areas
(Department Heads)
Arson / Fraud Litigation (Robert L. Brady
314-242-5273)
Business / Commercial Litigation (Steven H.
Schwartz 314-242-5280)
Construction Law (Matthew G. Koehler
314-242-5267)
Employment Law (Christine A. Vaporean
314-242-5337)
Environmental Insurance / Toxic Torts (A.J.
Bronsky 314-242-5324)
Health Care Liability (David P. Ellington
314-242-5329)
Insurance Law (Russell F. Watters
314-242-5252)
Product Liability (Brian R. Plegge
314-206-3049)
Transportation (Joseph R. Swift
314-242-5218)

Appellate (T. Michael Ward 314-242-5306)
Premises / Retail Liability (Bradley R.
Hansmann 314-242-5370)

Client Representations
Washington University
Cincinnati Insurance Company
Zurich American Insurance Company

Leading Officials
T. Michael Ward, Managing Principal
Kathy A. Johnson, Firm Administrator
Christine Vaporean, Hiring Partner
Donna Howard, Human Resources Manager
Lois LaDriere, Marketing Director
Scott Maschmann, Information
Systems Director
Christine A. Vaporean, Chair, Diversity
Committee, 314-242-5337

Bryan Cave LLP

One Metropolitan Square
211 North Broadway, Suite 3600
St. Louis, MO 63102-2750
Phone: 314-259-2000
Fax: 314-259-2020
Web Site: www.bryancave.com

2016 Total Lawyers: 967
2015 Total Lawyers: 1019

2016 Staff
Equity Partners: 202
Non-Equity Partners: 182
Associates: 321
Of Counsel: 54
Counsel: 115
Senior Counsel: 44
Staff Attorneys: 49

Offices: No. Attys.
Phoenix, AZ: 34

MISSOURI

Bryan Cave LLP (Continued)
Kansas City, MO: 67
Santa Monica, CA: 55
New York, NY: 129
Washington, DC: 46
London, England: 41
Irvine, CA: 33
Hong Kong, China: 5
Shanghai, China: 5
Jefferson City, MO: 4
Chicago, IL: 60
St. Louis, MO: 220
Hamburg, Germany: 13
San Francisco, CA: 29
Atlanta, GA: 88
Charlotte, NC: 11
Dallas, TX: 11
Paris, France: 13
Singapore: 3
Boulder, CO: 11
Colorado Springs, CO: 13
Denver, CO: 67
Frankfurt, Germany: 4
Miami, FL: 5

Hiring and Promotion
2015 Associates Hired: 67
2015 First-Year Hires: 32
Starting Salary for First-Year Assocs:
   $145,000 (CA, NY, Chicago, Dallas,
   Miami & Washington D.C.), $135,000
   (Atlanta, Charlotte & St. Louis), $130,000
   (CO, Phoenix & Kansas City)
2016 First-Year Hires (Est.): 27
2015 Equity Partners Named: 12
2015 Lateral Equity Partners: 6

Leading Practice Areas
(Department Heads)
Commercial Litigation (Kenneth Lee
   Marshall 415-675-3444)
Financial Services (James J. McAlpin Jr.
   404-572-6630)
Real Estate (James G. Buell 314-259-2373)
Transactions & Corporate Governance
   (Steven M. Baumer 314-259-2554)
Corporate Finance & Securities (Robert J.
   Endicott 314-259-2447)
Intellectual Property (Erik W. Kahn
   212-541-1143)
Tax Advice and Controversy (Paul E. Smith
   303-417-8508)
Labor and Employment (William J. Wortel
   312-602-5105)
Private Client (Stephen B. Daiker
   314-259-2604)
Bankruptcy, Restructuring & Creditors'
   Rights (Mark G. Stingley 816-391-7649)

Revenues and Profits
Revenues: $616,828,000
Profits: $162,824,000

Bryan Cave LLP (Continued)

Leading Officials
Therese D. Pritchard, Chair of the Firm,
   202-508-6252
Robert L. Newmark, St. Louis Office
   Managing Partner, 314-259-2568
David L. Fleisher, Chief Operating Officer,
   314-259-2011
Vincent Alfieri, Partner; also serves as the
   firmwide lateral hiring partner,
   212-541-2270
Thomas A. Grewe, Chief Legal Recruiting &
   Development Officer, 312-602-5122
Kathleen Flynn, Chief Marketing Officer,
   415-675-3539
Emma Cibelli, Director of Business
   Development, 212-541-2094
Constance O. Hoffman, Chief Information
   Officer, 314-259-2302
Judith L. Harris, Chief Library and Research
   Services, 314-259-2298
Lisa Demet Martin, Chief Diversity Officer,
   314-259-2125

Other Offices
One Kansas City Place
1200 Main Street
Suite 3800
Kansas City
MO
64105-2100
Phone: 816-374-3200
Fax: 816-374-3300
William Perry Brandt, Kansas City Office
   Managing Partner

120 Broadway
Suite 300
Santa Monica
CA
90401-2386
Phone: 310-576-2100
Fax: 310-576-2200
Jennifer A. Jackson, Los Angeles Office
   Managing Partner

1290 Avenue of the Americas
New York
NY
10104-3300
Phone: 212-541-2000
Fax: 212-541-4630
Steven M. Stimell, New York Office
   Managing Partner

One Metropolitan Square
211 N. Broadway
Suite 3600
St. Louis
MO
63102-2750
Phone: 314-259-2000
Fax: 314-259-2020
Therese D. Pritchard, Chair of the Firm;
Robert L. Newmark, St. Louis Office
   Managing Partner

Bryan Cave LLP (Continued)
161 North Clark Street
Suite 4300
Chicago
IL
60601-3315
Phone: 312-602-5000
Fax: 312-602-5050
Email: .
Joseph Q. McCoy, Chicago Office
   Managing Partner

One Atlantic Center
Fourteenth Floor
1201 W. Peachtree St., N.W.
Atlanta
GA
30309
Phone: 404-572-6600
Fax: 404-572-6999
G. Patrick Watson, Atlanta Office
   Managing Partner

1700 Lincoln Street
Suite 4100
Denver
CO
80203
Phone: 303-861-7000
Fax: 303-866-0200
Paul J. Lopach, Denver Office
   Managing Partner

Evans & Dixon

211 North Broadway
Suite 2500
St. Louis, MO 63101-2727
Phone: 314-621-7755
Fax: 314-621-3136
Web Site: www.evans-dixon.com

2016 Total Lawyers: 81
2015 Total Lawyers: 84

Greensfelder, Hemker & Gale, P.C.

10 South Broadway
Suite 2000
St. Louis, MO 63102
Phone: 314-241-9090
Fax: 314-241-8624
Web Site: www.greensfelder.com

2016 Total Lawyers: 151
2015 Total Lawyers: 149

2016 Staff
Associates: 50
Of Counsel: 24
Officers: 77

Offices: No. Attys.
St. Louis, MO: 124
Belleville, IL: 15
Chicago, IL: 12

MISSOURI

Greensfelder, Hemker & Gale, P.C. (Continued)

Hiring and Promotion
2015 Associates Hired: 16
2015 First-Year Hires: 4
Starting Salary for First-Year
  Assocs: $110,000
2016 First-Year Hires (Est.): 6

Leading Practice Areas
(Department Heads)
Litigation (David M. Harris 314-241-9090)
Corporate and Business (Tracy R. Ring
  314-241-9090)
Health Law (Kathy H. Butler 314-241-9090)
Employment and Labor (Kevin T.
  McLaughlin 314-241-9090)
Trusts and Estates (Keith A. Herman
  314-241-9090)
Construction Law (Andrew W. Manuel
  314-241-9090)
Intellectual Property (Kara E. F. Cenar
  312-419-9090)
Real Estate Law (James E. Adkins
  314-241-9090)
Employee Benefits (Douglas S. Neville
  314-241-9090)
Environmental Law (Gregory C. Mollett
  314-241-9090)
Bankruptcy & Creditors' Rights (Cherie
  Macdonald 618-257-7308)
Franchise & Distribution (Dawn M. Johnson
  314-241-9090)

Client Representations
SSM Healthcare
Schnuck Markets Inc.

Leading Officials
Timothy R. Thornton, Chief
  Executive Officer
Heather L. Henry, Chief Operating Officer
Abby L. Risner, Recruiting Committee Chair
Sarah L. Allen, Director of Administration
  and Human Resources
Michael T. Andrews, Chief
  Marketing Officer
Brad L. Vaughn, Director of M.I.S.
Katie Hahn, Library Manager
Christopher A. Pickett, Chief
  Diversity Officer

Husch Blackwell LLP

190 Carondelet Plaza
Suite 600
St. Louis, MO 63102
Phone: 314-480-1500
Fax: 314-480-1505
Email: info@husch.com
Web Site: www.husch.com

2016 Total Lawyers: 700
2015 Total Lawyers: 590

Lashly & Baer, P.C.

714 Locust Street
St. Louis, MO 63101
Phone: 314-621-2939
Fax: 314-621-6844
Email: info@lashlybaer.com
Web Site: www.lashlybaer.com

2016 Total Lawyers: 46
2015 Total Lawyers: 45

2016 Staff
Equity Partners: 29
Associates: 9
Of Counsel: 6

Offices: No. Attys.
St. Louis: 46

Hiring and Promotion
2015 Associates Hired: 7
Starting Salary for First-Year
  Assocs: $75,000
2016 First-Year Hires (Est.): 0
2015 Equity Partners Named: 0

Leading Practice Areas
(Department Heads)
Litigation 20% (Kenneth C. Brostron & Mark
  H. Levison 314-621-2939)
Health Care 15% (Richard D. Watters &
  Stuart J. Vogelsmeier 314-621-2939)
Business & Corporate 15% (John Fox Arnold
  & Michael D. Regan 314-621-2939)
Education 10% (Kenneth C. Brostron & Lisa
  O. Stump 314-621-2939)
Governmental & Public Agencies 10% (John
  Fox Arnold & Kenneth C. Brostron
  314-621-2939)
Real Estate 5% (John Fox Arnold & Michael
  D. Regan 314-621-2939)
Personal Injury 5% (Andrew G. Toennies
  314-621-2939)
Estate Planning 5% (Rhonda A. O'Brien &
  Nelson H. Howe, II 314-621-2939)
Product Liability/Toxic Tort 5% (Stephen L.
  Beimdiek & Matthew J. Eddy
  314-621-2939)
Labor & Employment 5% (James C. Hetlage
  314-621-2939)
Transportation 5% (Kevin L. Fritz, John S.
  McCollough & Patrick E. Foppe
  314-621-2939)

Client Representations
Metro
Health Care Services Group
Rockwood School District

Leading Officials
John Fox Arnold, Chairman, 314-621-2939
Kenneth C. Brostron, President,
  314-621-2939
Kara M. Brostron, Office Manager,
  314-621-2939
Kenneth C. Brostron, President,
  314-621-2939
Kara M. Brostron, Office Manager,
  314-621-2939
Kathleen Wilson, Network Administrator,
  314-621-2939
Lisa O. Stump, Member, 314-621-2939

Lathrop & Gage LLP

2345 Grand Boulevard
Suite 2200
Kansas City, MO 64108
Phone: 816-292-2000
Fax: 816-292-2001
Email: info@lathropgage.com
Web Site: www.lathropgage.com

2016 Total Lawyers: 323
2015 Total Lawyers: 317

2016 Staff
Equity Partners: 84
Non-Equity Partners: 82
Associates: 74
Of Counsel: 73
Staff Attorneys: 4

Offices: No. Attys.
Kansas City, MO: 122
Overland Park, KS: 45
Springfield, MO: 17
Jefferson City, MO: 4
Boulder, CO: 13
Denver, CO: 30
Los Angeles, CA: 10
Chicago, IL: 19
Boston, MA: 16
St. Louis: 32

Hiring and Promotion
2015 Associates Hired: 31
2015 First-Year Hires: 12
2016 First-Year Hires (Est.): 22
2015 Equity Partners Named: 9
2015 Lateral Equity Partners: 8

Leading Practice Areas
(Department Heads)
Business Litigation 16% (Richard N. Bien/
  James Moloney 816-460-5520
  816.460.5561)
Intellectual Property Litigation 13% (David
  R. Barnard 816.460.5869)
Intellectual Property Transactional 11%
  (Justin Poplin 913.451.5130)
Corporate 8% (Wallace E. Brockhoff /
  Thomas W. Greaves 816.460.5825
  816.460.5818)
Labor & Employment 7% (David C. Vogel /
  Beth A. Schroeder 816.460.5611
  310.789.4611)
Real Estate 7% (Lewis A.Heaven/ Larry B.
  Huebner 913-451-5119 913-451-5120)
Banking and Creditors' Rights Litigation 6%
  (Brian T. Fenimore/ Justin Nichols
  816.460.5525 816.460.5516)
Environmental 6% (Thomas A. Ryan / Jessica
  E. Merrigan 816-460-5822 816.460.5706)
Wealth Strategies 6% (James B. Betterman /
  Ruth J. Brackney 913-451-5102
  913-451-5104)
Product Liability 5% (Joseph Reid / Peter F.
  Daniel 417-877-5916 816.460.5702)

Client Representations
Caterpillar Financial Services Corporation
Burlington Northern Santa Fe Railway Co.
Gyrodata, Inc.

MISSOURI

Lathrop & Gage LLP (Continued)

Leading Officials
Mark A. Bluhm , Firm CEO, 816-292-2000
Bill Migneron, COO, 816-292-2000
Brian Fries, Hiring Partner, 816-292-2000
Cheri Rhodes, Recruiting Director,
816-292-2000
Lisa Simon, Chief Client Development
Officer, 816-292-2000
Gillian Power, Chief Information Officer,
816-292-2000
Brian Larios, Director of Knowledge
Resources, 816-292-2000
Dionne King, Diversity and Associate
Development Manager, 816-292-2000

Lewis, Rice & Fingersh, L.C.

600 Washington Avenue
Suite 2500
St. Louis, MO 63101-1311
Phone: 314-444-7600
Fax: 314-241-6056
Web Site: www.lewisrice.com

2016 Total Lawyers: 166
2015 Total Lawyers: 153

Polsinelli

900 W. 48th Place
Suite 900
Kansas City, MO 64112
Phone: 816-753-1000
Fax: 816-753-1536
Email: polsinellimarketing@polsi
Web Site: www.polsinelli.com

2016 Total Lawyers: 800
2015 Total Lawyers: 747

2016 Staff
Equity Partners: 122
Non-Equity Partners: 345
Associates: 227
Of Counsel: 27
Senior Attorneys: 27
Counsel: 29
Staff Attorneys: 23

Offices: No. Attys.
Kansas City, MO: 243
St. Louis, MO: 112
Chicago, IL: 90
Denver, CO: 68
Dallas, TX: 46
Washington D.C.: 39
Phoenix, AZ: 37
Los Angeles, CA: 36
Atlanta, GA: 26
New York, NY: 17
San Francisco, CA: 18
Houston, TX: 13
Wilmington, DE: 7
Nashville, TN: 4
Boston, MA: 3
Overland Park, KS: 15
Chattanooga, TN: 5
Raleigh, NC: 4

Polsinelli (Continued)
St. Joseph, MO: 10
Other offices: 7

Hiring and Promotion
2015 Associates Hired: 57
2015 First-Year Hires: 15
2016 First-Year Hires (Est.): 20
2015 Equity Partners Named: 5
2015 Lateral Equity Partners: 5

Leading Practice Areas
(Department Heads)
Health Care Regulatory/Transactional 10%
(Matt Murer 312-873-3603)
Real Estate 10% (Chase Simmons
816-360-4207)
Corporate and Transactional 9% (Jon
Henderson 214-397-0016)
Science & Technology 7% (Pat Woolley
816-360-4280)
Commercial Litigation 7% (Stacy Carpenter
303-583-8237)
Real Estate Finance 7% (John Duncan
214-661-5560)
Labor & Employment Litigation 6% (Nancy
Rafuse 404-253-6002)
Products Liability & Toxic Tort 5% (Dennis
Dobbels 816-360-4312)
Loan Enforcement 3% (Brett Anders
816-360-4267)
Financial & Fiduciary Litigation 3% (Bob
Henderson 816-374-0530)

Revenues and Profits
Revenues: $409,949,000
Profits: $86,646,000

Client Representations
Catholic Health Initiatives
KeyBank
Olin Corporation

Leading Officials
W. Russell Welsh, Chairman, 816-753-1000
Julian Arredondo, Chief Financial Officer,
816-753-1000
W. Russell Welsh, Hiring Committee Chair,
816-753-1000
Dani Barnard, Chief Recruiting Officer,
202-626-8398
Allison Yurman, Chief Marketing Officer,
816-753-1000
Andrea Daebler, Chief Information Officer,
816-753-1000
Betty Sola, Manager of Library Services,
816-753-1000
Danielle Carr, Director of Diversity &
Inclusion, 314-889-7025

Other Offices
St. Louis, MO
100 S. Fourth Street
Suite 1000
St. Louis
MO
63102
Phone: 314-889-8000
Fax: 314-231-1776
Randy Gerber

Polsinelli (Continued)

Chicago, IL
161 N. Clark Street
Suite 4200
Chicago
IL
60601
Phone: 312-819-1900
Fax: 312-819-1910
Anthony Nasharr

Denver, CO
1515 Wynkoop Street
Suite 600
Denver
CO
80202
Phone: 303-572-9300
Fax: 303-572-7883
Jennifer Evans

Shook, Hardy & Bacon

2555 Grand Boulevard
Kansas City, MO 64108
Phone: 816-474-6550
Fax: 816-421-5547
Web Site: www.shb.com

2016 Total Lawyers: 505
2015 Total Lawyers: 505

Spencer Fane Britt & Browne LLP

1000 Walnut Street
Suite 1400
Kansas City, MO 64106
Phone: 816-474-8100
Fax: 816-474-3216
Web Site: www.spencerfane.com

2016 Total Lawyers: 178
2015 Total Lawyers: 136

2016 Staff
Equity Partners: 45
Non-Equity Partners: 33
Associates: 28
Of Counsel: 30

Offices: No. Attys.
Kansas City, MO: 48
St. Louis, MO: 30
Overland Park, KS: 20
Omaha, NE: 2
Denver, CO: 21
Jefferson City, MO: 2
Colorado Springs, CO: 1
Springfield, MO: 12

Hiring and Promotion
2015 Associates Hired: 13
2015 First-Year Hires: 5
Starting Salary for First-Year Assocs:
$90,000 to $105,000
2016 First-Year Hires (Est.): 4
2015 Equity Partners Named: 5

MISSOURI

Spencer Fane Britt & Browne LLP (Continued)

*Leading Practice Areas
(Department Heads)*
Litigation & Dispute Resolution 23.3% (Erik
O. Solverud 314-333-3904)
Real Estate 17.3% (Robert H. Epstein
314-333-3943)
Business Transactions 13.5% (Michael L.
McCann 816-292-8110)
Labor & Employment 10.0% (Ronald L. Fano
303-839-3820)
Financial Services 7.4% (Scott J. Goldstein
816-292-8218)
Environmental 7.3% (James T. Price
816-292-8228)
Employee Benefits 6.2% (Kenneth A. Mason
913-327-5138)
Municipal and Local Governments 4.1%
(Matthew R. Dalton 303-839-3706)
Estate Planning, Trusts & Estates 3.6% (Scott
E. Blakesley 816-292-8268)
Intellectual Property 2.7% (Kyle L. Elliott
816-292-8150)

Revenues and Profits
Revenues: $57,435,000
Profits: $25,325,000

Leading Officials
Patrick J. Whalen, Firm Chair, 816-292-8237
Scott L. Breeding, Chief Financial &
Administrative Officer, 816-292-8891
Lisa A. Epps, Partner, 816-292-8881
Courtney M. Bogaard, Chief Human
Resources Officer, 816-292-8309
Dawn C. Zerbs, Chief Business Development
Officer, 816-292-8162
Garry D. Sullivan, IS Director, 816-292-8124
Deanna L. Long, Director of Research &
Knowledge Management, 816-292-8187
Courtney M. Bogaard, Chief Human
Resources Officer, 816-292-8309

Stinson Leonard Street

1201 Walnut Street
Suite 2900
Kansas City, MO 64106
Phone: 816-842-8600
Fax: 816-691-3495
Email: info@stinson.com
Web Site: www.stinson.com

2016 Total Lawyers: 439
2015 Total Lawyers: 500

Thompson Coburn

One US Bank Plaza
St. Louis, MO 63101
Phone: 314-552-6000
Fax: 314-552-7000
Email: info@thompsoncoburn.com
Web Site: www.thompsoncoburn.com

2016 Total Lawyers: 380
2015 Total Lawyers: 372

MONTANA

Crowley Fleck PLLP

Transwestern Plaza II, Suite 500
490 North 31st Street
Billings, MT 59101-1288
Phone: 406-252-3441
Fax: 406-256-8526
Web Site: www.crowleyfleck.com

2016 Total Lawyers: 146
2015 Total Lawyers: 150

NEBRASKA

Baird Holm LLP

1500 Woodmen Tower
1700 Farnam Street
Omaha, NE 68102-2068
Phone: 402-344-0500
Fax: 402-344-0588
Email: info@bairdholm.com
Web Site: www.bairdholm.com

2016 Total Lawyers: 81
2015 Total Lawyers: 81

Cline Williams Wright Johnson & Oldfather

Sterling Ridge
12910 Pierce Street, Suite 200
Omaha, NE 68144-1105
Phone: 402-397-1700
Fax: 402-397-1806
Web Site: www.clinewilliams.com

2016 Total Lawyers: 55
2015 Total Lawyers: 53

Kutak Rock LLP

The Omaha Building
1650 Farnam Street
Omaha, NE 68102-2186
Phone: 402-346-6000
Fax: 402-346-1148
Web Site: www.kutakrock.com

2016 Total Lawyers: 510
2015 Total Lawyers: 471

Offices: No. Attys.
Atlanta, GA: 22
Chicago, IL: 8
Denver, CO: 87
Fayetteville, AR: 30
Irvine, CA: 18
Kansas City, MO: 33
Little Rock, AR: 22
Los Angeles, CA: 8
Oklahoma City, OK: 1
Omaha, NE: 172
Richmond, VA: 8
Scottsdale, AZ: 43
Washington, DC: 26
Wichita, KS: 1.00
Philadelphia, PA: 9.0
Minneapolis, MN: 12

Kutak Rock LLP (Continued)
Spokane, WA: 5
Rogers, AR: 5

Leading Officials
David A. Jacobson, Chairman
David L. Amsden, Vice Chairman
Jeanne G. Salerno, Director of Professional
Development
Kenneth M. Kroeger, Chief
Information Officer
Kim McKelvey, Director of Strategic Focus
and Director of Diversity

McGrath, North, Mullin & Kratz, P.C.

1601 Dodge Street
First National Tower, Suite 3700
Omaha, NE 68102
Phone: 402-341-3070
Fax: 402-341-0216
Web Site: www.megrathnorth.com

2016 Total Lawyers: 68
2015 Total Lawyers: 68

NEW HAMPSHIRE

Devine, Millimet & Branch, P.A.

P.O. Box 719
111 Amherst Street
Manchester, NH 03105-0719
Phone: 603-669-1000
Fax: 603-669-8547
Email: firm-info@dmb.com
Web Site: www.dmb.com

2016 Total Lawyers: 65
2015 Total Lawyers: 68

McLane Graf Raulerson & Middleton, P.A.

900 Elm Street
City Hall Plaza
Manchester, NH 03105
Phone: 603-625-6464
Fax: 603-625-5650
Web Site: www.mclane.com

2016 Total Lawyers: 98
2015 Total Lawyers: 91

Sheehan, Phinney, Bass & Green, Professional Association

1000 Elm Street, 17th Floor
P.O. Box 3701
Manchester, NH 03105
Phone: 603-668-0300
Fax: 603-627-8121
Email: info@sheehan.com
Web Site: www.sheehan.com

2016 Total Lawyers: 58
2015 Total Lawyers: 60

Archer & Greiner

One Centennial Square
33 East Euclid Ave
Haddonfield, NJ 08033
Phone: 856-795-2121
Fax: 856-795-0574
Email: webmaster@archerlaw.com
Web Site: www.archerlaw.com

2016 Total Lawyers: 177
2015 Total Lawyers: 175

Budd Larner, P.C.

150 John F. Kennedy Parkway
Short Hills, NJ 07078-2703
Phone: 973-379-4800
Fax: 973-379-7734
Email: info@budd-larner.com
Web Site: www.buddlarner.com

2016 Total Lawyers: 80
2015 Total Lawyers: 71

Chiesa Shahinian & Giantomasi PC

1 Boland Dr
West Orange, NJ 07052
Phone: 973-325-1500
Fax: 973-325-1501
Web Site: www.csglaw.com

2016 Total Lawyers: 138
2015 Total Lawyers: 130

Cole, Schotz, Meisel, Forman & Leonard, P.A.

Court Plaza North, 25 Main Street
25 Main Street
Hackensack, NJ 07601
Phone: 201-489-3000
Fax: 201-489-1536
Email: info@coleschotz.com
Web Site: www.coleschotz.com

2016 Total Lawyers: 124
2015 Total Lawyers: 124

Connell Foley LLP

85 Livingston Avenue
Roseland, NJ 07068
Phone: 973-535-0500
Fax: 973-535-9217
Email: firm@connellfoley.com
Web Site: www.connellfoley.com

2016 Total Lawyers: 115
2015 Total Lawyers: 140

Day Pitney LLP

One Jefferson Road
Parsippany, NJ 07054-6300
Phone: 973-966-6300
Fax: 973-966-1015
Web Site: www.daypitney.com

2016 Total Lawyers: 283
2015 Total Lawyers: 274

DeCotiis FitzPatrick & Cole

Glenpointe Center West
500 Frank W. Burr Blvd, Ste 31
Teaneck, NJ 07666
Phone: 201-928-1100
Fax: 201-928-0588

2016 Total Lawyers: 61
2015 Total Lawyers: 60

Gibbons

One Gateway Center
Newark, NJ 07102
Phone: 973-596-4500
Fax: 973-596-0545
Email: firm@gibbonslaw.com
Web Site: www.gibbonslaw.com

2016 Total Lawyers: 202
2015 Total Lawyers: 202

Giordano, Halleran & Ciesla, P.C.

125 Half Mile Road
Suite 300
Red Bank, NJ 07701
Phone: 732-741-3900
Web Site: www.ghclaw.com

2016 Total Lawyers: 54
2015 Total Lawyers: 54

Greenbaum, Rowe, Smith, & Davis, LLP

99 Wood Avenue South
Iselin, NJ 08830-2712
Phone: 732-549-5600
Fax: 732-549-1881
Email: info@greenbaumlaw.com
Web Site: www.greenbaumlaw.com

2016 Total Lawyers: 95
2015 Total Lawyers: 96

Lowenstein Sandler PC

65 Livingston Avenue
Roseland, NJ 07068-1791
Phone: 973-597-2500
Fax: 973-597-2400
Email: information@lowenstein.co
Web Site: www.lowenstein.com

2016 Total Lawyers: 310
2015 Total Lawyers: 299

McCarter & English

Four Gateway Center
100 Mulberry Street
Newark, NJ 07102-4056
Phone: 973-622-4444
Fax: 973-624-7070
Email: info@mccarter.com
Web Site: www.mccarter.com

2016 Total Lawyers: 410
2015 Total Lawyers: 410

McElroy, Deutsch, Mulvaney & Carpenter, LLP

1300 Mount Kemble Avenue
P.O. Box 2075
Morristown, NJ 07962-2075
Phone: 973-993-8100
Fax: 973-425-0161
Email: info@mdmc-law.com
Web Site: www.mdmc-law.com

2016 Total Lawyers: 275
2015 Total Lawyers: 228

Norris, McLaughlin & Marcus

721 Route 202-206, Suite 200
P.O. Box 5933
Bridgewater, NJ 08876-5933
Phone: 908-722-0700
Fax: 908-722-0755

2016 Total Lawyers: 135
2015 Total Lawyers: 134

Parker McCay P.A.

9000 Midlantic Drive
Suite 300
Mt. Laurel, NJ 08054
Phone: 856-596-8900
Fax: 856-596-9631
Email: info@parkermccay.com
Web Site: www.parkermccay.com

2016 Total Lawyers: 64
2015 Total Lawyers: 64

2016 Staff
Equity Partners: 15
Associates: 25
Of Counsel: 6
Counsel: 10

Offices: No. Attys.
Mount Laurel, NJ: 58
Atlantic City, NJ: 2
Hamilton, NJ: 10

Hiring and Promotion
2015 Associates Hired: 9
2015 First-Year Hires: 5
2016 First-Year Hires (Est.): 4
2015 Equity Partners Named: 0

Leading Practice Areas
(Department Heads)
Litigation 18% (Carolyn Sleeper
856-596-8900)
Public Finance 17% (Philip A. Norcross
856-596-8900)
Real Estate and Land Use 13% (Kevin D.
Sheehan 856-596-8900)
Municipal and Government 12% (John C.
Gillespie 856-596-8900)
Banking and Financial Services 12% (Gene
Mariano 856-696-8900)
Public Schools and Education 11% (Frank P.
Cavallo 856-596-8900)
Business/Corporate 9% (Mariel Giletto
856-596-8900)
Personal Injury 4% (Gary F. Piserchia
856-596-8900)

Parker McCay P.A. (Continued)

Leading Officials
Philip A. Norcross, Managing Shareholder &
CEO, 856-985-4021
Carolyn J. Rutsky, COO, 856-810-5808
Lora M. Foley, Shareholder, 856-985-4018
Jessica Milewski, Director of Attorney
Recruitment and Development,
856-985-4008
Anna Malandra, Director of Marketing,
856-810-5821
Christopher Sabol, Information Technology
Director, 856-810-5858
Doug McCollister, Librarian, 856-985-4094
Jessica Milewski, Director of Attorney
Recruitment and Development,
856-596-8900

Peckar & Abramson

70 Grand Ave
River Edge, NJ 07661
Phone: 201-343-3434
Fax: 201-343-6306
Email: jwhite@pecklaw.com
Web Site: www.pecklaw.com/

2016 Total Lawyers: 100
2015 Total Lawyers: 97

Porzio, Bromberg & Newman

100 Southgate Parkway
P.O. Box 1997
Morristown, NJ 07962-1997
Phone: 973-538-4006
Fax: 973-538-5146
Email: info@pbnlaw.com
Web Site: www.pbnlaw.com

2016 Total Lawyers: 85
2015 Total Lawyers: 90

2016 Staff
Equity Partners: 14
Non-Equity Partners: 21
Associates: 17
Of Counsel: 14
Counsel: 19

Offices: No. Attys.
Morristown, NJ - Home Office: 64
New York, NY: 7
Princeton, NJ: 4
Westborough, MA: 2
Washington, DC: 8

Hiring and Promotion
2015 Associates Hired: 6
Starting Salary for First-Year
Assocs: $120,000
2016 First-Year Hires (Est.): 0
2015 Equity Partners Named: 2

Porzio, Bromberg & Newman (Continued)

Leading Practice Areas
(Department Heads)
Intellectual Property 19.41% (Robert G.
Shepherd 609-524-1822)
Wealth Management 16.23% (Phillip J. Siana
973-889-4149)
Real Estate 15.98% (Michael L Rich
973-889-4329)
Life Sciences Compliance,
Commercialization and Regulatory
Counseling 10.38% (John P. Oroho
973-889-4302)
Employment 10.35% (Vito A. Gagliardi, Jr.
973-889-4151)
Bankruptcy and Financial Restructuring
8.82% (Warren J. Martin Jr.
973-889-4006)
Commercial Litigation 7.85% (Diane F.
Averell 973-889-4150)
Corporate and Securities 6.86% (Christopher
F. Schultz 646-348-6755)
Product Liability & Mass Tort 4.12% (Roy A.
Cohen 973-889-4235)

Revenues and Profits
Revenues: $51,215,394
Profits: $3,829,688

Client Representations
El du Pont de Nemours & Company
Schindler Elevator Company
Georgia-Pacific LLC

Leading Officials
D. Jeffrey Campbell, Managing Principal,
973-889-4201
Karen E. Moore-Negast, Executive Director,
973-889-4242
Diane F. Averell, Lateral Recruitment
Committee Chair, 973-889-4150
Carole T. Mecca, Director of Attorney
Services, 973-889-4274
Tuyet T. Dorr, Director of Marketing and
Client Services, 973-889-4279
Paul C. Wittekind, Director of Information
Technology Services, 973-889-4328
Janice M. Schouten, Librarian, 973-889-4368
Renee L. Davis, Diversity Manager,
973-889-4206

Other Offices
100 Southgate Parkway
P.O. Box 1997
Morristown, NJ 07962-1997
Phone: 973-538-4006
Fax: 973-538-5146
Email: info@pbnlaw.com
D. Jeffrey Campbell, Managing Principal

Riker Danzig Scherer Hyland & Perretti LLP

Headquarters Plaza
One Speedwell Avenue
Morristown, NJ 07962-1981
Phone: 973-538-0800
Fax: 973-538-1984
Email: info@riker.com
Web Site: www.riker.com

2016 Total Lawyers: 137
2015 Total Lawyers: 219

2016 Staff
Equity Partners: 39
Non-Equity Partners: 12
Associates: 57
Of Counsel: 7
Counsel: 23
Staff Attorneys: 1

Offices: No. Attys.
Trenton, NJ: 1
Morristown, NJ: 131
New York, NY: 6

Hiring and Promotion
2015 Associates Hired: 21
2015 First-Year Hires: 4
Starting Salary for First-Year
  Assocs: $130,000
2016 First-Year Hires (Est.): 5
2015 Equity Partners Named: 2
2015 Lateral Equity Partners: 1

Leading Practice Areas
(Department Heads)
Commercial Litigation 26%% (Glenn A.
  Clark 973-451-8400)
Insurance 16%% (Brian E. O'Donnell
  973-451-8555)
Products Liability 13%% (Kelly S. Crawford
  973-451-8417)
Environmental 7%% (Dennis J. Krumholz
  973-451-8454)
Governmental Affairs 6%% (Mary Kathryn
  Roberts 609-394-6600)
Corporate 4%% (Jason Navarino
  973-451-8440)
Labor & Employment 4%% (Scott A.
  Ohnegian 973-451-8551)
Bankruptcy & Reorganization 4%% (Dennis
  J. O'Grady 973-451-8485)
Real Estate 4%% (Nicholas Racioppi
  973-451-8492)
Tax and Trusts & Estates 3%% (Robert C.
  Daleo 973-451-8421)

Client Representations
Johnson & Johnson
Casino Reinvestment Development Authority
Mitsui Sumitomo

Riker Danzig Scherer Hyland & Perretti LLP *(Continued)*

Leading Officials
Glenn A Clark, Managing Partner
Timothy P. Carr, Director of Administration
  and Chief Financial Officer
Edwin F. Chociey, Jr., Hiring Partner
Alison Feldman Walsh, Director of
  Recruitment
Richelle J. Delavan, Director of Practice
  Development
Karen B. Brunner, Director of
  Library Services
Glenn A. Clark, Managing Partner,
  973-451-8400

Sills Cummis & Gross

The Legal Center
One Riverfront Plaza
Newark, NJ 07102
Phone: 973-643-7000
Fax: 973-643-6500
Email: sillsmail@sillscummis.com
Web Site: www.sillscummis.com

2016 Total Lawyers: 136
2015 Total Lawyers: 138

2016 Staff
Equity Partners: 27
Non-Equity Partners: 32
Of Counsel/Associates: 77

Leading Officials
Steven E. Gross, Chairman of the Firm,
  973-643-5080
R. Max Crane, Managing Partner,
  973-643-5055
James Duffy, Chief Operating Officer,
  973-643-6612
Joshua Howley and Diane Lavenda, Hiring
  Committee Co-Chairs, 973-643-7000
Rachel Mayerson, Director of Recruiting,
  973-643-4769
Marcia Jeffers, Chief Marketing Officer,
  973-643-4215
Amy Davis, Director of Marketing,
  973-643-4285
Jennifer Johnson, Director of Information
  Services, 973-643-2013
Teresa Wrenn, Director of Library Services,
  973-643-6098

Stark & Stark

993 Lenox Dr
Building Two
Lawrenceville, NJ 08648
Phone: 609-896-9060
Fax: 609-895-7395
Email: info@stark-stark.com
Web Site: www.stark-stark.com

2016 Total Lawyers: 97
2015 Total Lawyers: 105

2016 Staff
Equity Partners: 32
Non-Equity Partners: 28
Associates: 32
Of Counsel: 3
Senior Attorneys: 2

Stark & Stark *(Continued)*

Offices: No. Attys.
Lawrenceville, NJ: 75
Marlton, NJ: 9
Yardley, PA: 10
Morristown, NJ: 3

Hiring and Promotion
2015 Associates Hired: 4
2015 First-Year Hires: 1
2016 First-Year Hires (Est.): 0
2015 Equity Partners Named: 4

Leading Practice Areas
(Department Heads)
Personal Injury 25% (John A. Sakson)
Litigation 20% (Lewis J. Pepperman)
Real Estate, Zoning & Land Use 10% (Gary
  S. Forshner)
Workers' Compensation 8% (Vicki
  W. Beyer)
Bankruptcy & Creditors' Rights 7% (Timothy
  P. Duggan)
Community Associations 6% (A.
  Christopher Florio)
Business & Corporate 6% (Rachel L. Stark)
Family Law 6% (John S. Eory)
Securities 5% (Thomas D. Giachetti)
Trusts & Estates 4% (Steven L. Friedman)

Leading Officials
Michael G. Donahue, Managing Shareholder
Michael G. Donahue, Managing Shareholder
Gregory Deatz, Chief Operating Officer
Bonnie Brenner, Director of Human
  Resources & Facilities
Jim Jarrell, Director of Marketing & Practice
  Development
Tom Kline, Director of Information
  Technology
Diversity & Inclusion Committee

Other Offices
993 Lenox Drive
Lawrenceville
NJ
08648

Waters, McPherson, McNeill, P.C.

300 Lighting Way
7th Floor
Secaucus, NJ 07096
Phone: 201-863-4400
Fax: 201-863-2866
Web Site: web.lawwmm.com

2016 Total Lawyers: 30
2015 Total Lawyers: 29

NEW JERSEY

Wilentz, Goldman & Spitzer P.A.

90 Woodbridge Center Drive
Suite 900, Box 10
Woodbridge, NJ 07095-0958
Phone: 732-855-6400
Fax: 732-855-6117
Email: webmaster@wilentz.com
Web Site: www.newjerseylaw.com

2016 Total Lawyers: 113
2015 Total Lawyers: 109

NEW MEXICO

Hinkle, Hensley, Shanor & Martin

400 Penn Plaza
Suite 700
Roswell, NM 88201
Phone: 505-622-6510
Fax: 505-623-9332
Web Site: www.hinklelawfirm.com

2016 Total Lawyers: 38
2015 Total Lawyers: 36

Keleher & McLeod, PA

P.O. Box AA
Albuquerque, NM 87103-1626
Phone: 505-346-4646
Fax: 505-346-1370
Web Site: www.keleher-law.com

2016 Total Lawyers: 31
2015 Total Lawyers: 32

Miller, Stratvert & Torgerson, P.A.

500 Marquette,
Suite 1000
Albuquerque, NM 87125-0687
Phone: 505-842-1950
Fax: 505-243-4408
Email: info@mstlaw.com
Web Site: www.mstlaw.com

2016 Total Lawyers: 31
2015 Total Lawyers: 30

Modrall, Sperling, Roehl, Harris & Sisk, P.A.

500 Fourth Street N.W., Suite 1000
P.O. Box 2168
Albuquerque, NM 87103-2168
Phone: 505-848-1800
Fax: 505-848-9710
Web Site: www.modrall.com

2016 Total Lawyers: 62
2015 Total Lawyers: 79

Rodey, Dickason, Sloan, Akin & Robb, P.A.

201 Third Street N.W.
Suite 2200
Albuquerque, NM 87102
Phone: 505-765-5900
Fax: 505-768-7395
Email: info@rodey.com
Web Site: www.rodey.com

2016 Total Lawyers: 65
2015 Total Lawyers: 70

2016 Staff
Equity Partners: 47
Associates: 8
Of Counsel: 10

Offices: No. Attys.
Albuquerque: 58
Santa Fe: 7

Hiring and Promotion
2015 Associates Hired: 4
2015 First-Year Hires: 1
2016 First-Year Hires (Est.): 0
2015 Equity Partners Named: 1

Leading Practice Areas
(Department Heads)
Litigation 75% (David W. Bunting 505-766-7545)
Business 25% (Justin A. Horwitz 505-768-7317)

Client Representations
University of California/Los Alamos National Laboratory
University of New Mexico
Presbyterian Healthcare Services

Leading Officials
Charles Vigil
Monty Morton
Aaron Viets
Cathy Lopez, Human Resources Manager
Jose Blanton
Jim McCue
Tisa Neff
Ellen Skrak, Diversity Committee Chair, 505-768-7732

Other Offices
Albuquerque
201 Third St NW
Albuquerque
NM
87102
Phone: 505-765-5900
Fax: 505-768-7395
Email: info@rodey.com
Charles J. Vigil

Sutin, Thayer & Browne A Professional Corporation

6565 Americas Parkway NE
Two Park Square, Suite 1000
Albuquerque, NM 87110
Phone: 505-883-2500
Fax: 505-888-6565
Email: stbao@sutinfirm.com
Web Site: sutinfirm.com

2016 Total Lawyers: 26
2015 Total Lawyers: 33

2016 Staff
Equity Partners: 29
Associates: 5
Of Counsel: 2
Counsel: 4

Offices: No. Attys.
Albuquerque: 36
Santa Fe: 4

Hiring and Promotion
2015 Associates Hired: 6
2016 First-Year Hires (Est.): 1
2015 Equity Partners Named: 8

Leading Practice Areas
(Department Heads)
General Commercial Litigation 40% (Ben Thomas 505-883-2500)
Commercial Transaction 40% (Jean Moore 505-883-2500)
Domestic Relations 20% (Ben Thomas 505-883-2500)

Client Representations
Wells Fargo
Bank of Albuquerque
Farm Credit of New Mexico

Leading Officials
Jay D. Rosenblum, President & CEO
Anne P. Browne, Vice President & CAO
Andrew Simons, Hiring Partner
Andrew Simons, Recruiting Director
Kelly Brewer, Director of Marketing & Communications
Dana Scott, Chief Technology Officer
Richard McGoey, Librarian
Andrew Simons, Chair, Recruiting

NEW YORK

Anderson Kill & Olick, P.C.

1251 Avenue of the Americas
42nd Floor
New York, NY 10020-1182
Phone: 212-278-1000
Fax: 212-278-1733
Email: marketing@andersonkill.co
Web Site: www.andersonkill.com

2016 Total Lawyers: 81
2015 Total Lawyers: 84

NEW YORK

Barclay Damon

One Park Place
300 South State Street
Syracuse, NY 13202
Phone: 315-425-2700
Fax: 315-425-2701
Email: reachus@barclaydamon.com
Web Site: www.Barclaydamon.com

2016 Total Lawyers: 275
2015 Total Lawyers: 275

2016 Staff
Equity Partners: 71
Non-Equity Partners: 57
Associates: 79
Of Counsel: 54
Counsel: 14

Offices: No. Attys.
Syracuse, NY: 80
Albany, NY: 39
Buffalo, NY: 105
Rochester, NY: 28
New York, NY: 3
Toronto, Ontario: 1
Washington, DC: 2
Boston, MA: 7
Elmira, NY: 6
Clarence, NY: 4

Hiring and Promotion
2015 Associates Hired: 9
2015 First-Year Hires: 5
Starting Salary for First-Year
Assocs: $80,000
2016 First-Year Hires (Est.): 3
2015 Equity Partners Named: 1

Leading Practice Areas
(Department Heads)
Intellectual Property 15% (Douglas J. Nash
315-425-2828)
Energy 12% (Richard R. Capozza
315-425-2710)
Torts & Products Liability Defense 11%
(Matthew J. Larkin, Thomas J. Drury
315-425-2805, 716-858-3845)
Corporate 9% (James J. Canfield, Christopher
T. Greene 315-425-2763, 716-858-3730)
Litigation 9% (Jon P. Devendorf
315-425-2724)
Real Property Tax & Condemnation 6%
(Mark R. McNamara 716-566-1536)
Trusts & Estates 5% (Marcy Robinson
Dembs, Jennifer G. Flannery
315-425-2740, 716-858-3701)
Health Care & Human Services 5% (Melissa
Zambri, Susan A. Benz 518-429-4229,
716-858-3812)
Public Finance 4% (M. Cornelia Cahill
518-429-4296)
Labor & Employment 4% (Laurence B.
Oppenheimer 716-566-1575)

Client Representations
Energy & Utility Companies
High Tech Manufacturers
Health Care Providers

Barclay Damon (Continued)

Leading Officials
John P. Langan, Managing Partner,
315-425-2754
Jeffrey B. Koehne, Executive Director,
315-425-2700
Christopher J. Centore, Hiring Partner,
315-425-2756
Margaret Q. Black, Director of Human
Resources, 315-425-2712
Christopher J. Harrigan, Director of
Marketing, 315-425-2772
Richard R. Capozza, Chief Marketing
Officer, 315-425-2710
Peter R. Hotchkiss, Director of Information
Technology, 315-425-2789
Elaine M. Knecht, Director of Information
Resources, 716-566-1595
Sheila A. Gaddis, Partner, Diversity Partner,
585-295-4357

Other Offices
One Park Place
300 South State Street
Syracuse
New York
13202
Phone: 315-425-2700
Fax: 315-425-2701
Email: reachus@barclaydamon.com
Gabriel M. Nugent, Syracuse Office
Managing Director

Avant Building
200 Delaware Avenue
1200
Buffalo
New York
14202
Phone: 716-856-5500
Fax: 716-856-5510
Email: reachus@barclaydamon.com
James P. Domagalski, Peter S. Marlette
Co-Managing Directors

Bond, Schoeneck & King

One Lincoln Center
Syracuse, NY 13202-1355
Phone: 315-218-8000
Fax: 315-218-8100
Email: webadmin@bsk.com
Web Site: www.bsk.com

2016 Total Lawyers: 264
2015 Total Lawyers: 228

2016 Staff
Associates: 62
Of Counsel: 22
Senior Counsel: 23
Equity Members: 126
Non-Equity Members: 31

Offices: No. Attys.
Syracuse, NY: 100
Albany, NY: 28
Buffalo, NY: 44
Garden City, NY: 15
Ithaca, NY: 2
New York City, NY: 21
Oswego, NY: 3

Bond, Schoeneck & King (Continued)
Rochester, NY: 32
Utica, NY: 2
Overland Park, KS: 4
Naples, FL: 13

Hiring and Promotion
2015 Associates Hired: 22
2015 First-Year Hires: 7
Starting Salary for First-Year Assocs:
$90,000 + $5,000 signing bonus
2016 First-Year Hires (Est.): 5
2015 Equity Partners Named: 23
2015 Lateral Equity Partners: 19

Leading Practice Areas
(Department Heads)
Labor & Employment Law 29% (Larry P.
Malfitano 315-218-8331)
Business Transaction/Commercial Law 17%
(Robert Kirchner 315-218-8319)
Litigation 13% (John H. Callahan
315-218-8292)
Property 11% (Robert R. Tyson
315-218-8221)
Estate & Financial Planning 7% (Martin A.
Schwab 315-218-8143)
Intellectual Property (Patent, Trademark,
Copyright) 4% (George R. McGuire
315-218-8515)
Sports Law/NCAA 4% (Michael S. Glazier
913-234-4413)
Higher Education & School Law 3% (Philip
J. Zaccheo 315-218-8113)
Environmental Law 3% (Virginia C. Robbins
315-218-8182)
Bankruptcy 3% (Stephen A. Donato, Joseph
Zagraniczny 315-218-8336,
315-218-8220)
Taxation 2% (Paul W. Reichel
315-218-8135)
Bonding 2% (Matthew N. Wells
315-218-8174)
Securities 1% (Matthew N. Wells
315-218-8174)
Local Government 1% (Raymond A. Meier
315-738-1223)

Client Representations
Syracuse University
KeyBank National Association
AngioDynamics, Inc.

Leading Officials
Kevin M. Bernstein, Chair, Management
Committee, 315-218-8329
Gary S. Goodwin, Executive Director,
315-218-8194
Suzanne O. Galbato, Chair, Recruiting
Committee, 315-218-8370
Ann E. Perrone, Recruiting Coordinator,
315-218-8376
Kathleen B. Leach, Director of Marketing
Services, 315-218-8379
Jean M. Hay, I.T. Director, 315-218-8601
Maureen T. Kays, Director of Information
Services, 315-218-8161
Sanjeeve K. DeSoyza, Member,
518-533-3206

NEW YORK

Bressler Amery & Ross

17 State Street
34th Floor
New York, NY 10004
Phone: 212-425-9300

2016 Total Lawyers: 161
2015 Total Lawyers: 141

Cadwalader, Wickersham & Taft

One World Financial Center
New York, NY 10281
Phone: 212-504-6000
Fax: 212-504-6666
Email: cwtinfo@cwt.com
Web Site: www.cadwalader.com

2016 Total Lawyers: 430
2015 Total Lawyers: 448

2016 Staff
Equity Partners: 49
Non-Equity Partners: 49
Associates: 267.7
Counsel: 82.7

Offices: No. Attys.
New York, NY: 229.5
Washington, DC: 87.4
London, UK: 50
Charlotte, NC: 42.5
Hong Kong: 23
Beijing, China: 8
Houston, TX: 3
Brussels, Belgium: 5

Hiring and Promotion
2015 Associates Hired: 91
2015 First-Year Hires: 48
Starting Salary for First-Year Assocs:
$160,000 (NY/DC/NC)
2016 First-Year Hires (Est.): 34
2015 Equity Partners Named: 6
2015 Lateral Equity Partners: 2

Cadwalader, Wickersham & Taft (Continued)

Leading Practice Areas
(Department Heads)
Capital Markets (Michael S. Gambro
212-504-6825)
Corporate (Christopher T. Cox
212-504-6888)
Financial Restructuring (Mark C. Ellenberg,
Gregory M. Petrick 202-862-2238,
+44-0-20-7170-8688)
Litigation (Louis M. Solomon 212-504-6600)
Regulation (Steven D. Lofchie, Richard M.
Schetman 212-504-6700, 212-504-6906)
Private Client (Dean C. Berry 212-504-6944)
Tax (Linda Z. Swartz 212-504-6062)

Intellectual Property (Christopher A. Hughes
212-504-6891)
Antitrust (Charles F. Rule 202-862-2420)
Business Fraud (Kenneth L. Wainstein
202-862-2474)
Private Equity (Ron Hopkinson
212-504-6789)
Energy & Commodities (Paul J. Pantano, Jr.
202-862-2410)
Health Care (Kathy H. Chin, Paul Mourning
212-504-6542, 212-504-6216)
Real Estate (William P. McInerney
212-504-6118)
Finance (Steven N. Cohen 212-504-6276)

Client Representations
Advised Salix Pharmaceuticals, Ltd. in its
$15.6 billion sale to Valeant
Pharmaceuticals International, Inc.
Represented Deutsche Bank as initial
purchaser in the first-ever short duration
CLO with limited reinvestment provisions
Represented Eli Lilly & Company in
connection with securing Federal Trade
Commission clearance for the company's
acquisition of Novartis Animal Health

Leading Officials
Patrick T. Quinn, Managing Partner,
212-504-6067
Mitchel Sekler, Executive Director,
212-504-6690
Paul W. Mourning, Hiring Partner,
212-504-6216
Susan H. Harlow, Director of Legal
Recruitment, 212-504-6565
Robert J. Robertson, 212-504-6897
Thomas Baldwin, Chief Information Officer,
212-504-6540
Rissa Peckar, Director of Library Services,
212-504-6767
Sonnia Shields, Director of Diversity,
212-504-5700

Other Offices
700 Sixth St., N.W.
Washington
DC
20001
Phone: 202-862-2200
Fax: 202-862-2400
Email: cwtinfo@cwt.com
Charles (Rick) Rule, Managing Partner

Cadwalader, Wickersham & Taft (Continued)

Dashwood House
69 Old Broad Street
London
UK
EC2M 1QS
Email: cwtinfo@cwt.com
Gregory Petrick, Managing Partner

Cahill Gordon & Reindel LLP

80 Pine Street
New York, NY 10005-1702
Phone: 212-701-3000
Fax: 212-269-5420
Email: marketing@cahill.com
Web Site: www.cahill.com

2016 Total Lawyers: 253
2015 Total Lawyers: 283

Carter, Ledyard & Milburn LLP

2 Wall Street
New York, NY 10005
Phone: 212-732-3200
Fax: 212-732-3232
Email: info@clm.com
Web Site: www.clm.com

2016 Total Lawyers: 88
2015 Total Lawyers: 97

Certilman Balin Adler & Hyman, LLP

90 Merrick Avenue
East Meadow, NY 11554
Phone: 516-296-7000
Fax: 516-296-7111
Email: info@certilmanbalin.com
Web Site: www.certilmanbalin.com

2016 Total Lawyers: 74
2015 Total Lawyers: 68

Chadbourne & Parke LLP

30 Rockefeller Plaza
New York, NY 10112
Phone: 212-408-5100
Fax: 212-541-5369
Email: newyork@chadbourne.com
Web Site: www.chadbourne.com

2016 Total Lawyers: 340
2015 Total Lawyers: 363

Offices: No. Attys.
New York, NY: 186
Washington, DC: 59
Moscow: 15
London: 31
Los Angeles, CA: 7
Beijing: 2
Warsaw: 25

NEW YORK

Chadbourne & Parke LLP (Continued)
Kyiv: 10
Dubai: 13
Sao Paulo: 5
Istanbul: 8
Mexico City: 2

Hiring and Promotion
2015 Associates Hired: 33

Leading Practice Areas
(Department Heads)
Corporate (J. Allen Miller +1
  (212) 408-5454)
Project Finance (Keith Martin +1
  (202) 974-5674)
Litigation (Abbe David Lowell +1
  (202) 974-5605)
Product Liability Litigation (Mary T.
  Yelenick +1 (212) 408-5493)
Tax (William G. Cavanagh +1
  (212) 408-5388)
Insurance/Reinsurance (David M. Raim +1
  (202) 974-5625)
Intellectual Property (Paul J. Tanck +1
  (212) 408-1116)
Real Estate (Lawrence R. Plotkin +1
  (212) 408-5323)
Bankruptcy (Howard Seife +1
  (212) 408-5361)

Leading Officials
Andrew A. Giaccia, Managing Partner,
  212-408-1046
Supria B. Kuppuswamy, Manager of
  Diversity Initiatives, 212-408-1152

Other Offices
1200 New Hampshire Avenue, N.W.
Washington, DC 20036
Phone: 202-974-5600
Fax: 202-974-5602

Cleary Gottlieb Steen & Hamilton

One Liberty Plaza
New York, NY 10006-1470
Phone: 212-225-2000
Fax: 212-225-3999
Web Site: www.cgsh.com

2016 Total Lawyers: 1200
2015 Total Lawyers: 1200

Clifford Chance US LLP

31 W. 52nd St.
New York, NY 10019
Phone: 212-878-8000
Fax: 212-878-8375
Web Site: www.cliffordchance.com

2016 Total Lawyers: 3300
2015 Total Lawyers: 3300

Cowan, Liebowitz & Latman, P.C.

114 West 47th Street
New York, NY 10036
Phone: 212-790-9200
Fax: 212-575-0671
Email: law@cll.com
Web Site: www.cll.com

2016 Total Lawyers: 43
2015 Total Lawyers: 48

2016 Staff
Equity Partners: 14
Associates: 12
Of Counsel: 11
Senior Attorneys: 1
Senior Counsel: 1
Staff Attorneys: 4

Offices: No. Attys.
New York, NY: 43
Customs, Int'l Cargo & Regulatory
  Compliance: 1

Hiring and Promotion
2015 Associates Hired: 5
2016 First-Year Hires (Est.): 0
2015 Equity Partners Named: 0

Leading Practice Areas
(Department Heads)
Trademark & Copyright 50% (Lynn Fruchter
  212-790-9207)
Litigation 20% (Richard Mandel
  212-790-9291)
Patent 15% (Mark Montague 212-790-9252)
Business & Personal 10% (Peter Porcino
  212-790-9208)
Customs 5% (C.J. Erickson 212-790-9274)

Client Representations
Various defendants in the Converse sneaker
  ITC trade dress proceeding
Successful opposition against High School
  World Series
Successful appeal decision in DELMONICO
  restaurant concurrent use proceeding

Leading Officials
Jonathan Z. King, 212-790-9238
Lauren Fragola, 212-790-9288
Deborah K. Squiers, 212-790-9211
Joel Karni Schmidt, 212-790-9244
Laurence W. Greene, 212-790-9229
Robert Gooch, 212-790-9269

Cravath, Swaine & Moore LLP

Worldwide Plaza
825 Eighth Avenue
New York, NY 10019
Phone: 212-474-1000
Fax: 212-474-3700
Web Site: www.cravath.com

2016 Total Lawyers: 503
2015 Total Lawyers: 463

Cravath, Swaine & Moore LLP (Continued)

2016 Staff
Equity Partners: 88
Non-Equity Partners: 1
Associates: 389
Of Counsel: 1
Senior Attorneys: 24

Offices: No. Attys.
New York, NY: 461
London, UK: 42

Hiring and Promotion
2015 Associates Hired: 126
2015 First-Year Hires: 96
2016 First-Year Hires (Est.): 87
2015 Equity Partners Named: 2

Leading Practice Areas
(Department Heads)
Corporate 51% (William V. Fogg)
Litigation 40% (Sandra C. Goldstein)
Tax 7% (Stephen L. Gordon)
Trusts & Estates 2% (Daniel L. Mosley)

Client Representations
Credit Suisse
Mylan
Republic of Argentina

Leading Officials
C. Allen Parker, Presiding Partner
Donna G. Rosenwasser, Executive Director
Eric L. Schiele; Karin A. DeMasi, Hiring
  Partner, Corporate; Hiring
  Partner, Litigation
Lauren D. Campbell; Lisa A. Kalen, Director
  of Legal Personnel and Recruiting;
  Director of Legal Recruiting
Deborah B. Farone, Director of Business
  Development and Communications
Jeffrey Franchetti, Director of Information
  Technology
Deborah S. Panella, Director of Library &
  Knowledge Management Services
Kiisha J.B. Morrow, Head of Diversity

Cullen and Dykman

177 Montague Street
Brooklyn, NY 11201-3611
Phone: 718-855-9000
Fax: 718-855-4282
Web Site: www.cullenanddykman.com

2016 Total Lawyers: 138
2015 Total Lawyers: 143

Curtis, Mallet-Prevost, Colt & Mosle LLP

101 Park Avenue
New York, NY 10178-0061
Phone: 212-696-6000
Fax: 212-697-1559
Email: info@cm-p.com
Web Site: www.cm-p.com

2016 Total Lawyers: 280
2015 Total Lawyers: 270

NEW YORK

D'Amato & Lynch

Two World Financial Center
New York, NY 10281
Phone: 212-269-0927
Fax: 212-269-3559
Email: dlmis1@aol.com
Web Site: www.damato-lynch.com

2016 Total Lawyers: 58
2015 Total Lawyers: 55

Davis & Gilbert

1740 Broadway
New York, NY 10019
Phone: 212-468-4800
Fax: 212-468-4888
Email: info@dglaw.com
Web Site: www.dglaw.com

2016 Total Lawyers: 119
2015 Total Lawyers: 118

Davis Polk & Wardwell

450 Lexington Avenue
New York, NY 10017
Phone: 212-450-4000
Fax: 212-450-3800
Web Site: www.davispolk.com

2016 Total Lawyers: 933
2015 Total Lawyers: 827

2016 Staff
Equity Partners: 146
Associates: 678
Counsel: 93

Offices: No. Attys.
New York: 642
Washington DC: 38
Menlo Park: 45
London: 52
Paris: 13
Madrid: 5
Hong Kong: 87
Beijing: 16
Tokyo: 8
São Paulo: 11

Hiring and Promotion
2016 First-Year Hires (Est.): 122

Leading Officials
Thomas J. Reid, Managing Partner

Other Offices
New York
642

Debevoise & Plimpton LLP

919 Third Avenue
New York, NY 10022
Phone: 212-909-6000
Fax: 212-909-6836
Email: mailbox@debevoise.com
Web Site: www.debevoise.com

2016 Total Lawyers: 660
2015 Total Lawyers: 660

Dechert LLP

1095 Avenue of the Americas
New York, NY 10036-6797
Phone: 212-698-3500
Fax: 212-698-3599
Web Site: www.dechert.com

2016 Total Lawyers: 965
2015 Total Lawyers: 907

DLA Piper

1251 Avenue of the Americas
New York, NY 10020-1104
Phone: 212-335-4500
Fax: 212-335-4501
Email: info@dlapiper.com
Web Site: www.dlapiper.com

2016 Total Lawyers: 3527
2015 Total Lawyers: 3329

Emmet, Marvin & Martin, LLP

120 Broadway
32nd Floor
New York, NY 10271
Phone: 212-238-3000
Fax: 212-238-3100
Email: postmaster@emmetmarvin.co
Web Site: www.emmetmarvin.com

2016 Total Lawyers: 52
2015 Total Lawyers: 54

Epstein Becker & Green P.C.

250 Park Avenue
New York, NY 10177-1211
Phone: 212-351-4500
Fax: 212-661-0989
Web Site: www.ebglaw.com

2016 Total Lawyers: 300
2015 Total Lawyers: 300

Hiring and Promotion
2016 First-Year Hires (Est.): 0
2015 Equity Partners Named: 0

Leading Practice Areas
(Department Heads)
1. Health Care and Life Sciences
2. Labor and Employment
3. Employee Benefits
4. Litigation
5. Corporate Services

Epstein Becker & Green P.C. (Continued)

Leading Officials
Mark E. Lutes, Chair
Carmine Iannaccone
Steven Di Fiore, Chief Operating Officer
Amy Simmons, Director of Legal Recruiting
and Professional Development
Amanda Schneider, Chief Planning Officer
Carrie Valiant, Member

Fitzpatrick, Cella, Harper & Scinto

1290 Avenue of the Americas
New York, NY 10104-3800
Phone: 212-218-2100
Fax: 212-218-2200
Email: info@fitzpatrickcella.com
Web Site: www.fitzpatrickcella.com

2016 Total Lawyers: 139
2015 Total Lawyers: 136

2016 Staff
Equity Partners: 53
Associates: 77
Of Counsel: 6
Counsel: 3

Offices: No. Attys.
Washington, DC: 21
New York, NY: 112
Costa Mesa, CA: 6

Hiring and Promotion
2015 Associates Hired: 13
2015 First-Year Hires: 8
Starting Salary for First-Year
Assocs: $160,000
2016 First-Year Hires (Est.): 7
2015 Equity Partners Named: 3

Leading Practice Areas
(Department Heads)
Litigation (Scott K. Reed 212-218-2227)
Patent Prosecution (Anthony M. Zupcic
212-218-2240)
PTO Contested Proceedings (Justin J. Oliver
202-721-5423)
Trademarks (Timothy J. Kelly 212-218-2262)
Licensing & Transactions (Robert H. Fischer
212-218-2254)
Due Diligence (Raymond R. Mandra
212-218-2235)
ITC Section 337 Litigation (Edmund J.
Haughey, Michael P. Sandonato
202-721-5489, 212-2182217)
Copyrights (Timothy J. Kelly 212-218-3480)

Client Representations
Client Novartis and LTS: Fitzpatrick Once
Again Successfully Defends Patent Related
To Exelon® Transdermal Patches
Client Canon:Fitzpatrick Obtains Another
General Exclusion Order from ITC for
Longtime Client Canon
Client Johnson Outdoors: Fitzpatrick Obtains
Final Determination of Section 337
Violation on Behalf of Johnson Outdoors

NEW YORK

Fitzpatrick, Cella, Harper & Scinto (Continued)

Leading Officials
Ha Kung Wong, Hiring Partner,
212-218-2571
Nicole Cohen, Director of Recruiting,
212-218-2252
Linda Lee Ficano, Director of Business
Development & Marketing, 212-218-2284
Wei Ma, Director of Information Technology,
212-218-2158
Jeffrey Cohan, Head Librarian, 212-218-2103
Tara Byrne, Partner, 212-218-2207

Fragomen, Del Rey, Bernstein & Loewy

7 Hanover Square
New York, NY 10004
Phone: 212-688-8555
Web Site: www.fragomen.com

2016 Total Lawyers: 480
2015 Total Lawyers: 391

Fried, Frank, Harris, Shriver & Jacobson LLP

One New York Plaza
New York, NY 10004
Phone: 212-859-8000
Fax: 212-859-4000
Web Site: www.friedfrank.com

2016 Total Lawyers: 414
2015 Total Lawyers: 414

2016 Staff
Equity Partners: 104
Non-Equity Partners: 20
Associates: 288

Offices: No. Attys.
Washington, D.C.: 75
London: 31
New York: 297
Frankfurt: 7
Hong Kong: 1

Hiring and Promotion
Starting Salary for First-Year Assocs: New
York and Washington DC - $180,000

Revenues and Profits
Revenues: $504,300,000
Profits: $22,600,000

Leading Officials
David J. Greenwald, Chairman
Don Smith, Director of Diversity
and Inclusion

Other Offices
1001 Pennsylvania Avenue, N.W.
Suite 800
Washington, D.C. 20004-2505
Phone: 202-639-7000
Fax: 202-639-700 ext. 348
John T. Boese, Matt T. Morley, Alan
S. Kaden

Greenberg Traurig, LLP

MetLife Building
200 Park Avenue
New York, NY 10166
Phone: 212-801-9200
Fax: 212-801-6400
Web Site: www.gtlaw.com

2016 Total Lawyers: 1991
2015 Total Lawyers: 1868

2016 Staff
Equity Partners: 950
Associates: 651
Of Counsel: 169
Senior Counsel: 2
Staff Attorneys: 58
Directors 38

Offices; No. Attys.
Miami, FL: 184
Washington, DC: 106
Atlanta, GA: 95
Phoenix, AZ: 44
Fort Lauderdale, FL: 70
Los Angeles, CA: 83
McLean, VA: 45
West Palm Beach, FL: 29
Orlando, FL: 38
Chicago, IL: 152
Boston, MA: 63
Denver, CO: 57
Tallahassee, FL: 16
Philadelphia, PA: 33
Boca Raton, FL: 16
Wilmington, DE: 12
Morristown, NJ: 76
Amsterdam, The Netherlands: 33
Albany, NY: 24
Dallas, TX: 38
Houston, TX: 61
East Palo Alto, CA: 19
Las Vegas, NV: 35
Sacramento, CA: 22
Tampa, FL: 23
Shanghai, China: 13
Austin, TX: 23
Westchester County, NY: 24
London, UK: 50
San Francisco, CA: 19
New York, NY: 212
Irvine, CA: 23
Mexico City: 54
Warsaw, Poland: 65
Seoul, South Korea: 1
Tel Aviv, Israel: 5
Tokyo: 6

Hiring and Promotion
Starting Salary for First-Year Assocs:
Greenberg Traurig is in 36 markets and
pays market rates in each.
2016 First-Year Hires (Est.): Confidential
2015 Equity Partners Named: N/A

Greenberg Traurig, LLP (Continued)

Leading Practice Areas
(Department Heads)
Corporate & Securities (Gary M. Epstein
305-579-0500)
Litigation (Alan Mansfield; Philip R.
Sellinger 212-801-9200; 973-360-7900)
Real Estate (Robert J. Ivanhoe; Corey E.
Light 212-801-9200; 312-456-8400)
Tax, Trusts & Estates (Tax: Martin Kalb,
Peter van Langeveld, Barbara T. Kaplan,
Trusts & Estates: Diana Zeydel
305-579-0500; +31 (0) 20 301 7300;
212-801-9200)
Governmental Affairs (Tom Bond, Harold N.
Iselin 512-320-7200; 518-689-1400)
Intellectual Property (Alan Sutin; Mark R.
Galis 212-801-9200; 312-456-8400)
Environmental (Kerri Barsh; David
Mandelbaum; David Weinstein
305-579-0500; 215-988-7800;
813-318-5701)
Business Reorganization & Financial
Restructuring (Mark D. Bloom, Keith J.
Shapiro, Nancy Mitchell 305-579-0537;
312-456-8400; 212-801-9200)
Entertainment (Joel A. Katz 678-553-2100)
Labor & Employment (Jonathan Sulds, Peter
Zinober, David Long-Daniels
212-801-9200; 813-318-5700;
678-553-2100)

Revenues and Profits
Revenues: $1,270,700,000

Client Representations
Williams-Yulee v. Florida Bar (Case
No. 131499)
Greenberg Traurig Represents Nomad
Holdings in 2.6 billion Acquisition of
Iglo Foods
Greenberg Traurig Serves as Lead M&A
Counsel in Amaya Gamings $4.9B
Acquisition of Rational Group

Leading Officials
Richard A. Rosenbaum, Chief Executive
Officer, 212-801-9200
Cesar L. Alvarez/Matt Gorson, Co-Chairman,
305-579-0500
Jill Perry, Managing Director, 212-801-9231
Brad. Kaufman, 561-650-7900
Janet McKeegan, Director of Recruiting,
305-579-0500
Jill Perry, Chief Marketing Officer,
212-801-9231
Julie Amos, Senior Director of Marketing &
Business Development, 678-553-2100
Jay Nogle, Chief Information Officer,
703-749-1300
Marlene, Gebauer, 973-360-7900
Nikki Lewis Simon, Director of Client
Development and Corporate Social
Responsibility, 305-579-0500

NEW YORK

Greenberg Traurig, LLP (Continued)

Other Offices
Greenberg Traurig, LLP - New
York Office
200 Park Avenue
MetLife Building
New York
NY
10166
Phone: 212-801-9200
Fax: 212-801-6400
Stephen L. Rabinowitz and Nancy Mitchell,
Co-Managing Shareholders; Warren Karp
& Ed Wallace, Co-Chairmen

Greenberg Traurig, P.A. - Miami Office
333 S.E. 2nd Avenue
Suite 4400
Miami
FL
33131
Phone: 305-579-0500
Fax: 305-579-0717
Richard Giusto and Jaret Davis,
Co-Managing Shareholders

Washington, D.C. Office
2101 L Street, N.W.
Suite 1000
Washington, D.C.
20037
Phone: 202-331-3100
Fax: 202-331-3101
Laura Klaus and Sanford Saunders,
Co-Managing Shareholders

Greenberg Traurig, LLP - Los
Angeles Office
1840 Century Park East
Suite 1900
Los Angeles
CA
90067
Phone: 310-586-7700
Fax: 310-586-7800
Jeff Scott, Managing Shareholder

Greenberg Traurig, LLP - Atlanta Office
Terminus 200, 3333 Piedmont Road NE
Suite 2500
Atlanta
GA
30305
Phone: 678-553-2100
Fax: 678-553-2212
Ernest Greer and Theodore Blum,
Co-Managing Shareholders

Greenberg Traurig - Chicago Office
77 West Wacker Drive
Suite 3100
Chicago
IL
60601
Phone: 312-456-8400
Fax: 312-456-8435
Paul T. Fox and John Gibbons, Co-Managing
Shareholders; Keith J. Shapiro, Chairman

Greenberg Traurig, LLP (Continued)

Greenberg Traurig, LLP - Boston Office
One International Place
Boston
MA
02110
Phone: 617-310-6000
Fax: 617-310-6001
Terence McCourt & John Pappalardo,
Co-Managing Shareholders

Greenberg Traurig, LLP - New
Jersey Office
200 Park Avenue
P.O. Box 677
Florham Park
NJ
07932
Phone: 973-360-7900
Fax: 973-301-8410
Philip Sellinger & Geoffrey Berman,
Co-Managing Shareholders

Greenberg Traurig, LLP - Fort
Lauderdale Office
401 East Law Olas Boulevard
Suite 2000
Fort Lauderdale
FL
33301
Phone: 954-765-0500
Fax: 354-735-1477
Glenn Goldstein, Managing Shareholder

Greenberg Traurig, LLP - Denver office
1200 17th Street - The Tarbor Center
2400
Denver
CO
80202
Phone: 303-572-6500
Fax: 303-572-6540
David Palmer, Managing Shareholder

Greenberg Traurig, LLP - Houston office
1000 Louisiana Street
1700
Houston
TX
77002
Phone: 713-374-3500
Fax: 713-374-3505
Mary-Olga Lovett and Doug Atnipp,
Co-Managing Shareholders

Greenberg Traurig Maher LLP
200 Grays Inn Road
7th Floor
London, WC1X 8HF
United Kingdom
Phone: 440-203-349 ext. 8700
Fax: 440-207-900 ext. 3632
Paul Maher, Chairman; Fiona Adams and
Cate Sharp, Co-Managing Shareholders

Greenberg Traurig, S.C.
Paseo de la Reforma No. 265 PH1
Colonia Cuauhtemoc
Mexico, D.F. C.P.
06500
Phone: 525-550-290 ext. 000
Fax: 525-550-290 ext. 002
Jose Raz Guzman, Managing Shareholder

Greenberg Traurig, LLP (Continued)

Greenberg Traurig Grzesiak sp.k.
Stock Exchange Building
ul. Ksica 4
Warsaw
Poland
00-498
Phone: 482-269-061 ext. 00
Fax: 482-269-062 ext. 22
Jarosaw Grzesiak, Managing Shareholder

Hahn & Hessen LLP

488 Madison Avenue
New York, NY 10022
Phone: 212-478-7200
Fax: 212-478-7440
Web Site: www.hahnhessen.com

2016 Total Lawyers: 43
2015 Total Lawyers: 43

Hancock Estabrook, LLP

1500 AXA Tower I
100 Madison Street
Syracuse, NY 13202
Phone: 315-565-4500
Fax: 315-565-4600
Web Site: www.hancocklaw.com

2016 Total Lawyers: 56
2015 Total Lawyers: 55

Offices: No. Attys.
Albany, NY: 1
Syracuse, NY: 54

Hiring and Promotion
2015 Associates Hired: 1
2015 First-Year Hires: 1
2016 First-Year Hires (Est.): 0

Leading Practice Areas
(Department Heads)
Litigation (Daniel B. Berman 315-565-4500)
Environmental (Doreen A. Simmons
315-565-4500)
Real Estate (Steven R. Shaw 315-565-4500)
Catherine A. Diviney (Health Care
315-565-4500)
Labor & Employment (John F. Corcoran
315-565-4500)
Richard E. Scrimale (Business
315-565-4500)
Tax, Trusts & Estates & Elder Law (Michael
C. Corp 315-565-4500)

Leading Officials
Janet C. Callahan, Managing Partner,
315-565-4500
Daniel W. Waldron, Chief Financial Officer,
315-565-4500
Lindsey H. Hazelton, Hiring Partner,
315-565-4500
Lisa A. Nardone, Firm Administrator,
315-565-4500
Carrie T. Ryder, Marketing Director,
315-565-4500
Mary Lou Haines, Information Technology
Director, 315-565-4500
Donna Byrne, Head Librarian, 315-565-4500
Manuel Arroyo, Diversity Officer

OF COUNSEL 700

NEW YORK

Hancock Estabrook, LLP (Continued)

Other Offices
1500 AXA Tower I, 100 Madison St.
Syracuse
NY
13202
Phone: 315-565-4500
Fax: 315-565-4600

Harris Beach PLLC

99 Garnsey Road
Pittsford, NY 14534
Phone: 585-419-8800
Fax: 585-419-8811
Email: info@harrisbeach.com
Web Site: www.harrisbeach.com

2016 Total Lawyers: 210
2015 Total Lawyers: 210

2016 Staff
Equity Partners: 77
Non-Equity Partners: 41
Associates: 72
Of Counsel: 10
Counsel: 2
Senior Counsel: 25

Offices: No. Attys.
Rochester, NY: 94
New York, NY: 37
Buffalo, NY: 31
Albany, NY: 19
Syracuse, NY: 14
Ithaca, NY: 7
Newark, NJ: 14
Saratoga Springs, NY: 5
White Plains NY: 7
Uniondale, NY: 10
New Haven, CT: 1
Melville: 8

Hiring and Promotion
2015 Associates Hired: 22
2015 First-Year Hires: 4
Starting Salary for First-Year Assocs: Varies,
based on capabilities, prior experience, and
office location.
2016 First-Year Hires (Est.): 10
2015 Equity Partners Named: 2

Harris Beach PLLC (Continued)

Leading Practice Areas
(Department Heads)
Business & Commercial Litigation 17%
(Philip G. Spellane, Douglas Foss
585-419-8800)
Public Finance and Economic Development
15% (Shawn M. Griffin, Charles I.
Schachter 585-419-8800)
Labor & Employment 10.4% (Daniel J.
Moore 585-419-8800)
Mass Tort & Industry Wide Litigation 6.6%
(Cynthia Weiss Antonucci, Abbie L.
Eliasberg Fuchs 212-687-0100)
Commercial Real Estate 6.5% (Charles W.
Russell 585-419-8800)
Medical & Life Sciences 6% (Frederick H.
Fern, Judi Abbott Curry 212-687-0100)
Corporate 5% (David M. Clar 585-419-8800)
Intellectual Property 4% (Neal L. Slifkin
585-419-8800)
Government Compliance and Investigations
3% (Thomas A. DeSimon, Terrance P.
Flynn, Karl J. Sleight 585-419-8800)
Health 3% (Heidi S. Gregory 585-419-8800)

Leading Officials
James A. Spitz Jr., CEO, 585-419-8800
William H. Kedley, COO, 585-419-8800
Thomas Abbott, CFO, 585-419-8800
Scott D. Piper, Hiring Committee Chair,
585-419-8800
Mario Domanti, Director of Human
Resources, 585-419-8800
Hilary C. Guthrie, Chief Business
Development Officer, 585-419-8800
Richard A. Shutts, Chief Information Officer,
585-419-8800
Marie Cavalruso, Director of Libraries and
Research Services, 585-419-8800
Munesh Patel, Chair of Council on Inclusion
and Diversity, 585-419-8800

Harter Secrest & Emery

1600 Bausch & Lomb Place
Rochester, NY 14604
Phone: 585-232-6500
Fax: 585-232-2152
Web Site: www.hselaw.com

2016 Total Lawyers: 129
2015 Total Lawyers: 129

2016 Staff
Equity Partners: 56
Non-Equity Partners: 1
Associates: 49
Of Counsel: 15
Senior Counsel: 1
Staff Attorneys: 1

Offices: No. Attys.
Rochester, NY: 105
Buffalo, NY: 20
Albany, NY: 2
Corning, NY: 1
New York, NY: 1

Harter Secrest & Emery (Continued)

Hiring and Promotion
2015 Associates Hired: 8
2015 First-Year Hires: 4
Starting Salary for First-Year
Assocs: $90,000.
2016 First-Year Hires (Est.): 4
2015 Equity Partners Named: 2

Leading Practice Areas
(Department Heads)
Corporate/M&A (Tyler J. Savage)
Trial (Peter H. Abdella)
Immigration (Frank A. Novak)
Employee Benefits and Executive
Compensation (Paul W. Holloway)
Intellectual Property (Brian B. Shaw)
Trusts and Estates (Martin W. O'Toole)
Real Estate (Kelly A. Pronti)
Environmental, Land Use and Zoning (Kelly
A. Pronti)
Government Affairs (Donald S. Mazzullo)
Labor and Employment (Jeffrey J. Calabrese)
Government Investigations (Brian
M. Feldman)
Private Equity and Venture Capital (William
A. Hoy)
Securities and Capital Markets (Alexander
R. McClean)
Health Care and Human Services (Richard
T. Yarmel)
Higher Education (Theresa A. Conroy)

Leading Officials
Craig S. Wittlin, Managing Partner
David A. Higgins, Chief Financial Officer
Mark R. Wilson, Hiring Partner
Elizabeth E. Hofmeister, Director of Legal
Recruiting and Development
Nicole L. Kershaw, Director of Business
Development
Beth A. LaRocca, Director of Information
Technology
Lisa M. Pipia, Manager of
Information Services
Megan K. Dorritie, Diversity Partner

Hawkins, Delafield & Wood

1 Chase Manhattan Plaza
42nd Floor
New York, NY 10005
Phone: 212-820-9300
Web Site: www.hawkins.com

2016 Total Lawyers: 87
2015 Total Lawyers: 82

Herrick, Feinstein LLP

Two Park Avenue
New York, NY 10016
Phone: 212-592-1400
Fax: 212-592-1500
Web Site: www.herrick.com

2016 Total Lawyers: 140
2015 Total Lawyers: 143

A-85

NEW YORK

Herrick, Feinstein LLP (Continued)

2016 Staff
Equity Partners: 34
Non-Equity Partners: 23
Associates: 44
Senior Attorneys: 2
Counsel: 37

Offices: No. Attys.
New York, NY: 116
Newark, NJ: 21

Hiring and Promotion
2015 Associates Hired: 9
2015 First-Year Hires: 4
Starting Salary for First-Year Assocs:
$150,000 (NY), $135,000 (NJ)
2016 First-Year Hires (Est.): 3
2015 Equity Partners Named: 0

Leading Practice Areas
(Department Heads)
Real Estate (Belinda G. Schwartz
(212) 592-1544)
Litigation (Therese M. Doherty and Ronald J.
Levine (212) 592-1516 and 609-452-3801)
Corporate (inc. Internet & Tech.) (Irwin A.
Kishner and Stephen D. Brodie
212-592-1435, 212-592-1452)
Tax and Personal Planning (Louis Tuchman
(212) 592-1490)
Sports (Irwin A. Kishner, Daniel A. Etna and
John R. Goldman 212-592-1435,
212-592-1557 and 212-592-1460)
Art Law (Howard N. Spiegler and Lawrence
M. Kaye 212-592-1444 and 212-592-1410)
Employment Law (Carol M. Goodman and
Mara B. Levin 212-592-1465 and
212-592 -1458)
Government Relations (Kevin Fullington and
Elizabeth Holtzman 212-592-1442 and
(212) 592-1421)
Insurance (Alan R. Lyons 212-592-1539)
Restructuring and Bankruptcy (Stephen B.
Selbst 212-592-1405)

Revenues and Profits
Revenues: $115,630,861
Profits: $31,530,606

Client Representations
Represented the heirs of Russian artist
Kazimir Malevich in the $34 million sale of
Suprematism, 18th Construction, and the
$38 million sale of Mystic Suprematism.
Represented a consortium of four large
financial services companies on the sale of
333,000 square-feet of South Street
Seaport development rights to the Howard
Hughes Corporation.
Represented an affiliate of New York City
Football Club in negotiations with the City
of New York for the financing,
construction, development and build-out of
a new soccer stadium.

Herrick, Feinstein LLP (Continued)

Leading Officials
Irwin A. Kishner , Executive Committee
Chair, 212-592-1435
George J. Wolf, Jr., Managing Director, Exec
Comm, 212-592-1431
Carol Goodman, Hiring Partner,
212-592-1465
Alexis Zager, Manager of Legal Recruitment,
212-498-5300
Bernadette DeCelle, Director of Marketing,
212-498-5600
Marcus Ienaro, Director of Information
Technology, 212-498-6400
Georgia Sussman, Manager of Professional
Development, 212-498-5240

Herzfeld & Rubin, P.C.

125 Broad Street
New York, NY 10004
Phone: 212-471-8500
Fax: 212-344-3333
Web Site: www.herzfeld-rubin.com

2016 Total Lawyers: 66
2015 Total Lawyers: 64

Hinman, Howard & Kattell, LLP

700 Security Mutual Building
80 Exchange Street
Binghamton, NY 13902
Phone: 607-723-5341
Fax: 607-723-6605
Web Site: www.hhk.com

2016 Total Lawyers: 75
2015 Total Lawyers: 73

Hodgson Russ

The Guaranty Building
140 Pearl Street, Suite 100
Buffalo, NY 14202-4040
Phone: 716-856-4000
Fax: 716-849-0349
Email: info@hodgsonruss.com
Web Site: www.hodgsonruss.com

2016 Total Lawyers: 206
2015 Total Lawyers: 207

2016 Staff
Equity Partners: 89
Non-Equity Partners: 43
Associates: 33
Of Counsel: 2
Senior Attorneys: 29
Senior Counsel: 6

Offices: No. Attys.
New York, NY: 25
Albany, NY: 13
Saratoga Springs, NY: 4
Toronto, ON: 2
Buffalo, NY: 158

Hodgson Russ (Continued)

Hiring and Promotion
2015 Associates Hired: 10
2015 First-Year Hires: 6
Starting Salary for First-Year Assocs:
$95,000 (Buffalo), $130,000 (New York);
plus $7,500 bonus
2016 First-Year Hires (Est.): 6
2015 Equity Partners Named: 5

Leading Practice Areas
(Department Heads)
Corporate & Securities 12.1% (Kenneth P.
Friedman 716-848-1279)
Real Estate & Finance 12.1% (Sujata
Yalamanchili 716-848-1657)
State & Local Tax 11.2% (Christopher L.
Doyle 716-848-1458)
Labor & Employment 5.9% (John J.
Christopher 716-848-1471)
Intellectual Property & Technology Law
5.9% (Ranjana Kadle 716-848-1628)
Insurance Defense (Torts, Insurance &
Product Liability) 5.8% (Michael E.
Maxwell 716-848-1495)
Federal / International Tax 5.8% (Thomas W.
Nelson 716-848-1453)
Estates & Trusts 5.2% (Katherine E. Cauley
716-848-1522)
Bankruptcy/Commercial Litigation 4.2%
(Garry M. Graber 716-848-1273)
Environmental Litigation 3.2% (Paul D.
Meosky 716-848-1482)
Employee Benefits 3.2% (Arthur A.
Marrapese 716-848-1751)
Immigration 2.5% (Margot M. Watt
716-848-1353)

Client Representations
M&T Bank
Moog
First Niagara Bank

Leading Officials
Daniel C. Oliverio, Chair, 716-848-1433
John P. Amershadian, President,
716-848-1277
Paul V. Hartigan, COO, 716-848-1215
Ryan K. Cummings, Hiring Partner,
716-848-1665
Diane K. Scott, Director of Human
Resources, 716-848-1240
Linda M. Schineller, Director of Marketing &
Business Development, 716-848-1610
Kathleen K. Krieger-Erbes, Chief
Information Officer, 716-848-1613
Joan Taulbee, Head Librarian, 716-848-1282
Peter C. Godfrey, Partner, 716-848-1246

Other Offices
The Guaranty Building
140 Pearl Street, Suite 100
Buffalo, NY 14202-4040
Phone: 716-856-4000
Fax: 716-849-0349
Managing Partner: John P.
Amershadian, President

Holland & Knight LLP

31 W. 52nd St, 12th Floor
New York, NY 10019
Phone: 212-513-3200
Fax: 212-385-9010
Email: info@hklaw.com
Web Site: www.hklaw.com

2016 Total Lawyers: 1200
2015 Total Lawyers: 1106

Hughes Hubbard & Reed LLP

One Battery Park Plaza
New York, NY 10004-1482
Phone: 212-837-6000
Fax: 212-422-4726
Email: info@hugheshubbard.com
Web Site: www.hugheshubbard.com

2016 Total Lawyers: 324
2015 Total Lawyers: 343

Jackson Lewis LLP

One North Broadway, 15th Floor
White Plains, NY 10601
Phone: 914-328-0404
Fax: 914-328-1882
Web Site: www.jacksonlewis.com

2016 Total Lawyers: 769
2015 Total Lawyers: 784

Jaeckle Fleischmann & Mugel, LLP

The Avant Building Suite 900
200 Delaware Avenue
Buffalo, NY 14202
Phone: 716-856-0600
Fax: 716-856-0432
Email: office@jaeckle.com
Web Site: www.jaeckle.com

2016 Total Lawyers: 48
2015 Total Lawyers: 45

Kaye Scholer LLP

425 Park Avenue
New York, NY 10022
Phone: 212-836-8000
Fax: 212-836-8689
Web Site: www.kayescholer.com

2016 Total Lawyers: 400
2015 Total Lawyers: 394

Kelley Drye & Warren LLP

101 Park Avenue
New York, NY 10178
Phone: 212-808-7800
Fax: 212-808-7897
Web Site: www.kelleydrye.com

2016 Total Lawyers: 300
2015 Total Lawyers: 300

Kenyon & Kenyon LLP

One Broadway
New York, NY 10004-1007
Phone: 212-425-7200
Fax: 212-425-5288
Email: info@kenyon.com
Web Site: www.kenyon.com

2016 Total Lawyers: 56
2015 Total Lawyers: 123

Kramer Levin Naftalis & Frankel LLP

1177 Avenue of the Americas
New York, NY 10036
Phone: 212-715-9100
Fax: 212-715-8000
Email: marketing@kramerlevin.com
Web Site: www.kramerlevin.com

2016 Total Lawyers: 345
2015 Total Lawyers: 375

Ladas & Parry LLP

1040 Avenues of the Americas
New York, NY 10018
Phone: 212-708-1800
Fax: 212-246-8959
Web Site: www.ladas.com

2016 Total Lawyers: 57
2015 Total Lawyers: 59

Latham & Watkins

885 Third Ave
New York, NY 10022-4834
Phone: 212-906-1200
Fax: 212-751-4864
Email: webmaster@lw.com
Web Site: www.lw.com

2016 Total Lawyers: 2300
2015 Total Lawyers: 2000

Lester, Schwab, Katz & Dwyer

100 Wall Street 27th Floor
New York, NY 10005-3701
Phone: 212-964-6611
Fax: 212-267-5916
Web Site: www.lskdnylaw.com

2016 Total Lawyers: 59
2015 Total Lawyers: 59

Mendes & Mount, LLP

750 Seventh Avenue
New York, NY 10019-6829
Phone: 212-261-8000
Fax: 212-261-8750
Email: info@mendes.com
Web Site: www.mendes.com

2016 Total Lawyers: 84
2015 Total Lawyers: 84

Milbank, Tweed, Hadley & McCloy

1 Chase Manhattan Plaza
New York, NY 10005-1413
Phone: 212-530-5000
Fax: 212-530-5219
Web Site: www.milbank.com

2016 Total Lawyers: 659
2015 Total Lawyers: 623

Milberg LLP

One Pennsylvania Plaza
49th Floor
New York, NY 10119-0165
Phone: 212-594-5300
Fax: 212-868-1229
Web Site: www.milberg.com

2016 Total Lawyers: 37
2015 Total Lawyers: 45

Morgan Lewis & Bockius

101 Park Ave
New York, NY 10178-0060
Phone: 212-309-6000
Fax: 212-309-6001
Email: info@morganlewis.com
Web Site: www.morganlewis.com

2016 Total Lawyers: 1876
2015 Total Lawyers: 1862

Morrison Cohen LLP

909 Third Ave
New York, NY 10022
Phone: 212-735-8600
Fax: 212-735-8708
Web Site: www.morrisoncohen.com

2016 Total Lawyers: 102
2015 Total Lawyers: 96

2016 Staff
Equity Partners: 42
Non-Equity Partners: 22
Associates: 34
Of Counsel: 1
Senior Counsel: 3

Offices: No. Attys.
New York, NY: 102

Hiring and Promotion
2015 Associates Hired: 12
2016 First-Year Hires (Est.): 0
2015 Equity Partners Named: 0

Leading Officials
David A. Scherl, Chairman and
Managing Partner
Stephen Long, Director of Marketing

Moses & Singer LLP

The Chrysler Building
405 Lexington Avenue, #12
New York, NY 10174
Phone: 212-554-7800
Fax: 212-554-7700
Web Site: www.mosessinger.com

2016 Total Lawyers: 97
2015 Total Lawyers: 87

2016 Staff
Senior Attorneys: 51
Counsel: 13
Staff Attorneys: 23

Offices: No. Attys.
New York, NY: 100

Leading Practice Areas
(Department Heads)
Litigation 33% (Jay Fialkoff 212-554-7850)
Corporate 20% (Dean Swagert
212-554-7816)
Entertainment 20% (Eric Bergner
212-554-7855)
Banking 15% (Michael Avidon
212-554-7854)
Bankruptcy 8% (Alan Kolod 212-554-7866)
Tax/Trust & Estate 4% (Gideon Rothschild
212-554-7806)

Moses & Singer LLP (Continued)

Leading Officials
Jay Fialkoff, Managing Partner,
212-554-7850
Alan Kolod, Chairman, 212-554-7866
Mark Parry, Hiring Partner, 212-554-7876
Vincent Mazzocco, Administrator,
212-554-7571
Eileen Alterbaum, Marketing Manager,
212-554-7583
Eddie Rivera, MIS Director, 212-554-7555
Maria Osterman, Head Librarian,
212-554-7560

Other Offices
The Chrysler Building
405 Lexington Avenue
New York, NY 10174-1299
Phone: 212-554-7800
Fax: 212-554-7700

Mound, Cotton, Wollan & Greengrass

One Battery Park Plaza
24 Whitehall Street
New York, NY 10004
Phone: 212-804-4200
Fax: 212-344-8066

2016 Total Lawyers: 86
2015 Total Lawyers: 94

Nixon Peabody LLP

437 Madison Avenue
New York, NY 10022
Phone: 212-940-3000
Fax: 212-940-3111
Email: nixonpeabody@nixonpeabody
Web Site: www.nixonpeabody.com

2016 Total Lawyers: 700
2015 Total Lawyers: 672

Olshan, Frome & Wolosky LLP

Park Avenue Tower
65 East 55th St
New York, NY 10022
Phone: 212-451-2300
Fax: 212-451-2222
Web Site: www.olshanlaw.com

2016 Total Lawyers: 87
2015 Total Lawyers: 86

Otterbourg PC

230 Park Avenue
New York, NY 10169
Phone: 212-661-9100
Fax: 212-682-6104
Web Site: www.otterbourg.com

2016 Total Lawyers: 50
2015 Total Lawyers: 51

Patterson Belknap Webb & Tyler

1133 Avenue of the Americas
New York, NY 10036
Phone: 212-336-2000
Fax: 212-336-2222
Email: info@pbwt.com
Web Site: www.pbwt.com

2016 Total Lawyers: 192
2015 Total Lawyers: 200

2016 Staff
Equity Partners: 53
Associates: 130
Of Counsel: 5
Counsel: 10
Staff Attorneys: 2

Offices: No. Attys.
New York, NY: 200

Hiring and Promotion
2015 Associates Hired: 16
2015 First-Year Hires: 14
Starting Salary for First-Year
Assocs: $160,000
2016 First-Year Hires (Est.): 17
including clerks
2015 Equity Partners Named: 3
2015 Lateral Equity Partners: 1

Leading Officials
William F. Cavanaugh, Jr. and Lisa E.
Cleary, Co-Chairs
Lisa E. Cleary, Managing Partner
Michael J. Greis, Executive Director
Robert W. Lehrburger, Hiring Partner
Robin L. Klum, Director of Professional
Development
Lisa Smith, Deputy Executive Director &
Director of Client Relations
Robert Holloway, Director of
Information Services
Edward Brandweis, Head Librarian
Peter C. Harvey, Travis J. Tu, and Richard R.
Upton, Co-Chairs, Diversity Committee

Paul, Weiss, Rifkind, Wharton & Garrison LLP

1285 Avenue of the Americas
New York, NY 10019-6064
Phone: 212-373-3000
Fax: 212-757-3990
Email: mailbox@paulweiss.com
Web Site: www.paulweiss.com

2016 Total Lawyers: 817
2015 Total Lawyers: 741

Phillips Lytle LLP

One Canalside
125 Main Street
Buffalo, NY 14203-2887
Phone: 716-847-8400
Fax: 716-852-6100
Email: info@phillipslytle.com
Web Site: www.phillipslytle.com

2016 Total Lawyers: 185
2015 Total Lawyers: 186

2016 Staff
Equity Partners: 76
Non-Equity Partners: 6
Associates: 44
Of Counsel: 36
Senior Attorneys: 19
Counsel: 3
Senior Counsel: 1

Offices: No. Attys.
Buffalo, NY: 126
Rochester, NY: 24
Jamestown, NY: 4
New York City: 16
Garden City, NY: 2
Albany, NY: 5
Kitchener Ontario Canada: 2
Washington, DC: 6

Hiring and Promotion
2015 Associates Hired: 14
2015 First-Year Hires: 8
Starting Salary for First-Year
   Assocs: $100,000
2016 First-Year Hires (Est.): 6
2015 Equity Partners Named: 6
2015 Lateral Equity Partners: 1

Leading Practice Areas
(Department Heads)
Litigation (Defense) 23% (Kevin J. English
   716-847-5447)
Medical Device/Pharmaceuticals 22%
   (Tamar P. Halpern 716-847-5441)
Banking & Financial Services 15% (Deborah
   A. Doxey 585-238-2058)
Corporate 12% (David J. Murray
   716-847-5453)
Real Estate 12% (Albert M. Mercury
   585-238-2031)
Telecommunications 5% (Douglas W.
   Dimitroff 716-847-5408)
Health Law 3% (William P. Keefer
   716-847-5488)
Family Wealth Planning 3% (Sharon L. Wick
   716-847-7025)
Bankruptcy & Creditors' Rights 2% (William
   J. Brown 716-847-7089)
Labor & Employment 2% (Linda T.
   Prestegaard 585-238-2029)
Environmental 2% (David P. Flynn
   716-847-5473)

Client Representations
Ford Motor Credit Company
DuPont
AT&T

Phillips Lytle LLP (Continued)

Leading Officials
David J. McNamara, Managing Partner,
   716-847-5457
Brian H. Eckert, Executive Director,
   716-847-7087
Sandra E. Langs, Human Resources and
   Professional Development Director,
   212-508-0463
Sandra E. Langs, Human Resources and
   Professional Development Director,
   212-508-0463
Rebecca E. Farbo, Chief Marketing Officer,
   716-847-8307
David M. Powers Jr., Director of IT,
   716-504-5787
Kristine D. Westphal, Information Services
   Manager, Library, 716-847-5470
Sandra E. Langs, Human Resources and
   Professional Development Director,
   212-508-0463

Other Offices
Buffalo
   One Canalside, 125 Main Street
   Buffalo
   NY
   14203-2887
Phone: 716-847-8400
Fax: 716-852-6100
Email: info@phillipslytle.com
David J. McNamara, Managing Partner

Phillips Nizer LLP

666 Fifth Avenue
New York, NY 10103-0084
Phone: 212-977-9700
Fax: 212-262-5152
Web Site: www.phillipsnizer.com

2016 Total Lawyers: 68
2015 Total Lawyers: 68

2016 Staff
Equity Partners: 17
Non-Equity Partners: 19
Associates: 8
Counsel: 14
Senior Counsel: 10

Offices: No. Attys.
New York, NY: 63
Garden City, NY: 2
Hackensack, NJ: 2
East Hampton: 1

Hiring and Promotion
2015 Associates Hired: 3
2015 First-Year Hires: 1
2016 First-Year Hires (Est.): 0
2015 Equity Partners Named: 2
2015 Lateral Equity Partners: 2

Phillips Nizer LLP (Continued)

Leading Practice Areas
(Department Heads)
General Commercial Litigation 24%
   (Mark Elliot)
Corporate/Securities - General 15%
   (Monte Engler)
Wills, Trusts, Estates & Probate 14%
   (Donald Perry)
Commercial/Residential Real Estate 13%
   (Marc Landis)
Domestic Relations/Family Law 11%
   (Elliot Wiener)
Tax 5% (Tiberio Schwartz)
Labor & Employment 5% (Marc
   Zimmerman)
Intellectual Property 4% (Thomas
   Jackson/Barry Fishkin)
Environmental 2% (Martin
   Wasser/Jon Brooks)
International Law 1% (Michael Galligan)

Leading Officials
Marc A. Landis / Perry S. Galler, Managing
   Partner / Administrative Partner,
   212-977-9700
Mark A. Landis, Managing Partner,
   212-977-9700
Mary Jane Craig, Human Resources Director,
   212-977-9700
Stacy Salmon, Marketing Director,
   212-977-9700
Diane Dangolovich, IT Director,
   212-977-9700
Mark Schwartz, Head Librarian,
   212-977-9700
Michael Galligan, Partner, 212-977-9700

Other Offices
666 Fifth Avenue
New York, NY 10103-0084
Phone: 212-977-9700
Fax: 212-262-5152
Email: mlandis@phillipsnizer.com
Marc A. Landis, Managing Partner

Pillsbury Winthrop Shaw Pittman LLP

1540 Broadway
New York, NY 10036-4039
Phone: 212-858-1000
Fax: 212-858-1500
Email: info@pillsburylaw.com
Web Site: www.pillsburylaw.com

2016 Total Lawyers: 700
2015 Total Lawyers: 667

Proskauer Rose LLP

11 Times Square
8th Avenue & 41st Street
New York, NY 10036-8299
Phone: 212-969-3000
Fax: 212-969-2900
Web Site: www.proskauer.com

2016 Total Lawyers: 700
2015 Total Lawyers: 700

NEW YORK

Pryor Cashman LLP

7 Times Square
New York, NY 10036-6569
Phone: 212-421-4100
Fax: 212-326-0806
Web Site: www.pryorcashman.com

2016 Total Lawyers: 144
2015 Total Lawyers: 144

2016 Staff
Associates: 48
Of Counsel: 11
Counsel: 3
Senior Counsel: 3
Partners: 79

Offices: No. Attys.
New York City: 138
Los Angeles: 6

Hiring and Promotion
2015 Associates Hired: 10
2016 First-Year Hires (Est.): 2
2015 Lateral Equity Partners: 6

Leading Practice Areas
(Department Heads)
Litigation 60% (Donald S. Zakarin
212-326-0108)
Entertainment, Media and Communications
30% (James A. Janowitz 212-326-0873)
Intellectual Property 20% (Brad D. Rose
212-326-0875)
Real Estate 20% (Wayne B. Heicklen
212-326-0854)
Labor & Employment, Executive
Compensation, ERISA and Employee
Benefits 15% (Ronald H. Shechtman,
Edward J. Rayner 212-326-0102,
212-326-0110)
Family Law 15% (Judith Poller
212-326-0130)
Corporate, Banking & Finance 10% (Eric M.
Hellige, Lawrence Remmel 212-326-0846,
212-326-0881)
Immigration Law 10% (Colleen L. Caden
212-326-0147)
Bankruptcy, Reorganization and Creditors
Rights 5% (Richard Levy, Jr.
212-326-0886)
Tax, Trust & Estates 5% (Eric B.
Woldenberg, Richard L. Kay
212-326-0865, 212-326-0844)

Client Representations
Pryor Cashman represented approximately
two dozen actors from the hit Broadway
musical "Hamilton" in a deal that will bring
the original cast members a share of the
smash musical's profits.
Pryor Cashman Wins Appeal For Devon Aoki
and Steven Aoki In Trust Dispute
Regarding Benihana Assets
Pryor Cashman Wins Second Circuit Appeal
In Significant Art Law Case Involving
Egon Schiele Drawing - October 11, 2012
- Law360

Pryor Cashman LLP (Continued)

Leading Officials
Gideon Cashman, Chairman, 212-326-0172
Ronald H. Shechtman, Managing Partner,
212-326-0102
Susan Locker, Executive Director,
212-326-0124
Philip R. Hoffman, Hiring Partner,
212-326-0192
Oris Diaz, Lateral Recruiting Manager,
212-326-0434
Michael Mellor, Director of Marketing,
212-326-0176
SAME AS ABOVE
Michael L. Cannizzaro, Director of
Information Technology, 212-326-0420
Celia M. Mondesir, Librarian, 212-326-0135

Rivkin Radler LLP

926 RXR Plaza
Uniondale, NY 11556-0111
Phone: 516-357-3000
Fax: 516-357-3333
Web Site: www.rivkinradler.com

2016 Total Lawyers: 165
2015 Total Lawyers: 152

Roberts & Holland LLP

Worldwide Plaza
825 Eighth Avenue
New York, NY 10019-7416
Phone: 212-903-8700
Fax: 212-974-3059
Web Site: www.robertsandholland.com

2016 Total Lawyers: 35
2015 Total Lawyers: 32

Ropes & Gray LLP

1211 Avenue of the Americas
New York, NY 10036
Phone: 212-596-9000
Fax: 212-596-9090
Email: contactus@ropesgray.com
Web Site: www.ropesgray.com

2016 Total Lawyers: 1257
2015 Total Lawyers: 1266

2016 Staff
Equity Partners: 313
Associates: 803
Senior Attorneys: 26
Counsel: 67
Senior Counsel: 4
Staff Attorneys: 20
Legal Counsultants 12
Senior Career Associates 12

Offices: No. Attys.
Boston, MA: 541
New York, NY: 294
Washington, DC: 80
Silicon Valley, CA: 36
San Francisco, CA: 58
Chicago, IL: 56

Ropes & Gray LLP (Continued)
Hong Kong: 48
London, England: 112
Tokyo, Japan: 13
Shanghai, China: 22
Seoul, South Korea: 6

Hiring and Promotion
Starting Salary for First-Year
Assocs: $160,000

Leading Practice Areas
(Department Heads)
Intellectual Property Litigation
Private Equity Transactions
Government Enforcement
Finance
Intellectual Property Rights Management
Investment Management
Business & Securities Litigation
Tax
Health Care
Securities & Public Companies

Revenues and Profits
Revenues: $1,390,000,000

Leading Officials
R. Bradford Malt, Chair
David Chapin, Managing Partner
Richard Batchelder, Hiring Partner
Marijane Benner Browne, Director of Lateral
Partner Recruitment
Timothy Larimer, Chief of Marketing
Communications
Andrew Murray-Brown, Chief Business
Development Officer
Marsha Stein, Chief Information Officer
Tracy Brown, Diversity Manager

Other Offices
Washington, DC
2099 Pennsylvania Avenue NW
Washington, DC
20006
Phone: 202-508-4600
Fax: 202-508-4650
Douglas Hallward-Driemeier

London
60 Ludgate Hill
London
EC4M 7AW
Phone: 203-122-1100
Fax: 203-122-1101
Michael Goetz

San Francisco
Three Embarcadero Center
San Francisco
CA
94111-4006
Phone: 415-315-6300
Fax: 415-315-6350
Rick Gallagher

Chicago
191 North Wacker Drive
32nd Floor
Chicago
IL
60606
Phone: 312-845-1200
Fax: 312-845-5500
Asheesh Goel

NEW YORK

Ropes & Gray LLP (Continued)

Boston
800 Boylston Street
Boston
MA
02199
Phone: 617-951-7000
Fax: 617-951-7050
R. Newcomb Stillwell & Diane Patrick

Schulte Roth & Zabel LLP

919 Third Avenue
New York, NY 10022-3902
Phone: 212-756-2000
Fax: 212-756-5955
Web Site: www.srz.com

2016 Total Lawyers: 357
2015 Total Lawyers: 347

2016 Staff
Equity Partners: 93
Associates: 193
Of Counsel: 9
Counsel: 54
Staff Attorneys: 7
Visiting Attorney 1

Offices: No. Attys.
New York, NY: 319
Washington, DC: 20
London, England: 18

Hiring and Promotion
2015 Associates Hired: 60
2015 First-Year Hires: 35
2015 Equity Partners Named: 8
2015 Lateral Equity Partners: 8

Leading Practice Areas
(Department Heads)
Corporate - Investment Management (Paul N. Roth 212-756-2450)
Litigation (Robert Abrahams/Martin L. Perschetz/Howard Schiffman 212-756-2355 212-756-2247 202-729-7461)
Corporate - M&A and Securities Group (John M. Pollack/Richard A. Presutti 212-756-2372 212-756-2063)
Corporate - Finance (Frederic L. Ragucci 212-756-2409)
Business Reorganization (Adam C. Harris 212-756-2253)
Individual Client Services (William D. Zabel 212-756-2351)
Real Estate (Jeffrey A. Lenobel 212-756-2444)
Employment & Employee Benefits (Mark E. Brossman/Ronald E. Richman 212-756-2050 212-756-2048)
Environmental (Howard B. Epstein 212-756-2596)
Corporate - Str. Finance & Derivatives Group (Craig Stein/Paul N. Watterson/Boris Ziser 212-756-2390 212-756-2563 212-756-2140)

Revenues and Profits
Revenues: $405,500,000
Profits: $198,000,000

Schulte Roth & Zabel LLP (Continued)

Client Representations
Advised Orchard Brands Corporation in its acquisition by holding company Capmark Financial Group Inc. (now known as Bluestem Group Inc.) for $410M in cash.
Represented 170 former partners of Dewey & LeBoeuf LLP in a victory in a major lawsuit brought by a past landlord for over $200 million.
Represented Oxford Properties Group in the closing of over $5B in financing for flagship office tower 30 Hudson Yards & the 650,000-square-foot Shops & Restaurants at Hudson Yards, a $15B NYC project.

Leading Officials
Brian F. Schare, Chief Operating Officer, 212-756-2386
Alissa K. Golden, Director of Legal Recruiting, 212-610-7185
Linda C. Sparn, Director of Marketing & Business Development, 212-610-7409
Will McDonald, Director of Information Technology, 212-610-7057
Bryn Bowen, Director of Information Services, 212-610-7139
Taleah Jennings, Partner, 212-756-2454

Seward & Kissel LLP

One Battery Park Plaza
New York, NY 10004
Phone: 212-574-1200
Fax: 212-480-8421
Email: sknyc@sewkis.com
Web Site: www.sewkis.com

2016 Total Lawyers: 171
2015 Total Lawyers: 153

Shearman & Sterling LLP

599 Lexington Avenue
New York, NY 10022
Phone: 212-848-4000
Fax: 212-848-7179
Web Site: www.shearman.com

2016 Total Lawyers: 850
2015 Total Lawyers: 850

Simpson Thacher & Bartlett LLP

425 Lexington Avenue
New York, NY 10017
Phone: 212-455-2000
Fax: 212-455-2502
Web Site: www.simpsonthacher.com

2016 Total Lawyers: 958
2015 Total Lawyers: 865

2016 Staff
Equity Partners: 187
Associates: 601
Counsel: 83

Offices: No. Attys.
Palo Alto, CA: 76

Simpson Thacher & Bartlett LLP (Continued)
London, England: 95
Hong Kong: 36
Los Angeles, CA: 28
Tokyo, Japan: 11
Washington, DC: 49
Sao Paulo, Brazil: 5
Beijing, China: 9
Houston, TX: 19
Seoul, South Korea: 5
New York, NY: 627

Hiring and Promotion
2015 Associates Hired: 171
2015 First-Year Hires: 121
Starting Salary for First-Year Assocs: $180,000
2016 First-Year Hires (Est.): 123
2015 Equity Partners Named: 9

Leading Practice Areas
(Department Heads)
Corporate 54%
Litigation 35%

Revenues and Profits
Revenues: $1,278,151,846
Profits: $648,182,986

Client Representations
JPMorgan Chase
Blackstone
Kohlberg Kravis Roberts

Leading Officials
William R. Dougherty, Chairman, Executive Committee
Alden Millard; Lynn Neuner, Administrative Partners
Michael Hersch, Executive Director
Gregory T. Grogan, Lori E. Lesser and Elizabeth A. Cooper, Co-Chairs, Recruiting
Amy Claydon, Director, Legal Recruiting
Danzey Burnham, Chief of Global Business Development
Michael Donnelly, Chief Information Officer
Sheila Sterling, Director, Library
Natalia Martin, Director of Diversity

Other Offices
2475 Hanover Street
Palo Alto
CA
94304
Phone: 650-251-5000
Fax: 650-251-5002
Jeff Ostrow

CityPoint
One Ropemaker Street
London
England
EC2Y 9HU
Phone: +44-020-7275 ext. 6500
Fax: +44-020-7275 ext. 6502
Gregory Conway

Skadden, Arps, Slate, Meagher & Flom LLP and Affiliates

Four Times Square
New York, NY 10036
Phone: 212-735-3000
Fax: 212-735-2000
Email: info@skadden.com
Web Site: www.skadden.com

2016 Total Lawyers: 1700
2015 Total Lawyers: 1700

Stroock & Stroock & Lavan LLP

180 Maiden Lane
New York, NY 10038-4982
Phone: 212-806-5400
Fax: 212-806-6006
Web Site: www.stroock.com

2016 Total Lawyers: 305
2015 Total Lawyers: 289

2016 Staff
Equity Partners: 93
Associates: 98
Of Counsel: 22
Senior Attorneys: 43
Senior Counsel: 49

Offices: No. Attys.
Los Angeles, CA: 36
Miami, FL: 25
Washington, DC: 20
New York, NY: 224

Hiring and Promotion
2015 Associates Hired: 44
2015 First-Year Hires: 14
Starting Salary for First-Year Assocs:
  $160,000 (New York)
2016 First-Year Hires (Est.): 14
2015 Equity Partners Named: 10
2015 Lateral Equity Partners: 6

Stroock & Stroock & Lavan LLP (Continued)

Leading Practice Areas
(Department Heads)
Litigation 26% (Alan M. Klinger, Charles G. Moerdler 212-806-5818, 212-806-3648)
Corporate 24% (Stuart H. Coleman 212-806-6049)
Real Estate 20% (Brian Diamond, Leonard Boxer, Jeffrey R. Keitelman 212-806-5569, 212-806-5565, 202-739-2810)
Financial Restructuring 10% (Kristopher M. Hansen 212-806-6056)
Intellectual Property 6% (Steven B. Pokotilow 212-806-6663)
Financial Services Litigation 4% (Julia B. Strickland 310-556-5806)
Tax 4% (Jeffrey D. Uffner 212-806-6001)
Employment Law and Benefits 2% (Howard S. Lavin, Steven W. Rabitz 212-806-6046, 212-806-6568)
National Security/CFIUS/Compliance 2% (Chris Griner 202-739-2850)
Personal Client Services 2% (Anita S. Rosenbloom 212-806-6026)

Revenues and Profits
Revenues: $266,700,000

Client Representations
JP Morgan
Goldman Sachs & Co.
AIG

Leading Officials
Stuart H. Coleman, Co-Managing Partner, 212-806-6049
Alan M. Klinger, Co-Managing Partner, 212-806-5818
Steven Gamesik, Executive Director, 212-806-5757
Claude G. Szyfer, Hiring Partner, 212-806-5934
Halle Schargel, Director of Legal Personnel, 212-806-6640
Brian J. Kegelman, Assistant Director of Communications, 212-806-5772
Kermit Wallace, Chief Information Officer, 212-806-6089
Anita S. Rosenbloom, Chair of Diversity Committee, 212-806-6026

Sullivan & Cromwell

125 Broad Street
New York, NY 10041
Phone: 212-558-4000
Fax: 212-558-3588
Email: fergusc@sullcrom.com
Web Site: www.sullcrom.com

2016 Total Lawyers: 797
2015 Total Lawyers: 800

Weil, Gotshal & Manges LLP

767 Fifth Avenue
New York, NY 10153-0119
Phone: 212-310-8000
Fax: 212-310-8007
Web Site: www.weil.com

2016 Total Lawyers: 1100
2015 Total Lawyers: 1100

White & Case LLP

1155 Avenue of the Americas
New York, NY 10036-2787
Phone: 212-819-8200
Fax: 212-354-8113
Web Site: www.whitecase.com

2016 Total Lawyers: 1990
2015 Total Lawyers: 1860

Willkie Farr & Gallagher

787 Seventh Avenue
New York, NY 10019-6099
Phone: 212-728-8000
Fax: 212-728-8111
Web Site: www.willkie.com

2016 Total Lawyers: 650
2015 Total Lawyers: 650

Wilson, Elser, Moskowitz, Edelman & Dicker LLP

150 East 42nd Street
New York, NY 10017
Phone: 212-490-3000
Fax: 212-490-3038
Email: info@wilsonelser.com
Web Site: wilsonelser.com

2016 Total Lawyers: 818
2015 Total Lawyers: 785

Windels Marx Lane & Mittendorf, LLP

156 West 56th Street
New York, NY 10019
Phone: 212-237-1000
Fax: 212-262-1215
Email: wmlm@windelsmarx.com
Web Site: windelsmarx.com.

2016 Total Lawyers: 136
2015 Total Lawyers: 135

Moore & Van Allen PLLC

100 N. Tryon Street
Suite 4700
Charlotte, NC 28202
Phone: 704-331-1000
Fax: 704-331-1159
Web Site: www.mvalaw.com

2016 Total Lawyers: 291
2015 Total Lawyers: 282

2016 Staff
Equity Partners: 79
Non-Equity Partners: 86
Associates: 75
Of Counsel: 5
Counsel: 34
Staff Attorneys: 12

Offices: No. Attys.
Charlotte, NC: 247
Research Triangle Park, NC: 13
Charleston, SC: 31

Hiring and Promotion
2015 Associates Hired: 18
2015 First-Year Hires: 10
2016 First-Year Hires (Est.): 8
2015 Equity Partners Named: 4
2015 Lateral Equity Partners: 2

*Leading Practice Areas
(Department Heads)*
Financial Services (James W. Hovis &
Thomas L. Mitchell 704-331-1047 &
704-331-1086)
Business (E. Beauregarde Fisher III & Jeremy
H. Godwin 704-331-1006 &
704-331-3520)
Litigation (Alton L. Gwaltney, Scott M. Tyler
& David E. Fox 704-331-1008,
704-331-2463 & 919-286-8069)
Information Technology & E-commerce
(Henry B. Ward, III 704-331-3566)
Tax & Estates (Neill G. McBryde
704-331-1094)
Commercial Real Estate (Jeffrey W. Glenney
& B. Palmer McArthur 704-331-1016 &
704-331-3545)
Taxation (William H. Moore, Jr.
704-331-1052)
Bankruptcy & Restructuring (David L. Eades
704-331-1044)
International (Scott D. Syfert 704-331-1138)
Intellectual Property (Dickson M. Lupo,
Arlene D. Hanks 704-331-3589,
919-286-8078)

Moore & Van Allen PLLC (Continued)

Leading Officials
Ernest W. Reigel, Chairman
Jim Hovis & Arlene Hanks & Don Meyer,
Managing Partners
Matt Gillespie, Executive Director
Amy Johnson, Carolyn Meade, Mark Nebrig,
Hiring Partners
Patti Oswald, Director of Human Resources
and Professional Recruiting
Nancy Smith, Marketing Director & Co-Head
of Public Affairs
Walter Price, Managing Director & Co-Head
of Public Affairs
William Ferguson, Director of
Information Systems
Tamara Acevedo, Manager of Research &
Knowledgement Management
Valecia McDowell, Amy Johnson,
Member, Member

Parker Poe Adams & Bernstein LLP

Three Wells Fargo Center
401 South Tryon Street, Suite 3000
Charlotte, NC 28202
Phone: 704-372-9000
Fax: 704-334-4706
Email: info@parkerpoe.com
Web Site: www.parkerpoe.com

2016 Total Lawyers: 200
2015 Total Lawyers: 200

Poyner Spruill LLP

301 Fayetteville Street, Suite 1900
Raleigh, NC 27601
Phone: 919-783-6400
Fax: 919-783-1075
Email: contact@poyners.com
Web Site: www.poynerspruill.com

2016 Total Lawyers: 94
2015 Total Lawyers: 104

Robinson Bradshaw

101 North Tryon Street
Suite 1900
Charlotte, NC 28246
Phone: 704-377-2536
Fax: 704-378-4000
Web Site: www.robinsonbradshaw.com

2016 Total Lawyers: 127
2015 Total Lawyers: 127

2016 Staff
Equity Partners: 90
Associates: 25
Of Counsel: 12

Offices: No. Attys.
Charlotte, NC: 113
Rock Hill, SC: 3
Chapel Hill, NC: 11

Robinson Bradshaw (Continued)

Hiring and Promotion
2015 Associates Hired: 6
2015 First-Year Hires: 3
2016 First-Year Hires (Est.): 4
2015 Equity Partners Named: 5

*Leading Practice Areas
(Department Heads)*
Antitrust and Trade Regulation (Lawrence C.
Moore III 704-377-8303)
Employment and Labor (Angelique R.
Vincent-Hamacher & Julian H. Wright Jr.
704-377-8357)
Finance and Capital Markets (Jeffrey A.
Henson 704-377-8342)
Health Care (Matthew S. Churchill & John B.
Garver III 704-377-8388)
Intellectual Property and Technology (Bob
Bryan & Kelly Luongo Loving
704-377-8310)
Complex Commercial Litigation (Robert E.
Harrington 704-377-8387)
Mergers and Acquisitions (Mark O. Henry
704-377-8128)
Private Equity (Mark O. Henry
704-377-8128)
Public Finance (Alice Pinckney Adams
704-377-8393)
Real Estate Development and Finance (T.
Thomas Gates 704-377-8360)

Client Representations
EnPro Industries, Inc.
Fresenius Medical Care North America
Wells Fargo & Company

Leading Officials
Allen K. Robertson, Managing Partner,
704-377-8368
Alan K. Menius, Executive Director,
704-377-8315
Henry H. Ralston & Adam K. Doerr, Hiring
Partner, 704-377-8313
Susan K. Floyd, Attorney Recruiting
Administrator, 704-377-8141
Chantal Sheaffer, Marketing
Communications Manager, 704-377-8161
Geoffrey S. Rhodes, Director of Information
Technology, 704-377-8188
Stephanie Nance, Director of Library
Services, 704-350-7171
D. Blaine Sanders, Chair, Diversity and
Inclusion Committee, 704-377-8344

Other Offices
Charlotte Office
101 N. Tryon Street
1900
Charlotte
NC
28246
Phone: 704-377-2536
Fax: 704-378-4000

NORTH CAROLINA

Smith, Anderson, Blount, Dorsett, Mitchell & Jernigan, LLP

150 Fayetteville Street, Suite 2300
P. O. Box 2611
Raleigh, NC 27602-2611
Phone: 919-821-1220
Fax: 919-821-6800
Email: info@smithlaw.com
Web Site: smithlaw.com

2016 Total Lawyers: 128
2015 Total Lawyers: 125

Smith Moore Leatherwood LLP

300 North Greene Street
Suite 1400
Greensboro, NC 27401
Phone: 336-378-5200
Fax: 336-378-5400

2016 Total Lawyers: 216
2015 Total Lawyers: 218

Ward and Smith, P.A.

1001 College Court
Post Office Box 867
New Bern, NC 28563-0867
Phone: 252-672-5400
Fax: 252-672-5477
Web Site: www.wardandsmith.com

2016 Total Lawyers: 91
2015 Total Lawyers: 92

2016 Staff
Equity Partners: 44
Associates: 23
Counsel: 24

Offices: No. Attys.
Greenville, NC: 17
Wilmington, NC: 15
Raleigh, NC: 23
New Bern, NC: 24
Asheville, NC: 11

Hiring and Promotion
2015 Associates Hired: 5
2016 First-Year Hires (Est.): 0
2015 Equity Partners Named: 2

Ward and Smith, P.A. (Continued)

Leading Practice Areas
(Department Heads)
Litigation 36% (William S. Durr
  828-348-6062)
Business Law 26% (Lee C. Hodge
  252-672-5430)
Trusts and Estates 14% (John R. Sloan
  910-794-4805)
Creditors' Rights 10% (Paul A. Fanning
  252-215-4027)
Real Estate 6% (Samuel B. Franck
  910-794-4835)
Intellectual Property 5% (Angela P. Doughty
  252-672-5471)
Labor and Employment 3% (S. McKinley
  Gray, III 252-672-5476)

Client Representations
First-Citizens Bank & Trust Company
Hewlett-Packard
Johns Hopkins Technology Transfer

Leading Officials
A. Charles Ellis and Kenneth R. Wooten,
  Managing Directors, 252-672-5452
Michael R. Epperson, Executive Director and
  Chief Operating Officer, 252-672-5483
Teresa R. Harper, Human Resources
  Coordinator, 252-672-5540
Laura V. Hudson, Director of Marketing and
  Business Development, 919-277-9118
Christopher S. Romano, Chief Information
  Officer, 252-672-5494
Whitney A. Beal, Library Coordinator,
  252-672-5508
Michael D. Christman, Director of Human
  Resources, 252-672-5551

Womble Carlyle Sandridge & Rice, PLLC

One West Fourth Street
Winston-Salem, NC 27101
Phone: 336-721-3600
Web Site: www.wcsr.com

2016 Total Lawyers: 550
2015 Total Lawyers: 550

OHIO

Baker & Hostetler LLP

Cleveland, OH
Web Site: www.bakerlaw.com

2016 Total Lawyers: 950
2015 Total Lawyers: 900

Benesch, Friedlander, Coplan & Aronoff LLP

200 Public Square
Suite 2300
Cleveland, OH 44114-2378
Phone: 216-363-4500
Fax: 216-363-4588
Web Site: www.beneschlaw.com

2016 Total Lawyers: 176
2015 Total Lawyers: 140

2016 Staff
Equity Partners: 53
Non-Equity Partners: 54
Associates: 61
Of Counsel: 9
Staff Attorneys: 3

Offices: No. Attys.
Cleveland, OH: 120
Columbus, OH: 25
Wilmington, DE: 8
Shanghai, China: 1
Indianapolis, IN: 18
Hackensack, NJ: 2

Hiring and Promotion
2015 Associates Hired: 19
2015 First-Year Hires: 5
Starting Salary for First-Year Assocs:
  $105,000 (Base Salary), $5,000 (Stipend)
2016 First-Year Hires (Est.): 5-6
2015 Equity Partners Named: 2
2015 Lateral Equity Partners: 1

Leading Practice Areas
(Department Heads)
Litigation 28% (Eric Zalud/Joe Castrodale
  216-363-4500)
Corporate 16% (Megan Mehalko/Rick
  Tracanna 216-363-4500)
Real Estate/Environmental 13% (Jeff Wild
  216-363-4500)
IP 9% (Mike Stovsky 216-363-4500)
Health Care 6% (Frank Carsonie
  614-223-9300)
Public Finance 5% (Stephen Grassbaugh
  614-223-9300)
Public Law 3% (Rob Zimmerman
  216-363-4500)
Labor & Employment 3% (Mike Buck/Eric
  Baisden 216-363-4500)
Commercial Finance 3% (Ross Kirchick
  216-363-4500)

Revenues and Profits
Revenues: $81,000,000
Profits: $26,900,000

OHIO

Benesch, Friedlander, Coplan & Aronoff LLP (Continued)

Leading Officials
Gregg Eisenberg, Managing Partner,
216-363-4500
John H. Banks, COO/CFO, 216-363-4526
Joe Tegreene, Hiring Committee Chair,
216-363-4643
Laura Dutt, Director of Talent Acquisition
and Development, 216-363-4500
Jeanne Hammerstrom, Chief Marketing and
Legal Recruiting Officer, 216-363-4500
Liz Boehm, Director of Business
Development, 216-363-4500
Jerry Justice, Chief Information Officer,
216-363-4432
Andrew Gates, Librarian, 216-363-4500

Other Offices
Cleveland, Ohio
200 Public Square
2300
Cleveland
OH
44114
Phone: 216-363-4500
Fax: 216-363-4588
Gregg Eisenberg

Bricker & Eckler, LLP

100 South Third Street
Columbus, OH 43215-4291
Phone: 614-227-2300
Fax: 614-227-2390
Email: info@bricker.com
Web Site: www.bricker.com

2016 Total Lawyers: 140
2015 Total Lawyers: 145

2016 Staff
Equity Partners: 64
Non-Equity Partners: 19
Associates: 36
Of Counsel: 3
Senior Attorneys: 8
Senior Counsel: 11
Staff Attorneys: 5

Offices: No. Attys.
Columbus, OH: 114
West Chester, OH: 14
Cleveland, OH: 7
Marietta, OH: 1

Hiring and Promotion
2015 Associates Hired: 8
2015 First-Year Hires: 2
Starting Salary for First-Year
Assocs: $110,000
2016 First-Year Hires (Est.): 6
2015 Equity Partners Named: 3
2015 Lateral Equity Partners: 1

Bricker & Eckler, LLP (Continued)

Leading Practice Areas
(Department Heads)
Health Care 16.6% (James Flynn
614-227-8855)
Litigation 15.3% (Nelson Reid
614-227-8812)
Real Estate 11.3% (Stephen Intihar
614-227-2376)
Regulated Industries 9.8% (Maria Armstrong
614-227-8821)
Education 9.3% (Laura Anthony
614-227-2366)
Public Finance 9.0% (Becky Princehorn
614-227-2302)
Business, Tax & Estates 8.9% (Tom
Washbush 614-227-7742)
Employment 7.4% (James G. Petrie
614-227-2373)
Construction 7.0% (Jack Rosati, Jr.
614-227-2321)
Creditor's Rights and Bankruptcy 4.0% (Ken
Johnson 614-227-2322)

Revenues and Profits
Revenues: $62,575,091
Profits: $24,249,560

Leading Officials
Kurt A. Tunnell, Managing Partner,
614-227-8837
Jim Hughes, Administrative Partner,
614-227-2365
Katherine Murphy, Chief Operating Officer,
614-227-2393
Natalie Furniss, Recruiting Committee Chair,
614-227-8918
Elizabeth K. Wetherby, Chief Human
Resources Officer, 614-227-8840
Carole Chidester, Director of Practice
Development, 614-227-8829
Ahmad Sinno, Chief Information Officer,
614-227-8882
Susan M. Lowe, Director of Library Services,
614-227-8845
Frank Merrill, Partner, 614-227-8871

Brouse McDowell

388 S. Main Street
Suite 500
Akron, OH 44311
Phone: 330-535-5711
Fax: 330-253-8601
Email: brouse@brouse.com
Web Site: www.brouse.com

2016 Total Lawyers: 74
2015 Total Lawyers: 77

Buckingham, Doolittle & Burroughs, LLC

3800 Embassy Parkway
Suite 300
Akron, OH 44333
Phone: 330-376-5300
Fax: 330-258-6559
Email: bdb@bdblaw.com
Web Site: www.bdblaw.com

2016 Total Lawyers: 66
2015 Total Lawyers: 64

2016 Staff
Equity Partners: 27
Non-Equity Partners: 21
Associates: 11
Of Counsel: 2
Staff Attorneys: 1
Contract Attorneys 2

Offices: No. Attys.
Canton, OH: 11
Cleveland, OH: 13
Akron, OH: 39

Hiring and Promotion
2015 Associates Hired: 1
2015 First-Year Hires: 1
Starting Salary for First-Year Assocs: Varies
2016 First-Year Hires (Est.): 1
2015 Equity Partners Named: 0

Leading Practice Areas
(Department Heads)
Litigation 35% (Patrick Keating)
Business 20% (Robert W. Malone)
Trusts & Estates 18% (David W. Woodburn)
Health & Medicine 13% (Dirk E.
Riemenschneider)
Real Estate & Construction 8% (Nicholas
T. George)
Employment & Labor 6% (Susan C. Rodgers)

Client Representations
Cleveland Clinic Health Systems
Red Bull North America
Struktol Company of America

Leading Officials
John P. Slagter, Managing Partner of Firm
David L. Drechsler (Cleveland); Joseph J.
Feltes (Canton); William L. Caplan
(Akron), Managing Partner
Timothy McEldowney , Chief
Financial Officer
Deborah Jordan, Director of
Information Systems
Tami Whiteleather, Human Resources &
Benefits Manager

OHIO

Calfee, Halter & Griswold LLP

The Calfee Building
1405 East 6th Street
Cleveland, OH 44114
Phone: 216-622-8200
Fax: 216-241-0816
Email: Info@calfee.com
Web Site: www.calfee.com

2016 Total Lawyers: 165
2015 Total Lawyers: 175

Climaco, Wilcox, Peca, Tarantino & Garofoli LPA

55 Public Square
Suite 1950
Cleveland, OH 44113
Phone: 216-621-8484
Fax: 216-771-1632
Web Site: www.climacolaw.com

2016 Total Lawyers: 11
2015 Total Lawyers: 11

Coolidge Wall

33 West First Street
Suite 600
Dayton, OH 45402
Phone: 937-223-8177
Fax: 937-223-6705
Email: coolinfo@coollaw.com
Web Site: coollaw.com

2016 Total Lawyers: 32
2015 Total Lawyers: 32

Crabbe, Brown & James

500 South Front St
Suite 1200
Columbus, OH 43215
Phone: 614-228-5511
Fax: 614-229-4559
Email: dmazzanti@cbjlawyers.com
Web Site: cbjlawyers.com

2016 Total Lawyers: 23
2015 Total Lawyers: 27

2016 Staff
Equity Partners: 10
Non-Equity Partners: 1
Associates: 6
Of Counsel: 5
Senior Attorneys: 1

Offices: No. Attys.
Columbus, Ohio: 23

Crabbe, Brown & James (Continued)

Hiring and Promotion
2015 Associates Hired: 1
2015 First-Year Hires: 1
Starting Salary for First-Year Assocs:
  $60,000 - $65,000
2016 First-Year Hires (Est.): 2
2015 Equity Partners Named: 1

Leading Practice Areas
(Department Heads)
Insurance 17%
General Litigation 17%
Workers Compensation 10%
Corporate Business Law 10%
Zoning/Real Estate 10%
Lobbying 10%
Corporate Governance 5%
Product Liability 5%
Trusts/Estates 5%
Employment Labor Law 5%
Bankruptcy 3%
Intellectual Property 3%

Revenues and Profits
Revenues: $6,500,000

Client Representations
National Fraternal Order of Police
The Ohio State University
Central Ohio Transit Authority

Leading Officials
Jeffrey M. Brown
Doreen Mazzanti, Operations Manager
Jeffrey M. Brown
Doreen Mazzanti
Jeffrey M. Brown
Doreen Mazzanti
Jeffrey M. Brown, Managing Partner

Dinsmore & Shohl LLP

255 East Fifth Street
Suite 1900
Cincinnati, OH 45202
Phone: 513-977-8200
Fax: 513-977-8141
Email: www.dinsmore.com
Web Site: www.dinsmore.com

2016 Total Lawyers: 621
2015 Total Lawyers: 572

2016 Staff
Equity Partners: 163
Non-Equity Partners: 160
Associates: 168
Of Counsel: 112
Staff Attorneys: 18

Offices: No. Attys.
Lexington, KY: 55
Columbus, OH: 74
Dayton, OH: 49
Charleston, WV: 26
Pittsburgh, PA: 33
Cincinnati, OH: 222
Morgantown, WV: 14
Wheeling, WV: 9
Frankfort, KY: 3
Washington, DC: 11

Dinsmore & Shohl LLP (Continued)
Philadelphia, PA: 8
Lewisburg, WV: 2
Chicago, IL: 16
Covington, KY: 4
Denver, CO: 9
Huntington WV: 30
Louisville, KY: 71
Ann Arbor, MI: 3
Mystic, CT: 1
Philadelphia Downtown, PA: 4
San Diego, CA: 4
Troy, MI: 13

Hiring and Promotion
2015 Associates Hired: 47
2015 First-Year Hires: 24
Starting Salary for First-Year
  Assocs: $115,000
2016 First-Year Hires (Est.): 22
2015 Equity Partners Named: 2

Leading Practice Areas
(Department Heads)
Tort and Environmental 17% (Linsey W.
  West/Timothy D. Hoffman 513-977-8358;
  937-449-2847)
Business Acquisitions & Securities 15%
  (Susan B. Zaunbrecher 513-977-8171)
Commercial Litigation 13% (Brian S.
  Sullivan 513-977-8233)
Tax, Benefits & Family Wealth Planning 9%
  (Ben F. Wells 513-977-8108)
Public Finance 9% (John Merchant/J.H.
  Mahaney 513-977-3224; 513-977-7320)
Employment 7% (Michael S. Glassman
  513-977-8255)
Real Estate Development, Leasing &
  Ownership 5% (Richard B. Tranter
  513-977-8684)
IP Licensing and Enforcement 4% (Joshua A.
  Lorentz 513-977-8564)
Healthcare, Lobbying & Public Policy 3%
  (Thomas W. Hess 614-227-4260)
Business Restructuring 3% (Kim Martin
  Lewis 513-977-8259)

Revenues and Profits
Revenues: $219,700,000
Profits: $97,500,000

Client Representations
Skechers, USA
Children's Hospital
Toyota

Leading Officials
George H. Vincent, Firm Chair - Board of
  Directors, 513-977-8367
George H. Vincent, Managing Partner,
  513-977-8367
Suellen Young, Executive Director,
  513-977-8257
Alan A. Abes, Recruiting Committee Chair,
  513-977-8149
Jennifer Stark, Director of Legal Recruitment,
  513-977-8488
Jennifer Davenport, Director of Marketing,
  513-977-8160
Juanene L. Wong, Chief Information Officer,
  513-977-8147
MaryJo Merkowitz, Librarian, 513-977-8146
Marty R. Dunn, Partner, 513-977-8209

OHIO

Dinsmore & Shohl LLP (Continued)

Other Offices
101 S.Fifth St.
2500 National City Tower
Louisville
KY
40202
Phone: 502-581-800
Fax: 502-581-8111
John Selent

191 West Nationwide Blvd
Suite 300
Columbus
OH
43215
Phone: 614-628-6880
Fax: 614-628-6890
Charles E. Tleknor III

Lexington Financial Center
250 W. Main St
Suite 1400
Lexington
Kentucky
40507
Phone: 859-425-1000
Fax: 859-425-1099
Chauncey Curtz

Eastman & Smith

P.O. Box 10032
One SeaGate, 24th Floor
Toledo, OH 43604-1558
Phone: 419-241-6000

2016 Total Lawyers: 70
2015 Total Lawyers: 76

Frost Brown Todd LLC

3300 Great American Tower
301 East Fourth Street
Cincinnati, OH 45202
Phone: 513-651-6800
Fax: 513-651-6981
Email: info@fbtlaw.com
Web Site: www.frostbrowntodd.com

2016 Total Lawyers: 489
2015 Total Lawyers: 470

2016 Staff
Equity Partners: 156
Non-Equity Partners: 150
Associates: 62
Senior Attorneys: 79
Staff Attorneys: 46

Offices: No. Attys.
Columbus, OH: 42
Nashville, TN: 27
Florence, KY: 8
Charleston, WV: 5
Cincinnati, OH: 145
West Chester, OH: 19
Indianapolis, IN: 57
Louisville, KY: 139
Pittsburgh, PA: 10

Frost Brown Todd LLC (Continued)
Dallas, TX: 8
Ashland, VA: 3
Lexington, KY: 37

Hiring and Promotion
2015 Associates Hired: 32
2015 First-Year Hires: 13
2016 First-Year Hires (Est.): 15
2015 Equity Partners Named: 8
2015 Lateral Equity Partners: 7

Leading Practice Areas
(Department Heads)
Finance and Real Estate 18.2% (David S. Bence 513-651-6428)
Business Litigation 11.6% (Theresa Canaday 502- 568-0369)
Labor and Employment 9.9% (David A. Skidmore, Jr. 513-651-6185)
Tax and Benefits 7.8% (Scott W. Dolson 502-568-0203)
Product, Tort and Insurance Litigation 7.2% (Eric Riegner 317- 237-3821)
Intellectual Property 6.5% (Ann G. Schoen 513-651-6128)
Regulated Business 6.2% (Steven J. Ellcessor 614-559-7225)
Business Combinations and Capital Transactions 5.4% (James A. Giesel 502-568-0307)
Privately Held Business and Wealth Planning 4.8% (Jeremy A. Hayden 513-651-6912)
Bankruptcy 3.8%

Leading Officials
John R. Crockett, III, Chairman of the Firm, 502-568-0258
George E. Yund, Managing Member of the Firm, 513-651-6824
Jill B. Burton, Chief Operating Officer, 502-568-0351
Scott Phillips, Member/Recruiting Committee Chair, 513-870-8206
Karen Laymance, Director of Attorney Recruiting & Development, 513-651-6875
Catherine Marquardt, Director of Firm and Client Communications, 502-568-0375
D. Paul Bromwell, Chief Information Officer, 513-651-6404
Tracie Tiegs, Library Manager
Kimberly S. Amrine, Member of the Firm and Director of Diversity, 513-651-6952

Other Offices
400 West Market Street, 32nd Floor
Louisville
KY
40202-3363
Phone: 502-589-5400
Fax: 502-581-1087
Email: info@fbtlaw.com
Geoff White, Member in Charge of the Louisville Office

3300 Great American Tower
301 East Fourth Street
Cincinnati
OH
45202-4182
Phone: 513-651-6800
Fax: 513-651-6981
Email: info@fbtlaw.com
George E. Yund - Managing Member of the Firm; Chris Habel - Member in Charge of the Cincinnati Office

Frost Brown Todd LLC (Continued)
201 North Illinois Street
Suite 1900
Indianapolis
IN
46204
Phone: 317-237-3800
Fax: 317-237-3900
Email: info@fbtlaw.com
Healther Wilson - Member in Charge of the Indianapolis Office

---

Gallagher Sharp LLP

1501 Euclid Avenue
Sixth Floor, Bulkley Building
Cleveland, OH 44115
Phone: 216-241-5310
Fax: 216-241-1608
Email: info@gallaghersharp.com
Web Site: www.gallaghersharp.com

2016 Total Lawyers: 52
2015 Total Lawyers: 52

2016 Staff
Equity Partners: 16
Non-Equity Partners: 18
Associates: 16
Of Counsel: 2

Offices: No. Attys.
Toledo, OH: 3
Detroit, MI: 4
Cleveland, OH: 45

Hiring and Promotion
2015 Associates Hired: 5
2015 First-Year Hires: 2
2016 First-Year Hires (Est.): 1
2015 Equity Partners Named: 0

Leading Practice Areas
(Department Heads)
General Litigation 20% (Thomas J. Cabral 216-522-1172)
Professional Liability 18% (Monica A. Sansalone 216-522-1154)
Insurance 12% (John Travis 216-522-1590)
Transportation 12% (Thomas E. Dover 216-522-1060)
Mass Torts 12% (Kevin C. Alexandersen 216-522-1098)
Product Liability 10% (Joseph W. Pappalardo 216-522-1320)
Business and Employment 10% (Timothy T. Brick 216-522-1157)
Appellate 6% (Colleen A. Mountcastle 216-522-1058)

Leading Officials
Timothy T. Brick, Managing Partner, 216-241-5310
Monica A. Sansalone, Executive Committee
Thomas J. Cabral, Executive Committee
Todd M. Haemmerle, Hiring Partner
Jeanne M. Kostelnik, Director of Client Services, 216-522-1082
Steven J. Wunderle, Chief Information Officer, 216-522-1061
Stephanie L. Cruz, Administrator, 216-522-1698

OHIO

Graydon Head & Ritchey LLP

1900 Fifth Third Center
511 Walnut Street
Cincinnati, OH 45202-3157
Phone: 513-621-6464
Fax: 513-651-3836
Email: info@graydon.com
Web Site: www.graydon.com

2016 Total Lawyers: 68
2015 Total Lawyers: 76

Hahn Loeser & Parks LLP

200 Public Square
Suite 2800
Cleveland, OH 44114-2316
Phone: 216-621-0150
Fax: 216-241-2824
Email: marketing@hahnlaw.com
Web Site: www.hahnlaw.com

2016 Total Lawyers: 118
2015 Total Lawyers: 128

2016 Staff
Equity Partners: 37
Non-Equity Partners: 38
Associates: 30
Of Counsel: 7

Offices: No. Attys.
Cleveland, OH: 64
Akron, OH: 13
Columbus, OH: 15
Naples, FL: 10
Fort Myers, FL: 6
San Diego, CA: 10
Chicago, IL: 7

Hiring and Promotion
2015 Associates Hired: 14
2015 First-Year Hires: 5
Starting Salary for First-Year Assocs:
$110,000 (Ohio), $105,000 (Florida),
$120,000 (California)
2016 First-Year Hires (Est.): 1
2015 Equity Partners Named: 3
2015 Lateral Equity Partners: 1

Hahn Loeser & Parks LLP (Continued)

*Leading Practice Areas
(Department Heads)*
Business Practice (Stanley R. Gorom III
216-274-2461, 216-274-2559)
Creditors' Rights, Reorganization and
Bankruptcy (Daniel A. DeMarco, Rocco I.
Debitetto 216-274-2432, 216-274-2383,
216-274-2374)
Government Relations (Craig O. White
216-274-2278, 216-274-2231)
Intellectual Property & Technology (Arland
T. Stein, R. Eric Gaum 614-233-5104,
330-237-4539)
Labor & Employment Law (Steven E. Seasly
216-274-2366)
Litigation (Stephen A. Goldfarb, Robert J.
Fogarty, Rob Remington 216-274-2314,
216-274-2291, 216-274-2208)
Patent, Trademark and Copyright (Arland T.
Stein, R. Eric Gaum 614-233-5104,
330-237-4539)
Construction (Rob Remington 216-274-2208)
Estate Planning , Wealth Transfer &
Preservation (Arthur E. Gibbs, Stephen H.
Gariepy, Andrew J. Krause 239-552-2990,
216-274-2253, 216-274-2224,
239-254-2902)
Health Care (Arthur L. Cobb 216-274-2270)

Client Representations
Cliffs Natural Resources, Inc.
Fidelity National Finance, Inc./Chicago Title
Insurance Company/Security Title Agency
Lincoln Electric

Leading Officials
Lawrence E. Oscar, Chief Executive Officer,
216-274-2229
Timothy J. McEldowney, Chief Operating
Officer, 216-274-2276
Eric B. Levasseur, Recruiting Committee
Chair, 216-274-2346
Jodi L. Bosak, Legal Personnel & Recruiting
Manager, 216-274-2284
Meggan A. Fallon , Digital & Internal
Communications Manager , 216-274-2390
Gary R. Knowland, Chief Information
Officer, 216-274-2305
Beth A. Langton , Director of Library
Services, 216-274-2246
Craig Owen White, Partner, 216-274-2231

Other Offices
Cleveland, OH
200 Public Square
Suite 2800
Cleveland
OH
44114
Phone: 216-621-0150
Fax: 216-241-2824
Lawrence E. Oscar

Keating Muething & Klekamp PLL (KMK Law)

One East Fourth Street
Suite 1400
Cincinnati, OH 45202
Phone: 513-579-6400
Fax: 513-579-6457
Email: info@kmklaw.com
Web Site: www.kmklaw.com

2016 Total Lawyers: 106
2015 Total Lawyers: 107

2016 Staff
Equity Partners: 38
Non-Equity Partners: 22
Associates: 25
Of Counsel: 6
Senior Attorneys: 15

Offices: No. Attys.
Cincinnati, OH: 106

Hiring and Promotion
2015 Associates Hired: 7
2015 First-Year Hires: 36
Starting Salary for First-Year Assocs: 2016
Base salary plus bonus ≈ $123,000
2016 First-Year Hires (Est.): 4
2015 Equity Partners Named: 1

*Leading Practice Areas
(Department Heads)*
Litigation 31% (Daniel E. Izenson
513-579-6400)
Corporate 24% (D. Brock Denton, James M.
Jansing and Edward E. Steiner
513-579-6400)
Real Estate 16% (Daniel P. Utt
513-579-6400)
Labor 7% (G. Randall Ayers 513-579-6400)
Bankruptcy 7% (Robert G. Sanker
513-579-6400)
Employee Benefits 4% (Lisa Wintersheimer
Michel 513-579-6400)
Estate Planning & Trusts 4% (Joseph P.
Rouse 513-579-6400)
Financing 3% (James M. Jansing
513-579-6400)
Securities 2% (Edward E. Steiner
513-579-6400)
Family Law 2% (Mary Ellen Malas
513-579-6400)

Client Representations
Cintas Corporation
American Financial Group, Inc.
Fifth Third Bank

OHIO

Keating Muething & Klekamp PLL (KMK Law) (Continued)

Leading Officials
Paul V. Muething, Managing Partner, 513-579-6400
Rachael A. Rowe, Executive Partner, 513-579-6400
David A. Custer, Executive Director, 513-579-6460
Brian P. Muething, Hiring Partner, 513-639-3814
Susan M. Kurz, Director of Client Services and Marketing, 513-579-6544
Richard E. Wills, Chief Information Officer, 513-579-6588
Meribeth H. Sewell, Director of Information Resources, 513-639-3901
Adrienne J. Roach, Partner, 513-579-6487

Kegler, Brown, Hill & Ritter

65 East State Street
Capitol Square, Suite 1800
Columbus, OH 43215-4294
Phone: 614-462-5400
Fax: 614-464-2634
Email: info@keglerbrown.com
Web Site: www.keglerbrown.com

2016 Total Lawyers: 75
2015 Total Lawyers: 84

Lane, Alton & Horst LLC

Two Miranova Place, Suite 500
Columbus, OH 43215-7052
Phone: 614-228-6885
Fax: 614-228-0146
Email: lane@lanealton.com
Web Site: www.lanealton.com

2016 Total Lawyers: 25
2015 Total Lawyers: 23

McDonald Hopkins LLC

600 Superior Avenue, East
Suite 2100
Cleveland, OH 44114-2653
Phone: 216-348-5400
Fax: 216-348-5474
Email: info@mcdonaldhopkins.com
Web Site: www.mcdonaldhopkins.com

2016 Total Lawyers: 137
2015 Total Lawyers: 139

2016 Staff
Equity Partners: 50
Non-Equity Partners: 33
Associates: 43
Of Counsel: 11

Offices: No. Attys.
Cleveland, OH: 78
Detroit, MI: 18
Columbus, OH: 5
West Palm Beach, FL: 13

McDonald Hopkins LLC (Continued)
Chicago, IL: 18
Miami, FL: 5

Hiring and Promotion
2015 Associates Hired: 14
2015 First-Year Hires: 4
2016 First-Year Hires (Est.): 0
2015 Equity Partners Named: 0

Leading Practice Areas
(Department Heads)
Litigation 34% (William O'Neill 216-348-5400)
Corporate Law 32% (Chuck Zellmer 216-348-5400)
Tax & Benefits 13% (Jeffrey Consolo 216-348-5400)
Intellectual Property 13% (David Cupar 216-348-5400)
Business Restructuring/Business Law 8% (Stephen Gross 216-348-5400)

Leading Officials
Carl J. Grassi, President, 216-348-5400
William Lindow, Jr., Executive Director, 216-348-5400
Michael Latiff, Hiring Partner, 248-646-5070
Jennifer Blaga, Director of Recruiting, 216-348-5400
Deborah W. Kelm, Director of Marketing, 216-348-5400
Laura Mansour, 216-348-5400
Michael Melillo, Librarian, 216-348-5400
Michele Kantor, Member, 312-280-0111

Porter Wright Morris & Arthur LLP

41 South High Street
Suite 2800-3200
Columbus, OH 43215
Phone: 614-227-2000
Fax: 614-227-2100
Web Site: www.porterwright.com

2016 Total Lawyers: 203
2015 Total Lawyers: 203

Roetzel & Andress, A Legal Professional Association

222 S. Main Street
Akron, OH 44308
Phone: 330-376-2700
Fax: 330-376-4577
Email: inquiries@ralaw.com
Web Site: www.ralaw.com

2016 Total Lawyers: 177
2015 Total Lawyers: 171

2016 Staff
Equity Partners: 109
Associates: 50
Of Counsel: 18

Offices: No. Attys.
Columbus, OH: 23
Naples, FL: 16
Fort Myers, FL: 10

Roetzel & Andress, A Legal Professional Association (Continued)
Toledo, OH: 5
Cincinnati, OH: 3
Washington, DC: 1
Orlando, FL: 14
Akron, OH: 52
Fort Lauderdale, FL: 7
Chicago, IL: 19
Cleveland, OH: 26

Hiring and Promotion
2015 Associates Hired: 16
2015 First-Year Hires: 4
Starting Salary for First-Year Assocs: varies by location
2016 First-Year Hires (Est.): 3
2015 Equity Partners Named: 15
2015 Lateral Equity Partners: 12

Leading Practice Areas
(Department Heads)
Business Litigation 21% (Paul Giordano 239-338-4267)
Real Estate 18% (Brian Moore 330-849-6616)
Business Services 18% (Clint Gage 954-759-2760)
Labor & Employment 12% (Doug Spiker 216-696-7125)
Medical Defense 10% (Anna Moore Carulas 216-615-7401)
Products and Transportation 8% (Ron Lee 330-549-6648)
Government Relations / Public Law 7% (Lewis Adkins 216-615-4842)
Creditors' Rights 6% (Glenn Jensen 407-835-8549)

Revenues and Profits
Revenues: $77,500,000

Client Representations
Marathon Petroleum Company, LLC
Wells Fargo Bank
ProAssurance

Leading Officials
Jeffrey J. Casto, Chairman and Chief Executive Officer, 330-849-6643
Joe Maslowski, Chief Operating Officer/Chief Financial Officer, 330-849-6626
Mike Yashko, Recruiting Partner, 239-338-4249
Eric Fleming, Director of Human Resources & Recruiting, 330-849-6754
Wendy Castorena, Director of Business Development & Marketing, 330-762-7725
Jeffrey J. Farkas, Chief Information Officer, 330-849-6673
Bobbie Feigenbaum, Director of Research and Reference, 330-762-7614
Lewis W. Adkins, Jr., Partner, 216-615-4842

Other Offices
222 S. Main Street
Akron
OH
44308
Phone: 330-376-2700
Fax: 330-376-4577
Email: inquires@ralaw.com
Bradley Wright

OHIO

Shumaker, Loop & Kendrick, LLP

1000 Jackson Street
Toledo, OH 43604-5573
Phone: 419-241-9000
Fax: 419-241-6894
Web Site: www.slk-law.com

2016 Total Lawyers: 245
2015 Total Lawyers: 241

2016 Staff
Equity Partners: 123
Non-Equity Partners: 51
Associates: 52
Of Counsel: 10
Counsel: 1
Staff Attorneys: 7
Contract Attorney: 1

Offices: No. Attys.
Toledo, OH: 90
Tampa, FL: 70
Charlotte, NC: 35
Columbus, OH: 14
Sarasota, FL: 36

Hiring and Promotion
2015 Associates Hired: 10
2015 First-Year Hires: 3
2016 First-Year Hires (Est.): 3
2015 Equity Partners Named: 11
2015 Lateral Equity Partners: 5

Leading Practice Areas
(Department Heads)
Litigation 41% (John C. Barron, Mard D.
Wagoner, Jr., Jaime Austrich, William H.
Sturges, Anthony J. Abate 419-321-1275,
419-321-1412, 813-227-2273,
704-945-2163, 941-364-2707)
Corporate/Transactional 26% (Philip S.
Chubb, James I. Rothschild, Darrell C.
Smith, Gregory C. Yadley 704-945-2165,
419-321-1223, 813-227-2226,
813-227-2238)
Real Estate 10% (Sharon M. Fulop, C.
Graham Carothers, Jan W. Pitchford
419-321-1419, 813-227-2349,
941-364-2710)
Health 6% (Jenifer A. Belt, Erin S. Aebel,
Ronald A. Christaldi 419-321-1222,
813-227-2357, 813-221-7152)
Estate Planning/Probate 4% (David J.
Rectenwald, Cheryl L. Gordon, William R.
Swindle 419-321-1407, 941-364-2706,
813-221-7430)
Employment and Labor 3% (Jennifer B.
Compton, W. Jan Pietruszka, Mechelle
Zarou 941-364-2754; 813-227-2245,
419-321-1460)
Environmental 3% (Louis E. Tosi
419-321-1397)
ERISA, Tax & Benefits 3% (Eric D. Britton,
William R. Swindle 419-321-1348,
813-221-7430)
Financial Institutions 2% (Mark D. Hildreth,
Martin D. Werner 941-364-2747,
419-321.1394)
Intellectual Property 2% (J. Todd
Timmerman, W. Thad Adams
813-227-2243, 704-945-2901)

Shumaker, Loop & Kendrick, LLP (Continued)

Leading Officials
Thomas P. Dillon and Benjamin R. Hanan,
Co-Chairs, Management Committee,
419-241-9000
Peter E. Krebs, Hiring Partner, 419-241-9000
ext. 1379
Linda B. Vandercook, Director of
Professional Development & Recruitment,
419-241-9000 ext. 1324
Jennifer Malin, Director of Marketing,
813-229-7600 ext. 2258
Erin W. Hawk (Ohio), Erica M. Shea
(Florida), Heidi H. Team (North Carolina),
Chief Business Development Officer,
614-463-9441 ext. 4428
Thomas Dangelo, Chief Information Officer,
419-241-9000 ext. 1276
Barbara B. Avery, Head Librarian,
419-241-9000 ext. 1239
C. Graham Carothers, Sharon M. Fulop,
Co-Chairs, Diversity and Inclusion
Committee, 813-229-1660 ext. 2349

Other Offices
Home - Toledo, OH
1000 Jackson Street
Toledo,
OH
43604
Phone: 419-241-9000
Fax: 419-241-6894
Thomas P. Dillon

Tampa, FL
Bank of America Plaza, 101 East
Kennedy Boulevard
Suite 2800
Tampa
FL
33602
Phone: 813-229-7600
Fax: 813-229-1660
Julio C. Esquivel

Squire Patton Boggs

4900 Key Tower
127 Public Square
Cleveland, OH 44114
Phone: 216-479-8500
Fax: 216-479-8780
Web Site: www.squirepattonboggs.com

2016 Total Lawyers: 1550
2015 Total Lawyers: 1350

Strauss & Troy, A Legal Professional Association

The Federal Reserve Building
150 East Fourth Street
Cincinnati, OH 45202-4018
Phone: 513-621-2120
Fax: 513-241-8259
Email: info@strausstroy.com
Web Site: www.strausstroy.com

2016 Total Lawyers: 54
2015 Total Lawyers: 49

Taft Stettinius & Hollister LLP

425 Walnut Street
Suite 1800
Cincinnati, OH 45202-3957
Phone: 513-381-2838
Fax: 513-381-0205
Email: msarakatsannis@taftlaw.co
Web Site: www.taftlaw.com

2016 Total Lawyers: 400
2015 Total Lawyers: 403

2016 Staff
Equity Partners: 141
Non-Equity Partners: 105
Associates: 94
Of Counsel: 29
Senior Attorneys: 1
Senior Counsel: 3

Offices: No. Attys.
Cincinnati, OH: 98
Cleveland, OH: 53
Columbus, OH: 42
Dayton, OH: 19
Covington, KY: 4
Indianapolis, IN: 103
Phoenix, AZ: 1
Chicago, IL: 86
Ann Arbor, MI: 2

Hiring and Promotion
2015 Associates Hired: 14
2015 First-Year Hires: 9
Starting Salary for First-Year Assocs: $8,000
bar study stipend + $120,000 (Chicago),
$110,000 (Cincinnati & Cleveland),
$105,000 (Columbus & Indianapolis),
$100,000 (Dayton)
2016 First-Year Hires (Est.): 11
2015 Equity Partners Named: 5
2015 Lateral Equity Partners: 3

Leading Practice Areas
(Department Heads)
Litigation (Thomas Barnard, David Butler,
Russell Sayre, David Wallace,
James Wilson)
Business & Finance (Michael Cramarosso,
Jeffrey Schloemer, James Strain)
Environmental (Kim Burke, Frank Deveau)
Health & Life Sciences (Dave Bromund,
Catherine Dunlay)
Intellectual Property/Patent (Margaret
Lawson, James Coles, Robert Schneider)
Labor & Employment (Gregory Rogers, Fred
Ungerman, Jr. & Doreen Canton)
Private Client (Carl Murway,
Susan Wheatley)
Business Restructuring, Bankruptcy &
Creditors' Rights (Timothy Hurley,
Michael O'Neil)
Real Estate (Kathryn Kovitz Arnold, Stephen
Griffith, Jr., William Phillips)
Tax (David Tavolier)

Revenues and Profits
Revenues: $136,000,000

Client Representations
U.S. Bank
Duke Energy
TriHealth

OHIO

Taft Stettinius & Hollister LLP (Continued)

Leading Officials
Thomas T. Terp, Managing Partner,
513-357-9354
Alan Pickett, Executive Director,
513-357-9410
Ralph Caruso, Co-Chair Legal Recruiting &
Professional Development Committee,
317-713-3463
Lisa Watson, Chief Recruiting &
Development Officer, 317-713-3502
Susan Kilkenny, Chief Marketing Officer,
317-713-3476
Brian Clayton, Chief Information Officer,
513-357-9424
Stephanie Woebkenberg, 513-357-9416
Jeffrey Schloemer, Partner-Chair, Diversity
Committee, 513-357-9609

Other Offices
Taft Stettinius & Hollister LLP
One Indiana Square
Suite 3500
Indianapolis
IN
46204-5198
Phone: 317-713-3500
Fax: 317-713-3699
Email: hicks@taftlaw.com
Robert J. Hicks

Taft Stettinius & Hollister LLP
200 Public Square
Suite 3500
Cleveland
OH
44114-2302
Phone: 216-241-2838
Fax: 216-241-3707
Email: sobryan@taftlaw.com
Stephen M. O'Bryan

Taft Stettinius & Holllister LLP
111 Wacker Dr
2800
Chicago
IL
60601
Phone: 312-527-4000
Fax: 312-527-4011
Email: alicata@taftlaw.com
Anthony R. Licata

Taft Stettinius & Hollister LLP
425 Walnuut Street
1800
Cincinnati
OH
45202
Phone: 513-381-2838
Fax: 513-381-0205
Email: zimmerman@taftlaw.com
James Zimmerman

Thompson Hine LLP

3900 Key Center
127 Public Square
Cleveland, OH 44114
Phone: 216-566-5500
Fax: 216-566-5800
Email: info@ThompsonHine.com
Web Site: www.thompsonhine.com

2016 Total Lawyers: 369
2015 Total Lawyers: 375

Ulmer and Berne LLP

1660 West 2nd Street, Suite 1100
Cleveland, OH 44113-1448
Phone: 216-583-7000
Fax: 216-583-7001
Email: infocleveland@ulmer.com
Web Site: www.ulmer.com

2016 Total Lawyers: 151
2015 Total Lawyers: 165

Vorys, Sater, Seymour and Pease

52 East Gay Street
PO Box 1008
Columbus, OH 43215
Phone: 614-464-6400
Fax: 614-464-6350
Email: info@vorys.com
Web Site: www.vorys.com

2016 Total Lawyers: 375
2015 Total Lawyers: 363

Weston Hurd LLP

The Tower at Erieview
1301 East 9th Street, Suite 1900
Cleveland, OH 44114-1862
Phone: 216-241-6602
Fax: 216-621-8369
Email: RWetzel@westonhurd.com
Web Site: www.westonhurd.com

2016 Total Lawyers: 57
2015 Total Lawyers: 51

2016 Staff
Equity Partners: 29
Non-Equity Partners: 8
Associates: 8
Of Counsel: 5
Staff Attorneys: 1

Offices: No. Attys.
Cleveland, Ohio: 42
Columbus, Ohio: 8
Beachwood, Ohio: 1

Hiring and Promotion
2015 Associates Hired: 3
2016 First-Year Hires (Est.): 1
2015 Equity Partners Named: 0

Weston Hurd LLP (Continued)

Leading Officials
Carolyn M. Cappel, Managing Partner,
216-241-6602
Randy Wetzel, Director of Finance &
Administration, 216-241-6602
Fred J. Arnoff, Hiring Partner, 216-241-6602
Maria Murphy, Marketing Manager,
216-687-3383
Greg Thompson, Litigation Support
Specialist, 216-241-6602

OKLAHOMA

Conner & Winters LLP

4000 One Williams Center
Tulsa, OK 74172
Phone: 918-586-5711

2016 Total Lawyers: 110
2015 Total Lawyers: 110

Crowe & Dunlevy, A Professional Corporation

20 North Broadway, Suite 1800
Oklahoma City, OK 73102-8273
Phone: 405-235-7700
Fax: 405-239-6651
Email: jeanette.stanton@crowedun
Web Site: www.crowedunlevy.com

2016 Total Lawyers: 130
2015 Total Lawyers: 127

Fellers Snider

Chase Tower
100 N. Broadway, Suite 1700
Oklahoma City, OK 73102
Phone: 405-232-0621
Fax: 405-232-9659
Email: info@FellersSnider.com
Web Site: www.FellersSnider.com

2016 Total Lawyers: 43
2015 Total Lawyers: 45

2016 Staff
Equity Partners: 28
Associates: 7
Of Counsel: 10

Offices: No. Attys.
Oklahoma City, OK: 32
Tulsa, OK: 12

Hiring and Promotion
2015 First-Year Hires: 1
2016 First-Year Hires (Est.): 1
2015 Equity Partners Named: 2

Leading Officials
Brent M. Johnson, President
Jay Walter, Shareholder
Jennyfer R. Guebert, Director of Marketing
Samuel Lincoln, Systems Administrator
Liz Davies, Associate, 405-232-0621

OKLAHOMA

GableGotwals

1100 ONEOK Plaza
100 West Fifth Street
Tulsa, OK 74103-4217
Phone: 918-595-4800
Fax: 918-595-4990
Email: info@gablelaw.com
Web Site: www.gablelaw.com

2016 Total Lawyers: 90
2015 Total Lawyers: 91

2016 Staff
Associates: 15
Of Counsel: 20
Shareholders 55

Offices: No. Attys.
Tulsa, Oklahoma: 63
Oklahoma City, Oklahoma: 27

Hiring and Promotion
2015 Associates Hired: 8
2015 First-Year Hires: 6
2016 First-Year Hires (Est.): 5
2015 Equity Partners Named: 8
2015 Lateral Equity Partners: 2

Leading Practice Areas
(Department Heads)
Oil & Gas 30% (Terry D. Ragsdale, Rob F. Robertson 918-595-4800 405-235-5500)
Business Litigation 20% (David E. Keglovits, Rob F. Robertson 918-595-4800 405-235-5500)
Corporate/Mergers & Acquisitions 15% (John D. Dale, Jeffrey D. Hassell 918-595-4800)
Commercial/Bankruptcy 10% (Jeffrey D. Hassell, Sidney K. Swinson 918-595-4800)
Health Care 10% (Robert Glass 918-595-4800)
Utilities 8% (Eric R. King 405-235-5500)
Estate & Probate/Guardianship 4% (Sheppard F. Miers, Jr. 918-595-4800)
Labor & Employment 3% (Chris Thrutchley 918-595-4800)

Client Representations
ONEOK, Inc.
ChevronTexaco
JP Morgan Chase Bank, N.A.

Leading Officials
David E. Keglovits, CEO, 918-595-4800
Sidney K. Swinson, President, 918-595-4800
Melissa Bogle, Business Development, 918-595-4800
Ellen Adams, Tom Hutchison, Recruiting Co-Chairs, 918-595-4800
Shelley Bradley, Recruiting Coordinator, 918-595-4800
Melissa Bogle, Manager of Development, 918-595-4800
Don Lovy, Technology Manager, 918-595-4800
Tonja Hitchcock, 918-595-4800
Jordan B. Edwards, Chair Diversity Committee, 918-595-4800

Hall, Estill, Hardwick, Gable, Golden & Nelson, P.C.

320 South Boston Avenue
Suite 200
Tulsa, OK 74103
Phone: 918-594-0400
Fax: 918-594-0505
Email: firminformation@hallestil
Web Site: www.HallEstill.com

2016 Total Lawyers: 127
2015 Total Lawyers: 122

2016 Staff
Equity Partners: 79
Non-Equity Partners: 7
Associates: 19
Of Counsel: 22

Offices: No. Attys.
Tulsa, OK: 79
Oklahoma City, OK: 39
Northwest Arkansas: 5
Nashville, TN: 1
Denver, CO: 3

Hiring and Promotion
2015 Associates Hired: 4
2015 First-Year Hires: 3
Starting Salary for First-Year Assocs: $100,000
2016 First-Year Hires (Est.): 4
2015 Equity Partners Named: 5
2015 Lateral Equity Partners: 3

Leading Practice Areas
(Department Heads)
Litigation 32.94% (Mark K. Blongewicz 918-594-0451)
Corporate & Commercial 16.13% (Michael D. Cooke 918-594-0414)
Energy & Natural Resources 11.33% (J. Kevin Hayes 918-594-0460)
Intellectual Property 8.24% (Phillip L. Free, Jr. 405-553-2878)
Labor & Employment 7.81% (J. Patrick Cremin 918-594-0594)
Real Estate 6.80% (B. Kenneth Cox, Jr. 918-594-0418)
Bankruptcy & Collections 5.72% (Steven W. Soule 918-594-0466)
Tax, Estates & ERISA 5.42% (Kenneth L. Hunt 918-594-0420)
Real Estate 3.98% (Gregory Alberty 918-594-0805)
Environmental 1.63% (D. Kenyon Williams, Jr. 918-594-0519)

Client Representations
AES Shady Point
Williams Companies
The Bankers Bank

Hall, Estill, Hardwick, Gable, Golden & Nelson, P.C. (Continued)

Leading Officials
Michael D. Cooke, Firm Chair, 918-594-0414
Robert P. Morris, Executive Director, 918-594-0535
Sarah E. Hansel, Hiring Committee Chair, 918-594-0814
Lari L. Gulley, Director of Business Development & Recruitment, 918-594-0552
Lari L. Gulley, Marketing Director, 918-594-0552
Michael Hamilton, Top technology Manager, 918-594-0562
Rebekah Henry, 918-594-0502
Janice L. Pierce, Director of Human Resources & Diversity, 918-594-0833

Other Offices
320 South Boston Avenue
Suite 200
Tulsa, OK 74103
Phone: 918-594-0400
Fax: 918-594-0505
Email: firminformation@hallestill.com
Michael D. Cooke

McAfee & Taft, A Professional Corporation

211 North Robinson
Tenth Floor, Two Leadership Square
Oklahoma City, OK 73102
Phone: 405-235-9621
Fax: 405-235-0439
Web Site: www.mcafeetaft.com

2016 Total Lawyers: 177
2015 Total Lawyers: 180

2016 Staff
Equity Partners: 100
Associates: 44
Of Counsel: 33

Offices: No. Attys.
Oklahoma City, OK: 147
Tulsa, OK: 30

Hiring and Promotion
2015 Associates Hired: 9
2015 First-Year Hires: 7
Starting Salary for First-Year Assocs: $100,000
2016 First-Year Hires (Est.): 6
2015 Equity Partners Named: 7

OKLAHOMA

McAfee & Taft, A Professional Corporation (Continued)

Leading Practice Areas (Department Heads)
Litigation 24% (Brad Donnell 405-235-9621)
Business Transitions 13% (Josh Smith 405-235-9621)
Labor and Employment Law 12% (Charlie Plumb 405-235-9621)
Tax 9% (Spencer Haines 405-235-9621)
Intellectual Property 8% (Rachel Blue 405-235-9621)
Real Estate 7% (Mike Nordin 405-235-9621)
Employee Benefits 6% (Brandon Long 405-235-9621)
Health Care 5% (Greg Frogge 405-235-9621)
Aviation 4% (Erin Van Laanen 405-235-9621)

Revenues and Profits
Revenues: $84,013,238
Profits: $39,443,166

Client Representations
Devon Energy Corporation
Tyson Foods
Oklahoma City Thunder

Leading Officials
Michael F. Lauderdale, Managing Director, 405-235-9621
Matthew Bown, Chief Operating Officer, 405-235-9621
Rodney Hansinger, Hiring Partner, 405-235-9621
Judy Cross, Recruiting Director, 405-235-9621
Robin Croninger, Marketing Director, 405-235-9621
Mark Bradley, I.T. Director, 405-235-9621
Mike Davis, Head Librarian, 405-235-9621

OREGON

Ater Wynne LLP

1331 NW Lovejoy St
Suite 900
Portland, OR 97209-3280
Phone: 503-226-1191
Fax: 503-226-0079
Web Site: www.aterwynne.com

2016 Total Lawyers: 29
2015 Total Lawyers: 36

Bullivant Houser Bailey PC

300 Pioneer Tower
888 S.W. Fifth Avenue, Suite 300
Portland, OR 97204-2017
Phone: 503-228-6351
Fax: 503-295-0915
Email: clientservices@bullivant.
Web Site: www.bullivant.com

2016 Total Lawyers: 53
2015 Total Lawyers: 54

Bullivant Houser Bailey PC (Continued)

2016 Staff
Equity Partners: 34
Associates: 15
Of Counsel: 4

Offices: No. Attys.
Portland, OR: 29
Seattle, WA: 13
San Francisco, CA: 11

Hiring and Promotion
2015 Associates Hired: 5
2015 First-Year Hires: 3
2016 First-Year Hires (Est.): 0
2015 Equity Partners Named: 5
2015 Lateral Equity Partners: 2

Leading Practice Areas (Department Heads)
Commercial Litigation 21% (Thomas L. Hutchinson 503-499-4582)
Insurance Law 20% (Matthew J. Sekits 206-521-6452)
Personal & Catastrophic Injury Litigation 12% (Jeanne F. Loftis 503-499-4601)
Product Liability 10% (Jeanne F. Loftis 503-499-4601)
Professional Liability / D&O 10% (Joel Wilson 503-499-4469)
Asbestos Litigation 7% (Jeanne F. Loftis 503-499-4601)
Admiralty & Maritime 5% (Marilyn Raia 415-352-2721)
Intellectual Property 5% (Michael M. Ratoza 503-499-4695)
Construction 5% (Kyle D. Sciuchetti 503-499-4611)
Appellate 5% (Jerret E. Sale 206-521-6418)

Leading Officials
Loren Podwill, Firm President, 503-499-4620
Julia Burroughs, Director of Operations, 503-499-4524
Jill Valentine, Attorney Services Administrator, 503-499-4558
Mark Reber, Director of Marketing and Client Development, 503-499-4487
Julia Burroughs, Director of Operations, 503-499-4524
Laurie Daley, Librarian, 503-499-4603

Miller Nash Graham & Dunn LLP

3400 U.S. Bancorp Tower
111 S.W. Fifth Avenue
Portland, OR 97204
Phone: 503-224-5858
Fax: 503-224-0155
Email: clientservices@millernash.com
Web Site: www.millernash.com

2016 Total Lawyers: 159
2015 Total Lawyers: 155

Schwabe, Williamson & Wyatt

1211 SW 5th Avenue Suite 1900
Portland, OR 97204
Phone: 503-222-9981
Fax: 503-796-2900
Email: info@schwabe.com
Web Site: www.schwabe.com

2016 Total Lawyers: 165
2015 Total Lawyers: 166

Stoel Rives LLP

900 SW Fifth Avenue
Suite 2600
Portland, OR 97204
Phone: 503-224-3380
Fax: 503-220-2480
Email: webmaster@stoel.com
Web Site: www.stoel.com

2016 Total Lawyers: 410
2015 Total Lawyers: 400

Tonkon Torp LLP

888 S.W. Fifth Avenue
Suite 1600
Portland, OR 97204
Phone: 503-221-1440
Fax: 503-274-8779
Web Site: www.tonkon.com

2016 Total Lawyers: 84
2015 Total Lawyers: 87

PENNSYLVANIA

Babst, Calland, Clements and Zomnir, P.C.

Two Gateway Center
603 Stanwix Street, Sixth Floor
Pittsburgh, PA 15222
Phone: 412-394-5400
Fax: 412-394-6576
Email: info@babstcalland.com
Web Site: www.babstcalland.com

2016 Total Lawyers: 125
2015 Total Lawyers: 129

2016 Staff
Equity Partners: 26
Non-Equity Partners: 39
Associates: 52
Of Counsel: 2
Senior Counsel: 3
Staff Attorneys: 3

Offices: No. Attys.
Pittsburgh, PA: 107
State College, PA: 3
Sewell, NJ: 1
Charleston, WV: 10
Canton, OH: 2
Washington, DC: 2

THE LAWYER'S ALMANAC

PENNSYLVANIA

Babst, Calland, Clements and Zomnir, P.C. (Continued)

Hiring and Promotion
2015 Associates Hired: 13
Starting Salary for First-Year
  Assocs: $100,000
2016 First-Year Hires (Est.): 0
2015 Equity Partners Named: 6
2015 Lateral Equity Partners: 5

Leading Practice Areas
(Department Heads)
Energy and Natural Resources (Joseph K.
  Reinhart/Bruce F. Rudoy 412-394-5452,
  412-253-8815)
Litigation (Leonard Fornella 412-394-6533)
Construction (D. Matthew Jameson III
  412-394-5491)
Corporate and Commercial (Sara M.
  Antol/Laure Stone 412-394-5412,
  412-394-5420)
Land Use (Blaine A. Lucas/Stephen L.
  Korbel 412-394-5657, 412-394-5627)
Creditors' Rights and Insolvency (David W.
  Ross 412-394-6558)
Environmental (Donald C. Bluedorn
  II/Lindsay P. Howard 412-394-5450,
  412-394-5444)
Employment and Labor (Richard J. Antonelli
  412-394-6440)
Title (Bruce F. Rudoy 412-253-8815)
Real Estate (Marcia L. Grimes
  412-394-5418)

Leading Officials
Chester R. Babst III, Managing Shareholder,
  412-394-5407
Dennis Yates, Executive Director,
  412-394-5413
Chester R. Babst III, Managing Shareholder
Lori Dunlap, Chief Marketing Officer,
  412-394-5684
W. Andrew Richards, Director of Information
  Technology, 412-394-6970
Mary Stacy, Librarian, 412-394-6534
Chester R. Babst III, Managing Shareholder,
  412-394-5407

Ballard Spahr

1735 Market Street
51st Floor
Philadelphia, PA 19103-7599
Phone: 215-665-8500
Fax: 215-864-8999
Email: lawyers@ballardspahr.com
Web Site: www.ballardspahr.com

2016 Total Lawyers: 528
2015 Total Lawyers: 528

Barley Snyder LLP

126 East King Street
Lancaster, PA 17602
Phone: 717-299-5201
Fax: 717-291-4660
Email: barley@barley.com
Web Site: www.barley.com

2016 Total Lawyers: 72
2015 Total Lawyers: 65

2016 Staff
Equity Partners: 34
Associates: 12
Of Counsel: 19

Offices: No. Attys.
Lancaster, PA: 35
York, PA: 12
Reading, PA: 13
Hanover, PA: 1
Malvern, PA: 4

Hiring and Promotion
2015 Associates Hired: 3
2015 First-Year Hires: 3
2016 First-Year Hires (Est.): 3
2015 Equity Partners Named: 0

Leading Practice Areas
(Department Heads)
Corporate/Business (John T. Reed
  717-399-1531)
Labor/Employment/Employee Benefits
  (Jennifer L. Craighead 717-399-1523)
Litigation (Paul Minnich 717-852-4976)
Banking/Finance (Don Geiter 717-399-4154)
Real Estate/Environmental/Municipal
  (Michael W. Davis/Caroline Hoffer
  717-399-1534)
Trusts & Estates (Brian Ott 610-898-7158)
Intellectual Property (Sal Anastasi
  610-722-3899)

Leading Officials
Jeffrey D. Lobach, Managing Partner,
  717-852-4979
Bert Kramer, COO, 717-399-1509
Dorothy L. Rund, Human Resources
  Director, 717-399-1565
Jenna Wagner, Marketing Director,
  717-399-1573
Erin Saylor, Director of Business
  Development, 717-399-2160
Richard Shepherd, Director of IT,
  717-399-2174
Rose Lowther, Director of Knowledge
  Development & Special Projects,
  717-553-1045

Blank Rome LLP

One Logan Square
130 North 18th Street
Philadelphia, PA 19103-6998
Phone: 215-569-5500
Fax: 215-569-5555
Email: webmaster@BlankRome.com
Web Site: www.BlankRome.com

2016 Total Lawyers: 619
2015 Total Lawyers: 540

Blank Rome LLP (Continued)

2016 Staff
Equity Partners: 172
Non-Equity Partners: 138
Associates: 220
Of Counsel: 89

Offices: No. Attys.
Philadelphia, PA: 198
Boca Raton, FL: 5
Princeton, NJ: 13
Cincinnati, OH: 3
New York, NY: 143
Washington, DC: 142
Wilmington, DE: 9
San Francisco, CA: 1
Los Angeles, CA: 42
Houston, TX: 38
Shanghai, China: 2
Tampa, FL: 5
Pittsburgh, PA: 7
Fort Lauderdale, FL: 11

Hiring and Promotion
Starting Salary for First-Year Assocs:
  $150,000 (PHL); $155,000 (DC);
  $160,000 (NY)

Leading Practice Areas
(Department Heads)
Intellectual Property and Technology
  (Timothy D. Pecsenye; Charles R. Wolfe,
  Jr.; David Cabello; Jeffrey Sherwood
  215-569-5619; 202-772-5841;
  713-632-8696; 202-420-3602)
Corporate, Securities, and M&A (Louis M.
  Rappaport; Alan F. Lieblich
  215-569-5647; 215-569-5693)
Maritime & International Trade (John D.
  Kimball; Jonathan K. Waldron
  212-885-5259; 202-772-5964)
Finance, Restructuring, and Bankruptcy
  (Regina Stango Kelbon; Robert B. Stein
  302-425-6424; 215-569-5507;
  212-885-5206)
Real Estate (Pelayo Coll; Samuel M. Walker
  215-569-5654; 212-885-5493)
Corporate Litigation: Commercial Litigation
  (Harris N. Cogan; Daniel E. Rhynhart;
  Adrienne C. Rogrove 212-885-5566;
  215-569-5371; 609-750-2648)
White Collar Defense and Investigations
  (Carlos F. Ortiz; Shawn Wright
  609-750-2641; 202-772-5968)
Energy, Environmental, & Mass Torts
  (Margaret A. Hill; Robert P. Scott
  215-569-5331; 713-228-6607)
Labor and Employment (Scott F. Cooper
  215-569-5487)
Insurance Coverage (Kevin J. Bruno; James
  Murray 212-885-5580; 202-420-3409)

Revenues and Profits
Revenues: $345,000,000

Blank Rome LLP (Continued)

Leading Officials
Alan J. Hoffman, Chairman and Managing
Partner, 215-569-5505
Lawrence F. Flick II, Partner, 212-885-5556
Julie Dressing, Chief Human Resources
Officer, 202-772-5873
Hans T. Haglund, Chief Business
Development and Marketing Officer,
202-772-5863
Laurence Liss, Chief Technology Officer,
215-569-5749
Mary Newman, Director of Library and
Research Services, 215-569-5490
Christopher A. Lewis, Chief Officer for
Diversity and Inclusion, 215-569-5793

Other Offices
The Chrysler Building
405 Lexington Avenue
New York
NY
10174
Phone: 212-885-5000
Fax: 212-885-5001
Email: webmaster@blankrome.com
Norman S. Heller; Robert J. Mittman

Farragut Square
1825 Eye Street NW
Washington
DC
20006
Phone: 202-420-2200
Fax: 202-420-2201
Email: webmaster@blankrome.com
Gregory F. Linsin, James Kelly

Buchanan Ingersoll & Rooney

One Oxford Centre
301 Grant Street, 20th Floor
Pittsburgh, PA 15219
Phone: 412-562-8800
Fax: 412-562-1041
Email: info@bipc.com
Web Site: www.bipc.com

2016 Total Lawyers: 528
2015 Total Lawyers: 528

Christie Sullivan & Young PC

1880 JFK Boulevard
Tenth Floor
Philadelphia, PA 19103
Phone: 215-587-1600
Fax: 215-587-1699
Web Site: www.epmy.com

2016 Total Lawyers: 21
2015 Total Lawyers: 29

Cohen & Grigsby, P.C.

625 Liberty Avenue
Pittsburgh, PA 15222-3152
Phone: 412-297-4900
Fax: 412-209-0672
Email: info@cohenlaw.com
Web Site: www.cohenlaw.com

2016 Total Lawyers: 152
2015 Total Lawyers: 152

Cozen O'Connor

1900 Market Street
Philadelphia, PA 19103
Phone: 215-665-2000
Fax: 215-665-2013
Email: postmaster@cozen.com
Web Site: www.cozen.com

2016 Total Lawyers: 620
2015 Total Lawyers: 620

Dickie, McCamey & Chilcote

Suite 400
Two PPG Place
Pittsburgh, PA 15222
Phone: 412-281-7272
Fax: 412-392-5367
Email: info@dmclaw.com
Web Site: www.dmclaw.com

2016 Total Lawyers: 167
2015 Total Lawyers: 163

Dilworth Paxson LLP

1500 Market Street, Suite 3500 E
Philadelphia, PA 19102
Phone: 215-575-7000
Fax: 215-575-7200
Web Site: www.dilworthlaw.com

2016 Total Lawyers: 95
2015 Total Lawyers: 103

2016 Staff
Equity Partners: 29
Non-Equity Partners: 32
Associates: 24
Of Counsel: 10
Special Counsel 1

Offices: No. Attys.
Philadelphia, PA: 79
Cherry Hill, NJ: 12
Harrisburg, PA: 2
Wilmington, DE: 2

Hiring and Promotion
2015 Associates Hired: 2
Starting Salary for First-Year
Assocs: $115,000
2015 Equity Partners Named: 0

Dilworth Paxson LLP (Continued)

Leading Practice Areas
(Department Heads)
Taxation & ERISA (John W. Schmehl)
Municipal Finance (Marc A. Feller)
Trusts & Estates (John R. Latourette)
Labor & Employment (Marjorie Obod)
Mergers & Acquisitions (Graham R. Laub)
Real Estate (Joseph F. Kessler)
Bankruptcy (Anne Marie P. Kelley, James
M. Matour)
Corporate & Business (Roger F. Wood,
Barbara T. Ilsen)
Commercial Litigation (Thomas S. Biemer,
Gregory F. Cirillo)
Capital Markets

Client Representations
PNC Bank
Hunter Roberts Construction Group
Pennsylvania Department of Human Services

Leading Officials
Ajay Raju, Chairman/CEO, 215-575-7000
Lawrence G. McMichael, Chairman of
Professional Practice, 215-575-7000
Richard P. Shappell, Chief Financial Officer,
215-575-7000
Michael Czerpak, Director of Operations,
215-575-7000
Peter Dunn, Director of Client Relations and
Communication , 215-575-7000
Ali Sethi , IT Director, 215-575-7000
Karen Anello, Chief Knowledge Officer,
215-575-7000
Marjorie McMahon Obod, Chair of Diversity,
215-575-7000

Drinker Biddle & Reath LLP

One Logan Square
Suite 2000
Philadelphia, PA 19103-6996
Phone: 215-988-2700
Fax: 215-988-2757
Web Site: www.drinkerbiddle.com

2016 Total Lawyers: 600
2015 Total Lawyers: 605

Duane Morris LLP

30 South 17th Street
Philadelphia, PA 19103-4196
Phone: 215-979-1000
Fax: 215-979-1020
Web Site: www.duanemorris.com

2016 Total Lawyers: 775
2015 Total Lawyers: 757

2016 Staff
Equity Partners: 121
Non-Equity Partners: 225
Associates: 235
Of Counsel: 77
Senior Counsel: 60

Offices: No. Attys.
Chicago, IL: 51
Washington, D.C.: 40

PENNSYLVANIA

Duane Morris LLP (Continued)
Miami, FL: 21
Newark, NJ: 20
Boston, MA: 29
San Francisco, CA: 63
Wilmington, DE: 11
London, England: 12
Atlanta, GA: 22
Houston, TX: 14
New York, NY: 99
Pittsburgh, PA: 7
San Diego, CA: 34
Philadelphia, PA: 212
Lake Tahoe, CA: 3
Las Vegas, NV: 3
Los Angeles, CA: 12
Baltimore, MD: 15
Singapore: 28
Ho Chi Minh City, Vietnam: 4
Hanoi, Vietnam: 5
Boca Raton, FL: 15
Cherry Hill, NJ: 23
Silicon Valley, CA: 9
Oman: 1
Myanmar: 3
Bangor: 5
Shanghai: 2

Hiring and Promotion
2015 Associates Hired: 62
2015 First-Year Hires: 12
2016 First-Year Hires (Est.): 19
2015 Equity Partners Named: 11
2015 Lateral Equity Partners: 3

Leading Practice Areas
(Department Heads)
Trial (Matthew A. Taylor)
Corporate Law (Brian P. Kerwin)
Business Reorganization and Financial
  Restructuring (Rudolph Di Massa, Jr.)
Intellectual Property (L. Norwood
  "Woody" Jameson)
Employment, Labor, Benefits & Immigration
  (Thomas G. Servodidio)
Health Law (David E. Loder)
Real Estate (George J. Kroculick)
Energy, Environment & Resources (Thomas
  M. Berliner)
Wealth Planning (Michael D. Grohman)

Revenues and Profits
Revenues: $434,500,000

Client Representations
Cisco Systems, Inc.
TD Bank
SAP

Leading Officials
John J. Soroko, Chairman
Charles J. O'Donnell, Chief
  Operating Officer
Amee R. McKim, Director of Legal
  Recruitment
Mark P. Messing, Chief Marketing Officer
Brett Arnold, Business Development Director
John J. Sroka, Chief Information Officer
Christine A. Scherzinger, Director of Library
  & Research Services
Joseph K. West, Partner and Chief
  Diversity Officer

Duane Morris LLP (Continued)

Other Offices
New York
1540 Broadway
New York
NY
10036
Phone: 212-692-1000
Fax: 212-692-1020
Email: mdgrohman@duanemorris.com
Michael Grohman

San Francisco
One Market, Spear Tower
San Francisco
CA
94105
Phone: 415-957-3000
Fax: 415-957-3001
Email: shsutro@duanemorris.com
Stephen H. Sutro

Philadelphia
30 South 17th Street
Philadelphia
PA
19103
Phone: 215-979-1000
Fax: 215-979-1020
Email: soroko@duanemorris.com
John J. Soroko

Chicago
190 South LaSalle Street
3700
Chicago
IL
60603
Phone: 312-499-6700
Fax: 312-499-6701
Email: DBYelin@duanemorris.com
David B. Yelin

Eckert Seamans Cherin & Mellott, LLC

600 Grant Street
44th Floor
Pittsburgh, PA 15219
Phone: 412-566-6000
Fax: 412-566-6099
Email: info@eckertseamans.com
Web Site: www.eckertseamans.com

2016 Total Lawyers: 353
2015 Total Lawyers: 363

Fox Rothschild LLP

2000 Market St.
20th Floor
Philadelphia, PA 19103
Phone: 215-299-2000
Fax: 215-299-2150
Web Site: www.foxrothschild.com

2016 Total Lawyers: 773
2015 Total Lawyers: 662

Harvey, Pennington, LTD

1800 JFK Blvd
Suite 1300
Philadelphia, PA 19103
Phone: 215-563-4470
Fax: 215-568-1044
Email: info@harvpenn.com
Web Site: www.harvpenn.com

2016 Total Lawyers: 8
2015 Total Lawyers: 14

K&L Gates LLP

K&L Gates Center
210 Sixth Avenue
Pittsburgh, PA 15222-2613
Phone: 412-355-6500
Fax: 412-355-6501
Email: info@klgates.com
Web Site: www.klgates.com

2016 Total Lawyers: 2000
2015 Total Lawyers: 2000

Keevican, Weiss, Bauerle & Hirsch, LLC

11th Floor, Federated Investors Tower
1001 Liberty Ave
Pittsburgh, PA 15222
Phone: 800-232-0812
Fax: 412-355-2609
Email: info@kwbhlaw.com
Web Site: www.kwbhlaw.com

2016 Total Lawyers: 18
2015 Total Lawyers: 20

2016 Staff
Equity Partners: 4
Non-Equity Partners: 7
Of Counsel: 2
Counsel: 6
Senior Counsel: 1

Offices: No. Attys.
Pittsburgh, PA: 20

Hiring and Promotion
Starting Salary for First-Year
  Assocs: $80,000
2016 First-Year Hires (Est.): 0
2015 Equity Partners Named: 0
2015 Lateral Equity Partners: 1

Leading Practice Areas
(Department Heads)
M&A 35% (Leo A. Keevican 412-355-2604)
Banking 30% (James F. Bauerle
  412-355-2605)
Corporate 20% (Leo A. Keevican
  412-355-2604)
Litigation 10% (Michael D. Yablonski
  412-355-2620)
Employment Law 2.5% (James F. Bauerle
  412-355-12605)
Intellectual Property 2.5% (Jeffrey D.
  Mulrooney 412-355-2634)

Keevican, Weiss, Bauerle & Hirsch, LLC (Continued)

Leading Officials
Leo A. Keevican, Jr., Managing Director,
  412-355-2604
Sherry A. Gibb, Executive Director,
  412-355-2610
Sherry A. Gibb, Acting HR Director,
  412-355-2610
Kelly Felsing, Marketing Director,
  412-355-2644
Robert Keresztury, IT Director,
  412-355-8502

Klehr, Harrison, Harvey, Branzburg & Ellers LLP

1835 Market Street
Suite 1400
Philadelphia, PA 19103
Phone: 215-568-6060
Fax: 215-568-6603
Web Site: www.klehr.com

2016 Total Lawyers: 82
2015 Total Lawyers: 82

Lavin, O'Neil, Cedrone & DiSipio

190 North Independence Mall West
Suite 500
Philadelphia, PA 19106
Phone: 215-627-0303
Fax: 215-627-2551
Email: info@lavin-law.com
Web Site: www.lavin-law.com

2016 Total Lawyers: 51
2015 Total Lawyers: 51

2016 Staff
Equity Partners: 25
Associates: 23
Of Counsel: 3

Offices: No. Attys.
Philadelphia, PA: 44
New York, NY: 5
Mt. Laurel, NJ: 1
Rochester, NY: 1

Hiring and Promotion
2015 Associates Hired: 8
2015 First-Year Hires: 2
2016 First-Year Hires (Est.): 3

Leading Officials
Basil A. DiSipio, Managing Partner
Martin Mack, Manager of Administration
William Person, Manager of
  Finance/Controller
Kevin Hollingsworth, Technology Manager
LaWanda Dyson White, Esq

Margolis Edelstein

Curtis Center
Independence Square West, Suite 400E
Philadelphia, PA 19106-3337
Phone: 215-922-1100
Fax: 215-922-1772
Email: jbrown@margolisedelstein.
Web Site: www.margolisedelstein.com

2016 Total Lawyers: 108
2015 Total Lawyers: 109

Offices: No. Attys.
983 Third Street, Beaver, PA 15009: 1
170 S. Independence Mall W., Philadelphia,
  PA: 41
100 Century Parkway, Mount Laurel, NJ
  08054: 15
525 William Penn Place, Pittsburgh, PA
  15219: 21
P.O. Box 628 Hollidaysburg, PA
  16648-9998: 2
3510 Trindle Rd. Camp Hill, PA 17011: 5
300 Delaware Avenue Suite 800 Wilmington,
  DE 19801: 5
400 Connell Dr., Ste. Berkeley Heights, NJ: 7

Hiring and Promotion
2015 Associates Hired: 3
2015 First-Year Hires: 3
2015 Equity Partners Named: 3

Leading Practice Areas
(Department Heads)
General Defense 20% (Catherine Straggas,
  Zygmunt Bialkowski, Rolf Kroll
  215-931-5835, 570-342-4231,
  717-760-7502)
Labor/Employment Practices 15%
  (Christopher Tinari, Colleen Ready,
  Charles Saul 215-931-5895,
  856-727-6013, 412-355-4961)
CPA, D&O, Misc Prof Liability 10%
  (Thomas Gebler, Dianne Wainwright, Paul
  Carbon, 412-355-4975, 412-281-4256,
  908-790-7771)
Workers' Compensation 10% (Joseph
  Bekelja, Michele Hodak 215-931-5807,
  856-727-6009)
Governmental Entity Defense 10% (Carol
  Murphy, Rolf Kroll, Charles Saul
  215-931-5881, 717-760-7502)

Leading Officials
Michael McKenna, Managing Partner,
  215-931-5811
James Brown, Partner, 215-931-5821

Marshall Dennehey Warner Coleman & Goggin

2000 Market Street, Suite 2300
Philadelphia, PA 19103
Phone: 215-575-2600
Fax: 215-575-0856
Email: bbbuchanan@mdwcg.com
Web Site: www.marshalldennehey.com

2016 Total Lawyers: 503
2015 Total Lawyers: 505

Marshall Dennehey Warner Coleman & Goggin (Continued)

2016 Staff
Equity Partners: 273
Associates: 171
Of Counsel: 4
Senior Counsel: 25
Special Counsel 30

Offices: No. Attys.
Philadelphia, PA: 135
Cherry Hill, NJ: 53
Pittsburgh, PA: 35
Roseland, NJ: 42
Scranton, PA: 23
Harrisburg, PA: 22
Wilmington, DE: 23
Doylestown, PA: 4
Tampa, FL: 7
Erie, PA: 4
Orlando, FL: 13
Cleveland, OH: 8
Ft. Lauderdale, FL: 22
Jacksonville, FL: 12
King of Prussia, PA: 37
New York, NY: 32
Long Island, NY: 14
Cincinnati, OH: 4
Allentown, PA: 12
Westchester, NY: 7

Hiring and Promotion
2015 Associates Hired: 34
2015 First-Year Hires: 8
2015 Equity Partners Named: 19
2015 Lateral Equity Partners: 5

Leading Practice Areas
(Department Heads)
General Liability 27% (Howard P. Dwoskin
  215-575-2664)
Professional Liability 20% (Christopher E.
  Dougherty 215-575-2733)
Health Care 20% (T. Kevin FitzPatrick
  610-354-8252)
Architectural, Engineering & Construction
  Defects Litigation 10% (John H. Osorio
  856-414-6007)
Workers' Compensation 7% (Niki T. Ingram
  215-575-2704)
Asbestos & Environmental 6% (Daniel J.
  Ryan 215-575-2740)
Product Liability 5% (Eric A. Weiss
  215-575-2676)
Employment Law 5% (Ronda K. O'Donnell
  215-575-2697)
Securities & Investments Professional
  Liability 5% (Andrew W. Davitt
  215-575-2679)
Vehicular Products Liability 3% (Eric A.
  Weiss 215-575-2676)

Client Representations
AIG
CNA
Liberty Mutual

PENNSYLVANIA

Marshall Dennehey Warner Coleman & Goggin (Continued)

Leading Officials
Thomas A. Brophy, Esq., President & CEO, 215-575-2748
Thomas A. Brophy, Esq., 215-575-2748
Liz Brown, Chief Operating Officer, 215-575-2848
Butler Buchanan, III, Esq., Hiring Partner, 215-575-2661
Joseph S. Goldshear, Director of Marketing & Business Development, 215-575-3561
Roger Bonine, Director of Information Technology, 215-575-2730
Colleen Bannon, Esq., Director of Legal Information Resources, 215-575-2825
Butler Buchanan, III, Esq., 215-575-2661

Other Offices
Woodland Falls Corporate Park
200 Lake Drive East
Suite 300
Cherry Hill
NJ
08002
Phone: 856-414-6000
Fax: 856-414-6077
Email: rlgoldstein@mdwcg.com
Richard L. Goldstein, Esquire

McNees Wallace & Nurick LLC

100 Pine Street
P.O. Box 1166
Harrisburg, PA 17108-1166
Phone: 717-232-8000
Fax: 717-237-5300
Email: info@mcneeslaw.com
Web Site: www.mcneeslaw.com

2016 Total Lawyers: 130
2015 Total Lawyers: 132

2016 Staff
Equity Partners: 59
Non-Equity Partners: 10
Associates: 27
Of Counsel: 34

Offices: No. Attys.
Harrisburg, PA: 95
Washington, DC: 1
State College, PA: 2
Lancaster, PA: 21
Columbus, OH: 9
Scranton, PA: 2

Hiring and Promotion
2015 Associates Hired: 8
2015 First-Year Hires: 5
2016 First-Year Hires (Est.): 5
2015 Equity Partners Named: 6
2015 Lateral Equity Partners: 1

McNees Wallace & Nurick LLC (Continued)

Leading Practice Areas (Department Heads)
Business 24% (Bradley J. Gunnison / Timothy M. Finnerty 717-232-8000)
Litigation 23% (James P. DeAngelo 717-232-8000)
Energy & Environmental 14% (Robert A. Weishaar, Jr. 202-898-5700)
Intellectual Property 13% (Michael A. Doctrow / Bruce J. Wolstoncroft 717-232-8000)
Real Estate 10% (Steven J. Weingarten 717-232-8000)
Financial Services and Public Finance 10% (Daniel J. Malpezzi / Donna L. Kreiser 717-232-8000)
Labor & Employment 9% (Brian F. Jackson / Eric N. Athey 717-232-8000)
Automotive Dealership 7% (Stephen A. Moore 717-232-8000)

Leading Officials
David M. Kleppinger, Chairman, 717-232-8000
Richard C. Burtnett, Chief Operating Officer, 717-232-8000
Susan E. Bruce, Hiring Committee Chairman, 717-232-8000
Daphne C. Moore, Director of Human Resources, 717-232-8000
Iris Jones, Chief Business Development & Marketing Director, 717-232-8000
Mark Golicher, Director of Technology, 717-232-8000
Kate Pettegrew, Director of Information Center, 717-232-8000

Meyer, Darragh, Buckler, Bebenek & Eck, P.L.L.C.

600 Grand St
Suite 4850
Pittsburgh, PA 15219
Phone: 412-261-6600
Fax: 412-471-2754
Email: info@mdbbe.com
Web Site: www.mdbbe.com

2016 Total Lawyers: 18
2015 Total Lawyers: 18

Meyer, Unkovic & Scott LLP

535 Smithfield Street
Suite 1300
Pittsburgh, PA 15222
Phone: 412-456-2800
Web Site: www.muslaw.com

2016 Total Lawyers: 53
2015 Total Lawyers: 54

Montgomery, McCracken, Walker & Rhoads, LLP

123 South Broad Street
28th Floor
Philadelphia, PA 19109
Phone: 215-772-1500
Fax: 215-772-7620
Web Site: www.mmwr.com

2016 Total Lawyers: 118
2015 Total Lawyers: 117

Obermayer Rebmann Maxwell & Hippel LLP

Centre Square West
1500 Market Street, Suite 3400
Philadelphia, PA 19102-2101
Phone: 215-665-3000
Fax: 215-665-3165
Email: info@obermayer.com
Web Site: www.obermayer.com

2016 Total Lawyers: 108
2015 Total Lawyers: 112

2016 Staff
Equity Partners: 41
Non-Equity Partners: 14
Associates: 37
Of Counsel: 14
contract attorneys 2

Offices: No. Attys.
Philadelphia, PA: 87
Pittsburgh, PA: 2
Cherry Hill, NJ: 5
Harrisburg, PA: 5
Wilmington, DE: 1
Denver, CO: 1
Altoona, PA: 1
West Conshohocken, PA: 3
New York, NY: 1

Hiring and Promotion
2015 Associates Hired: 10
2015 First-Year Hires: 2
Starting Salary for First-Year Assocs: $115,000
2016 First-Year Hires (Est.): 2
2015 Equity Partners Named: 1

PENNSYLVANIA

Obermayer Rebmann Maxwell & Hippel LLP (Continued)

Leading Practice Areas
(Department Heads)
Litigation 28% (Thomas A. Leonard, Robert I Whitelaw, Jeffrey S. Batoff 215-665-3220, 215-665-3206, 215-665-3064)
Business and Finance 17% (David A. Nasatir, Paul N. Allen, Anastasius Efstratiades 215-665-3036, 215-665-3016, 215-665-3030)
Labor Relations and Employment Law 14% (Joseph J. Centeno; Larry Besnoff 215-665-3017, 215-665-3126)
Family Law 8% (David L. Ladov, Robert I Whitelaw 267-675-4976, 215-665-3206)
Creditors' Rights, Bankruptcy & Financial Reorganization 5% (Edmond M. George 215-665-3140)
Trusts and Estates 5% (Nina B. Stryker 215-665-3057)
Environmental 4% (Joseph J. McGovern 215-665-3058)
Health Care 3% (Lawrence J. Tabas 215-665-3158)
Regulatory, Administrative & Gaming 1% (Martin Weinberg 215-665-3196)

Client Representations
WND

Leading Officials
Thomas A. Leonard, Firm Chair, 215-665-3220
Mathieu J. Shapiro, Managing Partner, 215-665-3014
Andrew S. Frey, Chief Operating Officer, 215-665-3163
Matthew A. Green, Hiring Partner, 215-665-3122
Matthew A. Green, Recruiting Director, 215-665-3122
Sharen Nocella, Chief Marketing Officer, 215-665-3151
Edwin L. Rosenberger, Jr., Chief Technology Officer, 215-665-3015
Gregory C. Weyant, Head Librarian, 215-665-3181
Min S. Suh, Esquire, Diversity Coordinator, 215-665-3050

Pepper Hamilton LLP

3000 Two Logan Square
Eighteenth and Arch Streets
Philadelphia, PA 19103-2799
Phone: 215-981-4000
Fax: 215-981-4750
Email: phinfo@pepperlaw.com
Web Site: www.pepperlaw.com

2016 Total Lawyers: 498
2015 Total Lawyers: 510

2016 Staff
Associates: 221
Of Counsel: 46
Partners 231

Offices: No. Attys.
Washington, DC: 33

Pepper Hamilton LLP (Continued)
Detroit, MI: 17
Berwyn, PA: 27
Pittsburgh, PA: 30
Harrisburg, PA: 12
Wilmington, DE: 16
New York, NY: 35
Princeton, NJ: 27
Philadelphia, PA: 239
Orange County, CA: 8
Boston, MA: 35
Los Angeles, CA: 14
Silicon Valley, CA: 5

Hiring and Promotion
2015 Associates Hired: 53
2015 First-Year Hires: 15
Starting Salary for First-Year Assocs: $115,000-$160,000
2016 First-Year Hires (Est.): 12
2015 Equity Partners Named: 2
2015 Lateral Equity Partners: 2

Leading Practice Areas
(Department Heads)
Corporate & Securities 19% (Brian M. Katz 215-981-4193)
Commercial Litigation 18% (Matthew H. Adler/Jan P. Levine 215-981-4802; 215-981-4714)
Health Effects Litigation 18% (Sean P. Fahey 215-981-4296)
Intellectual Property 14% (William D. Belanger/Raymond A. Miller 617-204-5101;412-454-5813)
Financial Services 8% (John M. Ford/Henry Liu 215-981-4009 202-220-1217)
White Collar 6% (Thomas M. Gallagher 215-981-4068)
Construction 4% (Michael P. Subak 215-981-4503)
Bankruptcy & Reorganization 3% (Todd A. Feinsmith/David M. Fournier 617-204-5145 302-777-6565)
Real Estate 3% (Matthew J. Swett 215-981-4788)
Tax 2% (Joan C. Arnold 215-981-4362)

Revenues and Profits
Revenues: $388,667,000
Profits: $179,800,000

Leading Officials
Thomas M. Gallagher, Chair, Executive Committee, 215-981-4068
Thomas J. Cole, Jr., Managing Partner, 215-981-4507
Daniel J. Boland, Hiring Partner, 215-981-4399
Margaret A. Suender, Senior Director of Professional Development & Recruitment, 215-981-4657
Daniel Pulka, Chief Marketing Officer, 215-981-4461
Josette L. Marsh, Director of IS/Technology, 215-981-4270
Robyn L. Beyer, Director of Library Services, 215-981-4100
Kassem L. Lucas, Partner in Charge, Diversity, 215-981-4426

Pepper Hamilton LLP (Continued)

Other Offices
3000 Two Logan Square
Eighteenth and Arch Streets
Philadelphia
PA
19103-2799
Phone: 215-981-4000
Fax: 215-981-4750
Email: phinfo@pepperlaw.com
Thomas J. Cole, Jr., Managing Partner

Post & Schell

Four Penn Center
1600 John F. Kennedy Boulevard
Philadelphia, PA 19103
Phone: 215-587-1000
Fax: 215-587-1444
Web Site: www.postschell.com

2016 Total Lawyers: 134
2015 Total Lawyers: 121

2016 Staff
Associates: 54
Principals 67

Offices: No. Attys.
Philadelphia: 64
Lancaster: 14
Allentown: 10
Harrisburg: 19
Pittsburgh: 8
Princeton, NJ: 1
Washington, DC: 5

Hiring and Promotion
2015 Associates Hired: 14
2015 First-Year Hires: 1
Starting Salary for First-Year Assocs: N/A
2016 First-Year Hires (Est.): 0
2015 Equity Partners Named: 0
2015 Lateral Equity Partners: 2

PENNSYLVANIA

Post & Schell (Continued)

*Leading Practice Areas
(Department Heads)*
Construction, Government Contracts &
Surety Law (Kenneth L. Sable (co-chair)
717-612-6036)
Construction, Government Contracts &
Surety Law (Gary A. Wilson (co-chair)
202-661-6956)
Energy (Michael W. Gang (co-chair)
717-612-6026)
Energy (David B. MacGregor (co-chair)
215-587-1197)
Environmental (Paul R. McIntyre (co-chair)
215-587-1150)
Environmental (Stephen C. Jones (co-chair)
215-587-1128)
Health Care (Paula G. Sanders
717-612-6027)
White Collar Defense (Ronald L. Levine
215-587-1071)
Employment & Employee Relations (Sidney
R. Steinberg 215-587-1140)
Insurance Law (Richard L. McMonigle, Jr.
215-587-1019)
Professional Liability Defense (Donald N.
Camhi 215-587-1015)
Workers' Compensation (Jonathan C. Ascher
412-577-2982)
Casualty Litigation (Daniel S. Altschuler
215-587-1107)

Client Representations
Elonis v. United States
PPL Corporation
Thomas Jefferson University
Hospitals System

Leading Officials
A. James Johnston, President and Chief
Executive Officer, 215-587-1000 ext. 1099
N/A
Stephen A. Schell, Jr., Chief Operating
Officer, 215-587-1000 ext. 1068
Andrew W. Allison, General Counsel and
Chief Compliance Officer, 215-587-1000
ext. 1059
Andrew W. Allison, Chief Compliance
Officer, 215-587-1000 ext. 1059
Michael J. Baltes, Chief Marketing and
Communications Officer, 215-587-1000
ext. 1195
N/A
Louis J. Mazzio, Jr., Chief Technology
Officer, 215-587-1000 ext. 1498
N/A
Andrew W. Allison, General Counsel and
Chief Compliance Officer, 215-587-1000
ext. 1059

Rawle & Henderson LLP

**1339 Chestnut Street
The Widener Building, 16th Floor
Philadelphia, PA 19107
Phone: 215-575-4200
Fax: 215-563-2583
Email: info@rawle.com
Web Site: www.rawle.com**

2016 Total Lawyers: 108
2015 Total Lawyers: 112

2016 Staff
Equity Partners: 12
Non-Equity Partners: 25
Associates: 45
Of Counsel: 26

Offices: No. Attys.
Philadelphia, PA: 64
Harrisburg, PA: 5
Pittsburgh, PA: 12
Marlton, NJ: 4
New York, NY: 11
Wilmington, DE: 5
Wheeling, WV: 1
Mineola, NY: 6

Hiring and Promotion
2015 Associates Hired: 21
2015 First-Year Hires: 3
2016 First-Year Hires (Est.): 1
2015 Equity Partners Named: 0

*Leading Practice Areas
(Department Heads)*
Environmental/Toxic Tort 15% (Peter J.
Neeson 215-575-4320)
Transportation Commercial Motor Vehicle
Defense 15% (Timothy J. Abeel
215-575-4280)
Medical Professional Liability 15% (John J.
Snyder 215-575-4220)
Product Liability 13% (Thomas A. Kuzmick
215-575-4262)
Casualty & Premises Liability 13% (John H.
McCarthy 215-575-4359)
Catastrophic Loss 10% (John J. Snyder
215-575-4220)
Workers Compensation 8% (Claudio DiPaolo
215-575-4343)
Professional Liability - Engineers, Architects
5% (Robert A. Fitch 212-323-7070)
Commercial Litigation 3% (David
Rosenbaum 215-575-4378)
Appellate 3% (Carl D. Buchholz
215-575-4235)

Client Representations
Kyle Deitrich v. Ward Sand & Materials, et
als, Docket No.: BUR-L-213-13,
Burlington County Superior Court, NJ,
defense verdict
Bernice Byrd, et al. v. Martin Felix Cabrera,
et al., Court of Common Pleas of
Philadelphia County, PA, August Term,
2014, No. 01366, defense verdict
Richard Wager v. Pelham Union Free School
District et al., Supreme Court of the State
of New York, Westchester County, Index
No. 68572/12, summary judgment

Rawle & Henderson LLP (Continued)

Leading Officials
James Cardell, Executive Director,
215-575-4310
Timothy J. Abeel, Recruiting Chairman,
215-575-4280
Nancy P. Mangini, HR & Office Manager,
215-575-4288
Stephen Davis, Marketing Director,
215-575-4240
James J. Begola, IT Manager, 215-575-4335
Research Assistant, Law Librarian,
215-575-4200
Timothy J. Abeel, Recruiting Chairman,
215-575-4280

Reed Smith LLP

**225 Fifth Avenue
Pittsburgh, PA 15219
Phone: 412-288-3131
Fax: 412-288-3063
Email: reedsmith@reedsmith.com
Web Site: www.reedsmith.com**

2016 Total Lawyers: 1880
2015 Total Lawyers: 1712

Saul Ewing LLP

**Centre Square West
1500 Market Street, 38th Floor
Philadelphia, PA 19102-2186
Phone: 215-972-7777
Fax: 215-972-7725
Email: Lawyers@saul.com
Web Site: www.saul.com**

2016 Total Lawyers: 270
2015 Total Lawyers: 270

Schnader Harrison Segal & Lewis LLP

**1600 Market Street
Suite 3600
Philadelphia, PA 19103-7286
Phone: 215-751-2000
Fax: 215-751-2205
Email: info@schnader.com
Web Site: www.schnader.com**

2016 Total Lawyers: 143
2015 Total Lawyers: 180

Stevens & Lee

**111 North Sixth Street
P.O. Box 679
Reading, PA 19603-0679
Phone: 610-478-2182
Fax: 610-371-8517
Email: attys@stevenslee.com
Web Site: www.stevenslee.com**

2016 Total Lawyers: 150
2015 Total Lawyers: 146

PENNSYLVANIA

Stradley Ronon Stevens & Young, LLP

2005 Market Street, Suite 2600
Philadelphia, PA 19103
Phone: 215-564-8000
Fax: 215-564-8120
Email: gbagin@stradley.com
Web Site: www.stradley.com

2016 Total Lawyers: 193
2015 Total Lawyers: 184

Swartz, Campbell & Detweiler

50 South 16th Street, Floor 28
2 Liberty Place
Philadelphia, PA 19102
Phone: 215-564-5190
Fax: 215-299-4301
Web Site: www.schwartzcampbell.com

2016 Total Lawyers: 86
2015 Total Lawyers: 86

Tucker Arensberg, P.C.

1500 One PPG Place
Pittsburgh, PA 15222
Phone: 412-566-1212
Fax: 412-594-5619
Email: tapc@tuckerlaw.com
Web Site: www.tuckerlaw.com

2016 Total Lawyers: 86
2015 Total Lawyers: 86

2016 Staff
Equity Partners: 43
Associates: 28
Of Counsel: 8
Counsel: 2
Senior Counsel: 2

Offices: No. Attys.
Pittsburgh, PA: 74
Harrisburg, PA: 6
Lewistown, PA: 2

Hiring and Promotion
2015 Associates Hired: 6
2015 First-Year Hires: 2
Starting Salary for First-Year Assocs: Decline
to disclose
2016 First-Year Hires (Est.): 2
2015 Equity Partners Named: 3
2015 Lateral Equity Partners: 1

Tucker Arensberg, P.C. (Continued)

*Leading Practice Areas
(Department Heads)*
Litigation 30% (Jonathan McAnney
412-594-5584)
Banking & Finance 20% (Eric M. Schumann
& Daniel J. Perry 412-594-5600 &
412-594-3901)
Insolvency & Creditors 10% (Beverly Weiss
Manne 412-594-5525)
Labor & Employment 10% (Robert L.
McTiernan & Homer L. Walton
412-594-5528 & 412-594-5657)
Estates & Trusts 5% (Charles J. Vater
412-594-5556)
Healthcare 5% (Paul Welk 412-594-5536)
Technology/Intellectual Property 5% (Ralph
F. Manning & Kristin Biedinger
412-594-5540 & 412-594-3916)
Municipal & School 5% (Thomas P. Peterson
& John T. Vogel 412-594-3914 &
412-594-5622)
Real Estate 5% (Steve Bovan, Irv Firman, Pat
Rodella 412-594-5607 & 412-594-5557,
412-594-3950)
Workers' Compensation 5% (Kenneth
Scholtz 412-594- 3903)

Client Representations
PNC Financial Service Group, Inc.
Verizon
Duquesne Light Company

Leading Officials
Thomas P. Peterson, Managing Shareholder,
412-594-3914
Robert Webb, COO, 412-594-5517
Irving Firman, 412-594-5557
Pamela J. Maxson, SPHR, Director of Human
Resources, 412-594-5512
Allysn Hurley, CMO, 412-594-3919
Alan Martin, MIS Director, 412-594-5549
Karen Eriksen, Librarian, 412-594-5601

PUERTO RICO

Fiddler, Gonzalez & Rodriguez, P.S.C.

254 Munoz Rivera Avenue
6th Floor
Hato Rey, PR 00918
Phone: 787-753-3113
Fax: 787-759-3123
Email: fiddler@fgrlaw.com
Web Site: www.fgrlaw.com

2016 Total Lawyers: 44
2015 Total Lawyers: 63

McConnell Valdes LLC

270 Munoz Rivera Avenue
Hato Rey
San Juan, PR 00918
Phone: 787-759-9292
Fax: 787-759-9225
Email: webmaster@mcvpr.com
Web Site: www.mcvpr.com

2016 Total Lawyers: 109
2015 Total Lawyers: 107

2016 Staff
Equity Partners: 30
Non-Equity Partners: 14
Associates: 24
Of Counsel: 12
Counsel: 28

Offices: No. Attys.
San Juan, Puerto Rico: 107

Hiring and Promotion
2016 First-Year Hires (Est.): 0
2015 Equity Partners Named: 0

*Leading Practice Areas
(Department Heads)*
Corporate (Samuel T. Cespedes, Jr.
787-250-2610)
Environmental, Energy & Land Use (Carlos
Fernandez-Lugo 787-250-5669)
Labor & Employment Law (Alfredo
Hopgood-Jovet 787-250-5689)
Litigation (Juan A. Marques 787-250-2619)
Tax (Isis Carballo 787-250-5691)
Tax (Yamary Gonzlez 787-250-5687)
Real Estate & Finance (Salvador F. Casellas
787-250-5613)

Leading Officials
Arturo J. Garcia-Sola, Managing Director.
787-250-5632
Miguel Rivera-Arce, Recruiting Partner.
787-250-5634
Teruca Sola, Marketing Director.
787-250-5150
Betzaida Velez, Head Librarian.
787-250-5147

RHODE ISLAND

Adler Pollock & Sheehan P.C.

One Citizens Plaza, 8th Floor
Providence, RI 02903-1345
Phone: 401-274-7200
Fax: 401-751-0604
Email: contactaps@apslaw.com
Web Site: www.apslaw.com

2016 Total Lawyers: 57
2015 Total Lawyers: 57

2016 Staff
Equity Partners: 28
Associates: 14
Of Counsel: 1
Counsel: 14

Offices: No. Attys.
Boston, MA: 9

Adler Pollock & Sheehan P.C. (Continued)
Providence, RI: 48

Hiring and Promotion
2015 Associates Hired: 4
2015 First-Year Hires: 1
2015 Equity Partners Named: 0

Leading Practice Areas
(Department Heads)
Commercial Litigation 40% (Patricia K. Rocha)
Corporate/Securities/Finance 20% (Stephen Geanacopoulos)
Product Liability/Toxic Tort 10% (John A. Tarantino)
Real Estate Law 6% (Robert I. Stolzman / Jonathan M. Sachs)
Government Relations 6% (Richard R. Beretta)
Employment/Labor 5% (Robert P. Brooks)
Hospitals/Health Care 4% (Patricia K. Rocha)
Energy & Utilities 3% (Alan M. Shoer)
Insurance Defense 3% (Mark O. Denehy)
Environmental 3% (Alan M. Shoer)

Leading Officials
John A. Tarantino, Firm Chair
Robert P. Brooks, Managing Partner
Nicholas F. Rago, Executive Director
Jeffrey K. Techentin, Recruiting Director
Toni Bianco, Marketing Manager
Paul R. Dumaine, Head Librarian
Robert P. Brooks, Chair Diversity Committee

Hinckley, Allen & Snyder P.C.

50 Kennedy Plaza, Suite 1500
Providence, RI 02903
Phone: 401-274-2000
Fax: 401-277-9600
Email: firm@haslaw.com
Web Site: www.haslaw.com

2016 Total Lawyers: 155
2015 Total Lawyers: 147

Haynsworth Sinkler Boyd, P.A.

1201 Main Street, 22nd Floor
P.O. Box 11889
Columbia, SC 29211
Phone: 803-779-3080
Fax: 803-765-1243
Web Site: www.sinklerboyd.com

2016 Total Lawyers: 115
2015 Total Lawyers: 108

McNair Law Firm, P.A.

1221 Main Street, Suite 1800
Columbia, SC 29211
Phone: 803-799-9800
Fax: 803-799-9804
Email: WCorley@mcnair.net
Web Site: www.mcnair.net

2016 Total Lawyers: 107
2015 Total Lawyers: 110

Motley Rice LLC

28 Bridgeside Blvd.
Mount Pleasant, SC 29464
Phone: 843-216-9000
Fax: 843-216-9450
Web Site: www.motleyrice.com

2016 Total Lawyers: 75
2015 Total Lawyers: 75

Leading Practice Areas
(Department Heads)
Occupational Disease
Securities Fraud
Environmental
Aviation
Anti-Terrorism
Pharmaceutical Drugs
Medical Devices
Human Rights
Toxic Exposure
Antitrust
Consumer Fraud
Catastrophic Personal Injury & Wrongful Death
Nursing Home Abuse & Neglect
Mass Transportation Personal Injury & Wrongful Death
Whistleblower

Leading Officials
Joseph F. Rice, Co-founder, 843-216-9000

Nelson Mullins Riley & Scarborough

1320 Main Street
Meridian, 17th Floor
Columbia, SC 29201
Phone: 803-799-2000
Fax: 803-256-7500
Email: info@nelsonmullins.com
Web Site: www.nelsonmullins.com

2016 Total Lawyers: 505
2015 Total Lawyers: 496

Nexsen Pruet

1230 Main Street
Suite 700
Columbia, SC 29201
Phone: 803-771-8900
Fax: 803-253-8277
Web Site: www.nexsenpruet.com

2016 Total Lawyers: 200
2015 Total Lawyers: 193

2016 Staff
Equity Partners: 73
Non-Equity Partners: 37
Associates: 30
Of Counsel: 3
Counsel: 43
Senior Counsel: 5
Staff Attorneys: 2

Offices: No. Attys.
Columbia, SC: 68
Charleston, SC: 26
Greenville, SC: 21
Hilton Head, SC: 4
Myrtle Beach, SC: 5
Charlotte, NC: 25
Greensboro, NC: 23
Raleigh, NC: 21

Hiring and Promotion
2015 Associates Hired: 8
2016 First-Year Hires (Est.): 2
2015 Equity Partners Named: 5

Leading Practice Areas
(Department Heads)
Real Estate (Franklin Daniels)
Business Litigation (Val Stieglitz)
Employment & Labor (David Dubberly)
Tax (Fred Kingsmore)
Health Care (Matthew Roberts)
Corporate (Marcus Knight)
Banking & Finance (Patrick Brown)
Intellectual Property (Marcus Knight)
Construction (Harper Heckman)
Bankruptcy & Creditors' Rights (Christine Myatt)

Leading Officials
John A. Sowards, Chairman
Mike Brittingham, Managing Member of Operations
Jean Anne Ferner, Chief Administrative Officer
David Gossett, Managing Member of Professionals
Tushar V. Chikhliker, Recruiting and Retention Committee Chair
Ashley Pace, Director of Business & Practice Development
Jeff Brewer, Chief Information Officer
Chris Wolf, Head Librarian
Tushar V. Chikhlikar, Diversity Committee Chair

Other Offices
1230 Main Street
Suite 700
Columbia, SC 29201
Phone: 803-771-8900
Fax: 803-253-8277
John A. Sowards

TENNESSEE

Baker, Donelson, Bearman, Caldwell & Berkowitz, P.C.

165 Madison Avenue
Suite 2000
Memphis, TN 38103
Phone: 901-526-2000
Fax: 901-577-2303
Email: web@bakerdonelson.com
Web Site: www.bakerdonelson.com

2016 Total Lawyers: 692
2015 Total Lawyers: 690

2016 Staff
Equity Partners: 219
Non-Equity Partners: 107
Associates: 167
Of Counsel: 82
Senior Counsel: 36
Staff Attorneys: 54
Senior Public Policy Advisors: 7
Public Policy Advisors: 1
Contract Attorneys: 2
Advisors 17

Offices: No. Attys.
Memphis, TN: 96
Nashville, TN: 109
Chattanooga, TN: 48
Jackson, MS: 76
Washington, DC: 39
Knoxville, TN: 22
Johnson City, TN: 14
Atlanta, GA: 78
Birmingham, AL: 61
New Orleans, LA: 58
Mandeville, LA: 6
Baton Rouge, LA: 18
Macon, GA: 3
Montgomery, AL: 1
Houston, TX: 25
Orlando, FL: 19
Ft. Lauderdale, FL: 12
Tallahassee, FL: 5
Jacksonville, FL: 2

Hiring and Promotion
2015 Associates Hired: 38
2015 First-Year Hires: 15
2016 First-Year Hires (Est.): 18
2015 Equity Partners Named: 11
2015 Lateral Equity Partners: 7

Leading Officials
Ben C. Adams, Jr., Chief Executive Officer
Jennifer Keller, Chief Operating Officer
James M. Hughes, Executive Director
Ben C. Adams, Jr., Hiring Partner
Rebecca Simon, Director of Attorney
    Recruitment
Jeff Hirka, Marketing Director
Adam Severson, Chief Marketing & Business
    Development Officer
John D. Green, Chief Information Officer
Rebecca Bowman, Director of
    Research Services
Mark Baugh, Diversity Committee Chair

Baker, Donelson, Bearman, Caldwell &
Berkowitz, P.C. (Continued)

Other Offices
First Tennessee Bank
165 Madison Avenue
Suite 2000
Memphis
TN
38103
Phone: 901-526-2000
Fax: 901-577-2303
Mark Glover, Office Managing Shareholder

Baker Donelson Center
211 Commerce Street
Suite 800
Nashville
TN
37201
Phone: 615-726-5600
Fax: 615-726-0464
Scott Carey, Office Managing Shareholder

One Eastover Center
100 Vision Drive
Suite 400
Jackson
MS
39211
Phone: 601-351-2400
Fax: 601-351-2424
Scott Pedigo, Office Managing Shareholder

Wells Fargo Tower
420 20th Street North
Suite 1400
Birmingham
AL
35203
Phone: 205-328-0480
Fax: 205-322-8007
Andy Rotenstreich, Office Managing
    Shareholder

Monarch Plaza
3414 Peachtree Street
Suite 1600
Atlanta
GA
30326-1164
Phone: 404-577-6000
Fax: 404-221-6501
Gary Barnes, Office Managing Shareholder

New Orleans
201 St. Charles Avenue
Suite 3600
New Orleans
LA
70170-3600
Phone: 504-566-5200
Fax: 504-636-4000
Nancy Degan, Office Managing Shareholder

Bass, Berry & Sims PLC

150 Third Avenue South
Suite 2800
Nashville, TN 37201
Phone: 615-742-6200
Fax: 615-742-6293
Email: info@bassberry.com
Web Site: www.bassberry.com

2016 Total Lawyers: 290
2015 Total Lawyers: 230

Chambliss Bahner & Stophel

Liberty Tower
605 Chestnut St., Ste. 1700
Chattanooga, TN 37450
Phone: 423-756-3000
Fax: 423-265-9574
Web Site: www.chamblisslaw.com

2016 Total Lawyers: 57
2015 Total Lawyers: 55

King & Ballow

1100 Union Street Plaza
315 Union Street
Nashville, TN 37201
Phone: 615-259-3456
Fax: 615-254-7907
Web Site: www.kingballow.com

2016 Total Lawyers: 22
2015 Total Lawyers: 25

Leitner, Williams, Dooley & Napolitan, PLLC

200 W. ML King Blvd, Suite 500
Tallan Building
Chattanooga, TN 37402
Phone: 423-265-0214
Fax: 423-266-5490
Email: lwdn@leitnerfirm.com
Web Site: www.leitnerfirm.com

2016 Total Lawyers: 60
2015 Total Lawyers: 69

2016 Staff
Equity Partners: 33
Associates: 18
Of Counsel: 9

Offices: No. Attys.
Chattanooga, TN: 24
Knoxville, TN: 13
Nashville, TN: 10
Memphis, TN: 11
Atlanta, GA: 2

Hiring and Promotion
2015 Associates Hired: 6
2015 First-Year Hires: 3
2016 First-Year Hires (Est.): 2
2015 Equity Partners Named: 4

TENNESSEE

Leitner, Williams, Dooley & Napolitan, PLLC (Continued)

Leading Officials
M. Andrew Pippenger, Managing Partner
C. Christopher Brown, Hiring Partner
Mary Gadd, Marketing Director
Charles W. Poss, Head Librarian
C. Christopher Brown, Member,
865-523-0404

Miller & Martin

Volunteer Building - Suite 1200
832 Georgia Avenue
Chattanooga, TN 37402-2289
Phone: 423-756-6600
Fax: 423-785-8480
Email: lori.pilon@millermartin.c
Web Site: www.millermartin.com

2016 Total Lawyers: 131
2015 Total Lawyers: 133

2016 Staff
Equity Partners: 59
Non-Equity Partners: 25
Associates: 21
Of Counsel: 26

Offices: No. Attys.
Chattanooga, TN: 82
Nashville, TN: 2
Atlanta, GA: 46

Hiring and Promotion
2015 Associates Hired: 7
2015 First-Year Hires: 9
Starting Salary for First-Year Assocs:
$95,000-$128,700
2016 First-Year Hires (Est.): 1
2015 Equity Partners Named: 4
2015 Lateral Equity Partners: 3

Leading Practice Areas
(Department Heads)
Litigation 32.96% (James Williams
423-756-6600)
Corporate 32.45% (Pat Murphy
423-756-6600)
Real Estate 15.74% (Tom Hayslett
423-756-6600)
Employment 4.89% (John Bode
423-756-6600)
Commercial 2.43% (Bill Dupre
423-756-6600)
Estates & Trusts 1.51% (Don Morton
423-756-6600)
Trademark 1.45% (Stephen Stark
423-756-6600)
Bankruptcy 1.42% (Craig Smith
423-756-6600)
Tax 1.20% (Jim Tramonte 423-756-6600)
Patent 1.08% (Stephen Stark 423-756-6600)

Revenues and Profits
Revenues: $57,972,985
Profits: $23,649,824

Client Representations
Coca-Cola Refreshments, Inc.
Life Care Centers of America
FDIC

Miller & Martin (Continued)

Leading Officials
Jim Haley, Chairman
David Hetzel, Executive Director
Karen Smith, Michael Kohler, Hiring
Committee Chairs
Caitlin Ross, Assistant Director of
Human Resources
Robyn Charles, Director of Marketing
Lori Pilon, Practice Development Manager
Kym Weaver, Director of Information
Systems and Technology
Ginny Hughes, Head Librarian
Jim Haley, Diversity Committee Chair

Waller Lansden Dortch & Davis

511 Union Street
Suite 2700
Nashville, TN 37219
Phone: 615-244-6380
Fax: 615-244-6804
Email: kathleen.caillouette@wall
Web Site: www.wallerlaw.com

2016 Total Lawyers: 200
2015 Total Lawyers: 198

TEXAS

Andrews Kurth LLP

600 Travis Street
Suite 4200
Houston, TX 77002
Phone: 713-220-4200
Fax: 713-220-4285
Email: webmaster@andrewskurth.co
Web Site: www.andrewskurth.com

2016 Total Lawyers: 328
2015 Total Lawyers: 397

2016 Staff
Equity Partners: 69.10
Non-Equity Partners: 96.65
Associates: 116.64
Of Counsel: 24.26
Senior Attorneys: 7.50
Counsel: 13.50

Offices: No. Attys.
Houston, TX: 170.25
Dallas, TX: 59.13
Austin, TX: 28.1
New York, NY: 21.44
The Woodlands, TX: 9.48
London, England: 3.9
Washington, DC: 20.96
Beijing, China: 5.4
Dubai, UAE: 6
Research Triangle Park, NC: 3

Hiring and Promotion
2015 Associates Hired: 29
2015 First-Year Hires: 15
Starting Salary for First-Year
Assocs: $180,000
2016 First-Year Hires (Est.): 17
2015 Equity Partners Named: 14
2015 Lateral Equity Partners: 5

Andrews Kurth LLP (Continued)

Leading Practice Areas
(Department Heads)
Litigation (Tom Taylor/John Shely
713-220-4200)
Corporate Securities (Mike O'Leary/David
Buck 713-220-4200)
Bankruptcy (Robin Russell/Paul Silverstein
713-220-4200)
Business Transactions (Darren Inoff
713-220-4200)
Public Law (Gene Locke/Rick Witte
713-220-4200)
Intellectual Property (Jeff Dodd
713-220-4200)
Environmental (Lisa Shelton 512-320-9200)
Tax (Tom Ford 713-220-4200)
Labor (Marc Katz 214-659-4400)
Energy (Ken Wiseman 202-662-2700)

Leading Officials
Tom Perich, Chairman, 713-220-4268
Robert V. Jewell, Managing Partner,
713-220-4358
Jeffrey E. Spiers, Partner & Executive
Director, 713-220-4103
Tammy Brennig/Tom Sage/Courtney
Cochran Butler, Hiring Partner,
713-220-4424
Kendall Lowery, Director of Attorney
Employment, 713-220-4580
Ashley Nelly, Director of Marketing
Operations, 713-220-4410
Deborah Grabein, Director of Business
Development, 713-220-4629
Lynn McGuire, CIO, 713-220-4537
Margo Davis, Manager of Library Services,
713-220-4094
Elizabeth Campbell, Partner & Chief
Diversity Officer, 713-220-4646

Other Offices
Dallas
1717 Main Street
Suite 3700
Dallas
TX
75201
Phone: 214-659-4400
Fax: 214-659-4401
Email: webmaster@andrewskurth.com
Mark Solomon

Baker Botts LLP

One Shell Plaza
910 Louisiana Street
Houston, TX 77002-4995
Phone: 713-229-1234
Fax: 713-229-1522
Web Site: www.bakerbotts.com

2016 Total Lawyers: 725
2015 Total Lawyers: 725

TEXAS

Bracewell LLP

711 Louisiana Street
Suite 2300
Houston, TX 77002-2770
Phone: 713-223-2300
Fax: 713-221-1212
Web Site: www.bracewelllaw.com

2016 Total Lawyers: 465
2015 Total Lawyers: 465

2016 Staff
Equity Partners: 102
Non-Equity Partners: 109
Associates: 131
Of Counsel: 1
Counsel: 41

Offices: No. Attys.
Houston, TX: 155
Connecticut: 8
Dubai, UAE: 7
Washington, DC: 43
Dallas, TX: 28
Austin, TX: 27
London, England: 21
San Antonio, TX: 12
New York, NY: 47
Seattle, WA: 11

Hiring and Promotion
2015 Associates Hired: 23

Leading Practice Areas
(Department Heads)
Litigation 30% (Stephen Crain
713-223-2300)
Corporate 14% (Greg Bopp 713-223-2300)
Energy 11% (G. Alan Rafte 713-223-2300)
Banking and Finance 9% (Dewey J.
Gonsoulin Jr. 713-223-2300)
Financial Restructuring 7% (Evan Flaschen
860-947-9000)
Labor & Employment 6% (Robert Sheeder
214-468-3800)
Securities 6% (Charles Still and William
Anderson 713-223-2300)
Intellectual Property 5% (Constance
Rhebergen 713-223-2300)
Real Estate 5% (Aaron Roffwarg
713-223-2300)
Government Relations 5% (Scott Segal
202-828-5800)

Revenues and Profits
Revenues: $337,508,813

Client Representations
Kinder Morgan
Wells Fargo
Apache

Bracewell LLP (Continued)

Leading Officials
Patrick C. Oxford, Chairman, 713-223-2300
Gregory M. Bopp, Managing Partner,
713-223-2300
Brenda Cook Cialone, COO, 713-223-2300
Ryan Holcomb and Bryan Dumesnil, Hiring
Partner, 713-223-2300
Jean Lenzner, Director, Attorney
Employment, 713-223-2300
Paul Grabowski, Chief Marketing Officer,
713-223-2300
Kristine Holland, Senior Director of Business
Development, 860-947-9000
Kirk Scruggs, Chief Information Officer,
713-223-2300
Sean Luman, Director, Knowledge
Management, 713-223-2300
Marredia Rogers, Manager, Diversity,
713-223-2300

Other Offices
Dallas
1445 Ross Avenue
Suite 3800
Dallas
TX
75202-2711
Phone: 214-468-3800
Fax: 214-468-3888
K. Brock Bailey

Houston
711 Louisiana Street
Suite 2300
Houston
TX
77002
Phone: 713-223-2300
Fax: 713-221-1212
Gregory M. Bopp

Washington, DC
2001 M Street, NW
Suite 900
Washington
DC
20036-3310
Phone: 202-828-5800
Fax: 202-223-1225
Mark K. Lewis

New York
1251 Avenue of the Americas
49th Floor
New York
NY
10020
Phone: 212-508-6100
Fax: 212-508-6101
Daniel S. Connolly

Cantey & Hanger, L.L.P.

600 West 6th Street
Suite 300
Fort Worth, TX 76102
Phone: 817-877-2800
Fax: 817-877-2807
Web Site: www.canteyhanger.com

2016 Total Lawyers: 62
2015 Total Lawyers: 62

Carrington, Coleman, Sloman & Blumenthal L.L.P.

901 Main St
Suite 5500
Dallas, TX 75202
Phone: 214-855-3000
Fax: 214-855-1333
Web Site: www.carringtoncoleman.com

2016 Total Lawyers: 48
2015 Total Lawyers: 50

2016 Staff
Equity Partners: 22
Associates: 17
Of Counsel: 7
Senior Counsel: 2

Offices: No. Attys.
Dallas: 48

Hiring and Promotion
2015 Associates Hired: 1
2015 First-Year Hires: 1
2016 First-Year Hires (Est.): 0
2015 Equity Partners Named: 4
2015 Lateral Equity Partners: 4

Leading Practice Areas
(Department Heads)
Business Litigation (Cathy Altman
214-855-3083)
Employment (Mike Birrer 214-855-3113)
Health Care (Rodney Lawson 214-855-3054)
Securities and Directors and Officers (Bruce
Collins 214-855-3018)
Transactions and Counseling (Charles Jordan
214-855-3021)
Intellectual Property (Mark Howland
214-855-3010)
Oil and Gas (Richard Rohan 214-855-3043)
Business Ownership Disputes (Tim Gavin
214-855-3012)
Family Wealth (Charles Jordan
214-855-3021)
Corporate (Bret Madole 214-855-3034)
Real Estate and Construction (Neal Suit
214-855-3046)

Leading Officials
None
Bruce W. Collins, Managing Partner,
214-855-3018
Gregory R. Grass, Chief Operating Officer,
214-855-3094
Kelli Hinson, Hiring Partner, 214-855-3110
Andrea Glover, Human Resources & Talent
Acquisition Manager, 214-855-3536
Bill Bourland, Director of Client Service &
Business Development, 214-855-3566
Scott Hampton, Director of Information
Services, 214-855-3355
Mike Birrer, Partner, 214-855-3113

THE LAWYER'S ALMANAC

TEXAS

Chamberlain Hrdlicka White Williams & Aughtry

1200 Smith Street
Suite 1400
Houston, TX 77002
Phone: 713-658-1818
Fax: 713-658-2553
Email: chwwm@chamberlainlaw.com
Web Site: www.chamberlainlaw.com

2016 Total Lawyers: 117
2015 Total Lawyers: 114

Cowles & Thompson, P.C.

901 Main Street
Suite 3900
Dallas, TX 75202
Phone: 214-672-2000
Fax: 214-672-2020
Email: info@cowlesthompson.com
Web Site: www.cowlesthompson.com

2016 Total Lawyers: 28
2015 Total Lawyers: 32

Gardere Wynne Sewell LLP

3000 Thanksgiving Tower
1601 Elm Street
Dallas, TX 75201-4761
Phone: 214-999-3000
Fax: 214-999-4667
Web Site: www.gardere.com

2016 Total Lawyers: 230
2015 Total Lawyers: 233

2016 Staff
Equity Partners: 72
Non-Equity Partners: 64
Associates: 70
Of Counsel: 8
Senior Attorneys: 10
Staff Attorneys: 9

Offices: No. Attys.
Dallas: 131
Houston: 73
Austin: 19
Mexico City: 10

Hiring and Promotion
2015 Associates Hired: 13
2015 First-Year Hires: 7
2015 Equity Partners Named: 3

Gardere Wynne Sewell LLP (Continued)

Leading Practice Areas
(Department Heads)
Litigation 35.1% (Scott L. Davis, Geoffrey H. Bracken 214.999.4511, 713.276.5739)
Corporate 23.5% (Michael H. Newman, Daniel L. Cohen 214.999.4716, 713.276.5860)
Tax 8.9% (James Howard 713.276.5391)
Intellectual Property 8.7% (Andre M. Szuwalski 214.999.4795)
Real Estate 8.1% (Kevin L. Kelley 214.999.4503)
Government Affairs (including Environmental) 6.4% (Kimberly A. Yelkin 512.542.7001)
Labor and Employment 5.3% (Carrie B. Hoffman 214.999.4262)
Financial Restructuring and Reorganization 4.0% (John P. Melko 713.276.5727)

Leading Officials
Holland N. O'Neil, Chair of the Board of Directors, 214-999-4961
Shawn Adams, Executive Director, 214-999-4844
Jenn Falls, Director of Recruiting and Professional Development, 214-999-4206
Christy Tedesco, Director of Marketing and Business Development, 214-999-4057
Kenneth Orgeron, Chief Information Officer, 214-999-4958
Juan M. Alcala, /Dwight M. Francis, Partners; Co-Chairs, Diversity Committee, 214-999-3000

Other Offices
2000 Wells Fargo Plaza
1000 Louisiana St.
77002
Houston
TX
77002
Phone: 713-276-5500
Fax: 713-276-5555
Claude Treece, Operating Partner

Graves, Dougherty, Hearon & Moody, P.C.

401 Congress Avenue
Suite 2200
Austin, TX 78701
Phone: 512-480-5600
Email: gdhm@gdhm.com
Web Site: www.gdhm.com

2016 Total Lawyers: 69
2015 Total Lawyers: 69

Gray, Reed & McGraw, a Professional Corporation

1300 Post Oak Boulevard
Suite 2000
Houston, TX 77056
Phone: 713-986-7000
Fax: 713-986-7100
Web Site: www.grayreed.com

2016 Total Lawyers: 127
2015 Total Lawyers: 125

2016 Staff
Equity Partners: 30
Non-Equity Partners: 30
Associates: 58
Of Counsel: 6
Staff Attorneys: 1

Offices: No. Attys.
Houston: 65
Dallas: 60

Hiring and Promotion
2015 Associates Hired: 10
2015 First-Year Hires: 4
Starting Salary for First-Year Assocs: 130,000
2016 First-Year Hires (Est.): 4
2015 Equity Partners Named: 5
2015 Lateral Equity Partners: 3

Leading Practice Areas
(Department Heads)
Litigation 30% (James Ormiston)
Corporate 20% (Dan Kroll)
Energy 10% (Paul Yale)
Intellectual Property 10% (David Henry)
Healthcare 5% (Andrew Meyercord)
Real Estate 5% (Terry Thornton)
Tax 5% (Tom Rhodus)
Employment 5% (Ruth Ann Daniels)
Bankruptcy 5% (Jason Brookner)
Family Law 3% (Kyle Sanders)
Trusts & Estates 2% (Greg Sampson)

Revenues and Profits
Revenues: $50,000,000
Profits: $20,000,000

Leading Officials
J. Cary Gray, President
Mark Gargiulo, Chief Operating Person
James Ormiston/Ken Stone, Hiring Committee Chair
Olga Alvarado, Director of Human Resources
Michael Blachly, Director of Client Development
Jason Rodriguez, Director of IT
Monika Miura
Terry Thornton, Chair, Diversity Committee

Other Offices
1601 Elm Street
Suite 4600
Dallas
TX
75201
Phone: 214-954-4135
Fax: 214-954-1332

A-116

TEXAS

Haynes and Boone, LLP

2323 Victory Blvd
Suite 700
Dallas, TX 75219
Phone: 214-651-5000
Fax: 214-651-5940
Web Site: www.haynesboone.com

2016 Total Lawyers: 587
2015 Total Lawyers: 558

Jackson Walker LLP

2323 Ross Avenue
Suite 600
Dallas, TX 75201
Phone: 214-953-6000
Fax: 214-953-5822
Email: jwextmarketing@jw.com
Web Site: www.jw.com

2016 Total Lawyers: 362
2015 Total Lawyers: 365

2016 Staff
Equity Partners: 98
Non-Equity Partners: 135
Associates: 88
Of Counsel: 9
Senior Attorneys: 13
Senior Counsel: 19

Offices: No. Attys.
Dallas, TX: 136
Houston, TX: 84
Austin, TX: 98
San Antonio, TX: 31
Fort Worth, TX: 17
San Angelo, TX: 3
Texarkana: 1

Hiring and Promotion
2015 Associates Hired: 28
2015 First-Year Hires: 12
2015 Equity Partners Named: 0

Revenues and Profits
Revenues: $221,500,000
Profits: $84,000,000

Client Representations
Crescent Real Estate Equities
Bank of America
Reliant Energy

Leading Officials
Wade Cooper, Managing Partner
Jeremy Brewer, Chief Financial Officer
James S. Ryan, Statewide Hiring Partner
Bridgette Stahlman, Director of
Lateral Recruiting
Barbara Malin, Chief Business Development
and Marketing Officer
Greg Lambert, Chief Knowledge
Services Officer
Bruce Ruzinsky, Diversity Committee
Chairperson

Jackson Walker LLP (Continued)

Other Offices
1401 McKinney Street
Ste. 1900
Houston, TX 77010-4008
Phone: 713-752-4200
Fax: 713-752-4221
Kurt Nondorf, Managing Partner

100 Congress Avenue
Ste. 1100
Austin, TX 78701-4099
Phone: 512-236-2000
Fax: 512-236-2002
Matt Dow, Managing Partner

Kelly, Hart & Hallman LLP

201 Main Street
Suite 2500
Fort Worth, TX 76102
Phone: 817-332-2500
Fax: 817-878-9280
Web Site: www.khh.com

2016 Total Lawyers: 155
2015 Total Lawyers: 151

2016 Staff
Equity Partners: 56
Non-Equity Partners: 39
Associates: 46
Of Counsel: 8
Senior Counsel: 6

Offices: No. Attys.
Fort Worth, TX: 115
Austin, TX: 17
Midland, TX: 11
New Orleans, LA: 10
Baton Rouge, LA: 2

Hiring and Promotion
2015 Associates Hired: 10
2015 First-Year Hires: 5
Starting Salary for First-Year Assocs:
$140,000-$150,000
2016 First-Year Hires (Est.): 3
2015 Equity Partners Named: 8
2015 Lateral Equity Partners: 3 non

Leading Practice Areas
(Department Heads)
Litigation (Bill Warren/Hugh Connor
817-878-3564)
Real Estate & Finance (Chad Key/Alan Hegi
817-878-3555)
Oil & Gas/Energy (Todd Spake
817-878-3592)
Corporate & Securities (Benton Cantey
817-878-3559)
Environmental & Water Law (Monica Jacobs
512-495-6405)
Appellate (Marianne Auld 817-878-3543)
Banking & Finance (Dan Settle
817-878-3536)
Labor & Employment (Henry Robinson
817-878-3558)
Bankruptcy/Business Reorganization
(Michael McConnell 817-878-3569)
Tax, Trusts & Estates (Chester Grudzinski
817-878-3584)

Kelly, Hart & Hallman LLP (Continued)

Leading Officials
Dee Kelly Jr, Managing Partner
Kristi Hudson, CFO
Dee Kelly Jr.
Marcus Mungioli
Mary Schlegel, Director of Marketing
Mike Reese, IT Director
Cheryl Leb and DeMarcus Gordon, Partners
and Co-Chairs of the Diversity Committee,
817-332-2500

Kemp Smith, P.C.

221 North Kansas
Suite 1700
El Paso, TX 79901
Phone: 915-533-4424
Fax: 915-546-5360
Email: ksdh@kempsmith.com
Web Site: www.kempsmith.com

2016 Total Lawyers: 41
2015 Total Lawyers: 43

Locke Lord LLP

2200 Ross Avenue
Suite 2200
Dallas, TX 75201
Phone: 214-740-8000
Fax: 214-740-8800
Web Site: www.lockelord.com

2016 Total Lawyers: 823
2015 Total Lawyers: 876

McGinnis, Lochridge & Kilgore, LLP

600 Congress Ave
Suite 2100
Austin, TX 78701
Phone: 512-495-6000
Fax: 512-495-6093
Email: info@mcginnislaw.com
Web Site: www.mcginnislaw.com

2016 Total Lawyers: 59
2015 Total Lawyers: 63

MehaffyWeber, P.C.

2615 Calder Avenue, Suite 800
Post Office Box 16
Beaumont, TX 77704
Phone: 409-835-5011
Fax: 409-835-5177
Web Site: www.mehaffyweber.com

2016 Total Lawyers: 31
2015 Total Lawyers: 30

TEXAS

Munsch Hardt Kopf & Harr, P.C.

3800 Lincoln Plaza
500 N. Akard Street
Dallas, TX 75201-6659
Phone: 214-855-7500
Email: ctedesco@munsch.com
Web Site: www.munsch.com

2016 Total Lawyers: 115
2015 Total Lawyers: 115

Naman, Howell, Smith & Lee

400 Austin Avenue
Suite 800
Waco, TX 76703-1470
Phone: 254-755-4100
Fax: 254-754-6331
Email: info@namanhowell.com
Web Site: www.namanhowell.com

2016 Total Lawyers: 63
2015 Total Lawyers: 72

Norton Rose Fulbright

Fulbright Tower
1301 McKinney, Suite 5100
Houston, TX 77010
Phone: 713-651-5151
Fax: 713-651-5246
Email: info@fulbright.com
Web Site: www.nortonrosefulbright.com/us

2016 Total Lawyers: 3622
2015 Total Lawyers: 3800

2016 Staff
Associates: 1533
Partners 1153
Counsel, Of Counsel, Trainees, etc. 936

Offices: No. Attys.
Austin: 75
Dallas: 124
Denver: 9
Houston: 218
Los Angeles: 50
Minneapolis: 18
New York: 122
Pittsburgh-Southpointe: 4
San Antonio: 48
St. Louis: 10
Washington, DC: 74
Abu Dhabi: 6
Bahrain: 3
Dubai: 34
Riyadh: 8
Bogota: 22
Caracas: 37
Rio de Janeiro: 3
Amsterdam: 42
Brussels: 11
Frankfurt: 51
Greece (Athens & Piraeus): 29
Hamburg: 24
Kazakhstan: 10

Norton Rose Fulbright (Continued)
London: 704
Moscow: 34
Munich: 68
Paris: 111
Milan: 41
Warsaw: 30
Calgary: 149
Montreal: 183
Ottawa: 48
Quebec: 63
Toronto: 198
Brisbane: 72
Melbourne: 137
Perth: 49
Sydney: 213
Bangkok: 15
Beijing: 6
Hong Kong: 87
Jakarta: 18
Shanghai: 10
Singapore: 77
Tokyo: 13
Cape Town: 35
Durban: 34
Johannesburg: 187
Casablanca: 1
Dar es Salaam: 6

Leading Officials
Linda L. Addison, US Managing Partner ,
212-318-3000
Doug Wabner, Chair, US Hiring Committee,
214-855-8000
Leslie Rice, Chief of Attorney Recruiting and
Development , 713-651-5518
Catherine Austin , Chief Marketing Officer ,
713-651-5151
Edie Dillon, Chief Information Officer,
713-651-5151
Saskia Mehlhorn, Director of Knowledge
Management & Library Services,
713-651-5151
Lisa Genecov, Chair, Diversity and Inclusion
Committee, 214-855-8000

Other Offices
New York
666 Fifth Avenue
New York
NY
10103
Phone: 212-318-3000
Fax: 212-318-3400
Email:
steven.suzzan@nortonrosefulbright.com
Steven Suzzan, New York Partner-in-Charge

Washington, DC
799 9th Street NW
Suite 1000
Washington, DC
20001
Phone: 202-662-0200
Fax: 202-662-4643
Email:
stephen.mcnabb@nortonrosefulbright.com
Stephen M. McNabb, Washington, DC
Partner-in-Charge

Norton Rose Fulbright (Continued)

Austin
98 San Jacinto Boulevard
Suite 1100
Austin
TX
78701
Phone: 512-474-5201
Fax: 512-536-4598
Email:
stacey.martinez@nortonrosefulbright.com
Stacey A. Martinez, Austin Partner-in-Charge

Dallas
2200 Ross Avenue
Suite 3600
Dallas
TX
75201
Phone: 214-855-8000
Fax: 214-855-8200
Email:
jon.skidmore@nortonrosefulbright.com
Jonathan B. Skidmore, Dallas
Partner-in-Charge

Houston
Fulbright Tower, 1301 McKinney
Suite 5100
Houston
TX
77010
Phone: 713-651-5151
Fax: 713-651-5246
Email: carter.crow@nortonrosefulbright.com
Carter Crow, Houston Partner-in-Charge

Montreal
1 Place Ville Marie
Suite 2500
Montreal
Quebec
H3B 1R1
Phone: 514-847-4747
Fax: 514-286-5474
Email:
solomon.sananes@nortonrosefulbright.com
Solomon Sananes, Managing Partner -
Montreal office

Quebec
2828 Boulevard Laurier
Suite 1500
Quebec
Quebec
G1V 0B9
Phone: 418-640-5000
Fax: 418-640-1500
Email:
carl.tremblay@nortonrosefulbright.com
Carl Tremblay, Managing Partner -
Quebec office

Calgary
400 3rd Avenue SW
Suite 3700
Calgary
Alberta
T2P 4H2
Phone: 403-267-8222
Fax: 403-264-5973
Email:
brad.hayden@nortonrosefulbright.com
Bradley Hayden, Managing Partner -
Calgary office

TEXAS

Norton Rose Fulbright (Continued)

Toronto
Royal Bank Plaza, 200 Bay Street
Suite 3800
Toronto
Ontario
M5J 2Z4
Phone: 416-216-4000
Fax: 416-216-3930
Email:
andrew.fleming@nortonrosefulbright.com
Andrew Fleming, Managing Partner -
Toronto office

Hong Kong
38/F Jardine House, 1 Connaught Place
Central
Hong Kong SAR
Email: phillip.john@nortonrosefulbright.com
Phillip John, Head of North Asia

Singapore
One Raffles Quay, 34-02 North Tower
Singapore
048583
Phone: 656-223-7311
Fax: 656-224-5758
Email: jeff.smith@nortonrosefulbright.com
Jeff Smith, Head of South East Asia

Melbourne
RACV Tower, 485 Bourke Street
Level 15
Melbourne
VIC
3000
Email: peter.cash@nortonrosefulbright.com
Peter Cash, Head, Melbourne office

Los Angeles
555 South Flower Street
Forty-First Floor
Los Angeles
CA
90071
Phone: 213-892-9200
Fax: 213-892-9494
Email:
peter.mason@nortonrosefulbright.com
Peter H. Mason, Los Angeles
Partner-in-Charge

Sydney
Grosvenor Place, 225 George Street
Level 18
Sydney
NSW
2000
Email:
felicity.rourke@nortonrosefulbright.com
Felicity Rourke, Head, Sydney office

Brisbane
111 Eagle Street
Level 21
Brisbane
QLD
4000
Email:
peter.schmidt@nortonrosefulbright.com
Peter Schmidt, Head, Brisbane office

Norton Rose Fulbright (Continued)

Johannesburg
15 Alice Lane
Johannesburg
Gauteng
2196
Email: rob.otty@nortonrosefulbright.com
Rob Otty, Managing Director

Paris
ParisEight, 40, rue de Courcelles
Paris
France
75008
Email:
george.paterson@nortonrosefulbright.com
George Patterson, Head, Paris office

Munich
Theatinerstrasse 11
Munich
Germany
80333
Email:
ralf.springer@nortonrosefulbright.com
Ralf Springer, Head of Germany

London
3 More London Riverside
London
United Kingdom
SE1 2AQ
Email:
martin.scott@nortonrosefulbright.com
Martin Scott, Managing Partner, EMEA

Frankfurt
Taunustor 1 (TaunusTurm), 60310
Frankfurt am Main
Frankfurt
Germany
Email:
thomas.hopf@nortonrosefulbright.com
Thomas Hopf, Head of Frankfurt

Strasburger & Price

901 Main Street
Suite 4400
Dallas, TX 75202-3794
Phone: 214-651-4300
Fax: 214-651-4330
Email: info@strasburger.com
Web Site: www.strasburger.com

2016 Total Lawyers: 209
2015 Total Lawyers: 212

Thompson & Knight

One Arts Plaza
1722 Routh Street, Suite 1500
Dallas, TX 75201
Phone: 214-969-1700
Fax: 214-969-1751
Web Site: www.tklaw.com

2016 Total Lawyers: 263
2015 Total Lawyers: 295

Vinson & Elkins

First City Tower
1001 Fannin Street, Suite 2500
Houston, TX 77002
Phone: 713-758-2222
Fax: 713-758-2346
Email: information@velaw.com
Web Site: www.velaw.com

2016 Total Lawyers: 621
2015 Total Lawyers: 625

Winstead PC

500 Winstead Building
2728 N. Harwood Street
Dallas, TX 75701
Phone: 214-745-5400
Fax: 214-745-5390
Email: stipton@winstead.com
Web Site: www.winstead.com

2016 Total Lawyers: 335
2015 Total Lawyers: 344

UTAH

Callister, Nebecker & McCoullogh PC

Zions Bank Building, Ste 900
10 East South Temple
Salt Lake City, UT 84133
Phone: 801-530-7300
Fax: 801-364-9127
Web Site: www.cnmlaw.com

2016 Total Lawyers: 41
2015 Total Lawyers: 41

2016 Staff
Equity Partners: 30
Associates: 3
Of Counsel: 3

Offices: No. Attys.
Salt Lake City, UT: 36

Hiring and Promotion
2015 Associates Hired: 1
2015 First-Year Hires: 1
Starting Salary for First-Year
Assocs: $90,000
2016 First-Year Hires (Est.): 1
2015 Equity Partners Named: 1

UTAH

Callister, Nebeker & McCoullogh PC (Continued)

*Leading Practice Areas
(Department Heads)*
Litigation 28% (James Gilson 801-530-7300)
Estate and Tax Planning 21% (David Parkinson 801-530-7300)
Corporate Law 18% (Paul Shaphren 801-530-7300)
Real Estate 7% (J. Taylor Fox 801-530-7300)
Banking and Finance 5% (Jeff Fillmore 801-530-7300)
ERISA/ Employee benefits 5% (Waldon Lloyd 801-530-7300)
Collections 3% (Zach Shields 801-530-7300)
Trademarks 2% (John Rees 801-530-7300)
Municipal Law 2% (Shane Topham 801-530-7300)
Environmental Law 1% (Brian Burnett 801-530-7300)

Revenues and Profits
Revenues: $13,252,000

Client Representations
UEP
Zions Bank

Leading Officials
Leland S. McCullough, Chairman
T. Richard Davis, President
Bret J Leifson, Firm Administrator
Michael Stanger, Recruiting Chairman
Mark Gardiner, IT Director
Michael Hurst, Librarian

Jones Waldo Holbrook & McDonough PC

170 So. Main Street, Suite 1500
Salt Lake City, UT 84101-1644
Phone: 801-521-3200
Fax: 801-328-0537
Email: info@joneswaldo.com
Web Site: www.joneswaldo.com

2016 Total Lawyers: 96
2015 Total Lawyers: 75

Parr Brown Gee and Loveless, A Professional Corporation

185 South State Street
Suite 800
Salt Lake City, UT 84111
Phone: 801-532-7840
Fax: 801-532-7750
Web Site: www.parrbrown.com

2016 Total Lawyers: 69
2015 Total Lawyers: 64

Parsons Behle & Latimer, A Professional Law Corporation

201 South Main Street
Suite 1800
Salt Lake City, UT 84111-2218
Phone: 801-532-1234
Fax: 801-536-6111
Email: awaters@parsonsbehle.com
Web Site: www.parsonsbehlelaw.com

2016 Total Lawyers: 136
2015 Total Lawyers: 136

Ray Quinney & Nebeker P.C.

36 South State Street
Suite 1400
Salt Lake City, UT 84111
Phone: 801-532-1500
Fax: 801-532-7543
Email: rqn@rqn.com
Web Site: www.rqn.com

2016 Total Lawyers: 105
2015 Total Lawyers: 105

Snow, Christensen & Martineau

10 Exchange Place
11th Floor
Salt Lake City, UT 84111
Phone: 801-521-9000
Fax: 801-363-0400
Web Site: www.scmlaw.com

2016 Total Lawyers: 53
2015 Total Lawyers: 55

2016 Staff
Equity Partners: 36
Associates: 13
Of Counsel: 6

Offices: No. Attys.
Salt Lake City, UT: 51
St. George, UT: 3

Hiring and Promotion
2015 Associates Hired: 2
2015 First-Year Hires: 2
2016 First-Year Hires (Est.): 0
2015 Equity Partners Named: 2
2015 Lateral Equity Partners: 2

Leading Officials
Pres.Andrew M. Morse, Managing Partner, 801-521-9000
Scott Young, Recruiting Director, 801-521-9000

Van Cott Bagley Cornwall & McCarthy

36 South State St., Suite 1900
Salt Lake City, UT 84111
Phone: 801-532-3333
Fax: 801-534-0058
Web Site: www.vancott.com

2016 Total Lawyers: 67
2015 Total Lawyers: 38

VIRGINIA

Christian & Barton, LLP

909 East Main Street
Suite 1200
Richmond, VA 23219
Phone: 804-697-4100
Fax: 804-697-6112
Web Site: www.cblaw.com

2016 Total Lawyers: 40
2015 Total Lawyers: 41

2016 Staff
Associates: 7
Partners 26
Counsel 7

Offices: No. Attys.
Richmond, VA: 40

Hiring and Promotion
2016 First-Year Hires (Est.): 2
2015 Equity Partners Named: 0

*Leading Practice Areas
(Department Heads)*
Corporate (Peter E. Broadbent , Jr. 804-697-4100)
Litigation (Michael W. Smith 804-697-4100)
Energy & Telecommunications (Louis R. Monacell 804-697-4100)
Trusts & Estates (William J. Newman 804-697-4100)

Client Representations
First Hospital Corporation
Norfolk Southern
Chesapeake Bank

Leading Officials
Michael W. Smith, Firm Chair
Michael J. Quinan, Managing Partner
Robert W. Rideout, Jr., Firm Administrator
David B. Lacy, Recruiting Committee Chair
Jennifer M. McLemore, Client Development Chair
John Campbell, Systems Administrator
Michelle Wilson, Head Librarian

VIRGINIA

Hirschler Fleischer

The Edgeworth Building
2100 East Cary Street
Richmond, VA 23223
Phone: 804-771-9500
Fax: 804-644-0957
Email: info@hf-law.com
Web Site: www.hf-law.com

2016 Total Lawyers: 82
2015 Total Lawyers: 74

Kaufman & Canoles, A Professional Corporation

150 W. Main Street, Suite 2100
Post Office Box 3037
Norfolk, VA 23514
Phone: 757-624-3000
Fax: 757-624-3169
Email: webmaster@kaufcan.com
Web Site: www.kaufcan.com

2016 Total Lawyers: 97
2015 Total Lawyers: 97

2016 Staff
Equity Partners: 60
Non-Equity Partners: 6
Associates: 13
Of Counsel: 15

Offices: No. Attys.
Richmond, VA: 14
Williamsburg, VA: 14
Virginia Beach, VA: 11
Newport News, VA: 13
Chesapeake, VA: 2
Hampton, VA: 2
Norfolk, VA: 56

Hiring and Promotion
2015 Associates Hired: 3
2015 First-Year Hires: 1
2016 First-Year Hires (Est.): 2
2015 Equity Partners Named: 2
2015 Lateral Equity Partners: 1

Client Representations
Wheeler Real Estate Investment Trust
Harbor Group
Wells Fargo

Leading Officials
William R. Van Buren III, Chairman
Dale E. Hower, Director of Administration
Nicole Naidyhorski, Marketing Director,
  757-624-3295
Sandra J. Stovall, Chief Information Officer,
  757-624-3121
Laurie Claywell, Director of Library Services
Stanley G. Barr, Member, 757-624-3274

Other Offices
150 W. Main Street, Suite 2100
Norfolk, VA 23510
Phone: 757-624-3000
Fax: 757-624-3169
Email: webmaster@kaufcan.com
William R. Van Buren III, Chairman

McCandlish Holton PC

1111 East Main Street, Suite 2100
P. O. Box 796
Richmond, VA 23218
Phone: 804-775-3100
Fax: 804-775-3800
Web Site: www.lawmh.com

2016 Total Lawyers: 23
2015 Total Lawyers: 32

2016 Staff
Equity Partners: 10
Non-Equity Partners: 4
Associates: 6
Of Counsel: 3

Offices: No. Attys.
Richmond, VA: 32

Hiring and Promotion
2015 Associates Hired: 2
2015 First-Year Hires: 1
2016 First-Year Hires (Est.): 1
2015 Equity Partners Named: 0

Leading Practice Areas
(Department Heads)
Worker's Compensation (Scott Ford)
Immigration (Mark Rhoads)
Business (Thomas McCandlish)
General Litigation (Scott Ford)
Real Estate (Peter Henderer)
Employee Benefits/Tax (Thomas Foster)

Leading Officials
Thomas W. McCandlish, Chariman
Mark B. Rhoads, President
Kelly D. Higgs, Administrator
Peter L. Henderer, Director

McGuireWoods

Gateway Plaza
800 East Canal Street
Richmond, VA 23219
Phone: 804-775-1000
Fax: 804-775-1061
Web Site: www.mcguirewoods.com

2016 Total Lawyers: 1120
2015 Total Lawyers: 1099

2016 Staff
Equity Partners: 205
Non-Equity Partners: 236
Associates: 325
Counsel: 131
Senior Counsel: 40
Staff Attorneys: 75

Offices: No. Attys.
Austin, TX: 5
Houston, TX: 22
Dallas, TX: 23
Richmond, VA: 229
Chicago, IL: 105
Tysons, VA: 47
Charlotte, NC: 186
Jacksonville, FL: 27
Pittsburgh, PA: 30
New York, NY: 37

McGuireWoods (Continued)
Baltimore, MD: 24
Washington, DC: 49
Atlanta, GA: 52
Charlottesville, VA: 21
Norfolk, VA: 7
Brussels, Belgium: 10
London, UK: 35
Raleigh, NC: 29
Wilmington, NC: 6
Los Angeles, CA - Century City: 64
Los Angeles, CA - Downtown: 4

Hiring and Promotion
2015 Associates Hired: 82
2015 First-Year Hires: 19
Starting Salary for First-Year Assocs:
  $155,000
  (Aus,Dallas,Hous,Chicago,LA,NY,Tysons,DC)
  $140,000 (Atl, Balt, Char, Richmond);
  $135,000 (Pitts, Ral); $125,000
  (Charlottesville); $120,000 (Norfolk,
  Wilmington); $110,000 (Jacksonville)
2016 First-Year Hires (Est.): 19
2015 Equity Partners Named: 11
2015 Lateral Equity Partners: 4

Leading Practice Areas
(Department Heads)
Business and Securities Litigation 8.7% (J.
  William Boland 804-775-4374)
Real Estate and Land Use 8.2% (John T.
  Grieb 404-443-5717)
Debt Finance 8.0% (Robert W. Cramer
  704-343-2015)
Labor and Employment 7.4% (Joel H. Spitz
  312-750-5704)
Specialty Corporate Practices 6.5% (David B.
  Whelpley Jr. 704-343-2312)
Complex Commercial Litigation 5.8%
  (Leonard J. Marsico 412-667-7987)
Financial Services Litigation 5.8% (Bradley
  R. Kutrow 704-343-2049)
Tax and Employee Benefits 5.6% (Craig D.
  Bell 804-775-1179)
Government, Regulatory and Criminal
  Investigations 4.7% (John D. Adams
  804-775-4744)
Restructuring and Insolvency 4.3% (Dion W.
  Hayes 804-775-1144)

Client Representations
Bank of America Corporation
Dominion Resources Inc.
Sprint Corporation

Leading Officials
Richard Cullen, Chairman, 804-775-1009
Thomas E. Cabaniss, Managing Partner,
  804-775-4733
Robert J. Couture, Executive Director,
  804-775-1048
Peter Covington, Hiring Partner,
  704-343-2074
J.D. Neary, Director of Professional
  Development and Attorney Recruiting,
  804-775-1360
Jospeh Calve, Chief Marketing and Business
  Development Officer, 212-548-2124
Gregg Sutfin, Chief Information Officer,
  804-775-7500
David Mason, Information Services Manager,
  804-775-7863
Jacquelyn Stone, Chair of the Diversity
  Committee, 804-775-1046

VIRGINIA

McGuireWoods (Continued)

Other Offices
Richmond
800 East Canal Street
Richmond
VA
23219
Phone: 804-775-1000
Fax: 804-775-1061
George Keith Martin

Chicago
77 West Wacker Drive
Suite 4100
Chicago
IL
60601-1818
Phone: 312-849-8100
Fax: 312-849-3690
Amy Manning

Charlotte
201 N. Tryon St.
Suite 3000
Charlotte
NC
28202
Phone: 704-343-2000
Fax: 704-343-2300
Scott P. Vaughn

Los Angeles - Century City
1800 Century Park East
8th Floor
Los Angeles
CA
90067
Phone: 310-315-8200
Fax: 310-315-8210
Richard Grant

Atlanta
1230 Peachtree Street N.E.
Suite 2100
Atlanta
GA
30309-3534
Phone: 404-443-5500
Fax: 404-443-5599
Hilary Jordan

Oblon, McClelland, Maier & Neustadt, LLP

1940 Duke Street
Alexandria, VA 22314
Phone: 703-413-3000
Fax: 703-413-2220
Email: oblonpat@oblon.com
Web Site: www.oblon.com

2016 Total Lawyers: 94
2015 Total Lawyers: 101

Sands Anderson Marks & Miller, PC

1111 East Main Street
Suite 2400
Richmond, VA 23218-1998
Phone: 804-648-1636
Fax: 804-783-7291
Email: marketing@sandsanderson.c
Web Site: www.sandsanderson.com

2016 Total Lawyers: 50
2015 Total Lawyers: 66

Watt, Tieder, Hoffar & Fitzgerald

8405 Greensboro Drive
Suite 100
McLean, VA 22102
Phone: 703-749-1000
Fax: 703-893-8029
Email: contactus@wthf.com
Web Site: www.wthf.com

2016 Total Lawyers: 53
2015 Total Lawyers: 52

Willcox & Savage, P.C.

440 Monticello Ave, Suite 2200
Norfolk, VA 23510-2197
Phone: 757-628-5500
Fax: 757-628-5566
Email: mshearon@wilsav.com
Web Site: www.willcoxsavage.com

2016 Total Lawyers: 64
2015 Total Lawyers: 62

Williams Mullen

200 South 10th Street
Williams Mullen Center, Suite 1600
Richmond, VA 23219
Phone: 804-420-6000
Fax: 804-420-6507
Email: ask@williamsmullen.com
Web Site: www.williamsmullen.com

2016 Total Lawyers: 230
2015 Total Lawyers: 239

Woods Rogers PLC

Wells Fargo Tower, Suite 1400
10 South Jefferson Street
Roanoke, VA 24038
Phone: 540-983-7600
Fax: 540-983-7711
Email: mail@woodsrogers.com
Web Site: www.woodsrogers.com

2016 Total Lawyers: 59
2015 Total Lawyers: 63

WASHINGTON

Davis Wright Tremaine LLP

1201 Third Avenue, Suite 2200
Seattle, WA 98101-3045
Phone: 206-622-3150
Fax: 206-757-7700
Email: info@dwt.com
Web Site: www.dwt.com

2016 Total Lawyers: 548
2015 Total Lawyers: 524

Foster Pepper PLLC

1111 Third Avenue
Suite 3400
Seattle, WA 98109-3299
Phone: 206-447-4400
Fax: 206-447-9700
Web Site: www.foster.com

2016 Total Lawyers: 133
2015 Total Lawyers: 125

2016 Staff
Associates: 30
Of Counsel: 15
Members (Partners) 80

Hiring and Promotion
2015 Associates Hired: 7
2016 First-Year Hires (Est.): 7
2015 Equity Partners Named: 0
2015 Lateral Equity Partners: 3

Garvey Schubert Barer

1191 Second Avenue
Suite 1800
Seattle, WA 98101-2939
Phone: 206-464-3939
Fax: 206-464-0125
Web Site: www.gsblaw.com

2016 Total Lawyers: 119
2015 Total Lawyers: 125

Gordon, Thomas, Honeywell, Malanca, Peterson & Daheim, LLP

1201 Pacific Avenue
Wells Fargo Plaza, Suite 2100
Tacoma, WA 98402
Phone: 253-620-6500
Fax: 253-620-6565
Web Site: www.gth-law.com

2016 Total Lawyers: 43
2015 Total Lawyers: 53

Helsell Fetterman LLP

1001 Fourth Avenue
Suite 4200
Seattle, WA 98154
Phone: 206-292-1144
Fax: 206-340-0902
Email: hf@helsell.com
Web Site: www.helsell.com

2016 Total Lawyers: 32
2015 Total Lawyers: 36

Karr Tuttle Campbell

701 Fifth Ave
Ste 3300
Seattle, WA 98104
Phone: 206-223-1313
Fax: 206-682-7100
Email: blarson@karrtuttle.com
Web Site: www.karrtuttle.com

2016 Total Lawyers: 52
2015 Total Lawyers: 53

Lane Powell

1420 Fifth Avenue, Suite 4200
P.O. Box 91302
Seattle, WA 98111-9402
Phone: 206-223-7000
Fax: 206-223-7107
Email: info@lanepowell.com
Web Site: www.lanepowell.com

2016 Total Lawyers: 200
2015 Total Lawyers: 172

2016 Staff
Equity Partners: 64
Non-Equity Partners: 41
Associates: 43
Of Counsel: 6
Senior Attorneys: 18

Offices: No. Attys.
Seattle, WA: 109
Portland, OR: 58
Anchorage, AK: 5

Hiring and Promotion
2015 Associates Hired: 10
2015 First-Year Hires: 2
Starting Salary for First-Year
Assocs: $120,000
2016 First-Year Hires (Est.): 2
2015 Equity Partners Named: 3
2015 Lateral Equity Partners: 2

Lane Powell (Continued)

Leading Practice Areas
(Department Heads)
Complex Litigation 39% (John Devlin,
Barbara Duffy, Charles Huber, Thomas
Sondag, Katie Matison 206-223-6280,
206-223-7944, 206-233-7265,
503-778-2111, 206-223-7029)
Corporate Finance/M&A 13% (Thomas
Grohman, Jeffrey Wolfstone
206-223-7044, 503-778-2153)
Intellectual Property 12% (Kenneth Davis
503-778-2121)
Labor and Employment 8% (Laura Morse, D.
Michael Reilly 206-223-7063,
206-223-7051)
Construction 6% (Grant Degginger
206-223-7390)
Real Estate 5% (Michael Silvey
503-778-2195)
Creditors' Rights 5% (Gregory Fox
206-223-7129)
Taxation/International 5% (Lewis Horowitz
206-223-7401)
Estate Planning 5% (Gail Mautner, Mary Lee
Moseley 206-223-7099, 206-223-7132)
Immigration 2% (Diane Butler
206-223-7715)

Revenues and Profits
Revenues: $91,500,000
Profits: $27,910,000

Client Representations
Wells Fargo Bank N.A.
Nordstrom, Inc.
Bank of America

Leading Officials
Charles W. Riley, President, 206-223-7959
Thomas W. Sondag, Vice President,
503-778-2111
Randy L. Leitzke, Chief Operating Officer,
205-223-7061
Gwendolyn C. Payton, Recruitment
Committee Chair, 206-223-7746
Len Roden, Manager of Attorney Recruiting,
206-223-6123
Lori A. Foleen, Director of Marketing,
503-778-2193
Sanjiv N. Kripalani, Director of Business
Development, 503-778-2109
David Fairchild, Director of Information
Technology, 206-223-6124
Karen Helde, Director of Library and
Resources, 206-223-7741
Gail E. Mautner, Shareholder and Diversity
Committee Chair, 206-223-7099

Other Offices
Seattle
1420 Fifth Avenue
Suite 4200
Seattle
WA
98111-9402
Phone: 206-223-7000
Fax: 206-223-7107
Email: info@lanepowell.com
Charles W. Riley, Jr., President; Thomas W.
Sondag, Vice-President

Lane Powell (Continued)

Portland
601 S.W. Second Avenue
Suite 2100
Portland
OR
97204
Phone: 503-778-2100
Fax: 503-778-2200
Email: info@lanepowell.com
Charles W. Riley, Jr., President; Thomas W.
Sondag, Vice-President

Ogden Murphy Wallace, P.L.L.C.

901 Fifth Ave.
Suite 3500
Seattle, WA 98164-2059
Phone: 206-447-7000
Fax: 206-447-0215
Email: info@omwlaw.com
Web Site: www.omwlaw.com

2016 Total Lawyers: 49
2015 Total Lawyers: 45

2016 Staff
Equity Partners: 19
Non-Equity Partners: 13
Associates: 9
Of Counsel: 8

Offices: No. Attys.
Seattle, WA: 39
Wenatchee, WA: 10

Hiring and Promotion
2015 Associates Hired: 4
2015 First-Year Hires: 1
2016 First-Year Hires (Est.): 0
2015 Equity Partners Named: 0

Leading Practice Areas
(Department Heads)
Commercial Litigation 20% (Jeff Dunbar
206-447-7000)
Healthcare 20% (David Schoolcraft
206-447-7000)
Municipal Law 20% (Jim Haney
206-447-7000)
Product Liability 15% (Geoff Bridgman
206-447-7000)
Mergers & Acquisitions 10% (Dave
Ellenhorn 206-447-7000)
Tax 10% (Leslie Pesterfield 206-447-7000)
Bankruptcy 5% (Mike Wickstead
206-447-7000)

Revenues and Profits
Revenues: $16,058,593
Profits: $6,390,527

Client Representations
Overlake Hospital Medical Center
Lockheed Shipbuilding
Travelers Insurance Company

WASHINGTON

Ogden Murphy Wallace, P.L.L.C. (Continued)

Leading Officials
Donald W. Black, Chair
Geoffrey J. Bridgman, Managing Member
Adam D. Nelson, Executive Director
Angela Summerfield, Hiring Member
Angela Summerfield, Recruiting Member
Adam D. Nelson, Marketing Director
Eric McCammon, Director of Information
Technology
Amy Madigan, Librarian

Perkins Coie

1201 Third Avenue
Suite 4800
Seattle, WA 98101-3099
Phone: 206-359-8000
Fax: 206-359-9000
Email: perkins@perkinscoie.com
Web Site: www.perkinscoie.com

2016 Total Lawyers: 1000
2015 Total Lawyers: 992

Williams Kastner

601 Union Street
Suite 4100
Seattle, WA 98101-2380
Phone: 206-628-6600
Fax: 206-628-6611
Email: info@williamskastner.com
Web Site: www.williamskastner.com

2016 Total Lawyers: 72
2015 Total Lawyers: 72

WEST VIRGINIA

Bowles Rice LLP

600 Quarrier Street
P.O. Box 1386
Charleston, WV 25301
Phone: 304-347-1100
Fax: 304-343-2867
Web Site: www.bowlesrice.com

2016 Total Lawyers: 124
2015 Total Lawyers: 137

2016 Staff
Equity Partners: 49
Non-Equity Partners: 17
Associates: 33
Of Counsel: 8
Senior Attorneys: 7
Counsel: 10

Offices: No. Attys.
Charleston, WV: 60
Martinsburg, WV: 14
Morgantown, WV: 22
Parkersburg, WV: 14
Winchester, VA: 2
Southpointe, PA: 6
Wheeling, WV: 3

Bowles Rice LLP (Continued)

Hiring and Promotion
2015 Associates Hired: 4
2015 First-Year Hires: 3
2016 First-Year Hires (Est.): 3
2015 Equity Partners Named: 0

Leading Practice Areas
(Department Heads)
Energy 20% (Seth Wilson 304-285-2531)
Business Litigation 20% (Stuart McMillan
304-264-4222)
Corporate & Commercial Services 13% (Tom
Heywood 304-347-1711)
General Torts & Insurance Defense 10%
(Aaron Boone 304-347-1110)
Tax 9% (David DeJarnett 304-420-5510)
Real Estate 7% (Stephen Mathias
304-264-4234)
Employment Law 7% (Mark Dellinger
304-347-1701)
Banking & Financial Services 5% (Sandra
Murphy 304-347-1131)
Mass & Toxic Torts 5% (Diana Johnson
304-347-1723)
Education 4% (Howard Seufer
304-347-1776)

Leading Officials
Thomas A. Heywood, Managing Partner,
304-347-1702
Judy Margolin, Executive Director,
304-347-1156
Ben Thomas, Recruiting Committee Chair,
304-347-1121
Barbara Joseph, Marketing & Client Services
Director, 304-347-2138
Scott Ball, Technology Director,
304-347-1729
Richard Smith, Head Librarian,
304-347-1180
Jill Hall, Diversity Partner, 304-347-1128

Jackson Kelly PLLC

500 Lee Street East, Suite 1600
Charleston, WV 25301
Phone: 304-340-1000
Fax: 304-340-1130
Email: info@jacksonkelly.com
Web Site: www.jacksonkelly.com

2016 Total Lawyers: 188
2015 Total Lawyers: 188

2016 Staff
Equity Partners: 73
Non-Equity Partners: 25
Associates: 51
Of Counsel: 25
Staff Attorneys: 4
Part-time Attorneys 2.71

Offices: No. Attys.
Charleston, WV: 94
Morgantown, WV: 22
Lexington, KY: 17
Martinsburg, WV: 5
Washington, D.C.: 7
Denver, CO: 18
Wheeling, WV: 9
Clarksburg, WV: 1

Jackson Kelly PLLC (Continued)
Pittsburgh, PA: 9
Indiana: 6
Akron, OH: 3

Hiring and Promotion
2015 Associates Hired: 7

Leading Officials
Michael D. Foster, Managing Member,
304-340-1238
James Lowen, Executive Director,
304-340-1137
Mary Hendrix, Director of Marketing and
Business Development, 304-340-1065
Gale Donelson, Technology Manager,
304-340-1399

Robinson & McElwee LLP

700 Virginia Street
Fifth Third Center, Suite 400
Charleston, WV 25301
Phone: 304-344-5800
Fax: 304-344-9566
Web Site: www.ramlaw.com

2016 Total Lawyers: 44
2015 Total Lawyers: 37

Spilman Thomas & Battle, PLLC

300 Kanawha Boulevard, East
PO Box 273
Charleston, WV 25301-0273
Phone: 304-340-3800
Fax: 304-340-3801
Email: stb@spilmanlaw.com
Web Site: spilmanlaw.com

2016 Total Lawyers: 126
2015 Total Lawyers: 126

Steptoe & Johnson PLLC

400 White Oaks Boulevard
Bridgeport, WV 26330
Phone: 304-933-8000
Fax: 304-933-8183
Email: info@steptoe-johnson.com
Web Site: www.steptoe-johnson.com

2016 Total Lawyers: 328
2015 Total Lawyers: 328

2016 Staff
Equity Partners: 66
Non-Equity Partners: 66
Associates: 83
Of Counsel: 74
Staff Attorneys: 17

Offices: No. Attys.
Wheeling, WV: 18
Huntington, WV: 15
Columbus, OH: 21
Bridgeport, WV: 59
Lexington, KY: 4
Charleston, WV: 70
Morgantown, WV: 32

WEST VIRGINIA

Steptoe & Johnson PLLC (Continued)
Meadville, PA: 11
Southpointe, PA: 17
The Woodlands, TX: 19
Denver, CO: 10
Martinsburg, WV: 9
Louisville, KY: 10

Hiring and Promotion
2015 Associates Hired: 17
2015 First-Year Hires: 12
Starting Salary for First-Year Assocs:
$75,000-$85,000
2016 First-Year Hires (Est.): 6
2015 Equity Partners Named: 3
2015 Lateral Equity Partners: 2

Leading Officials
Susan S. Brewer, CEO, 304-598-8103
Richard J. Mackessy, Chief Operating
Officer, 304-933-8130
Michael D. Mullins, Recruiting Committee
Chairperson, 304-353-8157
Michele Bendekovic, Director of Recruiting
& Professional Development,
304-598-5362
Betsy Beorn Spellman, Chief Marketing
Officer, 304-933-8377
Mark D. Combs, Chief Information Officer,
304-933-8140
Krista A. Ford, Director of Library Services,
304-933-8198
Susan S. Brewer, CEO, 304-598-8103

Other Offices
400 White Oaks Boulevard
Bridgeport, WV 26330
Phone: 304-933-8000
Fax: 304-933-8183
Email: info@steptoe-johnson.com
Gary W. Nickerson, Managing Member

Chase Tower
Eighth Floor
Charleston, WV 25326-1588
Phone: 304-353-8000
Fax: 304-353-8180
Email: info@steptoe-johnson.com
Bryan R. Cokeley, Managing Member

WISCONSIN

Boardman & Clark LLP

1 South Pinckney Street, Suite 410
P.O. Box 927
Madison, WI 53701
Phone: 608-257-9521
Fax: 608-283-1709
Web Site: www.boardmanlawfirm.com

2016 Total Lawyers: 67
2015 Total Lawyers: 67

2016 Staff
Equity Partners: 36
Associates: 10
Of Counsel: 10
Staff Attorneys: 11

Offices: No. Attys.
Madison, WI: 62

Boardman & Clark LLP (Continued)
Baraboo, WI: 2
Lodi, WI: 1
Poynette, WI: 1
Fennimore, WI: 1

Hiring and Promotion
2015 Associates Hired: 4
2015 First-Year Hires: 2
Starting Salary for First-Year
Assocs: $62,000
2016 First-Year Hires (Est.): 1-2
2015 Equity Partners Named: 3
2015 Lateral Equity Partners: 1

Leading Practice Areas
(Department Heads)
General Corporation & Business 15% (Jon C,
Nordenberg 608-257-9521)
Litigation - Insurance 11% (Claude J. Covelli
608-257-9521)
Municipal Law 11% (Anita T. Gallucci
608-257-9521)
Banking 9% (John E. Knight 608-257-9521)
School Law 9% (Michael J. Julka
608-257-9521)
Litigation - General 7% (Claude J. Covelli
608-257-9521)
Labor/Employment Law 6% (Robert E.
Gregg 608-257-9521)
Real Estate 6% (Richard L. Schmitt
608-257-9521)
Estate Planning 6% (Carl J. Rasmussen
608-257-9521)
Patent & Trademark 5% (Christopher J.
Hussin 608-257-9521)

Revenues and Profits
Revenues: $18,906,722
Profits: $6,951,016

Leading Officials
Richard A. Heinemann, Chair, Executive
Committee
Kathy J. Pline, Executive Director
Frank C. Sutherland
Anita T. Gallucci, Chair Recruiting
Committee
Nick Sayers, Communications Director
N/A
David Skrede, IT Manager
Carol Schmitt, Librarian
Jennifer S. Mirus, Partner

Davis & Kuelthau, S.C.

111 East Kilbourn Avenue
Suite 1400
Milwaukee, WI 53202
Phone: 414-276-0200
Fax: 414-276-9369
Email: info@dkattorneys.com
Web Site: www.dkattorneys.com

2016 Total Lawyers: 65
2015 Total Lawyers: 65

2016 Staff
Equity Partners: 28
Non-Equity Partners: 6
Associates: 8
Of Counsel: 9
Senior Attorneys: 8
Staff Attorneys: 1

Davis & Kuelthau, S.C. (Continued)

Offices: No. Attys.
Milwaukee, WI: 39
Green Bay, WI: 13
Brookfield, WI: 8

Hiring and Promotion
2016 First-Year Hires (Est.): 0
2015 Equity Partners Named: 0

Leading Practice Areas
(Department Heads)
Labor and Employment (James M. Kalny
920-431-2223)
Business and Corporate (Scott E. Fiducci
414-225-1428)
Civil and Commercial Litigation (Matthew R.
McClean 414-225-1420)
Real Estate (Joseph E. Tierney IV
414-225-1471)
Estate Planning (Charles G. Maris
262-792-2424)
Mergers & Acquisitions (Scott E. Fiducci
414-225-1428)
Employee Benefits (Kelly S. Kuglitsch
414-225-1428)
Intellectual Property (Joseph S. Heino
414-225-1452)
Municipal Labor Counsel (James M. Kalny
920-431-2223)
School and Higher Education (Mary S.
Gerbig 920-431-2242)

Leading Officials
Kathy L. Nusslock, Chief Operating Officer
and President, 414-225-1447
Kathy Nusslock, 414-225-1447
Pagette K. Fischer, Director of Marketing &
Business Development, 414-225-1466
Brian F. Langenbach, Director of Information
Services, 414-225-1457
Beverly G. Butula, Director of Library
Services, 414-225-1721
Kathy Nusslock, Chief Operating Officer and
Firm President, 414-225-1447

Dewitt Ross & Stevens

Two East Mifflin St
Suite 600
Madison, WI 53703
Phone: 608-255-8891
Fax: 608-252-9243
Email: info@dewittross.com
Web Site: www.dewittross.com

2016 Total Lawyers: 122
2015 Total Lawyers: 109

2016 Staff
Equity Partners: 54
Non-Equity Partners: 48
Associates: 16
Staff Attorneys: 4

Offices: No. Attys.
Brookfield, WI: 17
Madison, WI: 72
Minneapolis, MN: 33

WISCONSIN

Dewitt Ross & Stevens (Continued)

Hiring and Promotion
2015 Associates Hired: 4
2015 First-Year Hires: 4
Starting Salary for First-Year
    Assocs: $80,000
2016 First-Year Hires (Est.): 2
2015 Equity Partners Named: 11
2015 Lateral Equity Partners: 6

Leading Practice Areas
(Department Heads)
Corporate 18%
Environmental 14%
Intellectual Property 13%
Litigation (General) 10%
Lobbying 8%
Labor 7%
Estates & Trusts 6%
Family Law 5%
Family Law 5%
Real Estate 3%

Revenues and Profits
Revenues: $37,910,559
Profits: $16,143,215

Leading Officials
Bradley Raaths, Shareholder
Bradley Fulton, Managing Partner
Greg Harper, Firm Administrator
Bradley Fulton, Managing Partner
Michelle M. Friedman, Marketing Manager
Suzanne Arbet, IT Director
Richard Hendricks, Reasearch Librarian
Matthew Gentz, Controller

Other Offices
Two East Mifflin Street
Madison
WI
53703
Phone: 608-255-8891
Fax: 608-252-9243
Email: info@DewittRoss.com
Bradley C. Fulton

Foley & Lardner, LLP

777 East Wisconsin Avenue
Milwaukee, WI 53202-5367
Phone: 414-271-2400
Fax: 414-297-4900
Web Site: www.foley.com

2016 Total Lawyers: 839
2015 Total Lawyers: 900

Michael Best & Friedrich

100 East Wisconsin Avenue
Suite 3300
Milwaukee, WI 53202-4108
Phone: 414-271-6560
Fax: 414-277-0656
Email: info@michaelbest.com
Web Site: www.michaelbest.com

2016 Total Lawyers: 225
2015 Total Lawyers: 215

2016 Staff
Equity Partners: 80
Non-Equity Partners: 49
Associates: 64
Of Counsel: 9
Senior Counsel: 11
Staff Attorneys: 4
Senior Partners 8

Offices: No. Attys.
Milwaukee, WI: 101
Chicago, IL: 31
Madison, WI: 53
Waukesha, WI: 13
Manitowoc, WI: 6
Washington DC: 13
Salt Lake City, UT: 13
Austin, TX: 2

Hiring and Promotion
2015 Associates Hired: 16
2015 First-Year Hires: 9
Starting Salary for First-Year
    Assocs: $120,000
2015 Equity Partners Named: 5

Leading Practice Areas
(Department Heads)
Intellectual Property 38% (Daniel S. Jones
    414-271-6560)
Transactional 29% (Michael S. Green
    414-271-6560)
Litigation 17% (Daniel J. Vaccaro
    414-271-6560)
Labor and Employment Relations 16% (Jos
    A. Olivieri 414-271-6560)

Revenues and Profits
Revenues: $114,300,000
Profits: $39,400,000

Leading Officials
David A. Krutz, Firm Managing Partner,
    414-271-6560
L. David Lentz, Chief Operating Officer,
    414-271-6560
William G. Kellner, Director, Human
    Resources, 414-271-6560
Susan L. Hollender, Director, Marketing and
    Business Development, 414-271-6560
Alan W. Ciochon, Chief Information Officer,
    414-271-6560
Candace Hall Slaminski, Director,
    Information and Research Services,
    414-271-6560
Lori S. Meddings , Partner, 414-271-6560

Michael Best & Friedrich (Continued)

Other Offices
Madison WI
One South Pinckney Street
Suite 700
Madison
WI
53703
Phone: 608-257-3501
Fax: 608-283-2275
Mary C. Turke, Office Managing Partner

Quarles & Brady LLP

411 East Wisconsin Avenue
Suite 2040
Milwaukee, WI 53202
Phone: 414-277-5000
Fax: 414-271-3552
Web Site: www.quarles.com

2016 Total Lawyers: 694
2015 Total Lawyers: 536

Reinhart Boerner Van Deuren s.c.

1000 North Water Street
Suite 1700
Milwaukee, WI 53202
Phone: 414-298-1000
Fax: 414-298-8097
Web Site: www.reinhartlaw.com

2016 Total Lawyers: 215
2015 Total Lawyers: 204

2016 Staff
Equity Partners: 89
Non-Equity Partners: 49
Associates: 61
Of Counsel 16

Offices: No. Attys.
Milwaukee, WI: 153
Madison, WI: 33
Denver, CO: 1
Waukesha, WI: 16
Rockford, IL: 8
Phoenix, AZ: 1
Chicago, IL: 3

Hiring and Promotion
2015 Associates Hired: 6
2015 First-Year Hires: 7
Starting Salary for First-Year
    Assocs: $120,000
2016 First-Year Hires (Est.): 9
2015 Equity Partners Named: 0

WISCONSIN

Reinhart Boerner Van Deuren s.c. (Continued)

Leading Practice Areas
(Department Heads)
Banking & Bankruptcy (David B. Schulz;
Peter C. Blain 414-298-8326,
414-298-8129)
Business Law (Lawrence J. Burnett; Albert S.
Orr 414-298-8175, 414-298-8209)
Employee Benefits (Steven D. Huff
414-298-8126)
Health Care (Tracey L. Klein 414-298-8156)
Labor & Employment (Christopher P.
Banaszak 414-298-8320)
Litigation (Allen C. Schlinsog, Jr.
414-298-8214)
Real Estate (Jerome M. Janzer; Deborah C.
Tomczyk 414-298-8180; 414-298-8331)
Tax (Michael G. Goller 414-298-8336)
Trusts & Estates (Jennifer R. D'Amato
414-298-8319)
Intellectual Property (Jeffery J. Makeever
815-654-5620)

Client Representations
Associated Banc-Corp
Kohler Co.
Joy Global Underground Mining, LLC

Leading Officials
Jerome M. Janzer, Chief Executive Officer,
414-298-8180
Andrew E. Quackenboss, Chief Financial
Officer, 414-298-8250
Christopher P. Rechlicz, Chair, Attorney
Recruiting, 414-298-8368
Sandy Faull, Manager, Attorney Recruiting,
414-298-8528
Andrew Narrai, Chief Marketing Officer,
414-298-8710
Jerry Bishop, Director of Technology,
414-298-8416
Carol Bannen, Director, Information
Resource Center, 414-298-8253
Mark Cameli, Chair, Diversity Committee,
414-298-8155

Other Offices
Milwaukee
1000 N. Water Street
1700
Milwaukee
WI
53202
Phone: 414-298-1000
Fax: 414-298-8097
Email: jjanzer@reinhartlaw.com
Jerome M. Janzer (this is not a new office, but
is an office with 50 or more attorneys)

von Briesen & Roper, s.c.

411 East Wisconsin Avenue
Suite 1000
Milwaukee, WI 53202
Phone: 414-276-1122
Fax: 414-276-6281
Email: info@vonbriesen.com
Web Site: www.vonbriesen.com

2016 Total Lawyers: 151
2015 Total Lawyers: 141

OF COUNSEL 700 | International Offices

ARGENTINA

Cleary Gottlieb Steen & Hamilton

Buenos Aires
+54 11 5556 8900
CGSH International Legal Services, LLP-Sucursal Argentina
Avda. Quintana 529, 4to piso
Total Lawyers: 7

AUSTRALIA

Jones Day

Christopher J. Ahern
Aurora Place, Level 41
88 Phillip Street
Tel: 61-2-8272-0500
Fax: 61-2-8272-0599
Total Lawyers: 49

Chris Ahern
Level 17, Alluvion
58 Mounts Bay Road
Tel: 61-8-6214-5700
Total Lawyers: 1

Norton Rose Fulbright

Brisbane
Peter Schmidt
Level 21, 111 Eagle Street
Total Lawyers: 72

Canberra
Vince Sharma
60 Marcus Clarke Street, Level 6
Total Lawyers: 5

Melbourne
Peter Cash
Level 15, RACV Tower, 485 Bourke Street
Total Lawyers: 137

Perth
Chris McLeod
Level 39, 108 St. Georges Terrace
Total Lawyers: 49

Sydney
Felicity Rourke
Level 18, Grosvenor Place, 225 George Street
Total Lawyers: 213

Pillsbury Winthrop Shaw Pittman LLP

Sydney
Level 10
7 Macquarie Place
Sydney , NSW 2000, Australia
Total Lawyers: 5

Quinn Emanuel Urquhart & Sullivan LLP

Quinn Emanuel Urquhart & Sullivan LLP (Sydney)
Michael Mills
Level 15, 111 Elizabeth Street
Total Lawyers: 8

AUSTRALIA (Continued)

Sidley Austin LLP

Sydney
Level 10, 7 Macquarie Place
Total Lawyers: 14

Skadden, Arps, Slate, Meagher & Flom LLP and Affiliates

Sydney
Adrian J. S. Deitz
Level 13, 131 Macquarie Street
NSW 2000
Total Lawyers: 6

Sullivan & Cromwell

John E. Estes
101 Collins Street
Melbourne 3000, Australia
Tel: 613-9635-1500
Fax: 613-9654-2422
Total Lawyers: 6

John E. Estes
Level 27, The Chifley Tower
2 Chifley Square
Sydney, New South Wales 2000, Australia
Tel: 61-2-8227-6700
Fax: 61-2-8227-6750
Total Lawyers: 3

AUSTRIA

DLA Piper

DLA Piper Weiss-Tessbach Rechtsanwalte GmbH
Claudine Vartian, Country Managing Partner
Schottenring 14 A-1010
Total Lawyers: 52

Skadden, Arps, Slate, Meagher & Flom LLP and Affiliates

Vienna
Rainer K. Wachter
Schwarzenbergplatz 6
1030
Total Lawyers: 3

BELGIUM

Cadwalader, Wickersham & Taft

Brussels
Alec J. Burnside
Avenue d'Auderghem 22-28
Total Lawyers: 5

BELGIUM

Cleary Gottlieb Steen & Hamilton
Brussels
+32 2 287 2000
Rue de la Loi 57
Total Lawyers: 71

Dechert LLP
Dechert LLP
480 Avenue Louise
Box 13A IT Tower
Total Lawyers: 15

Dentons
Brussels
Joan Burns
Avenue Louise 65
bte 11
Total Lawyers: 2

DLA Piper
DLA Piper UK LLP
Bob Martens
106 Avenue Louise
Total Lawyers: 87

DLA Piper UK LLP
Bob Martens
Uitbreidlingstraat 2 B-2600
Total Lawyers: 17

Finnegan, Henderson, Farabow, Garrett & Dunner
Brussels Office
Anthony C. Tridico, Ph.D., Managing Partner
Avenue Louise 326, Box 37
Brussels, Belgium B-1050
+32 2 646 03 53
+32 2 646 21 35 fax
Total Lawyers: 2

Foley & Lardner, LLP
Brussels
Avenue Louise 480
Brussels, B1050
Belgium
Total Lawyers: 2

Gibson, Dunn & Crutcher
Brussels
Peter Alexiadis, Partner in Charge
Avenue Louise 480
1050
Total Lawyers: 15

Hunton & Williams
Brussels Office
Wim Nauwelaerts
Park Atrium, Rue des Colonies 11
Total Lawyers: 10

BELGIUM (Continued)

Jones Day
Bernard E. Amory
Rue de la Regence
Regentschapsstraat 4
Tel: 32-2-645-14-11
Fax: 32-2-645-14-45
Total Lawyers: 38

K&L Gates LLP
Brussels
Martin Lane
The View Building
Rue de l'Industrie 26/38
Total Lawyers: 9

Keller and Heckman LLP
Brussels Office
Avenue Louise 54
1050
Brussels, Belgium
Total Lawyers: 5

Kelley Drye & Warren LLP
Brussels
André Van Landuyt
106 Avenue Louise, 1050 Brussels
Total Lawyers: 1

Mayer Brown
Brussels
Dr. Jens Peter Schmidt
Total Lawyers: 19

McDermott Will & Emery
McDermott Will & Emery/Stanbrook LLP
Philip Bentley, Partner-in-Charge
Rue Pure Eudore Devroye 245
1150 Brussels
Belgium
Total Lawyers: 10

McGuireWoods
Brussels, Belgium
Hubert Andre-Dumont
rue des Colonies 56 (bte 3)
1000 Brussels, Belgium
Total Lawyers: 10

Norton Rose Fulbright
Brussels
Christian Filippitsch
Avenue Louise 489
Total Lawyers: 11

O'Melveny & Myers LLP
Brussels
Riccardo Celli
Blue Tower
Avenue Louise 326
1050 Brussels, Belgium
Total Lawyers: 10

BELGIUM

Quinn Emanuel Urquhart & Sullivan LLP
Quinn Emanuel Urquhart & Sullivan LLP (Brussels)
Nadine Herrmann
rue Breydel 34
Total Lawyers: 3

Shearman & Sterling LLP
Brussels
Hans Jürgen Meyer-Lindemann, Managing Partner
Avenue des Arts 56
B-1000 Bruxelles
Belgium

Sheppard, Mullin, Richter & Hampton
Brussels
Curt Dombek
Place du Champ de Mars 2
Marsveldplein
Total Lawyers: 1

Sidley Austin LLP
Brussels
NEO Building
Rue Montoyer 51 Montoyerstraat
B-1000
Total Lawyers: 30

Skadden, Arps, Slate, Meagher & Flom LLP and Affiliates
Brussels
Frederic Depoortere
523 avenue Louise
Box 30
1050
Total Lawyers: 12

Wilmer Cutler Pickering Hale and Dorr
Bastion Tower, Place du Champ de Mars/Marsveldplein 5
Total Lawyers: 10

Wilson Sonsini Goodrich & Rosati
Brussels
Bastion Tower, Level 21
5 Place du Champ de Mars
1050 Brussels, Belgium
Total Lawyers: 7

Winston & Strawn LLP
Winston & Strawn LLP
Peter Crowther
Wetstraat/Rue de la Loi 82 1040
Total Lawyers: 1

BRAZIL

Cleary Gottlieb Steen & Hamilton
Sao Paulo
+55 11 2196 7200
Consultores em Direito Estrangeiro
Rua Funchal, 418, 13 Andar
Total Lawyers: 4

BRAZIL (Continued)

Davis Polk & Wardwell
So Paulo
Total Lawyers: 11

Gibson, Dunn & Crutcher
Sao Paulo
Lisa Alfaro, Partner in Charge
Rua Funchal, 418, 35 andar
SP 04551-060
Total Lawyers: 2

Jones Day
Luis Riesgo
Edificio Plaza Iguatemi
Avenida Brigadeiro Faria Lima, 2277, 5® andar
Jardim Paulistano
Tel: 5511-3018-3939
Fax: 5511-3018-3938
Total Lawyers: 9

K&L Gates LLP
Sao Paulo
Elwood Collins
Rua Iguatemi 151, conjunto 281
Ed. Spazio Faria Lima
Total Lawyers: 1

Mayer Brown
Rio de Janeiro
Total Lawyers: 78
Sao Paolo
Total Lawyers: 82

Milbank, Tweed, Hadley & McCloy
Sao Paulo
Andrew Jánszky
Rua Colombia, 325
Jardim América
Total Lawyers: 7

Norton Rose Fulbright
Rio de Janeiro
Andrew Haynes and Glenn Faass
Rua Lauro Muller, 116, Suite 4405, Torre do Rio Sul, Botafogo
Total Lawyers: 3

Shearman & Sterling LLP
Sao Paulo
Robert Ellison, Managing Partner
Avenida Brigadeiro Faria Lima, 3400
Sao Paulo - SP, 04538-132
Brazil

Simpson Thacher & Bartlett LLP
Sao Paulo
Avenue Presidente Juscelino Kubitschek, 1455
Total Lawyers: 5

BRAZIL

Skadden, Arps, Slate, Meagher & Flom LLP and Affiliates

Sao Paulo
Richard S. Aldrich, Jr.
Av. Brigadeiro Faria Lima
3311 - 7º andar
04538-133
Total Lawyers: 5

BULGARIA

DLA Piper

Rizova & Partners Law Firm (part of DLA Piper)
Anna Rizova-Clegg
7 Pozitano Str BG-1301
Total Lawyers: 13

CANADA

Barclay Damon

Toronto
James P. Domagalski, Peter S. Marlette
130 King Street West
Suite 1800
Total Lawyers: 1

Burns & Levinson LLP

Burns & Levinson Canada Co.
Leonard M. Gold
1250 Rene Levesque Blvd. West
Suite 2200
Montreal, Quebec, H3B 4W8
Total Lawyers: 1

Cozen O'Connor

Toronto
Christopher Reain
One Queen Street East
Suite 1920
Toronto, Ontario
Canada
Total Lawyers: 3

Dickinson Wright PLLC

Dickinson Wright LLP
Mark S. Shapiro
199 Bay Street
2200
Total Lawyers: 45

Dorsey & Whitney LLP

Dorsey & Whitney Toronto
Richard Raymer
Brookfield Place 161 Bay Street, TD Canada Trust Tower
Suite 4310
Total Lawyers: 5

Dorsey & Whitney Vancouver
Jeffrey A. Peterson
777 Dunsmuir Street, P.O. Box 10444, Pacific Centre
Suite 1605
Total Lawyers: 2

CANADA (Continued)

Hodgson Russ

George J. Eydt, Esq.
150 King Street West
Suite 2309
P.O. Box 30
Toronto, Ontario, Canada M5H 1J9
Total Lawyers: 2

Littler

Toronto, Ontario
Sari Springer
181 Bay Street
Suite 3210
Total Lawyers: 8

Miller, Canfield, Paddock and Stone, P.L.C.

Windsor
Jennifer L. Shilson
433 Ouellette Avenue, Suite 300
Windsor, Ontario, Canada N9A6R4
Total Lawyers: 18

Toronto
John D. Leslie
Brookfield Place
TD Canada Trust Tower
161 Bay Street, 27th Floor
Toronto, Ontario, Canada M5J 2S1
Total Lawyers: 3

Norton Rose Fulbright

Montreal
Solomon Sananes
1 Place Ville Marie
Suite 2500
Total Lawyers: 183

Ottawa
Pierre-Paul Henrie
45 O'Connor Street
Suite 1500
Total Lawyers: 48

Quebec
Carl Tremblay
2828 Boulevard Laurier
Suite 1500
Total Lawyers: 63

Toronto
Andrew Fleming
200 Bay Street
Suite 3800
Total Lawyers: 198

Calgary
Bradley Hayden
400 3rd Avenue SW
Suite 3700
Total Lawyers: 149

Phillips Lytle LLP

Phillips Lytle
Richard E. Honen
The Communitech Hub
151 Charles Street West
Suite 152, The Tannery
Total Lawyers: 2

CANADA

Shearman & Sterling LLP

Toronto
Christopher J. Cummings, Managing Partner
Commerce Court West
Suite 4405
P.O. Box 247
Toronto, Ontario M5L 1E8
Canada

Skadden, Arps, Slate, Meagher & Flom LLP and Affiliates

Toronto
Christopher W. Morgan
222 Bay Street
Suite 1750
P.O. Box 258
M5K 1J5
Total Lawyers: 11

CHINA

Akin Gump Strauss Hauer & Feld LLP

Beijing
William Rosoff, Partner in Charge
B12 Jianguomenwai Avenue
Suite 06, EF Floor, Twin Towers (East)
Phone: 86-10-8567-2200
Fax: 86-10-8567-2201
Total Lawyers: 4

Andrews Kurth LLP

Beijing Office
Tim Unger
Room 2007, Capital Mansion
No. 6 Xin Yuan Nan Lu, Chao Yang District
Beijing, China 100004
Total Lawyers: 5.4

Armstrong Teasdale LLP

Armstrong Teasdale LLP
Steve Yu - Managing Attorney of China Office
1376 Nan Jing Xi Lu
Shanghai Centre - Suite 718
Shanghai, China
011-8621-6279-8866
Total Lawyers: 4

Benesch, Friedlander, Coplan & Aronoff LLP

Benesch Friedlander Coplan & Aronoff LLP
Lianzhong Pan
Kerry Centre Tower 1, Suite 3002
1515 W. Nanjing Road
Total Lawyers: 1

Blank Rome LLP

Blank Rome - Shanghai
45F Two IFC
8 Century Avenue
Total Lawyers: 2

CHINA (Continued)

Bryan Cave LLP

Shanghai
Zhongdong Zhang
Suite 918-921, One Corporate Avenue
222 Hubin Road, Huangpu District
Total Lawyers: 5

Cadwalader, Wickersham & Taft

Beijing
Rocky Lee
2301 China Central Place Tower 2
No. 79 Jianguo Road
Total Lawyers: 8

Carroll, Burdick & McDonough LLP

Beijing
No. 6 Jia Chaowai Street, Chaoyang District
Room 05, Floor 9, Tower D, Vantone Center
Total Lawyers: 2

Cleary Gottlieb Steen & Hamilton

Beijing
+86 10 5920 1000
Twin Towers - West (23rd Floor)
12 B Jianguomen Wai Da Jie
Chaoyang District
Total Lawyers: 8

Davis Polk & Wardwell

Beijing
Total Lawyers: 16

Hong Kong
Total Lawyers: 87

Davis Wright Tremaine LLP

Davis Wright Tremaine LLP
Ron (Rongwei) Cai, Partner-in-Charge
Suite 640, East Tower
Shanghai Centre
1376 Nanjing Xi Lu
Shanghai, China 200040
Total Lawyers: 8

Debevoise & Plimpton LLP

E. Drew Dutton
22/F Jin Mao Tower
88 Century Boulevard
Pudong New District
Shanghai 200121, China
Total Lawyers: 5

Dechert LLP

Dechert LLP Beijing Representative Office US
1 Guanghua Road, Chaoyang District
Suite 1218, South Tower
Total Lawyers: 6

Dechert LLP
27/F Henley Building, 5 Queen's Road
Total Lawyers: 15

CHINA

DLA Piper

DLA Piper UK LLP
Alastair Da Costa, Managing Director, Asia
36/F Shanghai World Financial Center
100 Century
Avenue, Pudong
Total Lawyers: 21

DLA Piper UK LLP
Alastair Da Costa, Managing Director, Asia
20th Floor, South Tower Beijing Kerry Center 1
Guanghua Road Chaoyang District
Total Lawyers: 18

Dorsey & Whitney LLP

Dorsey & Whitney Hong Kong
John Chrisman
88 Queensway
Suite 3008 One Pacific Place
Total Lawyers: 15

Dorsey & Whitney Shanghai
Peter Corne
No. 1155 Fang Dian Road
Suite 807- 808, Kerry Parkside
Total Lawyers: 3

Beijing
Frank Hong
Twin Towers, B12, Jianguomenwai Avenue
Suite 1101A, West Tower
Total Lawyers: 2

Duane Morris LLP

Duane Morris & Selvam LLP
Leon Yee
No 1501 Century Avenue
Unit 303B, Soho Century Plaza
Total Lawyers: 2

Faegre Baker Daniels

Bing Wang, Office Leader
No. 1 Jian Guo Men Wai Avenue
Office 2, China World Trade Center, Suite 1919
Total Lawyers: 1

John Grobowski, Office Leader
1601 Nanjing Road West
Suite 2702, Park Place
Total Lawyers: 10

Fenwick & West LLP

Fenwick & West Shanghai
Eva Wang (+86 21 8017 1212, ewang@fenwick.com)
No. 1155 Fang Dian Road
Unit 908
9th Floor, Kerry Parkside Office
Total Lawyers: 8

Finnegan, Henderson, Farabow, Garrett & Dunner

Shanghai Office
Esther H. Lim, Managing Partner
Mirae Asset Tower, 28/F Unit A-B
No. 166 Lujiazui Ring Road, Pudong
Shanghai, China 200120
+86 21 6194 2000
+86 21 6194 2018 fax
Total Lawyers: 2

CHINA (Continued)

Foley & Lardner, LLP

Shanghai
Suite 2201, Jin Mao Tower
88 Century Boulevard
Total Lawyers: 4

Fredrikson & Byron, P.A.

Brinton Scott
6F 4, Aurora Plaza
99 Fucheng Road
Pudong
Shanghai, China
200120
Total Lawyers: 2

Garvey Schubert Barer

Beijing
Leo C. Peng lpeng@gsblaw.com 8610.8529.9880
820 South Tower
Beijing Kerry Center
1 Guang Hua Road
Chaoyang District
Beijing, PRC 100020
Total Lawyers: 3

Gibson, Dunn & Crutcher

Beijing
Fang Xue, Partner in Charge
China Central Place
Unit 1301, Tower 1
No. 81 Jianguo Road
Chaoyang District,100025
Total Lawyers: 3

Hong Kong
Kelly Austin, Partner in Charge
32/F Gloucester Tower
The Landmark
15 Queen's Road Central
Total Lawyers: 15

Greenberg Traurig, LLP

Greenberg Traurig
George Qi and Dawn Zhang
Rooms 3125-3141
Shanghai Central Plaza
381 Huai Hai Zhong Lu
Total Lawyers: 13

Hunton & Williams

Beijing Office
Edward B. Koehler
517-520 South Office Tower, Beijing Kerry Centre, No. 1
Guanghua Road
Total Lawyers: 3

Jones Day

H. John Kao
3201 China World Tower 1
No. 1 Jianguomenwai Avenue
Tel: 86-10-5866-1111
Fax: 86-10-5866-1122
Total Lawyers: 10

Peter J. Wang
27 Zhongshan Dong Yi Road
4th Floor
Tel: 86-21-2201-8000
Fax: 86-21-5298-6569
Total Lawyers: 21

K&L Gates LLP

Shanghai Office
David Tang
Suite 3708, Park Place
1601 Nanjing Road West, Jing An District
Total Lawyers: 5

Beijing Office
David Tang
Suite 1009-1011 Tower C1, Oriental Plaza
No 1 East Chang An Avenue
Total Lawyers: 8

Kaye Scholer LLP

Yinxi Fu-Tomlinson
Suites 3806-3811 CITIC Square
1168 Nanjing Xi Lu
Shanghai 200041
People's Republic of China
Total Lawyers: 3

Keller and Heckman LLP

Shanghai Office
Suite 3604, The Bund Center
222 Yan' An Dong Lu
Shanghai 200002
China
Total Lawyers: 4

Kirkland & Ellis

Shanghai
Kirkland & Ellis International LLP
11th Floor, HSBC Building
8 Century Avenue
Pudong New District
Total Lawyers: 6

Beijing
Kirkland & Ellis International LLP
29th Floor, China World Office 2
No. 1 Jian Guo Men Wai Avenue
Total Lawyers: 5

Loeb & Loeb LLP

Beijing, PR China
Lawrence Venick
Suite 4301, Tower C, Beijing Yintai Center
2 Jianguomenwai Dajie, Chaoyang District
Total Lawyers: 3

Mayer Brown

Beijing
Ian K. Lewis
Total Lawyers: 24

Hong Kong
Connie Yu
Total Lawyers: 215

Milbank, Tweed, Hadley & McCloy

Beijing
Anthony Root
15th Floor, Tower 2 China Central Place
79 Jinguo Road
Chaoyang District
Beijing, China
Total Lawyers: 3

Miller, Canfield, Paddock and Stone, P.L.C.

Shanghai
Yanping Wang
29/F, Shanghai Kerry Centre
1515 Nanjing West Road
Shanghai, 200040
Total Lawyers: 2

Nixon Peabody LLP

Shanghai
David Cheng, Partner
Nixon Peabody LLP
Plaza 66, 63rd Floor (Suite 6302)
1266 Nan Jing West Road
Shanghai, China 200040
86 21 6137 5500
Total Lawyers: 2

Norton Rose Fulbright

Beijing
Phillip John
19/F China World Tower, No. 1 Jianguomenwai Ave.
Total Lawyers: 6

Hong Kong
Phillip John
38/F Jardine House, 1 Connaught Place
Total Lawyers: 87

Shanghai
Sun Hong
27/F, Plaza 66 II, 1277 Nanjing Road West
Total Lawyers: 10

O'Melveny & Myers LLP

Beijing
Howard Zhang
31/F, China World Tower 1
1 Jianguomenwai Avenue
Beijing, 100004 P.R.C.
China
Total Lawyers: 12

Shanghai
Kurt Berney
Plaza 66, 37th Floor
1266 Nanjing Road West
Shanghai 200040, P.R.C.
China
Total Lawyers: 18

Paul, Hastings, Janofsky & Walker LLP

Mitchell Dudek
Suite 2301 23rd Floor
Hong Kong New World Tower
300 Huai Hai Middle Road
Shanghai, 200021
China
Total Lawyers: 33

CHINA

David Livdahl
Suite 1101
China World Tower 1
1 Jianguomenwai Avenue
Beijing, 100004
China
Total Lawyers: 14

Paul, Weiss, Rifkind, Wharton & Garrison LLP

Beijing
Unit 3601, Fortune Plaza Office Tower A
No. 7 Dong Sanhuan Zhonglu
Chao Yang District
Beijing 100020, China

Perkins Coie

Beijing
Michael House
1 Guang Hua Road, Chao Yang
Unit 2518-2521
South Office Tower
District
Total Lawyers: 1

Shanghai
Aaron Winiger
16F, Hang Seng Bank Tower
1000 Lujiazui Ring Road
Pudong New Area
Total Lawyers: 1

Reed Smith LLP

Beijing
Hugh Scogin
1101 China World Office 1
1 Jianguomenwai Avenue
Chaoyang District
Total Lawyers: 11

Shanghai
Jay Yan
52nd Floor
Whelock Square
No. 1717 Nanjing Road West
Jing An District
Shanghai City 200040
Total Lawyers: 9

Ropes & Gray LLP

Hong Kong
41st Floor, One Exchange Square
8 Connaught Place
Total Lawyers: 48

Shanghai
36F, Park Place
1601 Nanjing Road West
Total Lawyers: 22

Shearman & Sterling LLP

Beijing
Alan Seem, Managing Partner
12th Floor East Tower, Twin Towers
B-12 Jianguomenwai Dajie
Beijing, 100022, China

CHINA (Continued)

Shanghai
Andrew Ruff, Managing Partner
11th Floor, Platinum
233 Taicang Road
Shanghai, 200020
China

Sheppard, Mullin, Richter & Hampton

Shanghai
Don Williams
26th Floor, Wheelock Square
1717 Nanjing Road West
Total Lawyers: 10

Beijing
Jim Zimmerman
15F, China World Office 1
No. 1 Jian Guo Men Wai Avenue
Chaoyang District
Total Lawyers: 8

Sidley Austin LLP

Shanghai
5 Corporate Avenue
150 Hubin Road
Suite 2009
Total Lawyers: 10

Beijing
Oriental Plaza
No. 1 East Chang An Avenue
1 Dong Cheng District
Suite 608, Tower C2
Total Lawyers: 14

Simpson Thacher & Bartlett LLP

Beijing
3901 China World Tower
1 Jian Guo Men Wai Avenue
Total Lawyers: 9

Skadden, Arps, Slate, Meagher & Flom LLP and Affiliates

Beijing
Jon L. Christianson
30/F Tower 2
China World Trade Center
No. 1 Jianguomenwai Ave.
100004
Total Lawyers: 9

Shanghai
Gregory G.H. Miao
Plaza 66, Tower 1
36th Floor
1266 Nanjing West Road
200040
Total Lawyers: 5

Sullivan & Cromwell

The Beijing Representative Office of Sullivan & Cromwell LLP
Robert Chu
Suite 501, China World Trade Center
No. 1 Jianguo Menwai Avenue
Beijing 100004, China
Tel: 86-10-5923-5900
Fax: 86-10-5923-5950
Total Lawyers: 5

CHINA

Troutman Sanders LLP

Hong Kong
Eric Szweda, Office Managing Partner
8 Connaught Place, Central
Two Exchange Square, 34th Floor
852-2533-7888

Shanghai
Edward Epstein, Office Managing Partner
1168 Nanjing West Road
23rd Floor, Citic Square
Shanghai, 200041
86-21-6133-8989

Beijing
Allen Tzo Ching Shyu, Office Managing Partner
1 Jianguomenwai Dajie
Suite 3610, China World Office 2
China World Trade Centre
Beijing 100004
86-10-6535-1788

Vinson & Elkins

Beijing
Paul C. Deemer
20/F, Beijing Silver Tower
No. 2 Dong San Huan Bei Lu, Chaoyang District
Beijing 100027, China
Total Lawyers: 11

Shanghai
David M. Blumental and Paul C. Deemer
5/F, The Center
989 Chang Le Road
Shanghai 200031 China
Total Lawyers: 13

Weil, Gotshal & Manges LLP

Beijing
Steven Xiang, Partner
1 Jianguomenwai Avenue
2011 China World Office 2
Beijing 100004
China
Total Lawyers: 4

Shanghai
Steven Xiang, Partner
38/f Tower 2 Plaza 66
1366 Nan Jing Road West
Shanghai 200040
China
Total Lawyers: 11

Williams Kastner

Duan & Duan
Charles Duan
88 Zun Yi Nan Road
17th Floor
Shanghai, China
Total Lawyers: 1

Wilmer Cutler Pickering Hale and Dorr

1206 North Tower, 1 Guanghua Road, Chaoyang District
Total Lawyers: 5

CHINA (Continued)

Wilson Sonsini Goodrich & Rosati

Wilson Sonsini Goodrich & Rosati
Jin Mao Tower
38F, Unit 01-04
88 Century Boulevard
Pudong, Shanghai 200121
People's Republic of China
Total Lawyers: 7

Winston & Strawn LLP

Winston & Strawn LLP
Brinton Scott
Unit 1802
Azia Center
1233 Lujiazui Ring Road
Total Lawyers: 6

Winston & Strawn LLP
David Hall-Jones
Suite 718
China World Tower 1
1 Jianguomenwai Ave
Total Lawyers: 1

COLOMBIA

Norton Rose Fulbright

Bogota
Mauricio Zagarra-Cayon
Edificio K2 7 Piso, Calle 97A
#9A-50
Total Lawyers: 22

CZECH REPUBLIC

Becker & Poliakoff, P.A.

Becker & Poliakoff
Martin Klimpl
Prague
Czech Republic
Total Lawyers: 15

DLA Piper

DLA Piper Prague LLP
Manesova 5 CZ-12000 Praha
Total Lawyers: 18

Weil, Gotshal & Manges LLP

Prague
Karel Muzikar, Partner
Charles Bridge Center
Krizovnicke nam 193/2
110 00 Prague 1
Czech Republic
Total Lawyers: 31

FRANCE

Bryan Cave LLP

Paris
Rémy Blain
78 Avenue Raymond Poincaré
Total Lawyers: 13

OF COUNSEL 700

FRANCE

Cleary Gottlieb Steen & Hamilton
Paris
+33 1 40 74 68 00
12, rue de Tilsitt
Total Lawyers: 104

Davis Polk & Wardwell
Paris
Total Lawyers: 13

Debevoise & Plimpton LLP
Pierre Clermontel
21 avenue George V
75008 Paris, France
Total Lawyers: 45

Dechert LLP
Dechert LLP
32 rue de Monceau
Total Lawyers: 63

DLA Piper
DLA Piper UK LLP
Jean-Philippe Sorba
15-17 rue Scribe
Total Lawyers: 52

Foley Hoag LLP
Foley Hoag AARPI
Isabelle de Jussieu
39, rue du Colisée
Total Lawyers: 2

Fried, Frank, Harris, Shriver & Jacobson LLP
Paris
75, Boulevard Haussmann
Total Lawyers: 0

Gibson, Dunn & Crutcher
Paris
Bernard Grinspan, Partner in Charge
166 rue du Faubourg Saint-Honore
75008
Total Lawyers: 19

Hughes Hubbard & Reed LLP
Merrikay S. Hall and Jose Rosell
47, Avenue Georges Mandel
75116 Paris, France

Jones Day
Sophie Hagege
2 Rue Saint-Floretin
Tel: 33-1-56-59-39-39
Fax: 33-1-56-59-39-38
Total Lawyers: 104

FRANCE (Continued)

K&L Gates LLP
Paris Office
Martin Lane
116 avenue des Champs-Elysées
Total Lawyers: 14

Keller and Heckman LLP
Paris Office
120 rue la Boetie
Total Lawyers: 1

Nixon Peabody LLP
Paris
Arnaud de Senilhes, Partner
Nixon Peabody
32, rue de Monceau
75008 Paris, France
33 0 1 70 72 36 01
Total Lawyers: 26

Norton Rose Fulbright
Paris
George Paterson
ParisEight, 40, rue de Courcelles
Total Lawyers: 111

Paul, Hastings, Janofsky & Walker LLP
Dominique Borde
96, boulevard Haussmann
Paris, 75008
France
Total Lawyers: 38

Quinn Emanuel Urquhart & Sullivan LLP
Quinn Emanuel Urquhart & Sullivan LLP (Paris)
Philippe Pinsolle
25 rue Balzac
Total Lawyers: 7

Reed Smith LLP
Paris
Benoit Charot
42
Avenue Raymond Poincare
75782 Paris Cedex 16
Total Lawyers: 46

Ropers, Majeski, Kohn, & Bentley, P.C.
Paris
Francois Laugier
4 rue Saint Florentin
Total Lawyers: 1

Shearman & Sterling LLP
Paris
Emmanuel Gaillard, Managing Partner
114, avenue des Champs-Elysées
75008 Paris, France

FRANCE

Skadden, Arps, Slate, Meagher & Flom LLP and Affiliates

Paris
Pierre Servan-Schreiber
68, rue du Faubourg Saint-Honore
75008
Total Lawyers: 22

Sullivan & Cromwell

William D. Torchiana
24, rue Jean-Goujon
75008 Paris, France
Tel: 011-331-73 04 10 00
Fax: 011-331- 73 04 10 10
Total Lawyers: 33

Weil, Gotshal & Manges LLP

Paris
Claude Serra, Partner
2, rue de la Baume
75008 Paris
France
Total Lawyers: 58

Winston & Strawn LLP

Winston & Strawn SELARL
Gilles Bigot
40 - 48 rue Cambon
CS 71234
75039 Paris Cedex 01
Total Lawyers: 27

GEORGIA

Dechert LLP

Dechert Georgia LLC
34 Chavchavadze Avenue
Pixel Building 7th Floor
Total Lawyers: 3

DLA Piper

DLA Piper Georgia LP
Melikishvili Street #10
Total Lawyers: 12

GERMANY

Akin Gump Strauss Hauer & Feld LLP

Frankfurt
James Terry, Partner in Charge
OpernTurm
Bockenheimer Landstraße 2-4
Phone: 49 69-677766-0
Fax: 49 69-677766-100
Total Lawyers: 4

Bryan Cave LLP

Hamburg
Eckart Budelmann
Hanseatic Trade Center
Am Sandtorkai 77
Total Lawyers: 13

GERMANY (Continued)

Frankfurt
Tobias Fenck
Main Building
Taunusanlage 18
Total Lawyers: 4

Carroll, Burdick & McDonough LLP

Böblingen
Herrenberger Strasse 12
Total Lawyers: 6

Cleary Gottlieb Steen & Hamilton

Frankfurt
+49 221 97103 0
Main Tower
Neue Mainzer Strasse 52
Total Lawyers: 39

Cologne
+49 221 80040 0
Theodor-Heuss-Ring 9
Total Lawyers: 22

Debevoise & Plimpton LLP

Dr. Thomas Schurrle
Borsencenter, Taubenstrasse 7-9
60313 Frankfurt am Main, Germany
Total Lawyers: 11

Dechert LLP

Dechert LLP
Tower 185
Friedrich-Ebert-Anlage 35-37
Total Lawyers: 15

Dechert LLP
Erika-Mann-Straße 5
Total Lawyers: 15

DLA Piper

DLA Piper UK LLP
Hohenzollernring 72
Total Lawyers: 53

DLA Piper UK LLP
Westhafenplatz 1
Total Lawyers: 47

DLA Piper UK LLP
Jungfernstieg 7
Total Lawyers: 31

DLA Piper UK LLP
Isartorplatz 1
Total Lawyers: 12

Fish & Richardson

Munich, Germany
Highlight Business Towers
Mies-van-der-Rohe
Strasse 8
D-80 807
Munich, Germany
Total Lawyers: 6

GERMANY

Fried, Frank, Harris, Shriver & Jacobson LLP

Frankfurt
Taunusanlage 18, 60325 Frankfurt am Main
Total Lawyers: 7

Gibson, Dunn & Crutcher

Munich
Michael Walther, Partner in Charge
Hofgarten Palais, Marstallstrasse 11
80539
Total Lawyers: 15

Jones Day

Friederike Goebbels
Prinzregentenstr. 11
Tel: 49-89-20-60-42-200
Fax: 49-89-20-60-42-293
Total Lawyers: 29

Sandra-Christiane Kamper
Thurn-und-Taxis-Platz 6
Nextower
Tel: 49-69-9726-3939
Fax: 49-69-9726-3993
Total Lawyers: 44

Ulrich G.H. Brauer
Breite Strasse 69
Tel: 49-211-5406-5500
Fax: 49-211-5406-5501
Total Lawyers: 19

K&L Gates LLP

Frankfurt Office
Dr. Rüdiger von Hülst
OpernTurm
Bockenheimer Landstrasse 2-4
60306 Frankfurt am Main
Total Lawyers: 21

Berlin Office
Dr. Rüdiger von Hülst
Markgrafenstrasse 42
D 10117
Total Lawyers: 42

Kaye Scholer LLP

Gottfried Freier
Schillerstrasse 19
60313 Frankfurt am Main, Germany
Total Lawyers: 16

King & Spalding, LLP

Frankfurt
Ariane Kuhnke
Taunusanlage 1
60329 Frankfurt am Main

Kirkland & Ellis

Munich
Kirkland & Ellis International LLP
Maximilianstrasse 11
Total Lawyers: 37

GERMANY (Continued)

Ladas & Parry LLP

Munich, Germany
Dachauerstrasse 37

McDermott Will & Emery

McDermott Will & Emery Rechtsanwalte Steuerberater LLP
Dirk Pohl, Partner-in-Charge
Nymphenburger Str. 3
80335 Muenchen
Germany
Total Lawyers: 26

McDermott Will & Emery Rechtsanwalte Steuerberater LLP
Konstantin Gunther, Partner-in-Charge
Stadttor 1
40219 Duesseldorf
Germany
Total Lawyers: 15

Milbank, Tweed, Hadley & McCloy

Frankfurt
Rainer Magold
Taunusanlage 15
60325
Frankfurt am Main, Germany
Total Lawyers: 13

Munich
Rolf Fueger
Maximilianstrasse 15
(Maximilianhoefe)
80589
Munich, Germany
Total Lawyers: 23

Norton Rose Fulbright

Munich
Ralf Springer
Theatinerstrasse 11
Total Lawyers: 68

Frankfurt
Thomas Hopf
Taunustor 1
Total Lawyers: 51

Hamburg
Klaus von Gierke
Bleichenbrucke 10
Total Lawyers: 24

Ogletree, Deakins, Nash, Smoak & Stewart, P.C.

Berlin
Ryan King
Fasanenstraße 77 10623 Berlin, Germany
Total Lawyers: 8

Quinn Emanuel Urquhart & Sullivan LLP

Quinn Emanuel Urquhart & Sullivan LLP (Hamburg)
Nadine Herrmann
An der Alster 3
Total Lawyers: 18

Quinn Emanuel Urquhart & Sullivan (Mannheim)
Dr. Marcus Grosch LL.M. (Yale)
MallstraBe 42
Total Lawyers: 7

GERMANY

Quinn Emanuel Urquhart & Sullivan LLP (Munich)
Dr. Marcus Grosch LL.M. (Yale)
Oberanger 28
Total Lawyers: 8

Reed Smith LLP

Munich
Stefan Kugler
Funf Hofe
Theatinerstrasse 8
80333 Munchen
Total Lawyers: 28

Shearman & Sterling LLP

Düsseldorf
Rainer Wilke; Markus S. Rieder, Co-Managing Partners
Breite Strasse 69
D-40213 Düsseldorf, Germany

Frankfurt
Rainer Wilke; Markus S. Rieder, Co-Managing Partners
Gervinusstrasse 17
D-60322 Frankfurt am Main, Germany

Munich
Rainer Wilke; Markus S. Rieder, Co-Managing Partners
Oberanger 28
D-80331 München, Germany

Skadden, Arps, Slate, Meagher & Flom LLP and Affiliates

Munich
Walter R. Henle
Karl-Scharnagl-Ring 7
80539
Total Lawyers: 8

Frankfurt
Hilary S. Foulkes
An der Welle 3
60322
Total Lawyers: 20

Smith, Gambrell & Russell

Smith, Gambrell & Russell
Stefan M. Tiessen
Sonnenberger Str. 60
Total Lawyers: 1

Sullivan & Cromwell

Wolfgang Feuring
Neue Mainzer Strasse 52
60311 Frankfurt am Main, Germany
Tel: 011-4969-42-72-52-00
Fax: 011-4969-42-72-52-10
Total Lawyers: 17

Weil, Gotshal & Manges LLP

Frankfurt
Gerhard Schmidt, Partner
Taunusanlage 1 (Skyper)
60329 Frankfurt
Germany
Total Lawyers: 26

GERMANY (Continued)

Munich
Gerhard Schmidt, Partner
Maximilianhofe
Maximilianstrasse 13
80539 Munich
Germany
Total Lawyers: 21

Wilmer Cutler Pickering Hale and Dorr

Ulmenstrasse 37-39
Total Lawyers: 27

Friedrichstr. 95
Total Lawyers: 25

GREECE

Norton Rose Fulbright

Greece (Athens & Piraeus)
Dimitri Sofianopoulos
Building K1, 175 01 Delta Paleo Faliro
Total Lawyers: 30

Reed Smith LLP

Piraeus
John Reece
Akti Miaouli
17-19
185 35 Piraeus
Total Lawyers: 9

HONG KONG

Akin Gump Strauss Hauer & Feld LLP

Hong Kong
Sebastian Rice, Partner in Charge
The Landmark, 15 Queen's Road Central
Units 1801-08 & 10, 18th Floor Gloucester Tower
Phone: 852-3694-3000
Fax: 852-3694-3001
Total Lawyers: 20

Bryan Cave LLP

Hong Kong
Kristi Swartz
11th Floor, Club Lusitano
16 Ice House Street
Total Lawyers: 5

Cadwalader, Wickersham & Taft

Hong Kong
Rocky Lee
100 Queen's Road Central
Suite 2702, 27th Floor
Total Lawyers: 23

Carroll, Burdick & McDonough LLP

Hong Kong
Suite 5904, 59/F, Central Plaza
18 Harbour Road
Wan Chai
Total Lawyers: 4

Cleary Gottlieb Steen & Hamilton

Hong Kong
+852 2521 4122
Bank of China Tower, 39th Floor
One Garden Road
Total Lawyers: 47

Debevoise & Plimpton LLP

Andrew M. Ostrognai
13/F Entertainment Building
30 Queens Road Central
Hong Kong, SAR China
Total Lawyers: 12

DLA Piper

DLA Piper Hong Kong
Alastair Da Costa, Managing Director, Asia
40th Floor, Bank of China Tower
1 Garden Road
Total Lawyers: 77

Goodwin Procter LLP

Hong Kong
Yash Rana
One Exchange Square, 8 Connaught Place Central
Suite 2801
Total Lawyers: 10

Jones Day

Robert L. Thomson
31st Floor, Edinburgh Tower
The Landmark, 15 Queen's Road Central
Tel: 852-2526-6895
Fax: 852-2868-5871
Total Lawyers: 53

K&L Gates LLP

Hong Kong Office
David Tang
44th Floor, Edingburgh Tower, The Landmark
15 Queen's Road Central
Total Lawyers: 32

Kirkland & Ellis

Hong Kong
Kirkland & Ellis International LLP
26th Floor, Gloucester Tower
The Landmark
15 Queen's Road Central
Total Lawyers: 73

Loeb & Loeb LLP

Hong Kong
Benny Pang
3 Connaught Road Central
21st floor, CCB Tower
Total Lawyers: 2

Milbank, Tweed, Hadley & McCloy

Hong Kong
Anthony Root
3007 Alexandra House
18 Chater Road
Central
Hong Kong
Total Lawyers: 11

O'Melveny & Myers LLP

Hong Kong
Michael Moser
31st Floor, AIG Tower
1 Connaught Road Central
Hong Kong
Total Lawyers: 18

Paul, Hastings, Janofsky & Walker LLP

Neil Torpey
21-22/F Bank of China Tower
1 Garden Road
Bank of China
Hong Kong, China
Total Lawyers: 59

Paul, Weiss, Rifkind, Wharton & Garrison LLP

Hong Kong
Hong Kong Club Building, 12th Floor
3A Chater Road, Central
Hong Kong

Quinn Emanuel Urquhart & Sullivan LLP

Quinn Emanuel Urquhart & Sullivan LLP (Hong Kong)
John Rhie
1307-1308 Two Exchange Square, 8 Connaught Place
Total Lawyers: 4

Reed Smith LLP

Hong Kong
Ivy Cheung
20th Floor
Alexandra House
18 Charter Road
Total Lawyers: 87

Shearman & Sterling LLP

Hong Kong
Matthew Bersani, Managing Partner
12/F, Gloucester Tower
The Landmark
15 Queen's Road Central, Central
Hong Kong, China

Sidley Austin LLP

Hong Kong
39/F Two International Finance Center
8 Finance Street
Total Lawyers: 81

HONG KONG

Simpson Thacher & Bartlett LLP

Hong Kong
ICBC Tower
3 Garden Road, Central
Total Lawyers: 36

Skadden, Arps, Slate, Meagher & Flom LLP and Affiliates

Hong Kong
Alan G. Schiffman
42/F, Edinburgh Tower
The Landmark
15 Queen's Road Central
Total Lawyers: 58

Sullivan & Cromwell

Chun Wei
28th Floor
Nine Queen's Road Central
Hong Kong, SAR China
Tel: 852-2826-8688
Fax: 852-2522-2280
Total Lawyers: 16

Vinson & Elkins

Hong Kong
James L. Cuclis
10th Floor, Gloucester Tower, The Landmark
15 Queen's Road
Central, Hong Kong, China
Total Lawyers: 13

Weil, Gotshal & Manges LLP

Hong Kong
Akiko Mikumo, Partner
29th Floor Gloucester Tower
The Landmark
15 Queen's Road Central
Hong Kong
Total Lawyers: 13

Wilson Sonsini Goodrich & Rosati

Hong Kong
5 Queen's Road Central
10/F Henley Building
Unit 1001
Total Lawyers: 5

Winston & Strawn LLP

Winston & Strawn LLP
David Hall-Jones
1 Garden Road
42nd Floor, Bank of China Tower
Total Lawyers: 21

HUNGARY

DLA Piper

Horvath & Partners Law Firm
Alkotas U.50 H-1123
Total Lawyers: 37

HUNGARY (Continued)

Weil, Gotshal & Manges LLP

Budapest
David S. Dederick, Partner
Bank Center Granite Tower
Szabadsag ter 7
H-1054
Budapest, Hungary
Total Lawyers: 18

INDIA

Jones Day

Associate Office
Anand S. Pathak
1st Floor, Dr. Gopal Das Bhavan
28, Barakhamba Road
Tel: 91-11-4139-3939
Fax: 91-11-2335-0416
Total Lawyers: 17

INDONESIA

Norton Rose Fulbright

Jakarta (Associate office: Susandarini & Partners)
Tasdikiah Siregar
Level 33, Equity Tower, Sudirman Central Business District
Total Lawyers: 18

IRELAND

Dechert LLP

Dechert LLP
Riverside Two
Sir John Rogerson's Quay
Total Lawyers: 8

ISRAEL

Greenberg Traurig, LLP

Greenberg Traurig, P.A.
Gary Epstein
One Azrieli Center
Round Tower, 30th Floor, 132 Menachem Begin Road
Total Lawyers: 5

ITALY

Cleary Gottlieb Steen & Hamilton

Rome
+39 06 69 52 21
Piazza di Spagna 15
Total Lawyers: 38

Milan
+39 02 72 60 81
Via San Paolo 7
Total Lawyers: 33

DLA Piper

Studio Legale Tributario Associato
Via Gabrio Casati 1 (Piazza Cordusio)
Total Lawyers: 74

ITALY

Studio Legale Tributario Associato
Frederico Sutti, Regional Managing Partner
Via dei Due Macelli 66-00187
Total Lawyers: 27

Jones Day

Marco Lombardi
Via Turati, 16/18
Tel: 39-02-7645-4001
Fax: 39-02-7645-4400
Total Lawyers: 39

K&L Gates LLP

Milan
Giampaolo Salsi
Piazza San Marco, 1
Total Lawyers: 10

McDermott Will & Emery

McDermott Will & Emery Studio Legale Associato
Massimo Trentino, Partner-in-Charge
Via A. Ristori, 38
00197 Rome
Italy
Total Lawyers: 16

Norton Rose Fulbright

Milan
Nicolo Juvara
Piazza San Babila 1
Total Lawyers: 41

Paul, Hastings, Janofsky & Walker LLP

Roberto Cornetta
Via Palestro, 24
Milan, 20121
Italy
Total Lawyers: 17

Shearman & Sterling LLP

Rome
Domenico Fanuele, Managing Partner
Via Borgognona, 17
00187 Roma, Italy

Milan
Domenico Fanuele, Managing Partner
Corso Venezia 16
20121 Milano, Italy

JAPAN

Davis Polk & Wardwell

Tokyo
Total Lawyers: 8

DLA Piper

DLA Piper Tokyo Partnership Gaikokuho Kyodojigyo, Jimusho
Alastair Da Costa, Managing Director, Asia
Meiji Selmei Kan 7F 2-1-1 Marunouchi Chiyoda-ku
Total Lawyers: 16

JAPAN (Continued)

Finnegan, Henderson, Farabow, Garrett & Dunner

Tokyo Office
Naoki Yoshida, Managing Partner
33rd Floor, Shiroyama Trust Tower
3-1, Toranomon 4-chome
Minato-ku, Tokyo, Japan 105-6033
+813 3431 6943
+813 3431 6945 fax
Total Lawyers: 2

Foley & Lardner, LLP

Tokyo
4-3-1 Toranomon Minato-Ku
Tokyo, 105-6015
Japan
Total Lawyers: 2

Greenberg Traurig, LLP

Greenberg Traurig Tokyo Law Offices are operated by GT Tokyo
Horitsu Jimusho
Koji Ishikawa
15th Floor, Tokyo Bankers Club Building
1-3-1, Marunouchi, Chiyoda-ku,
100-0005
Total Lawyers: 6

Hughes Hubbard & Reed LLP

Yasuo Okamoto
Akasaka Tokyu Building 6F
2-14-3 Nagata-cho, Chiyoda-ku
Tokyo 100-0014 Japan

Hunton & Williams

Tokyo Office
Pacific Century Place 8F, 1-11-1 Marunouchi, Chiyoda ku
Total Lawyers: 3

Jones Day

Masatomo Suzuki
Kamiyacho Prime Place
1-17, Toranomon 4-chome
Tel: 81-3-3433-3939
Fax: 81-3-5401-2725
Total Lawyers: 48

K&L Gates LLP

Tokyo Office
Ryan Dwyer
Kasumigaseki Common Gate West Tower 35F
3-2-1 Kasumigaseki, Chiyoda-ku
Total Lawyers: 15

Milbank, Tweed, Hadley & McCloy

Tokyo
Gary Wigmore
Fukoku Seimei Building
2-2, Uchisaiwaicho 2-chome
Chiyoda-ku, 100-0011
Tokyo, Japan
Total Lawyers: 7

JAPAN

Norton Rose Fulbright
Tokyo
Jeremy Gibb and Eiji Kobayashi
Otemachi First Square East, Tower 18F
Total Lawyers: 13

O'Melveny & Myers LLP
Tokyo
Naosuke Fujita
Meiji Yasuda Seimei Building, 11th Floor
2-1-1, Marunouchi
Chiyoda-ku
Tokyo 100-0005, Japan
Total Lawyers: 28

Oblon, McClelland, Maier & Neustadt, LLP
Oblon Spivak LLP
Tokyo Ginko Kyokai Building 16th Floor
3-1, Marunouchi 1-chome
Chiyoda-ku
Total Lawyers: 2

Paul, Hastings, Janofsky & Walker LLP
Edward S. Johnson
34th floor Ark Mori Building
P.O. Box 577
12-32 Akasaka 1-chome
Minato-Ku Tokyo, 107-6034
Japan
Total Lawyers: 42

Paul, Weiss, Rifkind, Wharton & Garrison LLP
Tokyo
Fukoku Seimei Building, 2nd Floor
2-2 Uchisaiwaicho 2-chome
Chiyoda-ku
Tokyo 100 0011, Japan

Pillsbury Winthrop Shaw Pittman LLP
Toyko
5F
Fuerte Kojimachi Bldg.
7-25 Kojimachi 1-chome
Chiyoda-ku
Tokyo 102-0083, Japan
Total Lawyers: 4

Quinn Emanuel Urquhart & Sullivan LLP
Quinn Emanuel Urquhart & Sullivan LLP (Toyko)
Ryan Goldstein
NBF Hibiya Bldg., 25F 1-1-7,
Uchisaiwai-cho
Total Lawyers: 3

Ropes & Gray LLP
Tokyo
Yusen Building 2F
3-2 Marunouchi 2-Chome
Total Lawyers: 13

JAPAN (Continued)

Shearman & Sterling LLP
Tokyo
Masahisa Ikeda, Managing Partner
Fukoku Seimei Building, 5th floor
2-2-2 Uchisaiwaicho
Chiyoda-ku, Tokyo, 100
Japan

Sidley Austin LLP
Tokyo
Marunouchi Building 23F
4-1, Marunouchi 2-chome
Total Lawyers: 13

Simpson Thacher & Bartlett LLP
Tokyo
Ark Hills Sengokuyama Mori Tower
41st Floor
Total Lawyers: 11

Skadden, Arps, Slate, Meagher & Flom LLP and Affiliates
Tokyo
Michael J. Mies
Izumi Garden Tower
21st Floor
1-6-1 Roppongi
Minato-ku 106-6021
Total Lawyers: 24

Sughrue Mion, PLLC
Yoshi Kishimoto
AIG Building
14F, 1-1-3 Marunouchi
Chiyoda-ku, Tokyo 100-0005 Japan
Total Lawyers: 2

Sullivan & Cromwell
Stanley F. Farrar, Izumi Akai
Otemachi First Square
5-1, Otemachi 1-chome
Chiyoda-ku, Tokyo 100-0004, Japan
Tel: 813-3213-6140
Fax: 813-3213-6470
Total Lawyers: 10

Vinson & Elkins
Tokyo
James E.B. Atkin
Marunouchi Kitaguchi Building
18th Floor, 1-6-5 Marunouchi
Chiyoda-ku, Tokyo 100-0005, Japan
Total Lawyers: 5

KAZAKHSTAN

Dechert LLP
Dechert Kazakhstan Limited
43 Dostyk Avenue
Fourth Floor
Total Lawyers: 10

KAZAKHSTAN

Norton Rose Fulbright

Almaty
Yerzhan Kumarov
3rd Floor, 32A Manas Street
Total Lawyers: 10

Reed Smith LLP

Astana
Dinara Jarmukhanova
Total Lawyers: 1

KINGDOM OF BAHRAIN

Norton Rose Fulbright

Bahrain
Joanne Emerson Taqi
48th Floor, West Tower, Bahrain Financial Harbour
Total Lawyers: 3

KOREA

Greenberg Traurig, LLP

Greenberg Traurig LLP
Chang Joo Kim
84 Taepyeongno 1-ga
Seoul Finance Center, 23F
Jung-gu
Foreign Legal Consultant Office
Total Lawyers: 1

Ropes & Gray LLP

Seoul
POSCO P&S Tower, 21F, 134 Teheran-ro, Gangnam-gu
Ropes & Gray Foreign Legal Consultant Office
Total Lawyers: 6

Sheppard, Mullin, Richter & Hampton

Seoul
Seth Kim
West Tower 23rd Floor Mirae Asset Center 1 Building
26 Euljiro 5-gil, Jung-gu
Total Lawyers: 5

Simpson Thacher & Bartlett LLP

Seoul
25th Floor, West Tower Mirae Asset Center 1 Building
26 Eulji-ro 5-Gil, Jung-Gu
Total Lawyers: 5

LUXEMBOURG

Dechert LLP

Dechert LLP
Avocats la Cour
74 Rue de Merl
B.P. 709
Total Lawyers: 7

MEXICO

Fredrikson & Byron, P.A.

Patrick Kelly, Luis Resendiz
Av. Batallon de San Patricio
109 Sur, Piso 6, #602
Col. Valle Oriente
San Pedro Garza García, N.L. C.P.
Montery 66260 Mexico

Gardere Wynne Sewell LLP

Gardere, Arena y Asociados, S.C.
Roberto Arena Reyes Retana
Torre Esmeralda II Blvd.
Manuel A. Camacho No. 36-1802
Lomas de Chapultepec
Mexico, D.F. Mexico 11000
Mexico
Total Lawyers: 10

Greenberg Traurig, LLP

Greenberg Traurig, S.C.
José Raz Guzmán
Paseo de la Reforma No. 265 PH1
Colonia Cuauhtemoc
Total Lawyers: 54

Jones Day

Fernando de Ovando
Paseo de la Reforma 342
Piso 30
Colonia Juarez
Tel: 52-55-3000-4000
Fax: 52-55-3000-4040
Total Lawyers: 40

Littler

Mexico City, Mexico
Rolando Santos
Park Plaza – Torre 1, Av. Javier Barros Sierra No.
540 Piso 7, Col. Santa Fe, Del. Álvaro Obregón
Total Lawyers: 18

Monterrey, Mexico
Rolando Santos
Rufino Tamayo No. 100 Piso 2
San Pedro Garza García
Total Lawyers: 8

Mayer Brown

Mexico City
Total Lawyers: 2

Miller, Canfield, Paddock and Stone, P.L.C.

Monterrey
Alberto J. Murga
Calz. del Valle #400 L. 62
Col. del Valle
San Pedro Garza Garcia, N.L., C.P. 66220
Total Lawyers: 2

MEXICO

Ogletree, Deakins, Nash, Smoak & Stewart, P.C.

Mexico City
Mary Lou Baxter
Mexico City Torre del Ángel Paseo de la Reforma 350 Pisos 10 y
11. Col.
Total Lawyers: 5

Strasburger & Price

Strasburger & Price, SC
Julian D. Nihill
Prolongacion Paseo de la Reforma (No. 600/201-A)
Col. Santa Fe Pena Blanca
01210 Mexico, D.F.
Total Lawyers: 1

MOROCCO

Norton Rose Fulbright

Casablanca
Alain Malek
Immeuble Merbouha, 10 bis rue Ali Abderrazak
Total Lawyers: 1

MYANMAR

Duane Morris LLP

Selvam & Partners Limited
Art Selvam
10 Bo Yar Zar Street, Kyaukkone
Total Lawyers: 3

NORWAY

DLA Piper

Advokatfirma DLA Piper Norway DA
Espen Moe
Olav Vs gate 4
PO Box 1364 Vika, N0-0114
Total Lawyers: 74

OMAN

Duane Morris LLP

Dr. Said Al Mashaikhi & Partner Law Firm, a GCC representative of
Duane Morris
Dr. Said Al Mashaikhi
Building No: 1540, Way No. 2724
8th Floor, Al Gazal Tower
Total Lawyers: 1

POLAND

DLA Piper

DLA Piper Wiater Sp.K.
Krzysztof Wiater, PhD
Warsaw Financial Centre Ul Emilii Plater 53
Total Lawyers: 42

POLAND (Continued)

Greenberg Traurig, LLP

Greenberg Traurig Grzesiak sp.k.
JarosÅ,aw Grzesiak
Stock Exchange Building
ul. Ksiazeca 4
00-498
Total Lawyers: 65

K&L Gates LLP

Warsaw Office
Maciej Jamka
Al. Jana Pawla II 25
Total Lawyers: 37

Miller, Canfield, Paddock and Stone, P.L.C.

Warsaw
Andrzej Chelchowski and Konrad B. Marciniuk
ul. Nowogrodzka 11, 5th Floor
00-513 Warsaw, Poland
Total Lawyers: 14

Gdynia
Wojciech Babicki
ul. Batorego 28-32
81-366 Gdynia, Poland
Total Lawyers: 6

Wroclaw
Karolina Figura
ul. Szewska 8
50-122, Wroclaw, Poland
Total Lawyers: 1

Norton Rose Fulbright

Warsaw (Norton Rose Fulbright Piotr Strawa and Partners,
Limited Partnership)
Piotr Strawa
Metropolitan Building, Plac Pilsudskiego 2
Total Lawyers: 30

Weil, Gotshal & Manges LLP

Warsaw
Pawel A. Rymarz, Partner
Warsaw Financial Center
ul. Emilii Plater 53
00-113 Warsaw
Poland
Total Lawyers: 35

QATAR

K&L Gates LLP

Doha
Michael Johns
Qatar Financial Centre Branch
31st Floor, Tornado Tower Al Funduq Street
PO Box 26100 West Bay
Total Lawyers: 2

ROMANIA

DLA Piper

Marian Dinu Law Office
Marian Dinu
Metropolis Center
89-97 Grigore Alesandrescu Str.
East Wing, 1st Floor Sector 1
Total Lawyers: 21

RUSSIA

Akin Gump Strauss Hauer & Feld LLP

Moscow
Natalia Baratiants, Partner in Charge
Geneva House
7 Petrovka Street
Phone: 7-495-783-7700
Fax: 7-495-783-7701
Total Lawyers: 26

Cleary Gottlieb Steen & Hamilton

Moscow
+7 495 660 8500
Paveletskaya Square 2/3
Total Lawyers: 39

Debevoise & Plimpton LLP

Dmitri V. Nikiforov
Business Center "Mokhovaya"
Ulitsa Vozdvizhenka
4/7 Stroyeniye 2
Moscow 125009
Total Lawyers: 17

Dechert LLP

Dechert Russia LLC
ul. Gasheka 7 str. 1
Total Lawyers: 17

DLA Piper

DLA Piper Rus Limited
Leontievsky pereulok, 25
Total Lawyers: 51

DLA Piper Rus Limited
Nevsky pr., 28, bld. A (Zinger House)
Total Lawyers: 32

Jones Day

Vladimir Lechtman
Ducat III, 12th Floor
6 Gasheka Street
Tel: 7-495-648-9200
Fax: 7-495-648-9201
Total Lawyers: 10

K&L Gates LLP

Moscow Office
Martin Lane
Lesnaya Street, 5
Building B, 4th Floor
Total Lawyers: 8

RUSSIA (Continued)

Norton Rose Fulbright

Moscow
Anatoly Andriash and Valentina Gluhovskaya
White Square Office Center, Butyrsky Val str. 10, Bldg. A
Total Lawyers: 34

Quinn Emanuel Urquhart & Sullivan LLP

Quinn Emanuel Urquhart & Sullivan LLP (Moscow)
Ivan Marisin
Paveletskaya Plaza, Paveletskaya Square, 2/3
Total Lawyers: 4

Skadden, Arps, Slate, Meagher & Flom LLP and Affiliates

Moscow
Bruce M. Buck; Pranav L. Trivedi
Ducat Place III
Gasheka Street 6
125047
Total Lawyers: 15

Vinson & Elkins

Moscow
Natalya V. Morozova
Lesnaya Plaza
4th Lesnoy Pereulok, 4, 4th Floor
125047 Moscow Russia
Total Lawyers: 1

Winston & Strawn LLP

Winston & Strawn LLP
Nikolai Krylov
26, Valovaya, 9th Floor
115054
Moscow
Total Lawyers: 4

SAUDI ARABIA

Jones Day

Yusuf Giansiracusa
29 Prince Mishari Bin Abdulaziz St.
Sulaymaniyah District
PO Box 26668
Tel: 966-11-462-8866
Total Lawyers: 2

Yusuf Giansiracusa
King's Road Tower, Floor 31
King Abdulaziz Road
PO Box 1512
Tel: 966-2-616-3939
Total Lawyers: 5

Yusuf Giansiracusa
Al-Hugayet Tower
PO Box 1759
Tel: 966-3-849-6602
Total Lawyers: 3

SAUDI ARABIA

Norton Rose Fulbright

Riyadh (Mohammed Al-Ghamdi Law Firm in association with
Fulbright & Jaworski LLP
John C. Bohem Jr.
Mawhiba Center, 3rd Floor, Olaya Main Street
Total Lawyers: 8

Vinson & Elkins

Saudi Arabia
Looaye M. Al-Akkas
The Law Office of Looaye M. Al-Akkas in Association with Vinson
& Elkins LLP
Kingdom Tower, 49th Floor
2239 Oroubah Road
Olaya, Unit No. 9
Total Lawyers: 3

SINGAPORE

Akin Gump Strauss Hauer & Feld LLP

Singapore
Robert M. Griffin, Jr., Partner in Charge
2 Shenton Way
#16-01 SGX Centre 1
One Raffles Place Tower 2
Phone:65 6579.9000
Fax: 65 6579.9009
Total Lawyers: 7

Bryan Cave LLP

Singapore
David R. Stepp
20 Anson Road. #16-02
Total Lawyers: 3

Butler Snow

Singapore
Kurt G. Rademacher
10 Collyer Quay #40-21
Ocean Financial Centre
Total Lawyers: 1

DLA Piper

DLA Piper Singapore Pte. Ltd.
Alastair Da Costa, Managing Director, Asia
80 Raffles Place
#4801 UOB Plaza 1
Total Lawyers: 21

Duane Morris LLP

Duane Morris & Selvam LLP
Eduardo Ramos-Gomez
16 Collyer Quay
17-00
Total Lawyers: 28

Gibson, Dunn & Crutcher

Singapore
Jai Pathak, Partner in Charge
One Raffles Quay
Level #37-01, North Tower
048583
Total Lawyers: 13

SINGAPORE (Continued)

Jones Day

Sushma Jobanputra
3 Church Street
14-02 Samsung Hub
Tel: 65-6538-3939
Fax: 65-6536-3939
Total Lawyers: 25

K&L Gates LLP

Singapore Office
David Tang
10 Collyer Quay
#37-01 Ocean Financial Centre
Total Lawyers: 12

Mayer Brown

Singapore
Kevin R. Owen
Total Lawyers: 8

Milbank, Tweed, Hadley & McCloy

Singapore
David Zemans
30 Raffles Place
#14-00 Chevron House
048622
Singapore
Total Lawyers: 15

Norton Rose Fulbright

Singapore
Jeff Smith
One Raffles Quay, 34-02 North Tower
Total Lawyers: 77

Reed Smith LLP

Singapore
Bee Lan Ho
10 Collyer Quay
Ocean Financial Center
Total Lawyers: 11

Shearman & Sterling LLP

Singapore
Bill McCormack, Managing Partner
6 Battery Rd. #25-03
Singapore 049909
Singapore

Sidley Austin LLP

Singapore
Six Battery Road
Level 31
Total Lawyers: 28

SINGAPORE

Skadden, Arps, Slate, Meagher & Flom LLP and Affiliates

Singapore
Rajeev P. Duggal
9 Temasek Boulevard
Suite 29-01
Suntec Tower Two
038989
Total Lawyers: 7

SLOVAKIA

DLA Piper

DLA Piper Weiss-Tessbach Rechtsanwalte GmbH
Suche myto 1 SK-811 03
Total Lawyers: 11

SOUTH AFRICA

Norton Rose Fulbright

Cape Town (Norton Rose Fulbright South Africa incorporated as
Deneys Reitz Inc.)
Rob Otty
8 Riebeek Street, 10th Floor
Total Lawyers: 35

Durban (Norton Rose Fulbright South Africa incorporated as Deneys
Reitz Inc.)
Craig Woolley
3 Pencarrow Crescent, La Lucia Ridge
Total Lawyers: 34

Johannesburg (Norton Rose Fulbright South Africa incorporated as
Deneys Reitz In
Rob Otty
15 Alice Lane
Total Lawyers: 187

SPAIN

Davis Polk & Wardwell

Madrid
Total Lawyers: 5

DLA Piper

DLA Piper Spain S.L.
Juan Picon
Paseo de la Castellana, 35-2
Total Lawyers: 69

Jones Day

Mercedes Fernandez
Paseo de Recoletos 37-41
5th Floor
Tel: 34-91-520-39-39
Fax: 34-91-520-39-38
Total Lawyers: 30

SWITZERLAND

Akin Gump Strauss Hauer & Feld LLP

Geneva
Jonathan Ivinson, Partner in Charge
54 Quai Gustave Ador
Phone: 41-22-787-4000
Fax: 41-22-787-4010
Total Lawyers: 8

Dentons

Zurich - Bloch & Partner in Assoc. w/ SNR Denton
Robert Schlup
Bahnhofstrasse 3
CH6340 Baar/Zug
Total Lawyers: 3

Shook, Hardy & Bacon

Shook, Hardy & Bacon
118 Rue du Rhône

Sidley Austin LLP

Geneva
Rue du Pré-de-la-Bichette 1
Total Lawyers: 19

TAIWAN

Finnegan, Henderson, Farabow, Garrett & Dunner

Taipei Office
Douglas S. Weinstein, Managing Partner
12D, 167 DunHua North Road
Taipei, Taiwan 105, R.O.C.
+886 2 2712 7001
+886 2 2712 7080 fax
Total Lawyers: 1

Jones Day

Jack J.T. Huang
8th Floor
2 Tun Hwa South Rd., Section 2
Tel: 886-2-7712-3399
Fax: 886-2-2704-6791
Total Lawyers: 35

K&L Gates LLP

Taipei Office
James Chen
30/F 95 Tun Hwa S. Road, Sec 2
Total Lawyers: 16

Perkins Coie

Taipei
Chun Ng
Taipei 101 Tower
Suite F, 45th Floor
No. 7, Sec. 5, Xinyi Road

TAIWAN

Pillsbury Winthrop Shaw Pittman LLP

Taipei
10F
No. 32
Section 3
Ren-Ai Road
Taipei 106, Taiwan

Winston & Strawn LLP

Winston & Strawn LLP
John Alison
13F., No. 1, SongGao Rd.
Xinyi Dist.
Total Lawyers: 4

TANZANIA

Norton Rose Fulbright

Dar es Salaam
Adam Lovett
180 Msasani Bay, 3rd Floor
Total Lawyers: 6

THAILAND

DLA Piper

DLA Piper (Thailand) Limited
Alastair Da Costa, Managing Director, Asia
47th Floor, Unit 4707, Empire Tower
195 South Sathorn Road, Yannawa, Sathorn
Total Lawyers: 25

Hunton & Williams

Bangkok Office
Edward B. Koehler
Q.House Lumpini Building, 1 South Sathorn Road,
Thungmahamek, Sathorn
34th Floor
Total Lawyers: 29

Mayer Brown

Bangkok
Maythawee Sarathai
Total Lawyers: 4

Norton Rose Fulbright

Bangkok
Somboon Kitiyansub
Sindhorn Building, Tower 2, Floor 14, 130-132 Wireless Road
Total Lawyers: 15

THE NETHERLANDS

DLA Piper

DLA Piper Nederland N.V.
Frans Stibbe
Gebouw Meerpare Amstelveenseweg 638
1081 JJ
Total Lawyers: 118

THE NETHERLANDS (Continued)

Greenberg Traurig, LLP

Greenberg Traurig
Allard Huizing
Leidseplein 29, Hirsch Building
Total Lawyers: 33

Jones Day

Luc Houben
Museumplein 17
PO Box 51204
Tel: 31-20-3054200
Total Lawyers: 18

Norton Rose Fulbright

Amsterdam
Daphne Broerse
24th Floor, Rembrandt Tower, Amstelplein 1
Total Lawyers: 42

TURKEY

DLA Piper

DLA Piper Danismanlik Hizmetleri Avukatik Ortaklii
Buyukdere Cad. No. 127, 5th Floor
34394 Esentepe
Total Lawyers: 1

Herrick, Feinstein LLP

Istanbul, Turkey
Barbaros Karaahmet
Trump Towers II Kustepe Mah., Mecidiyeky Cad.
No: 12, 18. Kat
34387
Total Lawyers: 5

UKRAINE

DLA Piper

DLA Piper Ukraine LLC
77 A Chervonoarmiyska Str. 4th Floor
Total Lawyers: 29

UNITED ARAB EMIRATES

Akin Gump Strauss Hauer & Feld LLP

Abu Dhabi
Natasha Kohne and Chadi A. Salloum, Partners in Charge
Abu Dhabi Global Market Square, Al Sila Tower
21st Floor
P.O. Box 55069
Phone: 971-2-406-8500
Fax: 971-2-406-8511
Total Lawyers: 11

Dubai
Marc C. Hammerson, Partner in Charge
Boulevard Plaza, Tower Two
23rd Floor
P.O. Box 120109
Phone: 971-4-317-3000
Fax: 971-4-409-6850
Total Lawyers: 2

UNITED ARAB EMIRATES

Andrews Kurth LLP

Andrews Kurth (Middle East) JLT
Hugh Fraser
45th Floor
Mazaya Business Avenue, BB2
Jumeirah Lakes Towers
P.O. Box 111587
Total Lawyers: 6

Bracewell LLP

Dubai
Chris Williams
Emirates Towers Offices
Level 29, P.O. Box 6750
Total Lawyers: 6

Dechert LLP

Dechert LLP
Unit 501, Level 5
Precinct Building 2
Dubai International Financial Centre
PO Box 506675
Total Lawyers: 16

DLA Piper

Level 6, Building 6
Emaar Square
PO Box 121662
Total Lawyers: 59

Gibson, Dunn & Crutcher

Dubai
Paul Harter, Partner in Charge
Building 5, Level 4
Dubai International Financial Centre
P.O. Box 506654
Total Lawyers: 15

Jones Day

Sheila L. Shadmand
Al Fattan Currency, Tower 1, Floor 33
Dubai International Financial Centre
P.O. Box 506662
Tel: 971-4-709-8484
Fax: 971-4-709-8499
Total Lawyers: 11

K&L Gates LLP

Dubai Office
Michael Johns
Currency House, Level 4
Dubai International Financial Centre
PO Box 506826
Total Lawyers: 11

Norton Rose Fulbright

Abu Dhabi
David Baylis
15th Floor Al Sila Tower
Total Lawyers: 6

UNITED ARAB EMIRATES (Continued)

Dubai
Patrick Bourke and John C. Boehm Jr.
4th Floor, Gate Precinct Building 3, Dubai International
Financial Center
Total Lawyers: 34

Reed Smith LLP

Abu Dhabi
Vince Gordan
Golden Falcon Tower
19th Floor
Hamdan St.
P.O. Box 46904
Total Lawyers: 10

Dubai
Vince Gordan
5th Floor
Building 10
Gate Village
PO Box 506548
Duabi International FInancial Centre
Total Lawyers: 7

Shearman & Sterling LLP

Abu Dhabi
Philip B. Dundas, Jr., Managing Partner
Butti Al Otaiba Building
13th floor, Suite 1302
Sheikh Khalifa St., P.O. Box 2948
Abu Dhabi, United Arab Emirates

Vinson & Elkins

Dubai
Ayman H. A. Khaleq
P.O. Box 504945
Emirates Towers Offices, Floor 10
Sheikh Zayed Road
Total Lawyers: 12

Abu Dhabi
Lewis Jones
P.O. Box 60935
Al Bateen Complex, Tower C-2, Suite 202
Bainunah (34th) Street
Total Lawyers: 10

Weil, Gotshal & Manges LLP

Dubai
Joseph Tortorici, Partner
Gate Village 10, Level 3, Office 30
Dubai International Financial Centre
P.O. Box 506781
Total Lawyers: 2

Winston & Strawn LLP

Winston & Strawn LLP
Stephen Jurgenson
Al Saada Street
Index Tower, Suite 516
Dubai International Financial Centre
P.O. Box 507024
Total Lawyers: 5

Akin Gump Strauss Hauer & Feld LLP

London
Sebastian Rice, Managing Partner and James Roome, Senior Partner
Ten Bishops Square
Eighth Floor
Phone: 44-20-7012-9600
Fax: 44-20-7012-9601
Total Lawyers: 97

Andrews Kurth LLP

Andrews Kurth (UK) LLP
Melanie Willems
16 Old Bailey
London EC4M 7EG, UK
Total Lawyers: 3,9

Bracewell LLP

London
Julian Nichol
Tower 42, 25 Old Broad Street
Total Lawyers: 17

Bryan Cave LLP

London
Carol R. Osborne
88 Wood Street
Total Lawyers: 41

Butler Snow

London
Brad F. Westerfield
25 Southampton Buildings
Total Lawyers: 4

Cadwalader, Wickersham & Taft

London
Gregory Petrick
69 Old Broad Street
Total Lawyers: 50

Cleary Gottlieb Steen & Hamilton

London
+44 20 7614 2200
City Place House
55 Basinghall Street
Total Lawyers: 79

Cozen O'Connor

London
Richard Allen
9th Floor, Fountain House
130 Fenchurch Street
London, England
United Kingdom
Total Lawyers: 5

Cravath, Swaine & Moore LLP

London
David Mercado
City Point
One Ropemaker Street
London EC2Y 9HR
Total Lawyers: 42

Davis Polk & Wardwell

London
Total Lawyers: 52

Debevoise & Plimpton LLP

James C. Scoville
Tower 42, Old Broad Street,
London EC2N 1HQ, England
Total Lawyers: 70

Dechert LLP

Dechert LLP
160 Queen Victoria Street
Total Lawyers: 117

DLA Piper

DLA Piper UK LLP
Victoria Square House
Victoria Square
Total Lawyers: 109

DLA Piper Scotland LLP
Simon Rae
Rutland Square
Total Lawyers: 43

DLA Piper Scotland LLP
Simon Rae
249 West George St
Total Lawyers: 31

DLA Piper UK LLP
Neil McLean
Princess Exchange
Princess Square
Total Lawyers: 158

DLA Piper UK LLP
Philip Rooney
India Buildings Water Street
Total Lawyers: 62

DLA Piper UK LLP
Catherine Usher
3 Noble Street
Total Lawyers: 363

DLA Piper UK LLP
Simon Woolley
101 Barbirolli Square Bridgewater
Total Lawyers: 124

DLA Piper UK LLP
Stephen Sly
1 St. Paul's Place
Total Lawyers: 86

Dorsey & Whitney LLP

Dorsey & Whitney London
Tim Maloney
199 Bishopsgate
Total Lawyers: 27

Duane Morris LLP

Duane Morris
Alexander M. Geisler & Susan A. Laws
10 Chiswell Street
2nd Floor
Total Lawyers: 12

UNITED KINGDOM

Faegre Baker Daniels
Paul Finlan, Office Leader
7 Pilgrim Street
Total Lawyers: 20

Fredrikson & Byron, P.A.
Richard Weiner
Wedlake Bell
52 Bedford Row
London, England
WC1R 4LR
United Kingdom

Fried, Frank, Harris, Shriver & Jacobson LLP
London
41 Lothbury
EC2R 7HF
Total Lawyers: 31

Gibson, Dunn & Crutcher
London
James Cox, Jeffrey Trinklein, Co-Partners in Charge
Telephone House
2-4 Temple Avenue
EC4Y 0HB
Total Lawyers: 78

Goodwin Procter LLP
London
David Evans
Tower 42, 25 Old Broad Street
Total Lawyers: 21

Greenberg Traurig, LLP
Greenberg Traurig Maher LLP
Paul Maher
200 Gray's Inn Road
7th Floor
Total Lawyers: 50

Hinshaw & Culbertson LLP
London
Raenu Barod
No. 1 Cornhill
Total Lawyers: 1

Hunton & Williams
London Office
Bridget C. Treacy
30 St. Mary Axe
Total Lawyers: 13

Jenner & Block LLP
London, UK
Charlie Lightfoot
25 Old Broad Street
Total Lawyers: 9

UNITED KINGDOM (Continued)

Jones Day
Luc Houben
21 Tudor Street
London EC4Y 0DJ, United Kingdom
Tel: 44-20-7039-5959
Fax: 44-20-7039-5999
Total Lawyers: 175

K&L Gates LLP
London Office
Tony Griffiths
One New Change
Total Lawyers: 140

Katten Muchin Rosenman LLP
Katten Muchin Rosenman UK LLP
Daniel S. Huffenus
1-3 Frederick's Place
Old Jewry
London, England
United Kingdom

Kaye Scholer LLP
Andrew Harris
Fifth Floor
140 Aldersgate Street
London EC1A 4HY, England
Total Lawyers: 10

Kirkland & Ellis
London
Kirkland & Ellis International LLP
30 St Mary Axe
Total Lawyers: 145

Ladas & Parry LLP
London, United Kingdom
1-2 Bolt Court
London EC4A 3DQ

Lane Powell
12 Leadenhall St
Lloyds Building - Gallery 4
London, EC3V, 1LP, England

Locke Lord LLP
London
Elisabeth Harper
Suite 785, One Lime Street
Total Lawyers: 0

McDermott Will & Emery
McDermott Will & Emery UK LLP
Doron Ezickson, Partner-in-Charge
7 Bishopsgate
London EC2N 3AR
United Kingdom
Total Lawyers: 68

UNITED KINGDOM	UNITED KINGDOM (Continued)

McGuireWoods

McGuireWoods London LLP
Philip Newhouse
11 Pilgrim Street
EC4V 6RN
Total Lawyers: 35

Milbank, Tweed, Hadley & McCloy

London
Russell Jacobs
10 Gresham Street
EC2V 7JD
London
United Kingdom
Total Lawyers: 51

Mintz Levin Cohn Ferris Glovsky and Popeo

Julian Crump
The Rectory
9 Ironmonger Lane
London EC2V 8EY, England
Total Lawyers: 6

Nixon Peabody LLP

London
Roland Diniz, Counsel
Nixon Peabody International LLP
Hillgate House
26 Old Bailey
London, United Kingdom EC4M 7HQ
44 0 20 7653 9760
Total Lawyers: 4

Norton Rose Fulbright

London
Martin Scott
3 More London Riverside
Total Lawyers: 704

O'Melveny & Myers LLP

London
Chris Ashworth
Warwick Court
5 Paternoster Square
London, EC4M 7DX, England
Total Lawyers: 35

Ogletree, Deakins, Nash, Smoak & Stewart, P.C.

London
Ryan King
Fourth Floor, Thavies Inn House
3-4 Holborn Circus
Total Lawyers: 4

Paul, Hastings, Janofsky & Walker LLP

Mark Eagan
88 Wood Street
London, EC2V 7AJ
United Kingdom
Total Lawyers: 42

Paul, Weiss, Rifkind, Wharton & Garrison LLP

London
Alder Castle, 10 Noble Street
London, EC2V 7 JU, United Kingdom

Phelps Dunbar LLP

London - Visiting Attorney Office Only
Sue Colley 011-44-207-929-4765
1 Lime Street
Suite 725, Level 7

Pillsbury Winthrop Shaw Pittman LLP

London
25 Old Broad St.
Tower 42, Level 23
London EC2N 1HQ, England
Total Lawyers: 13

Quinn Emanuel Urquhart & Sullivan LLP

Quinn Emanuel Urquhart & Sullivan LLP (London)
Richard East, Sue Prevezer
One Fleet Place
Total Lawyers: 28

Reed Smith LLP

London
Richard Swinburn
The Broadgate Tower
20 Primrose Street
Total Lawyers: 296

Ropes & Gray LLP

London
60 Ludgate Hill
Total Lawyers: 112

Schulte Roth & Zabel LLP

Schulte Roth & Zabel LLP
Christopher Hilditch
One Eagle Place
Total Lawyers: 18

Shearman & Sterling LLP

London
Anthony J. Ward, Managing Partner
Broadgate West
9 Appold Street
London EC2A 2AP
United Kingdom

Sheppard, Mullin, Richter & Hampton

London
Jamie Mercer
25 Southampton Buildings
Total Lawyers: 1

Shook, Hardy & Bacon

Shook, Hardy & Bacon
25 Cannon Street

Sidley Austin LLP
London
Woolgate Exchange
25 Basinghall Street
Total Lawyers: 117

Simpson Thacher & Bartlett LLP
London
Citypoint
One Ropemaker Street
Total Lawyers: 95

Skadden, Arps, Slate, Meagher & Flom LLP and Affiliates
London
Bruce M. Buck
40 Bank Street
Canary Wharf
E14 5DS
Total Lawyers: 111

Sullivan & Cromwell
Vanessa K. Blackmore, Robert M. Schlein
1 New Fetter Lane
London EC4A 1AN, England
United Kingdom
Tel: 011-4420-7959-8900
Fax: 011-4420-7959-8950
Total Lawyers: 73

Sullivan & Worcester
Sullivan & Worcester UK LLP
Geoff Wynne
Tower 42, 25 Old Broad Street
Total Lawyers: 8

Vedder Price
London, United Kingdom
Karen Haines
4 Coleman Street
Total Lawyers: 10

Vinson & Elkins
London
Alexander Msimang
CityPoint, 33rd Floor
One Ropemaker Street
London EC2Y 9UE, England
Total Lawyers: 39

Weil, Gotshal & Manges LLP
London
Michael Francies, Partner
One South Place
London EC2M 2WG
United Kingdom
Total Lawyers: 85

Williams Mullen
A. Patrick Giles, Of Counsel
The Lanterns, Bridge Lane
London SW11 3AD, England
Total Lawyers: 1

Wilmer Cutler Pickering Hale and Dorr
25 Western Avenue, Milton Park
Total Lawyers: N/A
Alder Castle, 10 Noble Street
Total Lawyers: 10
49 Park Lane
Total Lawyers: 41

Wilson, Elser, Moskowitz, Edelman & Dicker LLP
Andrew Hinton
65 Fenchurch Street
London, EC3M 4BE, England
Total Lawyers: 4

Winston & Strawn LLP
Winston & Strawn LLP
Peter Crowther
1 Ropemaker Street
London EC2Y 9AW
Total Lawyers: 19

Zelle Hofmann Voelbel & Mason LLP
London, UK
Jason Reeves
Total Lawyers: 1

Greenspoon Marder, P.A.
Jose Domingo Paoli
Torre Provincial "A"
Piso 8
Avenida Francisco de Miranda
Cavacas, Vanezuela
Total Lawyers: 10

Littler
Caracas, Venezuela
Juan Carlos Varela
Avenida Blandin
Centro San Ignacio, Torre Kepler, Piso 9, Ofic 9-2
Total Lawyers: 12
Valencia, Venezuela
Juan Carlos Varela
Torre Platinum (B.O.D.), Oficina 14-1, Piso 14
Urb. San José de Tarbes, Av. 96, Nro. 138-41
Total Lawyers: 7

Norton Rose Fulbright
Caracas
Carlos Fernandez-Smith
Centro San Ignacio Torre, Copernico, Piso 8
Total Lawyers: 37

VIETNAM

Duane Morris LLP

Duane Morris Vietnam LLC
Eduardo Ramos-Gomez
83B Ly Thuong Kiet Street
13th Floor
Total Lawyers: 5

Duane Morris Vietnam LLC
Eduardo Ramos-Gomez
29 Le Duan Street
Suite 1503/04
Total Lawyers: 4

Mayer Brown

Hanoi
John M. Marsden
Total Lawyers: 4

Ho Chi Minh City
John M. Marsden
Total Lawyers: 5

OF COUNSEL 700

Alphabetical List of the Top Firms

The following is an alphabetical index of all the firms appearing in the main survey that begins on page 13. Included is the main telephone number for the home (or largest) office of each firm

Firm Name	City	No. of Lawyers 2016/2015	Phone No.	Rank 2016/2015
Adams and Reese LLP	New Orleans, LA	293/293	504-581-3234	151/149
Adler Pollock & Sheehan P.C.	Providence, RI	57/57	401-274-7200	483/485
Akerman LLP	Orlando, FL	665/611	407-423-4000	70/78
Akin Gump Strauss Hauer & Feld LLP	Washington, DC	924/926	202-887-4000	41/35
Allen Matkins	Los Angeles, CA	193/197	949-851-5435	203/202
Andrews Kurth LLP	Houston, TX	328/397	713-220-4200	138/116
Armstrong Teasdale LLP	St. Louis, MO	233/219	314-621-5070	177/184
Babst, Calland, Clements and Zomnir, P.C.	Pittsburgh, PA	125/129	412-394-5400	303/294
Baker, Donelson, Bearman, Caldwell & Berkowitz, P.C.	Memphis, TN	692/690	901-526-2000	69/63
Barclay Damon	Syracuse, NY	275/275	315-425-2700	163/158
Becker & Poliakoff, P.A.	Fort Lauderdale, FL	147/147	954-987-7550	257/256
Benesch, Friedlander, Coplan & Aronoff LLP	Cleveland, OH	176/140	216-363-4500	224/269
Best Best & Krieger	Riverside, CA	182/171	951-686-1450	216/222
Beveridge & Diamond, P.C.	Washington, DC	100/99	202-789-6000	345/356
Bingham Greenebaum Doll LLP	Indianapolis, IN	188/210	317-635-8900	210/189
Blank Rome LLP	Philadelphia, PA	619/540	215-569-5500	82/87
Boardman & Clark LLP	Madison, WI	67/67	608-257-9521	443/452
Bond, Schoeneck & King	Syracuse, NY	264/228	315-218-8000	170/179
Bose McKinney & Evans LLP	Indianapolis, IN	99/109	317-684-5000	349/330
Bowles Rice LLP	Charleston, WV	124/137	304-347-1100	304/276
Bracewell LLP	Houston, TX	465/465	713-223-2300	106/103
Braun Kendrick Finkbeiner	Saginaw, MI	33/33	989-498-2100	544/550
Brown & James, P.C.	St. Louis, MO	110/110	314-421-3400	325/324
Bryan Cave LLP	St. Louis, MO	967/1019	314-259-2000	36/29
Bullivant Houser Bailey PC	Portland, OR	53/54	503-228-6351	496/496
Burnham Brown	Oakland, CA	30/37	510-444-6800	555/544
Burns & Levinson LLP	Boston, MA	128/126	617-345-3000	294/300
Butler Snow	Ridgeland, MS	327/321	601-948-5711	140/141
Callister, Nebeker & McCoullogh PC	Salt Lake City, UT	41/41	801-530-7300	531/538
Caplin & Drysdale, Chartered	Washington, DC	65/70	202-862-5000	450/440
Carmody Torrance Sandak & Hennessey LLP	Waterbury, CT	74/71	203-573-1200	424/436
Carrington, Coleman, Sloman & Blumenthal L.L.P.	Dallas, TX	48/50	214-855-3000	512/513
Carroll, Burdick & McDonough LLP	San Francisco, CA	63/68	415-989-5900	462/445
Cassiday Schade LLP	Chicago, IL	106/106	312-641-3100	332/339
Chaffe McCall, LLP	New Orleans, LA	61/61	504-585-7000	470/477
Chapman and Cutler LLP	Chicago, IL	225/240	312-845-3000	182/171

Firm Name	City	No. of Lawyers 2016/2015	Phone No.	Rank 2016/2015
Christian & Barton, LLP	Richmond, VA	40/41	804-697-4100	535/538
Clark Hill PLC	Detroit, MI	357/344	313-965-8300	127/135
Clausen Miller	Chicago, IL	102/108	312-855-1010	342/334
Cowan, Liebowitz & Latman, P.C.	New York, NY	43/48	212-790-9200	524/519
Crabbe, Brown & James	Columbus, OH	23/27	614-228-5511	566/569
Cravath, Swaine & Moore LLP	New York, NY	503/463	212-474-1000	96/104
Cummings & Lockwood LLC	Stamford, CT	62/65	203-327-1700	464/459
Davis, Brown, Koehn, Shors & Roberts	Des Moines, IA	79/79	515-288-2500	411/413
Davis Graham & Stubbs LLP	Denver, CO	140/140	303-892-9400	266/269
Davis & Kuelthau, S.C.	Milwaukee, WI	65/65	414-276-0200	450/459
Davis Polk & Wardwell	New York, NY	933/827	212-450-4000	40/48
Dewitt Ross & Stevens	Madison, WI	122/109	608-255-8891	307/330
Dickinson Wright PLLC	Detroit, MI	421/388	313-223-3500	111/121
Dilworth Paxson LLP	Philadelphia, PA	95/103	215-575-7000	360/348
Dinsmore & Shohl LLP	Cincinnati, OH	621/572	513-977-8200	79/82
Dorsey & Whitney LLP	Minneapolis, MN	547/530	612-340-2600	89/89
Duane Morris LLP	Philadelphia, PA	775/757	215-979-1000	54/53
Epstein Becker & Green P.C.	New York, NY	300/300	212-351-4500	146/143
Fennemore Craig	Phoenix, AZ	191/190	602-916-5000	207/206
Fenwick & West LLP	Mountain View, CA	396/376	650-988-8500	119/123
Finnegan, Henderson, Farabow, Garrett & Dunner	Washington, DC	353/353	202-408-4000	129/133
Fish & Richardson	Boston, MA	367/367	617-542-5070	125/127
Fisher Phillips	Atlanta, GA	340/300	404-231-1400	133/143
Fitzpatrick, Cella, Harper & Scinto	New York, NY	139/136	212-218-2100	271/279
Foley Hoag LLP	Boston, MA	267/250	617-832-1000	168/168
Fox Rothschild LLP	Philadelphia, PA	773/662	215-299-2000	55/66
Fried, Frank, Harris, Shriver & Jacobson LLP	New York, NY	414/414	212-859-8000	113/112
Frost Brown Todd LLC	Cincinnati, OH	489/470	513-651-6800	103/101
GableGotwals	Tulsa, OK	90/91	918-595-4800	372/379
Gallagher & Kennedy, P.A.	Phoenix, AZ	75/87	602-530-8000	419/387
Gallagher Sharp LLP	Cleveland, OH	52/52	216-241-5310	500/505
Gibson, Dunn & Crutcher	Los Angeles, CA	1253/1243	213-229-7000	20/20
Gordon Feinblatt LLC	Baltimore, MD	66/66	410-576-4000	447/455
Gray Plant Mooty	Minneapolis, MN	186/170	612-632-3000	214/224
Greenberg Glusker	Los Angeles, CA	86/86	310-553-3610	382/391
Greenberg Traurig, LLP	New York, NY	1991/1868	212-801-9200	10/10
Greensfelder, Hemker & Gale, P.C.	St. Louis, MO	151/149	314-241-9090	250/252
Gunster	West Palm Beach, FL	177/170	561-655-1980	220/224
Hahn Loeser & Parks LLP	Cleveland, OH	118/128	216-621-0150	311/296
Hall, Estill, Hardwick, Gable, Golden & Nelson, P.C.	Tulsa, OK	127/122	918-594-0400	296/309
Hand Arendall LLC	Mobile, AL	65/69	251-432-5511	450/442
Hanson Bridgett	San Francisco, CA	162/162	415-777-3200	237/232
Harris Beach PLLC	Pittsford, NY	210/210	585-419-8800	188/189
Harter Secrest & Emery	Rochester, NY	129/129	585-232-6500	293/294
Herrick, Feinstein LLP	New York, NY	140/143	212-592-1400	266/262

Firm Name	City	No. of Lawyers 2016/2015	Phone No.	Rank 2016/2015
Hill, Farrer & Burrill LLP	Los Angeles, CA	42/41	213-620-0460	529/538
Hinshaw & Culbertson LLP	Chicago, IL	525/459	312-704-3000	92/105
Honigman Miller Schwartz and Cohn LLP	Detroit, MI	282/257	313-465-7000	157/166
Howard & Howard Attorneys PLLC	Royal Oak, MI	140/138	248-645-1483	266/274
Hunton & Williams	Washington, DC	746/761	202-955-1500	60/52
Jackson Kelly PLLC	Charleston, WV	188/188	304-340-1000	210/208
Jackson Walker LLP	Dallas, TX	362/365	214-953-6000	126/128
Jaffe, Raitt, Heuer & Weiss, P.C.	Southfield, MI	116/106	248-351-3000	315/339
Jenner & Block LLP	Chicago, IL	500/450	312-222-9350	98/106
Jones Walker LLP	New Orleans, LA	380/386	504-582-8000	120/122
Kaufman & Canoles, A Professional Corporation	Norfolk, VA	97/97	757-624-3000	354/361
Keating Muething & Klekamp PLL (KMK Law)	Cincinnati, OH	106/107	513-579-6400	332/336
Keller and Heckman LLP	Washington, DC	73/74	202-434-4100	428/428
Kelly, Hart & Hallman LLP	Fort Worth, TX	155/151	817-332-2500	245/249
Kilpatrick Townsend & Stockton LLP	Atlanta, GA	650/630	404-815-6500	74/73
Kirkland & Ellis	Chicago, IL	1686/1607	312-862-2000	16/16
Knobbe Martens Olson & Bear, LLP	Irvine, CA	281/272	949-760-0404	158/161
Kramer, Deboer, Endelicato & Keane	Woodland Hills, CA	16/18	818-657-0255	577/582
Kutak Rock LLP	Omaha, NE	510/471	402-346-6000	93/100
Lashly & Baer, P.C.	St. Louis, MO	46/45	314-621-2939	514/527
Latham & Watkins	New York, NY	2300/2000	212-906-1200	8/8
Lavin, O'Neil, Cedrone & DiSipio	Philadelphia, PA	51/51	215-627-0303	504/510
Leitner, Williams, Dooley & Napolitan, PLLC	Chattanooga, TN	60/69	423-265-0214	474/442
Lester, Schwab, Katz & Dwyer	New York, NY	59/59	212-964-6611	476/481
Lewis Roca Rothgerber LLP	Phoenix, AZ	290/233	602-262-5311	154/175
Liskow & Lewis, A Professional Law Corporation	New Orleans, LA	134/132	504-581-7979	284/288
Littler	San Francisco, CA	993/1037		33/28
Lowndes, Drosdick, Doster, Kantor & Reed	Orlando, FL	89/94	407-843-4600	375/372
Manatt, Phelps & Phillips	Los Angeles, CA	349/356	310-312-4000	131/132
Marshall Dennehey Warner Coleman & Goggin	Philadelphia, PA	503/505	215-575-2600	96/94
Mayer Brown	Chicago, IL	1583/1583	312-782-0600	17/17
McAfee & Taft, A Professional Corporation	Oklahoma City, OK	177/180	405-235-9621	220/214
McCandlish Holton PC	Richmond, VA	23/32	804-775-3100	566/553
McConnell Valdes LLC	San Juan, PR	109/107	787-759-9292	327/336
McDonald Hopkins LLC	Cleveland, OH	137/139	216-348-5406	274/273
McGlinchey Stafford	New Orleans, LA	203/187	504-586-1200	191/209
McNees Wallace & Nurick LLC	Harrisburg, PA	130/132	717-232-8000	290/288
Michael Best & Friedrich	Milwaukee, WI	225/215	414-271-6560	182/187
Miles & Stockbridge P.C.	Baltimore, MD	230/238	410-727-6464	178/173
Miller, Canfield, Paddock and Stone, P.L.C.	Detroit, MI	277/280	313-963-6420	161/155
Miller & Martin	Chattanooga, TN	131/133	423-756-6600	288/285

Firm Name	City	No. of Lawyers 2016/2015	Phone No.	Rank 2016/2015
Milling Benson Woodward LLP	New Orleans, LA	30/27	504-569-7000	555/569
Mitchell, McNutt, & Sams, P.A.	Tupelo, MS	34/32	662-842-3871	541/553
Moore & Van Allen PLLC	Charlotte, NC	291/282	704-331-1000	153/153
Morris Polich & Purdy	Los Angeles, CA	79/84	213-891-9100	411/398
Morrison Cohen LLP	New York, NY	102/96	212-735-8600	342/367
Moss & Barnett, P.A.	Minneapolis, MN	62/61	612-877-5000	464/477
Motley Rice LLC	Mount Pleasant, SC	75/75	843-216-9000	419/425
Much Shelist, P.C.	Chicago, IL	86/89	312-521-2000	382/383
Neal, Gerber & Eisenberg LLP	Chicago, IL	137/137	312-269-8000	274/276
Norton Rose Fulbright	Houston, TX	3622/3800	713-651-5151	2/2
Ober, Kaler, Grimes & Shriver, P.C.	Baltimore, MD	112/112	410-685-1120	323/321
Obermayer Rebmann Maxwell & Hippel LLP	Philadelphia, PA	108/112	215-665-3000	328/321
Ogden Murphy Wallace, P.L.L.C.	Seattle, WA	49/45	206-447-7000	511/527
Ogletree, Deakins, Nash, Smoak & Stewart, P.C.	Atlanta, GA	783/736	404-881-1300	52/58
Parker McCay P.A.	Mt. Laurel, NJ	64/64	856-596-8900	457/462
Peckar & Abramson	River Edge, NJ	100/97	201-343-3434	345/361
Pepper Hamilton LLP	Philadelphia, PA	498/510	215-981-4000	101/93
Phelps Dunbar LLP	New Orleans, LA	266/266	504-566-1311	169/164
Phillips Lytle LLP	Buffalo, NY	185/186	716-847-8400	215/210
Phillips Nizer LLP	New York, NY	68/68	212-977-9700	439/445
Polsinelli	Kansas City, MO	800/747	816-753-1000	50/55
Porter Wright Morris & Arthur LLP	Columbus, OH	203/203	614-227-2000	191/193
Porzio, Bromberg & Newman	Morristown, NJ	85/90	973-538-4006	391/381
Post & Schell	Philadelphia, PA	134/121	215-587-1000	284/310
Procopio, Cory, Hargreaves & Savitch LLP	San Diego, CA	152/151	619-238-1900	248/249
Pryor Cashman LLP	New York, NY	144/144	212-421-4100	261/261
Rawle & Henderson LLP	Philadelphia, PA	108/112	215-575-4200	328/321
Reid and Riege, P.C.	Hartford, CT	45/47	860-278-1150	517/520
Reinhart Boerner Van Deuren s.c.	Milwaukee, WI	215/204	414-298-1000	187/192
Richards, Layton & Finger	Wilmington, DE	143/132	302-651-7700	263/288
Riker Danzig Scherer Hyland & Perretti LLP	Morristown, NJ	137/219	973-538-0800	274/184
Robins Kaplan LLP	Minneapolis, MN	219/226	612-349-8500	185/182
Robinson Bradshaw	Charlotte, NC	127/127	704-377-2536	296/298
Rodey, Dickason, Sloan, Akin & Robb, P.A.	Albuquerque, NM	65/70	505-765-5900	450/440
Roetzel & Andress, A Legal Professional Association	Akron, OH	177/171	330-376-2700	220/222
Ropers, Majeski, Kohn, & Bentley, P.C.	Redwood City, CA	90/94	650-364-8200	372/372
Ropes & Gray LLP	New York, NY	1257/1266	212-596-9000	19/19
Rubin and Rudman LLP	Boston, MA	74/74	617-330-7000	424/428
Schulte Roth & Zabel LLP	New York, NY	357/347	212-756-2000	127/134
Secrest, Wardle, Lynch, Hampton, Truex, and Morley, P.C.	Troy, MI	68/66	248-851-9500	439/455
Sheppard, Mullin, Richter & Hampton	Los Angeles, CA	750/655	213-620-1780	57/68
Sherman & Howard L.L.C.	Denver, CO	189/176	303-297-2900	209/217

Firm Name	City	No. of Lawyers 2016/2015	Phone No.	Rank 2016/2015
Shook, Hardy & Bacon	Kansas City, MO	505/505	816-474-6550	94/94
Shulman, Rogers, Gandal, Pordy & Ecker, P.A.	Potomac, MD	95/99	301-230-5200	360/356
Shumaker, Loop & Kendrick, LLP	Toledo, OH	245/241	419-241-9000	173/170
Sidley Austin LLP	Chicago, IL	1918/1825	312-853-7000	12/13
Sills Cummis & Gross	Newark, NJ	136/138	973-643-7000	278/274
Simpson Thacher & Bartlett LLP	New York, NY	958/865	212-455-2000	38/43
Stark & Stark	Lawrenceville, NJ	97/105	609-896-9060	354/342
Steptoe & Johnson PLLC	Bridgeport, WV	328/328	304-933-8000	138/140
Stone Pigman Walther Wittmann LLC	New Orleans, LA	61/57	504-581-3200	470/485
Stroock & Stroock & Lavan LLP	New York, NY	305/289	212-806-5400	145/151
Sullivan & Worcester	Boston, MA	162/167	617-338-2800	237/226
Taft Stettinius & Hollister LLP	Cincinnati, OH	400/403	513-381-2838	117/114
Tucker Arensberg, P.C.	Pittsburgh, PA	86/86	412-566-1212	382/391
Verrill Dana	Portland, ME	134/115	207-774-4000	284/318
Ward and Smith, P.A.	New Bern, NC	91/92	252-672-5400	369/378
Warner Norcross & Judd LLP	Grand Rapids, MI	227/222	616-752-2000	181/183
Wilmer Cutler Pickering Hale and Dorr	Washington, DC	1112/1113	202-663-6000	24/22
Winston & Strawn LLP	Chicago, IL	891/888	312-558-5600	44/40
Winthrop & Weinstine	Minneapolis, MN	124/116	612-604-6400	304/316
Wyatt, Tarrant & Combs, LLP	Louisville, KY	182/199	502-589-5235	216/200

B. ONLINE LEGAL RESEARCH
Online Legal Research Resources

The Internet offers a wealth of law-related materials, finding aids and primary legal resources that are useful for conducting legal research. The following is a list of some of the more noteworthy of these Internet offerings. The descriptions that accompany the Internet addresses for these sites are usually short and do not reflect, in many cases, the full contents or menus of these sites. Consequently, each of the resources listed below should be explored fully in order to determine the extent to which they may be useful to you. We have made every effort to ensure that the listings are correct and up-to-date, but given the highly dynamic nature of the Internet, we cannot guarantee their accuracy or currency. The inclusion of a particular site in the following list is not an indication that it is supported or endorsed by the author or publisher of this list. Likewise, given that the sites presented here represent a fraction of all the law-related sites on the Internet, the exclusion of a particular site is not an indication that it might not be worthy or useful for legal research.

Although there are numerous law-related sites on the Internet, with the number growing rapidly every day, the sites collected here are intended primarily to be good starting points for legal research of United States law. Thus, the list which follows includes sites that provide access to primary source materials, indexes of hyperlinked legal sites, or sites devoted to substantive legal areas or sites that combine these features in a particularly useful manner. Sites devoted primarily to legal services, legal employment, law firm management and technology, laws and policies govern-ing the Internet, law firm homepages, law schools, legal self-help, law-related orga-nizations, legal trivia, law-related mailing lists and discussion groups, and other law-related sites that do not offer significant resources for conducting legal research are not included. Additionally, the listed sites are "national" in scope and do not focus on one state or jurisdiction. Many of the listed sites, however, do provide links to legal materials from specific states or jurisdictions.

For ease of use, the following sites are organized by the following categories: General Legal, Meta-Indexes and Search Engines, Federal Government/Legislative, Judiciary, Miscellaneous Reference, and Specific Legal Practice Areas/Topics.

A Word Regarding the Alphabetization of the Listed Sites: Except for the category, Specific Legal Practice Areas/Topics, a web site within a category is listed in alphabetical order by its name. If the first word of the name is *The*, the article *The* is *not* included in the alphabetization; that is, *The Information Center* is alphabetized as though its name started with *I*, not the *T*, and it will show as *Information Center*. Sites listed under the category Specific Legal Practice Areas/Topics are organized alphabetically by specific legal practice area and/or topic. Under each legal area or topic, a site is then listed in alphabetical order by its name. Again, if the first word of the site's name is *The*, the article *The* is discounted in the alphabetization and will not show in the site's name.

GENERAL LEGAL

American Bar Association—ABA Network

http://www.americanbar.org

This site contains the ABA's Legal Technology Resource Center, at *www.americanbar.org/groups/departments_offices/legal_technology_resources .html,* and information about ABA entities, among others. It provides links to other legal research and information resources on the Internet, and is arranged by the following categories: federal resources, state resources, international resources, other research resources, finding a lawyer, law practice technology, news and information, legal associations, legal education, and legal employment. The site also has a legal research "jumpstation" entitled the ABA LawLink, which provides access to legal research from the ABA and other online associations.

ALM Media's law.com

http://www.law.com/

ALM Media Properties' law.com is a leading news and information network. Besides daily law news headlines and top stories, this site links to legal practice areas, bar results, law librarians, a legal career center, legal seminars, legal research and legal resources, courts, case law, attorneys, court reporters, expert witnesses, and much more. Law.com links legal professionals to more than 20 national and regional legal publications online, including *The American Lawyer, The National Law Journal, New York Law Journal*, and *Legal Times*, and delivers top legal news electronically to a growing national and international audience of subscribers each day on The Newswire Law.com recently partnered with The National Law Journal to publish a list entitled America's Elite Trial Lawyers, which names the top 50 firms that have won victories in complex causes of action and that have a significant impact on the law. The site also includes a comprehensive listing of legal blogs.

Cornell University's Legal Information Institute

http://www.law.cornell.edu

The LII is known as a leading provider of public legal information. The database provides opinions of the United States Supreme Court handed down since 1990, together with over 600 earlier decisions selected for their historic importance, over a decade of opinions of the New York Court of Appeals, and the full United States Code. It also contains libraries in two important areas: legal ethics and social security, and a series of topic pages and Internet listings for approximately 100 areas of law.

The LII also partnered with eLangdell to produce eBooks of the Federal Rules, and now provides the first three volumes of its evolving collection.

FedWorld

http://fedworld.ntis.gov

FedWorld.Gov, a program of the United States Department of Commerce, is a gateway to government information. The site allows searches of 30 million government web pages as well as provides links to the top government websites, government research and development reports, and Supreme Court decisions.

State Web Locator

http://www.statelocalgov.net/

State and Local Government on the Net is a state-by-state guide to state, country, and city government information on the Internet, including links to individual state home pages and executive and legislative branch listings for each state. To date, it has links to more than 11,500 state and local government websites.

Galaxy: Law

http://www.galaxy.com/directory/29787/Law.htm

Galaxy is one of the oldest searchable directories on the Internet. It is also one of the Web's largest directories, with over 3.2 million listings, covering about 680,000 categories. This site links to a variety of legal resources and law collections and is useful as a searchable general index to some of the more significant legal materials available on the Internet.

Internet Law Library

http://www.lawguru.com/ilawlib/index.php

Formerly the U.S. House of Representatives' Internet Law Library, this site links to federal, state, and international codes and statutes. The federal laws are arranged by original published source or by agency, and the laws of all jurisdictions are arranged by subject. The site also links to international treaties, and directories of law schools, attorneys, and the legal profession, as well as reviews of law books.

Internet Law Library

http://www.lawresearch.com

This site has 20,000 legal resources links available for free, 50,000 available to legal professionals on a trial basis, and 1,000,000 for a fee. The free links are arranged by categories such as U.S. federal law, U.S. law by state, law firm directory, law and ethics, historical documents of the law, law discussion groups, and more. Also available are global news, financial, economic, and investment links.

Public Legal Internet Legal Research Group

http://www.ilrg.com

An index of more than 4,000 select web sites, in 238 nations, islands, and territories, this site is a comprehensive resource of information concerning law and the legal profession, with an emphasis on the United States. The site claims that it includes only the most substantive legal resources. Major categories include the legal profession, academia, and legal research. The site also includes a form database with more than 2000 free forms and documents.

'Lectric Law Library

http://www.lectlaw.com

This user-friendly and fun online law library contains a wealth of resources including an online law encyclopedia with the capacity to search law-related words, terms and phrases; information arranged by topic and substantive areas of the law; link indexes to other Internet law resources; law-related news items; legal information for those involved in or thinking of starting a business; legal and business forms (claims to be the "Net's biggest collection of legal forms"); a collection of legal information for "lay people"; a collection of information of interest to judges, attorneys, and paralegals; resources on the study of law; materials from selected legal periodicals; and even lawyer jokes, courtroom bloopers, and other legal trivia. It even has an extensive collection of law-related software and e-texts.

LegalEthics.Com

http://www.legalethics.com

A comprehensive searchable listing of Internet legal resources by category and topic, with an emphasis on ethics, this site has links to bar associations, law journals, select law schools, Internet legal issues, legal publishers, law-related lists, as well as miscellaneous legal and nonlegal resources helpful to the practicing attorney.

Legal Information Institute, Cornell Law School

http://www.law.cornell.edu

The LII is known as a leading provider of public legal information. The database provides opinions of the United States Supreme Court handed down since 1990, together with over 600 earlier decisions selected for their historic importance, over a decade of opinions of the New York Court of Appeals, and the full United States Code. It also contains libraries in two important areas: legal ethics and social security, and a series of topic pages and Internet listings for approximately 100 areas of law. The LII also partnered with eLangdell to produce eBooks of the Federal Rules, and now provides the first three volumes of its evolving collection.

LLRX.com Research Guide-Law Library Resource Xchange

http://www.llrx.com/

LLRX.com works with recognized law librarians, attorneys, information technology specialists, and legal technology consultants in reporting important up-to-date legal news and producing information on a broad range of technology-related issues. LLRX.com focuses on the following types of information: technology and legal research; Congressional activities involving technology, research, and libraries; reviews of legal and nonlegal Web sites for researchers; international and comparative law guides by authors worldwide; technology training resources; and seminar materials presented at leading legal technology conferences. The site also offers a monthly installment of new articles, guides, and topical resources. Readers can be alerted to the topics and authors featured via monthly e-mails. LLRX has links to: *beSpacific* (authored by the founder of LLRX.com, Sabrina I. Pacifici)—a monitoring blog on breaking legal, technology, and research-related news, which includes daily updates on issues, such as copyright, privacy, censorship, the Patriot Act, ID theft, and freedom of information; and *9-11 News and Legal Resources, Information and Related Services* (edited and compiled by Sabrina I. Pacifici). The site also provides reviews of software and online legal applications and database services; resources for intranets, Web sites, and knowledge management systems; and books on legal and library technology topics.

Lycos: Your Personal Internet Guide

http://www.lycos.com

When you type "law" into the search query, this site points to, evaluates, ranks and describes some of the Internet's top law-related sites. It is an excellent jumping-off point for legal research and access to a wealth of law-related information.

Northern California Association of Law Libraries—Web Resources by Subject Area

http://www.nocall.org/resources

The Northern California Association of Law Libraries has compiled California-specific web resources for both its members and the public. Links are organized according to category and include state administrative offices and departments, bar associations, codes, laws and regulations, information specific to the courts, academic and public law libraries, library associations, academic and public libraries, legal support, and regional newspapers.

Reflaw—Washburn University School of Law

http://www.washlaw.edu/reflaw/reflaw.html

In addition to having a full-text search capability, this site has extensive links to the American Association of Law Librarian's AALLNET, bar associations, bar exam information, continuing legal education, directories, experts/consultants, federal law, federal documents, foreign law, law firms, law jobs, law journals, law library catalogs, law schools, legal forms, organizations, law books, legal software, publishers, state law, legal reference, and more.

Re: QUEST dot Net™—Law

http://www.re-quest.net/government/law/index.htm

A choice collection of some of the top legal research sites currently on the Internet—everything from law schools to legal forms to legal humor, from legal employment to general law sites, from consumer law to experts, Internet fraud, and much more. It also provides links to federal and state government websites.

Rutgers Law Library

camlaw.rutgers.edu/law-library

This site includes more than 1.2 million volumes of periodicals, case reporters, statutes, and treatises on Anglo-American law. It is a U.S. Government Document Depository Library, and also has substantial holdings of international organization documents and international, foreign, and comparative law materials. The law library has also digitized over 4,800 documents regarding U.S. Congressional hearings and committee prints. It also contains extensive linked lists of other law library online catalogs, U.S. and foreign law schools, a quick guide to Internet legal research, materials on law school admission, legal education, the bar examination, professional organizations, law firms, topics arranged by subject, and more. The site also hosts the blog Quo Vadis?, which discusses legal topics and issues. (camdenlaw.wordpress.com)

VersusLaw

http://www.versuslaw.com

VersusLaw, Inc. of Bellevue, Washington, is a leading provider of legal research material. The original focus of VersusLaw was to provide the legal community with in-depth information on legal malpractice and professional ethics through its monthly journal entitled, *Lawyers Liability Review* (LLR), which continues to be published, both in print and electronic form. Since 1992, VersusLaw has been providing online legal services to subscribers, drawing from comprehensive and continuously updated databases of decisions from the U.S. Supreme Court, federal circuit courts, federal district courts, state appellate courts, as well as other selected legal resources. VersusLaw also partners with Legal Research Center, Inc.

Yahoo!—Government: Law

http://www.yahoo.com/Law

Search for "law" on Yahoo!'s search engine and an exhaustive list of links to sites by substantive topic and to organizations, newsletters, libraries, law schools, law firms and legal agencies, countries, cases, institutes, journals, judicial branch, and more. It is part of the Yahoo search engine.

Yale Law School

http://library.law.yale.edu/research/legal-databases
http://library.law.yale.edu/foreign_resources

The Lillian Goldman Law Library provides a comprehensive list of research databases as well as domestic, foreign, international and transnational topic databases. Categories include historical research, legislative history, newspapers, statistical databases, and Supreme Court databases. The library also houses an extensive guide for foreign, international, and transnational legal research.

META-INDEXES

All Law—Legal Information, Links and Resources

http://www.alllaw.com

Another very extensive searchable index. Besides typical legal categories, such as law firms, bar associations, federal law, legal forms, law schools, and practice areas, this site also lets you search categories such as comics, general magazines, home and garden, shopping, and weather, just to name a few.

American Law Sources Online (ALSO!)

http://www.lawsource.com/also

This is a comprehensive listing of U.S., Canadian, and Mexican legal resources, both those in print and available on the Internet. Thus, this site is useful in determining if a particular resource is online and linking to it. If a given source is available in more than one Internet database, links to the alternative are also provided.

Fastcase

www.fastcase.com

Fastcase is a next-generation legal research service that provides comprehensive and search libraries, which include both federal and state primary law, cases, statutes, regulations, court rules, and constitutions. The site also contains a newspaper archive, legal forms, and a PACER search of federal filings through its content partners. Additional tools include a sorting function for research and visualization of search results to see best results instantly."

FindLaw—Learn About the Law

www.public.findlaw.com

This site is an excellent legal search engine and allows users to search only sites that contain legal information, leading to better search results and time saved for legal researchers. This site also permits users to limit searches to particular servers, such as those of a particular state, those of the U.S. government, or those of foreign countries. It is comprised of two sites, one of which is customized for legal professionals.

FindLaw-Law, Lawyers, and Legal Resources

http://www.findlaw.com

This is a superior searchable directory (index) of links, which allows users to search any type of information on a wide range of legal subjects. Among the categories listed are: legal subjects; laws: cases and codes; CLE online; lawyer jobs; U.S. federal and state resources; lawyer marketing; law office and practice; legal organizations; reference resources; forms; business resources; legal resources for the public (everything from landlord-tenant to consumer law to traffic tickets); foreign and international law; community message boards; legal news; document library; and more. This site is also known for its searchable Supreme Court decisions, from 1893 to the present, and also provides the ability to search for a lawyer or law firm.

Gavel2Gavel

http://www.re-quest.net/g2g/index.htm

Gavel2Gavel, one of the oldest online law libraries, offers fully annotated links to legal and governmental resources and directories. This site caters to legal professionals, law students, and lay people alike, and is meant to help convey legal information in an easy-to-use manner. In sending a user to a link, the site contains a fully annotated description of each resource together with a view of its current URL.

Hieros Gamos (HG)—Law and Legal Research Center

http://www.hg.org

This law and government information site strives to make law, government, and related information easily accessible to customers. HG.org claims that its site is one of the most visited non-subscription legal sites on the Internet. It contains more than four million pages of edited content, a directory of law firms and networks, an expert witness directory, and thousands of articles and information on law schools, employment postings, more than 4,000 videos, and links to governments and agencies around the world.

Legal Research Page

http://www.lawguru.com/search/lawsearch.html

The site provides access to free legal research on more than 535 legal search engines and tools. It bills itself as the world's largest free database of legal questions and answers. A user can find answers to over 100,000 previously asked legal questions or can ask entirely new questions from a network of over 3,500 law firms from around the world. Attorneys can join the attorney network for free. *LawGuru.com* also has a law library, legal employment and jobs details, legal forms, and law articles. In addition to its free access sites, various subscriber plans permit users to access U.S. Supreme Court decisions, federal cases, and state appellate cases.

Loislaw Libraries on Fastcase

www.fastcase.com

Loislaw Connect provides full-text searching of thousands of case and statute databases that have millions of documents. The site is a comprehensive primary research site with enhanced functionality that publishes case law, statutory law, constitutions, administrative law, court rules, and other authority for all 50 states and D.C., plus the most important federal law libraries. All Loislaw law libraries are exact duplications of the official law. New case law and legislative acts are typically available within 24 to 72 hours of their receipt from the courts and legislature or other designated official source. Loislaw Connect also has a citation research service, GlobalCite™, and a continuous search service, LawWatch™, that searches for documents specified by your search criteria and delivers found documents to you by e-mail. A specially structured service is available for law schools and law students. Expanded content includes extensive bankruptcy case law, tax law opinions rulings, and legal forms. Loislaw's treatise libraries have now been combined with Fastcase's legal research tools.

Meta-Index for U.S. Legal Research

http://www1.umn.edu/humanrts/lawform-new.html

This site provides searchable indexes to do legal research on the Internet. Main categories are: judicial opinions; legislation; federal regulation; and other legal sources.

FEDERAL GOVERNMENT/LEGISLATIVE

Code of Federal Regulations

http://www.gpo.gov/fdsys

This searchable text of the entire Code of Federal Regulations is provided as a service of the U.S. Government Publishing Office. Access to the code is provided under the "Browse" heading, along with access to the Federal Register, the United States Code, and United States Courts opinions.

FedLaw

http://www.thecre.com/fedlaw/default.htm

This site is designed to assist with research of federal, legal, and regulatory issues. It links to various legal and regulatory data, including federal laws, rules, and regulations, federal judicial decisions, resources relating to arbitration and mediation, general research and references sources, professional associations, and legal-related how-to locations.

Fed World Information Network

fedworld.ntis.gov

This is the National Technical Information Service's guide to federal government resources, including U.S. Government Reports from all agencies, U.S. Department of Commerce information products, the GPO (Government Printing Office) Access Service—with free tools to search the Congressional Record, Federal Register, congressional bills and government documents—U.S. Treasury, Federal Energy Regulatory Commission, Internal Revenue Service, and other U.S. government information servers.

Internal Revenue Service

http://www.irs.ustreas.gov; http://www.irs.gov

> Our tax dollars fund this site, which is chock-full of tax-related information and resources, including tax statistics, individual tax information, tax information for businesses, electronic tax services, taxpayer assistance and education, tax regulations in English, and IRS newsstand, forms and publications, what's hot, and more.

Law Library of Congress

www.loc.gov/law/

> This is an entry point for several extensive legal databases, including the Guide to Law Online, an annotated hypertext guide to legal sources worldwide (including the United States), which is accessible through the "Research & Reports" link. The "Research and Reports" link also contains a link to Legal Research Guides.

Library of Congress

www.loc.gov

> This is the Library of Congress home page link to THOMAS, a full-text, searchable legislative information service, to the Global Legal Information Network (GLIN) (*see above*), a database of national laws from around the world that includes a Guide to Law Online, to the Copyright Office—for forms and information—and to various other resources.

U.S. Congress on the Internet

congress.gov

> This site is provided through the Library of Congress. It has the full text of the Congressional Record; full text of all versions of House and Senate bills searchable by keywords or by bill number for the 101st through the most recent Congress; the Congressional Record Index; digests, and legislative histories of bills and amendments searchable by keyword, index term, bill/amendment number, sponsor/cosponsor, or committee/subcommittee; hot legislation as selected by legislative analysts; the U.S. Constitution; and links to the House, the Senate, the Library of Congress, Government Printing Office, General Accounting Office, Congressional Budget Office, Architect of the Capitol, and more.

United States Department of Justice

http://www.justice.gov

> Information on the Department of Justice (DOJ) can be obtained by organizational structure, alphabetically by organization name, or by

topic. DOJ issues, news, Freedom of Information Act resources, publications, U.S. Attorneys Manual, documents, and topics of interest are also accessible, as are other federal government and criminal justice information sources.

USA.Gov—Government Made Easy

http://www.usa.gov

This is the official U.S. gateway to all government information. It connects to millions of Web pages from the federal government; state, local, and tribal governments; and foreign nations. Most of these pages are not available on commercial Web sites. The site includes links to everything from federal forms and phone directories to social security information, small business resources, grants, government jobs, and much more.

U.S. Code—Office of the Law Revision Counsel

http://uscode.house.gov

This searchable database of the U.S. Code, a consolidation and codification by subject matter of the general and permanent laws of the United States, is provided by the Office of the Law Revision Counsel, which prepares and promulgates the U.S. Code.

U.S. Tax Code On-Line

http://www.fourmilab.ch/ustax/ustax.html

This is a hyperlinked and searchable version of the complete U.S. tax code, Title 26 of the U.S. Code—the Internal Revenue Code—searchable by subtitles, chapters, subchapters, parts, sections, and so forth.

JUDICIARY

Federal Court Opinions—The Georgetown University Law Library

http://www.ll.georgetown.edu/federal/judicial/index.cfm

This site contains links to databases of opinions for the U.S. Supreme Court, the U.S. Courts of Appeals (including the U.S. Court of Appeals for the Armed Forces), U.S. District Courts, and related sites, such as the Administrative Office of the Courts, the United States Department of Justice, and the United States Sentencing Commission.

Federal Judicial Center

http://www.fjc.gov

> This site provides access to the Federal Judicial Center's publications, a directory of offices and divisions, phone numbers, and links to the federal courts.

Federal Judiciary

http://www.uscourts.gov

> Maintained by the Administrative Office for the U.S. Courts on behalf of the U.S. Courts, this site links to all the federal courts and related agencies, publications and directories related to the work of the federal judiciary, employment opportunities, and the latest news and developments affecting the federal courts.

National Center for State Courts

http://www.ncsc.org

> This site contains information on some of the most successful technology applications in the courts, including case management, video conferencing, imaging, personal computers, voice technologies, and kiosks; court security; state court homepages; state judicial salaries; court and law-related Internet sites; internet search tools; and other courts-related matters.

MISCELLANEOUS REFERENCE

Law Library Resource Xchange—Court Rules, Forms, and Dockets

http://www.llrx.com/courtrules

> The Law Library Resource Xchange provides many links to more than 1400 sources for state and federal court rules, forms, and dockets. The user can browse, or search by keyword.

Martindale-Hubbell

http://www.martindale.com

> Here you can search a list of more than one million lawyers and law firms in more than 160 countries. Other features include state bar association profiles, a calendar of events, such as meetings and conferences of interest to the legal profession, a state-by-state compendium of CLE requirements, academic and professional profiles on law schools and faculty, and other valuable resources. The site also covers all aspects of management in the

legal marketplace, a professional legal staff directory, full-text articles and features organized by topic, a comprehensive collection of association links, and much more.

People and Organizations Working with Law in the U.S.

http://www.law.cornell.edu/directories.html

Here you can find directories for law organizations, legal publishers, paralegals, law firms, judges, and so forth. A new lawyer directory also allows access to lawyers by practice areas or by state or metro area.

FindLaw for Law Students

http://stu.findlaw.com

Findlaw provides free full text search of online law journals and an e-mail notification of new articles. The site also has law review editorial addresses of 101 law reviews, law school resources, bar exam information, and more.

WashLaw WEBLaw Schools

http://www.washlaw.edu/lawschools/

This is a good list of U.S. and international law schools, with links where available and addresses, telephone, and fax information. Also provided are links to other sites that list law schools.

FindLaw Lawyer Directory

http://lawyers.findlaw.com

With a searchable directory of over one million lawyers and legal professionals, FindLaw attempts to simplify the hiring of legal counsel by providing tips and practical advice on how to find and interview potential counsel. This site facilitates locating information about law firms, government offices, corporate law offices, and lawyers in the United States and Canada on all areas of the law. The site also has an extensive searchable database of materials covering more than 400 legal topics, most prominently on commercial issues, taxation, bankruptcy, real estate, intellectual property law, estate planning, health law, family law, and employment law.

SPECIFIC LEGAL PRACTICE AREAS/TOPICS

Advance Directives:

Caring Connections

http://www.caringinfo.org/

> Legal developments regarding living wills, medical powers of attorney, and downloadable advance directives for all 50 states.

Alternative Dispute Resolution:

American Arbitration Association

http://www.adr.org

> This is a good site for research on alternative dispute resolution (ADR), providing information on ADR law, rules, and procedures, publications, a roster of neutrals, a directory of regional offices, a list of focus areas, such as labor and employment, and more.

Bankruptcy:

The Bankruptcy LawTrove[SM]

http://www.lawtrove.com/bankruptcy

> This is an excellent list of links relating to bankruptcy law, from the Bankruptcy Code and Bankruptcy Rules to U.S. Supreme Court decisions and case law from all the circuits. Other resources include bankruptcy-related federal government locations, statistics, advice, books, articles, and more.

Bankrupt.com

http://www.bankrupt.com

> As its name implies, this site is devoted to providing bankruptcy-related laws, materials, and news items and new archives. It has a worldwide directory of bankruptcy and insolvency professionals, an online directory of bankruptcy clerks, books and periodicals dealing with bankruptcy, and U.S. and international resource materials, such as local bankruptcy rules, among others.

Copyrights, Patents, and Trademarks (See Intellectual Property)

Consumer Law:

Consumer Law Resources

http://www.re-quest.net/g2g/topics/consumer

This site provides links to federal consumer laws, consumer law-related federal agencies, and relevant Web resources.

Continuing Legal Education:

CLE-Online

http://www.cleonline.com

Offers continuing legal education programming in the form of online CLE seminars to attorneys and other professionals.

CLEreg

http://www.clereg.org

This site has a directory of state CLE administrators, accreditation applications, state-by-state requirements for applicants, a table of types of law classifications, and other CLE-related links.

CrimeLynx—The Criminal Defense Practitioner's Guide through the Internet

http://www.crimelynx.com

This site contains links for criminal defense research, experts, investigation, and crime policy. It also contains a criminal justice center for both professionals and the community.

Cyberspace Law/Electronic Commerce:

International Cyberspace Law Research Guide

http://www.law.georgetown.edu/library/research/guides/cyberspace.cfm

Georgetown Law Library provides this guide, which covers resources involving the Internet, cybercrime, privacy, e-commerce, and cyberwarfare. It also provides resources arranged by subtopic, journal articles, treaties and treaty bodies, foreign law, and current events.

Disabilities:

Americans with Disabilities Act Library

http://www.jan.wvu.edu/links/adalinks.htm

This site provides an assortment of links to the Americans with Disabilities Act (ADA) and disability-related sites, including the U.S. Department of Justice, the full text of the ADA and its regulations, ADA legal resources, and much more.

Estate Planning:

Law & Estate Planning Sites on the Internet

http://www.estateplanninglinks.com

This site provides information on and links to substantive law and tax law pertaining to trusts and wills, elder law, and related Web sites.

Cornell Law School—Legal Information Institute

http://www.law.cornell.edu/

Input "estate planning" into this search page and the site will provide you with links to definitions, related provisions of the United States Code, the Code of Federal Regulations, and United States Supreme Court decisions.

Family Law and Divorce:

Divorce Net: Family Law Advice on Divorce

http://www.divorcenet.com/resources/family

This site, published by NOLO, provides advice on a number of family law practice issues and links to family law resources, interactive bulletin boards dealing with everything from child support to custody and visitation, to domestic violence and parental abduction/child recovery, as well as to general online legal resources and state-by-state family law resources, including articles, more than 20,000 forms, local counsel, and so on.

Environmental Law:

Environmental Law Institute (ELI)

http://www.eli.org

ELI is an internationally recognized, independent nonprofit research and education center. ELI conducts policy studies on the environment and advances environmental protection by improving law, policy, and management. ELI has extensive education programs, publications, and provides technical assistance worldwide.

Immigration Law:

Immigration Home Page[SM]

http://www.lawcom.com/immigration

As its name suggests, this site has information on and links to immigration law materials, from visas to employer sanctions.

Intellectual Property—Copyright, Patents, and Trademarks:

Bitlaw: A Resource on Technology Law

http://www.bitlaw.com/

BitLaw provides information on intellectual property legal issues relating to technology law, containing nearly 4,000 pages on patent, copyright, trademark, and Internet legal issues. It also provides resources for the production of computers, software, and bits.

Copyright Clearance Center: Copyright Central

http://www.copyright.com/

This site provides a comprehensive overview of copyright issues, including licensing information on non-text works.

Copyright Website

http://www.benedict.com

Copyright-related fundamentals, registration materials, leading edge copyright and intellectual property Internet issues, fair use, public domain, source documents and resources, and even famous copyright infringements and cases can all be accessed from this site. The site also includes audio, video, and digital samples and has a Copyright Wizard that enables copyrighting of online assets—online.

KuesterLaw Technology Law Resource—Patent, Copyright, Trademark

http://www.kuesterlaw.com

This continually-updated website is intended to be a comprehensive resource available on the Internet for information related to technology law, especially IP law (patents, copyright, and trademarks). In addition to its extensive links to IP sites, this site also has numerous worldwide government links and links to technology lawyers and law firms.

There is also a link to an intellectual property blog entitled *AwakenIP.com*, which contains further information of interest.

United States Copyright Office

http://www.copyright.gov

Covered in this federal government site are topics ranging from copyright basics, copyright registration, how to search Copyright Office records— and the ability to actually search these records, licensing, Copyright Office announcements and regulations, and Copyright Arbitration Royalty Panels, to international copyright issues and Internet resources related to copyright.

U.S. Patent and Trademark Office

http://www.uspto.gov

> This site provides access to the U.S. Patent Database through hyperlinked patent classifications, and enables a search of U.S. patent full text and image or bibliographic data and an AIDS patent database. Also available are general patent and trademark information, the U.S. Trademark Electronic Search System (TESS) with over three million trademarks, forms, current PTO announcements and pending public hearings, USPTD services, information and acquisitions, an electronic business center, as well as links to intellectual property and general legal Internet resources.

International Law:

United Nations: International Law

http://www.un.org/en/law

> This site discusses the United Nation's work in upholding international law and links to United Nations bodies, specific topics of international law, international courts and tribunals, and legal resources.

Electronic Resource Guide for International Law

http://www.asil.org/resources/electronic-resource-guide-erg

> Developed by the American Society of International Law, this site provides a comprehensive collection of options for researching international law on the Internet. Links are provided for selected websites as well as international organizations, government agencies, human rights and humanitarian law, library catalogs, articles and periodicals, and research guides.

Lillian Goldman Law Library

http://library.law.yale.edu/foreign_resources

> The Lillian Goldman Law Library provides a comprehensive list of research databases for foreign, transnational, and international legal research, including a country by country guide to foreign law research, a foreign and international tax law research guide, a foreign and comparative law research guide, and an Islamic law research guide.

Legal Ethics:

LegalEthics.com: State Ethics Resources

http://www.legalethics.com

> This site offers links and references to state-by-state ethics rules, regulations, and articles relating to the Internet and the practice of law. The

focus of the site is to help attorneys find information and resources relating to their ethical obligations.

Mental Health Law:

Bazelon Center for Mental Health Law

http://www.bazelon.org

This site has the latest developments, legislative and judicial updates, and links for the legal advocacy for the civil rights and human dignity of people with mental disabilities.

Multimedia Law:

Multimedia Law

http://bailiwick.lib.uiowa.edu/journalism/mediaLaw/copyright.html

This site finds resources on the legal and business aspects of doing business on the Internet, interactive media, electronic and information commerce, and the digital distribution of intellectual property. Information on copyright law is also included, as well as governmental and statutory links.

Multimedia Law—WashLaw

http://www.washlaw.edu/subject/multimedia.html

This resource page provides links to multimedia law-related websites, listservs, and research guides.

World Legal Information Institute

http://www.worldlii.org/

This site contains 1743 databases from 123 countries via 14 legal information institutes, and includes numerous international databases in collaboration with members of the Free Access to Law Movement. Its catalog provides links to more than 15,000 law-related web sites in every country in the world. It also contains links to international legal information institutes.

Probate *See Estate Planning above*

Securities Law:

SEC Filings and Forms (EDGAR)

http://www.sec.gov/edgar.shtml

This is the online searchable database and information for EDGAR, the Electronic Data Gathering, Analysis, and Retrieval system, which performs automated collection, validation, indexing, acceptance, and forwarding of submissions by companies and others who are required by law to file forms with the U.S. Securities and Exchange Commission (SEC).

Securities Law and Compliance Center

http://www.seclaw.com/centers/lawcent.shtml

This site has many links to the securities laws, rules and regulations, securities law reports, proposals and comments, state blue sky laws, important securities-related court decisions, broker information, NASD rules, and SEC publications and releases. This site is also a part of The Securities Law Home Page (*www.seclaw.com*), which also provides securities-related news stories, commodities laws, investor, arbitration and mediation information, law-related web sites, and finance-related web sites.

Securities Lawyer's Deskbook

http://lawblogs.uc.edu/sld

This site contains information intended to assist lawyers in the practice of corporate and securities law. Included are the texts of the federal securities laws and their accompanying rules, regulations (AC), (BTR), (G), (S-K) (S-B) (S-T) (S-X) (S-P) (SHO), (M and ATS), (M-A), (NMS), (FD), and forms.

Taxation *(See also Estate Planning above):*

Essential Links to Taxes

http://www.el.com/elinks/taxes

This site provides online taxpayer tips and information on income tax preparation assistance, tax rules, tax code, financial planners and tax preparers, forms, publications, instructions, and more.

Tax Prophet

http://www.taxprophet.com

Combining snappy graphics with a plethora of links to tax sites and other legal and nonlegal Web resources, this site is a good starting point for tax research.

Technology Law *(See also Cyberspace Law/Electronic Commerce and select listings under Intellectual Property above)*

TechLaw Journal Home Page, Top Stories

http://www.techlawjournal.com

> This site provides up-to-date news, records, and analysis of legislation, litigation, and regulation affecting the computer and Internet industry. There is also a calendar of upcoming cases, conferences, and the Federal Communications Commission's schedule.

Trade Secrets:

Trade Secrets Institute

tsi.brooklaw.edu

> Brooklyn Law School has launched the Trade Secrets Institute to provide a comprehensive collection of case law, legislative, and regulatory action throughout the United States. The Institute has developed a first of its kind database that will allow users to access documents, briefs, motions, and timelines for open cases, along with updates on legislative or regulatory action pertaining to trade secrets.

Trial Practice:

American Association for Justice

http://www.justice.org

> This site provides litigation support and networking services for AAJ (American Association for Justice, formerly Association of Trial Lawyers of America) members. Updated frequently, the Exchange provides litigation support services and tracks trial-level data, including case abstracts and summaries, verdict and settlement data, articles, references, and supplies links to experts, on a multitude of litigation topics, such as: discovery abuse, insurance bad faith, medical malpractice, motor vehicle cases, premises liability, products liability, professional negligence, and toxic torts. AAJ members have access to thousands of depositions, pleadings, and other court documents, and attorney contact information on similar matters and customized case-specific research.

C. LAW FIRM SERVICES AND PERSONNEL

American Association of Law Libraries
Executive Board (2016-2017)

President
Ron E. Wheeler, Jr.
Director of the Law Library &
    Information Resources
Suffolk University Law Library
120 Tremont St
Boston, MA 02108-4977
Phone: (617) 305-3005
Fax: (617) 723-3164
Email: rewheeler@suffolk.edu

Vice President/President-Elect
Gregory R. Lambert
Chief Knowledge Services Officer
Jackson Walker L.L.P.
1401 McKinney St. Suite 1900
Houston, TX 77010-1900
Phone: (713) 752-4357
Fax: (713) 308-4143
Email: glambert@jw.com

Secretary
Katherine K. Coolidge, Esq.
659 S. Washington St.
Belchertown, MA 01007
Phone: (413) 531-9313
Email: kkcoolidge@charter.net

Treasurer
Jean W. Willis
Assistant Director for Support Services
Sacramento County Public Law
    Library
609 9th Street

Sacramento, CA 95814
Phone: (916) 874-8917
Fax: (916) 244-0699
Email: jwillis@saclaw.org

Past President
Keith Ann Stiverson
Director of the Library/Senior Lecturer
IIT Chicago-Kent College of Law
565 West Adams St.
Chicago, IL 60661-3652
Phone: (312) 906-5610
Fax: (312) 906-5679
Email: kstivers@kentlaw.iit.edu

Board Members
John W. Adkins
Director of Libraries
San Diego Law Library
1105 Front St
San Diego, CA 92101-3999
Phone: (619) 685-6567
Fax: (619) 239-1563
Email: jadkins@sdlawlibrary.org

Mary Jenkins Law Librarian &
    Director
Hamilton County Courthouse 1000
    Main St.
Cincinnati, OH 45202
Phone: (513) 946-5300
Fax: (513) 946-5252

Emily R. Florio
Library Services Manager
Finnegan, Henderson, Farabow,
  Garrett & Dunner, LLP
901 New York Ave NW
Washington, DC 20001-4435
Phone: (202) 216-5374
Fax: (202) 408-4400
Email: emily.florio@finnegan.com

Mary E. Matuszak
Director of Library Services
New York County District Attorney's
  Office
1 Hogan PL Fl 8
New York, NY 10013-4311
Phone: (212) 335-4292
Fax: (212) 335-4266
Email: matuszakm@dany.nyc.gov

Meg Kribble
Research Librarian & Outreach
  Coordinator
Harvard Law School Library
1545 Massachusetts Ave.
Cambridge, MA 02138-2903
Phone: (617) 495-5493
Email: mkribble@law.harvard.edu

Donna Nixon
Electronic Resources and Access
  Services Librarian
University of North Carolina at Chapel
  Hill
CB #3385 160 Ridge Road
Chapel Hill, NC 27599-3385
Phone: (919) 843-9280
Fax: (919) 962-2294
Email: dnixon@email.unc.edu

Chapter Presidents
(2016-2017)

Arizona Association of Law Libraries (AZALL)
Lidia Koelbel
Discussion forum:
asall@azallnet.org
Website:http://www.aallnet.org/chapter/azll/

Association of Law Libraries of Upstate New York (ALLUNY)
Laura Suttell
Discussion forum:
listserv@listserv.syr.edu
Website:http://www.aallnet.org/chapter/alluny/

Atlanta Law Libraries Association (ALLA)
Christina Glon
Discussion forum:
    http://share.aallnet.org/read/?forum=alla
Website: http://atlantalawlibraries.org/

Chicago Association of Law Libraries (CALL)
Todd T. Ito
Discussion forum: call@aallnet.org
http://new.chicagolawlib.org/

Colorado Association of Law Libraries (CoALL)
Andrea L. Hamilton
Discussion forum: coall@aallnet.org
http://www.aallnet.org/chapter/coall/

Dallas Association of Law Librarians (DALL)
Edward T. Hart
Discussion forum:
dall@aallnet.org
http://www.dallnet.org/

Greater Philadelphia Law Library Association (GPLLA)
Benjamin Carlson
Discussion forum: gplla-l@lishost.net
http://www.gplla.org

Houston Area Law Librarians (HALL)
Joseph Lawson
Discussion forum:
    hall-1@listserv.uh.edu
http://www.houstonarealawlibrarians.com/

Law Librarians Association of Wisconsin, Inc. (LLAW)
Elana Olson
Discussion forum:
    llaw@aallnet.org
http://www.aallnet.org/chapter/llaw/

Law Librarians of New England (LLNE)
Elaine Apostola
Discussion forum: llne@aallnet.org
http://llne.org

Law Librarians of Puget Sound (LLOPS)
Anna L. Endter
Discussion forum: llops@aallnet.org
http://llops.org/

Law Librarians Society of Washington, D.C., Inc. (LLSDC)
Andrew Martin
Discussion forum: llsdc@aallnet.org
http://www.llsdc.org/

---

* Reprinted with permission of the American Association of Law Libraries, Chicago, Illinois.

Law Libraries Association of Alabama (LLAA)
Della H. Darby
Discussion forum:
llaa@aallnet.org
Website: www.aallnet.org/chapter/
llaa/

Law Library Association of Greater New York (LLAGNY)
Sarah E. Kagen
Discussion forum:
llagny@llagny.org
http://www.llagny.org/

Law Library Association of Maryland (LLAM)
Charles A. Pipins, II
Discussion forum: llam@aallnet.org
http://llamonline.org/

Michigan Association of Law Libraries (MichALL)
Leanna Simon
Discussion forum:
MICHALL@AALLNET.ORG
http://www.aallnet.org/chapter/michall/

Mid-America Association of Law Libraries (MAALL)
Jennifer S. Prilliman
Discussion forum: maall@aallnet.org
http://www.aallnet.org/chapter/
maall/

Minnesota Association of Law Libraries (MALL)
Neal R. Axton
Discussion forum:
mall-l@aallnet.org
http://mall.wildapricot.org

New Jersey Law Librarians Association (NJLLA)
Joanne Murphy
Discussion forum:
listserv@aall.wuacc.edu
http://njlla.org/

New Orleans Association of Law Librarians (NOALL)
Brian Barnes
Discussion forum:
listserv@assocdir.wuacc.edu
http://www.aallnet.org/chapter/noall/

Northern California Association of Law Libraries (NOCALL)
Michael Ginsborg
Discussion forum:
nocall-list@aallnet.org
http://www.nocall.org

Ohio Regional Association of Law Libraries (ORALL)
Robert R. Myers, Jr.
Discussion forum:
orall@listserv.nku.edu
http://orall.org/

San Diego Area Law Libraries (SANDALL)
Michele A.R Villagran
Discussion forum:
sandall@aallnet.org
http://www.sandallnet.org/

Southeastern Chapter of the American Association of Law Libraries (SEAALL)
Michelle Cosby
Discussion forum:
seaall-l@aallnet.org
http://www.aallnet.org/chapter/seaall/

Southern California Association of Law Libraries (SCALL)
Stefanie A. Frame
Discussion forum:
scall@aallnet.org
http://scallnet.org/

Southern New England Law Librarians Association (SNELLA)
Anne Rajotte
Discussion forum:
snella@aallnet.org
http://www.snella.info/

Southwestern Association of Law Libraries (SWALL)
Mike Martinez, Jr.
Discussion forum:
SWALL-L@listserv.UH.EDU
http://www.aallnet.org/chapter/swall/

Virginia Association of Law Libraries (VALL)
Patricia Petroccione
Discussion forum:
VALL-L@aallnet.org
http://vall.pbworks.com/

Western Pacific Chapter of the American Association of Law Libraries (WestPac)
Mari Cheney
Discussion forum:
westpac-L@willamette.edu
http://www.aallnet.org/chapter/westpac/

Western Pennsylvania Law Library Association (WPLLA)
Patricia Roncevich
Discussion forum:
wplla@aallnet.org
http://www.aallnet.org/chapter/wplla/

Association of Legal Administrators
Board of Directors (2016-2017)
As of 5/17/2016

Laura J. Broomell, CLM
President
Greene Espel PLLP
Suite 2200
222 S. 9th St.
Minneapolis, MN 55402-1415
Work Phone: (612) 373-8395
Fax: (612) 373-0929

Gary T. Swisher, II, CLM
President-Elect
Clark Partington
Suite 800
125 W. Romana St.
Pensacola, FL 32501-5856
Work Phone: (850) 208-7053
Fax: (850) 432-7340

Teresa J. Walker
Past President
Waller Lansden Dortch
& Davis, LLP
Suite 2700
511 Union St.
Nashville, TN 37219-1760
Work Phone: (615) 244-6380
Fax: (615) 244-6804

Karen Glowacki
Region 1 Director
Sherin and Lodgen LLP
101 Federal St.
Boston, MA 02110
Work Phone: (617) 646-2116
Fax: (617) 646-2222

Vicki L. Smith-Bilt, CLM, SPHR,
SHRM-SCP
Region 2 Director
Greenberg Traurig, PA
Suite 4400
333 SE 2nd Ave.
Miami, FL 33131
Work Phone: (305) 579-0765
Fax: (305) 961-5867

Julie S. Logan, SPHR, SHRM-SCP
Region 3 Director
Husch Blackwell LLP
Suite 600
190 Carondelet Plaza
St. Louis, MO 63105-3441
Work Phone: (314) 480-1549
Fax: (314) 480-1670

James Louis Cornell, III
Region 4 Director
Graves Dougherty Hearon
& Moody, PC
Suite 2200
401 Congress Ave.
Austin, TX 78701-3744
Work Phone: (512) 480-5696
Fax: (512) 536-9996

April L. Campbell, JD
Region 5 Director
Perkins Coie LLP
Suite 4900
1201 3rd Ave.
Seattle, WA 98101-3099
Work Phone: (206) 359-3766
Fax: (206) 359-4766

---

[*] Reprinted with permission of the Association of Legal Administrators, Chicago, Illinois.

Mark A. Bridgeman, CLM, CRM
At-Large Director
U.S. Attorney's Office
Northern District of Illinois
Suite 500
219 S. Dearborn St.
Chicago, IL 60604
Work Phone: (312) 886-2953

Katie J. Bryant, CLM
At-Large Director
Udall Shumway PLC
Suite 101
1138 N. Alma School Rd.
Mesa, AZ 85201
Work Phone: (480) 461-5345
Fax: (480) 833-9392

Debra Lynn Elsbury, CLM
At-Large Director
Threlkeld & Associates
Suite 400
50 S. Meridian St.
Indianapolis, IN 46204-3539
Work Phone: (317) 655-5200
Fax: (317) 655-3150

Shaun M. Morrison
Region 6 Director
Allen Matkins Leck Gamble
Mallory & Natsis LLP
Suite 1800
1901 Avenue of the Stars
Los Angeles, CA 90067
Work Phone: (310) 788-2400
Fax: (310) 788-2410

Oliver P. Yandle, JD, CAE
Executive Director (Non-voting)
Association of Legal Administrators
Suite 110S
8700 W. Bryn Mawr Avenue
Chicago, IL 60631-3512
Work Phone: (847) 267-1570
Fax: (847) 267-1329

Alicia M. Coleman
Staff Liaison
Association of Legal Administrators
Suite 110S
8700 W. Bryn Mawr Avenue
Chicago, IL 60631-3512
Work Phone: (847) 267-1381
Fax: (847) 267-1329

Lawyers' Associations

720 Strategies

AAL USA, Inc. (a client of Maynard Cooper & Gale PC)

ABA Center on Children and the Law

Abbot Group (a client of Kirstein & Young PLLC.)

Academy of Hospitality Industry Attorneys

Academy of Legal Studies in Business

Academy of Legal Studies in Business: Mid-Atlantic

Academy of Legal Studies in Business: Midwest Chapter

Academy of Legal Studies in Business: North Atlantic Chapter

Academy of Legal Studies in Business: Northeast Chapter

Academy of Rail Labor Attorneys

Access to Courts Inititative, Inc.

Adamy Valuation Advisors

Adjutants General Association of the United States

Advocates, Inc. DC

Akerman LLP PAC

Alabama Association for Justice

Alabama Defense Lawyers Association

Alabama District Attorney's Association

Alabama Sheriffs Association

Alabama State Bar

Alaska Bar Association

Alaska Maritime Prevention & Response Network a client of Lindsay Hart, LLP

Albietz & Samuel Law Corporation

Albritton Law Firm

Alliance for Fair Trade with India (AFTI)

Alliance for International and Cultural Exchange (a client of Sixkiller Consulting)

Alliance for Justice

Alliance to Prevent Fraudulent Attacks on Patents

Alston & Bird PAC

American Academy of Adoption Attorneys

American Academy of Appellate Lawyers

American Academy of Estate Planning Attorneys

American Academy of Forensic Sciences

American Academy of Matrimonial Lawyers

American Academy of Psychiatry and the Law

American Agricultural Law Association

American Arbitration Association

American Arbitration Association - New England Region

American Association for Justice

American Association for Justice Political Action Committee (AAJ PAC)

American Association for Paralegal Education

American Association of Attorney-Certified Public Accountants

American Association of Jewish Lawyers and Jurists

American Association of Law Libraries

American Association of Legal Nurse Consultants

American Association of Legal Nurse Consultants - Connecticut Chapter

American Association of Public Welfare Attorneys

American Association of Visually Impaired Attorneys

American Bail Coalition

American Bar Association

American Bar Association Section on Legal Education

American Board of Trial Advocates

American Board of Trial Advocates - Alabama Chapter

American Board of Trial Advocates - Arkansas Chapter

American Board of Trial Advocates - California Chapter Coast

American Board of Trial Advocates - Connecticut Chapter

American Board of Trial Advocates - Delaware Chapter

American Board of Trial Advocates - Georgia Chapter

American Board of Trial Advocates - Hawaii Chapter

American Board of Trial Advocates - Illinois Chapter

American Board of Trial Advocates - Indiana Chapter

American Board of Trial Advocates - Louisiana Chapter

American Board of Trial Advocates - Maine Chapter

American Board of Trial Advocates - Maryland Chapter

American Board of Trial Advocates - Massachusetts Chapter

American Board of Trial Advocates - Michigan Chapter

American Board of Trial Advocates - Minnesota Chapter

American Board of Trial Advocates - Mississippi Chapter

American Board of Trial Advocates - Montana Chapter

American Board of Trial Advocates - Nebraska Chapter

American Board of Trial Advocates - New Hampshire Chapter

American Board of Trial Advocates - New Mexico Chapter

American Board of Trial Advocates - North Dakota Chapter

American Board of Trial Advocates - Ohio Chapter

American Board of Trial Advocates - Oklahoma Chapter

American Board of Trial Advocates - Oregon Chapter

American Board of Trial Advocates - Rhode Island Chapter

American Board of Trial Advocates - South Carolina Chapter

American Board of Trial Advocates - South Dakota Chapter

American Board of Trial Advocates - Tennessee Chapter

American Board of Trial Advocates - Utah Chapter

American Board of Trial Advocates - Washington Chapter

American Board of Trial Advocates - West Virginia Chapter

American Board of Trial Advocates - Wyoming Chapter

American Center for Civil Justice

LAWYERS' ASSOCIATION

American Civil Liberties Union (ACLU)

American Civil Liberties Union of the National Capital Area

American College of Bankruptcy

American College of Construction Lawyers

American College of Legal Medicine

American College of Mortgage Attorneys

American College of Real Estate Lawyers

American College of Tax Counsel

American College of Trial Lawyers

American College of Trust and Estate Counsel

American Continental Group, LLC

American Court & Commercial Newspapers

American Criminal Justice Association Lambda Alpha Epsilon

American Escrow Association

American Foreign Law Association

American Freedom Innovations, LLC

American Health Lawyers Association

American Immigration Lawyers Association

American Inns of Court

American Institute of Parliamentarians

American Intellectual Property Law Association

American Judges Association

American Judicature Society

American Justice Partnership

American Land Title Association

American Law Firm Association International

American Law Institute

American Probation and Parole Association

American Property Tax Counsel

American Psychology-Law Society

American Rivers (a Client of Capitol Strategies LLC)

American Security Action Fund

American Society for Legal History

American Society for Political and Legal Philosophy

American Society of Access Professionals

American Society of Comparative Law

American Society of Criminology

American Society of International Law

American Society of Law, Medicine and Ethics

American Society of Medical Association Counsel

American Society of Notaries

American Society of Questioned Document Examiners

American Society of Trial Consultants

American Tort Reform Association

Americans for Responsible Solutions

Americans for Responsible Solutions PAC

Americans Tired of Lawsuit Abuse

Amsterdam & Peroff

Analytix LLC (a client of Balch & Bingham LLP)

Anderson/Madison County Corporation for Economic Dev'elopment (a client of Ferguson Group)

Arizona Association of Defense Counsel

Arizona Court Reporters Association

Arizona Criminal Justice Commission

Arizona Supreme Court

Arizona Trial Lawyers Association

Arizona Women Lawyers Association - Maricopa Chapter

Arkansas Bar Association

Arkansas Court Reporters Association

Arkansas Sheriffs Association

Arkansas Trial Lawyers Association

Armed Forces Special Agents Association

Arundel Gateway MD LLC

ASC Advocacy Committee (a client of Cauthen Forbes & Williams)

Asian American Justice Center

Asian Americans Advancing Justice | AAJC

Associated Industries of Missouri

Association for Continuing Legal Education

Association for Financial Counseling and Planning Education

Association of Administrative Law Judges

Association of American Law Schools

Association of Attorney-Mediators

Association of Commercial Finance Attorneys

Association of Corporate Counsel

Association of Defense Counsel of Northern California and Nevada

Association of Defense Trial Attorneys

Association of Eminent Domain Professionals

Association of Family and Conciliation Courts

Association of Family and Conciliation Courts - Colorado Chapter

Association of Institutional Investors (a client of McGuireWoods LLP)

Association of Legal Administrators

Association of Legal Administrators, Capital Chapter

Association of Life Insurance Counsel

Association of Litigation Support Professionals

Association of Paroling Authorities International

Association of Real Estate License Law Officials

Association of State Prosecutors

Association of Transportation Professionals

Astigarraga Davis

AT&T - Law and Government Affairs

Attorney General of Ecuador

Attorneys for EB-5 Accountability

Attorneys Information Exchange Group (AIEG)

Auburn University(a Client of Cauthen Forbes and Williams)

Babcock and Wilcox (a client of McBee Strategic Consulting)

Bailey Perrin Bailey LLP

Baker Donelson

Baker, Donelson, Bearman, Caldwell & Berkowitz, P.C. PAC (Baker Donelson PAC)

Ballard, Spahr, Andrews & Ingersoll LLP

Baron & Budd

Barrack, Rodos, and Bacine

Bassford, Lockhart, Truesdell & Briggs, P.A.

Bateman Gibson LLC

Batten and Associates, Inc.

Battle Mountain Band Council

Becker & Poliakoff LLP

Beech Street Capital (a client of Cauthen Forbes & Williams)

Bell & Brigham

Bell-Pottinger Sans Frontieres

Belluck & Fox

Ben Barnes Group, LP

Benjamin Droz

Bennet & Bennet, PLLC

Bentham Capital

Berger & Montague

Bette J. Grahame

BGI-Shenzhen

BGI-Shenzhen (a client of O'Melveny & Myers LLP)

BGR Government Affairs

Bickel and Brewer

Bingham McCutchen LLP

Bingham McCutchen LLP PAC

Bipartisan Policy Center Advocacy Network Inc (a client of Capitol Solutions)

Bird Law Group

Bisher Al-Rawi

Black Entertainment and Sports Lawyers Association

Black, Kelly, Scruggs & Healey

BlueMountain Capital Management LLC (a client of DCI Group)

Bluestone Law, LLC

Boies Schiller & Flexner, LLP

Bone, McAllistar & Norton

Bose McKinney & Evans

Brady Campaign to Prevent Gun Violence

Braverman Kaskey & Caprara

Bricker & Eckler LLP

Broad and Cassel

Brooklyn Center for Law and Justice, Inc.

Brooklyn Navy Yards Cogeneration Partners, LLP

Brown & Associates

Brown Greer PLC

Brown McCarroll LLP

Buchanan Ingersoll and Rooney PC Committee for Effective Government (BIR-PC PAC)

Buckeye State Sheriffs' Association

Build Our New Bridge Now Corporation

Cahill & Goetsch, P.C.

California Association of Public Administrators, Public Guardians and Public Conservators

California Applicants' Attorney Association

California Association of Administration of Justice Educators

California Association of Highway Patrolmen

California Association of Legal Support Professionals

California Association of Licensed Investigators

California Attorneys for Criminal Justice

California Attorneys, Administrative Law Judges and Hearing Officers in State Employment

California Bail Agents Association

California Court Association, Inc.

California Defense Counsel

California Department of Justice

California Deposition Agency & Reporters Association

California District Attorneys Association

California Employment Lawyers Association

California Judges Association

California Land Title Association

California Official Court Reporters Association

California Peace Officers Association

California Public Defenders Association

California Rural Legal Assistance, Inc.

California Society for Healthcare Attorneys

California State Costal Conservancy (a client of Carmen Group, Inc.)

California Women Lawyers

California Workers' Compensation Defense Attorney's Association

California, Attorney General's Office of the State of

Calpers (a client of Williams & Jensen, PLLC)

Campaign for Tobacco Free Kids

Campaign Legal Center Inc.

Canon Law Society of America

Capital Region International Airport Authority (a client of Ferguson Group)

Capital Strategies Inc.

Capitol Advocacy Group, LLC

Capshaw DeRieux LLP

Carlton Lynch Ltd.

Casa De Esperanza

Catholic Charities Archdiocesan Legal Network

Catholic Charities of the Diocese of Harrisburg, PA

Cauthen & Associates

CCH Corsearch

Celerant Government Services, Inc.

Center for Children's Law and Policy

Center for Civic Education

Center for Dispute Settlement

Center for Inclusion at UPMC

Center for Law and Education

Center for Law and Social Policy

Center for the Study of Responsive Law

Charles Cronin

Charles T. Dillon

Charleston School of Law

Chevalier, Allan & Lichman

Children's Alliance

Chip B. Lewis

Christensen & Jensen, P.C.

Christian Legal Society

Christian Legal Society's Center for Law & Religious Freedom

Christopher McDonnell

Cincinnati Park Board

Citizens for Civil Justice Reform

Citizens for Law and Order

Civil Justice Reform Group

CJ Lake, LLC

Clark Consulting

Clark County Bar Association

Clark Herman and Associates

Class Plaintiff in Payment Card Interchange Fee and Merchant Discount Antitrust

Clerkship Directors in Internal Medicine

Clifford Chance US LLP

Clifford Law Offices

Coalition for Group Legal Services

Coalition for Juvenile Justice

Coalition for Uniform Product Liability Law

Coalition of Fort Hood Heroes

Coblence & Associates

Coblence & Associates (a client of TwinLogic Strategies)

Cohen & Slamowitz LIP

Cohen, Placitella & Roth

Colorado Association of Law Libraries

Colorado Bar Association

Colorado District Attorneys Council

Colorado Regional Center

Colorado Trial Lawyers Association

Colorado Womens Bar Association

Columbia Financial Advisors Incorporation

Commercial Law League of America

Committee to Support the Antitrust Laws

Common Good

Complete Discovery Source Inc.

ComStock Advisors

Conference of Chief Justices

Conference of State Court Administrators

Conference of Western Attorneys General

Conference on Consumer Finance Law

Congressional Committee on Law Enforcement and Public Safety

Congressional Legislative Staff Association

Connecticut Bar Association

Connecticut Chapter of the National Academy of Elder Law Attorneys

Connecticut Judges Association

Connecticut Trial Lawyers Association

Connecticut, Office of the Attorney General of the State of

Conrad & Scherer

Constitutional Accountability Center

Consumer Attorney Services (CAS) The McCann Law Group, LLP

Consumer Attorneys of California

Consumers for Choice

Copyright Society of the U.S.A.

Corbiere Trust Company Ltd. as Trustee of the Corbiere Trust

Corcoran & Johnston

Cors & Bassett, LLC

Council for Court Excellence

Council for Employment Law Equity (CELE)

Council of Juvenile Court Judges of Georgia

Council of Superior Court Judges of Georgia

Council on Governmental Ethics Laws

Council on Labor Law Equality

County Recorders' Association of California

Court Information Technology Officer Consortium

Courtroom Television Network (COURT TV)

Coyote Springs Investment, Llc. (a Client of Lionel Sawyer & Collins)

Crime and Justice Institute at Community Resources for Justice

Crowell & Moring LLP

Crowley Fleck, PLLP

Cruz Enverga & Raboca

CS Global Partners

CT Corporation

Cunningham, Bounds LLC

Customs and International Trade Bar Association

Dalton & Dalton P.C.

Dan L. Carter

Dan Tuttle

Daniel Richter

Darkness to Light

David and Lucile Packard Foundation (a client of McDermott Will & Emery)

David Balto

Davis Polk & Wardwell LLP

Davis Wright Political Action Committee

Dawn Sims

DC Legal Advisory Group

Dean M. Trafelet

Deborah S. Griffin

Defense Research Institute

Defense Trial Counsel of Indiana

Delaware State Bar Association

Delaware Trial Lawyers Association

Delaware Violent Crimes Compensation Board

Delta Theta Phi

Democratic Attorneys General Association

Denton US LLP PAC

Deposition Reporters Association of California

Dickstein and Zerbi

Dickstein Shapiro LLP Political Action Committee

Dill Dill Carr Stonebraker

District of Columbia Bar

DLA Piper LLP (US) (for The Ounce of Prevention)

DLA Piper US LLP Political Action Committee (DLA Piper PAC)

Dorsey National Fund PAC

Dreier Stein Kahan Browne Woods George LLP

Drinker Biddle PAC

Duff Phelps LLC

Dupont & Radlauer, LLP

Durkovic Law Firm

Dwight D. Opperman Institute of Judicial Administration

Earthjustice Legal Defense Fund

Eastern District of Texas Bar Association

Eastman & Eastman

Eaves Law Firm

EB-5 Attorney Group

Economic Development Strategies, Inc.

Ed Cowle

Education Law Association

Edwards Angell Palmer & Dodge LLP

Egan, Fitzpatrick & Malsch, PLLC

Eisai Inc (a client of Crossroads Strategies LLC)

Electronic Signature and Records Association

Employment Law Alliance

Energy Bar Association

Environmental Law & Policy Center

Environmental Law Institute

Environmetal Defense Action Fund

Equa Terra Public Sector, LLC.

Equal Justice Works

ERI, Inc. (a client of Quinn Racusin (a client of Cloakroom Advisors LLC))

ERI, Inc. (a client of Quinn, Racusin & Gazzola Chartered)

Eric D. Green Resolutions, LLC

Ernst & Young PAC

Ernster Law Offices for Southern California Regional Rail Authority

Estate of Ethel Mary Kendall

Eugene Scott LLC

EWyatt Consulting, LLC

Example Client

FCA North America Holdings LLC

Federal Administrative Law Judges Conference

Federal Bar Association

Federal Communications Bar Association

Federal Judges Association

Federal Judges Association (client of Patton Boggs LLP)

Federal Magistrate Judges Association

Federation of Defense and Corporate Counsel

Felicia Smith Law Office, P.C.

Fennemore Craig, P.C.

Fenton, City of (a client of Ferguson Group)

Fincher, Denmark & Minnifield, LLC

Finger, Parker, Brown and Roemer LLP

First Focus

FIsheries Survival Fund (a client of The Raben Group)

Florida Admiralty Trial Lawyers Association, Inc.

Florida Association for Women Lawyers

Florida Association of Court Clerks and Comptrollers

Florida Association of Criminal Defense Lawyers

Florida Association of DUI Programs

Florida Conference of Circuit Judges

Florida Court Reporters Association

Florida Defense Lawyers Association

Florida Justice Association

Florida Juvenile Justice Association

Florida Prosecuting Attorneys Association

Florida Public Defender Association, Inc.

Foley & Lardner Political Fund PAC

Food and Drug Law Institute

Ford Motor Credit Company (Legal Department)

Forster & Garbus, Llp.

Francois Deloche

Fraternal Order of Police of Ohio

Fredericks, Peebles & Morgan LLP

Freedom Now

Freedom of Information Clearinghouse

Freedom to Work Advocacy Fund, Inc.

Frente

Friends of Casa of Greater Los Angeles

Friends of L.A. Courthouse

Friends of the National Museum of the American Latino

Friends of the Ninth Circuit

Fuentes Consulting Group

Gallagher, Millage & Gallagher PLC

GBS-CIDP Foundation International

Genentech (a client of Cauthen Forbes & Williams)

General Capacitor (a client of Edington, Peel & Associates, Inc.)

Genworth Financials, Inc. (a client of McGuireWoods LLP)

George Igler

Georgia Association of Chiefs of Police

Georgia Association of Criminal Defense Lawyers

Georgia Trial Lawyers Association

Georgia, Office of the Attorney General of the State of

Gerald Fast and Carson & Coil, P.C.

Gerald N. Unger, MD, JD, LLM

Ghazi Abu Nahl

Girardi & Keese

Giving Institute

Gladys and Walter Counts

Gold Coast Florida Regional Center

Goldberg Segalla LLP

Goldberg, Godles, Wiener & Wright

Gordman-Leverich Partnership, LLC

Gordon Thomas Honeywell LLP

Grassroots Solutions Inc.

Gray Plant Mooty Law Firm

Greater Orlando Aviation Authority (a client of Alcalde & Fay)

Greenberg Traurig, P.A. PAC

Grey, Clark, Shih & Associates Ltd.

Groom Law Group Chartered Political Action Committee

Gross & Welch, P.C., L.L.O.

Guatemala Ministry of Justice

Hahn & Hessen LLP

Hall Render Stark Law Correction Coalition

HALT-An Organization of Americans for Legal Reform

Hammack, Barry, Thaggard & May, LLP

Hankin, Persson & Darnell

Harkins Cunningham LLP

Harper Meyer Perez & Hagen LLP

Harris, Beach & Wilcox

Harvard University Law School (MA)

Hastings and Associates

Hauck Strategies LLC

Hawaii Association for Justice

Hawaii State Bar Association

Hefner, Stark & Marois LLP

HELP, Inc.

Hemenway Associates

Heninger Garrison Davis, LLC

Herbert Smith LLP

HH Macaulay Center for Advancement of Democracy

Hill & Knowlton, Inc.

Hispanic National Bar Association

Hobby Distillers Association

Hogan Lovells Political Action Committee

Holland & Knight Committee for Effective Government PAC

HollyFrontier Corporation (a client of Crossroads Strategies LLC)

Honeywell International (a client of Akin Gump)

Hooper, Lundy and Bookman

Horty, Springer & Mattern

Housing and Development Law Institute

Human Rights First

Idaho Association of Counties

Idaho Prosecuting Attorneys Association

Idaho State Bar

Idaho Trial Lawyers Association

Idaho, Office of the Attorney General of the State of

Illinois Association of Defense Trial Counsel

Illinois Court Reporters Association

Illinois Crime Victim Compensation Bureau

Illinois Probation and Court Services Association, Inc

Illinois State Bar Association

Illinois Trial Lawyers Association

Indian American Muslim Council

Indian Law Resource Center

Indiana Prosecuting Attorneys Council

Indiana State Bar Association

Indiana Trial Lawyers Association

Indiana Violent Crime Victim Compensation Fund

Indiana State Guardianship Association

Indiana, Office of the Attorney General of the State of

Inman, Steinberg, Nye & Stone

Innovation Alliance

Institute for Justice

Institute for Public Representation

Intellectual Property Owners Association

Inter-American Bar Association

International Academy of Trial Lawyers

International Association for Insurance Law - United States Chapter

International Association of Attorneys and Executives in Corporate Real Estate

International Association of Bedding and Furniture Law Officials

International Association of Defense Counsel

International Association of Law Enforcement Firearms Instructors, Inc.

International Association of Official Human Rights Agencies

International Association of Privacy Professionals

International Counsel Bureau

International Foundation for Electoral Systems (IFES)

International Intellectual Property Alliance

International Law Institute

International Law Students Association

International Municipal Lawyers Association

International Pension and Employee Benefits Lawyers Association

International Practice Management Association

International Society of Barristers

International TechneGroup Inc.

International Technology Law Association

International Trade Commission Trial Lawyers Association

International Underwriting Association of London(a client of DLA Piper LLP (US))

Investment Adviser Association

Iowa Association for Justice

Iowa Crime Victim Assistance Division

Iowa State Bar Association

Iraqi Refugee Assistance Project

Ireland, Carroll & Kelley, P.C.

ITT Educational Services, Inc. (a client of Lanny J Davis & Associates)

Ivanyan & Partners

J. David Pena & Associates

J. P. Morgan Partners

Jackson Fishcher Gilmour & Dobbs, PC

Jackson Lewis LLP

Jacobson Buffalo Magnuson Anderson and Hogen P.C.

James C. Barker, P.C.

James Cooper-Hill, PC

James I. Mcconnell, Esq.

James T. Bruce III

Jamil El-Banna

Jay Rosenthal

JB Advocacy LLC

JBC International Trade Development PAC

JBG Companies

Jean Henry Ceant

Jefferson Orchards Inc.

Jennifer Fletcher

Jerome J. Schlichter

JK Harris & Company, LLC

Joe Mentor

Joel S Walter

John A. DeVierno, Attorney at Law

John J. McDermott, PLLC

John L. Loeb

Jones Walker L.L.P. PAC

Judge Advocates Association

Judge David L. Bazelon Center for Mental Health Law

Judicial Watch, Inc.

Justice Consensus Action Network

Justice Research and Statistics Association

K&L Gates LLP PAC

Kamlet, Shepherd, Reichert & Maes LLP

Kansas Association for Justice

Kansas Bar Association

Kansas County and District Attorneys Association

Kaplan, Strangis and Kaplan, P.A.

Kari Technologies International

Kaskol Group

Katharine Armstrong, Inc.

Kathleen H. Jarmiolowski Esq, LLC

Kaufman & Canoles

Keep The Change, LLC

Kelley Drye & Warren LLP

Kellogg, Huber, Hansen, Todd, Evans & Figel P.L.L.C.

Ken Bailey Law Firm

Kenneth R. Boiarsky

Kentucky Association of Criminal Defense Lawyers

Kentucky Association of Health Care Facilities

Kentucky Bar Association

Kentucky County Judge Executive Association

Kentucky Court Reporters Association

Kentucky Jailers Association

Kentucky Justice Association

Kentucky Sheriffs Association

Kenyon & Kenyon Law Firm

Keys Lobbying and Consulting Firm, LLC

KidsVoice (a client of Roetzel & Andress)

KiOR(a client of Federal Solutions LLC)

Kirby, McInerney & Squire, LLP

Kohlberg, Kravis Roberts and Company (client of Akin, Gump, Strauss, Hauer & Feld, LLP)

Kohn Swift & Graf, P.C.

Koonz, McKinney, Johnson, Depaolis, & Lightfoot

Korein Tillery

Krane Distribution LLC

Kreindler and Kreindler

KSE Focus

Kuykendall & Associates, PC

Kyle House Group

Kyowa Seni Company Ltd.

Kyowa Seni Company Ltd. (a client of Florence Rostami Law LLC)

Labaton Sucharow, LLP

Lakin Law Firm

Land Title Association of Colorado

Landmark Legal Foundation Center for Civil Rights

Lankford & Reed, PLLC

Laquidara & Edwards, P.A.

Large Public Power Council (a client of Van Ness Feldman)

Law and Society Association

Law Council of America

Law Librarians Society of Washington D.C.

Law Office of Steven R. Donziger, PC

Law Offices of Eugene Vamos

Law Offices of James Scott Farrin

Law Offices of Kristy Hernandez

Law Offices of Peter Angelos

Law Offices of Quin D. Dodd

Law School Admission Council

Lawler Strategies, LLC

Lawyers' Committee for Civil Rights Under Law

Lawyers Committee on Nuclear Policy

Lawyers for Children of America

Lawyers for Civil Justice

Lead Class Counsel In re Black Farmers Discrimination Litigation

Leaf & Associates, LLC

Legacy Consulting Group

Legal Action Center

Legal Action of Wisconsin Inc.

Legal Marketing Association

Legal Netlink Alliance

Legal Services Corporation

Legi\X Company

Legislative Strategies and Solutions, LLC

Leibowitz & Associates, P.A.

Lexington Law Firm

Lexis Nexis (a client of Card & Associates)

Life Changing Experiences

Linebarger, Goggen, Blair & Simpson L.L.P.

Lionel Sawyer & Collins PAC

Livermore Fitzgerald Kunin Doyle & Associates Inc.

Locke Lord (a client of Friedkin Group)

Long Beach Transit (a client of Ferguson Group)

Louisiana Association for Justice

Louisiana Association of Criminal Defense Lawyers

Louisiana Association of Defense Counsel

Louisiana Clerks of Court Association

Louisiana District Attorneys Association

Louisiana Notary Association

Louisiana State Bar Association

Lower Passaic River Study Area Cooperating Parties Group

LSI Federal

M. J. Bradley & Associates, LLC

Magna Services of America (a client of Akin Gump)

Maia Topuria

Maine State Bar Association

Manatt, Phelps & Phillips, LLP

Manding Control

Maples and Calder

Marcus Wide at Grant Thornton

Marianne Test

Maritime Law Association of the U.S.

MARSS SAM

Maryland Association for Justice

Maryland Chiefs of Police Association

Maryland Criminal Defense Attorneys Association

Maryland State Bar Association

Maryland, Office of the Attorney General of the State of

Massachusetts Academy of Trial Attorneys

Massachusetts Bar Association

Massachusetts District Attorneys Association

Massey & Bowers

Maynard, Cooper and Gale, P.C. PAC

McDermott Will & Emery PAC

McGovern & Associates

Mcguirewoods LLP PAC

McKenzie & Hart

McKissack & McKissack

McKool Smith

McMillan Metro P.C.

Mead & Hunt

Mendocino Redwood Company (a client of Resources Law Group)

Mentor Law Group

Meridian River Development (a client of Saxon, Gilmore, Carraway & Gibbons, P.A.)

Merit Systems Protection Board Professional Association

Michael Best & Friedrich

Michelman and Robinson

Michigan Association for Justice

Michigan Association of Professional Court Reporters

Michigan Counseling Association

Michigan Defense Trial Counsel

Michigan Prosecuting Attorneys Coordinating Council

Michigan Works! Association

Michigan, Office of the Attorney General of the State of

Migrant Legal Action Program

Mike Daniels

Miller & Chevalier Chartered Political Action Committee ('Miller & Chevalier PAC')

Mingo Zuniga

Minnesota Association for Justice

Minnesota Defense Lawyers Association

Minnesota Paralegal Association

Minnesota State Association of Narcotics Investigators

Minnesota State Bar Association

Minnesota Women Lawyers

Minnesota World's Fair Bid Committee

Minority Business Enterprise Legal Defense and Education Fund

Mississippi Association for Justice

Mississippi Defense Lawyers Association

Missouri Association of Criminal Defense Lawyers

Missouri Association of Prosecuting Attorneys

Missouri Association of Trial Attorneys

Missouri Organization of Defense Lawyers

MOB LLC

Modern Markets Initiative

Mohrman & Kaardal, PA

Montana Association of Clerks and Recorders

Montana Defense Trial Lawyers

Montana Sheriffs and Peace Officers Association

Montana Trial Lawyers Association

MorphoTrust USA

Morris Manning & Martin, LLP

Moshe Margareten

Motley Rice, LLC

Mountain States Employers Council

Mr. Tiangang Sun (a Client of Alvarez-Glasman & Colvin)

Ms. Debbie Blangiardo

MTBE Litigation

Multifamily Lenders Council

NAACP Legal Defense and Educational Fund, Inc.

Nadine Chatman Consulting Firm LLC

NALP - The Association for Legal Career Professionals

NALS

Napoli Shkolnik PLLC

National Abstinence Education Association

National Academy of Arbitrators

National Academy of Elder Law Attorneys, Inc.

National Alliance of Forest Owners (a client of McGuireWoods LLP)

National American Indian Court Judges Association

National Arbitration Forum (ADR Forum)

National Asian Pacific American Bar Association

National Asian Pacific American Legal Consortium

National Association for Court Management

National Association of Assistant United States Attorneys

National Association of Attorneys General

National Association of Bar Executives

National Association of Bar-Related Title Insurers

National Association of Blacks in Criminal Justice

National Association of Bond Lawyers

National Association of College and University Attorneys

National Association of Consumer Advocates

National Association of Consumer Bankruptcy Attorneys

National Association of County Civil Attorneys

National Association of Criminal Defense Lawyers

National Association of Drug Court Professionals

National Association of Estate Planners and Councils

National Association of Forensic Economics

National Association of Immigration Judges

National Association of Judiciary Interpreters and Translators

National Association of Latino Elected and Appointed Officials

National Association of Legal Assistants

National Association of Legal Investigators

National Association of Legal Search Consultants

National Association of Minority and Women Owned Law Firms

National Association of Professional Process Servers

National Association of Railroad Trial Counsel

National Association of Retail Collection Attorneys

National Association of Retired and Senior Volunteer Program Directors

National Association of Shareholder and Consumer Attorneys

National Association of State Boating Law Administrators

National Association of Subrogation Professionals

National Association of Women Judges

National Association of Women Lawyers

National Bar Association

National Black Caucus of State Legislators

National Black Law Students Association

National Center for State Courts

National College of Probate Judges

National Committee for a Human Life Amendment

National Community Action Agency

National Conference of Appellate Court Clerks

National Conference of Bankruptcy Judges

National Conference of Bar Examiners

National Conference of Bar Foundations

National Conference of Bar Presidents

National Conference of Black Lawyers

National Conference of Commissioners on Uniform State Laws

National Conference of Federal Trial Judges

National Conference of Insurance Legislators

National Conference of Specialized Court Judges

National Conference of State Legislatures

National Conference of Women's Bar Associations

National Consumer Law Center

LAWYERS' ASSOCIATION

National Council of Juvenile and Family Court Judges

National Council of Legislators from Gaming States

National Council on Crime and Delinquency

National Court Reporters Association

National Criminal Justice Association

National Defender Investigator Association

National Disability Rights Network

National District Attorneys Association

National Domestic Violence Hotline

National Elder Law Foundation

National Employment Law Council

National Employment Lawyers Association - Georgia Chapter

National Employment Lawyers Association (NELA)

National Foundation for Women Legislators

National Good Government Fund PAC

National Health Law Program

National Institute for Citizen Education in the Law

National Judges Association

National Juvenile Court Services Association

National Labor Relations Board Professional Association

National Law Center on Homelessness and Poverty

National Lawyers Guild

National Legal Aid and Defender Association

National Legal and Policy Center

National Lesbian, Gay, Bisexual and Transgender Bar Association

National Network of Estate Planning Attorneys

National Notary Association

National Organization for the Reform of Marijuana Laws (NORML)

National Organization of Consumer Credit Attorneys

National Organization of Social Security Claimants' Representatives

National Paralegal Association

National Partnership for Hospice Innovation

National Registered Agents, Inc.

National Rifle Association Institute for Legislative Action

National Right to Work Legal Defense Foundation

National Senior Citizens Law Center

National Structured Settlements Trade Association

National Verbatim Reporters Association

National Veterans Legal Services Program

National Whistleblowers Legal Defense and Education Fund

National White Collar Crime Center

National Women's Law Center

Native American Rights Fund

Natural Resources Defense Council

Nebraska Association of Trial Attorneys

Nebraska Council of School Attorneys

Nebraska Counseling Association

Nebraska Criminal Defense Attorneys Association

Nebraska State Bar Association

Neighborhood Legal Services Program

Nelson Mullins Riley & Scarborough LLP Federal Political Committee PAC

Nelson, Mullins, Riley & Scarborough

Ness, Motley, Loadholt, Richardson & Poole

Nevada Court Reporters Association

Nevada Justice Association

Nevada, Office of the Attorney General

New Hampshire Association for Justice

New Hampshire Bar Association

New Jersey State Bar Association

New Jersey Taxicab Association (NJTCA)

New Mexico Criminal Defense Lawyers Association

New Mexico Defense Lawyers Association

New Mexico District Judges Association

New Mexico Trial Lawyers Association and Foundation

New York County Lawyers' Association

New York Office of Victim Services

New York State Association of Criminal Defense Lawyers

New York State Bar Association

New York State Court Clerks Association

New York State Defenders Association

New York State Magistrates Association

New York State Sheriffs' Association

New York State Supreme Court Officers Association

New York State Trial Lawyers Association

New York Women's Bar Association

Nexus Services

Nicholson & Sands LLP

Nicolay & Dart

Nineveh Council of America

Nix, Patterson & Roach, LLP

Nordman Cormany Hair and Compton, LLP

Norris, McLaughlin and Marcus, PA

North Carolina Advocates for Justice

North Carolina Association of Defense Attorneys

North Carolina Bar Association

North Carolina Department of Justice

North Carolina Law Enforcement Officers Association

North Carolina State Bar

North Dakota Association for Justice

North Dakota States Attorney Association

NorthWestern Energy (a client of Cauthen Forbes & Williams)

Norwalk Redevelopment Agency (a client of Brown Rudnick)

Nossaman Political Action Committee

NTHDC (a client of Saxon, Gilmore, Carraway & Gibbons, P.A.)

Objet Ltd.

Office of the People's Counsel, District of Columbia

Ohio Association for Justice

Ohio Association of Chiefs of Police

Ohio Association of Civil Trial Attorneys

Ohio Association of Criminal Defense Lawyers

Ohio Association of Municipal Court Clerks

Ohio Court Reporters Association

Ohio Creditors Attorneys Association

Ohio Crime Prevention Association

Ohio Motor Carriers Labor Relations Association

Ohio Prosecuting Attorneys Association

Ohio Recorders Association

Ohio Regional Association of Law Libraries

Ohio State Bar Association

Ohio, Office of the Attorney General of the State of

Oikos Intentional Community

Oklahoma Association for Justice

Oklahoma Association of Defense Counsel

Oklahoma Bar Association

Oklahoma Sheriffs Association

Olsson Frank and Weeda PC Fund For American Values PAC

LAWYERS' ASSOCIATION

O'Melveny and Myers LLP Political Action Committee

Omni Air International Inc a client of Akin Gump

Oregon Association of Defense Counsel

Oregon Criminal Defense Lawyers Association

Oregon State Bar

Oregon Trial Lawyers Association

Oregon Women Lawyers Association

Orrick Herrington & Sutcliffe, LLP Federal PAC

Orrick, Herrington & Sutcliffe LLP

Osborn Law PC

Osen, LLC

Otten, Johnson, Robinson, Neff & Ragonetti

Our Generation Inc.

Ovarian Cancer National Alliance

Palaereo Inc.

Pan Am 103 Lockerbie Plaintiff's Committee

Park Strategies, LLC

Parker, Bunt and Ainsworth

Parsons, Behle & Latimer

Parties with claims before the

Patent and Trademark Office Society

Patent Office Professional Association

Patient Rights Watch

Patton Boggs PAC

Paul Hastings LLP Political Action Committee

Paul, Weiss, Rifkind, Wharton & Garrison LLP

Peace Officers Association of Georgia

Pennsylvania Association for Justice

Pennsylvania Association for Marriage and Family Therapy

Pennsylvania Association of Criminal Defense Lawyers

Pennsylvania Association of Notaries

Pennsylvania Bar Association

Pennsylvania Chiefs of Police Association

Pennsylvania Coalition Against Rape(PCAR)

Pennsylvania Court Reporters Association

Pennsylvania Defense Institute

Pennsylvania District Attorneys Association

Pennsylvania Gives

Pennsylvania Midstream Association

Perles Law Firm, P.C.

Pew Charitable Trusts(a Client of The Joseph Group, LLC)

Phi Alpha Delta

PhRMA (a client of Cauthen Forbes & Williams)

Plaintiff Class in Roeder et al v. Iran

Plaintiff's Steering Committee/Chinese Drywall

Pods Enterprises, Inc.(a client of Quarles & Brady LLP)

Polaris Consulting, LLC

Policy Studies, Inc.

Poorman-Douglas, Inc.

Porter & Korvick PA

Porter and Korvick, P.A.

Powers Pyles Sutter & Verville PC PAC

Practising Law Institute

Pray, Walker, Jackman, Williamson and Marlar

Pre-Paid Legal Services, Inc.

Prince, Yeates & Geldzahler, P.C.

Product Liability Alliance, The

Product Liability Information Bureau

Product Liability Prevention and Defense Group

Professional Advocacy Association of Texas

Professional Bail Agents of the United States

Professional Fiduciary Association of California

Prospect Silicon Valley

ProVest, LLC

Provost Umphrey Law Firm, LLP

Public DefenderService for the District of Columbia

Public Interest Lobbying Council

Public Interest Projects/The Atlantic Philanthropies

Public Investors Arbitration Bar Association

Quantum Research International, Inc. (a Cleint of Maynard Cooper & Gale PC)

Quinn, Racusin & Gazzola Chartered

Rafe Pomerance

Ranchers-Cattlemen Action Legal Fund, United Stockgrower of America

Rapiscan Systems Inc (a client of Holland & Knight LLP)

Rawlings & Associates PLLC

Real Estate Bar Association for Massachusetts

ReCommunity

Recorders Association of Missouri

Red White & Blue LLC

Reed Elsevier Inc. PAC

Regional Housing Legal Services

Regulatory Affairs Professionals Society

Rehabilitation Innovation Centers Coalition

Remy, Thomas & Moose, LLP

Reporters Committee for Freedom of the Press

Republican National Lawyers Association

Retired Participants of the W.W.E.

Retired Players of the NHL

Retirement Clearinghouse

Rhode Island Association for Justice

Rhode Island Bar Association

Rhode Island Crime Victim Compensation Program

Richard Hebert

Richard Sokoloff Attorney at Law

Richard W. Miller

Rider Bennett, LLC

Robert A. Roe Associates

Robert Amsterdam

Robert J. Brassell, Jr.

Robertson, Monagle & Eastaugh

Robins Kaplan PAC

Robins, Kaplan, Miller & Ciresi, LLP

Robinson & Foster

Robinson Walker LLC

Rodney Alexander, LLC

Roetzel & Andress Company LPA FSL PAC

Rosenthal & Watson

Rothstein, Donatelli, Hughes, Dahlstrom, Schoenburg & Frye, LLP

Rural Air Service Alliance, Inc.

Rust Consulting Inc.

Sabin Bermant & Gould LLP

Sackler Brinkmann & Hughes

Safe Skies For All

Salman Abdulrahman Alansari

Sandler, Travis and Rosenberg, P.A. Political Action Committee

Sarcoma Foundation of America

Save Ontario Shores, Inc.

Schnader Harrison Segal & Lewis

Schneider Kleinick Weitz & Damashek

Schwabe, Williamson & Wyatt

Schwartz Law Firm

Scribes-The American Society of Legal Writers

Scruggs Millette Lawson Bozeman & Dent

SEARCH Group, Inc.

Securities Litigation Reform Coalition

SEIU California State Council

Seventh Circuit Bar Association

Shahintaj Bakhtiar and Ghollam Nikbin

Shainis & Peltzman, Chartered

Shook, Hardy & Bacon PAC

Short, Elliot, and Hendrickson

Sidley Austin, LLP (a client of Cargill DMB Redwood City Saltworks)

Siff & Associates PLLC

Sigue Corporation

Silverman-Santucci

Simmons Cooper Law Firm (client of Integrated Solutions Group)

Simmons Cooper, LLC

Simmons Cooper, LLC (client of The Washington Group)

Simmons Hanly Conroy (FKA Simmons Browder Gianaris Angelides & Barnerd LLC)

Simpson Thacher & Bartlett LLP (a Client of CoStar Group, Inc.)

Simpson, Thacher and Bartlett

Siritzky Law, PLLC

SJSolutions PLLC

Skadden Arps Political Action Committee

Skadden, Arps, Slate, Meagher & Flom LLP

Slinshot

Smokerise International Group LTD

Snow Christensen & Martineau

Social Security Law Group, LLP

Society of American Law Teachers

Society of Maritime Arbitrators

Somach, Simmons & Dunn

Sorenson Center at Univ of Utah

Sorini, Samet & Associates

Soule, Bradtke, and Lambert

South Carolina Association for Justice

South Carolina Association of Criminal Defense Lawyers

South Carolina Bar

South Carolina Civil Justice Coalition

South Carolina Defense Trial Attorneys Association

South Carolina Law Enforcement Officers' Association

South Carolina Troopers Association

South Dakota Defense Lawyers Association

South Dakota State's Attorney's Association

South Dakota Trial Lawyers Association

South Dakota, Office of the Attorney General of the State of

Southeastern Legal Foundation

Southern States Police Benevolent Association

Southern Strategy Group of Northern Louisiana

Southington Water Department, Town of (a client of Ferguson Group)

Special Committee for Workplace Product Liability Reform

Spencer & Syed LLC

Spokane Tribal Business Council

Sports Lawyers Association

Sprenger & Lang, PLLC

State Bar Association of North Dakota

State Bar of Arizona

State Bar of California

State Bar of Georgia

State Bar of Michigan

State Bar of Montana

State Bar of Nevada

State Bar of New Mexico

State Bar of South Dakota

State Bar of Texas

State Bar of Wisconsin

State Capital Group

Stien Consulting, LLC

Stinson Leonard Street LLP

Stockamp and Associates

Stokes, Bartholomew, Evans and Petree

Stoll Stoll Berne Lokting & Shlachter, P.C.

Strategic Solutions Washington

Stratford, City of (a client of Brown Rudnick LLP.)

Strathspey Crown

Street Law Inc.

Student Press Law Center

Sutton Solicitors

TAEUS Global Licensing

Tahirih Justice Center

Tampa Housing Authority (a client of Saxon, Gilmore, Carraway & Gibbons, P.A.)

Tau Epsilon Rho Law Society

Tauzin Consultants, LLC

Taxpayers Against Fraud

Taylor Lomeyer PC PAC

Taylor Shellfish Company, Pac. Seafood & PCSGA (a client of Plauche & Carr LLP)

TechLaw Group

Ted B. Lyon and Associates

Telecommunications Law Professionals PLLC

Tennessee Alliance for Legal Services

Tennessee Association For Justice

Tennessee Association of Criminal Defense Lawyers

Tennessee Association of Professional Bail Agents

Tennessee Bar Association

Tennessee County Attorney's Association

Tennessee District Attorneys General Conference

Tennessee Paralegal Association

Tennessee Sheriffs' Association

Texas Association of Defense Counsel

Texas Counseling Association

Texas Criminal Defense Lawyers Association

Texas District and County Attorneys Association

Texas Trial Lawyers Association

Texas Young Lawyers Association

The Advocacy Center at ISC

The American Association of Code Enforcement

The American Association of Nurse Attorneys

The American Bar Association Rule of Law Initiative

The Association of Reporters of Judicial Decisions

The Bagley Group LLC

The BAR Association of the District of Columbia

The Brennan Center/NYU School of Law

The Castano Group

The Center for Regulatory Effectiveness

The Century Council (client of The Washington Group)

The Chase Law Firm

The Chestnut Firm

The Citizen's Assembly, Inc

The Clark Estates, Inc.

The Commercial Energy Working Group

The Committee for Justice

The Council for Economic Opportunities in Greater Cleveland

The Criminal Justice Policy Foundation

The Estate of Ms. Vernell Albert

The False Claims Act Legal Center

The Federalist Society for Law and Public Policy Studies

The FGA Group LLC

The Fiorentino Group

The Florida Bar

The Garretson Resolution Group

The Group Legal Services Association

The Harold Ford Group

The Infilaw System

The Institute for Legal Reform - U.S. Chamber of Commerce

The Institute of Legal Reform - U.S. Chamber of Commerce (a client of C2 Group)

The International Human Rights Law Group

The International Legal Honor Society of Phi Delta Phi

The Jones Firm

The Law Offices of Michael Kahn

The Mannino Law Firm

The Marsh Law Firm PLLC

The Mentor Network (a client of Raben Group)

The Mississippi Bar

The Missouri Bar

The National Association of Crime Victim Compensation Boards

The National Federation of Paralegal Associations, Inc.

The National Football League (a client of Gephardt Group, LLC)

The Neuroscience Center Foundation of Florida (a client of Brown Rudnick)

The New Jersey Association for Justice

The PROGRAM for Offenders Inc.

The Puerto Rico Equality Forum

The Response Industry Coalition (a client of Blank Rome LLP)

The Sentencing Project

The Settlement Law Group

The Victory Group, Inc.

The Ware Firm

The Weinberg Group

Thompson Cobb Bazilio & Associates Inc.

Thompson West

Thomson West

Thornton & James

TIAA-CREF (a client of McGuireWoods LLP)

Tiangang Sun (a client of The Gorman Law Firm)

Timber REIT (a client of NAREIT (a client of McGuireWoods LLP))

Tindall & Foster P.C.

Tohono O'odham Nation (a client of Dentons US LLP)

Tompkins & Davidson LLP

Tort Reform Institute

Trails Act Landowners/Plaintiffs

Transportation Lawyers Association

Tremont Public Advisors, LLC

Triadvocates, LLC

Trial Lawyers Association of Metropolitan DC

Trial Lawyers for Public Justice, P.C.

Tuca Zbarcea & Associatii

TWSHO Inc.

U.S. Chamber Institute for Legal Reform

U.S. Education Servicing, LLC (a Client of The Cormac Group)

U.S. Tamil Political Action Council (USTPAC)

United States Court Reporters Association

United States Trade Law Study Group

University of Notre Dame (IN)

Utah Association for Justice

Utah Paralegal Association

Utah Sheriff's Association

Utah State Bar

Van Ness Feldman, P.C. Political Action Committee

Van Scoyoc Associates, Inc.

Van Scoyoc Associates, Inc. PAC

Van Scoyoc Kelly & Roberts PLLC

Vanek, Vickers & Masini

Veritas LLC

Vermont Association for Justice

Vermont Association of Criminal Defense Lawyers

Vermont Bar Association

Vermont Law School

Vermont Police Association

Vern Clark & Associates

Virginia Association of Defense Attorneys

Virginia Bar Association

Virginia Court Reporters Association

Virginia State Bar

Virginia Trial Lawyers Association

Virtualaw LLC

Vulcan Materials Company (a client of Hogan Lovells US LLP)

Waesche, Sheinbaum, and O'Regan

Waite, Schneider, Bayless & Chesley Company, L.P.A.

Ward & Olivio

Washington Association of Criminal Defense Lawyers

Washington Association of Prosecuting Attorneys

Washington Defender Association

Washington Defense Trial Lawyers

Washington Legal Clinic for the Homeless

Washington Legal Foundation

Washington State Association for Justice

Washington State Association of Municipal Attorneys

Washington State Bar Association

Washington State Process Servers Association

Watts and Associates

Weatherly LLC

Wells Fargo Advisors, LLC

West Virginia Association for Justice

West Virginia Bar Association

West Virginia State Bar

West Virginia, Office of the Attorney General of the State of

Weston Benshoof

Wexler & Walker Public Policy Associates PAC

White Star International, Inc.

Wildlaw

Wilke, Fleury, Hoffelt, Gould & Birney, LLP

William S. Bach

William Wachtel

Williams & Jensen PLLC Political Action Committee

Williams Bailey Law Firm LLP

Windwright, LLC

Winston & Strawn Political Action Committee

Wisconsin Association for Justice

Wisconsin Association of Criminal Defense Lawyers

Wisconsin Court Reporters Association

Wisconsin Defense Counsel

Wisconsin, Office of the Attorney General of the State of

Wolf, Rifkin, Shapiro, Schulman & Rabkin, LLP

Women's Bar Association of Illinois

Women's Bar Association of Massachusetts

Women's Bar Association of the District of Columbia

Woodbury & Kesler

Worby, Groner, Edelman & Napoli, Bern LLP

Work College Consortium

Work College Consortium (a client of Arent Fox LLP)

Workers Injury Law & Advocacy Group (a client of Forscey and Stinson LLC)

Workers' Injury Law and Advocacy Group

World Jurist Association

World Trade Center Properties LLC (a client of Wachtell, Lipton, Rosen & Katz)

Wright Ginsberg Brusilow PC

Wright, Lindsey & Jennings

Wyoming Highway Patrol Association

Wyoming State Bar

Wyoming Trial Lawyers Association

Wyoming, Office of the Attorney General of the State of

Xanga.com (client of Katten Muchin Roseman LLP)

Zell & Cox Law, P.C.

Zelle, Hofman, Voelbel, Mason & Gette LLP

D. EDUCATION

Mandatory Continuing Legal Education

This section provides information regarding state mandatory continuing legal education (MCLE) requirements. Currently, there are 45 states, plus the Commonwealth of Puerto Rico, Guam, the Northern Mariana Islands, and the Virgin Islands that have a MCLE program that requires attorneys admitted to the bar in the MCLE state to acquire a minimum number of MCLE credits over a given period of time. This section provides the mailing and Internet address and telephone number(s) for the organization and administrator within an MCLE state responsible for overseeing lawyer compliance with the state's MCLE requirements. The rules governing MCLE for each state follow. In most instances, these rules were passed by the state's highest court. These rules were provided by the respective MCLE authorities and are current as of September 2017. For further detailed information regarding a state's MCLE requirements and regulations, please use the compilation of addresses and telephone numbers listed below to contact the appropriate MCLE administrator.

Addresses and Telephone Numbers of MCLE Administrators

(as of May 11, 2016)*

STATE MCLE CONTACTS

Alabama
Ms. Angela Parks
Director Regulatory Programs
Alabama State Bar
415 Dexter Ave
Montgomery, AL 36101
334/269-1515 x2122
334/261-6310 FAX
angela.parks@alabar.org/
www.alabar.org

Alaska
Ms. Ingrid Varenbrink
MCLE Administrator
Alaska Bar Association
550 W 7th Ave Ste 1900
Anchorage, AK 99501
907/272-7469
907/272-2932 FAX
ingrid@alaskabar.org
www.alaskabar.org

Arizona
Ms. Carolyn de Looper
Membership Administration &
 Services Manager
State Bar of Arizona
4201 N 24th St Ste 100
Phoenix, AZ 85016-6266
602/340-7327
602/271-4930 FAX
carolyn.delooper@staff.azbar.org
www.myazbar.org/MCLE/

Arkansas
Ms. Dana L. Rowlett
Deputy Director
Arkansas Supreme Court
Office of Professional Programs
2100 Riverfront Dr Ste 110
Little Rock, AR 72202-1747
501/374-1855
501/374-1853 FAX
dana.rowlett@arkansas.gov
www.courts.state.ar.us/opp/con
tinue_legal.cfm

California
Ms. Dino DiLoreto
The State Bar of California
Office of Certification
180 Howard Street
San Francisco, CA 94105
415/538-2121
415/538-2180 FAX
providers@calbar.ca.gov
www.calbar.ca.gov

Colorado
Mr. James C. Coyle
Colorado Supreme Court
Board of Continuing Legal &
 Judicial Education
Ralph L. Carr Judicial Center
1300 Broadway Ste 510
Denver, CO 80203
303/928-7771
www.coloradosupremecourt.com

Delaware
Ms. Margot Millar
Executive Director
Commission on CLE of the
 Supreme Court of Delaware
The Renaissance Centre
405 N King St Ste 420
Wilmington, DE 19801
302/651-3941
302/651-3939 FAX
margot.millar@state.de.us
www.courts.delaware.gov/cle

Florida
Ms. Jessica R. Malloy
Education Compliance &
 Accreditation Manager
The Florida Bar
651 E Jefferson Street
Tallahassee, FL 32399-2300
850/561-3180
850/561-5660 FAX
jmalloy@flabar.org
www.floridabar.org/cler

Georgia
Mr. Jeffery R. Davis
Executive Director
State Bar of Georgia
MCLE Programs
104 Marietta St NW, Ste 100
Atlanta, GA 30303
404/527-8710
404/527-8717 FAX
http://www.gabar.org

Hawaii
Ms. Debbie Blanton
MCLE Administrator
Hawaii State Bar Association
1100 Alakea St, Ste 1000
Honolulu, HI 96813
808/537-91868
808/527-7936 FAX
dblanton@hsba.org
www.hsba.org

Idaho
Ms. Annette Strauser
MCLE Administrator
Idaho State Bar
PO Box 895
Boise, ID 83701-0895
208/334-4500 x1886
208/334-4515 FAX
astrauser@isb.idaho.gov
www.isb.idaho.gov

Illinois
Ms. Karen Litscher Johnson
Director, MCLE Board of the
 Supreme Court of Illinois
200 W Madison St Ste 3420
Chicago, IL 60606
312/924-2420
mcle@mcleboard.org
www.mcleboard.org

Indiana
Ms. Julia L. Orzeske
Executive Director
Indiana Supreme Court
Indiana Commission for CLE
30 S Meridian St Ste 950
Indianapolis, IN 46204
317/232-1943
317/233-1442 FAX
jorzeske@courts.state.in.us
www.state.in.us

Iowa
Mr. Paul H. Wieck, II, Director
Iowa Office of Professional Regulation
Commission on CLE
1111 E Court Ave
Des Moines, IA 50319
515/725-8100
515/246-8032 FAX
paul.wieckii@iowacourts.gov
www.iowacourts.gov

Kansas
Ms. Shelly Sutton
Executive Director
Kansas CLE Commission
400 S Kansas Ave Ste 202
Topeka, KS 66603
785/357-6510
shelly.sutton@kscle.org
www.kscle.org

Kentucky
Ms. Mary Beth Cutter
Director for CLE
Kentucky Bar Association
514 W Main St
Frankfort, KY 40601-1883
502/564-3795 x231
502/564-3225
mcutter@kybar.org
www.kybar.org

Louisiana
Ms. Kitty Hymel
MCLE Administrator
Louisiana Supreme Court
 Committee on MCLE
2800 Veterans Memorial Blvd
Suite 355
Metairie, LA 70002-6130
800/518-1518 Toll Free
504/828-1414
504/828-1416 FAX
kittyh@lascmcle.org
www.lascmcle.org

Maine
Ms. Susan Adams
CLE Coordinator
Maine Board of Overseers of the Bar
PO Box 527
Augusta, ME 04332-0527
207/623-1121
207/623-4175 FAX
sadams@mebaroverseers.org
www.mecle.com

Minnesota
Ms. Liz Vanderbeek
CLE/BLC Administrator
Minnesota State Board of CLE
180 E 5th St Ste 950
St. Paul, MN 55101
651/297-7100
651/296-5866 FAX
lvanderbeek@mbcle.state.mn.us
www.mbcle.state.mn.us

Mississippi
Ms. Tracy Graves
CLE Administrator
Mississippi Commission on CLE
PO Box 369
Jackson, MS 39205-0369
601/576-4622
601/576-4733
tgraves@courts.ms.us
www.courts.ms.gov/cle_/

Missouri
Mr. Christopher C. Janku
Director of Programs
The Missouri Bar
PO Box 119
Jefferson City, MO 65102-2355
573/638-2233
573/635-2811 FAX
cjanku@mobar.org
mcle@mobar.org
www.mobar.org

Montana
Ms. Kathy Powers
MCLE Administrator
Montana Commission of CLE
7 W 6th Ave Ste 2B
PO Box 577
Helena, MT 59624
406/442-7660
406/442-7763 FAX
cle@montanabar.org
www.mtcle.org

Nebraska
Ms. Carole McMahon-Boies
Director, Judicial Branch
 Education
521 S 14th St Ste 200
Lincoln, NE 68508
402/471-3072
402/471-3071 FAX
carol.mcmahon-
boies@nebraska.gov
www.mcle.ne.gov

Nevada
Ms. Laura Bogden
Executive Director
Nevada CLE Board
457 Court St 2nd Fl
Reno, NV 89501
775/329-4443
775/329-4291 FAX
nevadacleboard@sbcglobal.net
www.nvcleboard.org

Revised: 05/11/2016

* Reprinted with permission of ALI CLE.

STATE MCLE CONTACTS

New Hampshire
Joanne M. Hinnendael
Director of CLE
New Hampshire Bar Association
2 Pillsbury St Ste 300
Concord, NH 03301-3502
603/224-6942
603/224-2910 FAX
jhinnendael@nhbar.org
www.nhbar.org

New Jersey
Supreme Court of New Jersey
Board of Attorney Certification CLE
25 Market St
Trenton, NJ 08625-0979
609/984-3077
BAC.mailbox@judiciary.state.nj.us
www.judiciary.state.nj.us/cle

New Mexico
Ms. Anita J. Otero
Court Regulated Programs Director
New Mexico MCLE
PO Box 93070
Albuquerque, NM 87199
505/821-1980
505/821-0220 FAX
mcle@nmmcle.org
www.nmmcle.org

New York
Ms. Elise Anne Geltzer
New York State Unified Court System
25 Beaver St Rm 888
New York, NY 10004
877/697-4253
212/428-2974 FAX
cle@courts.state.ny.us
www.courts.state.ny.us

North Carolina
Ms. Debra P. Holland
Assistant Director, Board of CLE
North Carolina State Bar
PO Box 26148
Raleigh, NC 27611
919/733-0123
919/821-9168 FAX
dholland@ncbar.gov
www.nccle.org

North Dakota
Ms. Justine Rowinski, Director
North Dakota CLE Commission
504 N Washington St.
Bismarck, ND 58501
701/255-1404
701/224-1621 FAX
www.sband.org

Ohio
Ms. Susan Christoff, Director
The Supreme Court of Ohio
Commission on CLE
65 S Front St FL5
Columbus, OH 43215-3431
614/387-9327
614/387-9323 FAX
susan.christoff@sc.ohio.gov
www.supremecourt.ohio.gov/att
orneyservices/cle.default.asp

Oklahoma
Ms. Beverly S. Petry
MCLE Administrator
Oklahoma Bar Association
PO Box 53036
Oklahoma City, OK 73152
405/416-7009
405/416-7089 FAX
beverlyp@okbar.org
www.okbar.org

Oregon
Ms. Denise Cline
MCLE Program Manager
Oregon State Bar
16037 SW Upper Boones Ferry Rd
Tigard, OR 97281-1935
503/620-0222
503/598-6915 FAX
dcline@osbar.org
www.osbar.org

Pennsylvania
Mr. Daniel Levering
CLE Administrator
Pennsylvania CLE Board
601 Commonwealth Ave
Ste 3400
Harrisburg, PA 17106-2495
717/231-3250
717/231-3251 FAX
800/497-2253
dlevering@pacle.org
www.pacle.org

Puerto Rico
Jose Campos-Perez
Supreme Court of Puerto Rico
CLE Programs
PO Box 190917
San Juan PR 00919-0917
(787)641-6604
Fax: (787)641-6602
www.ramajudicial.pr/sistema/su
premo/PEJC/index.htm

Rhode Island
Ms. Holly Hitchcock, M. Ed.
Executive Director MCLE
Rhode Island Supreme Court
MCLE Commission
John E. Fogarty Judicial Annex
24 Weybosset St., 3rd Floor
Providence, RI 02903
401/222-4942
401/222-4302 FAX
www.courts.ri.gov

South Carolina
Ms. Mary A. Germack
Executive Director
The Supreme Court of South
Carolina Commission on CLE &
Specialization
PO Box 2138
Columbia, SC 29202
803/799-5578
803/799-4118 FAX
commcle@bellsouth.net
www.commcle.org

Tennessee
Ms. Judy Bond-McKissack
Executive Director
Tennessee Commission on CLE &
Specialization
221 Fourth Ave. North, Ste. 300
Nashville, TN 37219
615/741-3096
615/532-2477 FAX
info@cletn.com
www.cletn.com

Texas
Ms. Nancy R. Smith
Director of MCLE
State Bar of Texas
PO Box 13007
Austin, TX 78711-3007
515/427-1806
800/204-2222 x1806
515/427-4123 FAX
nsmith@texasbar.com
www.texasbar.com/mcle

Utah
Ms. Sydnie W. Kuhre
MCLE Board Director
Utah Supreme Court Board of CLE
Utah Law & Justice Center
645 South 200 East, Ste. 312
Salt Lake City, UT 84111-3834
801/531-9077
801/531-0660 FAX
skuhre@utahbar.org
www.utahbar.org

Vermont
Ms. Martha I. Hicks-Robinson, Director
Vermont Judiciary
Board of Bar Examiners,
Character & Fitness
MCLE
111 State Street, Suite 9B
Montpelier VT 05609-0701
(802)828-3281
Fax: (802)828-6550
Martha.Hicks-Robinson@state.vt.us
www.vermontjudiciary.org

Virginia
Ms. Gale M. Cartwright
Director of MCLE
Virginia State Bar
1111 E. Main St., Ste. 700
Richmond, VA 23219-3565
804/775-0577
804/775-0544 FAX
mcle@vsb.org
www.vsb.org

Virgin Islands
Ms. Hinda Carbon
Executive Director
Virgin Islands Bar Association
PO Box 4108
Christiansted, VI 00822
340/778-7497
340/773-5060 FAX
executivedirector@vibar.org

Washington
Ms. Renata Garcia
MCLE Manager
Washington State Bar
Association
1325 4th Ave., Ste 600
Seattle, WA 98101-2539
206/727-5912
206/727-8313 FAX
renatag@wsba.org
www.wsba.org

West Virginia
Ms. Hope L. Gresham
MCLE Coordinator
The West Virginia State Bar
2000 Deitrick Blvd
Charleston, WV 25311-1231
304/553-7238
304/558-2467 FAX
greshamh@wvbar.org
www.wvbar.org

Wisconsin
Ms. Jacquelyn B. Rothstein
Director
Board of Bar Examiners
Mail: PO Box 2748
Madison, WI 53701-2748
Shipping: 110 E. Main St.,
Ste. 715, Tenney Building
Madison, WI 53703-3328
608/266-9760
608/266-1196 FAX
jacquelyn.rothstein@wicourts.gov
tammy.mcmillen@wicourts.gov
www.wicourts.gov

Wyoming
Ms. Marie Ellis, CLE Director
Wyoming State Bar
4124 Laramie St
PO Box 109
Cheyenne, WY 82003-0109
307/632-9061
307/632-3737 FAX
mellis@wyomingbar.org
www.wyomingbar.org

Revised: 05/11/2016

Table of State MCLE Requirements

State MCLE Requirements

State	Requirements
Alabama	12 hours per calendar year, 1 hour of which must be ethics New admittees must take a mandatory six-hour professionalism course within the first 12 months of admission Reporting deadline: January 31
Alaska	3 hours per calendar year, including professional responsibility, workplace ethics, law office management, attention to cases and clients, time management, malpractice prevention, collegiality, general attorney wellness, and professionalism, plus nine hours encouraged of voluntary CLE Reporting deadline: February 1
Arizona	15 credits per educational year (July 1 through June 30), with a minimum of three hours in the area of professional responsibility, which includes, among other topics, ethics, professionalism, malpractice prevention, substance abuse, attorneys' fees, and client development Reporting deadline: September 15
Arkansas	12 credits per reporting period (July 1 through June 30), 1 hour of which must be ethics, which may include professionalism Reporting deadline: August 31
California	25 hours per three-year compliance period (February 1 to January 31 of the third year), including at least 4 hours of ethics in the legal profession, 1 hour dealing with the elimination of bias in the legal profession, and 1 hour of education regarding prevention, detection, and treatment of substance abuse or mental illness Reporting deadline: No later than the day following January 31 of the compliance period

Colorado	45 hours for each three-year compliance period, with at least 7 hours pertaining to ethics Reporting deadline: At the time of payment of a registration fee, submission of an affidavit showing the units of CLE completed is required; no later than January 31 following the end of the compliance period, each attorney or judge must submit a final affidavit if the MCLE board's records do not show that the attorney or judge has completed the hourly requirement for the compliance period
Delaware	24 hours for each two-year compliance period, including 4 hours enhanced ethics Reporting deadline: December 31 of the reporting year
Florida	30 hours for every three years, including 5 hours in legal ethics, professionalism, substance abuse, or mental illness awareness Reporting deadline: no later than the last day of a member's applicable reporting period
Georgia	12 hours each year, including one hour of ethics and one hour of professionalism; trial attorneys must also include 3 hours of trial practice Reporting deadline: March 31
Guam	10 hours per calendar year, with two hours of ethics or professionalism Reporting deadline: January 31
Hawaii	3 hours each calendar year, and at least one credit of ethics every three years (included in annual requirement) Reporting deadline: December 31
Idaho	30 hours in each three-year period, including at least 2 hours on legal ethics or professional responsibility Reporting deadline: On or before February 1 in the year immediately following the calendar year within which the attorney is required to complete the requirements
Illinois	30 hours during a two-year reporting period, with at least 6 hours in professional responsibility Reporting deadline. July 31: submission of certification within 31 days after the end of the reporting period

Indiana

36 hours in each three-year period with a 6 credit minimum each year, including at least 3 hours in ethics
Reporting deadline: December 31 of three-year period

Iowa

15 hours per calendar year, including at least 3 hours, every two calendar years, in ethics
Reporting deadline: On or before March 10 of each year

Kansas

12 hours in each period (July 1 to June 30), including 2 hours in ethics and professional responsibility, but no more than 8 hours may be earned in a single day
Reporting deadline: attendance at a CLE activity must be reported within 30 days; if annual report provided to an attorney corresponds with the attorney's records, no action needs to be taken; if changes are necessary, instructions and forms are included with the transcript

Kentucky

12 hours per educational year (July 1 to June 30), including at least 2 hours in ethics
Reporting deadline: On or before August 10 following the educational year

Louisiana

12.5 hours per calendar year, including 1 hour in legal ethics and 1 hour in professionalism
Reporting deadline: January 31 of the following calendar year

Maine

11 hours for each calendar year, with at least 1 hour in ethics or professional responsibility Reporting deadline:August 31 of the following year along with the annual registration statement

Minnesota

45 hours per three-year reporting period, including at least 3 hours in ethics or professional responsibility; at least 2 hours in the elimination of bias in the legal profession and the practice of law; no more than 6 hours in law office management; and no more than 6 hours of credit for pro bono legal representation
Reporting deadline: by August 31 of the three-year reporting period

Mississippi

12 hours per reporting year (August 1 through July 31), including 1 hour in legal ethics, professional responsibility, professionalism, malpractice prevention, substance abuse, or mental health

Reporting deadline: On or before August 15 of each year

Missouri

15 hours per reporting year (July 1 through June 30), including at least 2 hours in professionalism, ethics, or malpractice prevention every three years Reporting deadline: On or before July 31

Montana

15 hours per reporting year (April 1 through March 31), plus two hour of legal ethics/professionalism every year Reporting deadline: May 15

Nebraska

10 hours per calendar year, including 2 credits in professional responsibility Reporting deadline: On or before January 20 of the annual reporting period

Nevada

12 hours per calendar year, including at least 2 hours in ethics and professional responsibility, and 1 hour of substance abuse, addictive disorders, or mental health credit every 3 years Reporting deadline: On or before March 1

New Hampshire

12 hours per reporting year (July 1 to June 30), including at least 2 hours of ethics and/or professionalism, substance abuse, malpractice prevention, or attorney-client relations and 6 hours of live programming Reporting deadline: On or before October 1

New Jersey

24 hours per two-year reporting period, including 4 hours in ethics and/or professionalism, with additional mandatory requirements for newly admitted lawyers Reporting deadline: March 31: certification of compliance at the end of the compliance period

New Mexico

12 hours per calendar year, including 2 credits in ethics/professionalism Reporting deadline: May 1

New York

24 hours per two-year reporting period, including at least 4 hours in ethics and professionalism Reporting deadline: Submission of certification along with submission of biennial attorney registration statement

North Carolina

12 hours per calendar year, including at least 2 hours in ethics, professional responsibility or professionalism; at least once every three calendar years, 1 hour in substance abuse, or debilitating mental conditions Reporting deadline: The last day of February

North Dakota

45 hours per each three-year reporting period, including 3 hours in ethics Reporting deadline: June 30

Northern Mariana Islands

20 hours per two year period; reporting deadline of February 15

Ohio

24 hours per each two-year reporting period, including at least 2.5 hours in professional conduct and ethics
Reporting deadline: On or before January 31 for the preceding two calendar years

Oklahoma

12 hours per calendar year, including at least 1 hour in legal ethics, professional responsibility, or legal malpractice prevention
Reporting deadline: February 15, unless exempted as provided

Oregon

45 hours every three years, including 6 hours in ethics, one hour of which must be on reporting child abuse; and 3 hours on elimination of bias
Reporting deadline: January 31 of the year immediately following the reporting period

Pennsylvania

12 hours per compliance period, including at least 2 hours of ethics
Reporting deadline: as assigned for each compliance group

Puerto Rico

24 hours per compliance period, with 4 hours in ethics
Reporting deadline: no later than 30 days following the end of the compliance period

Rhode Island

10 hours per reporting period (one year), including 2 hours in ethics
Reporting deadline: June 30

South Carolina

14 hours per reporting period (March 1 through the last day of February), including at least 2 hours in legal ethics; once every three reporting periods, one hour in substance abuse or mental health issues
Reporting deadline: on or before March 1

Tennessee

15 hours per calendar year, including 3 hours in ethics and professionalism
Reporting deadline: receipt on or before March 1

Texas

15 hours per compliance year (based on attorney's birth month), including at least 3 hours in legal ethics/professional responsibility
Reporting deadline: Attorneys must correct the annual verification report, if necessary, and all corrections/additions to the records must be completed, filed, and received on or before the last day of the attorney's birth month

Utah	24 hours per two-year period (July 1 through June 30), including at least 3 hours of ethics or professional responsibility, one hour of which must be in the area of professionalism and civility Reporting deadline: On or before July 31 of alternate years
Vermont	20 hours for each two-year compliance period (July 1 to June 30 of the second year), including at least 2 hours in legal ethics Reporting deadline: No later than July 1 following the end of each applicable reporting period
Virginia	12 hours per reporting year (November 1 through October 31), including 2 hours in legal ethics or professionalism Reporting deadline: By December 15
Virgin Islands	12 hours per calendar year, including at least 2 hours in legal ethics or professionalism Reporting deadline: On or before December 31 of each calendar year
Washington	45 hours per three-year reporting period ending December 31 of the third year, including at least 6 hours in ethics and professional responsibility, and 15 hours of law and legal procedure per 3-year period Reporting deadline: February 1 following the end of the three-year reporting period
West Virginia	24 hours per two-year period (July 1 to June 30 of the second year), including at least 3 hours in legal ethics, office management, substance abuse, or elimination of bias in the legal profession Reporting deadline: on or before July 31 following the end of the two-year period
Wisconsin	30 hours per two-year period (January 1 to December 31 of the second year), including at least 3 hours in legal ethics and professional responsibility Reporting deadline: on or before February 1 following the last day of the reporting period
Wyoming	15 hours per calendar year, including 2 hour of legal ethics Reporting deadline: on or before January 30

Source: State MCLE rules

ALABAMA

ALABAMA STATE BAR
RULES FOR MANDATORY CONTINUING LEGAL EDUCATION

RULE 1.   MCLE Commission

There is hereby established the Mandatory Continuing Legal Education Commission of the Alabama State Bar (the "MCLE Commission"). The MCLE Commission shall consist of nine members. The members shall be chosen from, and elected by, the members of the Board of Bar Commissioners, and shall serve at its pleasure.

The MCLE Commission shall have the following duties:

A. To exercise general supervisory authority over the administration of these rules.

B. To adopt regulations consistent with these rules.

REGULATIONS

1.1   The chairman of the MCLE Commission shall be appointed by the President of the Alabama State Bar ("ASB") from among the nine members of the MCLE Commission elected by the members of the Board of Bar Commissioners. The members of the MCLE Commission may select a member to be recommended to the president as chairman.

1.2   The MCLE Commission shall elect by majority vote a vice chairman and secretary from among its members.

1.3   The MCLE Commission may organize itself into committees of not fewer than three voting members for the purpose of considering and deciding matters submitted to them, except five affirmative votes shall be necessary for any action under Rule 8 (Noncompliance and Sanctions; Late Fees).

1.4   Replacement members, if and as necessary, shall be voted upon and recommended by the MCLE Commission to the nominating committee of the Board of Bar Commissioners for approval by the Board of Bar Commissioners.

1.5   The MCLE Commissioners shall meet no fewer than four times per year, and at any other time or times deemed necessary or advisable, upon reasonable notice of such meeting.

1.6   Members of the MCLE Commission shall be reimbursed for their actual direct travel expenses to the same extent as ASB employees when such travel is authorized by the Board of Bar Commissioners or by the president of the ASB.

1.7   The MCLE Commission shall designate an executive director and such other staff as may be deemed necessary and, further, may delegate executive authority to such director or staff to conduct the business of the MCLE Commission within the scope of these rules and regulations, subject at all times, however, to continuing review by the MCLE Commission.

RULE 2.   Scope of these Rules; Waivers and Exemptions.

A.   Scope.

Except as provided herein, these rules shall apply to every person whose qualification to practice law is subject to the *Code of Alabama* (1975), § 40-12-49 (occupational licenses), § 34-3-17 (qualified lawyers holding public office), and § 34-3-18 (lawyers not engaged in active practice), and shall be applicable for the compliance year beginning January 1, 2013.

B.   Waivers.

The MCLE Commission may waive the requirements of these rules for a period of one year or longer, upon a finding of undue hardship, or of extenuating circumstances beyond the control of the attorney seeking such waiver, which prevent him or her from complying in any reasonable manner with these rules. Upon expiration of the waiver, the MCLE Commission may impose any additional MCLE requirements as may be deemed appropriate under the circumstances.

C.   Exemptions.

1.   New Admittee. An attorney holding an occupational license is exempt from the requirement of these rules for the balance of the year during which he or she was first admitted to practice.

2.   Public Office.   All attorneys who by Constitution, law or regulation, are prohibited from the private practice of law by virtue of their occupation of public office, shall be exempt from these rules for the entire calendar year(s) during which they hold such office. Also exempt are members of the United States Senate, the United States House of Representatives, the Armed Forces, the Senate of Alabama (and its secretary), and the Alabama House of Representatives (and its clerk). This exemption DOES NOT apply to those attorneys serving as assistant or deputy attorneys general and district attorneys, assistant or deputy district attorneys, and public defenders.

3.   Age.   An attorney holding an occupational license is exempt from the requirements of these rules for the year in which he or she is begins receiving Social Security Benefits, or reaches the age of 65, whichever occurs first.

REGULATIONS

2.1   Nonresident attorneys from other jurisdictions who are temporarily admitted to practice in Alabama pursuant to *Rule VII of the Rules Governing Admission to the Alabama State Bar (pro hac vice rules)* shall not be subject to these rules.

2.2   An attorney who is exempt during the calendar year in which he or she was first admitted to the Alabama State Bar may earn up to 12 MCLE credits during the calendar year of admission, which may be carried over to the next compliance year if the attorney reports the credits on his or her annual report of compliance no later than February 15. Credits earned prior to the attorney's admission date to the Alabama State Bar may not be claimed.

2.3   Attorneys serving as judicial law clerks or judicial staff attorneys who are prohibited from the private practice of law for any part of a calendar year are exempt from the MCLE requirement for that year.

2.4.   An attorney who is exempt from these rules on the basis of age shall notify the MCLE Commission in writing of his or her claim of such exemption.

2.5.   Special Members of the Alabama State Bar are not subject to the MCLE requirement except as provided in Rule 2.C.2.

2.6.   An attorney seeking a waiver of these rules shall submit such request in writing on forms approved by the MCLE Commission.

2.7.   An attorney who maintains a residence and a principal office for the practice of law in a state other than Alabama which requires Mandatory Continuing Legal Education (MCLE), and who can demonstrate compliance with the MCLE requirements of that state, is exempt from these rules, except as provided in Rules 7 and 9.

RULE 3.   CLE Requirement

> Each attorney subject to these rules shall complete a minimum of 12 hours of approved continuing legal education annually, 1 hour of which shall be on the subject of ethics or professionalism.
>
> This requirement may be satisfied either by attendance at an ASB-approved course or by completion of any other ASB-approved continuing legal education activity.

REGULATIONS

3.1   A minimum of 6 credit hours of the 12 credit hours required annually must be earned through attendance at live ASB-approved programs.

3.2   This requirement may be satisfied through teaching an approved continuing legal education activity. Presentations supported by thorough, high quality, readable and carefully prepared written materials qualify for MCLE credit on the basis on six credits for each hour of presentation. Presentations accompanied by brief outlines, or not accompanied by substantial written materials, shall not satisfy this requirement. When a presentation is made by a panel, the credit will be divided equally among the panel members, unless the MCLE Commission is advised otherwise.

3.3   Repeat presentations shall satisfy this requirement to the extent of one-half the credits available for an initial presentation, provided each lawyer shall receive at least one credit for each hour of individual presentation or service on a panel.

3.4   This requirement may be satisfied through teaching a course in an ABA- or AALS-approved law school or any other law school approved by the MCLE Commission. The MCLE Commission will award six hours of MCLE credit for each hour of academic credit awarded by the law school for the course. For purposes of these rules, Miles College of Law and Birmingham School of Law are considered approved law schools.

3.5   This requirement may be satisfied by authoring a significant research article that is accepted for publication in a national law journal. Whether the article is significant will be determined by the executive director. The MCLE Commission will award twelve hours of MCLE credit upon publication of the article.

3.6.   This requirement may be satisfied through service as a bar examiner in Alabama or in any the sister state. The MCLE Commission shall award twelve hours of MCLE credit annually for such service during a given year.

3.7.   This requirement may be satisfied through formal enrollment and education of a postgraduate nature, either for credit or by audit, in an accredited law school. The MCLE Commission will award one credit for each credit hour so earned.

3.8   The MCLE Commission shall award two hours of MCLE credit to attorneys who attend the annual business meeting of the Alabama State Bar.

RULE 4.   Qualification of Course Sponsors

A.   To be eligible for accreditation, all MCLE course sponsors shall have been engaged in approved continuing legal education activities during the two years immediately preceding any application for accreditation and shall have sponsored at least five separate courses which would qualify for course approval under these rules.

B.   A qualifying sponsor shall apply to the MCLE Commission for approval of an individual MCLE activity that meets the standards set forth in these Rules.

C.   A qualifying sponsor may apply to the MCLE Commission for accreditation as a pre-approved sponsor. Such accreditation shall constitute prior approval of all MCLE activities to be offered by that sponsor, provided the sponsor and the activity meet the standards set forth in these rules.

D.   The MCLE Commission shall promulgate regulations to establish the procedures whereby sponsors are accredited, for imposing sanctions including amendment, revocation or suspension of accreditation, and to establish additional minimum standards for sponsors and activities as may be deemed necessary from time to time. A sponsor's status shall be subject to ongoing review by the MCLE Commission.

REGULATIONS

4.1   Applications for status as a pre-approved sponsor shall be accompanied by a fee of $250.00

4.2   Sponsors other than pre-approved sponsors shall submit a fee of $50.00 with each application for accreditation of an MCLE activity.

4.3   An attorney may submit an application for accreditation of an MCLE activity for which accreditation was not sought by the sponsor. Such an application shall be accompanied by a fee of $25.00.

4.4   Sponsors of approved MCLE activities shall refrain from advertising or encouraging the use of their products or services during the activity. Sponsors shall seek participants' opinions regarding their adherence to this policy. Failure to adhere to this policy shall be ground for withdrawal of accreditation of the MCLE activity.

4.5   Program sponsors may advertise in their informational brochures and program materials that the activity has been accredited by the MCLE Commission.

4.6   At the conclusion of an approved activity, each participating attorney shall complete an evaluation questionnaire addressing the quality, effectiveness and usefulness of the particular activity. If requested, copies of the questionnaires shall be forwarded to the MCLE Commission. Sponsors shall maintain the questionnaires for a period of 90 days following a program.

RULE 5:   **Minimum Standards for Approval**

A.   To be approved for credit, MCLE activities must meet the following requirements:

1.   Applications for approval of an MCLE activity must be submitted at least thirty (30) days in advance of the activity.

2.   The activity must have significant intellectual or practical content and its primary objective must be to increase the participant's professional competence as an attorney. The activity may not be designed primarily for non-lawyers.

3.   The activity must deal primarily with substantive legal issues, practice management, professional responsibility or ethical obligations of attorneys. Whenever possible, ethical implications of practice management subject matter shall be included.

4.   The activity must be offered by a sponsor having substantial, recent experience in providing mandatory continuing legal education activities or a demonstrated ability to organize and effectively present mandatory continuing legal education activities. Demonstrated ability arises partly from the extent to which individuals with legal training or educational experience are involved in the planning, instruction and supervision of the activity.

5.   The activity must be conducted by an individual or group qualified by practical or academic experience. The program must be conducted substantially as planned, including the named advertised participants, subject to emergency withdrawals and alterations.

6.   Thorough, high-quality, readable, and carefully prepared written materials must be made available to all participants, in hard copy or electronic medium, at or before the time of presentation of the activity, unless the absence of such materials is reasonable and has been pre-approved by the MCLE Commission.

7.   The activity must be conducted in an appropriate and suitably equipped physical setting, conducive to learning.

8.   The cost of the activity must be reasonably related to the subject matter, instructional level, and location.

B.   Approval may be given for activities where electronically recorded or reproduced material is used only if a qualified instructor is available to comment and answer questions at the time of the broadcast. Satellite and teleconference programs must have either telephone connections to instructors at the broadcast location or an instructor present at the receiving site to comment and answer questions.

C.   Web-based programs will be eligible for approval only if the participant's attendance is randomly monitored and verified by the sponsor during the program.

D.   No MCLE credit will be awarded for self-study programs.

REGULATIONS

5.1   The MCLE Commission will advise the applicant seeking accreditation whether the activity is approved or disapproved within 30 days of the receipt of the completed application and fee. Applicants denied accreditation may appeal the decision by submitting a letter of appeal to the MCLE Commission within 15 days of receipt of notice of denial.

5.2   No application for accreditation by either sponsor or a participant will be approved more than sixty (60) days after the close of the program year (December 31).

5.3   Web-based MCLE programs shall be limited to six hours of MCLE credit per year. On-demand web-based programs, which are not offered in real-time, shall be subject to the 6 credit hour limit. Synchronous, real-time webcasts and webinars may be considered live programs under these rules, and not subject to the 6 credit hour limit, only if the program allows instructors and participants to communicate directly via text or teleconference. Teleconferences shall be treated as live programs under these rules.

5.4   Attorneys desiring credit for an activity attended outside Alabama may be required to complete an evaluation questionnaire furnished by the MCLE Commission and to return it within a reasonable time following the conclusion of the activity.

5.5   Activities that cross academic lines, such as accounting-tax seminars, may be considered for approval.

5.6   When a law firm is the course sponsor, at least 50% of the instruction must be provided by persons not affiliated with the law firm sponsor. A qualified instructor not affiliated with the law firm sponsor must be present for all audio or videotaped replays of the live program.

5.7   Program materials without legal citations or explanatory notations shall be considered deficient.

5.8   Attorneys who have a permanent physical disability or limitation that makes attendance at approved MCLE activities inordinately difficult may file a request for a permanent substitute activity in lieu of attendance and shall set out in that request continuing legal education plans tailored to the attorney's specific interests and physical abilities. Any such request shall be accompanied by a physician's statement addressing the necessity for such alternative activity. The MCLE Commission shall review and approve or disapprove the proposed plan on an individual basis and in an expeditious manner.

RULE 6.   **Application of MCLE Credits**

A.   Credit will be awarded only for participation in MCLE activities that have been approved by the MCLE Commission.

B.   A maximum of 12 hours, including 1 ethics hour, in excess of the minimum annual requirement may be carried forward for credit in the succeeding year. Credits may be carried forward for one year only.

C.   An instructional hour will, in all events, contain at least sixty (60) minutes.

REGULATIONS

6.1   Program attendance and the number of program hours attended shall be confirmed by program sponsors for each attorney attending an accredited activity. Attorney attendance must be reported to the executive director within 30 days of the conclusion of the activity.

6.2.   No credit will be awarded for introductory remarks, meal breaks or business meetings during an accredited activity.

RULE 7. **Annual Reporting**

A.   As soon as practicable after January 31 of each year, the executive director shall cause to be prepared an annual report of compliance for each attorney subject to these rules for the prior year.

B.   By February 15 of each year, each attorney subject to these rules shall certify the accuracy of his or her individual annual report of compliance to the MCLE Commission, in such form as shall be prescribed by the MCLE Commission.

REGULATIONS

7.1   Any report sent by regular, certified, registered or express mail of the United States Postal Service and postmarked by February 15 (or the next business day if February 15 is a Saturday, Sunday or holiday) will be considered timely filed. Untimely reports received without the required late filing fee will be returned to the submitting attorney, who shall continue to be deemed non-compliant until all applicable late fees are paid.

7.2   The MCLE Commission may permit amendments of annual reports of compliance through March 1 of the year immediately succeeding the compliance year. Requests for such amendments must be in writing and must provide specific details of each proposed amendment. All credits, however, must be earned by December 31 of the reporting year, unless a deficiency plan is filed.

7.3   Requests for late amendments (after March 1 of the year immediately succeeding the compliance year) may be considered by the MCLE Commission on a case-by-case basis. Such requests must be in writing and must comply with the requirements of Regulation 7.2 above. Successive requests for late amendments will not be considered without a showing of good cause.

7.4   On or before February 15 of each year, each attorney who is exempt from these rules but who wishes to receive credit for courses attended, shall submit a report, in such form as the MCLE Commission shall prescribe, detailing such attorney's completion of any hours of instruction, including reference to hours earned during the preceding calendar year and hours to be carried forward for the current year.

7.5   The files and records of the MCLE Commission are confidential and shall not be disclosed except in furtherance of the duties of the MCLE Commission; however, strictly statistical abstracts may be compiled from those records for public information.

RULE 8. Noncompliance and Sanctions; Late Fees

A.   An attorney who fails to earn twelve hours of approved MCLE credits by December 31 of a particular year will be deemed noncompliant for that year.

B.   On or before February 15, any attorney deemed non-compliant for the prior compliance year shall submit to the MCLE Commission a plan for curing the deficiency by March 1, on the form prescribed by the MCLE Commission.

C.   Completion of an approved deficiency plan shall be reported by the non-compliant attorney to the MCLE Commission no later than March 15. Failure to complete an approved deficiency plan by March 1 and/or to submit the required report and fee by March 15 shall result in the imposition of sanctions.

D.   As soon as practicable after April 15 of each year, the executive director shall furnish to the Office of General Counsel of the Alabama State Bar a list of those attorneys who have failed to comply with Rule 3 and/or Rule 8 for further discipline.

E.   Successive requests for approval of a deficiency plan will not be considered without a showing of good cause.

F.   As soon as practicable after January 31 of each year, the executive director shall cause to be furnished to the Office of General Counsel of the Alabama State Bar a list of those attorneys who have failed to complete the professionalism course required by Rule 9 for further discipline.

REGULATION

8.1   Deficiency plans submitted pursuant to this rule shall be subject to the provisions of Regulation 7.1.

8.2   Any attorney who is deemed non-compliant shall pay a $100 Late Compliance Fee.

8.3   Any attorney who certifies his or her annual report of compliance after the February 15 deadline shall pay a $100 Late Filing Fee. This payment shall accompany any report submitted by mail, or in the case of online certification, such late filing fee must be received within 10 days of the late certification date.

8.4   Any attorney who fails to timely complete an approved deficiency plan, or who fails to timely report the completion of an approved deficiency plan, shall pay a $100 Late Reporting Fee.

8.5   A request for an extension of the March 15 deadline for earning credits under an approved deficiency plan may be considered if: (1) the request is made in writing and good cause is shown, as determined by the MCLE Commission, in its sole discretion, and (2) the request is accompanied by a fee of $100.00. This fee is in addition to the late compliance fee, the late filing fee, and any other late fee that may be due. No extensions will be granted beyond April 1.

8.6   In order to make a showing of good cause pursuant to Rule 8.E, after the approval of two successive deficiency plans, an attorney shall appear before a panel consisting of the executive director, a representative of the MCLE Commission and a representative of the Office of General Counsel, to explain why a further deficiency plan should be granted. The attorney shall be notified in writing of the decision of the panel.

Rule 9.   Professionalism

A.   Within twelve months of being admitted to the Alabama State Bar, every lawyer subject to these Rules shall complete a three hour course in professionalism.

B.   Lawyers claiming an exemption under Rule 2 shall likewise be exempt from the requirements of this rule so long as they remain exempt. Lawyers must complete the course in professionalism during the calendar year following the year in which the exempt status ends.

C.   This rule shall be waived for any attorney serving on active duty with the United States Armed Forces.

D.   Violations of this Rule shall be governed by Rule 8.

ALASKA

RULE 65.   Continuing Legal Education.

(a) Mandatory Continuing Legal Education.

In order to promote competence and professionalism in members of the Association, the Alaska Supreme Court and the Association require all members to engage in Mandatory Ethics Continuing Legal Education (MECLE). Every active member of the Alaska Bar Association shall complete at least three credit hours per year of approved MECLE. Qualifying educational topics may include professional responsibility, workplace ethics, law office management, attention to cases and clients, time management, malpractice prevention, collegiality, general attorney wellness, and professionalism.

(b) Voluntary Continuing Legal Education.

In addition to MECLE, the Alaska Supreme Court and the Association encourage all members to engage in Voluntary Continuing Legal Education (VCLE). Every active member of the Alaska Bar Association should complete at least nine credit hours per year of approved VCLE.

Commentary. The Alaska Supreme Court and the Association are convinced that CLE contributes to lawyer competence and benefits the public and the profession by assuring that attorneys remain current regarding the law, the obligations and standards of the profession, and the management of their practices. To protect the public, ensure that lawyers remain mindful of their obligations to their clients, and to address the area about which the Association receives the majority of questions from and complaints about lawyers, the Supreme Court is imposing a mandatory requirement for ethics CLE on all active Bar members. The ethics topics that qualify for MECLE are intended to be comprehensive, as conveyed by the examples in subsection (a) of this rule. Moreover, to help ensure that lawyers can easily and readily meet the MECLE requirements, the Association has agreed to provide at least three hours per year of approved MECLE at no cost to members. The Supreme Court has also concluded that Voluntary Continuing Education on additional subject areas is valuable to lawyers and should be encouraged. This rule uses incentives to encourage lawyers to participate in VCLE.

The Supreme Courts goal in imposing MECLE and mandatory reporting of all CLE is to encourage a substantial increase in attendance at CLE courses and participation in activities that earn MECLE and VCLE credit, with resulting enhancement of lawyer services to clients. This rule refines the former VCLE rule, and continues the pilot project begun in 1999. At the end of three years, the Supreme Court will again assess the project's results, including recommendations and statistics provided by the Association, and will determine whether an expanded mandatory CLE program is necessary.

(c) Carryforward of Credit Hours.

An active Bar member may carry forward from the previous reporting period a maximum of 12 credits (3 MECLE credits and 9 VCLE credits). To be carried forward, the credit hours must have been earned during the calendar year immediately preceding the current reporting period.

(d) Mandatory Reporting.

By February 1 of each year, each member must certify on a form prescribed by the Association whether the member has completed the required minimum of three hours of approved MECLE during the preceding year or carried over from the prior year as provided in subsection (c) of this rule. The member must also certify whether the member has completed nine hours of approved VCLE during the preceding year or carried over from the prior year as provided in subsection (c). If the member has completed fewer than nine hours of VCLE, the member must also estimate and report the estimated number of VCLE hours completed. A member shall maintain records of approved MECLE hours for the two most recent reporting periods, and these records shall be subject to audit by the Association on request.

Commentary. The Supreme Court has adopted this mandatory reporting requirement to ensure that Bar members report CLE activities to the Association. This will ensure that the Association and the Court can assess the effectiveness of the rule by determining what percentage of lawyers are earning CLE credit hours in excess of the minimum, and what percentage are earning VCLE credit hours, even if the hours are less than the nine hours that this rule encourages.

The record of approved MECLE hours that members are required to maintain under subsection (d) may be any documentation, including contemporaneous journal entries or timekeeping entries, whether paper or electronic, that serves to establish that the member earned the credit hours.

(e) Incentives for VCLE.

Only members who complete at least nine hours of VCLE are eligible to participate in the Alaska Bar Association's Lawyer Referral Service. If a member does not complete at least nine hours of VCLE, that fact may be taken into account in any Bar disciplinary matter relating to the requirements of Alaska Rule of Professional Conduct 1.1. The Association shall make a members record of compliance with VCLE available to the Alaska Judicial Council for its consideration in connection with a members candidacy for any judicial office or other position for which the Council screens and nominates candidates. The Association shall publish annually, and make available to members of the public, a list of attorneys who have complied with this rule's MECLE requirements and satisfied this rules minimum recommendations for VCLE. The Association may adopt other incentives to encourage compliance with the VCLE recommendations.

(f) Time Extensions.

A member may file a written request for an extension of time for compliance with this rule. A request for extension shall be reviewed and determined by the Association.

(g) CLE Activities.

The MECLE and VCLE standards of this rule may be met either by attending approved courses or completing any other continuing legal education activity approved for credit under these rules. If the approved course or activity or any portion of it relates to ethics as described in (a) of this rule, the member may claim MECLE credit for the course or activity or for the ethics-related portion of it. Any course or continuing legal education activity approved for credit by a jurisdiction, other than Alaska, that requires continuing legal education is approved for credit in Alaska under this rule. The following activities are approved for credit when they meet the conditions set forth in this rule:

(1) preparing for and teaching approved MECLE and VCLE courses and participating in public service broadcasts on legal topics; credit will be granted for up to two hours of preparation time for every one hour of time spent teaching;

(2) studying audio or video tapes or other technology-delivered approved MECLE and VCLE courses;

(3) writing published legal articles in any publication or articles in law reviews or specialized professional journals;

(4) attending substantive Section or Inn of Court meetings;

(5) participating as a faculty member in Youth Court;

(6) attending approved in-house continuing legal education courses;

(7) attending approved continuing judicial education courses;

(8) attending approved continuing legal education courses including local bar association programs and meetings of professional legal associations;

(9) participating as a mentor in a relationship with another member of the Alaska Bar Association for the purpose of training that other member in providing effective pro bono legal services;

(10) participating as a member of the Alaska Bar Association Law Examiners Committee, the Alaska Bar Association Ethics Committee, the Alaska Rules of Professional Conduct Committee, or any standing rules committees appointed by the Alaska Bar Association or the Alaska Supreme Court; and

(11) participating as a member of an Area Discipline Division or an Area Fee Dispute Resolution Division.

(h) Approval of CLE Programs.

The Association shall approve or disapprove all education activities for credit. CLE activities sponsored by the Association are deemed approved. Forms for approval may be submitted electronically.

(1) An entity or association must apply to the Board for accreditation as a CLE provider. Accreditation shall constitute prior approval of MECLE and VCLE courses offered by the provider, subject to amendment, suspension, or revocation of such accreditation by the Board.

(2) The Board shall establish by regulation the procedures, minimum standards, and any fees for accreditation of providers, in-house continuing legal education courses, and publication of legal texts or journal articles, and for revocation of accreditation when necessary.

(i) Effective Date; Reporting Period; Inapplicability to New Admittees.

(1) This rule will be effective January 1, 2008. The reporting period will be the calendar year, from January 1st to December 31st, and the first calendar year to be reported will be the year 2008. Any ethics or other CLE credits earned from January 1, 2007 to December 31, 2007 may be held over and applied to the reporting period for the year 2008.

(2) This rule does not apply to a new member of the Alaska Bar Association during the calendar year in which the member is first admitted to the practice of law in Alaska.

(Added by SCO 1366 effective September 2, 1999; amended by SCO 1640 effective January 1, 2008; and by SCO 1756 effective October 14, 2011)

RULE 66. Noncompliance with Continuing Legal Education Requirements; Suspension.

(a) Notice of Noncompliance.

Within 30 days after the deadline for filing the certification form described in Rule 65(d), the Association shall send a notice of noncompliance to each member whose certificate shows that the MECLE requirement has not been met, or who has failed to file the completed certification form. Within 30 days after receiving a notice of noncompliance, the member shall either remedy the noncompliance, demonstrate that the notice of non-compliance was issued erroneously, or submit an affidavit of compliance, if the member asserts that the information on the certification form contained an error.

(b) Suspension for Noncompliance with Mandatory Ethics Continuing Legal Education Requirement or Noncompliance with Requirement to Report MECLE and VCLE.

(1) Any member who has not complied with the MECLE requirement in Rule 65(a) or with the mandatory reporting of MECLE and VCLE requirement in Rule 65(d), and who has not remedied the noncompliance as provided in subsection (a) of this rule, shall be notified in writing by certified or registered mail that the Executive Director shall, after 15 days from the date of the notice, petition the Supreme Court of Alaska for an order suspending the member for noncompliance.

(2) A member suspended under this subsection shall not be reinstated until (A) the member has complied with the MECLE requirement and the mandatory reporting requirement; (B) the member has paid a reinstatement fee in an amount set by the Board; (C) the member has paid any dues accruing during suspension; and (D) the Executive Director has certified the members compliance to the Alaska Supreme Court.

(SCO 1640 effective January 1, 2008)

ARIZONA

RULE 45. **Mandatory Continuing Legal Education Rules of the Supreme Court of Arizona**

Effective January 1, 2015

(a) Continuing Legal Education Requirements.

1. Every active member of the bar, not exempted, shall complete a minimum of fifteen hours of continuing legal education activity in each educational year. An educational year shall begin on July 1 and end on the following June 30.

2. A minimum of three hours of continuing legal education activity each educational year shall be in the area of professional responsibility. Professional responsibility includes instruction in legal and judicial ethics, professionalism, and malpractice prevention, and may include such topics as substance abuse, including causes, prevention, detection and treatment alternatives, attorneys' fees, client development, law office economics and practice, alternatives to litigation for managing conflict and resolving disputes, stress management, and the particular responsibilities of public lawyers, judges, and in-house counsel, to the extent that professional responsibility is directly addressed in connection with these topics.

3. Except as otherwise provided in this rule, every active member of the bar, not exempted shall, between July 1, 1999 and June 30, 2004, satisfy the requirements of subsection (a)(2) of this Rule, in whole or in part for any educational year or succeeding year falling within that period, by completing the state bar course on professionalism or an equivalent course on the principles of professionalism approved or licensed by the Board of Governors of the State Bar of Arizona for this purpose.

   a. The requirements of this subsection shall be considered to have been fulfilled (i) by all members of the bar who have previously completed, or who do complete, such a course in satisfaction of the requirements of Rule 34(e) of these Rules, (ii) by all foreign legal consultants who have previously completed, or who do complete, such a course in satisfaction of the requirements of Rule 33(f)(9) of these Rules, or (iii) by all members of the bar who have previously completed a course on the principles of professionalism approved by the Board of Governors of the State Bar of Arizona as satisfying the requirements of this subsection.

   b. Active members of the bar who neither reside nor practice law in Arizona shall be exempt from completing such a course, except that any such member shall complete one within twelve (12) months of becoming a resident of or commencing the practice of law in Arizona, or in accordance with such other schedule as may be established by the Board of Governors.

c. The Board of Governors may, in its discretion, establish a schedule of dates earlier than June 30, 2004, by which designated categories of active members of the bar shall satisfy the requirements of this subsection.

4. An active member of the bar, not exempted, who serves as an arbitrator under Rule 73, Arizona Rules of Civil Procedure, is eligible for two hours of continuing legal education activity credit in lieu of financial compensation otherwise available under A.R.S. § 12-133(g) or local rule for service as an arbitrator. Such credit shall be included in the maximum number of hours allowed for self-study and shall be awarded under procedures approved by the Board of Governors.

5. An active member of the bar, not exempted, who provides pro bono service to the poor or near poor through an approved legal services organization, as defined in Rule 38(e), is eligible for one hour of continuing legal education credit for every five hours of pro bono service provided, up to a maximum of five hours per educational year of continuing legal education credit. Such credit shall be included in the maximum number of hours allowed for self-study and shall be reported in the attorney's annual affidavit of compliance.

6. An active member of the bar, not exempted, who serves as an arbitrator for a fee dispute resolution under the auspices of the State Bar Fee Arbitration Committee is eligible for one hour of continuing legal education activity credit for each hearing actually conducted, up to a maximum of two hours credit in any one educational year. This credit shall be applied to the required three hours of activity in the area of professional responsibility mandated for that educational year.

(b) Exemptions.

1. Inactive and Retired Members. An inactive or retired member of the bar shall be exempt from the requirements of section (a), if the lawyer is inactive or retired during the entire educational year. An active member who transfers to inactive or retired status is exempt during the educational year in which the transfer occurs.

2. Court Personnel: Retired Judges Subject to Assignment To Judicial Service. Court administrators, court clerks, and other court personnel who are active members and who are also subject to the educational requirements of the Council on Judicial Education and Training (COJET), will be deemed to have complied with the requirements of section (a) upon the filing of an affidavit of compliance as required in section (c). Retired judges subject to assignment to judicial service pursuant to A.R.S. § 38-813 who are active members and do not maintain an office separate from their residence, and no substantial part of whose activities consists of the active representation of clients outside the

judge's family, will be deemed to have complied with the requirements of section (a) upon the filing of an affidavit of compliance with the educational requirements of COJET.

3. **Active Members at Least 70 Years Old Before January 1, 2009.** An active member who both has been admitted to practice in Arizona and has attained the age of 70 before January 1, 2009, shall be exempt from the requirements of section (a).

4. **New Admittees.** A lawyer newly admitted between January 1 and June 30 need not comply with the requirements of section (a) for that educational year. A lawyer newly admitted between July 1 and December 31 shall comply with the requirements of section (a) for that educational year by completing two-thirds of the requirement.

5. **Out-of-State Compliance.** An active member of the bar who resides in another MCLE jurisdiction, and who is subject to and complying with the MCLE requirements for that jurisdiction, shall be exempted from the requirements of section (a) for the educational year in question. However, any member exempted under this section must satisfy the requirements of section (c).

6. **Other Exemptions.** Upon application and showing of undue hardship, the MCLE Committee may exempt an active member from the requirements of section (a) or extend the deadline for compliance for a period of not more than one year. Any consideration for additional time past one year based on a continuing hardship, would require a new application.

(c) Affidavit of Compliance.

On or before September 15 of each calendar year, every member who was active during the educational year, and not otherwise exempted, shall file with the board a completed affidavit or certification of compliance demonstrating full compliance with this rule. As an alternative to filing a written certificate, the board may allow certification to be filed electronically in a method and form as approved by the board. The affidavit will be considered timely received if the envelope in which it is mailed is postmarked on or before September 15, or if the affidavit is date-stamped received by State Bar personnel on or before the close of business September 15.

(d) Delinquent Compliance Fee and Delinquent Affidavit Filing Fee.

1. *Delinquent Compliance Fee.* A member who was active during the educational year and not otherwise exempted and who fails to complete the requirements of section (a) by the end of the educational year shall be deemed delinquent. Failure to obtain the required 15 hours of continuing legal education credit by the June 30 deadline will result in the following delinquency fees:

   a. If CLE requirements are completed between July 1 and July 31, a delinquent compliance fee of $33.00 is assessed.

b. If CLE requirements are completed between August 1 and August 31, a delinquent compliance fee of $67.00 is assessed.

c. If CLE requirements are completed between September 1 and September 15, a delinquent compliance fee of $133.00 is assessed.

d. If CLE requirements are completed after September 15, a delinquent compliance fee of $166.00 is assessed.

Such fees shall be in addition to any fee for delinquent filing of the affidavit required by section (c) as set forth below in sub § 2. Failure to complete the requirements of section (a) by September 15 may result in a motion for summary suspension pursuant to section (h) of this rule.

2. *Delinquent Affidavit Filing Fee*. An affidavit not filed when due under sections (b)(5) or (c) shall be deemed delinquent. A member who was active during the educational year and not otherwise exempted shall be subject to the following delinquent filing fees:

a. Members who file their affidavits between September 16 and October 15 will be assessed a delinquent filing fee of $133.00.

b. Members who file their affidavits between October 16 and November 15 will be assessed a delinquent filing fee of $166.00.

c. Members who file their affidavits after November 16 will be assessed a delinquent filing fee of $200.00.

Failure to file the affidavit by December 15 may result in a motion for summary suspension pursuant to section (h) of this rule.

(e) Status Changes.

1. Return from Inactive or Retired Status to Active Status. Before a member will be permitted to change status from inactive or retired to active, that member must show completion of hours of continuing legal education activity equivalent to those required in section (a) of this rule for each of the last two years for which the member was on inactive or retired status.

2. Any inactive, retired, or judicial member who transfers to active status shall comply with the educational requirements of section (a) of this rule in effect for the educational year in which such transfer occurs.

(f) Records.

Every active member, not exempted, shall maintain records (as defined in Regulation 101(l)) evidencing participation in continuing legal education for each education year. The lawyer shall preserve these records for two years after the filing of the affidavit.

(g) Audits of Compliance.

Each year the board shall randomly select a designated number of active members, except those exempt under section (b)(2) of this rule, to audit for compliance with this rule.

(h) Regulation Authority.

The administration of the continuing legal education requirements and the audits of compliance as provided by this rule shall be in accordance with regulations established by the board.

(i) Summary Suspension.

Upon notice of the state bar pursuant to Rule 62, any member who fails to comply with this rule for any educational year in which he or she was an active member and not otherwise exempted may be summarily suspended by order of the board, provided that a notice by certified mail, return receipt requested, of such noncompliance shall have been sent to the member, mailed to his or her last address of record in the State Bar office, at least 30 days prior to such suspension. The member may be reinstated upon completion of the continuing legal education activity requirements for each educational year in which the member was suspended with proof of cure, payment of a reinstatement fee of $100.00, all delinquency fees pursuant to section (d) of this rule and in accordance with Rule 64(f) of these rules.

(j) Confidentiality of Records.

Unless otherwise directed by the board, the file, records, and proceedings, as they relate to or arise out of any failure of any active member to satisfy the requirements of the rule, shall be deemed confidential to the same extent as bar disciplinary proceedings and shall not be disclosed except in furtherance of the duties of the board or upon the request of the active member affected or as they may be introduced in evidence or otherwise produced in proceedings under the rule.

(k) Immunity from Civil Suit.

Communications to the court, state bar, or committee thereof relating to compliance with this rule and testimony given in compliance proceedings shall be absolutely privileged conduct, and no civil action predicated thereon may be instituted against any witness. Members of the board, MCLE Committee, and staff shall be immune from suit for any conduct in the course of their official duties to the extent permitted by law.

ARKANSAS

Rule 1. Continuing Legal Education Board

1.(A) There is hereby established the Arkansas Continuing Legal Education Board (hereinafter referred to as the Board). The Board shall be composed of nine voting members, appointed by the Arkansas Supreme Court, all of whom are resident members of the Bar of Arkansas. In addition, the Dean of each Arkansas law school accredited by the American Bar Association shall be an ex-officio member, without vote.

1.(B) There shall be at least one Board member from each of the four congressional districts.

1.(C) All subsequent appointments shall be made by the Arkansas Supreme Court for terms of three years. Board members may be reappointed, but may serve no more than two terms of three years. The Arkansas Supreme Court shall fill all vacancies, with the appointee to serve the remaining term, for such position, subject to reappointment in accord with this paragraph. Any Board member whose term expires shall continue in office until his successor is appointed and qualified.

1.(D) The Board shall, annually, by majority vote, elect a Chairman from among its voting members. The Director of the Office of Professional Programs for the Arkansas Supreme Court shall serve as Secretary, without a vote. Board members shall be entitled to reasonable reimbursement for expenses and such per diem compensation as the Court may from time to time direct.

1.(E) The Board shall have the following duties and responsibilities:

Exercise general supervisory authority over these rules, to include the imposition of sanctions for noncompliance with these rules, as well as the implementation and administration of these rules;
Adopt regulations consistent with these rules, to be submitted to the Arkansas Supreme Court for approval prior to their implementation;
The Board may appoint committees as may be necessary to efficiently administer these rules; however, all matters concerning sanctions for noncompliance with these rules shall be the duty and responsibility of the
Board.

In cases of extreme hardship due to mental or physical disability, the Board may approve a substitute plan by which individuals may meet the requirements of these rules; and
Such other specific grants of authority as may be set out in these rules.
1.(F) A majority of all voting Board members shall constitute a quorum.

Rule 2. Scope

(A) Except as noted elsewhere in Rule 2, these rules shall apply to every member of the Bar of Arkansas, including all levels of the State and Federal Judiciary, and all attorneys who may be suspended during any reporting period due to nonpayment of license fee or action by the Supreme Court Committee on Professional Conduct. When used in the course of these rules, the word attorney shall include judges.

(B) Exemptions: Any attorney or Judge who attains age 70 or completes 40 years of licensure as an Arkansas lawyer, during any given reporting period, is exempt from all requirements of the Arkansas Rules for Minimum Continuing Legal Education (hereinafter referred to as CLE) for that reporting period as well as all subsequent reporting periods.

(C) Non Resident Attorneys:

(1) Attorneys who are members of the Bar of Arkansas, but reside outside this State, are required to meet the minimum continuing legal education requirements of their resident state. Such attorneys shall complete annual certification forms to that effect. These forms will be filed with the Arkansas Continuing Legal Education Board on or before the October 31 which succeeds the reporting period in question. Such certifications shall be subject to verification through the agency which administers the continuing legal education program for such resident state. In the event an attorney is a member of the Bar of Arkansas, yet resides in a state or foreign jurisdiction where there is no continuing legal education requirement, such attorneys shall be annually required to file with the Arkansas Continuing Legal Education Board a certification form confirming that fact. This form shall be filed on or before the October 31 which succeeds the reporting period in question. Further, in the event an attorney returns to the practice of law in the State of Arkansas from a state where there has been no continuing legal education requirement that attorney shall be required, by the end of the first reporting period after the attorney's return, to acquire thirty-six (36) hours of accredited continuing legal education.

(2) Nonetheless, an Arkansas licensed attorney or judge who resides: in a state which does not require continuing legal education; in a foreign jurisdiction; or, in a state which requires continuing legal education but is not licensed in that state and is therefore prohibited from participating in the continuing legal education program of that state, may remain current as regards Arkansas CLE requirements. Such attorneys may do so by meeting the twelve (12) hour requirement as set out in Rule 3.(A). The Secretary shall obtain from such attorneys appropriate documentation to confirm compliance with the Arkansas CLE program. In the event attorneys are in compliance with Rule 3(A) during the reporting period preceding their return to the practice of law in Arkansas, they shall not be subject to the thirty-six (36) hour requirement mentioned in paragraph 2.(C)(1) above. In the event an attorney has elected to remain current, yet fails to acquire 12 hours of approved CLE during any reporting period, that attorney shall be subject to the sanctions of Rule 6. 2.(D)

(D) Inactive Status:

(1) At anytime during a reporting period, an attorney on active status, with the exception of sitting judges, may take inactive status for the purpose of those rules. Such status may be secured by filing a petition in accord with Section 25 A.(7) of the Procedures of the Arkansas Supreme Court Regulating Professional Conduct of Attorneys at Law (Procedures) or its successor provision. By taking inactive status, the attorney shall be exempt from the minimum educational requirements of rule 3 for that reporting period and subsequent reporting periods.

(2) An attorney may return to active practice by petition filed as set forth in Section 23 of the Procedures or its successor provision.

(3) Such attorneys shall be required to obtain thirty-six (36) hours of qualified continuing legal education between the date of return to active status (which is the date the reinstatement fee is received by the Board) and the end of the next succeeding reporting period.

(E) Readmission/Reinstatement

(1) An attorney who is re-admitted to the Bar of Arkansas following voluntary resignation, voluntary surrender in lieu of discipline, or order of disbarment shall be required by the end of the next year's reporting period following the attorney's readmission to acquire thirty-six (36) hours of accredited continuing legal education, with at least three (3) of the required hours being in ethics.

(2) This thirty-six (36) hour requirement shall also apply to any attorney who is reinstated by the Board of Law Examiners following non-payment of license fees for a period of more than three (3) years and to attorneys whose license has been suspended by the Committee on Professional Conduct for a period of at least three (3) years.

History: Amended and substituted July 9, 1990; amended January 13, 1992, effective March 1, 1992; amended June 27, 1994, effective July 1, 1994; amended June 27, 2002; amended November 30, 2006, effective January 1, 2007; amended and effective October 10, 2013.

Rule 3. Minimum Educational Requirements

3.(A) Every member of the Bar of Arkansas, except as may be otherwise provided by these rules and, excepting those attorneys granted voluntary inactive status by the Arkansas Supreme Court Committee on Professional Conduct, shall complete 12 hours of approved continuing legal education during each reporting period as defined by Rule 5.(A) below. Of those 12 hours, at least one hour shall be ethics, which may include professionalism as defined by Regulation 3.02. In addition, an attorney or judge may carry over accredited hours in accord with the provisions of Rule 5.(A), including one hour of ethics which may be carried forward to the succeeding reporting period.

3.(B) This minimum requirement must be met through courses conducted by sponsors approved by the Board, or individual courses that have been approved by the Board, or such other programs, courses, or other educational materials that the Board may approve pursuant to Rule 4.

3.(C) An hour of continuing legal education shall include at least sixty minutes of instruction, exclusive of meals,introductions, or other non-educational activities.

3.(D) The Board is authorized and encouraged to consider the requirement of particular course content, such as professional or judicial ethics, as part of the minimum educational requirement.

Rule 4. Accreditation

4.(A) The Board shall be the exclusive authority for accreditation of continuing legal education sponsors or programs. However, the Board may delegate to a subcommittee, in accord with Rule 1.(E)(3), the authority to review submissions by new sponsors. Further, the Board may delegate to its Secretary the authority to approve or deny programs submitted by previously accredited sponsors, or by sponsors who have previously had individual program(s) approved by the Board. The Board, through its Secretary, shall provide an annual report to the Arkansas Supreme Court which shall reflect summary information with regard to program approvals or denials, attorney suspension information, and such other matters as the Board may direct.

4.(B) Approval of Accredited Sponsors:

An organization, or entity, may seek Board designation as an accredited sponsor;
In order to receive such a designation the organization or entity must establish to the satisfaction of the Board that it is regularly engaged in offering continuing legal education and is recognized as a provider of continuing legal education on a national basis;
Subsequent to designation as an accredited sponsor, programs offered by that sponsor outside this State shall be approved provided such courses meet the requirements of Rule 4.(C);
Programs conducted by sponsors accredited in another state or by a national continuing legal education accrediting body may be approved, provided the Secretary is satisfied that the sponsor meets the requirements of this Rule; and,
Accredited sponsors must abide by all reasonable requests for information or course materials from the Board, or its Secretary, and the Board reserves the right to withdraw accredited sponsor designation for failure to meet the requirements of these rules.
4.(C) Individual course or activity approval:
The Board may, upon application, approve continuing legal education courses or activities provided such courses meet the following standards:

The course must contribute directly to professional competence of attorneys and judges, or to their education with respect to professional or ethical obligations;
Course presenters must have the necessary experience or academic skills to conduct the course effectively;
Prior to, during, or after the course, each attendee must be provided with written course materials of a quality and quantity which indicate that adequate time has been devoted to the speaker's preparation and that the written
materials will be of value to the attendees in the course of their practice. In the event written materials are not provided before, or during the program, the program will not be subject to pre-approval by the Board. In the event materials are submitted after the program, the Board will make a determination as to what, if any, credit shall be
given for the course;

The course must be presented in a suitable setting, which provides attendees with adequate writing surfaces, provided that the Secretary is satisfied that the course substantially complies with the requirements of Rule 4.(C);

During activities presented by means of videotape, audiotape, or other such systems, there must be an opportunity to ask questions of course faculty or a qualified commentator;

The sponsor must encourage participation by attorneys as planners, authors, panelists, or lecturers;

The sponsor must make available to the Board, or its Secretary, upon request, information concerning the course, which might include a list of attendees or individual affidavits signed by attendees, the course brochure, a description of the method or manner of presentation, and a set of all written materials pertinent to the course; and

The course must be subject to evaluation before, during, and after presentation.

4.(D) The Board is authorized and encouraged to grant approval to all sources of continuing legal education which meet the relevant standards of Rule 4.(C), including: publication of law related articles in legal journals; preparation of bar examination materials; preparation for, and conduct of, approved continuing legal education courses; participation in regularly scheduled courses conducted by American Bar Association accredited law schools; and "In House" educational programs conducted by law firms or other law related entities. The Board shall also be authorized to determine the amount of approved hours such activities are worth and may limit the number of such hours that may be applied to the minimum requirement.

4.(E) It is presumed that sponsor accreditation, or individual program accreditation, will be sought well in advance of the event. However, the Board may accredit a sponsor or individual program after the event.

4.(F) In the event the Secretary denies approval of an individual course or sponsor, the aggrieved sponsor may, in writing, request that the Board review such denial.

Rule 5. Reporting

5.(A) Credit for approved continuing legal education hours will be given for courses or activities conducted from July 1 through June 30 of each year, and for the purposes of these rules, this period of time shall be known as the "reporting period." If an attorney or a judge acquires, during such reporting period, approved continuing legal education in excess of twelve (12) hours, the excess credit may be carried forward and applied to the education requirement for the succeeding reporting period only. The maximum number of CLE hours one may carry forward is twelve (12), which may include one hour of ethics.

5.(B) Sponsors may be required to report attendance to the Board or its Secretary. Such reports may be required promptly after completion of each program or activity. Attorneys may also report approved activities using a certificate approved by the Board.

5.(C) The Board, through its Secretary, shall maintain current records of CLE attendance for each attorney to whom these rules apply. Pursuant to Board regulation, they shall be made available to such attorneys.

5.(D) During the course of the reporting period, the Board, through its Secretary, may provide interim reports by first class mail to those attorneys subject to the 12 hour requirement of Rule 3.(A). Such reports will state the number of approved CLE hours each attorney has of record with the Board. On or before July 31 after the conclusion of the immediately preceding reporting period, the Board, through its Secretary, shall provide a final report by first class mail to those attorneys. The number of approved CLE hours stated in the interim and final reports shall be presumed correct unless the attorney notifies the Board otherwise. If the final report shows acquisition of 12 or more approved CLE hours during the reporting period, the attorney shall be deemed to be in compliance with these rules and need not take any further action for the immediately preceding reporting period.

In the event the final report reflects that an attorney has failed to meet the 12 hour requirement of Rule 3.(A), the final report will be accompanied by an acknowledgment of deficiency form. Such attorneys shall sign the acknowledgment of deficiency form and file it with the Board on or before the following August 31. Subsequently, such attorneys shall cure any deficiency by December 1 and provide appropriate documentation to the Board no later than the following December 15. CLE hours reported to the Board pursuant to the acknowledgment of deficiency shall first be applied to the deficiency and any remaining hours will be applied to the current reporting period.

Attorney members of the National Guard or reserves of any branch of the Armed Forces which are mobilized during the reporting period by Gubernatorial or Presidential order shall have an additional 180 days to meet each of the respective filing requirements set forth in the preceding paragraph. Such entitlement shall be based upon appropriate documentation to establish the date of mobilization and the date of release from active duty. Upon request of an affected attorney who is entitled to the relief set forth in this paragraph, the Board may grant additional extensions of time in order to meet the respective filing requirements set forth in the preceding paragraphs. The Board may also waive any of the various fees set forth in Regulation 5.01 of the Regulations of the Board. (Amended by per curiam order May 6, 2004.)

5.(E) The Board is authorized to assess costs against delinquent attorneys in the form of a reasonable fee for filing late and filing a deficiency plan.

5.(F) Newly admitted attorneys shall be subject to the twelve hour minimum requirement during the reporting period that follows the reporting period in which they are admitted.

5.(G) All filings pursuant to Rule 5 will be made with the Secretary to the Arkansas Continuing Legal Education Board, unless the Board directs otherwise. In addition, all such filings that require the signature of an attorney shall be subject to the requirements of Rule 8.4 of the Model Rules of Professional Conduct for Lawyers or its successor rule.

Rule 6. Noncompliance And Sanctions

6.(A) If an attorney to whom these rules apply either fails: to file timely the acknowledgement of deficiency or cure the deficiency as required by Rule 5.(D); or, to file timely an out of state certification form in accord with Rule 2.(C), the attorney shall not be in compliance with these rules.

6.(B) Within 30 days after an attorney fails to comply with any provision of the preceding paragraph, the Board, through its Secretary, shall serve a notice of noncompliance on the affected attorney. Such notice shall be sent by first class mail to the address the attorney maintains with the office of the Arkansas Supreme Court Clerk.

6.(C) The notice shall contain a statement of the nature of the noncompliance. The attorney must, within 30 days of the date of the notice of noncompliance, provide the Board written evidence that the attorney is either in compliance or has corrected the noncompliance.

6.(D) If within the allotted time as set out in paragraph 6.(C) above, the attorney fails either to provide written evidence of compliance or that the noncompliance has been corrected, the Board, through its Secretary, shall serve a notice of intent to suspend upon the affected attorney. Such notice shall be mailed to the address the attorney maintains with the Clerk of the Arkansas Supreme Court. The notice shall be sent by certified mail, return receipt requested. Such notice shall apprise the attorney that his or her Arkansas law license shall be considered for suspension at the next regularly scheduled meeting of the Board. Such notice shall be sent at least 20 days prior to that meeting. Upon written request of the attorney, a hearing shall be conducted at that meeting.

6.(E) Hearing Procedure:

The Board, in the performance of its responsibilities under these rules, shall have the authority to request issuance of summons or subpoena from the Office of the Supreme Court Clerk, and the Clerk shall issue same. Such requests shall be signed by the Chairman of the Board, or its Secretary.
Witnesses may be sworn by the Board Chair or any member acting in his or her stead, or by any individual authorized to administer oaths, and upon request, a record shall be made at the expense of the attorney. Such hearings are civil in nature and the standard for decision is preponderance of the evidence.
The hearing shall be open to the public.
After the hearing, the Board may retire to executive session to deliberate. Thereafter, its decision shall be publicly announced and, if not unanimous, there shall be a statement of votes by individual members.
The Board shall take action by a majority vote of the voting members present.
6.(F) Authorized dispositions at Board meeting subsequent to service of notice of intent to suspend:

The Board may dismiss the matter if records in possession of the Board show that the attorney has achieved compliance. However, such dismissal may be made contingent upon payment of a delinquency assessment as authorized by Rule 5.(E) and the regulations adopted pursuant to that rule; or,
The Board may enter an order deferring further action for no more than 90 days to allow the attorney to achieve compliance. Subsequent to the period of deferment, the Board may suspend the attorney in accordance with Rule 6.(F)(3), or, dismiss the action in accord with the preceding paragraph, or, take such other permissible actions it may deem appropriate; or,
The Board may suspend the license of the attorney subject to reinstatement pursuant to paragraph 6.(H) below. Such suspension shall become effective on the date of filing of the notice and order of suspension with the Arkansas Supreme Court Clerk. (Hereinafter referred to as "The Order of Suspension.")
6.(G) Promptly after a Board vote of suspension, the Secretary shall notify the affected attorney by way of certified mail, return receipt requested. In addition, the Secretary shall promptly file the order of suspension with the Clerk of the Arkansas Supreme Court and notify

Arkansas state judges of general jurisdiction and the United States District Court Clerk.

Attorneys who are suspended may request a stay of such suspension pending a hearing by the Board. Such a request shall be made in conjunction with a petition for reinstatement. The request shall be presented to the Board, through its Secretary, in the form required by Rule 6.(H). Such submissions shall be ruled upon by the Board Chairperson, or a member designated by the Chairperson. To be considered for review, the petition for reinstatement and request for stay must either:

establish that the attorney had obtained the requisite number of CLE hours, or filed the appropriate documents, to be in compliance on or before the vote of suspension on that attorney; or,

confirm that subsequent to the vote of suspension, but prior to filing the petition for reinstatement and request for stay, the attorney had obtained the requisite number of CLE hours to be in compliance or had filed appropriate documents to achieve compliance. Any request for stay of suspension must contain an affirmation by the attorney that he or she has not engaged in the practice of law subsequent to receipt of notification of suspension or actual knowledge of suspension, whichever is earlier.

6.(H) An attorney who has been suspended pursuant to these rules who desires reinstatement shall file a petition for reinstatement (which in appropriate cases may incorporate a request for stay of suspension) with the Secretary of the Board. The petition shall be sworn and properly acknowledged by a notary public or any official authorized to take oaths. The petition may include the applicant's reason(s) for noncompliance, state that the applicant is presently in compliance, or provide any other material information pertinent to the applicant's petition. The petition must contain an affirmation that the petitioner has not engaged in the practice of law subsequent to receipt of notification of suspension or actual knowledge of suspension, whichever is earlier. The petitioner may request a hearing before the Board. In such case, a hearing will be conducted in accordance with the provisions set out in Rules 6.(E) and 6.(F), and Section 6 of the regulations. In the event the attorney is reinstated, the Board may set additional educational requirements as a condition of reinstatement and may assess reinstatement fees and late filing fees consistent with its regulations.

Rule 7. Appeals

7.(A) Final determinations as to accreditation of a sponsor by the Secretary or a committee of the Board shall, upon request of the aggrieved sponsor, be reviewed by the Board. There shall be no further review of such determinations.

7.(B) Final determinations by the Board, which result in suspension of an attorney, may be appealed to the Arkansas Supreme Court. Such appeal shall be heard de novo on the record from the Board proceedings.

7.(C) To effect an appeal, the suspended attorney shall file the record with the Supreme Court Clerk within thirty days from the entry of order of suspension. The appellant shall bear the cost of record preparation.

Source URL: https://courts.arkansas.gov/rules-and-administrative-orders/rules-for-minimum-continuing-legal-education

CALIFORNIA

DIVISION 4. MINIMUM CONTINUING LEGAL EDUCATION

Chapter 1 Purpose and scope

Rule 2.50 Purpose of MCLE

Rules for Minimum Continuing Legal Education (MCLE) require active members of the State Bar of California to remain current regarding the law, the obligations and standards of the legal profession, and the management of their practices. A member's involuntary enrollment as inactive for failing to comply with these rules is public information available on the State Bar Web site.

Rule 2.50 adopted effective January 1, 2008.

Rule 2.51 Definitions

(A)   An "MCLE activity" is continuing legal education that the State Bar approves as meeting standards for MCLE credit.

(B)   A "provider" is an individual or entity approved by the State Bar to grant MCLE credit for an MCLE activity.

(C)   "MCLE credit" is the number of credit hours that a member may claim to meet the requirements of these rules.

(D)   A "credit hour" is sixty minutes actually spent in an MCLE activity, less any time for breaks or other activities that lack educational content. A credit hour is reported to the nearest quarter hour in decimals.

(E)   An "approved jurisdiction" is recognized by the State Bar as having MCLE requirements that substantially meet State Bar standards for MCLE activities and computing MCLE credit hours in a manner acceptable to the State Bar. Approved jurisdictions are listed on the State Bar Web site.

(F)   A "participatory activity" is an MCLE activity for which the provider must verify attendance. Participatory activities may be presented in person or delivered by electronic means.

(G)   A "self-study activity" is any MCLE activity identified in Rule 2.83. Self-study activities may be presented in person or delivered by electronic means.

Rule 2.51 adopted effective January 1, 2008; amended effective July 1, 2014.

Rule 2.52 MCLE Activities

To receive MCLE credit, a member must complete an MCLE activity that meets State Bar standards.

(A)   The MCLE activity must relate to legal subjects directly relevant to members of the State Bar or have significant current professional and practical content.

(B)   The presenter of the MCLE activity must have significant professional or academic experience related to its content.

(C)   Promotional material must state that the MCLE activity is approved for MCLE credit or that a request for approval is pending; specify the amount of credit offered; and indicate whether any of the credit may be claimed for required MCLE in legal ethics, elimination of bias, or competence issues.

(D)   If the activity lasts one hour or more, the provider must make substantive written materials relevant to the MCLE activity available either before or during every MCLE activity. Any materials provided online must remain online for at least thirty calendar days following the MCLE activity.

(E)   Programs and classes must be scheduled so that participants are free of interruptions.

Rule 2.52 adopted effective January 1, 2008; amended effective January 1, 2013; amended effective July 1, 2014.

Rule 2.53 New members

(A)   A new member is permanently assigned to a compliance group on the date of admission.

(B)   The initial compliance period for a new member begins on the first day of the month in which the member was admitted. It ends when the period ends for the compliance group. If the initial period is less than the period for the compliance group, the required credit hours may be reduced as provided in these rules.[1]

(C)   A new member may not claim credit for education taken before the initial compliance period.

Rule 2.53 adopted effective January 1, 2008.

Rule 2.54 Exemptions

---

[1] Rule 2.72 (C).

(A)   The following active members are exempt from MCLE requirements, provided they claim the exemption in their assigned compliance periods using My State Bar Profile online or an MCLE Compliance Form:

    (1)   officers and elected officials of the State of California;

    (2)   full-time professors at law schools accredited by the State Bar of California or the American Bar Association;

    (3)   those employed full-time by the State of California as attorneys or administrative law judges on a permanent or probationary basis, regardless of their working hours, who do not otherwise practice law; and

    (4)   those employed full-time by the United States government as attorneys or administrative law judges on a permanent or probationary basis, regardless of their working hours, who do not otherwise practice law.

(B)   Members whom this rule exempts by reason of their employment with the State of California or the United States government may provide pro bono legal services through a California qualified legal services project or a qualified support center[2], or through a legal services project or support center that primarily provides legal services without charge to indigent persons in another jurisdiction and is funded by the Legal Services Corporation or the Older Americans Act or receives funding administered by the jurisdiction's interest on lawyers trust accounts program.

Rule 2.54 adopted effective January 1, 2008; amended effective November 4, 2011.

Rule 2.55 Modifications

A member prevented from fulfilling the MCLE requirement for a substantial part of a compliance period because of a physical or mental condition, natural disaster, family emergency, financial hardship, or other good cause may apply for modification of MCLE compliance requirements. The State Bar must approve any modification.

Rule 2.55 adopted effective January 1, 2008.

<u>Chapter 2. Compliance</u>

Rule 2.70 Compliance groups

---

[2] Business & Professions Code § 6213.

A member is permanently assigned to one of three compliance groups on the basis of the first letter of the member's last name at the date of admission.[3] The three groups are A-G, H-M, and N-Z. The member remains in the compliance group despite any subsequent change of last name.

Rule 2.70 adopted effective January 1, 2008.

Rule 2.71 Compliance periods

A compliance period consists of thirty-six months. It begins on the first day of February and ends three years later on the last day of January. The three compliance groups begin and end their compliance periods in different years. A member must report MCLE compliance no later than the day following the end of the compliance period. The report must be made online using My State Bar Profile or with an MCLE Compliance Form. Fees for noncompliance are set forth in the Schedule of Charges and Deadlines.

Rule 2.71 adopted effective January 1, 2008.

Rule 2.72 Requirements

(A)   Unless these rules indicate otherwise, a member who has been active throughout a thirty-six-month compliance period must complete twenty-five credit hours of MCLE activities. No more than twelve and a half credit hours may be self-study.[4] Total hours must include no less than 6 hours as follows:

    (1)   at least four hours of legal ethics;

    (2)   at least one hour dealing with the recognition and elimination of bias in the legal profession and society by reason of, but not limited to, sex, color, race, religion, ancestry, national origin, physical disability, age, or sexual orientation; and

    (3)   at least one hour of education addressing substance abuse or other mental or physical issues that impair a member's ability to perform legal services with competence.

(B)   Required education in legal ethics, elimination of bias, or competence issues may be a component of an approved MCLE activity that deals with another topic.

(C)   A member may reduce the required twenty-five hours in proportion to the number of full months the member was inactive or exempt in the thirty-six-month

---

[3] A historical exception exists. When the MCLE program was established in 1992, members were permanently assigned to compliance groups on the basis of their last names at the time, regardless of any different last names they might have used previously.
[4] Rule 2.83.

compliance period. Up to half the reduced hours may be self-study.[5] A tool for applying this formula is available at the State Bar Web site.

(D)   Excess credit hours may not be applied to the next compliance period.[6]

Rule 2.72 adopted effective January 1, 2008; amended effective July 1, 2014.

Rule 2.73 Record of MCLE

For a year after reporting MCLE compliance, a member must retain and provide upon demand and to the satisfaction of the State Bar

(A)   a provider's certificate of attendance;

(B)   a record of self-study that includes the title, provider, credit hours, and date of each MCLE activity; or

(C)   proof of exempt status.

Rule 2.73 adopted effective January 1, 2008; amended effective July 1, 2014.

Chapter 3. MCLE Activities approved for MCLE credit

Rule 2.80 Attending programs and classes

A member may claim MCLE credit for attending a MCLE activity, such as a lecture, panel discussion, or law school class, in person or by technological means.

Rule 2.80 adopted effective January 1, 2008.

Rule 2.81 Speaking

A member may claim participatory MCLE credit for speaking at an approved MCLE activity.

(A)   A principal speaker, who is responsible for preparing and delivering a program or class and its related materials, may claim

(1)   actual speaking time multiplied by four for the first presentation; or

(2)   actual speaking time only for each time a presentation is repeated without significant change.

(B)   A panelist may claim

---

[5] Rule 2.83.
[6] But see Rule 2.93.

(1)   either of the following for the first panel presentation:

    (a)   scheduled individual speaking time multiplied by four, plus the actual time spent in attendance at the remainder of the presentation; or

    (b)   when times have not been scheduled for individual speakers, an equal share of the total time for all speakers multiplied by four plus the actual time spent in attendance at the remainder of the presentation.

(2)   actual speaking time only for each time a presentation is repeated without significant change.

(C)   A member who introduces speakers or serves as a moderator may claim only the MCLE credit available to any attendee.

Rule 2.81 adopted effective January 1, 2008; amended effective July 1, 2014.

Rule 2.82 Teaching

A member may claim participatory MCLE credit for teaching a law school course.

(A)   A member assigned to teach a course may claim no more than the credit hours granted by the law school multiplied by twelve or actual speaking time for required MCLE in legal ethics, elimination of bias, or competence issues.

(B)   A guest lecturer or substitute teacher may claim

    (1)   actual speaking time multiplied by four for the first presentation; or

    (2)   actual speaking time only for each time a presentation is repeated without significant change.

Rule 2.82 adopted effective January 1, 2008; amended effective July 1, 2014.

Rule 2.83 Self-study

A member may claim up to half the credit hours required in a compliance period for

(A)   completing MCLE activities for which attendance is not verified by a provider and the MCLE activities were prepared within the preceding five years;

(B)   taking an open- or closed-book self-test and submitting it to a provider who returns it with a grade and explanations of correct answers; or

(C)   authoring or co-authoring written materials that

      (1)   have contributed to the member's legal education;

      (2)   have been published or accepted for publication; and

      (3)   were not prepared in the ordinary course of employment or in connection with an oral presentation at an approved MCLE activity.

Rule 2.83 adopted effective January 1, 2008; amended effective July 1, 2014.

Rule 2.84 Legal specialization

A member may claim MCLE credit for educational activities that the California Board of Legal Specialization approves for certification or recertification.

Rule 2.84 adopted effective January 1, 2008; amended effective July 1, 2014.

Rule 2.85 Education taken while physically out of state

(A)   A member may claim MCLE credit for an MCLE activity authorized by an approved jurisdiction if it meets the requirements of these rules and if the member attends or does the MCLE activity outside California. A member may not claim credit for such an activity, including self-study, when physically present in California unless the State Bar has specifically approved it.

(B)   A member who qualifies for an MCLE activity authorized by an approved jurisdiction may claim the amount of credit authorized by the jurisdiction. No special procedure is required to claim the credit.

Rule 2.85 adopted effective January 1, 2008; amended effective July 1, 2014.

Rule 2.86 Member credit request

A member may apply for MCLE credit for an educational activity directly relevant to the member's practice but not otherwise approved if the activity substantially meets State Bar standards. The application must be submitted with the appropriate fee.

Rule 2.86 adopted effective January 1, 2008; amended effective July 1, 2014.

Rule 2.87 Bar examinations and MPRE

A member may not claim MCLE credit for preparing for or taking a bar examination or the Multistate Professional Responsibility Examination (MPRE).

Rule 2.87 adopted effective January 1, 2008.

Chapter 4. Noncompliance

Rule 2.90 Definition

Noncompliance is failure to

(A)   complete the required education during the compliance period or an extension of it;

(B)   report compliance or claim exemption from MCLE requirements;

(C)   keep a record of MCLE compliance[7]; or

(D)   pay fees for noncompliance.

Rule 2.90 adopted effective January 1, 2008.

Rule 2.91 Notice of noncompliance

(A)   A member who is sent a notice of noncompliance must comply with its terms or be involuntarily enrolled as inactive. An inactive member is not eligible to practice law.

(B)   If the notice requires the member to complete credit hours for the previous compliance period, any excess credit hours may be counted toward the current compliance period.

Rule 2.91 adopted effective January 1, 2008.

Rule 2.92 Enrollment as inactive for MCLE noncompliance

A member who fails to comply with a notice of noncompliance is enrolled as inactive and is not eligible to practice law. The enrollment is administrative and no hearing is required.

Rule 2.92 adopted effective January 1, 2008.

Rule 2.93 Reinstatement following MCLE noncompliance

Enrollment as inactive for MCLE noncompliance terminates when a member submits proof of compliance and pays noncompliance fees. Credit hours that exceed those required for compliance may be counted toward the current period.

Rule 2.93 adopted effective January 1, 2008.

---

[7] Rule 2.73.

COLORADO

STATE OF COLORADO
SUPREME COURT
BOARD OF CONTINUING LEGAL AND JUDICIAL EDUCATION
1300 Broadway, Suite 510
Denver, Colorado 80203
(303) 928-7771

RULES AND REGULATIONS GOVERNING
MANDATORY CONTINUING LEGAL AND JUDICIAL EDUCATION
FOR THE STATE OF COLORADO

(As adopted by the Colorado Supreme Court, August 14, 1978
and amended through September 1, 2014)

RULE 260: MANDATORY CONTINUING LEGAL AND JUDICIAL EDUCATION

PREAMBLE: STATEMENT OF PURPOSE

As society becomes more complex, the delivery of legal services likewise becomes more complex. The public rightly expects that practicing attorneys, in their practice of law, and judges, in the performance of their duties, will continue their legal and judicial education throughout the period of their service to society. It is the purpose of these rules to make mandatory a minimum amount of continuing legal education for practicing attorneys and judges in order to foster and promote competence and professionalism in the practice of law and the administration of justice.

RULE 260.1: DEFINITIONS

(1)   The "Board" is the Board of Continuing Legal and Judicial Education.

(2)   "Continuing legal education" is any legal, judicial or other educational activity accredited by the Board.

(3)   An attorney in "inactive status" is one who has elected such status pursuant to Rule 227A.

(4)   "Registered attorney" is an attorney who has paid the registration fee required by Rule 227A for the current year and who is not on inactive status or suspended by the Supreme Court from the practice of law.

(5)   "Judge" is a judge who is subject to the jurisdiction of the Commission on Judicial Qualifications or the Denver County Court Judicial Qualifications Commission.

(6)   "These rules" refer to rules numbered 260.1 through 260.7 of the Rules of Civil Procedure.

(7)   A "unit" of continuing legal education is a measurement factor combining time and quality assigned by the Board to all or part of a particular continuing legal educational activity.

RULE 260.2: MINIMUM EDUCATIONAL REQUIREMENTS

(1)   Every registered attorney and every judge shall complete 45 units of continuing legal education during each applicable three-year compliance period as provided in these rules.

(2)   At least seven of the 45 units will be devoted to continuing legal education specifically addressed to legal or judicial ethics.

(3)   All registered attorneys admitted after January 1, 1979 shall become subject to the minimal educational requirements set forth in these rules on the date of their initial admission to the bar of the State of Colorado. Their first compliance period shall begin on that date and end on December 31 of the third full calendar year following the year of admission.

(4)   This subsection 4 is repealed and replaced by 201.14(3).

(5)   Upon being reinstated pursuant to Paragraphs (3) or (8) of Rule 227A, any registered attorney who has been suspended under Paragraph (2) of Rule 227A, shall become subject to the minimal educational requirements set forth in these rules on the date of reinstatement. The first compliance period shall begin on that date and end on December 31 of the third full calendar year following the year of reinstatement, provided the date of reinstatement is more than one year after the date of suspension or transfer to inactive status. Otherwise, the compliance period shall be the same as it would have been absent the suspension or transfer.

(6)   Units of continuing legal education completed after the adoption of this rule by the Supreme Court and prior to January 1, 1979 may be used to meet the minimum educational requirement for the first applicable compliance period. Units of continuing legal education completed in excess of the required units of continuing legal education in any applicable compliance period may not be used to meet the minimum educational requirements in any succeeding compliance period.

COLORADO

RULE 260.3: BOARD OF CONTINUING LEGAL AND JUDICIAL EDUCATION

(1)   There is established a Board of Continuing Legal and Judicial Education which shall consist of nine members appointed by the Supreme Court. Six of the members shall be registered attorneys, at least one of whom shall also be a judge, and three of the members shall be non-attorneys. At least one of the registered attorneys shall be under the age of 35 when he or she is appointed. Members shall serve three-year terms; except that of the members initially appointed, three shall serve for one year, three shall serve for two years, and three shall serve for three years. The Supreme Court shall appoint one of the members to serve as chairperson at its pleasure. In the event of a vacancy, a successor shall be appointed for the unexpired term of the member whose office is vacated. Membership on the Board may be terminated as to any member by the Supreme Court at its pleasure. The members shall be entitled to reimbursement for reasonable travel, lodging and other expenses incurred in the performance of official duties.

(2)   The Board shall employ an Executive Director and such other staff as may be necessary to assist it in performing its functions and shall pay all expenses reasonably and necessarily incurred by it under a budget approved by the Supreme Court.

(3)   The Board shall administer the program of mandatory continuing legal education established by these rules. It may formulate rules and regulations and prepare forms not inconsistent with these rules pertaining to its functions and modify or amend the same from time to time. All such rules, regulations and forms and any modifications or amendments thereto shall be submitted to the Supreme Court and shall be made known to all registered attorneys and judges. Those rules, regulations and forms shall automatically become effective on the 28th day following submission unless they shall be suspended by the Supreme Court prior to that date.

RULE 260.4: ACCREDITATION

(1)   Continuing legal education must be educational activity which has as its primary objective the increase of professional competence of registered attorneys and judges. The activity must be an organized activity dealing with subject matter directly related to the practice of law or the performance of judicial duties. The Board shall accredit a broad variety of educational activities which meet these requirements.

(2)   Formal classroom instruction or educational seminars which meet the requirements of Paragraph (1) above lend themselves very well to the fulfillment of the educational requirement imposed by these rules and will be readily accredited by the Board. However, it is not intended that compliance with these rules will impose any undue hardship upon any registered attorney or judge by virtue of the fact that he or she may find it difficult because of age or other reasons to attend such activities. Consequently, in addition to accrediting classroom activities and seminars at centralized locations, the Board shall attempt to promote and accredit such educational activities as video tape and audio tape presentations; preparation of articles, papers, books, and other such written materials; self-administered courses and testing; and other meritorious learning experiences. The Board shall to the extent possible make all educational activities reasonably available throughout Colorado. In cases of incapacity because of poor health, the Board may defer the requirements set forth in these rules for individual attorneys. Deferral does not constitute a waiver.

(3)   The educational activity required by these rules will be in addition to teaching on a regular basis in which particular registered attorneys or judges may engage. Pursuant to Paragraph (6) below, the Board will determine whether a registered attorney's or judge's teaching qualifies for accreditation.

(4)   The Board shall assign an appropriate number of units of credit to each educational activity it shall accredit. Generally, a unit of credit shall be the equivalent to attending 50 minutes of a formal classroom lecture with accompanying textual material.

(5)   The Board may accredit as a sponsoring agency any organization which offers continuing legal education activities. All of the activities sponsored by such agency which conform to the requirements of these rules and such additional rules and regulations as the Board may adopt from time to time shall be accredited. Accreditation extended by the Board to any sponsoring agency shall be reviewed by the Board at least annually.

(6)   The Board shall develop criteria for the accreditation of individual educational activities and shall in appropriate cases accredit qualifying activities of such nature. Although such accreditation will generally be given before the occurrence of the educational activity, the Board may in appropriate cases extend accreditation to qualified activities which have already occurred.

(7)   The Board shall make available a list of all educational activities accredited by it, together with the units of credit assigned to each activity, which may be undertaken by registered attorneys or judges.

(8)   In furtherance of the purposes and objectives of this Rule to promote competence and professionalism in the practice of law and the administration of justice, the Board shall consider, in accrediting programs and educational activities, the contribution the program will make to the competent and professional practice of law by lawyers in this state or to the competent and professional administration of justice. To this end, the Board may review course content, presentation, advertising, and promotion to ascertain that the highest standards of competence and professionalism are being promoted. The Board may withhold accreditation for any program that does not meet these standards, or the contents or promotion of which would be scandalous or unprofessional.

RULE 260.5: EXEMPTIONS

Any registered attorney shall be exempt from the minimum educational requirements set forth in these rules for the years following the year of the attorney's 65th birthday.

RULE 260.6: COMPLIANCE

(1)   The mandatory continuing legal education requirement imposed by these rules shall take effect January 1, 1979. To aid administrative implementation of the requirement, the Board shall divide all registered attorneys into three groups of approximately equal numbers. The first group shall be required to complete 15 units of continuing legal education during the first year, and thereafter all registered attorneys in the first group shall complete 45 units of continuing legal education during each subsequent three-year compliance period. The second group shall be required to complete 30 units of continuing legal education during the first two years, and thereafter all registered attorneys in the second group shall complete 45 units of continuing legal education during each subsequent three-year compliance period. The third group shall be required to complete 45 units of continuing legal education during the first three years, and thereafter all registered attorneys and judges in the third group shall complete 45 units of continuing legal education during each subsequent three-year compliance period. All registered attorneys admitted to the bar within the two calendar years preceding January 1, 1979 and all judges shall be placed in the third group.

(2)   Commencing with the date set forth in Paragraph (1) above, the Board shall send to each registered attorney and judge an Affidavit for the reporting of compliance with these rules. It shall be in such form as will allow the reporting of progress towards fulfilling the units required during each applicable compliance period, as such units are earned.

(3)   At the time of payment of the registration fee required by Rule 227A or Rule 227B, each registered attorney and each judge shall submit an Affidavit showing the units of continuing legal education completed since the date such registered attorney or judge became subject to these rules or the date an Affidavit was last filed, whichever shall be later.

(4)   No later than January 31st following the end of each applicable compliance period, each registered attorney and each judge shall submit a final Affidavit showing the total units of continuing legal education completed during such period, if the Board's records do not show that the attorney or judge has completed the requirements for that compliance period.

(5)   In the event a registered attorney or judge shall fail to complete the required units at the end of each applicable compliance period, the final Affidavit may be accompanied by a specific plan for making up the deficiency of units necessary within 119 days (17 weeks) after the date of the final affidavit. WHEN FILED, THE PLAN SHALL BE ACCOMPANIED BY A MAKE-UP PLAN FILING FEE, THE AMOUNT OF WHICH SHALL BE DETERMINED BY THE BOARD ANNUALLY AND WHICH SHALL BE USED TO COVER THE COSTS OF PROCESSING THE PLAN. Such plan shall be deemed accepted by the Board unless within 14 days after the receipt of such final affidavit the Board notifies the affiant to the contrary. Full completion of the affiant's plan shall be reported by affidavit to the Board not later than 14 days following such 119-day period. Failure of the affiant to complete the plan within such 119-day period shall invoke the sanctions set forth in Paragraph (6).

(6)   In the event that any registered attorney or judge shall fail to comply with these rules in any respect, the Board shall promptly notify such registered attorney or judge of the nature of the noncompliance by a statement of noncompliance. The statement shall advise the registered attorney or judge that within 14 days either the noncompliance must be corrected or a request for a hearing before the Board must be made, and that upon failure to do either, the statement of noncompliance shall be filed with the Supreme Court.

(7)   If the noncompliance is not corrected within 14 days, or if a hearing is not requested within 14 days, the Board shall promptly forward the statement of noncompliance to the Supreme Court which may impose the sanctions set forth in Paragraph (10).

(8)   If a hearing before the Board is requested, such hearing shall be held within 28 days after the request by the full Board or one or more of the members of the Board as it shall designate, provided that the presiding member at the hearing must be a registered attorney or judge. Notice of the time and place of the hearing shall be given to the registered attorney or judge at least 14 days prior thereto. The registered attorney or judge may be represented by counsel. Witnesses shall be sworn; and, if requested by the registered attorney or judge, a complete electronic record shall be made of all proceedings had and testimony taken. The presiding member shall have authority to rule on all motions, objections and other matters presented in connection with the hearing. The hearing shall be conducted in conformity with the Colorado Rules of Civil Procedure, and the practice in the trial of civil cases, except the registered attorney or judge involved may not be required to testify over his or her objection. The chairman of the Board shall have the power to compel, by subpoena issued out of the Supreme Court, the attendance of witnesses and the production of books, papers, correspondence, memoranda and other records deemed necessary as evidence in the hearing.

(9)   At the conclusion of the hearing, the member or members of the Board who conducted the hearing shall make findings of fact and shall determine whether the registered attorney or judge involved has complied with the requirements of these rules and, if it determines there was noncompliance, whether there was reasonable cause for noncompliance. A copy of such findings and determination shall be sent to the registered attorney or judge, involved. If it is determined that compliance has occurred, the matter shall be dismissed; and the Board's records shall be made to reflect such compliance. If it is determined that compliance has not occurred, the Board shall proceed as follows:

(a) If the Board determines that there was reasonable cause for noncompliance, the registered attorney or judge shall be allowed 14 days within which to file with the Board a specific plan for correcting the noncompliance within 119 days (17 weeks). Such plan shall be deemed accepted by the Board unless within 14 days after its receipt the Board notifies the registered attorney or judge to the contrary. Full completion of the plan shall be reported by Affidavit to the Board not later than 14 days following such 119-day (17 weeks) period. If the registered attorney or judge shall fail to file an acceptable plan, or shall fail to complete and certify completion of the plan within such 119-day period, the Board shall proceed as set forth in paragraph (b) as though it had determined that there was not reasonable cause for noncompliance.

(b) If the Board determines that there was not reasonable cause for noncompliance, a record of the matter, which must include a copy of the findings and determination, shall be promptly filed with the Supreme Court. If requested by the Board, registered attorney or judge, the record shall include a transcript of the hearing prepared at the expense of the requesting party.

(10)   Upon receipt of a statement of noncompliance upon which a hearing was not requested or upon receipt of the record of a Board hearing, the Supreme Court shall enter such order as it shall deem appropriate, which may include an order of summary suspension from the practice of law until the further order of the Court in the case of registered attorneys or referral of the matter to the Commission on Judicial Qualifications or the Denver County Court Judicial Qualifications Commission in the case of judges.

(11)   Any registered attorney who has been suspended pursuant to Paragraph (2) of Rule 227A, or who has elected to transfer to inactive status pursuant to Paragraph (7) of Rule 227A, shall be relieved thereby from the requirements of these rules. Upon being reinstated pursuant to Paragraphs (3) or (7) of Rule 227A, the compliance period for such registered attorney shall commence on the date of reinstatement and end on December 31 of the third full calendar year following the year of reinstatement, provided the date of reinstatement is more than one year after the date of suspension or transfer to inactive status, or such lesser period as the Board may determine. Otherwise, the compliance period shall be the same as it would have been absent the suspension or transfer. No registered attorney or judge shall be permitted to transfer from active status to inactive status and vice versa or to become suspended and then reinstated to circumvent the requirements of these rules.

(12) All notices given pursuant to these rules shall be sent by certified mail, return receipt requested, to the registered address of the registered attorney or judge maintained by the Clerk of the Supreme Court pursuant to Rule 227A or Rule 227B.

(13) Any attorney who has been suspended for noncompliance pursuant to Rule 260.6(10) may be reinstated by order of the Court upon a showing that the attorney's current continuing legal education deficiency has been made up. The attorney shall file with the Board three (3) copies of a petition seeking reinstatement, addressed to the Supreme Court. The petition shall state with particularity the accredited programs of continuing legal education which the attorney has already completed, including dates of their completion, by which activity the attorney earned sufficient units of credit to make up the deficiency which was the cause of the attorney's suspension. The petition shall be accompanied by a reinstatement filing fee, the amount of which shall be determined by the Board annually and which shall be used to cover the costs associated with noncompliance. The Board shall file a properly completed petition, accompanied by the Board's recommendation, with the Clerk of the Supreme Court within 14 days after receipt.

RULE 260.7: CONFIDENTIALITY

The files, records and proceedings of the Board, as they relate to the compliance or noncompliance of any registered attorney or judge with the requirements of these rules, shall be confidential and shall not be disclosed except upon written request or consent of the registered attorney or judge affected or as directed by the Supreme Court.

RULE 260.8: DIRECT REPRESENTATION AND MENTORING IN PRO BONO CIVIL LEGAL MATTERS

(1) A lawyer may be awarded a maximum of nine (9) units of general credit during each three-year compliance period for providing uncompensated pro bono legal representation to an indigent or near-indigent client or clients in a civil legal matter, or mentoring another lawyer or a law student providing such representation.

(2) To be eligible for units of general credit, the civil pro bono legal matter in which a lawyer provides representation must have been assigned to the lawyer by: a court; a bar association or Access to Justice Committee-sponsored program; an organized non-profit entity, such as Colorado Legal Services, Metro Volunteer Lawyers, or Colorado Lawyers Committee whose purpose is or includes the provision of pro bono representation to indigent or near-indigent persons in civil legal matters; or a law school. Prior to assigning the matter, the assigning court, program, entity, or law school shall determine that the client is financially eligible for pro bono legal representation because (a) the client qualifies for participation in programs funded by the Legal Services Corporation, or (b) the client's income and financial resources are slightly above the guidelines utilized by such programs, but the client nevertheless cannot afford counsel.

(3) Subject to the reporting and review requirements specified herein, (a) a lawyer providing uncompensated, pro bono legal representation shall receive one (1) unit of general credit for every five (5) billable-equivalent hours of representation provided to the indigent client; (b) a lawyer who acts as a mentor to another lawyer as specified in this Rule shall be awarded one (1) unit of general credit per completed matter; and (c) a lawyer who acts as a mentor to a law student shall be awarded two (2) units of general credit per completed matter. A lawyer will not be eligible to receive more than nine (9) units of general credit during any three-year compliance period via any combination of pro bono representation and mentoring.

(4) A lawyer wishing to receive general credit units under this Rule shall submit to the assigning court, program, or law school a completed Form 8. As to mentoring, the lawyer shall submit Form 8 only once, when the matter is fully completed. As to pro bono representation, if the representation will be concluded during a single three-year compliance period, then the lawyer shall complete and submit Form 8 only once, when the representation is fully completed. If the representation will continue into another three-year compliance period, then the applying lawyer may submit an interim Form 8 seeking such credit as the lawyer may be eligible to receive during the three-year compliance period that is coming to an end. Upon receipt of an interim or final Form 8, the assigning court, program, entity, or law school shall in turn report to the Board the number of general CLE units that it recommends be awarded to the reporting lawyer under the provisions of this Rule. It shall recommend an award of the full number of units for which the lawyer is eligible under the provisions of this Rule, unless it determines after review that such an award is not appropriate due to the lawyer's lack of diligence or competence, in which case it shall recommend awarding less than the full number of units or no units. An outcome in the matter adverse to the client's objectives or interests shall not result in any presumption that the lawyer's representation or mentoring was not diligent or competent. The Board shall have final authority to issue or decline to issue units of credit to the lawyer providing representation or mentoring, subject to the other provisions of these Rules and Regulations, including without limitation the hearing provisions of Regulation 108.

COLORADO

(5) A lawyer who acts as a mentor to another lawyer providing representation shall be available to the lawyer providing representation for information and advice on all aspects of the legal matter, but will not be required to file or otherwise enter an appearance on behalf of the indigent client in any court. Mentors shall not be members of the same firm or in association with the lawyer providing representation to the indigent client.

(6) A lawyer who acts as a mentor to a law student who is eligible to practice law under C.R.S. §§ 12-5-116 to -116.5 shall be assigned to the law student at the time of the assignment of the legal matter with the consent of the mentor, the law student, and the law school. The matter shall be assigned to the law student by a court, a program or entity as described in Rule 260.8(2), or an organized student law office program administered by his or her law school, after such court, program, entity, or student law office determines that the client is eligible for pro bono representation in accordance Rule 260.8(2). The mentor shall be available to the law student for information and advice on all aspects of the matter, and shall directly and actively supervise the law student while allowing the law student to provide representation to the client. The mentor shall file or enter an appearance along with the law student in any legal matter pursued or defended for the client in any court. Mentors may be acting as full-time or adjunct professors at the law student's law school at the same time they serve as mentors, so long as it is not a primary, paid responsibility of that professor to administer the student law office and supervise its law-student participants.

REGULATIONS OF THE COLORADO BOARD OF CONTINUING LEGAL AND JUDICIAL EDUCATION

REGULATION 101. PREAMBLE

These regulations are adopted pursuant to Rule 260 of the Colorado Rules of Civil Procedure. They provide a framework for accrediting a wide variety of continuing legal education activities. It is the intent of these regulations that each Colorado attorney and judge has ample opportunity to participate in educational activities that fit individual professional needs.

REGULATION 102. CONTINUING LEGAL EDUCATION REQUIREMENT

(a) For registered attorneys in groups 1 and 2 (see Rule 260.6), units of continuing legal education in excess of the required 15 units for 1979 or 30 for 1979-80, respectively, may not be used to satisfy the requirements of the first full three-year compliance period. Similarly for registered attorneys in groups 1 and 2, units of continuing legal education completed between August 14, 1978, when Rule 260 was adopted by the Supreme Court, and January 1, 1979, when the Rule is effective, may be used to satisfy only the requirements for 1979 or 1979-80, respectively.

(b) For registered attorneys in groups 1 and 2, the requirement regarding continuing legal education specifically addressed to legal or judicial ethics will not be effective until the start of the first full three-year compliance period.

(c) The requirements of Rule 260 and these Regulations will not be applied to lawyers from other jurisdictions who are admitted for a case or proceeding.

REGULATION 103. STANDARDS FOR ACCREDITATION

Continuing legal education must be educational activity which has as its primary objective the increase of professional competence of registered attorneys and judges. The activity must be an organized activity dealing with subject matter directly related to the practice of law or the performance of judicial duties.

(a) The Board shall accredit formal and individualized course work and teaching and research activity applying the standards set forth below. Individual attorneys, judges or sponsors seeking accreditation of other types of educational activity should apply, in writing, to the Board, for accreditation, before undertaking such activities. Before making a final determination concerning the accreditation of activity other than those enumerated above, the Board shall formulate standards and promulgate rules in a manner consistent with the provisions of Rule 260.3(3).

(b)   Courses will be accredited only if they are offered by a sponsor recognized as eligible. In order to be recognized, a sponsor must have either (1) substantial, recent experience in offering continuing legal education, or (2) demonstrated ability to organize and present effectively continuing legal education. Demonstrated ability arises partly from the extent to which individuals with legal training or educational experience are involved in the planning, instruction, or supervision of continuing legal education activities.

(c)   Courses and other activities will not be accredited if attendance is limited to the members of a particular law firm, corporation or other business entity. This requirement will not apply, however, to professional associations, or activities sponsored by an agency for the benefit of registered attorneys or judges who are employees of a local, state or federal governmental unit.

(d)   Each faculty member must be qualified by practical or academic experience to teach the subject he or she covers.

(e)   Thorough, high quality written materials must be distributed to all attendees at or before the time the course is presented. A mere agenda will not be sufficient.

(f)   Formal courses must be conducted in a setting physically suitable to the educational activity of the program. A suitable writing surface should be provided where feasible.

(g)   The Board shall accredit teaching activities of registered attorneys and judges, upon written application by individuals engaged in such activities, provided the activity contributes to the continuing legal education of the applicant and other attorneys or judges. In addition, the Board may accredit educational activity of attorneys and judges who present programs to a public audience, provided the program's primary purpose is to inform the individuals in that audience about the workings of the Colorado judiciary and the functions of judges and courts.

(h)   The Board shall accredit research activities of registered attorneys and judges, upon written application by individuals engaged in such activities, provided the activity (1) has produced published findings in the form of articles, chapters, monographs or books, personally authored, in whole or part, by the applicant; (2) contributes substantially to the continuing legal education of the applicant and other attorneys or judges; and (3) is not done in the ordinary course of the practice of law, the performance of judicial duties, or other regular employment.

(i)   The Board shall accredit committee research activities of registered attorneys and judges, upon written application by individuals engaged in such activities, provided the activity (1) has produced written materials, personally authored, in whole or part, by the applicant on behalf of a committee, qualified under this regulation; (2) contributes substantially to the continuing legal education of the applicant and other attorneys and judges; and (3) is not done in the ordinary course of the practice of law, the performance of judicial duties, or other regular employment. In order to be qualified under this regulation, a committee must be recognized as such by the Board and have as its primary purpose and effect activity which has substantial educational value to attorneys and judges outside the committee.

(j)   In addition to formal courses, conducted in a class or seminar setting, the Board shall accredit individualized continuing legal education activity, provided the activity (1) is a structured course of study, (2) is organized by a sponsor recognized as eligible, (3) includes the use of thorough, high-quality written materials, available to any registered attorney or judge completing the course, and (4) incorporates some other educational medium, such as video or audio tapes, correspondence work, testing, or individual conferences, as deemed appropriate by the Board, (in order to receive accreditation for its individualized educational programs, a sponsor shall agree to maintain and supply the Board with a record of persons obtaining such programs from the sponsor) or (5) is a self-administered course of study. Anyone requesting credit for this type of activity shall submit a written proposal on the Board's Form 7 detailing the nature of the activity at least forty-five days before commencing such activity. The course of study must involve substantial active participation in an educational endeavor which is beneficial to the applicant's practice and is not part of the applicant's ordinary practice of law. A written work product evidencing the learning experience will ordinarily be required from the person seeking credit. The maximum credit available for this type of activity is nine hours during any one compliance period.

(k)   Formal, classroom type programs will be accredited only if a completed application for accreditation is filed with the Board at least fifteen days before the program's starting date. A non-refundable fee of fifty dollars ($50) shall accompany each application sent by a sponsoring agency. A separate application and fee must be provided for each presentation of a live program. Upon a showing of good cause, the Board may extend accreditation even if the timely filing requirement is not met, but a one hundred dollar ($100) fee will be charged to sponsors who fail to comply with this requirement. Video replays of a live program shall be subject to a ten dollar ($10) accreditation fee per replay date, and shall be submitted for accreditation at the same time as the live program. The fee for any program sponsored by a governmental agency, local bar association or non-profit organization shall be twenty-five dollars ($25), but a fifty dollar ($50) fee will be charged if the application is submitted less than fifteen days before the program's starting date. A qualifying non-profit under this provision must be a non-profit organization that acts as a legal service provider providing free or reduced cost legal services to indigent or near-indigent clients.

(l)   The Sponsor of a formal, classroom type program, offered in Colorado and accredited by the Board, shall distribute at the program, to each Colorado attorney and judge in attendance, a copy of the Board's official Notice of Accreditation of the program. In cases where the Notice includes provisions for Colorado attorneys and judges to report their CLE credits earned at the program to the Board, the sponsor shall

(1) provide a means at the program for individuals to submit a completed Notice and Report to the sponsor,
(2) transmit, by a secure means, all completed Notices and Reports to the Board, within (10) ten days after the program.

REGULATION 104. CREDITS; COMPUTATION

(a)   Credit will be given only for completion of continuing legal education activities that have (1) been previously accredited by the Board, or (2) been afforded retroactive credit by the Board.

(b)   Generally, credit for formal course work shall be awarded on the basis of one (1) unit for each fifty (50) minutes actually spent in attendance at an accredited activity after August 14, 1978. Credit will not be allowed for any program which in its entirety lasts less than 50 minutes exclusive of question and answer periods.

(c)   The units of credit assigned to a course merely reflect the maximum that may be earned through attendance. Only actual attendance by the registered attorney or judge earns credit.

(d)   Credit will not be given for time spent for introductory remarks, coffee and luncheon breaks, keynote speeches, business meetings, or question and answer periods following a presentation.

(e)   Credit will not be given for any course attended in preparation for admission to practice law in any jurisdiction.

(f)   In awarding credit for teaching, the Board shall take into account the following factors: (1) teaching content and level; (2) teaching methodology; (3) personal preparation by the individual applicant, including time spent; (4) originality of preparation with the individual applicant; and (5) supplemental course materials personally prepared by the individual applicant.

(g)   In awarding credit for research activity, under Regulations 103(h) and 103(i), the Board shall consider the following factors: (1) the content, level and length of the published findings or committee papers; (2) the originality of the published findings or committee papers with the individual applicant; and (3) the nature of the publication in which they appear, if any.

(h)   In awarding credit for individualized educational activities, under Regulation 103(j), the Board shall consider the following factors: (1) the nature of the structured, individualized activities comprising the course of study; (2) the time normally required to complete those activities; and (3) the extent to which the individual educational activity of a registered attorney or judge, completing the program, is evaluated by the sponsor. Generally, if the structured activity consists of listening to or watching the electronic replay of a lecture, the Board shall award credit in the same manner as for attendance at a live lecture. In order to claim credit for individualized educational activity, an attorney shall engage in such activity in a physical setting conducive to intellectual concentration and effective study.

REGULATION 105. Deleted by court action - year 1984.

REGULATION 106. PROCEDURE FOR ACCREDITATION

(a)   In order to apply for accreditation of a continuing legal education activity, a registered attorney, judge or sponsoring agency shall submit to the Board all information called for by the appropriate form (See Appendix).

    (1) Application for accreditation of a formal course shall be made on Form 1.
    (2) Application for recognition of a sponsor as eligible shall be made on Form 2.
    (3) Application for accreditation of a filmed or electronic replay of a formal course that has already been accredited shall be made on Form 3.
    (4) Application for accreditation of an individualized continuing legal educational activity shall be made on Form 4.
    (5) Application for accreditation of teaching activity shall be made on Form 5.
    (6) Application for accreditation of research activity shall be made on Form 6.

(b)   Accreditation shall be granted or denied in accordance with the provisions of Regulation 108 herein.

(c)   As to a course that has been accredited, the sponsoring agency may announce in informational brochures or registration materials: "This course has been accredited by the Colorado Board of Continuing Legal and Judicial Education for a maximum of ___ units of credit".

REGULATION 107. DELEGATION

(a)   To facilitate the orderly and prompt administration of Rule 260 and these Regulations, and to expedite the processes of course approval and the interpretation of these Regulations, the Executive Director may act on behalf of the Board under Rule 260 and these Regulations.

(b)   The Chairman of the Board may act on behalf of the Board under Rule 260 and these Regulations.

REGULATION 108. EXECUTIVE DIRECTOR'S DETERMINATIONS AND REVIEW

(a)   Pursuant to guidelines established by the Board, the Executive Director shall, in response to written requests for accreditation of courses or interpretations of these Regulations, make a written response describing the action taken. The Executive Director may seek a determination of the Board before making such response.

(b)   Any adverse determination and all questions of interpretation of these Regulations or Rule 260 by the Executive Director shall be subject to review by the Board upon written application by the person adversely affected. The registered attorney, judge or sponsoring agency affected may present information to the Board in writing or in person or both. If the Board finds that the Executive Director has incorrectly interpreted the facts, the provisions of Rule 260, or the provisions of these Regulations, it may take such action as may be appropriate. The Board shall advise the registered attorney, judge or sponsoring agency affected of its findings and any action taken.

REGULATION 109. MAKE-UP PLANS

(a)   Any plan for making up a deficiency filed after December 31, pursuant to Rule 260.6(5), shall include only activities which have already been accredited by the Board at the time such plan is filed.

(b)   The plan shall be specific and include the names and locations of such accredited activities, the number and type of credits that will be earned, and the dates on which such credits will be earned.

(c)   The number and type of credits to be earned shall be sufficient to make-up the deficiency.

(d)   The credits shall be earned not later than May 31 of the year following the end of the compliance period.

COLORADO

(e)   The make-up plan shall be accompanied by a check or money order, payable to the Supreme Court CLE Board, in the amount of one hundred dollars ($100) pursuant to Rule 260.6(5), if filed by the January 31 reporting deadline as set forth in Rule 260.6(4). If a make-up plan is submitted after the deadline, the plan shall be accompanied by a check or money order, payable to the Supreme Court CLE Board, in the amount of two hundred dollars ($200) at the time of filing.

(f)   Any make-up plan filed in accordance with these criteria shall be deemed accepted by the Board.

REGULATION 110. Deleted by court action - year 1986.

REGULATION 111. FEES

(a)   Any registered attorney or judge who fails to comply with Rule 260.6(4) shall be subjected to a one hundred dollar ($100) late reporting fee. This late reporting fee shall increase to two hundred dollars ($200) on March 1 immediately following the end of the registered attorney's or judge's compliance period.

(b)   Petitions for reinstatement from suspension for failure to comply with Rule 260 shall be accompanied by a check or money order in the amount of one hundred dollars ($100).

APPENDIX: ACCREDITATION FORMS TO BE USED IN CONJUNCTION WITH REGULATION 106(a)

FORM 1, and the supporting documents filed with it, provide basic information about formal class-room type programs. The Board needs this information to determine whether a program should be accredited and how much credit, if any, it should be awarded.

(a)   Program sponsors should file a Form 1 for each program attended by Colorado attorneys or judges. The Board encourages sponsors to do this but cannot make them. Attorneys seeking credit for attending such programs should also encourage sponsors to file. Attorneys, for whom attendance is conditioned upon program accreditation, should make their views clear to sponsors, even to the extent of telling the sponsor that they will not attend unless the sponsor obtains accreditation before the program takes place. This is especially important with regard to programs held IN Colorado (see Regulation 103(k) and 103(l)).

(b)   If the sponsor fails to file Form 1, and an individual wishes to claim credit for attendance, the only practical alternative is for the attorney or judge to file Form 1. If accreditation is critical to the individual, and if the sponsor is unlikely to file, the attorney or judge should file Form 1 at least 15 days before the program takes place (see Regulation 103(k)).

(c)   A separate Form 1 must be filed for each program seeking accreditation.

(d)   Form 1 must be accompanied by a brochure or other printed description of the program. The document must include: a statement of the faculty's qualifications; a clear outline of the program's content; and a detailed schedule of events indicating how time segments are spent and clearly distinguishing between breaks, meal times and substantive educational sessions.

FORM 1A is used to apply for accreditation of a graduate legal study course or program.

FORM 2 need be filed only on behalf of sponsors who have not yet been "recognized" by Colorado as a qualified sponsor of continuing legal education. "Recognition" is a pre-requisite to accreditation of individual programs. The Board has recognized over 500 sponsors. Many are not yet recognized. To determine if a sponsor has been recognized, contact the Board. An unrecognized sponsor should file Form 2 on its own behalf. If it does not, where feasible, an individual attorney or judge should do so.

FORM 3 is used to apply for accreditation of an electronic replay of a live program, where the live program has already been accredited. Form 3 should only be used where the replay is conducted by a recognized sponsor, in a formal seminar setting, open to all attorneys or judges, where written materials are distributed. Form 3 should not be used to apply for accreditation of individualized, home study programs.

FORM 4 is used to apply for accreditation of individualized or home-study programs. Form 4 must be filed by the sponsors of the program. If a Colorado attorney or judge wishes to claim credit for a particular home-study program that has not been accredited, the individual should encourage the sponsor to apply for Colorado accreditation by providing the sponsor with a copy of Form 4.

FORM 5 must be filed by an individual attorney or judge, who wishes to claim credit for teaching activity which contributes to the continuing legal education of <u>both</u> the applicant and other attorneys or judges.

(a)   Upon receipt of Form 5, the Board awards credit for teaching, which meets the accreditation standards, on the basis of at least 2 units of credit for each hour of lecture time. To claim this minimal credit, completion of the front of Form 5 is all that is required.

(b)   If the teaching activity does not consist of lecturing, or if the applicant wishes to apply for additional credit beyond the minimal standard, completion of Form 5 on <u>both</u> sides is required.

(c)   The Board provides applicants with written notice of the disposition of teaching accreditation requests. If you as an applicant do not receive notice within 30 days after application, contact the Board.

(d)   Individuals may claim credit for teaching only to the extent that they have received notice of the Board's accreditation of their individual activity.

FORM 6 must be filed by an individual attorney or judge who wishes to claim credit for research activity that has resulted in "publication". Form 6A must be filed by an individual attorney or judge who wishes to claim credit for Committee research. The research must contribute to the continuing legal education of <u>both</u> the applicant and other attorneys or judges.

(a)   Form 6 or 6A must be accompanied by the written work-product of the research, i.e. a copy of either the publication or the committee paper.

(b)   Those seeking credit for committee research should first check with the Board or the committee chairperson to determine if the committee has been "qualified" by the Board.

(c)   The Board provides applicants with written notice of the disposition of research accreditation requests. If you, as an applicant, do not receive notice within 30 days after application, contact the Board.

(d)   Individuals may not claim credit for research if they have not received written notice of the Board's accreditation of their individual activity.

FORM 7 must be filed by an individual attorney or judge who wishes to claim credit for a self-administered course of study.

(a)   The course of study must involve active participation in an educational endeavor that is beneficial to the applicant's practice and is not part of the applicant's ordinary practice of law.

(b)   Form 7 must be submitted at least forty-five (45) days in advance of the activity to allow appropriate time for review and consideration.

(c)   Individuals may not claim credit for an individual course of study if they have not received written notice of the Board's accreditation of their individual activity.

(d)   The maximum credit available for a self-administered course of study is nine credit hours during any one compliance period.

FORM 8 must be filed by an individual attorney or judge who wishes to claim credit for pro bono legal representation or for mentoring another lawyer or law student providing such representation. The maximum credit available for pro bono/mentoring is nine credits hours during any one compliance period.

DELAWARE

THE DELAWARE RULES FOR CONTINUING LEGAL EDUCATION

Effective January 1, 2016

Rule 1. Purpose

The Supreme Court of the State of Delaware has determined it is in the best interest of the public and the administration of justice that members of the Delaware Bench and Bar maintain their international reputation of professionalism and competence through continuing legal education. These Rules establish the expectations of the Court for the process of continuing legal education and establish a Commission to assist in their implementation, interpretation and enforcement.

Rule 2. Definitions

(A) "Accredited sponsor" means an organization whose entire continuing legal education program has been accredited by the Commission;

(B) "Attorney" means any member of the Bar of the Delaware Supreme Court, excluding judicial officers;

(C) "CLE" means Continuing Legal Education;

(D) "Commission" means the Commission on Continuing Legal Education;

(E) "Compliance Year" means the year in which the Attorney reaches the December 31 reporting deadline;

(F) "Court" means the Supreme Court of the State of Delaware;

(G) "DSBA" means the Delaware State Bar Association;

(H) "Enhanced Ethics" means both legal and judicial ethics. It also means professionalism, which is a broader concept embodying an attitude and a dedication to ethics, civility, skill, businesslike practices and a focus on service, which encompasses obligations to other Attorneys, obligations toward legal institutions, and obligations to the public whose interests Attorneys must serve;

(I) "Fundamentals Program" means the series of basic courses in legal practice, the subjects of which the Commission will establish;

(J) "In-House Program" means a continuing legal education activity sponsored by a law firm, corporation, governmental agency, or similar entity for the education of its employees or members;

(K) "Judicial Commissioner" means the judicial representative on the Commission under Rule 3(A);

(L) "Judicial Officer" means any member of the Bar of the Delaware Supreme Court appointed to serve as a judge, commissioner, master in chancery or justice of the peace on a Delaware state court;

(M) "Senior Attorney" means every Attorney who has been a member of the Bar of the Supreme Court in any State and in the District of Columbia in good standing for 40 or more years. An Attorney who has been a member of another state's bar has the burden of verifying the 40 or more year status to the satisfaction of the Commission.

(N) "Transcript" means the report prescribed by Rule 5 for verification compliance.

(O) "Uniform Application" means the Uniform Application for the Accreditation of a Continuing Legal Education Activity as approved by the Continuing Legal Education Regulators Association (CLEreg);

(P) "Verification Year" means the year in which the Attorney must verify the accuracy of the CLE transcript.

Rule 3. Commission on Continuing Legal Education

(A) **Commission Members:** The Commission on Continuing Legal Education is established and shall consist of 7 members appointed by the Supreme Court for a term of 3 years. The terms shall be staggered so that no more than 3 members' terms shall end in the same year. The 7 members of the Commission shall include at least one member of the judiciary and a lawyer from each county. The Commission members shall serve without compensation. Four voting members shall constitute a quorum at any meeting.

(B) **Officers:** The Court shall appoint 1 member of the Commission as Chair and 1 member as Vice Chair. The Executive Director of the Commission shall serve as Secretary.

(C) **Executive Director:** The Executive Director shall be selected and employed by the Court.

(D) **Ex-Officio Members:** The following shall serve as ex-officio members of the Commission, but shall have no vote: The Supreme Court Administrator or the Administrator's designee, the Executive Director and the Director of Continuing Legal Education of the DSBA, the Dean of Widener University Delaware Law School or the Dean's designee, and the Executive Director of the Commission.

(E) **Powers and Duties:** In addition to administering and interpreting these Rules, the Commission shall be responsible for:

(1) Managing the availability of quality continuing legal educational courses and activities to members of the Bench and Bar;

(2) Determining the number of credit hours to be allowed for any continuing legal educational course or activity;

(3) Producing the Court's annual Pre-Admission Conference;

(4) Approving the curriculum for Fundamentals courses offered pursuant to these Rules and providing guidance for the creation of these courses;

(5) Providing policy statements regarding courses, activities, credits and the interpretation of these Rules;

(6) Recommending to the Court an assessment to be paid by Attorneys concurrently with the annual registration required by Supreme Court Rule 69;

(7) Publishing a schedule of fees to be charged organizations sponsoring continuing legal education programs as a condition of accreditation for attendees to receive Delaware continuing legal education credit;

(8) Reporting annually to the Court on the activities of the Commission.

Rule 4. Educational Requirements

(A) **Attorneys Generally**: Each Attorney shall complete a minimum of 24 approved CLE credit hours during each two-year period. At least 12 of those credits must be earned by attending, in person, live CLE approved courses also attended by other lawyers from other law firms, organizations or governmental agencies (It is the intent of this requirement that each lawyer have the opportunity to interact with other lawyers from other organizations during the CLE activity). In addition, during the two-year period, at least 4 of the 24 approved CLE credit hours shall consist of approved Enhanced Ethics credits. If more than 24 approved CLE credit hours have been earned during the two-year period, up to 20 of the excess hours may be carried forward and applied to the requirement for the next two-year period. Enhanced Ethics credits cannot be carried forward as Enhanced Ethics, but may be carried forward as general CLE credits.

(B) **Judicial Officers:** Judicial Officers shall comply with the Educational Requirements of Rule 4(A) or 4(C) as appropriate, based on years admitted to the Bar as outlined in Rule 2(M).

(C) **Senior Attorneys:** Senior Attorneys shall be subject to these Rules, except that the number of hours required of a Senior Attorney shall be 12 hours during each two-year period, of which a minimum of 2 hours shall be from instruction in Enhanced Ethics. At least 6 of those credits must be earned by attending, in person, live CLE approved courses also attended by other lawyers from other law firms, organizations or governmental agencies.

(D) **Newly Admitted Attorneys:** The CLE requirement for a newly admitted Attorney shall begin on January 1st of the year after which he/she is admitted to the Bar of the Court. In addition, as to any newly admitted Attorney admitted after December 1, 2015, within four years from that January 1st, the Attorney must attend all of the following Fundamental courses: (1) Fundamentals of Lawyer-Client Relations (2) Fundamentals of Family Law; (3) Fundamentals of Real Estate; (4) Fundamentals of Civil Litigation; (5) Fundamentals of Will Drafting and Estate Administration; (6) Fundamentals of Law Practice Management and Technology; and (7) Fundamentals of Criminal Law and Procedure. Only Fundamental courses offered by the DSBA shall be eligible for approval for this requirement. Attendance at these courses shall be credited towards the Attorney's minimum continuing legal education obligation.

(E) Applicants to the Delaware Bar: Applicants who have passed the Delaware Bar Examination must attend the Court's two-day Pre-Admission Conference. However, if the applicant has been admitted to the Bar of another state for at least five years prior to the date of passing the Delaware Bar Examination, that applicant will be required to attend only Day One of the Pre-Admission Conference.

(F) Attorneys Resuming Active Practice: The CLE requirement for Attorneys resuming active practice shall begin on January 1st of the year after which active practice has been resumed. Attorneys admitted after December 1, 2015 who are resuming active practice and who have not completed the Fundamentals requirements for Newly Admitted Attorneys, are required to do so. This obligation to complete Fundamentals shall not apply to Attorneys admitted prior to December 1, 2015. Any Attorney resuming active practice after being inactive for more than 10 years, however, shall complete Fundamentals of Lawyer-Client Relations within the first compliance period following resumption of active practice. (This obligation applies even though the Attorney may have completed Fundamentals of Lawyer-Client Relations prior to becoming inactive.)

(G) Exemptions: The following Attorneys and Judicial Officers shall be exempt from these Rules:

(1) Any Attorney or Judicial Officer who has filed a Certificate of Retirement pursuant to the Supreme Court Rule 69(f);

(2) Any Attorney holding an elected public office of this State or the United States and who certifies to the Commission by affidavit that the Attorney is not engaged in the practice of law, and whose application for exemption has been approved by the Commission;

(3) Any Attorney or Judicial Officer who becomes an inactive member of the Bar pursuant to Supreme Court Rule 69(d)(i);

(4) Members of the federal judiciary;

(5) Any Attorney suspended by the Court.

(H) Comity: An Attorney whose principal office is located within another mandatory CLE state, who is licensed to practice law in that state and who is in compliance with the CLE requirements of that state and so certifies on the Transcript, shall be deemed in compliance with these Rules.

Rule 5. Verification Requirements for Attorneys

(A) When Attorneys' Credits Shall be Completed: Attorneys admitted to the Delaware Bar in even-numbered years shall complete the CLE credits required by December 31 of even-numbered years; Attorneys admitted in odd-numbered years shall complete the CLE credits required by December 31 of odd-numbered years. Attorneys failing to complete the required CLE credits on or before December 31 of the Compliance Year, must nevertheless verify the Transcript on or before March 31st of the Verification Year accompanied by a specific plan for making up the deficiency, as provided in Rule 10.

(B) When Attorneys Shall Verify Transcripts: Attorneys who are required to complete their CLE credits in a given year shall verify the accuracy of their Transcripts maintained on the Commission website no later than March 31st, of the following year. This is called the Verification Year. Transcripts will be available for review and verification on the Commission website after February 1st of the Verification Year.

(C) Penalties for Late Verification of Transcripts: Attorneys failing to verify their Transcripts by March 31st of the Verification Year shall be fined $300. An additional fine of $100 per month will be added to the initial fine for Attorneys failing to verify their Transcripts by May 1st of the Verification Year. Payment shall be made on the same day as the late Transcript is verified. The Commission may waive all or any part of the penalty for good cause shown.

(D) Audits of Transcripts: The Executive Director shall develop a means for selection of no fewer than 5% of the Transcripts received in each year for purposes of verification. The Executive Director shall cause each of the selected Transcripts to be subjected to any or all of the following verification procedures:

(1) Comparing the Transcript to the Commission's records to assure that each listed course was actually accredited and that appropriate applications were submitted and approved for any activities for which the submitting Attorney sought credit;

(2) Asking the Attorney to submit evidence of attendance at courses or participation in activities claimed on the Transcript;

(3) Communicating with a course or activity provider to obtain verification of the Attorney's participation;

(4) Obtaining an approved copy of the Attorney's most recent compliance report from another mandatory CLE state if the Attorney is claiming compliance under the comity clause of Rule 4.

If the Verification procedures produce reason to believe that an Attorney has submitted a false Transcript or other false information to the Commission, the Executive Director shall bring such information promptly to the attention of the Commission. The late filing of a Transcript may subject the Attorney to a CLE audit.

Rule 6. Attendance Records.

(A) Obligation of the Provider: The program provider shall create and maintain, for at least 3 years, records of attendance at the courses.

(1) Within 45 days after the date on which the program ends, the provider shall submit to the Commission a list of attendees for each activity. This list shall include:

(a) the course identification number as assigned by the Commission;

(b) the full name of each attendee;

(c) the Delaware Supreme Court identification number of each attendee, as available; and

(d) the number of credit hours to which each attendee is entitled, based upon the total number of credit hours approved by the Commission. This number should indicate how many of the credit hours were in Enhanced Ethics.

These records may be submitted to the Commission in writing or by electronic transmission in a format approved by the Commission. The Commission may require verified statements as to the accuracy of the reports it receives. To ensure accuracy, providers should have a representative present to properly record attendance on a sign-in sheet.

(2) In addition to the records submitted to the Commission, the provider shall provide each attendee with a certificate of attendance. This certificate shall include:

(a) the name, address and telephone number of the sponsoring organization;

(b) the course identification number as assigned by the Commission;

(c) the complete title of the course attended;

(d) the date(s), city and state of the course attended;

(e) the total number of credit hours approved by the Commission for the particular course;

(f) the total number of credit hours attended by the Attorney, including a statement of the number of these hours that were in Enhanced Ethics; and

(g) the name and signature of the provider's authorized representative.

The certificate of attendance shall be given to the attendee before the attendee leaves the seminar site. If this is not possible, the certificate of attendance shall be sent to the attendee as soon as possible after the seminar.

(B) **Obligation of the Attorney**: The Attorney should keep copies of all attendance certificates, course outlines, agendas, cancelled checks, receipts, travel vouchers, and the like, verify attendance, for 3 years after finalization of the approved Transcript. The Commission may periodically request an Attorney to produce independent verification of attendance.

Rule 7. Credit Hours and Accreditation Standards.

(A) **Credit Hours:** CLE credit hours shall be computed by the following formula: Total minutes /60 = total credit hours). Credit hours shall be rounded to the nearest 1/10th of an hour. Unless otherwise provided in these Rules, only legal education shall be included in computing the total hours of actual instruction. Programs may be split into accredited and non-accredited hours. Non-instructional portions of programs, such as breaks and introductory remarks, shall not be included in the credit computation. Business meetings or portions of programs devoted to the business of the presenting group do not qualify for credit.

(B) Accreditation Standards: The Commission shall approve continuing legal education activities consistent with the following standards:

(1) They shall have significant intellectual or practical content and the primary objective shall be to increase the participant's professional competence as a lawyer or a judge;

(2) They shall constitute an organized program of learning dealing with matters directly related to the practice of law, the exercise of judicial responsibility, professional responsibility, law office management, use of technology, or the ethical obligations of lawyers or judges;

(3) Credit may be given for continuing legal education activities where (i) in person or televised live instruction is used or (ii) mechanically or electronically recorded or reproduced material is used in an organized program;

(4) Continuing legal education materials are to be offered, and activities conducted, by an individual or group qualified by practical or academic experience in a setting physically suitable to the educational activity of the program;

(5) Thorough, high quality, and carefully prepared written materials should be made available to all who attend the course. It is recognized that written materials are not suitable or readily available for some types of subjects; the absence of written materials should, however, be the exception and not the rule.

(C) Activities for which CLE Credit Will Not be Approved: The Commission will not approve for CLE credit:

(1) Courses designed to review or refresh recent law school graduates or other Attorneys in preparation for any bar examination;

(2) Activities for which the Attorney has already received credit in another form, including attendance (e.g., an Attorney who prepared materials and received credit for presenting a seminar may not also receive credit for the publication of those materials, or for attendance during the time spent speaking at the seminar). However, (1) the Attorney may receive credit for attending portions of the seminar which the Attorney did not teach, and (2) the Attorney may receive credit notwithstanding that the Attorney also seeks or receives CLE credit for the activity from another State in which the Attorney is a member of the Bar.

(D) Disabilities and Special Circumstances: An Attorney who has a disability or some other special circumstance, which makes attendance at continuing legal education activities inordinately difficult for a substantial period of time, may file a request with the Commission for a permanent substitute program in lieu of attendance, or a temporary substitute program in lieu of attendance during the period of the disability or special circumstances. The Attorney shall state in writing to the Commission the reasons for the request and a proposal for a continuing legal education plan tailored to the Attorney's circumstances. The

Commission shall promptly review the request, seek such additional information as appropriate and approve or disapprove such plans on an individual basis.

Rule 8. Accreditation of Sponsors and Programs.

(A) **Accredited Sponsors:** The Commission may designate qualified organizations or persons (other than law firms, legal departments of corporations or government agencies) as Accredited Sponsors. While in good standing, any program of continuing legal education organized and conducted by the Accredited Sponsor shall be an accredited course, provided the program and the Accredited Sponsor complies with these Rules. Any person or organization seeking to become an Accredited Sponsor shall apply by filing with the Commission a completed Form 3 together with a filing fee of $250. To maintain Accredited Sponsor status, a Form 3-A together with a filing fee of $250 shall be filed annually. Filing fees may be waived when the approved continuing legal education activities are free of charge to all attendees or are presented under the supervision of the Delaware State judiciary. The Commission may re-evaluate the status of an Accredited Sponsor and revoke the accreditation for any reason the Commission deems appropriate.

(B) **Accreditation of Individual Courses:** The Commission may, on its own initiative, or upon application by any Attorney or the sponsor provider of any course, approve credit for all or a portion of a course that otherwise complies with these Rules. Application for accreditation of an individual program shall be on the Uniform Application if made by a program provider, and on Form 4 if made by an Attorney. Applications made by a program provider shall be accompanied by a $50 filing fee. Applications may be submitted before or after presentation of the program; however, if application for course approval is made by an Attorney before attendance, the Attorney shall submit a certificate of attendance within 45 days after the date on which the program ends. The Commission may request additional information from any applicant.

(C) **Accreditation for Non-Law Courses:** The Commission may approve credit for non-law courses necessary or appropriate to an Attorney's legal practice upon the Attorney's application.

(D) **Accreditation for Recorded or Electronically Broadcasted Courses:** The Commission may approve credit for recorded or electronically broadcasted courses that otherwise comply with these Rules, provided that the sponsor demonstrates objective means to verify that the Attorney has in fact completed the program (i.e., the Attorney's objective assertion of completion is necessary for credit, but not sufficient). Applications shall be made on the uniform application with an additional application fee of $25.00. The Commission may request additional information from any applicant. If the presentation is recorded from a previously presented course, the original course must have taken place no more than two years before the date of the presentation for which credit is being sought.

(E) **Accreditation of In-House Courses:** The Commission may approve credit for In-House courses that otherwise comply with these Rules.

Rule 9. Accreditation of Activities

(A) **Scholarly Writing:** The Commission may approve credit for uncompensated scholarly writing and publication. Applications shall be made by the Attorney on Form 7. The Commission may request additional information from any applicant.

    (1)   **What Must Be Included in the Application:** The application for credit hours for such materials must include:

    (a) A copy of the material for which credit is sought;

    (b) The name and address of any other person participating in the writing or presentation of the content of the material, and a statement of the extent to which that person contributed to the content of the material;

    (c) An estimate of the number of hours the Attorney expended preparing the material, and a description of the hours expended;

    (d) With regard to published material, the name and address of the publisher and a statement that (a) the written material will be published in a publication having distribution to at least 300 lawyers, (b) the material is an original work and (c) the author(s) received no compensation for writing it.

    (2)   **Other Conditions and Considerations:**

    (a) Only uncompensated scholarly writing qualifies for credit. Payment to the Attorney's firm constitutes payment to the Attorney. Reimbursement of out-of-pocket expenses is not considered compensation. If an Attorney donates all compensation for a scholarly writing to the Delaware Bar Foundation he/she may receive credit.

    (b) Credit hours may be allocated to writing and publication, at the election of the author, in the year in which the work is accepted for publication, or publication actually occurs.

    (c) If the work is not published, the Attorney may, in the Commission's discretion, receive credit for the preparation of the unpublished material.

    (d) The Commission will determine the number of credit hours to be allocated to the writing and publication of the work and will notify the applicant promptly on making its determination. As a general guideline: articles in general circulation newspapers and periodicals generally will not receive credit; a brief published piece worthy of credit in the Commission's judgment receives 2.5 credit hours; substantive articles appearing in professional newspapers and periodicals such as the Delaware Lawyer that evidence research and analysis generally receive five credit hours. Law review articles, books or chapters of published works are eligible for more credit, in the Commission's discretion.

(B) Instruction in or Participation in the Presentation of Accredited Courses: The Commission may approve credit for uncompensated teaching in an approved continuing legal education activity, accredited law school, college or university. Applications shall be made by the

Attorney on Form 8. The Commission may request additional information from any applicant.

(1) If a number of Attorneys seek credit for the same course, one application may be submitted on behalf of all. In the absence of an agreement between co-presenters, available credit shall be divided equally among them. Course moderators who do not otherwise teach in the program, but who participate in the program, shall receive credit for 1.5x the time of attendance of the portion of the program moderated.

(2) Only uncompensated teaching qualifies for credit. Compensation to the teaching Attorney's firm constitutes compensation to the Attorney. Reimbursement of out-of-pocket expenses is not considered payment for teaching. An Attorney who donates compensation for teaching to the Delaware Bar Foundation may receive teaching credit.

(3) Presentations accompanied by thorough, high quality, readable and carefully prepared written materials approved by the Commission will be awarded CLE credit, provided the Attorney certifies that the Attorney did the research and prepared the written materials for the presentation. For repeat presentations, Attorneys will be awarded one-half of the credit hours received for the initial presentation.

(C) **Court Appointed Commissions:**

(1) **The Commission may approve credit for Court appointed commissions, including the following:**

(a) Service on the Board on Professional Responsibility: Members of the Board on Professional Responsibility and the Preliminary Review Committee will receive 4 Enhanced Ethics credits for each year of service;

(b) Service as an appointed Presenter in any investigation or proceeding before the Court on the Judiciary, or as Special Disciplinary Counsel shall be applicable towards satisfaction of the biannual requirement for instruction in Enhanced Ethics;

(c) Service on the Board of Bar Examiners: Members will receive 12 credits (including 2 Enhanced Ethics for each year of service. Associate members and Secretaries will receive 6 credits (including 1 Enhanced Ethics) for each year of service;

(d) Service on the Board on Unauthorized Practice of Law, to the extent it requires significant research in the law, legal writing or drafting;

(e) Service on the Lawyers' Fund for Client Protection shall receive 2 Enhanced Ethics Credits for each year of service;

(f) Service on the Board of Examining Officers for the Court on the Judiciary.

(2)   **Applications must include:**

(a) A description of the activity for which credit is sought, including an identification of the commission involved;

(b) A statement of the number of hours expended in the activity;

(c) A description of the substantive legal work performed including, for example, contributions to the substance of a continuing legal education program, or research in the law performed;

(d) A copy of any written materials produced by the applicant, as a result of the activity;

(e) Upon receipt of an application, the Commission will determine whether the applicant shall receive credit for the activity and the number of credit hours allocated to it. The Commission shall notify the applicant promptly of its determination.

(D) Pro Bono Legal Services:

(1) The Commission may approve credit for entirely uncompensated Pro Bono Legal Services, and Special Court Appointments, provided:

(a) The services are performed pursuant to (i) appointment of the Attorney by a Delaware court, including the United States District Court for the District of Delaware; or, (ii) an assignment of a matter to the Attorney by Delaware Volunteer Legal Services, Inc., Community Legal Aid Society of Delaware, Inc., the Office of the Child Advocate, or Legal Services Corporation of Delaware, Inc., or (iii) services performed at outreach events such as an accredited law school's "Wills for Heroes" days; or (iv) any service performed that is determined by the Commission to be eligible for CLE credit under this section.

(b) Credit may be earned at a rate of one hour of CLE credit for every six hours of legal services performed, provided the work performed on the matter was totally uncompensated. Credit is limited to 6 credits per two-year compliance period.

(2) Applications must include:

(a) A description of the activity for which credit is sought, including an identification of the organization, committee, or association involved;

(b) A statement of the number of hours expended in the activity;

(c) A description of the substantive legal work performed including, for example, contributions to the substance of a continuing legal education program, or research in the law performed;

(d) A copy of any written materials produced by the applicant, as a result of the activity.

Rule 10. Noncompliance

(A) Attorneys:

(1) False Statements: If the Commission has reason to believe that an Attorney has submitted a false Transcript or other false information to the Commission, it shall forward the Attorney's name to Disciplinary Counsel for investigation and shall notify the Attorney it has done so.

(2) Notice of Noncompliance:

(a) In the event an Attorney shall fail to complete the required credits by December 31 of the Compliance Year, the Attorney shall submit to the Commission a specific plan for making up the deficiency of necessary credits by April 30 of the Verification Year. Submission of the make-up plan must be included with the online Transcript verification. The plan shall be deemed accepted by the Commission unless, within 30 days after the receipt of the Transcript, the Commission notifies the Attorney to the contrary. The Attorney shall report full completion of the plan by May 15 through the Commission website by marking the online plan entries as complete and forwarding copies of the program attendance certificates to the Commission. If the Attorney fails to complete the plan by April 30 of the Verification Year, or to report completion of the plan by May 15 of the Verification Year, within 120 days, the Commission shall send the Attorney a notice of noncompliance informing the Attorney that unless the Attorney presents satisfactory evidence of compliance within 20 days of the date of the notice, the Commission will file a statement of noncompliance with Disciplinary Counsel. An Attorney shall be required to pay to the Commission $10.00 for each business day that the Attorney's make-up plan has not been fully completed and reported to the Commission beginning on May 16 of the Verification Year, to and including the date of filing. The Commission may waive all or any part of this penalty for good cause shown;

(b) In the event that an Attorney shall fail to comply with these Rules in any respect, the Commission shall send a notice of noncompliance. The notice shall specify the nature of the noncompliance and state that unless the noncompliance is corrected, or satisfactory evidence of compliance is submitted within 20 days of the date of the notice, the Commission will file a statement of noncompliance with Disciplinary Counsel;

(c) Before sending an Attorney a notice of noncompliance, the Commission may request the Attorney to submit additional information to enable the Commission to evaluate the Attorney's compliance with these Rules.

(B) Judicial Officers:

(1) Compliance with the requirements of Rule 4(A) or 4(C) by judicial officers shall be

considered as the maintenance of professional competence pursuant to Canon 3A(1) of the Delaware Judges' Code of Judicial Conduct;

(2) If in the sole judgment of the Judicial Commissioner any judicial officer fails satisfactorily to comply with these Rules in any respect, the Judicial Commissioner shall take such action as the Judicial Commissioner deems appropriate to induce compliance. If compliance satisfactory to the Judicial Commissioner is not obtained, the Judicial Commissioner shall refer the matter to the Chief Justice for appropriate action to induce compliance.

Rule 11. Confidentiality

Unless directed otherwise by the Supreme Court, the files, records and proceedings of the Commission, as they relate to or arise out of any failure of any Attorney to satisfy the requirements of these Rules, shall be deemed confidential and shall not be disclosed, except in furtherance of the duties of the Commission or upon the request of the Attorney affected or as they may be introduced in evidence or otherwise produced in proceedings under these Rules.

Rule 12. Review.

(A) **Petitions to the Commission:** Any Attorney, provider or other person aggrieved by any decision or action of the Commission may petition the Commission for relief within 30 days from the date of mailing of the notice of the action of the Commission. The petition may be accompanied by supporting evidence or documentation including affidavits and may include a request for a hearing. If a hearing is requested, the Commission may conduct a hearing at which the aggrieved party may present evidence and argument in support of the petition.

(B) **Petitions to the Supreme Court:** If the Commission denies such petition as a whole or in part, and if such action affects the substantial rights of the person claimed to be aggrieved, the person may petition the Supreme Court for relief by serving 2 copies thereof upon the Executive Director of the Commission and by filing 6 copies with the Clerk of the Supreme Court, such service and filing to be accomplished within 30 days of the action of the Commission. No petition shall be accepted unless the provisions of this paragraph have been timely fulfilled.

(C) **Supreme Court Review:** The Supreme Court may summarily refuse a petition which does not affect the substantial rights of the person claimed to be aggrieved. Appeals from the Commission's action to the Supreme Court shall be briefed, argued and determined from the record of the matter before the Commission and not by means of a hearing de novo. Findings by the Commission relating to disputed issues of fact and credibility will not be reversed by the Supreme Court so long as they are supported by substantial evidence.

FLORIDA

RULE 6-10.1 CONTINUING LEGAL EDUCATION REQUIREMENT

(a) Preamble. It is of primary importance to the public and to the members of The Florida Bar that attorneys continue their legal education throughout the period of their active practice of law. To accomplish that objective, each member of The Florida Bar (hereinafter referred to as "member") shall meet certain minimum requirements for continuing legal education.

(b) Reporting Requirement. Each member except those exempt under rule 6-10.3(c)(4) and (5) shall report compliance with continuing legal education requirements in the manner set forth in the policies adopted for administration of this plan.

(c) Fees. The board of governors of The Florida Bar may require a reasonable fee to be paid to The Florida Bar in connection with each member's report concerning compliance with continuing legal education requirements.

(d) Rules. The board of legal specialization and education of The Florida Bar shall adopt policies necessary to implement continuing legal education requirements subject to the approval of the board of governors.

[Revised: 08-01-2006]

RULE 6-10.2 ADMINISTRATION

(a) Board of Legal Specialization and Education. The board of legal specialization and education shall administer the continuing legal education requirements as herein provided. Any member affected by an adverse decision of the board of legal specialization and education may appeal as provided in rule 6-10.5.

(b) Delegation of Authority. The board of legal specialization and education may delegate to the staff of The Florida Bar any responsibility set forth herein, except that of granting a waiver or exemption from continuing legal education requirements.

(c) Scope of Board of Legal Specialization and Education Activities. The board of legal specialization and education shall cooperate with and answer inquiries from staff pertaining to continuing legal education requirements and make recommendations to the board of governors concerning continuing legal education requirements, including but not limited to:

(1) approved education courses;

(2) approved alternative education methods;

(3) number of hours' credit to be allowed for various education efforts;

(4) established educational standards for satisfaction and completion of approved courses;

(5) additional areas of education and/or practice approved for credit under continuing legal education requirements;

(6) modification or expansion of continuing legal education requirements;

(7) adoption of additional standards or regulations pertaining to continuing legal education requirements;

(8) amount of reporting or delinquency fees; and

(9) general administration of continuing legal education requirements.

(d) Maintenance of Records. The Florida Bar shall maintain a record of each member's compliance with continuing legal education requirements.

[Revised: 08-01-2006]

RULE 6-10.3 MINIMUM CONTINUING LEGAL EDUCATION STANDARDS

(a) Applicability. Every member except those exempt under rule 6-10.3(c)(4) and (5) shall comply and report compliance with the continuing legal education requirement.

(b) Minimum Hourly Continuing Legal Education Requirements. Each member shall complete a minimum of 30 credit hours of approved continuing legal education activity every 3 years. Five of the 30 hours must be in approved legal ethics, professionalism, bias elimination, substance abuse, or mental illness aware-ness programs. Courses offering credit in professionalism must be approved by the center for professionalism. These 5 hours are to be included in, and not in addition to, the regular 30-hour requirement. If a member completes more than 30 hours during any reporting cycle, the excess credits cannot be carried over to the next reporting cycle.

(c) Exemptions. Eligibility for an exemption, in accordance with policies adopted under this rule, is available for;

(1) active military service;

(2) undue hardship;

(3) nonresident members not delivering legal services or advice on matters or issues governed by Florida law;

(4) members of the full-time federal judiciary who are prohibited from engaging in the private practice of law;

(5) justices of the Supreme Court of Florida and judges of the district courts of appeal, circuit courts, and county courts, and such other judicial officers and employees as may be designated by the Supreme Court of Florida; and,

(6) inactive members of The Florida Bar.

(d) Course Approval. Course approval shall be set forth in policies adopted pursuant to this rule. Special policies shall be adopted for courses sponsored by governmental agencies for employee attorneys that shall exempt such courses from any course approval fee and may exempt such courses from other requirements as determined by the board of legal specialization and education.

(e) Accreditation of Hours. Accreditation standards shall be set forth in the policies adopted under this rule. If a course is presented or sponsored by or has received credit approval from an organized state bar (whether integrated or voluntary), such course shall be deemed an approved course for purposes of this rule if the course meets the criteria for accreditation established by policies adopted under this rule.

(f) Full-time Government Employees. Credit hours shall be given full-time government employees for courses presented by governmental agencies. Application for credit approval may be submitted by the full-time government attorney before or after attendance, without charge.

(g) Skills Training Preadmission. The board of legal specialization and education may approve for CLER credit a basic skills or entry level training program developed and presented by a governmental entity. If approved, credit earned through attendance at such course, within 8 months prior to admission to The Florida Bar, shall be applicable under rule 6-10.3(b).

[Revised: 02-01-2010]

RULE 6-10.4   REPORTING REQUIREMENTS

(a) Reports Required. Each member except those exempt under rule 6-10.3(c)(4) and (5) shall file a report showing compliance or noncompliance with the continuing legal education requirement. Such report shall be in the form prescribed by the board of legal specialization and education.

(b) Time for Filing. The report shall be filed with The Florida Bar no later than the last day of such member's applicable reporting period as assigned by The Florida Bar.

[Revised: 02-01-2010]

RULE 6-10.5   DELINQUENCY AND APPEAL

(a) Delinquency. If a member fails to complete and report the minimum required continuing legal education hours by the end of the applicable reporting period, the member shall be deemed delinquent in accordance with rule 1-3.6, Rules Regulating The Florida Bar.

(b) Appeal to the Board of Governors. A member deemed delinquent may appeal to the board of governors of The Florida Bar. Appeals to the board of governors shall be governed by the policies promulgated under these rules.

(c) Appeal to the Supreme Court of Florida. A decision of the board of governors may be appealed by the affected member to the Supreme Court of Florida. Such review shall be by petition for review in accordance with the procedures set forth in rule 9.100, Florida Rules of Appellate Procedure.

(d) Exhaustion of Remedies. A member must exhaust each of the remedies provided under these rules in the order enumerated before proceeding to the next remedy.

(e) Tolling Time for Compliance. An appeal shall toll the time a member has for showing compliance with continuing legal education requirements.

[Revised: 02-01-2010]

RULE 6-10.6   REINSTATEMENT

A member deemed delinquent for failure to meet the continuing legal education requirement may be reinstated in accordance with rule 1-3.7, Rules Regulating The Florida Bar.

[Revised: 02-01-2010]

RULE 6-10.7   CONFIDENTIALITY

Unless directed otherwise by the Supreme Court of Florida, the files, records, and proceedings of the board of legal specialization and education, as they relate to or arise out of any failure of a member to satisfy the continuing legal education requirements, shall be deemed confidential and shall not be disclosed, except in the furtherance of the duties of the board of legal specialization and education or upon request of the member, in writing, or as they may be introduced in the evidence or otherwise produced in proceedings under these rules. Nothing herein shall be construed to prohibit The Florida Bar from advising that a member has been suspended from the active practice of law for failure to meet continuing legal education requirements.

[Revised: 08-01-2006]

RULE 6-10.8   DISCIPLINARY ACTION

The board of legal specialization and education may refer misrepresentation of a material fact concerning compliance with or exemption from continuing legal education requirements for disciplinary proceedings under chapter 3 or chapter 4 of the Rules Regulating The Florida Bar.

[Revised: 08-01-2006]

GEORGIA

Rule 8-101. Purpose.

It is of utmost importance to members of the Bar and to the public that attorneys maintain their professional competence throughout their active practice of law. To that end, these rules establish the minimum requirements for continuing legal education.

Rule 8-102. Definition.

(a) "Accredited sponsor" shall mean an organization whose entire continuing legal education program has been accredited by the Commission on Continuing Lawyer Competency. A specific, individual continuing legal education activity presented by such a sponsor constitutes an approved legal education activity.

(b) "Active member" shall include any person who is licensed to practice law in the State of Georgia and who is an active member of the State Bar of Georgia, but shall not include the Governor, Lieutenant Governor, Speaker of the House of Representatives, other Constitutional Executive Officers elected statewide, members of the Georgia Senate and the Georgia House of Representatives, United States Senators and Representatives, and shall not include judges who are prohibited by law, statute, or ordinance from engaging in the practice of law.

(c) "Commission" shall mean the Commission on Continuing Lawyer Competency (CCLC).

(d) "Inactive member" shall mean a member of the State Bar who is on inactive status.

(e) "Supreme Court" shall mean the Supreme Court of Georgia.

(f) "Year" shall mean the calendar year.

Rule 8-103. Commission on Continuing Lawyer Competency.

(A) Membership, Appointment and Terms:

There is established a permanent commission of the State Bar of Georgia known as the Commission on Continuing Lawyer Competency. The Commission shall consist of sixteen (16) members, six (6) of whom shall be appointed by the Supreme Court of Georgia and six (6) by the Board of Governors of the State Bar of Georgia, one (1) shall be designated by the Executive Committee of the State Bar of Georgia, one (1) shall be the chair of the Board of Trustees of the Institute of Continuing Legal Education in Georgia or his or her designee, one (1) shall be designated by the Chief Justice's Commission on Professionalism, and one (1) shall be designated by the President of the Young Lawyers Division of the State Bar of Georgia. Members shall be members of the State Bar of Georgia. Members of the Commission appointed by the Supreme Court of Georgia and by the Board of Governors of the State Bar shall be appointed for staggered three (3) year terms and until their successors are appointed, except that the initial appointed members of the Commission shall consist of four (4) members appointed for a term of one (1) year, four (4) members appointed for a term of two (2) years, and four (4) members appointed for a term of three (3) years. The appointed members of the initial Commission shall be appointed half by the Supreme Court and half by the Board of Governors of the State Bar of Georgia. No member appointed by the Supreme Court or the Board of Governors may serve more than two (2) consecutive terms as a member of the Commission, and no such member may be reappointed otherwise to the Commission until he or she has been inactive as a Commission member for three (3) consecutive years. Members of the Commission designated by the Executive Committee, the chair of the Board of Trustees of the Institute of Continuing Legal Education, the Chief Justice's Commission on Professionalism, and the President of the Young Lawyers Division shall each serve for a term of one (1) year. No person so designated to the Commission may serve more than three (3) consecutive terms as a member of the Commission, and no such member may be redesignated otherwise to the Commission until he or she has been inactive as a Commission member for three (3) consecutive years.

The Commission shall designate each year one of its members to serve as Chairperson. The Executive Director of the State Bar of Georgia, the Executive Director of the Institute of Continuing Legal Education of Georgia, the Executive Director of the Chief Justice's Commission on Professionalism, and the Executive Director of the Commission shall serve as ex-officio members of the Commission, but shall have no vote. The Executive Director of the Commission shall serve as Secretary of the Commission.

Rule 8-104.   Education Requirements and Exemptions.

(A) Minimum Continuing Legal Education Requirement.

Each active member shall complete a minimum of twelve (12) hours of actual instruction in an approved continuing legal education activity during each year. If a member completes more than twelve (12) hours in a year, the excess credit may be carried forward and applied to the education requirement for the succeeding year only.

(B) Basic Legal Skills Requirement.

(1) Except as set out in subsections (a) and (b) below, any newly admitted active member admitted after June 30, 2005, must complete in the year of his or her admission or in the next calendar year the State Bar of Georgia Transition Into Law Practice Program, and such completion of the Transition Into Law Practice Program shall satisfy the mandatory continuing legal education requirements for such newly admitted active member for both the year of admission and the next succeeding year.

(a) Any newly admitted active member, who has practiced law in another United States jurisdiction other than Georgia for two or more years immediately prior to admission to practice in this state, may be exempted from completing the Transition Into Law Practice Program upon the submission, within three months of admission, of an affidavit to the Commission on Continuing Lawyer Competency. The affidavit shall provide the date or dates of admission in every other state in which the member is admitted to practice and a declaration that the newly admitted member has been actively engaged in the practice of law for two or more years immediately prior to admission in this state. Upon submission of a satisfactory affidavit, the newly admitted active member shall be required to complete the annual twelve hours of instruction in approved continuing legal education activity beginning at the start of the first full calendar year after the date of admission. Any newly admitted active member, who has practiced law in another United State jurisdiction other than Georgia for two or more years immediately prior to admission to practice in this state and who does not timely file the required affidavit, shall be required to complete the Transition Into Law Practice Program as set out above.

(b) Any newly admitted active member, who is a judicial law clerk or who begins a clerkship within three months of admission, shall not be subject to the requirement of completing the Transition Into Law Practice Program during the period of the judicial clerkship. Within thirty days of admission to the State Bar or within thirty days of the beginning of the clerkship if said clerkship begins within three months after admission, the member shall provide written notice to the Commission on Continuing Lawyer Competency of the date of entry into the clerkship position. Judicial law clerks are required to complete the annual twelve hours of regular instruction in approved continuing legal education courses beginning at the start of the first full calendar year after the date of admission. Within thirty days of the completion of the clerkship, the member shall provide written notice to the Commission on Continuing Lawyer Competency of the date of such completion. The member must complete, in the year the clerkship was concluded, or the next calendar year, the Georgia Transition Into Law Practice Program. Such completion of the Transition Into Law Practice Program shall satisfy the mandatory continuing legal education requirements for such member for both the year of completion of the clerkship and the next succeeding calendar year.

(2) Each active member, except those participating in the Georgia Transition Into Law Practice Program, shall complete a minimum of one (1) hour of continuing legal education during each year in the area of ethics. This hour is to be included in, and not in addition to, the twelve-hour (12) requirement. If a member completes more than one (1) hour in ethics during the calendar year, the excess ethics credit may be carried forward up to a maximum of two (2) hours and applied to the ethics requirement for succeeding years.

(3) Each active member, except those participating in the Georgia Transition Into Law Practice Program, shall complete a minimum of one (1) hour of continuing

legal education during each year in an activity of any sponsor approved by the Chief Justice's Commission on Professionalism in the area of professionalism. This hour is to be included in, and not in addition to, the twelve-hour (12) requirement. If a member completes more than one (1) hour in professionalism during the calendar year, the excess professionalism credit may be carried forward up to a maximum of two (2) hours and applied to the professionalism requirement for succeeding years.

(4) Confidentiality of Proceedings.

(a) The confidentiality of all inquiries to, decisions of, and proceedings by the Transition Into Law Practice Program shall be respected. No disclosure of said inquiries, decisions and proceedings shall be made in the absence of the agreement of all participating.

(b) Except as expressly permitted by these rules, no person connected with the Transitions Into law Practice Program operated under the auspices of the Standards of the Profession Committee of the Commission on Continuing Lawyer Competency shall disclose any information concerning or comments on any proceeding under these rules.

(c) The Transition Into Law Practice Program operated under the auspices of the Standards of the Profession Committee of the Commission on Continuing Lawyer Competency may reveal private records when require by law, court rule, or court order.

(d) Any records maintained by the Transition Into Law Practice Program operated under the auspices of the Standards of the Profession Committee of the Commission on Continuing Lawyer Competency, as provided herein, shall be available to Counsel for the State Bar only in the event the State Bar or any department thereof receives a discovery request or properly executed subpoena requesting such records.

(C) Exemptions.

(1) An inactive member shall be exempt from the continuing legal education and the reporting requirements of this Rule.

(2) The Commission may exempt an active member from the continuing legal education, but not the reporting, requirements of this rule for a period of not more than one (1) year upon a finding by the Commission of special circumstances unique to that member constituting undue hardship.

(3) Any active member over the age of seventy (70) shall be exempt from the continuing legal education requirements of this rule, including the reporting requirements, unless the member notifies the Commission in writing that the member wishes to continue to be covered by the continuing legal education requirements of this rule.

(4) Any active member residing outside of Georgia who neither practices in Georgia nor represents Georgia clients shall be exempt, upon written application to the Commission, from the continuing legal education, but not the reporting, requirements of this rule during the year for which the written application is made. This application shall be filed with the annual report.

(5) Any active member of the Board of Bar Examiners shall be exempt from the continuing legal education but not the reporting requirement of this Rule.

(D) Requirements for Participation in Litigation.

(1) Prior to appearing as sole or lead counsel in the Superior or State Courts of Georgia in any contested civil case or in the trial of a criminal case, any participant in the Transition Into Law Practice Program admitted to practice after June 30, 2005, shall complete the mandatory Advocacy Experiences of the Transition Into Law Practice Program set forth in Regulation (5) hereunder. The mandatory Advocacy Experiences shall be completed as part of the Mentoring Plan of Activities and Experiences, except that up to three (3) of the five (5) mandatory Advocacy Experiences may be obtained after completion of 60% of the credit hours required for law school graduation and prior to admission to practice. At least two (2) of the mandatory Advocacy Experiences must be completed as part of the Mentoring Plan of Activities and Experiences.

(2) Each active member who appears as sole or lead counsel in the Superior or State Courts of Georgia in any contested civil case or in the trial of a criminal case in 1990 or in any subsequent calendar year, shall complete for such year a minimum of three (3) hours of continuing legal education activity in the area of trial practice. A trial practice CLE activity is one exclusively limited to one or more of the following subjects: evidence, civil practice and procedure, criminal practice and procedure, ethics and professionalism in litigation, or trial advocacy. These hours are to be included in, and not in addition to, the 12-hour (twelve) requirement. If a member completes more than three (3) trial practice hours, the excess trial practice credit may be carried forward and applied to the trial practice requirement for the succeeding year only.

Rule 8-105.   Annual Report.

The Commission shall provide at the end of each year to all nonexempt active members an Annual Report of their CLE record in such form as the Commission shall prescribe.

A member whose record contains credit for unearned hours shall report corrections on or before January 31st. A member whose record fails to include credit for earned hours may report corrections on or before January 31st.

Rule 8-106. Hours and Accreditation.

(A) Hours. The Commission shall designate the number of hours to be earned by participation, including, but not limited to, teaching in continuing legal education activities approved by the Commission.

(B) Accreditation Standards: The Commission shall approve continuing legal education activities consistent with the following standards:

(1) They shall have significant intellectual or practical content, and the primary objective shall be to increase the participant's professional competence as a lawyer;

(2) They shall constitute an organized program of learning dealing with matters directly related to the practice of law, professional responsibility or ethical obligations of lawyers;

(3) Credit may be given for continuing legal education activities where (a) live instruction is used or (b) mechanically or electronically recorded or reproduced material is used if a qualified instructor is available to comment and answer questions;

(4) Continuing legal education materials are to be prepared, and activities conducted, by an individual or group qualified by practical or academic experience in a setting physically suitable to the educational activity of the program;

(5) Thorough, high quality, and carefully prepared written materials should be distributed to all attendees at or before the time the course is presented. It is recognized that written materials are not suitable or readily available for some types of subjects; the absence of written materials for distribution, should, however, be the exception and not the rule;

(6) The Commission may issue from time to time a list of approved accredited sponsors deemed by it to meet the requirements set forth in this Rule. Any other sponsor desiring to be approved for accredited sponsor status must file an application with the Commission with such program material and information as the Commission may require;

(7) Any accredited sponsor must keep and maintain attendance records of each continuing legal education program sponsored by it, which shall be furnished to the Commission upon its request.

Rule 8-107. Grace Period and Noncompliance.

(A) Grace Period

(1) Members who are deficient in their CLE, fees, or other requirements at the end of a calendar year are entitled to an automatic grace period until March 31st of the succeeding year to make up their deficiency. This does not change the requirement that members file their annual report by January 31st.

(2) Members who remain deficient on April 1st of the succeeding year shall pay a late CLE fee in an amount to be set by the Commission.

(B) Noncompliance

(1) Notice. Members who remain deficient in their CLE, annual report filing, fees, or other requirements on April 1st of the succeeding year are in noncompliance. The Commission shall so notify the members by first class mail to the member's current address contained in the membership records of the State Bar of Georgia. Service or actual receipt is not a prerequisite to actions authorized by these Rules.

(2) Hearing. Members may contest their noncompliance by requesting a hearing before the Commission. The request should be in writing, contain the reasons for their contest, and be made within 60 days of the date of the notice of noncompliance mailed by the Commission. The Commission shall hear the matter at its next meeting. No action will be taken while hearings are pending.

(3) Report. The Commission shall report to the Supreme Court those members who remain in noncompliance after the time to request hearings has expired or any requested hearings have been held.

(4) Supreme Court of Georgia Action. Upon receipt from the Commission of a report of noncompliance, the Supreme Court of Georgia shall enter an order it deems appropriate including an allowance of additional time for compliance or summary suspension from the practice of law until further order of the Court.

Rule 8-108.   Reinstatement.

An active member suspended under the provisions of these rules may be reinstated by the Court upon motion of the Commission and upon a showing that the delinquency has been corrected and payment to the Commission of a uniform reinstatement fee fixed by the Commission.

Rule 8-109.   Confidentiality.

Records of the Commission are not confidential.

Rule 8-110.   Immunity.

The State Bar, its employees, the Standards of the Profession Committee members and advisory, the Commission on Continuing Lawyer Competency, its employees, members and advisory, the Chief Justice's Commission on Professionalism, its employees, members, and advisors shall be absolutely immune from civil liability of all acts in the course of their official duties.

Rule 8-112. Foreign Law Consultants.

Foreign law consultant members of the State Bar of Georgia shall be subject to and shall comply with the provisions of this Part VIII in the same manner and to the extent as active members of the State Bar of Georgia.

Rule 8-712.   Foreign Law Con-[illegible]

[illegible] in a [illegible] qualified member in the State Bar of [illegible] shall be subject to and
shall comply with the provisions of this Rule [illegible] in the same manner and to the
extent as active members of the State Bar." (Feb 1, [illegible])

Section 1 - Purpose.

Continuing professional education of lawyers serves to improve the administration of justice and benefit the public interest. Regular participation in Continuing Legal Education programs will enhance the professional skills of practicing lawyers, afford them periodic opportunities for professional self-evaluation, and improve the quality of legal services rendered to the public. All active members of the Guam Bar shall participate in the requisite number of hours, as set forth in this Rule, of further legal study throughout the period of their active practice of law, and failure to do so shall result in their suspension from membership in the Guam Bar.

Section 2 - Appointment of the Guam Bar Association for the Administration of this Rule.

(a) The Supreme Court of Guam hereby appoints the Guam Bar Association to administer this Rule.

(b) The Guam Bar Association shall have the following duties:

1.   Accept the certification forms to be filed annually by each active member of the Guam Bar.
2.   Conduct a compliance audit following the end of each reporting period.
3.   Review and approve Continuing Legal Education courses and activities.
4.   Report at least annually to the Supreme Court of Guam.

Section 3 - Continuing Legal Education (CLE) Requirement.

(a) **Annual Requirement.** Every active member of the Guam Bar shall complete and certify attendance at a minimum of ten (10) hours per year of approved Continuing Legal Education ("CLE") courses of which at least two (2) hours shall be in the area of legal ethics or professionalism. Each member shall complete the required CLE courses during the period of January 1 through December 31 of the same year. An "active member" is defined as a person who has active status in the Guam Bar Association. The annual credit requirement for lawyers who are active members for only a portion of the year shall be prorated at a rate of one-half (½) credit per month he or she claims active status, or any portion of a month thereof. (Amended 12/12/03 pursuant to an Order in Administrative Proceeding No. AP03-004)

(b) **Carry-Over.** In an effort to provide flexibility in fulfilling the annual requirement, a one year carry-over of credit hours is permitted, so that accrued credit hours in excess of one year's requirement may be carried forward from one year to meet the requirement for the next year. A member may carry forward a maximum of six (6) credit hours, two of which, if earned in legal ethics or professionalism, may be counted toward the two (2) hours required in legal ethics or professionalism. Hours in excess of the minimum requirements defined in this Rule may not be carried forward for credit beyond the one year provided for in this Rule. (Amended 12/12/03 pursuant to an Order in Administrative Proceeding No. AP03-004)

(c) **Prior Attendance.** Credit will not be given for CLE hours accumulated prior to admission to the Guam Bar.

(d) **Approved Courses and Activities.** The CLE requirement may be met either by attending courses or completing any other continuing legal education activity automatically approved for credit as provided in this Rule. Self-study, including the use of approved video or audio tapes, computer based resources, or participation in legal educational activities involving correspondence technology, in-house law firm continuing legal education efforts, teaching, and participation in a committee of the Guam Bar Association or the Supreme Court of Guam may be considered for credit when they meet the conditions set forth in this Rule. Credit shall not be given for activities not specifically enumerated in Section 7 of this Rule. (Amended 12/26/02 pursuant to Promulgation Order No. 02-010)

Section 4 - Reporting CLE Credit.

(a) **Reporting Requirement.** Unless exempt as provided in this Rule, each active member shall submit to the Guam Bar Association, on or before January 31 of each year, a Certification of Attendance certifying that the member has attended mandatory Continuing Legal Education course(s) for the minimum number of hours required during the previous year ending December 31. No member may submit a Certification of Attendance after January 31 without approval of the Supreme Court of Guam upon written request by the member.

(b) **Approved Forms.** A member may submit a Certification of Attendance form provided to the attendees at the CLE course(s) or, in the alternative, the form entitled "Attorney Application for CLE Credit/Certification of Attendance" attached as Appendix 1 to this Rule.

(c) **Responsibility of Members.** Every active member shall be responsible for ascertaining whether or not the particular course satisfies the requirements of this Rule.

Section 5 - Exemptions.

(a) **New Members.** A newly admitted member shall be exempted from filing a certification for the reporting period in which he or she is first admitted. A newly admitted member is a person who has never previously been a member of the Guam Bar Association.

(b) **Waivers.** A member who has been granted a waiver from compliance with the requirements of this Rule shall be exempted from filing a certification for the period for which the waiver is granted.

1.   A member seeking a waiver from the requirements for a reporting year must submit a written petition, together with any appropriate or required material or documentation (e.g. doctors' letter, medical records), to the Supreme Court of Guam.

2.   A member should, whenever practicable, file his or her petition prior to the January 31 reporting deadline for the year the member seeks a waiver. Failure to file a petition in a timely manner may be considered by the Supreme Court in determining whether to grant a waiver.

3.   A waiver shall not be granted unless good cause is shown.

4.   The filing of any petition for waiver will toll the running of any time limit set forth in this Rule up to, but not to exceed, thirty (30) days.

(c) **Extensions.** A member who has been granted an extension from compliance with the requirements of this Rule shall be exempted from filing a certification for the period for which the extension is granted.

1.   A member seeking an extension from the requirements for a reporting year must submit a written petition, together with any appropriate or required material or documentation (e.g. doctors' letter, medical records), to the Supreme Court of Guam.

2.   A member should, whenever practicable, file his or her petition prior to the January 31 reporting deadline for the year the member seeks an extension. Failure to file a petition in a timely manner may be considered by the Supreme Court in determining whether to grant an extension.

3.   An extension shall not be granted unless good cause is shown.

4.   The filing of any petition for extension will toll the running of any time limit set forth in this Rule up to, but not to exceed, thirty (30) days.

Section 6 - Sanctions.

(a) **Self-Reporting.** This Rule establishes a self-reporting system.

(b) **Annual Auditing.** Following the annual reporting deadline, the Guam Bar Association shall conduct a random audit of at least 15% of the active members to determine compliance with this Rule.

(c) **Notice of Delinquency.** In conducting the random audit, the Guam Bar Association shall send a Notice of Delinquency to each member found to have violated this Rule for the prior year just ended and may, in its discretion, include in any Notice of Delinquency any prior year or years in which a member is found to have violated this Rule.

(d) **Cure.** Within ninety (90) days following the mailing of the Notice of Delinquency, the member shall submit a Certificate of Attendance, certifying that he or she has taken course hours necessary to meet the annual requirements of the Rule for the relevant year or years, along with a payment of a delinquency fee of $300.00 for each year of delinquency.

(e) **Failure to Cure.** If the member fails to submit the requisite Certification of Attendance sufficient to permit retroactive compliance with the Rule, the Guam Bar Association shall file a Notice of Non-Compliance with the Supreme Court of Guam.

(f) **Automatic Suspension.** Failure to take steps to certify compliance with this Rule within ninety (90) days of the mailing of the Notice of Delinquency shall result in automatic suspension by the Supreme Court of Guam.

(g) **Reinstatement.** In order to be reinstated, a member suspended for violating this Rule shall file a petition for reinstatement with the Supreme Court of Guam along with a reinstatement fee of $300.00 which shall be in addition to the delinquency fee of $300 for each year of delinquency which must be paid to the GBA pursuant to Section 6(d). The petition for reinstatement shall include a Certification of Attendance certifying that the suspended attorney has completed the course hours necessary to meet the annual requirements of this Rule for the relevant year or years.

(h) **Continuing Responsibility.** A suspension for violating this Rule shall not relieve the delinquent member of his annual responsibility to attend CLE programs or to pay his dues to the Guam Bar Association.

(i) **Representations by Members.** A member who makes a materially false statement in any document filed with the Guam Bar Association or the Supreme Court of Guam shall be subject to appropriate disciplinary action.

Section 7 - Approved Educational Activities.

(a) **Courses automatically approved.** The following CLE courses will be automatically approved for credit.

1. Live CLE programs offered by the federal or local judiciary in Guam or the Commonwealth of the Mariana Islands, or by the Guam or Commonwealth of the Northern Mariana Islands Bar.

2. Self-study courses listed for automatic approval by the Guam Bar Association. (See Section 7(c) of this Rule, below).

3. Courses or activities approved by the highest court of another jurisdiction or its designee, the American Bar Association, or a state bar association.

4. Courses or activities offered by a provider accredited by the official CLE committee of another jurisdiction or a national CLE accrediting body.

5. Up to 5 general CLE hours each reporting year for completion of qualifying pro bono

activities during the same reporting year, on a ratio of 5 pro bono hours to 1 general CLE hour, so long as a pro bono program, properly adopted by the Supreme Court of Guam, is in effect during all or part of the relevant reporting year.

(b) In-office CLE. Courses offered by law firms, either individually or with the other law firms, corporate legal departments, government attorneys, or similar entities, primarily for the education of their members may be approved for credit. Members who seek credit for in-office courses shall submit, with the required certification of attendance form, the program schedule or agenda and course syllabus or statement describing the subject matter. If the program does not cover a recognized legal topic, the member must attach a statement of how the course relates to his or her practice.

(c) Self Study. In addition to formal courses conducted in a class or seminar setting, approved self-study courses involving the use of video or audio tapes, computer resources (e.g. CD-ROM and internet), or correspondence courses (e.g. satellite and teleconference) may be used to satisfy the credit requirements of this Rule. Members who seek credit for self-study courses shall submit, with the required certification of attendance form, the program schedule or agenda and course syllabus or statement describing the subject matter. If the program does not cover a recognized legal topic, the member must attach a statement of how the course relates to his or her practice. The Guam Bar Association shall make available to the members of the Association a list of self-study courses that will be automatically approved for credit.

(d) Teaching or Lecturing. Members who teach legal courses or deliver lectures on law, whether to other attorneys or to members of the general public, may be given credit for the time spent in preparation and time spent teaching or lecturing. Members who seek credit for teaching or lecturing shall submit, with the required certification of attendance form, the course syllabus, lecture outline or statement describing the subject matter. If the program does not cover a recognized legal topic, the member must attach a statement of how the course relates to his or her practice. Once credit has been given for teaching a course or delivering a lecture, no further credit shall be given for a subsequent delivery of the same material to a different audience.

(e) Service on Guam Bar Association Committee or Supreme Court of Guam Committees. Members who are officers of the Guam Bar Association or sit on and actively participate in a committee of the Guam Bar Association or Supreme Court of Guam may be given credit for such participation. Members who seek credit for such participation shall submit, with the required certification of attendance form, a statement describing the officer's or committee's tasks, the scope of the member's participation and the number of hours actually expended attending meetings or working on assigned tasks. No more than two credit hours attributed to participation as an officer or a committee member may be used to satisfy the annual CLE requirement. (Amended 12/26/02 pursuant to Promulgation Order No. 02-010)

(f) Other Activities Not Contemplated by this Rule.

Subject to the discretion of the GBA's CLE Committee, activities not addressed in this Section may be eligible for CLE credit. Members shall submit any such requests for credit to the Committee, in the same manner as requests for approval are to be submitted pursuant to Section 7(b)-(d), specifically articulating the basis on which credit might be allowed.

Section 8 - Standards for Approval of Courses.

(a) General Standards. To be approved for credit, the CLE course or activity must satisfy the following:

    1.   The activity must have significant intellectual or practical content with the primary objective of increasing the participant's professional competence as a lawyer;

    2.   The activity must deal primarily with substantive legal issues, legal skills, practice issues, or legal ethics and professional responsibility.

(b) Legal Ethics or Professionalism Standards. In order to satisfy the legal ethics or professionalism credit requirement, the course or activity shall be devoted to the study of judicial or legal ethics and professional responsibility or professionalism, and shall include discussion of applicable judicial conduct codes, disciplinary rules, or statements of professionalism.

(c) The following activities shall not be accredited:

    1.   Activities that would be characterized as dealing primarily with personal self-improvement unrelated to professional competence as a lawyer;

    2.   Activities designed primarily to sell services or equipment; or

    3.   Repeat live, video, audio, or CD-ROM CLE courses for which the member has already obtained CLE credit in the same or any past reporting year.

Section 9 - Effective Date.

The effective date of this Rule shall be March 8, 2002. All active members are required to complete four (4) hours of CLE courses for the year 2002. Starting in 2003, and every year thereafter, unless otherwise ordered by this court, active members shall complete the total number of CLE court hours as required in this Rule.

HAWAII

RULE 22. MANDATORY CONTINUING LEGAL EDUCATION

(a) Mandatory Continuing Legal Education.

Except as otherwise provided herein, every active member of the Bar shall complete at least 3 credit hours of approved continuing legal education (CLE) during each annual reporting period. "Continuing legal education," or "CLE," is any legal educational activity or program that is designed to maintain or improve the professional competency of lawyers or to expand an appreciation and understanding of the ethical and professional responsibility of lawyers and is approved for credit by the Hawai'i State Bar, including those listed in Rule 22(b) of these Rules.

(b) Ethics and Professional Responsibility Minimum.

At least once every 3 years every active member shall complete 1 hour of approved ethics or professional responsibility education. This credit hour shall count toward the annual CLE requirement. "Ethics or professional responsibility education" means those courses or segments of courses devoted to: (1) the Rules of Professional Conduct; (2) the professional obligations of the lawyer to the client, the judicial system, the public and other lawyers; (3) substance abuse and its effects on lawyers and the practice of law; or (4) client trust administration, bias awareness and prevention, and access to justice.

(c) Carry Forward of Credit Hours.

A member may carry forward from the previous reporting period a maximum of 3 excess CLE credit hours. To be carried forward, the credit hours must have been earned during the calendar year immediately preceding the current reporting period.

(d) Mandatory Certification, Reporting, and Record Keeping.

Each active Bar member shall certify on the annual registration form whether the member is in compliance with this Rule by reporting the number of approved credit hours of Continuing Legal Education completed in the previous year, including the specific number of hours of ethics or professional responsibility education, and shall maintain certification records for the three most recent reporting periods. These records shall be subject to audit by the Hawai'i State Bar. Non-cooperation with an audit shall be deemed noncompliance with this Rule.

(e) Courses and Activities.

The requirements of this Rule may be met, subject to prior approval as set out in sections (f) and (g) of this Rule, by:

(1) attending approved courses or activities, including but not limited to, presentations conducted in-house or for Inns of Court, bar sections, professional legal organizations, and the like;

(2) preparing for and teaching approved professional education or judicial education courses or activities. Two hours of preparation time may be certified or reported for each 50 minutes of time spent teaching, i.e. 3 hours may be claimed for teaching a 50 minute course;

(3) completing approved professional education courses or activities; and

(4) writing scholarly legal articles that comply with Regulation 3 of the Continuing Legal Education Regulations of the State Board of Continuing Legal Education and are published in a bar journal, law review, book, bar association or similarly recognized journal, or other legal publication may qualify for 2 credit hours per 1500 published words per year.

(f) Approved Courses or Activities.

Courses and activities sponsored by the Hawai'i State Bar, the American Bar Association, or the National Organization of Bar Counsel qualify for CLE credit under this Rule.

(g) Approval and Accreditation Authorization.

The Hawai'i State Bar is authorized to approve or disapprove:

(1) other educational courses and activities for CLE credit and

(2) applications by an entity for accreditation as a course or activity provider. Approved courses and activities may include, but are not limited to, courses and activities conducted in-house or sponsored by Inns of Court, bar sections or other professional legal organizations. Accreditation shall constitute prior approval of CLE courses offered by the provider, subject to amendment, suspension, or revocation of such accreditation by the Hawai'i State Bar. The Hawai'i State Bar shall establish the procedures, minimum standards, and fees for approval of specific courses and activities or accreditation of providers and for revocation of such approval or accreditation.

(h) Full-time Judges.

Federal judges, magistrate judges, bankruptcy judges, U.S. Court of Federal Claims judges and administrative law judges are exempt from the requirements of this Rule. Full-time state judges shall participate for at least 3 hours each year in a program of judicial education approved by the Committee on Judicial Education. Full-time state judges who are unable to attend, in person, a program approved by the Committee on Judicial Education or who are excused from that program shall comply with this requirement by such other means as the supreme court approves. Full-time state judges shall report the number of approved judicial education hours attended on the judges' annual financial disclosure form.

(i) Inactive members.

Inactive members of the Bar who subsequently elect active status shall complete and report 3 hours of approved CLE, including 1 hour of approved ethics or professional responsibility education, within 3 months of electing active status. These CLE hours shall fulfill the requirements of Rule 22(a). CLE credits completed during the year prior to the reporting year, or in the reporting year, although completed while on inactive status, may be credited toward completing this requirement.

(j) Newly licensed members.

Each person licensed to practice law who elects active status in the year in which he or she is licensed shall not be required to comply with the required 3 CLE hours mandated by section (a) of this Rule for that year. Nothing herein, however, shall modify the obligations imposed by Rule 1.14 of these rules, that requires completion of a specific Hawai'i Professionalism course, distinct from general CLE courses, sponsored jointly by the Hawai'i State Bar and the Supreme Court and offered only bi-annually. Failure to complete the Hawai'i Professionalism course in a timely manner will result in automatic administrative suspension. *See* Rule 1.14(c) of these Rules.

(k) Good Cause Exemption or Modification.

An active member may apply to the Hawai'i State Bar for good cause exemption or modification from the CLE requirement. Members seeking an exemption or modification shall furnish substantiation to support their application as requested by the Hawai'i State Bar. Good cause shall exist when a member is unable to comply with the CLE requirement because of illness, medical disability, or other extraordinary hardship or extenuating circumstances that are not willful and are beyond the member's control.

(Adopted effective January 1, 2010. Amended effective July 1, 2010; July 1, 2012; January 1, 2015.)

IDAHO

*SECTION IV
Mandatory Continuing Legal Education
(*Section IV rescinded and replaced 3-17-14 – effective 5-2-14)

RULE 400. Statement of Purpose. It is important to the public and members of the Bar that attorneys who are engaged in the active practice of law in Idaho continue their legal education. Continuing legal education enables attorneys to acquire new knowledge and skill sets and understand current trends and legal issues. These rules establish the minimum requirements for that continuing legal education.

RULE 401. Definitions. As used in these Rules, the following terms have the meanings set forth below:
(a) **Accredited Activity.** A course, video, recording or other activity approved for CLE credit by the Board or its designee.
(b) **Active or Active Member.** A member of the Bar as defined in I.B.C.R. 301.
(c) **Attendance.** Being present in an audience, either in person or through an electronic medium, at a live Accredited Activity at the time the course is actually presented, or engaging in self-study using an accredited recorded program under Rule 404(a).
(d) **Bar.** Idaho State Bar.
(e) **Bar Counsel.** Legal counsel for the Board.
(f) **Board.** Board of Commissioners, the duly elected governing body of the Bar.
(g) **Canceled.** Status of an attorney as defined in I.B.C.R. 301.
(h) **Certificate of Compliance.** Form certifying an attorney's compliance with applicable CLE requirements.
(i) **CLE.** Continuing legal education.
(j) **Court or Supreme Court.** Supreme Court of the State of Idaho.
(k) **Credit Hour.** Sixty (60) minutes of actual attendance at an Accredited Activity, rounded to the nearest quarter of an hour.
(l) **Executive Director.** The chief administrative officer of the Bar.
(m) **House Counsel or House Counsel Member.** A member of the Bar as defined in I.B.C.R. 301.
(n) **I.B.C.R.** Idaho Bar Commission Rules.
(o) **New Admittee Credit-Approved (NAC-Approved).** An Accredited Activity addressing Idaho practice, procedure, and/or ethics that has been designated by the Bar as NAC-Approved in accordance with standards adopted by the Board.
(p) **New Attorney Program.** The NAC-Approved Accredited Activity described in Rule 402(f).
(q) **Resigned.** Status of an attorney as defined in I.B.C.R. 301.
(r) **Rules.** Section IV of the I.B.C.R.
(s) **State.** State of Idaho.

RULE 402. Education Requirement - Report. Except as provided in Rule 408, all Active and House Counsel Members shall complete and report CLE credits as provided in this section.
(a) **Minimum Requirements.**
(1) Active and House Counsel Members shall complete a minimum of thirty (30) credit hours of Accredited Activity in every three (3) year reporting period.
(2) Beginning with the attorney's next full reporting period after the effective date of these Rules and thereafter, at least three (3) CLE credits shall be in courses on legal ethics or professional responsibility, as approved by the Board or its designee. Such courses may include discussion of the Idaho Rules of Professional Conduct, professionalism and civility, client trust account administration and legal malpractice prevention.

(3) No more than fifteen (15) of the required thirty (30) credits may be self-study credits.
(4) Attorneys holding themselves out as specialists or certified specialists, as provided in Section X of the I.B.C.R., shall comply with the requirements of the applicable certifying organization for completion of CLE credits in the specialty area.
(5) Fulfillment of the credit requirements specified in subsections (1) through (4) above may be concurrent.
(b) **Reporting Period.**
(1) **General.** Except as provided in subsection (2), the reporting period for Active and House Counsel Members shall be every three (3) calendar years.
(2) **Exceptions.**
(A) Upon an attorney's admission to the Bar as an Active or House Counsel Member, the reporting period shall begin on the date of admission and end on December 31 of the third full calendar year following admission.
(B) The reporting period for an attorney who transfers to active status under I.B.C.R. 306 shall begin on the effective date of the transfer and end on December 31 of the third full calendar year following transfer, provided:
(i) Any CLE credits obtained to satisfy transfer requirements shall not apply to the new reporting period; and
(ii) The reporting period for an attorney who transfers to Active status after less than one (1) year on another status shall be the same reporting period that was applicable prior to the attorney's transfer from Active status.
(C) The reporting period for an attorney whose license has been reinstated under I.B.C.R. 305 shall be the same reporting period that was applicable prior to the license cancelation, provided that any CLE credits obtained to satisfy requirements for reinstatement shall not apply to the reporting period.
(c) **Certificate of Compliance.** An attorney who is required to complete CLE credits under subsection (a) shall submit a written Certificate of Compliance, on a form prescribed by the Board, verifying the attorney's CLE compliance for the applicable reporting period.
(1) **Content.** The Certificate of Compliance shall set forth the record of the attorney's compliance with these Rules during the reporting period and shall contain at least:
(A) A list of the Accredited Activities attended;
(B) The dates of attendance;
(C) The sponsoring organization;
(D) The hours attended, rounded to the nearest quarter of an hour; and
(E) The attorney's signature, under penalty of perjury.
(2) **Place of Submission.** The Certificate of Compliance shall be submitted to the Executive Director.
(3) **Time of Submission.** The Certificate of Compliance shall be submitted on or before February 1 of the year immediately following the conclusion of the reporting period.
(d) **Verification of Compliance.** The Executive Director shall cause up to ten percent (10%) of the Certificates of Compliance

submitted pursuant to subsection (c) to be randomly reviewed to verify compliance.

(e) **Exemptions.** Exemptions from all or part of the CLE requirements of subsection (a) may be granted as follows:

(1) **Eligibility.** An exemption may be granted:

(A) Upon a finding by the Executive Director of special circumstances constituting an undue hardship for the attorney;

(B) Upon verification of the attorney's disability or severe or prolonged illness, in which case all or a specified portion of CLE credits may be earned through self-study; or

(C) To attorneys over the age of seventy-two (72) years.

(2) **Request for Exemption.** An attorney may request an exemption by submitting a written request to the Executive Director setting forth the grounds for the exemption.

(3) **Time for Submission.** A request for an exemption must be submitted to the Executive Director at least sixty (60) days prior to the end of the attorney's three (3) year reporting period.

(f) **New Admittee Education Requirement.** Commencing on the date of admission to the Bar as an Active or House Counsel Member and within one (1) year thereafter, attorneys shall complete and report the following CLE credits:

(1) **NAC-Approved CLE Credits.** Attorneys shall complete at least ten (10) NAC-Approved CLE credits, which shall be counted towards satisfying the thirty (30) credit requirement set forth in subsection (a)(1).

(2) **Idaho Substantive Law Requirement.** Of the ten (10) NAC-Approved CLE credits required in subsection (f)(1), attorneys shall complete Accredited Activities addressing Idaho law on ethics, civil and criminal procedure, and community property. The Board shall approve and administer the Accredited Activities that satisfy the Idaho substantive law requirements of this Rule.

(3) **New Attorney Program.** An attorney who has actively practiced law for less than three (3) years prior to admission to the Bar shall also complete the New Attorney Program, which shall consist of an introduction to practice, procedure and ethics. The New Attorney Program CLE credits shall count towards satisfying the NAC-Approved CLE credit requirement in subsection (f)(1).

(4) **Extension.** An attorney may request an extension of time to complete these requirements by filing a written petition with the Executive Director within one (1) year of admission as an Active or House Counsel Member. The Executive Director may grant the extension upon a showing by the attorney that completion of these requirements would cause a substantial hardship.

(5) **Noncompliance.** An attorney's failure to complete these requirements shall be grounds for a finding of noncompliance under Rule 406.

RULE 403. Accreditation.

(a) **Standards.** Accreditation of CLE activities shall be consistent with the following standards:

(1) The activity shall have significant intellectual or practical content, and the primary objective shall be to increase the attorney's professional competence and ability to deliver quality legal services in an efficient, competent and ethical manner;

(2) The activity shall constitute an organized program of learning that addresses matters directly related to the practice of law, professional responsibility or ethical obligations of attorneys, provided:

(A) Courses included in the curriculum of a college or university undergraduate degree program do not qualify for accreditation as a CLE activity; and

(B) An attorney may receive credit for attendance at a non-legal educational program if the subject of that program relates specifically to the attorney's area of practice. For example, credit may be given for attendance at a medical-related program if the attorney's practice includes medical malpractice;

(3) The activity shall be conducted by an individual or group qualified by practical or academic experience in the covered subjects;

(4) The activity may include video, digital content or other presentation formats;

(5) Materials used in the activity shall be thorough and of high quality, and should be distributed to participants prior to or during the activity; and

(6) The activity may address law practice management to promote the efficient and competent delivery of legal services; however, no CLE credit shall be approved for marketing, client cultivation, general time management or stress reduction, computer training that is not specific to attorneys, general business topics, or vendor-sponsored activities designed solely to promote products or services.

(b) **Accreditation.** A person or organization may apply for accreditation of a CLE activity by filing with the Executive Director a written application on a form prescribed by the Board.

(1) **Contents of Application.** The application shall contain:

(A) The name of the sponsoring organization;

(B) A description of the CLE activity;

(C) Detailed descriptions of the subjects covered in the CLE activity;

(D) The name and qualifications of each presenter;

(E) The time schedule of a live CLE activity or the length, in minutes, of a recorded CLE activity;

(F) The name of the person or organization requesting accreditation;

(G) The date and location of a live CLE activity or, if the CLE activity is recorded, the date and location that the attorney completes the CLE activity for self-study credit; and

(H) For a recorded CLE activity used for self-study credit, the date the activity was produced or initially recorded.

(2) **Time of Filing.**

(A) The application may be filed prior to the CLE activity.

(B) An application filed more than thirty (30) days after the CLE activity is completed may be rejected as untimely.

(3) **Attendance Roster.** Upon completion of an Accredited Activity, the sponsor shall forward to the Bar an attendance roster specifying the number of credits earned by each attorney participant.

(4) **In-House and Self-Study Programs.** In-house or self-study programs that satisfy the requirements of subsection (a) may qualify for CLE credit upon written application.

RULE 404. Credit for CLE Activity.

Attorneys may earn CLE credits for Accredited Activities that meet the standards of Rule 403(a), as follows:

(a) **Credit for Attendance.**

(1) **General.** One (1) credit hour will be given for each hour the attorney actually attends an Accredited Activity.

(2) **Exceptions.** No credit will be given for:

(A) Time spent in introductory remarks, coffee and food breaks, business meetings, or other activities that do not involve educational aspects of the CLE activity; or

(B) Any course attended in preparation for, or prior to, admission to the practice of law, provided that credit will be given for NAC-Approved CLE credits as provided under Rule 402(f).

(3) **Self-Study Programs.**

(A) Credits for self-study programs are limited to no more than one-half of the total credits for each reporting period.

(B) Self-study programs include viewing or listening to legal educational programs that meet the standards set forth in Rule 403(a) and that were produced within the previous five (5) years.

(C) A CLE activity will be deemed a self-study program unless:

(i) Three (3) or more participants attend the CLE activity; and

(ii) The participants have access to the presenter during the CLE activity or, in the case of a video, audio or other recording, a moderator is present during the CLE activity who is qualified to answer attendees' questions about the CLE topic.

(b) **Credit for Teaching.**

(1) Except as otherwise provided below, an attorney who teaches an Accredited Activity shall receive three (3) credit hours for each hour of teaching.

(2) No credit will be given for:

(A) Preparation time;

(B) Time spent in introductory remarks, coffee and food breaks, business meetings, or other activities that do not involve educational aspects of the CLE activity;

(C) Presentations by attorneys that include the promotion of goods or services; or

(D) CLE activities for which the attorney is directly compensated other than as an honorarium or for expenses.

(3) An attorney who teaches an activity that meets the accreditation standards under Rule 403(a) that is directed primarily to nonlawyers shall receive only one (1) credit hour for each hour of teaching.

(4) For panel presentations, credit shall be calculated by multiplying the course hours by three (3) and dividing by the number of panel members.

(c) **Credit for Published Legal Writing.**

(1) Published legal writing authored by attorneys may qualify for CLE credit as set forth below.

(2) Credit may be given if the writing:

(A) Contributes to the attorney's legal education;

(B) Is intended for an attorney audience; and

(C) Is an original writing that is published, in print or electronically, in a professional legal journal or publication.

(3) No credit will be given for:

(A) A writing that is prepared in the ordinary course of the attorney's employment or practice of law;

(B) Written materials prepared as part of a CLE course;

(C) A writing for which the attorney is directly compensated, other than as an honorarium;

(D) A writing prepared for or on behalf of a client or prospective client or for marketing purposes; or

(E) Editing or rewriting.

(4) Credit for writing will be as follows:

(A) One (1) credit hour will be given for each one thousand (1,000) words, provided that any writing submitted for credit shall include a minimum of one thousand (1,000) words;

(B) Attorneys are limited to a maximum of six (6) total credits for writing for each reporting period;

(C) Credits will be applied in the year in which the writing is actually published; and

(D) A writing that is co-authored by one or more attorneys is eligible for credit in proportion to the percentage of work contributed by each attorney.

(5) An attorney requesting credit for a published writing under this subsection shall include with the request a copy of the writing, a word count, and the name and address of the publisher. If the attorney is a co-author, the request shall also include a statement indicating the percentage of work contributed by the attorney.

(d) **Carryover Credit.** No credit for attending or teaching a CLE activity shall apply to a reporting period other than the reporting period in which the credit is earned.

RULE 405. Processing Applications for Accreditation.

Applications for accreditation under Rule 403(b) shall be submitted to the Executive Director.

(a) **Application Fee.** All applications for accreditation of CLE activities shall be accompanied by a forty dollar ($40) application fee, provided:

(1) Applications submitted by non-profit sponsors for live CLE activities that are two (2) hours or less in length and held in Idaho shall be accompanied by a twenty dollar ($20) application fee; and

(2) No application fee is required for accreditation applications submitted by the Supreme Court, the Bar and its sections or district bar associations, the Idaho Law Foundation, Inc., or individual members of the Bar.

(b) **Credit Approval or Denial.** The Executive Director shall:

(1) Examine and evaluate all applications for accreditation following the standards established by Rule 403(a);

(2) Approve or deny all or any portion of a CLE activity for which accreditation is sought; and

(3) Determine the number of credit hours allowed for each CLE activity.

(c) **Decision.** The Executive Director shall provide written notice of the determination to approve or deny an accreditation application to the respective person or organization.

(1) **Contents of Notice.**

(A) If the application is denied, the notice shall state the reason for the denial and advise the applicant of the right to seek review of the decision.

(B) If the application is approved, the notice shall state the number of credit hours allowed for the CLE activity.

(2) **Timing of Notice.** The notice shall be provided within twenty-one (21) days following receipt of the application.

(d) **Review.** Any person or organization whose application for accreditation of a CLE activity has been denied may seek review of the Executive Director's decision by filing a written request with the Board, stating the reasons for the review request.

(1) **Time for Filing.** Any request for review of the Executive Director's decision shall be filed within fourteen (14) days of the notice.

(2) **Additional Information.** The applicant may present additional information to the Board for its consideration.

(3) **Decision of Board.** Following its review of the record, the Board shall issue a decision and advise the applicant of that decision. The decision of the Board is final.

RULE 406. Noncompliance.

(a) **Grounds.** The following are grounds for a finding of noncompliance under these Rules:

(1) Failure to complete the minimum CLE requirements under Rule 402(a);

(2) Failure to submit a Certificate of Compliance under Rule 402(c);

(3) Failure to complete the requirements of Rule 402(f); or

(4) Failure to complete the CLE requirement under I.B.C.R. 306(a)(1)(E) or any additional CLE credits required by the Board following Transfer to Active status.

(b) **Notice.** The Executive Director shall give, or cause to be given, written notice to each attorney who fails to comply with the CLE requirements of Rule 402 or I.B.C.R. 306. Such notice shall advise that:

(1) If the attorney has failed to complete the requirements of Rule 402(f), the Supreme Court will be notified to cancel the attorney's license and remove the attorney's name from the list of attorneys entitled to practice law in Idaho;

(2) If the attorney has failed to complete the CLE requirement under Rule 402(a) or (c):

   (A) The attorney must complete the CLE requirement by March 1 under I.B.C.R. 305; and

   (B) If the attorney fails to complete the CLE requirement by the March 1 deadline, the Supreme Court will be notified to cancel the attorney's license and remove the attorney's name from the list of attorneys entitled to practice law in Idaho; or

(3) If the attorney has failed to complete the CLE requirement under I.B.C.R. 306:

   (A) The attorney must complete the CLE requirement within thirty (30) days; and

   (B) If the attorney fails to complete the CLE requirement by the thirty (30) day deadline, the Supreme Court will be notified to cancel the attorney's license and remove the attorney's name from the list of attorneys entitled to practice law in Idaho.

(c) **Cure of Defect.** An attorney may cure noncompliance with CLE requirements under I.B.C.R. 306 or Rule 402(a) or (c) by:

(1) Completing the minimum CLE requirements by the deadline contained in the Executive Director's notice under subsection (b);

(2) Paying the MCLE late fee under I.B.C.R. 304(e)(2), if applicable; and

(3) Submitting a Certificate of Compliance to the Executive Director certifying compliance with the CLE requirements.

(d) **Cancelation for Noncompliance.** The license of an attorney who fails to comply with the CLE requirements may be canceled pursuant to I.B.C.R. 305.

(e) **False Report.** If the Executive Director has reason to believe that an attorney has filed a false Certificate of Compliance under these Rules, the attorney's name shall be forwarded to Bar Counsel for review of the attorney's conduct under the Idaho Rules of Professional Conduct.

RULE 407. Confidentiality.

The files, records and proceedings of the Board relating to an attorney's failure to comply with these Rules are confidential and shall not be disclosed except in furtherance of the Board's duties, upon request by the affected attorney, or as the files, record and proceedings may be introduced in evidence or otherwise produced in proceedings taken in accordance with these Rules.

RULE 408. Idaho Attorneys Licensed in Other States.

Except as otherwise provided in subsection (c) below, an attorney licensed in Idaho and also in another jurisdiction that requires attorneys to comply with mandatory CLE requirements may comply with the CLE requirements under these Rules as follows:

(a) **General.** An attorney whose principal office for the practice of law is not in Idaho may comply with the CLE reporting rules by filing a compliance report, on a form prescribed by the Board, certifying that:

(1) The attorney is subject to the mandatory CLE credit requirements in the jurisdiction where his or her principal office for the practice of law is located;

(2) The attorney complied with that jurisdiction's mandatory CLE requirements within the past three (3) years by submission and approval of the required credits; and

(3) The attorney is currently in compliance with the mandatory CLE credit requirements in that jurisdiction.

(b) **Certificate of Compliance.** An attorney submitting a compliance report under subsection (a) must provide a mandatory CLE certificate of compliance, or similar verification, from the other jurisdiction that includes the following information:

(1) Confirmation that the attorney is in compliance with the mandatory CLE requirements;

(2) The attorney's current mandatory CLE reporting period;

(3) The date that the attorney's previous mandatory CLE reporting period ended; and

(4) Confirmation that the attorney complied with the mandatory CLE requirements by submission of approved credits during the previous reporting period.

(c) **Exceptions.**

(1) Satisfaction of CLE requirements in Alaska or Hawaii does not satisfy Idaho mandatory CLE requirements.

(2) Attorneys licensed in other jurisdictions are not exempted from the requirement to complete the requirements of Rule 402(f).

(3) Attorneys claiming specialty certification shall comply with Rule 402(a)(3), provided that such attorneys may conform their reporting period to that of the jurisdiction in which their principal place of business is located.

(4) Attorneys who transferred to Active status under I.B.C.R. 306 shall comply with the CLE requirements applicable to the Transfer.

ILLINOIS

PART C. MINIMUM CONTINUING LEGAL EDUCATION

Preamble

The public contemplates that attorneys will maintain certain standards of professional competence throughout their careers in the practice of law. The following rules regarding Minimum Continuing Legal Education are intended to assure that those attorneys licensed to practice law in Illinois remain current regarding the requisite knowledge and skills necessary to fulfill the professional responsibilities and obligations of their respective practices and thereby improve the standards of the profession in general.

Rule 790. Title and Purpose

These rules shall be known as the Minimum Continuing Legal Education Rules ("Rules"). The purpose of the Rules is to establish a program for Minimum Continuing Legal Education ("MCLE"), which shall operate as an arm of the Supreme Court of Illinois.

Adopted September 29, 2005, effective immediately.

Rule 791. Persons Subject to MCLE Requirements

(a) Scope and Exemptions

These Rules shall apply to every attorney admitted to practice law in the State of Illinois, except for the following persons, who shall be exempt from the Rules' requirements:

(1) All attorneys on inactive or retirement status pursuant to Supreme Court Rules 756(a)(5) or (a)(6), respectively, or on inactive status pursuant to the former Supreme Court Rule 770 or who have previously been placed on voluntarily removed status by the Attorney Registration and Disciplinary Commission ("ARDC");

(2) All attorneys on disability inactive status pursuant to Supreme Court Rules 757 or 758;

(3) All attorneys serving in the office of justice, judge, associate judge, or magistrate of any federal or state court;

(4) All attorneys serving in the office of judicial law clerk, administrative assistant, secretary, or assistant secretary to a justice, judge, associate judge or magistrate of any federal court or any court of the State of Illinois, or in any other office included within the Supreme Court budget that assists the Supreme Court in its adjudicative responsibilities, provided that the exemption

applies only if the attorney is prohibited by the terms of his or her employment from actively engaging in the practice of law;

(5) All attorneys licensed to practice law in Illinois who are on active duty in the Armed Forces of the United States, until their release from active military service and their return to the active practice of law;

(6) An attorney otherwise subject to this rule is entitled to an exemption if the attorney meets all of these criteria:

  (i) the attorney is a member of the bar of another state which has a comparable minimum continuing legal education requirement or is licensed to practice law under a limited license issued by another state which has a comparable minimum continuing legal education requirement;

  (ii) the individual attorney's only or primary office is in that other state or, if the attorney has no office, the individual attorney's only or primary residence is in that state;

  (iii) the attorney is required by that state to complete credits to be in compliance with the continuing legal education requirements established by court rule or legislation in that state; and

  (iv) the attorney has appropriate proof that he or she is in full compliance with the continuing legal education requirements established by court rule or legislation in that state; and

(7) In rare cases, upon a clear showing of good cause, the Minimum Continuing Legal Education Board ("Board") may grant a temporary exemption to an attorney from the Minimum Continuing Legal Education ("MCLE") requirements, or an extension of time in which to satisfy them. Good cause for an exemption or extension may exist in the event of illness, financial hardship, or other extraordinary or extenuating circumstances beyond the control of the attorney. Attorneys denied a temporary exemption or extension may request reconsideration of the initial decision made by the Director of MCLE ("Director") by filing a request in a form approved by the Board (or a substantially similar form) no later than 30 days after the Director's initial decision. The Director shall decide the request for reconsideration within 30 days of its receipt, and promptly notify the attorney. If the Director denies the request, the attorney shall have 30 days from the date of that denial to submit an appeal to the full Board for consideration at its next scheduled Board meeting. Submission of a request for reconsideration or an appeal does not stay any MCLE compliance deadlines or MCLE fee payments.

(b) Full Exemptions

An attorney shall be exempt from these Rules for an entire reporting period applicable to that attorney, if:

(1) The attorney is exempt from these Rules pursuant to paragraphs (a)(1), (a)(2), (a)(3), (a)(4),(a)(5), or (a)(6), on the last day of that reporting period; or

(2) The attorney is exempt from these Rules pursuant to paragraphs (a)(1), (a)(2), (a)(3), (a)(4), (a)(5), or (a)(6), for at least 365 days of that reporting period; or

(3) The attorney receives a temporary exemption from the Board pursuant to paragraph (a)(7), for that reporting period.

(c) Partial Exemptions

An attorney who is exempt from these Rules for more than 60, but less than 365, days of a two-year reporting period, and who is not exempt for the entire reporting period pursuant to paragraph (b), shall be required to earn one-half of the CLE activity hours that would otherwise be required pursuant to Rules 794(a) and (d).

(d) Nonexemptions

An attorney who is exempt from these Rules for less than 61 days during a two-year reporting period, and who is not exempt for the entire reporting period pursuant to paragraph (b), shall be required to earn all of the CLE activity hours required pursuant to Rules 794(a) and (d).

(e) Resuming Active Status

An attorney who was exempt from these Rules, pursuant to paragraphs (b)(1) or (b)(2), above, for the attorney's last completed reporting period because the attorney was on inactive, retirement or disability inactive status pursuant to Supreme Court Rules756(a)(5) or (a)(6), 757 or 758, shall upon return to active status, have 24 months to complete the deferred CLE requirements, not to exceed two times the requirement for the current two-year reporting period, in addition to the CLE credit required for the current two-year reporting period.

(f) Attorneys on Discipline Status

Paragraphs (f)(1) and (2) shall apply to attorneys on discipline status for reporting periods ending June 30, 2012, and thereafter.

(1) Discipline Imposed Pursuant to Rules 770(a), (b), (c) and (e)

    (i) An attorney whose discipline is imposed pursuant to Rules 770(a), (b), (c) and (e) is not required to comply with the MCLE requirements for any reporting period in which the discipline is in effect.

    (ii) If the attorney is reinstated to the master roll by order of the Supreme Court ("Court"), the attorney must thereafter earn no less than 30 hours of MCLE credit and no more than 90 hours of MCLE credit which will be set by the MCLE Board based on the length of the attorney's discipline and whether credits need to be earned for the current reporting period. Those MCLE credits shall be earned and reported to the MCLE Board no later than 365 days after entry of the order reinstating the attorney to the master roll. The attorney shall contact the MCLE Board promptly after entry of the order reinstating the attorney to the master roll to establish the number of credits that need to be earned by the attorney. The attorney may apply any MCLE credits earned while the discipline imposed pursuant to Rules 770(a), (b), (c) or (e) was in effect. If the attorney does not earn the needed credits and report no later than 365 days after entry of the order reinstating the attorney to the master roll, the attorney shall pay a late fee, in an amount as set by the Board in the Court-approved fee schedule, and the attorney shall be referred to the ARDC pursuant to Rule 796(e). A reinstated attorney then needs to comply with the MCLE requirements for the two-year reporting period that begins after the attorney's reinstatement and all reporting periods thereafter.

(2) Discipline Pursuant to Rules 770(d), (f), (g) and (h)

An attorney whose discipline is imposed pursuant to Rules 770(d), (f), (g) and (h) is required to comply with the MCLE requirements for all reporting periods in which the discipline is in effect.

(g) Foreign Legal Consultants

Beginning with the reporting period ending June 30, 2012 and thereafter, the MCLE Rules do not apply to foreign legal consultants licensed under Rule 712.

Adopted September 29, 2005, effective immediately; amended December 6, 2005, effective immediately; amended February 10, 2006, effective immediately; amended September 27, 2011, effective immediately; amended December 7, 2011, effective immediately; amended June 5, 2012, eff. immediately.

Rule 792. The MCLE Board

(a) Administration

The administration of the program for MCLE shall be under the supervision of the Minimum Continuing Legal Education Board ("Board").

(b) Selection of Members; Qualifications; Terms

(1) The Board shall consist of nine members, appointed by the Supreme Court ("Court"). At least one member may be a nonattorney and at least one member shall be a circuit court judge. The Executive Director of the Supreme Court Commission on Professionalism and the Administrator of the Attorney Registration and Disciplinary Commission shall serve as ex-officio members in addition to the nine members appointed by the Court but shall have no vote.

(2) To be eligible for appointment to the Board, an attorney must have actively practiced law in Illinois for a minimum of 10 years.

(3) Three members, including the chairperson, shall initially be appointed to a three-year term. Three members shall be appointed to an initial two-year term, and three members shall be appointed to an initial one-year term. Thereafter, all members shall be appointed or reappointed to three-year terms.

(4) Board members shall be limited to serving three consecutive three-year terms.

(5) No individual may be appointed to the Board who stands to gain financially, directly or indirectly, from accreditation or other decisions made by the Board.

(6) Any member of the Board may be removed by the Court at any time, without cause.

(7) Should a vacancy occur, the Court shall appoint a replacement to serve for the unexpired term of the member.

(8) Board members shall serve without compensation, but shall be reimbursed for reasonable and necessary expenses incurred in performing their official duties, including reasonable travel costs to and from Board meetings.

(9) The chairperson and vice-chairperson shall be designated by the Court. Other officers shall be elected by the members of the Board at the first meeting of each year.

(c) Powers and Duties

The Board shall have the following powers and duties:

(1) To recommend to the Court rules and regulations for MCLE not inconsistent with the rules of the Court and these Rules, including fees sufficient to ensure that the MCLE program is financially self-supporting; to implement MCLE rules and regulations adopted by the Court; and to adopt forms necessary to insure attorneys' compliance with the rules and regulations.

(2) To meet at least twice a year, or more frequently as needed, either in person, by conference telephone communications, or by electronic means. Six members of the Board shall constitute a quorum for the transaction of business. A majority of the quorum present shall be required for any official action taken by the Board.

(3) To accredit commercial and noncommercial continuing legal education ("CLE") courses and activities, and to determine the number of hours to be awarded for attending such courses or participating in such activities.

(4) To review applications for accreditation of those courses, activities or portions of either that are offered to fulfill the professional responsibility requirement in Rule 794(d)(1) for conformity with the accreditation standards and hours enumerated in Rule 795, exclusive of review as to substantive content. Those courses and activities determined to be in conformance shall be referred to the Supreme Court Commission on Professionalism for substantive review and approval as provided in Rules 799(c)(5) and (d)(6)(i). Professional responsibility courses or activities approved by both the Commission on Professionalism and the MCLE Board as specified in this subsection shall be eligible for accreditation by the MCLE Board.

(5) To submit an annual report to the Court evaluating the effectiveness of the MCLE Rules and the quality of the CLE courses, and presenting the Board's recommendations, if any, for changes in the Rules or their implementation, a financial report for the previous fiscal year, and its recommendations for the new fiscal year. There shall be an independent annual audit of the MCLE fund as directed by the Court, the expenses of which shall be paid out of the fund. The audit shall be submitted as part of the annual report to the Court.

(6) To coordinate its administrative responsibilities with the Attorney Registration and Disciplinary Commission ("ARDC"), and to reimburse expenses incurred by the ARDC attributable to enforcement of MCLE requirements.

(7) To take all action reasonably necessary to implement, administer and enforce these rules and the decisions of the MCLE Director, staff and Board.

(8) To establish policies and procedures for notification and reimbursement of course fees, if appropriate, in those instances where course accreditation is withheld or withdrawn.

(d) Administration

The Board shall appoint, with the approval of the Supreme Court, a Director of MCLE ("Director") to serve as the principal executive officer of the MCLE program. The Director, with the Board's authorization, will hire sufficient staff to administer the program. The Board will delegate to the Director and staff authority to conduct the business of the Board within the scope of this Rule, subject to review by the Board. The Director and staff shall be authorized to acquire or rent physical space, computer hardware and software systems and other items and services necessary to the administration of the MCLE program.

(e) Funding

The MCLE program shall initially be funded in a manner to be determined by the Court. Thereafter, funding shall be derived solely from the fees charged to CLE providers and from late fees and reinstatement fees assessed to individual attorneys. This schedule of CLE provider fees, late fees, and reinstatement fees must be approved by the Court, and any reference in these Rules to a fee assessed or set by the

Board means a fee based on the Court-approved fee schedule. The Board may elect to charge fees up to the amount approved by the Court and the Board may, as it deems appropriate, charge fees less than the amount approved by the Court.

Adopted Sept. 29, 2005, eff. immediately. Amended Dec. 6, 2005, eff. immediately; June 5, 2007, eff. immediately; Nov. 23, 2009, eff. Dec. 1, 2009; Sept. 27, 2011, eff. immediately; Jan. 17, 2013, eff. immediately; Nov. 19, 2015, eff. immediately.

Rule 793. Requirement for Newly-Admitted Attorneys

(a) Scope

Except as specified in paragraph (f), every Illinois attorney admitted to practice on or after October 1, 2011, must complete the requirement for newly-admitted attorneys described in paragraph (c).

(b) Completion Deadline

The requirements established in paragraphs (c), (f) and (h) must be completed one year after the newly-admitted attorney's admission to practice in Illinois.

(c) Elements of the Requirement for Newly-Admitted Attorneys

The requirement for newly-admitted attorneys includes three elements:

(1) A Basic Skills Course of no less than six hours covering topics such as practice techniques and procedures under the Illinois Rules of Professional Conduct, client communications, use of trust accounts, attorneys' other obligations under the Court's Rules, required record keeping, professional responsibility topics (which may include professionalism, diversity issues, mental illness and addiction issues and civility) and may cover other rudimentary elements of practice. The Basic Skills Course must include at least six hours approved for professional responsibility credit. An attorney may satisfy this requirement by participating in a mentoring program approved by the Commission on Professionalism pursuant to Rule 795(d)(12); and

(2) At least nine additional hours of MCLE credit. These nine hours may include any number of hours approved for professional responsibility credit;

(3) Reporting to the MCLE Board as required by Rule 796.

(d) Exemption From Other Requirements

During this period, the newly-admitted lawyer shall be exempt from the other MCLE requirements. A newly-admitted attorney may earn carryover credit as established by Rule 794(c)(2).

(e) Initial Reporting Period

The newly admitted attorney's initial two-year reporting period for complying with the MCLE requirements contained in Rule 794 shall commence, following the deadline for the attorney to complete the newly-admitted attorney requirement, on the next July 1 of an even-numbered year for lawyers whose last names begin with a letter A through M, and on the next July 1 of an odd-numbered year for lawyers whose last names begin with a letter N through Z.

(f) Prior Practice

(1) Attorneys admitted to the Illinois bar before October 1, 2011

The newly-admitted attorney requirements of Rule 793(c) do not apply to attorneys who are admitted in Illinois before October 1, 2011, and after practicing law in other states for a period of one year or more. Attorneys shall report this prior practice exemption to the MCLE Board under Rule 796. Thereafter, such attorneys will be subject to MCLE requirements under the appropriate schedule for each attorney.

(2) Attorneys admitted to the Illinois bar on October 1, 2011, and thereafter

The newly-admitted attorney requirements of Rule 793(c) do not apply to attorneys who: (i) were admitted in Illinois on October 1, 2011, and thereafter; and (ii) were admitted in Illinois after practicing law in other states for a period of at least one year in the three years immediately preceding admission in Illinois. Instead, such attorneys must complete 15 hours of MCLE credit (including four hours of professional responsibility credits) within one year of the attorney's admission to practice in Illinois. Such attorneys shall report compliance with this requirement to the MCLE Board under Rule 796. Thereafter, such attorneys will be subject to the MCLE requirements under the appropriate schedule for each attorney.

(g) Approval

The Basic Skills Course shall be offered by CLE providers, including "in-house" program providers, authorized by the MCLE Board after its approval of the provider's planned curriculum and after approval by the Commission on Professionalism of the professional responsibility credit. Courses shall be offered throughout the state and at reasonable cost.

(h) Applicability to Attorneys Admitted after December 31, 2005, and before October 1, 2011

Attorneys admitted to practice after December 31, 2005, and before October 1, 2011, have the option of completing a Basic Skills Course totaling at least 15 actual hours of instruction as detailed under the prior Rule 793(c) or of satisfying the requirements of paragraph (c).

Adopted September 29, 2005, effective immediately; amended September 27, 2011, effective immediately.

Rule 794. Continuing Legal Education Requirement

(a) Hours Required

Except as provided by Rules 791 or 793, every Illinois attorney subject to these Rules shall be required to complete 20 hours of CLE activity during the initial two-year reporting period (as determined on the basis of the lawyer's last name pursuant to paragraph (b), below) ending on June 30 of either 2008 or 2009, 24 hours of CLE activity during the two-year reporting period ending on June 30 of either 2010 or 2011, and 30 hours of CLE activity during all subsequent two-year reporting periods.

(b) Reporting Period

The applicable two-year reporting period shall begin on July 1 of even-numbered years for lawyers whose last names begin with the letters A through M, and on July 1 of odd-numbered years for lawyers whose last names begin with the letters N through Z.

(c) Carryover of Hours

(1) For attorneys with two-year reporting periods

All CLE hours may be earned in one year or split in any manner between the two-year reporting period.

(i) If an attorney earns more than the required CLE hours in the two-year reporting periods of July 1, 2006, through June 30, 2008, or July 1, 2007, through June 30, 2009, the attorney may carry over a maximum of 10 hours earned during that period to the next reporting period, except for professional responsibility credits referred to in paragraph (d).

(ii) If an attorney earns more than the required CLE hours in the two-year reporting periods of July 1, 2008, through June 30, 2010, or July 1, 2009, through June 30, 2011, and all reporting periods thereafter, the attorney may carry over to the next reporting period a maximum of 10 hours, including hours approved for professional responsibility credit. Professional responsibility credit carried over to the next reporting period may be used to meet the professional responsibility requirement of the next reporting period.

(2) For newly-admitted attorneys subject to Rule 793

(i) For an attorney admitted to practice in Illinois on January 1, 2006, through June 30, 2009, such newly-admitted attorney may carry over to his or her first two-year reporting period a maximum of 10 CLE hours (except for professional responsibility credits referred to in paragraph (d)) earned after completing the newly-admitted attorney requirement pursuant to Rule 793.

(ii) For an attorney admitted to practice in Illinois on July 1, 2009, and thereafter, such newly-admitted attorney may carry over to his or her first two-year reporting period a maximum of 15 CLE hours earned in excess of those required by Rule 793(c) or Rule 793(f)(2) if those excess hours were earned after the attorney's admission to the Illinois bar and before the start of the attorney's first two-year reporting period. Those carryover hours may include up to six hours approved for professional responsibility credit. Professional responsibility credit carried over to the next reporting period may be used to meet the professional responsibility requirement of the next reporting period.

(3) An attorney, other than a newly admitted attorney, may carry over to his or her first two-year reporting period a maximum of 10 CLE activity hours (except for professional responsibility credits referred to in paragraph (d)) earned between January 1, 2006, and the beginning of that period.

(d) Professional Responsibility Requirement

(1) A minimum of four of the total hours required for the first two reporting periods must be in the area of professionalism, diversity issues, mental illness and addiction issues, civility, or legal ethics. Beginning with the reporting periods ending on June 30 of either 2012 or 2013, in which 30 hours of CLE are required, and for all subsequent reporting periods, a minimum of six of the total CLE hours required must be in such areas.

(2) Such credit may be obtained either by:

(i) Taking a separate CLE course or courses, or participating in other eligible CLE activity under these Rules, specifically devoted to professionalism, diversity issues, mental illness and addiction issues, civility, or legal ethics; or

(ii) Taking a CLE course or courses, or participating in other eligible CLE activity under these Rules, a portion of which is specifically devoted to professionalism, diversity issues, mental illness and addiction issues, civility, or legal ethics credit. Only that portion of a course or activity specifically devoted to professionalism, diversity issues, mental illness and addiction issues, civility, or legal ethics shall receive CLE credit for the professional responsibility requirement of this paragraph.

Adopted September 29, 2005, effective immediately; amended October 1, 2010, effective immediately; amended September 27, 2011, effective immediately.

Rule 795. Accreditation Standards and Hours

(a) Standards

Eligible CLE courses and activities shall satisfy the following standards:

(1) The course or activity must have significant intellectual, educational or practical content, and its primary objective must be to increase each participant's professional competence as an attorney.

(2) The course or activity must deal primarily with matters related to the practice of law.

(3) The course or activity must be offered by a provider having substantial, recent experience in offering CLE or demonstrated ability to organize and effectively present CLE. Demonstrated ability arises partly from the extent to which individuals with legal training or educational experience are involved in the planning, instruction and supervision of the activity.

(4) The course or activity itself must be conducted by an individual or group qualified by practical or academic experience. The course or activity, including the named advertised participants, must be conducted substantially as planned, subject to emergency withdrawals and alterations.

(5) Thorough, high quality, readable and carefully prepared written materials should be made available to all participants at or before the time the course is presented, unless the absence of such materials is recognized as reasonable and approved by the Board.

(6) Traditional CLE courses or activities shall be conducted in a physical setting conducive to learning. The course or activity may be presented by remote or satellite television transmission, telephone or videophone conference call, videotape, film, audio tape or over a computer network, so long as the Board approves the content and the provider, and finds that the method in question has interactivity as a key component. Such interactivity may be shown, for example, by the opportunity for the viewers or listeners to ask questions of the course faculty, in person, via telephone, or on-line; or through the availability of a qualified commentator to answer questions directly, electronically, or in writing; or through computer links to relevant cases, statutes, law review articles, or other sources.

(7) The course or activity must consist of not less than one-half hour of actual instruction, unless the Board determines that a specific program of less than one-half hour warrants accreditation.

(8) A list of the names of all participants for each course or activity shall be maintained by the provider for a period of at least three years. The provider shall issue a certificate, in written or electronic form, to each participant evincing his or her attendance. Such lists and certificates shall state the

number of CLE hours, including professionalism, diversity issues, mental illness and addiction issues, civility, or legal ethics CLE hours, earned at that course or activity.

(b) Accredited CLE Provider

The Board may extend presumptive approval to a provider for all of the CLE courses or activities presented by that provider each year that conform to paragraph (a)'s Standards (1) through (8), upon written application to be an "Accredited Continuing Legal Education Provider." Such accreditation shall constitute prior approval of all CLE courses offered by such providers. However, the Board may withhold accreditation or limit hours for any course found not to meet the standards, and may revoke accreditation for any organization which is found not to comply with standards. The Board shall assess an annual fee, over and above the fees assessed to the provider for each course, for the privilege of being an "Accredited Continuing Legal Education Provider."

(c) Accreditation of Individual Courses or Activities

(1) Any provider not included in paragraph (b) desiring advance accreditation of an individual course or other activity shall apply to the Board by submitting a required application form, the course advance accreditation fee set by the Board, and supporting documentation no less than 45 days prior to the date for which the course or activity is scheduled. Documentation shall include a statement of the provider's intention to comply with the accreditation standards of this Rule, the written materials distributed or to be distributed to participants at the course or activity, if available, or a detailed outline of the proposed course or activity and list of instructors, and such further information as the Board shall request. The Board staff will advise the applicant in writing within 30 days of the receipt of the completed application of its approval or disapproval.

(2) Providers denied approval of a course or activity shall promptly provide written notice of the Board's denial to all attorneys who requested Illinois MCLE credit for the course. Providers denied approval of a course or activity or individual attorneys who have attended such course or activity may request reconsideration of the Board's initial decision by filing a form approved by the Board no later than 30 days after the Board's initial decision. The Director shall consider the request within 30 days of its receipt, and promptly notify the provider and/or the individual attorney. If the Director denies the request, the provider shall have 30 days from the date of that denial to submit an appeal to the Board for consideration at the next scheduled Board meeting. Submission of a request for reconsideration or an appeal does not stay any MCLE submission deadlines or fee payments.

(3) Providers who do not seek prior approval of their course or activity may apply for approval for the course or activity after its presentation by submitting an application provided by MCLE staff, the supporting documentation described above, and the accreditation fee set by the Board.

(4) A list of the names of participants shall be maintained by the provider for a period of three years. The provider shall issue a certificate, in written or electronic form, to each participant evincing his or her attendance. Such lists and certificates shall state the number of CLE hours, including professionalism, diversity issues, mental illness and addiction issues, civility, or legal ethics CLE hours, earned at that course or activity.

(5) An attorney may apply to the Illinois MCLE Board for accreditation of an individual out-of-state CLE course if the following provisions are satisfied: (i) the attorney participated in the course either in person or via live audio or video conference; (ii) (a) for a course held in person in a state with a comparable MCLE requirement, the course must be approved for MCLE credit by that state; or (b) for a course held in person in a state or the District of Columbia without a comparable MCLE requirement, the course must be approved for MCLE credit by at least one other state with a comparable MCLE requirement; or (c) for a course attended by live audio or video conference, the course must be approved for MCLE credit by at least one other state with a comparable MCLE requirement; and (iii) the course provider has chosen not to seek accreditation of the course for Illinois MCLE credit.

(d) Nontraditional Courses or Activities

In addition to traditional CLE courses, the following courses or activities will receive CLE credit:

(1) "In-House" Programs. Attendance at "in-house" seminars, courses, lectures or other CLE activity presented by law firms, corporate legal departments, governmental agencies or similar entities, either individually or in cooperation with other such entities, subject to the following conditions:

(i) The CLE course or activity must meet the rules and regulations for any other CLE provider, as applicable.

(ii) Specifically, the course or activity must have significant intellectual, educational or practical content, its primary objective must be to increase the participant's professional competence as an attorney, and it must deal primarily with matter related to the practice of law, professionalism, diversity issues, mental illness and addiction issues, civility or ethical obligations of attorneys. No credit will be afforded for discussions relating to the handling of specific cases, or issues relating to the management of a specific law firm, corporate law department, governmental agency or similar entity.

(iii) The course or activity shall be submitted for approval on an individual course or activity basis rather than on a Presumptively Accredited Continuing Legal Education Provider basis.

(iv) The application, including all written materials or an abstract thereof, should be filed with the Board at least 30 days prior to the date on which the course or activity is to be held in order for a prior determination of acceptability to be made. However, prior approval by the Board shall not be required.

(v) Only courses or activities that have at least five attorney participants shall qualify for CLE credit. The attorneys need not be associated with the same firm, corporation or governmental agency.

(vi) Experienced attorneys must contribute to the teaching, and efforts should be made to achieve a balance of in-house and outside instructors.

(vii) The activity must be open to observation, without charge, by members of the Board or their designates.

(viii) The activity must be scheduled at a time and location so as to be free of interruptions from telephone calls and other office matters.

(ix) A list of the names of participants shall be maintained by the provider for a period of three years. The provider shall issue a certificate, in written or electronic form, to each participant evincing his or her attendance. Such lists and certificates shall state the number of CLE hours, including professionalism, diversity issues, mental illness and addiction issues, civility, or legal ethics CLE hours, earned at that activity.

(x) The Board may impose a fee, similar to the fees assessed on traditional CLE providers, on the provider of an in-house program for programs involving payments to the provider.

(2) Law School Courses. Attendance at J.D. or graduate level law courses offered by American Bar Association ("ABA") accredited law schools, subject to the following conditions:

(i) Credit ordinarily is given only for courses taken after admission to practice in Illinois, but the Board may approve giving credit for courses taken prior to admission to practice in Illinois if giving credit will advance CLE objectives.

(ii) Credit towards MCLE requirements shall be for the actual number of class hours attended, but the maximum number of credits that may be earned during any two-year reporting period by attending courses offered by ABA accredited law schools shall be the minimum number of CLE hours required by Rules 794(a) and (d).

(iii) The attorney must comply with registration procedures of the law school, including the payment of tuition.

(iv) The course need not be taken for law school credit towards a degree; auditing a course is permitted. However, the attorney must comply with all law school rules for attendance, participation and examination, if any, to receive CLE credit.

(v) The law school shall give each attorney a written certification evincing that the attorney has complied with requirements for the course and attended sufficient classes to justify the awarding of course credit if the attorney were taking the course for credit.

(3) Bar Association Meetings. Attendance at bar association or professional association meetings at which substantive law, matters of practice, professionalism, diversity issues, mental illness and addiction issues, civility, or legal ethics are discussed, subject to the requirements for CLE credit defined in paragraphs (a)(1) through (a)(2) above. The bar or professional association shall maintain a list of the names of all attendees at each meeting for a period of three years and shall issue a certificate, in written or electronic form, to each participant evincing his or her attendance. Such lists and certificates shall state the number of CLE hours, including professionalism, diversity issues, mental illness and addiction issues, civility, or legal ethics CLE hours, earned at that meeting.

(4) Cross-Disciplinary Programs. Attendance at courses or activities that cross academic lines, such as accounting-tax seminars or medical-legal seminars, may be considered by the Board for full or partial credit. Purely nonlegal subjects, such as personal financial planning, shall not be counted towards CLE credit. Any mixed-audience courses or activities may receive credit only for sessions deemed appropriate for CLE purposes.

(5) Teaching Continuing Legal Education Courses. Teaching at CLE courses or activities during the two-year reporting term, subject to the following:

(i) Credit may be earned for teaching in an approved CLE course or activity. Presentations shall be counted at the full hour or fraction thereof for the initial presentation; a repeat presentation of the same material shall be counted at one-half; no further hours may be earned for additional presentations of the same material.

(ii) Time spent in preparation for a presentation at an approved CLE activity shall be counted at six times the actual presentation time.

(iii) Authorship or coauthorship of written materials for approved CLE activities shall qualify for CLE credit on the basis of actual preparation time, but subject to receiving no more than 10 hours of credit in any two-year reporting period.

(6) Part-Time Teaching of Law Courses. Teaching at an ABA-accredited law school, or teaching a law course at a university, college, or community college, subject to the following:

(i) Teaching credit may be earned for teaching law courses offered for credit toward a degree at a law school accredited by the ABA, but only by lawyers who are not employed full-time by a law school. Full-time law teachers who choose to maintain their licenses to practice law are fully subject to the MCLE requirements established herein, and may not earn any credits by their ordinary teaching assignments. Presentations shall be counted at the full hour or fraction thereof for the initial presentation; a repeat presentation of the same material shall be counted at one-half; no further hours may be earned for additional presentations of the same material. Teaching credit may be earned by appearing as a guest instructor, moderator, or participant in a law school class for a presentation which meets the overall guidelines for CLE courses or activities, as well as for serving as a judge at a law school moot court argument. Time spent in preparation for an eligible law school activity shall be counted at three times the actual presentation time. Appearing as a guest speaker before a law school assembly or group shall not count toward CLE credit.

(ii) Teaching credit may be earned for teaching law courses at a university, college, or community college by lawyers who are not full-time teachers if the teaching involves significant intellectual, educational or practical content, such as a civil procedure course taught to paralegal students or a commercial law course taught to business students. Presentations shall be counted at the full hour or fraction thereof for the initial presentation; a repeat presentation of the same material shall be counted at one-half; no further hours may be earned for additional presentations of the same material.

(7) Legal Scholarship. Writing law books and law review articles, subject to the following:

(i) An attorney may earn credit for legal textbooks, casebooks, treatises and other scholarly legal books written by the attorney that are published during the two-year reporting period.

(ii) An attorney may earn credit for writing law-related articles in responsible legal journals or other legal sources, published during the two-year reporting period, that deal primarily with matters related to the practice of law, professionalism, diversity issues, mental illness and addiction issues, civility, or ethical obligations of attorneys. Republication of any article shall receive no additional CLE credits unless the author made substantial revisions or additions.

(iii) An attorney may earn credit towards MCLE requirements for the actual number of hours spent researching and writing, but the maximum number of credits that may be earned during any two-year reporting period on a single publication shall be one-half the minimum number of CLE hours required by Rules 794(a) and (d). Credit is accrued when the eligible book or article is published, regardless whether the work in question was performed in the then-current two-year reporting period. To receive CLE credit, the attorney shall maintain contemporaneous records evincing the number of hours spent on a publication.

(8) Pro Bono Training. Attendance at courses or activities designed to train lawyers who have agreed to provide pro bono services shall earn CLE credit to the same extent as other courses and seminars.

(9) Bar Review Courses. Attendance at bar review courses before admission to the Illinois Bar shall not be used for CLE credit.

(10) Reading Legal Materials. No credit shall be earned by reading advance sheets, newspapers, law reviews, books, cases, statutes, newsletters or other such sources.

(11) Activity of Lawyer-to-Lawyer Mentoring. Lawyers completing a comprehensive year-long structured mentoring program, as either a mentor or mentee, may earn credit equal to the minimum professional responsibility credit during the two-year reporting period of completion, provided that the mentoring plan is preapproved by the Commission on Professionalism, the completion is attested to by both mentor and mentee, and completion occurs during the first three years of the mentee's practice in Illinois. For reporting periods ending in 2011 or earlier, the maximum number of professional responsibility credit hours shall be four. Beginning with the reporting periods ending on June 30 of either 2012 or 2013, in which 30 hours of CLE are required, the maximum number of credit hours available shall be six.

(e) Credit Hour Guidelines

Hours of CLE credit will be determined under the following guidelines:

(1) Sixty minutes shall equal one hour of credit. Partial credit shall be earned for qualified activities of less than 60 minutes duration.

(2) The following are not counted for credit: (i) coffee breaks; (ii) introductory and closing remarks; (iii) keynote speeches; (iv) lunches and dinners; (v) other breaks; and (vi) business meetings.

(3) Question and answer periods are counted toward credit.

(4) Lectures or panel discussions occurring during breakfast, luncheon, or dinner sessions of bar association committees may be awarded credit.

(5) Credits are determined by the following formula: Total minutes of approved activity *minus* minutes for breaks (as described in paragraph (e)(2)) *divided by* 60 *equals* maximum CLE credit allowed.

(6) Credits merely reflect the maximum that may be earned. Only actual attendance or participation earns credit.

(f) Financial Hardship Policy

The provider shall have available a financial hardship policy for attorneys who wish to attend its courses, but for whom the cost of such courses would be a financial hardship. Such policy may be in the form of scholarships, waivers of course fees, reduced course fees, or discounts. Upon request by the Board, the provider must produce the detailed financial hardship policy. The Board may require, on good cause shown, a provider to set aside without cost, or at reduced cost, a reasonable number of places in the course for those attorneys determined by the Board to have good cause to attend the course for reduced or no cost.

Adopted September 29, 2005, effective immediately; amended October 4, 2007, effective immediately; amended October 12, 2010, effective immediately; amended September 27, 2011; amended Feb. 6, 2013 effective immediately.

Rule 796.   Enforcement of MCLE Requirements

(a) Reporting Compliance

(1) Notice of Requirement to Submit MCLE Certification

The MCLE Board shall send to attorneys as set forth in (i), (ii) and (iii) below a notice of requirement to submit an MCLE certification ("Initial MCLE Notice"). The attorney's certification shall state whether the attorney complied with these Rules, has not complied with these Rules or is exempt.

(i) Newly-admitted attorney requirement
        On or before the first day of the month preceding the end of an attorney's newly-admitted attorney requirement reporting period, the Director shall mail or email to the attorney, at a mailing or email address maintained by the ARDC, an Initial MCLE Notice.

(ii) Two-year reporting period and deferred credits requirements

On or before May 1 of each two-year reporting period, the Director shall mail or email to the attorney, at a mailing or email address maintained by the ARDC, an Initial MCLE notice.

(iii) Attorneys Known to be Exempt or Removed for MCLE Noncompliance

An Initial MCLE Notice need not be sent to an attorney known by the Director to be fully exempt from these Rules pursuant to Rule 791(b) or to an attorney who has already been removed from the master roll of attorneys due to the attorney's failure to comply with the MCLE requirements for two consecutive reporting periods or more.

(2) Every Illinois attorney who is either subject to these Rules or who is sent an MCLE Initial Notice shall submit a certification to the Board, by means of the Board's online reporting system or other means specified by the Director, within 31 days after the end of the attorney's reporting period. It is the responsibility of each attorney on the master roll to notify the ARDC of any change of address or email address. Failure to receive an Initial MCLE Notice shall not constitute an excuse for failure to file the certification.

(b) Failure to Report Compliance

Attorneys who fail to submit an MCLE certification within 31 days after the end of their reporting period, or who file a certification within 31 days after the end of their reporting stating that they have not complied with these Rules during the reporting period, shall be mailed or emailed a notice by the Director to inform them of their noncompliance. Attorneys shall be given 61 additional days from the original certification due date provided in Rule 796(a)(2) to achieve compliance and submit a certification, by means of the Board's online reporting system or other means specified by the Director, stating that they have complied with these Rules or are exempt. The Director shall not send a notice of noncompliance to attorneys whom the Director knows, based on the status of the attorneys' licenses as inactive, retirement, disability inactive, judicial or military with the ARDC, are fully exempt from these Rules.

(c) Grace Period

Attorneys given additional time pursuant to paragraph (b) to comply with the requirements of these Rules may use that "grace period" to attain the adequate number of hours for compliance. Credit hours earned during a grace period may be counted toward compliance with the previous reporting period requirement, and hours in excess of the requirement may be used to meet the current reporting period's requirement. No attorney may receive more than one grace period with respect to the same reporting period, and the grace period shall not be extended if the Director fails to send, or the attorney fails to receive, a notice pursuant to paragraph (b).

(d) Late Fees

(1) Attorneys who are not fully exempt under Rule 791(a)(1), (2), (3) or (5) and who, for whatever reason, fail to submit an MCLE certification pursuant to Rule 796(a)(2) within 31 days after the end of their reporting period, and who are sent a notice of noncompliance from the Director pursuant to paragraph (b), shall pay a late fee, in an amount to be set by the Board. The Director shall not assess a late fee to an attorney whom the Director knows, based on the status of the attorney's license as inactive, retirement, disability inactive, judicial or military with the ARDC, are fully exempt from these Rules.

(2) Attorneys who submit an MCLE certification to the Board within 31 days after their reporting period ends and who certify that they failed to comply with these Rules during the applicable reporting period, shall pay a late fee, in an amount to be set by the Board that is less than the late fee imposed pursuant to paragraph (d)(1).

(e) Failure to Comply or Failure to Report

The Director shall refer to the ARDC the names of attorneys who were mailed or emailed a notice of noncompliance and who, by the end of their grace periods, failed either: (1) to comply or to report compliance with the requirements of these Rules to the MCLE Board; or (2) to report an exemption from the requirements of these Rules to the MCLE Board. The Director shall also refer to the ARDC the names of attorneys who, by the end of their grace period, failed to pay any outstanding MCLE fee. The ARDC shall then send notice, by mail or email, to any such attorneys that they will be removed from the master roll on the date specified in the notice, which shall be no sooner than 21 days from the date of the notice, because of their failure to comply or report compliance, failure to report an exemption, or failure to pay an outstanding MCLE fee. The ARDC shall remove such attorneys from the master roll of attorneys on the date specified in the notice unless the Director certifies before that date that an attorney has complied. Such removal is not a disciplinary sanction.

(f) Recordkeeping and Audits

(1) Each attorney subject to these Rules shall maintain, for three years after the end of the relevant reporting period, certificates of attendance received pursuant to Rules 795(a)(8), (c)(4), (d)(1)(ix), (d)(2)(v), (d)(3), as well as sufficient documentation necessary to corroborate CLE activity hours earned pursuant to Rules 795(d)(4) through (d)(9).

(2) The Board may conduct a reasonable number of audits, under a plan approved by the Court. At least some of these audits shall be randomly selected, to determine the accuracy of attorneys' certifications of compliance or exemption. With respect to audits that are not randomly selected, in choosing subjects for those audits the Board shall give increased consideration to attorneys who assumed inactive or

retirement status under Supreme Court Rule 756(a)(5) or (a)(6), and were thereby fully or partially exempt from these Rules pursuant to Rule 791(b) or (c), and who subsequently resumed active status.

(3) The ARDC may investigate an attorney's compliance with these Rules only upon referral from the Director; the ARDC will not investigate an attorney's compliance with these Rules as part of its other investigations. When the Director refers a matter to the ARDC, the investigation, and any resulting prosecution, shall be conducted in accordance with the rules pertaining to ARDC proceedings.

(g) Audits That Reveal an Inaccurate Certification

(1) If an audit conducted pursuant to paragraph (f)(2) reveals that the attorney was not in compliance with or exempt from these Rules for any reporting period for which the attorney had filed a certification of compliance or exemption, the Director shall provide the attorney with written notice containing: (i) the results of the audit, specifying each aspect of the Rules with which the attorney did not comply or the reason why the attorney is not exempt; (ii) a summary of the basis of that determination; and (iii) a deadline, which shall be at least 30 days from the date of the notice, for the attorney to file a written response if the attorney objects to any of the contents of the notice.

(2) After considering any response from the attorney, if the Board determines that the attorney filed an inaccurate certification, the attorney shall be given 60 days in which to file an amended certification, together with all documentation specified in paragraph (f)(1), demonstrating full compliance with the applicable MCLE requirements. The attorney also shall pay a late fee in an amount to be set by the Board. The assessment of a late fee is not a disciplinary sanction.

(3) If the results of the audit suggest that the attorney willfully filed a false certification, the Board through its Director shall provide that information to the ARDC.

(h) Reinstatement

An attorney who has been removed from the master roll due to noncompliance with these Rules may be reinstated by the ARDC, upon recommendation of the Board. Such recommendation may be made only after the removed attorney files a certification which the Board determines shows full compliance with the applicable MCLE requirements for each reporting period for which the attorney was removed from the master roll due to MCLE noncompliance. To be reinstated, the attorney shall pay a reinstatement fee for each reporting period for which the attorney was removed from the master roll due to MCLE noncompliance with the request, in an amount to be set by the Board. The Board may elect to cap the total amount of the reinstatement fee when an attorney has been removed from the master roll due to MCLE noncompliance in more than six consecutive reporting periods. The attorney must also meet any further conditions and pay any additional fees as may be required by Rule 756. The removed attorney may attain the necessary credit hours during the period of removal to meet the requirements for the years of noncompliance. Excess hours earned during the period of removal, however, may not be counted towards meeting the current or future reporting periods' requirements.

Adopted Sept. 29, 2005, eff. immediately. Amended Oct. 5, 2006, eff. immediately; Sept. 27, 2011, eff. immediately; Nov. 19, 2015, eff. Feb. 1, 2016.

Rule 797. Confidentiality

All files, records and proceedings of the Board must be kept confidential, and may not be disclosed except (a) in furtherance of the duties of the Board, (b) upon written request and consent of the persons affected, (c) pursuant to a proper subpoena *duces tecum*, or (d) as ordered by a court of competent jurisdiction.

Adopted September 29, 2005, effective immediately.

Rule 798. Reserved

INDIANA

Rule 29. Mandatory Continuing Legal Education

SECTION 1. PURPOSE.

The purpose of this Rule is to establish minimum continuing legal education requirements for each Attorney admitted to the Bar of the State of Indiana. The minimum continuing education requirements for an Attorney who serves as a Judge in the State of Indiana shall be governed by the provisions of Admission and Discipline Rule 28.

SECTION 2. DEFINITIONS.

As used in this Rule:

(a) Approved Courses shall mean those Substantive Legal Courses and those Non Legal Subject Matter Courses (as defined below) which are approved under the Commission's Accreditation Policies in the Guidelines to this Rule.

(b) Attorney shall mean a person who has been admitted to practice law in the State of Indiana and whose name appears in the files of the Board of Law Examiners as provided under Admission and Discipline Rule 4. The term Attorney includes a state or federal administrative law judge.

(c) Bar shall mean the Indiana Bar and includes those persons who are Attorneys under subsection (b) above.

(d) Business Day shall mean Monday, Tuesday, Wednesday, Thursday, and Friday of each week but shall not include Federal or Indiana state holidays.

(e) Clerk shall mean Clerk of the Indiana Supreme Court, Court of Appeals and Tax Court.

(f) Commission shall mean the Indiana Commission For Continuing Legal Education created by Section 4 of this Rule.

(g) Commissioner shall mean a person who is a member of the Commission.

(h) Educational Period shall mean a three-year period during which an Attorney must complete thirty-six (36) hours of Approved Courses. Educational Periods shall be sequential, in that once an Attorney's particular three-year period terminates, a new three-year period and thirty-six hour minimum shall commence.

(i) [Deleted, eff. January 1, 2011]

(j) Non Legal Subject Matter (NLS) Courses shall mean courses that the Commission approves for Non Legal Subject Matter credit pursuant to

Section 3(a) of this Rule because, even though they lack substantive legal content, they nonetheless enhance an attendee's proficiency in the attorney's practice of law.

(k) Supreme Court shall mean the Supreme Court of the State of Indiana.

(l) Year shall mean calendar year unless otherwise specified in this Rule.

(m) Professional Responsibility Credits shall mean credits for topics that specifically address legal ethics or professional responsibility.

(n) Distance Education shall mean instructional delivery that does not constrain the student to be physically present in the same location as the instructor and does not require an attendant at the learning site to monitor attendance.

SECTION 3. EDUCATION REQUIREMENTS.

(a) Every Attorney, except as provided below, shall complete no less than six (6) hours of Approved Courses each year and shall complete no less than thirty-six (36) hours of Approved Courses each Educational Period. At least three (3) hours of Approved Courses in professional responsibility shall be included within the hours of continuing legal education required during each three year Educational Period. Such hours may be integrated as part of a substantive program or as a free standing program. No more than twelve (12) hours of the Educational Period requirement shall be filled by Non Legal Subject Matter Courses. No more than six (6) hours of the Educational Period requirement shall be filled through interactive Distance Education. No more than three (3) hours of the Educational Period requirement shall be filled through in-house education programs in accordance with the Guidelines. All credits for a single educational activity will be applied in one (1) calendar year.

(b) Attorneys admitted to the Indiana Bar before December 31, 1998, on the basis of successfully passing the Indiana Bar examination, shall have a grace period of three (3) years commencing on January 1 of the year of admission and then shall commence meeting the minimum yearly and Educational Period requirements thereafter. Attorneys admitted after December 31, 1998, shall commence meeting the yearly and Educational Period requirements starting on January 1 after the year of their admission by completing programs designated by the Commission as appropriate for new lawyers.

For Attorneys admitted after December 31, 1998, at least six (6) of the thirty-six (36) Educational Period requirements shall be satisfied by attending an Applied Professionalism Program for Newly Admitted Attorneys which has been accredited by the Commission.

(c) Attorneys admitted on foreign license or Attorneys who terminate their inactive status shall have no grace period. Their first three-year Educational Period shall commence on January 1 of the year of admission or termination of inactive status.

(d) In recognition of the nature of the work, commitment of time, and the benefit of Attorney participation in the Indiana General Assembly, during an Attorney's Educational Period, for each calendar year in which the Attorney serves as a member of the Indiana General Assembly for more than six (6) months, the Attorney's minimum number of continuing legal education hours for that Educational Period shall be reduced by six (6) hours.

SECTION 4. COMMISSION FOR CONTINUING LEGAL EDUCATION.

(a) Creation of the Commission. A commission to be known as the Indiana Commission For Continuing Legal Education is hereby created and shall have the powers and duties hereinafter set forth. The Commission shall consist of eleven (11) Commissioners.

(b) Appointment of Commissioners and Executive Director. All Commissioners and the Executive Director shall be appointed by the Supreme Court.

(c) Diversity of Commissioners. It is generally desirable that the Commissioners be selected from various geographic areas and types of practice in order to reflect the diversity of the Bar and consideration should be given to the appointment of one (1) non-lawyer public member. The three (3) geographic divisions used for selecting Judges for the Indiana Court of Appeals in the First, Second and Third Districts may be used as a model for achieving geographic diversity.

(d) Terms of Commissioners. Commissioners shall be appointed for five (5) year terms. All terms shall commence on January 1 and end on December 31. Any Commissioner who has served for all or part of two (2) consecutive terms shall not be reappointed to the Commission for at least three (3) consecutive years.

SECTION 5. ORGANIZATION OF THE COMMISSION.

(a) Election of Officers. At the first meeting of the Commission after each December 1, the Commissioners shall elect from the membership of the Commission a Chair who shall preside at all meetings, a Vice Chair who shall preside in the absence of the Chair, a Secretary who shall be responsible for giving notices and keeping the minutes of the meetings of the Commission and a Treasurer who shall be responsible for keeping the records of account of the Commission.

(b) Meetings. The Commission shall meet at least twice each year at times and places designated by the Chair. The Chair, the Executive Committee or any six (6) Commissioners may call special meetings of the Commission.

(c) Notices. The Secretary shall send notice of each meeting of the Commission, stating the purposes of the meeting, to all Commissioners at least five (5) business days before the meeting. Commissioners may waive notice of a meeting by attending the meeting or by delivering a written waiver to the Secretary either before or after the meeting.

(d) Quorum. Six (6) Commissioners shall constitute a quorum for the transaction of business. The Commission shall act by a majority of the Commissioners constituting the quorum. Commissioners may participate in meetings of the Commission and committees thereof by telephone or other similar device.

(e) Vacancies. Any vacancy on the Commission shall be filled as soon as practical and the new Commissioner so appointed shall serve out the unexpired term of the Commissioner being replaced.

(f) Executive Committee. The officers of the Commission described in subsection (a) of this Section shall comprise the Executive Committee which shall have the power to conduct all necessary business of the Commission that may arise between meetings of the full Commission. Three (3) officers of the Commission shall constitute a quorum of the Executive Committee, and the Executive Committee shall act by a vote of a majority of the officers constituting the quorum. All action taken by the Executive Committee shall be reported to the full Commission at its next meeting.

(g) Other Committees. The Commission may appoint such other committees having such powers and duties as the Commission may determine from time to time.

SECTION 6. POWERS AND DUTIES OF THE COMMISSION AND EXECUTIVE DIRECTOR.

(a) In addition to the powers and duties set forth in this Rule or Rule 28, the Commission shall have the power and duty to:

(1) Approve all or portions of individual educational activities which satisfy the legal education requirements of this Rule.

(2) Approve Sponsors who meet the Requirements of Section 4 of the Commission's Guidelines and whose educational activities satisfy the legal education requirements of this Rule. The Judicial Conference and all seminars conducted by the Judicial Center shall be approved for credit.

(3) Determine the number of credit hours allowed for each educational activity.

(4) Establish an office to provide administrative and financial record-keeping support of the Commission and to employ such persons, sponsors, or providers as the Commission may in its discretion determine to be necessary to assist in administering matters solely of a ministerial nature under this Rule.

(5) Review this Rule and Commission Guidelines from time to time and make recommendations to the Supreme Court for changes.

(6) Upon approval of the Supreme Court publish proposed guidelines and procedures through West Publishing Company and Res Gestae and file the proposed guidelines and procedures with the Clerk.

(7) Provide quarterly financial reports and an annual report of the Commission activity to the Chief Justice of the Supreme Court. A proposed budget for the coming fiscal year (July 1-June 30) shall be submitted to the Chief Justice no later than May 1 of each year.

(8) Do all other things necessary and proper to carry out its powers and duties under this Rule.

(9) Perform all other duties as set forth in Indiana Admission and Discipline Rule 30 and the Indiana Alternative Dispute Resolution Rules.

(b) In addition to the powers and duties set forth in this Rule, the Executive Director shall have the power and the duty to:

(1) Administer the Commission's work.

(2) Appoint, with the approval of the Commission, such staff as may be necessary to assist the Commission to carry out its powers and duties under this Rule.

(3) Supervise and direct the work of the Commission's staff.

(4) Supervise the maintenance of the Commission's records.

(5) Enforce the collection of fees that attorneys, sponsors, mediators and independent certifying organizations must pay pursuant to this Rule, Admission and Discipline Rule 28, Admission and Discipline Rule 30 and the Indiana Alternative Dispute Resolution Rules.

(6) Enforce the continuing legal education requirements of Judges and Attorneys under this Rule.

(7) Assist the Commission in developing guidelines.

(8) Perform such other duties as may be assigned by the Commission in the furtherance of its responsibilities hereunder.

SECTION 7. SOURCES AND USES OF FUNDS.

(a) The Indiana Supreme Court shall periodically designate a portion of the registration fee charged to attorneys pursuant to Admission and Discipline Rule 2 to be used for the operations of the Commission on Continuing Legal Education. The Executive Director of the Commission shall deposit such funds into an account designated "Supreme Court Continuing Legal Education Fund."

(b) Disbursements from the fund shall be made solely upon vouchers signed by or pursuant to the direction of the Chief Justice of this Court.

(c) The Supreme Court shall specifically approve all salaries to be paid out of Continuing Legal Education Fund.

(d) Not later than May 1 of each year, the Commission shall submit for approval by the Supreme Court an operating budget for July 1 to June 30 of the following fiscal year.

(e) Commissioners shall be paid one hundred dollars ($100) for each meeting of the Commission they attend and be reimbursed for expenses in accordance with guidelines established by the State of Indiana.

SECTION 8. EXEMPTIONS AND OTHER RELIEF FROM THE RULE.

(a) An Attorney shall be exempted from the educational requirements of the Rule for such period of time as shall be deemed reasonable by the Commission upon the filing of a verified petition with the Commission and a finding by the Commission that special circumstances unique to the petitioning Attorney have created undue hardship. Subsequent exemptions may be granted.

(b) An Attorney who is physically impaired shall be entitled to establish an alternative method of completing the educational requirements of this Rule upon the filing of a verified petition with the Commission and a finding by the Commission that the alternative method proposed is necessary and consistent with the educational intent of this Rule. Any petition filed under this subsection shall contain a description of the physical impairment, a statement from a physician as to the nature and duration of the impairment, a waiver of any privileged information as to the impairment, and a detailed proposal for an alternative educational method.

(c) An Attorney shall be exempt from the educational and reporting requirements of this Rule if the Attorney has filed an affidavit of inactivity or a retirement affidavit under Section (c) or (d) of Rule 2. An Attorney who has been inactive for less than a year, and desires to resume active status, shall complete any balance of his or her yearly Educational Period requirements as of the date of inactive status.

(d) An Attorney who believes that he or she will be unable to make timely compliance with the educational requirements imposed by this Rule may seek relief from a specific compliance date by filing a verified petition with the Commission. The petition shall set forth reasons from which the Commission can determine whether to extend such compliance date. A petition seeking such an extension of time must be filed as much in advance of the applicable compliance date as the reasons which form the basis of the request afford. The Commission, upon receipt and consideration of such petition, shall decide if sufficient reasons exist, and may grant an extension for such period of time as shall be deemed reasonable by the Commission. In no event shall such an extension be granted beyond the time when the next compliance date, as required by the Rule, occurs.

SECTION 9. ANNUAL REPORTING TO ATTORNEYS.

(a) On or before September 1 of each year, the Commission shall mail or electronically transmit to each Attorney, a statement showing the Approved Courses which the Attorney e is credited on the records of the Commission with having attended during the current year and the current Educational Period. This statement will be sent to the mail or e-mail address for the Attorney listed on the Roll of Attorneys maintained by the Clerk. An Attorney shall at all times keep his or her mailing or e-mail address current with the Roll of Attorneys. If the Attorney has completed the minimum hours for the year or Educational Period, the statement will so reflect and inform the Attorney that he or she is currently in compliance with the education requirements of the Rule. It shall not be a defense to noncompliance that an Attorney has not received an annual statement. Additional statements will be provided to an Attorney upon written request and a five dollar ($5.00) fee made payable to the Continuing Legal Education Fund.

If the statement shows the Attorney is deficient in educational hours, but the Attorney believes he or she is in compliance for the year or Educational Period the Attorney shall file a letter of explanation, a Sponsor certification of course attendance, a personal affidavit of attendance, and an application for course accreditation. All fees must be included with the submission. The documents required by this subsection shall be filed by December 31 of the year or Educational Period in question unless an extension of time to file the same has been granted by the Commission. When an Attorney has resolved the above discrepancies, the Commission shall issue a statement showing that the Attorney is in compliance with the Rule for the year or Educational Period. In the event credit is not granted, the Attorney shall have thirty (30) days after written notification of that fact to comply with the educational requirements or appeal the determination pursuant to Section 11. Failure to do so will result in referral to the Supreme Court for suspension.

(b) If the statement incorrectly reflects that the Attorney has completed the minimum hours for the year or the Educational Period, then it shall be the duty of the Attorney to notify the Commission and to complete the educational requirements mandated by this Rule.

(c) All fees must be paid in order for an Attorney to be considered in compliance with this Rule.

SECTION 10. SANCTIONS AND REINSTATEMENTS.

(a) Sanctions. On January 1, a one hundred fifty dollar ($150.00) late fee accrues against each Attorney who has not met his/her yearly or Educational Period requirements for the period ending December 31st of the previous year. On February 1 of each year the Commission shall mail or electronically transmit a notice assessing a one hundred fifty dollar ($150.00) late fee to those Attorneys who are shown as not having completed the yearly or Educational Period requirements. The Commission will consider the Attorney delinquent for CLE until both certification of attendance at a CLE program and payment of the late fee are received. Late fees and surcharges are to be deposited by the Commission immediately upon receipt. If the delinquent Attorney has not fulfilled the yearly or Educational Period requirements at the time the Court issues an order suspending that Attorney, the delinquency fee is forfeited. If the Attorney is reinstated to the practice of law pursuant to the provisions of Admission and Discipline Rule 29(10) within one (1) year of suspension, any forfeited late fee shall be credited toward the reinstatement fee. A one hundred dollar ($100.00) surcharge will be added to the late fee for each consecutive year for which an Attorney fails to timely comply with CLE requirements.

On May 1 of each year, a list of those Attorneys still failing to complete the yearly or Educational Period requirements will be submitted to the Supreme Court for immediate suspension from the practice of law. These Attorneys will suffer the suspension of their license to practice law and all related penalties until they are reinstated.

(b) Reinstatement Procedures. An Attorney suspended shall be automatically reinstated upon petition to the Commission and payment of a two hundred dollar ($200.00) reinstatement fee in addition to any applicable surcharge. The petition must demonstrate the petitioner's compliance according to the following reinstatement schedule:

(1) for a suspension of one (1) year or less the petitioner must, between the date of suspension and the date of the petition for reinstatement:

(i) complete the hours required to satisfy the deficiency which resulted in the suspension; and

(ii) complete six (6) additional hours of Approved Courses in a separate course or courses;

(2) for a suspension of more than one (1) year a petitioner must, between the date of suspension and the date of the petition for reinstatement:

(i) complete the hours required to satisfy the deficiency which resulted in the suspension;

(ii) complete thirty-six (36) hours of Approved Courses, twelve (12) hours of which must have been completed within the last twelve (12) month period prior to the date of the petition; and

(iii) begin a new Educational Period as of January 1st of the year of reinstatement pursuant to Section 3(a) of this Rule.

The Commission shall issue a statement reflecting reinstatement which shall also be sent to the Clerk to show on the Roll of Attorneys that the Attorney is in good standing. An Attorney suspended by the Supreme Court who continues to practice law shall be subject to the sanctions for the unauthorized practice of law.

Extensions to provide course attendance certifications for courses which were timely taken may be granted for good cause shown; extensions of time to complete educational requirements are not permitted except under Section 8 of this Rule. Providing or procuring of false certifications of attendance at educational courses shall be subject to appropriate discipline under the Admission and Discipline Rules.

SECTION 11. APPEALS REGARDING COMMISSION RECORDS.

Any Attorney who disagrees with the records of the Commission in regard to the credits recorded for the Attorney during the current year or Educational Period and is unable to resolve the disagreement pursuant to Section 9 of this Rule, may petition the Commission for a determination as to the credits to which the Attorney is entitled. Petitions pursuant to this Section must be received by the Commission within thirty (30) days of the Commission's written notification that credit has not been granted and shall be considered by the Commission at its next regular or special meeting, provided that the petition is received by the Commission at least ten (10) business days before such meeting. The Attorney filing the petition shall have the right to attend the Commission meeting at which the petition is considered and to present relevant evidence and arguments to the Commission. The rules of pleading and practice in civil cases shall not apply, and the proceedings shall be informal. The determination of the Commission shall be final as to the number of credits for the Attorney and shall be appealable directly to the Supreme Court. In the event of a good faith dispute pursuant to this Section, the educational and reporting deadlines of this Rule shall be extended until thirty (30) days after the full Commission has ruled on the disputed issue, or if an appeal is taken, until thirty (30) days after the Supreme Court has ruled on the disputed issue.

SECTION 12. PETITIONS.

Any petition filed with the Commission pursuant to this Rule shall be in writing and shall be signed and verified by the Attorney seeking relief. The petition shall be sent by registered or certified mail to the attention of the Executive Director at the Commission's offices at the address shown on the most recent statements or Commission's web page pursuant to Section 9 of this Rule.

SECTION 13. CONFIDENTIALITY.

Unless otherwise directed by the Supreme Court or by another court having jurisdiction, the files, records, and proceedings of the Commission, as they may relate to or arise out of an Attorney, Mediator, or Sponsor attempting to satisfy the continuing legal educational requirements of this Rule, or the requirements of the Indiana Alternative Dispute Resolution Rules shall be confidential and shall not be disclosed except in furtherance of the duties of the Commission or upon the request of the Attorney, Mediator, or Sponsor affected.

SECTION 14. CONFLICT OF INTEREST.

A member, agent or administrator of the Commission shall abstain from participating in any decision involving a sponsor or provider of educational services of which he or she is an officer. A member, agent or administrator of the Commission shall not be an employee of an entity principally engaged in sponsoring or providing continuing legal education services."

IOWA

CHAPTER 41

CONTINUING LEGAL EDUCATION FOR LAWYERS

RULE 41.1 Purpose. Only by continuing their legal education throughout their period of the practice of law can attorneys fulfill their obligation competently to serve their clients. Failure to do so shall be grounds for disciplinary action by the supreme court. This chapter establishes minimum requirements for such continuing legal education and the means by which the requirements shall be enforced. [Court Order April 9, 1975; November 9, 2001, effective February 15, 2002]

Rule 41.2 Continuing legal education commission.

41.2(1) There is hereby established a commission on continuing legal education consisting of 12 members. The supreme court shall appoint to the commission ten resident members of this state who are currently licensed to practice law in the state of Iowa, and two residents of this state who are not lawyers. The court shall designate from among the members of the commission a chair who shall serve as such at the pleasure of the court. Of the members first appointed to the commission four shall serve a term of three years, four shall serve a term of four years, and four shall serve a term of five years. Members thereafter appointed, except for those appointed to fill unexpired terms, shall be appointed for a term of three years. No member shall serve more than two consecutive complete terms as a member of the commission. The supreme court shall adopt rules and regulations governing the operations and activities of the commission.

41.2(2) The commission shall have the following duties:

a. To exercise general supervisory authority over the administration of this chapter.

b. To accredit courses, programs, and other educational activities which will satisfy the educational requirements of this chapter; all being subject to continuous review by the commission.

c. To foster and encourage the offering of such courses, programs and educational activities.

d. To submit to the supreme court proposed rules and regulations [FN1] not inconsistent with this chapter to govern the operations and activities of the commission.

e. Subject to the approval of the supreme court, to employ such persons as it deems necessary for the proper administration of this chapter.

f. To make recommendations to the supreme court concerning this chapter and the enforcement thereof; to present an annual budget and a recommended annual fee for costs of administering this chapter.

g. To report promptly to the supreme court concerning any violation of this chapter by any member of the bar of this state.

h. On March 1 of each year, and at such additional times as the supreme court may order, the commission shall file with the supreme court a written report reviewing in detail the activities of the commission during the preceding calendar year together with an audit of commission funds certified by a certified public accountant licensed to practice in Iowa.

41.2(3) Members of the commission shall not be compensated but shall be reimbursed for expenses incurred by them in the performance of their duties upon vouchers approved by the supreme court.

[Renumbered from Rule 123.2 and amended Nov. 9, 2001, eff. Feb. 15, 2002. Amended, eff. Feb. 22, 2002; Dec. 5, 2007, eff. Dec. 5, 2007]

Rule 41.3   Continuing legal education requirement.

41.3(1) Each attorney admitted to practice in this state shall complete a minimum of 15 hours of legal education accredited by the commission, during each calendar year. The commission is authorized, pursuant to guidelines established by the supreme court, to determine the number of hours for which credit will be given for particular courses, programs or other legal education activities. Under rules to be promulgated by the supreme court, an attorney may be given credit in one or more succeeding calendar years, not exceeding two such years, for completing more than 15 hours of accredited education during any one calendar year.

41.3(2) The 15 hours required by rule 41.3(1) shall include a minimum of 3 hours, every two calendar years, devoted exclusively to the area of legal ethics. Excess hours of education devoted to legal ethics can be carried over for purposes of the annual 15-hour requirement under rule 41.3(1) but cannot be carried over beyond the two-year period for the special legal ethics requirement under this rule.

41.3(3) Commencing July 1, 2002, up to 6 hours of the 15 hours required by rule 41.3(1) each calendar year may be obtained through completion of computer-based legal education accredited by the commission. [Court Order April 9, 1975; December 6, 1978; January 8, 1988; November 9, 2001, effective February 15, 2002; February 22, 2002; February 21, 2012]

Rule 41.4   Annual fee and report by attorneys to commission.

41.4(1) On or before March 1 of each year, each attorney admitted to practice in this state shall pay to the commission a prescribed fee for costs of administering this chapter.

41.4(2) On or before March 1 of each year, each attorney admitted to practice in this state shall make a written report to the commission, in such form as the commission shall prescribe, concerning completion of accredited legal education during the preceding calendar year; provided, however, that an attorney shall not be required to comply with this rule nor comply with the continuing legal education requirements set forth in rule 41.3 for the year during which the attorney was admitted to practice. Each annual report shall be accompanied by proof satisfactory to the commission that the attorney has met the requirements for continuing legal education for the calendar year for which such report is made.

41.4(3) Each attorney admitted to practice in this state shall make a written report to the commission, in such form as the commission shall prescribe, concerning completion of accredited legal ethics education. The report is to be filed on or before March 1 following completion of each two-year period under the requirement. An attorney shall not be required to comply with this requirement for the year of admission to practice.

41.4(4) All attorneys who fail by March 1 of each year to file the annual report or to pay the prescribed fee shall, in addition, pay a penalty as set forth in the following schedule if either the annual report is filed or the prescribed fee is paid after March 1. The penalty fees collected shall be used to pay the costs of administering this chapter, or for such other purposes within the Office of Professional Regulation as the supreme court may direct.

Penalty Schedule:

If Filed:	Penalty:
After March 1 but before April 2	$100
After April 1 but before May 2	$150
After May 1	$200

41.4(5) The commission may prescribe in electronic format for the annual report and require submission of the report in that form.

[Renumbered from Rule 123.4 and amended Nov. 9, 2001, eff. Feb. 15, 2002. Amended April 25, 2008, eff. April 25, 2008, and Jan. 1, 2009; June 5, 2008, eff. July 1, 2008; Jan. 19, 2010, eff. Jan. 19, 2010]

Rule 41.5 Penalty for failure to satisfy continuing legal education requirements.

41.5(1) Attorneys who fail to comply with the provisions of rule 41.4 or who file a report showing on its face that they have failed to complete the required number of hours of continuing legal education may have their right to practice law suspended by the supreme court, provided that at least 15 days prior to such suspension, notice of such delinquency has been served upon them in the manner provided for the service of original notices in Iowa R. Civ. P. 1.305 or has been forwarded to them by restricted certified mail, return receipt requested, addressed to them at their last-known address. Such attorneys shall be given the opportunity during said 15 days to file in the office of professional regulation an affidavit disclosing facts demonstrating their noncompliance was not willful and tendering such documents and sums and penalties which, if accepted, would cure the delinquency, or to file in duplicate in the office of professional regulation a request for hearing to show cause why their license to practice law should not be suspended. A hearing shall be granted if requested. If, after hearing, or failure to cure the delinquency by satisfactory affidavit and compliance, an attorney is suspended, the attorney shall be notified thereof by either of the two methods above provided for notice of delinquency.

41.5(2) Any attorney suspended pursuant to this chapter shall do all of the following:

a. Within 15 days in the absence of co-counsel, notify clients in all pending matters to seek legal advice elsewhere, calling attention to any urgency in seeking the substitution of another lawyer.

b. Within 15 days deliver to all clients being represented in pending matters any papers or other property to which they are entitled or notify them and any co-counsel of a suitable time and place where the papers and other property may be obtained, calling attention to any urgency for obtaining the papers or other property.

c. Within 30 days refund any part of any fees paid in advance that have not been earned.

d. Within 15 days notify opposing counsel in pending litigation or, in the absence of such counsel, the adverse parties, of the suspension and consequent disqualification to act as a lawyer after the effective date of such discipline.

e. Within 15 days file with the court, agency, or tribunal before which the litigation is pending a copy of the notice to opposing counsel or adverse parties.

f. Keep and maintain records of the steps taken to accomplish the foregoing.

g. Within 30 days file proof with the supreme court and with the Iowa Supreme Court Attorney Disciplinary Board of complete performance of the foregoing, and this shall be a condition for application for readmission to practice.

41.5(3) Any attorney suspended pursuant to this chapter shall refrain, during such suspension, from all facets of the ordinary law practice including, but not limited to, the examination of abstracts; consummation of real estate transactions; preparation of legal briefs, deeds, buy and sell agreements, contracts, wills and tax returns; and acting as a fiduciary. Such suspended attorney may, however, act as a fiduciary for the estate, including a conservatorship or guardianship, of any person related to the suspended attorney within the second degree of affinity or consanguinity.

41.5(4) In addition, any attorney who willfully fails to comply with this chapter may be subject to disciplinary action as provided in chapter 35 of the Iowa Court Rules, upon report filed by the commission with the disciplinary board.

41.5(5) For good cause shown, the commission may, in individual cases involving hardship or extenuating circumstances, grant waivers of the minimum educational requirements or extensions of time within which to fulfill the same or make the required reports. [Renumbered from Rule 123.5 and amended Nov. 9, 2001, eff. Feb. 15, 2002. Amended April 20, 2005, eff. July 1, 2005; April 25, 2008, eff. April 25, 2008; June 5, 2008, eff. July 1, 2008]

Rule 41.6   Confidentiality.

Unless otherwise directed by the supreme court, the files, records and proceedings of the commission, as they relate to or arise out of any failure of any attorney to satisfy the requirements of this chapter, shall be deemed confidential and shall not be disclosed, except in furtherance of its duties or upon the request of the attorney affected, or as they may be introduced in evidence or otherwise produced in proceedings taken in accordance with this chapter. [Court Order April 9, 1975; November 9, 2001, effective February 15, 2002]

Rule 41.7   Inactive practitioners. A member of the bar who is not engaged in the practice of law in the state of Iowa as defined in Iowa Ct. R. 39.7, upon application to the commission, may be granted a waiver of compliance with this chapter and obtain a certificate of exemption. No person holding such certificate of exemption shall practice law in this state until reinstated. The supreme court will make rules and regulations governing the continuing legal education requirements for reinstatement of attorneys who, for any reason, have not theretofore been entitled to practice law in this state for any period of time subsequent to their admission to the bar. [Court Order April 9, 1975; November 9, 2001, effective February 15, 2002]

Rule 41.8   Application of this chapter. This chapter shall apply to every person licensed to practice law in the state of Iowa. [Court Order April 9, 1975; November 9, 2001, effective February 15, 2002]

Rule 41.9   Compliance with Iowa rules of professional conduct.

41.9(1) Each lawyer describing the lawyer's practice as permitted by Iowa Rs. of Prof'l Conduct 32:7.4(a) and (c) shall report annually the lawyer's compliance with the eligibility requirements of Iowa R. of Prof'l Conduct 32:7.4(e) on a form approved by the commission. A lawyer may report compliance with the requirement for percentage or hours of practice by providing a statement of compliance.

41.9(2) In reporting compliance with the continuing legal education requirements, the lawyer shall identify the specific courses and hours that apply to each designated or indicated field of practice. The lawyer may obtain up to six hours of the continuing legal education requirement for each designated or indicated field of practice through completion of computer-based legal education courses accredited by the commission.

41.9(3) If, due to hardship or extenuating circumstances, a lawyer is unable to complete the hours of accredited continuing legal education during the preceding calendar year as required by rule 32:7.4(e), the lawyer may apply to the commission for an extension of time in which to complete the hours. No extension of time shall be granted unless written application for the extension is made on a form prescribed by the commission. An extension of time shall not exceed a period of six months immediately following the last day of the year in which the requirements were not met.

41.9(4) The portion of the report required by this rule shall be considered public information. [Court Order April 20, 2005, effective July 1, 2005]

Rule 41.10   Reinstatement from suspension

41.10(1) An attorney who has been suspended for failure to pay the annual fee, complete required continuing legal education, or file the annual report required by rule 41.4 may be reinstated upon a showing that such failure was not willful and by filing such report showing completion of all continuing legal education required by Iowa Court Rules 41.3 and 42.2 through the end of the last complete reporting year. An attorney seeking reinstatement after suspension for failure to comply with the provisions of this rule shall pay all delinquent fees and late filing penalties due under rule 41.4 and a reinstatement fee of $100.00.

41.10(2) An attorney who applies for reinstatement from suspension under the provisions of chapter 35 of the Iowa Court Rules shall first file the annual report required by rule 41.4 showing completion of all continuing legal education required by Iowa Court Rules 41.3 and 42.2 through the end of the last complete reporting year, pay all fees and late filing penalties due under rule 41.4 and unpaid at the time of the suspension, and pay a reinstatement fee of $100.00. The commission may grant an attorney additional time after the effective reinstatement date, on such terms and conditions as it may prescribe, to complete and furnish evidence of compliance with these continuing legal education requirements.

[Adopted April 25, 2008, eff. April 25, 2008]

Rule 41.11   Denial of reinstatement for failure to comply with certain obligations

41.11(1) Denial of reinstatement for failure to comply with an obligation owed to or collected by the Centralized Collection Unit of the Department of Revenue. The supreme court may deny a lawyer's application for reinstatement under rule 41.7 or 41.10 for failure to comply with an obligation owed to or collected by the Centralized Collection Unit of the Department of Revenue. The procedure shall be governed by rule 35.22.

41.11(2) Denial of reinstatement for failure to comply with an obligation owed to or collected by the College Student Aid Commission. The supreme court may deny a lawyer's application for reinstatement under Rule 41.7 or 41.10 for failure to comply with an obligation owed to or collected by the College Student Aid Commission. The procedure shall be governed by Rule 35.20.

41.11(3) Denial of reinstatement for failure to comply with a support order. The supreme court may deny a lawyer's application for reinstatement under Rule 41.7 or 41.10 for failure to comply with a support order. The procedure shall be governed by Rule 35.19.

[Court Order June 5, 2008, effective July 1, 2008; February 20, 2012]

Rule 41.12   Basic skills course requirement

41.12(1) Every Iowa lawyer admitted to practice by examination after December 31, 2008 must complete a Basic Skills Course. The course must be completed within one year of the newly admitted lawyer's date of admission to practice in Iowa.[*] The course may be completed after the last day of the bar examination that resulted in admission. If the course is completed after the last day of the bar examination, but the applicant fails the examination, the applicant will remain in compliance with this rule so long as the applicant passes the next examination offered.

41.12(2) The Basic Skills Course must total at least eight actual hours of instruction and include at least one actual hour qualifying for credit in the area of legal ethics. The course shall include instruction on Iowa law selected from at least eight of the following topic areas:

> Civil Procedure
>
> Criminal Law
>
> Criminal Procedure
>
> Family Law
>
> Guardianships, Conservatorships, Trusts, and Powers of Appointment
>
> Business Entities
>
> Probate
>
> Torts
>
> Contracts

---

[*] As an interim implementation provision, lawyers admitted during calendar year 2009 must complete the Basic Skills Course within two years of the newly admitted lawyer's date of admission to practice in Iowa.

Real Estate Transactions

Ethics and Professionalism

41.12(3) Newly admitted lawyers shall be entitled to claim credit for attendance at an accredited Basic Skills Course against the continuing legal education requirements of rules 41.3 and 42.2, but are not exempt from reporting and fee payment duties of rule 41.4.

41.12(4) A lawyer who fails to complete the Basic Skills Course within one year of the date of admission may have the right to practice law suspended under the provisions of rule 41.5.

41.12(5) The commission may, in individual cases involving hardship or extenuating circumstances, grant waivers of the Basic Skills Course requirement or extensions of time in which to complete the Basic Skills Course.

41.12(6) The Basic Skills Course may be offered by any provider of continuing legal education, but must be reviewed and accredited by the Commission on Continuing Legal Education as provided in rule 42.4. The Basic Skills Course may be conducted in installments over time, and may be offered by computer-based transmission as provided in rule 42.3. Any provider of the Basic Skills Course is required to report attendance in the manner specified by the commission.

[Adopted Oct. 9, 2009, eff. Oct. 9, 2009. Amended Nov. 24, 2010, eff. Nov. 24, 2010]

KANSAS

RULES RELATING TO
CONTINUING LEGAL EDUCATION

PURPOSE AND SCOPE

It is essential to the public and the legal profession that attorneys admitted to practice law in Kansas maintain and increase their professional competence by continuing their legal education. These rules establish minimum requirements for continuing legal education necessary to remain authorized to practice law in this state.

RULE 801
CONTINUING LEGAL EDUCATION COMMISSION

(a)   **The Commission.** There is hereby created the Continuing Legal Education Commission.

(b)   **Duties and Responsibilities.** The Commission is responsible for the administration of Rules 801 through 811, subject to the supervision of the Supreme Court. The authority of the Commission includes: (1) accrediting providers and programs and determining the number of hours of CLE credit to be given for participating in a program; (2) granting or withdrawing approval of all or less than all programs of a provider; (3) receiving and considering reports of attorneys; (4) granting waivers and extensions of time to complete requirements; (5) giving notices and certifications required by these rules; and (6) adopting guidelines necessary to implement or administer these rules.

(c)   **Composition.** The Commission shall consist of nine members appointed by the Supreme Court. All attorney members must be registered under Supreme Court Rule 208. The members must include: (1) five practicing attorneys, at least one of whom has been admitted to practice law in Kansas for fewer than 10 years; (2) a faculty representative from each of the University of Kansas and Washburn University Schools of Law; (3) one nonattorney member; and (4) a justice or judge.

(d)   **Term of Service.** Appointment as a Commission member is for a 3-year term. The Supreme Court will appoint a new member to fill a vacancy on the Commission occurring during a term. A new member appointed to fill a vacancy serves the unexpired term of the previous member. No member may serve more than two consecutive 3-year terms, except that a member initially appointed to serve an unexpired term may serve two consecutive 3-year terms thereafter.

(e)   **Meetings.** The Commission may meet at such times and places as it determines. Five members constitute a quorum for the transaction of business.

(f)   **Election of Officers.** At the first Commission meeting held in each annual compliance period, the Commission must elect from its members a chairman, a vice chairman, and a secretary.

(g)   **Expenses.**   Members of the Commission and Commission staff shall be reimbursed for actual and necessary expenses they incur in travel to and from Commission meetings and for authorized travel in connection with Commission business.

(h)   **Confidentiality.** Unless otherwise directed by the Supreme Court, the files, records, and proceedings of the Commission which relate to or arise out of the failure of an attorney to satisfy continuing legal education requirements are confidential and must not be disclosed except in furtherance of the Commission's duties or on request of the attorney affected. However, anonymous statistical abstracts may be drawn from the files, records, and proceedings.

(i)   **Staff.** The Commission may employ an Executive Director and other necessary staff and may delegate to the director or staff the authority to conduct the business of the Commission under these Rules and Commission guidelines, subject to review by the Commission.

(j)   **Contact Information for Commission.** The Commission's mailing address is Kansas Continuing Legal Education Commission, Attn: Executive Director, 400 S. Kansas Ave., Ste. 202, Topeka, Kansas 66603. The Commission's telephone number is 785-357-6510. The Commission's website address is www.kscle.org.

RULE 802
DEFINITIONS

(a) **"Active practitioner"** means an attorney who is required to pay the annual registration fee imposed by Supreme Court Rule 208 for the current registration period and who is not on inactive status or suspended or disbarred by the Supreme Court from the practice of law.

(b) **"Approved program"** means a continuing legal education program that has been accredited by the Commission.

(c) **"CLE Commission"** or **"Commission"** means the governing body created by Rule 801(a).

(d) **"Compliance period"** means the period of 1 year from July 1 through June 30.

(e) **"Continuing legal education program"** or **"CLE program"** means a legal educational program, course, or activity designed to maintain or improve the professional competency of practicing attorneys.

(f) **"Ethics"** means the standards set by the Kansas Rules of Professional Conduct with which a lawyer must comply to remain authorized to practice law in Kansas and in good standing.

(g) **"Guidelines"** means a Commission document that:

> (1) prescribes administrative requirements for CLE programs which are not set forth in these rules; and

(2) is available to attorneys on the Commission's website.

(h) **"Inactive practitioner"** means an attorney who has elected inactive status pursuant to Supreme Court Rule 208 and has registered as an inactive attorney with the CLE Commission.

(i) **"In-house CLE program"** means traditional programming given for a select private audience **from the same law firm, corporation, or single governmental entity, and not open for attendance** by other members of the legal community generally. The term includes a program offered by invitation and a program not advertised to a broad attorney population.

(j) **"Law practice management programming"** means programming specifically designed for lawyers on non-substantive topics that deal with means and methods for enhancing the quality and efficiency of an attorney's service to the attorney's clients.

(k) **"Nontraditional programming"** means CLE programming accessed solely by an individual attorney, including: teleconference, internet-based conference, audiotape, videotape, CD, podcast, CD-ROM, DVD, or another format approved by the Commission and defined in its Guidelines for Nontraditional Programming.

(l) **"Professionalism"** means conduct consistent with the tenets of the legal profession by which a lawyer demonstrates civility, honesty, integrity, character, fairness, competence, ethical conduct, public service, and respect for the rules of law, the courts, clients, other lawyers, witnesses, and unrepresented parties.

(m) **"Rules"** means the Rules Relating to Continuing Legal Education, together with any amendments thereto, adopted by the Kansas Supreme Court.

(n) **"Traditional programming"** includes:

(1) **"Live Classroom Setting"** - A CLE program presented in a suitable classroom setting devoted to the program.

(2) **"Satellite"** - A live CLE program broadcast to a classroom setting or a central viewing or listening location advertised to a broad attorney population. There must be a live connection to the speaker to comment and answer questions. As long as the program is advertised, there is no minimum attendance requirement.

(3) **"Video Replay"** - A recorded CLE program presented in a suitable classroom setting or in a central viewing location advertised to a broad attorney population. The attorney must be able to contact the moderator, either in-person or by telephone or email, to comment or ask questions. As long as the program is advertised, there is no minimum attendance requirement.

RULE 803
MINIMUM REQUIREMENTS

(a)   **Credit Hours.** An active practitioner must earn a minimum of 12 CLE credit hours at approved programs in each compliance period (July 1 to June 30). Of the 12 hours, at least 2 hours must be in the area of ethics and professionalism.

(b)   **Carryover Credit.** If an active practitioner completes CLE credit hours at approved programs during a compliance period exceeding the number of hours required by subsection (a) and the practitioner complies with the requirements of Rule 806, the practitioner may carry forward to the next compliance period up to 10 unused general attendance credit hours from the compliance period during which the credit hours were earned. However, ethics and professionalism credit hours in excess of the 2-hour requirement in subsection (a) may be carried forward as general attendance credit hours but not as ethics and professionalism credit. CLE credit hours approved for teaching, authorship, or law practice management credit do not qualify for carryover credit.

(c)   **Reporting.** CLE credit hours at an approved program for each attorney must be reported to the Commission in the form and manner the Commission prescribes.

(d)   **Exemptions.** The following attorneys are not required to fulfill the CLE requirement in subsection (a):

   (1)   An attorney newly admitted to practice law in Kansas during the period prior to the first compliance period beginning after admission to practice.

   (2)   An attorney during the time the attorney is on retired or inactive status pursuant to Supreme Court Rule 208 and registered on inactive status with the CLE Commission.

   (3)   All active and retired federal and state judges or justices, bankruptcy judges, and full-time magistrates of the United States District Court for the District of Kansas who are not engaged in the practice of law. Federal and state administrative judges are not eligible for this exemption.

   (4)   An attorney exempted by the Commission for good cause pursuant to subsection (e).

(e)   **Exemptions for Good Cause.** The Commission may grant an exemption to the strict requirement of these rules to complete continuing legal education because of good cause, *e.g.* disability or hardship. A request for exemption must be submitted to the Commission in writing with full explanation of the circumstances necessitating the request. An attorney with a disability or hardship that affects the attorney's ability to attend CLE programs may file annually a request for a substitute program in lieu of attendance and must propose a substitute program the attorney can complete. The Commission must review and approve or disapprove a substitute program on an individual basis. An attorney who receives approval of a substitute program is responsible for the annual CLE fee required by Rule 808.

(f)   **Legislative Service.** An attorney serving in the Kansas Legislature may, on request, receive a reduction of 6 of the 10 general attendance credit hours required for the compliance period in which the attorney serves.

(g)   **Accommodation for Attorneys Employed Out-of-Country.** An attorney employed full time outside the United States for a minimum of 8 months during the compliance period may, upon written request and preapproval, complete the annual CLE requirement by nontraditional programming.

RULE 804
ACCREDITATION OF PROGRAMMING

(a)   **Provider Traditional Programming Approval.** A provider sponsoring a continuing legal education program by traditional programming may request prior accreditation of the CLE program for CLE credit. The Commission recommends the provider submit to the Commission, at least 60 days before the program, an application for approval of CLE activity and any other information required by the Commission. An application by a provider must be accompanied by a $25 nonrefundable filing fee. The Commission must notify the applicant of the status of its review of the application not later than 30 days after the Commission receives it. A program is not approved until the applicant is notified of approval. The program must be advertised only as pending approval, as required by Rule 805(a), and may not be advertised as approved until a notice of accreditation/affidavit is received. The time limit in this subsection does not apply to an in-house CLE program, which is governed by Rule 806(i).

(b)   **Individual Attorney Traditional Course Approval.** An attorney seeking CLE credit for attendance at a traditional CLE program that was not previously accredited must submit to the Commission an application for approval of CLE activity and any other information required by the Commission. The Commission must notify the applicant of the status of its review of the request not later than 30 days after the Commission receives it. A program is not approved until the applicant is notified of approval.

(c)   **Interdisciplinary CLE.** CLE credit may be earned for a program that crosses academic lines (*e.g.*, accounting-tax) if it is pertinent to an individual attorney's practice. See Rule 806(j).

(d)   **Nontraditional Programming Course Approval.** An application for approval of CLE credit for nontraditional programming must be submitted to the Commission by the provider in the form prescribed by the Commission, and the program must comply with the Guidelines for Nontraditional Programming. An application for approval of a live nontraditional program must be accompanied by a $25 nonrefundable filing fee. An application for approval of an on-demand nontraditional program must be accompanied by a $100 nonrefundable filing fee and will be valid until the expiration of the compliance period.

(e)   **Notice of Accreditation/Affidavit.** Upon approving a program for CLE credit, the Commission will issue to the applicant a notice of accreditation/affidavit. A provider must

D-141

distribute the appropriate Kansas affidavit to all attorneys seeking Kansas CLE credit. A provider holding an in-state program is responsible for distributing the appropriate Kansas affidavit for signature and for returning the executed affidavit to the CLE Commission within 30 days after the program. For an out-of-state program, the attorney is responsible for submitting the executed affidavit to the Commission within 30 days after the program. For nontraditional programming, the provider is responsible for submitting an attendance roster to the CLE Commission within 30 days after the program in the approved format.

(f)   **Appeal of Determination.** If an application for approval of CLE credit for a CLE program is denied, the applicant may appeal the decision to the Commission by submitting a letter of appeal within 30 days after notice of the denial was mailed. No other appeal may be taken.

(g)   **Standards.** To be accredited, a CLE program must comply with the following requirements:

(1) CLE credit must be awarded on the basis of 1 credit hour for each 50 minutes actually spent in attendance at instructional activities, exclusive of introductory remarks, meals, breaks, or other noneducational activities. One-half credit hour must be awarded for attendance of at least 25 but less than 50 minutes. No credit may be claimed for smaller fractional units.

(2) The program must have significant intellectual or practical content designed to promote lawyer competence and deal primarily with matters related to the practice of law, ethics and professionalism, or law practice management.

(3) The program must be presented by a person or persons qualified by practical or academic experience to present the subject. In most instances, legal subjects should be presented by lawyers.

(4) Thorough, high quality, readable, useful, and carefully prepared instructional materials must be made available to all participants at or before the time the program is presented, unless the Commission approves the absence of instructional materials as reasonable. A brief outline without citations or explanatory notations is not sufficient. Instructional materials must satisfy the criteria set forth in the Guidelines for Instructional Materials.

(5) For traditional programming, the program must be presented in or broadcast to a suitable classroom setting or central viewing or listening location devoted to the program. Generally, credit will not be approved for after-dinner type speeches.

(6) Integration of ethics or professionalism instruction into substantive law topics is encouraged, but integrated material does not count toward the 2-hour minimum annual ethics and professionalism requirement.

KANSAS

RULE 805
PROVIDER RESPONSIBILITY

(a) **Marketing prior to approval.** A provider of a CLE program for which accreditation has been sought but not yet approved may announce: "Application for CLE approval of this activity in Kansas is currently pending. Attorneys wanting to know the CLE approval status of a program should contact the sponsor."

(b) **Filing Affidavits.** See Rule 804(e).

(c) **Late Filing of Affidavit by Provider.** A provider of an accredited in-state CLE program held on or before June 30 of a compliance period must file the affidavits for the program which must be received in the Commission office or postmarked by July 31. If not filed timely, the provider is responsible for the fees set forth in Rule 807(c).

(d) **Audit of Activities.** A provider must allow a Commission member or staff to attend, free of charge, any continuing legal education program to audit compliance with these rules. Such attendance does not qualify for mandatory continuing legal education credit for the Commission member or staff.

(e) **Evaluations.** At the conclusion of an approved program, each participating attorney must be given the opportunity to complete an evaluation form addressing the quality, effectiveness, and usefulness of the program. The Commission may request copies of the evaluations.

(f) **Record Retention.** A provider must keep on file for a minimum of 3 years attendance records and evaluation summaries for a program.

RULE 806
CREDIT FOR PARTICIPATION

(a) **Carryover Credit.** Affidavits reporting hours that are to be carried forward pursuant to Rule 803(b) must be received in the CLE Commission office or postmarked by July 31 and reflect attendance during the compliance period in which they were earned. An application or affidavit received after that date will not qualify as carryover credit but will be applied to the compliance period in which the hours were earned, if accompanied by the fee required by Rule 807(c).

(b) **Credit for Attendance.** The number of credit hours assigned to an approved program reflects the maximum that may be earned by attending the entire program. Only actual attendance earns CLE credit. No attorney may receive more than 8 hours of credit in 1 day of CLE attendance.

(c) **Course or Program Formats.** An approved program may include traditional and nontraditional programming.

(d)   **Credit for Teaching.** Up to 5 CLE credit hours will be awarded for each 50 minutes spent teaching an approved program. The applicant must file an application for approval of teaching credit which outlines program content, teaching methodology, and time spent in preparation and instruction. In determining the number of credit hours to award, the Commission will calculate time spent in preparation and teaching. For example, an attorney who spends 150 minutes preparing a program and 50 minutes teaching it will be awarded 4 credit hours. One-half credit hour may be awarded for teaching at least 25 but less than 50 minutes. No credit may be claimed for smaller fractional units. A repeat presentation may qualify for additional credits, limited to time actually spent updating the presentation and teaching. Because teaching credit is awarded as an incentive to attorneys to benefit the legal profession, instruction must be directed toward an audience composed primarily of attorneys. Credit will not be awarded for teaching undergraduate, graduate, or law school classes.

(e)   **Credit for Authorship.** Credit may be awarded for authorship of legal publications. The author must complete an application for approval of authorship credit. Credit will be awarded if the applicant's research (1) has produced a published article, chapter, monograph, or book, personally authored, in whole or part, by the applicant, and (2) contributes substantially to the continuing legal education of the applicant and other attorneys. One credit hour may be awarded for each 50 minutes spent directly in preparing the publication. Publication must occur during the compliance period for which credit is requested. An article, chapter, monograph, or book directed to a nonattorney audience, while resulting in self-improvement as a form of self-study, does not qualify for authorship credit.

(f)   **Credit for Attendance Prior to Being Admitted to Practice Law in Kansas.** Credit will not be given for any CLE program attended before the applicant was admitted to practice law in Kansas.

(g)   **Credit for Attending Law School Course.** Credit may be earned for postgraduate education by enrollment in a course, either for credit or by audit, from a law school approved by the American Bar Association. The Commission will award 1 credit hour for each 50 minutes of class attendance.

(h)   **Duplicate Attendance.** Attendance at a program that an attorney has attended previously during the compliance period will not be accepted for continuing legal education credit.

(i)   **In-House CLE program.** An in-house CLE program, to receive approval, must meet all of the following requirements:

(1) The activity must meet the standards for program approval in Rule 804.

(2) The law firm, corporation, or single governmental entity for which the activity is offered must assume responsibility for accreditation.

(3) An application for approval of CLE credit must be received by the Commission not later than 30 days before the in-house CLE program. The activity must be open to in-person monitoring/observation by any Commission member or staff.

(4) The activity must be scheduled at a time and location so that attorneys attending are free of interruptions from telephone calls and other office matters.

(5) No more than 5 CLE credit hours may be earned by an attorney in any compliance period through in-house CLE programs.

(j) **Interdisciplinary Programming.** CLE credit may be earned for a program that crosses academic lines (*e.g.*, accounting-tax) if it is pertinent to an individual attorney's practice. An Application for Approval of CLE Activity must be submitted pursuant to Rule 804(b) and include a statement describing how the program is beneficial to the attorney's practice.

(k) **Law Practice Management Programming.** An attorney may receive CLE credit for participation in an accredited CLE program as defined in the Guidelines for Accreditation of Law Practice Management Programming. Law practice management credit is limited to a maximum of 2 hours of general attendance credit in any compliance period.

(l) **Nontraditional Programming Limitation.** Credit for nontraditional programming is limited to a maximum of 5 hours of credit per compliance period.

(m) **Self-Study Prohibition.** Self-study programming is not accreditable.

RULE 807
REPORTING REQUIREMENTS AND NONCOMPLIANCE FEE

(a) **Annual Report.** The Commission will issue an annual report in August for the preceding compliance period for each attorney subject to the Commission's jurisdiction. If the report is accurate, the attorney is not required to respond; the report will be filed automatically as the attorney's annual report. If the report is not accurate, the attorney must notify the Commission within 30 days of the issuance of the report.

(b) **Failure to Comply.** If it appears an attorney has not earned the minimum number of CLE credit hours required for a compliance period, the Commission must send notice of the apparent noncompliance to the attorney at the attorney's last known address by certified mail, return receipt requested. Not later than 30 days after mailing of the notice, the attorney, to avoid suspension from the practice of law, must cure the failure to comply or show cause for an exemption.

(c) **Attendance Affidavits.** All affidavits of attendance for a compliance period must be postmarked not later than July 31 immediately following the compliance period.

(d) **Noncompliance Fee.** An attorney must pay a noncompliance fee of $75 if:

(1) an attendance affidavit is postmarked on or after August 1; or

(2) the attorney fails to complete the hours required under Rule 803(a) within the compliance period.

(e)   **Address Change.** An attorney must notify the Commission within 30 days after a change of the attorney's address.

RULE 808
FEES

(a)   **Annual CLE Fee.** An active practitioner must pay an annual CLE fee to fund administration of these rules. The Commission may determine the amount of the annual fee, with approval by the Supreme Court.

(b)   **Notice of Fee.** On or before June 1 of each year, the Commission must mail a statement of the amount of the annual CLE fee to be paid for the next compliance period to each attorney then authorized to practice law in this state at the attorney's last known address.

(c)   **Failure to Receive Notice.** Failure of an attorney to receive a statement pursuant to subsection (b) does not excuse the attorney from paying the required fee.

(d)   **Due Date and CLE Late Fee.** The annual CLE fee is due on July 1 and is delinquent if not paid before August 1. A fee postmarked on or after August 1 of the year in which the fee is due must be accompanied by a $50 late fee.

(e)   **Attorney Returning to Practice.** An attorney who is reinstated to active status after a period of disbarment or suspension and an attorney who is returning to active status after a period of time on inactive status must pay the annual CLE fee required by subsection (a) for the current compliance period, together with any other fee required for reinstatement, prior to the attorney's return to active status.

(f)   **Active Status with Attorney Registration and CLE.** Payment of the annual CLE fee and any applicable late fee is a prerequisite to completing registration as an active attorney under Supreme Court Rule 208.

(g)   **Returned Check.** A service fee of the maximum amount allowed by law will be assessed for a check returned unpaid to the CLE Commission.

RULE 809
SUSPENSION FROM THE PRACTICE OF LAW

(a)   **Reasons for suspension.** An attorney who is required to file a report of CLE credit hours and does not do so, who fails to meet the minimum requirements of these rules, or who fails to pay the annual CLE registration fee will be suspended from the practice of law in this state.

(b) **Notice of Noncompliance.** The Commission must notify an attorney who appears to have failed to meet the requirements of these rules that the attorney's name will be certified to the Supreme Court for suspension from the practice of law in this state, unless the attorney shows cause why the certification should not be made. Notice must be sent to the attorney at the attorney's last known address by certified mail, return receipt requested. Thirty days after the notice is mailed, if no hearing is requested pursuant to subsection (c), the Commission must certify to the court, for an order of suspension, the name of the attorney who has not met the requirements of these rules.

(c) **Hearing.** An attorney to whom the Commission has sent notice of noncompliance pursuant to subsection (b) may, not later than 30 days after the date the notice was mailed, file with the Commission a request for a hearing, stating the issues the attorney raises. The Commission must grant a timely request for a hearing to consider the issues raised by the attorney. The attorney's name must not be certified to the Supreme Court for suspension unless suspension is recommended by the Commission after the hearing. The Commission must provide for a record and the costs thereof when needed.

RULE 810
REINSTATEMENT PROCEDURE FOR INACTIVE PRACTITIONER

(a) **Request for Reinstatement.** An inactive practitioner seeking to become an active practitioner must submit to the Commission a written request for reinstatement. This request is in addition to the request to the Kansas Supreme Court for reinstatement required by Supreme Court Rule 208.

(b) **Required Fees.** In addition to any amount to be paid to the Clerk of the Appellate Courts under Supreme Court Rule 208, a request for reinstatement submitted to the Commission by an inactive practitioner must be accompanied by a check or money order payable to the Kansas Continuing Legal Education Commission for the annual CLE fee for the current compliance period plus a change of status fee of $25.

(c) **Required Hours.** Any inactive practitioner reinstated to the practice of law in Kansas must earn a minimum of twelve (12) continuing legal education credit hours during the registration period in which such attorney is reinstated.

RULE 811
REINSTATEMENT PROCEDURE FOR SUSPENDED PRACTITIONER

(a) **Suspended less than 1 year.** A suspended practitioner returning from suspension of less than one year must:

(1) submit to the Commission a written request for reinstatement, accompanied by a check or money order payable to the Kansas Continuing Legal Education Commission for a reinstatement fee of $100;

(2) between the date of suspension and the date of reinstatement, complete any hours required to satisfy any deficiency in CLE requirements under Rule 803(a) and pay any fees incurred prior to suspension; and

(3) complete the annual CLE requirement under Rule 803(a) by the end of the compliance period in which the practitioner is reinstated; and

(4) complete prior to reinstatement any requirements imposed by the Attorney Registration Office under Rule 208(g)(3).

(b) **Suspended 1 year or more.** A suspended practitioner returning from suspension of 1 year or more must:

(1) submit to the Commission a written request for reinstatement, accompanied by a check or money order payable to the Kansas Continuing Legal Education Commission for a reinstatement fee of $100;

(2) between the date of suspension and the date of reinstatement, complete any hours required to satisfy any deficiency in CLE requirements under Rule 803(a) and pay any fees incurred prior to suspension;

(3) between the date of suspension and the date of reinstatement, complete an additional 12 hours of CLE credit, including 2 hours of ethics and professionalism, for each year during which the attorney was suspended, unless waived or modified by order of the Supreme Court; and

(4) complete the annual CLE requirement under Rule 803(a) by the end of the compliance period in which the attorney is reinstated; and

(5) complete prior to reinstatement any requirements imposed by the Attorney Registration Office under Rule 208(g)(3).

KENTUCKY

SCR 3.600 Continuing Legal Education Definitions

As used in SCR 3.605-3.695, the following definitions shall apply unless the context clearly requires a different meaning:

(1) "Approved activity" is a continuing legal education activity that meets the requirements set forth in SCR 3.650 and has been approved for credit by the CLE Commission.

(2) "Attorney Identification Number" is the 5 digit number assigned to each member of the Association upon admission.

(3) "Award" is the Continuing Legal Education Award.

(4) "Commission" is the Continuing Legal Education Commission.

(5) "Continuing legal education," or "CLE," is any legal educational activity which is designed to maintain or improve the professional competency of practicing attorneys and is accredited by the Commission.

(6) "Credit" is a unit for measuring continuing legal education.

(7) "Educational year" is the reporting period for mandatory continuing legal education and runs from July 1st each year through June 30th of the successive year.

(8) "Ethics, professional responsibility and professionalism" is the category by which "ethics credits" shall be earned and includes programs or seminars or designated portions thereof with instruction focusing on the Rules of Professional Conduct independently or as they relate to law firm management, malpractice avoidance, attorneys fees, legal ethics, and the duties of attorneys to the judicial system, the public, clients and other attorneys.

(9) "In-house activity" is an activity sponsored by a single law firm, single corporate law department, or single governmental office for lawyers who are members or employees of the firm, department or office.

(10) "Legal writing" is a publication which contributes to the legal competency of the applicant, other attorneys or judges and is approved by the Commission. Writing for which the author is paid shall not be approved.

(11) "Non-compliance" means not meeting continuing legal education requirements set forth in SCR 3.645 and SCR 3.640 and includes both lack of certification and lack of completion of activities prior to established time requirements.

(12) "Technological transmission" is a CLE activity delivery method other than live seminars and includes video tape, DVD, audio tape, CD-ROM, computer on-line services, or other appropriate technology as approved by the Commission.

HISTORY: Amended by Order 2013-12, eff. 1-1-2014; prior amendment eff. 3-1-12 (Order 2012-01); adopted by Order 2003-4, eff. 1-1-04

PRACTICE OF LAW

SCR 3.605 The commission; functions and membership

The Continuing Legal Education Commission shall consist of 7 attorneys, 1 of whom shall be from each appellate district of the Commonwealth as presently existing or hereafter created. Under the policy direction of the Court and the Board, the Commission shall be responsible for the administration and regulation of all continuing legal education programs and activities for the members of the Association.

HISTORY: Adopted by Order 2013-12, eff. 1-1-2014

KENTUCKY BAR ASSOCIATION
RULES OF THE SUPREME COURT OF KENTUCKY

PRACTICE OF LAW

SCR 3.610 Selection and tenure of the Commission; filling vacancies on the Commission

The Court shall appoint all members of the Commission from a list consisting of 3 times the number to be appointed submitted to the Court by the Board. A chairman shall be designated by the Court for such time as the Court may direct. Of the members first appointed, 3 shall be appointed for 1 year, 2 for 2 years and 2 for 3 years. Thereafter, appointments shall be made for a 3 year term. Members may be reappointed but no member shall serve more than 2 successive 3 year terms. Each member shall serve until a successor is appointed and qualified. Vacancies occurring through death, disability, inability or disqualification to serve or by resignation shall be filled for the vacant term in the same manner as initial appointments are made by the Court. Members of the Commission shall serve without compensation but shall be paid their reasonable and necessary expenses incurred in the performance of their duties. The Association shall have the responsibility of funding the Commission and any necessary staff who shall be employees of the Association.

HISTORY: Adopted by Order 2013-12, eff. 1-1-2014

KENTUCKY BAR ASSOCIATION
RULES OF THE SUPREME COURT OF KENTUCKY

PRACTICE OF LAW

SCR 3.615 Commission member qualifications

Each Commission member must be a citizen of the United States, licensed to practice law in the courts of this Commonwealth and have been a resident in the appellate district from which nominated for 2 years immediately preceding the appointment.

HISTORY: Adopted by Order 2013-12, eff. 1-1-2014

KENTUCKY BAR ASSOCIATION
RULES OF THE SUPREME COURT OF KENTUCKY

PRACTICE OF LAW

SCR 3.620 Commission quorum

A quorum consisting of at least 4 Commission members is required for conducting the business of the Commission.

HISTORY: Adopted by Order 2013-12 eff. 1-1-2014

SCR 3.625 Commission staff

The Commission shall be provided with a Director for Continuing Legal Education and sufficient administrative and secretarial assistants as are from time to time required. Selection and qualifications of the Director for Continuing Legal Education shall be determined by the Board except that the person selected shall be an attorney licensed to practice law in the courts of this Commonwealth. The Director for Continuing Legal Education shall be responsible to the Commission for the proper administration of the rules applying to the Commission and any regulations issued by the Commission.

HISTORY: Adopted by Order 2013-12 eff. 1-1-2014

KENTUCKY BAR ASSOCIATION
RULES OF THE SUPREME COURT OF KENTUCKY

PRACTICE OF LAW

SCR 3.630 Commission duties

The Commission shall be responsible for the administration of these continuing legal education rules, subject to policy approval and other direction by the Board and the Court. In discharging this responsibility, the Commission shall:

(1) Encourage and promote the offering of high quality continuing legal education.

(2) Conduct, sponsor, or otherwise provide high quality continuing legal education, specifically including, but not limited to, one 12 credit seminar in each Supreme Court District each year.

(3) Encourage and promote quality legal writing.

(4) Approve or deny promptly all applications provided for by these rules.

(5) Establish standards, procedures, and forms to evaluate applications made pursuant to these rules.

(6) Promulgate rules and regulations for the administration of the mandatory continuing legal education program subject to approval of the Board and the Court.

(7) Report annually, on or before September 15, and as otherwise required, to the Board and the Court on the status of continuing legal education in the Commonwealth. Such report shall include recommended changes to these rules and regulations and their implementation.

(8) Submit to the Board annually, on or before November 1, a recommended budget for the succeeding year with any recommended changes in annual membership dues to cover costs of administering these rules.

(9) Perform such other acts and duties, not inconsistent with these rules, as are necessary and proper to improve the continuing legal education programs within the Commonwealth. When in the course of undertaking the duties set forth above, the Commission receives information which may raise questions regarding a member's competence to represent clients or to otherwise practice law as defined at SCR 3.020, or which may raise any of the issues covered at SCR 3.165(b), the Commission has an affirmative duty to report such information to the Office of Bar Counsel for review by the Inquiry Commission.

HISTORY: Adopted by Order 2013-12, eff.1-1-2014

KENTUCKY BAR ASSOCIATION
RULES OF THE SUPREME COURT OF KENTUCKY

PRACTICE OF LAW

SCR 3.635 Kentucky Law Update seminars in each appellate district

(1) Each educational year, the Commission shall conduct a 12 credit continuing legal education seminar in each Supreme Court District. Subjects taught at each seminar shall include the latest Kentucky Supreme Court and Court of Appeals decisions, procedural rule changes, Federal Court decisions, legal ethics, professional responsibility and professionalism, Kentucky statutory changes and other subjects relating to improvements in basic legal skills. Each program shall include a minimum of 2 credits for subjects specifically addressing legal ethics, professional responsibility and professionalism.

(2) Registration for the Kentucky Law Update seminars shall be free to all members in good standing with the Association.

(3) Members may attend Kentucky Law Update seminars in any location. The maximum credit that may be earned for attending any 1 Kentucky Law Update seminar is 12 credits. However, if different tracks of programs are attended at different locations, additional credit may be approved by the Commission. Duplicate credits shall not be earned by attending the same program at different locations.

HISTORY: Adopted by Order 2013-12, eff. 1-1-2014

KENTUCKY BAR ASSOCIATION
RULES OF THE SUPREME COURT OF KENTUCKY

PRACTICE OF LAW

SCR 3.640 New Lawyer Program requirement

(1) Within 12 months following the date of admission as set forth on the certificate of admission, each person admitted to membership in the Association shall complete the New Lawyer Program requirement.

(2) At least twice each educational year, the Commission shall provide or cause to be provided a New Lawyer Program of not less than 12 credits. The Commission may in its discretion, accredit a New Lawyer Program proposed by other CLE providers.

(3) Continuing legal education credits for the New Lawyer Program shall be awarded in a number consistent with the award of credits for other continuing legal education programs.

(4) The New Lawyer Program shall include at least 2 hours of ethics, a course on law practice management and other subjects determined appropriate by the Commission.

(5) The Commission or other provider accredited under SCR 3.640(2) may charge a reasonable registration fee approved by the Court for the New Lawyer Program.

(6) Each individual attending the New Lawyer Program shall certify to the Director for CLE the completion of the Program on the attendance certificate provided for that purpose. Such certification shall be submitted to the Director for CLE upon completion of the program and in no case shall the certification be submitted later than 30 days after completion of the program. Continuing legal education credits awarded for the program shall be applied to the educational year in which the program is attended, and if applied to a year in which the individual so attending is otherwise exempt from CLE requirements under SCR 3.665(c), then said credits shall carry forward in accordance with SCR 3.645(3).

(7) A member required to complete the New Lawyer Program pursuant to paragraph (1) of this Rule may, upon application to and approval by the Commission, be exempted from the requirement if the member is admitted to practice in another jurisdiction for a minimum of 5 years, and will certify such prior admission to the Commission, or if the member has attended a mandatory new lawyer training program of at least 12 credits, including 2 ethics credits, offered by the state bar association of another jurisdiction and approved by the Director for CLE.

(8) The time for completion and certification set forth in paragraphs 1 and 6 of this Rule may, upon written application to and approval by the Commission or its designee, be extended. Written applications for an extension under this paragraph must be received by the Commission no later than 30 days after the member's deadline to complete the Program as set forth in paragraph (1) of this Rule. All applications must be signed by the member. The Commission may approve extensions for completing the Program under the following circumstances:

(a) Where the member demonstrates hardship or other good cause clearly warranting relief. Requests for relief under this subsection must set forth all circumstances upon which the request is based, including supporting documentation. In these circumstances, the member shall complete the requirement set forth in paragraphs (1) and (6) as soon as reasonably practicable as determined by the Commission or its designee; or

(b) Where the member fails to demonstrate hardship or other good cause clearly warranting relief, the member must pay a fee of $250.00 and complete the requirement set forth in paragraphs (1) and (6) at the next regularly scheduled New Lawyer Program.

(9) Non-compliance with the New Lawyer Program requirement: Failure to complete and certify attendance for the New Lawyer Program pursuant to this Rule shall be grounds for suspension from the practice of law in the Commonwealth or other sanctions as deemed appropriate by the Board.

(a) Ninety days prior to the end of the 12 month period all individuals not certifying completion of the New Lawyer Program pursuant to this Rule shall be notified in writing that the program must be completed before the end of the 12 month period, indicating the date.

(b) Names of all individuals not submitting certification of completion of the New Lawyer Program within the 12 month period or not being granted an extension of time, pursuant to paragraph (8) of this Rule, shall be submitted to the Board by the Director for CLE, certifying the member's failure to comply with the New Lawyer Program requirement.

(c) The Board shall cause to be sent to the member a notice of delinquency by certified mail, return receipt requested, at the member's bar roster address. Such notice shall require the attorney to show cause within 30 days from the date of the mailing why the attorney's license should not be suspended for failure to meet the New Lawyer Program requirement set forth in this Rule. Such response shall be in writing, sent to the attention of the Director of CLE, and shall be accompanied by costs in the amount of $50.00 payable to the Kentucky Bar Association.

(d) Unless good cause is shown by the return date of the notice, or within such additional time as may be allowed by the Board, the lawyer will be stricken from the membership roster as an active member of the KBA and will be suspended from the practice of law or will be otherwise sanctioned as deemed appropriate by the Board. A copy of the suspension notice shall be delivered by the Director of CLE to the member, the Clerk of the Kentucky Supreme Court, and in the case of suspension, to the Circuit Clerk of the district wherein the member resides for recording and indexing as required by SCR 3.480.

(e) A member suspended under this Rule may apply for restoration to membership under the provisions of SCR 3.500.

(f) A member may appeal to the Kentucky Supreme Court from such suspension order within 30 days of the effective date of the suspension. Such appeal shall include an affidavit showing good cause why the suspension should be set aside.

HISTORY: Adopted by Order 2013-12, eff. 1-1-2014

KENTUCKY BAR ASSOCIATION
RULES OF THE SUPREME COURT OF KENTUCKY

PRACTICE OF LAW

SCR 3.645 Continuing legal education requirements: compliance and certification

(1) Each educational year, as defined by SCR 3.600(7), every person licensed to practice law in this Commonwealth, not specifically exempted pursuant to the provisions of SCR 3.665, shall complete and certify a minimum of 12 credit hours in continuing legal education activities approved by the Commission, including a minimum of 2 credit hours devoted to "ethics, professional responsibility and professionalism" as defined by SCR 3.600(8). All continuing legal education activities must be completed by June 30 of each educational year.

>   (a) Integration of legal ethics, professional responsibility and professionalism issues into substantive law topics is encouraged, but will not count toward the 2 credit minimum annual requirement.
>   (b) It is the obligation of the attorney seeking credit to ensure the activity has been approved. Completion of a non-accredited activity shall be at the risk of the attorney.

(2) Certification of completion of approved CLE activities must be received by the Director for CLE no later than August 10th immediately following the educational year in which the activity is completed.

>   (a) Certification shall be submitted to the Director for CLE by the sponsor of the accredited activity or by individual attorneys on approved KBA forms, uniform certificates, or other format adopted by the Commission.
>   (b) Any certification submitted after the August 10th deadline shall be deemed past due. All past due reports shall be accompanied by a late filing fee of $50.00 per certificate to cover the administrative costs of recording credits to the prior year. All past due reports must be received by the Commission with the late fee no later than the close of the educational year (June 30th) immediately following the year during which the activity was completed. This deadline will not apply in instances where the member or former member is in the process of removing an exemption per SCR 3.665 (2) or attempting certification per SCR 3.685.
>   (c) Sponsors submitting certifications to the Director for CLE shall comply with all requirements set forth in SCR 3.660(6).

(3) A member who accumulates an excess over the 12 credit requirement may carry forward the excess credits into the 2 successive educational years for the purpose of satisfying the minimum requirement for those years. Carry-forward credits are limited to a total of 24 credits, including 4 ethics credits. All excess credits above a total of 24 credits will remain on the member's record but may not be carried forward.

(4) Failure to acquire a minimum of 12 credits, including 2 ethics credits, to meet the minimum, annual continuing legal education requirement and/or the associated certification requirements set forth herein, shall be grounds for suspension by the Board from the practice of law.

(5) Compliance and certification requirements concerning the New Lawyer Program requirement are set forth at SCR 3. 640(1) and (6).

HISTORY: Adopted by Order 2013-12, eff. 1-1-2014

KENTUCKY BAR ASSOCIATION
RULES OF THE SUPREME COURT OF KENTUCKY

PRACTICE OF LAW

SCR 3.650 Qualifying continuing legal education activity and standards

(1) Credit for completing qualifying continuing legal education activities, as set forth below in paragraphs 2 and 3 of this Rule, shall be calculated, reported and subject to the limitations set forth in SCR 3.655.

(2) A continuing legal education activity qualifies for accreditation if the Commission determines that the activity conforms to the following standards:

(a) The activity is an organized program of learning (including a course of study, workshop, symposium or lecture) which contributes directly to the legal competence of an attorney.

(b) The activity deals primarily with substantive legal issues directly related to the practice of law, or law practice management, and includes consideration of any related issues of ethics, professional responsibility, or professionalism.

(c) The activity has significant intellectual or practical content which is timely.

(d) The activity has as its primary objective to increase the participant's professional competence as an attorney. Activities designed primarily for non-lawyers do not qualify for accreditation.

(e) The activity must be offered by a sponsor having substantial, recent experience in offering continuing legal education. Demonstrated ability arises partly from the extent to which individuals with legal training or educational experience are involved in the planning, instruction and supervision of the activity.

(f) The activity itself must be taught and conducted by an individual or group qualified by practical or academic experience.

(g) The activity, including the named advertised participants, must be conducted substantially as planned, subject to emergency alterations.

(h) Thorough, high-quality, readable, timely, useful and carefully prepared written materials must be made available to all participants at or before the time the activity is presented. A brief outline without citations or explanatory notations is not sufficient.

(i) At the conclusion of the activity, each participating attorney must be given the opportunity to complete an evaluation questionnaire addressing the quality of the particular activity.

(j) The cost of the activity itself to participating attorneys must be reasonable considering the subject matter and instructional level.

(k) The activity may be presented live or by technological transmission as defined in SCR 3.600(12). Activities including audio components must have high quality audio reproductions so that listeners may easily hear the content of the activity. Activities including video components must have high quality video reproductions so that observers may easily view the content of the activity.

(l) In cases of an in-house activity, as defined in SCR 3.600(9), such activities may be approved if all standards set forth herein for accreditation are met. In addition, at least half the instruction hours must be provided by qualified persons having no continuing relationship or employment with the sponsoring firm, department or agency.

(3) Continuing legal education credit may be earned for the following additional activities subject to the limitations set forth in SCR 3.655:

(a) Teaching or participating as a panel member or seminar leader in an approved activity.

(b) Researching, writing or editing material to be presented at an approved activity.

(c) Publication of a legal writing as defined by SCR 3.600(10).

(d) Public speaking. Upon application, CLE credit may be earned by teaching or participating as a panel member, mock trial coach or seminar leader for law-related public service speeches to civic organizations or school groups. A maximum of 2 credits earned under this Rule per educational year may be applied to meet the annual minimum requirement. Speaking for which the member is paid shall not be approved. Written copies of presentations must accompany such applications; provided, however, that, where appropriate, a narrative summary of the material presented may be sufficient.
(e) Law school classes attended by a member, provided that the member registers for the class with the law school and completes the course as required by the terms of registration, for credit or by audit.

(4) The following categories of activities shall not qualify as a continuing legal education:
(a) Seminars or meetings sponsored by law firms or other organizations which are determined by the Commission to be in the nature of client development and do not meet the requirements set forth in SCR 3.650(2).
(b) Passing a bar exam for licensure to practice law in a state or jurisdiction.
(c) Bar review courses taken in preparation for bar examinations for admission to the highest court in a state or jurisdiction.
(d) Correspondence classes.
(e) Any activity completed prior to admission to practice in Kentucky except the program required pursuant to SCR 3.645(5) and 3.640(1).
(f) Undergraduate law or law-related classes.
(g) Programs taken in preparation for licensure exams for non-lawyer professionals.
(h) Business meetings or committee meetings of legal and law-related associations.

(5) Seminars designed for non-lawyer professionals which in, case-by-case situations, will benefit the lawyer by allowing clients improved services in unique areas of practice. Credits earned for this category of seminar or activity shall not count toward the 12 credit annual minimum requirement but may count toward continuing legal education award credits as determined by the Commission.

(6) Accreditation of activities may be withdrawn by the Commission in cases where there is evidence that any of the above standards and criteria have not been met or that circumstances surrounding the actual content or transmission of the activity are not as originally represented to the Commission during the application process such that withdrawal of accreditation is warranted.

HISTORY: Adopted by Order 2013-12, eff. 1-1-2014

PRACTICE OF LAW

SCR 3.655 Calculation and reporting of continuing legal education credits: formulas and limits

(1) All certifications and applications for credits shall be claimed on KBA forms, uniform certificates approved by the Commission, or other mechanism adopted by the Commission and shall be forwarded to the Director for CLE.

(2) Credits granted for continuing legal education activities vary depending on the nature of the activity. Credit will be granted, or is calculated, and in some instances limited, as set forth below.

(a) Members completing or participating in an approved activity will be granted 1 credit for each 60 minutes of actual instructional time. Instructional time shall not include introductory remarks, breaks, or business meetings held in conjunction with a continuing legal education activity.

(b) Members completing or participating in an accredited technologically transmitted, non-live activity will be granted credit as set forth in SCR 3.655(2)(a). A maximum of 6 credits may be applied to meet the annual minimum CLE requirement set forth in SCR 3.645. Credits earned by completing a non-live activity will be applied to the educational year in which such activity is completed. Activities presented by technological transmission with an attorney facilitator available for purposes of answering questions and leading discussions are considered "live." Live webinars and teleseminars are also considered "live" programs and are not subject to this limitation.

(c) Members teaching or participating as panel members or seminar leaders in an approved activity will be granted 1 credit for each 60 minutes of actual instructional time.

(d) Members may be granted preparation credit as follows:
(i) One credit for each 2 hours spent in preparation for teaching or participating as a panel member or seminar leader in an approved activity, up to a maximum of 12 credits per educational year.
(ii) One credit for each 2 hours spent researching, writing or editing material presented by another member at an approved continuing legal education activity, up to a maximum of 12 credits per educational year.

(e) Credit for attending a law school class as set forth in SCR 3.650 shall equal twice the number of semester or credit hours awarded by the law school for successful completion of the course for credit or by audit. Actual instruction time shall not be used to determine continuing legal education credit for attending law school classes.

(f) Members may earn credits for publication of qualified legal writing pursuant to SCR 3.650(3)(c), up to a maximum of 6 credits per year. One credit is granted for each 2 hours of actual preparation time including research, writing, and editing. Any excess credits, up to 20 hours, will be applied toward the award established in SCR 3.690. Applications for continuing legal education credit for a published legal writing shall be made as set forth in SCR 3.655(1) and shall be accompanied by a copy of the published legal writing for which credit is sought.

(g) The Commission shall grant a maximum of 2 credits to meet the annual minimum requirement for public speaking pursuant to SCR 3.650(3)(d).

HISTORY: Adopted by Order 2013-12, eff. 1-1-2014

KENTUCKY BAR ASSOCIATION
RULES OF THE SUPREME COURT OF KENTUCKY

PRACTICE OF LAW

SCR 3.660 Procedure for accreditation of continuing legal education activities and obligations of sponsors

(1) Educational activities may be approved for credit upon application to the Commission. Application for accreditation may be made by a member or former member without involving the sponsor, or application for accreditation may be made by an activity sponsor.

(2) Application for accreditation of continuing legal education activities shall be made by members, former members or activity sponsors using forms provided by the Association or using uniform applications adopted by the Association. Applications must provide all information required by the form in order to be reviewed. All applications shall be accompanied by the appropriate application fee as follows:

    (a) For applications submitted by sponsors for activities greater than 2 hours in length and submitted at least 30 days in advance of the activity, the fee is $50.00 per activity. If such application is submitted less than 30 days in advance of the activity, the fee is $100.00 per activity.

    (b) For applications submitted by sponsors for activities 2 hours or less in length and submitted at least 30 days in advance of the activity, the fee is $20.00 per activity. If such application is submitted less than 30 days in advance of the activity, the fee is $40.00 per activity.

    (c) For applications submitted by members or former members, regardless of length of activity and when submitted, the fee is $20.00 per activity.

    (d) Activities repeated on different dates or at different locations are separate activities and require separate applications and separate fees.

(3) Activity sponsors that apply for accreditation and receive approval prior to the activity may announce in advertising materials, "This activity has been approved by the Kentucky Bar Association Continuing Legal Education Commission for a maximum of XX.XX credits, including XX.XX ethics credits." Sponsors who have made application for accreditation of activities that have not yet been approved may announce in advertising materials, "Application for approval of this activity for a maximum of XX.XX credits, including XX.XX ethics credits, is PENDING before the Kentucky Bar Association Continuing Legal Education Commission." Sponsors may not advertise accreditation if accreditation has not been granted by the Commission and notice of such accreditation received by the sponsor.

(4) Technologically transmitted activities produced from live programs or studio productions must be accredited separately from the live or studio activity from which they were produced.

(5) Sponsors of accredited activities shall comply with the obligations and requirements set forth below.

    (a) Ensure that all education activities comply with SCR 3.650.

    (b) Permit Commission members and staff or their designees to monitor without payment of registration or other fees, any approved activity.

    (c) Utilize the activity code provided by the Kentucky Bar Association in its notification of accreditation in identifying the activity in all correspondence regarding the activity and provide the activity code to members for use in reporting credits.

    (d) Provide to each Kentucky attorney completing an approved activity a Commission approved credit reporting form and activity code. Credit reporting forms and activity numbers shall be made available to sponsors upon request from the Commission for use at approved activities.

(e) Collect credit reporting forms from Kentucky attorneys and submit to the Commission all forms received within 30 days of completion of the program. Failure to submit completed credit reporting forms within 30 days of the activity shall be accompanied by a late filing fee from the sponsor of $10.00 per form or certificate. Submit all attendance forms or certificates for activities held during the month of June no later than July 10th, immediately following the end of the educational year on June 30th. For programs held during June this provision of the rule supersedes the 30 day submission deadline provided above.

(f) Sponsors may submit member activity certifications to the Director of CLE as required by SCR 3.645(2), via electronic means so long as the sponsor maintains the member's original certification, or a copy thereof, on file for 2 subsequent educational years following the year in which the activity was completed.

HISTORY: Adopted by Order 2013-12, eff. 1-1-2014

KENTUCKY BAR ASSOCIATION
RULES OF THE SUPREME COURT OF KENTUCKY

PRACTICE OF LAW

SCR 3.665 Exemptions and removal of exemptions

(1) For each educational year, the following members of the Association shall be exempt from the requirements of SCR 3.645:

(a) In recognition of their positions, which prohibit the practice of law and have significant continuing education requirements by statute or rule of court as a result of the positions they hold, members who, during any portion of that educational year, are serving as:

(i) Justices, Judges, or Magistrates of the Commonwealth or Court of the United States; or

(ii) full-time administrative law judges for an agency of the United States or Commonwealth of Kentucky executive branch.

(b) Justices and Judges of the Commonwealth leaving the bench will be allowed to use accumulated Continuing Judicial Education credits toward the required CLE minimum, up to 12 credits, including 2 ethics, for the first year they are subject to the CLE requirement after leaving the bench.

(c) New lawyers who have been admitted less than 1 full educational year as of the June 30th deadline. Such members shall be subject to the New Lawyer Program requirement, as set forth in SCR 3.640.

(d) Members who are at least 75 years of age or at least 50 year members, including members who will become 75 years of age and those who become 50 year members within the educational year.

(2) Upon application to the Commission, the following members may be exempted from the requirements of SCR 3.645:

(a) Non-practice exemption: Members who do not practice law, as defined in SCR 3.020, within the Commonwealth and agree to refrain from such practice until the Commission approves an application for removal of the exemption.

(i) Non-practice exemptions shall not be effective retroactively unless the applicant certifies that he or she has not practiced law, as defined in SCR 3.020, within the Commonwealth, for all time periods covered by such exemption.

(ii) Practice of law as defined in SCR 3.020, within the Commonwealth, during the effective period of this exemption pursuant to SCR 3.665(2)(a) shall constitute the unauthorized practice of law. Information known by the Commission regarding the practice of law during any period for which a member has certified non-practice status pursuant to SCR 3.665(2)(a) is not confidential as provided by SCR 3.695 and shall be provided along with the member's continuing legal education transcript by the Director for CLE to the Office of Bar Counsel and the Inquiry Commission in writing.

(iii) A member seeking removal of a non-practice exemption shall be required to file a written application with the Commission, addressed to the Director for CLE, for the removal of said exemption. Required as an attachment to the application for removal of said exemption shall be certification of completion of sufficient continuing legal education credits to meet the minimum annual continuing legal education requirement for each educational year during which he or she was exempt, excluding the current educational year. In no case shall a member be required to certify completion of more than 12 credits, including applicable ethics credits, as a condition of removal of the exemption. Timely certification shall include only continuing legal education credits earned during the current educational year and 2 prior educational years. This Rule in no way affects the member's responsibility to complete the current year minimum annual education requirement by June 30th. The current year minimum educational requirement must be completed as set forth at SCR 3.645. The member shall be notified in writing, via certified mail, of the commission's action on the application for the removal of the exemption.

(iv) Application for removal of an exemption granted pursuant to SCR 3.665(2)(a) may not be made within 30 days of the granting of the exemption.

(b) Hardship exemption: Members who practice law within the Commonwealth, but demonstrate that meeting the requirements of SCR 3.645 would work an undue hardship by reason of disability, sickness, or other clearly mitigating circumstances.

(c) Military exemption: Any member who, for any portion of an educational year, was on active duty in the United States armed forces or whose spouse was on active duty in the United States armed forces for any portion of an educational year.

(3) Every member seeking an exemption from the mandatory continuing legal education requirement of SCR 3.645 pursuant to SCR 3.665(2) shall submit an application on forms provided by the Association or shall make other such written request providing information necessary for determination by the Commission of circumstances warranting exemption.

(4) Exemptions granted pursuant to SCR 3.665(2)(b) and (c) based on hardship or military service are considered temporary in nature unless specifically designated otherwise. In order to maintain an exemption based on a temporary hardship or military service, annual application is necessary. Failure to so certify will result in loss of the exempt status.

HISTORY: Adopted by Order 2013-12, eff. 1-1-2014

PRACTICE OF LAW

SCR 3.670 Extension of time requirements

(1) The time requirements associated with completion of continuing legal education and certification thereof, as set forth in SCR 3.645(1), may be extended by the Commission in case of hardship or other good cause clearly warranting relief. Requests for time extensions for completion of activities or certification thereof shall be made to the Commission in writing. All requests for time extension must be received by the Commission no later than the September 10th following the end of the educational year for which the time extension is sought. Requests must set forth all circumstances upon which the request is based, including supporting documentation. Applications for time extensions for completion of the New Lawyer Program may be submitted pursuant to SCR 3.640(8).

(2) A member who fails to complete the requirements of SCR 3.645 for any educational year, and who cannot show hardship or other good cause clearly warranting relief, may submit an application for a non-hardship extension of time in which to earn the annual minimum requirement. The application, which shall be made on KBA forms or by such other appropriate method approved by the Commission, must meet the following requirements:

    (a) Each application must contain a detailed plan for completing the annual requirement.

    (b) All required credits must be completed and reported by the September 10th deadline for the educational year for which an extension is sought.

    (c) The application must be submitted to the Director for CLE and received by the September 10th deadline for the educational year for which an extension is sought; and

    (d) The application must include the required application fee as set forth below:

        (i) $250.00 for the first year for which a non-hardship time extension is sought; or

        (ii) $350.00 for the second year for which a non-hardship time extension is sought; or

        (iii) $500.00 for the third year and all years thereafter for which a non-hardship time extension is sought.

        (iv) If a member does not seek a non-hardship time extension for 3 consecutive years, a subsequent non-hardship time extension thereafter sought will be considered the first such application and the fee schedule will begin again at the $250.00 level.

(3) Failure to comply with extended time requirements granted by the Commission pursuant to SCR 3.645 (1) or (2), including both completion of continuing legal education activities and certification thereof, shall subject the member to the sanctions of SCR 3.675: Suspension for Non-Compliance.

HISTORY: Adopted by Order 2013-12, eff. 1-1-2014

SCR 3.675 Non-compliance: procedure and sanctions

(1) As soon as practicable after August 20th of each year, the Commission shall notify a member in writing of existing delinquencies of record. The writing may consist of a computer generated form setting forth said delinquency. If any statement incorrectly reflects the continuing legal education status of the member it shall be the duty of the member to promptly notify the Commission of any claimed discrepancy in the education statement.

(2) If, by the first day of November immediately following, a member has neither certified completion by the June 30th immediately prior, of the minimum continuing legal education requirements set forth in SCR 3.645, nor applied for and satisfied the conditions of an extension under SCR 3.670 or exemption under SCR 3.665, the Commission shall certify the name of that member to the Board.

(3) The Board shall cause to be sent to the member a notice of delinquency by certified mail, return receipt requested, at the member's bar roster address. Such notice shall require the attorney to show cause within 30 days from the date of the mailing why the attorney's license should not be suspended for failure to meet the mandatory minimum CLE requirements of SCR 3.645. Such response shall be in writing, sent to the attention of the Director for CLE, and shall be accompanied by costs in the amount of $50.00 payable to the Kentucky Bar Association.

(4) Unless good cause is shown by the return date of the notice, or within such additional time as may be allowed by the Board, the lawyer will be stricken from the membership roster as an active member of the KBA and will be suspended from the practice of law or will be otherwise sanctioned as deemed appropriate by the Board. A copy of the suspension notice shall be delivered by the Director to the member, the Clerk of the Kentucky Supreme Court, the Director of Membership, and to the Circuit Clerk of the district wherein the member resides for recording and indexing as required by SCR 3.480.

(5) A member suspended under this Rule may apply for restoration to membership under the provisions of SCR 3.500.

(6) A member may appeal to the Kentucky Supreme Court from such suspension order within 30 days of the effective date of the suspension. Such appeal shall include an affidavit showing good cause why the suspension should be set aside.

HISTORY: Adopted by Order 2013-12, eff. 1-1-2014

KENTUCKY BAR ASSOCIATION
RULES OF THE SUPREME COURT OF KENTUCKY

PRACTICE OF LAW

SCR 3.680 Appeal of commission actions

(1) The Commission shall state the reason or reasons for any adverse Commission decision and shall notify the person or organization affected.

(2) Any person or organization may request in writing reconsideration of an adverse decision within 15 days of the notice of the decision. The Commission shall consider any pertinent material submitted and shall permit the aggrieved party the opportunity to appear at a meeting of the Commission for oral presentation of information to be considered.

(3) Any person or organization may appeal to the Board from an adverse decision of the Commission by filing a written notice in the Office of the Director within 30 days of the notice of the decision or of a refusal to reconsider a decision. The review of the Board shall be limited to the record considered by the Commission. The entire record, including a transcript of Commission proceedings, shall be submitted to the Board, with costs born by the unsuccessful party.

(4) Any person or organization may appeal to the Supreme Court of Kentucky from an adverse decision of the Board by filing a written petition, together with 10 copies, in the office of the Clerk of the Court, accompanied by a certificate of service on the Director and a filing fee of $100.00, within 30 days of the notice of the decision. The review of the Court shall be limited to the record considered by the Commission and the Board.

(5) Commission certification of non-compliance filed with the Board pursuant to SCR 3.640(9) or SCR 3.675 may not be appealed under Sections (3) and (4) of this Rule.

HISTORY: Adopted by Order 2013-12, eff. 1-1-2014

KENTUCKY BAR ASSOCIATION
RULES OF THE SUPREME COURT OF KENTUCKY

PRACTICE OF LAW

SCR 3.685 Continuing legal education requirements for restoration or reinstatement to membership: procedures

(1) Every former member, applying for or otherwise seeking restoration or reinstatement to membership pursuant to Rules 3.500 or 3.510, shall be required to have completed the minimum annual continuing legal education requirement for each year during which he or she was not a member in good standing, including any year prior to disbarment, suspension or withdrawal under threat of disbarment or suspension, during which the minimum annual continuing legal education requirement was not fulfilled. Completion of such credits shall be certified to the Commission as a condition precedent to reinstatement or restoration. In no case shall a member be required to attend more than 60 continuing legal education credits, including applicable ethics credits, as a condition precedent of restoration or reinstatement to membership.

(2) The application or affidavit of compliance submitted for restoration or reinstatement shall include certification from the Director for CLE of completion of continuing legal education activities as required by these Rules, or otherwise specified by the Commission or Court. Applicants or affiants shall request said certification from the Director for CLE in writing and shall submit with said written request a fee of $50.00 to cover the expense of the record search and certification. Applications or affidavits of compliance submitted for restoration or reinstatement which do not include the required certification of continuing legal education credits, including verification of fee payment for the certification, shall be considered incomplete and shall not be processed.

 (3) The requirements for completion of continuing legal education as a condition to restoration or reinstatement as set forth above may only be satisfied with credits earned in the current educational year during which the application is submitted and the preceding 2 educational years. Credits so earned shall be applicable to requirements imposed by the Commission upon application or other actions undertaken in pursuit of restoration or reinstatement.

(4) Approval of the application or provision of a certification for an affidavit of compliance shall satisfy the requirement of the applicant under SCR 3.645 for the current educational year.

(5) In the event that a new educational year begins after approval of the application or certification for an affidavit of compliance by the Commission, but prior to Supreme Court entry of an Order of Reinstatement or Restoration, or Registrar's certification of member's name to the active roster of membership the new year minimum continuing legal education requirement must be completed and the application updated before the reinstatement or restoration can proceed to the Board of Governors or to the Court, unless a maximum of 60 credits have been completed.

HISTORY: Adopted by Order 2013-12, eff.1-1-2014

KENTUCKY BAR ASSOCIATION
RULES OF THE SUPREME COURT OF KENTUCKY

PRACTICE OF LAW

SCR 3.690 Continuing Legal Education Award

(1) Any member who completes a minimum of 60 credit hours approved by the Commission within a period of 3 or fewer educational years, is eligible for a Continuing Legal Education Award which shall consist of a dignified certificate issued by the Association attesting to the educational accomplishment.

(2) The Commission shall notify the member and issue the award.

(3) Approved awards are valid for 1 year, beginning on the first day of July of the year of award notification.

(4) The validity of an award may be renewed for an additional year following the initial award date, in which the member who holds the award completes a minimum of 20 approved credits.

(5) Failure to earn 20 credits in any educational year following the initial award date shall disqualify the member from further renewals of that award. The member may only become eligible for another award by earning 60 approved credit hours in a period separate and distinct from the period for which a prior award was issued.

(6) Each member who holds a valid, unexpired award shall receive a 25% discount from the normal registration fee for the Kentucky Bar Association Annual Convention.

(7) The Association may publish annually in leading daily newspapers of general circulation throughout the Commonwealth an announcement of the members who during the preceding educational year have earned the Continuing Legal Education Award. The announcement shall describe the basis of the award and shall set forth in alphabetical order the name and geographical location of each recipient. A similar annual announcement may be included in the Kentucky Bench & Bar and on the Association website.

HISTORY: Adopted by Order 2013-12, eff. 1-1-2014

KENTUCKY BAR ASSOCIATION
RULES OF THE SUPREME COURT OF KENTUCKY

PRACTICE OF LAW

SCR 3.695 Commission records confidential

The files and records of the Commission shall be deemed confidential and shall not be disclosed except in furtherance of the duties of the Commission, as set forth at SCR 3.630, of the Board, upon request of the member affected, or as directed by the Supreme Court of Kentucky. This rule specifically excludes from confidentiality information provided by a member to the Commission as a part of a member's application for relief from the requirements of these rules.

HISTORY: Adopted by Order 2013-12, eff. 1-1-2014

LOUISIANA

STATEMENT OF PURPOSE

It is of primary importance to the members of the Louisiana State Bar Association (hereafter "Bar") and to the public that attorneys licensed to practice law in Louisiana keep current on changes and developments through continued legal education. These Rules establish the minimum requirements for continuing legal education.

Compliance with the continuing legal education (hereafter "CLE") requirements of these Rules is necessary to maintain a member's license to practice law in this State.

RULE 1. CONTINUING LEGAL EDUCATION COMMITTEE

(a) The Mandatory Continuing Legal Education Committee (hereinafter "Committee") shall consist of nine members. Five of the members shall be sitting or retired judges or attorneys and shall be appointed by the Court. Four of the members shall be attorneys appointed by the Louisiana State Bar Association.

(b) Initial appointments of Committee members following the 2006 amendments to these rules shall be for staggered terms. Thereafter, Committee members shall be appointed for three year terms of office. No appointee shall serve more than two (2) consecutive three (3) year terms. An appointment to fill any vacancies due to the death, resignation or disability of a member shall be for the unexpired term only.

(c) The Committee shall have the following duties:

(1) To exercise general supervisory authority over the administration of these Rules.

(2) To make and promulgate regulations that define, clarify, and assure prompt, accurate reporting of attendance at CLE activities.

(3) To inquire into and establish satisfactory procedures to ascertain the quality of programs, sponsors, and standards observed in CLE offered to members of the Bar.

(4) To grant or deny accreditation to, for the purpose of meeting the requirements of these Rules, any institution (hereafter "Sponsor") or any CLE course conducted within or without the State.

(5) To foster and encourage the offering of quality courses of CLE by qualified Sponsors at reasonable fees.

(6) To report annually and as otherwise required to the Supreme Court and to the Bar on the status of CLE within the State.

(7) To perform such other acts and duties, not inconsistent with these Rules, as are necessary and proper to improve the CLE programs within the State.

Added effective Jan. 1, 1988, amended effective January 1, 2007.

RULE 2. SCOPE AND EXEMPTIONS

These Rules shall apply to every attorney licensed to practice law (hereafter "Member"), except for the following persons who shall be exempt from the requirements of these Rules:

(1) All Members residing outside of the State and not engaged in the practice of law in Louisiana.

(2) All Members who demonstrate to the satisfaction of the Committee that meeting these requirements would work an undue hardship by reason of disability, sickness or other clearly mitigating circumstances.

(3) Active duty Members in the United States armed forces.

(4) Members of the United States Congress.

(5) All Members who have attained the age of sixty-five (65) years.

(6) All federal judges and magistrates.

(7) Members licensed to practice law in the State of Louisiana residing in the state but not engaged in the practice of law in Louisiana may qualify for restricted status and may be granted a waiver of compliance with the educational requirements of these rules. This exemption shall not apply to law clerks.

Added effective Jan. 1, 1988; amended effective June 14, 1991; amended effective Feb. 22, 1995.

RULE 3. CLE REQUIREMENT

(a) Each Member shall attend, or complete an approved substitute for attendance, a minimum of twelve and one half (12.5) hours of approved CLE each calendar year.

(b) Any newly admitted active Member shall, during the year of his or her admission through the next calendar year, attend twelve and one half (12.5) hours of approved CLE and not less than eight (8) of such hours shall concern legal ethics, professionalism, or law office management. A newly admitted active member is not required to comply with subsections (a) or (c). Law office management concerns knowledge and skill of office practice including courses on how to:

> Open and operate a client trust account;
>
> Establish a calendar (tickler) system;

Communicate with clients;

Set fee arrangements, send engagement letters, and establish billing procedures;

Avoid and/or obtain help for substance abuse problems;

Supervise staff;

Organize files;

Utilize a conflicts check system

Handle a disciplinary complaint

Terminate representation; and

Return files.

(c) Of the twelve and one half (12.5) hours of CLE required annually, not less than one (1) of such hours shall concern legal ethics, and not less than one (1) of such hours shall concern professionalism.

Legal ethics concerns the standard of professional conduct and responsibility required of a lawyer. It includes courses on professional responsibility and malpractice. It does not include such topics as attorneys' fees, client development, law office economics, and practice systems, except to the extent that professional responsibility is discussed in connection with these topics. Professionalism concerns the knowledge and skill of the law faithfully employed in the service of client and public good, and entails what is more broadly expected of attorneys. It includes courses on the duties of attorneys to the judicial system, courts, public, clients, and other attorneys; attorney competency; and pro bono obligations. Legal ethics sets forth the standards of conduct required of a lawyer; professionalism includes what is more broadly expected. The professionalism CLE requirement is distinct from, and in addition to, the legal ethics CLE requirement.

(d) Self-study credits shall be offered as an approved substitute to in-person attendance at CLE activities. Credit for self-study shall consist of participation in technological transmissions, including live or pre-recorded audio and/or audiovisual presentations and activities or other appropriate technology as approved by the MCLE Committee. Credit for attendance at such self-study courses shall be limited to four (4) hours annually.

(e) Except for CLE activities for which attendance cards are completed and forwarded by sponsors in accordance with Regulations 5.2.2 through 5.3.1, all Members shall submit to the Committee records pertaining to their compliance no later than January 31 of the following calendar year, pursuant to the conditions set forth in these Rules and Regulations.

(f) Louisiana state court judges shall be required to earn a minimum of 5 of the 12.5 hours of CLE required annually from programs sponsored by the Louisiana Judicial College, starting on January 1 of the year following their election to judicial office.

Added effective Jan. 1, 1988, amended effective July 12, 1996; amended effective Jan. 1, 1998, amended effective March 12, 2002, amended effective Jan. 1, 2003, amended effective June 5, 2003, amended effective April 4, 2012, amended effective January 1, 2013.

RULE 4. CREDITS

Credit will be given for attending CLE activities approved by the Committee.

Added effective Jan. 1, 1988.

RULE 5. ANNUAL REPORT

(a) On or before December 1 of each calendar year, the MCLE Committee will send to each member a preliminary report of compliance with the MCLE requirements for that year. The report will be mailed to the Members' primary registration statement address or preferred mailing address.

(b) Hours completed in any year in excess of the minimum number may be carried forward to satisfy the requirements for the year next following.

(c) On or before March 15 the MCLE Committee will forward to each non-complying Member a final transcript of compliance for the preceding calendar year. Such members shall correct any error(s) in the final transcript by forwarding to the MCLE Committee a written explanation of any such error(s) by March 31st. Members whose transcripts reflect compliance with the MCLE requirements of this Rule shall not receive a copy of their final transcript, but shall receive email notification reflecting such compliance

Amended and effective July 12, 1996; amended May 23, 1997, effective Jan. 1, 1998; amended and effective Dec. 10, 2001; amended Dec. 26, 2002, effective Jan. 1, 2003; amended and effective June 5, 2003; amended and effective June 29, 2007; amended and effective Nov. 6, 2007; amended and effective Sept. 18, 2014.

RULE 6. NONCOMPLIANCE AND SANCTIONS

(a) As soon as practical after January 31 of each year, the Committee shall compile the following:

(1) A list of those Members who have complied with Rule 3.

(2) A list of Members whose transcripts indicate that they have not complied with the requirements of Rule 3.

(b) The Committee shall then mail a notice of noncompliance with MCLE requirements to each attorney at the Member's official address of record. That attorney must, within sixty (60) days of the date the notice is mailed, furnish the Committee with the following:

(1) Documentary proof that the Member has complied with the requirements, or

(2) An affidavit or documentary proof setting forth the reasons for failure to comply with the requirements because of illness or other good cause, or

(3) Documentary proof indicating compliance with satisfactory substitutes to compensate for failure to comply timely.

(c) Any Member who fails to timely comply with the requirements of these Rules and Regulations for earning hours by the December 31st deadline or for reporting compliance by the January 31st deadline shall be assessed a delinquency penalty of $150.

Any Member, whether in regular practice or claiming an exemption, who has previously been noncompliant within the five years preceding the current reporting year will automatically incur an additional $50 penalty calculated at the rate of $50 per year for each noncompliant year within the five year period.

(d) Documentary proof of compliance furnished after the January 31 deadline must be accompanied by the delinquency penalty or documentary proof will not be accepted by the Committee.

(e) At the expiration of sixty (60) days from the date of notice to the Member, the Committee shall notify the Supreme Court of Louisiana of a Member's failure to furnish documentation as described in Rule 6(b) above, satisfactory to the Committee, to establish compliance or a valid excuse for noncompliance, or failure to comply with a satisfactory substitute, or failure to pay the delinquency penalty described in Rules 6(c) and (d) above, and shall request that the Court certify the Member ineligible to practice law. The Committee shall not request certification of ineligibility for a judge, but rather shall report to the Judiciary Commission any judge's failure to comply with the requirements of these rules.

(f) At any time after notice of noncompliance to the Supreme Court, a Member may file with the Committee documentary proof indicating compliance with Rule 3 of these Rules or compliance with satisfactory substitutes to compensate for failure to comply timely with such Rule; and if satisfactory to the Committee, it shall forthwith notify the Supreme Court for appropriate action, including reinstatement if the Member has been certified ineligible to practice law.

(g) Any Member affected adversely by a decision of the Committee, including a decision to request that the Supreme Court certify the Member ineligible to practice law, may apply for review of the decision by filing a written petition, with supporting materials, to the Supreme Court of Louisiana, within thirty (30) days of such adverse decision.

Added effective Jan. 1, 1988; amended effective Jan. 5, 1995; amended effective July 12, 1996, amended effective December 10, 2001, amended effective April 1, 2005, amended effective January 1, 2007, amended effective Oct. 11, 2007, amended effective July 26, 2011.

RULE 7.   FEES AND EXPENSES

(a) The Committee may contract with one or more Sponsors and may charge an application fee to Sponsors seeking approval of programs. All funds received from any contract or fees shall be used to defray the expenses of the Committee.

(b) Members of the Committee shall not be compensated but shall be reimbursed for expenses incurred by them in the performance of their duties, in accordance with reimbursement policies of the Office of the Judicial Administrator, Supreme Court of Louisiana.

Added effective Jan. 1, 1988; amended effective Jan. 5, 1995, amended effective January 1, 2007.

MAINE

RULE 5. Continuing Legal Education ("CLE")

(a) CLE Credit.

(1) Except as otherwise provided in this rule, every attorney required to register in accordance with these Rules shall complete 11 credit hours of approved CLE in each calendar year. At least one credit hour in each calendar year shall be primarily concerned with professionalism education. Qualifying professionalism education topics include professional responsibility, legal ethics, substance abuse and mental health issues, diversity awareness in the legal profession, and malpractice and bar complaint avoidance topics including law office and file management, client relations, and client trust account administration. If an attorney is subject to this rule for more than 3 months of a calendar year but for less than the entire year, the number of credits required for that year shall be prorated according to the number of full months of the year in which the attorney is subject to this rule. However, an attorney who has registered in emeritus attorney status is required to complete only seven credit hours of approved CLE in each calendar year, unless exempted from the requirements of CLE as provided by Rule 5(a)(5).

(2) An attorney who completes more than 11 credit hours in a calendar year may carry forward up to 10 credit hours to satisfy the requirement of the following year, provided that the ethics or professionalism education requirement of Rule 5(a)(1) is satisfied for each calendar year.

(3) The requirement of Rule 5(a)(1) may be met only by teaching (as provided in subsection (8)), attending courses or completing any CLE activity entitled to credit as provided in Rule 5(c) and (d); provided that no more than one half of the credit hours required in any reporting period may be earned through in-house courses, self-study, or a combination thereof.

(4) An attorney subject to this rule who is a member of the bar of another jurisdiction which has a mandatory CLE requirement satisfies the requirement of Rule 5(a)(1) if the attorney is in compliance with a CLE requirement established by court rule or statute in that jurisdiction. If the other jurisdiction does not require the equivalent of one professionalism education credit hour per year, the attorney must complete one approved professionalism education credit hour in each calendar year. An attorney subject to this rule who is a member of the bar of another jurisdiction must meet the requirement of Rule 5(a)(1) if CLE is not mandated by court rule or statute in the other jurisdiction.

(5) The following individuals otherwise subject to this rule are exempted from its requirements:

(A) attorneys in inactive status pursuant to Rule 4(e);

(B) full-time judges in any state or federal jurisdiction;

(C) full-time teachers in any law school approved by the American Bar Association;

(D) members of the armed forces of the United States who are on active duty outside of Maine;

(E) residents of another country unless they are practicing law in Maine;

(F) attorneys who have practiced 40 years or more, attained the age of 65 years, and are engaged in less than the full-time practice of law;

(G) legislators and members of Congress;

(H) attorneys serving as judicial law clerks; and

(I) emeritus attorneys.

In the discretion of the Board, any individual may be exempted from all or part of the requirements of this rule upon a showing of hardship or for other good cause pursuant to procedures to be established by the Board.

(6) An attorney subject to this rule will be exempted from the requirements of Rule 5(a)(1) during the year in which the attorney is admitted to the Maine Bar and during the following calendar year, if during the year of admission the attorney completes the Maine State Bar Association Bridging the Gap program.

(7) Except as provided in Rules 5(a)(8) and (9), credit is earned for the time of actual participation in an approved course or activity.

(8) An attorney subject to this rule who makes a presentation in an approved course or activity not offered for academic credit by the sponsoring institution will earn two hours of CLE credit for every 30 minutes of actual presentation at the approved course or activity if the attorney has prepared substantial written materials as defined by the Board to accompany the presentation. If substantial written materials have not been prepared, the attorney will earn one hour of CLE credit for every 30 minutes of actual presentation. An attorney who teaches a regularly scheduled law-related course offered for academic credit at an accredited post secondary educational institution will earn six hours of CLE credit under this rule for every hour of academic credit awarded by the institution for the course. An attorney who assists or participates in such a regularly scheduled course will earn one hour of CLE credit for every hour of actual participation, up to a maximum of six hours.

(9) An attorney subject to this rule who formally takes for credit or officially audits a regularly scheduled course offered for academic credit at a law school approved by the American Bar Association will earn four hours of CLE credit under this rule for every hour of academic credit awarded by the institution for the course, provided that the attorney attends at least 75% of the classes in the course and, if enrolled for academic credit, receives a passing grade.

(b) Reporting CLE Credit.

(1) An attorney subject to this rule shall, in connection with the filing of the registration documents required by Rule 4(a), submit an Annual Report to the Board providing the course title, date, location, sponsor, and number of credit hours of all courses or other activities taken for credit pursuant to Rule 5(a) during the preceding calendar year, or carried over from a prior year as provided in Rule 5(a)(2). If a reported course or other activity has not previously been approved in accordance with Rule 5(a), the attorney shall also submit the information required under section 5(c) to support a request for such approval. An attorney claiming exemption in accordance with Rules 5(a)(4) through 5(a)(6) shall state the ground of exemption in lieu of reporting the foregoing information.

(2) The Board may at any time ask an attorney to provide documentation supporting any information reported in accordance with Rule 5(b)(1).

(c) Courses and Other Activities Entitled to Credit.

(1) The Board shall maintain a list of approved sponsors. All publicly available courses or other publicly available CLE activities offered by approved sponsors are deemed automatically approved and entitled to credit upon payment of the requisite fees in accordance with Rule 5(a).

(2) All courses or other CLE activities sponsored or presented by any other individual or organization are entitled to credit for purposes of Rule 5(a) if the sponsor or the individual course or activity has been approved by the Board in accordance with Rule 5(a).

(3) The Board shall delegate all approval and other functions under this rule to the Board staff. Upon request, the Board shall review any decisions denying approval of any sponsor, individual course, or other CLE activity. The Board's determination of any such issue shall be final.

(d) Approval Procedure.

(1) *Sponsor Approval.* A sponsor may be approved by the Board upon payment of the requisite fees and submission of evidence establishing to the satisfaction of the Board:

(A) that the sponsor has been approved or accredited by a CLE accrediting authority established by court rule or statute in another state; or

(B) that, during the immediately preceding three years, the sponsor has sponsored at least six separate courses that comply with the requirements for individual course approval under Rule 5(d)(2).

The Board may at any time review the status of a sponsor or specific courses offered by a sponsor and may revoke approval if the status has changed or the courses offered by the sponsor do not comply with the requirements of Rules 5(c) and (d).

Requests for approval shall be submitted on a form prescribed by the Board, supplemented by such supporting documentation as would assist the Board in determining whether the sponsor meets the requirements of this rule.

(2) * Course Approval*. The Board may approve individual courses for credit under this rule upon written application from a non-approved sponsor or the submission of supporting documentation from an approved sponsor, together with the requisite fee.

An attendee may file such a request together with the requisite fee at any time up to and including the filing of the Annual Report under Rule 5(b) for the year for which credit is sought for the course. The Board shall grant the request if the Board is satisfied that the course meets the following criteria:

(A) the course or activity must contribute directly to the professional competence or skills of attorneys, or to their education with respect to their professional or ethical obligations and, where possible, should include a professionalism education component; and

(B) course leaders or lecturers and the authors of written materials must be persons sufficiently competent to accomplish the educational goals of the course.

The Board may, prior to granting approval, request any approved sponsor, non-approved sponsor, or attendee to submit further information concerning a course, including the brochure describing the course, a description of the method or manner of presentation of course materials, a statement as to the actual date and place of presentation and the number of persons in attendance, and a copy of the course materials.

(3) In-House and Self-Study CLE. Courses offered by law firms, either individually or jointly with other law firms, by corporate legal departments, or by similar entities employing attorneys, if such courses are provided primarily for the education of the sponsor's members or employees, and group or individual self-study courses involving the use of written materials, audio or video tapes, online, or other teaching methods and materials, may be approved for credit under Rule 5(d)(2) upon submission of evidence establishing to the satisfaction of the Board that:

(a) the course complies with the standards set forth in Rule 5(d)(2);

(b) experienced lawyers will contribute to the development or teaching of the course; and

(c) the course or self-study will be scheduled at a time and location that will be free of interruption.

The offering firm or other entity, an individual attendee, or any other individual seeking approval shall file information describing the course, activity or program, and a request for approval. Requests for approval shall be submitted using an

application form approved by the Board, supplemented by such supporting information as would assist the Board in determining whether the course, activity or
program meets the requirements of this rule. If a course or a program of self-study
consists of listening to or watching the video replay of a previously presented CLE
program, the Board shall allocate credit hours to the course in the same manner as
for a live program. For other courses or self-study activities, the Board shall
determine the amount of credit hours on the basis of program content and the
duration of the activity.

MINNESOTA

State of Minnesota

RULES of the BOARD of
CONTINUING LEGAL EDUCATION

Effective July 1, 2016

**Rules of the Minnesota
State Board of
Continuing Legal Education**

INDEX

E. Notice of Noncompliance Fee
F. Active Duty Military Service

10. Director's Determinations and Board Review
    A. Director's Determinations
    B. Board Review

11. Notice of Noncompliance
    A. Notice Required
    B. Service of Notice
    C. Contents of Notice
    D. Effect of Notice
    E. Board Hearing
    F. Decision
    G. Petition for Review

12. Restricted and Involuntary Restricted Status
    A. Election of Restricted Status
    B. Restrictions Imposed
    C. Transfer from Restricted Status to Active Status
    D. Transfer from Involuntary Restricted Status to Active Status
    E. Transfer from Involuntary Restricted Status to Voluntary Restricted Status

13. Retired Status
    A. Transfer from Active Status to Retired Status
    B. Transfer from Retired Status to Active Status

14. Emeritus Status
    A. Qualification
    B. Limitation of Practice
    C. Contents of Emeritus Affidavit Appendix IV
    D. Transfer to Emeritus Status
    E. Expiration of Emeritus Status
    F. Renewal of Emeritus Status

RULES OF THE MINNESOTA STATE BOARD
OF CONTINUING LEGAL EDUCATION

Rule 1. Purpose

The purpose of these Rules is to require that lawyers continue their legal education and professional development throughout the period of their active practice of law; to establish the minimum requirements for continuing legal education; to improve lawyers' knowledge of the law; and through continuing legal education courses, to address the special responsibilities that lawyers as officers of the court have to improve the quality of justice administered by the legal system and the quality of service rendered by the legal profession.

Rule 2. Definitions

In these Rules,

A. "Approved course" means a course approved by the Board.

B. "Approved legal services provider" means a legal services organization that meets at least one of the following criteria:

  (1) Funded by the Legal Services Corporation, or the Minnesota Legal Services Advisory Committee; or

  (2) Designated by the Minnesota Legal Services Advisory Committee as an approved legal service provider. Eligibility for designation is limited to:

   (a) Programs providing pro bono legal representation within 501(c)(3) nonprofit organizations that have as their primary purpose the furnishing of legal services to individuals with limited means.

   (b) Law firms, law libraries, or bar associations that conduct programs that have as their primary purpose the furnishing of legal services to individuals with limited means and are under the supervision of a pro bono coordinator or designated lawyer.

   (c) Law firms that provide pro bono legal services on behalf of a Minnesota Judicial Branch program, including but not limited to, the Guardian ad Litem Program.

C. "Board" means the State Board of Continuing Legal Education.

D. "Chairperson" means the Chairperson of the Board.

E. "Classroom setting" means a room, including an office, suitably appointed with chairs, writing surfaces, lecterns and other normal accouterments of a teaching room, which is exclusively devoted to the educational activity being presented.

F. "Course in ethics or professional responsibility" means a course or session within a course that deals with the Minnesota Rules of Professional Conduct, the ABA Model Rules of Professional Conduct, the rules of professional conduct or professional responsibility of other jurisdictions, or the opinions and case law arising from the application of any of the above-specified rules, including a course or session within a course that addresses in a specific way concepts such as professionalism, civility and ethical conduct in the practice of law and in the legal profession.

G. "Course in the elimination of bias in the legal profession and in the practice of law" means a course directly related to the practice of law that is designed to educate attorneys to identify and eliminate from the legal profession and from the practice of law biases against persons because of race, gender, economic status, creed, color, religion, national origin, disability, age or sexual orientation.

H. "Court" means the Supreme Court of the State of Minnesota.

I. "Director" means the Director of the Board.

J. "Emeritus status" is the status of a lawyer who has filed a Retirement Affidavit pursuant to Rule 2(C)(5) of the Rules of the Supreme Court on Lawyer Registration, is not on involuntary restricted status, has submitted an Affidavit of Emeritus Status Appendix IV showing compliance with the requirements of CLE Rule 14, and is authorized by Rule 14 to provide pro bono legal representation to a pro bono client when referred by an approved legal services provider. Emeritus status lawyers remain on restricted status.

K. "Established continuing legal education course sponsor," for the purposes of Rule 5B, is a person or entity regularly retained by firms or organizations for the purpose of presenting continuing legal education programs, which is completely independent of the firm or organization for whose members the continuing legal education course is presented.

L. "Fee" means funds made payable to the Minnesota State Board of Continuing Legal Education.

M. "In-house course" means a course sponsored by a single private law firm, a single corporation or financial institution, or by a single federal, state or local governmental agency for lawyers who are members or employees of any of the above organizations.

N. "Involuntary restricted status" means the status of a lawyer licensed in Minnesota who is not in compliance with the educational and reporting requirements of these Rules and who has been involuntarily placed in that status by order of the Court. See Rule 12 for additional provisions.

O. "Laboratory setting" means a mock courtroom, law office, negotiation table, or other simulated setting in which demonstrations are given, role-playing is carried out or lawyers' activities are taught by example or participation.

P. "Law and literature course" means a course that meets the requirements of Rules 4D and 5A, based upon a literary text and designed to generate discussion, insight, and learning about topics such as the practice of law, the history and philosophy of law, rhetoric, lawyers' professional or ethical responsibilities, professional development, and the elimination of bias in the legal profession and in the practice of law.

Q. "Moderator" means an individual, knowledgeable in the topic or topics addressed by the course, who guides the discussion and answers questions related to the material presented.

R. "On-Demand course" means archived CLE programming that meets all the requirements of Rule 5A and is available to participants at any time.

S. "Participant" means a lawyer licensed in Minnesota attending an approved course and actively engaged in the subject matter being presented.

T. "Pro bono client" means an individual, who is not a corporation or other organizational entity, and who has been referred to the lawyer by an approved legal services provider or by a state or federal court program.

U. "Pro bono legal representation" means providing legal representation to a pro bono client without compensation, expectation of compensation, or other direct or indirect pecuniary gain.

V. "Professional development course" means a course or session within a course designed to enhance the development and performance of lawyers by addressing issues such as career satisfaction and renewal, stress management, mental or emotional health, substance abuse, and gambling addiction. Professional development courses do not include individual or group therapy sessions.

W. "Restricted status" means the status of a lawyer licensed in Minnesota who has voluntarily chosen not to comply with the educational and reporting requirements of these Rules. See Rule 12 for additional provisions.

X. "Submit" means to communicate information to the Board office in writing or electronic submission:
   (1) through the Board's Online Attorney and Sponsor Integrated System (OASIS);
   (2) by regular U.S. Mail; or
   (3) by delivery.

Y. "Law office management course" is a course or session within a course designed to enhance the efficient and effective management of the law office by addressing topics of mentoring, staff development, and technology related to a law office.

Rule 3. State Board of Continuing Legal Education

A. **Membership of the Board.** The Court shall appoint twelve members and a Chairperson. The membership of the Board shall consist of:

   (1) 3 members of the public;
   (2) 1 member who is a district court judge;
   (3) 6 lawyer members who are nominated by the Minnesota State Bar Association; and
   (4) 3 lawyer members who are nominated by the Court.

B. **Terms of Members**. Appointments shall be for staggered 3-year terms, with no member serving more than two 3-year terms, and each member serving until a successor is appointed and qualifies.

C. **Officers of the Board**.

> **(1) Chairperson**. The Chairperson of the Board shall be appointed by the Court for such time as it shall designate and shall serve at the pleasure of the Court.
> **(2) Vice Chairperson**. A Vice Chairperson shall be designated by the Chairperson and shall maintain the minutes of meetings of the Board.

D. **Authority of the Board.** Subject to the general direction of the Court in all matters, the Board:

> **(1)** shall have supervisory authority over the administration of these Rules, shall approve courses and programs which satisfy the educational requirements of these Rules, and shall have authority to grant waivers of strict compliance with these Rules or extensions of time deadlines provided in these Rules in cases of hardship or other compelling reasons;
>
> **(2)** shall have supervisory authority over the administration of the Rules of the Supreme Court on Lawyer Registration; and
>
> **(3)** may adopt policies and forms not inconsistent with these Rules or the Rules of the Supreme Court on Lawyer Registration governing the conduct of business and performance of its duties.

E. **Board Procedures.** Robert's Rules of Order shall govern the conduct of Board meetings where practicable.

F. **Confidentiality.** Unless otherwise directed by the Court, the files, records, and proceedings of the Board, as they may relate to or arise out of any failure of an active lawyer to satisfy the continuing legal education requirements, shall be deemed confidential and shall not be disclosed except in furtherance of the Board's duties, or upon request of the lawyer affected, or as they may be introduced in evidence or otherwise produced in proceedings in accordance with these Rules.

G. **Persons with Disabilities.** It is the policy of the Board to administer these Rules in a manner consistent with state and federal laws prohibiting discrimination against persons with disabilities and to make reasonable modifications in any policies, practices, and procedures that might otherwise deny equal access to individuals with disabilities.

H. **Payment of Expenses.** The Chairperson, the Vice Chairperson and other members of the Board shall serve without compensation, but shall be paid reasonable and necessary expenses certified to have been incurred in the performance of their duties.

Rule 4.   Applying for Credit; Fees

A.   **Course Approval and Fee Information.** No segment of any course shall be approved in more than one credit category. In applying for course approval, a sponsoring agency or lawyer shall submit to the Board an application for course approval (see Appendix I) and include the following:

    (1) Name and contact information for the sponsor;

    (2) Title of the program under consideration;

    (3) City and state where the program is held;

    (4) Names and credentials of the speakers, including those of persons designated to act as moderators for video or satellite programs;

    (5) Type of presentation;

    (6) Agenda or course schedule showing beginning and ending times of each session and the date(s) on which the program is presented;

    (7) For each segment of the course, credit may be requested in one of the following categories:

        (a) Standard, including professional development and law office management
        (b) ethics and/or professional responsibility
        (c) elimination of bias

    (8) Fees.

        (a) A fee in the amount of $35 shall be paid when an application for course approval is submitted by means other than through the Board's Online Attorney and Sponsor Integrated System (OASIS).
        (b) A fee in the amount of $20 shall be paid when an application for course approval is submitted electronically through the Board's Online Attorney and Sponsor Integrated System (OASIS).
        (c) Fees for course approval may be subject to waiver under the provisions of Rule 3D(1).
        (d) A fee is not required when submitting an application for either of the following types of courses meeting Rule 4 and Rule 5 requirements:

            (i) a previously approved course that has been recorded and is replayed in its entirety with a live moderator present during the scheduled question and answer period of the program; or

            (ii) a live course 60 minutes or less in duration.

    (9) Expected audience or target audience to which the program is marketed; and

    (10) Such other information as the Board may require.

B. **Professional Responsibility or Ethics: General Treatment.** Every application for course approval must include:

    (1) A description of the general treatment of professional responsibility or ethical considerations; or

    (2) An explanation of why professional responsibility or ethical considerations are not included.

C. **Sanctions for Failure to Include Ethics.** If in the opinion of the Board, the general treatment of professional responsibility or legal ethics topics within courses approved as standard continuing legal education is inadequate without satisfactory explanation, the Board may refuse to grant full credit for all hours in attendance, impose a deduction from credit hours which would otherwise be granted, and in the case of persistent refusal to cover these topics, refuse to grant further credit for courses offered by the sponsor.

D. **Law and Literature.** A "law and literature course" that otherwise meets the course approval requirements set forth in Rule 5(A) will be approved for credit if the application for course approval includes the following:

    (1) A narrative describing the course learning goals and discussion topics.

    (2) Evidence that program registrants are instructed to read the designated literary text prior to attending the course.

No credit will be granted for the time that participants spend reading the designated literary text prior to attending the course.

E. **Notice of Credit.** The Board shall inform the sponsor or applicant of the number and type of credit hours granted or denied. This information will also be posted on the Board's website.

Rule 5. Standards for Course Approval

A. **General Standards.** A course must meet the following standards before approval is granted.

    (1) The course shall have current, significant intellectual or practical content, and shall be presented in a high-quality manner permitting participants to hear all of the audio and see all of the video portions of the program, including presentations, audience questions, responses to questions, embedded videos, and other program materials.

    (2) The course shall deal primarily with matter directly related to the practice of law, the professional responsibility or ethical obligations of lawyers, the elimination of bias in the legal profession and in the practice of law, law office management, or the professional development of lawyers.

(3) The course shall be taught by faculty members qualified by practical or academic experience to teach the specified subject matter. Legal subjects shall be taught by lawyers.

(4) Any written materials should be thorough, high quality, readable, carefully prepared, and distributed to all participants at or before the time the course is offered.

(5) The course shall be presented and attended in a suitable classroom or laboratory setting. A course presented via video recording, simultaneous broadcast, teleconference, or audiotape, or available on-demand or by podcast, may be approved provided that it complies with Rule 6D and a faculty member or moderator is accessible to all participants, either in person or via electronic means, allowing all participants to have access to and participate in the question and answer session. No course will be approved which involves solely correspondence work or self-study.

(6) Credit will not normally be given for speeches at luncheons or banquets.

(7) A list of all participants shall be maintained by the course sponsor and transmitted to the Board upon request, following the presentation of the course.

(8) Credit shall be awarded on the basis of one credit hour for each 60 minutes of instruction at an approved course.

(9) A lawyer shall not receive credit for any course attended before being admitted to practice law in Minnesota, but one so admitted may receive credit of one hour for each 60 minutes actually spent in attendance, for attending for credit or as an auditor, a regular course offered by a law school approved by the American Bar Association.

(10) Notwithstanding the provisions of paragraph (9) above, a person who takes approved courses or teaches in an approved course after sitting for the Minnesota Bar Examination, but before admission to practice, may claim credit for the courses taken or the teaching done, if he or she passes that bar examination.

B. **Standards for Course Approval for In-House Courses.**

(1) An in-house course as defined in Rule 2M will be approved if:

(a) The requirements of Rule 5A and other applicable Rules are met;

(b) 25% of the hours of approved instruction are taught by instructors having no continuing relationship or employment with the sponsoring firm, department, financial institution or agency; and

(c) Notice of the course is given to enough outside lawyers so that the audience can potentially be composed of at least 25% participants who are not lawyers working in or for the sponsoring firm, department, institution or agency.

   (2) An in-house course as defined in Rule 2M that is presented and controlled by an established continuing legal education course sponsor as defined in Rule 2K, may be approved for credit, notwithstanding the fact that the course does not comply with requirements of Rule 5B(1) (b) and (c) above.

   (3) An in-house course as defined in Rule 2M shall not be approved for credit if it is presented primarily for clients or clients' counsel.

Rule 6.   Special Categories of Credit

A.   **Ethics and Professional Responsibility.** To be approved for ethics credit, the courses or sessions within the courses approved must meet the following requirements:

   (1) Be at least 30 minutes in length; and

   (2) Be separately identified as ethics or professional responsibility on the course agenda and on the Course Approval Form at Appendix I.

B.   **Elimination of Bias in the Legal Profession and in the Practice of Law.** To be approved for elimination of bias credit, the courses or sessions within such courses approved must meet the following requirements:

   (1) Be at least 60 minutes in length;

   (2) Be identified on the application as fulfilling the elimination of bias requirement and be accompanied by a narrative describing how the course or sessions of the course meet one or more of the learning goals as described in the Course Approval Form at Appendix I;

   (3) Focus on issues in the legal profession and in the practice of law and not issues of bias in society in general; and

   (4) Not include courses on the substantive law of illegal discrimination unless such courses meet one or more of the learning goals for elimination of bias courses set forth in the Course Approval Form at Appendix I.

C.   **Pro Bono Legal Representation.** A lawyer may claim 1 hour of standard CLE credit for every 6 hours of pro bono legal representation as defined by Rule 2U that the lawyer provides to a pro bono client as defined by Rule 2T in a legal matter that has been referred to the lawyer by an approved legal services provider as defined by Rule 2B or by a state court or federal court program. No more than 6 hours of credit may be claimed per reporting period by a lawyer for pro bono legal representation. In order to receive CLE credit the lawyer must submit an Affidavit of Pro Bono Representation to the Board (see Appendix II).

D. **On-Demand Courses.** A lawyer may claim up to 15 hours of credit within the 45 hour CLE period for on-demand courses as defined in Rule 2R, subject to the following provisions:

    (1) The course meets all other requirements of Rules 2, 5, & 6;

    (2) The course sponsor agrees to have one or more faculty members accessible to all participants via electronic or other means through the 24 month period during which the program is approved for Minnesota CLE credit;

    (3) The course sponsor or course applicant completes and submits to the Board an Application for Course Approval; and

    (4) The approval for an on-demand course is valid for 24 months after the date of approval by the Board office.

Rule 7. Other Credit

A. **Teaching Credit.** Credit for teaching in an approved, live (not previously recorded) course shall be awarded to presenting faculty on the basis of one credit for each 60 minutes spent by the faculty preparing the presentation and materials for the course and teaching the course. No credit shall be awarded for teaching directed primarily to persons preparing for admission to practice law. A lawyer seeking credit for teaching and preparation for teaching shall submit to the Board all information called for on the Affidavit of CLE Compliance at Appendix III.

B. **Courses at Universities.** Courses that are part of a regular curriculum at a college or university, other than a law school, may be approved for a maximum of 15 hours per course when the lawyer requesting approval submits evidence supporting the conclusion that the course meets the Rule 5A(1) through (5) criteria and that it is directly related to the requesting lawyer's practice of law. Teaching credit shall not be awarded for courses approved under this paragraph.

C. **Retroactive Credit.** A lawyer, or a course sponsor, may seek retroactive approval of courses by submitting the necessary information and fees required in Rule 4A. (See Course Approval Form at Appendix I.)

Rule 8. Announcement of Approval

Any person may announce, as to an approved course: This course has been approved by the Minnesota State Board of Continuing Legal Education for _____ hours in the following category or categories of credit:

    (a) standard continuing legal education;

    (b) ethics or professional responsibility continuing legal education; or

    (c) elimination of bias continuing legal education.

Rule 9. Affidavit of CLE Compliance

A. **Contents of Affidavit.** To maintain active status, a lawyer shall report participation in no fewer than 45 credit hours of approved continuing legal education courses within a single reporting period that are in compliance with the provisions of Rule 9B. A lawyer may report the credits through the Board's Online Attorney and Sponsor Integrated System (OASIS) or by Affidavit of CLE Compliance (Appendix III). Effective July 1, 2010, the Affidavit of CLE Compliance (Appendix III) must be accompanied by a $10 processing fee. There is no processing fee for submission through OASIS.

B. **Special Categories of Credit.** Lawyers must report:

    (1) no fewer than 3 hours of approved courses in ethics or professional responsibility;

    (2) no fewer than 2 hours of approved courses in the elimination of bias in the legal profession and in the practice of law;

    (3) no more than 6 hours of credit for pro bono legal representation provided pursuant to Rule 6D and reported by Appendix II; and

    (4) no more than 15 hours of credit for on-demand courses.

C. **Timely Affidavit.** The affidavit must be received by the Board office or postmarked no later than August 31 following the close of the final year of the 3-year period specified by the Lawyer Registration Office as a lawyer's continuing legal education category. Electronic affidavits must be submitted on or before August 31.

D. **Late Affidavit Fee.** A lawyer who submits an Affidavit of CLE Compliance after the deadline specified in paragraph C above, but before issuance of a notice of noncompliance, shall submit along with the late affidavit a late filing fee in the amount of $75.00. This fee is payable notwithstanding the Board's grant of an extension of time. Additional late fees will not be charged for late affidavits filed within a single reporting period.

E. **Notice of Noncompliance Fee.** A lawyer who submits an Affidavit of CLE Compliance after the Board has issued a notice of noncompliance, but before the Court has issued an order placing the lawyer on involuntary restricted status, shall submit along with the affidavit a notice of noncompliance fee in the amount of $200.

F. **Active Duty Military Service.** A lawyer called to active duty military service who requests an extension of time to complete CLE requirements because of active duty military service shall be granted an extension of at least six months from the date of return from active duty status. Upon request, the Board shall grant a waiver of a late filing fee or a notice of non-compliance fee assessed as a result of the lawyer's active duty military status.

Rule 10. Director's Determinations and Board Review

A. **Director's Determinations.** The Director has the following authority and responsibility:

(1) To respond in writing to written requests for course approval, giving reasons for the determination;

(2) To grant credit to lawyers for participating in or teaching approved courses;

(3) To grant or deny requests for transfer, waiver, extension of time deadlines or interpretation of these Rules; and

(4) To inform the Board about determinations made since the Board's last meeting, together with observations and comments relating to matters under the Board's jurisdiction.

B. **Board Review.** A lawyer or sponsoring agency affected by an adverse determination of the Director may request Board review of the determination and may present information to the Board in writing and in person. The Board may take such action as it deems appropriate and shall advise the lawyer or sponsoring agency of its determination.

Rule 11. Notice of Noncompliance

A. **Notice Required.** The Director shall send a notice of noncompliance to any lawyer who:

(1) Fails to meet the requirements of these Rules; and

(2) Fails to request and obtain an extension of time in which to file an Affidavit of CLE Compliance as required by these Rules.

B. **Service of Notice.** The notice shall be sent by regular mail to the lawyer's address of record with the Lawyer Registration Office.

C. **Contents of Notice.** The notice shall state the nature of the noncompliance and shall inform the lawyer of the right to request a hearing within 30 days of the mailing of the notice, the right to be represented by counsel, and the right to present witnesses and evidence.

D. **Effect of Notice.** If no hearing is requested, the Director's determination of noncompliance shall become final and shall be reported to the Court with the recommendation that the lawyer be placed on involuntary restricted status.

E. **Board Hearing.** If a hearing is requested, the following apply:

(1) The Board may employ special counsel;

(2) The Chairperson shall preside at the hearing, which may be held before the entire Board or a committee appointed by the Chairperson, and shall make necessary rulings; and

(3) The hearing shall be recorded and a transcript shall be provided to the lawyer at a reasonable cost.

F. **Decision.** Following the hearing, the Board shall issue a written decision. If the lawyer is determined to be in noncompliance with these Rules, the Board may recommend to the Court that the lawyer be placed on involuntary restricted status or take other appropriate action.

G. **Petition for Review.** A lawyer who is adversely affected by the decision of the Board may appeal to the Court by filing a petition for review with the Clerk of Appellate Courts within 20 days of receipt by the lawyer of the decision together with proof of service of the petition on the Director. The petition shall state briefly the facts that form the basis for the petition and the lawyer's reasons for believing the Court should review the decision. Within 20 days of service of the petition, the Board shall serve and file a response to the petition and a copy of the final decision of the Board. Thereupon, the Court shall give such direction, hold such hearings and issue such orders as it may in its discretion deem appropriate.

Rule 12. Restricted and Involuntary Restricted Status

A. **Election of Restricted Status.** A lawyer duly admitted to practice in this state may elect restricted status as defined in Rule 2W by sending written notice of such election to the Director, except that a referee or judicial officer of any court of record of the State of Minnesota or lawyer employed and serving as attorney or legal counsel for any employer, including any governmental unit of the State of Minnesota, is not eligible to apply for restricted status. A lawyer on restricted status shall not be required to satisfy the educational and reporting requirements of these Rules.

B. **Restrictions Imposed.** A lawyer on restricted or involuntary restricted status shall be subject to the following provisions and restrictions:

(1) The lawyer may not engage in the practice of law or represent any person or entity in any legal matter or proceedings within the State of Minnesota other than himself or herself, except as provided in Rule 14.

(2) The name of the lawyer may not appear on law firm letterhead without a qualification that the lawyer's Minnesota license is restricted. A law firm name may continue to include the lawyer's name if the name was included prior to the lawyer's placement on restricted or involuntary restricted status. The lawyer may not be listed "of counsel" or otherwise be represented to clients or others as being able to undertake legal business.

(3) The lawyer may not have a financial interest in a law firm that is a professional corporation.

C. **Transfer from Restricted Status to Active Status.**

    (1) **Notice to Director and Fee.** Unless otherwise ordered by the Court, a lawyer on restricted status who desires to resume active status shall notify the Director in writing of the lawyer's intention to resume active status and submit a transfer fee of $125.

    (2) **Transfer Requirements.** A lawyer on restricted status shall be transferred to active status upon the Director's determination that the lawyer has fulfilled the requirements of (a) or (b) below:

        (a) **Automatic transfer requirements.** The lawyer has completed the number of CLE hours that the lawyer would have had to complete to meet reporting requirements and to be current on a proportional basis had the lawyer not been on restricted status, or

        (b) **Discretionary transfer requirements.** The lawyer has completed such lesser requirements as the Director determines are adequate provided that the number of hours completed total no fewer than 45 hours during the 3 years immediately preceding transfer. The Director will specify no more than 90 hours. Determinations will be made subject to the criteria set forth in paragraph (c) below. The Director shall report to the Board at its next meeting the terms and conditions upon which each transfer to active status was made.

        (c) **Discretionary transfer criteria.** The Director may transfer a lawyer to active status when the lawyer has fulfilled appropriate CLE conditions precedent or agreed to fulfill appropriate CLE conditions subsequent as determined by the Director. In making discretionary transfer decisions, the Director will take the following into consideration:

            i. The number of CLE hours the lawyer has taken in the past;

            ii. The lawyer's other educational activity;

            iii. The lawyer's practice of law in another jurisdiction;

            iv. The lawyer's law-related work other than the practice of law;

            v. Whether the lawyer acted reasonably in not anticipating the need to take the appropriate number of CLE hours before being transferred from active status; and

            vi. Whether the lawyer has demonstrated circumstances of hardship or other compelling reasons that show that the lawyer should be transferred to active status before completing the appropriate number of CLE hours.

(3) **Failure to Abide by Transfer Conditions.** A lawyer who fails to comply with the conditions of transfer shall be restored to restricted status upon notice from the Director sent by regular mail to the lawyer's last known address.

(4) **Appeal to the Board.** Upon written request from a lawyer, the Board shall review the Director's determination of transfer requirements and notify the lawyer in writing regarding the outcome of that review.

D. **Transfer from Involuntary Restricted Status to Active Status.**

(1) **Notice to Director and Fee.** Unless otherwise ordered by the Court, a lawyer on involuntary restricted status who desires to resume active status shall notify the Director in writing of the lawyer's intention to resume active status and submit a transfer fee of $250.

(2) **Transfer Requirements.** Unless otherwise ordered by the Court, the Director shall recommend to the Court that a lawyer on involuntary restricted status be transferred to active status upon the Director's determination that the lawyer has completed the number of CLE hours that the lawyer would have had to complete to meet reporting requirements and to be current on a proportional basis had the lawyer not been placed on involuntary restricted status, or that the lawyer has completed such lesser requirements as the Director determines are adequate provided that the number of hours completed total no fewer than 45 hours during the 3 years immediately preceding transfer. The Director will specify no more than 90 hours. The Director may recommend to the Court that a lawyer on involuntary restricted status be transferred to active status when the lawyer has fulfilled appropriate CLE conditions precedent or agreed to fulfill appropriate CLE conditions subsequent as determined by the Director. In making such a recommendation, the Director will take into consideration the discretionary transfer criteria in section (C)(2)(c) of this Rule.

(3) **Appeal to the Board.** Upon written request from a lawyer, the Board shall review the Director's determination of transfer requirements and notify the lawyer in writing regarding the outcome of that review.

E. **Transfer from Involuntary Restricted Status to Voluntary Restricted Status.** Unless otherwise ordered by the Court, a lawyer on involuntary restricted status who desires to transfer to restricted status shall notify the Director in writing and submit a transfer fee in the amount of $250.

Rule 13. Retired Status

A. **Transfer from Active Status to Retired Status.** A lawyer who files a Retirement Affidavit with the Lawyer Registration Office and who is placed on inactive status by the Lawyer Registration Office shall be transferred to voluntary restricted status by the CLE Board,

B. **Transfer from Retired Status to Active Status.** In addition to notifying the Lawyer Registration Office of the lawyer's intention to transfer to active status, a lawyer must satisfy the provision of Rule 12C before the Board returns the lawyer to active CLE status.

Rule 14. Emeritus Status

A. **Qualification.** A lawyer who has filed a Retirement Affidavit pursuant to Rule 2(C)(5) of the Rule s of the Supreme Court on Lawyer Registration and who has elected restricted status under the CLE Rules may elect emeritus status by complying with the requirements for emeritus status listed below.

B. **Limitation of Practice.** A lawyer on emeritus status is authorized solely to provide pro bono legal representation to a pro bono client in a matter referred to the lawyer by an approved legal services provider.

C. **Contents of Emeritus Affidavit Appendix IV**. Prior to representation as described by Rule 14B, the lawyer shall complete and submit to the Board an affidavit of emeritus status (Appendix IV) which shall include the following:

   (1) The list of approved CLE courses that the lawyer has attended or participated in during the 90-day period immediately preceding the submission of the emeritus affidavit, totaling no fewer than 5 credit hours of approved continuing legal education courses, and including:

   (a) 3 credit hours in approved courses in the substantive area of law in which the lawyer intends to be performing pro bono services;
   (b) 1 credit hour approved as ethics or professional responsibility; and
   (c) 1 credit hour approved as elimination of bias in the legal profession and in the practice of law;

   (2) A certification signed by the emeritus lawyer, affirming that if the lawyer provides pro bono representation in multiple areas such as in a brief advice clinic, the lawyer shall obtain the necessary training and resources to provide those services in a competent and ethical manner.

D. **Transfer to Emeritus Status.** When a lawyer submits an affidavit of emeritus status, the Board office shall verify the information and shall, for a period of three years, maintain a public posting on the Board's website listing the lawyer's name as being on emeritus status.

E. **Expiration of Emeritus Status.** Emeritus status shall expire three years from the date that the lawyer's name is posted. A lawyer shall not represent clients after expiration of the lawyer's emeritus status.

F. **Renewal of Emeritus Status.** Prior to the expiration of a lawyer's emeritus status, the lawyer may renew emeritus status by submitting to the Board an affidavit of emeritus status (Appendix IV) which shall include the following:
   (1) The list of approved CLE courses attended or participated in by the lawyer during the three-year period immediately preceding the submission of the emeritus

affidavit, totaling no fewer than 5 credit hours of approved continuing legal education courses, and including:

> **(a)** 3 credit hours in approved courses in the substantive area of law in which the lawyer intends to perform pro bono services;
>
> **(b)** 1 credit hour approved as ethics or professional responsibility; and
>
> **(c)** 1 credit hour approved as elimination of bias in the legal profession and in the practice of law.

(2) A certification signed by the emeritus lawyer, affirming that when lawyer provides pro bono representation in multiple areas such as in a brief advice clinic, lawyer shall obtain the necessary training and resources to provide those services in a competent and ethical manner.

MISSISSIPPI

STATE OF MISSISSIPPI
RULES AND REGULATIONS FOR
MANDATORY CONTINUING
LEGAL EDUCATION

1. Continuing Legal Education Commission.

2. Scope and Exemptions.

3. CLE Requirement.

4. Accreditation.

5. Annual Report.

6. Non-Compliance and Sanctions.

7. Sunset Review [Deleted].

STATE OF MISSISSIPPI
RULES AND REGULATIONS FOR
MANDATORY CONTINUING
LEGAL EDUCATION

Revised effective August 1, 1994

RULE 1. CONTINUING LEGAL EDUCATION COMMISSION

a. There is hereby established a Commission on Continuing Legal Education (hereinafter referred to as the Commission) consisting of nine (9) members who are resident members of the Bar of this state. The members shall be appointed by the Mississippi Supreme Court.

b. All appointments shall be for a term of three (3) years. Therefore, there shall be three (3) appointments each year, one from each state Supreme Court district. An appointment to fill any vacancy due to the death, resignation or disability of a member shall be for the unexpired term only.

c. The Commission shall have the following duties:

1. To exercise general supervisory authority over the administration of these rules.

2. To adopt, repeal and amend regulations consistent with these rules.

3. To make available for inspection by the Mississippi Supreme Court all minutes of the Commission, business records, and financial data.

d. **Financing**:

1. Sponsors of CLE programs to be held within the State of Mississippi shall, as a condition of accreditation, agree to remit a list of Mississippi attendees and to pay a fee of one dollar and fifty cents ($1.50) per credit hour for each State Bar member who attends the program and is subject to mandatory continuing legal education. Such lists and fees shall be submitted to the Commission within thirty (30) days of said program.

2. Individual attorneys who either attend approved CLE programs outside the State of Mississippi, or attend unapproved CLE programs within the State of Mississippi that would have been approved for credit except for failure of the sponsor to pay the fee described in the preceding paragraph, shall pay a fee of one dollar and fifty cents ($1.50) for each credit hour claimed. Such fees shall accompany the attorney's annual report of compliance to the Commission.

(Amended July 26, 2001)

Regulations

1.1   The Chairman of the Commission shall be elected by the nine (9) voting members of the Commission.

1.2   The Commission shall elect a Vice-Chairman and Secretary from among its members.

1.3   The Commission may organize itself into Committees of not fewer than three (3) voting members for the purpose of considering and deciding matters submitted to them, except five (5) affirmative votes shall be necessary for any action under Rule 6.

1.4   Members of the Commission in the performance of their official duties shall be reimbursed for expenses subject to reimbursement policies set by the Commission.

1.5   The Commission may designate such staff as may be necessary and may further delegate executive authority to such staff to conduct the business of the Commission within the scope of the Rules and Regulations, subject at all times, however, to continual review by the Commission.

RULE 2. SCOPE AND EXEMPTIONS

These rules shall apply to every attorney licensed to practice law in the State of Mississippi, except for the following persons who shall be exempt from the requirement of these rules:

a.   All attorneys shall be exempt from the requirement of these rules for the calendar year in which they are first admitted to practice.

b.   All attorneys licensed to practice law in the State of Mississippi residing outside of the state and not engaged in the practice of law in Mississippi.

c.   All attorneys licensed to practice law in the State of Mississippi residing in the state but not engaged in the practice of law in Mississippi.

d.   All full-time members of the United States Armed Forces.

e.   All of the Justices of the Mississippi Supreme Court, Circuit, Court of Appeals, Chancery, and County Judges, United States Magistrate Judges, Judges of the Bankruptcy Courts and the Judges of the Federal Courts. However, all members of the Judiciary are encouraged to attend and participate in continuing legal education programs.

f.   The Governor of the State of Mississippi.

g.   All members of the United States Senate and the United States House of Representatives.

h.   All members of the bar shall be exempt from the requirement of these rules on and after their seventieth birthday.

Regulations

2.1   Non-resident attorneys from other jurisdictions who are temporarily admitted to practice for a case or proceeding shall not be subject to these rules.

2.2   Any member of the Mississippi State Bar licensed to practice law in the State of Mississippi but not engaged in the practice of law in Mississippi shall endorse and claim the exemption on the Annual Report required by Rule 5.

2.3   Any full-time member of the U.S. Armed Forces shall endorse and claim the exemption on the Annual Report required by Rule 5.

RULE 3. CLE REQUIREMENT

Each attorney licensed to practice law in the State of Mississippi shall attend, or complete an approved substitute for attendance, a minimum or twelve (12) actual hours of approved Continuing Legal Education ("CLE") during each successive twelve (12) month period (the "CLE year") from and after August 1 of each year, of which one hour shall be in the area of legal ethics, professional responsibility, professionalism, malpractice prevention, substance abuse or mental health (the "ethics/professionalism hour").

Regulations

3.1   The number of hours required means that the attorney must actually attend twelve (12) instruction hours of CLE per CLE year, with no credit given for introductory remarks, breaks, meal breaks, keynote or luncheon speakers or business meetings.

3.2   CLE hours shall be computed by the following formula:

$$\frac{\text{Total minutes of actual instruction}}{60} = \text{Total hours}$$

(rounded to nearest 1/10 of an hour)

3.3   No attorney shall be permitted to claim more than six (6) hours of CLE credit through the use of satellite-transmitted or electronically recorded or reproduced material, even though same is presented by an accredited sponsor. As part of the six (6) hours an attorney may claim up to six (6) hours of CLE credit for telephone seminars and/or approved online programs. Seminars offered by satellite-transmittal, electronic reproduction, telephone or online programs must be approved by the Commission and must comply with Regulation 4.9. Approved online programs further must comply with Regulation 4.10.

3.4   Attorneys who have a permanent physical disability which makes attendance of CLE programs inordinately difficult may file a request for a permanent substitute program in lieu of attendance and shall therein set out continuing legal education plans tailored to their specific interests and physical ability. The Commission shall review and approve or disapprove such plans on an individual basis and without delay. Rejection of any requested substitute for attendance will be reviewed as provided in Rule 6 prior to any sanction being imposed.

3.5   Other requests for substituted compliance, partial waivers, or other exemptions for hardship or extenuating circumstances may be granted by the Commission upon written application of the attorney and may likewise be reviewed as provided in Rule 6.

3.6   No credit will be allowed for self-study, except as specifically approved under Regulation 3.3 for approved on-line programs and Regulation 4.10.

3.7   Twelve (12) hours of credit in excess of the minimum annual requirement may be carried forward for credit in the succeeding CLE year. Such hours must, however, be reported in the annual report of compliance for the CLE year in which they were completed and must be designated as hours to be carried forward. This regulation applies to attorneys claiming exemptions also. Ethics hours in excess of the one-hour requirement for the year may not be carried over to another year as ethics hours, although they may be carried over as regular hours.

3.8   The maximum number of hours which may be claimed for credit in any one seminar is 18.

3.9   Credit may be earned through teaching in an approved continuing legal education activity. Presentations accompanied by thorough, high quality, readable, and carefully prepared written materials will qualify for CLE credit on the basis of six (6) hours of credit for each instructional hour of presentation. Presentations accompanied by one or two page outlines or not accompanied by written materials will qualify for CLE credit on the basis of three (3) hours of credit per hour of presentation. Repeat presentations qualify for one half of the credits available for the initial presentation. A maximum of twelve (12) hours of CLE credit shall be earned from teaching pursuant to these regulations in any CLE year.

3.10   No credit will be allowed for teaching a continuing legal education activity if the instructor is compensated in any manner, excluding reimbursement of reasonable and necessary expenses. Contributions of honorariums to a public service organization such as the Mississippi Bar Foundation shall preclude this regulation.

3.11   Credits may also be earned through authorship of a law journal article on matters of law published by an ABA or AALS approved law school. The Commission will award six (6) hours of CLE credit for each such article published.

3.12 Credit may be earned through service as a member of the Mississippi Board of Bar Admissions or as a bar examiner. The Board of Bar Admissions will be awarded a maximum of six (6) hours of CLE credit per CLE year for writing and grading the Mississippi Essay Examination or for grading either the Multistate Essay Examination or Multistate Performance Test including attendance at the grading seminar, unless compensated for such service excluding reimbursement of reasonable and necessary expenses.

3.12.1 Credit may be earned through service as a member of the Committee on Professional Responsibility, as a member of the Ethics Committee, as a member of the Unauthorized Practice of Law Committee, or as a member of the Professionalism Committee of the Mississippi Bar. A member of the Committee on Professional Responsibility, the Ethics Committee, the Unauthorized Practice of Law Committee, or the Professionalism Committee will be awarded a maximum of one (1) hour of CLE ethics/professionalism credit per CLE year for service on those committees.

3.13 Credit may be earned through formal enrollment for audit or for credit for which regular fees are paid in an ABA or AALS accredited law school. Four (4) hours of CLE credit will be awarded for each credit hour of the particular course audited or taken for credit. A maximum of twelve (12) credit hours per CLE year will be awarded.

3.14 Credit may be earned through formal enrollment in a bar review course approved by the Commission. The attorney must already be admitted to practice in Mississippi or another state. Self-study bar review courses do not qualify for credit. A maximum of twelve (12) credit hours per CLE year will be awarded.

3.15 Credit may be earned through service as a member of the Supreme Court Advisory Committee on Rules. The Commission will award six (6) hours of CLE credit annually for service on this Committee.

3.16 Credit may be earned through service as a member of the Model Civil Jury Instructions Committee or the Model Criminal Jury Instruction Committee. The Commission will award six (6) hours of CLE credit annually for service on these committees.

3.17 Credit may be earned through service as Lieutenant Governor of the State of Mississippi or as a member of the Mississippi Legislature. The Commission will award six (6) hours of CLE credit annually to the Lieutenant Governor and to each attorney who certifies his/her membership in the Mississippi Senate or the House of Representatives.

3.18 Credit may also be earned through teaching a course in an ABA or AALS approved law school. The Commission will award six (6) hours of CLE credit for each hour of academic credit awarded by the law school for the course.

3.19   Full-time employees of a governmental department or agency may earn up to twelve (12) hours of credit per year by attending approved CLE activities offered by their governmental department or agency for its employees.

3.20   Part-time employees of a governmental department or agency may earn up to six (6) hours of credit per year by attending approved CLE activities offered by their governmental department or agency for its employees.

[Amended effective August 1, 1995; amended January, 1998; Regulations 3.3 and 3.6 amended effective December 9, 2004, to provide for approved online programs; Regulation 3.12.1 adopted effective December 9, 2004 to allow credit for service on Committee on Professional Responsibility and Ethics Committee of the Mississippi Bar; amended effective January 25, 2007, to add professionalism as an option for CLE credit; amended effective August 1, 2008, to increase the number of hours allowed for telephone seminars and online programs; amended effective July 1, 2009 to allow one (1) hour of CLE ethics/professionalism credit for service on the Mississippi Bar's Unauthorized Practice of Law Committee.]

RULE 4. ACCREDITATION

Credit will be given only for CLE programs approved by the Commission. Such approval normally must be sought and granted prior to the occurrence of the activity, but may be given retroactively.

Regulations

4.1   The following standards will govern the approval of continuing legal education activities by the Commission.

4.2   The activity must be effectively open to all attorneys licensed to practice law in the State of Mississippi, unless offered by a governmental department or agency for employees of the governmental department or agency. By making an application for approval by the Commission, the seminar sponsor consents to the seminar being listed on the calendar of upcoming CLE events disseminated by the Commission.

4.3   The activity must have significant intellectual or practical content and its primary objective must be to increase the participant's professional competence as an attorney.

4.4   The activity must deal primarily with matters related to the practice of law, professional responsibility or ethical obligations of attorneys.

4.5   The activity must be offered by a sponsor having substantial, recent experience in offering continuing legal education or demonstrated ability to organize and present effectively continuing legal education. Demonstrated ability arises partly from the extent to which individuals with legal training or educational experience are involved in the planning, instruction and supervision of the activity.

4.6   The activity itself must be conducted by an individual or group qualified by practical or academic experience. The program, including the named advertised participants, must be conducted substantially as planned, subject to emergency withdrawals and alterations.

4.7   Thorough, high quality, readable, and carefully prepared written materials must be made available to all participants at or before the time the course is presented, unless the absence of such materials is recognized as reasonable and approved by the Commission; mere outline without citations or explanatory notations will not be sufficient. Materials in an electronic format may be acceptable in lieu of printed material as long as the attorney consents to receive such material. Printed material must be made available to those attorneys for whom the electronic format is not satisfactory.

4.8   The activity must be conducted in a physical setting conducive to learning.

4.9   Activities offered by any sponsor must provide a qualified on-site moderator and question-and-answer session. Telephone seminars must be conducted "live," not pre-recorded, and must provide a question-and-answer session. As a minimum the activity must consist of not less than one (1) hour of actual instruction.

4.10   Each online program or online seminar will be reviewed for approval on a case by case basis. The course content, interactivity, as well as the effectiveness of the delivery method will be considered in the approval process. Applications for approval must be submitted by the sponsor and submitted 30 days prior to the beginning date of the program. Applications will not be approved retroactively. Sponsors must be able to verify attorney attendance and the number of hours attended. Attorney attendance must be reported to the Mississippi Commission on CLE immediately following the conclusion of the program.

4.11   Activities that cross academic lines, such as an accounting-tax seminar, may be considered for approval.

4.12   At the conclusion of an approved program or activity, each participating attorney must be given the opportunity to complete an evaluation questionnaire addressing the quality, effectiveness and usefulness of the particular activity. Within thirty (30) days of the conclusion of the activity, a summary of the results of the questionnaire must be forwarded to the Commission. If requested, copies of the questionnaires must also be forwarded to the Commission. Sponsors must maintain the questionnaires for a period of 90 days following a program pending a request for submission of them to the Commission.

4.13   The costs of the program itself to the participating attorney, apart from optional meals, lodging, travel, etc., must be reasonable considering the subject matter, instructional level, etc.

4.14   Continuing legal education activities sponsored by the following organizations (hereinafter referred to as Sponsors) are presumptively approved for credit, provided the standards set out in Regulations 4.1 through 4.13 are met.

Abbott & Weems "Recent Mississippi Law"
Accredited law schools (ABA or AALS)
Alabama Institute for CLE
American Academy of Hospital Attorneys
American Academy of Judicial Education
American Agricultural Law Association
American Association of Railroad Trial Counsel
American Bar Association and Bar Sections
American Bankers Association (legal programs only)
American Business Law Association
American Board of Trial Advocates
American College of Mortgages Attorneys
American College of Probate Counsel
American College of Real Estate Lawyers
American College of Trial Lawyers
American Corporate Counsel Association
American Institute for Justice
American Institute on Federal Taxation
American Intellectual Property Law Association
American Judicature Society
American Law Institute

American Society for Law and Medicine
Association of Insurance Attorneys
Association of Trial Lawyers of America
Bar Associations of Other States, the District of Columbia, Puerto Rico and Trust Territories
Boackle, K.F.
Bureau of National Affairs
Central Mississippi Legal Services
CLE International
Commercial Law League of America Fund for Public Education
Construction Education Management Corp. (legal programs only)
Copyright Society of the U.S.A.
Council of School Board Attorneys, MS School Boards Association
Court Practice Institute, Inc.
Credit Union National Association, Inc. (legal programs only)
Cumberland School of Law Institute for CLE
Defense Research Institute
East Mississippi Rural Legal Services
Eastern Mineral Law Foundation
Edison Electric Institute
Federal Bar Association
Federal Energy Bar Association
Federal Insurance Counsel
Federal Judicial Center
Federal Publications, Inc.
Food Marketing Institute
Government Institutes, Inc.
Gulf Coast Law Institute
International Association of Defense Counsel
International Association of Insurance Council
Jackson Young Lawyers Association
Law Journal Seminars Press
Legal Education Institute
Legal Sections, agency programs - U.S. and state government
Library of Congress - Legislative Service
Library of Congress (American Law Division)
Louisiana Trial Lawyers Association
Magnolia Bar Association
Maritime Law Association
Medi-Legal Institute
Memphis Bar Association

Mississippi Association of County Board Attorneys
Mississippi Bankruptcy Conference
Mississippi Bar Association, and Bar Sections, Local, County and Regional Bar Associations in Mississippi
Mississippi Chapter, Federal Bar Association
Mississippi College School of Law
Mississippi Defense Lawyers Association
Mississippi Institute of Continuing Legal Education
Mississippi Judicial College
Mississippi Law Institute
Mississippi Legal Services Coalition
Mississippi Municipal Attorneys Association
Mississippi Oil and Gas Lawyers Association
Mississippi Pro Bono Project
Mississippi Prosecutors College
Mississippi Society of Certified Public Accountants
Mississippi Tax Institute
Mississippi Trial Lawyers Association
Montgomery County, Maryland Bar Foundation
Motor Carrier Lawyers Association
National Association of Bond Lawyers
National Association of Attorneys General
National Association of College and University Attorneys
National Association of Criminal Defense Lawyers
National Association of Railroad Trial Counsel
National Bar Association
National Business Institute
National College of District Attorneys
National College of Juvenile Justice
National Contract Management Association
National District Attorneys Association
National Employment Law Institute
National Health Lawyers Association
National Institute for Trial Advocacy
National Institute of Municipal Law Officers
National Judicial College
National Legal Aid and Defender Association
National Organization of Social Security Claimants' Representatives
National Practice Institute
National Rural Electric Cooperative Association (legal programs only)

New Mexico Trial Lawyers
New Orleans Orthopaedic Clinic (legal programs only)
New York University School of Continuing Education in Law & Taxation
North Carolina Academy of Trial Lawyers
North Mississippi Rural Legal Services
Norton Institutes (CRR Publishing Co.)
National Association of Bond Lawyers
Patent Resources Group, Inc.
Practicing Law Institute
Prentice Hall Law and Business, Inc.
Professional Education Systems, Inc.
Professional Trial Lawyers Institute, Inc.
Rocky Mountain Mineral Law Foundation
Securities Industry Association (legal programs only)
South Mississippi Legal Services
Southeast Mississippi Legal Services
Southeastern Bankruptcy Law Institute, Inc.
Southern Federal Tax Institute, Inc.
Southwest Mississippi Legal Services
Southwestern Legal Foundation
Tennessee Association of Criminal Defense Lawyers
Tennessee Trial Lawyers Association
The National Center for Justice and the Rule of Law
The Southern California Tax & Estate Planning Forum
The Southern Trust School (Alabama)
Transportation Lawyers Association
Uniform Commercial Code Institute
University of Mississippi Center for Continuing Legal Education
U.S. League of Savings Association (legal programs only)
U.S. Department of Justice, Office of Legal Education
Veterans Administration (Office of General Counsel)
Westcott Communications

Other Sponsors may be added to this list as their identities and programs are confirmed by the Commission.

4.15   The Sponsor of an approved CLE activity may announce in informational literature or program materials as follows:

"THIS COURSE OR A PORTION THEREOF HAS BEEN APPROVED BY THE

MISSISSIPPI COMMISSION ON CONTINUING LEGAL EDUCATION FOR A MAXIMUM OF _____ HOURS OF CREDIT."

The sponsor of a CLE activity which has applied for but not received approval prior to the printing of informational literature or program materials may announce as follows:

"THE SPONSOR HAS APPLIED TO THE MISSISSIPPI COMMISSION ON CONTINUING LEGAL EDUCATION FOR APPROVAL OF THIS COURSE OR A PORTION THEREOF FOR A MAXIMUM OF _____ HOURS OF CREDIT."

4.16   The Commission may at any time reevaluate a program and revoke approval of the Sponsor or of a particular seminar.

4.17   Any Sponsor not included in Regulation 4.14 above, desiring approval of a course, program, or other activity, will apply to the Commission by submitting a required application form and supporting documentation no less than forty-five (45) days prior to the date for which the course or program is scheduled. The Commission will advise the applicant in writing by mail within thirty (30) days of the receipt of the completed application whether the activity is approved or disapproved. Applicants denied approval of a program or activity may appeal such a decision by submitting a letter of appeal to the Commission within fifteen (15) days of the receipt of the notice of the disapproval.

[Amended effective August 1, 1995; Regulations 4.7, 4.9 and 4.10 amended effective December 9, 2004 to allow limited use of approved on-line programs; amended effective July 1, 2009 to add two approved sponsors to Regulation 4.14.]

RULE 5. ANNUAL REPORT

On or before August 15 of each year, each attorney admitted to practice in the State, unless exempted from making a report under the provisions of Rule 2 hereof and regulations thereunder, shall make a written report to the Commission, in such form as the Commission shall prescribe, concerning his or her completion of accredited legal education during the CLE year having ended on July 31 of such year.

Regulations

5.1   On or before August 15 of each year, each attorney will submit a report on a form as the Commission shall provide concerning such attorney's completion of, exemption from or approved substitute for the minimum hours of instruction, including reference to hours earned during that CLE year and hours to be carried forward to the next CLE year.

5.2   The files and records of the Commission are deemed confidential and shall not be disclosed except in furtherance of the duties of the Commission; statistical abstracts may, however, be drawn therefrom in an anonymous fashion.

5.3   Each attorney failing to timely submit the reports of compliance required by Regulation 5.1 hereof shall, at the time of filing such report, pay a late fee to the Commission in the sum of Twenty-five Dollars ($25.00). The Commission shall treat all delinquently filed reports not accompanied by the late fee required hereunder as not having been filed.

RULE 6. NON-COMPLIANCE AND SANCTIONS

a.   As soon as practicable after August 15 of each year, the Commission shall compile the following:

1.   A list of attorneys who have filed annual reports of compliance for the next preceding CLE year ending July 31, as required by Rule 5, Mississippi Rules of Mandatory Continuing Legal Education.

2.   A list of attorneys who have filed annual reports of compliance on or before the next preceding July 31 indicating that they have not complied with the requirement of Rule 3, Mississippi Rules for Mandatory Continuing Legal Education.

3.   A list of attorneys who have failed to file annual reports of compliance for the next preceding CLE year as required by Rule 5, Mississippi Rules for Mandatory Continuing Legal Education.

b.   The Commission shall then serve, by certified mail, each attorney whose name appears upon the lists compiled by the Commission who has not complied with Rules 3 and 5, Mississippi Rules for Mandatory Continuing Legal Education, with an Order to Show Cause, within sixty (60) days, why the attorney's license should not be suspended. Said attorney shall furnish the Commission with an affidavit:

1.   Indicating that the attorney has complied with the requirement prior to expiration of the sixty (60) days, or

2.   Setting forth a valid excuse for failure to comply with the requirements because of illness or other good cause.

c.   At the expiration of sixty (60) days from the date of the Order to Show Cause, the Commission shall notify the Supreme Court of Mississippi of each attorney who fails to file an affidavit satisfactory to the Commission as described in (b)(1) and (b)(2) above and recommend appropriate sanctions to the Supreme Court, which may include, among others, that the attorney's license to practice law be suspended.

d.   At any time after notice of noncompliance to the Supreme Court, an attorney may file with the Commission an affidavit indicating compliance with Rule 3, Rules for Mandatory Continuing Legal Education and if satisfactory to the Commission, it shall forthwith notify the Supreme Court for appropriate action, including reinstatement.

e.   Administration of this program is complicated by attorneys who fail to comply with theses rules. Accordingly, the Commission and/or the Supreme Court is authorized to assess costs against such delinquent and/or non-filing attorneys in the form of a reasonable fee for filing late, filing an annual report reflecting a deficiency and/or not filing during the reporting period. Such costs can be increased proportionately by an attorney's late compliance or non-compliance for two successive CLE years.

RULE 7. SUNSET REVIEW

The sunset provision for the Rules was deleted by order entered October 5, 2006.

MISSOURI

15.01. Definitions

As used in this Rule 15 the following terms mean:

(a) "Accredited program or activity," a program or activity accredited by The Missouri Bar;

(b) "Board," the board of governors of The Missouri Bar;

(c) "Credit hour," at least 50 minutes of instruction or the equivalent;

(d) "Lawyer," a member of The Missouri Bar;

(e) "Reporting year," the 12 months between July first of one year and June 30th of the following year.

(Adopted December 3, 1986, effective January 1, 1987. Amended January 22, 1988, effective July 1, 1988. Amended October 18, 1988, effective November 1, 1988. Amended June 21, 2005, Amended January 1, 2006, Amended January 1, 2010.)

15.02 (RESERVED)

(Repealed by Order dated June 21, 1991.)

15.03. Duties of The Missouri Bar

The Missouri Bar shall:

(a) Exercise general supervisory authority over the administration of this Rule 15;

(b) Accredit programs and activities and sponsors that satisfy the requirements of this Rule 15;

(c) Foster and encourage the offering of accredited programs and activities;

(d) Report at least annually to this Court and the committee concerning the status of minimum continuing legal education in this state;

(e) Fund the administration of this Rule 15 through enrollment fees paid by members of The Missouri Bar; and

(f) Promulgate regulations necessary to implement this Rule 15. The regulations shall be consistent with the provisions of this Rule 15 and shall become effective 60 days after submission unless disapproved by this Court. This Court may promulgate, amend, revise, or rescind any regulation. Copies of this Rule 15 and the regulations thereto shall be published in a publication of general distribution to all lawyers and shall be furnished to interested parties upon request.

(Adopted Dec. 3, 1986, eff. Jan. 1, 1987. Amended Jan. 22, 1988, eff. July 1, 1988; Amended January 1, 2010.)

15.04. Accreditation of Programs, Activities and Sponsors

(a) The Missouri Bar may designate a sponsor of continuing legal education programs or activities as an "accredited sponsor" if the sponsor has substantial recent experience in offering continuing legal education or a demonstrable ability to organize and effectively present continuing legal education programs and activities.

(b) A program or activity may be an accredited program or activity if it directly contributes to the professional competency of lawyers or judges and has significant intellectual or practical content related to the development or practice of law, professional responsibility, or law office management.

(c) A program or activity offered by an accredited sponsor shall be an accredited program or activity. Continuing legal education programs and activities of identified sponsors may be accredited programs and activities if so designated by The Missouri Bar. Self-study, videotape, audiotape, or other similar programs or activities may be accredited programs and activities if so designated by The Missouri Bar.

(Adopted Dec. 3, 1986, eff. Jan. 1, 1987. Amended Jan. 22, 1988, eff. July 1, 1988, Amended January 1, 2010.)

15.05. Continuing Legal Education Requirements

(a) After July 1, 1988, except as provided in Rule 15.05(c), each lawyer shall complete and report during each reporting year at least 15 credit hours of accredited programs and activities. Credit hours of accredited programs and activities completed pursuant to Rule 15.05(e) and Rule 15.05(f) may be used to fulfill the requirements of Rule 15.05(a). Not more than six other credit hours may consist of self-study, videotape, audiotape or other similar programs or activities that are accredited programs or activities. A speaker at an accredited program or activity may receive credit for preparation time and presentation time. An author of written material published or to be published by an accredited sponsor or in a professional journal or as a monograph may receive credit for research time and composition time.

(b) For purpose of Rule 15.05(a), a lawyer reporting completion of more than 15 credit hours of accredited programs and activities during one reporting year may receive credit in the next succeeding reporting year for the excess credit hours.

(c) A lawyer is not required to complete or report any credit hours in the reporting year in which the lawyer is initially licensed to practice law in this state except as provided in

Rules 15.05(d) and 15.05(e). Any lawyer not an active judge who, during a reporting year, has neither engaged in the active practice of law in Missouri nor held himself out as an active practicing lawyer in Missouri shall not be required to complete or report any credit hours during that reporting year. Upon written application and for good cause shown, waivers or extensions of time of the credit hour or reporting requirements of this Rule 15 may be granted in individual cases or classes of cases involving hardship or extenuating circumstances.

(d) A person seeking admission under Rule 8.10 shall, prior to being issued a license, attend The Missouri Bar annual law update program or a continuing legal education program accredited as provided in this Rule 15 that has intellectual and practical content substantially equivalent to The Missouri Bar annual law update program. Attendance shall be no earlier than 12 months prior to the date the application for admission under Rule 8.10 is filed. The person shall report the completion of this requirement to the board of law examiners as the board shall specify.

(e) Each lawyer who:

(1) Between June 30, 1990 and July 1, 2009:

(a) Is admitted to practice law;

(b) Has a license to practice law reinstated, except any license reinstated as a matter of course pursuant to Rule 6.01; or

(c) Becomes an active lawyer after previously declaring inactive status as provided Rule 6.03;

shall complete at least three credit hours of accredited programs and activities devoted exclusively to professionalism, legal or judicial ethics, or malpractice prevention. Such programs and activities shall be completed within 12 months of the event requiring compliance with this Rule 15.05(e). Completion of this requirement shall be reported to The Missouri Bar as specified by The Missouri Bar;

(2) After June 30, 2009:

(a) Is admitted to practice law;

(b) Has a license to practice law reinstated, except any license reinstated as a matter of course pursuant to Rule 6.01; or

(c) Becomes an active lawyer after previously declaring inactive status as provided Rule 6.03;

shall complete at least two credit hours of accredited programs and activities devoted exclusively to professionalism, substance abuse and mental health, legal or judicial ethics, or malpractice prevention. Such programs and activities shall be completed within 12 months of the event requiring compliance with Rule 15.05(e). Completion of this requirement shall be reported to The Missouri Bar as specified by The Missouri Bar.

(f) For each professionalism compliance period:

(1) Between July 1, 1990 and June 30, 2008, each lawyer shall complete at least three credit hours of accredited programs and activities devoted exclusively to professionalism, legal or judicial ethics, or malpractice prevention. Such programs and activities shall be completed on or before June 30, 1993 and at least every three years thereafter. Completion of this requirement shall be reported to The Missouri Bar as specified by The Missouri Bar;

(2) On and after July 1, 2009, each lawyer shall complete and report at least 2 credit hours of accredited programs and activities devoted exclusively to professionalism, substance abuse and mental health, legal or judicial ethics, or malpractice prevention unless the lawyer has not actively practiced law in Missouri during the period or has given notice of inactive status pursuant to Rule 6.03. Completion of this requirement shall be reported to The Missouri Bar as specified by the Missouri Bar.

Credit hours of accredited programs and activities completed pursuant to Rule 15.05(e) may be used to fulfill the requirements of Rule 15.05(f).

Credit hours of accredited programs and activities devoted exclusively to professionalism, legal or judicial ethics, or malpractice prevention during the July 1, 2008 to June 30, 2009, reporting year shall apply to the professionalism compliance period for July 1, 2009 to June 30, 2010.

(g) Each judge of the family court division and each commissioner of the family court division shall complete not later than six months after designation or appointment a course of training in family law accredited by this Court's trial judge education committee. This requirement shall be in addition to the requirements contained in Rule 15.05(a), Rule 15.05(e), and Rule 15.05(f).

Each year thereafter, such judges and commissioners shall complete at least six hours of continuing legal education courses accredited by this Court's trial judge education committee relating to family court issues and law. The hours completed on an annual basis may be used to fulfill the requirements of Rule 15.05(a).

Completion of the requirements of this Rule 15.05(g) shall be reported to The Missouri Bar as specified by The Missouri Bar.

This Rule 15.05(g) shall apply to all reporting years beginning on or after July 1, 1993. This Rule 15.05(g) shall not apply to judges who are temporarily transferred or assigned to family court divisions; however judges who have met the requirements of this Rule 15.05(g) shall be preferred for such transfers and assignments.

(h) Each lawyer who is a member of the general assembly may report in each reporting year credit for 15 hours of continuing legal education for service during that reporting year's regular legislative session. Such credits shall not include credit for programs required by Rule 15.05(f).

(Adopted Dec. 3, 1986, eff. Jan. 1, 1987. Amended Jan. 22, 1988, eff. Jul. 1, 1988; Nov. 13, 1989; Dec. 11, 1989; Mar. 22, 1994; Dec. 17, 1996, eff. Jan. 1, 1997; May 14, 1999, eff. Jan. 1, 2000; eff. Jul. 1, 2002; Mar. 7, 2005, eff. Jul. 1, 2005; Nov. 16, 2009, eff. Jan. 1, 2010; Jun. 25, 2010, eff. Jan. 1, 2011; Amended Dec. 1, 2015, eff. Jul. 1, 2016.)

15.06. Reporting Requirements - Sanctions - Review

(a) On or before July 31st of each year after 1988, each lawyer shall report the number of credit hours of accredited programs or activities in which lawyer participated in the preceding reporting year, except that lawyers paying the annual enrollment fee under Rule 6.01(j)(3) for the entire reporting year and lawyers who have given notice of inactive status under Rule 6.03 are not required to report completion or exemption from the annual requirements of Rules 15.05(a) and 15.05(f). All lawyers must report completion of the requirement of Rule 15.05(e).

(b) Every lawyer failing to meet the requirements of this Rule 15 by September 30 shall be notified by mail addressed to the lawyer's last known address. The notice shall advise the lawyer that lawyer has not filed the required report or the required number of credit hours and that the lawyer, if subject to Rule 15, may file within 30 days of the date the notice was mailed information establishing compliance with this Rule 15. Within 30 days of the receipt of the information, it shall be determined if the lawyer has participated in the required number of credit hours of accredited programs or activities or if the lawyer is entitled to a waiver of the requirement or an extension of time to comply with the requirement. If it is determined that the lawyer has participated in the required number of credit hours, is entitled to waiver, or is entitled to an extension of time, the lawyer shall be so notified within 15 days of the decision. If it is determined that the lawyer has not participated in the required number of credit hours, is not entitled to a waiver and is not entitled to an extension of time, the lawyer shall be so notified.

(c) Every lawyer to whom a notice is sent pursuant to Rule 15.06b shall pay a late filing fee of $35.00. Payment of this fee shall accompany the late-filed information establishing compliance with Rule 15. Failure to pay the fee shall be considered a failure to comply with the requirements of Rule 15. The fee collected pursuant to Rule 15.06(c) shall be paid to The Missouri Bar for deposit in the advisory committee fund.

(d) Upon written request filed within 15 days of the date of notice to the lawyer of the decision concerning compliance with this Rule 15, a hearing shall be granted within 30 days of the date of the request. The hearing shall be held before a panel of three lawyers appointed by the president of The Missouri Bar. The lawyer shall be sent notice of the hearing at least 10 days prior to the hearing. At the hearing the lawyer may be represented by counsel, witnesses shall be sworn, and, if requested by the lawyer, a complete electronic record shall be made.

(e) Within fifteen days of the hearing it shall be determined if the lawyer has complied with this Rule 15. The lawyer shall be so notified within 5 days of the decision.

(f) On or before March 1, The Missouri Bar shall annually report to the clerk of this Court, the chief disciplinary counsel, and the Commission on Retirement, Removal and Discipline, as the case may be, the name of each lawyer not meeting the requirements of this Rule 15. Every lawyer so reported is automatically suspended from the practice of law on the date the report is received by the clerk of this Court. Any lawyer automatically suspended for failing to comply with this Rule 15 shall be retroactively reinstated as a matter of course upon certification to the clerk of this Court by The Missouri Bar that the lawyer is in full compliance with this Rule 15 within three years of the date of the lawyer's suspension and the payment of an additional $100 late fee. The late fee shall be paid to The Missouri Bar for deposit in the advisory committee fund. Any lawyer not reinstated as a matter of course shall apply for reinstatement as provided in Rule 5.28.

(Adopted Dec. 3, 1986, eff. Jan. 1, 1988. Amended Jan. 22, 1988, eff. July 1, 1988; Nov. 20, 1990, eff. July 1, 1991; Feb. 7, 1991, eff. July 1, 1991. Amended eff. Feb. 26, 1998. Amended February 3, 2005, eff. July 1, 2005. Amended March 1, 2006, eff. April 3, 2006, Amended January 1, 2010.)

15.07 [REPEALED]

Former Rule 15 was added December 3, 1986, effective January 1, 2987; implementation was stayed until July 1, 1988 by order of November 12, 1987. On January 22, 1988, new Rule 15 was adopted, effective July 1, 1988.

The repealed rule, which pertained to sources of funding, and the establishment of fees, was adopted December 3, 1986, effective January 1, 1987.

(Adopted Dec. 3, 1986, eff. Jan. 1, 1987; stayed by order dated Nov. 12, 1987, until July 1, 1988; new rule adopted Jan. 22, 1988, eff. July 1, 1988, repealing this section.)

MONTANA

RULES FOR CONTINUING LEGAL EDUCATION

Rule 1 – Purpose

These rules establish standards for the continuing legal education required of all persons licensed to practice law in the State of Montana. It is of primary importance to the members of the State Bar of Montana and to the public that attorneys continue their legal education throughout their active practice of law.

Rule 2 – Definitions

A. "Active Member" means any person who is licensed to practice law in the State of Montana and who pays "Active Member" dues to the State Bar of Montana.
B. "Approved Legal Education Activity" means an individual seminar, course, or other activity approved by the Commission.
C. "Commission" means the Montana Commission of Continuing Legal Education.
D. "Board of Trustees" means the Board of Trustees of the State Bar of Montana.
E. "Legislator Member" means a member of the State Bar of Montana who is holding office as a duly elected or appointed member of the Montana House of Representatives or the Montana Senate.
F. "Chairperson" means the chairperson of the Commission.
G. "Credit Hour" means sixty (60) minutes of approved legal education activity.
H. "Emeritus Members" are those who have been granted emeritus status under Article I, Section 3(g) of the By-Laws of the State Bar of Montana.
I. "Inactive Member" means any person who is licensed to practice law in the State of Montana and who pays "Inactive Member" dues to the State Bar of Montana.
J. "MCLE Administrator" is the person designated by the Commission, with the approval of the Executive Director of the State Bar of Montana.
K. "Rule" or "Rules" refers to the Rules for Continuing Legal Education.
L. "Reporting Year" means April 1st through March 31st.

Rule 3 - Commission

A. Membership, Appointment, and Terms.
The Commission consists of nine (9) members, six (6) of whom shall be admitted to practice law in the State of Montana, and three (3) of whom shall be residents of the State not admitted to the practice of law. The State Bar shall nominate and the Court shall appoint members for three-year terms. Each yearly class of members shall include two lawyers and one layperson. In addition, one member of the Montana Supreme Court shall serve as an ex-officio member of the Commission.

The Commission shall designate one of its attorney members to serve as Chairperson for a term of two years. A Commission member may serve no more than two consecutive terms as Chairperson. The MCLE Administrator shall serve as Secretary to the Commission. The Court may terminate membership on the Commission in accordance with the By-Laws of the State Bar. In the event of a vacancy, a successor will be appointed by the State Bar of Montana to serve the unexpired term. The successor will be given first consideration for appointment to a full term at the expiration of the interim appointment.

The Commission has authority to act when a quorum is present. A quorum of the Commission consists of five (5) or more of its members.

B. Powers of the Commission.

1. The Commission shall administer and interpret these Rules.

2. The Commission shall:

a. Determine whether, under Rules 6 and 7, all or portions of individual courses and programs not presented by an Accredited Sponsor are approved legal education activities;

b. Determine the number of credit hours allowed for each approved legal education activity, including those of Accredited Sponsors;

c. Designate Accredited Sponsors and annually review such designations;

d. Report annually to the Board of Trustees;

e. Assess annual affidavit filing fees to pay the reasonable and necessary costs of administering these rules, assess penalty fees for failure to file affidavits as required by Rule 5, assess a fee for the reinstatement to active practice of attorneys under Rule 12, assess sponsor fees, and assess other fees deemed necessary by the Commission;

f. Meet at least three times per year. The time, method, and place of meetings shall be at the discretion of the Commission, subject to these Rules; and

g. Place upon any member seeking to qualify under these rules the burden of proof.

h. Direct the State Bar of Montana to transfer attorneys not in compliance with Rule 5 from active status to inactive status.

3. The Commission may take other action deemed necessary to administer these rules.

C. Committees.

The chairperson may appoint one or more committees, which shall either be standing or ad hoc, as appropriate, but there shall be a standing committee known as the "Accreditation Committee", consisting of a least three (3) members of the Commission. The Accreditation Committee shall have the interim authority to determine requests for exemption or extension under Rule 4 and earned hours of accreditation under Rules 6 and 7.

D. Expenses of the Commission.

Members of the Commission shall not be compensated except for actual and necessary expenses incurred in the performance of Commission duties.

E.   Annual Budget.

The Commission shall submit an annual budget to the Board of Trustees for approval. Expenses of the Commission shall not exceed the annual budget approved by the Board of Trustees.

F.   MCLE Administrator.

The Commission may delegate its power to the MCLE Administrator pursuant to guidelines established by the Commission. At each meeting of the Commission, the MCLE Administrator shall report on all determinations made since the preceding meeting of the Commission.

G.   Authority.

The Commission shall operate, for administrative purposes only, under the general authority of the Board of Trustees. For all other purposes including amendments to the rules, recommendations for changes in the methods of operation, and reports on the effectiveness of enforcement, the Commission shall operate under the authority of the Court.

Rule 4 – Education Requirements, Exemptions, and Extensions

A. Active Member Minimum MCLE Requirements:

Each active member must earn a minimum of fifteen (15) credit hours of approved continuing legal education each reporting year. Of those fifteen (15) credit hours, at least ten (10) credit hours must be earned by attendance at interactive seminars as defined in Rule 7. No more than five (5) credit hours may be earned through "other methods" as defined in Rule 7.

Of the fifteen (15) credit hours of continuing legal education required each reporting year, at least two (2) credit hours must be in ethics. "Ethics" means the accepted principles of professional conduct and responsibility as established by the Montana Rules of Professional Conduct or established by other state or national rules of professional conduct for lawyers.

Approved programs on the relationship between substance abuse, chemical dependency, or debilitating mental illness as they relate to a lawyer's professional responsibilities, satisfy the requirement for ethics credits.

If a member earns more interactive credits than required in any year, the excess interactive credits may be carried forward and applied to satisfy the requirements of these rules in one or both of the next two reporting years. A maximum of thirty (30) interactive credit hours may be carried forward.

Credits, including ethics credits, earned in any reporting year by "other methods" as defined in Rule 7, may not be carried forward or applied to satisfy any requirement of these rules for any subsequent reporting year.

B. Emeritus Member Continuing Legal Education Requirement:

Each emeritus member shall complete a minimum of ten (10) credit hours of approved continuing legal education activity each year. Each of those ten (10) credit hours must be certified by a qualified provider of legal services, as defined in Section 3(g)(vi) of the By-laws of the State Bar of Montana, as training prescribed for emeritus lawyers and related to the field of law for which such lawyers provide legal services to persons unable to pay for such services. In addition, of the ten (10) credit hours, at least five (5) credit hours must be earned by attendance at interactive seminars as defined in Rule 7. No more than five (5) credit hours may be earned through "other methods" as defined in Rule 7.

If an emeritus member accumulates more interactive credits than required in a year, the excess interactive credits may be carried forward and applied to either or both of the next two succeeding years. Credits earned by "other methods" may not be carried forward. A maximum of twenty (20) interactive credit hours may be carried forward. Emeritus members are subject to the same requirements as active members for credit hours in ethics. All CLE filing fees shall be waived for emeritus members.

C. Inactive Member Continuing Legal Education Exemption:

An inactive member is exempt from the continuing legal education requirement of these rules.

D. Legislator Member and Governor Continuing Legal Education Exemption:

A legislator member or the Governor of the State of Montana is exempt from the continuing legal education requirement of these rules during his or her term of office as a member of the Montana House of Representatives, as a member of the Montana Senate, or as the Governor.

E. Judiciary Member Continuing Legal Education Exemption:

A full-time judge or retired judge eligible for temporary judicial assignment and not engaged in the practice of law is exempt from the continuing education requirement of these rules.

A full-time judge is an elected or appointed member of the Judiciary who devotes his or her full-time professional activity to his or her position as a judge. The Judiciary includes Montana Supreme Court justices, Montana district court judges, tribal judges, Montana water court judge, Montana workers' compensation judge, Montana justices of the peace, Montana city judges, Montana municipal judges, and federal administrative law judges, U.S. circuit court judges, U.S. district court judges, U.S. Magistrates, and U.S. bankruptcy judges.

F. Other Exemptions: Exemptions may be granted by the Commission as follows:

1. Exemptions due to special circumstances: Upon written and sworn application, accompanied by the annual filing fee required by Rule 3B2(e), the Commission may exempt an attorney from all or a portion of the continuing legal education requirement for a period of not more than one (1) year upon a finding by the Commission of special circumstances, unique to that member, constituting undue hardship. Such circumstances include:

a. Severe or prolonged illness or disability of the member that prevents the member from participating in approved continuing legal education activities. If the member is disabled or hospitalized, a sworn statement from another person who is familiar with the facts may be accepted;

b. Extended absence from the United States; or

c. Other extenuating circumstances.

2. An exemption may not be granted in successive years for the same or similar hardship.

3. Exemption during year of admission: An active member is exempt from the continuing legal education requirement of these rules during the balance of the reporting year during which he or she is admitted.

G. Waiver:

If an active member requests to become an inactive member after the Commission has notified the Court of noncompliance, the Commission may waive the continuing legal education requirement for the previous year.

H. Extensions:

The Commission may grant an extension of time for the reporting requirement of Rule 5, upon a finding by the Commission of special circumstances unique to that member constituting undue hardship.

I. Burden of Proof:

The burden is on the member to submit and satisfy the requirements of these rules.

Rule 5 – Reporting Requirements

A. Report.

On or before April 15 of each year, the Commission shall provide each active member, except those granted an exemption under Rule 4, a preliminary report of all CLE credits accumulated by that member in the previous reporting year. If the member finds the preliminary report to be inaccurate or incomplete, he or she shall provide corrections in writing to the CLE administrator by May 15. If the Commission determines the corrections incomplete or ambiguous, additional information may be required from the reporting member. The preliminary report, including Commission-approved corrections, if any, will be deemed the official report on June 1.

B. Fee.

The Commission shall require payment of a fee not to exceed twenty-five dollars ($25.00), which each reporting attorney must pay to defray the cost of maintaining records and enforcing the Rules. The prescribed fee shall accompany the Supreme Court License Tax and the State Bar of Montana Membership Dues submitted by each attorney. Failure to pay the prescribed fee constitutes noncompliance under Rule 12.

C. Noncompliance Fees.

In addition to the filing fee prescribed in Rule 3B2(e), attorneys deemed noncompliant who correct the deficiency on or before July 1, as provided in Rule 12A, shall be assessed an additional fee. Non-compliance after July 1 shall be governed by Rule 12.

D. Burden.

The burden is on the member to submit and satisfy the requirements of these rules, and failure to respond in a timely manner shall constitute noncompliance under Rule 12.

Rule 6 – Credit Hours and Accreditation Standards

A. Credit Hours.

The Commission shall designate the number of credit hours to be earned by participation in or teaching of approved continuing legal education activities.

Credit shall be earned on the basis of one (1) credit hour for each sixty (60) minutes actually spent by a member in attendance at an approved activity or in preparation for and teaching of an approved activity. Credit will not be earned for time spent in introductory remarks, coffee and luncheon breaks, or business meetings. Further, credit will not be earned for speeches presented at, or attendance at, luncheons or banquets. Repetition of an activity does not qualify for credit.

B. Accreditation and Accreditation Standards - General.

The Commission may approve continuing legal education activities when consistent with these Rules. The following standards as to content shall govern the approval of a continuing legal education activity:

1. It shall have significant legal content or application;

2. Its primary objective shall be to increase professional competence as a lawyer;

3. It shall constitute an organized program of learning dealing with matters directly related to the practice of law, professional conduct, or the ethical obligations of lawyers;

4. It shall be conducted by an individual or group qualified by practical or academic experience in a setting physically suited to the educational activity of the program; and

5. It should include thorough, high-quality, and carefully prepared written materials to be distributed to all attendees at or before the time the course is presented. While it is

recognized that written materials are not suitable or readily available for some types of subjects, the absence of written materials for distribution should be the exception and not the rule.

6. It shall not be offered on a basis that discriminates against attendees on account of race, color, sex, sexual orientation, culture, social origin or condition, or political or religious ideas.

C. The burden is on the member to submit and satisfy the requirements of these rules.

Rule 7 – Types of Programs and Activities that Qualify for Credit

A. All activities must meet the standards set forth in Rule 6B. The following methods of presentation will be considered for credit:

1. Interactive seminars - a minimum of ten (10) credit hours per year must be earned by attending interactive seminars. An interactive seminar is an activity where the instructor and at least four other participants are available to interact with each other for the purpose of further discussion or answering questions.

2. Other methods – a maximum of five (5) credit hours per year may be earned by participation in any one or a combination of the following other methods:

a. Using audio- or video-produced material;

b. Participating in online seminars that do not involve interaction with instructors and other participants;

c. Writing an article which appears in any *Law Review* published by an ABA-accredited law school;

d. Attending courses taught at an ABA-accredited law school subsequent to being admitted to the State Bar of Montana;

e. Teaching and preparing written materials for an approved activity. Repetition of such teaching activity does not qualify for credit;

f. Attending in-house courses offered by law firms, corporate legal departments, or similar entities primarily for the education of their employees or members. The standards set forth in Rule 6B are applicable to the approval of individual in-house courses. In addition, the following additional standards must be met:

i. An application for approval must be filed with the Commission before the date on which the course is to be held. The Applicant will be expected to furnish curriculum materials and a schedule and to provide assurances that client-related matters and case studies are not part of the credit hours being sought;

ii. The course must be attended by five (5) or more lawyers, including the instructor;

iii. The course must be scheduled at a time and location so as to be free of interruption from telephone calls and other office matters;

iv. The applicant must agree to permit any member of the Commission, or a designee of the Commission, including the MCLE Administrator, to be in attendance at the activity if deemed necessary by the Commission;

     g. Satisfactorily completing an approved self-study program; or

     h. Utilizing any other method if the applicant can demonstrate the activity has significant legal content and the primary objective of the activity is uniquely connected to the practice of law.

     3. The burden is on the member to submit and satisfy the requirements of these rules.

  B. The following will not be considered for credit:

     1. Bar Review Courses. Credit shall not be earned for any bar review course offered in any state or for any other course attended before admission to practice law in any state.

     2. Teaching at Educational Institutions. Teaching in scheduled activities of any educational institution by an attorney who has an employment relationship with the institution, either as an employee or as a contractor, or by an attorney who is a guest speaker on a regular basis is not an approved continuing legal education activity under this rule.

Rule 8 – Presumptive Accreditation

The Commission may recognize and presumptively accredit courses that have been accredited by *and* held in other states. The Commission will grant the same number of credits to each course that was granted in the state in which the course was presented. The Commission retains the right to reject accreditation of any course that it believes does not meet the standards set out in rule 6(B) or for which documentation of accreditation is not provided.

Rule 9 - Accreditation

A. A sponsor (other than an Accredited Sponsor) or an individual member may seek advance approval on a form provided by the Commission, accompanied with a filing fee in an amount to be determined by the Commission each year. The same procedure may be followed after presentation of the activity, except that, unless waived by the Commission, requests for approval of activities must be submitted before March 31 of the reporting year in which the activity was presented. Courses submitted after the March 31 deadline will incur a late filing fee not to exceed fifty dollars ($50.00). The Commission, with the MCLE Administrator, shall advise the applicant in writing whether the activity is approved and, if approved, the number of credit hours allowed.

B. Except as provided above, no credit will be recognized without application and approval. Any delay which takes place in making a determination on a request for approval does not relieve the member from compliance with the Rules.

Rule 10 Accredited Sponsors

A. An Accredited Sponsor is an organization designated as such by the Commission. Continuing legal education activities presented by an Accredited Sponsor are approved legal education activities.

B. An application for approval as an Accredited Sponsor shall be submitted annually on a form provided by the Commission and accompanied by a filing fee in an amount to be determined by the Commission each year. Applications shall be evaluated under criteria defined in Rules 6 and 7. A sponsor shall not be accredited unless it has offered five or more separate continuing legal education activities during the preceding year.

C. Upon approval as an Accredited Sponsor, the organization is exempt from the requirement of applying for approval of individual programs. Documentation for individual programs must be submitted prior to December 31 of the calendar year in which the activity was presented. Documentation submitted after the December 31 deadline will not be considered unless accompanied by a late filing fee not to exceed fifty dollars ($50.00). The Commission will determine the number of credit hours for each continuing legal education activity.

D. The Commission may at any time re-evaluate and revoke the status of an Accredited Sponsor if a program fails to meet either the accreditation standards set forth in Rule 6B or the methods of presentation set forth in Rule 7.

E. A list of organizations or groups which are approved as Accredited Sponsors of continuing legal education activities will be maintained by the MCLE Administrator in the office of the State Bar of Montana. A current list of Accredited Sponsors will be published in the *Montana Lawyer*.

Rule 11 – Appeals

An attorney or sponsoring agency disagreeing with a determination of the Commission, the Accreditation Committee, or the MCLE Administrator, other than the noncompliance provisions of Rule 12, shall submit his or her statement, together with supporting data, to the Commission. The Commission shall consider the matter at its next regular meeting. The Commission shall send written notice to the sponsoring agency or attorney advising of the date, time, and location of the meeting and advise that he or she has the right to appear at the meeting and present any evidence on his or her behalf. Consideration of the matter is not an adversarial or contested proceeding, and formal rules of evidence shall not apply. The Commission shall determine the matter by majority vote of those present and its decision shall be final.

Rule 12 – Noncompliance

A. Notice of Noncompliance.

The Commission shall, by June 1 of each year, send a written notice of noncompliance to each attorney who has not fulfilled the CLE requirements for the previous year as documented by the official report compiled through the procedure outlined in Rule 5. The notice of noncompliance shall describe the nature of the noncompliance and shall state that, unless the attorney files an acceptable update to the official report with the Commission by July 1 of that year showing that the noncompliance has been corrected and pays the appropriate fees, the Commission will direct the State Bar of Montana to transfer the attorney to inactive status until the noncompliance is corrected and the fees required by Rule 5 are paid.

B. Notice of Transfer.

No later than ten (10) Business days after July 1, the Commission shall furnish the names of the attorneys and the effective date of their transfers to inactive status to the named attorneys, to the Montana Supreme Court, to the Clerk of the Montana Supreme Court, to the Clerks of the District Courts of the State of Montana with the request that they provide a copy to the district judges in their judicial districts, to the Clerk of the Federal District Court of the District of Montana, with a request that the Clerk provide a copy to the United States District Judges in Montana and to the Clerk of the Circuit Court of Appeals of the Ninth Circuit.

C. Transfer Not Punishment.

The transfer of an attorney to inactive status pursuant to this Rule shall not be deemed a punishment or disciplinary action for purposes of the Montana Rules of Professional Conduct or the Montana Rules for Lawyer Disciplinary Enforcement.

D. Fee for Reinstatement.

An attorney transferred to inactive status pursuant to this Rule shall apply for reinstatement as provided in Section 3 of the By-Laws of the State Bar of Montana and shall pay to the State Bar of Montana a fee equal to the greater of two hundred dollars ($200.00) or the usual and customary fee charged by the State Bar of Montana for transferring a member from inactive to active status.

Rule 13 – CLE Requirement Upon Reinstatement to Active Status or After Suspension

This rule applies to an attorney transferred to inactive status in accordance with Rule 12 or suspended from the practice of law who applies for reinstatement to active practice.

The attorney may be reinstated by the Court upon the payment of all fees required by the Commission and certification by the Commission that the attorney has completed the minimum continuing legal education requirements. The attorney shall have completed fifteen (15) hours of approved continuing legal education for each 12-month period the attorney was on inactive status or suspended from the practice of law. The total continuing legal education requirement under all of the foregoing shall not exceed thirty (30) hours. The Commission may consider hours of approved continuing legal education that the attorney has completed within twenty-four months prior to the application for reinstatement.

Rule 14 – CLE Requirement Upon Change From Voluntary Inactive or Resigned Status to Active Status

This rule applies to an attorney who voluntarily switched from active to inactive status or who resigned membership in the State Bar and who applies for reinstatement to active status. Within 6 months of re-admission to active status by the Court, the attorney shall complete 15 hours of approved continuing legal education for each 12-month period of inactive or resigned status, not to exceed a total of 30 hours. The Commission may consider hours of approved continuing legal education which the member has completed within 24 months prior to the application for reinstatement to active status.

Attorneys who believe their occupations during inactive or resigned status are sufficient to warrant readmission to active status without being required to make up continuing legal education credits may submit petitions to the Court for such re-admission setting forth the grounds for re-admission.

If an active member requests to become an inactive member, the continuing legal education requirement may be waived for the preceding year.

Rule 15 – Confidentiality

Unless otherwise directed by the Supreme Court or these Rules, the files, records and proceedings of the Commission, as they relate to or arise out of any failure of any attorney to satisfy the requirements of these Rules, shall be deemed confidential and shall not be disclosed, except in furtherance of the duties of the Commission, upon the request of the Commission on Practice, or the attorney affected, or as introduced into evidence or otherwise produced in proceedings under these Rules. After the Commission directs the State Bar of Montana to transfer an attorney to inactive status, the matter becomes one of public record and is no longer confidential.

Approved by Montana Supreme Court April 3, 2013

NEBRASKA

Section 1: Mandatory Continuing Legal Education for Lawyers Rules

§ 3-401.1. Purpose and application.

By continuing their legal education throughout the period of their practice of law, attorneys can enhance their competence to serve their clients. Chapter 3, article 4, of the Nebraska Supreme Court Rules establishes minimum requirements for such continuing legal education (CLE) and the means by which the requirements shall be enforced. The mandatory CLE requirements of these rules shall apply to all active members of the Nebraska State Bar Association, unless otherwise provided herein. These rules shall become effective on July 1, 2009, except that those provisions mandating attorney compliance with the CLE requirements of the rules shall not become operative until January 1, 2010. Attendance at any accredited or approved CLE program, as approved by the Director of Judicial Branch Education (Director) as set forth in these rules, in the three (3) months preceding January 1, 2010, may apply toward CLE requirements for the first reporting period upon application of the attorney and approval of the Director.

§ 3-401.2. Definitions.

For purposes of Neb. Ct. R. §§ 3-401.1 through 3-402.3, the following definitions shall apply:

(A) Reporting period: The initial reporting period shall begin January 1, 2010. The reporting period shall be an annual period, based on a calendar year, in which attorneys shall complete the required hours of CLE.

(B) Commission: Nebraska Supreme Court Continuing Legal Education Commission.

(C) Credit hour: Sixty (60) minutes spent by an attorney in an accredited or approved instructional program designed for CLE. Credit may be claimed for less than one (1) credit hour.

(D) In-house activity: A CLE program given by, for, or to a select private audience, such as a law firm, corporation, government agency, or governmental entity, not open for admission to other members of the legal community generally. When determining whether a program is in-house activity, the Director shall consider the attendees and programming literature, not the sponsor of the education.

(E) Active member: An attorney as defined by Neb. Ct. R. § 3-803(B)(1).

(F) Inactive member: An attorney as defined by Neb. Ct. R. § 3-803(B)(2).

(G) Program sponsor: Any person or organization presenting or offering to present one or more individual CLE programs.

(H) Accredited CLE sponsor: A person or organization whose entire CLE program has been accredited pursuant to these rules.

(I) Faculty member: A person qualified by practical or academic experience to teach or present at a CLE program.

(J) Professional responsibility: As used herein, professional responsibility includes instruction in the following areas: legal ethics; professionalism; diversity in the legal profession; malpractice prevention; recognizing and addressing substance abuse and mental health issues in the legal profession; Nebraska Supreme Court Rules Relating to Discipline of Attorneys; ethical standards as they relate directly to law firm management; and duties of attorneys to the judicial system, public, clients, and other attorneys.

§ 3-401.2(C) amended November 16, 2011.

§ 3-401.3. CLE commission; administration.

(A) There is hereby established the Nebraska Supreme Court Continuing Legal Education Commission consisting of seven members. The Nebraska Supreme Court shall appoint to the commission six resident members of this state who are active members of the Nebraska State Bar Association licensed to engage in the practice of law in Nebraska. There shall be one such attorney member appointed from each of the six Nebraska Supreme Court judicial districts. The attorney members shall serve a term of three (3) years each. Of the six members initially appointed, two members shall serve for one (1) year, two members shall serve for two (2) years, and two members shall serve for three (3) years. The seventh member shall be a justice of the Nebraska Supreme Court appointed by the Chief Justice. No attorney member shall serve more than two consecutive terms as a member of the commission.

(B) The commission shall meet at such places and times as it determines. The members shall be entitled to reimbursement for reasonable travel, lodging, and other reasonable expenses incurred in the performance of duties relating to the commission.

(C) The Nebraska Supreme Court shall adopt rules governing the operations and activities of the commission.

(D) The administrator of the commission shall be the Director.

(E) The Director, on behalf of the commission, shall have the following duties with respect to CLE for attorneys:

(1) To exercise general administrative authority over the Nebraska Supreme Court program for CLE established by these rules;

(2) To accredit program sponsors, courses, programs, and other educational activities that will satisfy the educational requirements of these rules;

(3) To approve CLE activities other than accredited courses for credit toward the requirements of these rules;

(4) To establish and maintain a system for recording and monitoring attorney legal education credits required by these rules;

(5) To review and rule on attorney applications for waivers and extensions of time to the requirements of these rules;

(6) To notify attorneys pursuant to § 3-401.11 of their failure to comply with the requirements of these rules;

(7) To report promptly to the commission concerning any violation of these rules by any active member of the Nebraska State Bar Association;

(8) To set fees for sharing U.S. Postal mailing lists with CLE sponsors for correspondence with Nebraska attorneys.

(F) The Director, his or her representatives, and members of the CLE commission, and all others whose assistance is requested by any of the foregoing in connection with the enforcement of these rules, shall be immune from suit for any conduct in the course of their official duties under these rules.

§ 3-401.4. CLE requirement.

(A) Active members of the Nebraska State Bar Association admitted to engage in the active practice of law in this state shall complete a minimum of ten (10) hours of accredited or approved CLE in each annual reporting period. Of the ten (10) hours, at least two (2) hours shall be in the area of professional responsibility.

(B) CLE credit hours for each attorney shall be reported to the Director as set forth in these rules and in the manner prescribed by the Nebraska Supreme Court. Reporting shall be completed in electronic form using the MCLE on-line system.

(C) An attorney completing more than ten (10) CLE credit hours during the annual reporting period may receive credit in the next succeeding annual reporting period for the CLE credit hours earned in excess of ten (10) hours if the proposed carryover consists of regular/traditional credits earned in a setting in which the presenter is present with the attendees, and provided that the excess CLE credit hours carried over into the next succeeding annual reporting period may not exceed five (5) hours. CLE credit hours in the area of professional responsibility are an annual requirement, and those credit hours shall not roll over.

§ 3-401.4(C) amended November 12, 2009; § 3-401.4(B) amended November 16, 2011; § 3-401.4(C) amended March 28, 2012.

§ 3-401.5. Exemptions.

The following attorneys are exempt from CLE requirements as set forth by these rules:

(A) Attorneys during the time they are on inactive status pursuant to Neb. Ct. R. § 3-803(B)(2).

(B) Members of the U.S. Armed Forces under the following circumstances:

(1) Attorneys who are on continuous Active Military Service under title 10 or title 32 of the U.S. Code or State Active Duty under the jurisdiction of any state or territory of the United States for a period of at least six (6) months during the annual reporting period.

(2) Active component members or members of the reserve forces of the U.S. Military who are serving in excess of thirty (30) days but less than six (6) months of continuous active duty military service under title 10 or title 32 of the U.S. Code or State Active Duty under the jurisdiction of any state or territory of the United States. Upon release or discharge from service as described in this paragraph, said attorneys shall have either six (6) months or until the end of the annual reporting period, whichever is longer, to obtain the required CLE credits.

(C) All persons subject to mandatory judicial branch education pursuant to Neb. Ct. R.§ 1-501 et seq., including judges and attorneys.

(D) Attorneys who have been disbarred from the practice of law by order of the Nebraska Supreme Court.

(E) Newly admitted attorneys shall be subject to this article beginning January 1 of the year following admission to the Nebraska State Bar Association. Credit shall not be given for any courses attended before admission to the practice of law in Nebraska. Education credits obtained prior to when an attorney is subject to this article are not eligible for carry-forward to the next CLE period.

(F) Attorneys who have reached the year in which their 70th birthday occurs.

§ 3-401.5(F) adopted January 12, 2011; § 3-401.5(E) amended December 12, 2012; § 3-401.5(D) amended October 15, 2014.

§ 3-401.6. Accredited CLE sponsors: procedure for accreditation of sponsors.

An accredited CLE sponsor is a person or organization who has qualified as such under this rule. The programs of an accredited CLE sponsor shall be automatically approved for CLE credit so long as its status as an accredited CLE sponsor remains active, the $25 fee required by § 3-401.6(D) has been received by the Director no later than ten (10) days prior to the program being offered, the reporting requirements of § 3-401.9 have been agreed to by the sponsor, and there has been no revocation by the Director.

(A) An organization or person desiring to become an accredited CLE sponsor may apply for accreditation to the Director. Such application shall be submitted at least sixty (60) days prior to any educational activity. An accredited CLE sponsor's programs shall meet the educational standards of § 3-401.7. The Director may grant an application for accreditation as an accredited CLE sponsor if he or she is satisfied that the applicant's programs meet the standards set forth in § 3-401.7 and provided the applicant complies with the following:

(1) The person or organization submits to the Director, on a form approved for that purpose, information on CLE programs offered during the two (2) years immediately preceding the request for accredited CLE sponsor status. If the person or organization has been offering CLE courses for five (5) years or less, the Director may, at his or her discretion, request submission of course materials for inspection.

(2) The sponsor pays a one-time nonrefundable accreditation fee of $200.

(B) Accreditation is not approved until the sponsor is notified in writing by the Director.

(C) The Director may, at any time, reevaluate the programs being presented by an accredited CLE sponsor. If, after such reevaluation, the Director finds there is cause for revocation of the accreditation of a sponsor, he or she shall provide written notice of such cause to the sponsor and shall allow the sponsor fifteen (15) days to show cause to the Director why such accreditation should not be revoked. If such sponsor fails to adequately show cause why the accreditation should not be revoked, the Director may revoke the accreditation and shall promptly notify the sponsor of such decision. In addition, if the Director in his or her judgment concludes that a course fails to meet the educational standards for approval set forth in § 3-401.7, he or she may deny or withdraw approval for the course even though offered by an accredited sponsor.

(D) An accredited CLE sponsor shall pay a nonrefundable fee of $25 for each occasion a course or program is offered by that sponsor under these rules.

§ 3-401.6 amended November 12, 2009.

§ 3-401.7. Educational standards for CLE courses; application for approval of individual course by program sponsors other than accredited CLE sponsor.

(A) An individual CLE course offered by a program sponsor other than an accredited CLE sponsor may be approved for credit if the $50 application fee required by § 3-401.7(D) has been received by the Director, the reporting requirements of § 3-401.9 have been agreed to by the program sponsor, and the course meets the following educational standards:

(1) It has as its goal the teaching of a subject matter primarily related to the practice of law or to a discipline in which further education of attorneys would be beneficial to the practice of law.

(2) It constitutes an organized program of learning, including lectures, workshops, or symposiums, which contributes directly to the professional competency of an attorney.

(3) It pertains to legal subjects or other subject matters having significant intellectual or practical content relating to the practice of law or to the education of attorneys with respect to professional responsibility.

(4) It is conducted or taught by attorneys or other persons who have the necessary academic or practical skills to conduct the course effectively and who have special education, training, and experience by reason of which they should be considered knowledgeable concerning the subject matter of the program.

(5) Each attendee must be provided with written or electronic course materials that substantively pertain to the subject matter of the program and are of a quality and quantity that indicate adequate time has been devoted to their preparation and they will be of value to the attendees in the course of the practice of law.

(6) If the course involves the use of distance learning formats, including, but not limited to, archived video or audio programs, webcasts, telephone broadcasts, or simultaneous broadcasts, the credits shall be subject to the 5-hour annual cap set forth in § 3-401.8(A). Further, those not physically attending must have substantially the same opportunity for interaction with those teaching the course as they would if physically present at the same location. No credit will be given for archived video or audio programs whose content is more than one (1) year old.

(B) An organization or person, other than an accredited sponsor, desiring prior accreditation of a course or program shall apply for accreditation or approval to the Director at least forty-five (45) days before the activity. The application shall include a brief resume of the activity; its dates, subjects, and instructors and their qualifications; and a copy of the program outline, brochure, or other documentation upon which the Director can make a determination as to the credits. The Director shall approve or deny such application in writing within thirty (30) days of receiving the application.

(C) An attorney seeking credit for participation in an education course or program for which credits were not approved in advance by the Director shall submit the course for approval through the on-line system and include in the submission information from the sponsor outlining a brief resume of the activity; its dates, subjects, and instructors and their qualifications; and a copy of the sponsor's program outline, brochure, or other documentation upon which the Director can make a determination as to the credits to which the applicant is entitled. Within a reasonable time after receipt of the approval request and accompanying materials, not to exceed thirty (30) days, the Director shall assign the number of credits, if any, being granted through the on-line system. Attorneys affiliated with the education sponsor cannot submit the sponsor's activities for approval using their attorney user account credentials for the on-line system.

(D) A person or organization seeking accreditation of a course or program as a program sponsor under this section shall pay a nonrefundable application fee of $50 at the time of submitting the application to the Director. No application fee shall be required of an attorney who applies for accreditation solely as an attendee. The nonrefundable fee of $50 shall be submitted along with an approval request each occasion a course or program is offered by the sponsor under these rules.

§ 3-401.7(B) amended September 9, 2009; § 3-401.7(A)(6) amended December 8, 2010, effective January 1, 2011; § 3-401.7(A)(6) amended February 24, 2011; § 3-401.7(C) amended November 16, 2011; § 3-401.7(C) and (D) amended December 12, 2012.

§ 3-401.8. Limitations on credits based on class type and credit for activities other than attending accredited or approved courses.

Subject to the annual credit number limitations set forth below, which apply to all CLE activities, an attorney may receive CLE credit for activities other than attendance at courses offered by accredited CLE sponsors or individual courses approved under § 3-401.7. Credits earned in excess of the annual limit for the following class types will not carry over into the following year:

(A) Up to five (5) hours in the annual reporting period may be obtained through completion of computer-based legal education accredited by the Director.

(B) Up to five (5) hours in the annual reporting period may be obtained for approved "in-house" CLE programs as defined by § 3-401.2(D). "In-house" CLE must be approved by the Director and application for credit shall be in the manner prescribed by the Nebraska Supreme Court. In order for an in-house CLE program to be approved, the Director must approve it on application of the sponsor no fewer than thirty (30) days before the commencement of the program. The application must include a description of the dates, times, places, faculty members, and the subject matter of the program and an explanation of how the program meets the educational standards of § 3-401.7. In addition, the "in-house" program sponsor must agree to the reporting requirements of § 3-401.9, including payment of the sponsor's fee of $1 per approved credit hour for each attorney.

(C) Up to three (3) hours in the annual reporting period may be obtained for teaching pre-approved CLE programs. An attorney seeking credit for teaching approved CLE programs must make written application to the Director with an explanation of time spent in preparation of teaching the CLE materials. This credit shall be in addition to credit for attending the approved CLE program. No credit shall be given for teaching directed primarily to candidates for a law degree. No credit shall be given for teaching the same course on more than one occasion in a reporting period.

(D) Attendance at J.D.- or graduate-level law courses offered by American Bar Association (ABA)-accredited law schools, subject to the following conditions:

(1) Credit may be awarded for courses initiated and completed after admission to practice in Nebraska.

(2) Credit toward MCLE requirements shall be for the actual number of class hours attended, but the maximum number of credits that may be earned during any annual reporting period by attending courses offered by ABA-accredited law schools shall be the maximum annual CLE hours required by Neb. Ct. R. § 3-401.4.

(3) The course need not be taken for law school credit toward a degree; auditing a course is permitted. However, the attorney must comply with all law school rules for attendance, participation, and examination, if any, and complete the course to receive CLE credit.

(4) The law school shall give each attorney a written certification evincing that the attorney has complied with requirements for the course and has completed the course.

(E) Subject to the limitations listed above, for attendance at educational activities that are not approved in advance, provided that the attorney seeking credit submits to the Director a written report which shall include a brief resume of the activity; its dates, subjects, and instructors, and their qualifications; a copy of the program outline or brochure; and an explanation of how the activity meets the educational standards of § 3-401.7, and that the Director approves the credit.

§ 3-401.8(D) and (E) amended February 3, 2010; § 3-401.8 amended June 9, 2010; § 3-401.8(C) amended December 8, 2010, effective January 1, 2011; § 3-401.8 and (E) amended March 28, 2012; § 3-401.8(C) amended October 15, 2014.

§ 3-401.9. CLE sponsor reporting of attorney attendance; course promotional material requirements; attorney self-reporting of course completion.

(A) As a condition of accreditation pursuant to § 3-401.6 or program approval pursuant to § 3-401.7 or § 3-401.8(B), sponsors of CLE programs shall agree to remit to the Director an alphabetical list of Nebraska attorney attendees and shall pay to the Director a fee of $1 per approved credit hour for each Nebraska attorney who attends the program. This sponsor's fee, along with the list of attendees, shall be submitted to the Director in the manner provided by the Nebraska Supreme Court within thirty (30) days after the program is held.

(B) All accredited CLE sponsors qualified under § 3-401.6 and program sponsors of individual courses or programs approved under § 3-401.7 shall agree to the following as a condition of accreditation or program approval:

(1) An official record verifying all Nebraska attorneys' attendance at the activity shall be maintained by the sponsor for at least three (3) years after the completion date of the program.

(2) The sponsor shall include the attorney's name on the official record only if such attorney attended the program and there is verifiable proof of attendance at the educational activity.

(3) The official record of attendance shall state the name and bar number of the attorney, the date and location of the activity, and the title of the program attended along with the amount of CLE credit obtained from attendance at the activity.

(4) Sponsors shall provide a certificate of attendance to all attorneys attending CLE programming provided by the sponsor. The certificate of attendance shall state the date, location, title of the program, and the amount of CLE credit obtained from attendance at the activity.

(5) Accredited CLE sponsors and approved program sponsors shall include a statement in any materials promoting their approved educational activity, certifying that the sponsor is an accredited CLE sponsor or approved program sponsor under these rules. Examples: "[Sponsor] is an accredited CLE sponsor in the State of Nebraska" or "[Sponsor] certifies that this activity has been approved for CLE credit in the State of Nebraska."

(6) Sponsors shall not provide promotional material or other information to Nebraska attorneys that provides credit totals that differ from the credit total approved by the Nebraska MCLE Commission. In the case of distance learning courses lasting longer than 5 hours, and in the case of in-house programs, the course promotional material shall indicate the cap imposed upon such programs contained in §§ 3-401.8(A) and 3-401.8(B).

(C) Attorneys seeking CLE credit for any accredited or approved course involving distance learning formats, including, but not limited to, archived video or audio programs, webcasts, telephone broadcasts, simultaneous broadcasts, or computer-based legal education, as referenced in §§ 3-401.7(A)(6) and 3-401.8, or for any other similar accredited or approved course for which there will be no sponsor reporting, shall submit to the Director a written report of completion, signed by the attorney, which includes the name of or other identifying information regarding the course; information regarding the prior accreditation or approval of the course; the sponsor of the course, if applicable; the total time spent in study; and the date and location of completion.

§§ 3-401.9(B)(6) and (C) amended February 24, 2011.

§ 3-401.10. Report by attorneys to Director.

(A) On or before October 1 of each annual reporting period, the Director shall provide e-mail notification to all active attorneys to review their on-line accounts and make sure all education is reported in order to facilitate the timely filing of annual reports beginning December 1.

(B) On or before January 20 following the end of the annual reporting period, each attorney admitted to the active practice of law in this state shall make a report to the Director, through the use of the on-line MCLE system, evidencing completion of accredited or approved CLE, including professional responsibility education, during the preceding reporting period.

(C) Once an annual report is submitted through the on-line system, the CLE record for the attorney becomes final and cannot be modified. In the event an attorney chooses to rescind an annual report and refile for the year, the request to do so must be received by the MCLE Commission no later than January 31 following the end of the reporting period. A request to rescind and refile a report can only be processed upon the payment of a $25 fee to the MCLE Commission.

(D) All attorneys who fail by January 20 following the end of the annual reporting period to file the report shall pay a penalty of $25 by a credit card transaction through the on-line system.

§ 3-401.10(A) and (C) amended and (D) deleted November 16, 2011; § 3-401.10(B) and (C) amended and (D) adopted March 28, 2012.

§ 3-401.11. Sanction for failure to satisfy CLE requirements.

(A) Any attorney who fails to comply with the provisions of this rule or who files a report that does not comply with the MCLE requirements may have his or her right to practice law suspended by the Nebraska Supreme Court, provided that at least thirty (30) days prior to such suspension, the Director shall provide notice of noncompliance to the attorney by restricted certified mail, return receipt requested, addressed to the attorney at his or her last known address. The attorney shall be given forty-five (45) days to file with the Director such information, documents, sums, and penalties which, if accepted, would cure the delinquency.

(B) If compliance does not occur within forty-five (45) days as stated in § 3-401.11(A), a statement of noncompliance shall be filed by the Director with the commission. The commission shall enter an order to show cause why the attorney should not be suspended from the practice of law for failure to comply with these rules. A hearing may be requested by the attorney as set forth in § 3-402.3.

(C) If the commission finds that cause was not shown, a recommendation of suspension from the practice of law for failure to comply with these rules shall be made to the Nebraska Supreme Court by submission of the same to the Office of the Clerk of the Nebraska Supreme Court.

(D) The Nebraska Supreme Court shall enter an order to show cause why such attorney should not be suspended from the practice of law as an active member of the Nebraska State Bar Association. The Nebraska Supreme Court shall, after hearing thereon if requested, enter such an order as it may deem appropriate. If an order of suspension shall be entered, such attorney shall not practice law until restored to active status as set forth below.

§ 3-401.11(A) amended December 11, 2013.

§ 3-401.12. Reinstatement for inactive, resigned, retired, or suspended attorneys.

(A) Attorneys on inactive status as defined by § 3-401.2(F) and attorneys who have resigned or retired from the NSBA as of December 31 of any year who apply for reinstatement to active status during any subsequent calendar year shall be required to complete ten (10) hours of approved CLE in the twelve (12) months immediately preceding the application as a condition of reinstatement. Such hours of credit required shall include two (2) hours of professional responsibility education as defined by § 3-401.2(J) and shall be subject to the limitations based on class type as defined by § 3-401.8. In addition if the attorney transferred to an inactive status or resigned while not in compliance with MCLE requirements, the attorney must cure the noncompliance and pay any late fees for the delinquent report. Only those credits earned in the calendar year of reinstatement exceeding the required hours for reinstatement shall be counted toward the credit requirement for the year of reinstatement to active status.

(B) Attorneys suspended from the practice of law for more than 12 months for reasons other than those listed in § 3-401.12(C) shall be required to complete ten (10) hours of approved CLE in the twelve (12) months immediately preceding the application for reinstatement as a condition of reinstatement. Such hours of credit required shall include two (2) hours of professional responsibility education as defined by § 3-401.2(J) and shall be subject to the limitations based on class type as defined by § 3-401.8. Only those credits earned in the calendar year of reinstatement exceeding the ten (10) hours of credit required for reinstatement shall be counted toward the credit requirement for the year of reinstatement to active status.

(C) Attorneys suspended from the practice of law due to the failure to file a report of MCLE or for failing to pay mandatory assessments, prior to reinstatement to the practice of law in Nebraska, shall submit to the Nebraska Supreme Court a written request for reinstatement, together with a written statement from the Director which evidences the payment of any penalties as established by the these rules and the making up of any deficiency in the CLE requirements incurred prior to suspension or, if applicable, during the suspension. In no event shall the hours required for reinstatement exceed a total of 20 hours.

§ 3-401.12(A) amended April 21, 2011; § 3-401.12(A) and (B) amended December 12, 2012; § 3-401.12(C) deleted December 12, 2012; § 3-401.12 amended October 15, 2014; § 3-401.12(A) amended April 13, 2016.

§ 3-401.13. Extension of time; waivers.

(A) If, due to disability, hardship, or extenuating circumstances, an attorney is unable to complete the hours of accredited CLE during the preceding reporting period as required by § 3-401.4, the attorney may apply to the Director for an extension of time in which to complete the hours. Such request for extension of time shall be filed with the Director by December 1 of the end of the annual reporting period. No extension of time to complete CLE shall be granted unless written application for the extension is made in the manner prescribed by the Nebraska Supreme Court. An extension of time shall not exceed a period of six (6) months immediately following the last day of the year in which the requirements were not met.

(B) If, due to disability, hardship, or extenuating circumstances, an attorney is unable to meet the minimum required hours for CLE during the annual reporting period as required by § 3-401.4, the attorney may apply to the Director for a waiver of the minimum education requirements. Such request for waiver shall be filed with the Director by December 1 of the end of the annual reporting period. No waiver shall be granted unless written application for the waiver is made in the manner prescribed by the Nebraska Supreme Court. A waiver of the minimum educational requirements shall not exceed one (1) year or ten (10) credit hours. After one (1) year, the attorney may reapply for an extension of the waiver if such disability, hardship, or extenuating circumstances still exist.

(C) The press of business shall not be considered a disability, hardship, or extenuating circumstance.

§ 3-401.14. Confidentiality.

Unless otherwise directed by the Nebraska Supreme Court, the files, records, and proceedings of the Director and the commission, as they relate to the requirements of this article, shall be deemed confidential and shall not be disclosed, except in furtherance of the Director's or commission's duties or upon the request of the attorney affected, or as they may be introduced in evidence or otherwise produced in proceedings taken in accordance with these rules or as the records may relate to U.S. Postal mailing lists used exclusively to provide information on CLE programs to attorneys licensed in the State of Nebraska.

§ 3-401.15. Financing; purpose.

Funds collected pursuant to §§ 3-401.6 through 3-401.11 of these rules shall be used by the Director for the purpose of management and oversight of CLE as required by the Nebraska Supreme Court under its constitutional and inherent authority.

NEVADA

Rule 205. Definitions.

[As used in Rules 205 to 215, inclusive,] In these rules, unless the context or subject matter otherwise requires:

1. "Board" means the State of Nevada Board of Continuing Legal Education.

2. "Court" means the Supreme Court of the State of Nevada.

3. "Board of Governors" means the Board of Governors of the State Bar of Nevada.

4. "Active member" means an active member of the State Bar of Nevada. It also means any attorney who is subject to the same rules and regulations as an active member.

5. "Inactive member" means a member of the State Bar of Nevada in good standing but who is not an active member.

6. "Limited practice" means an attorney who does not qualify for active membership in the State Bar of Nevada but who is subject to continuing legal education requirements.

7. "Attorney subject to these rules" means any active, limited practice, or other attorney who is subject to continuing legal education requirements and who is not otherwise exempt pursuant to Rule 214.

8. "These rules" means Supreme Court Rules 205-215, inclusive, or any part thereof.

Added, eff. Feb. 19, 1982. As amended, eff. Dec. 30, 1983; Jan. 15, 2010.

Rule 206. Purpose.

It is of primary importance to the state bar and to the public that attorneys continue their legal education throughout the period of their practice of law or judicial service. Failure to do so constitutes grounds for action by the board, the court, and the state bar as provided herein. It is the purpose of these rules to establish minimum requirements of continuing legal education for attorneys subject to these rules and the means by which those requirements are to be enforced.

Added, eff. Feb. 19, 1982. As amended, eff. Dec. 30, 1983; Jan. 15, 2010.

Rule 207. Creation of board.

1. The board of continuing legal education is hereby created.

2. The board shall consist of seven (7) members, each of whom must be an active member. At least one (1) member must be concurrently serving as a member of the board

of governors. One (1) member must be concurrently serving as a member of the state judiciary. Each member of the board shall have one (1) vote.

3. Six (6) members of the board shall be appointed by the board of governors. The court shall appoint the member of the judiciary. The board shall select its own chair. The board may, in its discretion, appoint nonvoting ex officio members to serve in an advisory capacity only.

4. The terms of the members of the board are as follows:

(a) The term of each member shall be three (3) years; however, to ensure that no more than three (3) members' regular terms expire at once, the board of governors may, in its discretion, designate that an appointee's initial term shall be less than three (3) years.

(b) The term of each member expires on December 31 of the final year of the member's term.

Added, eff. Feb. 19, 1982. As amended, eff. Dec. 30, 1983; April 8, 2002; Jan. 15, 2010.

Rule 208. Powers and duties of board.

The board shall administer these rules. Without limiting the generality of this duty, the board has the following specific powers and duties:

1. To accredit individual courses and all or portions of programs of continuing legal education which, in the judgment of the board, will satisfy the educational requirements of these rules, according to regulations adopted by the board.

2. To grant accredited sponsorship status to certain sponsors of continuing legal education courses or programs, on such terms or conditions as the board may deem appropriate, according to regulations adopted by the board.

3. To determine the number of hours of credit each participant shall be entitled to receive for attendance or participation in each accredited course or educational activity, according to regulations adopted by the board.

4. To discover and encourage the offering of courses and programs which will satisfy the educational requirements of these rules, whether offered within or without the State of Nevada.

5. To adopt, publish, and enforce regulations pertinent to these powers and duties.

6. To adopt and publish forms to facilitate compliance with these rules and the board's regulations.

7. To adopt bylaws to govern the internal conduct of its affairs.

8. To make recommendations to the court concerning these rules.

9. To maintain its own offices and employ an executive director and other such persons as the board deems necessary for the proper administration of these rules.

10. To report at least annually to the board of governors and to the court concerning its activities. On the application of the board of governors or on its own motion, the court may order the board to review these rules or any of its regulations, forms, or bylaws and to report to the court concerning any proposed amendments thereto. Absent such a court order, the board may amend its regulations, forms, or bylaws without prior court approval.

11. To collect an annual fee from each attorney subject to these rules, and to assess fees and other penalties for noncompliance with these rules. All fees collected must be utilized for the cost of administration by the board of these rules.

12. To sue and be sued in its own name, and to carry out and defend the purposes, duties, and powers imposed upon or granted to the board in these rules. Individual members of the board, its executive director, and all staff persons assisting them shall have absolute immunity from civil liability for all acts undertaken in the course of their official duties pursuant to these rules.

13. To refer to the state bar for appropriate disciplinary action any attorney who engages in perceived illegal or unethical conduct in response to any of the requirements of these rules.

Added, eff. Feb. 19, 1982. As amended, eff. Jan. 1, 1994; Jan. 1, 2000; Jan. 15, 2010.

Rule 209. Expenses of board.

Members of the board shall serve without compensation, but each member is entitled to reimbursement by the board for actual and necessary expenses incurred in the performance of the member's duties.

Added, eff. Feb. 19, 1982. As amended, eff. Dec. 30, 1983; Jan. 15, 2010.

Rule 210. Minimum continuing legal education requirements.

To meet the annual minimum continuing legal education requirements imposed by these rules, each attorney subject to these rules must timely: submit an annual fee, complete the requisite number of credit hours, and submit an annual compliance report.

1. Annual Fee.

The amount of the annual fee is $40, made payable to the Nevada Board of Continuing Legal Education, and must be postmarked on or before March 1 of the year for which the fee is required to be paid.

2. Credit hours.

(a) Subject to the carry forward provisions of subparagraph (c), a minimum of twelve (12) hours of accredited educational activity, as defined by the regulations adopted by the board, must be completed by December 31 of each year. Of the twelve (12) hours, at least two (2) shall be exclusively in the area of ethics and professional conduct. At least one (1) hour every three (3) years shall be exclusively in the area of substance abuse, addictive disorders and/or mental health issues that impair professional competence. In a year in which the attorney is subject to the requirement in the area of substance abuse, addictive disorders and/or mental health issues that impair professional competence, the attorney shall complete at least nine (9) hours of general continuing legal education, at least two (2) hours exclusively in the area of ethics and professional conduct, and at least one (1) hour exclusively in the area of substance abuse, addictive disorders and/or mental health issues that impair professional competence; in the remaining two years of the three-year cycle, the attorney shall complete at least ten (10) hours of general continuing legal education and at least two (2) hours exclusively in the area of ethics and profes-sional conduct. Credit hours in the area of ethics and professional conduct, and credit hours in the area of substance abuse, addictive disorders and/or mental health issues that impair professional competence, shall be tracked separately from general educational credit hours.

(b) The three-year cycle for completion of the requirement regarding substance abuse, addictive disorders and/or mental health issues that impair professional competence shall be determined as follows:

(1) Attorneys subject to these rules must complete the requirement within the same calendar year that this amendment becomes effective; except that attorneys who com-pleted the requirement in the calendar year preceding this amendment shall receive credit as though they completed it within the same calendar year that this amendment becomes effective.

(2) Attorneys entitled to an exemption pursuant to Rule 214(1)(a) must complete the requirement within the same calendar year in which they are first subject to continuing legal education requirements.

(3) Attorneys who, for reasons other than an exemption pursuant to Rule 214(1)(a), become subject to these rules subsequent to or in the same calendar year that this amendment becomes effective, must complete the requirement within the same calendar year in which they become subject to these rules.

(c) Any attorney subject to these rules who completes more than twelve (12) hours of accredited educational activity in any calendar year may carry forward up to twenty (20) hours of excess credit and apply the same to the attorney's general educational require-ment for the next two (2) calendar years. Likewise, any attorney subject to these rules who completes more than two (2) hours of ethics and professional conduct credit in any calendar year may carry forward up to four (4) hours of excess credit and apply the same to the attorney's ethics and professional conduct educational requirement for the next two (2) calendar years.

(d) Any attorney subject to these rules who completes more than one (1) hour in the area of substance abuse, addictive disorders and/or mental health issues that impair professional competence in a three-year cycle may not carry forward the excess credit hours to the next three-year cycle, but may have the excess hour(s) credited toward the attorney's ethics and professional conduct requirement, subject to the carry forward provisions set forth in subparagraph (c) above. Excess hour(s) in the area of ethics and professional conduct may be credited toward the attorney's general educational requirement, subject to the carry forward provisions set forth in subparagraph (c) above.

3. Annual compliance report.

A properly completed and verified written compliance report must be submitted to the board, and must be postmarked on or before March 1 each year. The report must be submitted on a form to be provided by the board. The board shall, no later than six (6) weeks prior to the due date, send a compliance report form to each attorney subject to these rules. The report shall include the attorney's mailing address and shall state the attorney's compliance with the credit hour requirements during the preceding calendar year. It shall not be a defense to noncompliance that the attorney did not receive the compliance report form.

Added, eff. Feb. 19, 1982. As amended, eff. July 31, 1999; Jan. 15, 2010.; Feb. 11, 2013; April 21, 2014.

Rule 211. Reserved.

Repealed, eff. Jan. 15, 2010.

Rule 212. Penalties for noncompliance.

1. Procedure in event of noncompliance. An attorney who is subject to these rules and who fails to timely comply with their provisions shall be subject to the following:

(a) Extension fee for additional time to complete requisite continuing education credit hours. In the event that an attorney subject to the requirements of Rule 210(2) fails to complete the requisite continuing education credit hours by December 31, the board may grant, upon written request, an extension of time to March 1 to obtain credits to cure the deficiency from the preceding calendar year. The request for an extension of time must be accompanied by an extension fee of $50. The fee for an extension of time is separate from and in addition to the annual fee.

(b) Late fee for failure to timely pay annual fee or submit compliance report: notice of noncompliance. In the event that an attorney subject to the requirements of Rule 210 fails to meet the March 1 deadline for paying the annual fee and/or submitting the annual compliance report, the board shall assess a late fee of $100. The late fee is separate from and in addition to the annual fee and any other fees owed. The late fee shall be assessed in a notice of noncompliance, which shall be mailed by the board via first-class mail to the attorney's last known address on or about April 1. The notice of noncompliance shall:

(1) state the manner in which the attorney has failed, or appears to have failed, to comply with the requirements of Rule 210 resulting in a deficiency;

(2) advise the attorney that to cure the deficiency the attorney must comply with the applicable rules and pay all applicable fees including late fees; and

(3) advise the attorney that to avoid being the subject of a petition for suspension, the deficiency must be completely cured on or before May 1.

It shall not be a defense to noncompliance that the attorney did not receive the notice of noncompliance.

2. Petition for suspension. Failure to timely comply with the provisions of these rules shall result in the board placing the attorney's name on a petition to be filed with the court to have the attorney's status changed to CLE suspended and to be barred from practicing law in the State of Nevada until such time as the attorney is reinstated pursuant to Rule 213. The petition shall conform, to the extent practicable, to the requirements of NRAP 21 and shall be served on the attorney via certified mail to the attorney's last known address on or about June 1. It shall not be a defense to noncompliance that the attorney did not receive the petition.

3. Order to show cause. The court, after reviewing the petition, may order the attorney to show cause why the attorney's status should not be changed to CLE suspended and why the attorney should not be barred from practicing law in the State of Nevada until such time as the attorney is reinstated pursuant to Rule 213.

4. Consent to dismissal; increased penalties for repeat offenders.

(a) Consent to dismissal. In the event that an attorney who has been placed on a petition pursuant to subsection 2 demonstrates compliance with these rules prior to suspension by the court, the board may consent to dismissal of the petition with prejudice as to that attorney, subject to the payment of the requisite fee.

(b) Fee: penalties for repeat offenders. The fee for processing the consent to dismissal shall be as follows:

(1) $250 the first time an attorney has been placed on petition in the preceding five-year period.

(2) $350 the second time an attorney has been placed on petition in the preceding five-year period.

(3) $550 the third time an attorney has been placed on petition in the preceding five-year period.

(4) $850 the fourth time an attorney has been placed on petition in the preceding five-year period.

(5) $1,250 the fifth time an attorney has been placed on petition in the preceding five-year period.

The consent to dismissal fee is separate from and in addition to any other fees owed.

5. Order of CLE suspension; publication required; other requirements. If an attorney placed on petition and ordered to show cause under this rule fails to demonstrate cause as ordered, the court may order the attorney suspended for noncompliance with these rules. The order of suspension shall be published in the state bar's official publication. In the event that the court suspends an attorney for noncompliance with these rules, the attorney is not entitled to engage in the practice of law in the State of Nevada until such time as the attorney is reinstated under Rule 213. An attorney who is suspended for noncompliance with these rules must comply with Rule 115. If the attorney fails to comply with Rule 115, then the board shall proceed under Rule 118. The board shall also comply with Rule 121.1.

6. Multiple suspensions; referral to state bar. In the event that an attorney is suspended by the court for noncompliance with all or any portion of these rules more than once within a five-year period, that attorney shall be referred by the board to the state bar for appropriate disciplinary action.

Added, eff. Feb. 19, 1982. As amended, eff. Dec. 30, 1983; Jan. 1, 2000; Apr. 28, 2004; Mar. 1, 2007; Jan. 15, 2010.

Rule 213. Reinstatement to active status.

1. Application for reinstatement. If an attorney has been suspended as a result of noncompliance with all or any portion of these rules, the attorney may apply for reinstatement as follows:

(a) Application. The attorney must file with the board a reinstatement application, properly verified and fully and accurately completed, in a form approved by the board.

(b) Reinstatement fee. The reinstatement application must be accompanied by a fee of $500. The reinstatement fee is separate from and in addition to the annual fee required to be paid for the year in which reinstatement is sought.

(c) Reinstatement credits. The reinstatement application must be accompanied by proof that the attorney has completed a minimum of fifteen (15) hours of accredited educational activity, at least six (6) of which must be exclusively in the area of ethics and professional conduct within the period of twelve (12) months immediately preceding the filing of the application with the board. This requirement is separate from and in addition to the annual credit requirement of Rule 210(2).

2. Approval by the board. If the application for reinstatement appears satisfactory to the board, the board shall notify the clerk of the court and the state bar that the suspended attorney has completed the requirements for reinstatement, and, so long as the sole condition of reinstatement is compliance with Rule 213, the suspended attorney shall become automatically reinstated upon receipt by the clerk of the court of the notice from the board stating that the attorney has complied with the requirements of this rule.

Added, eff. Feb. 19, 1982. As amended, eff. Dec. 30, 1983; Jan. 1, 2000; Mar. 1, 2007; Jan. 15, 2010.

Rule 214. Exemptions.

1. The following attorneys are entitled to an exemption from the requirements of Rule 210:

(a) Any active member who has successfully completed the Nevada state bar examination in the present calendar year. The exemption shall be for the remainder of the calendar year in which the examination was successfully completed and the first full calendar year thereafter. Commencing on January 1 of the second calendar year after the successful completion of the examination, the active member becomes subject to these rules. Notwithstanding this exemption, each active member of the state bar, following admission, shall complete the Transitioning into Practice program.

(b) Any active member who is a full-time member of the federal judiciary.

(c) Any member of the state bar who, while not in default of the obligations imposed by these rules, has been voluntarily placed on inactive status; provided, however, that such voluntary placement must have been given in writing to the state bar and the board prior to the expiration of the applicable calendar year for which the exemption is claimed.

(d) Any active member who has attained the age of 70 years.

(e) Any active member who is deployed on full-time active duty in the armed forces of the United States, until the member's release from active military service and resumption of the practice of law.

2. The board, in its discretion, may grant an attorney subject to these rules an exemption upon circumstances constituting exceptional, extreme and undue hardship unique to the attorney, subject to the following:

(a) The attorney seeking the exemption shall promptly file with the board a verified application, specifying in detail the circumstances which the attorney believes afford a basis for an exemption;

(b) The board may, but need not, exempt the attorney from all or a portion of these rules; and

(c) The board may condition the exemption upon such terms and conditions, and limit the exemption or partial exemption to such period of time, as the board may deem appropriate.

Added, eff. Feb. 19, 1982. As amended, eff. May 6, 1990; Jan. 15, 2010; March 13, 2014.

Rule 215. Reporting change of address; penalty for failure to timely report.

1. Duty to notify of change of address. Every attorney subject to these rules shall maintain a permanent mailing address with the board to which all communications to the attorney shall be addressed. The attorney must advise the board of any change of address within thirty (30) days after such change. The obligations under this rule are separate and distinct from the requirements of Rule 79; therefore, compliance with Rule 79 is not deemed compliance with this rule.

2. Penalty for failure to timely report change of address. Failure to timely advise the board of a change of address pursuant to this rule shall result in assessment of a penalty of $150. The penalty for failure to timely report the attorney's change of address is separate from and in addition to any other fees collected by the board. It is also separate and distinct from any fees collected by the state bar under Rule 79. Failure to comply with the provisions of this rule is also a basis for the attorney's name being placed on a petition for suspension pursuant to Rule 212(2).

Added, eff. Feb. 19, 1982. As amended, eff. Jan. 1, 2000; Apr. 28, 2004; Jan. 15, 2010.

NEW HAMPSHIRE

RULE 53

As enacted 7/1/2016

53.1. NHMCLE REQUIREMENT

A. Purpose. Continuing legal education CLE improves the administration of justice and benefits the public interest. Regular participation in CLE programs strengthens the professional skills of practicing lawyers, affords them periodic opportunities for professional self-evaluation and enhances the quality of legal services rendered to the public. This Rule requires active members of the New Hampshire Bar to participate in additional legal study throughout their careers.

B. Amount Required

1. In General—Every person covered by this rule shall complete 720 minutes (twelve hours) of CLE in each reporting year. At least 120 minutes (two hours) of CLE shall be in the area of legal ethics, professionalism or the prevention of malpractice, substance abuse or attorney-client disputes.

2. Return to Active Membership Status—Lawyers who are suspended or have selected inactive membership status with the New Hampshire Bar Association for more than two (2) consecutive reporting years are required to complete 360 minutes of additional CLE upon returning to active membership status. Lawyers may complete the additional credits during the reporting year in which they return to active membership status or in the reporting year immediately preceding. Lawyers shall report completion of these credits by such method as the NHMCLE Board shall prescribe.

C. Reporting Year—The reporting year shall be the period from July 1 to June 30. The annual reporting date shall be July 1, and reporting shall be done in the manner specified in Rule 53.3.

D. Carry Over of Excess Minutes—If a lawyer has completed more than 720 minutes of CLE in a reporting year commencing after the effective date of this rule, the excess minutes may be used to fulfill the requirement of Rule 53.1(B) for the reporting year next following only. Ethics credits may be brought forward to meet the ethics requirement only when not utilized to meet any minimum requirement in the year earned.

E. Qualifying Activities—To satisfy the requirements of Rule 53, every person covered by this rule shall seek out educational activity of significant intellectual and practical content reasonably directed at maintaining or enhancing his or her professional knowledge, skills and values.

53.2. Lawyers Subject To or Exempt from Certification and Fulfillment Requirements

A. Annual Certification Requirement.

1. All lawyers in any New Hampshire Bar Association active membership status at any time during the reporting year must make an annual certification as prescribed in Rule 53.3. Such certification may, if applicable, indicate an exemption from the minimum credit requirements for the reporting period under provisions of Rule 53.2(B).

2. The certification requirement of this rule shall not apply to any full-time judge, full-time magistrate, full-time marital master, the state reporter appointed pursuant to RSA 505:1, or any full-time supreme, superior, and circuit court clerk or deputy clerk who occupies such position at any time during the reporting year.

3. The certification requirement of this rule shall not apply to any part-time judge, part-time magistrate, part-time marital master, or any part-time supreme, superior and circuit court clerk or deputy clerk; unless such individual was in the active practice of law at any time during the reporting year.

B. Exemptions From Minimum CLE Requirement.

1. Those exempt from annual certification requirements under Rule 53.2(A)(2) or 53.2(A)(3) are not required to meet the minimum CLE requirements of Rule 53.1(B) for that reporting year.

2. Lawyers first admitted to New Hampshire practice on or after January 1 of the reporting year are not required to meet the minimum CLE requirements of Rule 53.1(B) for that reporting year, but must do so in any subsequent reporting year during which they hold any New Hampshire Bar Association active membership status for an aggregated total of more than six (6) months during the reporting year.

3. Lawyers on active duty for the United States Armed Forces for more than three (3) months of the reporting year are not required to meet the minimum CLE requirements of Rule 53.1(B) for that reporting year.

4. Lawyers who change from any New Hampshire Bar Association active membership status to any inactive membership status before January 1 of any reporting period, and who maintain inactive membership status for the remainder of that reporting period are not required to meet the minimum CLE requirements of Rule 53.1(B) for that reporting year, but must do so in any subsequent reporting year during which they hold any New Hampshire Bar Association active membership status for an aggregated total of more than six (6) months during the reporting year.

5. Lawyers who are elected State or Federal officials not engaged in the practice of law during a reporting year are not required to meet the minimum CLE requirements of Rule 53.1(B) for that reporting year, but must do so in any subsequent reporting year during which they hold any New Hampshire Bar Association active membership status for an aggregated total of more than six (6) months during the reporting year.

6. Lawyers may be exempted from meeting the minimum CLE requirements of Rule 53.1B, in whole or in part, by the NHMCLE Board, upon petition, for compelling reasons. Such reasons may include, but are not limited to, physical or other disability which prevents compliance with this rule during the period of such disability.

53.3. Reporting And Certification of Compliance with Rule 53

A. On or before July 1 of each year, every lawyer having been in any New Hampshire Bar Association active membership status at any time during the immediately preceding July 1-June 30 reporting year and not exempt pursuant to Rule 53.2(A)(2) or 53.2(A)(3) shall file a Certification of Compliance with the NHMCLE Board, in such form as the NHMCLE Board shall prescribe, concerning either his or her completion of CLE during the previous reporting year, or the basis for his or her claim of exemption under Rule 53.2(B).

Lawyers may engage in and report CLE performed after the close of the reporting year and prior to the filing of a Certification of Compliance, provided that such CLE may not also be used to satisfy the requirement for the reporting year in which it is performed.

B. Each such lawyer shall maintain such records or certificates of attendance as may be required to substantiate his or her compliance or exemption for a period of two (2) years following the close of a reporting year.

C. The court shall assess each lawyer in New Hampshire Bar Association active membership status as of the assessment date an annual sum to support the administration of Rule 53.

D. Lawyers exempt under Rule 53.2(B) who wish to claim NHMCLE credit for activities completed during a reporting year for which such exemption applies (e.g., for purposes of carrying over such credits pursuant to Rule 53.1(D)) may do so by either (1) filing a Certification of Compliance for the reporting year in which the activity was completed, or (2) reporting such activities on the Certification of Compliance filed for the following reporting year if no exemption is then available.

E. The NHMCLE Board shall from time to time audit the Certifications of Compliance filed by lawyers in accordance with this rule to determine whether the information reported is accurate and/or to determine whether the activities reported are qualifying activities. The NHMCLE Board may select Certifications of Compliance for audit based on apparent deficiencies in the Certifications, or based on any other factor that the NHMCLE Board, in its discretion, deems appropriate. Certifications may also be selected for audit on a random basis. The NHMCLE Board shall notify a lawyer whose Certification of Compliance has been selected for audit of the reporting period or periods to be audited. The NHMCLE Board shall request that, within thirty (30) days of the notification, the lawyer provide information about the CLE activities reported and/or evidence to substantiate that the lawyer completed the CLE activities reported. If the information provided by the lawyer is insufficient to establish that the Certification of Compliance is accurate and/or that the activities reported are qualifying activities, the NHMCLE Board shall notify the lawyer of the issue(s) involved and invite the lawyer to submit a written response. If, upon consideration of the lawyer's response and any other facts and circumstances that the NHMCLE Board considers pertinent, the NHMCLE Board determines that a lawyer's Certification of Compliance is inaccurate and/or deficient, it shall determine whether the lawyer should be required to take remedial action, and if so, the remedial action required. The decision of the NHMCLE Board as to the remedial action required shall be final.

53.4. Sanctions And Appeal

A. Delinquency—

1. Notice of Delinquency—On August 1, following the annual reporting date, any lawyer not in compliance with this rule shall be assessed a delinquency fee by the NHMCLE Board. Thereafter, the Board shall send a notice to the lawyer notifying the lawyer of the delinquency fee and directing the lawyer to comply with this rule for the prior reporting period.

2. Final Demand for Compliance—On September 1 following the annual reporting date, any lawyer not in compliance with this rule shall be assessed an additional delinquency fee by the NHMCLE Board. Thereafter the Board shall send a second notice of delinquency to the lawyer notifying the lawyer of the additional delinquency fee and demanding that the lawyer comply with the rule for the prior reporting period. On or about September 15 following the annual reporting date, the NHMCLE Board shall report to the Supreme Court the name of any lawyer who still has not complied with the requirements of the rule, or who has failed to certify that the lawyer is exempt from the requirements and/or has not paid any outstanding delinquency fee. Upon receiving this report, the court shall initiate a proceeding to suspend the lawyer from the practice of law.

B. Reinstatement—

1. Upon correction of the delinquency and payment to the NHMCLE Board of the delinquency fee, the delinquent lawyer shall be recorded as in compliance by the NHMCLE Board. However, if the lawyer shall have been suspended due to such delinquency, the suspended lawyer must also submit a petition to the Supreme Court for reinstatement. The petition for reinstatement shall be accompanied by the required file fee.

2. If reinstatement is requested more than one year after the date of the order suspending the person from the practice of law in this State, then the request shall be accompanied by evidence of continuing competence and learning in the law, and evidence of continuing moral character and fitness. Said evidence shall be attached to the petition for reinstatement. If the evidence of continuing competence and learning in the law, and evidence of continuing moral character and fitness, are satisfactory to the court, the court may order reinstatement upon such conditions as it deems appropriate.

If the evidence of continuing competence and learning in the law is not satisfactory to the court, the court shall refer the petition for reinstatement to the professional conduct committee for review. The professional conduct committee shall review the petition and conduct such proceedings as it deems necessary to make a recommendation to the court as to whether the petition should be granted. The professional conduct committee shall file its recommendation and findings, together with the record, with the court. Following the submission of briefs, if necessary, and oral argument, if any, the court shall enter a final order.

If the evidence of continuing moral character and fitness is not satisfactory to the court, the court shall order the applicant to file with the committee on character and fitness and with the clerk of the supreme court the petition and questionnaire referred to in Supreme Court Rule 42 VI(c). Further proceedings shall be governed by Rule 42.

C. False Statements—Should the NHMCLE Board have reasonable grounds to believe that a lawyer has knowingly misrepresented his or her CLE activity, the Board shall notify the Attorney Discipline Office of the New Hampshire Supreme Court forthwith.

53.5. NHMCLE Board

A. Membership, Appointment and Terms of Board—The Supreme Court of the State of New Hampshire shall appoint a Minimum Continuing Legal Education Board consisting of ten (10) members as follows:

1. The President-Elect of the New Hampshire Bar Association—ex officio

2. An active or retired New Hampshire Supreme Court Justice

3. An active or retired New Hampshire Superior Court Judge, or an active or retired Circuit Court Judge

4. The Chair of the New Hampshire Bar Association Continuing Legal Education Committee—ex officio

5. Nominee of the New Hampshire Bar Association President

6. Four (4) lawyers admitted to the New Hampshire Bar Association, at least one of whom shall be a professor of law or other professional educator at the post-secondary level

7. The Executive Director of the New Hampshire Bar Association or designee—ex officio

Board members, other than ex officio members, shall serve a term of three (3) years or in the case of active members of the judiciary, until they no longer are on the court from which their appointment is derived, if sooner. Nothing in this section shall prohibit an active member of the judiciary whose term expires by reason of retirement from being appointed thereafter as a retired member of the judiciary.

B. Chair of Board—The Chair of the NHMCLE Board shall be designated by the Supreme Court from among the ten (10) members of the Board.

C. Other Officers—The NHMCLE Board shall elect a Vice Chair and Secretary from among its members.

D. Quorum—A quorum of the Board shall consist of five (5) members, and the act of a majority of such quorum shall constitute the lawful act of the Board.

E. Powers and Duties—The Board shall have the following powers and duties:

1. Administer this rule and establish appropriate committees for that purpose;

2. Adopt procedures and standards consistent with this rule and for its intended operation;

3. Report at least annually to the New Hampshire Bar Association and the Supreme Court; and

4. As provided in Rule 53.3(E), conduct audits of lawyers' Certifications of Compliance to determine whether the requirements of the rule are being met.

F. Confidentiality—The records of the Board are not confidential, other than those pertinent to exemptions pursuant to Rule 53.2(B)(6).

NEW JERSEY

RULE 1:42. Continuing Legal Education

1:42-1. Continuing Legal Education Required.

An attorney holding a license to practice in this State shall be required to participate in a program of continuing legal education in accordance with regulations adopted under these rules. In satisfaction of the continuing legal education requirement, attorneys shall participate in twenty-four hours of qualifying continuing legal education over a two-year period. Four of the twenty-four hours of credit shall be concentrated in the areas of ethics and/or professionalism. Attorneys shall demonstrate that they have satisfied the continuing legal education requirement by certifying to their compliance at the end of the two-year period in a manner prescribed by the Board on Continuing Legal Education. In addition, attorneys shall maintain all necessary records and documentation to demonstrate such compliance in accordance with regulations adopted under these Rules.

Note: Adopted December 18, 2009 to be effective immediately.

1:42-2. Board on Continuing Legal Education.

(a) Organization. The Supreme Court shall establish a Board on Continuing Legal Education to administer the program of continuing legal education in accordance with these rules. The Board shall consist of not more than eleven members of the bar of the State of New Jersey and shall be appointed by the Supreme Court. Three members of the Board must also be members of the Board on Attorney Certification. Additionally, one member shall be the annual designee of the New Jersey State Bar Association, and one shall be the annual designee of the New Jersey Commission on Professionalism in the Law. The Administrative Director of the Courts or the Administrative Director's designee shall serve as a non-voting member of the Board. Other than the designee of the New Jersey State Bar Association, the designee of the New Jersey Commission on Professionalism in the Law, and the Administrative Director or the Administrative Director's designee, members shall be appointed for three-year terms, with the terms of approximately one-third of those members expiring each year. No member who has served four full three-year terms successively shall be eligible for immediate reappointment. Members appointed to fill unexpired terms may be reappointed to four successive terms. The Supreme Court annually shall designate a chair and vice chair from among the members of the Board.

(b) Authority. The Board on Continuing Legal Education shall have the authority to administer the continuing legal education program including, without limitation, the following:

(1) to determine the courses and activities that qualify for continuing legal education credit under the program;

(2) to designate approved continuing legal education providers and approved courses and programs that shall qualify for continuing legal education credit;

(3) to monitor compliance with the program by continuing legal education providers and by attorneys;

(4) to promulgate regulations governing the continuing legal education program, subject to the approval of the Supreme Court;

(5) to establish a schedule of fees to be charged to continuing legal education providers and to attorneys to fund the administration of the program, subject to the approval of the Supreme Court;

(6) to cooperate with the Board on Attorney Certification in establishing and administering the continuing legal education requirement for certified attorneys under Rule 1:39-2(d); and

(7) to make recommendations to the Supreme Court regarding changes to Rule 1:42, to the Board's Regulations, or to the continuing legal education program.

(c) Quorum. One more than half of the sitting members of the Board shall constitute a quorum and all determinations of the Board shall be made by a majority of a quorum.

(d) Staffing and Funding. The day-to-day operations of the Board on Continuing Legal Education shall be performed by a staff operating under the supervision of the Supreme Court Clerk's Office. Staff salaries, benefits, and operational costs shall be funded from fees imposed in accordance with this rule and the Board's regulations. To the extent that the Board is not fully self-funding in any particular year, the additional funds necessary to maintain the operation of the continuing legal education program shall be provided by the Administrative Office of the Courts, subject to subsequent reimbursement by the Board from the program fees.

(e) Audit. The Board shall retain an auditor to conduct financial audits as recommended by the Administrative Director of the Courts.

Note: Adopted December 18, 2009 to be effective immediately.

1:42-3. Immunities.

Members of the Board on Continuing Legal Education, their lawfully appointed designees, and staff to the Board shall be absolutely immune from suit based on their respective conduct in performing their official duties.

Note: Adopted December 18, 2009 to be effective immediately.

New Mexico MCLE Rules

ARTICLE 1
Education Committees

18-101. Purpose and Title.
    A. Purpose. It is of primary importance to the members of the New Mexico State Bar and to the public that attorneys continue their legal education throughout the period of their active practice of law. These rules establish the requirements for minimum continuing legal education.
    B. Title. These rules shall be known as the Rules for Minimum Continuing Legal Education.

18-102. Minimum Continuing Legal Education Board.
    A. Board established.
        (1) There is hereby established a Minimum Continuing Legal Education Board to be appointed by the Supreme Court, consisting of nine members. The executive director of the State Bar of New Mexico shall be an ex-officio, non-voting member.
        (2) Each member of the board shall be a licensed active member of the State Bar of New Mexico who practices in this state and maintains such member's principal office in this state. The members shall be appointed for staggered three (3) year terms pursuant to Rule 23-106 NMRA.
        (3) The chairperson of the board shall be appointed by the court and shall serve at the pleasure of the court.
    B. Powers and duties of the board.
        (1) The board shall have general supervisory authority over implementing and supervising the minimum continuing legal education requirements for members of the State Bar of New Mexico. The board shall provide the procedure for assuring compliance and enforcement of the requirements set by the board in furtherance of these duties.
        (2) The board shall have specific duties and responsibilities, as follows:
            (a) to implement practice and procedures for the effective administration of these rules;
            (b) to accredit institutions that will provide courses and to approve programs which will satisfy the educational requirements of these rules;
            (c) to report annually on the activities and operations of the board to the Board of Bar Commissioners of the State Bar of New Mexico and the Supreme Court.
    C. Finances.
        (1) The board may establish reasonable fees, and such other requirements as may be necessary to carry out the program, subject to approval by the court. However, sanctions collected under Rule 18-301 NMRA not necessary to carry out the program may be transferred by the Court on an annual basis for administration of other Court regulated programs.
        (2) Members of the board shall serve without compensation, but shall be paid mileage and per diem consistent with the guidelines approved by the court for the judicial branch of government. The mileage and per diem shall be paid out of the funds collected by the board.
        (3) The board may establish such requirements as may be necessary to implement and carry out this program, including imposition of reasonable certification and filing fees, all subject to prior approval by the Supreme Court.
    D. Board Expenses. Subject to the approval of the Supreme Court, the board may appoint or contract for such services, equipment, facilities and staff as may be needed for the efficient administration of the board's work. Subject to the approval of the Supreme Court, the board shall fix the compensation of the staff appointed or contracted pursuant to this rule, and shall

promulgate policies for the orderly and efficient conduct of their duties. The salaries and other expenses pursuant to this rule shall be paid by the board out of the funds collected pursuant to paragraph C of this rule.

18-103. Judicial continuing education committee.

A. Committee established.

(1) There is hereby established a judicial continuing education committee to be appointed by the Supreme Court, consisting of nine (9) members.

(2) One member of the committee shall be an appellate court judge, six members shall be district court judges, and two members shall be metropolitan court judges. As much as feasible, the members shall be appointed with staggered terms. The Supreme Court may also appoint a justice to serve as the Court's liaison to the committee. The director of the Judicial Education Center shall provide staff support for the committee in the performance of its duties.

(3) The chairperson of the committee shall be appointed by and shall serve at the pleasure of the Supreme Court.

B. Powers and duties of the committee. The committee shall:

(1) adopt continuing judicial education requirements for state appellate, district and metropolitan court judges;

(2) approve judicial continuing legal education courses;

(3) recommend to the Judicial Education Center and to continuing legal education providers appropriate judicial continuing legal education programs, including the agenda for the annual judicial conclave.

(4) subject to Supreme Court approval, adopt regulations to implement the effective administration of the committee's duties; and

(5) monitor continuing judicial legal education compliance by judges subject to these rules.

ARTICLE 2
Continuing Education Requirements

18-201. Minimum educational requirements.

A. Hours required. Every active licensed member of the state bar shall complete twelve (12) hours of continuing legal education during each year as provided by these rules. *One hour of continuing legal education is equivalent to sixty (60) minutes of instruction.* This rule sets forth the requisite hours and categories of continuing legal education. Rule 18-204 NMRA sets forth the means by which the hours may be acquired.

B. Legal substantive credits. Ten (10) of the required twelve (12) hours may include legal subjects or subjects which relate to the individual attorney's practice of law. The hours shall be defined as general credits.

C. Legal ethics and professionalism credits. At least two (2) hours of the twelve (12) hours shall be devoted to board approved subjects dealing with legal ethics or professionalism. Excess ethics and professionalism credits shall be applied as follows:

1. first, to any deficit in general credits in the current compliance year;

2. second, to the next compliance year as carry-over ethics and professionalism credits;

3. third, to the next compliance year as carry-over general credits, subject to the limitations set forth in Paragraph D of this rule.

D. Carry-over. Any member may carry up to twelve (12) hours of excess credits earned in one (1) compliance year to the next compliance year only. Only two (2) ethics and professionalism credit may be carried-over as part of the twelve (12) hours of credits. Excess ethics and professionalism credits can be converted to be used toward the substantive (general) requirement. Self-study credit hours cannot be carried-over. No credit may be carried-over for more than one compliance year.

E. Judges. Judges, retired judges who are active licensed members of the state bar, domestic violence special commissioners and domestic relations hearing officers shall be required to complete the same number of hours of continuing legal education as other active licensed bar members. The means by which these individuals may satisfy their continuing legal education requirements are set forth in Rule 18-204 NMRA.

[As amended, effective May 1, 2011 for compliance year ending December 31, 2011 and subsequent compliance years.]

18-202. Exemptions and waivers.

A. Inactive members. An inactive member of the state bar shall be exempt from continuing legal education and reporting requirements of these rules.

B. Extensions and Waivers.

(1) Upon petition and a finding by the board of special circumstances constituting undue hardship, the board may provide an extension of time to complete the credit requirements of these rules.

(2) Upon a finding by the board of special circumstances constituting undue hardship and with approval by the Supreme Court, the board may grant a waiver to an active licensed member from the credit requirements of these rules.

C. U.S. military active duty. An active licensed member of the state bar who is in the armed services of the United States and who serves one hundred eighty (180) days or more in any year on full-time active duty is exempt from the minimum education requirements of Rule 18-201 NMRA during such year. In order to eligible for this exemption, the member must provide to the board a certification of military service and dates.

18-203. Accreditation; course approval; provider reporting

A. Accreditation. The board shall do the following:

(1) accredit institutions that have a history of providing quality continuing legal education;

(2) approve individual programs of continuing legal education. The content of the instruction provided may include, but not be limited to, live seminars, participation in education activities involving the use of computer-based resources, audiotapes and videotapes; and

(3) periodically review accredited institutions.

B. Accredited institutions and program provider requirements. Accredited institutions and program providers shall do the following:

(1) assure that each program addresses the ethical or professionalism implications where appropriate; provided, however, that only those portions of a program specifically approved or specified as granting ethics and professionalism credit shall be used to fulfill the attorneys' ethics and professionalism requirements;

(2) assure that the course has significant intellectual or practical content and that its primary objective is to increase the participant's professional competence as an attorney;

(3) assure that the curriculum offered relates to legal subjects or subjects which relate to the individual attorney's practice of law, including legal ethics and professionalism;

(4) assure that presenters for all programs are qualified by practical or academic experience to teach the subject to be covered;

(5) assure that legal subjects are normally taught by attorneys;

(6) assure that program faculty includes at least one lawyer, judge or full-time law professor;

(7) assure that thorough, high quality, current, readable, carefully prepared written materials are distributed to all participants at or before the time the course is offered; and

(8) assure that a level of activity is noted on the promotional materials following the guidelines listed below:

(a) Advanced. An advanced continuing legal education course should be designed for the practitioner who specializes in the subject matter of the course;

(b) Intermediate. An intermediate course is designed for the practitioner experienced in the subject matter, but not necessarily an expert. A survey course in which there have been recent, substantial changes will be deemed intermediate. In an intermediate course, some segment may be low intermediate or basic and others high or advanced. In those instances, the course taken as a whole will be considered intermediate;

(c) Basic. A basic course is designed for the practitioner with no experience or limited experience in the area of law with which the course deals. A survey course will be considered basic unless there are recent, significant changes in the law.

C. Announcement of approval. Providers shall announce, as to a program that has been given approval, that: "This course has been approved by the New Mexico Minimum Continuing Legal Education Board for _____ hours of credit".

D. Provider attendance lists. Pursuant to practices and procedures adopted by the board, all continuing legal education providers must, as a condition of accreditation or program approval, agree to provide the board a list of all New Mexico attorneys and judges who attended the continuing legal education program and the number of hours claimed by each participant. Such list, and any required credit filing fees, shall be provided within thirty (30) days of the program being held.

[As amended, effective May 1, 2011 for compliance year ending December 31, 2011 and subsequent compliance years.]

18-204. Earning Credits; Credit Types

A. Scope. This rule sets forth the means by which a member may acquire the credits required by Rule 18-201 NMRA.

B. Live program credit.

1) Credit for attending approved live programs shall be based on one (1) hour of credit for each sixty (60) minutes of actual instruction time, which may include the following:

(a) lecture;

(b) panel discussion;

(c) question-and-answer periods;

(d) film presentation; or

(e) time spent viewing videotapes or listening to audiotapes at an organized open enrollment program at which there is a moderator assigned to supervise the program and to foster discussion among participants, and provided that this program is approved as provided for in these rules.

(2) The individual seeking live program credit must not have previously received credit for the same program.

C. Self-study credit.

(1) Self-study general, or ethics and professionalism credits may be given for viewing videotapes or listening to audiotapes or participating in educational activities involving the use of computer-based resources, provided the following conditions are met:

(a) board approval is received prior to viewing, listening or participating;

(b) the self-study course is from an accredited provider and was produced within five (5) years from the date of viewing, listening or participating; or

(c) the self-study course is from an approved program and was produced within five (5) years from the date of viewing, listening or participating.

(2) Absent prior board approval in exceptional circumstances, no more than four (4) hours of credit may be given during one (1) compliance year for self-study activities.

(3) The individual seeking self-study credit must not previously have received self-study or live program credit for the same program.

(4) Self-study credits may be applied only to the continuing legal education requirements for the year in which they are earned, and may not be carried over to subsequent year requirements or backward to prior year requirements.

D. Speakers. Speakers who participate at an accredited providers' program or an approved program may receive credit for preparation time and presentation time, including credit for repeated presentations, within the following parameters:

(1) Speakers may receive credit for the actual presentation time.

(2) Speakers may receive up to three (3) hours of credit for preparation time for each presentation hour.

(3) For repeat presentations, the speaker may only receive credit for presentation time.

E. Publications.

(1) Credit for one (1) hour may be earned for each sixty (60) minutes spent authoring or co-authoring written material that is actually published in a legal periodical, journal, book or treatise approved by the board, provided that the following conditions are met:

(a) the material substantially contributes to the legal education or competency of the attorney and other attorneys; and

(b) the work is not done in the ordinary course of the attorney's practice of law or the performance of regular employment.

(2) Credit is given in the year the work is accepted for publication, or in which publication actually occurs.

(3) The maximum number of credits an attorney can earn for a publication is ten (10) general credits.

F. Other attorney reporting procedures. An attorney wishing to obtain approval for a program, for which the provider has not sought accreditation or has not properly reported attendees, shall comply with the practices and procedures established by the board.

G. Judges.

(1) In addition to other means set forth in this rule, judges, retired judges who are active licensed members of the state bar, domestic violence special commissioners and domestic relations hearing officers may satisfy the continuing legal education requirements of Paragraph F of Rule 18-201 NMRA by attending judicial education programs:

(a) provided by the Judicial Continuing Education Committee;

(b) approved by the Minimum Continuing Legal Education Board;

(c) provided by the Judicial Education Center; or

(d) approved by the Administrative Office of the Courts pursuant to the Rules Governing Judicial Education.

(2) Annual training for metropolitan, district and appellate court judges, domestic violence special commissioners and domestic relations hearing officers shall include appropriate training in understanding domestic violence, as determined by the Judicial Continuing Education Committee.

[As amended, effective May 1, 2011 for compliance year ending December 31, 2011 and subsequent compliance years.]

ARTICLE 3
Reporting

18-301. Compliance; reporting.

A. Initial compliance year. For members admitted on or after January 1, 1990 the initial compliance year shall be the first full compliance year following the date of admission.

B. Compliance year. For all active members not mentioned Paragraph A of this rule, the compliance year shall end December 31 of each year.

C. Credit reporting deadline. The deadline for reporting prior year credits earned is May 1 of each year following the December 31 compliance deadline. The May 1 reporting deadline:

(1) does not relieve an active licensed member from the compliance deadlines set forth in Paragraphs A and B of this rule;

(2) does not relieve an active licensed member from the procedures set forth in Paragraph B of Rule 18-202 NMRA for seeking an extension of time to complete the credit requirements of these rules or a waiver from the credit requirements of these rules;

(3) does not preclude the Supreme Court from taking disciplinary action pursuant to Paragraph G of this rule; and

(4) does not preclude sanctions for late compliance set forth in Paragraph H of this rule.

D. Annual report statement. The board shall prepare an annual report statement for each licensed active member of the state bar for the previous compliance year which shall be provided to each member no later than the last day of February of each year. This report shall include reference to hours earned during the compliance year that have been reported by active members and providers and any carryover hours from the previous compliance year. The annual report statement shall indicate whether the active member has completed credit requirements for the compliance year or whether the active member has a deficiency in credits. Any active member may notify the board of any errors or omission on their annual report statement.

E. Second notification of deficiency to active members. On or about April 1 of each year, the board shall prepare a letter for each active member of the state bar who continues to have a deficiency in credits for the previous compliance year. The letter will indicate that the active member has until April 30 of the present year to complete the necessary credit requirements for compliance.

F. Certification of deficiency. The board shall annually compile and certify to the Supreme Court a list of those members of the state bar who prior to May 1 following the December 31 compliance deadline have failed to comply with the requirements of these rules.

G. Citation to show cause. Whenever that board shall certify to the Supreme Court that any member of the state bar has failed or refused to comply with the provisions of these rules, the Clerk of the Supreme Court shall issue a citation to such member requiring the member to show cause before the court, within fifteen (15) days after service of such citation, why the member should not be suspended from the right to practice in the courts of this state. Service of such citation may be personal or by first class mail postage prepaid. The member's compliance with the provision of these rules on or before the return day of such citation shall be deemed sufficient showing of cause and shall serve to discharge the citation.

H. Sanctions. In addition to any disciplinary action taken by the Supreme Court pursuant to rules is subject to monetary sanctions as follows:

(1) Each active member who fails to complete the annual minimum educational requirements by December 31 of each year shall pay a fee of one hundred dollars ($100). The fee shall be assessed in the annual report statement provided to each member pursuant to paragraph A of this rule, and shall be paid no later than March 31. Payment of the one hundred dollar ($100) fee does not eliminate compliance year credit requirements.

(2) Each active member who, as of April 1, either continues to have deficiency in credits for the previous compliance year or fails to pay the fee assessed pursuant to Subparagraph (1) of this paragraph shall pay an additional fee of two hundred and fifty dollars ($250). That fee shall be paid no later than April 30. Payment of the two hundred fifty dollar ($250) fee does not eliminate compliance year credit requirements.

(3) The board shall include in the certifications to the Supreme Court, pursuant to Paragraph F of this rule, any member who has failed to pay any assessed fees prior to May 1.

(4) The board shall not waive any fees unless the member can prove that the member was in compliance with the minimum educational requirements prior to the applicable deadline.

18-302. Review and appeal.

A. Review by board. An attorney, judge or provider who is aggrieved by a decision of the board and who is unable to resolve the disagreement informally may petition the board to review the decision. The petition must be in writing and filed with the board within thirty (30) days from the date the decision was mailed to the petitioner. The petition must state briefly the facts supporting the petitioner's claim and may be accompanied by supporting evidence or documentation. The board may, in its discretion, request that the petitioner appear before the board.

B. Decision. The board shall review the petition and shall notify the petitioner of its final decision. The decision shall be based on a review of the petition and the records of the board.

C. Appeal. An attorney, judge or provider may petition the Supreme Court for modification or reversal of the decision of the board. The petition must be filed with the Court within thirty (30) days after the date of mailing of the final decision by the board and must be accompanied by a certificate of service on the board. Unless otherwise directed by the Court, within thirty (30) days after service of the petition, the board shall file with the Court a response to the petition and shall deliver the record considered by the board in this matter.

18-303.
Reinstatement.

If an attorney whose license to practice law has been suspended pursuant to these rules thereafter files a report with the board showing compliance with the requirements of Rule 18-301, the board shall promptly notify the Clerk of the Supreme Court, and recommend reinstatement.

NM MCLE
PO Box 93070
Albuquerque, NM 87199

505.821.1980
mcle@nmmcle.org
www.nmmcle.org

NEW YORK

CONTENTS

SUBPART B. MANDATORY CONTINUING LEGAL EDUCATION FOR NEWLY ADMITTED ATTORNEYS

PART 1500. MANDATORY CONTINUING LEGAL EDUCATION PROGRAM FOR ATTORNEYS IN THE STATE OF NEW YORK

SUBPART A. STRUCTURE OF PROGRAM

§1500.1 Scope

There shall be a mandatory continuing legal education program in the State of New York (hereinafter Program) which shall include a transitional legal education program for newly admitted attorneys, as set forth in Subpart B, and a legal education program for all other admitted attorneys, as set forth in Subpart C. A Continuing Legal Education Board shall accredit and oversee, as set forth in this Subpart, the courses, programs and other educational activities that will satisfy the requirements of the Program.

§1500.2 Definitions

(a) **Accredited Course or Program** is a continuing legal education course or program that has met the standards set forth in §1500.4(b) and has received advance accreditation approval by the Continuing Legal Education Board.

(b) **Accredited Provider** is a person or entity whose entire continuing legal education program has been accredited by the Continuing Legal Education Board, and who has been certified by the Continuing Legal Education Board as an accredited provider of continuing legal education courses and programs in accordance with §1500.4(c).

(c) **Ethics and Professionalism** may include, among other things, the following: the norms relating to lawyers' professional obligations to clients (including the obligation to provide legal assistance to those in need, confidentiality, competence, conflicts of interest, the allocation of decision making, and zealous advocacy and its limits); the norms relating to lawyers' professional relations with prospective clients, courts and other legal institutions, and third parties (including the lawyers' fiduciary, accounting and record-keeping obligations when entrusted with law client and escrow monies, as well as the norms relating to civility); the sources of lawyers' professional obligations (including disciplinary rules, judicial decisions, and relevant constitutional and statutory provisions); recognition and resolution of ethical dilemmas; the mechanisms for enforcing professional norms; substance abuse control; and professional values (including professional development, improving the profession, and the promotion of fairness, justice and morality).

(d) **Skills** must relate to the practice of law and may include, among other things, problem solving, legal analysis and reasoning, legal research and writing, drafting documents, factual investigation (as taught in courses on areas of professional practice), communication, counseling, negotiation, mediation, arbitration, organization and trial advocacy.

(e) **Law Practice Management** must relate to the practice of law and may encompass, among other things, office management, applications of technology, state and federal court procedures, stress management, management of legal work and avoiding malpractice and litigation.

(f)   **Areas of Professional Practice** may include, among other things, corporations, wills/trusts, elder law, estate planning/administration, real estate, commercial law, civil litigation, criminal litigation, family law, labor and employment law, administrative law, securities, tort/insurance practice, bankruptcy, taxation, compensation, intellectual property, municipal law, landlord/tenant, environmental law, entertainment law, international law, social security and other government benefits, and alternative dispute resolution procedures.

(g)   **Regulations and Guidelines** refers to the Regulations and Guidelines of the Continuing Legal Education Board set forth in Part 7500 of Volume 22 of the New York Codes, Rules and Regulations.

§1500.3   The Continuing Legal Education Board

(a)   **The Continuing Legal Education Board.**   The Continuing Legal Education Board (CLE Board) is hereby established.

(b)   **Board Composition.**   The CLE Board shall consist of 16 resident members of the bench and bar.   Three (3) members shall be chosen by each of the Presiding Justices of the Appellate Divisions, and four (4) members shall be chosen by the Chief Judge of the State of New York.   The Chief Judge shall designate the Chair.   Board members shall serve at the pleasure of the Administrative Board of the Courts.

(c)   **Quorum.** Nine (9) members shall constitute a quorum of the entire CLE Board.

(d)   **Term of Service.** The term of Board members shall be three years. Board members shall be appointed for no more than one three-year term.

(e)   **Duties and Responsibilities.** The CLE Board is authorized to: accredit providers of courses, programs, and other educational activities that will satisfy the requirements of the Program; determine the number of credit hours for which continuing legal education credit will be given for particular courses or programs; adopt or repeal regulations and forms consistent with these rules; examine course materials and the qualifications of continuing legal education instructors; consult and appoint committees in furtherance of its official duties as necessary; foster and encourage the offering of accredited courses and programs, particularly in geographically isolated regions; and report annually on its activities to the Chief Judge, the Presiding Justices of the Appellate Divisions and the Chief Administrator of the Courts.

(f)   **Expenses.** Members of the CLE Board shall serve without compensation but shall be reimbursed for their reasonable, actual and direct expenses incurred in furtherance of their official duties.

(g) **Confidentiality**. The files, records and proceedings of the CLE Board, as they relate to an attorney's satisfying the requirements of this Part, shall be confidential and shall not be disclosed except in furtherance of the duties of the Board or upon the request of the attorney affected, or as they may be introduced in evidence or otherwise produced in proceedings implementing this Part.

(h) **Appeal of Determinations**. Any person or organization aggrieved by a determination pursuant to this Part may seek administrative review of that determination pursuant to the Regulations and Guidelines adopted by the CLE Board.

§1500.4 Accreditation

(a) **Procedure**. Unless a provider has been granted Accredited Provider status pursuant to subdivision (c), accreditation of continuing legal education courses or programs must be sought at least 60 days prior to the occurrence of the course or program, except in extenuating circumstances and with prior permission of the CLE Board.

(b) **Standards**. Continuing legal education courses or programs to be accredited shall comply with the following guidelines:

(1) One (1) hour of continuing legal education credit shall consist of at least 50 minutes of instruction, exclusive of introductory remarks, meals, breaks, or other noneducational activities.

(2) The course or program must have significant intellectual or practical content and its primary objective must be to increase the professional legal competency of the attorney in ethics and professionalism, skills, practice management and/or areas of professional practice.

(3) The course or program shall be taught by instructors with expertise in the subject matter being taught and shall be specifically tailored to attorneys.

(4) The faculty of the course or program shall include at least one attorney in good standing, who shall actively participate in the course or program. *[effective January 1, 2008]*

(5) The course or program shall not be taught by a disbarred attorney, whether the disbarred attorney is the sole presenter or one of several instructors. *[effective August 2, 2007]*

(6) The continuing legal education course or program must be offered by a provider that has substantial, recent experience in offering continuing legal education to attorneys, or that has demonstrated an ability to effectively organize and present continuing legal education to attorneys. *[formerly 1500.4(b)(4)]*

(7) Thorough, high quality, readable and carefully prewritten materials must be made available to all participants at or before the time the course or program is presented, unless the absence of materials, or the provision of such materials shortly after the course or program, is pre-approved by the CLE Board. Written materials shall satisfy the criteria set forth in the Regulations and Guidelines. *[formerly 1500.4(b)(5)]*

(8) The cost of continuing legal education courses or programs to the participating attorney shall be reasonable. *[formerly 1500.4(b)(6)]*

(9) Providers must have a financial hardship policy as provided in the Regulations and Guidelines. *[formerly 1500.4(b)(7)]*

(10) The course or program must be conducted in a physical setting that is comfortable and conducive to learning. *[formerly 1500.4(b)(8)]*

(11) At the conclusion of the course or program, each participant must be given the opportunity to complete an evaluation questionnaire addressing the quality, effectiveness and usefulness of the particular course or program. A summary of the results of the survey(s) must be submitted to the CLE Board at the end of the calendar year in which the course or program was given. Providers must maintain the questionnaires for a period of four (4) years following the course or program. *[formerly 1500.4(b)(9)]*

(12) Providers of continuing legal education courses or programs shall provide a Certificate of Attendance to all persons completing the continuing legal education course or program. *[formerly 1500.4(b)(10)]*

(13) Providers of continuing legal education courses or programs must maintain an official attendance list of participants in the program, and the time, date, location, title, speaker(s) and amount of approved CLE credit for each course or program, for at least four (4) years after the completion date. *[formerly 1500.4(b)(11)]*

(14) Programs that satisfy these standards and that cross academic lines, such as accounting-tax seminars, may be considered for approval by the CLE Board. *[formerly 1500.4(b)(12)]*

(c) **Accredited Provider Status.**

(1) **Procedure.** Application may be made for Accredited Provider status by submitting the appropriate forms and materials to the CLE Board pursuant to CLE Board Regulations and Guidelines.

(2) **Requirements**. Accredited Provider status may be granted at the discretion of the CLE Board to applicants satisfying the requirements of this section and, as well, the following requirements:

(i) The provider has presented, within the prior three (3) years, separate programs of continuing legal education that meet the standards set forth in subdivision (b) and the Regulations and Guidelines of the CLE Board, or

(ii) The provider has demonstrated to the Board that its CLE activities have consistently met the standards set forth in subdivision (b) and the Regulations and Guidelines of the CLE Board.

Providers that meet the foregoing requirements may include bar associations, law schools, law firms and legal departments (including corporate, nonprofit and municipal and state law departments).

(3) **Duration of Accredited Provider Status**. Once a provider has been granted Accredited Provider status, the continuing legal education courses or programs sponsored by that provider are presumptively approved for credit for a period of three (3) years from the date of the grant of such status.

(4) **Accredited Provider Reports.** Providers granted Accredited Provider status shall file a written report with the CLE Board each year at a time fixed by the Board. The report shall describe the continuing legal education activities conducted during the prior 12 months and shall be in such detail and form as required by the Board and by the Regulations and Guidelines. The accredited status of a provider may be continued by filing an application for renewal with the Board before the end of the provider's accreditation period.

(5) **Renewal of Accredited Provider Status.** Renewal of Accredited Provider status shall be for periods of three (3) years. The CLE Board shall determine if there are pending or past breaches of these Rules or Regulations and Guidelines, and the Board, in its discretion, may condition renewal upon the provider meeting additional requirements specified by the Board.

(i) If an application for renewal is timely filed, the accredited status shall continue until the Board acts on the application.

(ii) If an application for renewal is not filed before the end of the provider's accreditation period, the provider's accredited status will terminate at the end of the period. Any application received thereafter shall be considered by the Board as an initial application for Accredited Provider status.

(6) **Revocation.** Accredited Provider status may be revoked by the Board if the reporting requirements of these Rules and Regulations and Guidelines are not met or, if upon review of the provider's performance, the CLE Board determines that the content of the course or program materials, the quality of the CLE activities, or the provider's performance does not meet the standards set forth in these Rules and Regulations and Guidelines. In such event, the CLE Board shall send the provider a 30-day notice of revocation by first class mail. The provider may request a review of such revocation, and the CLE Board shall determine the request within 90 days of receipt of such request. The decision of the CLE Board shall be final after such review.

(d) **Provider List.** A list of accredited providers whose continuing legal education courses or activities have been presumptively approved for credit shall be compiled and published periodically by the CLE Board. Lists shall be made available at each of the Appellate Divisions and at such other offices and electronic sites as the Chief Administrator of the Courts shall determine.

(e) **Announcement.** Providers who have received approval for continuing legal education courses and programs may indicate that their course or program has received CLE Board approval as follows:

> "This (transitional) continuing legal education course (or program) has been approved in accordance with the requirements of the Continuing Legal Education Board for a maximum of _____ credit hours, of which _____ credit hours can be applied toward the _____ requirement, and _____ credit hours can be applied toward the _____ requirement."

Where a program or segment of a program might reasonably be used to satisfy more than one category of instruction, e.g., either ethics or areas of professional practice, the approved provider may so indicate, but must state that duplicate credit for the same hour of instruction is not permitted; an election must be made by the attendee, and each hour may be counted as satisfying only one category of instruction. The following language may be used:

and an aggregate of ____ credit hours can be applied toward the ____ requirement or the ____ requirement.

§1500.5   Waivers, Modifications and Exemptions

(a) **Waivers and Modifications.**   The Continuing Legal Education Board may, in individual cases involving undue hardship or extenuating circumstances, grant waivers and modifications of Program requirements to attorneys, upon written request, in accordance with the Regulations and Guidelines established by the CLE Board and this Part.

(b) **Exemptions.**   The following persons shall be exempt from the requirements of New York's continuing legal education program:

(1) Subject to the requirements in §§1500.12(f) and 1500.22(n), attorneys who do not practice law in New York. Attorneys practice law pursuant to this section if, during the reporting period, they give legal advice or counsel to, or provide legal representation for, a particular body or individual in a particular situation in either

the public or private sector. The practice of law does not include the performance of judicial or quasi-judicial (e.g., administrative law judge, hearing officer) functions;

(2)　Full-time active members of the United States Armed Forces;

(3)　Attorneys with offices outside of New York who are temporarily admitted to practice in a court within New York for a case or proceeding;

(4)　Attorneys who certify that they are retired from the practice of law pursuant to §468-a of the Judiciary Law.

SUBPART B. MANDATORY CONTINUING LEGAL EDUCATION FOR NEWLY ADMITTED ATTORNEYS

§1500.10 Application

(a)   The requirements of this Subpart shall apply to all newly admitted attorneys, who are not exempt from these requirements pursuant to §1500.5(b), during the first two years after their admission to the Bar of the State of New York.

(b)   A newly admitted attorney is an attorney who has successfully passed the New York State Bar examination administered by the State Board of Law Examiners and who becomes duly admitted to the practice of law in New York after October 1, 1997.

(c)   Attorneys who have been engaged in the practice of law in another state, the District of Columbia, any territory of the United States or any foreign jurisdiction, for at least five (5) of the seven (7) years immediately preceding admission to the New York Bar, shall not be deemed newly admitted attorneys for the purposes of this Subpart, and shall be required to comply with the requirements of Subpart C to the extent they are applicable.

§1500.11   Statement of Purpose

Mandatory Continuing Legal Education for Newly Admitted Attorneys in the State of New York is a transitional continuing legal education program designed to help recent graduates and newly admitted attorneys become competent to deliver legal services at an acceptable level of quality as they enter practice and assume primary client service responsibilities. The Program seeks to help the newly admitted attorney establish a foundation in certain practical skills, techniques and procedures, which are and can be essential to the practice of law, but may not have been adequately addressed in law school. It includes courses targeting ethics and professionalism, skills, practice management and areas of professional practice.

§1500.12 Minimum Requirements

(a) **Credit Hours.** Each newly admitted attorney shall complete a minimum of 32 credit hours of accredited transitional education within the first two (2) years of the date of admission to the Bar. Sixteen (16) accredited hours shall be completed in each of the first two (2) years of admission to the Bar as follows:

-   Three (3) hours of ethics and professionalism;

-   Six (6) hours of skills; and

-   Seven (7) hours of law practice management and
    areas of professional practice.

Ethics and professionalism, skills, law practice management and areas of professional practice are defined in §1500.2. The ethics and professionalism and skills components may be intertwined with other courses.

(b)   **Carry-Over Credit.** Except as provided in section 1500.13(b)(2), a newly admitted attorney who accumulates more than the 16 hours of credit required in the first year of admission to the Bar may carry over to the second year of admission to the Bar a maximum of eight (8) credits. Six (6) credits in excess of the 16-hour requirement in the second year of admission to the Bar may be carried over to the following biennial reporting cycle to fulfill the requirements of Subpart C. Ethics and professionalism credit may not be carried over.

(c)   **Accredited Courses or Programs Only.** Transitional continuing legal education credit will be granted only for courses and programs approved as such by the CLE Board, except as provided in subdivision (d). No transitional continuing legal education course or program consisting of nontraditional formats, such as self-study, correspondence work, videotapes, audiotapes, motion picture presentations or on-line programs may be accepted for credit without prior permission from the CLE Board, except as provided in the Regulations and Guidelines.

(d)   **Other Jurisdictions.** Transitional continuing legal education courses approved by another state, the District of Columbia, any territory of the United States or any foreign jurisdiction with requirements meeting the standards adopted by the CLE Board shall count toward the newly admitted attorney's compliance with New York's transitional CLE Program requirements in accordance with the Regulations and Guidelines established by the CLE Board and this Part.

NEW YORK

(e)   **Post-Graduation/Pre-Admission.**   A maximum of 16 credit hours of approved transitional CLE courses taken from the date of graduation from law school up through the date of admission to the New York Bar may be applied toward a newly admitted attorney's first-year CLE Program requirements.   Credit hours in excess of 16 may not be carried over and applied toward the second-year CLE requirement.

(f)   **Obligations of Attorneys exempt from the Program Requirements.**

(1)   An attorney who is exempt from the requirements of this Program and who is required to comply with the continuing legal education requirements of another jurisdiction shall comply with those requirements and shall certify to this compliance on the attorney's biennial attorney registration statement.

(2)   An attorney who is exempt from the requirements of this Program and who is not required to comply with the continuing legal education requirements of another jurisdiction shall so certify on the attorney's biennial attorney registration statement.

(3)   An attorney who is exempt from the requirements of this Program and who thereafter ceases to be exempt and commences the practice of law in New York during the first two years after admission to the Bar shall be required to complete by the end of those two years 1.5 credit hours of accredited continuing legal education as set forth in section 1500.12(a), in any combination of categories set forth in said section, for each full month of the two-year period during which the attorney practices law in New York.

(4) An attorney who permanently ceases to practice law in New York while commencing or continuing the practice of law in another jurisdiction shall be exempt from the requirements of this Program for the year in which the permanent cessation from New York practice occurred, and shall comply with the requirements of any jurisdiction in which the attorney practices law during that year.

§1500.13 Reporting Requirements

(a) **Attorney Obligations.** Each newly admitted attorney subject to New York's transitional continuing legal education requirements shall retain the Certificate of Attendance for each approved transitional education course or program for at least four (4) years from the date of the course or program.

(b) **Certification.** (1) Except as otherwise authorized by this Part, each newly admitted attorney subject to New York's transitional continuing legal education requirements is required to certify along with the submission of his or her biennial attorney registration statement that the attorney has satisfactorily completed 32 credit hours of transitional continuing legal education (16 credit hours in the first year of admission to the Bar, 16 credit hours in the second year of admission to the Bar) and that the attorney has retained the Certificates of Attendance or other documentation required by the CLE Board for the accredited courses or programs.

(2)   A newly admitted attorney who is required to file his or her biennial attorney registration statement prior to completing the second year of admission to the Bar shall certify the actual number of credit hours of transitional continuing legal education completed at the time the statement is filed.   The attorney shall remain responsible for completing the 16 second-year credit hours of transitional continuing legal education by the end of that second year after admission, but may apply 12 of the 16 credit hours to fulfilling the requirements of Subpart C as set forth in §1500.22(b)(3).

§1500.14 Waivers or Modifications

(a)   A newly admitted attorney may apply in writing to the CLE Board for a waiver or modification of Program requirements based upon extenuating circumstances preventing the newly admitted attorney from complying with the requirements, in accordance with the Regulations and Guidelines established by the CLE Board and this Part.

(b)   Requests for extensions of time in which to complete Program requirements based upon extenuating circumstances shall be made pursuant to the procedures contained in the Regulations and Guidelines and shall not be granted for a period of greater than 90 days absent special circumstances.   If an extension is granted, the period of time by which a newly admitted attorney must complete the mandatory continuing legal education requirements applicable to all attorneys as set forth in Subpart C remains the same.

§1500.15 Noncompliance

The names of newly admitted attorneys who fail to comply with transitional continuing legal education requirements will be submitted to the Appellate Division for appropriate action.

§1500.16 Effective Date

Mandatory Continuing Legal Education for Newly Admitted Attorneys in the State of New York shall become effective on October 1, 1997.

SUBPART C. MANDATORY CONTINUING LEGAL EDUCATION FOR ATTORNEYS OTHER THAN NEWLY ADMITTED ATTORNEYS

§1500.20 Application

The requirements of this Subpart shall apply to all attorneys who have been duly admitted to the practice of law in New York, are not exempt from these requirements pursuant to §1500.5(b), and are not newly admitted attorneys subject to the requirements of Subpart B of this Part.

§1500.21 Statement of Purpose

It is of utmost importance to members of the Bar and to the public that attorneys maintain their professional competence by continuing their legal education throughout the period of their active practice of law. This Program establishes the minimum requirements for continuing legal education for attorneys other than newly admitted attorneys in New York State.

§1500.22 Minimum Requirements

(a) **Credit Hours.** Each attorney shall complete a minimum of 24 credit hours of accredited continuing legal education each biennial reporting cycle in ethics and professionalism, skills, law practice management or areas of professional practice, at least four (4) credit hours of which shall be in ethics and professionalism. Ethics and professionalism, skills, law practice management and areas of professional practice are defined in §1500.2. The ethics and professionalism components may be intertwined with other courses.

(b) **Biennial Reporting Cycle.**

(1) The biennial reporting cycle shall be the two-year period between the dates of submission of the attorney's biennial registration statement.

(2) An attorney shall comply with the requirements of this Subpart commencing from the time of the filing of the attorney's biennial attorney registration statement in the second calendar year following admission to the Bar.

(3) A newly admitted attorney whose transitional two year post-Bar admission period has not been completed as of the last day the attorney registration statement in paragraph (2) is required to be filed may apply 12 credit hours of the second-year accredited transitional education credits required in section 1500.12(a) to fulfilling the requirements of this Subpart.

(c) **Carry-Over Credit.** An attorney who accumulates more than the 24 hours of credit in any one biennial reporting cycle may carry over a maximum of six (6) credits to the next biennial reporting cycle.

(d) **Course or Program Formats.** Continuing legal education courses or programs may include traditional live classroom or audience settings; teleconferences; video conferences; satellite transmissions; videotapes; audiotapes; motion picture presentations; interactive video instruction; activities electronically transmitted from another location; self-study; correspondence work; and on-line computer courses.

(e) **Credit for Speaking and Teaching Activities.** Credit may be earned through speaking, teaching or participating in a panel in an accredited CLE program. Where teaching is done in tandem or by panel, teaching credit shall be given to all participants.

(f) **Credit for Teaching Law School Classes.** Credit may be earned through teaching in an ABA-accredited law school as may be permitted pursuant to the Regulations and Guidelines of the CLE Board.

(g) **Credit for Attending Law School Courses.** Credit may be earned for attending courses at an ABA-accredited law school after admission to practice in New York provided (i) the attorney is officially registered for the course, and (ii) the attorney completed the course as required by the terms of registration.

(h) **Credit for Judging Law Competitions.** Credit may be earned for preparing students for and judging law competitions, mock trials and moot court arguments, including those in high school, pursuant to the Regulations and Guidelines of the CLE Board.

(i) **Credit for Publications.** Credit may be earned, as may be permitted pursuant to the Regulations and Guidelines of the CLE Board, for legal research-based writing upon application to the CLE Board, provided the activity (i) produced material published or to be published, in print or electronically, in the form of an article, chapter or book written, in whole or in substantial part, by the applicant, and (ii) contributed substantially to the continuing legal education of the applicant and other attorneys.

(j) **Credit for Performing Pro Bono Legal Services.** Credit may be earned for performing uncompensated legal services for clients unable to afford counsel pursuant to (a) assignment by a court; or (b) a program, accredited by the CLE Board, of a bar association, legal services provider or other entity. Credit shall be awarded pursuant to the Regulations and Guidelines of the CLE Board, provided that no more than ten (10) hours of CLE credit may be earned in a two-year reporting period for performing pro bono legal services. An additional five (5) hours of CLE credit may be earned subject to the requirements and limitations set forth in the Regulations and Guidelines of the CLE Board. *[revised effective February 15, 2012]*

(k) **Accredited Courses, Programs and Activities Only.** Continuing legal education credit will be granted only for courses, programs and activities approved by the CLE Board, except where credit is extended as provided in subdivision (m).

(l) **Individual Course Approval.** An attorney seeking approval of a course or program that has not otherwise been approved shall apply to the CLE Board for approval in accordance with Board procedures. Such approval must be sought at least 60 days prior to the occurrence of the course or program, except in extenuating circumstances and only with prior permission of the Board.

(m) **Other Jurisdictions**. Continuing legal education courses approved by another state, the District of Columbia, any territory of the United States or any foreign jurisdiction with requirements meeting the standards adopted by the CLE Board shall count toward the attorney's compliance with New York's CLE Program requirements in accordance with the Regulations and Guidelines established by the CLE Board and this Part.

(n) **Obligations of Attorneys exempt from the Program Requirements.**

(1) An attorney who is exempt from the requirements of this Program and who is required to comply with the continuing legal education requirements of another jurisdiction shall comply with those requirements and shall certify this compliance on the attorney's biennial attorney registration statement.

(2) An attorney who is exempt from the requirements of this Program and who is not required to comply with the continuing legal education requirements of another jurisdiction shall so certify on the attorney's biennial attorney registration statement.

(3) An attorney who is exempt from the requirements of this Program and who thereafter ceases to be exempt and commences the practice of law in New York during a biennial reporting cycle shall be required to complete by the end of the reporting cycle one credit hour of accredited continuing legal education as set forth in section 1500.22(a), in any combination of categories set forth in said section, for each full calendar month of the biennial reporting cycle during which the attorney practices law in New York.

(4) An attorney who permanently ceases to practice law in New York while commencing or continuing the practice of law in another jurisdiction shall be exempt from the requirements of this Program for the reporting cycle in which the permanent cessation from New York practice occurred, and shall comply with the requirements of the jurisdiction in which the attorney practices law during that cycle.

1500.23 Reporting Requirements

(a) **Attorney Obligations**. Each attorney subject to New York's continuing legal education requirements shall retain the Certificate of Attendance or other documentation required by the Board for each approved education course, program or activity for at least four (4) years from the date of the course, program or activity.

(b) **Certification**. Except as otherwise authorized by this Part, each attorney subject to New York's continuing legal education requirements is required to certify along with the submission of his or her biennial attorney registration statement that the attorney has satisfactorily completed 24 credit hours of continuing legal education for the current biennial reporting cycle and that the attorney has retained the Certificates of Attendance or other documentation required by the CLE Board for the accredited courses, programs or activities.

§1500.24 Waivers or Modifications

(a) An attorney may apply in writing to the CLE Board for a waiver or modification of Program requirements based upon extenuating circumstances preventing the attorney from complying with the requirements, in accordance with the Regulations and Guidelines established by the CLE Board and this Part.

(b) Requests for extensions of time in which to complete Program requirements based upon extenuating circumstances shall be made pursuant to the procedures contained in the Regulations and Guidelines and shall not be granted for a period of greater than 90 days absent special circumstances. If an extension is granted, the period of time by which the attorney must complete the mandatory continuing legal education requirements of the next biennial reporting cycle remains the same.

§1500.25 Noncompliance

The names of attorneys who fail to comply with continuing legal education requirements will be submitted to the Appellate Division for appropriate action.

§1500.26 Effective Date and Transition

The requirements of this Subpart shall become effective on December 31, 1998. Compliance with the certification requirement shall commence with biennial attorney registration statements filed on or after January 1, 2000, as follows:

(1)   Attorneys who file their biennial registration statement in calendar year 2000 shall complete 12 credit hours of accredited continuing legal education as of the date of the filing in any combination of the categories set forth in §1500.22(a). Attorneys who accumulate more than 12 credit hours at the time of this filing may carry over a maximum of six (6) credit hours to the next biennial cycle;

(2)   Attorneys who file their biennial registration statement in calendar year 2001 must complete the full 24 credit hours of accredited continuing legal education as set forth in §1500.22(a).

Approved CLE credits earned from January 1, 1998, may be applied toward fulfilling the requirements for the initial biennial reporting cycle.

August 2, 2007

[Updated to include revised section 1500.22(j)]

NORTH CAROLINA

Section.1500 Rules Governing the Administration of the Continuing Legal Education Program

.1501 Scope, Purpose and Definitions

(a) Scope

Except as provided herein, these rules shall apply to every active member licensed by the North Carolina State Bar.

(b) Purpose

The purpose of these continuing legal education rules is to assist lawyers licensed to practice and practicing law in North Carolina in achieving and maintaining professional competence for the benefit of the public whom they serve. The North Carolina State Bar, under Chapter 84 of the General Statutes of North Carolina, is charged with the responsibility of providing rules of professional conduct and with disciplining attorneys who do not comply with such rules. The Revised Rules of Professional Conduct adopted by the North Carolina State Bar and approved by the Supreme Court of North Carolina require that lawyers adhere to important ethical standards, including that of rendering competent legal services in the representation of their clients.

At a time when all aspects of life and society are changing rapidly or becoming subject to pressures brought about by change, laws and legal principles are also in transition (through additions to the body of law, modifications and amendments) and are increasing in complexity. One cannot render competent legal services without continuous education and training.

The same changes and complexities, as well as the economic orientation of society, result in confusion about the ethical requirements concerning the practice of law and the relationships it creates. The data accumulated in the discipline program of the North Carolina State Bar argue persuasively for the establishment of a formal program for continuing and intensive training in professional responsibility and legal ethics.

It has also become clear that in order to render legal services in a professionally responsible manner, a lawyer must be able to manage his or her law practice competently. Sound management practices enable lawyers to concentrate on their clients' affairs while avoiding the ethical problems which can be caused by disorganization.

It is in response to such considerations that the North Carolina State Bar has adopted these minimum continuing legal education requirements. The purpose of these minimum continuing legal education requirements is the same as the purpose of the Revised Rules of Professional Conduct themselves to ensure that the public at large is served by lawyers who are competent and maintain high ethical standards.

(c) Definitions

(1) "Accredited sponsor" shall mean an organization whose entire continuing legal education program has been accredited by the Board of Continuing Legal Education.

(2) "Active member" shall include any person who is licensed to practice law in the state of North Carolina and who is an active member of the North Carolina State Bar.

(3) "Administrative Committee" shall mean the Administrative Committee of the North Carolina State Bar.

(4) "Approved activity" shall mean a specific, individual legal education activity presented by an accredited sponsor or presented by other than an accredited sponsor if such activity is approved as a legal education activity under these rules by the Board of Continuing Legal Education.

(5) "Board" means the Board of Continuing Legal Education created by these rules.

(6) "Continuing legal education" or "CLE" is any legal, judicial or other educational activity accredited by the board. Generally, CLE will include educational activities designed principally to maintain or advance the professional competence of lawyers and/or to expand an appreciation and understanding of the professional responsibilities of lawyers.

(7) "Council" shall mean the North Carolina State Bar Council.

(8) "Credit hour" means an increment of time of 60 minutes which may be divided into segments of 30 minutes or 15 minutes, but no smaller.

(9) "Inactive member" shall mean a member of the North Carolina State Bar who is on inactive status.

(10) "In-house continuing legal education" shall mean courses or programs offered or conducted by law firms, either individually or in connection with other law firms, corporate legal departments, or similar entities primarily for the education of their members. The board may exempt from this definition those programs which it finds

(A) to be conducted by public or quasi-public organizations or associations for the education of their employees or members;

(B) to be concerned with areas of legal education not generally offered by sponsors of programs attended by lawyers engaged in the private practice of law.

(11) A "newly admitted active member" is one who becomes an active member of the North Carolina State Bar for the first time, has been reinstated, or has changed from inactive to active status.

(12) "Participatory CLE" shall mean courses or segments of courses that encourage the participation of attendees in the educational experience through, for example, the analysis of hypothetical situations, role playing, mock trials, roundtable discussions, or debates.

(13) "Professional responsibility" shall mean those courses or segments of courses devoted to a) the substance, underlying rationale, and practical application of the Rules of Professional Conduct; b) the professional obligations of the lawyer to the client, the court, the public, and other lawyers; c) moral philosophy and ethical decision-making in the context of the practice of law; and d) the effects of stress, substance abuse and chemical dependency, or debilitating mental conditions on a lawyer's professional responsibilities and the prevention, detection, treatment, and etiology of stress, substance abuse, chemical dependency, and debilitating mental conditions. This definition shall be interpreted consistent with the provisions of Rule.1501(c)(4) or (6) above.

(14) "Professionalism" courses are courses or segments of courses devoted to the identification and examination of, and the encouragement of adherence to, non-mandatory aspirational standards of professional conduct which transcend the requirements of the Rules of Professional Conduct. Such courses address principles of competence and dedication to the service of clients, civility, improvement of the justice system, diversity of the legal profession and clients, advancement of the rule of law, service to the community, and service to the disadvantaged and those unable to pay for legal services.

(15) "Rules" shall mean the provisions of the continuing legal education rules established by the Supreme Court of North Carolina (Section.1500 of this subchapter).

(16) "Sponsor" is any person or entity presenting or offering to present one or more continuing legal education programs, whether or not an accredited sponsor.

(17) "Year" shall mean calendar year.

History Note: Authority—Order of the North Carolina Supreme Court, October 7, 1987, 318 N.C. 711.

Readopted Effective December 8, 1994

Amended March 6, 1997; March 3, 1999; June 7, 2001; March 3, 2005; March 8, 2007; October 9, 2008; August 25, 2011

.1502 Jurisdiction: Authority

The Council of the North Carolina State Bar hereby establishes the Board of Continuing Legal Education (board) as a standing committee of the council, which board shall have authority to establish regulations governing a continuing legal education program and a law practice assistance program for attorneys licensed to practice law in this state.

History Note: Authority—Order of the North Carolina Supreme Court, October 7, 1987, 318 N.C. 711.

Readopted Effective December 8, 1994

.1503 Operational Responsibility

The responsibility for operating the continuing legal education program and the law practice assistance program shall rest with the board, subject to the statutes governing the practice of law, the authority of the council, and the rules of governance of the board.

History Note: Authority—Order of the North Carolina Supreme Court, October 7, 1987, 318 N.C. 711.

Readopted Effective December 8, 1994

.1504 Size of Board

The board shall have nine members, all of whom must be attorneys in good standing and authorized to practice in the state of North Carolina.

History Note: Authority—Order of the North Carolina Supreme Court, October 7, 1987, 318 N.C. 711.

Readopted Effective December 8, 1994

.1505 Lay Participation

The board shall have no members who are not licensed attorneys.

History Note: Authority—Order of the North Carolina Supreme Court, October 7, 1987, 318 N.C. 711.

Readopted Effective December 8, 1994

.1506 Appointment of Members; When; Removal

The members of the board shall be appointed as of the quarterly meeting of the council. The first members of the board shall be appointed as of the quarterly meeting of the council following the creation of the board. Thereafter, members shall be appointed annually as of the same quarterly meeting. Vacancies occurring by reason of death, resignation, or removal shall be filled by appointment of the council at the next quarterly meeting following the event giving rise to the vacancy, and the person so appointed shall serve for the balance of the vacated term. Any member of the board may be removed at any time by an affirmative vote of a majority of the members of the council in session at a regularly called meeting.

History Note: Authority—Order of the North Carolina Supreme Court, October 7, 1987, 318 N.C. 711.

Readopted Effective December 8, 1994

.1507 Term of Office

Each member who is appointed to the board shall serve for a term of three years beginning as of the first day of the month following the date on which the appointment is made by the council. See, however, Rule .1508 of this subchapter.

History Note: Authority—Order of the North Carolina Supreme Court, October 7, 1987, 318 N.C. 711.

Readopted Effective December 8, 1994

.1508 Staggered Terms

It is intended that members of the board shall be elected to staggered terms such that three members are appointed in each year. Of the initial board, three members shall be elected to terms of one year, three members shall be elected to terms of two years, and three members shall be elected to terms of three years. Thereafter, three members shall be elected each year.

History Note: Authority—Order of the North Carolina Supreme Court, October 7, 1987, 318 N.C. 711.

Readopted Effective December 8, 1994

.1509 Succession

Each member of the board shall be entitled to serve for one full three-year term and to succeed himself or herself for one additional three-year term. Thereafter, no person may be reappointed without having been off the board for at least three years.

History Note: Authority—Order of the North Carolina Supreme Court, October 7, 1987, 318 N.C. 711.

Readopted Effective December 8, 1994

.1510 Appointment of Chairperson

The chairperson of the board shall be appointed from time to time as necessary by the council. The term of such individual as chairperson shall be one year. The chairperson may be reappointed thereafter during his or her tenure on the board. The chairperson shall preside at all meetings of the board, shall prepare and present to the council the annual report of the board, and generally shall represent the board in its dealings with the public.

History Note: Authority—Order of the North Carolina Supreme Court, October 7, 1987, 318 N.C. 711.

Readopted Effective December 8, 1994

.1511 Appointment of Vice-Chairperson

The vice-chairperson of the board shall be appointed from time to time as necessary by the council. The term of such individual as vice-chairperson shall be one year. The vice-chairperson may be reappointed thereafter during tenure on the board. The vice-chairperson shall preside at and represent the board in the absence of the chairperson and shall perform such other duties as may be assigned to him or her by the chairperson or by the board.

History Note: Authority—Order of the North Carolina Supreme Court, October 7, 1987, 318 N.C. 711.

Readopted Effective December 8, 1994

.1512 Source of Funds

(a) Funding for the program carried out by the board shall come from sponsor's fees and attendee's fees as provided below, as well as from duly assessed penalties for noncompliance and from reinstatement fees.

(1) Accredited sponsors located in North Carolina (for courses offered within or outside North Carolina), or accredited sponsors not located in North Carolina (for courses given in North Carolina), or unaccredited sponsors located within or outside of North Carolina (for accredited courses within North Carolina) shall, as a condition of conducting an approved activity, agree to remit a list of North Carolina attendees and to pay a fee for each active member of the North Carolina State Bar who attends the program for CLE credit. The sponsor's fee shall be based on each credit hour of attendance, with a proportional fee for portions of a program lasting less than an hour. The fee shall be set by the board upon approval of the council. Any sponsor, including an accredited sponsor, which conducts an approved activity which is offered without charge to attendees shall not be required to remit the fee under this section. Attendees who wish to receive credit for attending such an approved activity shall comply with Rule .1512(a)(2) below.

(2) The board shall fix a reasonably comparable fee to be paid by individual attorneys who attend for CLE credit approved continuing legal education activities for which the sponsor does not submit a fee under Rule .1512(a)(1) above. Such fee shall accompany the member's annual affidavit. The fee shall be set by the board upon approval of the council.

(b) Funding for a law practice assistance program shall be from user fees set by the board upon approval of the council and from such other funds as the council may provide.

History Note: Authority—Order of the North Carolina Supreme Court, October 7, 1987, 318 N.C. 711.

Readopted Effective December 8, 1994

.1513 FISCAL RESPONSIBILITY

All funds of the board shall be considered funds of the North Carolina State Bar and shall be administered and disbursed accordingly.

(a) Maintenance of Accounts: Audit - The North Carolina State Bar shall maintain a separate account for funds of the board such that such funds and expenditures therefrom can be readily identified. The accounts of the board shall be audited on an annual basis in connection with the audits of the North Carolina State Bar.

(b) Investment Criteria - The funds of the board shall be handled, invested and reinvested in accordance with investment policies adopted by the council for the handling of dues, rents, and other revenues received by the North Carolina State Bar in carrying out its official duties.

(c) Disbursement - Disbursement of funds of the board shall be made by or under the direction of the secretary-treasurer of the North Carolina State Bar pursuant to authority of the council. The members of the board shall serve on a voluntary basis without compensation, but may be reimbursed for the reasonable expenses incurred in attending meetings of the board or its committees.

(d) All revenues resulting from the CLE program, including fees received from attendees and sponsors, late filing penalties, late compliance fees, reinstatement fees, and interest on a reserve fund shall be applied first to the expense of administration of the CLE program including an adequate reserve fund; provided, however, that a portion of each sponsor or attendee fee, in an amount to be determined by the council, shall be paid to the Chief Justice's Commission on Professionalism and to the North Carolina Equal Access to Justice Commission for administration of the activities of these commissions. Excess funds may be expended by the council on lawyer competency programs approved by the council.

History Note: Authority - Order of the North Carolina Supreme Court, October 7, 1987, 318 N.C. 711.

Readopted Effective December 8, 1994

Amended December 30, 1998; November 5, 2015

.1514 Meetings

The annual meeting of the board shall be held in October of each year in connection with the annual meeting of the North Carolina State Bar. The board by resolution may set regular meeting dates and places. Special meetings of the board may be called at any time upon notice given by the chairperson, the vice-chairperson, or any two members of the board. Notice of meeting shall be given at least two days prior to the meeting by mail, telegram, facsimile transmission or telephone. A quorum of the board for conducting its official business shall be a majority of the members serving at a particular time.

History Note: Authority—Order of the North Carolina Supreme Court, October 7, 1987, 318 N.C. 711.

Readopted Effective December 8, 1994

.1515 Annual Report

The board shall prepare at least annually a report of its activities and shall present the same to the council one month prior to its annual meeting.

History Note: Authority—Order of the North Carolina Supreme Court, October 7, 1987, 318 N.C. 711.

Readopted Effective December 8, 1994

.1516 Powers, Duties, and Organization of the Board

(a) The board shall have the following powers and duties:

(1) to exercise general supervisory authority over the administration of these rules;

(2) to adopt and amend regulations consistent with these rules with the approval of the council;

(3) to establish an office or offices and to employ such persons as the board deems necessary for the proper administration of these rules, and to delegate to them appropriate authority, subject to the review of the council;

(4) to report annually on the activities and operations of the board to the council and make any recommendations for changes in the rules or methods of operation of the continuing legal education program;

(5) to submit an annual budget to the council for approval and to ensure that expenses of the board do not exceed the annual budget approved by the council;

(6) to administer a law office assistance program for the benefit of lawyers who request or are required to obtain training in the area of law office management.

(b) The board shall be organized as follows:

(1) Quorum—Five members shall constitute a quorum of the board.

(2) The Executive Committee—The executive committee of the board shall be comprised of the chairperson, a vice-chairperson elected by the members of the board, and a member to be appointed by the chairperson. Its purpose is to conduct all necessary business of the board that may arise between meetings of the full board. In such matters it shall have complete authority to act for the board.

(3) Other Committees—The chairperson may appoint committees as established by the board for the purpose of considering and deciding matters submitted to them by the board.

(c) Appeals—Except as otherwise provided, the board is the final authority on all matters entrusted to it under Section .1500 and Section .1600 of this subchapter. Therefore, any decision by a committee of the board pursuant to a delegation of authority may be appealed to the full board and will be heard by the board at its next scheduled meeting. A decision made by the staff pursuant to a delegation of authority may also be reviewed by the full board but should first be appealed to any committee of the board having jurisdiction on the subject involved. All appeals shall be in writing. The board has the discretion to, but is not obligated to, grant a hearing in connection with any appeal regarding the accreditation of a program.

History Note: Authority—Order of the North Carolina Supreme Court, October 7, 1987, 318 N.C. 711.

Readopted Effective December 8, 1994; Amended by council October 22, 2004; March 3, 2005

.1517 EXEMPTIONS

(a) Notification of Board. To qualify for an exemption for a particular calendar year, a member shall notify the board of the exemption in the annual report for that calendar year sent to the member pursuant to Rule .1522 of this subchapter. All active members who are exempt are encouraged to attend and participate in legal education programs.

(b) Government Officials and Members of Armed Forces. The governor, the lieutenant governor, and all members of the council of state, members of the United States Senate, members of the United States House of Representatives, members of the North Carolina General Assembly and members of the United States Armed Forces on full-time active duty are exempt from the requirements of these rules for any calendar year in which they serve some portion thereof in such capacity.

(c) Judiciary and Clerks. Members of the state judiciary who are required by virtue of their judicial offices to take an average of twelve (12) or more hours of continuing judicial or other legal education annually and all members of the federal judiciary are exempt from the requirements of these rules for any calendar year in which they serve some portion thereof in such judicial capacities. A full-time law clerk for a member of the federal or state judiciary is exempt from the requirements of these rules for any calendar year in which the clerk serves some portion thereof in such capacity, provided, however, that the exemption shall not exceed two consecutive calendar years and, further provided, that the clerkship begins within one year after the clerk graduates from law school or passes the bar examination for admission to the North Carolina State Bar whichever occurs later.

(d) Nonresidents. Any active member residing outside of North Carolina who does not practice in North Carolina for at least six (6) consecutive months and does not represent North Carolina clients on matters governed by North Carolina law shall be exempt from the requirements of these rules.

(e) Law Teachers. An exemption from the requirements of these rules shall be given to any active member who does not practice in North Carolina or represent North Carolina clients on matters governed by North Carolina law and who is:

(1) A full-time teacher at the School of Government (formerly the Institute of Government) of the University of North Carolina;

(2) A full-time teacher at a law school in North Carolina that is accredited by the American Bar Association; or

(3) A full-time teacher of law-related courses at a graduate level professional school accredited by its respective professional accrediting agency.

(f) Special Circumstances Exemptions. The board may exempt an active member from the continuing legal education requirements for a period of not more than one year at a time upon a finding by the board of special circumstances unique to that member constituting undue hardship or other reasonable basis for exemption, or for a longer period upon a finding of a permanent disability.

(g) Pro Hac Vice Admission. Nonresident attorneys from other jurisdictions who are temporarily admitted to practice in a particular case or proceeding pursuant to the provisions of G.S. 84-4.1 shall not be subject to the requirements of these rules.

(h) Senior Status Exemption. The board may exempt an active member from the continuing legal education requirements if

(1) the member is sixty-five years of age or older and

(2) the member does not render legal advice to or represent a client unless the member associates with another active member who assumes responsibility for the advice or representation.

(i) CLE Record During Exemption Period. During a calendar year in which the records of the board indicate that an active member is exempt from the requirements of these rules, the board shall not maintain a record of such member's attendance at accredited continuing legal education activities. Upon the termination of the member's exemption, the member may request carry over credit up to a maximum of twelve (12) credits for any accredited continuing legal education activity attended during the calendar year immediately preceding the year of the termination of the exemption. Appropriate documentation of attendance at such activities will be required by the board.

(j) Permanent Disability. Attorneys who have a permanent disability that makes attendance at CLE programs inordinately difficult may file a request for a permanent substitute program in lieu of attendance and shall therein set out continuing legal education plans tailored to their specific interests and physical ability. The board shall review and approve or disapprove such plans on an individual basis and without delay.

(k) Application for Substitute Compliance and Exemptions. Other requests for substitute compliance, partial waivers, other exemptions for hardship or extenuating circumstances may be granted by the board on a yearly basis upon written application of the attorney.

(l) Bar Examiners. Credit is earned through service as a bar examiner of the North Carolina Board of Law Examiners. The board will award 12 hours of CLE credit for the preparation and grading of a bar examination by a member of the North Carolina Board of Law Examiners.

History Note: Authority - Order of the North Carolina Supreme Court, October 7, 1987, 318 N.C. 711.

Readopted Effective December 8, 1994

Amended February 12, 1997; October 1, 2003; March 3, 2005; October 7, 2010; October 2, 2014; June 9, 2016"

.1518 Continuing Legal Education Program

(a) Annual Requirement. Each active member subject to these rules shall complete 12 hours of approved continuing legal education during each calendar year beginning January 1, 1988, as provided by these rules and the regulations adopted thereunder.

Of the 12 hours:

(1) at least 2 hours shall be devoted to the areas of professional responsibility or professionalism or any combination thereof; and

(2) effective January 1, 2002, at least once every three calendar years, each member shall complete an hour of continuing legal education instruction on substance abuse and debilitating mental conditions as defined in Rule .1602 (a). This hour shall be credited to the annual 12-hour requirement but shall be in addition to the annual professional responsibility/professionalism requirement. To satisfy the requirement, a member must attend an accredited program on substance abuse and debilitating mental conditions that is at least one hour long.

(b) Carryover. Members may carry over up to 12 credit hours earned in one calendar year to the next calendar year, which may include those hours required by paragraph (a)(1) above. Additionally, a newly admitted active member may include as credit hours which may be carried over to the next succeeding year any approved CLE hours earned after that member's graduation from law school.

(c) Professionalism Requirement for New Members. Except as provided in paragraph (d)(1), each active member admitted to the North Carolina State Bar after January 1, 2011, must complete the North Carolina State Bar Professionalism for New Admittees Program (PNA Program) in the year the member is first required to meet the continuing legal education requirements as set forth in Rule .1526(b) and

(c) of this subchapter. CLE credit for the PNA Program shall be applied to the annual mandatory continuing legal education requirements set forth in paragraph (a) above.

(1) Content and Accreditation. The State Bar PNA Program shall consist of 12 hours of training in subjects designated by the State Bar including, but not limited to, professional responsibility, professionalism, and law office management. The chairs of the Ethics and Grievance Committees, in consultation with the chief counsel to those committees, shall annually establish the content of the program and shall publish the required content on or before January 1 of each year. To be approved as a PNA Program, a sponsor must satisfy the annual content require-ments. At least 45 days prior to the presentation of a PNA Program, a sponsor must submit a detailed description of the program to the board for approval. Accredited sponsors shall not be exempt from the prior submission requirement and may not advertise a PNA Program until approved by the board. PNA Programs shall be specially designated by the board and no course that is not so designated shall satisfy the PNA Program requirement for new members.

(2) Evaluation. To receive CLE credit for attending a PNA Program, the partici-pant must complete a written evaluation of the program which shall contain questions specified by the State Bar. Sponsors shall collate the information on the completed evaluation forms and shall send a report showing the collated informa-tion, together with the original forms, to the State Bar when reporting attendance pursuant to Rule .1601(e)(1) of this subchapter.

(3) Timetable and Partial Credit. The PNA Program shall be presented in two six-hour blocks (with appropriate breaks) over two days. The six-hour blocks do not have to be attended on consecutive days or taken from the same provider; however, no partial credit shall be awarded for attending less than an entire six-hour block unless a special circumstances exemption is granted by the board. The board may approve an alternative timetable for a PNA program upon demonstration by the provider that the alternative timetable will provide an enhanced learning experience or for other good cause; however, no partial credit shall be awarded for attending less than the entire 12-hour program unless a special circumstances exemption is granted by the board.(4) Online and Prerecorded Programs. The PNA Program may be distributed over the Internet by live web streaming (webcasting) but no part of the program may be taken online (via the Internet) on demand. The program may also be taken as a prerecorded program provided the requirements of Rule .1604(d) of this subchapter are satisfied and at least one hour of each six-hour block consists of live programming.

(d) Exemptions from Professionalism Requirement for New Members.

(1) Licensed in Another Jurisdiction. A member who is licensed by a United States jurisdiction other than North Carolina for five or more years prior to admission to practice in North Carolina is exempt from the PNA Program requirement and must

notify the board of the exemption in the first annual report sent to the member pursuant to Rule .1522 of this subchapter.

(2) Inactive Status. A newly admitted member who is transferred to inactive status in the year of admission to the State Bar is exempt from the PNA Program requirement but, upon the entry of an order transferring the member back to active status, must complete the PNA Program in the year that the member is subject to the requirements set forth in paragraph (a) above unless the member qualifies for the exemption under paragraph (d)(1) of this rule.(3) Exemptions Under Rule .1517. A newly admitted active member who qualifies for an exemption under Rule .1517 of this subchapter shall be exempt from the PNA Program requirement during the period of the Rule .1517 exemption. The member shall notify the board of the exemption in the first annual report sent to the member pursuant to Rule .1522 of this subchapter. The member must complete the PNA Program in the year the member no longer qualifies for the Rule .1517 exemption or the next calendar year unless the member qualifies for the exemption under paragraph (d)(1) of this rule.

(e) The board shall determine the process by which credit hours are allocated to lawyers' records to satisfy deficits. The allocation shall be applied uniformly to the records of all affected lawyers and may not be appealed by an affected lawyer. History Note: Authority - Order of the North Carolina Supreme Court, October 7, 1987, 318 N.C. 711.Readopted Effective December 8, 1994 Amended February 12, 1997; December 30, 1998; March 3, 1999; November 6, 2001; October 1, 2003; March 11, 2010; August 25, 2011; March 6, 2014; March 5, 2015

.1519 Accreditation Standards

The board shall approve continuing legal education activities which meet the following standards and provisions.

(a) They shall have significant intellectual or practical content and the primary objective shall be to increase the participant's professional competence and proficiency as a lawyer.

(b) They shall constitute an organized program of learning dealing with matters directly related to the practice of law, professional responsibility, professionalism, or ethical obligations of lawyers.

(c) Credit may be given for continuing legal education activities where live instruction is used or mechanically or electronically recorded or reproduced material is used, including videotape or satellite transmitted programs.

Subject to the limitations set forth in Rule.1604(e) of this subchapter, credit may also be given for continuing legal education activities on CD-ROM and on a computer website accessed via the Internet.

(d) Continuing legal education materials are to be prepared, and activities conducted, by an individual or group qualified by practical or academic experience.

Credit shall not be given for any continuing legal education activity taught or presented by a disbarred lawyer except a course on professional responsibility (including a course or program on the effects of substance abuse and chemical dependency, or debilitating mental conditions on a lawyer's professional responsibilities) taught by a disbarred lawyer whose disbarment date is at least five years (60 months) prior to the date of the activity. The advertising for the activity shall disclose the lawyer's disbarment.

(e) Continuing legal education activities shall be conducted in a setting physically suitable to the educational activity of the program and, when appropriate, equipped with suitable writing surfaces or sufficient space for taking notes.

(f) Thorough, high quality, and carefully prepared written materials should be distributed to all attendees at or before the time the course is presented. These may include written materials printed from a computer presentation, computer website, or CD-ROM. A written agenda or outline for a presentation satisfies this requirement when written materials are not suitable or readily available for a particular subject. The absence of written materials for distribution should, however, be the exception and not the rule.

(g) Any accredited sponsor must remit fees as required and keep and maintain attendance records of each continuing legal education program sponsored by it, which shall be furnished to the board in accordance with regulations.

(h) Except as provided in Rules .1501 and .1604 of this subchapter, in-house continuing legal education and self-study shall not be approved or accredited for the purpose of complying with Rule .1518 of this subchapter.

(i) Programs that cross academic lines, such as accounting-tax seminars, may be considered for approval by the board. However, the board must be satisfied that the content of the activity would enhance legal skills or the ability to practice law.

History Note: Authority- Order of the North Carolina Supreme Court, October 7, 1987, 318 N.C. 711.Readopted Effective December 8, 1994

Amended March 1, 2001; October 1, 2003; February 5, 2009; March 11, 2010

.1520 Accreditation of Sponsors and Programs

(a) Accreditation of Sponsors. An organization desiring accreditation as an accredited sponsor of courses, programs, or other continuing legal education activities may apply for accredited sponsor status to the board. The board shall approve a sponsor as an accredited sponsor if it is satisfied that the sponsor's programs have met the standards set forth in Rule .1519 of this subchapter and regulations established by the board.

(b) Program Approval for Accredited Sponsors.

(1) Once an organization is approved as an accredited sponsor, the continuing legal education programs sponsored by that organization are presumptively approved for credit; however, application must be made to the board for approval. At least 50 days prior to the presentation of a program, an accredited sponsor shall file an application, on a form prescribed by the board, notifying the board of the dates and locations of presentations of the program and the sponsor's calculation of the CLE credit hours for the program.

(2) The board may at any time revoke the accreditation of an accredited sponsor for failure to satisfy the requirements of Rule .1512 and Rule .1519 of this subchapter, and for failure to satisfy the Regulations Governing the Administration of the Continuing Legal Education Program set forth in Section .1600 of this subchapter.

(3) The board shall evaluate a program presented by an accredited sponsor and, upon a determination that the program does not satisfy the requirements of Rule.1519, notify the accredited sponsor that the program is not approved for credit. Such notice shall be sent by the board to the accredited sponsor within 45 days after the receipt of the application. If notice is not sent to the accredited sponsor within the 45-day period, the program shall be presumed to be approved. The accredited sponsor may request reconsideration of an unfavorable accreditation decision by submitting a letter of appeal to the board within 15 days of receipt of the notice of disapproval. The decision by the board on an appeal is final.

(c) Unaccredited Sponsor Request for Program Approval.

(1) Any organization not accredited as an accredited sponsor that desires approval of a course or program shall apply to the board. The board shall adopt regulations to administer the accreditation of such programs consistent with the provisions of Rule .1519 of this subchapter. Applicants denied approval of a program may request reconsideration of such a decision by submitting a letter of appeal to the board within 15 days of receipt of the notice of disapproval. The decision by the board on an appeal is final.

(2) The board may at any time decline to accredit CLE programs offered by a non-accredited sponsor for a specified period of time, as determined by the board, for failure to comply with the requirements of Rule .1512, Rule.1519 and Section .1600 of this subchapter.

(d) Member Request for Program Approval. An active member desiring approval of a course or program that has not otherwise been approved shall apply to the board. The board that shall adopt regulations to administer approval requests consistent with the requirements Rule .1519 of this subchapter. Applicants denied approval of a program may request reconsideration of such a decision by submitting a letter of appeal to the board within 15 days of the receipt of the notice of disapproval. The decision by the board on an appeal is final.

(e) Records. The board may provide by regulation for the accredited sponsor, unaccredited sponsor, or active member for whom a continuing legal education program has been approved to maintain and provide such records as required by the board.

History Note: Authority- Order of the North Carolina Supreme Court, October 7, 1987, 318 N.C. 711.

Readopted Effective December 8, 1994

Amended February 27, 2003; March 3, 2005; October 7, 2010; March 6, 2014

.1521 Credit Hours

The board may designate by regulation the number of credit hours to be earned by participation, including, but not limited to, teaching, in continuing legal education activities approved by the board.

History Note: Authority—Order of the North Carolina Supreme Court, October 7, 1987, 318 N.C. 711.

Readopted Effective December 8, 1994

.1522 Annual Report and Compliance Period

(a) Annual Written Report. Commencing in 1989, each active member of the North Carolina State Bar shall provide an annual written report to the North Carolina State Bar in such form as the board shall prescribe by regulation concerning compliance with the continuing legal education program for the preceding year or declaring an exemption under Rule .1517 of this subchapter. The annual report form shall be corrected, if necessary, signed by the member, and promptly returned to the State Bar. Upon receipt of a signed annual report form, appropriate adjustments shall be made to the member's continuing legal education record with the State Bar. No further adjustments shall thereafter be made to the member's continuing legal education record unless, on or before July 31 of the year in which the report form is mailed to members, the member shows good cause for adjusting the member's continuing legal education record for the preceding year.

(b) Compliance Period. The period for complying with the requirements of Rule.1518 of this subchapter is January 1 to December 31. A member may complete the requirements for the year on or by the last day of February of the succeeding year provided, however, that this additional time shall be considered a grace period and no extensions of this grace period shall be granted. All members are encouraged to complete the requirements within the appropriate calendar year.

(c) Report. Prior to January 31 of each year, the prescribed report form concerning compliance with the continuing legal education program for the preceding year shall be mailed to all active members of the North Carolina State Bar.

(d) Late Filing Penalty. Any attorney who, for whatever reasons, files the report showing compliance or declaring an exemption after the due date of the last day of February shall pay a $75.00 late filing penalty. This penalty shall be submitted with the report. A report that is either received by the board or postmarked on or before the due date shall be considered timely filed. An attorney who is issued a notice to show cause pursuant to Rule .1523(b) shall pay a late compliance fee of $125.00 pursuant to Rule .1523(e) of this subchapter. The board may waive the late filing penalty or the late compliance fee upon a showing of hardship or serious extenuating circumstances or other good cause.

History Note: Authority—Order of the North Carolina Supreme Court, October 7, 1987, 318 N.C. 711.

Readopted Effective December 8, 1994

Amended October 1, 2003; March 3, 2005; March 2, 2006; October 9, 2008

.1523 Noncompliance

(a) Failure to Comply with Rules May Result in Suspension

A member who is required to file a report of CLE credits and does not do so or who fails to meet the minimum requirements of these rules, including the payment of duly assessed penalties and attendee fees, may be suspended from the practice of law in the state of North Carolina.

(b) Notice of Failure to Comply

The board shall notify a member who appears to have failed to meet the requirements of these rules that the member will be suspended from the practice of law in this state, unless the member shows good cause in writing why the suspension should not be made or the member shows in writing that he or she has complied with the requirements within the 30-day period after service of the notice. Notice shall be served on the member by mailing a copy thereof by registered or certified mail or designated delivery service (such as Federal Express or UPS), return receipt requested, to the last-known address of the member according to the records of the North Carolina State Bar or such later address as may be known to the person attempting service. Service of the notice may also be accomplished by (i) personal service by a State Bar investigator or by any person authorized by Rule 4 of the North Carolina Rules of Civil Procedure to serve process, or (ii) email sent to the email address of the member contained in the records of the North Carolina State Bar if the member sends an email from that same email address to the State Bar acknowledging such service.

(c) Entry of Order of Suspension Upon Failure to Respond to Notice to Show Cause

If a written response attempting to show good cause is not postmarked or received by the board by the last day of the 30-day period after the member was served with the notice to show cause upon the recommendation of the board and the Administrative Committee, the council may enter an order suspending the member from the practice of law. The order shall be entered and served as set forth in Rule .0903(c) of this subchapter.

(d) Procedure Upon Submission of a Timely Response to a Notice to Show Cause

(1) Consideration by the Board

If the member files a timely written response to the notice, the board shall consider the matter at its next regularly scheduled meeting or may delegate consideration of the matter to a duly appointed committee of the board. If the matter is delegated to a committee of the board and the committee determines that good cause has not been shown, the member may file an appeal to the board. The appeal must be filed within 30 calendar days of the date of the letter notifying the member of the decision of the committee. The board shall review all evidence presented by the member to determine whether good cause has been shown or to determine whether the member has complied with the requirements of these rules within the 30-day period after service of the notice to show cause.

(2) Recommendation of the Board

The board shall determine whether the member has shown good cause why the member should not be suspended. If the board determines that good cause has not been shown or that the member has not shown compliance with these rules within the 30-day period after service of the notice to show cause, then the board shall refer the matter to the Administrative Committee for hearing together with a written recommendation to the Administrative Committee that the member be suspended.

(3) Consideration by and Recommendation of the Administrative Committee

The Administrative Committee shall consider the matter at its next regularly scheduled meeting. The burden of proof shall be upon the member to show cause by clear, cogent, and convincing evidence why the member should not be suspended from the practice of law for the apparent failure to comply with the rules governing the continuing legal education program. Except as set forth above, the procedure for such hearing shall be as set forth in Rule .0903(d)(1) and (2) of this subchapter.

(4) Order of Suspension

Upon the recommendation of the Administrative Committee, the council may determine that the member has not complied with these rules and may enter an order suspending the member from the practice of law. The order shall be entered and served as set forth in Rule .0903(d)(3) of this subchapter.

(e) Late Compliance Fee

Any member to whom a notice to show cause is issued pursuant to paragraph (b) above shall pay a late compliance fee as set forth in Rule .1522(d) of this subchapter;

provided, however, upon a showing of good cause as determined by the board as described in paragraph (d)(2) above, the fee may be waived.

History Note: Authority- Order of the North Carolina Supreme Court, October 7, 1987, 318 N.C. 711.

Readopted Effective December 8, 1994

Amended March 7, 1996; March 6, 1997; February 3, 2000; October 1, 2003; October 9, 2008; August 23, 2012

.1524 Reinstatement

(a) Reinstatement Within 30 Days of Service of Suspension Order

A member who is suspended for noncompliance with the rules governing the continuing legal education program may petition the secretary for an order of reinstatement of the member's license at any time up to 30 days after the service of the suspension order upon the member. The secretary shall enter an order reinstating the member to active status upon receipt of a timely written request and satisfactory showing by the member that the member cured the continuing legal education deficiency for which the member was suspended. Such member shall not be required to file a formal reinstatement petition or pay a $250 reinstatement fee.

(b) Procedure for Reinstatement More that 30 Days After Service of the Order of Suspension

Except as noted below, the procedure for reinstatement more than 30 days after service of the order of suspension shall be as set forth in Rule.0904(c) and (d) of this subchapter, and shall be administered by Administrative Committee.

(c) Reinstatement Petition

At any time more than 30 days after service of an order of suspension on a member, a member who has been suspended for noncompliance with the rules governing the continuing legal education program may seek reinstatement by filing a reinstatement petition with the secretary. The secretary shall transmit a copy of the petition to each member of the board. The reinstatement petition shall contain the information and be in the form required by Rule .0904(c) of this subchapter. If not otherwise set forth in the petition, the member shall attach a statement to the petition in which the member shall state with particularity the accredited legal education courses which the member has attended and the number of credit hours obtained in order to cure any continuing legal education deficiency for which the member was suspended.

(d) Reinstatement Fee

In lieu of the $125.00 reinstatement fee required by Rule .0904(c)(4)(A), the petition shall be accompanied by a reinstatement fee payable to the board, in the amount of $250.00.

(e) Determination of Board; Transmission to Administrative Committee

Within 30 days of the filing of the petition for reinstatement with the secretary, the board shall determine whether the deficiency has been cured. The board's written determination and the reinstatement petition shall be transmitted to the secretary within five days of the determination by the board. The secretary shall transmit a copy of the petition and the board's recommendation to each member of the Administrative Committee.

(f) Consideration by Administrative Committee

The Administrative Committee shall consider the reinstatement petition, together with the board's determination, pursuant to the requirements of Rule.0902(c)-(f) of this subchapter.

(g) Hearing Upon Denial of Petition for Reinstatement

The procedure for hearing upon the denial by the Administrative Committee of a petition for reinstatement shall be as provided in Section.1000 of this subchapter.

History Note: Authority—Order of the North Carolina Supreme Court, October 7, 1987, 318 N.C. 711.

Readopted Effective December 8, 1994

Amended March 7, 1996; March 6, 1997; February 3, 2000; March 3, 2005

.1525 Reserved

.1526 Effective Date

(a) The effective date of these rules shall be January 1, 1988.

(b) Active members licensed prior to July 1 of any calendar year shall meet the continuing legal education requirements of these rules for such year.

(c) Active members licensed after June 30 of any calendar year must meet the continuing legal education requirements of these rules for the next calendar year.

History Note: Authority—Order of the North Carolina Supreme Court, October 7, 1987, 318 N.C. 711.

Readopted Effective December 8, 1994

.1527 Regulations

The following regulations (Section .1600 of the Rules of the North Carolina State Bar) for the continuing legal education program are hereby adopted and shall remain in effect until revised or amended by the board with the approval of the council. The board may adopt other regulations to implement the continuing legal education program with the approval of the council.

History Note: Authority—Order of the North Carolina Supreme Court, October 7, 1987, 318 N.C. 711.

Readopted Effective December 8, 1994

NORTH DAKOTA

NORTH DAKOTA RULES FOR CONTINUING LEGAL EDUCATION

Rule

1. Purpose.
2. State Commission for Continuing Legal Education.
3. Mandatory Continuing Legal Education, Report of Compliance.
4. Procedures and Penalty for Failure to Satisfy Educational Requirements.
5. Payment of Expenses.
6. Approved Course Work.
7. Judges Exempt.
8. Effective Dates.

Rule 1.   Purpose.

It is important to the Bar and to the public that attorneys continue their legal education throughout their active practice of law, and that attorneys who fail to do so should be prohibited from practicing law in the State of North Dakota.

Rule 2.   State commission for continuing legal education.

(a)   The Commission for Continuing Legal Education consists of seven members, one of whom shall be a chairman. Each member must be licensed to practice law in the State of North Dakota. The members of the Commission are appointed by the Board of Governors of the State Bar Association of North Dakota.

(b)   Members are appointed, for three-year terms.

(c)   A member may not serve more than two successive three-year terms. Each member serves until a successor is appointed and qualified. The chair of the Commission is appointed annually by the Board of Governors of the State Bar Association of North Dakota. The Board of Governors designates the Secretary-Treasurer of the Commission who has no vote. The chair and the other members of the Commission serve without compensation, but shall be paid their reasonable and necessary expenses incurred in the performance of their duties. The Secretary-Treasurer is allowed compensation for services, staff, and expenses as the Commission determines.

(d)   The Commission has general supervisory authority over the administration of these rules.

Rule 3.   **Mandatory Continuing Legal Education, Report of Compliance.**

    (a)   Except as qualified in section (b), each attorney duly admitted and licensed to practice in this State shall complete not less than 45 hours of approved course work in Continuing Legal Education during each three-year period the attorney is licensed in this State. Beginning in the 1993 reporting year, three hours of this forty-five hour triennial requirement shall be in the area of ethics or course work commonly considered professional responsibility, including coursework related to racial and ethnic diversity, gender equity, disability access, and the elimination of bias in the profession.

    (b)   A Report of Compliance, in the form set by the Commission, must be filed by each attorney with the Commission by July 30 after the close of each three-year reporting period for the attorney under the following schedule:

        (1)   The reporting periods for attorneys who were licensed to practice in this State prior to 1978 and who have secured an annual license to practice in this State every year since then are:
            (i)   from July 1, 1985, to June 30, 1988, for those whose last name in 1977 began with the letter A through G;
            (ii)   from July 1, 1986, to June 30, 1989, for those whose last name in 1977 began with the letter H through N; and
            (iii)   from July 1, 1984, to June 30, 1987, for those whose last name in 1977 began with the letter O through Z.

Subsequent reporting periods conclude on June 30 every three years thereafter.

        (2)   The reporting periods for all other attorneys begin on July 1 succeeding the date the attorney initially secures a license to practice in this State, or succeeding the date the attorney secures relicensure after a period of nonlicensure in this State of one or more years, and concludes on June 30th three years later. Subsequent reporting periods will conclude on June 30th every three years thereafter.

    (c)   Each attorney shall pay a fee not to exceed $25.00 as set by the Commission for expenses for operation of the Commission, to the State Bar Association of North Dakota -- Commission for Continuing Legal Education, at the time of filing the Report of Compliance.

Rule 4.   Procedures and penalty for failure to satisfy educational requirements.

    (a)   If an attorney fails to file a report, or the proof accompanying the report fails to establish to the satisfaction of the Commission that the attorney has complied with the minimum requirements for Continuing Legal Education, the Commission shall serve upon the attorney notice that the attorney has 60 days within which to comply with these rules or the requirements of the Commission and that failure to do so may result in a suspension of the attorney's right to practice law in this State. The attorney may request, within 20 days after issuance of the 60-day notice, the Commission to schedule a hearing at which the attorney may appear in person to discuss the Commission's determination of non-compliance.

        (i)   If a hearing is not timely requested and no proof of compliance is filed within 60 days of the date of the 60-day notice, it shall be deemed acquiescence by the attorney of the Commission's finding of non-compliance.

      (ii)   Upon the timely receipt of a request for hearing, the Commission shall set a date, time and place for hearing and notify the attorney of the hearing by first-class mail at least 10 days in advance of the hearing.

Unless compliance or good cause constituting extreme hardship is shown by the attorney within the 60 days set in the notice or, if requested, at the hearing, the Commission shall issue and file with the secretary-treasurer of the State Board of Law Examiners its findings of non-compliance and an order of suspension.

      (b)   An attorney not desiring licensure in North Dakota may request to be placed on inactive status. An attorney must make such a request in writing in the format in Appendix A no later than June 30 of the year in which the attorney's Report of Compliance is due. The request shall include a certification that the attorney is not subject to any pending discipline proceedings or investigations in any jurisdiction. Attorneys electing inactive status are not required to comply with continuing legal education reporting requirements.

      A lawyer not complying with the continuing legal education requirements and electing voluntary inactive status has special ethical concerns. An inactive lawyer may not represent any other person or business in legal matters or proceedings. The name of an inactive lawyer may not appear on a law firm letterhead without a qualification that the North Dakota license is inactive. A law firm name may continue to include the lawyer's name if the name was included prior to the lawyer's placement on inactive status. An inactive lawyer may not be listed as "of counsel" or otherwise be represented to clients or others as being able to undertake legal business.

      Law partners or associates knowingly allowing an inactive lawyer to continue practice violate the Rules of Professional Conduct. An inactive lawyer may not have a financial interest in a law firm that is a professional corporation except under a separation agreement allowing for payments to former partners or associates of a law firm. An inactive lawyer should promptly advise clients that the lawyer is unable to represent them and that they should retain other counsel.

      Reinstatement to active status from inactive status is governed by Rule 7 of the Admission to Practice Rules which allows the State Board of Law Examiners to examine the attorney's continuing legal education course work during the three-year period preceding the period of nonlicensure and the number of approved or approvable coursework hours received during the period of nonlicensure.

      (c)   Upon the filing of the Commission's findings of non-compliance and order of suspension with the secretary-treasurer of the State Board of Law Examiners, the attorney's license to practice law is suspended effective the 31st day of December after the order of suspension is filed with the secretary-treasurer of the State Board of Law Examiners. From that date forward the attorney is prohibited from engaging in the practice of law and is prohibited from securing a license to practice law in the State of North Dakota until the Commission issues and files with the secretary-treasurer of the State Board of Law Examiners findings of compliance and an order of reinstatement, or unless the attorney is relicensed under Rule 7 of the North Dakota Admission to Practice Rules. The order of suspension shall require the attorney to comply with Rule 6.3 of the North Dakota Rules for Lawyer Discipline pertaining to notification of clients regarding the suspension by December 31st unless an order of reinstatement has been entered.

At the time the order of suspension and findings of non-compliance are filed with the secretary-treasurer of the State Board of Law Examiners, the Commission shall serve, by certified mail -- return receipt requested, the findings of non-compliance and the order of suspension upon the attorney involved. At the same time the order of suspension and findings of non-compliance are filed with the secretary-treasurer of the State Board of Law Examiners a certified copy of the findings of non-compliance and the order of suspension shall be filed with the Clerk of the Supreme Court of the State of North Dakota.

(d)   If strict compliance by the attorney with the requirements of this rule is excused by the Commission because of a showing of extreme hardship, the Commission may extend the reporting period for the attorney or make other reasonable accommodations consistent with the spirit of these rules, subject to reasonable limitations and conditions as the Commission imposes.

(e)   An attorney subject to an order of suspension issued by the Commission may have his or her license to practice law reinstated by 1) completing the number of hours of approved coursework in Continuing Legal Education which the Commission has determined the attorney to be delinquent, 2) filing proof of such compliance with the Commission within one year from the date of issuance of the order of suspension, and 3) filing the proof of compliance with Rule 6.3 of the North Dakota Rules for Lawyer Discipline within the time period specified in Rule 6.3(f). If an attorney timely files proof of such compliance, the Commission shall issue and file with the secretary-treasurer of the State Board of Law Examiners and the Clerk of the Supreme Court of the State of North Dakota its findings of compliance and an order of reinstatement. Upon such filing with the secretary-treasurer of the State Board of Law Examiners, the attorney's license to practice and right to practice law in this State shall be reinstated, provided the attorney's certificate of admission to the bar has not otherwise been revoked or suspended by the Supreme Court.

(f)   Reports of compliance received after the issuance of a 60-day notice as described in subpart (a) and the reports of compliance of lawyers who have been granted extensions by the Commission, and which are in turn received by the Commission within the granted period of extension, shall be accompanied by a late filing fee of $25.00 made out to the North Dakota Commission for Continuing Legal Education in addition to the fee required by Rule 3(c). Reports received after the expiration of the 60-day notice period or after the expiration of an extension period shall be accompanied by a late filing fee of $75.00 made out to the North Dakota Commission for Continuing Legal Education in addition to the fee required by Rule 3(c).

(g)   The number of hours of approved coursework in Continuing Legal Education completed by an attorney in bringing the attorney into compliance with an order of suspension issued by the Commission, in the year succeeding the order, may not be applied to the number of hours reportable to the Commission by the attorney in the subsequent three-year reporting period applicable to the attorney.

(h)   An attorney whose license has been suspended, who does not qualify for a license under section (d), and who seeks licensure must file an application for a license with the State Board of Law Examiners in the manner prescribed in Rule 7 of the North Dakota Admission to Practice Rules.

(i)   Within 20 days of receipt of the Commission's order of suspension, any attorney aggrieved by a decision of the Commission may petition the North Dakota Supreme Court for review of the decision. Any petition filed with the Court must be accompanied by a signed affidavit stating that a copy of the petition had been sent by first-class mail to the Commission on or before the date of filing the petition. The filing of the petition and affidavit vacates the decision of the Commission. No transcript of the Commission's proceedings is required. The record on review consists of all relevant documents maintained by the Commission, the written decision of the Commission, and any other documents submitted by the attorney to the Commission. The attorney and Commission may submit briefs to the Court within 20 days after the filing of the petition. If requested by either the attorney or Commission within 10 days after the filing of the petition, the Court may set a hearing for oral arguments on the petition. The attorney has the burden of showing proof of compliance with these rules by a preponderance of the evidence.(Adopted on an emergency basis August 17, 1993; amended and re-approved February 2, 1994; amended effective November 1, 2000; August 1, 2001.)

Rule 5.   Payment of expenses.

The employees and members of the Commission are entitled to reimbursement for all necessary expenses incurred in the performance of their official duties. Each claim must be certified by the individual seeking payment.

Rule 6.   Approved course work.

(a)   The Commission determines what constitutes "approved course work." It may issue and publish advance guidelines or evaluate courses and supporting information as submitted for approval. It may also approve courses after they had been presented. Courses sponsored by the following organizations, and their associated entities, are presumptively approved:

(1)   State bar associations;
(2)   Accredited law schools;
(3)   American Bar Association;
(4)   American Law Institute;
(5)   Practicing Law Institute.

(b)   The Commission shall cooperate with the Continuing Legal Education Committee of the State Bar Association of North Dakota, the University of North Dakota School of Law, and other educational institutions within the State to promote Continuing Legal Education within the State.

(c)   The Commission shall publish quarterly, in the newsletter of the State Bar Association of North Dakota, a list of Continuing Legal Education courses and activities that are available to attorneys within the State of North Dakota, and may include courses available elsewhere.

Rule 7.   **Judges exempt.**

These rules do not apply to Judges who are prohibited by the Code of Judicial Conduct from engaging in the private practice of law. (Amended 3/24/87; 1/01/94)

Rule 8.   **Effective dates.**

The Commission for Continuing Legal Education was established on September 1, 1977. The remainder of the original rules became effective January 1, 1978, and all applications of the rules are prospective.

Rule 9.   Title and citation.

These rules are titled, "North Dakota Rules for Continuing Legal Education" and may be cited as "N.D.R. Continuing Legal Ed.""

EXPLANATORY NOTE

The North Dakota Rules for Continuing Legal Education were adopted July 27, 1977. Rules 1, 3 and 4 were subsequently amended as emergency rules December 1, 1986, and adopted as permanent rules March 24, 1987. Rule 7 was amended March 24, 1987. The above Rule incorporates the previous amendments adopted March 24, 1987, and those approved November 22, 1988, which were effective December 31, 1988. Rule 3 was further amended June 24, 1992. Emergency amendments to Rule 4 were adopted August 17, 1993, and subsequently amended and readopted February 2, 1994. Nonsubstantive amendments to the permanent rules were adopted February 2, 1994. Changes to the filing fee in Rule 3 were changed on November 1, 1998. Rule 4 was amended effective November 1, 2000, to include the language regarding notice to clients of the suspension as required in Rule 6.3 of the ND Rules for Lawyer Discipline.

2000

Rule 4: Incorporate reference to Rule 6.3 of the ND Rules for Lawyer Discipline requiring lawyers receiving a CLE suspension to provide clients with a notice of the suspension within 10 days of the suspension.

1993

Rule 4:   Amended to allow an inactive status for attorneys not planning on continuing the practice of law in ND. Included language concerning the ethical restraints placed upon the attorney and associated firm when placed on inactive status. Referenced to Rules of Admissions for obtaining license again.

Rule 7:   Deleted following language: "Rules of Judicial Conduct" and inserted: "Code of Judicial Conduct". Order of adoption issued 10/20/93...effective 01/01/94.

NORTHERN MARIANA ISLANDS

COMMONWEALTH RULES FOR
CONTINUING LEGAL EDUCATION

Section 1: Purpose

The purpose of these rules is to establish minimal continuing legal education requirements for each active lawyer admitted to the practice of law in the Commonwealth of the Northern Mariana Islands in order to maintain and increase professional competence.

Section 2: Committee on Continuing Legal Education (CLE)

(a)   The CNMI Bar Association President shall appoint a Continuing Legal Education Committee (CLEC) composed of three (3) members.

(b)   The CLEC shall have the following duties:

(1) Administer this rule; and

(2) Report at least annually to the CNMI Bar and the Commonwealth Supreme Court.

Section 3: Continuing Legal Education Requirement

(a)   Every active lawyer in the Commonwealth shall complete twenty (20) hours of Continuing Legal Education every two years. An active lawyer is defined as a person who has active status in the CNMI Bar Association. The reporting requirement for lawyers who are not active lawyers for the entire compliance period shall be prorated based upon the month of admission. Provided that, former full time judges or justices of the courts of the Commonwealth of the Northern Mariana Islands, who are now active members of the CNMI Bar Association, shall be exempt from any of the Continuing Legal Education requirements provided for in these rules.

(b)   The CLE requirement may be met by either attending courses or by completing any other continuing legal education activity approved for credit by the ABA, approved CLE in other US jurisdictions, the CLEC, or the Commonwealth Supreme Court. Self-study, including viewing approved videotapes, audiotapes, other means of electronic communication, teaching, writing for CLE publications, pro bono services in family court and criminal actions, participation in educational activities involving the use of computer-based resources, participation in conferences, seminars and/or training programs, the Bar Association's Mock Trial Program, and in-office law firm continuing legal education efforts, may be considered for credit when they meet the conditions set forth in this rule.

(c) In addition to the requirements under Section 3(a), every attorney admitted after July 1, 2002 shall attend and complete a course in Professionalism sponsored jointly by the Commonwealth Supreme Court and the CNMI Bar Association.

Section 4: Reporting CLE Credit

(a) CLE credits shall be reported annually every other year, in the even-numbered years on or before February 15th. The two calendar year period (January 1 to December 31) immediately preceding the even year reporting shall hereinafter be referred to as the reporting period. Five credit hours of approved CLE credits earned in one reporting period but not used during that reporting period may be carried to over to the next reporting period.

(b) A lawyer shall report approved activities in a statement of compliance which lists specifically courses taken, videotapes or audiotapes listened to, course of self-study, or pro bono work, the dates on which the activity took place, and the amount of time taken. The statement shall be certified as correct under penalty of perjury.

Section 5: Approved Educational Activities

(a) Educational Activities From Other Jurisdictions: Courses or activities offered by a provider accredited or approved by a CLEC in another jurisdiction or a national CLE accrediting body will be approved automatically for credit. CLE programs sponsored by the federal or local judiciary in the CNMI or Guam, or by the CNMI or Guam Bar Associations are automatically approved for credit. Attendance and participation in conferences, seminars and/or training programs not otherwise accredited or approved by any jurisdiction's CLEC committee may be approved for credit upon review by the CLEC.

(b) In-Office CLE: Courses offered by law firms, either individually or with other law firms, corporate legal departments, government attorneys or similar entities primarily for the education of their members may be approved for credit.

(c) Self-Study: In addition to formal courses conducted in a class or seminar setting, the CLEC shall accredit self-study classes involving the use of audio or videotapes, computers, or correspondence. The CLEC shall initially list those audio and videotapes available to attorneys located in the courts and law libraries which qualify for credit and shall circulate this list among the active attorneys.

(d) Teaching: A lawyer who teaches law classes or presents lectures on the law, whether to other lawyers or to members of the general public, shall be provided credit for his or her preparation time and teaching time. A one-time credit will be given for teaching such a course or lecture. No further credit shall be given for subsequent presentations of the same material to different audiences.

(e) Pro-Bono: A lawyer who renders pro bono legal services shall receive one credit hour for every four hours of legal services actually performed, not to exceed a total of five (5) CLE credits awarded for pro bono services in a calendar year or ten (10) per reporting period. A pro bono case is one taken initially with an agreement that there would be no charge for professional services. Credit for pro bono services will only be given for the period in which the work was performed.

(f) Bar Committees: Any member who sits on a bona fide Bar Committee, is an appointed or elected bar representative or is an Officer or Board Member of the Bar shall receive two (2) credits hour for each year of service. A maximum of four (4) credit hours per reporting period may be earned in this way.

(g) Writing a Professional Article: Any member who writes a professional article that is to be published may receive up to five credits per article.

(h) Mock Trial: The Bar Coordinator of the Mock Trial shall be given five (5) hours per year of service, with a maximum of ten (10) credit hours per reporting period. Mock-trial Attorney-Coaches shall be given one credit for every one hour of coaching up to a maximum of five (5) credit hours per year and a maximum of ten (10) CLE credits for each reporting period. Attorneys who sit as judges or jurors in the actual competition are eligible for one (1) credit hour per year and a maximum of two (2) per reporting period.

Section 6: Sanctions

(a) Notice of Delinquency: Within thirty (30) days after the annual reporting date the CLEC shall send each lawyer not in compliance with the requirement of this rule a notice of delinquency will post within the Bar's web site the names of the lawyers not in compliance with the requirements of this rule and mail via US Mail, return receipt requested, to each attorney, at the last mailing address provided to the Bar Association by the attorney, a notice of delinquency. A fee of $100 must be paid to the CNMI Bar Association by any attorney who files his or her report in a reporting year after the February 15 deadline. Filing a report that indicates on its face that the minimum CLE requirement has not been met shall be deemed a non-filing.

(b) Cure: Within ninety (90) days following the annual reporting date, the lawyer shall take steps necessary to meet the annual requirements of the rule for the prior reporting period, or submit a statement of compliance.

(c) Failure to Cure: After this ninety (90) day period, if the lawyer fails to report CLE credits sufficient to permit retroactive compliance with the rule or fails to submit a statement of compliance, the CLEC shall file a notice of noncompliance with the Commonwealth Supreme Court. An additional fee of $150 (total $250) must be paid to the CNMI Bar Association by any attorney who files his or her report in a reporting year after June 20.

(d)   Suspension and Reinstatement: Any order for suspension shall provide for reinstatement upon completion by the suspended attorney of the required hours as proven upon the lawyer's petition for reinstatement, complete payment of all fees as indicated above, and any other requirements the Supreme Court deems appropriate, including, but not limited to, payment of the Courts' and Bar Association's related costs. The petition for reinstatement shall be filed with the Commonwealth Supreme Court, with a copy provided to the CNMI Bar Association.

Section 7: Compliance

(a)   Record Keeping
        (1)   Every active member shall maintain records of participation in CLE activities for use in completing a compliance report and shall retain these records for a period of twelve months after the end of the member's reporting period.
        (2)   In furtherance of its audit responsibilities, the CLEC may ask to review an active member's records of participation in CLE activities. Records which may satisfy such a request include, but are not limited to, certificates of attendance or transcripts issued by sponsors, CLE record keeping forms, cancelled checks or other proof of payment for registration fees or audio or video tapes, course materials, notes or annotations to course materials, or daily calendars for the dates of CLE activities. With regard to individually screened audio or video presentations, contemporaneously made records of screening dates and times may be required.
        (3)   The CLEC is not required to maintain records of active members' participation in CLE activities, except as necessary to verify compliance with the CLE requirement.

(b)   Audits
        (1)   The CLEC may audit compliance reports selected because of facial defects or by random selection or other appropriate method.
        (2)   For the purpose of conducting audits, the CLEC may request and review records of participation in CLE activities reported by active members.
        (3)   Failure to adequately substantiate participation in CLE activities after request by CLEC shall result in disallowance of credits for the reported activity and assessment of the late filing fee(s) specified in Section 6.

(c) Noncompliance.

    (1)   Grounds. The following are considered grounds for a finding of non-compliance with these Rules:

        (i)   Failure to complete the CLE requirement for the applicable reporting period.

        (ii)   Failure to file a completed compliance report on time.

        (iii)   Failure to provide sufficient records of participation in CLE activities to substantiate credits reported, after request by the CLEC.

    (2)   Notice. In the event of a finding of noncompliance, the CLEC shall serve, by certified mail to the last mailing address provided to the Bar Association by the member, a written notice of noncompliance on the affected active member. The notice shall state the nature of the noncompliance and shall summarize the applicable rules regarding noncompliance and its consequences.

(d) Cure.

    (1)   Noncompliance for failure to file a completed compliance report by the due date can be cured by filing the completed report demonstrating completion of the CLE requirement during the applicable report period, together with the late fee specified Rule 6 above within ninety calendar days following mailing of the notice of noncompliance.

    (2)   Credit hours applied to a previous reporting period for the purpose of curing noncompliance may only be used for that purpose and may not be used to satisfy the CLE requirement for any other reporting period.

(e) Suspension. If the noncompliance is not cured within the deadline specified in this Rule, the name of the lawyer shall be recommended to the Supreme Court for suspension.

Section 8: Review and Enforcement

(a) Review.

    (1)   Decisions of the CLE Committee. A decision, other than a suspension recommended pursuant to Section 7(e), affecting any active member is final unless a request for review is filed with the CLEC within 30 days after notice of the decision is mailed. The request for review may be by letter and requires no special form, but it shall state the decision to be reviewed and give the reasons for review. The matter shall be reviewed by the Bar Association Board of Directors (BOD) at its next regular meeting. An active member shall have the right, upon request, to be heard, and any such hearing request shall be made in the initial letter.

(b) <u>Decisions of the CLE Committee.</u> A decision of the CLEC may be reviewed by the BOD on written request of the affected active member or sponsor.

(c) <u>Reinstatement.</u> An active member suspended for noncompliance with the CLE requirement shall be reinstated only upon completion of the CLE requirement, submission of completed compliance report to the bar, payment of the late filing fee of $250, and reinstatement fees, and compliance with the applicable provisions of the Rules of Procedure and any relevant orders of the Supreme Court.

Section 9: Citation

These rules may be cited as "Com.R.C.L.E. _____".

OHIO

RULE X. CONTINUING LEGAL EDUCATION

Section 1. Purpose; Construction.

(A) The purpose of this rule is to maintain and improve the quality of legal and judicial services in Ohio by requiring continuing legal education for Ohio attorneys and regulating the provision of continuing legal education to Ohio judges.

(B) This rule and regulations adopted under authority of this rule by the Supreme Court Commission on Continuing Legal Education shall be construed liberally to accomplish the purpose of this rule.

(C) As used in this rule, "judge" includes the Chief Justice and Justices of the Supreme Court.

Section 2. Supreme Court Commission on Continuing Legal Education.

(A)(1) There is hereby created the Supreme Court Commission on Continuing Legal Education, consisting of nineteen members appointed by the Supreme Court, as follows:

    (a) Twelve attorneys licensed to practice law in Ohio, one from each appellate district;

    (b) One dean or member of a law faculty engaged in full-time legal education in an Ohio law school;

    (c) Five judges;

    (d) One member who shall not be an attorney.

(2) Terms of office shall be three years. Members shall be eligible for reappointment, but shall not serve more than two full terms. A member appointed to fill a vacancy occurring prior to the expiration of the term shall hold office for the remainder of the unexpired term. If an attorney member no longer resides or practices in the district from which the attorney is appointed, if the educator or dean member is no longer engaged in full-time legal education in an Ohio law school, or if a judge member leaves office, the member shall be disqualified and a vacancy shall occur.

(3) Each year, the Commission shall elect a chair, a vice-chair, and other officers as are necessary. The Commission shall meet at the call of the chair or upon written request of a majority of the members. A majority of the members duly appointed and qualified constitutes a quorum. No action shall be taken by the Commission without the concurrence of a majority of the members constituting a quorum at that meeting.

(4) Members shall serve without compensation, but shall be reimbursed for expenses incurred in the performance of their official duties.

(B)(1) The Commission shall administer the continuing legal education requirements of this rule and Rule IV of the Rules for the Government of the Judiciary of Ohio, including promulgating regulations and performing other administrative functions necessary to carry out the duties of the Commission.

(2) The Director of Attorney Services or the Director's designee shall serve as Secretary of the Commission.

(3) The Commission shall accredit continuing legal education programs, activities, and sponsors and establish procedures for accreditation. The Commission, by regulation, may assess reasonable application fees for accreditation, sponsors that submit a program or activity for accreditation, or both.

(4) The Commission shall accredit mayor's court continuing education courses and sponsors pursuant to the Mayor's Court Education and Procedure Rules and establish procedures for accreditation.

(5) The Commission shall establish procedures for awarding credits toward the completion of the continuing legal education requirements of this rule and Gov. Jud. R. IV.

(6) The Commission shall endeavor to make accredited programs and activities on a variety of subjects available at a reasonable cost to attorneys and judges in all areas of the state.

(7) The Commission shall not sponsor programs and activities for continuing legal education.

(8) The Commission shall report, at least annually, to the Supreme Court concerning the activities of the Commission and the status of continuing legal education in the state.

(C) Commission operations shall be funded by the Attorney Services Fund established pursuant to Gov. Bar R. VI. All fees collected pursuant to this rule shall be deposited in the Attorney Services Fund.

(D) At the request of the Administrative Director of the Supreme Court, the Secretary of the Commission shall prepare and submit a proposed budget for approval by the Supreme Court.

(E) Records of the Commission shall be public records.

Section 3. Continuing Legal Education Requirements for Attorneys.

(A) *Total credit hours.* Each attorney admitted to the practice of law in this state and each attorney registered for corporate status pursuant to Gov. Bar R. VI, Section 3 shall complete a minimum of twenty-four credit hours of continuing legal education for each biennial compliance period.

(B) *Professional conduct credit hours.* As part of the minimum twenty-four credit hours of continuing legal education required by division (A) of this section, an attorney shall complete a minimum of two and one-half credit hours of instruction on one or any combination of the following professional conduct topics:

(1) Legal ethics, which shall include instruction on the Ohio Rules of Professional Conduct;

(2) Professionalism, which shall include instruction on the role of attorneys in promoting ethics and professionalism among attorneys by facilitating compliance with the requirements of the Ohio Rules of Professional Conduct, "A Lawyer's Creed," "A Lawyer's Aspirational Ideals," and the "Statement Regarding the Provision of Pro Bono Legal Services by Ohio Lawyers" adopted by the Supreme Court;

(3) Alcoholism, substance abuse, or mental health issues, which shall include instruction on any of their causes, prevention, detection, and treatment alternatives, as applicable;

(4) Access to justice and fairness in the courts and how these issues impact public trust and confidence in the judicial system and the perception of justice in Ohio, which shall include instruction on one or any combination of the following topics:

(a) Interacting with self-represented litigants;

(b) Encouraging pro bono representation;

(c) Accommodating language interpretation;

(d) Assuring fairness in matters of race, ethnicity, foreign origin, religion, gender, sexual orientation, disability, socio-economic status, or other relevant topics.

(C) *Single or multiple programs or activities.* The instruction related to professional conduct required by division (B) of this section may be obtained in a single program or activity or in separate programs or activities that include one or more of the subjects set forth in that division.

Section 4. Biennial Compliance Periods.

An attorney whose last name begins with a letter from A through L shall complete the number of continuing legal education credit hours required by Section 3 of this rule on or before December 31st of each odd-numbered year. An attorney whose last name begins with a letter from M through Z shall complete the number of continuing legal education credit hours required by Section 3 of this rule on or before December 31st of each even-numbered year. If the name of an attorney changes after the attorney is admitted to the practice of law or registers for corporate status pursuant to Gov. Bar R. VI, Section 3, the attorney shall remain in the same alphabetical grouping for purposes of meeting the requirements of this section.

Section 5. Allowance of Credit Hours.

(A) *Amount of credit hours.* Sixty minutes of actual instruction or other approved activity shall constitute one credit hour.

(B) *Continuing legal education teaching credit.* The Supreme Court Commission on Continuing Legal Education may allow up to three credit hours to an instructor for each credit hour taught in an approved continuing legal education program or activity the first time the program or activity is presented by that instructor, two credit hours for each credit hour taught as part of a panel presentation in an approved program or activity the first time the program or activity is presented by that instructor, and one credit hour for each credit hour taught in subsequent presentations of the same program or activity by that instructor, with a maximum of one-half the required credit hours for teaching during the biennial compliance period.

(C) *Law school teaching credit.* The Commission may allow one-half credit hour for each semester hour taught at a law school accredited by the American Bar Association. Prorated credit may be granted for quarter or trimester hours.

(D) *Publication of article or book credit.* The Commission may allow up to twelve credit hours for the publication of an article or book personally authored by the applicant, with a maximum of twelve credit hours for publications during a biennial compliance period.

(E) *Self-study credit.* The Commission may allow up to twelve credit hours for approved self-study during a biennial compliance period.

(F) *Law school course credit.* The Commission may allow three credit hours for each semester hour of a course taken at a law school accredited by the American Bar Association. Prorated credit may be granted for quarter or trimester hours.

(G) *Mayor's court education credit.* The Commission may allow one credit hour for every two credit hours of accredited mayor's court education completed by an attorney for the purpose of serving as a mayor's court magistrate pursuant to section 1905.05 of the Revised Code.

(H) *Pro bono credit*. The Commission may allow one credit hour for every six hours of pro bono legal service performed, with a maximum of six credit hours for service performed during a biennial compliance period. As used in this rule, "pro bono" means legal service provided to either a person of limited means or a charitable organization in which the legal service is assigned, verified, and reported to the Commission by any of the following:

(1) An organization receiving funding for pro bono programs or services from the Legal Services Corporation or the Ohio Legal Assistance Foundation;

(2) A metropolitan or county bar association;

(3) The Ohio State Bar Association;

(4) The Ohio Legal Assistance Foundation;

(5) Any other organization recognized by the Commission as providing pro bono programs or services in Ohio.

Section 6. Standards for Granting Credit Hours.

In establishing standards for the granting of credit hours for continuing legal education programs or activities, the Supreme Court Commission on Continuing Legal Education shall consider all of the following:

(A) The program or activity shall have significant intellectual or practical content and the primary objective shall be to improve the participant's professional competence as an attorney or judge;

(B) A program or activity for attorneys shall be an organized program of learning dealing with matters directly related to the practice of law, professional responsibility or ethical obligations, law office economics, or similar subjects that promotes the purposes of this rule. A program or activity for judges shall be an organized program of learning dealing with matters directly related to the law or judicial administration that promotes the purposes of Gov. Jud. R. IV.

(C) The program or activity may consist of live instruction or other methods as approved in advance by the Commission, including the use of self-study materials, and that are prepared and conducted by an individual or a group qualified by practical or academic experience;

(D) The program or activity shall be presented in a setting physically suited to the educational activity of the program or activity;

(E) The program or activity should include thorough, high-quality written materials.

Section 7. Proration of Credit Hours.

(A) *Attorney who becomes subject to rule during biennial compliance period.* An attorney who becomes subject to this rule during a biennial compliance period may have the continuing legal education requirements under Section 3 of this rule prorated by the Supreme Court Commission on Continuing Legal Education pursuant to CLE Regulation 305 for the biennial compliance period in which the attorney is subject to this rule.

(B) *Former inactive or retired attorney.* Upon registration as active, an attorney who was registered as inactive pursuant to Gov. Bar R. VI, Section 2 or as retired pursuant to former Gov. Bar R. VI, Section 3 may have the attorney's continuing legal education requirements under Section 3 of this rule prorated pursuant to CLE Regulation 305 for the biennial compliance period in which the attorney registers as active.

(C) *Attorney with military exemption.* An attorney who is granted a military exemption pursuant to Section 12(A)(1) of this rule and whose exemption is terminated may have the attorney's continuing legal education requirements under Section 3 of this rule prorated pursuant to CLE Regulation 305 for the prorated period in which the exemption ends.

(D) *Attorney exempt from rule for more than two years.* An attorney who was exempt for more than two years from the requirements of this rule pursuant to Section 12(A) of this rule may have the attorney's continuing legal education requirements prorated pursuant to CLE Regulation 305 for the biennial compliance period in which the exemption ends.

Section 8. Carryover of Credit Hours.

If the Supreme Court Commission on Continuing Legal Education determines that an attorney has timely completed in a biennial compliance period more than the number of continuing legal education credit hours required by Section 3 of this rule, the Commission may apply a maximum of twelve general credit hours to the next biennial compliance period.

Section 9. Newly-Admitted and Corporate Registered Attorneys.

(A) *Exemption from continuing legal education requirements.* An attorney newly admitted to the practice of law or registered for corporate status under Gov. Bar R. VI, Section 3 shall be exempt from the continuing legal educational requirements of Section 3 of this rule during the attorney's first biennial compliance period, provided that if the attorney is admitted to the practice of law or registered for corporate status during the second year of the attorney's biennial compliance period, the attorney shall be exempt during the biennial compliance period that follows the attorney's year of admission or year of initial corporate registration. However, the attorney shall complete the New Lawyers Training instruction in accordance with Section 14 of this rule by the deadline set forth in this division.

(B) *Exemption from New Lawyers Training*. The following newly admitted attorneys shall be exempt from the New Lawyers Training instruction requirements of Section 14 of this rule, but shall otherwise comply with the applicable requirements of this rule:

(1)

(2) Section 9.

(C) the continuing legal educational requirements of Section 3 of this rule because the attorney has been registered as inactive and subsequently registers as active, the attorney shall complete the New Lawyers Training instruction in accordance with Section 14 of this rule by the end of the biennial compliance period in which active status is reinstated or, if the attorney's exemption ends

An attorney registered as inactive pursuant to Gov. Bar R. VI, Section 2; An attorney admitted to the practice of law in Ohio pursuant to Gov. Bar R. I,

Attorney previously registered as inactive. If an attorney has been exempt from on or after July 1st of the second year of the attorney's biennial compliance period, by the end of the next biennial compliance period.

(D) *Termination of exemption*. If an attorney has been granted an exemption by the Supreme Court Commission on Continuing Legal Education pursuant to Section 12(A) of this rule, which exempts the attorney from completing the New Lawyers Training instruction in accordance with Section 14 of this rule, and the exemption is subsequently terminated, the attorney shall complete the New Lawyers Training instruction by the end of the biennial compliance period in which the exemption is terminated or, if the exemption ends on or after July 1st of the second year of the attorney's biennial compliance period, by the end of the next biennial compliance period.

Section 10. Magistrates.

(A) *Definition*. As used in this section, "magistrate" means an individual appointed by a court pursuant to Rule 53 of the Ohio Rules of Civil Procedure, Rule 40 of the Ohio Rules of Juvenile Procedure, Rule 14 of the Ohio Traffic Rules, or Rule 19 of the Ohio Rules of Criminal Procedure.

(B) *Credit hours*. As part of the continuing legal education requirements of this rule, a magistrate shall complete a minimum of ten credit hours of continuing legal education for each biennial compliance period that are offered by the Supreme Court of Ohio Judicial College and that do not consist solely of the classroom instruction on professional conduct required by Section 3(B) of this rule.

(C) *Registration*. Each magistrate shall register annually with the Secretary of the Supreme Court Commission on Continuing Legal Education in a manner authorized by the Commission.

Section 11. Acting Judges.

(A) *Definition*. As used in this section, an "acting judge" means a person appointed by a judge of a municipal or county court pursuant to sections 1901.10, 1901.12, or 1907.14 of the Revised Code.

(B) *Credit hours*. As part of the continuing legal education requirements of this rule, an acting judge shall complete a minimum of ten credit hours of continuing legal education instruction for each biennial compliance period that are offered by the Supreme Court of Ohio Judicial College that do not consist solely of the classroom instruction on professional conduct required by Section 3(B) of this rule.

(C) *Registration*. Each acting judge shall register annually with the Secretary of the Supreme Court Commission on Continuing Legal Education in a manner authorized by the Commission.

(D) *Emergency appointment*. Divisions (B) and (C) of this section shall not apply to an acting judge appointed due to both of the following reasons:

(1) An event or circumstance that is unforeseen and requires the appointing judge to be away from the court, including but not limited to a family illness or death;

(2) No acting judge who is registered pursuant to division (C) of this section is available or the application for a visiting judge or retired judge sitting by assignment of the Chief Justice of the Supreme Court would be impracticable.

(E) *Length of emergency appointment*. The appointment of an acting judge to whom division (D) of this section applies shall last no longer than twenty-four hours or until the conclusion of the next day the court regularly is open if the appointment is made on a weekend, holiday, or other day on which the court is not open.

Section 12. Exemptions.

(A) *Exemption by Commission*. Upon approval by the Supreme Court Commission on Continuing Legal Education, the following attorneys may be exempted from the requirements of Section 3 of this rule:

(1) An attorney on full-time military duty who does not engage in the private practice of law in Ohio;

(2) An attorney suffering from severe, prolonged illness or disability preventing participation in accredited continuing legal education programs and activities for the duration of the illness or disability;

(3) An attorney who has demonstrated special circumstances unique to that attorney and constituting good cause to grant an exemption for a period not to exceed one year and subject to any prorated adjustment of the continuing legal education requirements.

(B) *Substitute program or activity.* An attorney who, because of a permanent physical disability or other compelling reason, has difficulty attending programs or activities may request, and the Commission may grant, approval of a substitute program or activity.

(C) *Temporary certified attorney, foreign legal consultant, or pro hac vice admitted attorney.* A person certified to practice law temporarily pursuant to Gov. Bar R. IX, a foreign legal consultant registered pursuant to Gov. Bar R. XI, or an attorney registered with the Office of Attorney Services for pro hac vice admission pursuant to Gov. Bar R. XII shall be exempt from the requirements of this rule.

(D) *Federal judges and magistrate judges.* The following attorneys are exempt from the requirements of this rule while in office:

(1) United States judges appointed to office for life pursuant to Article III of the United States Constitution;

(2) (3) (E)

Section 13. Disciplined Attorneys.

An attorney against whom a definite or an indefinite suspension is imposed pursuant to Gov. Bar R. V shall complete one credit hour of continuing legal education for each month, or portion of a month, of the suspension. As part of the total credit hours of continuing legal education required under this section, the attorney shall complete one credit hour of the instruction related to professional conduct required by Section 3(B) of this rule for each six months, or portion of six months, of the suspension.

Section 14. New Lawyers Training.

(A) *Requirement.*

(1) Each attorney newly admitted to the practice of law or registered for corporate status under Gov. Bar R. VI, Section 3 shall complete a minimum of twelve credit hours of New Lawyers Training instruction in the time frame set forth in Section 9(A) of this rule. The twelve credit hours of instruction shall include both of the following:

(a) Three credit hours of instruction in professionalism, law office management, and client fund management consisting of sixty minutes of instruction on topics related to professional conduct, professional relationships, obligations of attorneys, or aspirational ideals of the profession; sixty minutes of instruction on topics related to fundamental law office management practices; and sixty minutes of instruction on topics related to client fund management;

(b) Nine credit hours of instruction in one or more substantive law topics that focus on handling legal matters in specific practice areas.

(2) An attorney newly admitted to the practice of law or registered for corporate status under Gov. Bar R. VI, Section 3 may satisfy the New Lawyers Training instruction requirement of division (A)(1) of this section by participating in and successfully completing the Supreme Court Lawyer to Lawyer Mentoring Program, provided the attorney also completes three credit hours of instruction on professionalism, law office management, and client fund management as required in division (A)(1)(a) of this section.

United States bankruptcy judges; United States magistrate judges.

Inactive and retired attorneys. An attorney registered as inactive pursuant to Gov. Bar R. VI, Section 2 or as retired pursuant to former Gov. Bar R. VI, Section 3 shall be exempt from the requirements of this rule.

(B) *Approval of activity.* To be approved by the Supreme Court Commission on Continuing Legal Education as a New Lawyers Training activity, the activity shall satisfy the following standards, together with any other standards as established by regulation of the Commission:

(1) The activity shall consist of live instruction in a setting physically suited to the educational activity of the program;

(2) The activity shall be a minimum of one hour in length;

(3) The activity shall include thorough, high-quality, written materials that emphasize

and include checklists of procedures to follow, practical instructions, and forms with guidance as to how they should be completed and when they should be used.

(C) *Carryover hours.* An attorney subject to Section 9(A) of this rule who completes more than the number of New Lawyers Training credit hours required under division (A)(1) of this section may be awarded a maximum of twelve general credit hours to the next biennial compliance period.

(D) *Awarding of general credit hours.* The Commission may award one credit hour of continuing legal education for every credit hour of New Lawyers Training instruction completed by an attorney not subject to Section 9(A) of this rule.

Section 15. Accreditation of Programs and Activities.

(A) *Accreditation procedures.* The Supreme Court Commission on Continuing Legal Education shall establish and publish written procedures for accreditation of continuing legal education programs and activities.

(B) *Accreditation term.* The Commission may establish the term for which the accreditation of a continuing legal education program or activity is effective. The Commission may renew accreditation of a program or activity.

(C) *Application decision.* The Commission shall render a decision on an application for accreditation of a continuing legal education program or activity within forty-five days after the date the Commission receives a completed application.

(D) *Prior approval.* The Commission may require prior approval of a continuing legal education program or activity.

(E) *Accreditation of out-of-state or national program or activity.* The Commission may accredit continuing legal education programs and activities of other states or national or state legal organizations.

(F) *Automatic accreditation.* The Commission may grant automatic accreditation for continuing legal education programs and activities offered by established sponsors, provided that the Commission shall monitor those programs and activities.

(G) *Notice and explanation of denial.* The Commission shall notify a continuing legal education program or activity sponsor if accreditation is not granted and explain the reasons for denial.

(H) *Calendar of programs and activities.* The Commission shall maintain a calendar of accredited continuing legal education programs and activities and shall make the calendar available on a regular basis.

(I) *Political involvement.* The Commission shall not accredit a continuing legal education program or activity, any proceeds from which are to be used to support a political party, political action committee, campaign committee of a candidate for public office, or candidate for public office.

Section 16. Evaluation of Programs and Activities.

(A) *Procedures for evaluation.* The Supreme Court Commission on Continuing Legal Education shall establish procedures for evaluating continuing legal education programs and activities offered under this rule.

(B) *Commission attendance at program or activity.* Commission representatives may attend any continuing legal education program or activity without notice or fee to evaluate the program or activity. No credit hours shall be awarded for attendance to evaluate a program or activity.

(C) *Revocation of accreditation.* The Commission may revoke accreditation for failure to comply with the requirements of this rule, regulations adopted pursuant to this rule, or for other good cause shown. An attorney or judge who attends an accredited continuing legal education program or activity for which accreditation is later revoked shall receive credit, provided the attendance occurred prior to notice of revocation.

Section 17. Sanctions for Failure to Comply.

(A) *Continuing legal education requirements.* An attorney, magistrate, or acting judge who fails to satisfy the applicable requirements of this rule, except for failure to complete the New Lawyers Training instruction as required by Section 14 of this rule, or a full-time judge, part-time judge, or retired judge who fails to satisfy the applicable mandatory continuing legal education requirements of this rule or Gov. Jud. R. IV shall be subject to one or both of the following sanctions:

(1) A monetary penalty;

(2) Suspension from the practice of law.

(B) *New Lawyers Training requirements.* An attorney who is required to complete the New Lawyers Training instruction as required by Section 14 of this rule and who, without good cause, fails to complete the requirements shall be suspended from the practice of law.

(C) *Sanctions.* When imposing a sanction for professional misconduct pursuant to Gov. Bar R. V, a monetary penalty imposed under this section shall not be considered as prior discipline but a suspension shall be considered as prior discipline.

Section 18. Enforcement Procedures.

(A) *Late compliance.* An attorney or judge who fails to meet the applicable requirements of this rule or Gov. Jud. R. IV, but does so within ninety days of the deadline set forth in Section 4 of this rule, shall be assessed a late fee in accordance with the late fee schedule in CLE Regulation 503.

(B) *Failure to comply.* An attorney or judge who fails to meet the applicable requirements of this rule or Gov. Jud. R. IV shall be notified of the apparent noncompliance by the Supreme Court Commission on Continuing Legal Education. The Commission shall send notice of the apparent noncompliance by regular mail to the attorney or judge at the most recent address provided by the attorney or judge to the Office of Attorney Services. The notice shall inform the attorney or judge that the attorney or judge will be subject to one or both of the sanctions set forth in Section 17 of this rule unless, on or before the date set forth in the notice, the attorney or judge either files evidence of compliance with the applicable requirements of this rule or Gov. Jud. R. IV or comes into compliance. The attorney or judge shall come into compliance by taking sufficient credit hours to meet the requirements and paying the late fee set forth in CLE Regulation 503 by the date set forth in the notice of apparent noncompliance. If the attorney or judge does not file evidence of compliance or come into compliance on or before the date set forth in the notice, the attorney or judge shall be subject to sanction as set forth in Section 17 of this rule. The Commission shall send the sanction order by certified mail to the attorney or judge at the most recent address provided by the attorney or judge to the Office of Attorney Services. The Supreme Court Reporter shall publish notice of the Commission's sanction orders in the *Ohio Official Reports* and the *Ohio State Bar Association Report.*

Section 19. Reinstatement.

(A) *Application.* An attorney or judge who is suspended under this rule may be reinstated to the practice of law by applying for reinstatement with the Supreme Court Commission on Continuing Legal Education. The application for reinstatement shall be in a manner authorized by the Commission and accompanied by evidence that the attorney or judge has satisfied the deficiency that was the cause of the suspension under this rule, a reinstatement fee of three hundred dollars, and payment of all fees assessed for noncompliance with this rule.

(B) *Order and notice.* Upon receipt of a completed application for reinstatement and verification that the attorney has fulfilled the registration requirements of Gov. Bar R. VI, the Secretary shall issue an order of reinstatement and send notice of the reinstatement to the attorney.

(C) *Publication.* Any sanction or reinstatement ordered by the Commission pursuant to this rule shall be published by the Supreme Court Reporter in the *Ohio Official Reports* and the *Ohio State Bar Association Report.* Certified copies of any sanction or reinstatement order entered by the Commission pursuant to this rule shall be sent to those persons or organizations named in Gov. Bar R. V, Section 17(D)(1).

Section 20. Effective Date.

(A) The effective date of this rule shall be July 1, 1988, except Section 3, which is effective January 1, 1989.

(B)(1) The amendments to Section 3 of this rule, adopted by the Supreme Court of Ohio on June 28, 1989, shall be effective on July 1, 1989.

(2) The amendments to Section 6 of this rule, adopted by the Supreme Court of Ohio on November 22, 1989, shall be effective on December 15, 1989.

(3) The amendments to Section 3 of this rule, adopted by the Supreme Court of Ohio on May 8, 1990, shall be effective on May 28, 1990.

(4) The amendments to Section 3 of this rule, adopted by the Supreme Court of Ohio on July 19, 1990, shall be effective on September 1, 1990 and shall apply to definite and indefinite suspensions imposed on or after that effective date.

(5) The amendments to Sections 3 and 4 of this rule, adopted by the Supreme Court of Ohio on October 16, 1990 and December 11, 1990, shall be effective January 1, 1991 and shall apply to all programs and activities conducted on or after that effective date.

(6) The amendments to Section 2 of this rule, adopted by the Supreme Court of Ohio on February 5, 1991, shall be effective on February 18, 1991.

(7) The amendments to Section 3 of this rule, adopted by the Supreme Court of Ohio on June 4, 1991, shall take effect on September 1, 1991.

(8) The amendments to Sections 1 to 7 of this rule, adopted by the Supreme Court of Ohio on October 8, 1991, shall take effect on January 1, 1992.

(C) The amendments to this rule adopted by the Supreme Court of Ohio on December 14, 1993 shall take effect on January 1, 1994.

(D) The amendments to Section 4 of this rule, adopted by the Supreme Court of Ohio on October 12, 1994, shall take effect on January 1, 1995.

(E) The amendments to Section 3 of this rule, adopted by the Supreme Court of Ohio on July 12, 1995, shall take effect on January 1, 1996.

(F) The amendments to Section 3 of this rule, adopted by the Supreme Court of Ohio on October 20, 1997, shall take effect on January 1, 1998.

(G) The amendments to Section 3 of this rule, adopted by the Supreme Court of Ohio on September 28, 1998, shall be effective on November 1, 1998.

(H) The amendments to Section 4 of this rule, adopted by the Supreme Court of Ohio on September 21, 1999, shall take effect on January 1, 2000.

(I) The amendment to Section 2 of this rule, adopted by the Supreme Court of Ohio on April 10, 2000, shall take effect on May 8, 2000.

(J) The amendments to Sections 3 (C)(2), 3 (H), and Section 5 of this Rule, adopted by the Supreme Court of Ohio on November 28, 2000 shall be effective on July 1, 2001.

(K) The amendments to Sections 2 and 3 of this rule, adopted by the Supreme Court of Ohio on December 11, 2001, shall take effect on January 21, 2002.

(L) The amendments to Section 3 (B)(2) and Section 4 (B)(1) of this rule, adopted by the Supreme Court of Ohio on April 22, 2002, shall be effective on July 1, 2002.

(M) The amendments to Section 3 (B)(2), Section 4 (A)(4) and Section 6 (C) of this rule, adopted by the Supreme Court of Ohio on July 20, 2004, shall be effective on September 1, 2004.

(N) The amendments to Section 6 (A)(1)(a) of this rule, adopted by the Supreme Court of Ohio on October 11, 2005, shall be effective on November 7, 2005.

(O) The amendments to this rule, adopted by the Supreme Court of Ohio on September 11, 2007, shall be effective on November 1, 2007, and shall apply to the 2008 reporting period and subsequent reporting periods, except that former sections 5, 6, 7, and 8 shall govern sanctions and enforcement procedures for the 2007 reporting period.

(P) The amendments to this rule adopted by the Supreme Court of Ohio on June 24, 2008, shall be effective November 1, 2008, and shall apply to attorneys admitted to the practice of law and attorneys initially registered for corporate status pursuant to Gov. Bar R. VI, Sec. 3, on or after November 1, 2008. These amendments shall not apply to attorneys registered for corporate status pursuant to Gov. Bar R. VI, Sec. 3, prior to November 1, 2008, who are subsequently admitted to the practice of law on or after November 1, 2008. Attorneys admitted to the practice of law or registered for corporate status prior to November 1, 2008, shall comply with former Sec. 3 of this rule.

(Q) The amendment to Section 3(H)(2) of this rule, adopted by the Supreme Court of Ohio on November 1, 2011, shall be effective December 1, 2011.

(R) The amendments to Section 3 of this rule, adopted by the Supreme Court of Ohio on September 11, 2012, shall be effective January 1, 2013.

(S) The amendments to Sections 3 through 20 of this rule, adopted by the Supreme Court of Ohio on October 23, 2012, shall be effective January 1, 2014, and apply to the biennial compliance period ending on December 31, 2014, and all subsequent biennial compliance periods. Former Sections 3 through 8 of this rule shall apply to the biennial compliance period ending on December 31, 2013, and all prior biennial compliance periods.

(T) The amendments to Sections 17 and 19 of this rule, adopted by the Supreme Court of Ohio on October 21, 2014, shall be effective January 1, 2015.

[Effective: July 1, 1988 and January 1, 1989; amended effective January 1, 1989; July 1, 1989; December 15, 1989; May 28, 1990; September 1, 1990; January 1, 1991; February 18, 1991; September 1, 1991; January 1, 1992; July 1, 1992; January 1, 1994; January 1, 1995; January 1, 1996; January 1, 1998; November 1, 1998; January 1, 2000; May 8, 2000; July 1, 2001; January 21, 2002; July 1, 2002, September 1, 2004, November 7, 2005; November 1, 2007; November 1, 2008; December 1, 2011; January 1, 2014; January 1, 2015.]

OKLAHOMA

Adopted and Promulgated by the Supreme Court of Oklahoma on the 17th day of January, 1986. Effective March 1, 1986. Amended to June, 2004.

RULE 1. MANDATORY CONTINUING LEGAL EDUCATION COMMISSION (MCLEC).

(a) There is hereby established a Mandatory Continuing Legal Education Commission (MCLEC) consisting of eleven (11) members who are resident members of the Bar of this State. The Executive Director of the Oklahoma Bar Association and the Director of Continuing Legal Education of the Oklahoma Bar Association shall be ex-officio members without vote. The remaining nine (9) members shall be appointed by the President of the Oklahoma Bar Association with the consent of the Board of Governors of the Oklahoma Bar Association.

(b) The MCLEC shall have the following duties:

(1) To exercise general supervisory authority over the administration of these rules.

(2) To adopt regulations consistent with these rules with approval of the Board of Governors.

(3) Report annually on the activities and operations of the Mandatory Continuing Legal Education Commission to the Board of Governors of the Oklahoma Bar Association and the Oklahoma Supreme Court.

(c) Five (5) Commissioners shall constitute a quorum of the MCLEC.

(d) A member of the MCLEC who misses three (3) consecutive regular meetings of the MCLEC, for whatever reason, shall automatically vacate the office.

RULE 2. SCOPE AND EXEMPTIONS.

(a) Except as provided herein these rules shall apply to every active member of the Oklahoma Bar Association as defined by Article II of the Rules Creating and Controlling the Oklahoma Bar Association.

(b) An attorney is exempt from the educational requirements of these rules for the calendar year during which he or she was first admitted to practice.

(c) All Judges who, during the entire reporting period, are by Constitution, law or regulation prohibited from the private practice of law, members of the United States Congress, members of the Oklahoma Legislature, the Attorney General of the State of Oklahoma and members of the armed forces on full-time active duty shall be exempt from the educational requirements of these rules.

(d) An attorney who attains the age of sixty-five years of age before or during the calendar year which is being reported is exempt from all requirements of these rules except as provided in Rule 5.

(e) An attorney who, during the entire reporting period, is a nonresident of the State of Oklahoma and did not practice law in the State of Oklahoma is exempt from the educational requirements of these rules.

(f) An attorney who files an affidavit with the Commission on Mandatory Continuing Legal Education of the Oklahoma Bar Association stating that the attorney did not practice law during the reporting period is exempt from the educational requirements of these rules.

(g) Any person claiming an exemption hereunder is required to file an annual report in compliance with these rules and regulations.

RULE 3. CONTINUING LEGAL EDUCATION (CLE) REQUIREMENT.

Each attorney subject to these rules pursuant to Rule 2 herein shall attend, or complete an approved substitute for attendance, a minimum of twelve (12) hours of approved continuing legal education each calendar year beginning January 1, 1986.

RULE 4. CREDITS.

(a) Credit will be given for CLE programs approved by the MCLEC.

(b) Hours in excess of the minimum annual requirement may be carried forward for credit only in the succeeding year.

RULE 5. ANNUAL REPORT.

On or before February 15th of each year, every active member of the Oklahoma Bar Association, who did not attain age 65 before or during the preceding calendar year, shall report in such a form as the MCLEC Shall prescribe concerning his or her completion of accredited legal education during the preceding calendar year or exemption from the requirements of these rules. An attorney reporting attainment of age sixty-five (65) need only make one (1) such annual report.

RULE 6. NONCOMPLIANCE AND SANCTIONS.

(a) As soon as practicable after February 15th of each year, the Commission on Mandatory Continuing Legal Education shall furnish to the Executive Director of the Oklahoma Bar Association (1) a list of those attorneys who have not reported for the calendar year ending the preceding December 31st as required by Rule 5, Rules for Mandatory Continuing Legal Education, and (2) a list of attorneys who have reported on or before February 15th indicating that they have not complied with the requirements of Rule 3, Rules of Mandatory Continuing Legal Education.

(b) For a member who fails to comply with the Rule 3 continuing legal education requirement by December 31st of each year, there shall be added an expense charge of $100.00. For a member who fails to comply with the Rule 5 annual report requirement by February 15th of each year, there shall be added an expense charge of $100.00. The Commission is authorized to, and may waive the expense charge for a late filing of the Rule 5 annual report upon finding by the Commission that the late filing was attributable to extreme hardship. Attorneys seeking a waiver shall do so by written application submitted to the Commission. The Commission is authorized to adopt, from time to time, policies and procedures as may be deemed appropriate for continuity in the exercise of the forgoing discretionary authority.

(c) The Executive Director of the Oklahoma Bar Association shall then serve by certified mail each attorney who has not complied with the Rules for Mandatory Continuing Legal Education, with an order to show cause, within sixty (60) days, why the attorney's license should not be suspended at the expiration of the sixty (60) days. Cause may be shown by furnishing the Board of Governors of the Oklahoma Bar Association with an affidavit by the attorney and a certificate from the MCLEC (a) indicating that the attorney has complied with the requirement prior to the expiration of the sixty (60) days or (b) setting forth a valid reason for failure to comply with the requirement because of illness or other good cause.

(d) At the expiration of sixty (60) days from the date of the order to show cause, if good cause is not shown, the Board of Governors shall file application with the Supreme Court recommending suspension of the delinquent's membership. Upon order of the Court, the attorney shall be so suspended and shall not thereafter practice law in this state until reinstated as provided herein. At any time within one (1) year after the order of suspension, an attorney may file with the Executive Director an affidavit by the attorney and a certificate from the MCLEC indicating compliance with the Rules for Mandatory Continuing Legal Education, and payment of a reinstatement fee of $500.00 and, if satisfactory to the Executive Director, the member will be restored to membership and the Executive Director will notify the Clerk and the Chief Justice of the Supreme Court and cause notice of reinstatement to be published in the Oklahoma Bar Journal.

(e) A suspended member who does not file an application for reinstatement within one (1) year from the date the member is suspended by the Supreme Court for noncompliance with the Rules for Mandatory Continuing Legal Education, shall cease automatically to be a member of the Association, and the Board of Governors shall file an application with the Supreme Court recommending the member be stricken from the membership rolls. Subsequent to the Order of the Court, if the attorney desires to become a member of the Association, the attorney shall be required to file with the Professional Responsibility Commission an affidavit by the attorney and a certificate from the MCLEC indicating compliance with the Rules for Mandatory Continuing Legal Education, including payment of all fees and charges, and the attorney must comply with Rule 11 of the Rules Governing Disciplinary Proceedings of the Oklahoma Bar Association.

RULE 7. REGULATIONS.

The following Regulations for Mandatory Continuing Legal Education are hereby adopted and shall remain in effect until revised or amended by the Mandatory Continuing Legal Education Commission with approval of the Board of Governors and the Oklahoma Supreme Court.

Regulation 1

1.1 The Mandatory Continuing Legal Education Commission shall consist of eleven (11) members as provided by Supreme Court rule. The Executive Director of the Oklahoma Bar Association and the Director of Continuing Legal Education of the Oklahoma Bar Association shall be ex-officio members without vote. Nine (9) members of the Commission shall be appointed by the President of the Oklahoma Bar Association with the consent of the Board of Governors. Initially three (3) appointed members shall serve one-year terms, three (3) appointed members shall serve two-year terms, and three (3) appointed members shall serve three-year terms. Thereafter, at the expiration of the stated terms, all members shall serve three-year terms. Members shall not serve more than two successive three-year terms.

1.2 The President of the Oklahoma Bar Association shall appoint the Chairman of the Commission on Mandatory Continuing Legal Education. The Commission on Mandatory Continuing Legal Education shall elect a Vice Chairman and Secretary from among its members.

1.3 The Commission may organize itself into committees of not fewer than four (4) voting members for the purpose of considering and deciding matters submitted to them, except five (5) affirmative votes shall be necessary for any action under Rule 6 of the Rules of the Supreme Court of the State of Oklahoma for Mandatory Continuing Legal Education.

1.4 Members of the Commission shall be reimbursed for their actual direct expenses incurred in travel when authorized by the Board of Governors or the President.

1.5 Support staff as may be required shall be employed by the Executive Director of the Oklahoma Bar Association in the same manner and according to the same procedure as other employees of the Oklahoma Bar Association within the funds available in the budget approved by the Supreme Court.

1.6 As used herein "MCLEC" and the "Commission" shall mean the Mandatory Continuing Legal Education Commission. "CLE" shall mean Continuing Legal Education. "MCLE" shall mean Mandatory Continuing Legal Education. "Rules" referred to shall mean and are the Rules of the Supreme Court of the State of Oklahoma for Mandatory Continuing Legal Education.

Regulation 2

2.1 Nonresident attorneys from other jurisdictions who are temporarily admitted to practice for a case or proceeding shall not be subject to the rules or regulations governing MCLE.

2.2 An attorney who is exempt from the MCLE requirement under Rule 2 shall endorse and claim the exemption on the annual report required by Rule 5 of said rules.

Regulation 3

3.1 Attorneys who have a permanent physical disability which makes attendance of CLE programs inordinately difficult may file a request for a permanent substitute program in lieu of attendance and shall therein set out continuing legal education plans tailored to their specific interest and physical ability. The Commission shall review and approve or disapprove such plans on an individual basis and without delay. Rejection of any requested substitute for attendance will be reviewed by the Board of Governors of the Oklahoma Bar Association prior to any sanction being imposed.

3.2 Other requests for substituted compliance, partial waivers, or other exemptions for hardship or extenuating circumstances may be granted by the Commission upon written application of the attorney and may likewise be reviewed by the Board of Governors and the Oklahoma Bar Association.

3.3 Credit may be earned through teaching in an approved continuing legal education program, or for a presentation substantially complying with the standards of Regulation 4 in a program which is presented to paralegals, legal assistants, and/or law clerks. Presentations accompanied by thorough, high quality, readable, and carefully prepared written materials will qualify for CLE credit on the basis of six (6) hours of credit for each hour of presentation.

3.4 Credit may also be earned through teaching a course in an ABA accredited law school or a course in a paralegal or legal assistant program accredited by the ABA. The Commission will award six (6) hours of CLE credit for each semester hour of academic credit awarded by the academic institution for the course.

3.5 Credit may also be earned through auditing of or regular enrollment in a college of law course at an ABA or AALS approved law school. The MCLE credit allowed shall equal a sum equal to three (3) times the number of credit hours granted by the college of law for the completion of the course.

3.6 The number of hours required means that the attorney must actually attend twelve (12) instructional hours of CLE per year with no credit given for introductory remarks, meal breaks, or business meetings. Of the twelve (12) CLE hours required the attorney must attend and receive one (1) instructional hour of CLE per year covering the area of professional responsibility or legal ethics or legal malpractice prevention. An instructional hour will in all events contain at least fifty (50) minutes.

3.7 Hours of credit in excess of the minimum annual requirement may be carried forward for credit only in the succeeding calendar year. Such hours must, however, be reported in the annual report of compliance for the year in which they were completed and in the year for which they are being claimed and must be designated as hours being carried forward.

Regulation 4

4.1.1 The following standards will govern the approval of continuing legal education programs by the Commission.

4.1.2 The program must have significant intellectual or practical content and its primary objective must be to increase the participant's professional competence as an attorney.

4.1.3 The program must deal primarily with matters related to the practice of law, professional responsibility or ethical obligations of attorneys.

4.1.4 The program must be offered by a sponsor having substantial, recent, experience in offering continuing legal education or demonstrated ability to organize and present effectively continuing legal education. Demonstrated ability arises partly from the extent to which individuals with legal training or educational experience are involved in the planning, instruction and supervision of the program.

4.1.5 The program itself must be conducted by an individual or group qualified by practical or academic experience. The program including the named advertised participants, must be conducted substantially as planned, subject to emergency withdrawals and alterations.

4.1.6 Thorough, high quality, readable, and carefully prepared written materials must be made available to all participants at or before the time the course is presented, unless the absence of such materials is recognized as reasonable and approved by the Commission. A mere outline without citations or explanatory notations will not be sufficient.

4.1.7 The program must be conducted in a comfortable physical setting, conducive to learning and equipped with suitable writing surfaces.

4.1.8 Approval may be given for programs where audiovisual recorded or reproduced material is used. Television video programs and motion picture programs with sound shall qualify for CLE credit in the same manner as a live CLE program provided:

a. the original CLE program was approved for CLE credit as provided in these regulations or the visual recorded program has been approved by the Commission under these rules, and

b. each person attending the visual presentation is provided written material as provided in Regulation 4.1.6 and

c. each program is conducted in a location as required in Regulation 4.1.7 and

d. there are a minimum of five (5) persons enrolled and in attendance at the presentation of the visually recorded program unless viewed at the Oklahoma Bar Center or sponsored by a county bar association in Oklahoma.

4.1.9 Programs that cross academic lines may be considered for approval.

4.2 Continuing legal education programs sponsored by the following organizations are presumptively approved for credit, provided that the standards set out in the Regulations 4.1.2 through 4.1.7 are met:

- American Association for Justice
- American Bankruptcy Institute*
- American Bar Association and Bar Sections
- American College of Real Estate*
- American Immigration Lawyers Association
- American Inns of Court*
- American Law Institute-American Bar Association Committee on Continuing Professional Education
- ALM
- Building Blocks, CLE
- Center for American & International Law (formerly Southwestern Legal Foundation)
- Cleveland County Bar Association*
- Commercial Law League of America*
- Defense Research Institutey
- Energy Bar Association*
- Executive Enterprises, Inc.*
- Federal Bar Association*
- Federal Deposit Insurance Corporation*
- Federal Public Defender*
- Garfield County Bar Association*
- Garvin County Bar Association*
- HB Litigation*
- International Municipal Lawyers Association* (formerly NIMLO)
- Kingfisher County Bar Association*
- LawProse Inc. *
- Law Seminars International, Inc.*
- Legal Aid Services of Oklahoma. Inc.*

- Mayes County Bar Association*
- Mediation Institute*
- Muskogee County Bar Association*
- National Academy of Continuing Legal Education*
- National Association of Attorneys General*
- National Association of College and University Attorneys*
- National Association of Criminal Defense Lawyers*
- National Association of Railroad Trial Counsel*
- NBI, Inc.*
- National Constitution Center Conferences
- National District Attorneys Association
- National Employment Law Institute*
- National Employment Lawyers Association
- National Institute of Trial Advocacy
- National Legal Aid and Defender Association*
- New York University School of Continuing and Professional Studies*
- Northwestern University School of Law
- Office of the Oklahoma Attorney General*
- Oklahoma Academy of Collaborative Professionals*
- Oklahoma Association of Defense Counsel*
- Oklahoma Association for Justice
- Oklahoma Association of Municipal Attorneys
- Oklahoma Baptist University Bench and Bar Association*
- Oklahoma Bar Association
- Oklahoma City Commercial Lawyers Association*
- Oklahoma City Criminal Defense Lawyers Association*
- Oklahoma City Mineral Lawyers Society*
- Oklahoma City Real Property Lawyers Association*
- Oklahoma City University Law School

- Oklahoma County Bar Association
- Oklahoma County Criminal Defense Lawyers Association
- Oklahoma County Public Defenders Office
- Oklahoma Criminal Defense Lawyer's Association*
- Oklahoma District Attorneys Council
- Oklahoma Municipal Judges Association*
- Oklahoma Planned Giving Council*
- OSU Tax Schools
- PESI Law and Accounting*
- Practicing Law Institute
- Rocky Mountain Mineral Law Foundation
- SEC Institute, Inc.*
- South Oklahoma City Lawyers Association*
- South Texas College Of Law Continuing Legal Education
- State Bar of Texas
- Sterling Education Services*
- Strafford Publications*
- Tax Forum*
- TRT, Inc.
- Tuesday Professional Tax Group*
- Tulsa County Bar Association
- Tulsa Employee Benefits Group *
- Tulsa Estate Planning Forum*
- Tulsa Pension Attorneys*
- Tulsa Tax Club
- Tulsa Title and Probate Lawyers Association *
- U.S. Air Force-Judge Advocate General School*
- U.S. Army-Judge Advocate General School*
- U.S. Department of Justice-Office of Legal Education*

- University of Houston Law Foundation
- University of Oklahoma College of Law
- University of Tulsa College of Law
- Washington County Bar Association*
- WealthCounsel, LLC*
- West Professional Development*
- Woodward County Bar Association
- Young Lawyers Division of the Oklahoma Bar Association

All other county bar associations in Oklahoma presenting seminars or programs that are co-sponsored by an organization that has presumptive approval as a CLE sponsor.

Added since the rules were approved by the Supreme Court January 17, 1986.

4.3 Approved seminars may be advertised in informational brochures and program materials provided by the sponsoring body. Organizations listed in Regulation 4.2 whose programs are presumptively approved shall give adequate notice that a program or seminar it conducts is not approved for MCLE credit in the event the program or seminar does not meet the standards set forth in Regulations 4.1.1 through 4.1.7.

4.4 The Commission may at any time re-evaluate and grant or revoke presumptive approval of a sponsor.

4.5 Any organization not included in Regulation 4.2 above, desiring approval of a course or program shall apply to the Commission by submitting an application on a form to be obtained from the Commission and supporting documentation at least forty-five (45) days prior to the date for which the course or program is scheduled. The Commission will advise the applicant in writing by mail within ten (10) days of the receipt of the completed application whether the program is approved or disapproved. Applicants denied approval of a program may appeal such a decision by submitting a letter of appeal to the Commission within fifteen (15) days of the receipt of the notice of disapproval.

4.6 An attorney desiring approval of a course or program which has not otherwise been approved shall apply to the Commission by submitting an application on a form to be obtained from the Commission and supporting documentation as follows:

1. If approval is requested before the course or program is presented the application and supporting documentation shall be submitted at least forty-five (45) days prior to the date for which the course or program is scheduled.

2. If approval is requested after the applicant has attended a course or program the application and supporting documentation shall be submitted within ninety (90) days after the date the course or program was presented or prior to the end of the calendar year in which the course or program was presented, whichever is earlier.

The Commission will advise the applicant in writing by mail within ten (10) days of the receipt of the completed application whether the program is approved or disapproved. Applicants denied approval of a program may appeal such a decision by submitting a letter of appeal to the Commission within fifteen (15) days of the receipt of the notice of disapproval.

4.7 The sponsor of an approved continuing legal education program may announce or indicate as follows:

This course has been approved by the Oklahoma Bar Association Mandatory Continuing Legal Education Commission for _____ hours of CLE credit, including _____ hours of legal ethics credit.

4.8 As soon as practicable but in any event on or before the earlier of (1) thirty (30) days following an approved legal education program or (2) January 10 of the succeeding year, the sponsor shall furnish to the Commission such attendance information in such format as the Commission shall direct.

An attorney desiring approval of a course or program which has not otherwise been approved shall apply to the Commission by submitting an application on a form to be obtained from the Commission and supporting documentation as follows:

a. If approval is requested before the course or program is presented the application and supporting documentation shall be submitted at least forty-five (45) days prior to the date for which the course or program is scheduled.

b. If approval is requested after the applicant has attended a course or program the application and supporting documentation shall be submitted within ninety (90) days after the date the course or program was presented or prior to the end of the calendar year in which the course or program was presented, whichever is earlier.

The Commission will advise the applicant in writing by mail within ten (10) days of the receipt of the completed application whether the program is approved or disapproved. Applicants denied approval of a program may appeal such a decision by submitting a letter of appeal to the Commission within fifteen (15) days of the receipt of the notice of disapproval.

Regulation 5

On or before February 15th of each year, every active member, under sixty-five (65) years of age, or the Oklahoma Bar Association shall submit a report in a form as the Commission shall provide concerning such attorney's completion of, exemption from or approved substitute for the minimum hours of instruction, including reference to hours earned during the preceding year and hours to be carried forward to the next year. An attorney reporting attainment of age sixty-five (65), need only make one (1) such annual report.

5.1 Commencing with calendar year 2004, the MCLEC shall deem a member to have fulfilled the reporting requirements and to have reported as required by the Rules of the Supreme Court of Oklahoma for Mandatory Continuing Legal Education if the official records of the OBA indicate the member is in compliance with the minimum educational requirements or exempt from compliance for the year in question.

Caveat: It shall remain the responsibility of each member to review the accuracy of the OBA records and reports, and to be assured that exemption or compliance is recognized by the MCLEC. Reports and records are available for member review by logging on to myOKBbar on the OBA website.

Regulation 6

Sponsors of the seminars or courses qualifying for Mandatory Continuing Legal Education credits shall keep records of attendance for a period of two (2) years following the date of the course or seminar.

SUBSTITUTED COMPLIANCE POLICIES

The following Policies have been adopted by the Mandatory Continuing Legal Education Commission which interpret and supplement the Rules and Regulations concerning substituted compliance with the Mandatory Continuing Legal Education requirements:

1. Approval for credit may be granted, on a course-by-course basis, for live interactive, audio-only teleconference courses such as those sponsored and provided by the American Bar Association.

2. Approval for credit may be granted, for no more than six hours MCLE credit per year, for computer-based or other technology-based legal education programs which otherwise meet the criteria established in the Rules of the Oklahoma Supreme Court for Mandatory Continuing Legal Education, Rule 7, Regulation 4, subject to standard course approval procedures and appropriate certification of course completion.

3. Other substitute forms of compliance may be granted for members with permanent or temporary physical disabilities (based upon a doctor's certification) which make attendance at regular approved CLE programs difficult or impossible, as set forth in Rule 7, Regulation 3.

4. If the CLE course provider has not secured course approval or rejection for MCLE credit in Oklahoma, the attorney attendee, in order to receive MCLE credit, must submit a request for MCLE credit and course approval on forms which will be supplied by the MCLE office, which application must be submitted with a $15 per course application fee.

OREGON

Oregon State Bar
Minimum Continuing Legal Education
Rules and Regulations
(As amended effective July 13, 2016)

Purpose

It is of primary importance to the members of the bar and to the public that attorneys continue their legal education after admission to the bar. Continuing legal education assists Oregon lawyers in maintaining and improving their competence and skills and in meeting their obligations to the profession. These Rules establish the minimum requirements for continuing legal education for members of the Oregon State Bar.

Rule One
Terms and Definitions

1.1 Active Member: An active member of the Oregon State Bar, as defined in Article 6 of the Bylaws of the Oregon State Bar.

1.2 Accreditation: The formal process of accreditation of activities by the MCLE Administrator.

1.3 BOG: The Board of Governors of the Oregon State Bar.

1.4 Accredited CLE Activity: An activity that provides legal or professional education to attorneys in accordance with MCLE Rule 5.

1.5 Executive Director: The executive director of the Oregon State Bar.

1.6 Hour or Credit Hour: Sixty minutes of accredited group CLE activity or other CLE activity.

1.7 MCLE Committee: The Minimum Continuing Legal Education Committee appointed by the BOG to assist in the administration of these Rules.

1.8 New Admittee: A person is a new admittee from the date of initial admission as an active member of the Oregon State Bar through the end of his or her first reporting period.

1.9 Regulations: Any regulation adopted by the BOG to implement these Rules.

1.10 Reporting Period: The period during which an active member must satisfy the MCLE requirement.

1.11 Retired Member: An active member who is over 65 years old and is fully retired from the practice of law.

1.12 Sponsor: An individual or organization providing a CLE activity.

1.13 Supreme Court: The Supreme Court of the State of Oregon.

Regulations to MCLE Rule 1
Terms and Definitions

1.100 Inactive Member. An inactive member of the Oregon State Bar, as defined in Article 6 of the Bylaws.

1.101 Suspended Member. A member who has been suspended from the practice of law by the Supreme Court.

1.110 MCLE Filings.

(a) Anything to be filed under the MCLE Rules shall be delivered to the MCLE Administrator, at 16037 SW Upper Boones Ferry Road, PO Box 231935, Tigard, Oregon, 97281-1935.

(b) Filing shall not be timely unless the document is actually received by the MCLE Administrator by the close of business on the day the filing is due.

(c) Timely filing of a completed compliance report as required by Rule 7.1 and 7.4(a)(2) is defined as the actual physical receipt of the signed report at the MCLE office, regardless of the date of posting or postmark, or the date of delivery to a delivery service of any kind. Reports may be delivered by facsimile or electronic transmission. If the due date for anything to be filed under the MCLE Rules is a Saturday or legal holiday, including Sunday, or a day that the Oregon State Bar office is closed, the due date shall be the next regular business day.

1.115 Service Method.

(a) MCLE Compliance Reports shall be sent to the member's email address on file with the bar, except that reports shall be sent by first-class mail (to the last designated business or residence address on file with the Oregon State Bar) to any member who is exempt from having an email address on file with the bar.

(b) Notices of Noncompliance shall be sent via regular mail and email to the member's last designated business or residence address on file with the Oregon State Bar and to the email address on file with the bar on the date of the notice. Email notices will not be sent to any member who is exempt from having an email address on file with the bar.

(c) Service by mail shall be complete on deposit in the mail.

1.120 Regularly Scheduled Meeting. A meeting schedule for each calendar year will be established for the BOG and the MCLE Committee, if one is appointed. All meetings identified on the schedule will be considered to be regularly scheduled meetings. Any other meeting will be for a special reason and/or request and will not be considered as a regularly scheduled meeting.

1.130 Reporting Period. Reporting periods shall begin on January 1 and end on December 31 of the reporting year.

1.140 Fully Retired. A member is fully retired from the practice of law if the member is over 65 years of age and does not engage at any time in any activity that constitutes the practice of law including, without limitation, activities described in OSB Bylaws 6.100 and 20.2.

Rule Two
Administration of Minimum Continuing Legal Education

2.1 Duties and Responsibilities of the Board of Governors. The Minimum Continuing Legal Education Rules shall be administered by the BOG. The BOG may modify and amend these Rules and adopt new rules subject to the approval of the Supreme Court. The BOG may adopt, modify and amend regulations to implement these Rules. The BOG may appoint an MCLE Committee to assist in the administration of these rules. There shall be an MCLE Administrator who shall be an employee of the Oregon State Bar.

2.2 Duties of the MCLE Administrator. The MCLE Administrator shall:

(a) Oversee the day-to-day operation of the program as specified in these Rules.

(b) Approve applications for accreditation and requests for exemption, and make compliance determinations.

(c) Develop the preliminary annual budget for MCLE operations.

(d) Prepare an annual report of MCLE activities.

(e) Perform other duties identified by the BOG or as required to implement these Rules.

2.3 Expenses. The executive director shall allocate and shall pay the expenses of the program including, but not limited to staff salaries, out of the bar's general fund.

Rule Three
Minimum Continuing Legal Education Requirement

3.1 Effective Date. These Rules, or any amendments thereto, shall take effect upon their approval by the Supreme Court of the State of Oregon.

3.2 Active Members.

(a) Minimum Hours. Except as provided in Rules 3.3 and 3.4, all active members shall complete a minimum of 45 credit hours of accredited CLE activity every three years as provided in these Rules.

(b) Ethics. At least six of the required hours shall be in subjects relating to ethics in programs accredited pursuant to Rule 5.5(a), including one hour on the subject of a lawyer's statutory duty to report child abuse or one hour on the subject of a lawyer's statutory duty to report elder abuse (see ORS 9.114). MCLE Regulation 3.300(d) specifies the reporting periods in which the child abuse or elder abuse reporting credit is required.

(c) Access to Justice. In alternate reporting periods, at least three of the required hours must be in programs accredited for access to justice pursuant to Rule 5.5(b).

3.3 Reinstatements, Resumption of Practice After Retirement and New Admittees.

(a) An active member whose reporting period is established in Rule 3.7(c)(2) or (d)(2) shall complete 15 credit hours of accredited CLE activity in the first reporting period after reinstatement or resumption of the practice of law in accordance with Rule 3.4. Two of the 15 credit hours shall be devoted to ethics.

(b) New admittees shall complete 15 credit hours of accredited CLE activity in the first reporting period after admission as an active member, including two credit hours in ethics, and ten credit hours in practical skills. New admittees must also complete a three credit hour OSB-approved introductory course in access to justice. The MCLE Administrator may waive the practical skills requirement for a new admittee who has practiced law in another jurisdiction for three consecutive years immediately prior to the member's admission in Oregon, in which event the new admittee must complete ten hours in other areas. After a new admittee's first reporting period, the requirements in Rule 3.2(a) shall apply.

3.4 Retired Members. A retired member shall be exempt from compliance with these Rules, provided the member files a compliance report for any reporting period during which the exemption is claimed certifying that the member was or became retired during the reporting period. A retired member shall not resume the practice of law, either on a full or part-time basis, without prior written notice to the MCLE Administrator.

3.5 Out-of-State Compliance.

(a) Reciprocity Jurisdictions. An active member whose principal office for the practice of law is not in the State of Oregon and who is an active member in a jurisdiction with which Oregon has established MCLE reciprocity may comply with these rules by filing a compliance report as required by MCLE Rule 7.1 accompanied by evidence that the member is in compliance with the requirements of the other jurisdiction and has completed the child abuse or elder abuse reporting credit required in ORS 9.114. MCLE Regulation 3.300(d) specifies the reporting periods in which the child abuse or elder abuse reporting credit is required.

(b) Other Jurisdictions. An active member whose principal office for the practice of law is not in the State of Oregon and is not in a jurisdiction with which Oregon has established MCLE reciprocity must file a compliance report as required by MCLE Rule 7.1 showing that the member has completed at least 45 hours of accredited CLE activities as required by Rule 3.2.

3.6 Active Pro Bono. Members who are in Active Pro Bono status pursuant to OSB Bylaw 6.101 are exempt from compliance with these Rules.

3.7 Reporting Period.

(a) In General. All active members shall have three-year reporting periods, except as provided in paragraphs (b), (c) and (d).

(b) New Admittees. The first reporting period for a new admittee shall start on the date of admission as an active member and shall end on December 31 of the next calendar year. All subsequent reporting periods shall be three years.

(c) Reinstatements.

(1) A member who transfers to inactive or Active Pro Bono status, is suspended, or has resigned and who is reinstated before the end of the reporting period in effect at the time of the status change shall retain the member's original reporting period and these Rules shall be applied as though the transfer, suspension, or resignation had not occurred.

(2) Except as provided in Rule 3.7(c)(1), the first reporting period for a member who is reinstated as an active member following a transfer to inactive or Active Pro Bono status or a suspension, disbarment or resignation shall start on the date of reinstatement and shall end on December 31 of the next calendar year. All subsequent reporting periods shall be three years.

(3) Notwithstanding Rules 3.7(c)(1) and (2), reinstated members who did not submit a completed compliance report for the reporting period immediately prior to their transfer to inactive or Active Pro Bono status, suspension or resignation will be assigned a new reporting period upon reinstatement. This reporting period shall begin on the date of reinstatement and shall end on December 31 of the next calendar year. All subsequent

reporting periods shall be three years.

(d) Retired Members.

(1) A retired member who resumes the practice of law before the end of the reporting period in effect at the time of the member's retirement shall retain the member's original reporting period and these Rules shall be applied as though the retirement had not occurred.

(2) Except as provided in Rule 3.7(d)(1), the first reporting period for a retired member who resumes the practice of law shall start on the date the member resumes the practice of law and shall end on December 31 of the next calendar year. All subsequent reporting periods shall be three years.

(3) Notwithstanding Rules 3.7(d)(1) and (2), members resuming the practice of law after retirement who did not submit a completed compliance report for the reporting period immediately prior to retirement will be assigned a new reporting period upon the resumption of the practice of law. This reporting period shall begin on the date of the resumption of the practice of law and shall end on December 31 of the next calendar year. All subsequent reporting periods shall be three years.

Regulations to MCLE Rule 3
Minimum Continuing Legal Education Requirement

3.200 Resumption of Law Practice By a Retired Member. The resumption of the practice of law by a retired member occurs when the member undertakes to perform any activity that would constitute the practice of law including, without limitation the activities described in OSB Bylaws 6.100 and 20.2.

3.250 Out-of-State Compliance. An active member seeking credit pursuant to MCLE Rule 3.5(b) shall attach to the member's compliance report filed in Oregon evidence that the member has met the requirements of Rules 3.2(a) and (b) with courses accredited in any jurisdiction. This evidence may include certificates of compliance, certificates of attendance, or other information indicating the identity of the crediting jurisdiction, the number of 60-minute hours of credit granted, and the subject matter of programs attended.

3.260 Reciprocity. An active member who is also an active member in a jurisdiction with which Oregon has established MCLE reciprocity (currently Idaho, Utah or Washington) may comply with Rule 3.5(a) by attaching to the compliance report required by MCLE Rule 7.1 a copy of the member's certificate of compliance with the MCLE requirements from that jurisdiction, together with evidence that the member has completed the child abuse or elder abuse reporting training required in ORS 9.114. No other information about program attendance is required. MCLE Regulation 3.300(d) specified the reporting periods in which the child abuse or elder abuse reporting credit is required.

3.300 Application of Credits.

(a) Legal ethics and access to justice credits in excess of the minimum required can be applied to the general or practical skills requirement.

(b) Practical skills credits can be applied to the general requirement.

(c) For members in a three-year reporting period, one child abuse or elder abuse reporting credit earned in a non-required reporting period may be applied to the ethics credit requirement. Additional child-abuse and elder abuse reporting credits will be applied to the general or practical skills requirement. For members in a shorter reporting period, child abuse and elder abuse reporting credits will be applied as general or practical skills credit. Access to Justice credits earned in a non-required reporting period will be credited as general credits.

(d) Members in a three-year reporting period are required to have 3.0 access to justice credits and 1.0 child abuse reporting credit in reporting periods ending 12/31/2012 through 12/31/2014, 12/31/2018 through 12/31/2020 and in alternate three-year periods thereafter. Members in a three-year reporting period ending 12/31/2015 through 12/31/2017, 12/31/2021 through 12/31/2023 and in alternate three-year periods thereafter are required to have 1.0 elder abuse reporting credit.

3.400 Practical Skills Requirement.

(a) A practical skills program is one which includes courses designed primarily to instruct new admittees in the methods and means of the practice of law. This includes those courses which involve instruction in the practice of law generally, instruction in the management of a legal practice, and instruction in particular substantive law areas designed for new practitioners. A practical skills program may include but shall not be limited to instruction in: client contact and relations; court proceedings; negotiation and settlement; alternative dispute resolution; malpractice avoidance; personal management assistance; the negative aspects of substance abuse to a law practice; and practice management assistance topics such as tickler and docket control systems, conflict systems, billing, trust and general accounting, file management, and computer systems.

(b) A CLE course on any subject matter can contain as part of the curriculum a portion devoted to practical skills. The sponsor shall designate those portions of any program which it claims is eligible for practical skills credit.

(c) A credit hour cannot be applied to both the practical skills requirement and the ethics requirement.

(d) A new admittee applying for an exemption from the practical skills requirement, pursuant to Rule 3.3(b), shall submit in writing to the MCLE Administrator a request for exemption describing the nature and extent of the admittee's prior practice of law sufficient for the Administrator to determine whether the admittee has current skills equivalent to the practical skills requirements set forth in this regulation.

3.500 Reporting Period Upon Reinstatement.
A member who returns to active membership status as contemplated under MCLE Rule 3.7(c)(2) shall not be required to fulfill the requirement of compliance during the member's inactive status, suspension, disbarment or resignation, but no credits obtained during the member's inactive status, suspension, disbarment or resignation shall be carried over into the next reporting period.

3.600 Introductory Course in Access to Justice.
In order to qualify as an introductory course in access to justice required by MCLE Rule 3.3(b), the three-hour program must meet the accreditation standards set forth in MCLE Rule 5.5(b) and include discussion of at least three of the following areas: race, gender, economic status, creed, color, religion, national origin, disability, age or sexual orientation.

Rule Four
Accreditation Procedure

4.1 In General.

(a) In order to qualify as an accredited CLE activity, the activity must be given activity accreditation by the MCLE Administrator.

(b) The MCLE Administrator shall electronically publish a list of accredited programs.

(c) All sponsors shall permit the MCLE Administrator or a member of the MCLE Committee to audit the sponsors' CLE activities without charge for purposes of monitoring compliance with MCLE requirements. Monitoring may include attending CLE activities, conducting surveys of participants and verifying attendance of registrants.

4.2 Group Activity Accreditation.

(a) CLE activities will be considered for accreditation on a case-by-case basis and must satisfy the accreditation standards listed in these Rules for the particular type of activity for which accreditation is being requested.

(b) A sponsor or individual active member may apply for accreditation of a group CLE activity by filing a written application for accreditation with the MCLE Administrator. The application shall be made on the form required by the MCLE Administrator for the particular type of CLE activity for which accreditation is being requested and shall demonstrate compliance with the accreditation standards contained in these Rules.

(c) A written application for accreditation of a group CLE activity submitted by or on behalf of the sponsor of the CLE activity shall be accompanied by the program sponsor fee required by MCLE Regulation 4.300. An additional program sponsor fee is required for a repeat live presentation of a group CLE activity.

(d) A written application for accreditation of a group CLE activity must be filed either before or no later than 30 days after the completion of the activity. An application received more than 30 days after the completion of the activity is subject to a late processing fee as provided in Regulation 4.300.

(e) The MCLE Administrator may revoke the accreditation of an activity at any time if it determines that the accreditation standards were not met for the activity. Notice of revocation shall be sent to the sponsor of the activity.

(f) Accreditation of a group CLE activity obtained by a sponsor or an active member shall apply for all active members participating in the activity.

4.3 Credit Hours. Credit hours shall be assigned in multiples of one-quarter of an hour. The BOG shall adopt regulations to assist sponsors in determining the appropriate number of credit hours to be assigned.

4.4 Sponsor Advertising.

(a) Only sponsors of accredited group CLE activities may include in their advertising the accredited status of the activity and the credit hours assigned.

(b) Specific language and other advertising requirements may be established in regulations adopted by the BOG.

Regulations to MCLE Rule 4
Accreditation Procedure

4.200 Group Activity Accreditation.

(a) Review procedures shall be pursuant to MCLE Rule 8.1 and Regulation 8.100.

(b) The number of credit hours assigned to the activity shall be determined based upon the information provided by the applicant. The applicant shall be notified via email or regular mail of the number of credit hours assigned or if more information is needed in order to process the application.

4.300 Sponsor Fees.

(a) A sponsor of a group CLE activity that is accredited for 4 or fewer credit hours shall pay a program sponsor fee of $40.00. An additional program sponsor fee is required for every repeat live presentation of an accredited activity, but no additional fee is required for a video or audio replay of an accredited activity.

(b) A sponsor of a group CLE activity that is accredited for more than 4 credit hours shall pay a program sponsor fee of $75. An additional program sponsor fee is required for every repeat live presentation of an accredited activity, but no additional fee is required for a video or audio replay of an accredited activity.

(c) Sponsors presenting a CLE activity as a series of presentations may pay one program fee of $40.00 for all presentations offered within three consecutive calendar months, provided:

> (i) The presentations do not exceed a total of three credit hours for the approved series; and

> (ii) Any one presentation does not exceed one credit hour.

(d) A late processing fee of $40 is due for accreditation applications that are received more than 30 days after the program date. This fee is in addition to the program sponsor fee and accreditation shall not be granted until the fee is received.

(e) All local bar associations in Oregon are exempt from payment of the MCLE program sponsor fees. However, if accreditation applications are received more than 30 days after the program date, the late processing fee set forth in MCLE Regulation 4.350(d) will apply.

4.400 Credit Hours.

(a) Credit hours shall be assigned to CLE activities in multiples of one-quarter of an hour or .25 credits and are rounded to the nearest one-quarter credit.

(b) Credit Exclusions. Only CLE activities that meet the accreditation standards stated in MCLE Rule 5 shall be included in computing total CLE credits. Credit exclusions include the following:

> (1) Registration

> (2) Non-substantive introductory remarks

> (3) Breaks exceeding 15 minutes per three hours of instruction

> (4) Business meetings

> (5) Programs of less than 30 minutes in length

4.500 Sponsor Advertising.

(a) Advertisements by sponsors of accredited CLE activities shall not contain any false or misleading information.

(b) Information is false or misleading if it:

> (i) Contains a material misrepresentation of fact or law or omits a fact necessary to make the statement considered as a whole not materially misleading;

(ii) Is intended or is reasonably likely to create an unjustified expectation as to the results to be achieved from participation in the CLE activity;

(iii) Is intended or is reasonably likely to convey the impression that the sponsor or the CLE activity is endorsed by, or affiliated with, any court or other public body or office or organization when such is not the case.

(c) Advertisements may list the number of approved credit hours. If approval of accreditation is pending, the advertisement shall so state and may list the number of CLE credit hours for which application has been made.

(d) If a sponsor includes in its advertisement the number of credit hours that a member will receive for attending the program, the sponsor must have previously applied for and received MCLE accreditation for the number of hours being advertised.

Rule Five
Accreditation Standards

5.1 Group CLE Activities. Group CLE activities shall satisfy the following:

(a) The activity must have significant intellectual or practical content with the primary objective of increasing the participant's professional competence as a lawyer; and

(b) The activity must deal primarily with substantive legal issues, legal skills, practice issues, or legal ethics and professionalism, or access to justice; and

(c) The activity must be offered by a sponsor having substantial, recent experience in offering continuing legal education or by a sponsor that can demonstrate ability to organize and effectively present continuing legal education. Demonstrated ability arises partly from the extent to which individuals with legal training or educational experience are involved in the planning, instruction, and supervision of the activity; and

(d) The activity must be primarily intended for presentation to multiple participants, including but not limited to live programs, video and audio presentations (including original programming and replays of accredited programs), satellite broadcasts and on-line programs; and

(e) The activity must include the use of thorough, high-quality written materials, unless the MCLE Administrator determines that the activity has substantial educational value without written materials.

(f) The activity must have no attendance restrictions based on race, color, gender, sexual orientation, religion, geographic location, age, handicap or disability, marital, parental or military status or other classification protected by law, except as may be permitted upon application from a provider or member, where attendance is restricted due to applicable state or federal law.

5.2 Other CLE Activities.

(a) Teaching Activities.

(1) Teaching activities may be accredited at a ratio of two credit hours for each sixty minutes of actual instruction.

(2) Teaching credit is allowed for accredited continuing legal education activities or for courses in ABA or AALS accredited law schools.

(3) Teaching other courses may also be accredited as a CLE activity, provided the activity satisfies the following criteria:

    (i)   The MCLE Administrator determines that the content of the activity is in compliance with other MCLE accreditation standards; and

    (ii)   The course is a graduate-level course offered by a university; and

    (iii)   The university is accredited by an accrediting body recognized by the U.S. Department of Education for the accreditation of institutions of postsecondary education.

(4) Credit shall not be given to an active member whose primary employment is as a full-time or part-time law teacher, but may be given to an active member who teaches on a part-time basis in addition to the member's primary employment.

(5) Teaching credit is not allowed for programs and activities for which the primary audience is nonlawyers unless the applicant establishes to the MCLE Administrator's satisfaction that the teaching activity contributed to the professional education of the presenter.

(6) No credit is allowed for repeat presentations of previously accredited courses unless the presentation involves a substantial update of previously presented material, as determined by the MCLE Administrator.

(b) Service as a Bar Examiner. Service as a bar examiner for Oregon may be accredited, provided that the service includes personally writing or grading a question for the Oregon bar exam during the reporting period. Up to six (6) credit hours may be earned for writing and grading a question, and up to three (3) credit hours may be earned for grading a question.

(c) Legal Research and Writing.

(1) Legal research and writing activities, including the preparation of written materials for use in a teaching activity may be accredited provided the activity satisfies the following criteria:

    (i)   It deals primarily with one or more of the types of issues for which group CLE activities can be accredited as described in Rule 5.1(b); and

    (ii)   It has been published in the form of articles, CLE course materials, chapters, or books, or issued as a final product of the Legal Ethics Committee or a final instruction of the Uniform Civil Jury Instructions Committee or the Uniform Criminal Jury Instructions Committee, personally authored or edited in whole or in substantial part, by the applicant; and

    (iii)   It contributes substantially to the legal education of the applicant and other attorneys; and

    (iv)   It is not done in the regular course of the active member's primary employment.

(2) The number of credit hours shall be determined by the MCLE Administrator, based on the contribution of the written materials to the professional competency of the applicant and other attorneys. One hour of credit will be granted for each sixty minutes of research and

writing, but no credit shall be granted for time spent on stylistic editing.

(d) Legal Ethics Service. A member serving on the Oregon State Bar Legal Ethics Committee, Client Security Fund Committee, Commission on Judicial Fitness & Disability, Oregon Judicial Conference Judicial Conduct Committee, Local Professional Responsibility Committees, State Professional Responsibility Board, and Disciplinary Board or serving as volunteer bar counsel or volunteer counsel to an accused in Oregon disciplinary proceedings may earn two ethics credits for each twelve months of service.

(e) Legislative Service. General credit hours may be earned for service as a member of the Oregon Legislative Assembly while it is in session.

(f) Service in Executive Branch Statewide Elected Office. Members serving as statewide elected officials in Oregon's Executive Branch, whose term in office includes all or part of a reporting period, are exempt from all MCLE requirements except those credits required in Rules 3.2(b) and (c).

(g) New Lawyer Mentoring Program (NLMP)

(1) Mentors may earn CLE credit for serving as a mentor in the Oregon State Bar's New Lawyer Mentoring Program.

(2) New lawyers who have completed the NLMP may be awarded CLE credits to be used in their first three-year reporting period.

(h) Jury instructions Committee Service. A member serving on the Oregon State Bar Uniform Civil Jury Instructions Committee or Uniform Criminal Jury Instructions Committee may earn two general credits for each 12 months of service.

(i) A member seeking credit for any of the activities described in Rule 5.2 must submit a written application on the form designated by the MCLE Administrator for Other CLE Activities.

5.3 Other Professionals. Notwithstanding the requirements of Rules 5.1(b) and (c) and 5.2, participation in or teaching an educational activity offered primarily to or by other professions or occupations may be accredited as a CLE activity if the MCLE Administrator determines that the content of the activity is in compliance with other MCLE accreditation standards. The MCLE Administrator may accredit the activity for fewer than the actual activity hours if the MCLE Administrator determines that the subject matter is not sufficient to justify full accreditation.

5.4 Attending Classes.

(a) Attending a class at an ABA or AALS accredited law school may be accredited as a CLE activity.

(b) Attending other classes may also be accredited as a CLE activity, provided the activity satisfies the following criteria:

(1) The MCLE Administrator determines that the content of the activity is in compliance with other MCLE accreditation standards; and

(2) The class is a graduate-level course offered by a university; and

(3) The university is accredited by an accrediting body recognized by the U.S. Department of Education for the accreditation of institutions of postsecondary education.

5.5 Ethics and Access to Justice.

(a) In order to be accredited as an activity in legal ethics under Rule 3.2(b), an activity shall be devoted to the study of judicial or legal ethics or professionalism, and shall include discussion of applicable judicial conduct codes, disciplinary rules, or statements of professionalism. Of the six hours of ethics credit required by Rule 3.2(b), one hour must be on the subject of a lawyer's statutory duty to report child abuse or elder abuse (see ORS 9.114). The child abuse reporting training requirement can be completed only by one hour of training by participation in or screening of an accredited program. MCLE Regulation 3.300(d) specifies the reporting periods in which the child abuse or elder abuse reporting credit is required.

(b) In order to be accredited as an activity pertaining to access to justice for purposes of Rule 3.2(c), an activity shall be directly related to the practice of law and designed to educate attorneys to identify and eliminate from the legal profession and from the practice of law barriers to access to justice arising from biases against persons because of race, gender, economic status, creed, color, religion, national origin, disability, age or sexual orientation.

(c) Portions of activities may be accredited for purposes of satisfying the ethics and access to justice requirements of Rule 3.2, if the applicable content of the activity is clearly defined.

5.6 Personal Management Assistance. Activities that deal with personal self-improvement may be accredited, provided the MCLE Administrator determines the self-improvement relates to professional competence as a lawyer.

5.7 Unaccredited Activities. The following activities shall not be accredited:

(a) Activities that would be characterized as dealing primarily with personal self-improvement unrelated to professional competence as a lawyer; and

(b) Activities designed primarily to sell services or equipment; and

(c) Video or audio presentations of a CLE activity originally conducted more than three years prior to the date viewed or heard by the member seeking credit, unless it can be shown by the member that the activity has current educational value.

(d) Repeat live, video or audio presentations of a CLE activity for which the active member has already obtained MCLE credit.

Regulations to MCLE Rule 5
Accreditation Standards

5.050 Written Materials.

(a) For the purposes of accreditation as a group CLE activity under MCLE Rule 5.1(e), written material may be provided in an electronic or computer-based format, provided the material is available for the member to retain for future reference.

(b) Factors to be considered by the MCLE Administrator in determining whether a group CLE activity has substantial educational value without written materials include, but are not limited to: the qualifications and experience of the program sponsor; the credentials of the program faculty; information concerning program content provided by program attendees or monitors; whether the subject matter of the program is such that comprehension and retention by members is likely without written materials; and whether accreditation previously was given for the same or substantially similar program.

5.100 Other CLE Activities. The application procedure for accreditation of Other CLE Activities shall be in accordance with MCLE Rule 5.2 and Regulation 4.300.

(a) With the exception of panel presentations, when calculating credit for teaching activities pursuant to MCLE Rule 5.2, for presentations where there are multiple presenters for one session, the number of minutes of actual instruction will be divided by the number of presenters unless notified otherwise by the presenter. Members who participate in panel presentations may receive credit for the total number of minutes of actual instruction. Attendance credit may be claimed for any portion of an attended session not receiving teaching credit.

(b) Credit for legislative service may be earned at a rate of 1.0 general credit for each week or part thereof while the legislature is in session.

(c) Members serving as Governor, Secretary of State, Commissioner of the Bureau of Labor and Industries, Attorney General and Treasurer during all or part of a reporting period are required to complete the minimum credit requirements in the following categories – ethics, access to justice, child abuse and elder abuse reporting – during the reporting periods set forth in MCLE Regulation 3.300(d). These members are exempt from any other credit requirements during the reporting period in which they serve.

(d) Members who serve as mentors in the Oregon State Bar's New Lawyer Mentoring Program (NLMP) may earn eight credits, including two ethics credits, upon completion of the plan year. If another lawyer assists with the mentoring, the credits must be apportioned between them.

(e) Upon successful completion of the NLMP, new lawyers may earn six general/practical skills credits to be used in their first three-year reporting period.

5.200 Legal Research and Writing Activities.

(a) For the purposes of accreditation of Legal Research and Writing, all credit hours shall be deemed earned on the date of publication or issuance of the written work.

(b) Legal Research and Writing that supplements an existing CLE publication may be accredited if the applicant provides a statement from the publisher confirming that research on the existing publication revealed no need for supplementing the publication's content.

5.250 Jury Instructions Committee Service. To be eligible for credit under MCLE Rule 5.2(g), a member of a jury instructions committee must attend at least six hours of committee meetings during the relevant 12-month period.

5.300 Personal Management Assistance. A program may be accredited as a personal management assistance program if it provides assistance with issues that could impair a lawyer's professional competence (examples include but are not limited to programs addressing alcoholism, drug addiction, burnout, procrastination, depression, anxiety, gambling or other addictions or compulsive behaviors, and other health and mental health related issues). A program may also be accredited as a personal management assistance program if it is designed to improve or enhance a lawyer's professional effectiveness and competence (examples include but are not limited to programs addressing time and stress management, career satisfaction and transition, and interpersonal/relationship skill-building).

5.400 Business Development and Marketing Activities. Activities devoted to enhancing profits or generating revenue through advertising and solicitation of legal business, whether denominated business development, client development, practice development, marketing or otherwise, shall not be accredited. Activities dealing with ethical issues relating to advertising and solicitation under applicable disciplinary rules may be accredited if it appears to the Administrator that the emphasis is on legal ethics rather than on business development or marketing.

5.500 Access to Justice. A program shall not be ineligible for accreditation as an access to justice activity solely because it is limited to a discussion of substantive law, provided the substantive law relates to access to justice issues involving race, gender, economic status, creed, color, religion, national origin, disability, age, or sexual orientation.

5.600 Independent Study. Members may earn credit through independent screening or viewing of audio-or video-tapes of programs originally presented to live group audiences, or through online programs designed for presentation to a wide audience. A lawyer who is licensed in a jurisdiction that allows credit for reading and successfully completing an examination about specific material may use such credits to meet the Oregon requirement. No credit will be allowed for independent reading of material selected by a member except as part of an organized and accredited group program.

5.700 In order to be accredited as a child abuse reporting or elder abuse reporting activity, the one-hour session must include discussion of an Oregon attorney's requirements to report child abuse or elder abuse and the exceptions to those requirements.

Rule Six
Credit Limitations

6.1 In General.

(a) Credit shall be allowed only for CLE activities that are accredited as provided in these Rules, and substantial participation by the active member is required. The MCLE Administrator may allow partial credit for completion of designated portions of a CLE activity.

(b) Except as provided in Rule 6.1(c), credit for a particular reporting period shall be allowed only for activities participated in during that reporting period.

(c) An active member may carry forward 15 or fewer unused credit hours from the reporting period during which the credit hours were earned to the next reporting period.

6.2 Teaching and Legal Research and Writing Limitation. No more than 15 credit hours shall be allowed for each legal research activity for which credit is sought under MCLE Rule 5.2(c) and no more than 20 hours of combined teaching and legal research and writing credit may be claimed in one three-year reporting period. Not more than 10 hours may be claimed in any shorter reporting period.

6.3 Personal Management Assistance Limitation. No more than 6 credit hours may be claimed in one three-year reporting period and not more than 3 hours may be claimed in a shorter reporting period for personal management assistance activities.

Regulations to MCLE Rule 6
Credit Limitations

6.100 Carry Over Credit. No more than six ethics credits can be carried over for application to the subsequent reporting period requirement. Ethics credits in excess of the carry over limit may be carried over as general credits. Child abuse and elder abuse education credits earned in excess of the reporting period requirement may be carried over as general credits, but a new child abuse or elder abuse reporting education credit must be earned in each reporting period in which the credit is required. Access to justice credits may be carried over as general credits, but new credits must be earned in the reporting period in which they are required. Carry over credits from a reporting period in which the credits were completed by the member may not be carried forward more than one reporting period.

6.200 Credits Earned in Excess of Credit Limitations. Any credits earned in excess of the credit limitations set forth in MCLE Rule 6.2 and 6.3 may not be claimed in the reporting period in which they are completed or as carry over credits in the next reporting period.

Rule Seven
Compliance

7.1 Reports. Every active member shall file a completed compliance report certifying completion of the member's MCLE requirement, on a form provided by the MCLE Administrator, on or before 5:00 p.m. on January 31 of the year immediately following the active member's reporting period.

7.2 Recordkeeping.

(a) Every active member shall maintain records of participation in CLE activities for use in completing a compliance report and shall retain these records for a period of twelve months after the end of the member's reporting period.

(b) The MCLE Administrator may maintain records of active members' participation in CLE activities as necessary to verify compliance with the MCLE requirement.

7.3 Audits.

(a) The MCLE Administrator may audit compliance reports selected because of facial defects or by random selection or other appropriate method.

(b) For the purpose of conducting audits, the MCLE Administrator may request and review records of participation in CLE activities reported by active members.

(c) Failure to substantiate participation in CLE activities in accordance with applicable rules and regulations after request by the MCLE Administrator shall result in disallowance of credits for the reported activity and assessment of the late filing fee specified in 7.5(f).

(d) The MCLE Administrator shall refer active members to the Oregon State Bar Disciplinary Counsel for further action where questions of dishonesty in reporting occur.

7.4 Noncompliance.

(a) Grounds. The following are considered grounds for a finding of non-compliance with these Rules:

(1) Failure to complete the MCLE requirement for the applicable reporting period.

(2) Failure to file a completed compliance report on time.

(3) Failure to provide sufficient records of participation in CLE activities to substantiate credits reported, after request by the MCLE Administrator.

(b) Notice. In the event of a finding of noncompliance, the MCLE Administrator shall send a written notice of noncompliance to the affected active member. The notice shall be sent via regular mail and email 30 days after the filing deadline and shall state the nature of the noncompliance and shall summarize the applicable rules regarding noncompliance and its consequences.

7.5 Cure.

(a) Noncompliance for failure to file a completed compliance report by the due date can be cured by filing the completed report demonstrating completion of the MCLE requirement during the applicable reporting period, together with the late fee specified MCLE Regulation 7.200, no more than 60 days after the notice of noncompliance was sent.

(b) Noncompliance for failure to complete the MCLE requirement during the applicable reporting period can be cured by doing the following no more than 60 days after the notice of noncompliance was sent:

> (1) Completing the credit hours necessary to satisfy the MCLE requirement for the applicable reporting period;

> (2) Filing the completed compliance report; and

> (3) Paying the late filing fee specified in MCLE Regulation 7.200.

(c) Noncompliance for failure to provide the MCLE Administrator with sufficient records of participation in CLE activities to substantiate credits reported can be cured by providing the MCLE Administrator with sufficient records, together with the late fee specified in MCLE Regulation 7.200, no more than 60 days after the notice of noncompliance was sent.

(d) Credit hours applied to a previous reporting period for the purpose of curing noncompliance as provided in Rule 7.5(b) may only be used for that purpose and may not be used to satisfy the MCLE requirement for any other reporting period.

(e) When it is determined that the noncompliance has been cured, the MCLE Administrator shall notify the affected active member that he or she has complied with the MCLE requirement for the applicable reporting period. Curing noncompliance does not prevent subsequent audit and action specified in Rule 7.3.

7.6 Suspension.
If the noncompliance is not cured within the deadline specified in Rule 7.5, the MCLE Administrator shall recommend to the Supreme Court that the affected active member be suspended from membership in the bar.

Regulations to MCLE Rule 7
Compliance

7.100. Member Records of Participation. In furtherance of its audit responsibilities, the MCLE Administrator may review an active member's records of participation in CLE activities. Records which may satisfy such a request include, but are not limited to, certificates of attendance or transcripts issued by sponsors, MCLE recordkeeping forms, canceled checks or other proof of payment for registration fees or audio or video tapes, course materials, notes or annotations to course materials, or daily calendars for the dates of CLE activities. For individually screened presentations, contemporaneous records of screening dates and times shall be required.

7.150 Sponsor Records of Participation. Within 30 days after completion of an accredited CLE activity, the sponsor shall submit an attendance record reflecting the name and Oregon bar number of each Oregon bar member attendee. The record shall be in a compatible electronic format or as otherwise directed by the MCLE Administrator.

7.200 Late Fees.

(a) The late fee for curing a failure to timely file a completed compliance report is $50 if the report is filed and the late fee is paid after the filing deadline and no more than 30 days after the mailing of the notice of noncompliance and $100 if the report is filed and the late fee is paid more than 30 days after the mailing of the notice of noncompliance but within the 60 day cure period; if additional time for filing is granted by the MCLE Administrator, the fee shall increase by $50 for every additional 30 days or part thereof.

(b) The late fee for not completing the MCLE requirement during the applicable reporting period is $200 if the requirement is completed after the end of the reporting period but before the end of the 60 day cure period; if additional time for meeting the requirement is granted by the MCLE Administrator, the fee shall increase by $50 for every additional 30 days or part thereof.

Rule Eight
Review and Enforcement

8.1 Review.

(a) Decisions of the MCLE Administrator. A decision, other than a suspension recommended pursuant to Rule 7.6, affecting any active member or sponsor is final unless a request for review is filed with the MCLE Administrator within 21 days after notice of the decision is mailed. The request for review may be by letter and requires no special form, but it shall state the decision to be reviewed and give the reasons for review. The matter shall be reviewed by the BOG or, if one has been appointed, the MCLE Committee, at its next regular meeting. An active member or sponsor shall have the right, upon request, to be heard, and any such hearing request shall be made in the initial letter. The hearing shall be informal. On review, the BOG or the MCLE Committee shall have authority to take whatever action consistent with these rules is deemed proper. The MCLE Administrator shall notify the member or sponsor in writing of the decision on review and the reasons therefor.

(b) Decisions of the MCLE Committee. If a decision of the MCLE Administrator is initially reviewed by the MCLE Committee, the decision of the MCLE Committee may be reviewed by the BOG on written request of the affected active member or sponsor made within 21 days of the issuance of the MCLE Committee's decision. The decision of the BOG shall be final.

(c) Suspension Recommendation of the MCLE Administrator. A recommendation for suspension pursuant to Rule 7.6 shall be subject to the following procedures:

(1) A copy of the MCLE Administrator's recommendation to the Supreme Court that a member be suspended from membership in the bar shall be sent by regular mail and email to the member.

(2) If the recommendation of the MCLE Administrator is approved, the court shall enter its order and an effective date for the member's suspension shall be stated therein.

8.2 Reinstatement. An active member suspended for noncompliance with the MCLE requirement shall be reinstated only upon completion of the MCLE requirement, submission of a completed compliance report to the bar, payment of the late filing and reinstatement fees, and compliance with the applicable provisions of the Rules of Procedure.

Regulations to MCLE Rule 8
Review and Enforcement

8.100 Review Procedure.

(a) The MCLE Administrator shall notify the active member or sponsor of the date, time and place of the BOG or MCLE Committee meeting at which the request for review will be considered. Such notice must be sent no later than 14 days prior to such meeting. If the request for review is received less than 14 days before the next regularly scheduled meeting, the request will be considered at the following regularly scheduled meeting of the BOG or MCLE Committee, unless the member or sponsor waives the 14 day notice.

(b) A hearing before the MCLE Committee may be recorded at the request of the active member or sponsor or the MCLE Committee. In such event, the party requesting that the matter be recorded shall bear the expense of such recording. The other party shall be entitled to a copy of the record of the proceedings at their own expense.

(c) The MCLE Administrator shall notify the active member or sponsor of the decision and the reasons therefor within 28 days of the date of the review. A decision of the MCLE Committee shall be subject to BOG review as provided in Rule 8.1.

Rule Nine
Waivers and Exemptions

Upon written request of a member or sponsor, the MCLE Administrator may waive in full or part, grant exemption from or permit substitute compliance with any requirement of these Rules upon a finding that hardship or other special circumstances makes compliance impossible or inordinately difficult, or upon a finding that the requested waiver, exemption or substitute compliance is not inconsistent with the purposes of these Rules. The request shall state the reason for the waiver or exemption and shall describe a continuing legal education plan tailored to the particular circumstances of the requestor.

Regulations to MCLE Rule 9
Waivers and Exemptions

9.100 Waivers and Exemptions . The MCLE Administrator will consider requests for waivers and exemptions from the MCLE Rules and Regulations on a case by case basis.

Rule Ten
Amendment

These Rules may be amended by the BOG subject to approval by the Supreme Court. Amendments may be proposed by the MCLE Committee, the executive director, or an active member. Proposed amendments shall be submitted and considered in compliance with any regulations adopted by the BOG.

PENNSYLVANIA

PENNSYLVANIA RULES FOR CONTINUING LEGAL EDUCATION

Rule 101. Title and Citation.

These rules shall be known as the Pennsylvania Rules for Continuing Legal Education and may be cited as "Pa.R.C.L.E. _____."

Rule 102. General.

(a) Purpose.

These rules are adopted to assure that lawyers admitted to practice in the Commonwealth of Pennsylvania continue their education to have and maintain the requisite knowledge and skill necessary to fulfill their professional responsibilities.

(b) Definitions.

Subject to any definitions contained in subsequent rules, the following words and phrases, when used in these rules shall have, unless the context clearly indicates otherwise, the following meanings:

"Active Lawyer": A member in good standing of the bar of the Supreme Court of Pennsylvania, who is not an active or senior member of the judiciary. A lawyer who is active for any part of a year must comply with these rules.

"Administrative Office": The Administrative Office of Pennsylvania Courts.

"Administrator": The head of the administrative staff of the Board.

"Board": The Continuing Legal Education Board established by these rules.

"CLE": Continuing legal education to be provided under these rules.

"Compliance Period": The twelve month time period assigned to a lawyer within which he or she must comply with their annual CLE requirement, except during the implementation period from July 1, 1992 through December 31, 1992.

"Fiscal Year": The fiscal year of the Board which shall end December 31.

"Provider": A corporation or association which has been accredited by the Board to provide continuing legal education under these rules or a corporation or association which provides one (1) or more continuing legal education courses approved by the Board.

"Supreme Court": The Supreme Court of Pennsylvania existing under Section 2 Article V of the Constitution of Pennsylvania.

"Verified Statement": A document filed with the Board or the Supreme Court under these rules containing statements of fact and a statement by the signatory that it is made subject to the penalties of 18 Pa.C.S.A. ss 4904 (relating to unsworn falsification to authorities).

(c) Gender; Number; Tense:

In these rules the masculine shall include the feminine, and the feminine shall include the masculine; the singular shall include the plural, and the plural, the singular; words used in the past or present tense shall include the future.

(d) Effective date:

These rules shall become effective on the first day of the sixth month following their adoption by the Supreme Court.

Rule 103. Board.

(a) Establishment.

The Supreme Court hereby establishes the Continuing Legal Education Board ("Board").

(b) Constituency.

The Board shall consist of ten (10) members appointed by the Supreme Court. Each member of the Board shall be an active member of the Bar of this Commonwealth with his or her primary residency in the Commonwealth of Pennsylvania.

(c) Organization.

The Supreme Court shall appoint from the members of the Board a chairman and a vice chairman. The Board may designate such other officers and form such other committees as it deems appropriate.

(d) Board Member Terms.

The regular term of members of the Board shall be for three (3) years, and no member may serve for more than two (2) consecutive three (3) year terms. The terms of a third of the members, as nearly as may be, shall expire at the end of the fiscal year. The terms of the first Board shall be staggered so that three (3) members shall be appointed for three (3) years, three (3) members for two (2) year terms, and three (3) members for a one (1) year term.

(e) Action by Board.

Five (5) Board members in office shall constitute a quorum. The Board shall act only with the concurrence of not less than five (5) Board members. The Board may adopt rules providing for the holding of teleconference meetings.

(f) Compensation and Expenses.

Board members shall receive no compensation for services provided under these rules. Board members shall be reimbursed by the Board for their reasonable and necessary expenses in attendance at meetings and in otherwise fulfilling their responsibilities

(g) Immunity.

The Board, and its members, employees and agents are immune from all civil liability for conduct and communications occurring in the performance of their official duties relating to the administration of the continuing legal education requirements.

Rule 104. Powers and Duties of the Board.

(a) To administer these rules;

(b) To adopt regulations and procedures consistent with these rules;

(c) To report to the Supreme Court at least annually and at such other times as the Supreme Court shall require;

(d) To recommend a budget for approval by the Supreme Court, to receive monies and to expend funds for operation of the Board to fulfill its duties under these rules;

(e) To employ an administrator and such other staff as may be required from time to time;

(f) To accredit providers of CLE;

(g) To approve the subjects which will receive credit for CLE requirements;

(h) To audit, examine, inspect, and review the operations of providers, including instructors, classes, curricula, teaching materials, facilities, income, and receipts from CLE to assure compliance with these rules and any rules adopted by the Board;

(i) To impose sanctions on providers where appropriate;

(j) To impose reasonable fees upon providers for support of Board operations and to reimburse the Board for expenditures relating to providers generally or to impose reasonable fees upon a provider for expenditures relating to such provider or its operation;

(k) To impose reasonable fees upon active lawyers to reimburse the Board for expenditures relating to active lawyers generally or to impose reasonable fees upon an active lawyer for expenditures relating to such active lawyer;

(l) Provided, however, that all fees imposed by the Board shall be approved by the Supreme Court;

(m) To issue subpoenas and cause testimony to be taken under oath in any investigation or proceeding before the Board, Board member(s), or hearing examiner appointed to the Board. All subpoenas shall be issued in the name and under the seal of The Pennsylvania Supreme Court and served as provided by the Pennsylvania Rules of Civil Procedure;

(n) To order the testimony of a witness be taken in deposition within or without this Commonwealth in the manner prescribed and extent required for the taking of depositions in civil actions.

Rule 105. Continuing Legal Education Requirement

(a) General Requirement

1. Every active lawyer shall annually complete, during the compliance period to which he or she is assigned, the CLE required by the Board pursuant to these rules and established in Board regulations.

2. CLE shall be on the subjects of:

(i) substantive law, practice and procedure

(ii) lawyer ethics and the rules of professional conduct

(iii) professionalism

(iv) substance abuse as it affects lawyers and the practice of law.

3. The minimum annual CLE requirement shall be nine (9) hours, effective September 1, 1994, and twelve (12) hours, effective September 1, 1995.

(b) Fulfillment Requirements.

The CLE requirement shall be fulfilled by attending the required number of CLE courses by providers or completing a CLE activity approved by the Board as sufficient to meet the CLE general requirement.

(c) Every newly admitted attorney shall attend the Bridge the Gap program, of at least four (4) credit hours, sponsored by approved Bridge the Gap CLE provider prior to his or her first compliance deadline.

Rule 106. Providers.

(a) Eligibility.

1. Accredited provider: A corporation or association may apply to the Board for accreditation as a CLE provider. Such accreditation shall constitute prior approval of CLE courses offered by such provider, subject to amendment, suspension or revocation of such accreditation by the Board.

2. Course provider: A corporation or association may apply to the Board for approval of CLE courses under Rule 107 and upon such approval, and while any course offered remains approved, such corporation or association shall be deemed a provider subject to these rules.

(b) Procedures for Accreditation.

The Board shall establish by rules the procedures for accreditation of accredited providers and for sanctions including the revocation of accreditation.

(c) Minimum Standards for Providers

1. A provider shall be an organization engaged in CLE which, during the two (2) years immediately preceding its application has sponsored at least five (5) separate courses which would comply with the requirements for course approval under these rules. A provider may be an ABA accredited law school or a bar association within the Commonwealth of Pennsylvania.

2. The Board may establish by regulations additional minimum standards for providers.

3. At all times a provider must:

a. Develop and implement methods to evaluate its course offerings to determine their effectiveness and the extent to which they meet the needs of lawyers, and, upon request from the Board, provide course evaluations by attendees;

b. If requested by the Board, a provider shall promptly submit information about the course including any brochure, advertisement or circular describing the course, a description of the method or manner of presentation of the course materials, and a set of any written, videotaped or audiotaped materials;

c. Provide courses consistent with the standards set forth in these rules and any rules adopted by the Board;

d. Make the course available to lawyers throughout the Commonwealth who are thought to be interested in the subject matter;

e. Pay the administrative or provider fees and appropriate attendee fee, if any, established by the Board.

(d) Bridge the Gap Providers.

Accredited providers may request Board approval to offer the Bridge the Gap program.

Rule 107. Minimum Standards for Course Approval.

To be approved for credit, a CLE course or activity must meet the following standards:

(a) The course shall be of intellectual or practical content;

(b) The course shall contribute directly to lawyers professional competence or skills, or to their education with respect to their professional or ethical obligations;

(c) If a course does not bear entirely on the general requirements for CLE or the practice of law or the substance of laws, practice or procedure or if the method of presenting the course is below minimum standards, the Board may assign partial credit;

(d) Each faculty member must possess the necessary practical or academic skills to conduct the course effectively. Subjects should normally be taught by lawyers or judges;

(e) While written materials need not be distributed for every course, thorough, high quality, readable, carefully prepared written materials should be distributed to all participants at or before the time the course is offered whenever practicable;

(f) The course shall be presented in a suitable setting devoted to the educational activity of the program. No CLE shall consist solely of television viewing in the home, correspondence work, or self study, except as the Board shall approve to accommodate the needs of the handicapped or incapacitated. Video, motion picture or audio tape presentations may be used provided a faculty person is in attendance at all presentations to comment and answer questions. Distance Learning programs may be approved if they meet interactive, technical and accreditation standards set forth by the Board;

(g) The course must be open to any lawyers thought to be interested in the subject matter;

(h) The Board shall adopt rules which will allow providers to obtain prior approval of CLE courses or which may allow providers to obtain post presentation approval of CLE courses subject to the right of the Board to adjust the credit as provided in subsection (c).

Rule 108. Credit for Continuing Legal Education Courses and Activity.

(a) Credit.

Participants shall receive credit of one (1) hour for each sixty (60) minutes actually spent in attendance at an approved course.

(b) Law school courses.

Courses by an ABA accredited law school, other than those required for a legal degree, which otherwise comply with these rules, shall qualify for credit.

(c) CLE credit for preparation.

The Board shall establish rules for credit to be given to faculty members for the preparation of CLE courses which qualify for credit under these rules. (Teaching Activity - Application for Course Preparation Credit)

(d) Carry over credits.

A balance of credit hours in excess of the current annual CLE requirement may be carried forward for the next two (2) succeeding years. No more than two times the current annual CLE requirement may be carried forward into the two (2) succeeding years.

(e) The number of credits earned by distance learning education that may be applied to the annual compliance requirement shall not exceed four (4). Commencing with the compliance period beginning on May 1, 2014, and to all compliance periods commencing thereafter, the number of credits earned by distance learning education that may be applied to the annual compliance requirement shall not exceed six (6).

Rule 109. Financing the Continuing Legal Education Board.

(a) Provider fee.

The cost of establishing, maintaining, and operating the Board shall be paid by providers through a fee per credit established by the Board and paid to the Board at the time of the filing of the enrollment form. In the discharge of its responsibility, the Board shall adjust as far as possible any fee schedule adopted so as to reduce the financial impact on lawyers in the early years of practice and the sole practitioner generally.

(b) Effect of non-payment.

If payment is not received by a due date to be established by the Board, a lawyer shall be deemed not to have fulfilled the lawyer CLE requirements, and the Board may impose sanctions on the provider, including revocation of accreditation.

(c) Audit.

The Board shall annually obtain an independent audit by a certified public accountant of the funds entrusted to it and their disposition and shall file a copy of the audit with the **Supreme Court.**

Rule 110. Reporting Responsibilities.

(a) Provider Report. Providers shall enroll attendees at CLE courses and shall file a written form with the Board or provide an electronic transmission to the Board listing all participants seeking CLE credit under these rules in a format approved by the Board within thirty (30) days of the date of presentation of the course. The Board shall require verified statements as to the accuracy of the reports it receives.

(b) CLE Compliance Report. The Board will notify each lawyer of his or her CLE status prior to the end of the compliance period to which the lawyer has been assigned and will provide a final compliance notice after the end of the compliance period.

(c) Assumed compliance. The lawyer whose Board report indicates compliance with the CLE requirement may assume that he or she is in compliance.

(d) Disputed reports. If a lawyer shall disagree with the enrollment or annual reporting forms, the lawyer shall within thirty (30) days of the date thereof notify the Board in writing setting forth the matter in dispute.

(e) Board review. The Board shall establish regulations providing for review of its determination of the CLE credits earned by a lawyer and for resolving disputes.

Rule 111. Lawyer Noncompliance.

(a) Notification. If a lawyer shall fail to comply with these rules or if a lawyer is determined by the Board to be deficient in his or her CLE requirement, such lawyer shall be so notified in writing by the Board of the nature of such noncompliance and shall be given sixty (60) days to remedy such noncompliance.

(b) Sanctions. If the Board finds the lawyer not in compliance with these rules or the regulations of the Board, it shall so report to the Supreme Court and recommend that the lawyer be placed on administrative suspension.

Rule 112. Reporting of Board.

The Board shall report to the Supreme Court the names of all lawyers who are not in compliance under these rules, the names of all lawyers reinstated hereunder, and the names of all lawyers who have been granted waivers and extensions of CLE requirements by the Board and the basis therefore.

Rule 113. Waivers and Extensions.

These rules shall be strictly enforced, but waivers of strict compliance with these rules or extensions of time deadlines provided in these rules may be made by the Board in cases of undue hardship or for other compelling reasons in accordance with the following:

(a) Waiver.

When a lawyer on active status, because of circumstances beyond his or her control, cannot in any reasonable manner meet the requirement for continuing education in any given reporting year, these rules may be waived, in whole or in part.

(b) Application for Waiver.

The application for waiver shall set forth the reason why the lawyer cannot comply with the minimum requirements of these rules; shall set forth the efforts made to comply; and shall be accompanied by a plan setting forth how the lawyer expects to continue his or her legal education during the period of time for which strict compliance is waived.

(c) Termination of Waiver.

Waivers may be granted by the Board for such period as the Board may determine. Upon termination of the waiver, the Board may make such additional educational requirements as it deems appropriate.

(d) Extensions of Time.

The Board may grant an extension of time for the completion of a lawyer's CLE requirements upon such terms as the Board shall require.

PUERTO RICO

RULES OF THE CONTINUING LEGAL
EDUCATION PROGRAM

TABLE OF CONTENTS

CHAPTER IV – PROVIDERS

CHAPTER V – PROCEDURES BEFORE THE BOARD

CHAPTER VI – COMPLIANCE BY LAW PROFESSIONALS

CHAPTER VII – ALTERNATIVE COMPLIANCE MECHANISMS AND OTHER PROVISIONS

RULES OF THE CONTINUING LEGAL EDUCATION PROGRAM

CHAPTER I   GENERAL PROVISIONS

RULE 1.   LEGAL BASIS

These Rules are promulgated by virtue of the authority vested in the Continuing Legal Education Board under Rule 8(d)(7) of the *Rules for Continuing Legal Education* adopted by the Supreme Court of Puerto Rico on June 30, 1998.

COMMENT

Rule 8(d)(7) of the *Rules for Continuing Legal Education* of June 1998 provides that the Continuing Legal Education Board will adopt the necessary rules to achieve the efficient administration of the continuing legal education program.

RULE 2.   TITLE

These Rules will be known as the *Rules of the Continuing Legal Education Program.*

COMMENT

The title of these Rules identifies the function delegated to the Board: to administer the continuing legal education program created by the Supreme Court for all lawyers who practice the legal and notarial profession in Puerto Rico.

RULE 3.   MISSION

The Supreme Court of Puerto Rico, by virtue of its inherent power to regulate the practice of law and the notarial profession in Puerto Rico, promulgated the *Rules for Continuing Legal Education* of June 30, 1998, to establish a mandatory continuing legal education program that would encourage and contribute to the professional advancement of every person engaged in the practice of Law. It also created the Continuing Education Board, the body to which it delegated the necessary functions to carry out this program and ensure compliance with the requirements established in the *Rules*.

One of the Board's basic functions is to certify that law professionals comply with their duty to take the legal education courses approved by the Board to achieve the intended goals. To accomplish this mission, therefore, there must be an efficiently managed continuing legal education program that will enable law professionals to keep up-to-date on caselaw, legislation, and doctrines, as well as on the skills needed to practice their profession at the highest levels of quality and competence.

The mechanisms established in these Rules allow the Board to achieve its mission and to perform the other tasks delegated to it. These rules also aim to facilitate compliance by law professionals with their ethical duty to maintain the highest degree of excellence and competence in the legal services they provide.

COMMENT

The rule states the purpose of the mandatory continuing legal education program established by the Supreme Court for law professionals actively engaged in the practice of their profession, as provided by Rules 1 and 2 of the 1998 *Rules.*

The mission set forth in this Rule is consistent with the functions delegated to the Board by the Supreme Court: to develop, administer, and assess the continuing legal education program as provided by Rule 8 of the 1998 *Rules.* It is also consistent with Canon 2 of Professional Ethics, which imposes on all law professionals the duty to attain a high degree of excellence and competence in their profession and to offer adequate assistance of counsel; these objectives must be achieved through their participation in educational programs that contribute to their professional advancement.

RULE 4.   APPLICABILITY

(A)   The provisions of these Rules apply to:

(1) any law professional admitted to legal and notarial practice in Puerto Rico, and to those who have been suspended by the Supreme Court from the practice of their profession, either temporarily or for a specific period of time;

(2) providers accredited by the Board to offer continuing legal education courses.

(B)   Any lawyer who has been permanently separated or indefinitely suspended from the legal profession by the Supreme Court and who voluntarily wishes to comply with the Continuing Legal Education Program requirements may do so; in that case, the Board must inform the Supreme Court every semester about the attorneys who comply with the provisions of these Rules.

(C)   The following are excluded from the provisions of these Rules:

     (1)   judges of the General Court of Justice of Puerto Rico, for the term of their office, and former Justices of the Supreme Court of Puerto Rico;

     (2)   judges of the Federal Court for the District of Puerto Rico, of the Bankruptcy Court, and federal magistrates, for the term of their office;

     (3)   law professionals who have any of the following characteristics:

     (a)   teach Law at universities accredited by the Supreme Court or by the American Bar Association, while performing that function;

     (b)   are inactive by reason of age or of physical or mental incapacity after the Supreme Court accepted their petition for voluntary separation from the practice of law in Puerto Rico;

     (c)   are exempted from payment of annual bar association dues by reason of incapacity to practice their profession under Section 10 of the Bar Association Rules, and who ask the Board to exempt them from compliance;

     (d)   apply before the Board and are granted exemption or deferral from the continuing legal education requirement for good cause for the term granted;

     (e)   have been permanently separated from the practice of their profession by the Supreme Court. If they are reinstated, it will be incumbent upon the Court to decide how they will comply with the provisions of these Rules;

     (f)   submit to the Board a certification from the Puerto Rico Bar Association stating that they are inactive members of the bar, as defined in Rule 5(13) of these Rules, during the time of inactivity. If reactivated, it will be incumbent upon the Court to decide how they will comply with the provisions of these Rules;

     (g)   are enjoined by legal mandate from practicing law during the statutory term.

(D)   Law professionals are under no obligation to comply with the continuing legal education requirement or with the provisions of these Rules during the two (2) years following the date of their initial admission to the practice of law.

COMMENT

Section (A)(1) is based on Rule 2 of the 1998 *Rules*, which establishes the general standard that continuing legal education will be mandatory for all law professionals who remain active after being duly admitted by the Supreme Court to the practice of the legal and notarial profession in Puerto Rico. The phrase "active lawyer" was defined in Rule 3 of the 1998 *Rules* as any person who, in addition to being duly admitted to the practice of law, is also a member of the Bar Association. Rule 5 of these Rules defines "law professional" as a professional authorized by the Supreme Court to practice the legal and notarial profession in Puerto Rico.

Section (A)(1) is also consistent with Rule 10 of the 1998 *Rules*, which requires that the law professional inform in the motion for reinstatement to active status that he or she continued to receive legal education during the term of his or her suspension and explain how this requirement was met. These provisions advise law professionals that their temporary suspension from the practice of the legal or notarial profession does not entail an automatic release from their obligation to receive continuing legal education. This is so because temporary suspension, unlike a court-ordered permanent separation from the legal profession, entails a high probability that reinstatement will be sought upon the lapse of the term fixed, as the case may be. Consequently, requiring that law professionals continue to receive legal education during the term of suspension and show how they met this requirement averts any interruption in their professional advancement and prevents retroactive compliance with the required continued legal education credit hours in a manner that could be burdensome. This rule also intends to stimulate law professionals to use this term to learn more about the ethical aspects that gave rise to his or her suspension. On the other hand, this rule is beneficial because it establishes an additional standard that may be considered by the Supreme Court when passing on the reinstatement petition.

Section (A)(2) extends the application of these Rules to providers of continuing legal education courses regarding all aspects of the implementation of this program. Providers are entities or institutions approved by the Supreme Court.

Section (C) of the rule includes a list of law professionals who were exempted from compliance with the continuing legal education requirement and with the provisions of these Rules. The exemption of judges from the Puerto Rico judicial system and the federal system is grounded on the fact that the Judiciary has its own particular continuing legal education needs that it must address through specialized courses and activities of its own. Pursuant to Rule 2 of the 1998 *Rules*, "[t]he [J]udiciary shall meet the minimum continuing legal education requirements determined by the administrative authorities of their respective systems."

Section (C)(3)(a) is based on Rule 7(b) of the 1998 *Rules*, which recognizes this alternative compliance mechanism. Professionals engaged in the teaching of Law at accredited universities are exempted because their teaching practice requires them to keep up to date on different subjects and because they are used as resources in continuing legal education activities. This section clarifies the Rule 7(b) text by providing that accredited universities are those recognized by the Supreme Court or by the American Bar Association. Applications for exemption from compliance by reason of teaching in other universities may be considered under section (C)(3)(d), which establishes exemptions for good cause.

Section (C)(3)(c) is based on Rule 3(b) of the 1998 *Rules*, which defines "inactive lawyer" as a law professional who has been exempted by the Bar Association from payment of the annual membership dues by reason of his or her incapacity to practice law. It is also based on Rule 8(d)(4) of the mentioned *Rules*, which authorizes the Board to consider applications for exemption filed by law professionals who are in this situation.

Section (C)(3)(d) adopts the provisions of Rule 8(d)(3) of the 1998 *Rules*, which grants the Board discretion to defer or exempt from compliance with the continuing legal education requirement for good cause.

Among the reasons that could be considered "good cause" for exemption from compliance with the provisions of these Rules is the situation of lawyers who practice law in United States jurisdictions that have established an equivalent board or accrediting entity for mandatory continuing legal education, and who are complying with said program.

Section (C)(3)(e) provides that the continuing legal education requirement does not apply to law professionals who have been permanently separated from the practice of their profession by the Supreme Court because in these cases, the probability of reinstatement in the near future is more remote. The second sentence of this section addresses the Board's concern that law professionals who are reinstated years after being suspended indefinitely will certainly lack the skills needed for the effective practice of their profession, inasmuch as they have been out of touch with it, and might place public interest and the interests of their clients at risk. The Board recommends that in these cases the Supreme Court, as a condition for reinstatement, should require those law professionals to take a specific legal training that would at least require them to take courses for one or more compliance periods.

Section (C)(3)(f) exempts law professionals who do not practice their profession but are still members of the Bar Association; provided that if they become active again, the Board may require them to comply with all or with some of the continuing legal education requirements under conditions that are different from those established in these Rules (for instance, they may have to comply with some or with all of the required credits within a shorter period of time).

Section (C)(3)(g) may apply to government officers or employees whose positions are regulated by a statute that enjoins them from practicing their profession during the time they hold office.

Section (D), which exempts new law professionals from compliance with the continuing legal education requirements during the first two (2) years following the date of their initial admission to the practice of law, addresses the fact that newly admitted law professionals have a clearer recollection of matters related to the legal and notarial practice because they recently passed the bar examination.

RULE 5.   DEFINITIONS

1. Reasonable Accommodation – A logical and reasonable adjustment of the requirements established in these Rules for the accreditation of continuous legal education [courses] in order to ameliorate the impact of a law professional's disability on his or her capacity to derive full and effective benefits from the courses, without said adjustment resulting in any of the following consequences:

    (a) fundamentally altering the objective of the mandatory continuing legal education program, which is to encourage and contribute to the lawyers' professional advancement through their full and effective utilization of the courses offered, as prescribed in the 1998 *Rules*;

    (b) imposing undue hardship on the Supreme Court and on the Board regarding the administrative function of certifying compliance with the continuing legal education requirements.

2. Authorized course – A continuing legal education course approved by the Board because it meets all the requirements established in Rule 11 of these Rules.

3. Continuing Legal Education Course – Any educational activity that addresses the professional advancement needs of law professionals and that is designed for the purpose of obtaining, developing, and preserving the knowledge and skills needed to practice the legal and notarial profession at the highest levels of quality and competence.

4. Director – The person designated to perform the function of Executive Director of the Board.

5. Effective disclosure – The act of announcing the course to be offered to all Bar Association members by publication in a daily newspaper of general circulation in Puerto Rico or by any other alternative means of disclosure.

6. Private professional institution – The private law firm, partnership, professional corporation, organization, or entity whose members are mainly engaged in the practice of law.

7. Public professional institution – Any organization or entity under an agency, department, corporation, instrumentality, entity or body of the three branches of state, federal, or municipal government.

8. Board – The Continuing Legal Education Board, the body in charge of administering and enforcing compliance with the continuing legal education requirements as established in the 1998 *Rules*.

9. Compliance period – The two (2)-year-period within which law professionals must complete twenty-four (24) credit hours of continuing legal education, as prescribed by Rule 6(a) of the 1998 *Rules*, and in keeping with the staggered mechanism to comply with Rule 28(D) of these Rules.

10. Law professional – Any lawyer duly authorized by the Supreme Court to practice law in Puerto Rico, except those admitted by courtesy.

11. Provider – Any natural or artificial person who offers continuing legal education courses, in keeping with Rules 11, 17, and 18 of these Rules.

12. 1998 *Rules* – The *Rules for Continuing Legal Education* adopted on June 30, 1998.

13. Inactive Bar Association Member – Law professional who does not practice his or her profession, but who remains a Bar Association member as certified by the Puerto Rico Bar Association.

COMMENT

After discussing the concept of effective disclosure and its implications within the context of the regulation and the purpose of the continuing legal education program, the Board members concluded that the publication of legal notices in a newspaper does not meet the Rule 16 course accreditation requirement.

Lawyers admitted by courtesy to practice law in Puerto Rico courts in special cases, as authorized by Rule 12(e) of the Rules of the Supreme Court of Puerto Rico, 4 L.P.R.A. App. XXI-A, are exempted from the application of these Rules.

CHAPTER II   CONTINUING EDUCATION BOARD

RULE 6.   MEMBERS: APPOINTMENT, POWERS, AND LIMITATIONS

(A)   Board members will be appointed as provided by Rule 8 of the 1998 *Rules.*

(B)   The Chair of the Board will have the power to designate from among its members an Acting Chair to substitute for him or her at any moment during his or her absence.

(C)   During his or her term of office, no member of the Board may be a provider or have a financial interest or share in the business of continuing legal education providers. Neither may a Board member participate as a resource in the activities carried out by providers under the continuing legal education program.

RULE 7.   MEETINGS

(A)   The Chair will call the Board meetings. He or she may delegate this faculty to the Executive Director of the Board.

(B)   The presence of four (4) Board members shall constitute a quorum. All decisions will be approved by a majority of those present.

(C)   Absent members may be consulted on matters that require immediate attention, whether by telephone, fax, or e-mail.

(D)   Meetings will be recorded when the Board so decides. Its deliberations will be confidential.

(E)   Minutes will be taken of each meeting. The minutes must include a summary of issues discussed and all the agreements reached by the Board.

(F)   Board members must attend all meetings or notify their absence if unable to attend.

(G)   Board members will go over the minutes and will raise any objection thereto in writing or by telephone, fax, or e-mail before the meeting, or in person during the meeting. If no objections are raised, the minutes will be deemed approved for all purposes, there being no need to bring up the issue again for consideration by the Board.

RULE 8.   EXECUTIVE DIRECTOR

The Chief Justice of the Supreme Court will appoint a Director, who will be in charge of the Board's direction and administration.

RULE 9.   FUNCTIONS OF THE DIRECTOR

The Director is the administrative officer of the Board in charge of implementing these Rules, and who will perform the necessary functions to do so, among which are the following:

(1)   certify and accredit providers;

(2)   approve continuing legal education courses;

(3)   keep under his or her custody and control all the documents, registries, records, and equipment;

(4)   issue certifications in keeping with these Rules;

(5)   direct, coordinate, and supervise the Board's administrative personnel;

(6)   prepare the minutes of Board meetings;

(7)   examine situations of noncompliance with the terms and requirements set forth in these Rules and recommend the pertinent action;

(8)   submit recommendations on any other matter related to the performance of his or her functions and the efficient administration of these Rules;

(9)   administer the scholarship fund established by the Board.

COMMENT

As a result of the discussions on course costs and on ways to make continuing legal education available to law professionals who can show financial hardship, the Board determined that in due time it will establish a scholarship fund with the income derived from the payment of the fees prescribed by these Rules. Section (9) of this rule authorizes the Director to administer said fund, which will accrue as allowed by the Board's operational budget.

CHAPTER III   CONTINUING LEGAL EDUCATION ACCREDITATION

RULE 10.   COURSE ACCREDITATION: REQUIREMENTS

To be accredited, every continuing legal education course must meet the following requirements:

(1)   have significant intellectual and practical content directly related to the practice of law or the notarial profession, or to the ethical duties and obligations of law professionals;

(2)   contribute directly to the development of professional competence or skills as applied to the practice of law or the notarial profession;

(3)   include printed or electronic educational materials that will be distributed to all participants;

(4)   its contents must show that providers have devoted adequate time to its preparation and that it will indeed be useful for the advancement of the profession;

(5)   be presented in a suitable setting conducive to a worthwhile educational experience, which provides participants with the necessary electronic or technical equipment and with adequate space for all registered participants;

(6)   give participants an opportunity to pose questions to the teaching resources or to qualified persons, whether in person, in writing, or through electronic or technological means.

RULE 11.   COURSE APPROVAL: REQUIREMENTS

(A)   At the provider's request

(1)   An application for course approval must be submitted by filling out the application form provided by the Board sixty (60) days prior to the date on which the course will be offered, unless the Board shortens this term for good cause.

(2)   The following information and attachments must be included with the application:

(a)   title and general description of the course;

(b)   location, date, and time;

(c)   duration of the course, contact hours;

(d)   time allotted for ethical or notarial aspects, where applicable;

(e)   outline of course contents;

(f)   names and professional credentials of teaching resources;

(g)   copies of the materials to be distributed or shown to participating law professionals;

(h)   course costs.

(3)   The application and attachments must show that the course meets the Rule 10 requirements and, if applicable, those of Rules 12, 13, and 15.

(4)   The Director's decision will be notified to the applicant provider within fifteen (15) days of submission of the application.

(5)   Within thirty (30) days following the date on which the course was offered, the provider must submit the following to the Board:

(a)   a list of the names of law professionals who took the course;

(b)   a certification stating that the course was available to the public and that it was offered as informed in the application; or, if there were changes, a description of such changes and an explanation on how these should not affect course approval;

(c)   in the form provided by the Board, a brief report of the course evaluation made by participating law professionals;

(d)   a $3.00 fee per each credit hour taken by each law professional.

(B)   At the law professional's request

(1)   A law professional may submit an application for approval or accreditation of a course regardless of whether the course was offered by a Certified Provider or by any other provider.

(2)   The application must be submitted in the form provided by the Board, which will include the following information:

(a)   a general description of the course and any materials made available by the provider explaining its contents, the name of the teaching resource, the location, date, and time, the number of contact hours, the registration fee, and the time allotted to course work on notarial practice or ethics, if applicable;

    (b)   any information on the provider that may help the Board evaluate the provider's background and history to determine whether to accept the application.

(3)   The petition and its attachments must show that the course meets the requirements established in Rule 10 of these Rules.

(4)   The application may not be submitted if more than six months have elapsed from the date the course was offered, except as provided in Rule 37 on retroactive accreditation.

(5)   The application must be accompanied by a fee equivalent to five per cent (5%) of the attendance fee or $15.00 per credit hour, whichever is less.

COMMENT

When evaluating applications for course approval, the Director must specifically follow up on aspects related to the reasonableness of course costs in section (A)(2)(h), in order to facilitate the attainment by all law professionals of the professional advancement sought by these Rules.

Section (B)(1) of this Rule allows law professionals to seek approval or accreditation of courses taken in other jurisdictions.

RULE 12.   IN-HOUSE COURSES OFFERED BY PRIVATE FOR-PROFIT OR NONPROFIT PROFESSIONAL INSTITUTIONS: REQUIREMENTS

(A)   Private for-profit or nonprofit professional institutions interested in offering to its members a course in order to have it accredited as a continuing legal education activity must meet the following requirements:

    (1)   submit an application as prescribed in Rule 11;

    (2)   include with the application the information and documents needed to show that the course meets Rule 10 requirements;

    (3)   show that the course will be offered at a reasonable cost, based on the fee regularly charged for a similar course in the Puerto Rico market;

    (4)   separate at least twenty-five percent (25%) of available spaces for outside law professionals who may be interested in taking the course as a continuing legal education activity;

    (5)   comply with the effective disclosure requirement provided in Rule 16 at least ninety (90) days before the start of the course;

(6) wait at least up to forty-five (45) days prior to the starting date of the course to begin admitting applications from outside participants (who are not associated with the private professional institution). If, at the time of admission, there are more applications from outside applicants than available spaces, the participants will be chosen at random; if, after being chosen, any of the outside participants cancels his or her participation or fails to send the payment on time, a substitute participant will be immediately chosen at random from the remaining outside applicants;

(7) within twenty (20) days after the course was offered:

(a) prove that the effective disclosure requirement provided in section (A)(5) of this Rule was met;

(b) inform: (i) the total number of spaces available and the number of spaces made available to persons outside the private institution ("public"); (ii) the names of persons unrelated to the private institution ("public") who applied for the course and the date each application was received, regardless of whether these persons were admitted or the application was timely filed; (iii) the number of persons admitted; (iv) the names of outside participants ("public") unrelated to the private professional institutions who were admitted, the date of admission, and the names of admitted in-house attendees; (v) the number of attendees; (vi) the names of outside attendees who were unrelated to the private professional institution ("public") and the names of the other attendees;

(c) comply with the Rule 11(A)(5) requirement.

(B) All courses approved under the provisions of section (A) of this Rule will receive credit for up to one third (1/3) of the total hours required for each compliance period.

COMMENT

Section (A) of this rule allows for the accreditation of in-house courses organized by law firms, partnerships, professional corporations, or private entities for their members, provided that the purpose of this activity is consistent with that of the mandatory continuing legal education program. Sections (A)(4), (5), (6), and (7) are grounded on the fact that private law firms and other private professional entities offer courses that might contribute to the advancement of non-member law professionals. The Board considered the standards established in other jurisdictions for the accreditation of these courses.

RULE 13. IN-HOUSE COURSES OFFERED BY PUBLIC PROFESSIONAL INSTITUTIONS: REQUIREMENTS

Public professional institutions interested in offering to their employees who are law professionals a course to have it accredited as a continuing legal education activity must meet the following requirements:

(1) submit an application in the form provided by the Board sixty (60) days before the start of the course;

(2) include the information and documents needed to show that the course meets Rule 10 requirements.

COMMENT

The Rule allows for the accreditation of in-house courses offered by public entities for the purpose of facilitating the provision of continuing legal education at a reasonable cost to law professionals in the public service. Once approved by the Board, these courses will receive 100% credit. As may be inferred from Rule 9(9) and its comment, the scholarship fund to be established in due time by the Board will provide law professionals who are in financial hardship, and professionals in the public service who can show financial hardship, with greater access to continuing legal education.

RULE 14. COMPUTATION OF CREDIT HOURS

The required twenty-four (24) credit hours of continuing legal education will be calculated as follows:

(1) one credit hour will consist of sixty (60) minutes of actual participation in continuing legal education activities;

(2) the time to be credited for courses offered only through nontraditional teaching and learning methods may not exceed one third (1/3) of the total credit hours required; to credit that time, the Board will examine the nature of the course, the time normally required to complete it, and the report rendered by the provider on the attendees' performance;

(3) the credit hours earned in excess of the total credit hours required may be credited to the next compliance period as long as they do not exceed twenty-four (24) credit hours.

COMMENT

Rule 6 of the 1998 *Rules* requires twenty-four (24) credit hours of continuing legal education in a period of two (2) years. Rule 3(e) of said *Rules* defines credit hours as the hours devoted to attending a course or seminar offered by a recognized sponsor, and provides that one credit hour will be computed on the basis of sixty (60) minutes.

Section (1) of this rule broadens that provision to clarify that the sixty (60) minutes refer to participation in activities involving legal education, obviously excluding the time devoted to activities unrelated to continuing legal education. Other jurisdictions provide specific standards in that regard: Rule 104(d) (Colorado); Rule 2 (Vermont); Rule 3(c) (Arkansas); Rule 3.5 (Alabama); and Section 5(a)(2) (Pennsylvania).

Section 9 of the American Bar Association Model Rules for [Minimum] Continuing Legal Education recognizes that credit may be awarded for courses taken by law professionals through nontraditional teaching and learning methods conducted outside the classroom setting, as long as they meet certain requirements. One of these requirements is to establish the maximum number of hours of continuing legal education completed in this manner for which credit may be awarded. The American Bar Association recommends that this number not exceed one-third (1/3) of the total continuing legal education credit hours required, and that other standards set forth in section (2) of this Rule be met.

Section (3) addresses an aspect of the computation of credit hours provided in Rule 6(a) of the 1998 *Rules*.

RULE 15.   COURSES OFFERED THROUGH NONTRADITIONAL TEACHING AND LEARNING METHODS

(A)   Courses that employ nontraditional teaching and learning methods such as correspondence, computers, video or audio recordings, or any other means, may receive continuing legal education credit subject to the limitations and requirements established in Rule 14(2) of these Rules.

(B)   The application for approval of these courses must meet the Rule 11(A)(1), (2), (3), and (5) requirements. The provider must explain how the course complies with the Rule 10 requirements, with the purpose of the compulsory continuing legal education program, and with these Rules.

(C)   The Board will make a case-by-case evaluation of these applications and may approve them at its discretion. All certified providers must submit these courses for prior approval by the Board.

COMMENT

Preapproval of courses under Rules 17(c) and 18(c) does not include these courses.

RULE 16. EFFECTIVE DISCLOSURE REQUIREMENT

(A)   Providers seeking approval of course accreditation may publish their course offering through any effective disclosure method addressed to law professionals who may be interested in taking these courses. Once the course is approved, the provider must announce it in keeping with the definition set forth in Rule 5(5).

(B)   The Board will announce the courses approved for credit through the Judicial Branch website based on the information contained in its administrative records, which must be constantly updated.

CHAPTER IV   PROVIDERS

RULE 17.   CERTIFIED PROVIDER: REQUIREMENTS; PROCEDURE

(A)   Requirements

A natural or artificial person who wishes to be licensed as a Certified Provider must meet the following requirements:

(1)   during the four (4) years following adoption of these Rules, offer continuing legal education courses that met accreditation requirements;

(2)   show that the mission of its continuing legal education program is the advancement of law professionals through legal education;

(3)   show that it is financially sound to support a continuing legal education program of the highest quality;

(4)   show that its activities are primarily directed at law professionals;

(5)   agree to comply with the mandatory Continuing Legal Education Program mission and purposes.

(B)   Procedure

The natural or artificial person who wishes to be licensed as a Certified Provider must submit an application provided by the Board with the following information:

(1)　the provider's name, address, telephone number, fax, and e-mail address;

(2)　the name and title of the contact person;

(3)　a description of each continuing legal education course or activity offered during the four (4) years preceding the application date, with the following information:

　　(a)　course title and description;

　　(b)　date and location;

　　(c)　registration costs;

　　(d)　a course syllabus or contents;

　　(e)　names of teaching resources and professional qualifications;

　　(f)　description of materials to be distributed to participants;

　　(g)　hours to be accredited;

　　(h)　distribution of credit hours by category or subject matter (i.e., substantive matters, matters related to the practice of law, exercises, questions);

　　(i)　the audience to which the course is addressed;

　　(j)　whether the course was announced as open to the public or as an in-house activity;

　　(k)　evaluation method for the course (participant critique, independent evaluator);

　　(l)　presentation format (classroom setting, videotape, closed circuit, simultaneous transmission; self-study, computer);

　　(m)　mechanism used to assess attendees' academic achievement;

(4)　attachments and documents to prove the information required in section B(3);

(5)　a description of its experience in the field of law, of its physical facilities, and of its preparation of the persons in charge of program organization, teaching, and supervision;

(6)　jurisdictions where it was granted a Certified Provider license, if any;

(7) if the provider is a corporation, it must include the Good Standing Certificate issued by the Department of State, a copy of the certificate of incorporation, of its corporate charter, and of the most recent annual report;

(8) a copy of the most recent audited financial statement;

(9) a certification stating that it has filed its income tax returns for the last five (5) years;

(10) an affidavit of compliance with the continuing legal education program mission and with all the other requirements established by the Supreme Court in these Rules and related provisions.

(C) Once the Certified Provider license is granted, the courses offered by the provider will be deemed preapproved after the provider notifies the Board as prescribed in Rule 11(A)(1), (2), (3), and (5). The Board, in the exercise of its authority, may deny approval of any course that does not meet the requirements of these Rules, in which case the provider will be notified sufficiently in advance. Noncompliance cases may entail revocation of the previously issued license.

(D) The Certified Provider license will remain in force for a period of two (2) years. Should the provider wish to continue having certified provider status, it must apply for renewal for each subsequent period.

COMMENT

The course is the main object of regulation of the mandatory continuing legal education program. The figure of the provider is framed within this general principle as it is regulated within the context of the certification to offer courses, thus making it easier to evaluate the vast number of courses that will be created in each compliance period. In Rule 18, the regulation makes a temporary distinction by reason of need, which allows the program to begin with a group of providers of proven experience in legal education while remaining equally focused on the Board's authority to supervise the courses offered by these providers. This course-by-course approval approach further allows the Board to rely on a flexible mechanism for on-the-spot certification of providers that meet the program's standards.

RULE 18.   PROVISIONAL CERTIFICATION OF PROVIDERS

(A) The Board, upon request, will issue a Provisional Certification of Provider status for a period of four (4) years to continuing legal education programs from law schools recognized by the Supreme Court and accredited by the

American Bar Association, the Eugenio María de Hostos Law School, and the Puerto Rico Bar Association.

(B)   The organizations or institutions mentioned above must submit an application along with the information required under Rule 17(B) of these Rules.

(C)   Once a Provisional Certification of Provider status is issued, the courses offered by these organizations and institutions will be deemed preapproved if they have been notified to the Board pursuant to the provisions of Rule 11(A)(1), (2), (3), and (5). The Board, in the exercise of its authority, may deny approval of any course that does not meet the requirements established in these Rules, in which case it will give the provider sufficient advance notice. Noncompliance may entail license revocation.

(D)   After the lapse of the provisional four (4)-year-period, these organizations and institutions will be at par with the other providers and may apply for a Certified Provider license under Rule 17.

COMMENT

The mechanism described in this Rule is adopted temporarily for the purpose of making easier the administration of the mandatory continuing legal education program at its early stages and allowing the Board to acquire greater experience as it goes along in the administration of the program. The result of this experience will subsequently enable the Board to decide whether this mechanism should be definitely adopted or whether it should be modified or eliminated.

RULE 19.   PROVIDERS' DUTIES REGARDING ACADEMIC ACHIEVEMENT

(A)   Every provider must make continuous, systematic evaluations regarding the achievement of educational goals, program design, teaching methods, contents of materials, and quality of teaching resources, among others.

(B)   At the Board's request, course providers will render a report on how the mechanisms used furthered academic achievement in its courses, program objectives, continued attendance, and the real and effective participation of the attendees.

(C)   The Board may verify the effectiveness of these mechanisms through the procedures it will establish for that purpose. Providers must keep for a period of five (5) years all documents and records related to their compliance with this rule for future examination by the Board.

COMMENT

Motivation is an essential element for effective academic achievement in legal education. Rule 6(b) of the 1998 *Rules* established this important element by requiring that measures be developed to encourage and determine the effectiveness of all courses offered.

In this sense, in order to achieve the goals of the mandatory continuing legal education program, and in view of the interest in attaining specific—not pro forma—compliance, it is of utmost importance to adopt the necessary and adequate mechanisms to guarantee academic achievement, without which it is not possible to maintain quality control in the courses offered and to make sure that each course meets the educational purpose for which it was designed. Demanding these mechanisms does not necessarily mean that participants will be required to take examinations or tests.

The subject of academic achievement was discussed and analyzed by Board members from different perspectives. It is a very complex matter whose implications require the consideration of numerous factors. As a result of those discussions, the Board recommends that providers be given time to establish standards and mechanisms for measuring the academic achievement obtained in their courses. They may benefit from the experience of providers from other jurisdictions and from guides such as the report *MCLE: A Coordinated Approach, Report and Recommendations*, The Association for Continuing Legal Education, American Law Institute, American Bar Association Committee on Continuing Professional Education (1997).

If after checking these mechanisms for a reasonable period of time it is determined that the expected academic goals are not being met, the Board may propose to the Supreme Court whatever recommendations it may deem necessary, such as considering the possibility of reducing the effective term of the Certified Provider license.

RULE 20.   TEACHING RESOURCES

(A)   All providers will establish the necessary mechanisms to guarantee that professors who participate as continuing legal education resources have the necessary qualifications, professional competence, and teaching skills to provide a worthwhile teaching experience.

(B)   At the time of approving the course, the Director will determine whether the provider complies with this rule.

COMMENT

The rule establishes the responsibility of all course providers to develop mechanisms that may enable them to have the best law professionals as teaching resources for their continuing legal education activities. The certification granted by the Court imposes on each provider the duty to make sure that every course offered for accreditation stimulates and contributes to the advancement of participating law professionals.

RULE 21. ACTIVITIES UNRELATED TO CONTINUING LEGAL EDUCATION

> If the provider combines a course with other noncreditable activities, it must state in the documents submitted the exact amount of time devoted to continuing legal education and the time allotted for other activities.

RULE 22. DUTY TO PROVIDE REASONABLE ACCOMMODATION

> All providers must make reasonable accommodation for any law professional who may seek such accommodation by reason of disability in order to comply with the mandatory continuing legal education requirement.

COMMENT

The Rule refers to the provider's duty to make reasonable accommodation as prescribed by the statutes that impose this obligation on all entities that render a public service. It is based on the Prohibition of Discrimination against the Disabled Act, Act No. 44 of July 2, 1985, as amended, 1 L.P.R.A. §501 *et seq.*, the Americans with Disabilities Act (ADA), Pub. L. 101-336, July 26, 1990, 42 U.S.C.A. §1201 *et seq.*, and sec. 9 of the American Bar Association's Model Rule for Minimum Continuing Legal Education. The disability must be one that is covered by the ADA provisions.

RULE 23. COURSE RECORDS

> (A) All providers must keep for a period of five (5) years the records of the courses offered for accreditation purposes and will make them available to the Board for its inspection upon request.
>
> (B) The records must include the following information, which is essential for granting accreditation to the continuing legal education courses:
>
> > (1) identification of the courses;

(2)   participating faculty;

(3)   roll of attendance bearing the signatures of course attendees;

(4)   course evaluation by attending law professionals;

(5)   issued certificates of participation and other related certifications;

(6)   use of technological or other mechanisms for individual or distance learning;

(7)   evaluation reports on academic achievement in the courses; and

(8)   any other relevant information.

CHAPTER V   PROCEDURES BEFORE THE BOARD

RULE 24.   APPLICATIONS

(A)   Any person interested in a Board determination may submit a written application for any of the following:

(1)   certified provider license under Rule 17;

(2)   provisional certification of provider status under Rule 18;

(3)   accreditation of courses under Rule 11(B);

(4)   exemption under Rule 4(C)(3)(c) and (d);

(5)   deferral under Rule 4(C)(3)(d);

(6)   any other request that may result from the application of these Rules.

(B)   Requirements:

(1)   The application must be submitted by way of a form provided by the Board, giving a clear and detailed description of the purpose and including the pertinent supporting documents. Absent a form, the interested person will determine the form of application, as long as it is in writing.

(2)   The application for Certified Provider status must include the information required in Rule 17.

(3)   The application for accreditation of courses must include the information required in Rule 11(B).

RULE 25. EVALUATION; DETERMINATION

(A) The Director will evaluate all duly submitted applications.

(B) The Director may deny incomplete applications or applications that do not meet the requirements set forth in these Rules.

(C) When examining the application, the Director may require additional information from the applicant.

(D) The Director may grant the application in whole or in part or may deny it. In either case, the Director must notify his or her decision to the applicant.

RULE 26. REVIEW OF DIRECTOR'S DETERMINATIONS

(A) Reconsideration:

Any person who disagrees with the Director's determination may seek reconsideration within fifteen (15) days after the determination was notified, stating the grounds for such disagreement. He or she may request an informal hearing, which may be held at the Director's discretion. The Director must adjudicate the petition for reconsideration within ten (10) days after the filing date of the petition.

(B) Appeal before the Board:

Any person who disagrees with the Director's determination on reconsideration may file an appeal before the Board within ten (10) days after the decision was notified.

(C) The above terms must be strictly complied with and may be extended for good cause, which must be set forth in the petition.

RULE 27. REVIEW BEFORE THE SUPREME COURT

Board decisions will be final. These decisions may be reviewed by the Supreme Court upon the filing of a petition for certiorari within ten (10) days after the Board decision was notified. Said term must be strictly complied with.

CHAPTER VI   COMPLIANCE BY LAW PROFESSIONALS

RULE 28. MINIMUM CREDIT HOURS; COMPLIANCE REPORT

(A) All law professionals must comply with the minimum credit hour requirements established in Rule 6 of the 1998 *Rules*. He or she must submit before the Board a compliance report in the form provided therefor as soon as he or she completes the twenty-four (24) credit hours of the applicable compliance period, but never later than thirty (30) days following the end of the period. This report may be submitted personally, by mail, by fax, or through any electronic means.

(B) All law professionals exempted under Rule 4(C) from compliance with the continuing legal education requirements must render a compliance report for each compliance period, indicating under which exemption he or she was not required to take the continuing legal education courses. Law professionals who requested and were granted an exemption from compliance must also render said report explaining the exemption that was granted.

(C) All law professionals must inform any change of home or mailing address in the compliance report.

(D) The Board will establish a staggered schedule to facilitate compliance with this Rule on different dates.

RULE 29. NOTICE OF NONCOMPLIANCE

Within thirty (30) days after the end of each compliance period, the Board will send a Notice of Noncompliance to all law professionals who have failed to submit the report required under Rule 28.

COMMENT

The rule reiterates the provisions of Rule 9(a) of the 1998 *Rules*, which requires that a Notice of Noncompliance be sent to law professionals who have failed to report the credit hours of continuing legal education courses taken during the compliance period.

RULE 30. LATE COMPLIANCE

All law professionals who fail to comply with their obligation to submit the report required by Rule 28 may file the report within thirty (30) days following the date on which the Notice of Noncompliance was given. The report must explain the reasons for such late compliance and must be accompanied by a $50.00 fee in check or money order.

COMMENT

Rule 9(b) of the 1998 *Rules* grants a 30-day term, counted from the date of Notice of Noncompliance, to inform the Board about the reasons for not submitting the report on time.

By virtue of the authority vested in the Board to adopt the rules necessary for the efficient administration of these Rules, it is provided that late compliance will automatically entail payment of a $50.00 late reporting fee, payable by check or money order, to cover the Board's operational expenses in the performance of its functions. Most of the jurisdictions surveyed provide for the payment of a fee for the late submission of the compliance report. See Rule 6-A - $50 (Alabama); Regulation 5.01 - $75 (Arkansas); Regulation 111(a) - $50 (Colorado); Rule 6(c) - $150 (Louisiana); Rule 9 C - $50 (Minnesota); section .1608(b) - $75 (North Carolina); section 18 - $100 (Pennsylvania).

RULE 31.   NONCOMPLIANCE; SUMMONS

(A)   If the law professional fails to submit the compliance report within the applicable term, the Director will summon him or her in writing to appear at an informal hearing.

(B)   The summons will include the following information: the purpose, the date and place of the hearing, and the period of noncompliance.

COMMENT

The rule is based on Rule 8(d)(2) and Rule 9(c) of the 1998 *Rules*, which authorize the Board to consider cases of noncompliance and to order the lawyer to appear in such cases.

RULE 32.   INFORMAL HEARING BEFORE THE DIRECTOR

(A)   The law professional summoned to an informal hearing for noncompliance must set forth the reasons for noncompliance and present whatever evidence he or she may have.

(B)   The Director will weigh the reasons for noncompliance and decide in accordance with the applicable rules and regulations.

(C)   In the event of nonappearance, the Board will forward the matter to the Supreme Court as provided in Rule 9 of the 1998 *Rules*.

(D)   Any determination made by the Director will be timely notified to the law professional in question.

COMMENT

Rule 8(d)(2) of the 1998 *Rules* authorizes the Board to consider noncompliance cases and to submit the pertinent reports after giving the affected persons an opportunity to be heard, while Rule 9(c) orders that cases of nonappearance of law professionals be referred to the Supreme Court.

CHAPTER VII   ALTERNATIVE COMPLIANCE MECHANISMS AND OTHER PROVISIONS

RULE 33.   PARTICIPATION AS TEACHING RESOURCES

Law professionals who participate as continuing legal education teaching resources will receive credit for performing that function when they submit their request to the Board along with the provider's certification attesting to their participation and the number of teaching hours.

RULE 34.   PUBLICATION OF LAW-RELATED WORKS

Law professionals who publish law-related books and articles in well-known law reviews will receive credit for these publications that will not exceed two (2) compliance periods when they submit their request to the Board accompanied by the pertinent evidence of publication and of the time devoted to it. It will be incumbent upon the Director, and ultimately upon the Board, to determine the number of credit-hours earned for said publication.

COMMENT ON RULES 33 AND 34:

Rules 33 and 34 are based on Rule 7 (a) and (b) of the 1998 *Rules*, which recognizes as alternative compliance mechanisms the publication of law-related books and articles in well-known law reviews, and the teaching of continuing legal education courses. A new requirement is added: law professionals must submit a request along with the pertinent documents to provide the Board with the necessary information that will allow it to determine how many hours will be credited.

RULE 35.   ADVANCED DEGREES

Law professionals who have completed a Master of Laws degree in a law school accredited by the Council of Higher Education will be exempted from taking continuing legal education courses for a period of two (2) years, to be counted from the date on which they obtained the degree. If the degree is that of Doctor of Juridical Science or its equivalent, Doctor of Law, the exemption period will be four (4) years, to be counted from the date on which they obtained the degree.

COMMENT

The rule is based on Rule 7(c) of the 1998 *Rules*, which recognizes the pursuit of postgraduate Law studies in universities recognized by the Puerto Rico Council of Higher Education as an alternative compliance mechanism. This provision seeks to stimulate the development and advancement of law professionals by way of courses through which the goals of the mandatory continuing legal education program are also fulfilled.

RULE 36. PARTICIPATION IN COMMISSIONS, BOARDS, SUPREME COURT COMMITTEES, AND AS BAR EXAMINATION ITEM-WRITERS AND GRADERS

(A)   Exemption from the terms of these Rules will be granted, for the term of their designation, to law professionals who serve in any of the following:

(1)   the Commission on Discipline and Disability Retirement of Judges of the Court of First Instance and the Circuit Court of Appeals;

(2)   the Committee on Character of Applicants for Admission to the Bar;

(3)   the Board of Bar Examiners;

(4)   the Continuing Legal Education Board;

(5)   the active standing and ad hoc advisory committees of the Secretariat of the Judicial and Notarial Conference;

(6)   the item-writing and grading committees of the general bar examination and the notarial law examination designated in conformance with the Rules for the Admission of Applicants to the Practice of Law and the Notarial Profession;

(7)   other committees, commissions or boards that, according to the Supreme Court, should be exempted from compliance with this Program.

RULE 37. RETROACTIVE ACCREDITATION

(A)   The Board will give credit to continuing legal education courses taken by law professionals during the three (3) years immediately preceding the effective date of these Rules.

(B)   To obtain credit, an application must be filed as provided in Rule 11(B)(1), (2), and (3), and a certification from the provider attesting to the law professional's participation in the courses must be included.

(C)   The Board reserves the right to determine whether these courses meet accreditation standards and may request any information it may deem relevant to such purposes.

RULE 38.   NOTICE OF THE DIRECTOR OR OF THE BOARD; SERVICE

All notices given by the Director or by the Board to law professionals and to the providers may be sent by regular mail, fax, or through electronic means.

COMMENT

The application of these Rules requires a high volume of communications and notices by the Director or by the Board to law professionals and providers. As an example, to facilitate the understanding of the structure of the Rules, a list of such notices is provided below:

To law professionals:

(1)   Total or partial course accreditation (Rule 11(B), or denial of accreditation (Rule 25(D), 26(B));

(2)   Request for additional information for course accreditation (Rule 25(C));

(3)   Accreditation for participation as teaching resource (Rule 33);

(4)   Accreditation for publication of law-related works (Rule 34);

(5)   Retroactive accreditation of courses (Rule 37);

(6)   Exemption from compliance with the continuing legal education requirement by reason of completion of postgraduate studies (Rule 35);

(7)   Exemption from compliance with the continuing legal education requirement by reason of participation in Supreme Court boards and committees and by reason of the services rendered as item-writers and graders of the General Bar Examination (Rule 36);

(8)   Notice of Noncompliance (Rule 29);

(9)   Summons to an informal hearing for failure to submit the Compliance Report (Rule 31);

(10)   Director's determination after the hearing (Rule 32 (D));

(11)   Notice of hearing on reconsideration (Rule 26(A));

(12)   Director's decision on reconsideration (Rule 26(A));

(13)   Board's decision on appeal (Rule 27);

(14)   Determination to refer to the Supreme Court the cases of noncompliance for failure to appear (Rule 32(C));

(15)   Exemption from compliance by reason of incapacity to practice the profession (Rule 4(C)(3)(c);

(16)   Exemption from compliance with the continuing legal education requirement for good cause (Rule 4(C)(3)(d));

(17)   Deferral from the continuing legal education requirement for good cause (Rule 4(C)(3)(d));

(18)   Any other communication related to the fulfillment of the continuing legal education requirements.

To providers:

(1)   Provisional Certification of Provider (Rule 18);
(2)   Certified Provider License (Rule 17);
(3)   Total or partial approval of courses (Rule 11(A));
(4)   Denial of application for course approval (Rule 11(A)(4), Rule 12, Rule 13, Rule 14, Rule 17(C), Rule 18(C), Rule 25(B) and (D));
(5)   Denial of application for Certified Provider status (Rule 17);
(6)   Approval of courses offered by private professional entities (Rule 12);
(7)   Approval of courses offered by public professional entities (Rule 13);
(8)   Request for reports on academic achievement (Rule 19(B));
(9)   Notice of document inspection (Rule 19(C));
(10) Failure to comply with the mechanisms to guarantee the best teaching resources (Rule 20(B));
(11) Director's decision on reconsideration (Rule 26);
(12) Board's decision on appeal (Rule 27);
(13) Revocation of license for failure to comply with the continuing legal education program (Rule 17(C), Rule 18(C));
(14) Request for additional information (Rule 25(C));
(15) Any other communication related to the fulfillment of the continuing legal education requirements.

RULE 39.   UNFORESEEN SITUATIONS

The Director, with the approval of the Chair of the Board, may take steps to address unforeseen situations in the manner that, in his or her judgment, best serves the interests of all the parties.

RULE 40.   SEPARABILITY CLAUSE

If, by virtue of legislation or judicial decision, any provision of these Rules is declared void or ineffective in whole or in part, said provision will be deemed as not included herein and will not affect the validity of the remaining provisions, which will continue to be in full force and effect.

RULE 41.   EFFECTIVE DATE

These Rules will become effective 18 months after their adoption.

PUERTO RICO

IN THE SUPREME COURT OF PUERTO RICO

In re Adoption of the Rules of the Continuing Legal Education Program	No. <u>ER-2005-04</u>	

RESOLUTION

San Juan, Puerto Rico, April 8, 2005

By virtue of the inherent power of this Court to regulate the practice of law in Puerto Rico, and by virtue of the authority vested in the Continuing Legal Education Board by Rule 8(d)(7) of the *Rules for Continuing Legal Education* adopted by the Supreme Court of Puerto Rico on June 30, 1998, the Court hereby promulgates these Rules of the Continuing Legal Education Program, which will become effective 18 months after their adoption. The complete text of these Rules is made a part of this Resolution.

The Court thanks the members of the Continuing Legal Education Board for their excellent work in the fulfillment of their commission. The Court further thanks the Puerto Rico Bar Association for its contribution and participation in the preparation of the Draft Rules presented by the Board.

This Resolution will become effective immediately.

To be published.

It was so agreed by the Court and certified by the Clerk of the Supreme Court. Justice Fuster Berlingeri issued a dissenting opinion.

(Sgd.)

Aida Ileana Oquendo Graulau
Clerk of the Supreme Court

D-419

RHODE ISLAND

Rule 3. Mandatory Continuing Legal Education

Preamble. It is of primary importance to the courts, the bar, and the public that attorneys continue their legal education in order to have and maintain the requisite knowledge and skill necessary to fulfill their professional responsibilities. This rule is adopted to establish a program of mandatory continuing legal education (MCLE) and to set standards and minimum requirements for that program.

3.1. Commission.

(a) The Supreme Court shall appoint a MCLE Commission which shall consist of eleven (11) members, two (2) of whom shall be justices of the Supreme Court who shall serve at the pleasure of the Supreme Court, two (2) of whom shall be justices of the trial courts, five (5) of whom shall be active members of the bar of this State, and two (2) of whom shall be members of the general public. The Supreme Court shall appoint one (1) of the members of the MCLE Commission as its chair.

(b) When the MCLE Commission is first selected, three (3) of its members shall be appointed for a term of one (1) year, three (3) for a term of two (2) years, and three (3) for a term of three (3) years. All terms thereafter shall be for three (3) years. Seven (7) members shall constitute a quorum.

(c) The MCLE Commission shall have the following powers and duties:

(1) to administer Sections 3.2 – 3.9 of this rule under the supervision of the Supreme Court;

(2) to adopt and promulgate, subject to the approval of the Supreme Court, such regulations and rules of procedure as the MCLE Commission determines are necessary to effectuate this rule;

(3) to designate any person, corporation, or other entity as a sponsor of approved MCLE courses, as provided herein;

(4) to approve courses for MCLE credit upon application of a sponsor, attorney, law firm, corporate legal department, or governmental agency, as provided herein;

(5) to refer attorneys who are not in compliance with this rule to the Supreme Court for the imposition of sanctions and removal from the Master Roll of Attorneys; and

(6) to set the fees required under this rule and any others that may be determined by the MCLE Commission to be necessary in order to contribute to the administrative costs of this program.

3.2. MCLE requirements.

(a) Except as provided in Section 3.2(b) of this rule, all attorneys admitted to practice in this state shall complete ten (10) hours of continuing legal education in each MCLE reporting year, at least two (2) hours of which shall be in the area of legal ethics. The MCLE reporting year shall be defined to include the period from July 1 to June 30.

(b) Section 3.2(a) of this rule shall not apply to:

(1) attorneys who are listed as inactive or retired on the Master Roll of Attorneys of the Supreme Court;

(2) attorneys holding a full-time federal, state, or municipal office and who are not engaged in the practice of law shall be exempt during their term(s) of office;

(3) federal and state court judges and magistrates whose judicial duties are full-time and who are not engaged in the practice of law;

(4) all newly admitted attorneys for the current and next full MCLE reporting year;

(5) attorneys who are seventy (70) years old or over, due to their stature in the profession. Although they are not required to participate in continuing legal education programs, attorneys in this category are encouraged to do so-;

(6) attorneys who are current members of the Rhode Island Board of Bar Examiners and the Committee on Character and Fitness, due to their unique contribution to the profession; and

(7) attorneys who are current members of the Commission on Judicial Tenure and Discipline are exempt from reporting two (2) ethics credits due to their unique contribution to the profession.

(c) The MCLE Commission is authorized to exempt attorneys from MCLE requirements under Section 3.2(a) for good cause shown.

3.3. "Rhode Island Bridge the Gap" requirement.

(a) Requirement – All newly admitted attorneys shall be required to take the one-day, mandatory "Rhode Island Bridge the Gap" course upon admission to the Rhode Island Bar unless at the time of admission he or she has been admitted in another jurisdiction for a period of three (3) years. The attorney shall submit a certificate of good standing to the MCLE Commission via the Rhode Island Supreme Court Attorney Portal attesting to the fact that he or she has been admitted in another jurisdiction for the prescribed period. No course substitution from other jurisdictions will be accepted for this requirement.

(b) Filing and Records – The course shall be taken by the end of the first full MCLE reporting year after the attorney is admitted to the Rhode Island Bar. On or before June 30 of that MCLE reporting year, each attorney shall file the date of attendance with the MCLE Commission via the Rhode Island Supreme Court Attorney Portal in such form as the Commission shall prescribe, documenting compliance with this requirement. Each attorney shall maintain such records as may be required to substantiate his or her compliance for a period of three (3) years following the close of each MCLE reporting year.

(c) Course Offering – The "Rhode Island Bridge the Gap" course shall be sponsored by the Rhode Island Bar Association or an educational institution approved by the Supreme Court. The course curriculum shall be approved by the MCLE Commission. The course shall be offered online as well. The fees for the course, whether in-person or online, shall be set by the Supreme Court as deemed necessary.

(d) No Exemptions or Extensions – Because the course will be offered online, there will be no exemptions or extensions granted by the MCLE Commission except in exceptional circumstances. An attorney may file a request for waiver or make up consideration to the MCLE Commission via the Rhode Island Supreme Court Attorney Portal with full explanation of the extraordinary circumstances supporting the request. The MCLE Commission shall review and approve or disapprove each request on an individual basis.

(e) No MCLE Credit – As this course contains mandatory content, the course shall not be applied toward any MCLE requirements.

(f) Failure to Comply – A newly admitted attorney who fails to fulfill the requirement under this section by June 30 following the end of the first full MCLE reporting year after the attorney is admitted to the Rhode Island Bar, shall be assessed a make up filing fee and shall be removed from the Master Roll of Attorneys without further notice. Any person whose name is not on the Master Roll and who practices law or who holds himself or herself out in any manner to the public or to another person as being competent, qualified, authorized, or entitled to practice law in this State is engaged in the unauthorized practice of law and may be subject to the disciplinary procedures of the Supreme Court.

1. An attorney whose name has been removed from the Master Roll for failure to comply with this rule may be reinstated upon completing the "Rhode Island Bridge the Gap" course and payment of the make up filing fee, plus reimbursement of the costs of collection, if any, within six (6) months of the initial filing deadline.

2. Any attorney whose name has been removed from the Master Roll for failure to comply with this rule for a period in excess of six (6) months shall file an application with the Supreme Court seeking reinstatement and provide a copy to the Supreme Court's Disciplinary Counsel and the MCLE Commission. The applicant for reinstatement shall submit an affidavit attesting that he or she has not been disciplined in this or any other jurisdiction, that the applicant is not the subject of any pending disciplinary charges, and that the applicant is not aware of any reason why the application should not be granted. Disciplinary Counsel shall provide the Supreme Court with a Report and Recommendation on the application within thirty (30) days.

3. An attorney in the practice of law in another jurisdiction who is removed from the Master Roll for failure to comply with this rule shall, in addition to any other prerequisite contained in these rules before being returned to the Master Roll, shall provide to the Supreme Court a certificate from the appropriate disciplinary tribunal of the jurisdiction in which he or she has been practicing law that (a) he or she is a member in good standing of the bar in such jurisdiction, and (b) that no disciplinary action is pending against him or her in said jurisdiction.

(g) Effective Date – This rule will take effect on July 1, 2012. Individuals admitted as a Rhode Island attorney on or after January 1, 2011 shall be subject to this Section 3.3. On July 1, 2012, individuals admitted as a Rhode Island attorney before January 1, 2011 shall be required to complete only the MCLE requirements set forth in Section 3.2.

3.4. Credits – Computation.

Credit shall be awarded on the basis of one (1) credit hour for each fifty (50) minutes of attendance at an approved course, program, or activity of legal education. Three (3) credit hours shall be awarded for each hour of teaching within an approved MCLE course, program, or activity, up to a maximum of six (6) credit hours per year.

3.5. Accredited sponsor approval.

(a) Any person, firm, organization or other entity may apply to the MCLE Commission for designation as an accredited sponsor of MCLE courses or activities via the Rhode Island Supreme Court Attorney Portal and in such manner as the Commission shall prescribe.

(b) A law firm, corporate legal department, or governmental agency may apply to the MCLE Commission for approval for credit of an in-house course or activity in such manner as the Commission shall prescribe. A minimum of seven (7) lawyers, including the instructor, must attend the course or activity for it to qualify for MCLE credit.

(c) The MCLE Commission may promulgate appropriate regulations establishing standards and procedures for approval of sponsors of MCLE courses or activities. The MCLE Commission shall have the authority to monitor and review programs and may revoke the approval of an accredited sponsor that fails to comply with this rule or with Commission regulations.

(d) In order to obtain and maintain approval, sponsors of MCLE courses or activities must comply with the following minimum requirements:

(1) The accredited sponsor must develop and implement methods to evaluate its course offerings to determine their effectiveness and, upon request from the MCLE Commission, provide course evaluations by attendees;

(2) The accredited sponsor must provide courses consistent with the standards for individual course approval as set forth in Section 3.76 of this rule;- and

(3) The accredited sponsor must apply for course approval thirty (30) days prior to the course date as well as report attorney attendance no later than thirty (30) days after the course date via the Rhode Island Supreme Court Attorney Portal.

3.6. Individual course approval.

An individual attorney may apply to the MCLE Commission for approval for credit of a continuing legal education course or activity in such manner as the Commission shall prescribe.

3.7. Standards.

A continuing legal education course, program, or activity shall meet the following minimum standards in order to be approved for MCLE credit:

(1) It shall be of significant intellectual and practical content such that it will contribute to the growth of an attorney's professional competence and skills;

(2) Its subject matter shall be directly or supportively relevant to the practice of law and/or legal ethics;

(3) It shall be conducted by a person or persons qualified professionally to present the subject matter involved;

(4) It shall be presented in a classroom, meeting room, or lecture hall conducive to a meaningful educational experience;

(5) Its content shall be presented in a multi-mode fashion, utilizing oral presentations supplemented with written hand-outs and texts. All materials shall meet the highest professional standards in terms of their timeliness, organization, and detail; and

(6) It shall utilize video and audio presentations only as an adjunct to oral and written presentations.

3.8. Filing for MCLE credit.

On or before June 30 of each year, each attorney shall document compliance with the MCLE requirements set forth in Section 3.2(a) of this rule or state the basis for his or her exemption under Section 3.2(b) via the Rhode Island Supreme Court Attorney Portal in such form as the MCLE Commission shall prescribe. Each attorney shall maintain such records as may be required to substantiate his or her compliance or exemption for a period of three (3) years following the close of each MCLE reporting year.

3.9. Failure to comply – Sanctions.

(a) Following the close of each MCLE reporting year the MCLE Commission shall send a notice of delinquency to each attorney deemed not in compliance with the filing or educational requirements of this rule for that reporting year. If the attorney has failed to fulfill the educational requirements of this rule, the attorney shall correct his or her failure to comply with the requirements within ninety (90) days of the date of the notice of delinquency or the attorney shall be subject to possible sanction by the Supreme Court. A fee shall be assessed for make up filing or for late filing. For any make up credits received after the ninety (90) day make up period has elapsed, the attorney shall be assessed double the published make up filing fee.

(b) If an attorney does not correct his or her failure to comply with the requirements of this rule within one hundred eighty (180) days of the date of the notice of delinquency, the attorney shall be removed from the Master Roll without further notice.

(c) An attorney whose name has been removed from the Master Roll for failure to comply with MCLE may be reinstated upon completing and filing the courses, payment of the make up filing fee, filing certification of proof with the MCLE Commission via the Rhode Island Supreme Court Attorney Portal, and payment of a reinstatement fee within six (6) months of the removal date.

(d) Any attorney whose name has been removed from the Master Roll for failure to comply with this rule for a period in excess of six (6) months shall file an application with the Supreme

Court seeking reinstatement and provide a copy to the Supreme Court's Disciplinary Counsel and the MCLE Commission. The applicant for reinstatement shall submit an affidavit attesting that he or she has not been disciplined in this or any other jurisdiction, that the applicant is not the subject of any pending disciplinary charges, and that the applicant is not aware of any reason why the application should not be granted. Disciplinary Counsel shall provide the Supreme Court with a Report and Recommendation on the application within thirty (30) days.

(e) An attorney in the practice of law in another jurisdiction who is removed from the Master Roll for failure to comply with this rule, in addition to any other prerequisite contained in these rules before being returned to the Master Roll, shall provide to the Supreme Court a certificate from the appropriate disciplinary tribunal of the jurisdiction in which he or she has been practicing law that (a) he or she is a member in good standing of the bar in such jurisdiction, and (b) that no disciplinary action is pending against him or her in said jurisdiction.

(f) An attorney removed from the Master Roll pursuant to this rule who thereafter comes into compliance shall file certification of proof with the MCLE commission via the Rhode Island Supreme Court Attorney Portal in such form as the Commission shall prescribe and shall also pay a reinstatement fee. An attorney aggrieved by the refusal of the MCLE Commission to approve his or her certification of proof may file a petition for review with the Supreme Court.

(g) In the event that an attorney resides outside the State of Rhode Island and certifies that he or she has not practiced law in this state during the preceding MCLE reporting year, the Supreme Court clerk, with the concurrence of the Chief Justice, may waive the MCLE requirements for that preceding year. In the event that an attorney resides within the State of Rhode Island, but certifies that he or she has not practiced law during the preceding MCLE reporting year and has performed no legal work for any client in Rhode Island during that year, the Supreme Court clerk, with the concurrence of the Chief Justice, may waive the MCLE requirements for that year. Provided, however, such attorneys must pay the annual registration fee required by Rule 1, Periodic Registration of Attorneys.

3.10. Effective date.

This rule will take effect immediately with respect to the appointment of the MCLE Commission and the performance by the Commission of the adoption and promulgation of regulations and rules of procedure, the designation of persons, corporations or other entities as sponsors of automatically approved MCLE courses, and the approval of specific courses for MCLE credits. This rule will take effect with respect to compliance by members of the bar beginning July 1, 1993. At the discretion of the MCLE Commission, credit may be given for courses taken in the 1993 calendar year prior to July 1.

Changes to these rules will take effect on July 1, 2012.

SOUTH CAROLINA

RULE 408
CONTINUING LEGAL EDUCATION AND SPECIALIZATION
PREAMBLE

In the modern legal environment, the law continues to grow more complex and it changes with increasing frequency. Continuing education is no longer a luxury, but is a necessity for all lawyers. Mindful of the improvements in the administration of justice that have resulted from our judicial continuing legal education and mandatory continuing legal education requirements, we believe that all judges and lawyers must meet certain minimum continuing legal education requirements if they are to maintain their competency. We have provided for the continuing legal education of elected and selected other judges in Rule 504. It is our intention that all members of the Bar and those judges (other than federal judges) who are not required to satisfy the requirements of Rule 504 shall fulfill the mandatory continuing legal education requirements specified in this Rule.

(a)   Continuing Legal Education Requirements.

(1)   **Annual Report of Compliance; Fees; Waiver and Suspension.** The reporting year under this rule shall run from March 1 through the last day in February. Reports of compliance for the reporting year shall be due not later than March 1, and shall be submitted to the Commission on Continuing Legal Education and Specialization (Commission) on a form prepared by the Commission along with a filing fee specified in the regulations of the Commission. The Commission may specify a penalty that must be paid if a person fails to timely file a report establishing compliance and/or pay the annual filing fee. For good cause shown, the Commission may, in individual cases involving extraordinary hardship or extenuating circumstances, waive or modify the requirements of this rule. When appropriate, and as a condition for any waiver or modification, the Commission may proportionally increase continuing legal education (CLE) requirements for the succeeding reporting year. A person who fails to comply with the CLE requirements of this rule will be suspended as provided by Rule 419, SCACR.

(2)   **Continuing Legal Education Requirements for Members of the South Carolina Bar.** Except as provided below, all members of the South Carolina Bar shall be required to attend at least fourteen (14) hours of approved CLE courses each reporting year. At least two (2) of the fourteen (14) hours required annually shall be devoted to legal ethics/professional responsibility (LEPR). At least once every three reporting years, the member must complete one (1) hour of LEPR devoted exclusively to instruction in substance abuse or mental health issues and the legal profession. The following members of the South Carolina Bar shall be exempt from these requirements:

(A)   specialists certified pursuant to this Rule who satisfy the CLE requirements of their specialty; provided, however, that at least two (2) hours of the CLE credits completed by certified specialists shall be devoted to LEPR. At least once every three (3) reporting years, the member must complete one (1) hour of LEPR devoted exclusively to instruction in substance abuse or mental health issues and the legal profession.

(B) members who are at least sixty (60) years old and have been admitted to practice law for thirty (30) or more years, and who apply to the Commission for this exemption. Further, any exemptions granted prior to June 23, 1994, shall remain in effect. Provided, however, that if a member who receives an exemption or is entitled to an exemption under this provision is suspended for a definite period of more than six (6) months under Rule 413, SCACR, this exemption shall not apply or be granted during the suspension period;

(C) inactive members, military members, and retired members.

(D) judicial members who are subject to the CLE requirements of Rule 504, SCACR.

(E) members who are federal judges or federal administrative law judges.

(F) limited members licensed under Rule 415, SCACR (Limited Certificate of Admission for Retired and Inactive Attorney Pro Bono Participation Program).

(3) **Continuing Legal Education Requirements for Foreign Legal Consultants.** As required by Rule 424, SCACR, all foreign legal consultants shall attend at least two (2) hours of approved CLE courses devoted to LEPR each reporting year.

(b) **Commission on Continuing Legal Education and Specialization.**

(1) **Membership and Terms of Office.** The Commission on Continuing Legal Education and Specialization shall consist of twelve (12) members. The Supreme Court shall appoint to the Commission: one (1) member of the Supreme Court or Court of Appeals; one (1) circuit court judge; one (1) family court judge; two (2) attorneys from each of the four (4) judicial regions established by order of the Chief Justice dated January 9, 1992; and one (1) additional attorney from Region II. Of the members first appointed to the Commission, four (4) shall serve a term of one (1) year; four (4) shall serve a term of two (2) years; and four (4) shall serve a term of three (3) years. Members thereafter appointed shall be appointed for three (3) years, but shall continue to serve until their successors are appointed. A member appointed to fill an unexpired term shall serve only to the completion of that term and until his or her successor is appointed. Except for the initial appointments to the Commission, the House of Delegates of the South Carolina Bar shall nominate up to two (2) members of the South Carolina Bar to fill each attorney position on the Commission. No person shall be appointed for more than two (2) consecutive terms. The Supreme Court shall appoint a chairperson and a secretary of the Commission from among the Commission's membership.

(2) **Duties.** Subject to the continuing jurisdiction of the Supreme Court, the Commission shall have general jurisdiction over all matters pertaining to mandatory continuing legal education and specialization in the practice of law and shall:

(A) administer the programs established pursuant to this Rule and Rule 504, SCACR;

(B) select fields of specialization in which South Carolina lawyers may be certified;

(C) appoint and supervise Specialization Advisory Boards, each consisting of at least five (5) lawyers practicing in the specialty field. Each Specialization Advisory Board shall be charged with the responsibility for establishing standards and procedures for certification, recertification and decertification of lawyers in specialty fields approved by the Commission;

(D) subject to the approval of the Supreme Court, make and publish rules, regulations, bylaws, standards and procedures implementing its duties. No proposed rule, regulation, by-law, set of standards or procedures, or any substantive amendment to the preceding shall be adopted by the Commission or any Specialization Advisory Board unless it is first published in the South Carolina Bar News or its successor publication for the information and comments of members of the Bar at least ninety (90) days prior to the proposed effective date. A public hearing shall be ordered by the Commission or Specialization Authorization Board upon receipt, at least ten (10) days prior to the effective date, of a petition for a hearing signed by at least ten (10) members of the Bar. Notice of the hearing shall be given in the South Carolina Bar News or its successor publication. An adopted rule, regulation, by-law, set of standards or procedures, or any substantive amendment to the preceding shall not become effective until it is filed with and approved by the Supreme Court. The final versions shall be included in any publication of the South Carolina Appellate Court Rules. The procedures contained in this paragraph shall not apply to internal operating procedures of the Commission;

(E) direct a staff headed by an Executive Director appointed by the Supreme Court. The staff shall assist the Commission and the Specialization Advisory Boards in administering this Rule, including processing applications for certified specialist status and for recertification, processing decertification orders, advising Specialization Advisory Boards on CLE course accreditation, providing information about the requirements of this Rule, assisting the Commission and Specialization Advisory Boards in preparing reports, and performing other administrative assignments as directed by the Commission; and

(F) report, at least annually, to the Supreme Court and the South Carolina Bar;

(G) may promulgate regulations approving organizations which certify lawyers as specialists in specialty fields in which the Supreme Court of South Carolina does not certify specialists.

(c) **Designation of Specialty Fields.**

(1) Subject to approval by the Supreme Court, the Commission may designate a specialty field and define the scope of practice of the field. The designation may be made by the Commission on its own initiative or upon the petition of 100 members of the Bar. Prior to the Commission's designation of a specialty field, notice of the proposed designation must be published in the South Carolina Bar News or its successor publication and at least one (1) public hearing relating to the proposed designation must be held.

In designating and defining a specialty field, the Commission shall consider:

(A)   whether the public interest would be served;

(B)   whether there is sufficient interest to warrant the designation;

(C)   whether appropriate standards of proficiency can be established for the specialty field;

(D)   whether there is satisfactory evidence of the existence or prospect of an adequate program of continuing legal education in the specialty field; and

(E)   whether the designation of the specialty field would fulfill the objectives and further the orderly growth of certified specialization in South Carolina.

(2)   No standard governing lawyer certification shall be approved which shall in any way limit the right of any certified lawyer to practice in all fields of law. Any lawyer, alone or in association with any other lawyer, shall have the right to practice in all fields of law, even though certified as a specialist in a particular field. No lawyer shall be required to attain certified specialist status before practicing in any designated specialty field. Any lawyer, alone or in association with any other lawyer, shall have the right to practice in any field of law, even though not certified under the program as a specialist in that field.

All requirements for and all benefits to be derived from certification as a specialist are individual and may not be fulfilled nor attributed to a law firm of which the specialist may be a member.

Participation in the specialization program shall be on a completely voluntary basis.

(d)   Specialization Advisory Boards. Each designated specialty field shall have a Specialization Advisory Board charged with the responsibility of establishing standards and procedures for the certification, recertification and decertification of lawyers in the specialty field. No rules or standards shall be adopted in contravention of the South Carolina Appellate Court Rules. Each Specialization Advisory Board shall:

(1)   make and publish reasonable and nondiscriminatory standards concerning education, experience and other relevant matters for the certification of lawyers as specialists in its specialty field;

(2)   provide procedures for investigating the qualifications of applicants and certificate holders;

(3)   make and publish reasonable and nondiscriminatory standards for recertification and decertification;

(4) recommend to the Supreme Court, for the issuance of certificates, lawyers who have qualified for certification in the designated specialty fields;

(5) make and publish rules, regulations and by-laws to implement its authority and duties;

(6) cooperate with the Supreme Court, the Commission and other agencies of the Court and the Bar in establishing and enforcing standards of professional conduct for certified lawyers;

(7) cooperate with the Special Committee on Specialization of the American Bar Association and with agencies in other states engaged in regulating legal specialization;

(8) accredit CLE courses to be taken by certified specialists for recertification, subject to the right of a certified specialist to appeal accreditation decisions to the Commission and from the Commission to the Supreme Court; and

(9) report, at least annually, to the Commission.

(e) **Minimum Standards for Specialist Certification.**

(1) To qualify for certification in a designated specialty field, an applicant must, at a minimum:

(A) be a regular member in good standing of the South Carolina Bar;

(B) submit the names of five (5) other attorneys who are familiar with the applicant's practice, not including attorneys who currently practice in the same law firm as the applicant, who can attest to the applicant's reputation for involvement and competency in the specialty field;

(C) have been engaged in the practice of law for at least five (5) years. If a Specialization Advisory Board finds that an applicant who has not been engaged in the practice of law for five (5) years has had specialized post-graduate education or concentrated experience in a particular area of practice and that the experience is equal to or greater than the experience the applicant would have gained in that area from five (5) years of practice, the Specialization Advisory Board may recommend to the Supreme Court that the requirement of five (5) years of practice be waived and that the applicant be certified as a specialist; and

(D) pay any fee required by the Commission.

(2) As determined by each Specialization Advisory Board, an applicant must:

(A) make a satisfactory showing of substantial involvement (i.e. actual performance) in the specialty field during a five (5) year period, or other reasonable period of not less than three (3) years, immediately preceding the application, which demonstrates according to objective and verifiable standards that the applicant has been substantially involved in the specialty field for which certification is sought; and

(B)   successfully complete a program of instruction approved by the Specialization Advisory Board; and

(C)   undergo and satisfactorily complete an examination approved and administered by the Specialization Advisory Board. The examination shall consist of oral and/or written parts and shall be designed to test the applicant's knowledge of and ability in the specialty field for which certification is sought.

(3)   "Substantial involvement" shall be defined by each Specialization Advisory Board as to its particular field of law from a consideration of the complexity and the extent of necessary devotion to the particular field of practice. It is intended to be a measurement of the actual experience within that particular field. It may be measured by any of several standards such as the time spent on legal matters within the specialty field, the number or type of matters handled within a certain period of time, the time spent in teaching the law of the specialty field, or any combination of these or other appropriate factors. However, within each specialty field, experience requirements shall be measured by objective standards.

(4)   The limit on the number of specialties in which a lawyer may be certified shall be determined by such practical limits as are imposed by the requirement of substantial involvement and such other standards as may be established by the Commission and approved by the Supreme Court as a prerequisite to certification.

(f)   Standards for Renewal of Certification. Renewal of certification in a designated specialty field shall be required every five (5) years. Each applicant for recertification must:

(1)   make a satisfactory showing of substantial involvement in the particular designated specialty field during the period of certification;

(2)   make a satisfactory showing of attendance, during the preceding period of certification, at a minimum of sixty (60) hours of continuing legal education in the designated specialty field for which certification was granted. Only attendance at courses accredited by the pertinent Specialization Advisory Board shall count as credit toward the mandatory continuing legal education requirement for certified specialists. The Specialization Advisory Boards shall determine the number of credit hours to be given for each course and the specialty field entitled to credit. On the application of any interested person, the Specialization Advisory Boards, with the assistance of the staff described in section (b)(2)(E) of this Rule, shall make a determination of the qualification of, and credit to be allowed for, particular continuing legal education courses; and

(3)   pay any fees prescribed by the Commission.

(g)   Revocation of Certification. The Specialization Advisory Board may revoke certification of any lawyer if the certification program for that field is terminated or if it is determined after a hearing, on appropriate notice, that:

(1) certification was granted contrary to the rules of the Specialization Advisory Board, the Commission, or the Supreme Court; or

(2) certification was granted to a lawyer who was not eligible to have been certified in a specialty or who made any false representation or misstatement of material fact; or

(3) the certified lawyer has failed to abide by all rules and regulations covering the program promulgated by the Specialization Advisory Board, as amended from time to time, including the continuing legal education requirement for maintenance of certified status; or

(4) the certified lawyer has failed to pay any fee prescribed by the Commission; or

(5) the certified lawyer no longer meets the qualifications established by a Specialization Advisory Board; or

(6) the lawyer fails to meet the standards of competence for his particular specialty. Competency in a specialty area shall be determined in the same manner violations of the Rules of Professional Conduct are determined by the Commission on Lawyer Conduct.

(h)   Right of Hearing and Appeal.

(1) Except for denial of certification because of failure to receive a passing grade on a specialty field's written examination, a lawyer who is refused certified status, renewal of certification, or whose certified status is revoked shall have the right to a hearing before the appropriate Specialization Advisory Board and the right to appeal the Advisory Board's ruling to the Commission under rules and regulations prescribed by the Commission and approved by the Supreme Court. The exhaustion of this right to appeal shall be a condition precedent to judicial review.

Under rules and regulations prescribed by the Commission and approved by the Supreme Court, an examination and grade review process shall be established for lawyers who fail to receive a passing grade on a specialty field's written examination.

(2) Except as provided otherwise with respect to the issue of whether a lawyer passed a specialty field's written examination, decisions of the Commission may be appealed to the Supreme Court under rules and regulations prescribed by the Commission and approved by the Supreme Court. Decisions of the Commission concerning whether a lawyer passed or failed a specialty field's written examination shall be final.

(i)   Responsibilities of Certified Specialists. When a client is referred by a lawyer to a lawyer who is certified under this program, on a matter within the lawyer's specialty field, the certified lawyer shall not take unfair advantage of the certification to enlarge the scope of the representation, and shall strictly comply with the requirements of the Rules of Professional Conduct.

Any certified specialist or any lawyer who holds himself or herself out as a specialist in a particular field shall be held to a standard of competence set by the Supreme Court for a certified specialist in that field.

(j)   Financing. Fees approved by the Commission shall be charged for filing applications for certification or renewal of certification by a Specialization Advisory Board, issuance of the certificate evidencing certified status and mandatory continuing legal education registration. The fees shall be reasonable and in an amount as may be necessary to defray the expense of administering the specialization and mandatory continuing legal education programs, and may be changed from time to time.

(k)   Confidentiality. The following records regarding lawyer specialization shall be confidential and shall not be disclosed except upon order of the Supreme Court of South Carolina:

(1)   All statements or other matter submitted by persons asked to provide a reference for an applicant seeking certification or recertification as a specialist; and

(2)   All files or records relating to any applicant who has been denied certification or recertification as a specialist.

Last amended by Order dated December 28, 2012, effective January 1, 2013.

RULE 21: RULE FOR MANDATORY CONTINUING LEGAL EDUCATION.

Section 1. Commission on Continuing Legal Education.

1.01. There is hereby established the Tennessee Commission on Continuing Legal Education and Specialization consisting of 11 members, to be appointed by the Supreme Court of Tennessee. Nine members shall be attorneys who are resident members of the Bar of this State (three of whom shall reside in each of the Grand Divisions of the State) and two shall be non-attorneys.

1.02. The Commission shall have the following duties:

(a) To exercise general supervisory authority over the administration of this Rule.

(b) To adopt regulations consistent with this Rule.

(c) To monitor developments in the operation of this rule, and to design, promulgate for discussion, test and recommend to this Court modifications to the Continuing Legal Education program in Tennessee as deemed appropriate by the Commission. In furtherance of this particular responsibility, the Commission may, with prior Court approval, from time to time, adopt by regulation, after notice and an opportunity to comment to the bar and CLE providers in Tennessee, new accreditation standards, evaluation programs, and other similar programs for trial periods not to exceed 42 months in duration.

1.03. All Commission members shall hold office for three (3) years and, until their successors are appointed, to staggered terms of office.

1.04. Any Commission vacancy shall be filled by the Supreme Court to serve until the expiration of the term in which the vacancy occurred. All members shall be eligible for reappointment for no more than one additional term.

1.05. Officers of the Commission shall consist of the Chairperson, Vice Chairperson, Secretary and Treasurer. The Chairperson shall be appointed by the Supreme Court. Each of the other officers shall be elected by members of the Commission during their first meeting of each calendar year.

1.06. Meetings of the Commission may be held at any time upon notification by any officer to the entire Commission. Votes may be cast concerning any action before the Commission by registering an affirmative or negative vote during a physical meeting, or by electronic or telephonic means, or mail.

1.07. A quorum of six (6) members shall be required for any Commission action. A majority of the members in attendance at any Commission meeting having a quorum, but no less than four (4) affirmative votes, shall be necessary to approve any action.

1.08. Members of the Commission shall receive no compensation for their services but may be reimbursed by the Commission for their incidental travel and other expenses in accordance with the allowances approved by the Administrative Office of the Courts.

1.09. The Court shall appoint an executive director of the Commission, who shall serve at the pleasure of the Court. Following his or her appointment by the Court, the executive director shall report to the Commission, which shall conduct regular performance evaluations of the executive director and report such evaluations to the Court. The executive director may engage such staff as may be necessary to conduct the business of the Commission within the scope of this Rule.

1.10. Communications to the Commission, any subcommittee thereof, or to the Commission's staff relating to the failure of any lawyer to comply with this Rule, or of any fraud upon the Commission shall be absolutely privileged, and no civil suit predicated thereon may be instituted against any complainant or a witness. Members of the Commission and its staff shall be immune from civil suit for any conduct in the course of their official duties.

Section 2. Scope and Exemptions.

TENNESSEE

2.01. This Rule shall apply to every person whose qualifications to practice law are subject to the Rules of Professional Conduct of the Supreme Court of Tennessee. The exemptions contained herein shall apply only to the mandatory continuing legal education requirements of this Rule.

2.02. The practice of law shall be defined as described in Rule 9, Setion 10.3(e).

2.03. An attorney may receive twelve (12) hours of general continuing legal education credit, and three (3) hours of ethics and professionalism credit, for passing the bar examination of any state, any examination required by a certification program approved under this Rule, or the examination for admission to practice before the United States Patent and Trademark Office. In addition, an attorney may receive three hours of ethics and professionalism credit for passing either the ethics portion of a bar examination of any state or the Multi-state Professional Responsibility Examination. The maximum credit to be earned by passing any and all bar examinations in a given compliance year is twelve (12) hours of general credit and three (3) hours of ethics/professionalism credit.

2.04. The Commission shall recognize the following exemptions:

(a) Nonresident attorneys from other jurisdictions who are temporarily admitted to practice for a case or proceeding shall not be subject to this Rule.

(b) Members of the Armed Forces on active duty shall not be subject to this Rule.

(c) An attorney shall not be subject to the requirements of the Rule after age seventy (70) upon filing a request with the Commission. This exemption shall not include the calendar year in which he or she becomes seventy (70) years of age. However, any attorney who reached age sixty-five (65) on or before December 31, 2014, but who was less than age seventy (70) on that date, shall continue to be exempt from the requirements of this Rule pursuant to the age-related exemption granted by the previous version of Rule 21.

(d) An attorney who is licensed to practice law in Tennessee but who resided outside of the State and did not practice law in Tennessee during the compliance year may request an annual exemption from this Rule.

(e) Full time law school professors who are not practicing law shall not be subject to this Rule.

(f) An attorney holding an elective office in the Executive or Legislative branches of government who is prohibited by law from practicing law is exempt while holding such office.

(g) All Justices, Judges, and Magistrate Judges of the federal system shall not be subject to the requirements of this Rule in view of their required comparable continuing legal education programs.

2.05. An attorney may petition the Commission for "Exceptional Relief" from this Rule, and may be granted Exceptional Relief upon majority vote of the Commission. An attorney applying for Exceptional Relief, including appropriate waivers, extensions of time, hardship and extenuating circumstances, shall file with the Commission a written statement showing cause why that individual should be considered for Exceptional Relief and shall specify in detail the particular relief being sought.

Section 3. Continuing Legal Education Requirement.

3.01. Unless otherwise exempted, each attorney admitted to practice law in the State of Tennessee shall obtain by December 31 of that calendar year a minimum of fifteen (15) hours of continuing legal education. Of those fifteen hours, three (3) hours shall be approved for ethics/professionalism credit ("EP credits") and twelve (12) hours shall be approved for general credit. The combined fifteen (15) hours shall include a minimum of five (5) in-classroom hours of CLE credit.

3.02. (a) An attorney that has a disability that prevents compliance with Section 3.01 may file a Petition for Exceptional Relief with the Commission. The request must include a statement from a medical provider in support of the relief requested. An attorney shall provide an updated statement of disability when filing his or her Annual Report Statement.

(b) Attorneys who have a disability which makes attendance of CLE programs inordinately difficult may file a request for a substitute program in lieu of attendance and shall therein set out continuing legal education plans tailored to their specific interests and physical abilities. The Commission shall review and approve or disapprove such plans on an individual basis. Denial of any requested substitute for attendance will be accompanied by reasons for the denial of the application and suggestions how the attorney might improve his or her application for an approved substitute for attendance.

Section 4. Continuing Legal Education Credits.

4.01. Credit will be given only for continuing legal education activities approved by the Commission.

4.02. Hours of credit in excess of the minimum annual requirement may be carried forward for credit in the succeeding calendar year, but only for the succeeding calendar year. EP credits in excess of the annual requirement will, to a maximum of three (3) hours, be carried forward to the subsequent year's EP requirement, but will not be used to satisfy any deficiency in the twelve (12) hour general requirement. Such hours must, however, be reported and paid. Any attorney required to earn CLE credits that receives an Annual Report Statement showing less than twelve (12) general credits and three (3) EP credits or that a fee is due shall sign and return the Annual Report Statement as directed in the statement.

4.03. (a) Credit may be earned through teaching in an approved continuing legal education activity. Presentations accompanied by thorough, high quality, readable and carefully prepared written materials will qualify for CLE credit on the basis of four (4) hours of credit for each hour of presentation. Presentations accompanied by less than five pages of outlines, or not accompanied by written materials, will qualify for CLE credit on the basis of two (2) credits per hour of presentation. Repeat presentations qualify for one-half of the credits awarded for the initial presentation. CLE credit is earned as of the date the CLE presentation occurs.

(b) Credit may also be earned through teaching in an approved law school, or teaching law-related courses offered for credit toward a degree at the undergraduate or graduate level in an approved college, university or community college. The Commission will award four (4) hours of CLE credit for each hour of academic credit awarded by the law school, college, university or community college for the course(s) taught.

4.04. Credit may be earned through formal enrollment and education of a postgraduate nature, either for credit or by audit, in an approved law school. The Commission will award one (1) credit hour for each hour of class attendance.

4.05. Credit may be earned through service as a bar examiner in Tennessee or in any of the sister states. The Commission will award twelve (12) hours of general CLE credit and three (3) hours of EP credit annually for the preparation and grading of one or more bar examination questions during a given compliance year.

4.06. The Commission will award three (3) hours of EP credit annually for service on the Board of Professional Responsibility or any of its hearing committees.

4.07. The Commission may, in its discretion, award:

(a) Up to one-half of the annual requirement to attorneys for participation as members of governmental commissions, committees, or other governmental bodies, at either the state or national level, involved in formal sessions for review of proposed legislation, rules or regulations.

(b) Up to one-half of the annual requirement (six (6) general hours and one and one-half (1.5) EP hours) for published writings concerning substantive law, the practice of law, or the ethical and professional responsibilities of attorneys if the writing is published in approved publications intended primarily for attorneys. Credit shall be awarded in the amount of one (1) hour for every 1,000 words, not including footnotes, endnotes or citations of authority. Credit shall not be awarded to a named author when the actual principal author was another person acting under the direction or supervision of the named author. In requesting credit under this subsection, the attorney shall provide the Commission with an affidavit stating the facts of authorship.

(c) An annual maximum of three (3) dual hours of CLE credits earned at the rate of one hour of credit for every five billable hours of pro bono legal representation provided through court appointment, an organized bar association program or an approved legal assistance organization, or of pro bono mediation services as required by Tennessee Supreme Court Rule 31 or the Federal Court Mediation Programs established by the United States District Courts in Tennessee. Credits awarded pursuant to this paragraph shall be exempt from the per-hour fee imposed by Section 8 of this Rule.

An "approved legal assistance organization" for the purposes of this section is an organization or professional association that provides pro bono legal services and that is approved by the Tennessee Supreme Court. An organization which receives funding from the Legal Services Corporation is presumptively approved under this section. Organizations or groups which do not provide legal assistance as their primary service or business but wish to develop an initiative or project designed specifically to provide pro bono legal services may apply to be approved by the Supreme Court under this section. Any organization seeking approval under this section must file a petition with the clerk of the Tennessee Supreme Court.

(d) Up to six (6) hours per year of dual credit for participation as a mentor or mentee in a program meeting standards established by the Commission, including programs sponsored by bar associations, law schools, law firms, or other appropriate governmental or organizational sponsors. To help facilitate establishment of mentoring programs, the Commission is authorized to provide for a program of training for mentors, whether through its own auspices or through those of other organizations, and to charge a reasonable fee for such training. With regard to mentors participating in a mentoring program sponsored by a governmental or non-profit organization, the Commission is authorized to provide such training at no charge. This subparagraph (d) shall take effect on July 1, 2013, and shall expire on December 31, 2016, unless affirmatively readopted by the Supreme Court.

(e) Up to one (1) year of CLE credit may be awarded for completion of a bar review course. An attorney shall not receive bar review credit and bar exam credit in the same compliance year.

4.08. A maximum of eight (8) hours of credit per year earned in a distance learning format approved by the Commission pursuant to section 5.01(f) may be applied to the annual requirements.

Section 5. Continuing Legal Education Providers.

5.01. The following standards will govern the approval by the Commission of continuing legal education activities:

(a) The activity must have significant intellectual or practical content and its primary objective must be to enhance the participant's professional competence as an attorney.

(b) The activity must deal primarily with matters related to substantive law, the practice of law, professional responsibility or ethical obligations of attorneys.

(c) The activity must be offered by a provider having substantial recent experience in offering continuing legal education or demonstrated ability to organize and present effectively continuing legal education. Demonstrated ability arises partly from the extent to which individuals with legal training or educational experience are involved in the planning, instruction and supervision of the activity.

(d) The activity itself must be conducted by an individual or group qualified by practical or academic legal experience. The program, including the named advertised instructors, must be conducted substantially as planned, subject to emergency withdrawals and alterations.

(e) Textual materials should be made available in written or electronic form to all participants at or before the time the course is presented, unless the absence of such materials is recognized as reasonable.

(f) The activity must be conducted in a physical setting that is conducive to learning or in a distance-learning format approved by the Commission.

(g) No activity consisting solely of the viewing or hearing of pre-recorded material may be awarded credit.

(h) Activities that cross academic lines, such as accounting-tax seminars, may be considered for approval.

5.02. Tennessee does not recognize presumptive approval status for providers.

5.03. Tennessee does not recognize presumptive approval for any activity or program.

5.04. The Commission may at any time re-evaluate a program and revoke specific approval of any particular seminar.

5.05. (a) Any provider desiring to advertise Commission approval of a course, program, or other activity, shall submit application for such permission and supporting documentation electronically or on the Uniform Application for Accreditation at least forty-five (45) days prior to the date on which the course or program is scheduled. Documentation shall include a statement of the provider's intention to comply with the accreditation standards of this Rule, copies of programs and written materials distributed to participants at the two most recently produced programs, if available, or an outline of the proposed program and list of instructors if the provider has not produced previous programs, and such further information as the Commission shall request. The staff of the Commission will advise the provider whether the activity is approved or disapproved in writing by mail or by electronic means within thirty (30) days of the receipt of the completed application.

(b) Providers denied approval of a program or activity may appeal such a decision by submitting a letter of appeal to the Executive Director within fifteen (15) days of the receipt of the notice of disapproval. Within thirty (30) days of the receipt of the appeal, the Executive Director shall make a new decision which shall be promptly delivered to the provider. Any adverse decision may be appealed to the full Commission for final decision.

(c) Any provider may submit to the Commission the Uniform Application for Accreditation seeking approval of a program after the program is conducted.

(d) An attorney licensed to practice in Tennessee who has attended an out-of-state CLE activity not approved in advance by the Commission may submit a detailed agenda and speaker biographies for the purpose of obtaining accreditation of the course after the program is conducted. All rules pertaining to course accreditation shall apply.

5.06. (a) The provider of a continuing legal education activity approved in advance may advertise or indicate approval of an activity, as follows: "This course has been approved by the Tennessee Commission on Continuing Legal Education for a maximum of _____ hours of credit."

(b) Any out-of-state provider that holds a program in Tennessee and does not obtain program accreditation shall include a statement on any program advertisement:

    (1) "This program is not accredited in Tennessee"; or

    (2) "We intend to seek accreditation for this program in Tennessee"; or

    (3) "This program is not being submitted for accreditation in Tennessee".

Section 6. Annual Report.

6.01. On or before January 31 of each year, the Commission shall prepare and mail an Annual Report Statement to each attorney covered by this Rule requesting information concerning the attorney's compliance with Section 3 of this Rule in the preceding calendar year. The Annual Report Statement shall be mailed to the attorney's address as shown in the most recent registration statement filed by the attorney pursuant to Supreme Court Rule 9, Section 10.1, or to the attorney's last known address.

6.02. On or before March 1, each attorney shall complete the Annual Report Statement, indicating his or her completion of, exemption from, or approved substitute for accredited continuing legal education during the preceding calendar year, and shall deliver the completed Annual Report Statement to the Commission. The completed Annual Report Statement shall disclose all CLE hours earned during the preceding calendar year, including any hours to be carried forward to the following year. Any attorney whose Annual Report Statement demonstrates compliance with Section 3 of this Rule, and whose Annual Report Statement demonstrates that all fees due the Commission for the preceding calendar year have been paid, shall be exempt from the requirement to sign and deliver to the Commission the Annual Report Statement described herein.

6.03. The files and records of the Commission are deemed confidential and shall not be disclosed except in furtherance of the duties of the Commission; statistical abstracts may, however, be drawn therefrom in an anonymous fashion.

Section 7. Noncompliance and Sanctions

7.01. By March 31 of each year, the Commission shall compile:

(a) A list of those attorneys who did not timely file an Annual Report Statement for the preceding calendar year; and

(b) A list of those attorneys who timely filed an Annual Report Statement indicating lack of compliance with the requirements of Section 3 of this Rule for the preceding calendar year; and

(c) A list of those attorneys who timely filed an Annual Report Statement indicating compliance with the requirements of Section 3 of this Rule for the preceding calendar year but who did not pay any and all fees due under Section 8.03 of this Rule.

7.02. On March 31 of each year, the Commission shall serve each attorney listed on any of the three foregoing lists a Notice of Non-completion requiring the attorney to remedy his/her deficiencies on or before May 31 of that year. The notice shall be served upon the attorney by registered or certified mail, return receipt requested, at the address shown in the most recent registration statement filed by the attorney pursuant to Supreme Court Rule 9, Section 10.1 or other last known address.

7.03. Each attorney to whom a Notice of Non-completion is issued shall pay to the Commission a non-completion fee of One Hundred Dollars ($100.00). Such non-completion fee shall be paid on or before May 31 of that year unless the attorney shows to the satisfaction of the Executive Director of the Commission that the Notice of Non-completion was erroneously issued, in which case no such fee is due.

7.04. Each attorney to whom a Notice of Non-completion is issued shall file an affidavit with the Commission on or before May 31 of that year showing that he or she has remedied his/her deficiencies. In the event an attorney fails to timely remedy his/her deficiencies or fails to timely file such affidavit, the attorney shall pay to the Commission, in addition to the non-completion fee, a delinquent compliance fee of Two Hundred Dollars ($200.00).

7.05. On July 1 of each year, the Commission shall prepare a draft Suspension Order listing all attorneys who were issued Notices of Non-completion and who failed to remedy their deficiencies by May 31. The Commission shall submit the draft Suspension Order to the Supreme Court for informational purposes. The Commission also shall mail a copy of the draft Suspension Order to each attorney named in the draft Order by registered or certified mail, return receipt requested, to the address shown in the most recent registration statement filed by the attorney pursuant to Supreme Court Rule 9, Section 10.1 or other last known address.

7.06. On or before August 10, each attorney listed in the draft Suspension Order may file an affidavit in a form acceptable to the Commission showing compliance with Section 3 of this Rule for the preceding calendar year. Upon the Commission's approval of such affidavit and upon the attorney's payment of all outstanding fees, the Commission shall remove the attorney's name from the list of potential suspensions contained in the draft Suspension Order.

7.07. On August 15, the Commission shall submit to the Supreme Court a final Suspension Order listing all attorneys with active Tennessee law licenses who failed to comply with this Rule for the preceding calendar year. Also on August 15, the Commission shall notify the Board of Professional Responsibility of the names of all licensed attorneys who have retired, taken inactive status, been suspended, or whose license to practice law in this state is otherwise inactive, and who failed to comply with the requirements of this Rule. The Supreme Court will review the final Suspension Order and, upon the Court's approval, shall enter the Suspension Order suspending the law license of each attorney listed in the order. The Board of Professional Responsibility shall not reactivate the license of any attorney whose license is suspended pursuant to this Rule until the Commission certifies completion of a program of remedial continuing legal education satisfactory to the Commission.

7.08. Each attorney named in the final Suspension Order entered by the Court or whose name is submitted to the Board of Professional Responsibility as ineligible for reactivation for failure to meet the requirements of this rule shall pay to the Commission a Five Hundred Dollar ($500) Suspension Fee as a condition of reinstatement of his or her law license. The suspension fee shall be paid in addition to the non-completion fee and the delinquent compliance fee.

7.09. Payment of all fees imposed in this section shall be a requirement for compliance with this Rule.

7.10. An attorney suspended or made ineligible for reactivation by the Commission pursuant to this Rule may file with the Commission an application for reinstatement demonstrating compliance with Section 3 of this Rule. If the application is satisfactory to the Commission, if the attorney is otherwise eligible for reinstatement, and if the attorney has paid in full all fees due under this Rule, the Commission will recommend to the Supreme Court that the Court reinstate the attorney's law license.

7.11. An attorney may request a hearing before the Commission in regard to a recommendation of suspension or a recommendation against reinstatement. Additionally, any attorney not finding suitable relief before the Commission may petition the Supreme Court for modification or reversal of actions of the Commission. [Added by order filed March 21, 2002.]

7.12. No attorney suspended under this Rule 21 may resume practice until reinstated by Order of the Supreme Court.

Section 8. Financing.

8.01. The Commission shall be adequately funded to enable it to perform its duties in a financially independent and responsible manner.

8.02. (a) Providers of CLE programs held within the State of Tennessee as a condition of accreditation shall agree to remit to the Commission an alphabetical list of attendees and to pay a fee of $2.00 per approved credit hour for paper filings and a fee of $1.00 per approved credit hour for electronic filings for each attorney licensed in Tennessee who attends the program. This provider's fee, along with the list of attendees, shall be submitted within thirty (30) days after the program is held.

(b) Information contained in the attendance report required by this section or any Commission requirement under this Rule, or obtained by the Commission through analysis or comparison of such reports or information shall be deemed confidential..

8.03. Attorneys attending approved out-of-state CLE programs, or other programs for which the sponsor does not report and pay the per-hour fee, shall be responsible for remitting their individual fees at the rate set under § 8.04. This fee shall be paid at the time of, and along with, the report of such hours.

8.04. The Commission will review the level of the fees at least annually and adjust the levels as necessary to maintain adequate finances for prudent operation of the Commission.

8.05. The Commission shall deposit all funds collected hereunder with the State Treasurer; all such funds including earnings on investments and all interest and proceeds from said funds, if any, are deemed to be, and shall be designated as, funds belonging solely to the Commission. Withdrawals from those funds shall only be made by the Commission for the purposes set forth in this Rule, and for such other purposes as this Court may from time to time authorize or direct.

Section 9. Effective Dates of the Rule.

9.01. The establishment of the program for Mandatory Continuing Legal Education for attorneys licensed in Tennessee took effect on January 1, 1987. This Rule shall continue until such time as the Supreme Court shall determine that its program is no longer in keeping with the Court's responsibility to the legal profession in Tennessee and the public which it serves.

Section 10. Annual CLE Compliance Summary.

10.01. Notwithstanding any other provision of this Rule to the contrary, the Commission shall publish an Annual CLE Compliance Summary of the activities of the Commission and the CLE reports and requests for exemption received by the Commission during the preceding compliance year. As part of this summary, the Commission shall report on the following topics:

(a) The number of courses approved and rejected for accreditation;

(b) The number of providers from whom lawyers holding a Tennessee license have received CLE credit;

(c) The number of general and dual credit hours earned by lawyers holding a Tennessee license, both in the aggregate and in the following general categories:

(1) traditional live or in-classroom programs;

(2) distance learning broken down by the following categories:

(i) online computer interactive;

(ii) webinars; and

(iii) telephone conference calls;

(3) pro bono legal representation;

(4) teaching;

(5) completion of a law-related course broken down by the following areas:

(i) bar review course;

(ii) bar exam; and

(iii) postgraduate course;

(6) service to the bar in the following areas:

(i) bar examiner;

(ii) governmental commissions, committees, or other governmental bodies;

(iii) Board of Professional Responsibility or as a hearing committee member;

(7) published author; and

(8) mentoring.

(d) The number of courses offered per provider and the attendance figures based on the categories above;

(e) The number of lawyers holding a Tennessee license who have been granted an exemption for the previous compliance year; and

(f) The number of requests for exceptional relief granted by the Commission during the previous compliance year.

The Commission shall also report generally on the substantive content areas in which CLE credits are being earned and reported. The Commission's report relating to the preceding compliance year shall be published on its website by September 1.

Section 11. Identification of Specialists.

11.01. Lawyers licensed to practice law in Tennessee may be certified as being a legal specialist by any organization that has been accredited by the American Bar Association's House of Delegates to award specialist certifications to lawyers.

11.02. Each lawyer who has received a certification as a specialist shall register the certification with the Commission. The Commission shall confirm that the certification presented by the specialist has been issued from an organization that has been accredited by the American Bar Association's House of Delegates to award specialist certifications to lawyers. However, the Commission shall have no authority to certify any lawyer practicing in this State as being a specialist in any area of law.

11.03. Upon confirmation that a lawyer has received a specialist certification from an appropriate certifying organization, the Commission shall record the following information in the form of a Roll of Certified Specialists:

(a) the lawyer's name;

(b) the lawyer's Board of Professional Responsibility registration number;

(c) the state and county in which the lawyer maintains the lawyer's principal office;

(d) the name, address, and current website of the certifying organization;

(e) the area or areas of law in which the lawyer has obtained a specialty certification; and

(f) the date on which the lawyer obtained the specialty certification.

11.04. Each lawyer shall renew the lawyer's registration annually with the Commission and, in so doing, shall represent that the specialty certification remains valid. If a lawyer's certification of specialty has expired, or is withdrawn or revoked for any reason, the lawyer must report such fact to the Commission within fifteen (15) days of the expiration, withdrawal or revocation. If a lawyer fails to renew the specialty certification, or if the lawyer notifies the Commission of the expiration, withdrawal or revocation of a specialty certification, the Commission shall immediately remove the lawyer's information from the Roll of Certified Specialists.

11.05. No lawyer shall at any time represent that the lawyer is a specialist in any area of law without first having a current registration of a valid certification on file with the Commission.

11.06. The Commission shall maintain the Roll of Certified Specialists, taking special care to ensure the accuracy and timeliness of information contained therein. The Commission shall also make the Roll of Certified Specialists available for public inspection and shall publish the Roll from time to time. The Commission may satisfy the obligation to publish the Roll of Certified Specialists by maintaining the Roll on the Commission's website.

11.07. The Commission, subject to the approval of the Court, may establish and collect reasonable fees from lawyers seeking to register, or re-register, any specialty certification to offset the costs of administering the procedures set forth in this Section

[As adopted by order filed September 25, 1986 and designated by orders entered Rule 21: September 26 and 29, 1986; and amended by orders entered June 22, 1988, July 25, 1988, October 5, 1988, March 1, 1991, and October 29, 1991, April 7, 1992, April 17, 1992, July 1, 1993, December 14, 1994, September 21, 2010, April 30, 2012, effective January 1, 2012, January 11, 2013, effective July 1, 2013, and by order filed August 30, 2013, effective January 1, 2014; Amended by order filed August 18, 2014; and by order filed December 16, 2014, effective January 1, 2015.]

TEXAS

TEXAS
MINIMUM CONTINUING LEGAL EDUCATION RULES
(Article XII, State Bar Rules)

Section 1. Purpose

The purpose of minimum continuing legal education requirements is to ensure that every active member of the State Bar of Texas pursues a plan of continuing legal education throughout his or her career in order to remain current on the law in our rapidly changing society.

Section 2. Definitions

(A)   "MCLE" means Minimum Continuing Legal Education.

(B)   "Committee" means the Committee on Minimum Continuing Legal Education.

(C)   "Committee member" is a member of the Committee on Minimum Continuing Legal Education.

(D)   "MCLE Department" means the departmental staff of the State Bar of Texas with the responsibility of administering all aspects of the MCLE program as determined by this Article and any regulations established pursuant hereto.

(E)   "The Director" means the Director of the MCLE Department of the State Bar of Texas.

(F)   "Continuing legal education activity" means any organized legal educational activity accredited by the Committee.

(G)   "CLE Credit Hours" means the actual amount of instruction time for an accredited continuing legal education activity expressed in terms of hours rounded to the nearest one-quarter hour. The number of CLE credit hours shall be based on sixty (60) minutes of instruction per hour, unless otherwise specified herein.

(H)   "Self-study" includes individual viewing or listening to audio, video, or digital media, reading written material, or attending organized in-office educational programs, or such other activities as may be approved by the Committee.

(I)   "Accredited sponsor" means any provider who receives presumptive approval of the Committee to conduct continuing legal education activities that satisfy the requirements of this Article.

(J)   "Accredited CLE Activity" means any CLE activity that receives MCLE accreditation under the MCLE Rules, Regulations, and accreditation criteria adopted by the MCLE Committee.

(K)   "MCLE compliance record" means the official record of a member's CLE credit hours earned during any MCLE compliance year that shall be maintained by the MCLE Department and used to verify a member's compliance with the MCLE requirements. It shall be the responsibility of each member to ensure that his/her MCLE compliance record is accurate and complete.

(L)   "MCLE compliance year" means the twelve (12) month period that begins each year on the first day of an attorney's birth month and ends on the last date of the month that immediately precedes the attorney's birth month in the following year.

(M)   "MCLE reporting month" means the birth month during which the attorney is required to show completion of CLE requirements. If an extension has been granted in accordance with the Article (Section 9), the reporting month shall mean the month immediately following the last date of the extension and shall replace the birth month for that current compliance year.

(N)   "MCLE Annual Verification Report" means the written report containing a listing of all CLE credit hours recorded in a member's MCLE compliance record for an MCLE compliance year. This report shall be furnished to each member annually by the MCLE Department.

(O)   "Preferred Address" means the member's physical address, post office box, E-mail address or other address, that is on file with the State Bar of Texas Membership department and that is designated as the member's preferred address for receiving written notifications.

(P)   "Secondary Address" means any or all of the member's physical addresses, post office boxes, E-mail addresses, or other addresses on file with the State Bar of Texas Membership department and that are not designated as the member's preferred address for receiving written notifications.

Section 3. Committee on Minimum Continuing Legal Education

(A)   There is hereby established the Committee which shall be composed of twelve (12) members. Nine (9) of the members shall be residents of this State who are active members of the State Bar, at least two (2) of whom shall be under the age of thirty-six (36) years as of June 1 of the year being appointed. Of the nine (9) attorney members, not more than two (2) shall be judges. The remaining three (3) members of the Committee shall be residents of this State who are not attorneys. The President-Elect, with the approval of the Board, shall appoint any Committee members whose term will begin at the beginning of the bar year during which he or she will be President. Should a vacancy on the Committee occur during the bar year, the President, with the approval of the Board, shall appoint a successor to fill the unexpired term. Each member of the Committee shall continue to serve until his or her successor is appointed and qualified. The President-Elect shall designate one (1) of the attorney members of the Committee to serve as chairperson during his or her term as President. The Board may remove a member of the Committee for good cause. No Committee member shall be appointed for more than two (2) terms. Committee members shall serve without compensation, but shall be reimbursed for reasonable and necessary expenses incurred in the performance of their official duties.

(B)   The State Bar shall employ such staff as may be necessary to perform the record keeping, auditing, reporting, accreditation, and other functions required by these rules.

(C)   The Committee, subject to these rules and such regulations as it may propose and may be adopted by the Board, shall administer the program of minimum continuing legal education established by this Article. It may propose regulations and prepare forms not inconsistent with this Article pertaining to its function and modify or amend the same from time to time. All such regulations, forms, modifications or amendments shall be submitted to the Board for approval and, upon such approval, shall be published in the Texas Bar Journal.

Section 4. Accreditation

(A)   The Committee shall develop criteria for the accreditation of continuing legal education activities and shall designate the number of hours to be earned by participation in such activities, as approved by the Committee. In order for an activity to be accredited, the subject matter must directly relate to legal subjects and the legal profession, including professional responsibility, legal ethics, or law practice management. The Committee may, in appropriate cases, extend accreditation to qualified activities that have already occurred. The Committee shall not extend credit to activities completed in the ordinary course of the practice of law, in the performance of regular employment, as a volunteer service to clients or the general public, as a volunteer service to government entities, or in a member's regular duties on a committee, section or division of any bar related organization. The Committee may extend accredited status, subject to periodic review, to a qualified sponsor for its overall continuing legal education curriculum. No examinations shall be required.

(B)   Self-study credit may be given for individual viewing or listening to audio, video, or digital media, reading written material, attending organized in-office educational programs or such other activities as may be approved by the Committee. No more than five (5) hours of credit may be given during any compliance year for self-study activities. Time spent viewing or listening to audio, video or digital media as an organized CLE activity approved by the Committee counts as conventional continuing legal education and is not subject to the self-study limitation.

(C)   Credit may be earned through teaching or participating in an accredited CLE activity. Credit shall be granted for preparation time and presentation time, including preparation credit for repeated presentations.

(D)   Credit may be earned through legal research-based writing upon application to the Committee provided the activity (1) produced material published or to be published in the form of an article, chapter, or book written, in whole or in part, by the applicant; (2) contributed substantially to the continuing legal education of the applicant and other attorneys; and (3) is not done in the ordinary course of the practice of law, the performance of regular employment, or as a service to clients.

(E)   The Committee may, in appropriate cases charge a reasonable fee to the sponsor for accrediting CLE activities.

(F)   A member who holds a full-time faculty position in any law school which is approved by the American Bar Association may be credited as fulfilling the requirements of this article, except as to the minimum requirements for CLE in legal ethics and professional responsibility. A member who holds a part-time faculty position in any such law school may claim participatory credit for the actual hours of class instruction time not to exceed twelve (12) hours per compliance year, except as to the minimum requirements for CLE in legal ethics and professional responsibility.

(G)   The Committee shall grant exemption from this Article to any emeritus member of the State Bar of Texas. (Emeritus as defined by the State Bar Act, Section 81.052 (e)).

(H)   Credit to meet the minimum educational requirement shall be extended to attorneys who are members of the Senate and House of Representatives of present and future United States and Texas Legislatures for each regular session in which the attorney member shall serve.

(I)   No credit shall be given for activities directed primarily to persons preparing for admission to practice law.

(J)   Credit, not to exceed thirty 30 hours in any compliance year, may be earned for attending a law school class after admission to practice in Texas provided (1) that the member officially registered for the class with the law school; and (2) that the member completed the course as required by the terms of registration. Credit for approved attendance at law school classes shall be for the actual number of hours of class instruction time the member is in attendance at the law school course.

Section 5. Compliance Year

(A)   Each member's compliance year shall begin on the first day of the month in which his or her birthday occurs.

(B)   The initial compliance year for each member shall be the 24-month period that begins on the first birth month following the date of admission.

Section 6. Minimum Educational Requirements

(A)   Every member shall complete fifteen (15) hours of continuing legal education during each compliance year as provided by this article. No more than five (5) credit hours may be given for completion of self-study activities during any compliance year.

(B)   At least three (3) hours of the fifteen (15) hours shall be devoted to legal ethics/professional responsibility subjects. One (1) of the three (3) legal ethics/professional responsibility hours may be completed through self-study.

(C)   All persons admitted, and any person who has been suspended, disbarred, or who has resigned pursuant to Article X of the State Bar Rules, or who has resigned pursuant to Article III of the State Bar Rules, or who has been suspended pursuant to Section 8 of this Article, or who has taken inactive status pursuant to Section 81.052, Texas Government Code, and who desires to return to active status shall be required, in addition to such other requirements as the State Bar Rules may contain, to comply with the requirements of Section 6(A) and 6(B) hereof.

(D)   Accredited continuing legal education and self-study completed within a 12-month period immediately preceding a member's initial compliance year may be used to meet the educational requirement for the initial compliance year. Exception: Credit for the educational activity entitled "The Guide to the Basics of Law Practice," sponsored by the Texas Center for Legal Ethics and Professionalism, completed anytime during the third year of law school or during the initial compliance year, may be used toward meeting the educational requirements for the initial compliance year.

(E)   Accredited continuing legal education and self-study completed during any compliance year in excess of the minimum fifteen (15) hour requirement for such period will be applied to the following compliance year's requirement. This carryover provision applies to one (1) year only.

Section 7. Credit Computation

(A)   Credit for attending accredited continuing legal education activities shall be based on net actual instruction time, which may include organized lecture, panel discussion, audio, video, and digital media presentations and organized question-and-answer periods.

Sponsors are encouraged to calculate the number of hours of credit that should be given for any activity offered, using the above guide, and indicate the number on the activity brochure. Fractional hours should be stated as decimals.

(B)   Credit for viewing or listening to audio, video, or digital media shall be based on the running time of the recordings.

(C)   Credit for reading approved material or attending in-office educational programs shall be based on actual time spent.

Section 8. Compliance

(A)   Two months prior to the end of the MCLE compliance year, the Director shall send an MCLE Annual Verification Report to each member's Preferred Address for who said MCLE compliance year applies. Upon receipt of the MCLE Annual Verification Report, the member shall review the report for accuracy and completeness. If the report accurately reflects the member's MCLE compliance record for the current MCLE compliance year, and if it shows that the minimum CLE credit hours requirements have been met, then no additional action is required by the member.   If the Report does not accurately and completely reflect a member's CLE credits, then the member shall correct his or her record according to the instructions on the Report. To avoid fines and/or suspension, all CLE credit hours, corrections and additions to the MCLE record shall be completed, filed and received by the MCLE Director on or before the end of the compliance year.

(B)   On or about the first day of the birth month, the Director shall make available to the member, a report of amendments that have been made to the MCLE record for the compliance year that ended immediately prior to said birth month.

The Director shall also notify any member who has not completed MCLE requirements for the compliance year that ended immediately prior to said birth month. A member, who has not completed his or her CLE requirements by the first day of the birth month, will receive an automatic grace period through the last day of the birth month to complete and report any remaining CLE credits. Members shall not be fined or penalized for completing and reporting CLE credits by the last day of the birth month (grace period).

(C)   On or about the twelfth (12th) day of the month immediately following a member's birth month, the Director shall notify all members who are in non-compliance for the MCLE compliance year just ended to advise such members of their non-compliance status. Such notice shall be in the form of a written notice, and sent to each member at the Preferred Address and via one (1) Secondary Address (if any) that is then on file with the Membership Department of the State Bar.

(D)   On or about the first (1st) day of the third month immediately following a member's birth month, the Director shall send final notice to any member who has not cured their non-compliance status. Such notice shall be in the form of a written notice, and sent to each member at the Preferred Address and via one (1) Secondary Address (if any) that is then on file with the Membership Department of the State Bar.

(E)   If by the last business day of the fourth month following the birth month (or reporting month if the member has been granted an extension in accordance with this article for completion of CLE requirements) the member has still not cured his or her non-compliance, the member shall be automatically suspended from the practice of law in Texas as directed by Order of the Supreme Court dated December 23, 2002.

(F)   Upon the execution of suspension, the Director shall cause to be sent a written notification to each member who is suspended from practice by the order. Said notification shall be sent to each member at his or her Preferred Address and via one (1) Secondary Address (if any) that is then on file with the Membership Department of the State Bar.

Section 9. Review and Appeal

(A)   A member may file a written request for exemption from compliance with any of the requirements of this Article, an extension of time for compliance, an extension of time to comply with a deficiency notice, or an extension of time to file an annual activity report. Such request for excuse or for extension shall be reviewed and determined by the Committee or by such members as the chairperson may, from time to time, designate. The member shall be promptly notified of the Committee's decision.

(B)   "Good cause" shall exist when a member is unable to comply with this Article because of illness, medical disability, or other extraordinary hardship or extenuating circumstances that were not willful on the part of the member and were beyond his or her control.

(C)   Should the decision of the Committee be adverse to the member, the member may request the Board of Directors of the State Bar to review the decision by making such request in writing to the Executive Director of the State Bar within thirty days of notification of the decision of the Committee. The Chairman of the Board may appoint a committee of the Board to review the decision of the Committee and make a recommendation to the Board. The decision shall be made by the Board.

(D)   Should the decision of the Board be adverse to the member, the member may appeal such decision by filing suit within thirty (30) days of notification of the Board's action, failing which the decision of the Board shall be final. Such suit shall be brought against the State Bar, and shall be filed in a district court in Travis County, Texas. Trial shall be de novo, but (1) the burden of proof shall be on the member appealing; (2) the burden shall be a preponderance of the evidence; and (3) the member shall prove the existence of "good cause" as defined herein. The trial court shall proceed to hear and determine the issue without a jury. Either party shall have a right to appeal.

(E)   Any suspension of a member under this Article shall be vacated during the administrative review process and while any suit filed is pending.

Section 10. Return to Former Status

Any member whose license to practice law has been suspended under the terms of this Article who after the date of suspension files an activity report with the MCLE Director showing compliance and who has paid all applicable fees associated with non-compliance and suspension, shall be entitled to have such suspension promptly terminated and be returned to former status. Return to former status shall be retroactive to the inception of suspension, but shall not affect any proceeding for discipline of the member for professional misconduct. The MCLE Director shall promptly notify the Clerk that a member formerly suspended under this Article has now complied with this Article.

Section 11. Exemption of Certain Judges

Judges subject to Supreme Court Order for Judicial Education dated August 21, 1985, Supreme Court Order for Judicial Education for Retired or Former District Judges dated July 2, 1986, and federal judicial officers, shall be exempt from these requirements.

Section 12. Confidentiality

A member who reports attendance credits individually to the MCLE Director, without the sponsoring organization's knowledge, automatically consents to release of his or her name to the sponsoring organization for the sole purpose of reconciling attendance records. Otherwise, the files, records and proceedings of the Committee, as they relate to the compliance or noncompliance of any member with the requirements of this Article, shall be confidential and shall not be disclosed except upon consent of the member affected or as directed in the course of judicial proceeding by a court of competent jurisdiction.

Section 13. Effective Date

The effective date of this Article shall be June 1, 1986.
The effective date of amendments to this Article shall be February 1, 2005.

UTAH

Article 4. Mandatory Continuing Legal Education

Rule 14-401. Purpose.

By continuing their legal education throughout the period of practice of law, lawyers can better fulfill their obligation to serve their clients competently. This article establishes minimum requirements for mandatory continuing legal education and the means by which the requirements are enforced.

Effective May 1, 2016.

Rule 14-402. Definitions.

As used in this article:

(a) "Active emeritus" or "active emeritus lawyer" means a lawyer who has been a member of the Bar for 50 years or who is 75 years of age as of July 1 of the current year and who qualifies for active emeritus status as defined under the Bar's rules, regulations and policies;

(b) "Active status" or "active status lawyer" means a lawyer who has elected to be on active status as defined under the Bar's rules, regulations and policies; state judges, federal judges and magistrates, court commissioners, active senior judges and active justice court judges, both full and part time, meet CLE requirements through the Administrative office of the Courts;

(c) "Admission on motion applicant or lawyer" means a lawyer who has applied for reciprocal admission as defined under Rule 14-705 or has been admitted as such;

(d) "Approved law school" means an ABA approved law school as defined under Rule 14-701;

(e) "Bar" means the Utah State Bar;

(f) "Bar Examination" means the Bar Examination as defined in Rules 14-710 and 14-711 and includes the UBE, regardless of where the UBE was taken;

(g) "Board" means the Utah State Board of Mandatory Continuing Legal Education as set forth in Rule 14-403;

(h) "Board of Bar Commissioners" means the governing board of the Bar;

(i) "Certificate of Compliance" means a written report evidencing a lawyer's completion of accredited CLE as required and defined under Rule 14-414;

(j) "CLE" means continuing legal education;

(j)(1) "Live CLE" means a CLE program presented in a classroom setting where the lawyer is in the same room as the presenter;

(j)(2) "Live Attendance" means in person attendance at a Utah state courthouse where a course is streamed by live audio-visual communication from another Utah state courthouse or from the Law and Justice Center;

(j)(3) "Self-Study CLE Program" means a program presented in a suitable setting where the lawyer can view approved self-study activities;

(k) "Comity Certificate" is a Certificate that is filed to show MCLE compliance with a reciprocal jurisdiction;

(l) "Compliance Cycle"- means the period of 2 years beginning July 1 through June 30;

(m) "Ethics" means standards set by the Utah Rules of Professional Conduct with which a lawyer must comply to remain authorized to practice law in Utah and remain in good standing;

(n) "Full exam" means all components of the Bar Examination as defined under Rule 14-710;

(o) "House Counsel" means a lawyer admitted with a restricted House Counsel license as defined in Rule 14-719, which is required and limits his or her practice of law to the business of his or her employer;

(p) "Inactive status" or "inactive status lawyer" means a lawyer who has elected to be on inactive status as defined under the Bar's rules, regulations and policies;

(q) "MCLE" means mandatory continuing legal education as defined under this article;

(r) "Multi-State Compliance Reciprocity" means Utah has established that MCLE compliance in certain states (Idaho, Oregon, Washington) may be used as MCLE compliance in Utah by an active lawyer whose principal practice is in one of the established reciprocal states;

(s) "New admittee" means a lawyer newly admitted to the Utah State Bar;

(t) "NLTP" means the New Lawyer Training Program as set forth in Rule 14-404 and Rule 14-808;

(u) "Presumptively approved sponsor" means those CLE sponsors or providers who qualify under the standards set forth in Rule 14-412;

(v) "Presumptive CLE accreditation" means those CLE courses or activities that qualify under the standards set forth in Rule 14-412;

(w) "Professionalism and Civility" means conduct consistent with the tenets of the legal profession by which a lawyer demonstrates civility, honesty, integrity, character, fairness, competence, ethical conduct, public service, and respect for the rules of law, the courts, clients, other lawyers, witnesses and unrepresented parties;

(x) "OPC" means the Bar's Office of Professional Conduct;

(y) "OPC ethics school" means the OPC biannual seminar on the Utah Rules of Professional Conduct which provides six CLE credit hours;

(z) "Supreme Court" means the Utah Supreme Court; and

(aa) "UBE Transfers" means applicants who gain admission by transferring a uniform bar exam score;

Effective May 1, 2016.

Rule 14-403.   Establishment and membership of Board.

There is hereby established by this Court a Board of Mandatory Continuing Legal Education. The Board consists of 15 members, all of whom are lawyers admitted to the Bar. Members are appointed for three-year terms, except that three members of the initial Board will be appointed for a one-year term and three members will be appointed for a two-year term. Each yearly class of members will include one member residing outside of Salt Lake County. No lawyer may serve more than two consecutive terms as a member of the Board.

Effective May 1, 2016.

Rule 14-404.   Active status lawyers: MCLE, NLTP, admission on motion, multi-state compliance reciprocity, house counsel and UBE requirements.

(a) Active status lawyers. Commencing with calendar year 2012, each lawyer admitted to practice in Utah must complete, during each two fiscal year period (July 1 through June 30), a minimum of 24 hours of Utah accredited CLE which must include a minimum of three hours of accredited ethics or professional responsibility. One of the three hours of ethics or professional responsibility must be in the area of professionalism and civility. Lawyers on inactive status are not subject to the requirements of this rule, or the NLTP requirements.

(a)(1) Lawyers on active status who reside in Utah and who are subject to the NLTP under Rule 14-808 must complete the NLTP requirements before the end of their first compliance cycle.

(b) NLTP. A lawyer who is obligated to and who successfully fulfills the requirements of the NLTP will receive 12 accredited MCLE hours for the reporting period ending June 30 of the second complete fiscal year following the lawyer's year of admission to the Bar. Twelve additional MCLE hours must also be completed during the lawyer's first compliance cycle, not including the New Lawyer Ethics program.

(b)(1) New Lawyer Ethics Program. New lawyers are required to attend the New Lawyer Ethics Program. This program satisfies the ethics requirement for the new lawyer's first compliance cycle.

(c) Admission on motion. A lawyer who fulfills the requirements of admission on motion as prescribed in Rule 14-705 satisfies the accredited MCLE requirements of this rule for the reporting cycle ending June 30 of the second complete fiscal year following the lawyer's year of admission. In addition, the admission on motion lawyer must pay the designated filing fee and must complete and certify no later than six months following the lawyer's admission that he or she has attended at least 15 hours of accredited CLE hours on Utah practice and procedure and ethics requirements as follows:

(c)(1) Nine credit hours must be comprised of accredited CLE courses on Utah practice and procedure.

(c)(2) Six credit hours must be comprised of the professional ethics course presented in OPC's ethics school.

(c)(3) Twelve of the 15 hours may be completed through self-study through the Bar's online CLE system. The 15 hours from (c)(1) and (c)(2) will apply towards the 24 hours required per two-year compliance cycle.

(d) Multi-State Reciprocity Compliance. An active lawyer whose principal practice of law is in a Multi-State Compliance Reciprocity State may elect to meet the MCLE requirements in that other state and use that state's MCLE compliance as compliance in Utah by filing a "Comity Certificate" for Utah CLE compliance.

(e) House Counsel lawyers. House Counsel lawyers must pay the designated filing fee and file with the MCLE Board by July 31 of each year a House Counsel Certificate signed by the jurisdiction where House Counsel maintains an active license evidencing that the lawyer has completed the hours of continuing legal education required of active lawyers in the jurisdiction where House Counsel is licensed. House Counsel lawyers that do not have a CLE requirement from the jurisdiction where House Counsel maintains an active license must complete 12 hours annually (July 1 – June 30) of Utah approved CLE to include 1 hour of legal ethics and 1 hour of professionalism/civility. At least half of the hours must be completed by attending live, in-person CLE.

(f) UBE Applicants. A lawyer who gains admission by transferring a UBE score and has less than two years of legal practice will comply with the New Lawyer Training Program. If the lawyer gains admission by transferring a UBE score and has less than two years of legal practice and receives a waiver of the New Lawyer Training Program because the lawyer lives out of the state, the lawyer will comply with the same rules as admission on motion lawyers. A lawyer who gains admission by transferring a UBE score and has more than 2 years of active practice will comply with the same rules as admission on motion lawyers. These lawyers must pay the designated filing fee and are required to complete and certify no later than six months following the lawyer's admission that he or she has attended at least 15 hours of accredited CLE hours on Utah practice and procedure and ethics requirements including the OPC's ethics school.

(g) Out-of-state CLE activities. CLE credit may be awarded for out-of-state activities that the Board determines meet standards in furthering a lawyer's legal education. The Board determines whether to accredit the activities and, if accredited, the number of hours of credit to allow for such activities. Out-of-state activities cannot substitute for the 15 mandatory CLE hours described in paragraph (c) and Rules14-705(b) and 14-705(b)(1).

(h) Activities that may be regarded as equivalent to state-sponsored self-study CLE may include, but are not limited to, viewing of approved CLE audio and video, and webcast presentations, computer interactive telephonic programs, writing and publishing an article in a legal periodical, part-time teaching in an approved law school, or delivering a paper or speech on a professional subject at a meeting primarily attended by lawyers, legal assistants, or law school students.

(i) A lawyer's application for accreditation of a CLE activity must be submitted in writing to the Board if the activity has not been previously approved for CLE credit in Utah.

Effective May 1, 2016.

Rule 14-405. MCLE requirements for lawyers on inactive status.

(a) Lawyers on inactive status are not subject to MCLE requirements while on inactive status.

(b) Return to active status. A lawyer on inactive status who returns to active status must complete the 24 hour MCLE requirement by June 30 of the fiscal year following his or her return to active status and may use CLE hours completed prior to activation to satisfy part or all of the MCLE requirement if those hours were completed during the CLE cycle in which the lawyer must complete the MCLE requirement.

(c) If a lawyer elects inactive status at the end of the licensing cycle (June 1-September 30) when his or her CLE reporting is due and elects to change back to active status within the first three months of the following licensing cycle, the lawyer will be required to complete the CLE requirement for the previous CLE reporting period before returning to active status.

Effective May 1, 2016.

Rule 14-406. MCLE requirements for lawyers on active military duty.

(a) Waiver. Lawyers who are serving or called to federal active military duty that will last for 90 concurrent days or longer during any portion of a compliance period will have MCLE requirements waived for that particular compliance period.

(b) Statement of compliance. Each lawyer serving or called to federal active military duty that will last for 90 concurrent days or longer must file with the Board a statement of compliance providing verification of the date the lawyer was called to federal active military duty. The statement of compliance is due by July 31 following the end of the compliance cycle in which the report is due.

Effective May 1, 2016.

Rule 14-407. MCLE requirements for lawyers on active emeritus status.

(a) Commencing with calendar year 2012, lawyers on active emeritus status must comply with MCLE requirements by participation in 12 hours of Utah accredited CLE during each two-fiscal-year (July 1 through June 30) compliance cycle.

(b) Alternative. In the alternative, lawyers on active emeritus status may work in conjunction with another Utah lawyer on active status in lieu of complying with the requirement of 12 hours of Utah accredited CLE. These lawyers must contact the MCLE Board Director prior to working with another active Utah lawyer. Lawyers on active emeritus status who elect to work in conjunction with another Utah lawyer on active status in lieu of complying with 12 hours of Utah accredited CLE must file with the Board a signed statement verifying that he or she has complied with the requirements of this rule by July 31 following the end of the compliance cycle in which the report is due.

(c) If an Emeritus lawyer elects inactive status at the end of the licensing cycle (June 1-September 30) when his or her CLE reporting is due and elects to change back to active status within the first three months of the following licensing cycle, the lawyer will be required to complete the active emeritus CLE requirement for the previous CLE reporting period before returning to active status.

Effective May 1, 2016.

Rule 14-408. Credit hour defined; application for approval.

(a) An hour of accredited CLE means 60 minutes of attendance in a one-hour period at an accredited CLE program.

(b) A lawyer or a sponsoring agency applying for approval of a CLE activity or program must submit to the Board all the necessary information required under this article.

Effective May 1, 2016.

Rule 14-409.   Self-study categories of accredited MCLE defined.

(a) Lecturing, teaching and panel discussions. Lawyers who lecture in an accredited CLE program will receive credit for three hours for each hour spent lecturing. No lecturing or teaching credit is available for participation in a panel discussion or for preparation time.

(b) Final published course schedule. The Board will determine the number of accredited CLE hours available for a program based on the final published course schedule.

(c) Equivalent CLE credit for certain self-study activities. Subject to the Board's determination, the Board will allow equivalent credit for such activities that further the purpose of this article and qualify for equivalency. Such equivalent activities may include, but are not limited to, viewing of approved CLE audio and video and webcast presentations, computer interactive telephonic programs, writing and publishing an article in a legal periodical, part-time teaching by a lawyer in an approved law school, or delivering a paper or speech on a professional subject at a meeting primarily attended by lawyers, legal assistants or law students. The number of hours of credit allowed for such activities and the procedures for obtaining equivalent credit will be determined specifically by the Board for each instance.

Effective May 1, 2016.

Rule 14-410.   Accreditation of MCLE; attendance; undue hardship and special accreditation.

(a) Accredited CLE activities provided by this article must:

(a)(1) have as their primary objective to increase lawyers' professional competency;

(a)(2) be comprised of subject matter directly related to the practice of law; and

(a)(3) comply with the specific requirements set forth in this article with respect to each activity.

(b) The Board shall assign an appropriate number of credit hours to each accredited CLE activity.

(c) Attendance. A lawyer may attend a course in person or by live, interactive audio-video communication from a Utah state courthouse to another Utah state courthouse or from the Law and Justice Center to a Utah state courthouse.

(c)(1) The total of all hours allowable for live, interactive webcasts that are broadcast from a Utah state courthouse to another Utah state courthouse or from the Law and Justice Center to a Utah state courthouse must be authorized by the Board.

(d) Ethics and professional responsibility courses. All courses or components of courses offered to fulfill the ethics and professional responsibility requirement under 14-404(a) must be specifically accredited by the Board.

(d)(1) Professionalism and Civility. All courses or components of courses offered to fulfill the professionalism and civility requirement under 14-404(a) must be specifically accredited by the Board.

(e) Undue hardship; special accreditation. Formal instruction or educational seminars which meet the requirements of paragraph (a) lend themselves well to the fulfillment of the educational requirement imposed by this article and will be readily accredited by the Board. It is not intended that compliance with this article will impose any undue hardship upon any lawyer because the lawyer may find it difficult to attend such activities because of health or other special reasons. In addition to accrediting formal instruction at centralized locations, the Board, in its discretion, may accredit such educational activities including, but not limited to, audio and video presentations, webcast, computer interactive telephonic programs, teaching, preparation of articles and other meritorious learning experiences as provided in this article.

Effective May 1, 2016.

Rule 14-411. Board accreditation of non-approved sponsor courses.

The Board in its discretion may accredit CLE courses or activities offered by non-approved sponsors if they meet the following standards.

(a) The course must be of intellectual or practical content and, where appropriate, should include an ethics or professional responsibility component.

(b) The course or activity must contribute directly to a lawyer's professional competence or skills, or the lawyer's professional ethical obligations.

(c) Course or activity leaders or lecturers must have the necessary practical or academic skills to conduct the course effectively.

(d) Prior to or during the course or activity, each attendee must be provided with written or electronic course materials of a quality and quantity which indicate that adequate time has been devoted to preparation and which are of value to lawyers in their practice of the law. One-hour courses or activities meet this requirement by providing an outline of the course or activity's content.

(e) The course or activity must be presented in an appropriate setting.

(f) The course or activity must be made available to lawyers throughout the state unless the sponsor demonstrates to the satisfaction of the Board that there is good reason to limit availability.

(g) A sponsor or attendee must submit to all reasonable requests for information related to the course or activity.

(h) A sponsor or attendee must submit a written request for accreditation on an approved form within 60 days prior to or following the course or activity. Sponsors who wish to advertise a course or activity as being accredited must submit a request for approval at least 60 days prior to the event.

(i) The sponsor must submit the registration list in an approved format and CLE fees if applicable within 30 days following the presentation of a course.

Effective May 1, 2016.

Rule 14-412.   Presumptively approved sponsors; presumptive MCLE accreditation.

(a) The Board may designate an individual or organization as a presumptively approved sponsor of accredited CLE courses or activities if they meet the following standards:

(a)(1) The sponsor must be either an approved law school or an organization engaged in CLE that has, during the three years immediately preceding its application, sponsored at least six separate courses that comply with the requirements for individual course accreditation under Rule 14-411. Status as a presumptively approved sponsor is subject to periodic review.

(a)(2) Presumptively approved sponsors are required to pay annual presumptive fees.

(a)(3) Within 60 days prior to offering a course, the sponsor must indicate on a Board-approved form that the course satisfies the provisions of Rule 14-411. The sponsor should also submit a copy of the brochure or outline describing the course, a description of the method or manner of presentation, and, if specifically requested by the Board, a set of materials.

(a)(4) The sponsor must submit the registration list in an approved format, and CLE fees if applicable within 30 days following the presentation of a course.

(a)(5) The sponsor must make its courses available to all lawyers throughout the state, unless it can demonstrate to the satisfaction of the Board that there is good reason to limit the availability.

(a)(6) The sponsor must submit to all reasonable requests for information and comply with this article.

(b) Denial of presumptively approved sponsor status. Notwithstanding a sponsor's compliance with paragraphs (a)(1) through (a)(6), the Board may deny designation as a presumptively approved sponsor if the Board finds there is just cause for denial.

(c) Revocation of presumptive approval. The Board may audit any sponsor having presumptive approval and may revoke the presumptive approval if it determines that the sponsor is offering, as accredited, courses which do not satisfy the standards established under Rule 14-411.

Effective May 1, 2016.

Rule 14-413.   MCLE credit for qualified audio and video presentations; webcasts; computer interactive telephonic programs; writing; lecturing; teaching; live attendance.

(a) Credit will be allowed for self-study with Board accredited audio and video presentations, webcasts or computer interactive telephonic programs in accordance with the following.

(a)(1) One hour of self-study credit will be allowed for viewing and/or listening to 60 minutes of audio or video presentations, webcasts or computer interactive telephonic programs in accordance with Rule 14-408(a).

(a)(2) No more than 12 hours of credit may be obtained through self-study with audio or video presentations, webcasts or computer interactive telephonic programs. Upon application to the Board, the Board may grant a waiver, permitting a lawyer on active status to obtain all required hours of credit through self-study, if the lawyer:

(a)(2)(A) does not reside in Utah; and

(a)(2)(B) is engaged in full-time volunteer work for a religious or charitable organization.

(b) Credit will be allowed for writing and publishing an article in a legal periodical in accordance with the following.

(b)(1) To be eligible for any credit, an article must:

(b)(1)(A) be written to address a lawyer audience;

(b)(1)(B) be at least 3,000 words in length;

(b)(1)(C) be published by a recognized publisher of legal material; and

(b)(1)(D) not be used in conjunction with a seminar.

(b)(2) Three credit hours will be allowed for each 3,000 words in the article. An application for accreditation of the article must be submitted at least 60 days prior to reporting the activity for credit. Two or more authors may share credit obtained pursuant to this paragraph in proportion to their contribution to the article. No more than 12 hours of credit may be obtained through writing and publishing an article or articles.

(c) Credit will be allowed for lecturing in an accredited CLE program, part-time teaching by a lawyer in an approved law school, or delivering a paper or speech on a professional subject at a meeting primarily attended by lawyers, legal assistants or law students in accordance with the following.

(c)(1) Lecturers in an accredited CLE program and part-time teachers may receive three hours of credit for each hour spent in lecturing or teaching as provided in Rule 14-408(a).

(c)(2) No lecturing or teaching credit is available for participation in a panel discussion.

(c)(3) No more than 12 hours of credit may be obtained through lecturing and part-time teaching.

(d) Credit will be allowed for lecturing and teaching by full-time law school faculty members in accordance with the following.

(d)(1) Full-time law school faculty members may receive credit for lecturing and teaching but only for lecturing and teaching accredited CLE courses.

(d)(2) No lecturing or teaching credit is available for participation in panel discussions.

(d)(3) No more than 12 hours of credit may be obtained through lecturing and teaching by full-time law school faculty members.

(e) Credit will be allowed for attendance at an accredited CLE program in accordance with the following.

(e)(1) Credit is allowed for attendance at an accredited CLE program in accordance with Rule 14-408(a).

(e)(2) A minimum of 12 CLE hours, with no maximum restriction, must be obtained through attendance at live in-person CLE programs.

(f) The total of all hours allowable under paragraphs (a), (b), (c), and (d) of this rule may not exceed 12 hours during a reporting period.

(g) No credit is allowed for self-study programs except as expressly permitted under paragraph (a).

Effective May 1, 2016.

Rule 14-414. Certificate of compliance; filing, late, and reinstatement fees; suspension; reinstatement.

(a) Certificate of compliance. On or before July 31 of alternate years, each lawyer subject to MCLE requirements must file a Certificate of Compliance with the Board, appropriately evidencing the lawyer's completion of accredited CLE courses or activities ending the preceding 30th day of June. The Certificate of Compliance must include the title of programs or the audio or video presentation, computer interactive webcast, telephonic program attended, viewed or listened to; the sponsoring entity; the number of hours in actual attendance at each program or the number of hours of such audio or video presentation; and other information as the Board requires.

(b) Filing fees, late fees and reinstatement fees.

(b)(1) Each lawyer shall pay a filing fee in the amount of $15 at the time of filing the Certificate of Compliance under paragraph (a).

(b)(2) Any lawyer who fails to complete the MCLE requirement by the June 30 deadline, or fails to file by the July 31 deadline will be assessed a $100 late fee.

(b)(3) Lawyers who fail to comply with the MCLE requirements but who file within a reasonable time, as determined by the Board and who are subject to an administrative suspension pursuant to Rule 14-415 will be assessed, in addition to the late fee, a $200 reinstatement fee and a $500 fee if the failure to comply is a repeat violation within the past 5 years.

(c) Maintaining proof of compliance. Each lawyer will maintain proof to substantiate the information provided on the filed Certificate of Compliance. The proof may contain, but is not limited to, certificates of completion or attendance from sponsors, certificates from course leaders, or materials related to credit. The lawyer must retain this proof for a period of four years from the end of the period for which the Certificate of Compliance is filed. Proof must be submitted to the Board upon written request.

(d) Failure to provide proof of compliance; rebuttable presumption. Failure by the lawyer to produce proof of compliance within 15 days after written request by the Board constitutes a rebuttable presumption that the lawyer has not complied with the MCLE requirements for the applicable time period.

(e) Verification period. The Board may, at any time within four years after the Certificate of Compliance has been filed, commence verification proceedings to determine a lawyer's compliance with this article.

Effective May 1, 2016.

Rule 14-415. Failure to satisfy MCLE requirements; notice; appeal procedures; reinstatement; waivers and extensions; deferrals.

(a) Failure to comply; petition for suspension. A lawyer who fails to comply with reporting provisions of Rule 14-414 will be assessed a late fee. A lawyer who fails to comply with Rule 14-414 or who files a Certificate of Compliance showing that he or she has failed to complete the required number of hours of MCLE will be notified that a petition for the lawyer's suspension from the practice of law will be submitted to the Supreme Court unless all requirements are completed and reported within 30 days.

(a)(1) The lawyer will have the opportunity during the 30-day period to file an affidavit with the Board disclosing facts demonstrating that the lawyer's noncompliance was not willful and to tender such documents that, if accepted, would cure the delinquency. A hearing before the Board will be granted if requested.

(a)(2) If, after a hearing or a failure to cure the delinquency by satisfactory affidavit and compliance, the lawyer is suspended by the Supreme Court, the lawyer will be notified by certified mail, return receipt requested.

(b) Reinstatement. A lawyer suspended by the Supreme Court under the provisions of this rule may be reinstated by the Court upon motion of the Board showing that the lawyer has cured the delinquency for which the lawyer has been suspended. If a lawyer has been suspended by the Supreme Court for non-compliance with this article, the lawyer must then comply with all applicable rules to be eligible to return to active or inactive status.

(c) Waivers and extensions of time. For good cause shown, the Board may use its discretion in cases involving hardship or extenuating circumstances to grant waivers of the minimum MCLE requirements or extensions of time within which to fulfill the requirements. Active Utah lawyers will not be granted a waiver of the CLE requirements in Utah if they are living outside of Utah and practicing law in other jurisdictions. These Active Utah lawyers must comply with the Utah CLE requirements or change from active to inactive status.

(d) Deferrals. The Board may defer MCLE requirements in the event of the lawyer's serious illness.

(e) Petition to appeal. Any lawyer who is aggrieved by any decision of the Board under this rule may, within 30 days from the date of the notice of decision, appeal to the Board by filing a petition setting forth the decision and the relief sought along with the factual and legal basis. Unless a petition is filed, the Board's decision is final.

(e)(1) The Board may approve a petition without hearing or may set a date for hearing. If the Board determines to hold a hearing, the lawyer will have at least 10 days notice of the time and place set for the hearing. Testimony taken at the hearing will be under oath. The Board shall enter written findings of fact, conclusions of law and the decision on each petition. A copy will be sent by certified mail, return receipt requested, to the lawyer.

(e)(2) The Board may grant the petitioner an extension of time within which to comply with this rule.

(e)(3) Decisions of the Board are final and are not subject to further contest, unless the decision was a denial of a request for a waiver or a recommendation of suspension of lawyer's license to practice.

(f) Appeal to Supreme Court. A decision denying a request for waiver or a decision to suspend the lawyer is final under paragraph (e)(3) unless within 30 days after service of the findings of fact, conclusions of law and decision, the lawyer files a written notice of appeal with the Supreme Court.

(f)(1) Transcripts. To perfect an appeal to the Supreme Court, the lawyer must, at the lawyer's expense, obtain a transcript of the proceedings from the Board. If testimony was taken before the Board, the Board will certify that the transcript contains a fair and accurate report of the proceedings. The Board will prepare and certify a transcript of all orders and other documents pertinent to the proceeding before it and file these promptly with the clerk of the Supreme Court. The matter will be heard by the Supreme Court under this article and other applicable rules.

(f)(2) The time set forth in this article for filing notices of appeal are jurisdictional. The Board or the Supreme Court, as to appeals pending before each such body, may, for good cause shown either extend the time for the filing or certification of any material or dismiss the appeal for failure to prosecute.

Effective May 1, 2016.

Rule 14-416. Lawyers on active status not practicing law in Utah; Lawyers on active status engaged in full-time volunteer work in remote locations.

(a) A lawyer on active status who is not engaged in the practice of law in Utah may, file and attach to his or her Utah Certificate of Compliance evidence showing that the lawyer has met the Utah MCLE requirements in Rule 14-404 with CLE courses accredited in the state in which the lawyer resides and practices. This may include certificates of compliance, certificates of attendance or other information indicating the identity of the accrediting jurisdiction.

(a)(1) The lawyer must attach to his or her Utah Certificate of Compliance a copy of the member's Certificate of Compliance with the MCLE requirements from that jurisdiction together with evidence that the member has completed a minimum of three hours of accredited ethics or professional responsibility. One of the three hours of ethics or professional responsibility must be in the area of professionalism and civility.

(a)(2) If the lawyer lives in a jurisdiction where there is not a CLE requirement, the lawyer must comply with the Utah CLE requirements or place his or her license on inactive status.

(b) Upon application by a lawyer on active status, the Board may grant a waiver of the MCLE requirements of Rule 14-404 and issue a certificate of exemption if the lawyer:

(b)(1) resides in a remote location outside of Utah where audio or video presentations or computer interactive telephonic programs sufficient to allow the lawyer to participate in CLE credit hours are not reasonably available to the lawyer; and

(b)(2) is engaged in full-time volunteer work for a religious or charitable organization.

Effective May 1, 2016.

Rule 14-417.   Miscellaneous fees and expenses.

(a) All fees under this article will be deposited in a special account of the Board and used to defray the costs of administering this article.

(b) A lawyer must pay an administrative fee of $25 for preparation and mailing of certificates of CLE compliance to other MCLE states, for filing of Reciprocal Certificates for lawyers admitted on motion to the Utah State Bar, or for filing of House Counsel Certificates of Compliance from the jurisdiction where the House Counsel maintains an active license. The Board may establish other fees to defer administrative costs related to requests for accreditation with Supreme Court approval.

(c) Members of the Board are not compensated, but will be reimbursed for reasonable and necessary expenses incurred in the performance of their duties under this article.

(d) All CLE sponsors who offer any course for Utah approved CLE credit must pay to the Board, within 30 days following the course, a fee of $1.50 per credit hour per attendee. The required fee must accompany the required registration list. The $1.50 per credit hour fee will cap at $15 per attendee.

(d)(1) All CLE sponsors that submit more than 50 programs annually must pay additional application fees to the Board.

(d)(2) All CLE sponsors that do not charge registration fees but submit more than 50 programs annually must pay to the Board additional application fees.

(d)(3) If the CLE sponsor is a government or non-profit agency that is offering a program free of charge, the fees may be waived.

(e) Any lawyer who is required by this article to apply to the Board for any special accreditation or approval of an educational activity must pay a fee of $10 at the time of application.

(f) Any lawyer subject to NLTP requirements must pay a separate and additional fee of $300 to the Bar as specified in the NLTP Manual.

(g) Presumptive providers are required to pay an annual fee. The presumptive provider fee must be paid by January 1st of each year and is good through December 31st of each year.

(g)(1) Presumptive providers that submit more than 50 applications annually will be required to pay additional presumptive fees.

Effective May 1, 2016.

VERMONT

STATE OF VERMONT

SUPREME COURT

Rules for Mandatory Continuing Legal Education
As of February 18, 2014

§ 1   Purpose

It is of primary importance to members of the Bar of the Supreme Court of Vermont and to the public that attorneys continue their legal education throughout the period of their active practice of law. These rules establish minimum requirements for continuing legal education.

§ 2   Definitions

As used in these Rules, the following definitions shall apply:

(a)   The "Board" shall mean the Vermont Board of Mandatory Continuing Legal Education.

(b)   The "Director" shall mean an employee of the Board.

(c)   "Rules" shall mean Rules for Mandatory Continuing Legal Education together with any subsequent amendments thereto, as adopted by the Supreme Court of the State of Vermont.

§ 3   Board of Continuing Legal Education

(a)   The Court shall appoint a Board to be known as the Board of Continuing Legal Education, consisting of seven members as follows:

(1)   One shall be a judge, active or retired, or a retired justice of the Supreme Court;

(2)   Four shall be attorneys admitted to the Bar of the Supreme Court; and

(3)   Two shall be laypersons, not admitted to the practice of law in this state.

For purposes of these rules, a quorum shall consist of four members, or all members not disqualified, whichever is the lesser.

(b)   Each term of office shall be four years and until a successor is appointed. Whenever a member resigns, or the office is otherwise vacant, the Court shall appoint a successor to fill the unexpired term. Appointments shall be made annually on June first. No member shall serve for more than two consecutive terms or parts thereof.

(c)   The chairperson and vice-chairperson shall be members designated by the Court annually on June first and shall so serve until their successors are designated.

(d)　In the performance of their duties, the members of the Board shall be reimbursed for reasonable and necessary expenses and shall receive per diem compensation equivalent to that provided by law for comparable boards and commissions. The commissioner of finance and information support shall issue a warrant for the compensation and expenses of each member of the Board when submitted on vouchers approved by the court administrator.

(e)　The Board shall have general supervisory authority over the administration of these rules. The Board shall accredit activity, within and without the state, which will satisfy the educational requirements of these rules; shall encourage the offering of such activity; shall determine and keep records of attorney compliance with these rules; shall report in writing to the Court the names of those who fail to meet the requirements of these rules; shall evaluate the effectiveness of mandatory continuing legal education in maintaining and improving the competence of members of the Bar; and shall monitor the continuing legal competence of members of the Bar and policies and procedures to maintain and improve that competency. The Board shall annually report in writing to the Court on December first its activities during the prior year and its recommendations, if any, relating to these rules and the maintenance of professional competence of attorneys admitted to the Bar of the Supreme Court.

§ 4　Minimum Educational Requirements

(a)　Every licensed attorney admitted to the Bar of the Supreme Court shall complete twenty hours of accredited continuing legal education during each two-year compliance period established by these rules.

(b)　At least two of the twenty hours required by paragraph (a), above, shall be devoted to continuing legal education specifically addressed to legal ethics. Courses that qualify for ethics credits should focus specifically on the Rules of Professional Conduct and their applicability to specific problems and situations lawyers face in their practice.

§ 5　Accreditation

(a)　Educational activity shall be eligible for accreditation to satisfy the requirements of these rules if it has significant intellectual and practical content directed at increasing the professional competence of attorneys and is of the nature listed below:

(1)　Law school or other classroom instruction or educational seminars with substantial written material available, whether conducted by live speakers, lecturers, panel members, video or audio tape presentation, in a classroom setting with a group of not fewer than three individuals. For the purposes of these rules, in order for a course to qualify as live credit, the instructor and attendee must participate simultaneously. For video replays or computer generated courses to count as live credit, an expert moderator needs to be monitoring to answer questions and/or lead discussion; or

(2)　Self-study meaning individually viewing prerecorded presentations and is limited to 10 hours per reporting period; or

(3)   With prior approval, independent study in supervised and graded courses.

(b)   In addition to the general standard described above, the following specific standards shall also be met by any course or activity for which credit is sought:

(1)   The course shall constitute an organized program of learning dealing with matter directly relating to the practice of law or to the professional responsibility and ethical obligations of a lawyer;

(2)   Each faculty member shall be qualified by practical or academic experience to teach the subject he or she covers;

(3)   Thorough, high quality, readable and carefully prepared written or printable materials should be distributed to all attendees at or before the time the course is presented. It is recognized that such materials are not suitable or readily available for some types of subjects; the absence of such materials should, however, be the exception and not the rule. Such material may be offered as an optional purchase by the course provider;

(4)   Courses should be conducted in a setting physically suitable to the educational activity of the program. A suitable writing surface should be provided where feasible and appropriate;

(5)   With prior approval supervised and graded self-study courses may be granted up to 10 hours of CLE credit per reporting period. Video, telephonic, audiotape and computer program courses may be approved up to 10 CLE credit hours per reporting period. In the event of unusual hardship or extenuating circumstances, additional credit may be granted for such activities at the Board's discretion;

(6)   Activities which involve the crossing of disciplinary lines, such as a medicolegal symposium or an accounting-tax law seminar, may be approved;

(7)   An in-house course is one sponsored by a private law firm, a corporate law department or a federal, state or local governmental agency primarily for lawyers who are members or employees of the firm, department or agency, and must meet all of the following requirements:

(i)   It must meet all of the requirements of the standards for approval of this Section of the Rules;

(ii)   It must be approved prior to its presentation;

(iii)   Matters pending in the firm or agency will not be the focus of the in-house course;

(iv)   At least three learners must be present for the in-house course, not including the presenter;

(v)   The presenter may be eligible for teaching credit under this section but may not also seek credit under any other applicable section of the Rules for the same in-house course, such as credit for preparation of the in-house course;

(8)   A video or audio tape presentation by an accredited sponsor shall not be considered an in-house course. An attorney, whether in-house in a law firm, corporate law department or whatever, may, for CLE credit, listen to and/or watch audio and/or video cassettes, accompanied by substantial written material, created by an accredited sponsor without the need to invite or have present any "outside" attorneys;

(9)   Credit will be allowed for non-paid scholarly writing and publication as follows (with prior approval):

(i)   Two and a half hours for 1000 published words;

(ii)   Five hours for 3000 published words. Earned hours may be prorated among multiple authors.

(10)   Credit is also allowed as follows:

(i)   service as acting judge - up to 3 hours per reporting period (no credit for preparation);

(ii)   reviewing small claims cases in superior court - up to 3 hours per reporting period (no credit for preparation);

(iii)   service as judge at moot court - up to 2 hours per reporting period (no credit for preparation);

(iv)   volunteer committee work - up to 2 hours per reporting period for approved committees (no credit for preparation);

(c)   In the event that unusual circumstances render it a hardship for an attorney to engage in a sufficient quantity of continuing legal education activity accreditable pursuant to subdivisions (1) or (2) of paragraph (a) above, the Board, in its discretion, may approve any alternate plan for continuing legal education which it finds satisfies the objectives of these rules.

(d)   Activity may be accredited upon an application made to the Board, containing such information as the Board in its discretion requires. Applications may be filed by a sponsoring agency or group, or by any participant. Applications for the accreditation of activity described above must be filed no later than 30 days after the course has ended. Applications for the accreditation of activity described in paragraph (c) above must be filed and approved before the educational activity has occurred. The following requirements shall apply:

      (1)   A member or sponsoring agency desiring approval of a continuing legal education activity not previously approved shall submit to the Board complete information concerning:

        (i)   The name and address of the sponsoring agency;

        (ii)   Title, date, location and fee of the course;

        (iii)   A list of faculty and their qualifications;

        (iv)   A description of course content and length of presentation;

        (v)   An indication as to any portion pertaining to legal ethics;

        (vi)   A description of the materials.

      (2)   Applications shall be in writing and required course information may be supplied by attaching a copy of the course brochure. The application must be received by the Director's office no later than thirty (30) days after the course has ended. An attorney who files a request for credit more than 30 days after the date of attendance must pay a $50.00 fee pending approval of the out-of-time request.

      (3)   Approval shall be granted or denied in accordance with the procedures set out herein.

      (4)   Approval may be granted for a specific course or a series of courses. Courses given annually may be approved on an ongoing basis subject to revocation after notice by the Board. A list of specifically approved courses shall be maintained by the Director.

      (e)   The Board shall assign a maximum number of credit hours to each accredited activity.

      (f)   The Board may refuse to accredit any activity which it finds is not eligible for accreditation pursuant to paragraphs (a) or (b) of this section or which it finds is sponsored by a group or individual lacking the ability or intention to produce continuing legal educational activity of the kind proposed of sufficiently high quality to improve or maintain an attorney's professional competence, or which it finds is not offered in a sufficiently organized fashion or under otherwise adequate circumstances to fulfill the objectives of these rules.

      (g)   In the event that an activity has been approved by the Board, the sponsor shall be entitled to so state and to state the maximum number of credit hours for which the activity has been approved.

      (h)   The Board may delegate the authority to determine applications for accreditation. In the event said authority is delegated, a denial of accreditation by the Board's delegate shall be subject, upon request of the grievant, to de novo review by the Board.

§ 6   Accumulation and Computation of Credit

(a)   Credit will be given only for participation in accredited activities, up to the maximum number of hours assigned by the Board to each activity.

(b)   Credit will be given for any course attended in preparation for admission to the practice of law in any jurisdiction.

(c)   Credit may be earned by teaching in accredited activities; however, no credit will be given for teaching which is part of an attorney's regular occupational activity, such as full-time instruction at a law school or college.

(d)   Credit may be earned by presenting formal education and/or informational programs to nonlawyers, including but not limited to student groups, which are designed to broaden public knowledge and understanding of the law, and/or increase public support and respect for the legal system – up to two (2) hours per reporting period. This section is not intended to award credit for instruction primarily aimed at the marketing of the presenter.

(e)   One (1) hour of credit shall consist of not less than sixty (60) minutes of attendance or teaching at an approved activity.

Credit hours will be rounded to the nearest quarter hour. Coffee breaks, keynote speeches and business meetings will not be allowed credit.

Credit will not be given for speeches presented at and attendance at luncheons and banquets.

Where a provider combines an educational program with a business meeting or other noncreditable program, it is the responsibility of the provider to indicate what portion of the program is intended to be educational and what portion is business or other noncreditable activity.

(f)   A teacher shall receive credit only for teaching at a course approved under these Rules. No credit shall be given for any teaching for which the attorney receives compensation other than for expenses. One hour of actual preparation time will be allowed for each actual hour of approved teaching, up to a maximum of five (5) hours of preparation time.

(g)   No CLE credit is allowed for any activity which an attorney received financial remuneration exceeding out-of-pocket expenses.

§ 7   Accreditation of Sponsoring Agencies

(a)   The Board may extend approval to a sponsoring agency for any of the continuing legal education activities sponsored by such agency which conform to the standards for approval. A sponsoring agency to which such general approval has been extended shall be known as an "accredited sponsor". A list of "accredited sponsors" shall be maintained by the Director.

(b)   An organization or person which desires accreditation as an "accredited sponsor" shall apply for accreditation to the Board stating its legal education history for the preceding two calendar years, including dates, subjects offered, total hours of instructions presented, and the names and qualifications of speakers. A primary consideration in the evaluation of such a request for status as an accredited sponsor shall be the previous experience of an agency in sponsoring and presenting continuing legal education activities.

(c)   Once a sponsoring agency has been granted the status of an "accredited sponsor," it shall be exempt from the requirement for prior approval set out above with respect to courses or activities which comply with the Board's standards for approval.

(d)   An accredited sponsor may seek an advisory opinion from the Director in any case where there is a question of whether an activity may be accredited or the amount of credit to be given. The Board may at any time reevaluate an accredited sponsor. If the Board finds there is a basis for consideration of revocation of the accreditation as an accredited sponsor, the Board shall give notice by certified mail to that sponsor of a hearing on possible revocation within 30 days prior to the hearing. The decision of the Board after the hearing will be final.

§ 8   Director's Determinations and Review

(a)   Pursuant to guidelines established by the Board, the Director shall, in response to written requests for approval of courses or accreditation of sponsors, awarding of credit for attending, teaching or participating in approved courses, waivers, extensions of time deadlines and interpretations of these Regulations, make a written response describing the action taken. The Director may seek a determination of the Board before rendering a decision. At each meeting of the Board the Director shall report on all adverse determinations made since the last meeting of the Board.

(b)   The Board shall review any adverse determination of the Director. The active member or the sponsoring agency affected may present information to the Board in writing. If the Board finds that the Director has incorrectly interpreted the facts or the provisions of the Rules, it may take such action as may be appropriate. The Board shall advise the active member or sponsoring agency affected of its findings and any action taken.

§ 9   Procedure

(a)   The continuing legal education requirement imposed by these rules shall be effective from and after June 1, 1999. For licensed attorneys admitted to practice after July 1, 1999, the reporting period shall commence on the date of admission and end on June 30th of the second full year following the year of admission. Continuing legal education courses taken as a requirement for admission to the Vermont bar will count toward the continuing legal education requirement during the first reporting period.

(b)   Before June 1 of each subsequent year, the Board shall cause to be sent to each attorney subject to reporting for that period a compliance form for the recording and reporting of compliance with these rules. The compliance form shall also be available on the Vermont judiciary's website.

(c)   No later than July 1st following the end of each applicable reporting period, each licensed attorney shall submit the compliance form attesting to the total hours of continuing legal education (a minimum of twenty hours) that the attorney has completed during such period.

(d)   In the event a licensed attorney fails to file the compliance form, files an incomplete compliance form, or files a form which does not demonstrate substantive compliance with the requirements of these rules, the Board shall promptly notify such attorney of the fact and nature of noncompliance, by certified or registered mail, return receipt requested. Failure of the Board to send timely notice shall not relieve the attorney of his or her duty to comply with the rules. The statement of noncompliance shall advise the attorney that the attorney must respond within fifteen days by:

(1)   filing the form which reflects compliance;

(2)   filing a makeup plan as described in § 10, below, along with the makeup plan filing fee; or

(3)   filing with the Board a written answer to the Board's notice of noncompliance.

(e)   If an answer pursuant to subdivision (3) of paragraph (d) above is filed and the answer does not admit noncompliance, the Board shall schedule a hearing on the question of compliance within thirty days of the filing. Notice of the date, time and place of said hearing shall be given to the attorney at least ten days prior thereto. The attorney shall bear the burden of establishing compliance with the substance of these rules. The attorney may be represented by counsel. Witnesses shall be sworn; and if requested by the attorney a complete electronic recording shall be made of all proceedings and all testimony taken. The chairperson, or other presiding member of the Board, shall have the authority to determine all motions, objections and other matters presented in connection with the hearing. The hearing shall be conducted in conformity with the Vermont Rules of Civil Procedure. The presiding officer of the Board and the attorney shall have the right to subpoena witnesses for said hearing. Application for a subpoena, including a subpoena duces tecum, shall be made to the Clerk of the Supreme Court, who shall issue the same.

(f)   Within thirty days of the conclusion of a hearing, the members of the Board who conducted the hearing shall make findings of fact determining whether the attorney has complied with the requirements of these rules. If the Board finds that compliance has occurred, the matter shall be dismissed, and the Board's records shall be amended to reflect such compliance. If it is determined that the attorney has not complied with these rules, the Board shall recommend suspension. The Board shall promptly forward said findings and recommendation to the Supreme Court.

(g)   In the event that an attorney fails to answer the Board's statement of noncompliance pursuant to paragraph (d), or files an answer which admits noncompliance, the Board shall promptly file a determination of noncompliance and a recommendation of suspension with the Supreme Court.

(h)   Upon the recommendation of the Board, the Court may enter an order suspending an attorney for noncompliance, or, if it determines that the Board's finding of noncompliance is not supported by the record, reverse the finding of noncompliance and remand the matter to the Board for further consideration, or, find compliance and order the Board's records amended to reflect compliance.

(i)   An attorney who has been suspended pursuant to order of the Court for noncompliance shall be deemed to be without a license to practice law pursuant to Administrative Order No. 41, Licensing of Attorneys, § 2 and, in the event the attorney should practice law during the period of suspension, the attorney may be punished for unauthorized practice of law.

(j)   Any attorney who has been suspended for noncompliance may be reinstated by order of the Court upon a showing that the attorney's continuing legal education deficiency has been made up. The attorney shall file with the Board a petition seeking reinstatement. The petition shall state with particularity the accredited continuing legal education activity which the attorney has completed including the dates of completion. The petition shall be accompanied by a reinstatement filing fee of $100.The Board shall determine whether the petition shows that compliance has been made, in which event it shall, as soon as possible file the petition, together with its recommendation of reinstatement, with the Supreme Court. If the Court finds the attorney eligible for licensure, or exempt therefrom, and that the record supports the Board's recommendation of reinstatement, it shall order reinstatement; otherwise, it may deny reinstatement or remand the matter to the Board for further consideration.

(k)   At any time when proceedings are pending, and before the Board makes a recommendation of suspension, the Board may, in its discretion, dismiss said proceedings upon the filing of a makeup plan by the attorney, if it finds that the makeup plan is in compliance with § 10 of these rules and that dismissal will serve the policy of these rules.

§ 10   Makeup Plans

(a)   An attorney who has failed to comply with the substantive requirements of these rules within the applicable compliance period may file a makeup plan, on his or her own initiative, or in response to a statement of noncompliance.

(b)   The makeup plan must contain a specific plan for correcting the attorney's noncompliance within 120 days from the date of filing. The plan shall be accompanied by a makeup plan filing fee of $50.00. The plan shall be deemed accepted by the Board unless within 30 days after its receipt the Board notifies the attorney to the contrary. Full completion of the plan shall be reported by the compliance form filed with the Board not later than 15 days following the 120-day period. If the attorney shall fail to file an acceptable plan, or shall fail to complete and report completion of the plan within the aforementioned 135 days, the Board shall proceed as set forth in paragraphs (d) through (k) of § 9 of these rules.

§ 11   Inactive Attorneys

(a)   An attorney who is exempt from licensure shall be relieved thereby from the requirements of these rules during the period of exemption of said attorney. Upon application for reinstatement and issuance of a license to practice law pursuant to Administrative Order No. 41, Licensing of Attorneys, the compliance period of the attorney shall commence on the date of reinstatement and end on June 30th of the same year as it would have been absent inactive status. No attorney shall be permitted to transfer from active status to inactive status and vice versa in order to circumvent the requirements of these rules.

(b)   The provisions of paragraph (a) above notwithstanding, an attorney who has been in inactive status for a period of three years or more shall be required before reinstatement to file with the Board the compliance form reflecting the completion of not less than twenty hours of accredited continuing legal education, including two hours of legal ethics and limited to ten hours of self-study courses within two years before the date upon which reinstatement is sought.

§ 12   Fees

All fees received pursuant to these rules shall be deposited in the General Fund.

Reporter's Notes – 2014 Amendment

Since the institution of the requirement of continuing legal education for attorneys admitted to practice law in Vermont, separate rules and regulations have governed. These rules and regulations defined the minimal educational requirements, how they could be met, and the process a sponsoring agency must follow in order to offer courses for CLE credit, among other things. The rules often overlapped with the regulations and some topics were discussed in both the rules and regulations. This created an often cumbersome process for attorneys seeking information on the requirements for continuing legal education. There is no distinction to be made between the rules and regulations, as the Vermont Supreme Court must approve of and administer both. Therefore, the Board of Mandatory Continuing Legal Education has consolidated the rules and regulations into one document, the Rules for Mandatory Continuing Legal Education. There have been no substantive changes to the rules or regulations during this rewrite. The change has been made in an effort to achieve simplicity and for the convenience of those governed by the rules.

VIRGINIA

17. Mandatory Continuing Legal Education Rule—

The Virginia Supreme Court hereby establishes a Mandatory Continuing Legal Education Program in the Commonwealth of Virginia.

A. Purpose:

Continuing professional education of lawyers serves to improve the administration of justice and benefit the public interest. Regular participation in Continuing Legal Education programs will enhance the professional skills of practicing lawyers, afford them periodic opportunities for professional self-evaluation and improve the quality of legal services rendered to the public. All active members of the Virginia State Bar shall participate in an additional amount of further legal study throughout the period of their active practice of law, and failure to do so shall result in their suspension from membership in the Virginia State Bar.

B. Continuing Legal Education Board:

A Continuing Legal Education Board shall be established for the purpose of administering the program.

(1) Appointment:

The Chief Justice of the Supreme Court shall appoint, after consultation with the Council, the members of the board who shall be members of the Bar and twelve in number. One member shall be designated by the Chief Justice as Chair and another as Vice chairman. Members shall serve terms of three years each, except that, initially, four members shall be appointed for terms of one year, four for terms of two years, and four for terms of three years. No member shall serve more than two consecutive terms but shall be eligible for reappointment after the lapse of one or more years following expiration of the previous term. The Executive Director of the Virginia State Bar shall be an ex officio member of the board.

(2) Notice of Meetings/Quorum:

The board shall meet on reasonable notice by the Chair, Vice chair or the Executive Director. Five members shall constitute a quorum and the action of a majority of a quorum shall constitute action of the board; however, new regulations or amendments shall be approved by a majority of the full membership of the board.

(3) Powers:

The board shall have those general administrative and supervisory powers necessary to effectuate the purposes of this Rule, including the power to adopt, following the advice and comment of Council, reasonable and necessary regulations consistent with this Rule. The effective date of any regulations or amendments to the regulations adopted by the board shall be as prescribed by the board, but in no event earlier than one hundred twenty (120) days following such adoption. The Council may reject any regulations or amendments to the regulations adopted by the board on or after July 1, 2010, by a 2/3 vote of those members of Council present and voting. Council's rejection of any regulations or amendments to the regulations shall have the effect of suspending the regulation or amendment until the Supreme Court has reviewed and approved, rejected, or modified the proposed regulation or amendment. The Virginia State Bar shall have the responsibility for funding the board and for enforcing Mandatory Continuing Legal Education requirements. The board may delegate to the Virginia State Bar staff as it deems appropriate to carry out its responsibilities under this Rule.

The board shall specifically have the following powers and duties:

(a) To approve CLE programs and sponsors;

(b) To establish procedures for the approval of Continuing Legal Education courses, whether those courses are offered within the Commonwealth or elsewhere. These procedures should include the method by which CLE sponsors could make application to the board for approval, and if necessary, make amendments to their application;

(c) To authorize sponsors of Continuing Legal Education programs to advertise that participation in their program fulfills the CLE requirements of this Rule;

(d) To formulate and distribute to all members of the Virginia State Bar appropriate information regarding the requirements of this Rule, including the distribution of a certification form to be filed annually by each active member.

C. Continuing Legal Education Requirements:

(1) All active members of the Virginia State Bar shall annually complete and certify attendance at a minimum of twelve (12) credit hours of approved Continuing Legal Education courses of which at least two (2) hours shall be in the area of legal ethics or professionalism, except those lawyers expressly exempted from the requirement by this Rule or by decision of the Continuing Legal Education Board; provided, however, that for the period July 1, 2001 through October 31, 2002, active members shall complete and certify attendance at a minimum of fifteen (15) credit hours of approved Continuing Legal Education courses of which at least two (2) hours shall be in the area of legal ethics or professionalism, except those lawyers expressly exempted from the requirement by this rule or by decision of the Continuing Legal Education Board. Each active member shall complete the required Continuing Legal Education courses each year during the period November 1 through October 31 of the following year; provided, however, the next completion period following June 30, 2001, shall be July 1, 2001 through October 31, 2002.

(2) In order to provide flexibility in fulfilling the annual requirement, a one year carryover of credit hours is permitted, so that accrued credit hours in excess of one year's requirement may be carried forward from one year to meet the requirement for

the next year. A member may carry forward a maximum of twelve (12) credit hours, two (2) of which, if earned in legal ethics or professionalism, may be counted toward the two (2) hours required in legal ethics or professionalism.

(3) Each active member of the Virginia State Bar shall be responsible for ascertaining whether or not a particular course satisfies the requirements of this Rule. Each member should exercise discretion in choosing those approved programs which are most likely to enhance professional skills and improve delivery of legal services.

D. Certificate of Attendance:

(1) Each active member of the Virginia State Bar shall certify prior to December 15 each year that such lawyer attended approved Mandatory Continuing Legal Education programs for the minimum number of hours required during the previous calendar year ending October 31; provided, however, the next certification deadline following July 31, 2001, shall be December 15, 2002. The failure to certify shall cause suspension of such lawyer's license to practice law. An untruthful certification shall subject the lawyer to appropriate disciplinary action.

E. Exemptions:

Each active member of the Virginia State Bar shall comply with this Rule except as follows:

(1) A newly admitted member shall be exempted from filing a certification for the completion period in which he or she is first admitted.

(2) A member who has obtained a waiver for good cause shown, as may be determined by the board, shall be exempted from filing a certification for the completion period for which the waiver is granted.

F. Activation or Reactivation:

A member of any category who wishes to become an active member of the Virginia State Bar shall furnish to the Secretary an affidavit stating that he or she has completed twelve (12) hours of Continuing Legal Education, including two (2) hours in legal ethics or professionalism within the previous twelve months. Thereafter, that member shall have the same completion period and certification deadline as other active members.

G. Credits:

(1) Credit will be given only for Continuing Legal Education courses or activities approved by the board.

(2) Hours in excess of the minimum requirements defined in this Rule may not be carried forward for credit beyond the one year provided for in the Rule.

(3) Credit will not be given for Continuing Legal Education hours accumulated prior to admission to the Virginia State Bar.

(4) Credit shall be given to active members of the Virginia State Bar who prepare course materials and who personally participate as instructors. The credit, as determined by the board, will reflect the time reasonably required for preparation of materials, as well as the actual time spent instructing.

H. Standards:

In evaluating specific programs for approval, consideration shall be given to the following factors:

(1) Whether the course tends to increase the participant's professional competence as a lawyer.

(2) The number of hours of actual presentation, lecture, or participation, so that the appropriate number of credit hours can be identified and published.

(3) The usage of written educational materials which reflect a thorough preparation by the provider of the course, and which assist course participants in improving their legal competence.

(4) To qualify for mandatory legal education credit, a course is not required to have a component on legal ethics or professionalism, although such components are encouraged. When topics on legal ethics or professionalism are offered, either as an entire course or component thereof, they must be clearly identified as such.

Updated: May 1, 2014

VIRGIN ISLANDS

Rule 208. MANDATORY CONTINUING LEGAL EDUCATION

Continuing professional education of lawyers serves to improve the administration of justice and benefit the public interest. Regular participation in Continuing Legal Education programs will enhance the professional skills of practicing lawyers, afford them periodic opportunities for professional self-evaluation, and improve the quality of legal services rendered to the public. All active members of the United States Virgin Islands shall participate in the requisite number of hours, as set forth in this Rule, of further legal study throughout the period of their active practice of law, and failure to do so shall result in their suspension from membership in the Virgin Islands' Bar.

(a) Appointment of the Virgin Islands Bar Association for the Administration of this Rule.

(1) The Supreme Court of the United States Virgin Islands hereby appoints the Virgin Islands Bar Association to administer these Rules. The Virgin Islands Bar Association shall create a Continuing Legal Education and Admissions Committee which shall be charged with the responsibility for implementation and administration of these rules

(2) The Virgin Islands Bar Association Committee Continuing Legal Education and Admissions shall have the following duties:

(A) Accept the certification forms to be filed annually by each active member of the Virgin Islands' Bar.

(B) Conduct a compliance audit during the month following the end of each reporting period.

(C) Review and approve Continuing Legal Education courses and activities.

(3) Report at least annually to the Supreme Court of Virgin Islands and quarterly to the Board of Governors of the V. I. Bar Association, on the operation, compliance and effectiveness of these Rules.

(b) Continuing Legal Education (CLE) Requirement.

(1) Annual Requirement. Every active member of the United States Virgin Islands Bar shall complete and certify attendance at a minimum of twelve (12) hours per year of approved Continuing Legal Education ("CLE") courses of which at least two (2) hours shall be in the area of legal ethics or professionalism. Each member shall complete the required CLE courses during the period of January 1 through December 31 of the same year. An "active member" is defined as a person who has active status in the Virgin Islands Bar Association. The annual credit requirement

for lawyers who are active members for only a portion of the year shall be prorated at a rate of one (1) credit per month he or she claims active status, or any portion of a month thereof.

(2) Carry-Over. In an effort to provide flexibility in fulfilling the annual requirement, a one year carry-over of credit hours is permitted, so that accrued credit hours in excess of one year's requirement may be carried forward from one year to meet the requirement for the next year. A member may carry forward a maximum of six (6) credit hours, two of which, if earned in legal ethics or professionalism, may be counted toward the two (2) hours required in legal ethics or professionalism. Hours in excess of the minimum requirements defined in this Rule may not be carried forward for credit beyond the one year provided for in this Rule.

(3) Prior Attendance. Credit will be given for CLE hours accumulated within the year prior to admission to the Virgin Islands Bar.

(4) Approved Courses and Activities. The CLE requirement may be met either by attending courses or completing any other continuing legaleducation activity automatically approved for credit as provided in this Rule. Self-study, including the use of approved video or audio tapes, computer based resources, or participation in legal educational activities involving correspondence technology, in-house law firm continuing legal education efforts, teaching, and participation in a committee of the Virgin Islands Bar Association or the Supreme Court of the United States Virgin Islands may be considered for credit when they meet the conditions set forth in this Rule. Credit shall not be given for activities not specifically enumerated in Section (g) of this Rule.

(c) Reporting CLE Credit.

(1) Reporting Requirement. Unless exempt as provided in this Rule, each active member shall submit to the Virgin Islands Bar Association, on or before January 31 of each year, a ertification of Attendance certifying that the member has attended mandatory Continuing Legal Education course(s) for the minimum number of hours required during the previous year ending December 31. No member may submit a Certification of Attendance after January 31 without approval of the Supreme of the United States Virgin Islands upon written request by the member.

(2) Approved Forms. A member may submit a Certification of Attendance form provided to the attendees at the CLE course (s) or, in the alternative, the form entitled Attorney Application for CLE Credit/Certification of Attendance attached as Appendix 1 to this Rule.

(3) Responsibility of Members. Every active member shall be responsible for ascertaining whether or not the particular course satisfies the requirements of this Rule.

(d) Exemptions.

(1) New Members. A newly admitted member shall not be exempt from filing a certification for the reporting period in which he or she is first admitted. A newly admitted member is a person who has never previously been a member of the Virgin Islands Bar Association, or any other bar association for less than a year.

(2) Waivers. A member who has been granted a waiver from compliance with the requirements of this Rule shall be exempted from filing a certification for the period for which the waiver is granted.

(A) A member seeking a waiver from the requirements for a reporting year must submit a written petition, together with any appropriate or required material or documentation (e.g. doctors' letter, medical records), to the Supreme Court of the United States Virgin Islands.

(B) A member should, whenever practicable, file his or her petition prior to the January 31 reporting deadline for the year the member seeks a waiver. Failure to file a petition in a timely manner may be considered by the Supreme Court in determining whether to grant a waiver.

(C) A waiver shall not be granted unless good cause is shown.

(D) The filing of any petition for waiver will toll the running of any time limit set forth in this Rule up to, but not to exceed, thirty (30) days.

(3) Extensions. A member who has been granted an extension from compliance with the requirements of this Rule shall be exempted from filing a certification for the period for which the extension is granted.

(A) A member seeking an extension from the requirements for a reporting year must submit a written petition, together with any appropriate or required material or documentation (e.g. doctors' letter, medical records), to the Supreme Court of the United States Virgin Islands.

(B) A member should, whenever practicable, file his or her petition prior to the January 31 reporting deadline for the year the member seeks an extension. Failure to file a petition in a timely manner may be considered by the Supreme Court in determining whether to grant an extension.

(C) An extension shall not be granted unless good cause is shown.

(D) The filing of any petition for extension will toll the running of any time limit set forth in this Rule up to, but not to exceed, thirty (30) days.

(e) Sanctions.

(1) Self-Reporting. This Rule establishes a self-reporting system.

(2) Annual Auditing. During the month following the annual reporting deadline, the Virgin Islands Bar Association shall conduct a random audit of at least 15% of the active members to determine compliance with this Rule.

(3) Notice of Delinquency. After completion of the random audit, the Virgin Islands Bar Association shall send a Notice of Delinquency to each member found to have violated this Rule for any prior year.

(4) Cure. Within ninety (90) days following the receipt of the Notice of Delinquency, the member shall submit a Certification of Attendance, certifying that he or she has taken course hours necessary to meet the annual requirements of the Rule for the relevant year, along with a payment of a delinquency fee of $50.00.

(5) Failure to Cure. If the member fails to submit the requisite Certification of Attendance sufficient to permit retroactive compliance with the Rule, the Virgin Islands Bar Association shall file a Notice of Non-Compliance with the Supreme Court of the United States Virgin Islands.

(6) Automatic Suspension. Failure to take steps to certify compliance with this Rule within ninety (90) days of receiving the Notice of Delinquency shall result in automatic suspension by the Supreme Court of the United States Virgin Islands.

(7) Reinstatement. In order to be reinstated, a member suspended for violating this Rule shall file a petition for reinstatement with the Supreme Court of the United States Virgin Islands along with a reinstatement fee of $200.00. The petition for reinstatement shall include a Certification of Attendance certifying that the suspended attorney has completed the course hours necessary to meet the annual requirements of this Rule for the relevant year.

(8) Continuing Responsibility. A suspension for violating this Rule shall not relieve the delinquent member of his annual responsibility to attend CL E programs or to pay his dues to the Virgin Islands Bar Association.

(9) Representations by Members. A member who makes a materially false statement in any document filed with the Virgin Islands Bar Association or the Supreme Court of the United States Virgin Islands shall be subject to appropriate disciplinary action.

(f) Approved Educational Activities.

(1) Courses automatically approved. The following CLE courses will be automatically approved for credit.

(A) Live CLE programs offered by the federal or local judiciary in the United States Virgin Islands , or by the Virgin Islands Bar Association. A live course is one where there is an instructor in the room with the participants.

(B) Self-study courses listed for automatic approval by the Virgin Islands Bar Association. (See Section 7(c) of this Rule, below).

(C) Courses or activities approved by the highest court of another jurisdiction or its designee, the American Bar Association, the National Bar Association, the American Law Institute or a state, the District of Columbia or territorial bar association.

(D) Courses or activities offered by a provider accredited by the official CLE committee of another jurisdiction or a national CLE accrediting body.

(2) In-office CLE. Courses offered by law firms, either individually or with other law firms, corporate legal departments, government attorneys, or similar entities, primarily for the education of their members may be approved for credit. Members who seek credit for in-office courses shall submit, with the required certification of attendance form, the program schedule or agenda and course syllabus or statement describing the subject matter. If the program does not cover a recognized legal topic, the member must attach a statement of how the course relates to his or her practice.

(3) Self Study. In addition to formal courses conducted in a class or seminar setting, approved self-study courses involving the use of video or audio tapes, computer resources (e.g. CD-ROM and internet), or correspondence courses (e.g. satellite and teleconference) may be used to satisfy the credit requirements of this Rule. Members who seek credit for self-study courses shall submit, with the required certification of attendance form, the program schedule or agenda and course syllabus or statement describing the subject matter. If the program does not cover a recognized legal topic, the member must attach a statement of how the course relates to his or her practice. The Virgin Islands Bar Association shall make available to the members of the Association a list of self-study courses that will be automatically approved for credit.

(4) Teaching or Lecturing. Members who teach legal courses or deliver lectures on law, whether to other attorneys or to members of the general public may be given credit for the time spent in preparation and time spent teaching or lecturing. A member seeking credit for teaching or lecturing must obtain prior approval from the Virgin Islands Bar Association. Members who seek credit for teaching or lecturing shall submit, with the required certification of attendance form, the course syllabus, lecture outline or statement describing the subject matter. If the program does not cover a recognized legal topic, the member must attach a statement of how the course relates to his or her practice. Once credit has been given for teaching a course or delivering a lecture, no further credit shall be given for a subsequent delivery of the same material to a different audience.

(5) Service on the Virgin Islands Bar Association Committees or Supreme Court of the United States Virgin Islands Committees, or in the Annual Moot Court Competition. Members who are officers of the Virgin Islands Bar Association or sit on and actively participate in a committee of the Virgin Islands Bar Association or federal or local Courts of the United States Virgin Islands may be given credit for such participation. Members who seek credit for such participation shall submit, with the required certification of attendance form, a statement describing the officer's or committee's tasks, the scope of the member's participation and the number of hours actually expended attending meetings or working on assigned tasks. No more than two credit hours attributed to participation as an officer or a committee member may be awarded for each committee activity to satisfy the annual CLE requirement. Participants in the Moot Court competition shall be awarded one

(1) credit hour for every six (6) 50-minute hours (300 minutes) of eligible service in the Moot Court competition. A maximum of four (4) CLE credit hours may be earned during any one reporting cycle for any of the above eligible activities.

(g) Standards for Approval of Courses.

(1) General Standards. To be approved for credit, the CLE course or activity must satisfy the following:

(A) The activity must have significant intellectual or practical content with the primary objective of increasing the participant's professional competence as a lawyer;

(B) The activity must deal primarily with substantive legal issues, legal skills, practice issues, or legal ethics and professional responsibility.

(2) Legal Ethics or Professionalism Standards. In order to satisfy the legal ethics or professionalism credit requirement, the course or activity shall be devoted to the study of judicial or legal ethics and professional responsibility or professionalism, and shall include discussion of applicable judicial conduct codes, disciplinary rules, or statements of professionalism.

(3) The following activities shall not be accredited:

(A) Activities that would be characterized as dealing primarily with personal self-improvement unrelated to professional competence as a lawyer;

(B) Activities designed primarily to sell services or equipment;

(C) Repeat live, video, audio, or CD-ROM CLE courses for which the member has already obtained CLE credit in the same reporting year.

(4) Standards for Approval of Program and Sponsors.

(A) An Approved CLE program or activity must be offered by a sponsor having substantial, recent, experience in offering continuing legal education or demonstrated ability to organize and present effectively continuing legal education. Demonstrated ability arises partly from the extent to which individuals with legal training or educational experience are involved in the planning, instruction and supervision of the program.

(B) The program or activity itself must be conducted by an individual or group qualified by practical or academic experience. The program, including the named advertised participants, shall be conducted substantially as planned, subject to emergency withdrawals and alterations.

(C) Thorough, high quality, readable and carefully prepared written materials shall be made available to all participants at or before the time the course is presented, unless the absence of such materials is recognized as reasonable and approved by the Committee. A mere outline without citations or explanatory notations shall not be sufficient.

(D) The program shall be conducted in a comfortable physical setting, conducive to learning and equipped with suitable writing surfaces.

(E) Approval may be given for programs where audio-visual recorded or reproduced material is used. Television, computer, videotape, audiotape, simultaneous broadcast, teleconference, computer network and motion picture programs with sound shall qualify for CLE credit in the same matter as a live CLE program provided: (a) the original CLE program was approved for CLE credit as provided in these rule or the visual recorded program has been approved by the Committee under these Rules; (b) each person attending the visual presentation is provided written material as provided in Rule 104 (g)(4)(C) each program is conducted in a location as required in Rule 104 (g)(4)(D); and (d) there are a minimum of three (5) persons enrolled and in attendance at the presentation of the visually recorded program.

(F) Programs that cross academic lines may be considered for approval.

5. Approved Sponsors:

Continuing legal education programs sponsored by the following organizations as well as all organizations in good standing with the Association of Continuing Legal Education Administrators (ACLEA) shall be presumptively approved for credit, provided that the standards set forth in the Regulation (g) (4). through (g)(7) are met:

Accredited Law Schools (ABA, AALS)

Administrative Conference on the United States

American Bar Association and Bar Sections and Divisions

American Judicature Society

American Law Institute-American Bar Association Committee on

Continuing Professional Education

Attorneys Liability Protection Society (ALPS)

American Association for Justice, formerly American Trial Lawyers

Association

Defense Research Institute

National Association of Attorneys General

National Bar Association and Bar Sections and Divisions

National College of Trial Advocacy

National District Attorneys Association

National Institute of Trial Advocacy

National Judicial College

Practicing Law Institute

U.S. Air Force-Judge Advocate General School

U. S. Army-Judge Advocate General School

U. S. Department of Justice-Office of Legal Education

U. S. Navy-Naval Justice School

Veterans Administration-Office of General Counsel

V. I. Bar Association and other state and territorial bar and trial lawyer associations

6. Approved seminars may be advertised in informational brochures and program materials provided by the sponsoring body. Organizations listed in Regulation 4.2 whose programs are presumptively approved shall give adequate notice that a program or seminar it conducts is not approved for MCLE credit in the event the program or seminar does not meet the standards set forth in Rules 104 (g)(4)(A) through Rule 104 (g)(4)(E)

7. The Committee may at any time re-evaluate and grant or revoke presumptive approval of a provider.

8 Any organization not included in Rule 104 (g) (5) above, desiring approval of a course or program shall apply to the Committee by submitting an application on a form to be obtained from the Committee and supporting documentation at least forty-five (45) days prior to the date for which the course or program is scheduled, together with any sponsorship fee as may be required by the Committee. The Committee will advise the applicant in writing by mail within ten (10) days of the receipt of the completed application whether the program is approved or disapproved. Applicants denied approval of a program may appeal such a decision by submitting a letter of appeal to the Committee within fifteen (15) days of the receipt of the notice of disapproval.

9. An attorney desiring approval of a course or program which has not otherwise been approved shall apply to the Committee by submitting an application on a form to be obtained from the Committee and supporting documentation as follows:

(A) If approval is requested before the course or program is presented the application and supporting documentation shall be submitted at least forty-five (45) days prior to the date for which the course or program is scheduled.

(B) If approval is requested after the applicant has attended a course or program the application and supporting documentation shall be submitted within ninety (90) days after the date the course or program was presented or prior to the end of the calendar year in which the course or program was presented, whichever is earlier.

(C) The Committee shall advise the applicant in writing by mail within ten (20) days of the receipt of the completed application whether the program is approved or disapproved. Applicants denied approval of a program may appeal such a decision by submitting a letter of appeal to the Committee within fifteen (20) days of the receipt of the notice of disapproval.

(D) The provider of an approved continuing legal education program may announce or indicate as follows:

The course has been approved by the V. I. Bar Association Committee on Legal Education and Admissions to the Bar for _____ hours of CLE credit.

(E) Within forty-five (45) days following an approved legal education program conducted in the Virgin Islands, the sponsor shall furnish the Executive Director of the of V. I. Bar Association a list of V. I. Bar Association attendees.

(h) Effective Date.

The effective date of this Rule shall be January 1, 2008. Starting January 1, 2008, and every year thereafter, unless otherwise ordered by this court, active members shall complete the total number of CLE course hours as required in this Rule.

WASHINGTON

RULE 11. MANDATORY CONTINUING LEGAL EDUCATION (MCLE)

(a) **Purpose.** Mandatory continuing legal education ("MCLE") is intended to enhance lawyers' legal services to their clients and protect the public by assisting lawyers in maintaining and developing their competence as defined in RPC 1.1, fitness to practice as defined in APR 22, and character as defined in APR 21. These rules set forth the minimum continuing legal education requirements for lawyers to accomplish this purpose.

(b) **Definitions.**

(1) "Activity" means any method by which a lawyer may earn MCLE credits.

(2) "Association" means the Washington State Bar Association.

(3) "Attending" means participating in an approved activity or course.

(4) "Calendar year" means a time period beginning January 1 and ending December 31.

(5) "Identical activity" means any prior course or other activity that has not undergone any substantial or substantive changes since last offered, provided or undertaken.

(6) "Lawyer" means an active member of the Association, a judicial member of the Association classified as an administrative law judge, and any other lawyer admitted to the limited practice of law in Washington who is required by the Admission and Practice Rules (APR) to comply with this rule.

(7) "Reporting period" means a three-year time period as assigned by the Association in which a lawyer must meet the education requirements of this rule.

(8) "Sponsor" means a provider of continuing legal education activities.

(c) **Education Requirements.**

(1) *Minimum Requirement.* Each lawyer must complete 45 credits of approved continuing legal education by December 31 of the last year of the reporting period with the following requirements:

(i) at least 15 credits must be from attending approved courses in the subject of law and legal procedure, as defined in section (f)(1); and

(ii) at least six credits must be in ethics and professional responsibility, as defined in section (f)(2).

(2) *Earning Credits.* A lawyer earns one credit for each 60 minutes of attending an approved activity. Credits are rounded to the nearest quarter hour. A lawyer may earn no more than eight credits per calendar day. A lawyer cannot receive credit more than once for an identical activity within the same reporting period.

(3) *New Lawyers.* Newly admitted lawyers are exempt for the calendar year of admission.

(4) *Military Personnel.* Military personnel in the United States Armed Forces may be granted an exemption, waiver or modification upon proof of undue hardship, which includes deployment outside the United States. A petition shall be filed in accordance with subsection (i)(5) of these rules.

(5) *Exemptions.* The following are exempt from the requirements of this rule for the reporting period(s) during which the exemption applies:

    (i) *Judicial Exemption.* Judicial members of the Association, except for administrative law judges;

    (ii) *Supreme Court Clerks.* The Washington State Supreme Court clerk and assistant clerk(s) who are prohibited by court rule from practicing law;

    (iii) *Legislative Exemption.* Members of the Washington State Congressional Delegation or the Washington State Legislature; and

    (iv) *Gubernatorial Exemption.* The Governor of Washington state.

(6) *Comity.* The education requirements in Oregon, Idaho and Utah substantially meet Washington's education requirements. These states are designated as comity states. A lawyer may certify compliance with these rules in lieu of meeting the education requirement by paying a comity fee and filing a Comity Certificate of MCLE Compliance from a comity state certifying to the lawyer's subjection to and compliance with that state's MCLE requirements during the lawyer's most recent reporting period.

(7) *Carryover Credits.* If a member completes more than the required number of credits for any one reporting period, up to 15 of the excess credits, two of which may be ethics and professional responsibility credits, may be carried forward to the next reporting period.

(d) MCLE Board

(1) *Establishment.* There is hereby established an MCLE Board consisting of seven members, six of whom must be active members of the Bar Association and one who is not a member of the Association. The Supreme Court shall designate one board member to serve as chair of the MCLE Board. The members of the MCLE Board shall be appointed by the Supreme Court. Appointments shall be staggered for a 3-year term. No member may serve more than two consecutive terms. Terms shall end on September 30 of the applicable year.

(2) *Powers and Duties.*

    (i) Rules and Regulations. The MCLE Board shall review and suggest amendments or make regulations to APR 11 as necessary to fulfill the

WASHINGTON

purpose of MCLE and for the timely and efficient administration of these rules and for clarification of education requirements, approved activities and approved course subjects. Suggested amendments are subject to review by the Association's Board of Governors and approval by the Supreme Court.

(ii) Policies. The MCLE Board may adopt policies to provide guidance in the administration of APR 11 and the associated regulations. The MCLE Board will notify the Board of Governors and the Supreme Court of any policies that it adopts. Such policies will become effective 60 days after promulgation by the MCLE Board.

(iii) Approve Activities. The MCLE Board shall approve and determine the number of credits earned for all courses and activities satisfying the requirements of these rules. The MCLE Board shall delegate this power to the Association subject to MCLE Board review and approval.

(iv) Review. The MCLE Board shall review any determinations or decisions regarding approval of activities made by the Association under these rules that adversely affect any lawyer or sponsor upon request of the lawyer, sponsor or Association. The MCLE Board may take appropriate action consistent with these rules after any such review and shall notify the lawyer or sponsor in writing of the action taken. The MCLE Board's decision shall be final.

(v) Fees. The MCLE Board shall determine and adjust fees for the failure to comply with these rules and to defray the reasonably necessary costs of administering these rules. Fees shall be approved by the Association's Board of Governors.

(vi) Waive and Modify Compliance. The MCLE Board shall waive or modify a lawyer's compliance with the education or reporting requirements of these rules upon a showing of undue hardship filed in accordance with these rules. The MCLE Board may delegate this power to the Association subject to (1) parameters and standards established by the MCLE Board, and, (2) review by the MCLE Board.

(vii) Approve Mentoring Programs. The MCLE Board shall approve mentoring programs that meet requirements and standards established by the MCLE Board for the purposes of awarding MCLE credit under these rules.

(viii) Audits for Standards Verification. The MCLE Board may audit approved courses to ensure compliance with the standards set forth in these rules.

(3) *Expenses and Administration.* Members of the MCLE Board shall not be compensated for their services but shall be reimbursed for actual and necessary expenses incurred in the performance of their duties according to the Association's expense policies. All expenses incurred and fees collected shall be

submitted on a budget approved by the Association's Board of Governors. The Association shall provide administrative support to the MCLE Board.

(e) Approved Activities. A lawyer may earn MCLE credit by attending, teaching, presenting or participating in activities approved by the Association. Only the following types of activities may be approved:

(1) Attending, teaching, presenting or participating in or at a course, provided that any pre-recorded audio/visual course is less than five years old;

(2) Preparation time for a teacher, presenter or panelist of an approved activity at the rate of up to five credits per hour of presentation time, provided that the presentation time is at least 30 minutes in duration;

(3) Attending law school courses with proof of registration or attendance;

(4) Attending bar review courses for jurisdictions other than Washington with proof of registration or attendance;

(5) Writing for the purpose of lawyer education, when the writing has been published by a recognized publisher of legal works as a book, law review or scholarly journal article of at least 10 pages, will earn one credit for every 60 minutes devoted to legal research and writing;

(6) Teaching law school courses, when the instructor is not a full-time law school professor;

(7) Providing pro bono legal services provided the legal services are rendered through a qualified legal services provider as defined in APR 8(e);

(8) Participating in a structured mentoring program approved by the MCLE Board provided the mentoring is free to the mentee and the mentor is an active member of the Association in good standing and has been admitted to the practice of law in Washington for at least five years. The MCLE Board shall develop standards for approving mentoring programs; and

(9) Judging or preparing law school students for law school recognized competitions, mock trials or moot court. The sponsoring law school must comply with all sponsor requirements under this rule.

(f) Approved Course Subjects. Only the following subjects for courses will be approved:

(1) *Law and legal procedure*, defined as legal education relating to substantive law, legal procedure, process, research, writing, analysis, or related skills and technology;

(2) *Ethics and professional responsibility*, defined as topics relating to the general subject of professional responsibility and conduct standards for lawyers and judges, including diversity and anti-bias with respect to the practice of law or the

legal system, and the risks to ethical practice associated with diagnosable mental health conditions, addictive behavior, and stress;

(3) *Professional development*, defined as subjects that enhance or develop a lawyer's professional skills including effective lawyering, leadership, career development, communication, and presentation skills;

(4) *Personal development and mental health,* defined as subjects that enhance a lawyer's personal skills, well-being and awareness of mental health issues. This includes, stress management, and courses about, but not treatment for, anxiety, depression, substance abuse, suicide and addictive behaviors;

(5) *Office management*, defined as subjects that enhance the quality of service to clients and efficiency of operating an office, including case management, time management, business planning, financial management, office technology, practice development and marketing, client relations, employee relations, and responsibilities when opening or closing an office;

(6) *Improving the legal system,* defined as subjects that educate and inform lawyers about current developments and changes in the practice of law and legal profession in general, including legal education, global perspectives of the law, courts and other dispute resolution systems, regulation of the practice of law, access to justice, and pro bono and low cost service planning; and

(7) *Nexus subject*, defined as a subject matter that does not deal directly with the practice of law but that is demonstrated by the lawyer or sponsor to be related to a lawyer's professional role as a lawyer.

(g) **Applying for Approval of an Activity.** In order for an activity to be approved for MCLE credit, the sponsor or lawyer must apply for approval as follows.

(1) *Sponsor.* A sponsor must apply for approval of an activity by submitting to the Association an application fee and an application in a form and manner as prescribed by the Association by no later than 15 days prior to the start or availability of the activity.

(i) *Late fee.* A late fee will be assessed for failure to apply by the deadline. The Association may waive the late fee for good cause shown.

(ii) *Repeating Identical Course.* A sponsor is not required to pay an application fee for offering an identical course if the original course was approved and the identical course is offered less than 12 months after the original course.

(iii) *Waiver of Application Fee.* The Association shall waive the application fee for a course if the course is offered for free by a government agency or nonprofit organization. This provision does not waive any late fee.

(2) *Lawyer.* A lawyer may apply for approval of an activity not already approved or submitted for approval by a sponsor by submitting to the Association an application in a form and manner as prescribed by the Association. No application fee is required.

(h) Standards for Approval. Application of the standards for approval, including determination of approved subject areas and approved activities in subsections (e) and (f) of this rule, shall be liberally construed to serve the purpose of these rules. To be approved for MCLE credit, all courses, and other activities to the extent the criteria apply, must meet all of the following criteria unless waived by the Association for good cause shown:

(1) A course must have significant intellectual or practical content designed to maintain or improve a lawyer's professional knowledge or skills, competence, character, or fitness;

(2) Presenters must be qualified by practical or academic experience or expertise in the subjects presented and not disbarred from the practice of law in any jurisdiction;

(3) Written materials in either electronic or hardcopy format must be distributed to all lawyers before or at the time the course is presented. Written materials must be timely and must cover those matters that one would expect for a professional treatment of the subject. Any marketing materials must be separate from the written subject matter materials;

(4) The physical setting must be suitable to the course and free from unscheduled interruption;

(5) A course must be at least 30 minutes in duration;

(6) A course must be open to audit by the Association or the MCLE Board at no charge except in cases of government-sponsored closed seminars where the reason is approved by the Association;

(7) Presenters, teachers, panelists, etc. are prohibited from engaging in marketing during the presentation of the course;

(8) A course must not focus directly on a pending legal case, action or matter currently being handled by the sponsor if the sponsor is a lawyer, private law firm, corporate legal department, legal services provider or government agency; and

(9) A course cannot have attendance restrictions based on race, color, national origin, marital status, religion, creed, gender, age, disability or sexual orientation.

(i) Lawyer Reporting Requirements.

(1) *Certify Compliance.* By February 1 of the year following the end of a lawyer's reporting period, a lawyer must certify compliance, including compliance by

comity certification, with the education requirements for that reporting period in a manner prescribed by the Association.

(2) *Notice.* Not later than July 1 every year, the Association shall notify all lawyers who are in the reporting period ending December 31 of that year, that they are due to certify compliance.

(3) *Delinquency.* A lawyer who does not certify compliance by the certification deadline or by the deadline set forth in any petition decision granting an extension may be ordered suspended from the practice of law as set forth in APR 17.

(4) *Lawyer Late Fee.* A lawyer will be assessed a late fee for either (i) or (ii) below but not both.

    (i) *Education Requirements Late Fee.* A lawyer will be assessed a late fee for failure to meet the minimum education requirements of this rule by December 31. Payment of the late fee is due by February 1, or by the date set forth in any decision or order extending time for compliance, or by the deadline for compliance set forth in an APR 17 pre-suspension notice.

    (ii) *Certification and Comity Late Fee.* A lawyer will be assessed a late fee for failure to meet the certification requirements or comity requirements by February 1. Payment of the late fee is due by the date set forth in any decision or order extending time for compliance or by the deadline for compliance set forth in an APR 17 pre-suspension notice.

    (iii) *Failure to Pay Late Fee.* A lawyer who fails to pay the MCLE late fee by the deadline for compliance set forth in an APR 17 pre-suspension notice may be ordered suspended from the practice of law as set forth in APR 17.

(5) *Petition for Extension, Modification or Waiver.* A lawyer may file with the MCLE Board an undue hardship petition for an extension, waiver and/or modification of the MCLE requirements for that reporting period. In consideration of the petition, the MCLE Board shall consider factors of undue hardship, such as serious illness, extreme financial hardship, disability, or military service, that affect the lawyer's ability to meet the education or reporting requirements. The petition shall be filed at any time in a form and manner as prescribed by the Association but a petition filed later than 30 days after the date of the APR 17 pre-suspension notice will not stay suspension for the reasons in the APR 17 pre-suspension notice.

(6) *Decision on Petition.* The MCLE Board shall as soon as reasonably practical notify the lawyer of the decision on a petition. A lawyer may request review of the decision by filing, within 10 days of notice of the decision, a request for a hearing before the MCLE Board.

(7) *Hearing on Petition.* Upon the timely filing of a request for hearing, the MCLE Board shall hold a hearing upon the petition.

(i) The MCLE Board shall give the lawyer at least 10 days written notice of the time and place of the hearing.

(ii) Testimony taken at the hearing shall be under oath and recorded.

(iii) The MCLE Board shall issue written findings of fact and an order consistent with these rules as it deems appropriate. The MCLE Board shall provide the lawyer with a copy of the findings and order.

(iv) The MCLE Board's order is final unless within 10 days from the date thereof the lawyer files a written notice of appeal with the Supreme Court and serves a copy on the Association. The lawyer shall pay to the Clerk of the Supreme Court any required filing fees.

(8) *Review by the Supreme Court.* Within 15 days of filing a notice with the Supreme Court for review of the MCLE Board's findings and order, after such a non-compliance petition hearing, the lawyer shall cause the record or a narrative report in compliance with RAP 9.3 to be transcribed and filed with the Bar Association.

(i) The MCLE Board chairperson shall certify that any such record or narrative report of proceedings contains a fair and accurate report of the occurrences in and evidence introduced in the cause.

(ii) The MCLE Board shall prepare a transcript of all orders, findings, and other documents pertinent to the proceeding before the MCLE Board, which must be certified by the MCLE Board chairperson.

(iii) The MCLE Board shall then file promptly with the Clerk of the Supreme Court the record or narrative report of proceedings and the transcripts pertinent to the proceedings before the MCLE Board.

(iv) The matter shall be considered by the Supreme Court pursuant to procedures established by order of the Court.

(v) The times set forth in this rule for filing notices of appeal are jurisdictional. The Supreme Court, as to appeals pending before it, may, for good cause shown (1) extend the time for the filing or certification of said record or narrative report of proceedings and transcripts; or (2) dismiss the appeal for failure to prosecute the same diligently.

(9) *Compliance Audits.* The Association may audit an individual lawyer's compliance certification to substantiate participation in the activities listed in the certification. The Association may request records from a lawyer or sponsor for the purpose of conducting the audit and the lawyer must comply with all such requests. Where facts exist that indicate a lawyer may not have participated in the activities certified to, the lawyer may be referred to the Association's Office of Disciplinary Counsel and/or credit for the activities may be rescinded.

(j) Sponsor Duties. All sponsors must comply with the following duties unless waived by the Association for good cause shown:

(1) The sponsor must not advertise course credit until the course is approved by the Association but may advertise that the course credits are pending approval by the Association after an application has been submitted. The sponsor shall communicate to the lawyer the number of credits and denominate whether the credits are "law and legal procedure" as defined under section (f)(1), "ethics and professional responsibility" as defined under section (f)(2), or "other," meaning any of the other subjects identified in sections (f)(3)-(7).

(2) The sponsor must provide each participant with an evaluation form to complete. The forms or the information from the forms must be retained for two years and provided to the Association upon request.

(3) The sponsor must submit an attendance report in a form and manner as prescribed by the Association and pay the required reporting fee no later than 30 days after the conclusion of the course. A late fee will be assessed for failure to report attendance by the deadline.

(i) *Waiver of Reporting Fee.* The Association shall waive the reporting fee for a course if the course is offered for free by a government agency or nonprofit organization. This provision does not waive any late fee.

(4) The sponsor must retain course materials for four years from the date of the course. Upon request of the Association, a sponsor must submit for review any written, electronic or presentation materials including copies of audio/visual courses.

(5) The sponsor must keep accurate attendance records and retain them for six years. The sponsor must provide copies to the Association upon request.

(6) The sponsor shall not state or imply that the Association or the MCLE Board approves or endorses any person, law firm or company providing goods or services to lawyers or law firms.

(7) *Accredited Sponsors.* The Association may approve and accredit sponsoring organizations as "accredited sponsors" subject to procedures and fees established by the Association. Accredited sponsors have the same duties as sponsors but have the additional responsibility of approving their own courses and determining appropriate MCLE credit in accordance with this rule. Accredited sponsors pay an annual flat fee for all course applications submitted in lieu of an application fee for each individual course.

(k) Confidentiality. Unless expressly authorized by the Supreme Court or by the lawyer, all files and records relating to a lawyer's individual MCLE requirements are confidential and shall be privileged against disclosure except as necessary to conduct an investigation, hearing, and appeal or review pursuant to these rules. This provision does not apply to the Association except that such records shall not be disclosed to Association staff responsible for creating or marketing CLE products.

WEST VIRGINIA

CHAPTER VII. RULES TO GOVERN MANDATORY CONTINUING LEGAL EDUCATION

1. Purpose. These rules establish minimum objective requirements, and the means by which such requirement shall be enforced, to satisfy every lawyer's obligation to continue his or her legal education throughout the period of his or her active practice.

2. Continuing Legal Education Commission. There is hereby established a Continuing Legal Education Commission ("Commission") to administer the program of mandatory continuing legal education established by these rules.

2.1 The Commission shall consist of nine members, at least seven of whom shall be active members of the state bar. It will elect its own chairperson.

2.2 Members of the Commission shall be appointed by the board of governors of the state bar and confirmed by the Supreme Court of Appeals. Any vacancy occurring on the Commission shall be filled by the same appointment procedure. Members shall continue to serve until their successors are appointed and confirmed notwithstanding any age restrictions.

2.3 At least three members of the Commission shall be under the age of 36 or admitted to The West Virginia State Bar for less than ten years.

2.4 Of the members first appointed, three shall be appointed for 1 year, three for 2 years and three for 3 years. Thereafter, appointments shall be for a 3-year term. No member may serve more than two consecutive 3-year terms. Terms shall expire on June 30 of the applicable year.

2.5 For any meeting of the Commission a majority of the duly appointed members shall constitute a quorum. Attendance of and participation in meetings may be by conference telephone or similar two-way electronic communications equipment.

2.6 The members of the Commission shall have judicial immunity from civil liability for acts or omissions occurring in the performance of their duties. Any member of the Commission may be removed by the Supreme Court of Appeals for cause, which may include failure to attend Commission meetings, disability or misconduct.

2.7 Members of the Commission shall serve without compensation, but each member is entitled to reimbursement for his or her actual and necessary expenses in the performance of Commission duties.

3. Powers and Duties of the Commission. The Commission shall administer the program of mandatory continuing legal education established by these rules and shall have the following powers and duties:

3.1 To accredit, pursuant to its rules and regulations, individual courses and all or portions of the entire continuing legal education program of specific sponsors which, in the judgement of the Commission, will satisfy the educational objectives of these rules.

3.2 To determine the number of credit hours to be allowed for each accredited course.

3.3 To grant conditional, partial or complete exemptions from the education requirements of these rules on an individual basis in cases of extreme hardship or extenuating circumstances.

3.4 To seek appropriate disciplinary action by the Supreme Court of Appeals in the case of any active member of the state bar failing to comply with the requirements of these rules.

3.5 To meet, conduct hearings and make determinations as required to administer the program of mandatory continuing legal education established by these rules.

3.6 To recommend reinstatement to active status in the case of any member of the state bar attaining compliance with the requirements of these rules after having been suspended from active status for noncompliance.

3.7 To submit annually a written report to the Supreme Court of Appeals and to the board of governors of the state bar of the Commission's activities during the preceding year and including any recommendations for changes in these rules.

3.8 To report to the board of governors of the state bar any significant deficiency in the availability of continuing legal education courses or programs within the State of West Virginia, considering the educational requirements of these rules.

3.9 To adopt, publish and enforce rules and regulations pertaining to its powers and duties.

4. Accreditation of Courses. Only the Commission may accredit courses and programs for purposes of the mandatory continuing legal education requirements established by these rules.

4.1 Courses (including video and audio tapes) from the continuing legal education programs sponsored by the following organizations are presumptively accredited until and unless the Commission determines otherwise:

Contact MCLE Coordinator for current list.

4.2 Courses sponsored by other organizations may be accredited by the Commission upon the request of an individual lawyer in accordance with the procedures, rules and regulations of the Commission pertaining to accreditation.

4.3 Continuing legal education courses or programs sponsored by other organizations may be accredited by the Commission upon the request of the organization in accordance with the procedures, rules and regulations of the Commission pertaining to accreditations.

4.4 To be accredited, a course shall have significant intellectual or practical content; it shall deal primarily with matter directly related to the practice of law (which includes professional responsibility and office practice); it shall be taught by persons who are qualified by practical or academic experience in the subjects covered and preferably should include the distribution of good quality written materials pertaining to the subjects covered.

4.5 One hour of credit for purposes of the mandatory continuing legal education requirements established by these rules shall be given for each period of fifty minutes of instruction in an accredited course. Based upon this standard, sponsors of accredited courses given in West Virginia shall include with their course materials a statement that, "This course or program qualifies for ____ hours of credit under the West Virginia Rules for Mandatory Continuing Legal Education."

4.6 The Commission may refuse to accredit or change or remove the accredited status of any sponsor which misrepresents the extent to which a course or program is qualified under these rules.

4.7 In cases where accreditation could not be reasonably obtained in advance for a given course, an individual lawyer may request, in accordance with the procedures, rules and regulations of the Commission, accreditation for a course after he or she has attended such course.

4.8 All decisions of the Commission concerning accreditation shall be final.

5. Minimum Continuing Legal Education Requirements. As a condition of maintaining his or her license to practice law in the State of West Virginia, every active member of the state bar shall satisfy the following minimum continuing legal education requirements:

5.1 During each of the first two fiscal years (July 1-June 30) following the adoption of these rules, each active member of the state bar shall complete a minimum of six hours of continuing legal education as approved by these rules or accredited by the Commission. Completion of such activities should be reported by the attorney no later than July 31 of each phase-in year.

5.2 After the above two-year phase-in period, each active member of the state bar shall complete a minimum of twenty-four hours of continuing legal education, as approved by these rules or accredited by the Commission, every two fiscal years. At least three of such twenty-four hours shall be taken in courses on legal ethics, office management, substance abuse and/or elimination of bias in the legal profession. On or before July 31, 1990, and every other July 31 thereafter, each attorney must file a report of completion of such activities. The Commission recommends that such report be completed on Form C--Certification of Completion of Approved MCLE Activity. Attorneys who exceed the minimum MCLE requirement may carry a maximum of six credit-hours forward to only the next reporting period, except that no carryover credits can be applied to the legal ethics, office management, substance abuse requirement and/or elimination of bias in the legal profession.

5.3A New graduates and new admittees, beginning July 1, 1999, are required to complete a mandatory Bridge-the-Gap seminar sponsored by the West Virginia State Bar within six months prior to admission or within twelve months after admission to the West Virginia State Bar. The mandatory Bridge-the-Gap seminar shall be recorded at least once per year. The Bridge-the-Gap course will be provided free of charge to new admittees as an audio tape or video tape or CD-Rom/DVD. MCLE credit shall be available for completing the mandatory Bridge-the-Gap seminar.

Any lawyer subject to this requirement who fails to complete the mandatory Bridge-the-Gap seminar within sixty days after written notice of noncompliance from the MCLE Commission shall have such lawyer's license to practice law in the State of West Virginia automatically suspended until such lawyer has complied with such requirement. Any member of the West Virginia State Bar otherwise in good standing who is suspended for failure to complete the mandatory Bridge-the-Gap program shall be reinstated as a member of the West Virginia State Bar upon completion of the mandatory course and fulfillment of other such administrative requirements.

Rule 5.3B Any lawyer not previously admitted to practice in West Virginia who is admitted during the first twelve months of any 24-month reporting period is required to complete 12 hours in approved MCLE activities including at least 3 hours in legal ethics, office management, or substance abuse before the end of the reporting period. Any lawyer not previously admitted during the second twelve months of any 24-month reporting period is exempt for that entire reporting period.

5.4 For good cause shown, the Commission may, in individual cases involving extreme hardship or extenuating circumstances, grant conditional, partial or complete exemptions of these minimum continuing legal education requirements. Any such exemption shall be reviewed by the Commission at least once during each reporting period, unless a lifetime conditional exemption has been granted.

5.5 Active but not practicing members, Justices of the Supreme Court of Appeals, Circuit Judges, Family Court Judges, Senior Status Justices, Senior Status Circuit Judges, the Clerk of the Supreme Court of Appeals, the Deputy Clerk of the Supreme Court of Appeals, and any other individuals as may hereafter, from time to time, be designated by the Supreme Court of Appeals, are not required to comply with these requirements.

5.6 [Transferred].

6. Obtaining Credits to Satisfy Mandatory Continuing Legal Education Requirements. Members of the state bar may obtain credit for purposes of the mandatory continuing legal education requirements established by these rules as follows:

6.1 One hour of credit may be obtained for each period of fifty minutes of instruction attended in an accredited course.

6.2 One hour of credit may be obtained for each period of fifty minutes of video cassette, videotape, or audio cassette instructions, providing that such video/audio tape is accredited by the Commission.

6.3 No more than half of the mandatory continuing legal education requirements may be satisfied by video/audio tape instructions.

6.4 Six hours of credit may be obtained for the teaching of an accredited course when the period of teaching lasts for at least fifty minutes. If the teacher participates in a panel discussion or teaches for a period of less than fifty minutes, three hours of credit may be obtained.

6.5 The Commission may give credit for the following forms of publication, including, but not limited to, publishing an article in the law review of an ABA-accredited law school; publishing an article in the official publication of the state bar; authorship or co-authorship of a book; contribution of a paper published in a legal society's annual, hardbound collection; publication of an article in a bar journal in another state; and contribution through either editing or authorship to periodic newsletters designed to serve the interests of specialists.

6.6 The Commission has authority to allocate the amount of credits to be given for publication in Paragraph 6.5 above.

6.7 The Commission may by its rules and regulations establish additional methods or standards for obtaining credits to satisfy the mandatory continuing legal education requirement.

7. Noncompliance and Sanctions. Noncompliance with the reporting or minimum continuing education requirements of these rules may result in the suspension of a lawyer's license to practice law until such lawyer has complied with such requirements.

7.1 As soon as practicable after July 1, the Commission shall notify all active members of the state bar who are not in compliance with the reporting or minimum continuing education requirements of these rules of the specific manner in which such member has failed, or appears to have failed, to comply with these rules. Any member of the state bar shall have until October 1 to correct such noncompliance or provide the Commission with proper and adequate information to establish that such member is in compliance with these rules. The following delinquency fee schedule for any lawyer requiring notice of noncompliance with reporting or minimum continuing legal education requirements is hereby established, effective July 1, 1990:

Form C, certificate of attendance or online submission not received by July 31:
    $50.00

Form C, certificate of attendance or online submission not received by October 1:
    $100.00

Form D or Form E (request for publication or teaching credit) not received by July 31:
    $50.00

An additional fee of $100.00 shall be paid upon application for reinstatement by those attorneys whose licenses have been suspended for failure to comply with the MCLE requirement. This fee is in addition to the reinstatement fee charged for suspension for non-payment of membership fees. The attorney will not be reinstated unless all outstanding fees have been paid.

MCLE credits, if reported on a delinquent Form C, will not be entered until all outstanding fees have been paid.

7.2 As soon as practicable after October 1, the Commission shall give notice, by certified or registered mail to the most recent address maintained on the records of the state bar, to any active member of the state bar who has still not established himself or herself to be in compliance with these rules for the preceding two year reporting period that after thirty days, the Commission will notify the Supreme Court of Appeals of such fact and request the Court to suspend such lawyer's license to practice law until such time as the lawyer has established that he or she has complied with the requirements of these rules for the preceding two year reporting period.

7.3 During such thirty day period, any lawyer having received a thirty day notice may demand a hearing before the Commission. Any such hearing shall be conducted within a reasonable period of time after receipt of the demand. At such hearing the lawyer shall have the burden of establishing either (a) that he or she is in fact in compliance with the requirements of these rules or (b) that he or she is entitled to an exemption. In the event such burden is not carried, the Commission shall by appropriate petition notify the Supreme Court of Appeals that the lawyer has failed to comply with the reporting or education requirements for the preceding two year reporting period and request the Court to enter an appropriate order suspending such lawyer's license to practice law in the State of West Virginia until such time as such lawyer has complied with such requirements. Any adverse decision by the Commission may be appealed to the Supreme Court of Appeals. In the event such lawyer does not prevail at such hearing or appeal, he or she shall be assessed with the costs thereof.

7.4 In the event no demand for a hearing is received within the thirty day period, the Commission shall by appropriate petition notify the Supreme Court of Appeals of the names of any members of the state bar who have failed to comply with the reporting or education requirements of these rules for the preceding two year reporting period and request the Court to enter an appropriate order suspending each such lawyer's license to practice law in the State of West Virginia until such time as such lawyer has complied with such requirements.

7.5 A lawyer who has not complied with the mandatory continuing legal education requirements by June 30 may thereafter obtain credits to be carried back to meet the requirements of the preceding two year reporting period. However, any credit obtained may only be used to satisfy the mandatory continuing legal education requirements for one reporting period.

7.6 No lawyer shall be permitted to make use of a transfer from active to inactive or active but not practicing membership in the state bar as a means to circumvent the requirements of these rules.

7.7 During the two year phase-in period all references in this section 7 to "two year reporting period" shall be read as "one year reporting period."

8. Confidentiality. The files, records, and proceedings of the Commission, as they relate to or arise out of the compliance or noncompliance of an active member of the state bar with the requirements of these rules, shall be deemed confidential and shall not be disclosed, except in furtherance of the Commission's duties, or upon written request of the lawyer affected, or as directed by the Supreme Court of Appeals.

9. Change to Active Status. Any person previously enrolled as an active member of the state bar who has been an inactive member of the state bar, suspended for nonpayment of dues, or suspended or disbarred by the Supreme Court of Appeals, shall demonstrate that he or she has complied with a minimum of twelve hours of continuing legal education, as approved by these rules or accredited by the Commission, at least three hours of which shall be taken in courses in legal ethics, office management, or substance abuse, within twelve months immediately preceding the application to change to active status. Effective July 1, 1994, any person previously enrolled as an active member of the state bar who has served as a Justice of the Supreme Court of Appeals or a Judge of a Circuit Court shall be exempt from this requirement.

9.1 Any lawyer who was suspended solely for the nonpayment of dues and who is returned to active status within six months of the date of suspension may be reinstated to active status by bringing the dues current and will not be required to submit any additional information regarding mandatory continuing legal education provided that the attorney has otherwise been in compliance with the continuing legal education requirements.

10. Judicial CLE. Members of the state bar recommended that a mandatory education plan, similar to the one outlined in these rules, be adopted for West Virginia judges, justices and magistrates.

WISCONSIN

SCR CHAPTER 31

CONTINUING LEGAL EDUCATION

SCR 31.01 Definitions.

In this chapter:

(1) "Board" means the board of bar examiners.

(1m) "CLE" means continuing legal education.

(2) "Committee" means a panel comprising at least 3 members of the board.

(3) (Repealed)

(4) "Hour" means a period of approved continuing legal education consisting of not less than 50 minutes.

(5) "Inactive member" means an inactive member of the state bar under SCR 10.03(3) and the bylaws of the state bar.

(6) "Lawyer" means an active member of the state bar under SCR 10.03(3) and the bylaws of the state bar and includes an active member under suspension other than a person under a form of suspension that will terminate only on order of the court or a person suspended pursuant to SCR 31.10(1).

(6m) "Repeated on-demand program" means an on-line program delivered over the Internet, consisting of a program previously approved by the board.

(7) "Reporting period" means the two-year period ending December 31 during which a lawyer must satisfy the Wisconsin continuing legal education requirement of SCR 31.02. The reporting period for a lawyer is determined by the year of his or her admission to the practice of law in Wisconsin. The reporting period for a lawyer admitted in an even-numbered year shall end on December 31 of each even-numbered year; the reporting period for a lawyer admitted in an odd-numbered year shall end on December 31 of each odd-numbered year.

(8) "State bar" means the state bar of Wisconsin.

(9) "Electronic CLE reporting system" means a web-based system established by the board of bar examiners through which lawyers may electronically file an original or amended report of their CLE compliance.

(10) "Electronic signature" means an electronic sound, symbol, or process attached to or logically associated with an electronically-filed CLE report that can be executed or adopted by the reporting lawyer with the intent to sign the document under oath or affirmation.

SCR 31.02 Attendance requirement.

(1) A lawyer shall attend a minimum of 30 hours of approved CLE during each reporting period.

(2) A lawyer shall attend a minimum of 3 of the 30 hours required under sub. (1) on the subject of legal ethics and professional responsibility in every reporting period.

SCR 31.03 Reporting requirement.

(1) A lawyer shall file a written report under oath or affirmation on designated CLE Form 1 with the board on or before the February 1 following the last day of the reporting period. The written report shall establish compliance with the attendance requirement of SCR 31.02.

(2) A lawyer who has not satisfied SCR 31.02 and completed the reporting requirement under sub. (1) by the close of business on the February 1 following the last day of the reporting period shall be assessed a late fee of $100.

(3) Lawyers may satisfy the reporting requirements of sub. (1) through the electronic CLE reporting system. Reports filed electronically must include the reporting lawyer's electronic signature, by which the lawyer avers under oath or affirmation that the information contained in the report is true.

(4) Electronically-filed reports are deemed filed when they are submitted to the electronic CLE reporting system, except that a late-filed report is deemed filed upon receipt of payment of the late fee.

SCR 31.04 Exemptions.

(1) A lawyer is exempt from the attendance and reporting requirements of this chapter in the year of his or her admission to the practice of law in Wisconsin.

(2) A lawyer who does not engage in the practice of law in Wisconsin at any time during the reporting period is exempt from the attendance requirement of SCR 31.02 but shall comply with the reporting requirement of SCR 31.03.

(3) A lawyer whose practice is principally in another jurisdiction that has mandatory CLE requirements and who is current in meeting those requirements is exempt from the attendance requirement of SCR 31.02, but shall comply with the reporting requirement of SCR 31.03.

SCR 31.05 Approved hours.

(1) Activities that are approved by the board either before or after the close of the reporting period may be used to satisfy the requirement of SCR 31.02. Lawyers claiming credit for activities that are not already approved must seek approval on a CLE Form 2 filed contemporaneously with their CLE Form 1.

(2)(a) Up to 15 hours of CLE reported on CLE Form 1 may be carried forward to the next reporting period if all of the following conditions are met:

1. The hours that are to be carried forward reflect attendance during the reporting period covered by the CLE Form 1.

2. These hours reflect attendance at courses that are approved by the board either before or after the close of the reporting period. Lawyers claiming credit for activities that are not already approved must seek approval on a CLE Form 2 filed contemporaneously with their CLE Form 1.

3. Repealed.

(b) Repealed.

(c) CLE programs approved by the board for legal ethics and professional responsibility may not be carried forward under this subsection for the purpose of fulfilling the legal ethics and professional responsibility requirement of SCR 31.02(2) but may be carried forward under par. (a).

(3) Teaching an approved continuing legal or judicial education activity or teaching a course in a law school approved by the American bar association may be used to satisfy the requirement of SCR 31.02. The board shall award 2 hours for each hour of presentation of the approved continuing legal or judicial education activity and one hour for each hour of presentation for teaching a course in a law school.

(4) Participation in an educational activity approved by the judicial education committee may be used to satisfy the requirement of SCR 31.02.

(5)(a) A repeated on-demand program may be used to satisfy the requirement of SCR 31.02, if all of the following conditions are met:

1. The repeated on-demand program is approved prior to being claimed for credit by a lawyer on CLE Form 1, and the lawyer must take the on-demand program no later than December 31 of the year after the year in which approval was given.

2. Sponsors of the approved on-demand on-line program must maintain a roster verifying the attendance of all attorneys logged-in and paying for the program and provide the roster to the board if requested.

(b) No more than 10.0 credits may be claimed for repeated on-demand programs during a lawyer's reporting period.

(c) No legal ethics and professional responsibility credit is allowed for a repeated on-demand program.

(d) Repeated on-demand programs may not be used for reinstatement, readmission, or reactivation.

(6) Each hour of service on the office of lawyer regulation preliminary review committee, special preliminary review panel, district committee or as an office of lawyer regulation special investigator may be used to satisfy the requirements of SCR 31.02, to a maximum of 3.0 hours of legal ethics and professional responsibility credit per reporting period, provided that the office of lawyer regulation maintains a roster verifying service and provides the roster to the board if requested.

SCR 31.06 Attendance and reporting requirements for persons upon reactivation or reinstatement.

The board shall determine the attendance and reporting requirements for a person who seeks to change from inactive to active membership in the state bar or for a person who seeks reinstatement following voluntary resignation from the state bar, license suspension that will terminate only on order of the court, or license revocation.

SCR 31.07 Standards for approval of CLE activities.

(1) The board shall designate the number of hours applicable to the requirement of SCR 31.02 for each approved CLE activity.

(2) The following standards shall govern the approval of CLE activities by the board:

(a) The primary objective of any CLE activity shall be to increase the attendee's professional competence as a lawyer.

(b) The CLE activity shall deal primarily with matters related to the practice of law, professional responsibility or ethical obligations of lawyers.

(c) Except for repeated on-demand programs, a mechanically or electronically recorded activity will be approved only if a qualified instructor is available to comment and answer questions.

(d) CLE materials shall be prepared by and activities shall be conducted by an individual or group qualified by practical or academic experience.

(e) CLE activities shall be accompanied by thorough, well-organized and readable written materials which are available to attendees at the time of presentation unless otherwise permitted by the board.

(f) The board may grant approval of an activity to an individual lawyer, although the activity itself does not satisfy SCR 31.07(2)(a) and (b), where the lawyer demonstrates to the satisfaction of the board the manner in which the activity increases his or her competence as a lawyer.

(3) The board may approve published legal writings for use toward the CLE requirement under rules it may adopt.

(4) An activity sponsored by a private law firm, corporate law department or federal, state or local government agency offered for lawyers connected with it may be approved if it meets the requirements set forth in sub. (2).

(5) The board shall not approve any CLE for legal ethics and professional responsibility credit unless that education has a minimum component of at least one continuous hour devoted to legal ethics and professional responsibility.

SCR 31.08 Procedure for approval of CLE activities.

(1) Any person desiring approval of a CLE activity shall submit all information required by the board.

(2) Following the presentation of an approved CLE activity, each sponsor shall promptly transmit to the board a list of all lawyers in attendance.

(3) The board may annually extend approval to a sponsor for all its activities which conform to SCR 31.07. An organization which desires the general program approval shall submit all information required by the board.

SCR 31.09 Delegation, determinations and review.

(1) The board may delegate the authority of the board under this chapter to a committee, to a member or to the staff of the board.

(2) The board or its delegate shall, in response to written requests for approval of courses, waivers, extensions of time or interpretation of this chapter, make a written response giving appropriate reasons for the determination within reasonable time.

(3) The board may review any action taken under this chapter at the written request of a lawyer or sponsor adversely affected by the action. Any request for review shall be made within 60 days after notice of the action taken has been sent by mail to the lawyer or sponsor.

SCR 31.10 Noncompliance.

(1) If a lawyer fails to comply with the attendance requirement of SCR 31.02, fails to comply with the reporting requirement of SCR 31.03(1), or fails to pay the late fee under SCR 31.03(2), the board shall

serve a notice of noncompliance on the lawyer. This notice shall advise the lawyer that the lawyer's state bar membership shall be automatically suspended for failing to file evidence of compliance or to pay the late fee within 60 days after service of the notice. The board shall certify the names of all lawyers so suspended under this rule to the clerk of the supreme court, all supreme court justices, all court of appeals and circuit court judges, all circuit court commissioners appointed under SCR 75.02(1) in this state, all circuit court clerks, all juvenile court clerks, all registers in probate, the executive director of the state bar of Wisconsin, the Wisconsin State Public Defender's Office, and the clerks of the federal district courts in Wisconsin. A lawyer shall not engage in the practice of law in Wisconsin while his or her state bar membership is suspended under this rule.

(2) If the board believes that a false report has been filed, the board may refer the matter to the office of lawyer regulation.

SCR 31.11 Reinstatement.

(1) Suspension of less than 3 consecutive years. (a) A lawyer whose suspension for noncompliance under SCR 31.10(1) has been for a period of less than 3 consecutive years may file a petition with the board for reinstatement to membership in the state bar. Payment in the amount of $100.00 and any applicable late fee shall accompany the petition.

(b) Within 60 days after service of a petition for reinstatement, the board shall make a determination regarding compliance. If the board determines that the lawyer is in compliance with all requirements under this chapter, it shall reinstate the lawyer's membership in the state bar. The board shall certify the names of all lawyers so reinstated to the clerk of the supreme court, all supreme court justices, all court of appeals and circuit court judges, all circuit court commissioners appointed under SCR 75.02(1) in this state, all circuit court clerks, all juvenile court clerks, all registers in probate, the executive director of the state bar of Wisconsin, the Wisconsin State Public Defender's Office, and the clerks of the federal district courts in Wisconsin.

(c) If the board denies a petition for reinstatement, the board shall serve a notice of denial on the lawyer. After denial, a hearing shall be held by the board only upon written petition of the lawyer made within 30 days of service of the notice of denial, which petition for hearing shall be served on the board. The board shall conduct the hearing within 60 days after service of the petition for hearing and shall make and serve its findings and recommendations on the lawyer within

60 days after the close of the hearing, and, if adverse to the lawyer, shall notify the supreme court of its action. If reinstatement is denied, the findings and recommendations of the board shall be reviewed by the supreme court only upon written petition by the lawyer filed within 30 days of the date of the action of the board.

(1m) Suspension of 3 or more consecutive years. (a) A lawyer whose suspension has been for a period of 3 or more consecutive years may file a petition for reinstatement with the supreme court and serve a copy on the board and the office of lawyer regulation. Separate payments in the amount of $200 each shall be made to the board of bar examiners and the office of lawyer regulation shall accompany the petition.

(b) Within 90 days after service of the petition, the board shall make a determination regarding compliance and file its finding with the supreme court.

(c) Within 90 days after service of the petition, the director of the office of lawyer regulation shall investigate the eligibility of the petitioner for reinstatement and file a response with the supreme court in support of or opposition to the petition.

(3) Petition for reinstatement. The petition for reinstatement shall state in detail the manner in which the lawyer has complied with all requirements under this chapter. Only verified attendance at sufficient hours of approved CLE activities for the period of suspension shall be considered full compliance with the attendance requirements of this chapter.

(4) Disciplinary suspension. A lawyer suspended as a result of disciplinary action following referral under SCR 31.10(2) may petition the supreme court for reinstatement under SCR 22.28.

SCR 31.12 Extensions and waivers.

(1) The board may extend time deadlines for completion of attendance and reporting requirements in cases of hardship or for other compelling reasons.

(2) The board may waive attendance and reporting requirements where to do otherwise would work an injustice.

SCR 31.13 Service; filing.

(1) Service under this chapter means a communication made by certified mail and is complete upon mailing. Service on a lawyer is sufficient if addressed to the lawyer's address last listed with the state bar. Service on the board is sufficient if addressed to the board at its office.

(2) A report or other communication to the board under this chapter is timely filed if any of the following is applicable:

(a) The report or other communication, together with the applicable fees, is received at the board's office within the time specified for filing.

(b) The report or other communication, together with the applicable fees, is sent to the board's office through the United States Postal Service by 1st class mail, including express or priority mail, postage prepaid, and bears a postmark, other than a commercial postage meter label, showing that the communication was mailed on or before the last day for filing.

(c) The report or other communication, together with the applicable fees, is delivered on or before the last day for filing to a 3rd-party commercial carrier for delivery to the board's office within 3 calendar days.

SCR 31.14 Rule-making authority.

The board may promulgate rules to carry out the purposes of this chapter.

Chapter repealed and recreated by S.Ct. Order July 1, 1986, effective January 1, 1987; May 10, 1988; January 1, 1989; October 17, 1990; January 1, 1991; February 1, 1991; October 24, 1991; December 10, 1992; November 18, 1994; December 3, 2008; January 6, 2009; June 1, 2009; September 10, 2009; June 14, 2013.

APPENDIX

Rules of the Board of Bar Examiners

DEFINITIONS

CLE 1.01
The year of an attorney's admission to the State Bar of Wisconsin shall be the year carried on the computer records of the State Bar unless the lawyer notifies the Board in writing prior to the end of his or her first reporting period that the State Bar data is incorrect and attaches supporting documentation.

CLE 1.02
Except for repeated on-demand programs, the minimum number of persons attending a course shall be two attendees and one moderator. Fewer than that number, and the course shall be deemed to be self-study and shall not be approved for CLE credit.

REPORTING REQUIREMENTS

CLE 3.01
The classification of State Bar of Wisconsin membership on the February 1 immediately following the end of the lawyer's reporting period will govern whether a report will be required. The Board will grant lawyers who change to inactive status after February 1 according to State Bar records a deferment of the 30 hours then due on receipt of a written request that is accompanied by the late fee then due and the written statement of the State Bar that the lawyer has in fact already converted his or her membership to inactive status. A request will be considered timely if received at the Board office by the close of business on the date that the lawyer's suspension is to go into effect pursuant to SCR 31.10(1); that is, the filing date established by that rule.

CLE 3.015
(1) Lawyers who have been in inactive status for less than 2 years, or have been voluntarily resigned from the State Bar for less than 2 years, must complete 30 hours of CLE (including 3 ethics hours) prior to resuming active status.

(2) Lawyers who have been in inactive status for more than 2 years, or have been voluntarily resigned from the State Bar for more than 2 years, must complete 60 hours of CLE (including 3 ethics hours) prior to resuming active status.

(3) Lawyers may satisfy the requirements of the above subsections if they demonstrate to the board that, during the entire time they were in inactive status, (i) they were admitted to the practice of law in another jurisdiction that had mandatory continuing legal education requirements, and (ii) they were current in meeting those requirements.

(4) Lawyers who resume active status must also satisfy the requirements of SCR 31.02 for the reporting period in which they are reactivated.

(5) CLE requirements under this section shall not be greater than they would have been if the lawyer had not been in inactive status.

CLE 3.02

(1) No late fee will be assessed against lawyers who complete their reporting and attendance requirements by the February 1 following the end of their reporting period.

(2) Lawyers who have been served with the notice of noncompliance set out in SCR 31.10(1) may avoid the automatic suspension therein described if, within 60 days after service, they (a) complete their reporting and attendance requirements and (b) pay the late fee.

CLE 3.03

Where CLE Form 1 appears in SCR Chapter 31, it shall also include written amendments of a CLE Form 1 previously filed for the same reporting period. Such amendments are subject to the same deadlines as the CLE Form 1.

EXEMPTIONS

CLE 4.01

Although a lawyer is exempt from attendance or reporting in the calendar year during which his or her admission falls, the lawyer may report on the CLE Form 1 due at the end of the first full two-year reporting period any approved hours up to a maximum of 15 that were attended between the date of admission and the end of the calendar year in which his or her admission to the practice of law occurred. Hours carried in under this provision may not be used to satisfy the legal ethics and professional responsibility requirement in accordance with SCR 31.05(2)(c).

APPROVED HOURS

CLE 5.01
Sponsors must provide a method for lawyers who have taken on-line on-demand programs to submit questions, and must provide answers supplied by instructors who are qualified by practical and academic experience with fifteen business days, at no additional cost.

CLE 5.02
(1) Applications for approval of on-line on-demand programs must be accompanied by
> (a) A copy of the on-line on-demand program on DVD;
> (b) A statement of the manner in which the sponsor intends to comply with CLE 5.01.

(2) Sponsors with general program approval under SCR 31.08(3) need not comply with the requirements of sub. (1).

CLE 5.03
Grading the essay portion of the Wisconsin bar exam may be used to satisfy the requirements of SCR 31.02, up to a maximum of six (6) credits per examination administration. No legal ethics and professional responsibility credits shall be awarded for grading the essay portion of the Wisconsin bar exam.

ATTENDANCE AND REPORTING REQUIREMENTS FOR PERSONS UPON REACTIVATION OR REINSTATEMENT

CLE 6.01
Compliance with CLE make up requirements shall be a prerequisite to reactivation of membership in the State Bar of Wisconsin.

STANDARDS FOR APPROVAL OF CONTINUING LEGAL EDUCATION ACTIVITIES

CLE 7.005

Except for repeated on-demand programs as defined in SCR 31.01(6m), self-study courses as defined in CLE 1.02, and courses explicitly disapproved in Wisconsin, courses approved for CLE credit by, and attended in, any other state or territory or the District of Columbia are deemed approved for the same number of hours and for the same purposes in Wisconsin. To take advantage of this section, lawyers must document the out-of-state approval in connection with filing their CLE Form 1.

CLE 7.01

The following portions of the program may not be counted for credit: breaks, business meetings, and similar non-academic activities.

CLE 7.02

Credit hours shall be rounded down to the nearest whole or half hour. Hours of credit shall be determined by the following formula: Total minutes minus nonacademic portions (breaks, business meetings) divided by 50 minutes equal the hours of CLE credit.

CLE 7.03

Approved hours merely reflect a maximum that may be earned through attendance. Only actual attendance by the lawyer may be used to satisfy the Wisconsin requirement.

CLE 7.04

Credit will not be allowed for any program which in its entirety lasts less than 50 minutes.

CLE 7.05

[Repealed.]

CLE 7.06

(1) A published legal writing is defined as material that satisfies all of the following criteria:

(a) It is in printed form as a book, a supplement or a pocket part to a book, or an article in a publication that is included in the *Index to Legal Periodicals*. For the purposes of this definition, systems manuals that are developed and offered for sale are deemed to be books;

(b) It is commercially available or distributed to at least 500 lawyers; and

(c) It satisfies the criteria set forth in SCR 31.07(2)(a) and (b) in that its objective is to increase the reader's professional competence as a lawyer, and in that its content must deal primarily with matters related to the practice of law, professional responsibility or ethical obligations of lawyers.

(2) Published legal writings specifically exclude the following:

(a) Compilations of materials written by others;

(b) Contributions to newsletters;

(c) Written materials that are developed and distributed at CLE activities in accordance with SCR 31.07(2)(e).

CLE 7.07

In order to request approval for a published legal writing, a CLE Form 4 and a copy of the published legal writing must be submitted by its author to the Board.

CLE 7.08

A lawyer may claim his or her actual preparation time up to a maximum of 15 hours for any approved published legal writing.

CLE 7.09

A lawyer may not claim in excess of 15 hours for all approved published legal writings in any one reporting period.

CLE 7.10

The only reporting period in which hours for an approved published legal writing may be claimed is that in which the writing was published.

PROCEDURE FOR APPROVAL OF CONTINUING LEGAL EDUCATION ACTIVITIES

CLE 8.01

Approval may be refused to a sponsor for any course which has previously been falsely advertised as approved by the Board of Bar Examiners.

CLE 8.02

General program sponsorship does not extend to activities in which the sponsor acts as the co-sponsor of an activity. Approval shall be sought by letter from the general program sponsor to the Board.

CLE 8.03

Any sponsor holding general program approval that fails to cooperate with the administrative requirements developed by the Board may have its general program approval revoked by the Board.

CLE 8.04

CLE Form 2 shall be submitted to the Board to initiate a request for course approval. The Board will accept a uniform national course approval request form at the discretion of its Board.

CLE 8.05

CLE Form 5, or CLE Form 2, shall be submitted to initiate a request for legal ethics and professional responsibility approval. The Board will accept a uniform national course approval request form at the discretion of its Board.

CLE 8.06

Program sponsors shall maintain a list of lawyers in attendance for a minimum of four (4) years. Attendance lists may be kept in hardcopy or stored in a retrievable electronic format.

REINSTATEMENT AFTER SUSPENSION
PURSUANT TO SCR 31.11

CLE 11.02

Petitions for reinstatement pursuant to SCR 31.11(1)(a) must be executed under oath or affirmation.

CLE 11.03

The number of hours required of a lawyer seeking reinstatement is 30 per previous reporting period up to a maximum of 60; in addition, the lawyer will be required to meet the requirement for the reporting period in which his or her reinstatement falls.

CLE 11.04

The Board will accept the election of the SCR 31.04(2) exemption, if appropriate, in satisfaction of its requirement for reinstatement only for the reporting period from which the suspension arose; that is, the exemption may not be used toward reinstatement for any reporting period subsequent to the reporting period from which the suspension arose.

EXTENSIONS AND WAIVERS

CLE 12.01

The Board will consider extensions for completion of attendance and reporting requirements only upon written request.

SERVICE; FILING

CLE 13.01

The Board will not accept facsimile transmissions in satisfaction of its filing requirements.

BOARD MEETINGS

CLE 14.01

As an agency of the Supreme Court, the Board is not subject to Subchapter V of Chapter 19 of the Wisconsin Statutes, relating to open meetings of governmental bodies. However, the Board posts the dates, locations and agendas of its meetings in its Internet web site and invites the public to attend its meetings. Members of the public are not allowed to attend meetings or parts of meetings that involve confidential matters. Examples of confidential matters include (i) individuals' applications for admission to the Wisconsin bar, (ii) hearings on admission applications and (iii) bar examination questions.

Adopted December 12, 1986, by the Board of Attorneys Professional Competence; amended July 8, 1988; December 9, 1988; March 23, 1990; September 21, 1990; March 22, 1991; December 12, 1991; May 14, 1992; May 3, 1994; August 25, 1994; November 14, 2001; January 23, 2002; August 17, 2004; January 29, 2007; January 11, 2008; December 3, 2008; May 1, 2009; September 23, 2011.

WYOMING

Rules for Continuing Legal Education of Members of the Wyoming State Bar

Rule 1. Purpose.

By continuing their legal education throughout their practice of law, attorneys can better fulfill their obligation to competently serve their clients. These rules establish minimum requirements for such continuing legal education and the means by which the requirements shall be enforced.

Rule 2. State Board of Continuing Legal Education.

(a) The Wyoming State Board of Continuing Legal Education, having been previously established, is hereby continued under these rules. The members of the Board are to be appointed by the Court. The Board shall consist of nine members, six of whom shall be members of the Wyoming State Bar and three of whom shall be residents of the state not admitted to the practice of law. Members shall be appointed for three-year terms.

(b) Each yearly class of members shall include two members of the bar and one layperson. No person may serve more than two consecutive terms as a member of the Board.

(c) Each year the Board shall designate one of the lawyer members to serve as chairperson. The executive director of the Wyoming State Bar, or designee, shall serve as the executive secretary of the Board.

(d) The Board shall elect a vice-chairperson from its membership who shall, in the event of the resignation, absence, incapacity or demise of the chairperson, act as chairperson until such time as the absence or incapacity has been removed or the Board designates a new chairperson.

(e) The Board has general supervisory authority over the administration of these rules.

(f) Five or more members of the Board shall constitute a quorum.

(g) All communications to or with the Board or any member thereof relating to matters governed by these rules, and all communications with either the Board or any member thereof relating to waiver of any part of these rules, whether by an attorney or by any person or agent acting for or on the behalf of an attorney, shall be transmitted through the office of the Wyoming State Bar unless otherwise directed in writing by the chair of the Board.

(h) All proceedings of the Board relating to applications for waivers or extensions under Rule 7 shall be confidential.

(i) Vouchers for expenses incurred by members of the Board shall be submitted to the executive director of the Wyoming State Bar. Mileage will be paid at the rate set by the Wyoming State Bar. Other expenses will be reimbursed at actual cost-incurred rates.

(Amended August 27, 2014, effective October 1, 2014; amended June 2, 2015, effective July 1, 2015)

Rule 3. Definitions.

For the purposes of these rules, the following definitions apply:

(a) "Attorney" means a member of the Wyoming State Bar who is required to complete continuing legal education as provided in these rules.

(b) The "Board" means the Wyoming State Board of Continuing Legal Education.

(c) "Court" means the Wyoming Supreme Court.

(d) An "hour" of accredited continuing legal education means 60 minutes in attendance at an accredited continuing legal education activity. Credit will be given to the nearest quarter of an hour.

(e) "Legal Ethics" means instruction in legal and judicial ethics and professional responsibility. It may include, but is not limited to, subjects dealing with duties of attorneys to the judicial system, court, public, clients and other attorneys; competency; pro bono work; substance abuse; attorney fees; and client development. It may also include subjects dealing with law office management to the extent professional responsibility is directly discussed in relation to that topic.

(f) "Mentor" is a lawyer who holds Active or Emeritus status with the Wyoming State Bar and has at least five (5) years of experience in the practice of law.

(g) "CLE Director" is the Continuing Legal Education Director, an employee of the Wyoming State Bar.

(h) "Reporting period" is the calendar year to which the continuing legal education requirement applies.

(Amended June 2, 2015, effective July 1, 2015)

Rule 4. Continuing legal education requirements and conditions.

(a) Requirements.

(1) Active Members: A minimum of 15 hours of continuing legal education including a total of two hours of legal ethics must be completed each calendar year.

(2) New Active Members: A minimum of 15 hours of continuing legal education including a total of two hours of legal ethics must be completed each calendar year.

(3) Emeritus Members: A minimum of seven (7) hours of continuing legal education including one hour of legal ethics must be completed each calendar year.

(4) New Admittees by Examination or UBE Score Transfer. Each new admittee by examination or by Uniform Bar Examination score transfer shall attend, within 12 months from the date of admission to the Wyoming State Bar, a six-hour continuing legal education course entitled "Pathways to Professional Practice." The Pathways course shall be conducted by the Wyoming State Bar and shall be available at least twice each year, at such times and places as the Wyoming State Bar may designate, and may be counted toward the 15 hours of continuing legal education that must be obtained pursuant to this rule.

(b) Continuing legal education credit may be obtained by attending or participating in a continuing legal education activity accredited by the CLE Director under these rules. Credits will not be granted for attending duplicate courses in the same calendar year.

(c) Hours completed in any year in excess of the minimum number, including legal ethics credits, may be carried forward for two years.

(d) Attorneys who lecture in a continuing legal education activity accredited or eligible for accreditation as provided in these Rules will receive credit for three hours for each hour spent lecturing. If an attorney lectures as part of a panel, the total length of the lecture will be divided by the number of panelists and that portion will be multiplied by three for instruction credit. Credit will not be granted for instructing duplicate courses in the same calendar year unless substantive changes are made in the program.

(e) The final published course schedule of an accredited continuing legal education activity shall be determinative of the number of hours of accredited continuing legal education available through such activity. In all other cases, the CLE Director will determine the number of hours of accredited continuing legal education available through such activity.

(f) To obtain continuing legal education credit, an attorney shall submit an application approved by the Board or apply online on the Wyoming State Bar website (www.wyomingbar.org) for each continuing legal education activity for which credit is sought. The application should be submitted within a reasonable time following participation in the activity. Applications submitted after March 1 for continuing legal education activities completed during the previous calendar year shall not be accepted.

(1) For continuing legal education activities which have received prior accreditation under Rule 6, no further documentation is required other than the application.

(2) For continuing legal education activities which have not received prior accreditation, the application shall include a brief description of the activity, its dates, subjects, instructors and their qualifications, a copy of the activity outline, activity

brochure and other documentation upon which the CLE Director can make a determination as to the qualifications of the activity and the number of credit hours to which the applicant is entitled. Within a reasonable time after receipt of the application and accompanying materials, CLE Director shall notify the attorney that the activity is not accredited or if the number of hours of credit approved is less than requested. Such notification shall be made by United States mail or by email to the address provided by such attorney to the Wyoming State Bar.

(g) The Wyoming State Bar shall maintain a record of the continuing legal education credits which have been accumulated for each attorney. On November 15 (or the next business day following) the Wyoming State Bar shall notify each attorney of the number of continuing legal education hours credited to that attorney for the current calendar year. Such notification shall be made by United States mail or by email to the address provided by such attorney to the Wyoming State Bar.

(Amended effective July 1, 2012; amended and effective December 14, 2012; amended September 17, 2013, effective January 1, 2014; amended May 13, 2014; effective May 13, 2014; amended August 27, 2014, effective October 1, 2014.)

(Amended effective July 1, 2012; amended and effective December 14, 2012; amended September 17, 2013, effective January 1, 2014; amended May 13, 2014; effective May 13, 2014; amended August 27, 2014, effective October 1, 2014; amended June 2, 2015, effective July 1, 2015

Rule 5. Standards for continuing legal education activity.

(a) A continuing legal education activity consisting of lecture (classroom) style instruction qualifies for accreditation, and the attorney participants, both attendees and faculty, are entitled to continuing legal education credit, if the CLE Director determines that:

(1) The activity constitutes an organized program of learning (including workshop or symposium) which contributes directly to the professional competency of an attorney;

(2) The activity pertains to legal subjects or other subject matters which integrally relate to the practice of law;

(3) The purpose of the activity is the education of professionals including attorneys;

(4) The activity is conducted or taught by attorneys, although it may also be conducted or taught in part by individuals who have special education, training and experience by reason of which they should be considered experts concerning the subject matter of the program; and

(5) The activity is accompanied by a paper, manual or written outline which substantively pertains to the subject matter of the program.

(b) Examples. The program's purpose must be the education of professionals, including attorneys, on legal topics or on non-legal topics which nevertheless integrally relate to the practice of law, such as

(1) A joint continuing legal education program sponsored, for instance, by accountants to which attorneys are invited and at which attorneys lecture on topics of interest to both accountants and attorneys would likely be accredited by the CLE Director, subject to the CLE Director's review of the specific course outline or program brochure.

(2) A meeting of doctors, lawyers, managed health care professionals and hospital administrators at which one or more attorneys lecture on topics of interest to all participants, such as legal concerns in the establishment of an HMO, malpractice, giving expert testimony, new federal laws and regulations for Medicaid/Medicare providers, would likely provide continuing legal education credit to attorney lecturers and to attorney attendees if the topics pertain to subject matters which integrally relate to the practice of law and contribute directly to the professional competency of an attorney.

(3) A meeting of public service commissioners and attorneys at which one or more attorneys lecture on topics such as new regulations, administrative rules, and/or laws would likely be accredited by the CLE Director if the topics pertain to subject matters which integrally relate to the practice of law and contribute directly to the professional competency of an attorney.

(4) A meeting of doctors at which one or more attorneys lecture on topics of interest to doctors, such as malpractice, court procedures or giving expert testimony would not qualify as continuing legal education credit to attorney lecturers or attendees, because the program was not intended for the continuing legal education of attorneys. Attorneys are expected to participate in such programs as a contribution to the community and to their profession. Other similar programs which would not ordinarily qualify for continuing legal education credit would include teaching a bar review course or presenting a seminar exclusively to records managers on "Law Enforcement Records Liability."

(5) Attending a course taught by engineers, for engineers, on topics which may be of vital interest to a product liability attorney would not provide continuing legal education credit to the attorney because the program was not intended for the continuing legal education of attorneys. Other programs which would not ordinarily qualify for continuing legal education credit include attending courses at a real estate school, attending a non-attorney workshop on juvenile delinquency or attending a non-attorney course on federal procurement.

(c) Time spent researching and writing articles that are published in a legal periodical including without limitation law reviews, legal newsletters, pamphlets, magazines or newspapers, consisting of case summaries, law updates and other subjects of interest to the legal community, qualifies for continuing legal education credit to a maximum of 15 hours in any calendar year. Authors of such articles applying for continuing legal education credit must submit a copy of the article, as published, with the approved form.

(d) An attorney may receive a maximum of five hours of legal education credit each calendar year for providing pro bono public service as defined in Rule 6.1 of the Wyoming Rules of Professional Conduct. Such credit may be received at the rate of one credit hour for each two hours of pro bono public service, including (1) performing pro bono public service, (2) acting as a mentor for another attorney who is performing pro bono public service, and (3) acting as a mentor for an eligible law student in accordance with Rule 9 of the Rules Governing the Wyoming State Bar and the Authorized Practice of Law.

(e) An attorney may receive a maximum of six hours of continuing legal education credit for self-study programs where audio, video or online material is used. No hours may be carried over to any subsequent years.

(f) Attorneys will not receive continuing legal education credit for any "for profit" activity such as authoring a book or treatise for a fee or commission or teaching a course for which payment of other than expenses is received.

(g) Identical activities will not be accredited unless they are held at least one year apart.

(Amended August 27, 2014, effective October 1, 2014; amended June 2, 2015, effective July 1, 2015)

Rule 6. Accreditation of continuing legal education activities.

(a) A sponsor may apply for accreditation of a continuing legal education program by submitting an application for accreditation on a form provided by the CLE Director and approved by the Board at least 30 days prior to the activity, along with an application fee established by the Board. The application fee established by the Board is subject to approval by the Court. The application shall state the dates, subjects offered, total minutes of instruction, names and qualifications of speakers and other pertinent information. Programs are approved for 12 months and must be re-submitted for approval, along with payment of an application fee established by the Board, every 12 months in order for the program to be accredited that year. The application fee will be waived for programs that are being offered free of charge.

(Amended September 17, 2013, effective January 1, 2014; amended June 2, 2015, effective July 1, 2015)

Rule 7. Hardship waivers and extensions.

(a) The Board may, in individual cases involving hardship grant waivers of the continuing legal educational requirements or extensions of time. Hardship may be shown by illness, medical disability or other extraordinary or extenuating circumstances beyond the control of the attorney, but generally will not include financial hardship or lack of time due to a busy professional or personal schedule. Requests for waivers or extensions of time shall be submitted in writing to the Board prior to March 1 of the year following the reporting period for which the request is being made, provided, however, that any such requests pertaining to the Pathways requirement set forth in Rule 4(a)(4) shall be submitted within 12 months of the date of the attorney's admission. The Board shall have discretion to review an untimely request if the attorney shows good and sufficient cause as to why the request was not submitted within the time required by this rule, and if the untimely request is submitted to the Board before a Recommendation for Suspension for Noncompliance has been submitted to the Court.

(b) Waivers of the continuing legal educational requirements may be granted by the Board for any period of time not to exceed one year. If the hardship or the extenuating circumstances upon which a waiver has been granted continue beyond the period of the waiver, the attorney must reapply for an extension of the waiver. The Board may, as a condition of any waiver granted, require the applicant to make up a certain portion or all of the continuing legal educational requirements waived by such methods as may be prescribed by the Board.

(c) Extensions of time within which to fulfill the continuing legal educational requirements may, in individual cases involving hardship or extenuating circumstances, be granted by the Board for a period not to exceed six months immediately following expiration of the year in which the requirements were not met. Hours of continuing legal educational requirement completed within an extension period will be applied first to the continuing legal educational requirements for the preceding year and will be applied to the current or following year only to the extent that the hours are not required to fulfill the continuing legal educational requirements for the preceding year.

(Amended April 3, 2007, effective June 1, 2007; amended August 27, 2014, effective October 1, 2014.)

(Amended April 3, 2007, effective June 1, 2007; amended August 27, 2014, effective October 1, 2014; amended June 2, 2015, effective July 1, 2015)

Rule 8.   Exemptions.

(a) An attorney is exempt from the provisions of Rule 4(a) during the calendar year in which the attorney is admitted to practice law in Wyoming; provided, however, that new admittees by examination or by Uniform Bar Examination score transfer must comply with the mandatory continuing legal education requirements set forth in Rule 4(a)(4).

(b) A member of the Wyoming State Bar who is honorary, inactive, honorary retired or retired, according to Article I, Section 3 of the Bylaws of the Wyoming State Bar, is exempt from the provisions of Rule 4, and is not required to obtain or report continuing legal education credit on a yearly basis.

(c) An attorney who is elected to state or national executive or legislative office is exempt from the provisions of Rule 4 if written request for exemption is made each year the office is held.

(d) member of the Board of Law Examiners is exempt from the provisions of Rule 4 if written request for exemption is made each year the attorney is a member of the Board of Law Examiners.

(Amended September 30, 2008, effective January 1, 2009; amended August 27, 2014, effective October 1, 2014; amended June 2, 2015, effective July 1, 2015)

Rule 9. Appeals to the Board.

In the event of denial, in whole or in part, of any application for continuing legal education credit, the attorney may, within 10 days after notification of denial request in writing that the Board reconsider the denial. The Board's decision upon reconsideration shall be final.

(Amended August 27, 2014, effective October 1, 2014.); amended June 2, 2015, effective July 1, 2015)

Rule 10. Penalties for failure to satisfy continuing legal education requirement.

(a) An attorney who has not complied with the applicable continuing legal education requirement by January 15 of the year following the reporting period shall be delinquent and shall be subject to a $300.00 delinquency fee. As soon as possible after January 15, the Wyoming State Bar shall send a Notice of Delinquency to each delinquent attorney. The Notice of Delinquency shall be sent by United States mail and email to the attorney at the official address listed with the Wyoming State Bar. Attorneys who are delinquent shall have until March 1 to submit applications for adequate credits to cure the delinquency, along with payment of a $300.00 delinquency fee payable to the Wyoming State Bar.

(b) As soon as possible after March 15, the Board, upon certification from the Wyoming State Bar that the requirements of Rule 4(a) and/or Rule 10(a) have not been met by the attorney, and that the Notice of Delinquency required by Rule 10(a) was timely sent to the attorney, shall forward a Recommendation for Suspension for Noncompliance with continuing legal education requirement to the Court for each attorney who failed to comply with the continuing legal education requirement for the previous calendar year, or for any delinquent attorney who has failed to pay the delinquency fee. For attorneys who have not complied with the Pathways requirement set forth in Rule 4(a)(4) within 12 months from the date of admission, the Recommendation for Suspension for Noncompliance shall be forwarded to the Court as soon as possible after the expiration of the 12 months. A copy of the

Recommendation for Suspension for Noncompliance shall be sent by certified mail, return receipt requested, addressed to the attorney at the official address listed with the Wyoming State Bar.

(c) Upon receipt of the Recommendation for Suspension for Noncompliance with the continuing legal education requirement, the Court shall issue an Order to Show Cause as to why the delinquent attorney's license to practice law in the State of Wyoming should not be suspended, sent by certified mail, return receipt requested, addressed to the attorney at the official address listed with the Wyoming State Bar. The delinquent attorney may file a response with the Court within 30 days of the date of the order to show cause by filing an original and six copies of such response with the clerk of the Court. The delinquent attorney shall also serve a copy of the response on the Board, together with a $300.00 noncompliance fee payable to the Wyoming State Bar. The $300.00 noncompliance fee is in addition to the delinquency fee provided in subsection (a) of this rule.

(d) If the attorney files a response to the Order to Show Cause and mails a copy of the response to the Board, the Wyoming State Bar shall submit any additional information to the Court within five (5) days of filing of the attorney's response.

(e) In the absence of good cause shown, an order of suspension from the practice of law for a period of one (1) year shall issue from the Court.

(Amended April 3, 2007, effective June 1, 2007; amended August 10, 2012, effective September 30, 2012; amended September 17, 2013, effective January 1, 2014; amended August 27, 2014, effective October 1, 2014; amended June 2, 2015, effective July 1, 2015)

Rule 11. Duties of suspended attorneys.

(a) Within 15 days of the date of an order of suspension, the suspended attorney shall notify the following persons by registered or certified mail, return receipt requested, of the attorney's suspension and the attorney's consequent inability to act as an attorney after the effective date of the suspension:

(1) All clients with pending matters in the State of Wyoming. The attorney shall advise clients to seek legal advice elsewhere and to obtain another attorney for litigated matters or administrative proceedings in the State of Wyoming.

(2) Any co-counsel who is involved in litigated matters or administrative proceedings in the State of Wyoming.

(3) The attorney for each adverse party or, in the absence of such counsel, the adverse party or parties in litigated matters or administrative proceedings in the State of Wyoming. The notice to parties shall state the place of residence of the client of the suspended attorney.

(4) All courts or administrative bodies in which the attorney has matters pending in the State of Wyoming.

(b) If an attorney has not filed a petition for reinstatement within six months from the date of the order, the attorney shall within 15 days deliver to all present and former clients all client files.

(c) A suspended attorney shall notify the client of all deadlines and scheduled court dates.

(d) A suspended attorney, after entry of the suspension order, shall not accept any new legal matters in the State of Wyoming. During the period from the entry date of the order to its effective date, the attorney may wind up and complete, on behalf of any client, all matters which were pending on the entry date.

(e) A suspended attorney shall return any unearned fees.

(f) Within 30 days after the effective date of the suspension order, the suspended attorney shall file with the Court and Board an affidavit showing that the attorney has fully complied with the provisions of the order and with this rule and stating the address where communications may thereafter be directed.

(g) A suspended attorney shall maintain records of the steps taken to comply with this rule.

(h) The provisions of this section are deemed to be incorporated into all orders of suspension. Failure to comply with any requirement of this section is punishable as contempt.

(i) Suspension under these rules shall not be considered as a disciplinary infraction.

(Amended April 3, 2007, effective June 1, 2007; amended August 10, 2012, effective September 30, 2012.)

Rule 12. Reinstatement.

The suspended member may be reinstated upon the filing of a petition for reinstatement within one (1) year of the date of the order of suspension, which petition shall be filed, along with six copies, with the Court. A copy of the petition shall also be provided to the Board. The petition shall be supported by an affidavit which shows: (1) that all past annual license fees, the current year's annual license fee and any late charges have been paid in full, in addition to all past and current annual fees for continuing legal education; (2) that the attorney is current on all mandatory continuing legal education requirements; (3) that there have been no claims or awards made in regard to an attorney on the client's security fund for which the fund has not been reimbursed; and (4) the attorney has complied with all other applicable conditions for reinstatement. The petition shall be accompanied by all appropriate fees for applicants for admission on motion. A response by the Board may be filed within twenty (20) days of the date of service of the petition for reinstatement.

If an attorney who is suspended from the practice of law for a continuing legal education delinquency has not petitioned for reinstatement within one (1) year of the date of the order of suspension, such attorney's membership in the Wyoming State Bar shall be terminated by order of the Court. Such attorney who thereafter seeks admission to the Wyoming State Bar shall comply with the admissions requirements set forth in the Wyoming Rules and Procedures Governing Admission to the Practice of Law.

(Amended August 27, 2014, effective October 1, 2014; amended June 2, 2015, effective July 1, 2015)

Rule 13.   Fees.

Each active member of the bar must pay an annual Continuing Legal Education fee in an amount established by the Board, subject to approval by the Court. This fee will be collected by the Bar at the time of the collection of the annual license fee, but will constitute a fee to be used only to defray the costs of administering the rules and regulations for continuing legal education and issuing annual reports. This fee is payable October 1 of each fiscal year and will be considered late on December 1.

(Amended August 27, 2014, effective October 1, 2014; amended June 2, 2015, effective July 1, 2015)

2015 Bar Examination Admission and Statistics

2015 STATISTICS

This section includes data, by jurisdiction, on the following categories for 2015:

- the number of persons taking and passing bar examinations;

- the number taking and passing bar examinations categorized by source of legal education;

- the number of and passage rates for first-time exam takers and repeaters, both overall and for graduates of ABA-approved law schools;

- the number of and passage rates for graduates of non-ABA-approved law schools by type of school;

- the number of attorney candidates taking and passing special Attorneys' Examinations; and

- the number of disbarred or suspended attorneys taking and passing examinations as a condition of reinstatement.

Also included are the following:

- a chart showing a longitudinal view of bar passage rates, both overall and for first-time takers, over a 10-year period;

- a five-year snapshot, by jurisdiction, of the number of persons admitted to the bar by examination, on motion, by transferred Uniform Bar Examination (UBE) score (data collection started by NCBE in 2013), and by diploma privilege, as well as the number of individuals licensed as foreign legal consultants; and

- a chart displaying relative admissions to the bar in 2015 by examination, on motion, and by diploma privilege.

Data for the first 10 charts were supplied by the jurisdictions. In reviewing the data, the reader should keep in mind that some individuals seek admission in more than one jurisdiction in a given year. The charts represent the data as of the date they were received from jurisdictions and may not reflect possible subsequent appeals or pending issues that might affect the overall passing statistics for a given jurisdiction. Statistics are updated to reflect any later changes received from jurisdictions and can be found on the NCBE website, www.ncbex.org.

The following national data are shown for the administrations of the Multistate Bar Examination (MBE) and the Multistate Professional Responsibility Examination (MPRE):

- summary statistics,
- score distributions,
- examinee counts over a 10-year period, and
- mean scaled scores over a 10-year period.

The use, by jurisdiction, is illustrated for the MBE, the MPRE, the Multistate Essay Examination (MEE), and the Multistate Performance Test (MPT).

* Reprinted with permission from the National Conference of Bar Examiners, Madison, Wisconsin. Originally published in *The Bar Examiner*, 85, no.1 (March 2016): 14-49.

BAR EXAMINATION STATISTICS
2015 STATISTICS CONTENTS

Persons Taking and Passing the 2015 Bar Examination

Jurisdiction	February			July			Total		
	Taking	Passing	% Passing	Taking	Passing	% Passing	Taking	Passing	% Passing
Alabama	261	112	43%	490	294	60%	751	406	54%
Alaska	60	39	65%	75	45	60%	135	84	62%
Arizona	455	266	58%	650	368	57%	1,105	634	57%
Arkansas	108	68	63%	222	145	65%	330	213	65%
California	4,761	1,882	40%	8,323	3,882	47%	13,084	5,764	44%
Colorado	360	222	62%	799	576	72%	1,159	798	69%
Connecticut	219	148	68%	432	323	75%	651	471	72%
Delaware	No February examination			188	124	66%	188	124	66%
District of Columbia	259	102	39%	296	130	44%	555	232	42%
Florida	1,461	758	52%	3,140	1,948	62%	4,601	2,706	59%
Georgia	552	303	55%	1,273	822	65%	1,825	1,125	62%
Hawaii	110	68	62%	182	125	69%	292	193	66%
Idaho	57	40	70%	116	79	68%	173	119	69%
Illinois	923	638	69%	2,234	1,687	76%	3,157	2,325	74%
Indiana	270	182	67%	495	364	74%	765	546	71%
Iowa	92	66	72%	227	195	86%	319	261	82%
Kansas	65	53	82%	109	83	76%	174	136	78%
Kentucky	195	135	69%	375	267	71%	570	402	71%
Louisiana	302	198	66%	698	432	62%	1,000	630	63%
Maine	57	37	65%	97	57	59%	154	94	61%
Maryland	607	284	47%	1,316	827	63%	1,923	1,111	58%
Massachusetts	689	390	57%	1,831	1,313	72%	2,520	1,703	68%
Michigan	537	313	58%	810	503	62%	1,347	816	61%
Minnesota	232	140	60%	672	521	78%	904	661	73%
Mississippi	98	70	71%	188	145	77%	286	215	75%
Missouri	303	236	78%	767	647	84%	1,070	883	83%
Montana	66	49	74%	112	69	62%	178	118	66%
Nebraska	39	23	59%	179	143	80%	218	166	76%
Nevada	222	135	61%	309	186	60%	531	321	60%
New Hampshire	48	27	56%	161	112	70%	209	139	67%
New Jersey	1,005	524	52%	2,946	2,060	70%	3,951	2,584	65%
New Mexico	93	74	80%	167	121	72%	260	195	75%
New York	3,997	1,713	43%	10,671	6,496	61%	14,668	8,209	56%

Persons Taking and Passing the 2015 Bar Examination *(continued)*

Jurisdiction	February			July			Total		
	Taking	Passing	% Passing	Taking	Passing	% Passing	Taking	Passing	% Passing
North Carolina	592	253	43%	1,210	703	58%	1,802	956	53%
North Dakota	44	24	55%	60	43	72%	104	67	64%
Ohio	411	262	64%	1,045	779	75%	1,456	1,041	71%
Oklahoma	107	72	67%	307	210	68%	414	282	68%
Oregon	250	159	64%	398	239	60%	648	398	61%
Pennsylvania	646	340	53%	1,799	1,280	71%	2,445	1,620	66%
Rhode Island	60	37	62%	154	98	64%	214	135	63%
South Carolina	249	158	63%	432	309	72%	681	467	69%
South Dakota	27	7	26%	73	49	67%	100	56	56%
Tennessee	361	195	54%	704	456	65%	1,065	651	61%
Texas	1,333	806	60%	2,987	1,985	66%	4,320	2,791	65%
Utah	129	103	80%	285	211	74%	414	314	76%
Vermont	40	19	48%	61	32	52%	101	51	50%
Virginia	484	287	59%	1,140	810	71%	1,624	1,097	68%
Washington	362	238	66%	814	618	76%	1,176	856	73%
West Virginia	91	62	68%	182	123	68%	273	185	68%
Wisconsin	87	63	72%	127	82	65%	214	145	68%
Wyoming	24	20	83%	57	40	70%	81	60	74%
Guam	10	6	60%	8	3	38%	18	9	50%
N. Mariana Islands	3	3	100%	3	3	100%	6	6	100%
Palau	No February examination			13	1	8%	13	1	8%
Puerto Rico[a]	512	160	31%	676	241	36%	1,188	401	34%
Virgin Islands	6	5	83%	21	15	71%	27	20	74%
TOTALS	24,331	12,574	52%	53,106	33,419	63%	77,437	45,993	59%

[a]Examinations in Puerto Rico are administered in March and September.

Persons Taking and Passing the 2015 Bar Examination by Source of Legal Education

Jurisdiction	ABA-Approved Law School			Non-ABA-Approved Law School[a]			Law School Outside the USA			Law Office Study		
	Taking	Passing	% Passing	Taking	Passing	% Passing	Taking	Passing	% Passing	Taking	Passing	% Passing
Alabama	458	353	77%	289	52	18%	4	1	25%	—	—	—
Alaska	133	84	63%	—	—	—	2	0	0%	—	—	—
Arizona	1,102	633	57%	1	1	100%	2	0	0%	—	—	—
Arkansas	330	213	65%	—	—	—	—	—	—	—	—	—
California	8,763[b,c]	4,642[b,c]	53%	2,090[b,c]	328[b,c]	16%	1,142	200	18%	3	2	67%
Colorado	1,150	795	69%	4	0	0%	5	3	60%	—	—	—
Connecticut	612	467	76%	38	4	11%	1	0	0%	—	—	—
Delaware	188	124	66%	—	—	—	—	—	—	—	—	—
District of Columbia	324	169	52%	27	4	15%	204	59	29%	—	—	—
Florida	4,600	2,706	59%	1	0	0%	—	—	—	—	—	—
Georgia	1,791	1,120	63%	24	0	0%	10	5	50%	—	—	—
Hawaii	290	192	66%	—	—	—	2	1	50%	—	—	—
Idaho	173	119	69%	—	—	—	—	—	—	—	—	—
Illinois	3,085	2,304	75%	—	—	—	72	21	29%	—	—	—
Indiana	765	546	71%	—	—	—	—	—	—	—	—	—
Iowa	318	261	82%	—	—	—	1	0	0%	—	—	—
Kansas	174	136	78%	—	—	—	—	—	—	—	—	—
Kentucky	570	402	71%	—	—	—	—	—	—	—	—	—
Louisiana	992	628	63%	—	—	—	8	2	25%	—	—	—
Maine	152	92	61%	2	2	100%	—	—	—	—	—	—
Maryland	1,895	1,097	58%	2	2	100%	26	12	46%	—	—	—
Massachusetts	2,210	1,609	73%	272	82	30%	38	12	32%	—	—	—
Michigan	1,342	814	61%	—	—	—	5	2	40%	—	—	—
Minnesota	904	661	73%	—	—	—	—	—	—	—	—	—
Mississippi	286	215	75%	—	—	—	—	—	—	—	—	—
Missouri	1,059	878	83%	1	1	100%	10	4	40%	—	—	—

[a]See page 28 for a breakdown of exam takers and passers from non-ABA-approved law schools by type of school.

[b]California does not recognize U.S. attorneys taking the General Bar Examination as being from either ABA-approved or non-ABA-approved law schools. This number of applicants (1,044 taking, 590 passing) is therefore omitted from either category. California's "U.S. Attorneys Taking the General Bar Exam" category is composed of attorneys admitted in other jurisdictions less than four years who must take, and those admitted four or more years who have elected to take, the General Bar Examination.

[c]Applicants under California's four-year qualification rule who did not earn J.D. degrees (42 taking, 2 passing) are not included in either the ABA-approved or non-ABA-approved category. California's four-year qualification rule allows applicants to take the General Bar Examination through a combination of four years of law study without graduating from a law school.

BAR EXAMINATION STATISTICS

Persons Taking and Passing the 2015 Bar Examination
by Source of Legal Education (*continued*)

Jurisdiction	ABA-Approved Law School			Non-ABA-Approved Law School[a]			Law School Outside the USA			Law Office Study		
	Taking	Passing	% Passing	Taking	Passing	% Passing	Taking	Passing	% Passing	Taking	Passing	% Passing
Montana	178	118	66%	—	—	—	—	—	—	—	—	—
Nebraska	218	166	76%	—	—	—	—	—	—	—	—	—
Nevada	523	319	61%	2	0	0%	6	2	33%	—	—	—
New Hampshire	192	132	69%	16	7	44%	1	0	0%	—	—	—
New Jersey	3,951	2,584	65%	—	—	—	—	—	—	—	—	—
New Mexico	260	195	75%	—	—	—	—	—	—	—	—	—
New York	9,893	6,752	68%	4	1	25%	4,754	1,454	31%	17	2	12%
North Carolina	1,802	956	53%	—	—	—	—	—	—	—	—	—
North Dakota	104	67	64%	—	—	—	—	—	—	—	—	—
Ohio	1,441	1,038	72%	—	—	—	15	3	20%	—	—	—
Oklahoma	414	282	68%	—	—	—	—	—	—	—	—	—
Oregon	644	398	62%	—	—	—	4	0	0%	—	—	—
Pennsylvania	2,436	1,619	66%	1	0	0%	8	1	13%	—	—	—
Rhode Island	213	135	63%	—	—	—	1	0	0%	—	—	—
South Carolina	681	467	69%	—	—	—	—	—	—	—	—	—
South Dakota	100	56	56%	—	—	—	—	—	—	—	—	—
Tennessee	833	566	68%	215	81	38%	17	4	24%	—	—	—
Texas	4,174	2,758	66%	6	3	50%	140	30	21%	—	—	—
Utah	413	313	76%	—	—	—	1	1	100%	—	—	—
Vermont	94	49	52%	—	—	—	—	—	—	7	2	29%
Virginia	1,615	1,096	68%	—	—	—	2	0	0%	7	1	14%
Washington	1,134	840	74%	—	—	—	31	10	32%	11	6	55%
West Virginia	271	185	68%	2	0	0%	—	—	—	—	—	—
Wisconsin	203	141	69%	3	3	100%	8	1	13%	—	—	—
Wyoming	81	60	74%	—	—	—	—	—	—	—	—	—
Guam	18	9	50%	—	—	—	—	—	—	—	—	—
N. Mariana Islands	6	6	100%	—	—	—	—	—	—	—	—	—
Palau	4	1	25%	—	—	—	9	0	0%	—	—	—
Puerto Rico	1,174	400	34%	14	1	7%	—	—	—	—	—	—
Virgin Islands	27	20	74%	—	—	—	—	—	—	—	—	—
TOTALS	66,763	42,988	64%	3,014	572	19%	6,529	1,828	28%	45	13	29%

[a]See page 28 for a breakdown of exam takers and passers from non-ABA-approved law schools by type of school.

First-Time Exam Takers and Repeaters in 2015[a]

Jurisdiction	2015 Administration	First-Timers			Repeaters		
		Taking	Passing	% Passing	Taking	Passing	% Passing
Alabama	February	129	78	60%	132	34	26%
	July	375	280	75%	115	14	12%
	Total	504	358	71%	247	48	19%
Alaska	February	37	31	84%	23	8	35%
	July	58	41	71%	17	4	24%
	Total	95	72	76%	40	12	30%
Arizona	February	302	199	66%	153	67	44%
	July	516	339	66%	134	29	22%
	Total	818	538	66%	287	96	33%
Arkansas	February	50	40	80%	58	28	48%
	July	186	141	76%	36	4	11%
	Total	236	181	77%	94	32	34%
California	February	1,524	723	47%	3,237	1,159	36%
	July	5,838	3,486	60%	2,485	396	16%
	Total	7,362	4,209	57%	5,722	1,555	27%
Colorado	February	226	159	70%	134	63	47%
	July	710	550	77%	89	26	29%
	Total	936	709	76%	223	89	40%
Connecticut	February	143	123	86%	76	25	33%
	July	368	297	81%	64	26	41%
	Total	511	420	82%	140	51	36%
Delaware	February			No February examination			
	July	150	109	73%	38	15	39%
	Total	150	109	73%	38	15	39%
Dist. of Columbia	February	163	86	53%	96	16	17%
	July	173	100	58%	123	30	24%
	Total	336	186	55%	219	46	21%
Florida	February	831	534	64%	630	224	36%
	July	2,687	1,851	69%	453	97	21%
	Total	3,518	2,385	68%	1,083	321	30%
Georgia	February	283	206	73%	269	97	36%
	July	1,067	784	73%	206	38	18%
	Total	1,350	990	73%	475	135	28%
Hawaii	February	58	46	79%	52	22	42%
	July	155	116	75%	27	9	33%
	Total	213	162	76%	79	31	39%
Idaho	February	33	27	82%	24	13	54%
	July	107	74	69%	9	5	56%
	Total	140	101	72%	33	18	55%
Illinois	February	549	442	81%	374	196	52%
	July	2,030	1,623	80%	204	64	31%
	Total	2,579	2,065	80%	578	260	45%
Indiana	February	166	126	76%	104	56	54%
	July	432	344	80%	63	20	32%
	Total	598	470	79%	167	76	46%

[a]First-time exam takers are defined as examinees taking the bar examination for the first time in the reporting jurisdiction. Repeaters are defined as examinees who have taken the bar examination in the reporting jurisdiction at least once prior to the listed administration.

First-Time Exam Takers and Repeaters in 2015[a] (continued)

Jurisdiction	2015 Administration	First-Timers			Repeaters		
		Taking	Passing	% Passing	Taking	Passing	% Passing
Iowa	February	57	47	82%	35	19	54%
	July	207	188	91%	20	7	35%
	Total	264	235	89%	55	26	47%
Kansas	February	45	38	84%	20	15	75%
	July	94	76	81%	15	7	47%
	Total	139	114	82%	35	22	63%
Kentucky	February	125	98	78%	70	37	53%
	July	321	243	76%	54	24	44%
	Total	446	341	76%	124	61	49%
Louisiana	February	120	75	63%	182	123	68%
	July	580	403	69%	118	29	25%
	Total	700	478	68%	300	152	51%
Maine	February	34	28	82%	23	9	39%
	July	85	54	64%	12	3	25%
	Total	119	82	69%	35	12	34%
Maryland	February	281	131	47%	326	153	47%
	July	1,123	776	69%	193	51	26%
	Total	1,404	907	65%	519	204	39%
Massachusetts	February	354	236	67%	335	154	46%
	July	1,589	1,256	79%	242	57	24%
	Total	1,943	1,492	77%	577	211	37%
Michigan	February	291	206	71%	246	107	43%
	July	638	461	72%	172	42	24%
	Total	929	667	72%	418	149	36%
Minnesota	February	120	88	73%	112	52	46%
	July	609	503	83%	63	18	29%
	Total	729	591	81%	175	70	40%
Mississippi	February	73	65	89%	25	5	20%
	July	162	132	81%	26	13	50%
	Total	235	197	84%	51	18	35%
Missouri	February	209	183	88%	94	53	56%
	July	712	620	87%	55	27	49%
	Total	921	803	87%	149	80	54%
Montana	February	33	27	82%	33	22	67%
	July	102	68	67%	10	1	10%
	Total	135	95	70%	43	23	53%
Nebraska	February	10	9	90%	29	14	48%
	July	171	140	82%	8	3	38%
	Total	181	149	82%	37	17	46%
Nevada	February	129	98	76%	93	37	40%
	July	245	168	69%	64	18	28%
	Total	374	266	71%	157	55	35%

[a]First-time exam takers are defined as examinees taking the bar examination for the first time in the reporting jurisdiction. Repeaters are defined as examinees who have taken the bar examination in the reporting jurisdiction at least once prior to the listed administration.

First-Time Exam Takers and Repeaters in 2015[a] (continued)

Jurisdiction	2015 Administration	First-Timers			Repeaters		
		Taking	Passing	% Passing	Taking	Passing	% Passing
New Hampshire	February	40	25	63%	8	2	25%
	July	148	107	72%	13	5	38%
	Total	188	132	70%	21	7	33%
New Jersey	February	517	311	60%	488	213	44%
	July	2,616	1,922	73%	330	138	42%
	Total	3,133	2,233	71%	818	351	43%
New Mexico	February	72	65	90%	21	9	43%
	July	153	119	78%	14	2	14%
	Total	225	184	82%	35	11	31%
New York	February	1,449	815	56%	2,548	898	35%
	July	8,586	6,045	70%	2,085	451	22%
	Total	10,035	6,860	68%	4,633	1,349	29%
North Carolina	February	248	137	55%	344	116	34%
	July	952	639	67%	258	64	25%
	Total	1,200	776	65%	602	180	30%
North Dakota	February	25	19	76%	19	5	26%
	July	51	42	82%	9	1	11%
	Total	76	61	80%	28	6	21%
Ohio	February	202	145	72%	209	117	56%
	July	931	743	80%	114	36	32%
	Total	1,133	888	78%	323	153	47%
Oklahoma	February	63	50	79%	44	22	50%
	July	275	203	74%	32	7	22%
	Total	338	253	75%	76	29	38%
Oregon	February	140	96	69%	110	63	57%
	July	336	227	68%	62	12	19%
	Total	476	323	68%	172	75	44%
Pennsylvania	February	320	219	68%	326	121	37%
	July	1,556	1,217	78%	243	63	26%
	Total	1,876	1,436	77%	569	184	32%
Rhode Island	February	35	25	71%	25	12	48%
	July	138	94	68%	16	4	25%
	Total	173	119	69%	41	16	39%
South Carolina	February	157	106	68%	92	52	57%
	July	372	279	75%	60	30	50%
	Total	529	385	73%	152	82	54%
South Dakota	February	11	5	45%	16	2	13%
	July	60	45	75%	13	4	31%
	Total	71	50	70%	29	6	21%
Tennessee	February	171	109	64%	190	86	45%
	July	589	436	74%	115	20	17%
	Total	760	545	72%	305	106	35%

[a]*First-time exam takers* are defined as examinees taking the bar examination for the first time in the reporting jurisdiction. *Repeaters* are defined as examinees who have taken the bar examination in the reporting jurisdiction at least once prior to the listed administration.

First-Time Exam Takers and Repeaters in 2015[a] (continued)

Jurisdiction	2015 Administration	First-Timers			Repeaters		
		Taking	Passing	% Passing	Taking	Passing	% Passing
Texas	February	725	503	69%	608	303	50%
	July	2,512	1,810	72%	475	175	37%
	Total	3,237	2,313	71%	1,083	478	44%
Utah	February	101	86	85%	28	17	61%
	July	263	203	77%	22	8	36%
	Total	364	289	79%	50	25	50%
Vermont	February	36	19	53%	4	0	0%
	July	48	29	60%	13	3	23%
	Total	84	48	57%	17	3	18%
Virginia	February	216	145	67%	268	142	53%
	July	1,001	757	76%	139	53	38%
	Total	1,217	902	74%	407	195	48%
Washington	February	201	151	75%	161	87	54%
	July	721	581	81%	93	37	40%
	Total	922	732	79%	254	124	49%
West Virginia	February	51	43	84%	40	19	48%
	July	151	115	76%	31	8	26%
	Total	202	158	78%	71	27	38%
Wisconsin	February	65	52	80%	22	11	50%
	July	105	79	75%	22	3	14%
	Total	170	131	77%	44	14	32%
Wyoming	February	17	15	88%	7	5	71%
	July	52	38	73%	5	2	40%
	Total	69	53	77%	12	7	58%
Guam	February	9	6	67%	1	0	0%
	July	7	3	43%	1	0	0%
	Total	16	9	56%	2	0	0%
N. Mariana Islands	February	3	3	100%	—	—	—
	July	3	3	100%	—	—	—
	Total	6	6	100%	—	—	—
Palau	February	No February examination					
	July	5	1	20%	8	0	0%
	Total	5	1	20%	8	0	0%
Puerto Rico[b]	February	176	51	29%	336	109	32%
	July	376	156	41%	300	85	28%
	Total	552	207	38%	636	194	31%
Virgin Islands	February	6	5	83%	—	—	—
	July	19	14	74%	2	1	50%
	Total	25	19	76%	2	1	50%
TOTALS	February	11,431	7,355	64%	12,900	5,219	40%
	July	43,516	31,130	72%	9,590	2,289	24%
	Total	54,947	38,485	70%	22,490	7,508	33%

[a]First-time exam takers are defined as examinees taking the bar examination for the first time in the reporting jurisdiction. Repeaters are defined as examinees who have taken the bar examination in the reporting jurisdiction at least once prior to the listed administration.

[b]Examinations in Puerto Rico are administered in March and September.

2015 First-Time Exam Takers and Repeaters
from ABA-Approved Law Schools[a]

Jurisdiction	2015 Administration	ABA First-Timers			ABA Repeaters		
		Taking	Passing	% Passing	Taking	Passing	% Passing
Alabama	February	77	61	79%	42	25	60%
	July	316	262	83%	23	5	22%
	Total	393	323	82%	65	30	46%
Alaska	February	37	31	84%	22	8	36%
	July	58	41	71%	16	4	25%
	Total	95	72	76%	38	12	32%
Arizona	February	301	198	66%	152	67	44%
	July	515	339	66%	134	29	22%
	Total	816	537	66%	286	96	34%
Arkansas	February	50	40	80%	58	28	48%
	July	186	141	76%	36	4	11%
	Total	236	181	77%	94	32	34%
California	February	672	331	49%	2,013	898	45%
	July	4,786	3,146	66%	1,292	267	21%
	Total	5,458	3,477	64%	3,305	1,165	35%
Colorado	February	224	158	71%	132	63	48%
	July	708	548	77%	86	26	30%
	Total	932	706	76%	218	89	41%
Connecticut	February	138	123	89%	63	23	37%
	July	360	296	82%	51	25	49%
	Total	498	419	84%	114	48	42%
Delaware	February	No February examination					
	July	150	109	73%	38	15	39%
	Total	150	109	73%	38	15	39%
Dist. of Columbia	February	105	62	59%	58	11	19%
	July	112	82	73%	49	14	29%
	Total	217	144	66%	107	25	23%
Florida	February	831	534	64%	630	224	36%
	July	2,687	1,851	69%	452	97	21%
	Total	3,518	2,385	68%	1,082	321	30%
Georgia	February	282	205	73%	256	97	38%
	July	1,059	780	74%	194	38	20%
	Total	1,341	985	73%	450	135	30%
Hawaii	February	57	45	79%	52	22	42%
	July	154	116	75%	27	9	33%
	Total	211	161	76%	79	31	39%
Idaho	February	33	27	82%	24	13	54%
	July	107	74	69%	9	5	56%
	Total	140	101	72%	33	18	55%
Illinois	February	538	437	81%	358	193	54%
	July	1,999	1,613	81%	190	61	32%
	Total	2,537	2,050	81%	548	254	46%
Indiana	February	166	126	76%	104	56	54%
	July	432	344	80%	63	20	32%
	Total	598	470	79%	167	76	46%

[a]First-time exam takers are defined as examinees taking the bar examination for the first time in the reporting jurisdiction. Repeaters are defined as examinees who have taken the bar examination in the reporting jurisdiction at least once prior to the listed administration.

BAR EXAMINATION STATISTICS

2015 First-Time Exam Takers and Repeaters from ABA-Approved Law Schools[a] (*continued*)

Jurisdiction	2015 Administration	ABA First-Timers			ABA Repeaters		
		Taking	Passing	% Passing	Taking	Passing	% Passing
Iowa	February	57	47	82%	34	19	56%
	July	207	188	91%	20	7	35%
	Total	264	235	89%	54	26	48%
Kansas	February	45	38	84%	20	15	75%
	July	94	76	81%	15	7	47%
	Total	139	114	82%	35	22	63%
Kentucky	February	125	98	78%	70	37	53%
	July	321	243	76%	54	24	44%
	Total	446	341	76%	124	61	49%
Louisiana	February	118	75	64%	181	122	67%
	July	577	402	70%	116	29	25%
	Total	695	477	69%	297	151	51%
Maine	February	33	27	82%	22	8	36%
	July	85	54	64%	12	3	25%
	Total	118	81	69%	34	11	32%
Maryland	February	272	198	73%	322	77	24%
	July	1,109	771	70%	192	51	27%
	Total	1,381	969	70%	514	128	25%
Massachusetts	February	285	207	73%	243	133	55%
	July	1,529	1,226	80%	153	43	28%
	Total	1,814	1,433	79%	396	176	44%
Michigan	February	290	205	71%	244	106	43%
	July	638	461	72%	170	42	25%
	Total	928	666	72%	414	148	36%
Minnesota	February	120	88	73%	112	52	46%
	July	609	503	83%	63	18	29%
	Total	729	591	81%	175	70	40%
Mississippi	February	73	65	89%	25	5	20%
	July	162	132	82%	26	13	50%
	Total	235	197	84%	51	18	35%
Missouri	February	207	181	87%	90	52	58%
	July	709	619	87%	53	26	49%
	Total	916	800	87%	143	78	55%
Montana	February	33	27	82%	33	22	67%
	July	102	68	67%	10	1	10%
	Total	135	95	70%	43	23	53%
Nebraska	February	10	9	90%	29	14	48%
	July	171	140	82%	8	3	38%
	Total	181	149	82%	37	17	46%
Nevada	February	129	98	76%	92	37	40%
	July	240	166	69%	62	18	29%
	Total	369	264	72%	154	55	36%

[a] *First-time exam takers* are defined as examinees taking the bar examination for the first time in the reporting jurisdiction. *Repeaters* are defined as examinees who have taken the bar examination in the reporting jurisdiction at least once prior to the listed administration.

2015 First-Time Exam Takers and Repeaters
from ABA-Approved Law Schools[a] (continued)

Jurisdiction	2015 Administration	ABA First-Timers			ABA Repeaters		
		Taking	Passing	% Passing	Taking	Passing	% Passing
New Hampshire	February	33	22	67%	6	2	33%
	July	144	105	73%	9	3	33%
	Total	177	127	72%	15	5	33%
New Jersey	February	517	311	60%	488	213	44%
	July	2,616	1,922	73%	330	138	42%
	Total	3,133	2,233	71%	818	351	43%
New Mexico	February	72	65	90%	21	9	43%
	July	153	119	78%	14	2	14%
	Total	225	184	82%	35	11	31%
New York	February	967	676	70%	1,419	626	44%
	July	6,533	5,183	79%	974	267	27%
	Total	7,500	5,859	78%	2,393	893	37%
North Carolina	February	248	137	55%	344	116	34%
	July	952	639	67%	258	64	25%
	Total	1,200	776	65%	602	180	30%
North Dakota	February	25	19	76%	19	5	26%
	July	51	42	82%	9	1	11%
	Total	76	61	80%	28	6	21%
Ohio	February	200	144	72%	203	115	57%
	July	929	743	80%	109	36	33%
	Total	1,129	887	79%	312	151	48%
Oklahoma	February	63	50	79%	44	22	50%
	July	275	203	74%	32	7	22%
	Total	338	253	75%	76	29	38%
Oregon	February	140	96	69%	108	63	58%
	July	336	227	68%	60	12	20%
	Total	476	323	68%	168	75	45%
Pennsylvania	February	319	219	69%	323	121	37%
	July	1,554	1,216	78%	240	63	26%
	Total	1,873	1,435	77%	563	184	33%
Rhode Island	February	35	25	71%	24	12	50%
	July	138	94	68%	16	4	25%
	Total	173	119	69%	40	16	40%
South Carolina	February	157	106	68%	92	52	57%
	July	372	279	75%	60	30	50%
	Total	529	385	73%	152	82	54%
South Dakota	February	11	5	45%	16	2	13%
	July	60	45	75%	13	4	31%
	Total	71	50	70%	29	6	21%
Tennessee	February	113	81	72%	138	63	46%
	July	511	406	79%	71	16	23%
	Total	624	487	78%	209	79	38%

[a]First-time exam takers are defined as examinees taking the bar examination for the first time in the reporting jurisdiction. Repeaters are defined as examinees who have taken the bar examination in the reporting jurisdiction at least once prior to the listed administration.

2015 First-Time Exam Takers and Repeaters
from ABA-Approved Law Schools[a] (continued)

Jurisdiction	2015 Administration	ABA First-Timers			ABA Repeaters		
		Taking	Passing	% Passing	Taking	Passing	% Passing
Texas	February	693	494	71%	600	300	50%
	July	2,431	1,793	74%	450	171	38%
	Total	3,124	2,287	73%	1,050	471	45%
Utah	February	100	85	85%	28	17	61%
	July	263	203	77%	22	8	36%
	Total	363	288	79%	50	25	50%
Vermont	February	36	19	53%	4	0	0%
	July	45	28	62%	9	2	22%
	Total	81	47	58%	13	2	15%
Virginia	February	215	144	67%	265	142	54%
	July	1,000	757	76%	135	53	39%
	Total	1,215	901	74%	400	195	49%
Washington	February	197	149	76%	150	84	56%
	July	698	570	82%	89	37	42%
	Total	895	719	80%	239	121	51%
West Virginia	February	50	43	86%	40	19	48%
	July	151	115	76%	30	8	27%
	Total	201	158	79%	70	27	39%
Wisconsin	February	63	51	81%	19	10	53%
	July	103	77	75%	18	3	17%
	Total	166	128	77%	37	13	35%
Wyoming	February	17	15	88%	7	5	71%
	July	52	38	73%	5	2	40%
	Total	69	53	77%	12	7	58%
Guam	February	9	6	67%	1	0	0%
	July	7	3	43%	1	0	0%
	Total	16	9	56%	2	0	0%
N. Mariana Islands	February	3	3	100%	—	—	—
	July	3	3	100%	—	—	—
	Total	6	6	100%	—	—	—
Palau	February	No February examination					
	July	1	1	100%	3	0	0%
	Total	1	1	100%	3	0	0%
Puerto Rico[b]	February	176	51	29%	326	108	33%
	July	376	156	41%	296	85	29%
	Total	552	207	38%	622	193	31%
Virgin Islands	February	6	5	83%	—	—	—
	July	19	14	74%	2	1	50%
	Total	25	19	76%	2	1	50%
TOTALS	February	9,773	6,762	69%	10,166	4,533	45%
	July	39,955	29,772	75%	6,869	1,921	28%
	Total	49,728	36,534	73%	17,035	6,454	38%

[a] First-time exam takers are defined as examinees taking the bar examination for the first time in the reporting jurisdiction. Repeaters are defined as examinees who have taken the bar examination in the reporting jurisdiction at least once prior to the listed administration.

[b] Examinations in Puerto Rico are administered in March and September.

2015 Exam Takers and Passers from Non-ABA-Approved Law Schools by Type of School

Jurisdiction	Conventional Law School[a]			Correspondence Law School[b]			Online Law School[c]		
	Taking	Passing	% Passing	Taking	Passing	% Passing	Taking	Passing	% Passing
Alabama	289	52	18%	—	—	—	—	—	—
Arizona	1	1	100%	—	—	—	—	—	—
California[d]	1,539	247	16%	159	30	19%	308	51	17%
Colorado	4	0	0%	—	—	—	—	—	—
Connecticut	38	4	11%	—	—	—	—	—	—
District of Columbia	15	3	20%	—	—	—	12	1	8%
Florida	1	0	0%	—	—	—	—	—	—
Georgia	24	0	0%	—	—	—	—	—	—
Maine	2	2	100%	—	—	—	—	—	—
Maryland	—	—	—	—	—	—	2	2	100%
Massachusetts	272	82	30%	—	—	—	—	—	—
Missouri	1	1	100%	—	—	—	—	—	—
Nevada	2	0	0%	—	—	—	—	—	—
New Hampshire	16	7	44%	—	—	—	—	—	—
New York	4	1	25%	—	—	—	—	—	—
Pennsylvania	1	0	0%	—	—	—	—	—	—
Tennessee	215	81	38%	—	—	—	—	—	—
Texas	6	3	50%	—	—	—	—	—	—
West Virginia	2	0	0%	—	—	—	—	—	—
Wisconsin	—	—	—	2	2	100%	1	1	100%
Puerto Rico	14	1	7%	—	—	—	—	—	—
TOTALS	2,446	485	20%	161	32	20%	323	55	17%

[a]*Conventional law schools* are fixed-facility schools that conduct instruction principally in physical classroom facilities.

[b]*Correspondence law schools* are schools that conduct instruction principally by correspondence.

[c]*Online law schools* are schools that conduct instruction and provide interactive classes principally by technological transmission, including Internet transmission and electronic conferencing.

[d]California applicants from non-ABA-approved law schools also include those who attended schools no longer in operation, composed of an unverifiable mixture of conventional, correspondence, and online schools. This number of applicants (84 taking, 0 passing) is therefore omitted from this chart.

BAR EXAMINATION STATISTICS

Attorneys' Examinations[a] in 2015

Jurisdiction	February			July			Total		
	Taking	Passing	% Passing	Taking	Passing	% Passing	Taking	Passing	% Passing
California	469	216	46%	413	144	35%	882	360	41%
Georgia	111	98	88%	124	96	77%	235	194	83%
Idaho	4	3	75%	4	4	100%	8	7	88%
Maine	18	16	89%	12	7	58%	30	23	77%
Maryland	78	65	83%	101	90	89%	179	155	87%
Rhode Island	22	17	77%	15	5	33%	37	22	59%
Vermont	40	19	48%	—	—	—	40	19	48%
N. Mariana Islands	2	2	100%	—	—	—	2	2	100%
TOTALS	744	436	59%	669	346	52%	1,413	782	55%

[a] *Attorneys' Examination* refers to a short form or other form of bar examination administered to attorneys admitted in other jurisdictions.

Examinations Administered to Disbarred or Suspended Attorneys as a Condition of Reinstatement in 2015[a]

Jurisdiction[b]	Taking	Passing	% Passing
Arizona	2	0	0%
California	48	1	2%
Georgia	1	0	0%
Kansas	1	1	100%
Kentucky	1	1	100%
Michigan	2	0	0%
Missouri	5	1	20%
New Hampshire	1	0	0%
North Dakota	1	0	0%
Texas	4	1	25%
Virginia	3	1	33%
TOTALS	69	6	9%

[a] The form of examination administered to disbarred or suspended attorneys varied among jurisdictions as follows: regular bar examination (8 jurisdictions), local component only (2 jurisdictions), Attorneys' Examination (1 jurisdiction).

[b] Florida reports only a subset of suspended attorneys who are required to take the Florida portion of the examination only. Disbarred and other suspended attorneys who are required to take the regular bar examination are reported with other test takers.

Ten-Year Summary of Bar Passage Rates, 2006–2015

Jurisdiction		2006	2007	2008	2009	2010	2011	2012	2013	2014	2015
Alabama	Overall	65%	64%	67%	65%	67%	65%	64%	64%	62%	54%
	First-Time	80%	78%	79%	77%	78%	77%	76%	78%	79%	71%
Alaska	Overall	62%	60%	70%	58%	71%	59%	67%	66%	66%	62%
	First-Time	75%	82%	80%	72%	81%	71%	78%	80%	78%	76%
Arizona	Overall	68%	70%	76%	73%	73%	70%	75%	73%	67%	57%
	First-Time	75%	78%	84%	80%	81%	76%	80%	78%	73%	66%
Arkansas	Overall	69%	70%	72%	67%	65%	71%	68%	65%	63%	65%
	First-Time	80%	80%	83%	74%	72%	84%	76%	76%	76%	77%
California	Overall	47%	49%	54%	49%	49%	51%	51%	51%	47%	44%
	First-Time	65%	66%	71%	66%	65%	67%	65%	65%	60%	57%
Colorado	Overall	68%	69%	73%	74%	74%	79%	77%	76%	74%	69%
	First-Time	76%	78%	83%	85%	83%	86%	84%	82%	78%	76%
Connecticut	Overall	75%	77%	78%	75%	71%	71%	73%	73%	75%	72%
	First-Time	83%	86%	87%	83%	81%	82%	82%	81%	86%	82%
Delaware	Overall	59%	62%	73%	63%	66%	67%	63%	72%	63%	66%
	First-Time	67%	71%	80%	71%	72%	73%	69%	78%	69%	73%
District of Columbia	Overall	51%	54%	56%	49%	41%	48%	51%	47%	40%	42%
	First-Time	72%	76%	70%	65%	60%	69%	68%	61%	57%	55%
Florida	Overall	64%	66%	71%	68%	69%	72%	71%	70%	65%	59%
	First-Time	75%	78%	81%	78%	78%	80%	79%	78%	72%	68%
Georgia	Overall	76%	75%	79%	76%	75%	76%	75%	76%	71%	62%
	First-Time	86%	85%	89%	86%	84%	85%	84%	85%	80%	73%
Hawaii	Overall	71%	70%	76%	76%	68%	75%	68%	73%	67%	66%
	First-Time	77%	82%	88%	86%	77%	83%	75%	81%	74%	76%
Idaho	Overall	79%	76%	72%	81%	78%	79%	80%	79%	68%	69%
	First-Time	85%	81%	80%	86%	83%	85%	86%	83%	73%	72%
Illinois	Overall	79%	82%	85%	84%	84%	83%	81%	82%	79%	74%
	First-Time	87%	89%	91%	91%	89%	89%	87%	88%	85%	80%
Indiana	Overall	76%	76%	78%	75%	75%	74%	72%	74%	69%	71%
	First-Time	84%	84%	84%	83%	81%	83%	79%	83%	79%	79%

Ten-Year Summary of Bar Passage Rates, 2006–2015 (*continued*)

Jurisdiction		2006	2007	2008	2009	2010	2011	2012	2013	2014	2015
Iowa	Overall	81%	83%	85%	88%	87%	84%	88%	88%	83%	82%
	First-Time	88%	89%	90%	93%	91%	90%	92%	93%	84%	89%
Kansas	Overall	82%	87%	86%	82%	84%	86%	84%	85%	82%	78%
	First-Time	90%	91%	89%	86%	90%	89%	89%	89%	86%	82%
Kentucky	Overall	73%	77%	77%	77%	77%	80%	76%	75%	76%	71%
	First-Time	82%	87%	83%	86%	82%	86%	82%	81%	81%	76%
Louisiana	Overall	70%	61%	62%	69%	61%	66%	59%	50%	62%	63%
	First-Time	76%	63%	66%	72%	65%	70%	63%	58%	69%	68%
Maine	Overall	73%	80%	86%	77%	88%	68%	68%	76%	71%	61%
	First-Time	81%	84%	91%	82%	89%	73%	73%	81%	76%	69%
Maryland	Overall	66%	67%	75%	69%	71%	74%	71%	73%	69%	58%
	First-Time	78%	76%	85%	78%	80%	81%	78%	80%	76%	65%
Massachusetts	Overall	77%	77%	80%	79%	81%	80%	77%	78%	73%	68%
	First-Time	87%	86%	89%	87%	88%	87%	83%	85%	81%	77%
Michigan	Overall	78%	76%	72%	81%	80%	76%	58%	62%	64%	61%
	First-Time	87%	86%	82%	89%	85%	82%	64%	69%	72%	72%
Minnesota	Overall	86%	88%	87%	85%	86%	88%	85%	85%	79%	73%
	First-Time	91%	93%	91%	90%	92%	93%	91%	90%	84%	81%
Mississippi	Overall	80%	81%	82%	78%	76%	73%	73%	77%	79%	75%
	First-Time	86%	88%	88%	85%	80%	81%	81%	85%	87%	84%
Missouri	Overall	82%	84%	87%	87%	86%	89%	89%	87%	84%	83%
	First-Time	88%	90%	91%	91%	90%	93%	92%	90%	87%	87%
Montana	Overall	91%	89%	91%	87%	89%	90%	91%	85%	65%	66%
	First-Time	92%	88%	92%	89%	93%	91%	93%	89%	70%	70%
Nebraska	Overall	80%	83%	84%	78%	81%	78%	73%	74%	70%	76%
	First-Time	83%	89%	89%	88%	90%	83%	83%	77%	77%	82%
Nevada	Overall	61%	60%	64%	60%	59%	65%	64%	61%	57%	60%
	First-Time	72%	74%	77%	73%	73%	76%	73%	73%	68%	71%
New Hampshire	Overall	77%	77%	88%	84%	80%	78%	82%	71%	81%	67%
	First-Time	82%	84%	88%	85%	82%	81%	84%	75%	86%	70%

Ten-Year Summary of Bar Passage Rates, 2006–2015 (*continued*)

Jurisdiction		2006	2007	2008	2009	2010	2011	2012	2013	2014	2015
New Jersey	Overall	73%	73%	77%	77%	76%	77%	71%	75%	71%	65%
	First-Time	81%	82%	85%	84%	82%	84%	78%	79%	76%	71%
New Mexico	Overall	86%	78%	85%	84%	81%	82%	84%	83%	83%	75%
	First-Time	91%	83%	92%	91%	88%	88%	89%	91%	88%	82%
New York	Overall	63%	64%	69%	65%	65%	64%	61%	64%	60%	56%
	First-Time	77%	77%	81%	77%	76%	76%	74%	76%	73%	68%
North Carolina	Overall	64%	65%	71%	67%	68%	70%	65%	59%	60%	53%
	First-Time	75%	76%	83%	77%	78%	80%	79%	69%	69%	65%
North Dakota	Overall	72%	69%	77%	80%	78%	83%	78%	72%	63%	64%
	First-Time	83%	79%	85%	87%	84%	85%	81%	80%	65%	80%
Ohio	Overall	74%	76%	79%	76%	78%	79%	76%	79%	73%	71%
	First-Time	83%	86%	88%	86%	86%	86%	84%	86%	81%	78%
Oklahoma	Overall	83%	85%	89%	80%	82%	83%	80%	81%	76%	68%
	First-Time	91%	91%	93%	87%	89%	88%	84%	86%	84%	75%
Oregon	Overall	72%	74%	71%	69%	68%	68%	72%	73%	65%	61%
	First-Time	80%	81%	78%	77%	75%	78%	81%	80%	73%	68%
Pennsylvania	Overall	71%	72%	77%	76%	74%	77%	73%	73%	71%	66%
	First-Time	83%	83%	87%	86%	83%	85%	82%	81%	81%	77%
Rhode Island	Overall	71%	75%	75%	74%	74%	69%	78%	71%	73%	63%
	First-Time	77%	79%	79%	78%	79%	74%	83%	76%	77%	69%
South Carolina	Overall	77%	79%	75%	72%	73%	73%	67%	75%	68%	69%
	First-Time	78%	82%	82%	78%	80%	77%	73%	79%	73%	73%
South Dakota	Overall	77%	85%	88%	83%	94%	94%	83%	87%	72%	56%
	First-Time	85%	89%	95%	90%	99%	94%	86%	91%	75%	70%
Tennessee	Overall	75%	71%	76%	68%	70%	69%	68%	73%	66%	61%
	First-Time	79%	80%	83%	77%	79%	77%	73%	82%	72%	72%
Texas	Overall	74%	76%	78%	78%	76%	80%	75%	80%	70%	65%
	First-Time	82%	84%	84%	85%	83%	86%	82%	85%	77%	71%
Utah	Overall	83%	81%	83%	83%	82%	84%	77%	82%	80%	76%
	First-Time	89%	85%	87%	89%	89%	88%	82%	87%	87%	79%

Ten-Year Summary of Bar Passage Rates, 2006–2015 *(continued)*

Jurisdiction		2006	2007	2008	2009	2010	2011	2012	2013	2014	2015
Vermont	Overall	68%	66%	65%	61%	76%	68%	65%	76%	67%	50%
	First-Time	78%	70%	79%	68%	87%	71%	69%	83%	75%	57%
Virginia	Overall	68%	67%	73%	69%	70%	72%	69%	71%	66%	68%
	First-Time	74%	76%	82%	76%	77%	79%	77%	77%	72%	74%
Washington	Overall	78%	77%	73%	67%	71%	66%	64%	76%	76%	73%
	First-Time	80%	78%	74%	69%	70%	67%	66%	82%	80%	79%
West Virginia	Overall	60%	63%	67%	73%	65%	74%	72%	68%	73%	68%
	First-Time	64%	74%	79%	81%	75%	83%	82%	76%	82%	78%
Wisconsin	Overall	78%	89%	89%	89%	90%	84%	83%	83%	74%	68%
	First-Time	82%	92%	92%	93%	92%	88%	86%	88%	81%	77%
Wyoming	Overall	72%	62%	64%	75%	71%	62%	53%	81%	72%	74%
	First-Time	74%	70%	67%	79%	75%	62%	60%	84%	78%	77%
Guam	Overall	75%	76%	75%	52%	80%	67%	57%	63%	68%	50%
	First-Time	70%	79%	73%	60%	90%	81%	60%	64%	77%	56%
N. Mariana Islands	Overall	88%	88%	83%	100%	63%	83%	100%	92%	88%	100%
	First-Time	88%	86%	83%	100%	57%	100%	100%	92%	88%	100%
Palau	Overall	27%	—	67%	17%	57%	25%	30%	63%	18%	8%
	First-Time	27%	—	50%	17%	67%	0%	38%	67%	15%	20%
Puerto Rico	Overall	46%	42%	44%	41%	42%	44%	36%	40%	39%	34%
	First-Time	57%	52%	52%	48%	50%	50%	45%	45%	45%	38%
Virgin Islands	Overall	73%	56%	76%	65%	71%	49%	64%	61%	73%	74%
	First-Time	70%	65%	84%	70%	77%	52%	70%	70%	77%	76%
AVERAGES	Overall	67%	67%	71%	68%	68%	69%	67%	68%	64%	59%
	First-Time	78%	79%	82%	79%	79%	79%	77%	78%	74%	70%

Admissions to the Bar by Type, 2011–2015

Jurisdiction	Admission by Examination					Admission on Motion/by Transferred UBE Score[a]				
	2011	2012	2013	2014	2015	2011	2012	2013	2014	2015
Alabama	516	533	465	461	408	32	—	38/—	30/10	36/10
Alaska	70	106	103	79	84	36	44	27	37/8	38/18
Arizona	506	629	722	683	635	183	145	176/8	171/38	153/47
Arkansas	260	253	242	219	212	47	55	60	47	56
California	6,627	6,846	7,008	6,726	6,150	—	—	—	—	—
Colorado	1,101	1,080	1,019	914	807	155	157	185/13	245/45	273/45
Connecticut	531	585	564	516	446	28	83	116	81	84
Delaware	122	147	148	122	99	—	—	—	—	—
District of Columbia	194	204	92	253	200	2,970	2,932	3,028	2,670	2,189
Florida	3,646	3,342	3,476	3,137	3,177	—	—	—	—	—
Georgia	1,165	1,144	1,245	1,297	1,029	123	124	132	178	176
Hawaii	208	219	206	203	188	—	—	—	—	—
Idaho	137	183	158	132	118	73	92	63/10	71/34	61/33
Illinois	2,793	2,786	2,944	2,676	2,327	135	191	240	293	198
Indiana	578	625	609	565	534	65	52	66	58	91
Iowa	335	364	328	294	262	96	79	88	97	93/1
Kansas	356	322	316	277	137	39	116	77	94	78/125
Kentucky	554	476	581	475	398	91	83	87	91	65
Louisiana	744	664	533	722	630	—	—	—	—	—
Maine	157	145	152	128	92	6	20	31	48	53
Maryland	1,653	1,685	1,742	1,637	1,382	—	—	—	—	—
Massachusetts	2,278	2,289	2,233	1,998	1,787	138	174	178	194	194
Michigan	979	878	1,061	1,011	849	120	138	187	192	233
Minnesota	732	825	796	752	662	191	233	215/17	200/48	201/76
Mississippi	252	248	265	233	205	34	33	40	35	27
Missouri	877	922	911	899	887	88	111	115/8	138/29	127/37
Montana	192	200	170	112	107	—	—	—/34	—/72	—/51
Nebraska	104	80	142	147	166	141	198	173/1	119/3	113/6
Nevada	542	550	343	319	321	—	—	—	—	—

[a]NCBE began collecting data for admission by transferred UBE score in 2013. Any persons admitted by transferred UBE score in 2011 (the first administration of the UBE, in which three jurisdictions administered the UBE) and 2012 (in which six jurisdictions administered the UBE) are included in those jurisdictions' admission on motion numbers.

BAR EXAMINATION STATISTICS

Admissions to the Bar by Type, 2011–2015 (*continued*)

Jurisdiction	Admission by Examination					Admission on Motion/by Transferred UBE Score[a]				
	2011	2012	2013	2014	2015	2011	2012	2013	2014	2015
New Hampshire	159	164	128	168	142	118	91	99/1	74/6	100/7
New Jersey	2,844	3,175	3,386	3,635	2,586	—	—	—	—	—
New Mexico	287	298	287	324	191	—	—	—	—	100/1
New York	9,309	9,046	9,698	10,273	8,261	546	613	553	476	606
North Carolina	1,032	1,094	997	1,102	956	69	76	94	107	116
North Dakota	67	102	85	76	64	128	185	174/8	132/28	102/53
Ohio	1,234	1,235	1,309	1,179	1,036	90	118	135	143	136
Oklahoma	411	510	392	328	278	54	73	71	69	72
Oregon	616	496	488	471	384	179	138	171	160	190
Pennsylvania	2,099	1,886	1,995	1,883	1,662	305	285	246	236	265
Rhode Island	185	204	201	158	175	—	—	—	—	—
South Carolina	508	526	598	469	494	—	—	—	—	—
South Dakota	74	87	91	52	62	22	23	30	22	31
Tennessee	681	668	858	709	616	140	124	153	135	125
Texas	3,097	2,988	3,356	2,892	2,805	379	408	480	533	541
Utah	545	390	424	441	437	61	53	53/22	61/43	67/44
Vermont	82	73	95	104	48	27	35	56	326	60
Virginia	1,411	1,577	1,528	1,224	1,050	41	43	62	98	202
Washington	923	935	1,006	910	856	225	232	318/29	484/69	819/84
West Virginia	224	221	208	185	181	83	73	66	53	61
Wisconsin	256	241	215	204	144	202	174	167	154	230
Wyoming	96	91	101	61	58	18	27	40/20	66/78	60/80
Guam	12	6	11	10	11	—	—	—	—	—
N. Mariana Islands	5	8	13	8	4	11	9	4	7	7
Palau	0	4	5	4	1	—	—	—	7	16
Puerto Rico	557	466	491	495	458	—	—	—	—	—
Virgin Islands	23	25	23	29	19	2	—	—	6	—
TOTALS	54,946	54,846	56,558	54,381	47,278	7,489	7,840	8,295/171	8,436/511	8,445/718

[a]NCBE began collecting data for admission by transferred UBE score in 2013. Any persons admitted by transferred UBE score in 2011 (the first administration of the UBE, in which three jurisdictions administered the UBE) and 2012 (in which six jurisdictions administered the UBE) are included in those jurisdictions' admission on motion numbers.

Admissions to the Bar by Type, 2011–2015 (*continued*)

Foreign Legal Consultants

Jurisdiction	2011	2012	2013	2014	2015
Arizona	—	1	1	—	—
California	3	4	13	17	14
Colorado	—	—	—	1	—
Delaware	1	—	—	—	—
District of Columbia	8	11	13	6	5
Florida	47	52	60	9	80
Georgia	—	1	2	1	1
Hawaii	—	—	—	1	—
Illinois	—	—	1	—	—
Massachusetts	1	—	1	1	2
Michigan	—	—	—	1	1
Minnesota	1	1	—	2	1
New Mexico	—	1	—	—	—
New York	23	36	26	36	36
North Carolina	—	—	—	1	1
Ohio	—	—	—	2	—
Pennsylvania	1	—	—	1	1
South Carolina	2	1	—	—	—
Texas	4	6	8	3	7
Virginia	—	—	1	—	3
Washington	—	1	2	3	2
TOTALS	91	115	128	85	154

Admission by Diploma Privilege[a]

Jurisdiction	2011	2012	2013	2014	2015
New Hampshire[b]	19	20	22	22	23
Wisconsin	462	463	461	417	407
TOTALS	481	483	483	439	430

[a]Diploma privilege is defined as an admissions method that excuses students from a traditional bar examination.

[b]Individuals are graduates of New Hampshire's Daniel Webster Scholar Honors Program, which is a two-year, performance-based program that includes clinical experience, portfolio review, and meetings with bar examiners.

BAR EXAMINATION STATISTICS

2015 Admissions to the Bar by Examination, on Motion, and by Diploma Privilege

(Note: Some jurisdictions have relatively low percentages of on-motion admissions, which may not be easily visible in this chart. Please refer to the accompanying chart on pages 34–36 for precise numbers.)

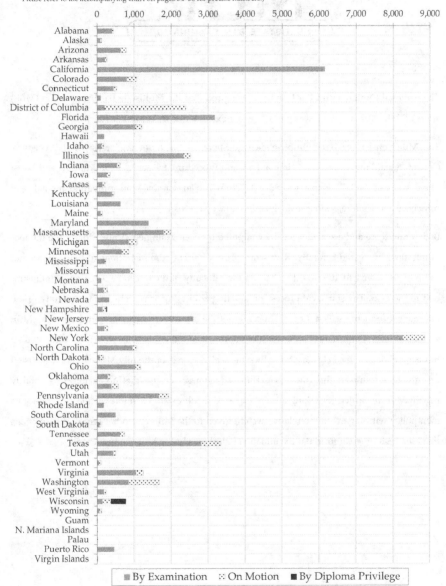

By Examination   ∴ On Motion   By Diploma Privilege

D-557

The National Conference of Bar Examiners has produced the Multistate Bar Examination (MBE) since 1972. In 2015, the MBE was part of the bar examination in 54 jurisdictions.

The MBE consists of 200 multiple-choice questions in the following areas: Civil Procedure, Constitutional Law, Contracts, Criminal Law and Procedure, Evidence, Real Property, and Torts. The purpose of the MBE is to assess the extent to which an examinee can apply fundamental legal principles and legal reasoning to analyze given fact patterns.

Both a raw score and a scaled score are computed for each examinee. A raw score is the number of questions answered correctly. Raw scores from different administrations of the MBE are not comparable, primarily due to differences in the difficulty of the questions from one administration to the next. The statistical process of equating adjusts for variations in the difficulty of the questions, producing scaled scores that represent the same level of performance across all MBE administrations. For instance, if the questions appearing on the July MBE were more difficult than those appearing on the February MBE, then the scaled scores for the July MBE would be adjusted upward to account for this difference. These adjustments ensure that no examinee is unfairly penalized or rewarded for taking a more or less difficult exam. Each jurisdiction determines its own policy with regard to the relative weight given to the MBE and other scores. (Jurisdictions that administer the Uniform Bar Examination [UBE] weight the MBE component 50%.)

BAR EXAMINATION STATISTICS

Jurisdictions Using the MBE in 2015

Key for Jurisdictions Using the MBE in 2015

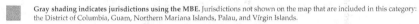

Gray shading indicates jurisdictions using the MBE. Jurisdictions not shown on the map that are included in this category: the District of Columbia, Guam, Northern Mariana Islands, Palau, and Virgin Islands.

No shading indicates jurisdictions not using the MBE. Jurisdiction not shown on the map that is included in this category: Puerto Rico.

2015 MBE
National Score Distributions[a]

MBE Scaled Score[b]	Percentage of Examinees	
	February (Mean = 136.2)	July (Mean = 139.9)
85	0.0	0.0
90	0.1	0.1
95	0.3	0.3
100	0.6	0.6
105	1.4	1.0
110	2.0	1.7
115	4.0	3.0
120	6.3	5.5
125	9.0	7.0
130	9.9	9.1
135	13.2	10.9
140	13.5	10.3
145	12.5	12.5
150	10.2	10.4
155	6.5	9.6
160	5.3	7.7
165	2.9	5.4
170	1.2	3.2
175	0.6	1.2
180	0.2	0.5
185	0.0	0.1
190	0.0	0.0

2015 MBE
National Summary Statistics
(Based on Scaled Scores)[a]

	February	July	2015 Total
Number of Examinees	22,396	48,384	70,780
Mean Scaled Score	136.2	139.9	138.7
Standard Deviation	15.1	16.1	15.9
Maximum	185.2	186.1	186.1
Minimum	63.5	47.7	47.7
Median	136.4	140.6	139.1

2015 MBE National Score Distributions[a]

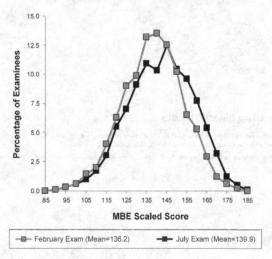

Legend: February Exam (Mean=136.2)   July Exam (Mean=139.9)

[a] The values reflect valid scores available electronically as of 12/8/2015.
[b] These data represent scaled scores in increments of 5. For example, the percentage reported for 135 includes examinees whose MBE scaled scores were between 130.5 and 135.4.

BAR EXAMINATION STATISTICS

MBE National Examinee Counts, 2006–2015[a]

	Number of Examinees		
	February	July	Year Total
2006	22,824	51,176	74,000
2007	22,250	50,181	72,431
2008	20,822	50,011	70,833
2009	18,868	50,385	69,253
2010	19,504	50,114	69,618
2011	20,369	49,933	70,302
2012	20,695	52,337	73,032
2013	21,578	53,706	75,284
2014	22,083	51,005	73,088
2015	22,396	48,384	70,780

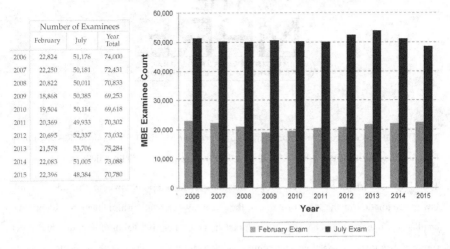

MBE National Mean Scaled Scores, 2006–2015[a]

	Mean Scaled Scores		
	February	July	Year Total
2006	137.5	143.3	141.5
2007	136.9	143.7	141.6
2008	137.7	145.6	143.3
2009	135.7	144.5	142.1
2010	136.6	143.6	141.7
2011	138.6	143.8	142.3
2012	137.0	143.4	141.6
2013	138.0	144.3	142.5
2014	138.0	141.5	140.4
2015	136.2	139.9	138.7

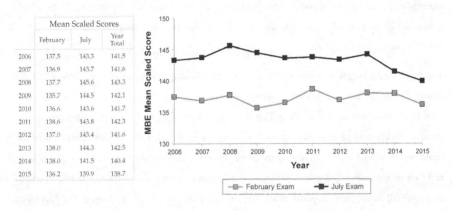

[a]The values reflect valid scores available electronically as of 12/8/2015.

D-561

THE
MPRE
MULTISTATE PROFESSIONAL
RESPONSIBILITY EXAMINATION

The National Conference of Bar Examiners has produced the Multistate Professional Responsibility Examination (MPRE) since 1980. In 2015, the MPRE was required in 53 jurisdictions.

The MPRE consists of 60 multiple-choice questions whose scope of coverage includes the following: regulation of the legal profession; the client-lawyer relationship; client confidentiality; conflicts of interest; competence, legal malpractice, and other civil liability; litigation and other forms of advocacy; transactions and communications with persons other than clients; different roles of the lawyer; safekeeping funds and other property; communications about legal services; lawyers' duties to the public and the legal system; and judicial conduct. The purpose of the MPRE is to measure the examinee's knowledge and understanding of established standards related to a lawyer's professional conduct.

The MPRE scaled score is a standard score. Standard scaled scores range from 50 (low) to 150 (high). The mean (average) scaled score was established at 100, based upon the performance of the examinees who took the MPRE in March 1999. The conversion of raw scores to scaled scores involves a statistical process that adjusts for variations in the difficulty of different forms of the examination so that any particular scaled score will represent the same level of knowledge from test to test. For instance, if a test is more difficult than previous tests, then the scaled scores on that test will be adjusted upward to account for this difference. If a test is easier than previous tests, then the scaled scores on the test will be adjusted downward to account for this difference. The purpose of these adjustments is to help ensure that no examinee is unfairly penalized or rewarded for taking a more or less difficult form of the test. Passing scores are established by each jurisdiction.

BAR EXAMINATION STATISTICS

Jurisdictions Using the MPRE in 2015
(with Pass/Fail Standards Indicated)

Key for Jurisdictions Using the MPRE in 2015

 **Gray shading indicates jurisdictions using the MPRE.** Jurisdictions not shown on the map that are included in this category: the District of Columbia (75), Guam (80), Northern Mariana Islands (80), Palau (75), and Virgin Islands (75).

No shading indicates jurisdictions not using the MPRE. Jurisdiction not shown on the map that is included in this category: Puerto Rico.

2015 MPRE
National Summary Statistics
(Based on Scaled Scores)[a]

	March	August	November	2015 Total
Number of Examinees	23,160	16,800	19,601	59,561
Mean Scaled Score	94.6	92.9	97.3	95.0
Standard Deviation	17.4	16.9	17.5	17.4
Maximum	150	149	150	150
Minimum	50	50	50	50
Median	96	92	99	96

2015 MPRE
National Score Distributions[a]

MPRE Scaled Score[b]	Percentage of Examinees		
	March (Mean = 94.6)	August (Mean = 92.9)	November (Mean = 97.3)
50	2.4	2.2	2.0
60	6.9	7.8	4.1
70	11.5	14.0	9.8
80	17.5	15.0	16.8
90	22.7	23.9	22.5
100	20.7	21.1	17.2
110	11.3	9.9	18.3
120	5.5	5.0	7.3
130	1.2	1.0	1.6
140	0.3	0.2	0.4
150	0.0	0.0	0.0

2015 MPRE National Score Distributions[a]

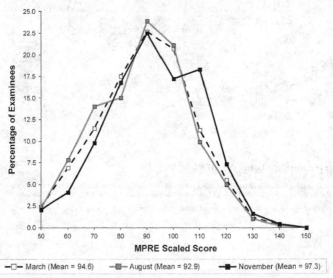

—□— March (Mean = 94.6)   —■— August (Mean = 92.9)   —■— November (Mean = 97.3)

[a]The values reflect valid scores available electronically as of 12/8/2015 on both standard and alternative forms of the MPRE.
[b]These data represent scaled scores in increments of 10. For example, the percentage reported for 70 includes examinees whose MPRE scaled scores were between 70 and 79.

BAR EXAMINATION STATISTICS

MPRE National Examinee Counts, 2006–2015[a]

	Number of Examinees			
	Mar./Apr.	Aug.	Nov.	Year Total
2006	21,684	15,986	23,308	60,978
2007	21,724	17,107	23,404	62,235
2008	20,288	16,536	23,568	60,392
2009	21,755	18,085	22,483	62,323
2010	22,478	18,641	23,345	64,464
2011	22,136	19,773	24,731	66,640
2012	24,280	19,028	23,191	66,499
2013	22,320	19,895	20,459	62,674
2014	22,957	17,699	19,888	60,544
2015	23,160	16,800	19,601	59,561

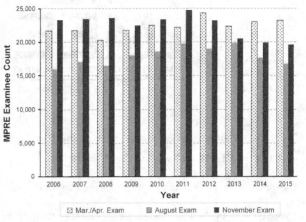

MPRE National Mean Scaled Scores, 2006–2015[a]

	Mean Scaled Scores			
	Mar./Apr.	Aug.	Nov.	Year Total
2006	98.6	96.9	98.1	98.0
2007	98.5	98.0	99.2	98.6
2008	98.9	95.6	97.9	97.6
2009	98.8	95.8	97.3	97.4
2010	97.4	95.7	97.2	96.8
2011	97.1	93.4	96.3	95.7
2012	99.3	95.8	97.2	97.6
2013	94.6	94.3	98.1	95.6
2014	93.1	93.1	94.5	93.6
2015	94.6	92.9	97.3	95.0

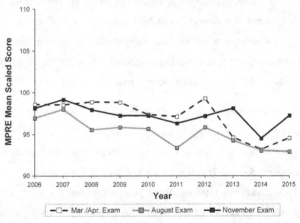

[a]The values reflect valid scores available electronically as of 12/8/2015 on both standard and alternative forms of the MPRE.

THE MEE

MULTISTATE ESSAY EXAMINATION

The National Conference of Bar Examiners has produced the Multistate Essay Examination (MEE) since 1988. In 2015, the MEE was used in 31 jurisdictions.

The MEE consists of six 30-minute questions per administration.

The purpose of the MEE is to test the examinee's ability to (1) identify legal issues raised by a hypothetical factual situation; (2) separate material which is relevant from that which is not; (3) present a reasoned analysis of the relevant issues in a clear, concise, and well-organized composition; and (4) demonstrate an understanding of the fundamental legal principles relevant to the probable solution of the issues raised by the factual situation. The primary distinction between the MEE and the Multistate Bar Examination (MBE) is that the MEE requires the examinee to demonstrate an ability to communicate effectively in writing.

Areas of law that may be covered on the MEE include the following: Business Associations (Agency and Partnership; Corporations and Limited Liability Companies), Civil Procedure, Conflict of Laws, Constitutional Law, Contracts, Criminal Law and Procedure, Evidence, Family Law, Real Property, Secured Transactions (UCC Article 9), Torts, and Trusts and Estates (Decedents' Estates; Trusts and Future Interests). Some questions may include issues in more than one area of law. The particular areas covered vary from exam to exam. Each jurisdiction determines its own policy with regard to the relative weight given to the MEE and other scores. (Jurisdictions that administer the Uniform Bar Examination [UBE] weight the MEE component 30%.)

BAR EXAMINATION STATISTICS

Jurisdictions Using the MEE in 2015

Key for Jurisdictions Using the MEE in 2015

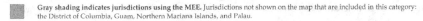

Gray shading indicates jurisdictions using the MEE. Jurisdictions not shown on the map that are included in this category: the District of Columbia, Guam, Northern Mariana Islands, and Palau.

No shading indicates jurisdictions not using the MEE. Jurisdictions not shown on the map that are included in this category: Puerto Rico and Virgin Islands. (The Virgin Islands will begin using the MEE in July 2016.)

*Kansas began using the MEE in February 2016.

† New York and Vermont will begin using the MEE in July 2016.

‡ South Carolina will begin using the MEE in February 2017.

D-567

THE MPT
MULTISTATE PERFORMANCE TEST

The National Conference of Bar Examiners has produced the Multistate Performance Test (MPT) since 1997. In 2015, the MPT was used in 41 jurisdictions.

NCBE offers two 90-minute MPT items per administration. A jurisdiction may select one or both items to include as part of its bar examination. (Jurisdictions that administer the Uniform Bar Examination [UBE] use two MPTs as part of their bar examinations.)

The MPT is designed to test an examinee's ability to use fundamental lawyering skills in a realistic situation. Each test evaluates an examinee's ability to complete a task that a beginning lawyer should be able to accomplish. The MPT requires examinees to (1) sort detailed factual materials and separate relevant from irrelevant facts; (2) analyze statutory, case, and administrative materials for applicable principles of law; (3) apply the relevant law to the relevant facts in a manner likely to resolve a client's problem; (4) identify and resolve ethical dilemmas, when present; (5) communicate effectively in writing; and (6) complete a lawyering task within time constraints. Each jurisdiction determines its own policy with regard to the relative weight given to the MPT and other scores. (Jurisdictions that administer the UBE weight the MPT component 20%.)

BAR EXAMINATION STATISTICS

Jurisdictions Using the MPT in 2015

Key for Jurisdictions Using the MPT in 2015

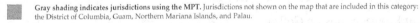 **Gray shading indicates jurisdictions using the MPT.** Jurisdictions not shown on the map that are included in this category: the District of Columbia, Guam, Northern Mariana Islands, and Palau.

No shading indicates jurisdictions not using the MPT. Jurisdictions not shown on the map that are included in this category: Puerto Rico and Virgin Islands. (The Virgin Islands will begin using the MPT in July 2016.)

*Kansas began using the MPT in February 2016.

† South Carolina will begin using the MPT in February 2017.

Association of American Law Schools 2016 Executive Committee

President

Kellye Y. Testy, University of Washington

President-Elect

Paul Marcus, College of William & Mary

Immediate Past President

Blake D. Morant, The George Washington University

Serving through 2016

Devon W. Carbado, University of California-Los Angeles

Vicki Jackson, Harvard University

Serving through 2017

Darby Dickerson, Texas Tech University

Avi Soifer, University of Hawai'i

Serving through 2018

Alicia Alvarez, The Univeristy of Michigan

Vincent Rougeau, Boston College

*Reprinted with permission from the Association of American Law Schools, Washington, D.C.

Association of American Law Schools Sections

Academic Sections

Administrative Law

Chair	Emily C. Hammond, The George Washington University Law School
	Phone: 336-758-5834
	E-mail: ehammond@law.gwu.edu
Chair-Elect	Linda D. Jellum, Mercer University School of Law
	Phone: (478) 301-5689
	E-mail: jellum_l@law.mercer.edu

Admiralty and Maritime Law

Chair	William V. Dunlap, Quinnipiac University School of Law
	Phone: (203) 582-3265
	E-mail: william.dunlap@quinnipiac.edu
Chair-Elect	Kristen van de Biezenbos, Texas Tech University School of Law
	Phone: (806) 742-3990
	E-mail: kristen.van-de-biezenbos@ttu.edu

Africa

Chair	Brian E. Ray, Cleveland-Marshall College of Law at Cleveland State University
	Phone: (216) 687-2528
	E-mail: brian.ray@law.csuohio.edu
Chair-Elect	W. Warren Hill Binford, Willamette University College of Law
	Phone: (503) 370-6758
	E-mail: wbinford@willamette.edu

Agency, Partnership, LLC's and Unincorporated Associations

Chair	Mohsen Manesh, University of Oregon School of Law
	Phone: (541) 346-3887
	E-mail: mohsen@uoregon.edu
Chair-Elect	Anne M. Tucker, Georgia State University College of Law
	Phone: 404. 413. 9179
	E-mail: amtucker@gsu.edu

---

* Reprinted with permission from the Association of American Law Schools, Washington, D.C.

Aging and the Law

Chair   Nina A. Kohn, Syracuse University College of Law
Phone: (315) 443-6565
E-mail: nakohn@law.syr.edu

Chair-Elect   Roberta K. Flowers, Stetson University College of Law
Phone: (727) 562-7863
E-mail: flowers@law.stetson.edu

Agricultural and Food Law

Chair   Susan Schneider, University of Arkansas, Fayetteville, Robert A. Leflar Law Center
Phone: (479) 575-4334
E-mail: sschneid@uark.edu

Chair-Elect   Michelle B. Nowlin, Duke University School of Law
Phone: 919-613-8502
E-mail: nowlin@law.duke.edu

Alternative Dispute Resolution

Chair   Cynthia J Alkon, Texas A&M University School of Law
Phone: (817) 212-3956
E-mail: calkon@law.tamu.edu

Chair-Elect   Jill I. Gross, Pace University Elisabeth Haub School of Law
Phone: (914) 422-4061
E-mail: jgross@law.pace.edu

Animal Law

Chair   Ani B. Satz, Emory University School of Law
Phone: (404) 712-9505
E-mail: asatz@emory.edu

Chair-Elect   Scott Hemphill, New York University School of Law
Phone: (212) 854-0593
E-mail: hemphill@nyu.edu

Antitrust and Economic Regulation

Chair   Hillary Greene, University of Connecticut School of Law
Phone: (860) 570-5211
E-mail: hillary.greene@uconn.edu

Chair-Elect   Scott Hemphill, New York University School of Law
Phone: (212) 854-0593
E-mail: hemphill@nyu.edu

Art Law

Chair   Sarah Burstein, University of Oklahoma College of Law
                   Phone: (405) 208-5337
                   E-mail: sarah.burstein@ou.edu

Chair-Elect   Tyler T. Ochoa, Santa Clara University School of Law
                   Phone: (408) 554-2765
                   E-mail: ttochoa@scu.edu

Biolaw

Chair   Oliver R. Goodenough, Vermont Law School
                   Phone: (802) 831-1231
                   E-mail: ogoodenough@vermontlaw.edu

Chair-Elect   Jonathan Kahn, Mitchell | Hamline School of Law
                   Phone: (651) 523-2948
                   E-mail: jonathan.kahn@mitchellhamline.edu

Business Associations

Chair   Usha R. Rodrigues, University of Georgia School of Law
                   Phone: (706) 542-5562
                   E-mail: rodrig@uga.edu

Chair-Elect   Michelle M. Harner, University of Maryland Francis King Carey School of Law
                   Phone: 410-706-4238
                   E-mail: mharner@law.umaryland.edu

Children and the Law

Chair   Annette R Appell, Washington University in St. Louis School of Law
                   Phone: 314-935-7912
                   E-mail: arappell@wulaw.wustl.edu

Chair-Elect   Rebecca Aviel, University of Denver Sturm College of Law
                   Phone: (303) 871-6521
                   E-mail: raviel@law.du.edu

Civil Procedure

Chair   Simona Grossi, Loyola Law School, Los Angeles
                   Phone: (213) 736-8140
                   E-mail: simona.grossi@lls.edu

Chair-Elect   Ira Steven Nathenson, St. Thomas University School of Law
                   Phone: (305) 474-2454
                   E-mail: inathenson@stu.edu

Civil Rights

Chair   Gilda Daniels, University of Baltimore School of Law
Phone: (410) 837-4607
E-mail: gdaniels@ubalt.edu

Chair-Elect   Cheryl Nelson Butler, Southern Methodist University, Dedman School of Law
Phone: (214) 768-2598
E-mail: cnbutler@smu.edu

Clinical Legal Education

Chair

Co-Chair   Eduardo R. Capulong, Alexander Blewett III School of Law at the University of Montana
Phone: (406) 243-6707
E-mail: eduardo.capulong@umontana.edu
Christine N. Cimini, Vermont Law School
Phone: (802) 831-1281
E-mail: ccimini@vermontlaw.edu

Chair-Elect

Co-Chair-
Elect   Lisa R. Bliss, Georgia State University College of Law
Phone: (404) 413-9131
E-mail: lbliss@gsu.edu

Commercial and Related Consumer Law

Chair   Nancy S. Kim, California Western School of Law
Phone: (619) 525-1693
E-mail: nsk@cwsl.edu

Chair-Elect   Pamela Foohey, Indiana University Maurer School of Law
Phone: (812) 855-1257
E-mail: pfoohey@indiana.edu

Comparative Law

Chair   Darren Rosenblum, Pace University Elisabeth Haub School of Law
Phone: (914) 422-4663
E-mail: drosenblum@law.pace.edu

Chair-Elect   Seval Yildirim, Whittier Law School
Phone: (714) 444-4141 (226)
E-mail: syildirim@law.whittier.edu

Conflict of Laws

Chair   Christopher A. Whytock, University of California, Irvine School of Law
Phone: (949) 824-0496
E-mail: cwhytock@law.uci.edu

Chair-Elect   Jamelle C. Sharpe, University of Illinois College of Law
Phone: (217) 244-1650
E-mail: jcsharpe@illinois.edu

Constitutional Law

Chair   Lauren Sudcall Lucas, Georgia State University College of Law
Phone: (404) 413-9258
E-mail: lslucas@gsu.edu

Chair-Elect   Rebecca E. Zietlow, University of Toledo College of Law
Phone: (419) 530-2872
E-mail: rebecca.zietlow@utoledo.edu

Contracts

Chair   Danielle K. Hart, Southwestern Law School
Phone: (213) 738-5720
E-mail: dhart@swlaw.edu

Chair-Elect   Val D. Ricks, South Texas College of Law
Phone: (713) 646-2944
E-mail: vricks@stcl.edu

Creditors' and Debtors' Rights

Chair   Anthony Casey, The University of Chicago, The Law School
Phone: (773) 702-9578
E-mail: ajcasey@uchicago.edu

Chair-Elect   Lea Krivinskas Shepard, Loyola University Chicago School of Law
Phone: (312) 915-6325
E-mail: lkrivinskas@luc.edu

Criminal Justice

Chair   Laurent Sacharoff, University of Arkansas, Fayetteville, Robert A. Leflar Law Center
Phone: (479) 575-4578
E-mail: lsacharo@uark.edu

Chair-Elect   Meghan J. Ryan, Southern Methodist University, Dedman School of Law
Phone: 214-768-2603
E-mail: meghanryan@mail.smu.edu

Defamation and Privacy

Chair   Dennis D. Hirsch, Capital University Law School
Phone: (614) 236-6685
E-mail: dhirsch@law.capital.edu

Chair-Elect   Lyrissa B. Lidsky, University of Florida Fredric G. Levin College of Law
Phone: (352) 273-0941
E-mail: lidsky@law.ufl.edu

Disability Law

Chair   William M. Brooks, Touro College, Jacob D. Fuchsberg Law Center
Phone: (631) 761-7086
E-mail: williamb@tourolaw.edu

Chair-Elect   Jessica L. Roberts, University of Houston Law Center
Phone: 713-743-2105
E-mail: jrobert6@central.uh.edu

East Asian Law and Society

Chair   Carole Silver, Northwestern University Pritzker School of Law
Phone: 312-503-1772
E-mail: c-silver@law.northwestern.edu

Chair-Elect   James V. Feinerman, Georgetown University Law Center
Phone: (202) 662-9030
E-mail: feinerma@law.georgetown.edu

Economic Globalization and Governance

No
information
available

Education Law

Chair   Laura McNeal, University of Louisville, Louis D. Brandeis School of Law
Phone: 502-852-8859
E-mail: laura.mcneal@louisville.edu

Chair-Elect   Aaron J. Saiger, Fordham University School of Law
              Phone: (212) 636-7736
              E-mail: asaiger@law.fordham.edu

Election Law

Chair   Michael J. Pitts, Indiana University Robert H. McKinney School of Law
              Phone: (317) 278-9155
              E-mail: mjpitts@iupui.edu

Chair-Elect   Franita Tolson, Florida State University College of Law
              Phone: (850) 644-7402
              E-mail: ftolson@law.fsu.edu

Employee Benefits and Executive Compensation

Chair   Regina T. Jefferson, The Catholic University of America, Columbus School of Law
              Phone: (202) 319-5025
              E-mail: jefferson@law.edu

Chair-Elect   Natalya Shnitser, Boston College Law School
              E-mail: natalya.shnitser@bc.edu

Employment Discrimination Law

Chair   Bradley A. Areheart, University of Tennessee College of Law
              Phone: (865) 974-6808
              E-mail: brad.areheart@tennessee.edu

Chair-Elect   Naomi Schoenbaum, The George Washington University Law School
              Phone: (202) 994-6261
              E-mail: nschoenbaum@law.gwu.edu

Environmental Law

Chair   Rebecca M. Bratspies, City University of New York School of Law
              Phone: (718) 340-4505
              E-mail: bratspies@law.cuny.edu

Chair-Elect   Robin K. Craig, University of Utah, S. J. Quinney College of Law
              Phone: (801) 585-5228
              E-mail: robin.craig@law.utah.edu

European Law

Chair   Roger J. Goebel, Fordham University School of Law
Phone: (212) 636-6844
E-mail: rgoebel@law.fordham.edu

Chair-Elect   Julie C. Suk, Benjamin N. Cardozo School of Law
Phone: (212) 790-0855
E-mail: jsuk@yu.edu

Evidence

Chair   Ann M. Murphy, Gonzaga University School of Law
Phone: (509) 868-9750
E-mail: murphya@gonzaga.edu

Chair-Elect   Andrew W. Jurs, Drake University Law School
Phone: 515-271-2067
E-mail: andrew.jurs@drake.edu

Family and Juvenile Law

Chair   Joel A. Nichols, University of St. Thomas School of Law
Phone: 651-962-4827
E-mail: joel.nichols@stthomas.edu

Chair-Elect   Jill Hasday, University of Minnesota Law School
Phone: (612) 626-6633
E-mail: jhasday@umn.edu

Federal Courts

Chair   Bradford R. Clark, The George Washington University Law School
Phone: (202) 994-2073
E-mail: bclark@law.gwu.edu

Chair-Elect   Curtis A. Bradley, Duke University School of Law
Phone: (919) 613-7179
E-mail: cbradley@law.duke.edu

Financial Institutions and Consumer Financial Services

Chair   Jennifer Taub, Vermont Law School
Phone: (802) 831-1107
E-mail: jtaub@vermontlaw.edu

Chair-Elect   Mehrsa Baradaran, University of Georgia School of Law
Phone: (706) 542-5294
E-mail: mehrsa@gmail.com

Graduate Programs for Non-U.S. Lawyers

Chair   Lauren Fielder, The University of Texas School of Law
Phone: (512) 471-5151
E-mail: lfielder@law.utexas.edu

Chair-Elect   John B. Thornton, Northwestern University Pritzker School of Law
E-mail: j-thornton@law.northwestern.edu

Immigration Law

Chair   Huyen T. Pham, Texas A&M University School of Law
Phone: (817) 212-3953
E-mail: hpham@law.tamu.edu

Chair-Elect   Rose Cuison Villazor, University of California, Davis, School of Law
Phone: (530) 752-4220
E-mail: rcvillazor@ucdavis.edu

Indian Nations and Indigenous Peoples

Chair   Michalyn Steele, Brigham Young University, J. Reuben Clark Law School
E-mail: steelem@law.byu.edu

Chair-Elect   Not available

Institutional Advancement

Chair

Co-Chair   Jill DeYoung, University of Iowa College of Law
Phone: (319) 335-9028
E-mail: jill-deyoung@uiowa.edu
Corley Raileanu, The Catholic University of America, Columbus School of Law
Phone: 202-319-4697
E-mail: raileanu@law.edu

Chair-Elect

Co-Chair   David Finley, Chapman University Dale E. Fowler School of
Elect   Law
E-mail: dfinley@chapman.edu
Allison Fry, Stanford Law School
Phone: (650) 725-9786
E-mail: aneumeister@law.stanford.edu

Insurance Law

Chair   Ezra Friedman, Northwestern University Pritzker School of Law
                 Phone: (312) 503-0230
                 E-mail: ezra-friedman@law.northwestern.edu

Chair-Elect   Allison K. Hoffman, University of California, Los Angeles
                 School of Law
                 Phone: (310) 206-5230
                 E-mail: hoffman@law.ucla.edu

Intellectual Property

Chair   Jessica Silbey, Northeastern University School of Law
                 Phone: (617) 305-6270
                 E-mail: j.silbey@neu.edu

Chair-Elect   Joe Miller, University of Georgia School of Law
                 Phone: (706) 542-7989
                 E-mail: getmejoe@uga.edu

International Human Rights

Chair   Milena Sterio, Cleveland-Marshall College of Law at Cleveland
                 State University
                 Phone: (216) 687-3852
                 E-mail: m.sterio@csuohio.edu

Chair-Elect   Timothy Webster, Case Western Reserve University School of
                 Law
                 E-mail: timothy.webster@case.edu

International Law

Chair   Shalanda H. Baker, University of Hawaii, William S. Richardson
                 School of Law
                 Phone: (808) 956-9345
                 E-mail: bakersh@hawaii.edu

Chair-Elect   Anastasia Telesetsky, University of Idaho College of Law
                 Phone: (208) 885-7510
                 E-mail: atelesetsky@uidaho.edu

Internet and Computer Law

Chair   Derek E. Bambauer, The University of Arizona James E. Rogers
                 College of Law
                 Phone: (520) 621-5499
                 E-mail: derekbambauer@email.arizona.edu

Chair-Elect	Margot Einan Kaminski, The Ohio State University, Michael E. Moritz College of Law
	Phone: (614) 292-2631
	E-mail: margot.kaminski@gmail.com

Islamic Law

Chair	Intisar A. Rabb, Harvard Law School
	Phone: (617) 998-9576
	E-mail: irabb@law.harvard.edu
Chair-Elect	Russell Powell, Seattle University School of Law
	Phone: (206) 398-4198
	E-mail: rpowell@seattleu.edu

Jewish Law

Chair	Timothy Daniel Lytton, Georgia State University College of Law
	Phone: (518) 445-2397
	E-mail: tlytton@gsu.edu
Chair-Elect	Noa Ben-Asher, Pace University Elisabeth Haub School of Law
	Phone: (914) 422-4545
	E-mail: nbenasher@law.pace.edu

Jurisprudence

Chair	Mary Anne Franks, University of Miami School of Law
	Phone: (305)284-5345
	E-mail: mafranks@law.miami.edu
Chair-Elect	Adil A. Haque, Rutgers Law School
	Phone: (973) 353-3264
	E-mail: ahaque@kinoy.rutgers.edu

Labor Relations and Employment Law

Chair	Michael Z. Green, Texas A&M University School of Law
	Phone: (817) 212-4140
	E-mail: mzgreen@law.tamu.edu
Chair-Elect	Danielle Weatherby, University of Arkansas, Fayetteville, Robert A. Leflar Law Center
	Phone: (479) 575-7959
	E-mail: dweath@uark.edu

Law and Anthropology

Chair	Khiara M. Bridges, Boston University School of Law
	Phone: (617) 358-6187
	E-mail: kmb73@bu.edu

Chair-Elect   Monica Eppinger, Saint Louis University School of Law
               Phone: (314) 977-4536
               E-mail: meppinge@slu.edu

Law and Economics

Chair   Jason S. Johnston, University of Virginia School of Law
               Phone: (434) 243-8552
               E-mail: jsj8q@virginia.edu

Chair-Elect   Jonah Gelbach, University of Pennsylvania Law School
               Phone: (215) 746-4574
               E-mail: jgelbach@law.upenn.edu

Law and Interpretation

Chair   Neil H. Cogan, Whittier Law School
               Phone: (714) 444-4141 (216)
               E-mail: ncogan@law.whittier.edu

Chair-Elect   Not available

Law and Mental Disability

Chair   Fredrick E. Vars, The University of Alabama School of Law
               Phone: (205) 348-0841
               E-mail: fvars@law.ua.edu

Chair-Elect   E. Lea Johnston, University of Florida Fredric G. Levin College
               of Law
               Phone: (352) 273-0794
               E-mail: johnstonl@law.ufl.edu

Law and Religion

Chair   Richard Albert, Boston College Law School
               Phone: 617-552-3930
               E-mail: richard.albert@bc.edu

Chair-Elect   Robin Fretwell Wilson, University of Illinois College of Law
               Phone: (217) 244-7582
               E-mail: wils@illinois.edu

Law and South Asian Studies

Chair   Manoj Mate, Whittier Law School
               Phone: 714-444-4141 (224)
               E-mail: mmate@law.whittier.edu

Chair-Elect   Priya Gupta, Southwestern Law School
               Phone: (213) 738-6777
               E-mail: psgupta@swlaw.edu

Law and Sports

Chair   Maureen A. Weston, Pepperdine University School of Law
         Phone: (310) 506-4676
         E-mail: mweston@pepperdine.edu

Chair-Elect   Ettie Ward, St. John's University School of Law
         Phone: (718) 990-6017
         E-mail: warde@stjohns.edu

Law and the Humanities

Chair   Rodger Daniel Citron, Touro College, Jacob D. Fuchsberg Law Center
         Phone: (631) 761-7115
         E-mail: rcitron@tourolaw.edu

Chair-Elect   Neil H. Cogan, Whittier Law School
         Phone: (714) 444-4141 (216)
         E-mail: ncogan@law.whittier.edu

Law and the Social Sciences

Chair   Douglas M. Spencer, University of Connecticut School of Law
         Phone: (860) 570-5437
         E-mail: douglas.spencer@uconn.edu

Chair-Elect   Victoria Sutton, Texas Tech University School of Law
         Phone: (806) 834-1752 (264)
         E-mail: vickie.sutton@ttu.edu

Law, Medicine and Health Care

Chair   Leslie P. Francis, University of Utah, S. J. Quinney College of Law
         Phone: (801) 581-4289
         E-mail: francisl@law.utah.edu

Chair-Elect   Elizabeth Pendo, Saint Louis University School of Law
         Phone: (314) 977-2767
         E-mail: ependo@slu.edu

Legal History

Chair   Anders Walker, Saint Louis University School of Law
         Phone: (314) 977-7447
         E-mail: awalke16@slu.edu

Chair-Elect   Mary Ziegler, Florida State University College of Law
         Phone: (850) 644-0364
         E-mail: mziegler@law.fsu.edu

Legal Writing, Reasoning and Research

Chair   Robert Brain, Loyola Law School, Los Angeles
                  Phone: (213) 736-8168
                  E-mail: bob.brain@lls.edu

Chair-Elect   Sabrina DeFabritiis, Suffolk University Law School
                  Phone: (617) 573-8108
                  E-mail: sdefabritiis@suffolk.edu

Legislation & Law of the Political Process

Chair   Richard Briffault, Columbia Law School
                  Phone: (212) 854-2638
                  E-mail: rb34@columbia.edu

Chair-Elect   Rebecca Kysar, Brooklyn Law School
                  E-mail: rebecca.kysar@brooklaw.edu

Litigation

Chair   Morris Ratner, University of California, Hastings College of the
                  Law
                  Phone: (415) 581-8853
                  E-mail: ratnerm@uchastings.edu

Chair-Elect   Katharine Traylor Schaffzin, The University of Memphis, Cecil
                  C. Humphreys School of Law
                  Phone: 901-678-1623
                  E-mail: k.schaffzin@memphis.edu

Mass Communication Law

Chair   Keith J. Bybee, Syracuse University College of Law
                  Phone: 315-443-9743
                  E-mail: kjbybee@maxwell.syr.edu

Chair-Elect   LaVonda N. Reed, Syracuse University College of Law
                  Phone: (315) 443-9578
                  E-mail: lareed@law.syr.edu

National Security Law

Chair   Sudha N. Setty, Western New England University School of Law
                  Phone: (413) 782-1431
                  E-mail: sudha.n.setty@gmail.com

Chair-Elect   Jennifer Daskal, American University, Washington College of
                  Law
                  Phone: (202) 274-4407
                  E-mail: jdaskal@wcl.american.edu

Natural Resources and Energy Law

Chair   Madeline June Kass, Thomas Jefferson School of Law
          Phone: (619) 961-4258
          E-mail: mkass@tjsl.edu

Chair-Elect   Gina Warren, Texas A&M University School of Law
          Phone: 817-212-3935
          E-mail: gswarren@law.tamu.edu

Nonprofit and Philanthropy Law

Chair   Garry W. Jenkins, The Ohio State University, Michael E. Moritz College of Law
          Phone: (614) 247-8338
          E-mail: jenkins.434@osu.edu

Chair-Elect   Roger Colinvaux, The Catholic University of America, Columbus School of Law
          Phone: (202) 319-5146
          E-mail: colinvaux@law.edu

North American Cooperation

Chair   Mark E. Wojcik, The John Marshall Law School
          Phone: (312) 987-2391
          E-mail: mwojcik@jmls.edu

Chair-Elect   Gerardo Puertas
          E-mail: gpuertas@fldm.edu.mx

Poverty Law

Chair   Jason Parkin, Pace University Elisabeth Haub School of Law
          Phone: (914) 422-4419
          E-mail: jparkin@law.pace.edu

Chair-Elect   Marc-Tizoc Gonzalez, St. Thomas University School of Law
          Phone: (305) 474-2441
          E-mail: mtgonzalez@stu.edu

Professional Responsibility

Chair   Barbara A. Glesner Fines, University of Missouri-Kansas City School of Law
          Phone: (816) 235-2380
          E-mail: glesnerb@umkc.edu

Chair-Elect   Susan S. Fortney, Texas A&M University School of Law
          Phone: 817-212-3902
          E-mail: sfortney@law.tamu.edu

Property Law

Chair   Ezra E.S. Rosser, American University, Washington College of Law

E-mail: erosser@wcl.american.edu

Chair-Elect   Donald J. Kochan, Chapman University Dale E. Fowler School of Law

E-mail: kochan@chapman.edu

Real Estate Transactions

Chair   Tanya D. Marsh, Wake Forest University School of Law

Phone: (336) 758-6059

E-mail: marshtd@wfu.edu

Chair-Elect   Kristen Barnes, University of Akron School of Law

Phone: (330) 972-7613

E-mail: barnes6@uakron.edu

Remedies

Chair   Andrew Hessick, University of Utah, S. J. Quinney College of Law

Phone: (801) 581-6833

E-mail: andy.hessick@law.utah.edu

Chair-Elect   Anthony J. Sebok, Benjamin N. Cardozo School of Law

Phone: (212) 790-0418

E-mail: sebok@yu.edu

Securities Regulation

Chair   Verity Winship, University of Illinois College of Law

Phone: (217) 244-8161

E-mail: vwinship@illinois.edu

Chair-Elect   Anita K. Krug, University of Washington School of Law

Phone: (206) 543-4145

E-mail: akrug@uw.edu

Sexual Orientation and Gender Identity Issues

Chair   Steven J. Macias, Southern Illinois University School of Law

Phone: (618) 453-8464

E-mail: smacias@law.siu.edu

Chair-Elect   Ann E. Tweedy, Mitchell | Hamline School of Law

Phone: 651-523-2076

E-mail: atweedy01@mitchellhamline.edu

Socio-Economics

Chair   Robert Cooter, University of California, Berkeley School of Law
Phone: (510) 642-0424
E-mail: rcooter@law.berkeley.edu

Chair-Elect   Thomas Earl Geu, University of South Dakota School of Law
Phone: (605) 677-6347
E-mail: thomas.geu@usd.edu

State and Local Government Law

Chair   Sara Bronin, University of Connecticut School of Law
Phone: (860) 570-5121
E-mail: sara.bronin@uconn.edu

Chair-Elect   Matthew J. Parlow, Marquette University Law School
Phone: 414.288.7842
E-mail: matthew.parlow@marquette.edu

Taxation

Chair   Stephen W. Mazza, University of Kansas School of Law
Phone: (785) 864-9266
E-mail: smazza@ku.edu

Chair-Elect   Lawrence A. Zelenak, Duke University School of Law
Phone: (919) 613-7267
E-mail: zelenak@law.duke.edu

Torts and Compensation Systems

Chair   Leslie Kendrick, University of Virginia School of Law
Phone: (434) 243-8633
E-mail: lck6s@virginia.edu

Chair-Elect   Christopher J. Robinette, Widener University Commonwealth
Law School
Phone: (717) 541-3993
E-mail: cjrobinette@widener.edu

Transactional Law and Skills

Chair   D. Gordon Smith, Brigham Young University, J. Reuben Clark
Law School
Phone: (801) 422-3233
E-mail: smithg@law.byu.edu

Chair-Elect   Brian JM Quinn, Boston College Law School
Phone: 617 552-2202
E-mail: bjmquinn@bc.edu

Trusts and Estates

Chair Alyssa A. DiRusso, Samford University, Cumberland School of Law
Phone: (205) 726-4325
E-mail: aadiruss@samford.edu

Chair-Elect Lee-ford Tritt, University of Florida Fredric G. Levin College of Law
Phone: (352) 273-0952
E-mail: tritt@law.ufl.edu

Administrative Sections

Academic Support

Chair Lisa Young, Seattle University School of Law
Phone: (206) 398-4000
E-mail: youngl@seattleu.edu

Chair-Elect Corie L. Rosen Felder, University of Colorado Law School
Phone: (303) 492-2781
E-mail: corie.rosen@colorado.edu

Associate Deans for Academic Affairs and Research

Chair Susan D. Rozelle, Stetson University College of Law
Phone: 727-562-7321
E-mail: srozelle@law.stetson.edu

Chair-Elect Viva Rivers Moffat, University of Denver Sturm College of Law
Phone: (303) 871-6508
E-mail: vmoffat@law.du.edu

Balance in Legal Education

Chair Susan L. Brooks, Drexel University Thomas R. Kline School of Law
Phone: 215 571 4784
E-mail: sb589@drexel.edu

Chair-Elect Jennifer A. Brobst, Southern Illinois University School of Law
Phone: 618-453-8702
E-mail: jbrobst@siu.edu

Continuing Legal Education

Chair Daniel McCarroll, University of Missouri-Kansas City School of Law
Phone: (816) 235-1649
E-mail: mccarrolld@umkc.edu

Chair-Elect   Jessica A. Justice Stolarik, West Virginia University College of Law
Phone: (304) 293-7497
E-mail: jessica.justice@mail.wvu.edu

Dean, for the Law School
Chair
Co-Chair   Craig M. Boise, Cleveland-Marshall College of Law at Cleveland State University
Phone: 216-687-2300
E-mail: c.boise@csuohio.edu
Rachel A. Van Cleave, Golden Gate University School of Law
Phone: (415) 442-6601
E-mail: rvancleave@ggu.edu

Co-Chair   J
Elect
Jane Byeff Korn, Gonzaga University School of Law
Phone: (509) 313-3700
E-mail: jkorn@lawschool.gonzaga.edu
Deanell Reece Tacha, Pepperdine University School of Law
Phone: (310) 506-4676
E-mail: deanell.tacha@pepperdine.edu

Graduate Programs for Non-U.S. Lawyers
Chair   Lauren Fielder, The University of Texas School of Law
Phone: (512) 471-5151
E-mail: lfielder@law.utexas.edu
Chair-Elect   John B. Thornton, Northwestern University Pritzker School of Law
E-mail: j-thornton@law.northwestern.edu

Institutional Advancement
Chair
Co-Chair   Jill DeYoung, University of Iowa College of Law
Phone: (319) 335-9028
E-mail: jill-deyoung@uiowa.edu
Corley Raileanu, The Catholic University of America, Columbus School of Law
Phone: 202-319-4697
E-mail: raileanu@law.edu

Chair-Elect

Co-Chair
Elect
David Finley, Chapman University Dale E. Fowler School of
Law
E-mail: dfinley@chapman.edu
Allison Fry, Stanford Law School
Phone: (650) 725-9786
E-mail: aneumeister@law.stanford.edu

International Legal Exchange

Chair
William H Byrnes, Texas A&M University School of Law
Phone: (817) 212-3969
E-mail: williambyrnes@law.tamu.edu

Chair-Elect
Mark E. Wojcik, The John Marshall Law School
Phone: (312) 987-2391
E-mail: mwojcik@jmls.edu

Law Libraries and Legal Information

Chair
Pauline M. Aranas, University of Southern California Gould
School of Law
Phone: (213) 740-6482
E-mail: paranas@law.usc.edu

Chair-Elect
Carol A Watson, University of Georgia School of Law
Phone: (706) 248-5721
E-mail: cwatson@uga.edu

Law School Administration and Finance

Chair
Debra J. Martin, Loyola Law School, Los Angeles
Phone: (213) 736-7420
E-mail: debra.martin@lls.edu

Chair-Elect
Michael S. Dean, Mercer University School of Law
Phone: (478) 301-2607
E-mail: dean_ms@law.mercer.edu

Part-Time Division Programs

Chair
Liam Skilling, University of Hawaii, William S. Richardson
School of Law
Phone: (808) 956-7966
E-mail: lskillin@hawaii.edu

Chair-Elect
Tracy L. Simmons, University of the Pacific, McGeorge School
of Law
Phone: (916) 549-7117
E-mail: tsimmons@pacific.edu

Post-Graduate Legal Education

Chair Aric K. Short, Texas A&M University School of Law
    Phone: (817) 212-4000
    E-mail: ashort@law.tamu.edu

Chair-Elect Deborah B. McGregor, Indiana University Robert H. McKinney School of Law
    Phone: (317) 274-2608
    E-mail: dmcgreg@iu.edu

PreLegal Education and Admission to Law School

Chair Shani Butts, The Catholic University of America, Columbus School of Law
    Phone: (202) 319-5151
    E-mail: butts@law.edu

Chair-Elect Michael W. Donnelly-Boylen, Roger Williams University School of Law
    Phone: (401) 254-4515
    E-mail: mdonnelly-boylen@rwu.edu

Pro-Bono & Public Service Opportunities

Chair Tara Casey, The University of Richmond School of Law
    Phone: (804) 289-8002
    E-mail: tcasey@richmond.edu

Chair-Elect Michele Storms, University of Washington School of Law
    Phone: (206) 543-4550
    E-mail: mestorms@uw.edu

Scholarship

Chair Eric C. Chaffee, University of Toledo College of Law
    Phone: (419) 530-2948
    E-mail: eric.chaffee@utoledo.edu

Chair-Elect Matthew T. Bodie, Saint Louis University School of Law
    Phone: 314-977-7507
    E-mail: mbodie@slu.edu

Student Services

Chair Macey Lynd Edmondson, University of Mississippi School of Law
    Phone: (662) 915-6819
    E-mail: maceye@olemiss.edu

Chair-Elect Albert Sturgeon, Pepperdine University School of Law
Phone: (310) 506-7695
E-mail: albert.sturgeon@pepperdine.edu

Teaching Methods

Chair Karin Mika, Cleveland-Marshall College of Law at Cleveland State University
Phone: (216) 687-5278
E-mail: k.mika@csuohio.edu

Chair-Elect Deborah Lee Borman, Northwestern University Pritzker School of Law
Phone: (312) 503-6748
E-mail: deborah.borman@gmail.com

Affinity Sections

Minority Groups

Chair Rose Cuison Villazor, University of California, Davis, School of Law
Phone: (530) 752-4220
E-mail: rcvillazor@ucdavis.edu

Chair-Elect Elena Marty-Nelson, Nova Southeastern University Shepard Broad College of Law
Phone: (954) 262-6186
E-mail: nelsone@nsu.law.nova.edu

New Law Professors

Chair Jennifer Carter-Johnson, Michigan State University College of Law
Phone: (517) 432-6989
E-mail: jcj@law.msu.edu

Chair-Elect Eugene D. Mazo, Rutgers Law School
Phone: (973) 353-5332
E-mail: emazo@kinoy.rutgers.edu

Women in Legal Education

Chair Rebecca E. Zietlow, University of Toledo College of Law
Phone: (419) 530-2872
E-mail: rebecca.zietlow@utoledo.edu

Chair-Elect Kerri L. Stone, Florida International University College of Law
Phone: (305) 348-1154
E-mail: stonek@fiu.edu

ASSOCIATION OF AMERICAN LAW SCHOOLS MEMBER SCHOOLS

University of Akron School of Law (AALS, 1974)

The University of Alabama School of Law (AALS, 1928)

Albany Law School (AALS, 1947)

American University, Washington College of Law (AALS, 1947)

Arizona State University Sandra Day O'Connor College of Law (AALS, 1969)

University of Arizona James E. Rogers College of Law (AALS, 1931)

University of Arkansas, Fayetteville, School of Law (AALS, 1927)

University of Arkansas at Little Rock, William H. Bowen School of Law (AALS, 1979)

University of Baltimore School of Law (AALS, 1988)

Baylor University Law School (AALS, 1938)

Boston College Law School (AALS, 1937)

Boston University School of Law (AALS, Charter Member)

Brigham Young University, J. Reuben Clark Law School (AALS, 1982)

Brooklyn Law School (AALS, 1973)

University at Buffalo School of Law, The State University of New York (AALS, 1937)

California Western School of Law (AALS, 1967)

University of California, Berkeley School of Law (AALS, 1912)

University of California, Davis, School of Law (AALS, 1968)

University of California, Hastings College of the Law (AALS, Charter Member, 1900-1927; 1949)

---

* Reprinted with permission from the Association of American Law Schools, Washington, D.C.

** "The," "The University of," and "University of" are discounted in alphabetizing the names of the law schools. For example, for purposes of alphabetization, "The University of Alabama School of Law" is listed as an "A" entry. If a law school is named after a person, that person's last name, not the first name, is used for alphabetization purposes. For example, "William Mitchell College of Law" is listed under the "M" entries. Names of law schools beginning with an abbreviation, such as "St." for "Saint" are alphabetized as though the abbreviation was spelled out.

University of California Irvine School of Law (AALS, 2016)

University of California, Los Angeles School of Law (AALS, 1952)

Capital University Law School (AALS, 1983)

Benjamin N. Cardozo School of Law, Yeshiva University (AALS, 1983)

Case Western Reserve University School of Law (AALS, Charter Member)

The Catholic University of America, Columbus School of Law (AALS, 1921)

Chapman University Dale E. Fowler School of Law (AALS, 2006)

University of Chicago, The Law School (AALS, 1902)

Chicago-Kent College of Law, Illinois Institute of Technology (AALS, 1951)

University of Cincinnati College of Law (AALS, Charter Member)

City University of New York School of Law (AALS, 2008)

Cleveland-Marshall College of Law at Cleveland State University (AALS, 1970)

University of Colorado Law School (AALS, Charter Member)

Columbia University Law School (AALS, Charter Member)

University of Connecticut School of Law (AALS, 1946)

Cornell Law School (AALS, Charter Member)

Creighton University School of Law (AALS, 1907)

University of Dayton School of Law (AALS, 1984)

University of Denver, Sturm College of Law (AALS, 1929)

DePaul University College of Law (AALS, 1924)

University of Detroit Mercy School of Law (AALS, 1934)

Drake University Law School (AALS, Charter Member)

Drexel University Thomas R. Kline School of Law (AALS, 2012)

Duke University School of Law (AALS, 1905-1919, under name of Trinity College, Department of Law; 1930)

Duquesne University School of Law (AALS, 1964)

Emory University School of Law (AALS, 1920)

University of Florida Fredric G. Levin College of Law (AALS, 1920)

Florida State University College of Law (AALS,1969)

Florida International University College of Law (AALS, 2009)

LAW SCHOOLS

Fordham University School of Law (AALS, 1936)

The George Washington University Law School (AALS, Charter Member)

The Antonin Scalia Law School at George Mason University (AALS, 1990)

Georgetown University Law Center (AALS, 1902)

University of Georgia School of Law (AALS, 1931)

Georgia State University College of Law (AALS, 1995)

Golden Gate University School of Law (AALS, 1980)

Gonzaga University School of Law (AALS, 1977)

Harvard Law School (AALS, Charter Member)

University of Hawaii William S. Richardson School of Law (AALS, 1989)

Maurice A. Deane School of Law at Hofstra University (AALS, 1972)

University of Houston Law Center (AALS, 1966)

Howard University School of Law (AALS, 1931)

University of Idaho College of Law (AALS, 1914)

University of Illinois College of Law (AALS, Charter Member)

Indiana University Robert H. McKinney School of Law (AALS, Charter Member)

Indiana University Maurer School of Law (AALS, Charter Member)

University of Iowa College of Law (AALS, Charter Member)

John Marshall Law School (AALS, 1979)

University of Kansas School of Law (AALS, Charter Member)

University of Kentucky College of Law (AALS, 1912)

Lewis and Clark Law School (AALS, 1973)

University of Louisville Louis D. Brandeis School of Law (AALS, 1933)

Louisiana State University, Paul M. Hebert Law Center (AALS, 1924)

Loyola University School of Law, Chicago (AALS, 1924)

Loyola Law School, Los Angeles (AALS, 1937)

Loyola University New Orleans College of Law (AALS, 1934)

University of Maine School of Law (AALS, Charter Member)

Marquette University Law School (AALS, 1912)

University of Maryland Francis King Carey School of Law (AALS, 1930)

McGeorge School of Law, University of the Pacific (AALS, 1974)

The University of Memphis Cecil C. Humphreys School of Law (AALS, 2001)

Mercer University Law School (AALS, 1923)

University of Miami School of Law (AALS, 1946)

The University of Michigan Law School (AALS, Charter Member)

Michigan State University College of Law (AALS, 1946)

University of Minnesota Law School (AALS, Charter Member)

University of Mississippi School of Law (AALS, 1929)

Mississippi College School of Law (AALS, 1990)

University of Missouri School of Law (AALS, Charter Member)

University of Missouri-Kansas City School of Law (AALS, 1938)

Mitchell | Hamline School of Law (AALS, 1982)

Alexander Blewett III School of Law at the University of Montana (AALS, 1914)

University of Nebraska College of Law (AALS, 1905)

University of Nevada, Las Vegas, William S. Boyd School of Law (AALS, 2004)

New England Law | Boston (AALS, 1998)

University of New Hampshire School of Law (AALS, 2014)

University of New Mexico School of Law (AALS, 1948)

New York Law School (AALS, 1974)

New York University School of Law (AALS, Charter Member)

North Carolina Central University School of Law (AALS, 2012)

Northern Illinois University College of Law (AALS, 1985)

Northern Kentucky University, Salmon P. Chase College of Law (AALS, 1984)

University of North Carolina School of Law (AALS, 1920)

University of North Dakota School of Law (AALS, 1910)

Northeastern University School of Law (AALS, 1945, closed 1956; Reopened 1968; 1970)

Northwestern University Pritzker School of Law (AALS, Charter Member)

Notre Dame Law School (AALS, 1924)

Nova Southeastern University Shepard Broad College of Law (AALS, 1989)

Ohio Northern University, Pettit College of Law (AALS, 1965)

The Ohio State University, Michael E. Moritz College of Law (AALS, Charter Member)

University of Oklahoma College of Law (AALS, 1911)

Oklahoma City University School of Law (AALS, 2003)

University of Oregon School of Law (AALS, 1919)

Pace University Elisabeth Haub School of Law (AALS, 1982)

University of Pennsylvania Law School (AALS, Charter Member)

The Pennsylvania State University – Dickinson Law (AALS, 1912-1924 resigned; 1934)

The Pennsylvania State University – Penn State Law (AALS, 2006)

Pepperdine University School of Law (AALS, 1980)

University of Pittsburgh School of Law (AALS, Charter Member)

University of Puerto Rico School of Law (AALS, 1948)

Quinnipiac University School of Law (AALS, 1985)

University of Richmond School of Law (AALS, 1920)

Roger Williams University School of Law (AALS, 2006)

Rutgers Law School (AALS, 1946)

Saint John's University School of Law (AALS, 1946)

Saint Louis University School of Law (AALS, 1924)

Saint Mary's University of San Antonio School of Law (AALS, 1949)

Saint Thomas University School of Law (AALS, 2001)

University of Saint Thomas School of Law (AALS, 2012)

Samford University, Cumberland School of Law (AALS, 1952)

University of San Diego School of Law (AALS, 1966)

University of San Francisco School of Law (AALS, 1937)

Santa Clara University School of Law (AALS, 1940)

Seattle University School of Law (AALS, 1974)

Seton Hall University School of Law (AALS, 1959)

University of South Carolina School of Law (AALS, 1924)

University of South Dakota School of Law (AALS, 1907)

Southern University Law Center (AALS, 2011)

South Texas College of Law (AALS, 1998)

University of Southern California, Gould School of Law (AALS, 1907)

Southern Illinois University School of Law (AALS, 1982)

Southern Methodist University, Dedman School of Law (AALS, 1929)

Southwestern Law School (AALS, 1974)

Stanford Law School (AALS, Charter Member)

Stetson University College of Law (AALS, 1931)

Suffolk University Law School (AALS, 1977)

Syracuse University College of Law (AALS, Charter Member)

Temple University, James E. Beasley School of Law (AALS, 1935)

University of Tennessee College of Law (AALS, Charter Member)

Texas Southern University, Thurgood Marshall School of Law (AALS, 2014)

Texas Tech University School of Law (AALS, 1969)

The University of Texas School of Law (AALS, 1907)

Texas A&M University School of Law (AALS, 2012)

University of Toledo College of Law (AALS, 1941)

Thomas Jefferson School of Law (AALS, 2008)

Touro College Jacob D. Fuchsberg Law Center (AALS, 1994)

Tulane University Law School (AALS, 1909)

The University of Tulsa College of Law (AALS, 1966)

University of Utah, S.J. Quinney College of Law (AALS, 1929)

Valparaiso University School of Law (AALS, 1930)

Vanderbilt University School of Law (AALS, 1910)

Vermont Law School (AALS, 1982)

Villanova University Charles Widger School of Law (AALS, 1957)

University of Virginia School of Law (AALS, 1916)

LAW SCHOOLS

Wake Forest University School of Law (AALS, 1935)

Washburn University School of Law (AALS, 1905)

Washington and Lee University School of Law (AALS, 1920)

University of Washington School of Law (AALS, 1909)

Washington University School of Law (AALS, Charter Member)

Wayne State University Law School (AALS, 1946)

West Virginia University College of Law (AALS, 1914)

Western New England University School of Law (AALS, 1981)

Whittier Law School (AALS, 1987)

Widener University Commonwealth Law School (AALS, 1989)

Widener University Delaware Law School (AALS, 1987)

Willamette University College of Law (AALS, 1946)

William & Mary Law School (AALS, 1936)

University of Wisconsin Law School (AALS, Charter Member)

University of Wyoming College of Law (AALS, 1923)

Yale Law School (AALS, Charter Member)

E. PROFESSIONAL PUBLICATIONS

LEGAL NEWSPAPERS

Akron Legal News
(mon to fri) (Law)
60 S Summit St, Akron, OH,
44308-1775;
gen tel (330) 376-0917; adv tel (330)
376-0917; gen fax (330) 376-7001;
gen e-mail aln97@apk.net; web site
www.akronlegalnews.com
Advertising Rate:
Open inch rate $11.00
News services:
AP.
Pres./Pub. John L.
Vice Pres./Gen. Mgr. Robert Heffern
Ed. Susan Maybury
Gen. Mngr. Jason Crosten

Bay County Legal News
(thur) (Law)
PO Box 278, Bay City, MI,
48707-0278,
Bay ; gen tel (989) 893-6344; adv tel
(989)893-6344; ed tel (989) 893-6344;
gen fax (989) 893-2991; adv fax (989)
893-2991; ed fax (989) 893-2991; gen
e-mail bcdem@sbcglobal.net; adv
e-mail bcdem@sbcglobal.
net; ed e-mail bcdem@sbcglobal.net;
web site bclegalnews.com
Circulation: 900(pd)
January 7, 2004

Advertising Rate:
Open inch rate $5.00
Established: 1892
Gen. Mgr. Carol DeVeau

Brooklyn Daily Eagle & Daily Bulletin
(mon to fri) (Law)
16 Court St Ste 1208, Brooklyn, NY,
11241-1012; gen tel (718) 858-2300;
gen fax (718) 858-8281; gen e-mail
publisher@brooklyneagle.net; web
site www.brooklyneagle.net
Advertising Rate:
Open inch rate $24.00
Pub. J.D. Hasty
Adv. Mgr. Patricia Higgins
Adv. Mgr., Legal Daniel Doctorow
Adv. Mgr., Special Projects Ted
Cutler
Sam Howe
Mng. Ed. Ron Geberer

Chicago Daily Law Bulletin
(mon to fri) (Law)
415 N State St, Chicago, IL,
60654-4674;
gen tel (312) 644-7800; gen fax (312)
644-4255; gen e-mail
displayads@lbpc.com; web
site www.lawbulletin.com
Advertising Rate:
Open inch rate $26.40 (Classified),
$2,588.00 (Full Page Display)

News services:
AP, NYT.
Chrmn. Lanning Macfarland
Pres./CEO Brewster Macfarland
Exec. Vice Pres. Neil Breen
James Banich
Consultant Bernie Judge
Adv. Sr. Dir., Sales/Mktg. Mark
Menzies
Mng. Ed. Stephen Brown
Fred Faulkner
Adam Music
Patrick Milhizer

Cincinnati Court Index
(mon to fri) (Law)
119 W Central Pkwy Fl 2,
Cincinnati, OH,
45202-1075; gen tel (513) 241-1450;
gen fax (513) 684-7821; gen e-mail
support@courtindex.com; web site
www.courtindex.com
Advertising Rate:
Open inch rate $9.00
News services:
AP.
Ed. Mark Veatty

Daily Commerce
(e-mon to fri) (Law)
PO Box 54026, Los Angeles, CA,
90054-0026, Los Angeles; gen tel
(213) 229-5300;
adv tel (213) 229-5511; ed tel (213)
229-5558; gen fax (213) 229 5481;
adv fax (213)
229 5481; ed fax (213) 229-5462;
gen e-mail
audreymiller@dailyjournal.com;
web site www.dailyjournal.com

Circulation: 1,254(pd)
September 24, 1998
Advertising Rate:
Open inch rate $12.00
News services:
AP, LAT-WP, NYT..
Established: 1888
Pub. Gerald L. Salzman
Adv. Rep. Audrey Miller
Circ. Mgr. Ray Chagolla
Ed. Lisa Churchill
Mgmt. Info Servs. Mgr. Ky Tu
Prodn. Mgr. Manuel Azuiler

Daily Commercial Record
(mon to fri) (Law)
706 Main St Bsmt, Dallas, TX,
75202-
3699; gen tel (214) 741-6366; gen
fax (214) 741-6373; gen e-mail dcr@
dailycommercialrecord.com; web site
www.dailycommercialrecord.com
Advertising Rate:
Open inch rate $14.76
Pub. E. Nuel Cates Jr.
Ed. Emily Cates

Daily Court Reporter
(mon to fri) (Law)
120 W 2nd St Ste 418, Dayton, OH,
45402-1602; gen tel (419) 470-8602;
gen fax (937) 341-5020; gen e-mail
info@thedailycourt.
com; web site www.dailycourt.com
Advertising Rate:
Open inch rate $12.00
News services:
American Court & Commercial
Newspapers.
Pres./Pub. Jeffrey Foster
Editorial Mgr. Virginia Steitz

Daily Court Review
(mon to fri) (Law)
PO Box 1889, Houston, TX,
77251-1889;
gen tel (713) 869-5434; ed tel (713)
869-5434; gen fax (713) 869-8887; ed
e-mail editor@dailycourtreview.com;
web site www.dailycourtreview.com
Advertising Rate:
Open inch rate $16.80
News services:
RN, National Newspaper
Association, Texas
Press Association.
Established: 1889
Pub. Tom Morin
Editor Michael Clements

Daily Journal of Commerce
(mon to fri) (Law)
921 SW Washington St Ste 210,
Portland,
OR, 97205-2810, Multnomah; gen
tel (503)
226-1311; adv tel (503) 226-1311; gen
fax (503) 226-1315; adv fax (503)
802-7219; ed fax (503) 802-7239;
gen e-mail
newsroom@djcoregon.com; adv
e-mail
rynni.henderson@djcoregon.com; ed
e-mail
stephanie.basalyga@djcoregon.com;
web site djcoregon.com
Group:
The Dolan Company
Advertising Rate:
Open inch rate $25.00
News services:
AP, RN, TMS.
Established: 1872
Digital Platform - Mobile:
Apple, Android
Ed. Stephanie Basalyga

Publisher/Vice President Rynni
Henderson

Daily Legal News
(mon to fri) (Law)
100 E Federal St Ste 126,
Youngstown,
OH, 44503-1834; gen tel (330)
747-7777;
gen fax (330) 747-3977; gen e-mail
john@
akronlegalnews.com; web site
www.dlnnews.com
Advertising Rate:
Open inch rate $5.00
Pres. John Burleson
Office Mgr. Kim Pierson
Adv. Dir. Ellen Dellaserra

Daily Record
(mon to fri) (Law)
3323 Leavenworth St, Omaha, NE,
68105-1900, Douglas; gen tel (402)
345-1303; gen fax (402) 345-2351;
gen e-mail
lhenningsen@omahadailyrecord.com;
adv
e-mail
diane@omahadailyrecord.com; ed
e-mail
lorraine@omahadailyrecord.com;
web
site www.omahadailyrecord.com
Advertising Rate:
Open inch rate $7.25
News services:
Associated Press, Creators Syndicate,
U.S. News Syndicate.
Established: 1886
Publisher Lynda K. Henningsen
Editor Lorraine Boyd

Production Brian Henningsen
Advertising (Classified, Display,
Website)
Diane Bilek
Legal Editor/Legal Notices Mary
Mosher
Legal Notice Judy Boyd
Note:
Bona fide paid circulation in
Douglas County
in excess of 300 copies, printed in
Omaha, NE

Daily Report
(mon to fri) (Law)
190 Pryor St SW, Atlanta, GA,
30303-3607;
gen tel (404) 521-1227; gen fax (404)
523-5924; gen e-mail
fcdr@amlaw.com; web site
www.dailyreportonline.com
Advertising Rate:
Open inch rate $1,800.00 (page)
Established: 1890
Office Mgr. Sarah Wagner
Adv. Dir. Mischelle Grant
Assoc. Pub. Ed Bean
Mng. Ed. Jonathan Ringel
Art. Dir. Jason Bennitt
Pub. Wayne Curtis

Finance and Commerce
(tues to sat) (Law)
730 2nd Ave S Ste 100, Minneapolis,
MN, 55402-5767, Hennepin; gen tel
(612) 333-4244; adv tel (612)
584-1545; ed tel (612)
584-1526; gen fax (612) 333-3243;
gen e-mail
info@finance-commerce.com; web
site www.finance-commerce.com
Advertising Rate:
Open inch rate $12.00

News services:
AP.
Established: 1887
Vice Pres./Pub. Steve Jahn
Bus. Mgr. Joann Barquest
Jeanne Reiland
Prodn. Mgr. Nancy Spangler

Fulton County Daily Report (Law)
190 Pryor St SW, Atlanta, GA,
30303-3685,
Fulton; gen tel (404) 521-1227; adv
tel
(404) 419-2870; adv fax (404) 419-
2819;
gen e-mail lsimcoe@alm.com; web
site
dailyreportonline.com
Group:
ALM
Circulation: 3,297(pd); 225(fr);
VAC
December 30, 2014
Digital Platform - Mobile:
Apple, Android, Windows,
Blackberry
Editor Ed Bean
Group Publisher Wayne Curtis
Systems Director Scott Pitman
Regional Editor-in-Chief George
Haj
Mng. Ed. Jonathan Ringel

Garfield County Legal News (Law)
302 E Maine Ave, Enid, OK,
73701-5746,
Garfield ; gen tel (580) 234-4739; adv
tel
(580) 234-4739; ed tel (580)
234-4739; gen fax (580) 237-3237;
adv fax (580) 237-3237;

ed fax (580) 237-3237; gen e-mail
info@
garfieldcountylegalnews.com; ed
e-mail
publisher@garfieldcountylegalnews.com;
web site
www.garfieldcountylegalnews.com
Advertising Rate:
$50.00 ($0.15 per word) (Notice to
Creditors)
Established: 1913

Miami Daily Business Review
(mon to fri) (Law)
PO Box 10589, Miami, FL,
33101-0589,
Miami-Dade; gen tel (305) 377-3721;
adv tel (305) 347-6623; ed tel (305)
347-6694; gen fax (305) 374-8474;
adv fax (305) 347-6644; ed fax (305)
347-6626; gen e-mail
DailyBusinessReview@alm.com; adv
e-mail
ccurbelo@alm.com; ed e-mail
dlyons@alm.
com; web site
www.dailybusinessreview.com
Group:
ALM Media
Advertising Rate:
Varies:
http://www.dailybusinessreview.com/
advertising.jsp;
N/A(Sun)
News services:
AP, Bloomberg, Florida News
Service. Established: 1926
Group Publisher, FL/GA/TX Chris
Mobley
Associate Publisher/Chief Financial
Officer Jeff Fried
Director of Advertising Carlos
Curbelo Editor-in-Chief David
Lyons Business Editor Jay Rees
Law Editor Catherine Wilson
Director of Creative Services John
Michael Rindo
Director of Operations & MIS
Guillermo Garcia
Web Adminstrator John Hernandez
Vice President/Miami-Dade Legal &
Court Relations Sookie Williams
Note:
See Daily Business Review editions
in Broward and Palm Beach, FL.

Missouri Lawyers Media (Law)
319 N 4th St Fl 5, 5th Floor, Saint
Louis,
MO, 63102-1907, St. Louis; gen tel
(314)
421-1880; adv tel (314) 558-3260; ed
tel
(314) 558-3220; gen fax (314)
621-1913;
adv fax (314) 421-7080; ed fax (314)
621-1913; gen e-mail
stephen.hughes@
molawyersmedia.com; adv e-mail
jadii.
castillo@molawyersmedia.com; ed
e-mail jill.
miller@molawyersmedia.com; web
site www.
molawyersmedia.com
Group:
The Dolan Company
Circulation: 4,500(pd); 10,820(fr)
October 1, 2013
Advertising Rate:
Full Page $2,200.00
Established: 1890

Digital Platform - Mobile:
Apple, Android, Windows
Digital Platform - Tablet:
Apple iOS, Android, Windows 7
Pub. S. Richard Gard
Production Mgr. John Reno
Managing Ed. Lora Wegman

New York Law Journal
(mon to fri) (Law)
120 Broadway Fl 5, New York, NY,
10271-1100; gen tel (212) 457-9400;
gen fax (212)
417-7705; gen e-mail
cservice@nylj.com;
web site www.nylj.com
Advertising Rate:
Open inch rate $99.40
News services:
AP.
Established: 10271
Pres./CEO William L. Pollak
CFO Eric Lundberg
Pub. George Dillehay
Adv. Vice Pres., Nat'l Steve Lincoln
Martha Sturgeon
Circ. Mktg. Mgr. Michael Bennett
Ed. in Chief Rex Bossert

Palm Beach Daily Business Review
(mon to fri) (Law)
1 SE 3rd Ave, Suite 900, Miami, FL,
33131-1700; gen tel (305) 377-3721;
adv
tel (305) 347-6623; ed tel (305)
347-6694;
gen fax (561) 820-2077; adv fax (305)
347-6644; ed fax (305) 347-6626; gen
e-mail
DailyBusinessReview@alm.com; adv
e-mail
ccurbelo@alm.com; ed e-mail
dlyons@alm.
com; web site

www.dailybusinessreview.com
Group:
ALM Media
Advertising Rate:
http://www.dailybusinessreview.com/
advertising.jsp;
N/A(Sun)
News services:
AP, Bloomberg, Florida News
Service.
Established: 1979
Group Publisher, FL/GA/TX Chris
Mobley
Associate Publisher/Chief Financial
Officer
Jeff Fried
Editor-in-Chief David Lyons
Vice President/Broward & Palm
Beach
Legals Deborah Mullin
Director of Advertising Carlos
Curbelo
Group Subscriptions Manager
Annette
Martinez
Web Administrator John Hernandez
Business Editor Jay Rees
Law Editor Cathy Wilson
Director of Client Development
Stephanie
Hemmerich
Audience Development Manager
Adam
Kaplan
Note:
See Daily Business Reviews editions
in
Broward and Miami, FL.

Pittsburgh Legal Journal
(mon to fri) (Law)
436 7th Ave Ste 4, Pittsburgh, PA,
15219-1827, Allegheny; gen tel (412)

402-6623;
gen fax 412-320-7965; gen e-mail
JPULICE@SCBA.ORG; web site
WWW.
PITTSBURGHLEGALJOURNAL.
COM
Group:
Pennsylvania NewsMedia
Association
Advertising Rate:
Open inch rate $8.75
Established: 1853
Exec. Dir. David Blaner

Saint Paul Legal Ledger
(mon to thur) (Law)
332 Minnesota St Ste E1432, Saint
Paul, MN, 55101-1309, Ramsey; gen
tel (651) 222-0059; ed tel (651)
602-0575; gen fax
(651) 222-2640; gen e-mail
steve.jahn@
finance-commerce.com; web site
www.legalledger.
com
Advertising Rate:
Open inch rate $12.00 (legal)
News services:
AP.
Established: 55101-1163
Pub. Patrick Boulay
Bus. Mgr. Barbara St. Martin
Adv. Mgr., Display Jay Kodytek
Bill Wolfe
Prodn. Supvr., Pressroom Mike
Wolfe

San Francisco Daily Journal
(mon to fri) (Law)
44 Montgomery St Ste 500, San
Francisco,
CA, 94104-4607; gen tel (415)

296-2400;
gen fax (415) 296-2440; web site
www.
dailyjournal.com
Advertising Rate:
Open inch rate $754.00 (quarter
page)
News services:
AP.
Ed. Linda Hubbell

St. Joseph Daily Courier
(mon to fri) (Law)
1020 S 10th St, Saint Joseph, MO,
64503-2407; gen tel (816) 279-3441;
gen fax
(816) 279-2091; gen e-mail
sjdailycourier@
sbcglobal.net
Pres./Pub. Bill Cunningham

St. Louis Daily Record
(mon to sat; S) (Law)
PO Box 88910, Saint Louis, MO,
63188-1910; gen tel (314) 421-1880;
adv tel (314)
421-1880; ed tel (314) 421-1880; gen
fax (314) 421-0436; adv fax (314)
421-7080; ed fax (314) 421-0436; gen
e-mail
editcopy@thedailyrecord.com; adv
e-mail
wildk@thedailyrecord.com; ed
e-mail will.
connaghan@molawyersmedia.com;
web site www.molawyers.com
Group:
Missouri Press Service, Inc.
Advertising Rate:
Open inch rate $6.56

News services:
R.N.
Pub. Richard Gard
Bus. Mgr. Amanda Passmore
Adv. Dir. Amy Burdge
Circ. Mgr. Stacey Fish
Richard Jackoway
Assoc. Ed. William B. Connaghan
Information Servs. Mgr. Robert
Doyle
Prodn. Mgr. John M. Reno

The Daily Commercial Recorder
(mon to fri) (Law)
P.O. Box 2171, San Antonio, TX,
78297, Bexar; gen tel (210) 250-2439;
gen fax (210) 250-2360; gen e-mail
dcr@primetimenewspapers.com; web
site www.
primetimenewspapers.com
Group:
Hearst Media Services
Advertising Rate:
Open inch rate $25.00
News services:
ACCN, Creator Syndicates,
LAT-WP, National
American Press Syndicate, NYT..
General Sales Manager Mickey
Urias

The Daily Events
(mon to fri) (Law)
PO Box 1, Springfield, MO,
65801-0001,
Greene; gen tel (417) 866-1401; gen
fax (417) 866-1491; gen e-mail
info@dailyevents.
com; web site
www.thedailyevents.com
News services:
American Court & Commercial
Newspapers.
Established: 1881

Editor Wendy Greyowl
Associate Editor Susan Barnes
Court Reporter Andrea Donohue
Circulation Manager Jasmin Adams
Court Reporter Lindsey Wheeler
Publisher Jeff Schrag

The Daily Journal
(mon to fri) (Law)
1114 W 7th Ave Ste 100, Denver, CO,
80204-4455; gen tel (303) 756-9995;
adv tel (303)
584-6737; ed tel (303) 584-6724; gen
fax (303) 756-4465; adv fax (303)
584-6717; ed fax (303) 756-4465; web
site colorado.
construction.com
Advertising Rate:
Open inch rate $25.20
Established: 1897Open inch rate
$25.20 John
Adv. Dir. John Rhoades
Adv. Mgr. Michael Branigan
Ed. Melissa Leslie
Mark Shaw

The Daily Legal News
(mon to fri) (Law)
501 Texas St Rm M103, Shreveport,
LA, 71101-5403; gen tel (318)
222-0213; web site
www.dailylegalnews.net
Advertising Rate:
Open inch rate $15.00/wk (3 1/2" x
1"), $25.00/2wk, $35.00/3wk
Pub. Lee Ann Bryce

*The Daily Legal News and Cleveland
Recorder*
(tues to sat) (Law)
2935 Prospect Ave E, Cleveland, OH,
44115-2688, Cuyahoga; gen tel (216)

696-3322; gen
fax (216) 696-6329; gen e-mail
dln@dln.com;
adv e-mail ads@dln.com; ed e-mail
editor@
dln.com; web site www.dln.com
Advertising Rate:
Open inch rate $16.00
News services:
AP, National Newspaper
Association, Ohio
Newspaper Association.
Established: 1885
Sec./Gen. Counsel John D. Karlovec
Controller Frederick Davis
Richard Karlovec
Mng. Ed. Jeffrey B. Karlovec
editor@dln.com Lisa Cech
Prodn. Mgr. Terry Machovina
Kurt Gutwein

The Daily News
(mon to fri) (Law)
193 Jefferson Ave, Memphis, TN,
38103-2339, Shelby; gen tel (901)
523-1561; adv
tel (901) 528-8122; ed tel (901)
523-8501;
gen fax (901) 526-5813; adv fax (901)
526-5813; ed fax (901) 526-5813; gen
e-mail
advertising@memphisdailynews.com;
adv
e-mail
leah@memphisdailynews.com; ed
e-mail
joverstreet@memphisdailynews.com;
web site
www.memphisdailynews.com
Group:
The Daily News Publishing Co.
Circulation: 1,000(pd); 2,000(fr);
USPS

Advertising Rate:
Open inch rate $13.50 (legal)
News services:
CNS.
Established: 1886
Publisher Eric Barnes
Marketing Director Leah Sansing
Associate Publisher/Exec. Ed. James
Overstreet

The Daily Record
(mon to fri) (Law)
PO Box 30006, Rochester, NY,
14603-3006; gen tel (585) 232-6920;
gen fax
(585) 232-2740; gen e-mail
kevin.momot@
nydailyrecord.com; web site www.
nydailyrecord.com
Advertising Rate:
Open inch rate $.90 (agency line),
$.75 (retail line)
News services:
American Court & Commercial
Newspapers,
National Newspaper Association.
Established: 14603-3006
Chrmn./CEO James P. Dolan
Vice Pres./Pub. Kevin Momot
CFO Scott Pollei
Tara Buck

The Daily Record
(mon to fri) (Law)
PO Box 3595, Little Rock, AR,
72203-3595, Pulaski; gen tel (501)
374-5103; gen fax (501) 372-3048;
gen e-mail bobby@dailydata.com;
adv e-mail jedwards@dailydata.com;
ed e-mail editor@dailydata.
com; web site www.dailyrecord.us

Circulation: 3,210(pd); 25(fr);
USPS
October 4, 2011
Advertising Rate:
Column Inch Rate - $20.00
News services:
NNS, TMS, DRNW, INS.
Established: 1925
Pres Don Bona
Pub. Bill F. Rector
Adv./Mktg. Dir. Jay Edwards
GM Bobby Burton
Comptroller Robin Hill

The Daily Record
(mon to sat; S) (Law)
405 E 13th St Ste 101, Kansas City,
MO, 64106-2830; gen tel (816)
931-2002; adv tel (816) 931-2002; gen
fax (816) 561-6675; adv fax (816)
561-6675; gen e-mail
mail@kcdailyrecord.com; adv e-mail
www.kcdailyrecord.com
Advertising Rate:
Open inch rate $9.80
Pub. Richard Gard
Bus. Mgr. Amanda Passmore
Kansas City Office Mgr. Peter
Crawford
Prodn. Mgr. John Reno

The Daily Record
(mon to fri) (Law)
PO Box 1062, Louisville, KY,
40201-1062;
gen tel (502) 583-4471; gen fax (502)
585-5453; gen e-mail
janicep@nacms-c.com
Advertising Rate:
Open inch rate $1.20 (legal line)
News services:
National Association of Credit
Management.
Established: 40201

Pub. Connie J. Cheak
Mng. Ed. Janice Prichard

The Daily Recorder
(mon to fri) (Law)
PO Box 1048, Sacramento, CA,
95812-1048;
gen tel (916) 444-2355; adv tel (800)
652-1700; gen fax (916) 444-0636;
gen e-mail
daily_recorder@dailyjournal.com; ed
e-mail jt_long@dailyjournal.com;
web site www.
dailyjournal.com
Advertising Rate:
Open inch rate $26.00
News services:
AP, dj.
Established: 1901
Pres./Pub. Jerry Salzman
Cor. Office Dir. Raymond Chagolla
Personnel Dir. Dorothy Salzman
Ed. Michael Gottlieb
Tom Barragan
Prodn. Designer Houay Keobouth

The Daily Reporter
(mon to fri) (Law)
PO Box 514033, Milwaukee, WI,
53203-3433;
gen tel (414) 276-0273; gen fax (414)
276-4416; adv fax (414) 276-8057; ed
fax (414)
276-4416; gen e-mail
news@dailyreporter.
com; web site
www.dailyreporter.com
Advertising Rate:
Open inch rate $12.30 (R.O.P. &
classified),
$1.75 (legal line)

News services:
AP.
Pres./CEO Stephen Staloch
Adv. Dir. Lisa Oertel
Associate Editor Dan Shaw

The Daily Territorial
(m-mon to fri) (Law)
3280 E Hemisphere Loop Ste 180,
Tucson,
AZ, 85706-5027, Pima; gen tel (520)
294-1200; adv tel (520) 294-1200; ed
tel (520) 294-1200; gen fax (520)
294-4040; adv fax (520) 294-4040; ed
fax (520) 295-4071;
gen e-mail editor@azbiz.com; adv
e-mail advertising@azbiz.com; ed
e-mail dhatfield@azbiz.com; web site
www.azbiz.com
Group:
Wick Communications Co Inc
Circulation: 753(pd);
Sworn
Advertising Rate:
Open inch rate $5.45
News services:
American Newspaper
Representatives Inc . . .
Established: 1966
Pub. Thomas Lee
Adv. Dir. Jill A'Hearn
Adv. Mgr., Legal Monica Akyol
Circ. Dir. Laura Horvath
Ed. David Hatfield
Art Dir. Andrew Arthur
Prodn. Mgr. Greg Day

The Inter-City Express
(mon to fri) (Law)
1109 Oak St Ste 103, Oakland, CA,
94607-4917; gen tel (510) 272-4747;
gen fax (510)
465-1576
Pub. Nell Fields

Adv. Dir. Dan Gougherty
Adv. Mgr., Legal Tonya Peacock
Ed. Tom Barkley
Ronald McNees

The Journal Record
(mon to fri) (Law)
PO Box 26370, Oklahoma City, OK,
73126-0370, Oklahoma; gen tel (405)
235-3100; adv tel (405) 278-2830; ed
tel (405) 278-2850;
gen fax (405) 278-6907; ed fax (405)
278-2890; ed e-mail
news@journalrecord.com;
web site www.journalrecord.com
Group:
The Dolan Company
Circulation: 2,509(pd); 69(fr);
VAC
December 31, 2012
Advertising Rate:
Open inch rate $18.62
News services:
AP, CSM, DMN.
Established: 1903
Bus. Mgr. Terri Vanhooser
Ed. Ted Streuli
Prodn. Mgr. Gary Berger
Advertising and Community
Relations
Managers Sunny Cearly
Pub. Joni Brooks

The Legal Intelligencer
(mon to fri) (Law)
1617 John F Kennedy Blvd Ste 1750,
Philadelphia, PA, 19103-1854, Del
Val; gen tel (215) 557-2300; adv tel
(215) 557-2359;
ed tel (215) 557-2489; gen fax (215)
557-2301; adv fax (215) 557-2301; ed
fax (215)

557-2301; gen e-mail
HGREZLAK@ALM.
COM; adv e-mail
dchalphin@alm.com; ed
e-mail hgrezlak@alm.com; web site
www.thelegalintelligencer.com
Group:
ALM Media
News services:
AP.
Established: 1843
Publisher Hal Cohen
Associate Publisher Donald
Chalphin
Note:
See media kit for market
information.

The Los Angeles Daily Journal
(mon to fri) (Law)
915 E 1st St, Los Angeles, CA,
90012-4042, Los Angeles; gen tel
(213) 229-5300; gen fax (213)
229-5481; ed fax (213) 229-5462; web
site www.dailyjournal.com
Advertising Rate:
Open inch rate $69.16 (page)
News services:
AP, NYT, CNS, McClatchy.
Chrmn. of the Bd. Charles T.
Munger Vice Chrmn. of the Bd. J.P.
Guerin Pub. Gerald Salzman
Adv. Dir. Audrey Miller
Ramond Chagolla
Ed. Martin Berg

The Record Reporter
(Mon`Wed`Fri) (Law)Maricopa; gen
tel (602) 417-9900; gen fax (602)
417-9910; gen e-mail
Diane_Heuel@dailyjournal.com;
adv e-mail
record_reporter@dailyjournal.com;
ed e-mail

Christopher_Gilfillan@recordreporter.
com ; web site
www.recordreporter.com
Group:
DAILY JOURNAL
CORPORATION
Established: 1914
Digital Platform - Mobile:
Apple, Android, Blackberry
Digital Platform - Tablet:
Apple iOS, Android, Blackberry
Tablet OS
Pub. Diane Heuel
Ed. Christopher Gilfillan

The Recorder
(mon to fri) (Law)
1035 Market St Ste 500, San
Francisco, CA, 94103-1650; gen tel
(415) 749-5400; adv tel
(415) 749-5444; gen fax (415)
749-5449; adv fax (415) 749-5566; ed
fax (415) 749-5549;
gen e-mail
recorder_editor@alm.com; web
site www.therecorder.com
Advertising Rate:
Open inch rate $3,200.00 (Full Page
Display)
News services:
AP.
Established: 1877
Pub. Chris Braun
Controller Janice Tang
Adv. Mgr., Classified Patrick Vigil
Adv. Mgr., Display Jim Tamietti
Robert Salapuddin
Adv. Coord., Display Heather
Ragsdale
Mktg. Dir. John Cosmides
Circ. Mgr. Ed Vergara
Scott Graham

Mng. Ed. Greg Mitchell
Prodn. Mgr./Art Dir. Tess Herrmann

The St. Louis Countian
(mon to sat; S) (Law)
319 N 4th St, Saint Louis, MO,
63102-1906; gen tel (314) 421-1880;
adv tel (314) 421-1880; ed tel (314)
421-1880; gen fax (314) 421-0436;
adv fax (314) 421-0436;
ed fax (314) 421-0436; adv e-mail
carol.prycma@thedailyrecord.com;
ed e-mail willc@thedailyrecord.com;
web site www.thedailyrecord.com
Advertising Rate:
Open inch rate $6.56
News services:
R N.
Pub. Richard Gard
Bus. Mgr. Amanda Passmore

Adv. Dir. Amy Burdge
Circ. Mgr. Stacey Fish
William B. Connaghan
Prodn. Mgr. John M. Reno

Tulsa Business & Legal News (Law)
315 S. Boulder, Tulsa, OK,
74103-4422,Tulsa; gen tel (918)
581-8306; adv tel
918581-8525; ed tel 918-581-8306;
gen e-mail news@tulsabusiness.com;
adv e-mail
legalnews@oklaweeklygroup.com; ed
e-mail news@tulsabusiness.com; web
site http://tulsabusiness.com
Group:
BH Media
Established: 1909
Editor Lesa Jones

F. AMERICAN BAR ASSOCIATION OFFICERS (2016-2017)

Chicago Offices
321 North Clark Street
Chicago, IL 60654-7598
(312) 988-5000
Fax: (312) 988-5528
www.americanbar.org

ABA Service Center
(800) 285-2221 or (312) 988-5522
Fax: (312) 988-5528
E-mail: *service@americanbar.org*

ABA Concierge
(866) 222-5078
E-mail: *ABAConcierge@americanbar.org*

Washington Office
Suite 400
1050 Connecticut Avenue, NW
Washington, DC 20036
(202) 662-1000
Fax: (202) 662-1032
www.americanbar.org

Information Services-Washington, D.C.
(202) 662-1010
All other inquiries: (800) 285-2221

The ABA Concierge program provides dedicated e-mail and telephone contact information to high-level members who need an escalation point if they are not receiving timely or adequate responses from ABA staff. All contacts will be acknowledged when received and answered within 24 hours. The ABA Concierge phone number and e-mail are not for routine matters. Routine questions should be sent to the Service Center at *service@americanbar.org* or (800) 285-2221.

BOARD OF GOVERNORS

OFFICERS

President:	Paulette Brown, Morristown, NJ
President-Elect:	Linda A. Klein, Atlanta, GA
Chair, House of Delegates:	Patricia Lee Refo, Phoenix, AZ
Secretary:	Mary T. Torres, Albuquerque, NM
Treasurer:	G. Nicholas Casey, Jr., Charleston, WV
Immediate Past President:	William C. Hubbard, Columbia, SC
Executive Director:	Jack L. Rives, Chicago, IL

SECTIONS AND DIVISIONS

ADMINISTRATIVE LAW AND REGULATORY PRACTICE

Chair:	Jeffrey A. Rosen, Washington, DC
Chair-Elect:	Renee M. Landers, Boston, MA
Vice-Chair:	John F. Cooney, Washington, DC
Last Retiring Chair:	Anna Williams Shavers, Lincoln, NE
Secretary:	Linda D. Jellum, Macon, GA
Budget Officer:	Edward J. Schoenbaum, Springfield, IL
Assistant Budget Officer:	Louis J. George, Washington, DC

ANTITRUST LAW

Chair:	Roxann E. Henry, Washington, DC
Chair-Elect:	William C. MacLeod, Washington, DC
Vice-Chair:	Jonathan M. Jacobson, New York, NY
Immediate Past Chair:	Howard Feller, Richmond, VA
Committee Officer:	Deborah A. Garza, Washington, DC
Consumer Protection	
Officer:	Thomas F. Zych, Sr., Cleveland, OH
Finance Officer:	Kevin J. O'Connor, Madison, WI
International Officer:	Jonathan Ian Gleklen, Washington, DC
Programs Officer:	Brian R. Henry, Atlanta, GA
Publications Officer:	Bernard A. Nigro, Jr., Washington, DC
Secretary/Communications Officer:	Anthony Chavez, Baytown, TX

BUSINESS LAW

Chair:	William B. Rosenberg, Montreal, QC, Canada
Chair-Elect:	William D. Johnston, Wilmington, DE
Vice-Chair:	Christopher J. Rockers, Kansas City, MO
Secretary:	Vicki O. Tucker, Richmond, VA
Budget Officer:	Linda J. Rusch, Seattle, WA
Content Officer:	Jonathan C. Lipson, Madison, WI
Immediate Past Chair:	Paul L. Lion III, Palo Alto, CA

CIVIL RIGHTS AND SOCIAL JUSTICE

Chair:	Lauren Stiller Rikleen, Wayland, MA
Chair-Elect:	Kirke Kickingbird, Oklahoma City, OK
Vice-Chair:	Robert N. Weiner, Washington, DC
Secretary:	Wilson Adam Schooley, La Mesa, CA
Treasurer:	John Paul Graff, Vancouver, WA
Past Chair:	Mark I. Schickman, San Francisco, CA

CRIMINAL JUSTICE

Chair:	Bernice B. Donald, Memphis, TN
Chair-Elect:	Matthew Frank Redle, Sheridan, WY
First Vice-Chair:	Morris Weinberg, Jr., Tampa, FL
Vice-Chairs-at-Large:	April Frazier-Camara, Memphis, TN
	Justine M. Luongo, New York, NY
	Martin Marcus, Bronx, NY
	Wayne S. McKenzie, New York, NY
	Michael R. Moore, Huron, SD
Past Chairs:	James E. Felman, Tampa, FL
	Cynthia E. Hujar Orr, San Antonio, TX
Budget Officer:	Ronald Goldstock, Larchmont, NY
Diversity Officer:	Matthew Frank Redle, Sheridan, WY

DISPUTE RESOLUTION

Chair:	Howard Herman, San Francisco, CA
Chair-Elect:	Nancy A. Welsh, Carlisle, PA
Vice-Chair:	Benjamin G. Davis, Toledo, OH
Budget Officer:	Harrie Samaras, West Chester, PA
CLE Officer:	Joan Stearns Johnsen, West Newton, MA
Immediate Past Chair:	Geetha Ravindra, Glen Allen, VA

ENVIRONMENT, ENERGY, AND RESOURCES

Chair:	Pamela Barker, Glendale, WI
Chair-Elect:	Seth A. Davis, Rye, NY
Vice-Chair:	John E. Milner, Jackson, MS
Secretary:	Jonathan W. Kahn, Toronto, ON, Canada

Budget Officer:	Michael J. Peare, Phoenix, AZ
Education Officer:	Amy L. Edwards, Washington, DC
Membership and Diversity	
Officer:	Karen Mignone, Westport, CT
Publications Officer:	Jeffery Scott Dennis, Washington DC
Immediate Past Chair:	Steven Thomas Miano, Philadelphia, PA

FAMILY LAW

Chair:	Greg J. Ortiz, Highlands Ranch, CO
Chair-Elect:	Mary T. Vidas, Philadelphia, PA
Vice-Chair:	Roberta S. Batley, Albuquerque, NM
Secretary:	Melissa J. Avery, Indianapolis, IN
Treasurer:	Deborah Akers-Parry, Cleveland, OH
Immediate Past Chair:	Lori W. Nelson, Salt Lake City, UT

GOVERNMENT AND PUBLIC SECTOR LAWYERS DIVISION

Chair:	Joan M. Burke, Cherry Hill, NJ
Chair-Elect:	Pauline A. Weaver, Fremont, CA
Vice-Chair:	Janet M. Coulter, Long Beach, CA
Secretary:	Susan N. Burke, Minneapolis, MN
Treasurer:	Sharon E. Pandak, Woodbridge, VA
Immediate Past Chair:	Gregory G. Brooker, Minneapolis, MN

HEALTH LAW

Chair:	William W. Horton, Birmingham, AL
Chair-Elect:	C. Joyce Hall, Jackson, MS
Vice-Chair:	Hilary Hughes Young, Austin, TX
Secretary:	Alexandria Hien McCombs, Addison, TX
Budget Officer:	Eugene Holmes, Burbank, CA
Immediate Past Chair:	Michael E. Clark, Houston, TX

INTELLECTUAL PROPERTY LAW

Chair:	Theodore H. Davis, Jr., Atlanta, GA
Chair-Elect:	Donna P. Suchy, Cedar Rapids, IA
Vice-Chair:	Scott Francis Partridge, Houston, TX
Secretary:	Susan E. McGahan, Bedminster, NJ
Financial Officer:	Kim R. Jessum, Langhorne, PA
Publications Officer:	Mark Kevin Dickson, South San Francisco, CA
CLE Officer:	Jonathan Hudis, Washington, DC
Membership Officer:	George Jordan III, Houston, TX
Immediate Past Chair:	Lisa A. Dunner, Washington, DC
Parliamentarian:	Jack C. Goldstein, Houston, TX

INTERNATIONAL LAW

Chair:	Lisa J. Savitt, Washington, DC
Chair-Elect:	Sara P. Sandford, Seattle, WA
Vice-Chair:	Steven M. Richman, Philadelphia, PA
Secretary/Operations Officer:	Lelia Mooney, Washington, DC
Immediate Past Chair:	Marcelo E. Bombau, Buenos Aires Argentina
Programs Officer:	Robert L. Brown, Louisville, KY
Communications Officer:	Ingrid Busson, New York, NY
Publications Officer:	Patrick L. Del Duca, Los Angeles, CA
Finance Officer:	Adam Benjamin Farlow, London UK
Liaison Officer:	Dixon F. Miller, Columbus, OH
Budget Officer:	William B T Mock, Jr., Chicago, IL
Membership Officer:	Marcos Rios, Las Condes, Santiago, Chile
Diversity Officer:	Lisa Ryan, San Francisco, CA
Policy/Government Affairs Officer:	David A. Schwartz, New York, NY
Rule of Law Officer:	Nancy Kaymar Stafford, Newport, RI
Technology Officer:	Marcela B. Stras, Washington, DC

JUDICIAL DIVISION

Chair:	Michael G. Bergmann, Chicago, IL
Chair-Elect:	Linda Strite Murnane, Leidschendam Netherlands
Vice-Chair:	Ann Breen-Greco, Chicago, IL
Immediate Past Chair:	David J. Waxse, Kansas City, KS

LABOR AND EMPLOYMENT LAW

Chair:	Wayne Norris Outten, New York, NY
Chair-Elect:	Gail Golman Holtzman, Tampa, FL
Vice-Chairs:	Donald David Slesnick II, Coral Gables, FL
	Joseph E. Tilson, Chicago, IL
Secretary:	Scott Adam Moss, Denver, CO
Secretary-Elect:	Thomas C. Goldstein, Bethesda, MD
Immediate Past Chair:	Joyce Margulies, Memphis, TN

LAW PRACTICE DIVISION

Chair:	Tom Bolt, St. Thomas, VI
Chair-Elect:	John E. Mitchell, Chicago, IL
Vice-Chair:	William Ferreira, Morristown, NJ
Secretary:	Katayoun M. Goshtasbi, San Diego, CA
Immediate Past Chair:	Robert Arthur Young, Bowling Green, KY

LAW STUDENT DIVISION

Chair:	Fabiani Alberto Duarte, Atlanta, GA
Vice-Chair/SBA:	Josephine Bahn, New York, NY
Vice-Chair:	Michael Dumas, Portland, ME
Secretary/Treasurer:	John Louros, Brooklyn, NY

LEGAL EDUCATION AND ADMISSIONS TO THE BAR

Chair:	Rebecca White Berch, Phoenix, AZ
Chair-Elect:	Gregory G. Murphy, Billings, MT
Vice-Chair:	Maureen O'Rourke, Boston, MA
Secretary:	Edward N. Tucker, Baltimore, MD
Immediate Past Chair:	Joan S. Howland, Minneapolis, MN

LITIGATION

Chair:	Steven A. Weiss, Chicago, IL
Chair-Elect:	Laurence Pulgram, San Francisco, CA
Vice-Chair:	Koji F. Fukumura, San Diego, CA
Secretary:	Mary L. Smith, Lansing, IL
Past Chairs:	William R. Bay, Saint Louis, MO
	Don Bivens, Phoenix, AZ
Immediate Past Chair:	Nancy Scott Degan, New Orleans, LA
Publications and Content Officer:	Mark A. Neubauer, Los Angeles, CA
Budget Officer:	James Arthur Reeder, Jr., Houston, TX
Revenue Officer:	Palmer G. Vance II, Lexington, KY

PUBLIC CONTRACT LAW

Chair:	David G. Ehrhart, Fort Worth, TX
Chair-Elect:	James A. Hughes, Arlington, VA
Vice-Chair:	Aaron P. Silberman, San Francisco, CA
Secretary:	Kara M. Sacilotto, Washington, DC
Budget and Finance Officer:	Jennifer L. Dauer, Sacramento, CA
Immediate Past Chair:	Stuart B. Nibley, Washington, DC

PUBLIC UTILITY COMMUNICATIONS AND TRANSPORTATION LAW

Chair:	Dynda Thomas, Cleveland, OH
Chair-Elect:	John J. Beardsworth, Jr., Richmond, VA
Vice-Chair:	Peter V. Lacouture, Providence, RI
Secretary:	Michael A. McGrail, Allentown, PA
Treasurer:	Mark Christopher Darrell, Saint Louis, MO
Immediate Past Chair:	Steven H. Brose, Washington, DC

REAL PROPERTY, TRUST, AND ESTATE LAW

Chair:	Robert J. Krapf, Wilmington, DE
Chair-Elect:	David J. Dietrich, Billings, MT
Trust and Estate Division Vice-Chair:	David M. English, Columbia, MO
Real Property Division Vice-Chair:	Elizabeth C. Lee, Washington, DC
Secretary:	Robert C. Paul, New York, NY
Immediate Past Chair:	Gideon Rothschild, New York, NY
Finance and Corporate Sponsorship Officer:	Stephanie Loomis-Price, Houston, TX

SCIENCE AND TECHNOLOGY LAW

Chair:	Cynthia H. Cwik, San Diego, CA
Chair-Elect:	Eileen Smith Ewing, Boston, MA
Vice-Chair:	David Z. Bodenheimer, Washington, DC
Secretary:	William B. Baker, Washington, DC
Budget Officer:	Garth Jacobson, Seattle, WA
Immediate Past Chair:	Michael Hawes, Houston, TX

SENIOR LAWYERS

Chair:	Louraine C. Arkfeld, Tempe, AZ
Chair-Elect:	William D. Missouri, Upper Marlboro, MD
Vice-Chair:	John Hardin Young, Rehoboth Bch, DE
Secretary:	Marvin S.C. Dang, Honolulu, HI
Budget Officer:	Llewelyn G. Pritchard, Seattle, WA
Immediate Past Chair:	John Michael Vittone, Silver Spring, MD

SOLO, SMALL FIRM AND GENERAL PRACTICE

Chair:	Stephen B. Rosales, Belmont, MA
Chair-Elect:	David H. Lefton, Cincinnati, OH
Vice-Chair:	Stephen Williams, Flemington, NJ
Secretary:	Melanie Bragg, Houston, TX
Budget Officer:	Stephen J. Curley, Stamford, CT
Immediate Past Chair:	Amy L. Meyerson, Weston, CT

STATE AND LOCAL GOVERNMENT LAW

Chair:	Donna Y. Frazier, Shreveport, LA
Chair-Elect:	Ellen F. Rosenblum, Salem, OR
Vice-Chair:	Robert H. Thomas, Honolulu, HI
Secretary:	Ronald J. Kramer, Chicago, IL
Immediate Past Chair:	James Charles Hanks, Des Moines, IA
Budget Officer:	Stephen Adnopoz, New York, NY
Content Coordinator:	Martha Harrell Chumbler, Tallahassee, FL
Editor, The Urban Lawyer:	Julie Marie Cheslik, Kansas City, MO
Editor, State and Local Law News:	Erica Levine Powers, Albany, NY

Government Law News, Monthly E-News Co-Editors:	Christopher Lake Brown, Mansfield, OH
	Craig R. Bucki, Buffalo, NY
	Michael Dumas, Portland, ME
CLE Coordinator:	Sorell Elizabeth Negro, Hartford, CT
Committee Coordinator:	Steven F. Stapleton, Grand Rapids, MI
Electronic Communications Coordinator:	Robert H. Thomas, Honolulu, HI
Sponsorship Director:	Lawrence E. Bechler, Madison, WI
Publications Director:	William J. Scheiderich, Spokane, WA
Membership Director:	Michael Thomas Kamprath, Ruskin, FL

TAXATION

Chair:	George C. Howell III, Richmond, VA
Chair-Elect:	William H. Caudill, Houston, TX
Vice-Chair/Administration:	Charles P. Rettig, Beverly Hills, CA
Vice-Chair/Committee Operations:	Thomas James Callahan, Cleveland, OH
Vice-Chair/Continuing Legal Education:	Joan C. Arnold, Philadelphia, PA
Vice-Chair/Government Relations:	Peter Blessing, Stamford, CT
Vice-Chair/Pro Bono and Outreach:	Carl Wells Hall III, Charlotte, NC
Vice-Chair/Publications	Julie A. Divola, San Francisco, CA
Secretary:	Catherine B. Engell, New York, NY
Assistant Secretary:	Katherine E. David, San Antonio, TX
Past Chair:	Armando Gomez, Washington, DC

TORT TRIAL AND INSURANCE PRACTICE

Chair:	G. Glennon Troublefield, Roseland, NJ
Chair-Elect:	John B. Cartafalsa, Jr., New York, NY
Vice-Chair:	Holly M. Polglase, Boston, MA
Secretary/Chief Diversity Officer:	Dorothea M. Capone, New York, NY
Finance Officer:	Loren D. Podwill, Portland, OR
Revenue Officer:	Robert J. Caldwell, Las Vegas, NV
Revenue Officer-Elect:	James A. Young, Tampa, FL
Immediate Past Chair:	Michael W. Drumke, Chicago, IL

YOUNG LAWYERS

Chair:	Lacy L. Durham, Dallas, TX
Chair-Elect:	Anna Romanskaya, San Diego, CA
Secretary:	Dana M. Hrelic, Hartford, CT
Treasurer:	Christina M. Liu, Chicago, IL
Assembly Speaker:	Stefan Palys, Phoenix, AZ
Assembly Clerk:	Shenique A. Moss, Lansing, MI
Immediate Past Chair:	Andrew M. Schpak, Portland, OR

G. STATE BAR ASSOCIATIONS

ALABAMA STATE BAR

415 Dexter Avenue (36104)
P.O. Box 671
Montgomery, AL 36104
(334) 269-1515
FAX: (334) 261-6310
Website: *www.alabar.org*

President:	Lee Copeland
President Elect:	Jon Cole Portis
Executive Director:	Keith B. Norman

ALASKA BAR ASSOCIATION

840 K Street, Suite 100
Anchorage, AK 99501
(907) 272-7469
FAX: (907) 272-2932
Website: *www.alaskabar.org*

President:	Nelson G. Page
President Elect:	Susan Cox
Executive Director:	Deborah O'Regan

STATE BAR OF ARIZONA

Suite 200
4201 N. 24th Street
Phoenix, AZ 85016-6288
(602) 252-4804
FAX: (602) 271-4930
Website: *www.azbar.org*

President:	Bryan B. Chambers
President Elect:	Lisa Loo
Executive Director:	John F. Phelps

ARKANSAS BAR ASSOCIATION

2224 Cottondale Lane
Little Rock, AR 72202
(501) 375-4606
FAX: (501) 375-4901
Website: *www.arkbar.com*
President: Eddie H. Walker, Jr.
President Elect: Denise Reid Hoggard
Executive Director: Karen Hutchins

STATE BAR OF CALIFORNIA

180 Howard Street, Floor 10
San Francisco, CA 94105-1639
(415) 538-2000
FAX: (415) 538-2305
Website: *www.calbar.ca.gov*
President: Heather Linn Rosing
President Elect: To Be Appointed
Executive Director: Elizabeth Rindskopf Parker

COLORADO BAR ASSOCIATION

9th Floor
1900 Grant Street
Denver, CO 80203
(303) 860-1115
FAX: (303) 894-0821
Website: *www.cobar.org*
President: Loren Michael Brown
President Elect: Patricia M. Jarzobski
Executive Director: Patrick Flaherty

CONNECTICUT BAR ASSOCIATION

30 Bank Street
P.O. Box 350
New Britain, CT 06050-0350
(860) 223-4400
FAX: (860) 223-4488
Website: *www.ctbar.org*
President: William H. Clendenen, Jr.
President Elect: Monte Frank
Executive Director: Douglas S. Brown

DELAWARE STATE BAR ASSOCIATION

405 N. King Street, Suite 100
Wilmington, DE 19801
(302) 658-5279
FAX: (302) 658-5212
Website: *www.dsba.org*
President: Richard A. Forsten
President Elect: Miranda D. Clifton
Executive Director: Rina Marks

THE DISTRICT OF COLUMBIA BAR

Suite 200
1101 K Street, NW
Washington, DC 20005-39908
(202) 737-4700
FAX: (202) 626-3471
Website: *www.dcbar.org*
President: Timothy K. Webster
President Elect: Annamaria Steward
Executive Director: Katherine A. Mazzaferri

BAR ASSOCIATION OF THE DISTRICT OF COLUMBIA

Suite 101
1016 16th Street, NW
Washington, DC 20036
(202) 223-6600
FAX: (202) 293-3388
Website: *www.badc.org*
President: Nancy Nunan
President Elect: Erin Marie Dunston
Executive Director: vacant

THE FLORIDA BAR

P.O.Box 389 (32302)
651 East Jefferson Street
Tallahassee, FL 32399-2300
(850) 561-5600
FAX: (850) 561-5826
Website: *www.flabar.org*
President: Ramon A. Abadin
President Elect: William J. Schifino, Jr.
Executive Director: John F. Harkness, Jr.

STATE BAR OF GEORGIA

Suite 100
104 Marietta Street, NW
Atlanta, GA 30303
(800) 334-6865
FAX: (404) 527-8717
Website: *www.gabar.org*
President: Robert J. Kauffman
President Elect: Rita A. Sheffey
Executive Director: Jeffrey Reese Davis

GUAM BAR ASSOCIATION

Supreme Court of Guam
Second Floor, Guam Judicial Center
120 West O'Brien Drive
Hogatna, Guam 96910
011/671/745-3118
FAX: 011/671/745-3400
Website: *www.guambar.org*

President:	Jehan'Ad G. Martinez
President Elect:	Michael A. Pangelinan
Executive Director:	Bruce A. Bradley

HAWAII STATE BAR ASSOCIATION

Alakea Corporate Tower
1100 Alakea Street, Suite 1000
Honolulu, HI 96813
(808) 537-1868
FAX: (808) 521-7936
Website: *www.hsba.org*

President:	Gregory K. Markham
Vice President/President Elect:	Jodi Lei Kimura Yi
Executive Director:	Patricia Mau-Shimizu

IDAHO STATE BAR

P.O. Box 895
525 W. Jefferson Street (83702)
Boise, ID 83701
(208) 334-4500
FAX: (208) 334-4515
Website: *www.idaho.gov/isb*

President:	Trudy H. Fouser
President Elect:	Tim Gresback
Executive Director:	Diane K. Minnich

ILLINOIS STATE BAR ASSOCIATION

Illinois Bar Center
424 S. Second Street
Springfield, IL 62701
(217) 525-1760
FAX: (217) 525-0712
Website: *www.illinoisbar.org*

President:	Umberto Davi
President Elect:	Vincent F. Cornelius
Executive Director:	Roger E. Craghead

INDIANA STATE BAR ASSOCIATION

One Indiana Square, Suite 530
Indianapolis, IN 46204
(317) 639-5465
FAX: (317) 266-2588
Website: *www.inbar.org*

President:	Jeff Ray Hawkins
President Elect:	Carol Marian Adinamis
Executive Director:	Thomas A. Pyrz

IOWA STATE BAR ASSOCIATION

625 East Court Avenue
Des Moines, IA 50309
(515) 243-3179
FAX: (515) 243-2511
Website: *www.iowabar.org*

President:	Bruce L. Walker
President Elect:	Arnold O. Kenyon III
Executive Director:	Dwight Dinkla

KANSAS BAR ASSOCIATION

1200 S.W. Harrison Street
P.O. Box 1037
Topeka, KS 66612
(785) 234-5696
FAX: (785) 234-3813
Website: *www.ksbar.org*
President: Natalie Gayle Haag
President Elect: Steve Six
Executive Director: Jordan Yochim

KENTUCKY BAR ASSOCIATION

514 West Main Street
Frankfort, KY 40601-1883
(502) 564-3795
FAX: (502) 564-3225
Website: *www.kybar.org*
President: Douglass Farnsley
President Elect: R. Michael Sullivan
Executive Director: John D. Meyers

LOUISIANA STATE BAR ASSOCIATION

601 St. Charles Avenue
New Orleans, LA 70130
(504) 566-1600
FAX: (504) 566-0930
Website: *www.lsba.org*
President: Mark A. Cunningham
President Elect: Darrel J. Papillion
Executive Director: Loretta L. Larsen

MAINE STATE BAR ASSOCIATION

124 State Street
P.O. Box 788
Augusta, ME 04332-0788
(207) 622-7523
FAX: (207) 623-0083
Website: *www.mainebar.org*

President:	David Levesque
President Elect:	Stephen D. Nelson
Executive Director:	Angela Pease Weston

MARYLAND STATE BAR ASSOCIATION

520 W. Fayette Street
Baltimore, MD 21201
(410) 685-7878
FAX: (410) 837-1016
Website: *www.msba.org*

President:	Pamila J. Brown
President Elect:	Harry C. Storm
Executive Director:	Paul V. Carlin

MASSACHUSETTS BAR ASSOCIATION

20 West Street
Boston, MA 02111-1218
(617) 338-0500
FAX: (617) 542-7947
Website: *www.massbar.org*

President:	Robert W. Harnais
President Elect:	Jeffrey N. Catalano
Executive Director:	Martin William Healy

STATE BAR OF MICHIGAN

306 Townsend Street
Lansing, MI 48933-2083
(517) 346-6330
FAX: (517) 482-6248
Website: *www.michbar.org*
President: Lori Iafret Buiteweg
President Elect: Lawrence Patrick Nolan, Sr.
Executive Director: Janét K. Welch

MINNESOTA STATE BAR ASSOCIATION

Suite 380
600 Nicollet Mall
Minneapolis, MN 55402
(612) 333-1183
FAX: (612) 333-4927
Website: *www.mnbar.org*
President: Michael W. Unger
President Elect: Robin Wolpert
Executive Director: Timothy Groshens

THE MISSISSIPPI BAR

643 N. State Street
P.O. Box 2168
Jackson, MS 39225-2168
(601) 948-4471
FAX: (601) 355-8635
Website: *www.msbar.org*
President: Roy Davies Campbell III
President Elect: W. Briggs Hopson III
Executive Director: Larry Houchins

THE MISSOURI BAR

326 Monroe Street
P.O. Box 119 (65102)
Jefferson City, MO 65101
(573) 635-4128
FAX: (573) 635-2811
Website: *www.mobar.org*
President: Erik A. Bergmanis
President Elect: To Be Appointed
Executive Director: Sebrina Annette Barrett

STATE BAR OF MONTANA

Suite 2B
7 West Sixth Avenue
P.O. Box 577
Helena, MT 59624
(406) 442-7660
FAX: (406) 442-7763
Website: *www.montanabar.org*
President: Matthew B. Thiel
Vice President: Vacant
Executive Director: Chris L. Manos

NEBRASKA STATE BAR ASSOCIATION

635 S. 14th Street, 2nd Floor
Lincoln, NE 68508
(402) 475-7091
FAX: (402) 475-7098
Website: *www.nebar.com*
President: Annie C. Martinez
President Elect: Robert F. Rossiter, Jr.
Executive Director: Elizabeth Marie Neeley

STATE BAR OF NEVADA

600 East Charleston Boulevard
Las Vegas, NV 89104
(702) 382-2200
FAX: (702) 382-2075
Website: *www.nvbar.org*
President: Laurence P. Digesti
President Elect: Bryan Scott
Executive Director: Kimberly Farmer

NEW HAMPSHIRE BAR ASSOCIATION

2 Pillsbury Street, Suite 300
Concord, NH 03301
(603) 224-6942
FAX: (603) 224-2910
Website: *www.nhbar.org*
President: Mary Elizabeth Tenn
President Elect: David Ruoff
Executive Director: Jeannine L. McCoy

NEW JERSEY STATE BAR ASSOCIATION

New Jersey Law Center
One Constitution Square
New Brunswick, NJ 08901-1500
(732) 249-5000
FAX: (732) 249-2815
Website: *www.njsba.com*
President: Miles S. Winder III
President Elect: Thomas Hoff Prol
Executive Director: Angela C. Scheck

STATE BAR OF NEW MEXICO

5121 Masthead, NE
P.O. Box 92860 (87199-2860)
Albuquerque, NM 87109
(505) 797-6000
FAX: (505) 828-3765
Website: *www.nmbar.org*
President: Mary Martha Chicoski
President Elect: J. Brent Moore
Executive Director: Joe Conte

NEW YORK STATE BAR ASSOCIATION

One Elk Street
Albany, NY 12207
(518) 463-3200
FAX: (518) 487-5517
Website: *www.nysba.org*
President: David P. Miranda
President Elect: Claire P. Gutekunst
Executive Director: David R. Watson

NORTH CAROLINA STATE BAR

217 E. Edenton Street
P.O. Box 25908
Raleigh, NC 27611
(919) 828-4620
FAX: (919) 821-9168
Website: *www.ncbar.com*
President: Ronald L. Gibson
President Elect: Margaret Hunt
Executive Director: L. Thomas Lunsford II

NORTH CAROLINA BAR ASSOCIATION

P.O. Box 3688
Cary, NC 27519
(919) 677-0561
FAX: (919) 677-0761
Website: *www.ncbar.org*
President: Shelby Duffy Benton
President Elect: Kearns Davis
Executive Director: Allan B. Head

STATE BAR ASSOCIATION OF NORTH DAKOTA

P.O. Box 2136
Bismarck, ND 58502-2136
(701) 255-1404
FAX: (701) 224-1621
Website: *www.sband.org*
President: Joseph A. Wetch, Jr.
President Elect: Charles G. DeMakis
Executive Director: Tony J. Weiler

NORTHERN MARIANA ISLANDS BAR ASSOCIATION

P.O. Box 504539 C.K.
Saipan, MP 96950
(670) 235-4529
FAX: (670) 235-4528
Website: *www.cnmibar.net*
President: Jennifer Dockter
President Elect: Lillian Ada Tenorio
Executive Director: Suzanne M. Steffy

OHIO STATE BAR ASSOCIATION

1700 Lake Shore Drive (43204)
P.O. Box 16562
Columbus, OH 43216-6562
(614) 487-2050
FAX: (614) 487-1008
Website: *www.ohiobar.org*
President: John D. Holschuh, Jr.
President Elect: Ronald S. Kopp
Executive Director: Mary Amos Augsburger

OKLAHOMA BAR ASSOCIATION

1901 N. Lincoln (73105)
P.O. Box 53036
Oklahoma City, OK 73152-3036
(405) 416-7000
FAX: (405) 416-7001
Website: *www.okbar.org*
President: David A. Poarch
President Elect: Garvin A. Isaacs, Jr.
Executive Director: John M. Williams

OREGON STATE BAR

16037 S.W. Upper Boones Ferry Road
P.O. Box 231935
Tigard, OR 97224
(503) 620-0222
FAX: (503) 598-6912
Website: *www.osbar.org*
President: Richard G. Spier
President Elect: R. Ray Heysell
Executive Director: Sylvia E. Stevens

PENNSYLVANIA BAR ASSOCIATION

100 South Street
P.O. Box 186
Harrisburg, PA 17101-0186
(800) 932-0311
FAX: (717) 238-1204
Website: *www.pabar.org*

President:	William Henry Pugh V
President Elect:	Sara A. Austin
Executive Director:	Barry Michael Simpson

PUERTO RICO BAR ASSOCIATION

Ponce de Leon Avenue
808 Stop II
P.O. Box 9021900
San Juan, PR 00902-1900
(787) 999-6294
FAX: (787) 724-2622

President:	Mark Anthony Bimbela
President Elect:	To Be Appointed
Executive Director:	Maria E. Hernandez-Torrales

RHODE ISLAND BAR ASSOCIATION

115 Cedar Street, Suite 2
Providence, RI 02903
(401) 421-5740
FAX: (401) 421-2703
Website: *www.ribar.com*

President:	Melissa E. Darigan
President Elect:	Armando Batastini
Executive Director:	Helen Desmond McDonald

SOUTH CAROLINA BAR

950 Taylor Street
P.O. Box 608
Columbia, SC 29201-0608
(803) 799-6653
FAX: (803) 799-4118
Website: *www.scbar.org*

President:	Anne S. Ellefson
President Elect:	William K. Witherspoon
Executive Director:	Robert S. Wells

STATE BAR OF SOUTH DAKOTA

222 E. Capitol Avenue
Pierre, SD 57501-2596
(605) 224-7554
FAX: (605) 224-0282
Website: *www.sdbar.org*

President:	Eric C. Schulte
President Elect:	Stephanie E. Johnson Pochop
Executive Director:	Thomas C. Barnett, Jr.

TENNESSEE BAR ASSOCIATION

Tennessee Bar Center
Suite 400
221 Fourth Avenue, N.
Nashville, TN 37219-2198
(615) 383-7421
FAX: (615) 297-8058
Website: *www.tba.org*

President:	William L. Harbison
President Elect:	Jason H. Long
Executive Director:	Allan F. Ramsaur

STATE BAR OF TEXAS

Suite 300
1414 Colorado (78701)
P.O. Box 12487
Austin, TX 78711-2487
(800) 204-2222
FAX: (512) 427-4100
Website: *www.texasbar.com*
President: Allan K. DuBois
President Elect: Frank E. Stevenson II
Executive Director: Michelle Hunter

UTAH STATE BAR

645 S. 200 East, #310
Salt Lake City, UT 84111-3834
(801) 531-9077
FAX: (801) 531-0660
Website: *www.utahbar.org*
President: Angelina Tsu
President Elect: Robert O. Rice
Executive Director: John C. Baldwin

VERMONT BAR ASSOCIATION

P.O. Box 100
Montpelier, VT 05601-0100
(802) 223-2020
FAX: (802) 223-1573
Website: *www.vtbar.org*
President: Jennifer Emens-Butler
President Elect: To Be Appointed
Executive Director: Robert Michael Paolini

VIRGIN ISLANDS BAR ASSOCIATION

2155 King Cross Street, Suite 2
Phoenix Business Court
P.O. Box 4108
Christiansted, Saint Croix, VI USA 00822
340/778-7497
FAX: 340/773-5060
Website: *www.vibar.org*

President:	Natalie Nelson Tang-How
President Elect:	John-Russell Bart Pate
Executive Director:	Hinda Carbon

VIRGINIA STATE BAR

Suite 700
1111 E. Main Street
Richmond, VA 23219-2800
(804) 775-0500
FAX: (804) 775-0501
Website: *www.vsb.org*

President:	Edward Weiner
President Elect:	Michael W. Robinson
Executive Director:	Karen A. Gould

VIRGINIA BAR ASSOCIATION

701 E. Franklin Street, #1120
Richmond, VA 23219
(804) 644-0041
FAX: (804) 644-0052
Website: *www.vba.org*

President:	Harry M. Johnson III
President Elect:	James Patrick Guy II
Executive Vice President:	Yvonne C. McGhee

WASHINGTON STATE BAR ASSOCIATION

Suite 600
1325 Fourth Avenue
Seattle, WA 98101-2539
(206) 443-9722
FAX: (206) 727-8319
Website: *www.wsba.org*
President: William Douglas Hyslop
President Elect: Robin L. Haynes
Executive Director: Paula Littlewood

WEST VIRGINIA BAR ASSOCIATION

1111 6th Avenue
P.O. Box 2162 (25722)
Huntington, WV 25701
(304) 522-2652
FAX: (304) 522-2795
Website: *wvbarassociation.org*
President: William J. Powell
President Elect: To Be Appointed
Executive Director: Pryce M. Haynes II

WEST VIRGINIA STATE BAR

2000 Deitrick Boulevard
Charleston, WV 25311
(304) 553-7220
FAX: (304) 558-2467
Website: *www.wvbar.org*
President: W. Michael Frazier
President Elect: John R. McGhee, Jr.
Executive Director: Anita R. Casey

STATE BAR OF WISCONSIN

5302 Eastpark Boulevard
P.O. Box 7158 (53707-7158)
Madison, WI 53718-2101
(608) 257-3838
FAX: (608) 257-5502
Website: *www.wisbar.org*

President:	Ralph M. Cagle
President Elect:	Francis W. Deisinger
Executive Director:	George C. Brown

WYOMING STATE BAR

4124 Laramie Street
P.O. Box 109
Cheyenne, WY 82003-0109
(307) 632-9061
FAX: (307) 632-3737
Website: *www.wyomingbar.org*

President:	Devon O'Connell Coleman
President Elect:	John A. Masterson
Executive Director:	Sharon Wilkinson

PART II
THE JUDICIARY

PART II

THE DREAM

H.   THE FEDERAL BENCH
The Federal Judicial System
Judicial Branch
The Supreme Court of the United States

http://www.supremecourt.gov

United States Supreme Court Building, One First Street NE., Washington, DC 20543
202-479-3000

Members

Title	Name
Chief Justice of the United States	John G. Roberts, Jr.
Associate Justice	Antonin Scalia
Associate Justice	Anthony M. Kennedy
Associate Justice	Clarence Thomas
Associate Justice	Ruth Bader Ginsburg
Associate Justice	Stephen G. Breyer
Associate Justice	Samuel A. Alito, Jr.
Associate Justice	Sonia Sotomayor
Associate Justice	Elena Kagan

Officers

Title	Name
Counselor to the Chief Justice	Jeffrey P. Minear
Clerk	Scott S. Harris
Court Counsel	Ethan V. Torrey
Curator	Catherine E. Fitts
Director of Information Technology	Robert J. Hawkins
Librarian	Linda Maslow
Marshal	Pamela Talkin
Public Information Officer	Kathleen L. Arberg
Reporter of Decisions	Christine L. Fallon

---

* Reprinted from the 2015 Edition (November) U.S. Government Manual and from *www.gpo.gov*.

Article III, section 1, of the Constitution of the United States provides that "[t]he judicial Power of the United States, shall be vested in one supreme Court, and in such inferior Courts as the Congress may from time to time ordain and establish."

The Supreme Court of the United States was created in accordance with this provision and by authority of the Judiciary Act of September 24, 1789 (1 Stat. 73). It was organized on February 2, 1790. Article III, section 2, of the Constitution defines the jurisdiction of the Supreme Court.

The Supreme Court comprises the Chief Justice of the United States and such number of Associate Justices as may be fixed by Congress, which is currently fixed at eight (28 U.S.C. 1). The President nominates the Justices with the advice and consent of the Senate. Article III, section 1, of the Constitution further provides that "[t]he Judges, both of the supreme and inferior Courts, shall hold their Offices during good Behaviour, and shall, at stated Times, receive for their Services, a Compensation, which shall not be diminished during their Continuance in Office."

http://www.supremecourt.gov/about/briefoverview.aspx

Court officers assist the Court in the performance of its functions. They include: the Counselor to the Chief Justice, the Clerk, the Court Counsel, the Curator, the Director of Information Technology, the Librarian, the Marshal, the Public Information Officer, and the Reporter of Decisions.

Appellate Jurisdiction

Various statutes, derived from the authority that the Constitution has given to Congress, confer appellate jurisdiction upon the Supreme Court. The basic statute effective at this time in conferring and controlling jurisdiction of the Supreme Court may be found in 28 U.S.C. 1251, 1253, 1254, 1257-1259, and various special statutes. Congress has no authority to change the original jurisdiction of this Court.

Court Term

http://www.supremecourt.gov/about/procedures.aspx

The term of the Court begins on the first Monday in October and lasts until the first Monday in October of the next year. Over the course of a term, approximately 10,000 petitions are filed for cases to be briefed before the Court. Moreover, each year, about 1,200 applications that can be acted upon by a single Justice while serving in the capacity of a Circuit Justice are filed.

Power To Make Rules

From time to time, Congress has conferred upon the Supreme Court power to prescribe rules of procedure to be followed by the lower courts of the United States.

Public Access

http://www.supremecourt.gov/visiting/visitorservices.aspx

The Supreme Court is open to the public from 9 a.m. to 4:30 p.m., weekdays, except on Federal holidays. Unless the Court or Chief Justice orders otherwise, the Clerk's office is open from 9 a.m. to 5 p.m., weekdays, except on Federal holidays. The library is open to members of the bar of the Court, attorneys for the various Federal departments and agencies, and Members of Congress.

For further information concerning the Supreme Court, contact the Public Information Office, United States Supreme Court Building, One First Street NE., Washington, DC 20543. Phone, 202-479-3211. http://www.supremecourt.gov

Lower Courts

Article III of the Constitution declares, in section 1, that the judicial power of the United States shall be invested in one Supreme Court and in "such inferior Courts as the Congress may from time to time ordain and establish." The Supreme Court has held that these constitutional courts "... share in the exercise of the judicial power defined in that section, can be invested with no other jurisdiction, and have judges who hold office during good behavior, with no power in Congress to provide otherwise."

United States Courts of Appeals

The courts of appeals are intermediate appellate courts created by act of March 3, 1891 (28 U.S.C. ch. 3), to relieve the Supreme Court of considering all appeals in cases originally decided by the Federal trial courts. They are empowered to review all final decisions and certain interlocutory decisions (18 U.S.C. 3731; 28 U.S.C. 1291, 1292) of district courts. They also are empowered to review and enforce orders of many Federal administrative bodies. The decisions of the courts of appeals are final except as they are subject to review on writ of certiorari by the Supreme Court.

The United States is divided geographically into 12 judicial circuits, including the District of Columbia. Each circuit has a court of appeals (28 U.S.C. 41, 1294). Each of the 50 States is assigned to one of the circuits. The territories and the Commonwealth of Puerto Rico are assigned variously to the first, third, and ninth circuits. There is also a Court of Appeals for the Federal Circuit, which has nationwide jurisdiction defined by subject matter. At present each court of appeals has from 6 to 28 permanent circuit judgeships (179 in all), depending upon the amount of judicial work in the circuit. Circuit judges hold their offices during good behavior as provided by Article III, section 1, of the Constitution. The judge senior in commission who is under 70 years of age (65 at inception of term), has been in office at least 1 year, and has not previously been chief judge, serves as the chief judge of the circuit for a 7-year term. One of the Justices of the Supreme Court is assigned as circuit justice for each of the 13 judicial circuits. Each court of appeals normally hears cases in panels consisting of three judges but may sit en banc with all judges present.

The judges of each circuit (except the Federal Circuit) by vote determine the size of the judicial council for the circuit, which consists of the chief judge and an equal number of circuit and district judges. The council considers the state of Federal judicial business in the circuit and may "make all necessary and appropriate orders for [its] effective and expeditious administration . . ." (28 U.S.C. 332).

The chief judge of each circuit may summon periodically a judicial conference of all judges of the circuit, including members of the bar, to discuss the business of the Federal courts of the circuit (28 U.S.C. 333). The chief judge of each circuit and a district judge elected from each of the 12 geographical circuits, together with the chief judge of the Court of International Trade, serve as members of the Judicial Conference of the United States, over which the Chief Justice of the United States presides. This is the governing body for the administration of the Federal judicial system as a whole (28 U.S.C. 331).

To obtain a complete list of judges, court officials, and official stations of the United States Courts of Appeals for the Federal Circuit, as well as information on opinions and cases before the court, consult the Judicial Circuit Web sites listed below.

List of Judicial Circuit Web Sites—United States Courts of Appeals

Circuit	URL
District of Columbia Circuit	http://www.cadc.uscourts.gov
First Circuit	http://www.ca1.uscourts.gov
Second Circuit	http://www.ca2.uscourts.gov
Third Circuit	http://www.ca3.uscourts.gov
Fourth Circuit	http://www.ca4.uscourts.gov
Fifth Circuit	http://www.ca5.uscourts.gov
Sixth Circuit	http://www.ca6.uscourts.gov
Seventh Circuit	http://www.ca7.uscourts.gov
Eighth Circuit	http://www.ca8.uscourts.gov
Ninth Circuit	http://www.ca9.uscourts.gov
Tenth Circuit	http://www.ca10.uscourts.gov
Eleventh Circuit	http://www.ca11.uscourts.gov

United States Court of Appeals for the Federal Circuit

This court was established under Article III of the Constitution pursuant to the Federal Courts Improvement Act of 1982 (28 U.S.C. 41, 44, 48), as successor to the former United States Court of Customs and Patent Appeals and the United States Court of Claims. The jurisdiction of the court is nationwide (as provided by 28 U.S.C. 1295) and includes appeals from the district courts in patent cases; appeals from the district courts in contract, and certain other civil actions in which the

United States is a defendant; and appeals from final decisions of the U.S. Court of International Trade, the U.S. Court of Federal Claims, and the U.S. Court of Appeals for Veterans Claims. The jurisdiction of the court also includes the review of administrative rulings by the Patent and Trademark Office, U.S. International Trade Commission, Secretary of Commerce, agency boards of contract appeals, and the Merit Systems Protection Board, as well as rulemaking of the Department of Veterans Affairs; review of decisions of the U.S. Senate Committee on Ethics concerning discrimination claims of Senate employees; and review of a final order of an entity to be designated by the President concerning discrimination claims of Presidential appointees.

http://www.cafc.uscourts.gov

The court consists of 12 circuit judges. It sits in panels of three or more on each case and may also hear or rehear a case en banc. The court sits principally in Washington, DC, and may hold court wherever any court of appeals sits (28 U.S.C. 48).

United States District Courts

The Nation's district courts are the trial courts of general Federal jurisdiction. These courts resolve disputes by determining the facts and applying legal principles to decide which party is right. Each State has at least one district court, and large States have as many as four. There are 89 district courts in the 50 States, plus one in the District of Columbia and another in the Commonwealth of Puerto Rico. Three other U.S. Territories also have courts that hear Federal cases: Guam and the Northern Mariana and Virgin Islands.

At present, each district court has from 2 to 28 Federal district judgeships, depending upon the amount of judicial work within its territory. Only one judge is usually required to hear and decide a case in a district court, but in some limited cases it is required that three judges be called together to comprise the court (28 U.S.C. 2284). The judge senior in commission who is under 70 years of age (65 at inception of term), has been in office for at least 1 year, and has not previously been chief judge, serves as chief judge for a 7-year term. There are 645 permanent district judgeships in the 50 States and 15 in the District of Columbia. There are seven district judgeships in Puerto Rico. District judges hold their offices during good behavior as provided by Article III, section 1, of the Constitution. However, Congress may temporary judgeships for a court with the provision that when a future vacancy occurs in that district, such vacancy shall not be filled. Each district court has one or more United States magistrate judges and bankruptcy judges, a clerk, a United States attorney, a United States marshal, probation officers, court reporters, and their staffs. The jurisdiction of the district courts is set forth in title 28, chapter 85, of the United States Code and at 18 U.S.C. 3231.

http://www.uscourts.gov/about-federal-courts/court-role-and-structure

Cases from the district courts are reviewable on appeal by the applicable court of appeals.

Territorial Courts

Pursuant to its authority to govern the Territories (Art. IV, sec. 3, clause 2, of the Constitution), Congress has established district courts in the territories of Guam and the Virgin Islands. The District Court of the Canal Zone was abolished on April 1, 1982, pursuant to the Panama Canal Act of 1979 (22 U.S.C. 3601 note). Congress has also established a district court in the Northern Mariana Islands, which is administered by the United States under a trusteeship agreement with the United Nations. These Territorial courts have jurisdiction not only over the subjects described in the judicial article of the Constitution, but also over many local matters that, within the States, are decided in State courts. The District Court of Puerto Rico, by contrast, is established under Article III, is classified like other "district courts," and is called a "court of the United States" (28 U.S.C. 451). There is one judge each in Guam and the Northern Mariana Islands, and two in the Virgin Islands. The judges in these courts are appointed for terms of 10 years.

For further information concerning the lower courts, contact the Administrative Office of the United States Courts, Thurgood Marshall Federal Judiciary Building, One Columbus Circle NE., Washington, DC 20544. Phone, 202-502-2600.

http://www.uscourts.gov/about-federal-courts/court-role-and-structure

United States Court of International Trade

This court was originally established as the Board of United States General Appraisers by act of June 10, 1890, which conferred upon it jurisdiction theretofore held by the district and circuit courts in actions arising under the tariff acts (19 U.S.C. ch. 4). The act of May 28, 1926 (19 U.S.C. 405a), created the United States Customs Court to supersede the Board; by acts of August 7, 1939, and June 25, 1948 (28 U.S.C. 1582, 1583), the court was integrated into the United States court structure, organization, and procedure. The act of July 14, 1956 (28 U.S.C. 251), established the court as a court of record of the United States under Article III of the Constitution. The Customs Court Act of 1980 (28 U.S.C. 251) constituted the court as the United States Court of International Trade.

The Court of International Trade has jurisdiction over any civil action against the United States arising from Federal laws governing import transactions. This includes classification and valuation cases, as well as authority to review certain agency determinations under the Trade Agreements Act of 1979 (19 U.S.C. 2501) involving antidumping and countervailing duty matters. In addition, it has exclusive jurisdiction of civil actions to review determinations as to the eligibility of workers, firms, and communities for adjustment assistance under the Trade Act of 1974 (19 U.S.C. 2101). Civil actions commenced by the United States to recover customs duties, to recover on a customs bond, or for certain civil penalties alleging fraud or negligence are also within the exclusive jurisdiction of the court.

The court is composed of a chief judge and eight judges, not more than five of whom may belong to any one political party. Any of its judges may be temporarily designated and assigned by the Chief Justice of the United States to sit as a court of appeals or district court judge in any circuit or district. The court has a clerk and deputy clerks, a librarian, court reporters, and other supporting personnel. Cases before the court may be tried before a jury. Under the Federal Courts Improvement Act of 1982 (28 U.S.C. 1295), appeals are taken to the U.S. Court of Appeals for the Federal Circuit, and ultimately review may be sought in appropriate cases in the Supreme Court of the United States.

The principal offices are located in New York, NY, but the court is empowered to hear and determine cases arising at any port or place within the jurisdiction of the United States.

For further information, contact the Clerk, United States Court of International Trade, One Federal Plaza, New York, NY 10278-0001. Phone, 212-264-2814.

http://www.cit.uscourts.gov

Judicial Panel on Multidistrict Litigation

The Panel, created by act of April 29, 1968 (28 U.S.C. 1407), and consisting of seven Federal judges designated by the Chief Justice from the courts of appeals and district courts, is authorized to temporarily transfer to a single district, for coordinated or consolidated pretrial proceedings, civil actions pending in different districts that involve one or more common questions of fact.

For further information, contact the Clerk, Judicial Panel on Multidistrict Litigation, Room G–255, Thurgood Marshall Federal Judiciary Building, One Columbus Circle NE., Washington, DC 20002-8041. Phone, 202-502-2800.

http://www.jpml.uscourts.gov

Special Courts

United States Court of Appeals for the Armed Forces

http://www.armfor.uscourts.gov
450 E Street NW., Washington, DC 20442-0001
202-761-1448 202-761-4672

This court was established under Article I of the Constitution of the United States pursuant to act of May 5, 1950, as amended (10 U.S.C. 867). Subject only to certiorari review by the Supreme Court of the United States in a limited number of cases, the court serves as the final appellate tribunal to review court-martial convictions of all the Armed Forces. It is exclusively an appellate criminal court, consisting of five civilian judges who are appointed for 15-year terms by the President with the advice and consent of the Senate.

The court is called upon to exercise jurisdiction to review the record in all cases extending to death; certified to the court by a Judge Advocate General of one of the Armed Forces; or petitioned by accused who have received a sentence of confinement for 1 year or more and/or a punitive discharge.

The court also exercises authority under the All Writs Act (28 U.S.C. 1651(a)).

In addition, the judges of the court are required by law to work jointly with the senior uniformed lawyer from each of the Armed Forces and two members of the public appointed by the Secretary of Defense to make an annual comprehensive survey, to report annually to the Congress on the operation and progress of the military justice system under the Uniform Code of Military Justice, and to recommend improvements wherever necessary.

For further information, contact the Clerk, United States Court of Appeals for the Armed Forces, 450 E Street NW., Washington, DC 20442-0001. Phone, 202-761-1448. Fax, 202-761-4672.

http://www.armfor.uscourts.gov

United States Court of Appeals for Veterans Claims

http://www.uscourts.cavc.gov
Suite 900, 625 Indiana Avenue NW., Washington, DC 20004-2950
202-501-5970 202-501-5848

The United States Court of Appeals for Veterans Claims, a court of record under Article I of the Constitution, was established on November 18, 1988 (38 U.S.C. 7251) and given exclusive jurisdiction to review decisions of the Board of Veterans' Appeals. Appeals concern veteran disability benefits, dependent educational assistance, survivor benefits, and pension benefits claims. In addition to its review authority, the Court has contempt authority, as well as the authority to compel action by the Secretary of Veterans Affairs, the authority to grant a petition for extraordinary relief under the All Writs Act (28 U.S.C. 1651), and the authority to make attorney fee determinations under the Equal Access to Justice Act (28 U.S.C. 2412). Decisions of the Court of Appeals for Veterans Claims are subject to review by the United States Court of Appeals for the Federal Circuit on questions of law and on writ of certiorari by the United States Supreme Court.

The Court consists of nine judges whom the President appoints with the advice and consent of the Senate for 15-year terms. One of the judges serves as chief judge.

The Chief Judge generally conducts a judicial conference every 2 years. The primary purpose of the conference, which involves the active participation of members of the legal community, attorneys, and practitioners admitted to practice before the Court, is to consider the business of the Court and to recommend means of improving the administration of justice within the Court's jurisdiction.

The Court is located in Washington, DC, but it is a court of national jurisdiction and may sit at any location within the United States.

Opinions issued by the Court, case information, and a current list of judges and officials of the United States Court of Appeals for Veterans Claims are available online.

For further information, contact the Clerk, United States Court of Appeals for Veterans Claims, Suite 900, 625 Indiana Avenue NW., Washington, DC 20004-2950. Phone, 202-501-5970. Fax, 202-501-5848 http://www.uscourts.cavc.gov

United States Court of Federal Claims

http://www.uscfc.uscourts.gov
717 Madison Place NW., Washington, DC 20439
202-357-6400

The United States Court of Federal Claims has jurisdiction over claims seeking money judgments against the United States. A claim must be founded upon the Constitution, an act of Congress, an Executive order, a contract with the United States, or Federal regulations. Judges are appointed by the President for 15-year terms, subject to Senate confirmation. Appeals are to the U.S. Court of Appeals for the Federal Circuit.

For further information, contact the Clerk's Office, United States Court of Federal Claims, 717 Madison Place NW., Washington, DC 20439. Phone, 202-357-6400.

http://www.uscfc.uscourts.gov

United States Tax Court

http://www.ustaxcourt.gov
400 Second Street NW., Washington, DC 20217-0002
202-521-0700

The United States Tax Court is a court of record under Article I of the Constitution of the United States (26 U.S.C. 7441). The court was created as the United States Board of Tax Appeals by the Revenue Act of 1924 (43 Stat. 336). The name was changed to the Tax Court of the United States by the Revenue Act of 1942 (56 Stat. 957). The Tax Reform Act of 1969 (83 Stat. 730) established the court under Article I and then changed its name to the United States Tax Court.

The court comprises 19 judges who are appointed by the President to 15-year terms and subject to Senate confirmation. The court also has varying numbers of both senior judges (who may be recalled by the chief judge to perform further judicial duties) and special trial judges (who are appointed by the chief judge and may hear and decide a variety of cases). The court's jurisdiction is set forth in various sections of title 26 of the U.S. Code.

The offices of the court and its judges are in Washington, DC. However, the court has national jurisdiction and schedules trial sessions in more than 70 cities in the United States. Each trial session is conducted by one judge, senior judge, or special trial judge. Court proceedings are open to the public and are conducted in accordance with the court's rules of practice and procedure and the rules of evidence applicable in trials without a jury in the U.S. District Court for the District of Columbia. A fee of $60 is charged for the filing of a petition. Practice before the court is limited to practitioners admitted under the court's rules of practice and procedure.

Decisions entered by the court, other than decisions in small tax cases, may be appealed to the regional courts of appeals and, thereafter, upon the granting of a writ of certiorari, to the Supreme Court of the United States. At the option of petitioners, simplified procedures may be used in small tax cases. Small tax cases are final and not subject to review by any court.

For further information, contact the Office of the Clerk of the Court, United States Tax Court, 400 Second Street NW., Washington, DC 20217-0002. Phone, 202-521-0700.

http://www.ustaxcourt.gov

Administrative Office of the United States Courts

http://www.uscourts.gov
One Columbus Circle NE., Washington, DC 20544
202-502-2600

Title	Name
Director	James C. Duff
Deputy Director	Jill C. Sayenga
Associate Director, Department of Administrative Services	George H. Schafer
Associate Director, Department of Program Services	Laura C. Minor
Associate Director, Department of Technology Services	Joseph R. Peters, Jr.
General Counsel	Sheryl L. Walter
Judicial Conference Secretariat Officer	Katherine H. Simon
Legislative Affairs Officer	Cordia A. Strom
Public Affairs Officer	David A. Sellers

The Administrative Office of the United States Courts supports and serves the nonjudicial, administrative business of the United States Courts.

ADMINISTRATIVE OFFICE OF THE UNITED STATES COURTS

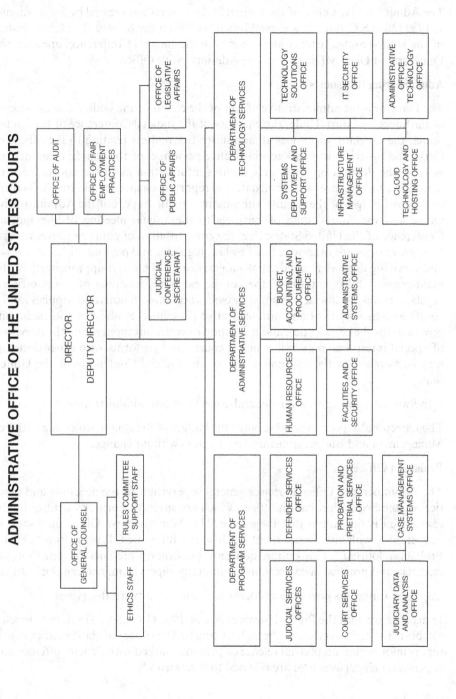

The Administrative Office of the United States Courts was created by act of August 7, 1939 (28 U.S.C. 601). It was established on November 6, 1939. The Chief Justice of the United States, after consultation with the Judicial Conference, appoints the Director and Deputy Director of the Administrative Office.

Administering the Courts

The Director is the administrative officer of the courts of the United States—except of the Supreme Court. Under the guidance of the Judicial Conference of the United States, the Director supervises all administrative matters relating to the offices of clerks and other clerical and administrative personnel of the courts; examines the state of the dockets of the courts, secures information as to the courts' need of assistance, and prepares statistical data and reports each quarter and transmits them to the chief judges of the circuits; submits an activities report of the Administrative Office and the courts' state of business to the annual meeting of the Judicial Conference of the United States; fixes the compensation of court employees whose compensation is not otherwise fixed by law; regulates and pays annuities to widows and surviving dependent children of judges; disburses moneys appropriated for the maintenance and operation of the courts; examines accounts of court officers; regulates travel of judicial personnel; provides accommodations and supplies for the courts and their clerical and administrative personnel; establishes and maintains programs for the certification and utilization of court interpreters and the provision of special interpretation services in the courts; and performs such other duties as may be assigned by the Supreme Court or the Judicial Conference of the United States.

http://www.uscourts.gov/about-federal-courts/judicial-administration

The Director also prepares and submits the budget of the courts, which the Office of Management and Budget transmits to Congress without change.

Probation Officers

The Administrative Office exercises general supervision of the accounts and practices of the Federal probation offices, which are subject to primary control by the respective district courts that they serve. The Administrative Office publishes, in cooperation with the Department of Justice's Bureau of Prisons, the "Federal Probation Journal." This online, quarterly publication presents current thought, research, and practice in corrections, community supervision, and criminal justice.

http://www.uscourts.gov/services-forms/probation-and-pretrial-services

In accordance with the Pretrial Services Act of 1982 (18 U.S.C. 3152), the Director establishes pretrial services in the district courts. The offices of these district courts report information on pretrial release of persons charged with Federal offenses and supervise such persons who are released to their custody.

Bankruptcy

According to the Bankruptcy Amendments and Federal Judgeship Act of 1984 (28 U.S.C. 151), the bankruptcy judges for each judicial district constitute a unit of the district court known as the bankruptcy court. The courts of appeals appoint bankruptcy judges in such numbers as authorized by Congress. These judges serve for a term of 14 years as judicial officers of the district courts.

This act placed jurisdiction in the district courts over all cases under title 11, United States Code, and all proceedings arising in or related to cases under that title (28 U.S.C. 1334). The district court may refer such cases and proceedings to its bankruptcy judges (as authorized by 28 U.S.C. 157).

http://www.uscourts.gov/services-forms/bankruptcy

The Director of the Administrative Office recommends to the Judicial Conference the duty stations of bankruptcy judges and the places they hold court, surveys the need for additional bankruptcy judgeships to be recommended to Congress, and determines the staff needs of bankruptcy judges and the clerks of the bankruptcy courts.

Federal Magistrate Judges

http://www.uscourts.gov/statistics-reports/us-magistrate-judges-judicial-business-2014

The Director of the Administrative Office exercises general supervision over administrative matters in offices of U.S. magistrate judges, compiles and evaluates statistical data relating to such offices, and submits reports thereon to the Judicial Conference. The Director reports annually to Congress on the business that has come before U.S. magistrate judges and also prepares legal and administrative manuals for the magistrate judges. In compliance with the act, the Administrative Office conducts surveys of the conditions in the judicial districts to make recommendations as to the number, location, and salaries of magistrate judges. The Judicial Conference then determines their number, location, and salaries, subject to the availability of appropriated funds.

Federal Defenders

The Criminal Justice Act (18 U.S.C. 3006A) establishes the procedure for the appointment of private panel attorneys in Federal criminal cases for individuals who are unable to afford adequate representation, under plans adopted by each district court. The act also permits the establishment of Federal public defender or Federal community defender organizations by the district courts in districts where at least 200 persons annually require the appointment of counsel. Two adjacent districts may be combined to reach this total.

http://www.uscourts.gov/services-forms/defender-services

Each defender organization submits to the Director of the Administrative Office an annual report of its activities along with a proposed budget or, in the case of community defender organizations, a proposed grant for the coming year. The Director is responsible for the submission of the proposed budgets and grants to the Judicial Conference for approval. The Director also makes payments to the defender organizations out of appropriations in accordance with the approved budgets and grants, as well as compensating private counsel appointed to defend criminal cases in the United States courts.

Budget, Accounting, and Procurement Office. Phone, 202-502-2000.
Court Services Office. Phone, 202-502-1500.
Defender Services Office. Phone, 202-502-3030.
General Counsel Office. Phone, 202-502-1100.
Human Resources Office. Phone, 202-502-3100.
Judicial Conference Executive Secretariat. Phone, 202-502-2400.
Judiciary Reporting and Analysis Division. Phone, 202-502-1440.
Judicial Services Office. Phone, 202-502-1800.
Legislative Affairs Office. Phone, 202-502-1700.
Probation and Pretrial Services Office. Phone, 202-502-1600.
Public Affairs Office. Phone, 202-502-2600.

For further information, contact the Administrative Office of the United States Courts, Thurgood Marshall Federal Judiciary Building, One Columbus Circle NE., Washington, DC 20544. Phone, 202-502-2600.

http://www.uscourts.gov/contact-us

Federal Judicial Center

http://www.fjc.gov
Thurgood Marshall Federal Judiciary Building, One Columbus Circle NE., Washington, DC 20002-8003
202-502-4000

Title	Name
Director	Jeremy D. Fogel
Deputy Director	John S. Cooke
Director, Editorial and Information Services Office	Sylvan A. Sobel
Director, Education Division	John S. Cooke, Acting
Director, Federal Judicial History Office	Clara Altman
Director, Information Technology Office	Esther DeVries
Director, Interjudicial Relations Office	Mira Gur-Arie
Director, Research Division	James B. Eaglin

THE FEDERAL JUDICIARY

The Federal Judicial Center is the judicial branch's agency for policy research and continuing education

The Federal Judicial Center was created by act of December 20, 1967 (28 U.S.C. 620), to further the development and adoption of improved judicial administration in the courts of the United States.

The Center's basic policies and activities are determined by its Board, which is composed of the Chief Justice of the United States, who is permanent Chair of the Board by statute, and two judges of the U.S. courts of appeals, three judges of the U.S. district courts, one bankruptcy judge, and one magistrate judge, all of whom are elected for 4-year terms by the Judicial Conference of the United States. The Director of the Administrative Office of the United States Courts is also a permanent member of the Board.

The Center develops and administers orientation and continuing education programs for Federal judges and defenders and nonjudicial court personnel, including probation officers, pretrial services officers, and clerks' office employees. It conducts research on and evaluates the Federal rules of practice and procedure, court management, and sentencing and its consequences. The Center produces research reports, training manuals, video programs, and computer-based training on the Federal courts; provides guidance and advice and maintains data and records relevant for documenting and conserving the history of the Federal courts; and cooperates with and assists other agencies and organizations in providing advice to improve the administration of justice in foreign courts.

http://www.fjc.gov/public/home.nsf/autoframe?openform&url_l=/public/home.nsf/inavgeneral?openpage&url_r=/public/home.nsf/pages/104

For general information on the Federal Judicial Center, including a directory of telephone and fax numbers for its component offices and divisions, use the link below.

Electronic Access

Selected publications, Federal judicial history databases, and educational resources are available on the Federal Judicial Center's Web site.

http://www.fjc.gov/library/fjc_catalog.nsf

Publications

Single copies of most Federal Judicial Center publications are available free of charge. Phone, 202-502-4153. Fax, 202-502-4077.

For further information, contact the Federal Judicial Center, Thurgood Marshall Federal Judiciary Building, One Columbus Circle NE., Washington, DC 20002-8003. Phone, 202-502-4000. http://www.fjc.gov

United States Sentencing Commission

http://www.ussc.gov
Suite 2-500, One Columbus Circle NE., Washington, DC 20002-8002
202-502-4500

Title	Name
Chair	Patti B. Saris
Vice Chair	Charles R. Breyer
Vice Chair	(vacancy)
Vice Chair	(vacancy)
Commissioner	Rachel E. Barkow
Commissioner	Dabney L. Friedrich
Commissioner	Wiiliam H. Pryor, Jr.
Commissioner (ex officio)	J. Patricia Wilson Smoot
Commissioner (ex officio)	Jonathan J. Wroblewski
Staff Director	Kenneth P. Cohen
Director, Office of Administration and Planning	Susan M. Brazel
Director, Office of Education and Sentencing Practice	Raquel Wilson, Acting
Director, Office of Legislative and Public Affairs	(vacancy)
Director, Office of Research and Data	Glenn R. Schmitt
General Counsel	Kathleen C. Grilli

The United States Sentencing Commission develops sentencing guidelines and policies for the Federal court system.

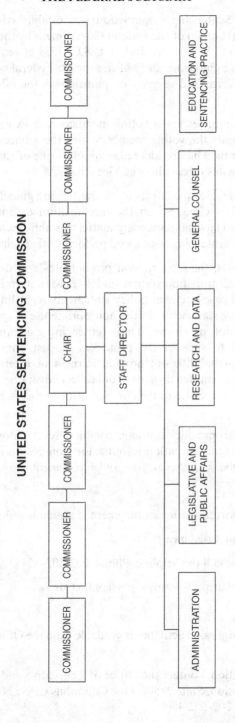

UNITED STATES SENTENCING COMMISSION

The United States Sentencing Commission was established as an independent agency in the judicial branch of the Federal Government by the Sentencing Reform Act of 1984 (28 U.S.C. 991 et seq. and 18 U.S.C. 3551 et seq.). The Commission establishes sentencing guidelines and policies for the Federal courts, advising them of the appropriate form and severity of punishment for offenders convicted of Federal crimes.

The Commission comprises seven voting members and two nonvoting members. The President appoints the voting members with the advice and consent of the Senate for 6-year terms. The President also appoints one of the voting members as the Chair and designates three others as Vice Chairs.

The Commission evaluates the effects of the sentencing guidelines on the criminal justice system, advises Congress on the modification or enactment of statutes pertaining to criminal law and sentencing matters, establishes a research and development program on sentencing issues, and performs other related duties.

In executing its duties, the Commission promulgates and distributes to Federal courts and to the U.S. probation system guidelines for determining sentences to be imposed in criminal cases, general policy statements regarding the application of guidelines, and policy statements on the appropriate use of probation and supervised release revocation provisions. These sentencing guidelines and policy statements are intended to support the principles of just punishment, deterrence, incapacitation, and rehabilitation; provide fairness in meeting the purposes of sentencing; avoid unwarranted disparity; and reflect advancement in the knowledge of human behavior as it relates to the criminal justice process. http://www.ussc.gov/about

The Commission also provides training, conducts research on sentencing-related issues, and serves as an information resource for Congress, criminal justice practitioners, and the public. http://www.ussc.gov/employment

Employment

Information on opportunities for employment is available online.

Guideline Application Assistance

For assistance, please call the helpline. Phone, 202-502-4545.

pubaffairs@ussc.gov http://www.ussc.gov/contact-us

Public Information

Information on Commission activities is available from the Office of Legislative and Public Affairs.

For further information, contact the Office of Legislative and Public Affairs, U.S. Sentencing Commission, Suite 2–500, One Columbus Circle NE., Washington, DC 20002-8002. Phone, 202-502-4500.

Locations and Judges of the U.S. Courts of Appeals

DISTRICT OF COLUMBIA CIRCUIT

Circuit Judges

Merrick B. Garland, Chief Judge
(202) 216-7460.
** Room 5409
Washington, D.C. 20001

Karen LeCraft Henderson
(202) 216-7370.
** Room 3118
Washington, D.C. 20001

Patricia A. Millett
(202) 216-7110.
**Washington, D.C. 20001

Nina Pillard
(202) 216-7120.
**Washington, D.C. 20001

Srikanth Srinivasan
(202) 216-7080.
**Washington, D.C. 20001

Judith W. Rogers
(202) 216-7260.
**Washington, D.C. 20001

David S. Tatel
(202) 216-7160.
** Room 3818
Washington, D.C. 20001-2866

Robert L. Wilkins
(202) 216-7240.
**Washington, D.C. 20001-2858

Brett M. Kavanaugh
(202) 216-7180.
**Washington, D.C. 20001-2866

Janice R. Brown
(202) 216-7220.
**Washington, D.C. 20001-2866

Thomas B. Griffith
(202) 216-7170.
** Room 3118
Washington, D.C. 20001

** United States Courthouse, 333 Constitution Avenue, N.W.
* Source: Almanac of the Federal Judiciary (Aspen Publishers).

Senior Circuit Judges

Harry T. Edwards
 (202) 216-7380.

** Room 5400
Washington, D.C. 20001-2866

David B. Sentelle
 (202) 216-7330.

** Room 5818
Washington, D.C. 20001-2866

Douglas H. Ginsburg
 (202) 216-7190.

** Room 5128
Washington, D.C. 20001-2866

A. Raymond Randolph
 (202) 216-7425.

5010 William B. Bryant U.S.
   Courthouse Annex
333 Constitution Avenue, N.W.
Washington, D.C. 20001-2866

Laurence H. Silberman
 (202) 216-7353.

** Room 3400
Washington, D.C. 20001-2866

Stephen F. Williams
 (202) 216-7210.

** Room 3800
Washington, D.C. 20001-2866

** United States Courthouse, 333 Constitution Avenue, N.W.

FIRST CIRCUIT-Maine, Massachusetts, New Hampshire, Puerto Rico, Rhode Island

Circuit Judges

Jeffrey R. Howard, Chief Judge (603) 225-1525	One Warren Rudman U.S. Courthouse 55 Pleasant Street Concord, NH 03301
David J. Barron (617) 748-9057	*Boston, Massachusetts 02210
William J. Kayatta, Jr. (207) 699-3600	*Boston, Massachusetts 02210
Sandra L. Lynch (617) 748-9014	*Suite 8710 Boston, Massachusetts 02210
Juan R. Torruella (787) 977-6146	Ochoa Building 500 Calle de la Tanca San Juan, Puerto Rico 00901
O. Rogeriee Thompson (401) 272-2960	*Suite 2500 Boston, Massachusetts 02210

---

* John Joseph Moakley U.S. Courthouse, One Courthouse Way

FIRST CIRCUIT-Maine, Massachusetts, New Hampshire, Puerto Rico, Rhode Island- *(Cont'd)*

Senior Circuit Judges

Michael Boudin
(617) 748-4431

*Suite 7710
Boston, Massachusetts 02210

Levin H. Campbell
(617) 748-9002

*Suite 6720
Boston, Massachusetts 02210

Conrad K. Cyr
(207) 941-8150

214 U.S. Courthouse
202 Harlow Street
Bangor, Maine 04401

Bruce M. Selya
(401) 752-7140

316 U.S. Courthouse
One Exchange Terrace
Providence, Rhode Island 02903-1270

Norman H. Stahl
(617) 748-4596

*Suite 8730
Boston, Massachusetts 02210

Kermit V. Lipez
(207) 822-0455

156 Federal Street
Portland, ME 04101

---

* John Joseph Moakley U.S. Courthouse, One Courthouse Way

SECOND CIRCUIT-Connecticut, New York, Vermont

Circuit Judges

Robert A. Katzmann, Chief Judge
(212) 857-2180

*Room 301
New York, New York 10007

Jose A. Cabranes
(203) 867-8782

U.S. Courthouse
141 Church Street
New Haven, Connecticut 06510-2030

Susan L. Carney
(212) 857-8500

U.S. Courthouse
157 Church St.
New Haven, CT 06510

Denny Chin
(212) 805-0200

U.S. Courthouse
500 Pearl Street, Room 1020
New York, NY 10007

Christopher Droney
(860) 240-2635

U.S. Courthouse
450 Main St.
Hartford, CT 06103

Peter W. Hall
(212) 857-8500

*New York, New York 10007

Dennis Jacobs
(212) 857-2150

*New York, NY 10007

Debra A. Livingston
(212) 857-8595

U.S. Courthouse
40 Centre Street
New York, NY 10007

Rosemary S. Pooler
(315) 448-0420

100 S. Clinton Street
Syracuse, New York 13261-7395

Reena Raggi
(718) 260-2490

U.S. Courthouse
225 Cadman Plaza East
Brooklyn, NY 11201

Richard C. Wesley
(585) 243-7910

Livingston County Government
Center
6 Court Street
Geneseo, NY 14454

---

* U.S. Courthouse, 40 Foley Square

SECOND CIRCUIT-Connecticut, New York, Vermont-*(Cont'd)*

Circuit Judges*(Cont'd)*

Gerard E. Lynch
(212) 857-2320

*New York, NY 10007

Raymond J. Lohier, Jr.
(212) 857-8500

*New York, NY 10007

Senior Circuit Judges

Guido Calabresi
(203) 773-2291

U.S. Courthouse
157 Church Street
New Haven, Connecticut 06510

John M. Walker, Jr.
(203) 773-2181

U.S. Courthouse
157 Church Street
New Haven, Connecticut 06510

Amalya Lyle Kearse
(212) 857-2250

*New York, New York 10007

Pierre N. Leval
(212) 857-2310

*Room 1901
New York, NY 10007

Jon O. Newman
(860) 240-3260

450 Main Street
Hartford, Connecticut 06103

---

* U.S. Courthouse, 40 Foley Square

SECOND CIRCUIT-Connecticut, New York, Vermont-*(Cont'd)*

Senior Circuit Judges-(Cont'd)

Ralph K. Winter
(203) 782-3682

U.S. Courthouse
141 Church Street
New Haven, Connecticut 06510

Barrington Daniels Parker, Jr.
(212) 857-8500

U.S. Courthouse
500 Pearl Street
New York, NY 10007

Robert D. Sack
(212) 857-2140

*New York, New York 10007

Chester J. Straub
(212) 857-2130

2530 United States Courthouse
500 Pearl Street
New York, NY 10007

---

* U.S. Courthouse, 40 Foley Square

THIRD CIRCUIT-Delaware, New Jersey, Pennsylvania, Virgin Islands

Circuit Judges

Theodore A. McKee, Chief Judge
(215) 597-9601

20614 U.S. Courthouse
601 Market Street
Philadelphia, Pennsylvania 19106

Thomas L. Ambro
(302) 573-6500

J. Caleb Boggs Federal Courthouse
844 N. King Street
Wilmington, Delaware 19801

Julio M. Fuentes
(973) 645-3831

Martin Luther King
Federal Building and U.S. Courthouse
50 Walnut Street
Newark, New Jersey 07102

Michael A. Chagares
(973) 368-6486

U.S. Courthouse
50 Walnut Street
Newark, New Jersey 07101

D. Brooks Smith
(814) 693-0570

Allegheny Professional Center, Suite 203
1798 Old Route 220 North
Ducansville, Pennsylvania 16635

Cheryl Ann Krause
(215) 597-2995

James A. Byrne U.S. Courthouse
601 Market Street
Philadelphia, PA 19106

D. Michael Fisher
(412) 208-7320

5360 United States Post Office and
Courthouse
700 Grant Street
Pittsburgh, Pennsylvania 15219

THIRD CIRCUIT-Delaware, New Jersey, Pennsylvania, Virgin Islands-*(Cont'd)*

Circuit Judges-(Cont'd)

Joseph A. Greenway, Jr.
(973) 622-4828

Frank R. Lautenberg U.S. Post Office
& Courthouse
Room 411, PO Box 999
Newark, NJ 07101

Thomas M. Hardiman
(412) 208-7440

United States Courthouse
700 Grant Street
Pittsburgh, PA 15219

Kent A. Jordan
(302) 573-6001

6325 Federal Building
Lockbox 10, 844 North King Street
Wilmington, DE 19801

L. Felipe Restrepo
(267) 299-7690

U.S. Courthouse
601 Market Street
Philadelphia, PA 19106

Patty Shwartz
(973) 645-6596

United States Post Office and
Courthouse Building
2 Federal Square, Room 477
Newark, NJ 07101

Thomas I. Vanaskie
(570) 207-5720

Federal Courthouse
Room 234
235 North Washington Avenue
Scranton, PA 18501

Senior Circuit Judges

Anthony J. Scirica
(215) 597-2399

22614 U.S. Courthouse
Independence Mall West
Philadelphia, Pennsylvania 19106

Dolores K. Sloviter
(215) 597-1588

18614 U.S. Courthouse
601 Market Street
Philadelphia, Pennsylvania 19106

Franklin S. Van Antwerpen
(610) 252-6522

The Holmes Building, 4th Floor
101 Larry Holmes Drive
Easton, Pennsylvania 18042

Walter K. Stapleton
(302) 573-6165

U.S. Courthouse
Lockbox 33, 844 King Street
Wilmington, Delaware 19801

THIRD CIRCUIT-Delaware, New Jersey, Pennsylvania, Virgin Islands-*(Cont'd)*

Senior Circuit Judges-(Cont'd)

Robert E. Cowen (609) 989-2188	207 United States Courthouse 402 East State Street Trenton, New Jersey 08608
Jane R. Roth (215) 597-7803	18316 United States Courthouse 601 Market St. Philadelphia, PA 19106
Leonard I. Garth (973) 645-6521	5040 Martin Luther King Jr Federal Building and United States Courthouse 50 Walnut St. Newark, N.J. 07102
Morton I. Greenberg (609) 989-0436	219 United States Courthouse 402 East State Street Trenton, New Jersey 08608
Richard Lowell Nygaard (814) 464-9640 (215) 597-2077	17 South Park Row Suite B-230 Erie, PA 16501 and 18613 United States Courthouse 601 Market Street Philadelphia, PA 19106
Marjorie O. Rendell (215) 597-3015	21613 U.S. Courthouse 601 Market Street Philadelphia, Pennsylvania 19106
Maryanne Trump Barry (973) 645-2133	U.S. Courthouse P.O. Box 999 50 Walnut Street Newark, New Jersey 07101

FOURTH CIRCUIT-Maryland, North Carolina, South Carolina, Virginia, West Virginia

Circuit Judges

William B. Traxler, Jr., Chief Judge (864) 241-2730	300 E. Washington Street, Suite 222 Greenville, South Carolina 29601-2431
James Harvie Wilkinson, III (434) 296-7063	255 West Main Street, Room 230 Charlottesville, Virginia 22902
James A. Wynn. Jr. (804) 916-2700	1100 East Main St. Richmond, VA 23219
Paul V. Niemeyer (410) 962-4210	U.S. Courthouse 101 West Lombard Street Baltimore, Maryland 21201
Diana Gribbon Motz (410) 962-3606	920 U.S. Courthouse 101 West Lombard Street Baltimore, Maryland 21201
Robert Bruce King (304) 347-3533	Robert C. Byrd U.S. Courthouse 300 Virgina Street, Ste. 7602 Charleston, West Virginia 25301
Dennis W. Shedd (803) 253-3688	1100 Laurel Street Columbia, South Carolina 29201-2431
Stephanie D. Thacker (304) 347-3516	Lewis F. Powell, Jr. U.S. Courthouse Annex 1100 East Main Street, Suite 617 Richmond, Virginia 23219-3517
Albert Diaz (704) 333-8025	U.S. Court of Appeals 1100 East Main Street Ste. 501 Richmond, Virginia 23219

FOURTH CIRCUIT-Maryland, North Carolina, South Carolina, Virginia, West Virginia-(Cont'd)

Circuit Judges-(Cont'd)

Allyson K. Duncan
(919) 782-2554

1100 East Main Street
Richmond, VA 23219

Henry F. Floyd
(864) 591-5300

U.S. Courthouse
201 Magnolia Street
Spartanburg, SC 29306

Roger L. Gregory
(804) 916-2607

212 Lewis F. Powell, Jr.
U.S. Courthouse
1000 E. Main Street
Richmond, Virginia 23219-3517

Pamela Harris
(804) 916-2700

Lewis F. Powell Jr. Courthouse &
Annex
1100 East Main Street, Suite 501
Richmond, VA 23219

G. Steven Agee
(804) 916-2700

1100 East Main St.
Richmond, VA 23219

Barbara Milano Keenan
(804) 916-2700

U.S. Courthouse
1100 East Main Street
Richmond, VA 23219

Senior Circuit Judge

Clyde H. Hamilton
(803) 765-5461

NationsBank Plaza, Suite 1250
1901 Main Street, Compartment 704
Columbia, South Carolina 29201

Andre Davis
(410) 962-0801

U.S. Courthouse
101 West Lombard Street
Baltimore, MD 21201

FIFTH CIRCUIT-Louisiana, Mississippi, Texas

Circuit Judges

Carl E. Stewart, Chief Judge (318) 676-3765	5226 United States Courthouse 300 Fannin Street Shreveport, LA 71101
Edith Hollan Jones (713) 250-5484	12505 U.S. Courthouse 515 Rusk Avenue Houston, Texas 77002
E. Grady Jolly (601) 608-4745	3.850 James O. Eastland U.S. Courthouse 245 East Court Street, Jackson, Mississippi 39201
W. Eugene Davis (337) 593-5280	800 Lafayette Street, Suite 5100 Lafayette, Louisiana 70501
Jerry E. Smith (713) 250-5101	12621 U.S. Courthouse 515 Rusk Avenue Houston, Texas 77002-2698
Edith Brown Clement (504) 310-8068	Room 200, 600 Camp Street New Orleans, Louisiana 70130
Gregg J. Costa (713) 250-5500	Bob Casey U.S. Courthouse 515 Rusk Street, Room 5300 Houston TX 77002-2600

FIFTH CIRCUIT-Louisiana, Mississippi, Texas-*(Cont'd)*

Circuit Judges-(Cont'd)

Edward C. Prado (210) 472-4060	U.S. Courthouse 755 E. Mulberry Ave, St. 350 San Antonio, Texas 78212-3186
James L. Dennis (504) 310-8000	219 John Minor Wisdom Courthouse 600 Camp Street New Orleans, Louisiana 70130
Priscilla R. Owen (512) 916-5167	Homer Thornberry Judicial Building 903 San Jacinto Boulevard, Rm. 434 Austin, Texas 78701-2450
Jennifer Walker Elrod (713) 250-7590	U.S. Courthouse 515 Rusk Avenue, Rm. 12014 Houston, TX 77002
Catharina Haynes (214) 753-2750	1100 Commerce St., Rm. 1264 Dallas, TX 75242
Stephen A. Higginson (504) 310-8228	U.S. Courthouse 600 Camp Street, Room 300 New Orleans, LA 70130-3425
Leslie H. Southwick (601) 608-4760	50 East Court St., Suite 3.750 Jackson, MS 39201
James E. Graves (601) 608-4775	501 E. Court St. Suite 3550 Jackson, MS 39201

FIFTH CIRCUIT-Louisiana, Mississippi, Texas-*(Cont'd)*

Senior Circuit Judges

Rhesa H. Barksdale
(601) 608-4730

3.800 James O. Eastland U.S. Courthouse
501 East Court Street
Jackson, Mississippi 39201

Fortunato P. Benavides
(512) 916-5796

Homer Thornberry Judicial Building, Suite 450
903 San Jacinto Boulevard
Austin, Texas 78701

Carolyn Dineen King
(713) 250-5750

11020 Bob Casey U.S. Courthouse
515 Rusk Avenue
Houston, Texas 77002

John M. Duhe, Jr.
(337) 593-5250

U.S. Courthouse
600 Camp Street
New Orleans, LA 70103

Patrick E. Higginbotham
(512) 916-5723

Homer Thornberry Judicial Building
903 San Jacinto Boulevard, Room 400
Austin, TX 78701

Thomas M. Reavley
(713) 250-5185

515 Rusk Avenue
Houston, TX 77002

Jacques L. Wiener, Jr.
(504) 310-8098

John Minor Wisdom U.S. Court of Appeals Building
600 Camp Street, Room 244
New Orleans, Louisiana 70130

SIXTH CIRCUIT-Kentucky, Michigan, Ohio, Tennessee

Circuit Judges

Ransey Guy Cole, Jr., Chief Judge
(614) 719-3350

127 United States Courthouse
85 Marconi Boulevard
Columbus, Ohio 43215

Alice M. Batchelder
(330) 764-6026

143 West Liberty Street
Medina, Ohio 44256

Danny J. Boggs
(502) 625-3900

220 United States Courthouse
601 West Broadway
Louisville, KY 40202

Karen Nelson Moore
(216) 357-7290

Carl B. Stokes United States
Courthouse
801 West Superior Avenue
Cleveland, OH 44113-1831

Julia Smith Gibbons
(901) 495-1265

970 Federal Building
167 North Main Street
Memphis, TN 38103

Eric L. Clay
(313) 234-5260

481 Theodore Levin United States
Courthouse
231 West Lafayette Boulevard
Detroit, MI 48226

John M. Rogers
(859) 233-2680

100 East Vine Street
Community Trust Bank Building
Suite 400
Lexington, Kentucky 40507

SIXTH CIRCUIT-Kentucky, Michigan, Ohio, Tennessee-*(Cont'd)*

Circuit Judges-*(Cont'd)*

Jeffrey S. Sutton
(614) 849-0134

260 U.S. Courthouse
85 Marconi Boulevard
Columbus, Ohio 43215

Deborah L. Cook
(330) 375-5412

433 Courthouse and Federal Building
Two South Main Street
Akron, Ohio 01410

Bernice Bouie Donald
(513) 564-7000

540 Potter Stewart U.S. Courthouse
100 East Fifth Street
Cincinnati, Ohio 45202

Richard A. Griffin
(513) 564-7000

540 Potter Stewart U.S. Courthouse
100 East 5th Street
Cincinnati, OH 45202

David W. McKeague
(517) 377-1563

Charles E. Chamberlain
Federal Building
315 West Allegan Street, Room 213
Lansing, Michigan 48933

Raymond M. Kethledge
(513) 564-7000

540 Potter Stewart U.S. Courthouse
100 East Fifth Street
Cincinnati, Ohio 45202

Jane Branstetter Stranch
(513) 564-7000

Potter Stewart U.S. Courthouse
100 East Fifth St.
Cincinnati, Ohio 45202

Helene N. White
(513) 564-7000

540 Potter Stewart U.S. Courthouse
100 East Fifth Street
Cincinnati, Ohio 45202

Senior Circuit Judges

Ronald Lee Gilman
(901) 495-1575

1176 Federal Building
167 North Main Street
Memphis, Tennessee 38103

Martha Craig Daughtrey
(615) 736-7678

300 U.S. Customs House
701 Broadway
Nashville, Tennessee 37203

James L. Ryan
(313) 234-5250

611 Theodore Levin U.S. Courthouse
231 West Lafayette Boulevard
Detroit, Michigan 48226

SIXTH CIRCUIT-Kentucky, Michigan, Ohio, Tennessee-*(Cont'd)*

Senior Circuit Judges-(Cont'd)

Damon J. Keith
(313) 234-5245

240 U.S. Courthouse
231 West Lafayette Boulevard
Detroit, Michigan 48226

Alan E. Norris
(614) 719-3330

328 U.S. Courthouse
85 Marconi Boulevard
Columbus, Ohio 43215

Eugene E. Siler, Jr.
(606) 877-7930

310 South Main Street
Suite 333
London, KY 40741

Richard F. Suhrheinrich
(517) 377-1513

241 Federal Building
315 West Allegan Street
Lansing, Michigan 48933

Ralph B. Guy, Jr.
(734) 741-2300

200 East Liberty Street
Room 226
Ann Arbor, MI 48104

Gilbert S. Merritt
(615) 736-5957

303 U.S. Customs House
701 Broadway
Nashville, Tennessee 37203

SEVENTH CIRCUIT-Illinois, Indiana, Wisconsin

Circuit Judges

Diane P. Wood, Chief Judge
(312) 435-5521

* Room 2602
Chicago, Illinois 60604-1803

Frank H. Easterbrook
(312) 435-5808

*Room 2746
Chicago, Illinois 60604

Joel M. Flaum
(312) 435-5626

*Room 2702
Chicago, Illinois 60604

Richard A. Posner
(312) 435-5806

*Room 2788
Chicago, Illinois 60604

Michael S. Kanne
(312) 435-5764

2447H Halleck Federal Building
4th and Ferry Streets
Lafayette, IN 47902

Ilana Diamond Rovner
(312) 435-5608

*Room 2774
Chicago, Illinois 60604

Ann C. Williams
(312) 435-5532

*Room 2612
Chicago, Illinois 60604

Diane S. Sykes
(414) 727-6988

716 United States Courthouse and
Federal Building
517 East Wisconsin Avenue
Milwaukee, WI 53202

David F. Hamilton
(312) 435-5850

330 Birch Bayh Federal Building
& U.S. Courthouse
46 East Ohio Street
Indianapolis, IN 46204

---

* Everett McKinley Dirksen U.S. Courthouse, 219 South Dearborn Street

SEVENTH CIRCUIT-Illinois, Indiana, Wisconsin-*(Cont'd)*

Senior Circuit Judges

William J. Bauer
(312) 435-5810

*Room 2754
Chicago, Illinois 60604

Kenneth F. Ripple
(574) 246-8150

208 U.S. Courthouse
204 South Main Street
South Bend, Indiana 46601-2122

Daniel A. Manion
(574) 246-8060

301 Federal Building
204 South Main Street
South Bend, Indiana 46601

---

* Everett McKinley Dirksen U.S. Courthouse, 219 South Dearborn Street

EIGHTH CIRCUIT-Arkansas, Iowa, Minnesota, Missouri, Nebraska, North Dakota, South Dakota

Circuit Judges

William Jay Riley, Chief Judge
(402) 661-7575

Roman L. Hruska Courthouse
111 South 18th Plaza, Suite 4303
Omaha, Nebraska 68102-1322

James B. Loken
(612) 664-5810

U.S. Courthouse, Suite 11W
300 South Fourth Street
Minneapolis, Minnesota 55415

Roger L. Wollman
(605) 330-6680

315 U.S. Courthouse
400 South Phillips Avenue
Sioux Falls, South Dakota 57104-6851

Diana E. Murphy
(612) 664-5820

11E U.S. Courthouse
300 South 4th Street
Minneapolis, Minnesota 55415

Lavenski R. Smith
(501) 324-7310

Richard S. Arnold U.S. Courthouse
600 West Capitol Ave., Ste. A502
Little Rock, AR 72201

Steven M. Colloton
(515) 284-6356

110 E. Court Avenue, Suite 461
Des Moines, Iowa 50309

Raymond W. Gruender
(314) 244-2820

Thomas S. Eagleton United States
Courthouse
111 South 10th Street, Suite 23-365
St. Louis, Missouri 63102

Jane Kelly
(319) 423-6110

111 7th Avenue S.E.
Cedar Rapids, IA 52401-2101

EIGHTH CIRCUIT-Arkansas, Iowa, Minnesota, Missouri, Nebraska, North Dakota, South Dakota-(*Cont'd*)

Circuit Judges-(*Cont'd*)

Bobby E. Shepherd
(870) 863-3173

W. Duane Benton
(816) 512-5815

Senior Circuit Judges

Michael J. Melloy
(319) 423-6080

Myron H. Bright
(701) 297-7260

Clarence Arlen Beam
(402) 437-1600

Kermit E. Bye
(701) 297-7270

David R. Hansen
(319) 364-5815

Pasco M. Bowman II
(816) 512-5800

Morris S. Arnold
(501) 324-6880

U.S. Courthouse
101 S. Jackson St.
El Dorado, AR 71730

1020 Charles Evans Whittaker United States Courthouse
400 East Ninth Street
Kansas City, MO 64106-2605

United States Courthouse & Federal Building
111 Seventh Avenue, S.E.
Cedar Rapids, IA 52401

Quentin N. Burdick United States Courthouse
Suite 340
655 First Avenue North
Fargo, ND 58102-4952

435 Federal Building
100 Centennial Mall North
Lincoln, Nebraska 68508

Quentin N. Burdick
U.S. Courthouse
655 1st Avenue North, Chambers 330
Fargo, North Dakota 58102-4952

United States Courthouse
221 Third Ave., SE; Suite 400
Cedar Rapids, IA 52401

10-50 Charles Evans Whittaker
U.S. Courthouse
400 East Ninth Street
Kansas City, Missouri 64106

Richard Sheppard Arnold U.S. Courthouse
600 W. Capital Avenue
Suite A414
Little Rock AR 72201

NINTH CIRCUIT-Alaska, Arizona, California, Guam, Hawaii, Idaho, Montana, Nevada, Northern Mariana Islands, Oregon, Washington

Circuit Judges

Sidney R. Thomas, Chief Judge (406) 657-5950	P.O. Box 31478 Billings, MT 59107-1478
Alex Kozinski (626) 229-7150	Richard H. Chambers Courthouse 125 South Grand Avenue Pasadena, California 91105
Carlos T. Bea (415) 556-3000	95 Seventh Street; Suite 205 San Francisco, CA 94103-1526
Morgan Christen (415) 355-8000	James R. Browning Courthouse 95 7th Street San Francisco, CA 94103
Richard R. Clifton (808) 522-7474	999 Bishop Street Suite 2010 Honolulu, HI 96813
Michelle T. Friedland (415) 355-8000	James R. Browning Courthouse 95 7th Street San Francisco, CA 94103
Harry Pregerson (818) 710-7791	21800 Oxnard Street, Suite 1140 Woodland Hills, California 91367-3633
Stephen Reinhardt (213) 894-3639	1747 U.S. Courthouse 312 North Spring Street Los Angeles, California 90012
Andrew D. Hurwitz (415) 355-8000	James R. Browning Courthouse 95 7th Street San Francisco, CA 94103
Diarmuid F. O'Scannlain (503) 833-5380	The Pioneer Courthouse 700 S.W. Sixth Avenue, Suite 313 Portland, OR 97204-1396
Sandra Segal Ikuta (626) 229-7250	Richard H. Chambers United States Courthouse 125 South Grand Avenue Pasadena, CA 91109

NINTH CIRCUIT-Alaska, Arizona, California, Guam, Hawaii, Idaho, Montana, Nevada, Northern Mariana Islands, Oregon, Washington-(*Cont'd*)

Circuit Judges-(*Cont'd*)

Milan D. Smith, Jr.
(310) 607-4020

U.S. Court of Appeals
Suite 2325
222 N. Sepulveda Blvd.
El Segundo, California 90245-5648

Mary Murguia
(415) 355-8000

James R. Browning Courthouse
95 7th Street
San Francisco, CA 94103

Barry G. Silverman
(602) 322-7330

Sandra Day O'Connor U.S.
Courthouse
401 West Washington Street SPC 78
Phoenix, Arizona 85003

William A. Fletcher
(415) 355-8140

95 7th Street
San Francisco, California 94103-1526

Susan P. Graber
(503) 326-7608

Pioneer Courthouse
555 S.W. Yamhill Street
Portland, Oregon 97204

Mary Margaret McKeown
(619) 557-5300

401 West A Street, Suite 2000
San Diego, California 92101

Johnnie B. Rawlinson
(702) 464-5670

333 Las Vegas Boulevard South,
Room 7072
Las Vegas, Nevada 89101

Kim McLane Wardlaw
(626) 229-7130

Richard H. Chambers
U.S. Courthouse
125 S. Grand Ave., Suite 500
Pasadena, California 91105

Ronald M. Gould
(206) 553-7344

William K. Nakamura U.S.
Courthouse
1010 5th Ave., Ste. 940
Seattle, WA 98104

NINTH CIRCUIT-Alaska, Arizona, California, Guam, Hawaii, Idaho, Montana, Nevada, Northern Mariana Islands, Oregon, Washington-*(Cont'd)*

Circuit Judges-(Cont'd)

Richard A. Paez
(626) 229-7180

Richard H. Chambers U.S.
  Courthouse
125 S. Grand Ave.
Pasadena, California 91105

Marsha S. Berzon
(415) 556-7800

95 Seventh Street
San Francisco, California 94103-1526

Jacqueline H. Nguyen
(213) 894-2554

U.S. Courthouse
312 N. Spring Street
Los Angeles, CA 90012

Richard C. Tallman
(206) 224-2250

William K. Nakamura U.S.
  Courthouse
1010 5th Avenue, Suite 902
Seattle, WA 98104-1130

Jay S. Bybee
(702) 464-5650

Lloyd B. George U.S. Courthouse
333 Las Vegas Boulevard, Suite 3099
Las Vegas, Nevada 89101

Consuelo Maria Callahan
(916) 930-4160

U.S. Courthouse
501 I Street
Sacramento, California 95814

Norman R. Smith
(415) 355-8000

United States Courthouse
95 Seventh Street
San Francisco, CA 94103

John B. Owens
(626) 229-7250

Richard H. Chambers Courthouse
125 South Grand Ave.
Pasadena, CA 91105

Paul J. Watford
(626) 229-7250

Richard H. Chambers U.S.
Courthouse
125 South Grand Ave.
Pasadena, CA 91105

NINTH CIRCUIT-Alaska, Arizona, California, Guam, Hawaii, Idaho, Montana, Nevada, Northern Mariana Islands, Oregon, Washington-(*Cont'd*)

Senior Circuit Judges

Mary M. Schroeder
(602) 322-7320

U.S. Courthouse, Suite 610
401 West Washington Street, SPC 54
Phoenix, Arizona 85003-2156

Raymond C. Fisher
(626) 229-7110

U.S. Courthouse
125 South Grand Avenue, Suite 400
Pasadena, California 91105

Alfred T. Goodwin
(626) 229-7100

506 United States Courthouse
125 South Grand Avenue
Pasadena, CA 91105

Procter Hug, Jr.
(775) 686-5949

708 Bruce Thompson
U.S. Courthouse
400 South Virginia Street
Reno, Nevada 89501-1948

Ferdinand F. Fernandez
(626) 229-7121

602 Richard H. Chambers U.S.
     Courthouse
125 South Grand Avenue
Pasadena, California 91105

J. Clifford Wallace
(619) 557-6114

4192 U.S. Courthouse
940 Front Street
San Diego, California 92101-8918

Jerome Farris
(206) 224-2260

1030 U.S. Courthouse
1010 Fifth Avenue
Seattle, Washington 98104-1181

NINTH CIRCUIT-Alaska, Arizona, California, Guam, Hawaii, Idaho,
Montana, Nevada, Northern Mariana Islands,
Oregon, Washington-*(Cont'd)*

Senior Circuit Judges-(Cont'd)

Dorothy W. Nelson
(626) 229-7400

Richard H. Chambers
U.S. Courthouse
125 South Grand Avenue, Suite 303
Pasadena, California 91105-1652

William C. Canby, Jr.
(602) 322-7300

612 Sandra Day O'Connor U.S.
Courthouse
401 West Washington Street SPC 55
Phoenix, Arizona 85003

John T. Noonan, Jr.
(415) 556-9636

95 Seventh St.
San Francisco, California 94103-1526

Stephen S. Trott
(208) 334-1612

667 U.S. Courthouse
550 West Fort Street
Boise, Idaho 83724-0040

Edward Leavy
(503) 833-5350

Pioneer Courthouse
700 S.W. Sixth Avenue, Suite 226
Portland, Oregon 97204

A. Wallace Tashima
(626) 229-7373

Richard H. Chambers U.S.
Courthouse, Suite 406
125 South Grand Avenue
Pasadena, California 91105

Andrew J. Kleinfeld
(907) 456-0564

Courthouse Square
250 Cushman Street, Suite 3-A
Fairbanks, Alaska 99701-4665

Michael D. Hawkins
(602) 322-7310

510 Sandra Day O'Connor U.S.
Courthouse
401 West Washington Street, SPC 47
Phoenix, Arizona 85003-2151

TENTH CIRCUIT-Colorado, Kansas, New Mexico, Oklahoma, Utah, Wyoming

Circuit Judges

Timothy M. Tymkovich, Chief Judge (303) 844-3157	Byron White U.S. Courthouse 1823 Stout Street Denver, Colorado 80257
Robert E. Bacharach (405) 609-5320	U.S. Courthouse 200 N.W. 4th Street Oklahoma City, OK 73102
Mary Beck Briscoe (785) 843-4067	645 Massachusetts Street, Suite 400 Lawrence, Kansas 66044
Paul J. Kelly, Jr. (505) 988-6541	120 United States Courthouse South Federal Place Santa Fe, NM 87501
Carlos F. Lucero (303) 844-2200	Byron White U.S. Courthouse 1823 Stout Street Denver, Colorado 80257
Carolyn B. McHugh (303) 335-2728	Byron White U.S. Courthouse 1823 Stout Street Denver, CO 80257
Harris L. Hartz (505) 843-6196	201 Third Street N.W., Suite 1870 Albuquerque, NM 87102
Neil M. Gorsuch (303) 844-3157	Byron White U.S. Courthouse 1823 Stout Street Denver, Colorado 80257
Nancy L. Moritz (303) 335-2728	Byron White U.S. Courthouse 1823 Stout Street Denver, CO 80257
Gregory Alan Phillips (303) 844-3157	Byron White U.S. Courthouse 1823 Stout Street Denver, CO 80257

TENTH CIRCUIT-Colorado, Kansas, New Mexico, Oklahoma, Utah, Wyoming-*(Cont'd)*

Circuit Judges-(Cont'd)

Jerome A. Holmes
(405) 609-5480

U.S. Courthouse
215 Dean A. McGee Ave. Room 315
Oklahoma City, OK 73102

Scott M. Matheson, Jr.
(303) 844-3157

The Byron White U.S. Courthouse
1823 Stout Street
Denver, CO 80257

Senior Circuit Judges

Michael R. Murphy
(801) 524-5955

5438 Wallace F. Bennett Federal
Building
125 South State Street
Salt Lake City, Utah 84138-1181

Terrence L. O'Brien
(307) 433-2400

2120 Capitol Avenue
Room 2141
Cheyenne, Wyoming 82001

Monroe G. McKay
(801) 524-5252

6012 Wallace F. Bennett Federal Building
125 South State Street
Salt Lake City, Utah 84138-1181

John C. Porfilio
(303) 844-6346

Byron White U.S. Courthouse
1823 Stout Street
Denver, Colorado 80257

Stephen H. Anderson
(801) 524-6950

4201 Wallace F. Bennett Federal Building
125 South State Street
Salt Lake City, Utah 84138-1102

TENTH CIRCUIT-Colorado, Kansas, New Mexico, Oklahoma, Utah, Wyoming-(Cont'd)

Senior Circuit Judges-(Cont'd)

Bobby R. Baldock
(575) 625-2388

P.O. Box 2388
Roswell, NM 88202

Wade Brorby
(307) 772-2885

P.O. Box 1028
Cheyenne, Wyoming 82003

Stephanie K. Seymour
(918) 699-4745

4562 United States Courthouse
333 West Fourth Street
Tulsa, OK 74103-3877

David M. Ebel
(303) 844-3800

109L Byron White U.S. Courthouse
1823 Stout Street
Denver, Colorado 80257

ELEVENTH CIRCUIT-Alabama, Florida, Georgia

Circuit Judges

Edward E. Carnes, Chief Judge
(334) 954-3580

United States Courthouse
One Church Street
Montgomery, AL 36104

Gerald B. Tjoflat
(904) 301-6570

*Atlanta, Georgia 30303

Jill A. Pryor
(404) 335-6100

*Atlanta, GA 30303

Julie E. Carnes
(404) 215-1510

U.S. Courthouse
75 Spring Street, S.W.
Atlanta, GA 30303

Frank Mays Hull
(404) 335-6550

*Room 300
Atlanta, Georgia 30303

Adalberto Jose Jordan
(305) 523-5560

400 North Miami Avenue
Miami, FL 33128

Stanley Marcus
(305) 536-4841

U.S. Courthouse
99 N.E. 4th Street, Room 1262
Miami, Florida 33132

Robin S. Rosenbaum
(305) 579-4430

Clerk's Office
99 N.E. 4th St., #1212
Miami, Florida 33132

Charles R. Wilson
(813) 301-5650
(813) 301-5659

Sam M. Gibbons U.S. Courthouse
801 North Florida Avenue
Tampa, Florida 33602-4511

William H. Pryor, Jr.
(205) 278-2030

1729 Fifth Avenue N., Suite 900
Birmingham, AL 35203

Beverly B. Martin
(404) 335-6100

U.S. Courthouse
56 Forsyth St., N.W.
Atlanta, GA 30303

---

* Elbert P. Tuttle Court of Appeals Building, 56 Forsyth Street, N.W.

ELEVENTH CIRCUIT-Alabama, Florida, Georgia-*(Cont'd)*

Senior Circuit Judges

J.L. Edmondson
(404) 335-6230

*Room 416
Atlanta, Georgia 30303

Susan H. Black
(904) 232-2496

300 N. Hogan St.
Jacksonville, Florida 32202

Phyllis A. Kravitch
(404) 335-6300

*Room 202
Atlanta, Georgia 30303

James C. Hill
(904) 232-2284

United States Courthouse
300 N. Hogan St.
Jacksonville, FL 32202

Peter T. Fay
(305) 536-5974

Federal Justice Building
Room 1255
99 N.E. Fourth Street
Miami, Florida 33132

Emmett R. Cox
(251) 690-2055

113 St. Joseph Street, Room 433
Mobile, Alabama 36602

R. Lanier Anderson, III
(478) 752-8101

*Atlanta, Georgia 30303

Joel F. Dubina
(334) 954-3560

United States Courthouse
One Church Street
Montgomery, AL 36104

---

* Elbert P. Tuttle Court of Appeals Building, 56 Forsyth Street, N.W.

UNITED STATES COURT OF APPEALS FOR THE FEDERAL CIRCUIT

Circuit Judges

Sharon Prost, Chief Judge
(202) 275-8000

*Washington, D.C. 20439

Pauline Newman
(202) 275-8000

*Washington, D.C. 20439

Alan D. Lourie
(202) 275-8580

*Washington, D.C. 20439

Timothy B. Dyk
(202) 275-8000

*Room 915
Washington, D.C. 20439

Kimberly Ann Moore
(202) 275-8000

*Washington, D.C. 20439

Kathleen O'Malley
(202) 275-8000

*Washington, D.C. 20439

Raymond T. Chen
(202) 275-8000

*Washington, D.C. 20439

Todd M. Hughes
(202) 275-8000

*Washington, D.C. 20439

Jimmie V. Reyna
(202) 275-8000

*Washington, D.C. 20005

Kara Farnandez Stoll
(202) 275-8000

*Washington, D.C. 20005

Richard G. Taranto
(202) 275-8000

*Washington, D.C. 20439

Evan J. Wallach
(202) 275-8000

*Washington, D.C. 20439

Senior Circuit Judges

Richard Linn
(202) 275-8000

*Washington, D.C. 20439

William C. Bryson
(202) 275-8000

*Washington, D.C. 20439

---

* Howard T. Markey National Courts Building, 717 Madison Place, N.W.

S. Jay Plager
(202) 275-8000

*Washington, D.C. 20439

Raymond C. Clevenger, III
(202) 275-8000

*Washington, D.C. 20439

Haldane Robert Mayer
(202) 275-8560

*Washington, D.C. 20439

Alvin A. Schall
(202) 275-8000

*Washington, D.C. 20439

---

* Howard T. Markey National Courts Building, 717 Madison Place, N.W.

Locations and Judges of the U.S. District Courts

ALABAMA, MIDDLE

W. Keith Watkins, Chief Judge

W. Harold Albritton, III, Senior Judge

Myron H. Thompson, Senior Judge

William R. Sawyer, Chief Bankruptcy Judge

Dwight H. Williams, Bankruptcy Judge

Charles S. Coody, Chief Magistrate Judge

Gray M. Borden, Magistrate Judge

Susan Russ Walker, Magistrate Judge

Wallace Capel, Jr., Magistrate Judge

Terry F. Moorer, Magistrate Judge

ALABAMA, NORTHERN

Karon Bowdre, Chief Judge
Abdul K. Kallon, District Judge
L. Scott Coogler, District Judge
Madeline H. Haikala, District Judge
Virginia E. Hopkins, District Judge
R. David Proctor, District Judge
William M. Acker, Jr., Senior Judge
Sharon Lovelace Blackburn, Senior District Judge
J. Foy Guin, Jr., Senior Judge
James Hughes Hancock, Senior Judge
Inge Prytz Johnson, Senior Judge
Robert B. Propst, Senior Judge
C. Lynwood Smith, Jr., Senior Judge
James J. Robinson, Chief Bankruptcy Judge
Jack Caddell, Bankruptcy Judge
Jennifer H. Henderson, Bankruptcy Judge
Clinton R. Jessup, Jr., Bankruptcy Judge
Tamara O. Mitchell, Bankruptcy Judge
Robert A. Armstrong, Jr., Magistrate Judge
Harwell G. Davis, III, Magistrate Judge
John E. Ott, Magistrate Judge
Terry Michael Putnam, Magistrate Judge
Staci G. Cornelius, Magistrate Judge

ALABAMA, SOUTHERN

William H. Steele, Chief Judge
Callie V. Granade, District Judge
Kristi K. DuBose, District Judge
Charles R. Butler, Jr., Senior Judge
William S. Shulman, Chief Bankruptcy Judge
Margaret A. Mahoney, Bankruptcy Judge
Jerry C. Oldshue, Jr., Bankruptcy Judge
Sonja Faye Bivins, Magistrate Judge
William E. Cassady, Magistrate Judge
Bert W. Milling, Jr., Magistrate Judge
Katherine P. Nelson, Magistrate Judge

ALASKA

Ralph Beistline, Chief Judge
Timothy Burgess, District Judge
Sharon L. Gleason, District Judge
John W. Sedwick, Senior Judge
H. Russel Holland, Senior Judge
James K. Singleton, Jr., Senior Judge
Donald MacDonald, IV, Chief Bankruptcy Judge
Herbert A. Ross, Bankruptcy Judge
Leslie C. Longenbaugh, Magistrate Judge
Deborah M. Smith, Magistrate Judge
Kevin F. McCoy, Magistrate Judge (Part-time)
Scott A. Oravec, Magistrate Judge (Part-time)
Matthew D. Jamin, Magistrate Judge (Part-time)

ARIZONA

Raner C. Collins, Chief Judge
Susan R. Bolton, District Judge
David G. Campbell, District Judge
Cindy Jorgenson, District Judge
G. Murray Snow, District Judge
Neil V. Wake, District Judge
Jennifer G. Zipps, District Judge
Diane J. Humetewa, District Judge
Steven P. Logan, District Judge
Rosemary Marquez, District Judge
Douglas L. Rayes, District Judge
James A. Soto, District Judge
John J. Tuchi, District Judge
Roslyn O. Silver, Senior Judge
David C. Bury, Senior Judge
Frederick J. Martone, Senior Judge
James A. Teilborg, Senior Judge
Paul G. Rosenblatt, Senior Judge
Stephen M. McNamee, Senior Judge
Frank R. Zapata, Senior Judge
Daniel Collins, Chief Bankruptcy Judge
Edward P. Ballinger, Jr., Bankruptcy Judge
Charles G. Case, II, Bankruptcy Judge
Scott H. Gan, Bankruptcy Judge
Eileen W. Hollowell, Bankruptcy Judge
James M. Marlar, Bankruptcy Judge
Brenda K. Martin, Bankruptcy Judge
George B. Nielsen, Jr., Bankruptcy Judge
Paul Sala, Bankruptcy Judge
Madeleine C. Wanslee, Bankruptcy Judge
Brenda M. Whinery, Bankruptcy Judge
Mark E. Aspey, Magistrate Judge

ARIZONA-*(Cont'd)*

Bridget S. Bade, Magistrate Judge

Leslie A. Bowman, Magistrate Judge

John Z. Boyle, Magistrate Judge

Michelle H. Burns, Magistrate Judge

John A. Buttrick, Magistrate Judge (Part-Time)

David K. Duncan, Magistrate Judge

Glenda E. Edmonds, Magistrate Judge

Hector C. Estrada, Magistrate Judge

D. Thomas Ferraro, Magistrate Judge

Bruce MacDonald, Magistrate Judge

Eric J. Markovich, Magistrate Judge

Jacqueline Marshall, Magistrate Judge

James F. Metcalf, Magistrate Judge

Charles R. Pyle, Magistrate Judge

Jacqueline Rateau, Magistrate Judge

Bernardo P. Velasco, Magistrate Judge

Edward C. Voss, III, Magistrate Judge

Eileen S. Willett, Magistrate Judge

ARKANSAS, EASTERN

Brian S. Miller, Chief Judge
J. Leon Holmes, District Judge
Kristine G. Baker, District Judge
Denzil P. Marshall, Jr., District Judge
James M. Moody, Jr., District Judge
Susan Webber Wright, Senior Judge
Bill Wilson, Senior Judge
Garnett Thomas Eisele, Senior Judge
Richard D. Taylor, Chief Bankruptcy Judge
Audrey R. Evans, Bankruptcy Judge
Ben T. Barry, Bankruptcy Judge
James G. Mixon, Bankruptcy Judge
Jerry W. Cavaneau, Magistrate Judge
Beth M. Deere, Magistrate Judge
Patricia S. Harris, Magistrate Judge
J. Thomas Ray, Magistrate Judge
H. David Young, Magistrate Judge
Jerome T. Kearney, Magistrate Judge
Joseph Volpe, Magistrate Judge

ARKANSAS, WESTERN

Paul K. Holmes, III, Chief Judge
Susan O. Hickey, District Judge
Timothy L. Brooks, District Judge
Harry F. Barnes, Senior Judge
Robert T. Dawson, Senior Judge
Jimm Larry Hendren, Senior Judge
Richard D. Taylor, Chief Bankruptcy Judge
Audrey R. Evans, Bankruptcy Judge
Ben T. Barry, Bankruptcy Judge
James G. Mixon, Bankruptcy Judge
Barry A. Bryant, Magistrate Judge
James R. Marschewski, Magistrate Judge
Erin L. Setser, Magistrate Judge
Beverly R. Stites, Magistrate Judge

CALIFORNIA, CENTRAL

George Herbert King, Chief Judge
Manuel L. Real, District Judge
Stephen V. Wilson, District Judge
David O. Carter, District Judge
Percy Anderson, District Judge
Cormac J. Carney, District Judge
Dean D. Pregerson, District Judge
Christina A. Snyder, District Judge
Virginia A. Phillips, District Judge
Dale S. Fischer, District Judge
R. Gary Klausner, District Judge
S. James Otero, District Judge
John F. Walter, District Judge
James V. Selna, District Judge
Michael W. Fitzgerald, District Judge
Dolly M. Gee, District Judge
Andrew J. Guilford, District Judge
Philip S. Gutierrez, District Judge
John A. Kronstadt, District Judge
Otis D. Wright, II, District Judge
George H. Wu, District Judge
Jesus G. Bernal, District Judge
Andre Birotte, Jr., District Judge
Beverly Reid O'Connell, District Judge
Fernando M. Olguin, District Judge
Josephine L. Staton, District Judge
Terry J. Hatter, Jr., Senior Judge
Robert J. Timlin, Senior Judge
William D. Keller, Senior Judge

CALIFORNIA, CENTRAL-*(Cont'd)*

Consuelo Bland Marshall, Senior Judge

Ronald S. W. Lew, Senior Judge

Valerie Baker Fairbank, Senior Judge

Peter H. Carroll, Chief Bankruptcy Judge

Alan M. Ahart, Bankruptcy Judge

Theodor C. Albert, Bankruptcy Judge

Neil W. Bason, Bankruptcy Judge

Catherine Bauer, Bankruptcy Judge

Sheri Bluebond, Bankruptcy Judge

Julia W. Brand, Bankruptcy Judge

Scott C. Clarkson, Bankruptcy Judge

Thomas B. Donovan, Bankruptcy Judge

Mark D. Houle, Bankruptcy Judge

Wayne E. Johnson, Bankruptcy Judge

Meredith A. Jury, Bankruptcy Judge

Victoria S. Kaufman, Bankruptcy Judge

Sandra R. Klein, Bankruptcy Judge

Robert N. Kwan, Bankruptcy Judge

Richard M. Neiter, Bankruptcy Judge

Robin L. Riblet, Bankruptcy Judge

Ernest Robles, Bankruptcy Judge

Barry Russell, Bankruptcy Judge

Deborah J. Saltzman, Bankruptcy Judge

Erithe A. Smith, Bankruptcy Judge

Maureen A. Tighe, Bankruptcy Judge

Mark S. Wallace, Bankruptcy Judge

Scott H. Yun, Bankruptcy Judge

Vincent P. Zurzolo, Bankruptcy Judge

Patrick J. Walsh, Chief Magistrate Judge

Paul L. Abrams, Magistrate Judge

David T. Bristow, Magistrate Judge

Jacqueline Chooljian, Magistrate Judge

Charles F. Eick, Magistrate Judge

Paul Game, Magistrate Judge

CALIFORNIA, CENTRAL-*(Cont'd)*

Jay C. Gandhi, Magistrate Judge
Stephen J. Hillman, Magistrate Judge
Kenley K. Kato, Magistrate Judge
Victor B. Kenton, Magistrate Judge
Louise A. LaMothe, Magistrate Judge
Alexander F. MacKinnon, Magistrate Judge
Douglas F. McCormick, Magistrate Judge
John E. McDermott, Magistrate Judge
Frederick F. Mumm, Magistrate Judge
Arthur Nakazato, Magistrate Judge
Oswald Parada, Magistrate Judge
Sheri N. Pym, Magistrate Judge
Alicia G. Rosenberg, Magistrate Judge
Jean P. Rosenbluth, Magistrate Judge
Alka Sagar, Magistrate Judge
Karen E. Scott, Magistrate Judge
Suzanne H. Segal, Magistrate Judge
Karen L. Stevenson, Magistrate Judge
Michael R. Wilner, Magistrate Judge
Andrew J. Wistrich, Magistrate Judge
Carla M. Woehrle, Magistrate Judge

CALIFORNIA, EASTERN

Morrison C. England, Jr., Chief Judge
Dale Drozd, District Judge
John A. Mendez, District Judge
Kimberly J. Mueller, District Judge
Lawrence J. O'Neill, District Judge
Troy L. Nunley, District Judge
Garland E. Burrell, Jr., Senior Judge
Anthony W. Ishii, Senior Judge
William B. Shubb, Senior Judge
Ronald H. Sargis, Chief Bankruptcy Judge
Robert S. Bardwil, Bankruptcy Judge
Philip H. Brandt, Bankruptcy Judge
Frederick E. Clement, Bankruptcy Judge
Christopher D. Jaime, Bankruptcy Judge
Christopher M. Klein, Bankruptcy Judge
Rene Lastreto, II, Bankruptcy Judge
W. Richard Lee, Bankruptcy Judge
Michael S. McManus, Bankruptcy Judge
David E. Russell, Bankruptcy Judge
Gary S. Austin, Magistrate Judge
Stanley A. Boone, Magistrate Judge
Edmund F. Brennan, Magistrate Judge
Allison Claire, Magistrate Judge
Carolyn K. Delaney, Magistrate Judge
Erica P. Grosjean, Magistrate Judge
Gregory G. Hollows, Magistrate Judge
Craig M. Kellison, Magistrate Judge
Barbara McAuliffe, Magistrate Judge
Kendall J. Newman, Magistrate Judge
Sheila K. Oberto, Magistrate Judge
Michael J. Seng, Magistrate Judge
Sandra M. Snyder, Magistrate Judge
Jennifer L. Thurston, Magistrate Judge

CALIFORNIA, NORTHERN

Phyllis Jean Hamilton, Chief Judge
William H. Alsup, District Judge
Jeremy D. Fogel, District Judge
Jeffrey S. White, District Judge
Edward M. Chen, District Judge
Edward J. Davila, District Judge
Haywood Stirling Gilliam, Jr., District Judge
Lucy H. Koh, District Judge
Yvonne Gonzalez Rogers, District Judge
Richard Seeborg, District Judge
Vince Girdhari Chhabria, District Judge
James Donato, District Judge
Beth Labson Freeman, District Judge
William H. Orrick, III, District Judge
John S. Tigar, District Judge
Susan Y. Illston, Senior Judge
Samuel Conti, Senior Judge
William W. Schwarzer, Senior Judge
Thelton E. Henderson, Senior Judge
Saundra Brown Armstrong, Senior Judge
Ronald M. Whyte, Senior Judge
Maxine M. Chesney, Senior Judge
Charles R. Breyer, Senior Judge
Claudia Wilken, Senior Judge
Alan Jaroslovsky, Chief Bankruptcy Judge
Hannah L. Blumenstiel, Bankruptcy Judge
Thomas E. Carlson, Bankruptcy Judge
Roger L. Efremsky, Bankruptcy Judge
M. Elaine Hammond, Bankruptcy Judge
Stephen L. Johnson, Bankruptcy Judge
William J. Lafferty, III, Bankruptcy Judge

CALIFORNIA, NORTHERN-*(Cont'd)*

Dennis Montali, Bankruptcy Judge

Charles D. Novack, Bankruptcy Judge

Arthur S. Weissbrodt, Bankruptcy Judge

Laurel Beeler, Magistrate Judge

Jacqueline S. Corley, Magistrate Judge

Nathanael M. Cousins, Magistrate Judge

Paul S. Grewal, Magistrate Judge

Maria-Elena James, Magistrate Judge

Sallie Kim, Magistrate Judge

Elizabeth D. Laporte, Magistrate Judge

Howard R. Lloyd, Magistrate Judge

Donna M. Ryu, Magistrate Judge

Joseph C. Spero, Magistrate Judge

Nandor J. Vadas, Magistrate Judge

Kandis A. Westmore, Magistrate Judge

Bernard Zimmerman, Magistrate Judge

CALIFORNIA, SOUTHERN

Barry Ted Moskowitz, Chief Judge
Marilyn L. Huff, District Judge
Larry A. Burns, District Judge
Roger T. Benitez, District Judge
John A. Houston, District Judge
William Q. Hayes, District Judge
Dana M. Sabraw, District Judge
Michael M. Anello, District Judge
Anthony J. Battaglia, District Judge
Cathy Ann Bencivengo, District Judge
Janis L. Sammartino, District Judge
Cynthia A. Bashant, District Judge
Gonzalo P. Curiel, District Judge
William B. Enright, Senior Judge
Jeffrey T. Miller, Senior Judge
M. James Lorenz, Senior Judge
Thomas J. Whelan, Senior Judge
Laura S. Taylor, Chief Bankruptcy Judge
Louise DeCarl Adler, Bankruptcy Judge
Christopher B. Latham, Bankruptcy Judge
Margaret M. Mann, Bankruptcy Judge
Jan M. Adler, Magistrate Judge
David H. Bartick, Magistrate Judge
Ruben B. Brooks, Magistrate Judge
Jill L. Burkhardt, Magistrate Judge
Karen S. Crawford, Magistrate Judge
Mitchell D. Dembin, Magistrate Judge
William V. Gallo, Magistrate Judge
Peter C. Lewis, Magistrate Judge
Barbara L. Major, Magistrate Judge
William McCurine, Jr., Magistrate Judge
Bernard G. Skomal, Magistrate Judge
Nita L. Stormes, Magistrate Judge

COLORADO

Marcia S. Krieger, Chief Judge
Robert Blackburn, District Judge
Christine M. Arguello, Distict Judge
Philip A. Brimmer, District Judge
Richard B. Jackson, District Judge
William J. Martinez, District Judge
Raymond P. Moore, District Judge
Wiley Young Daniel, Senior Judge
Lewis Thornton Babcock, Senior Judge
John Lawrence Kane, Jr., Senior Judge
Richard P. Matsch, Senior Judge
Michael E. Romero, Chief Bankruptcy Judge
Sidney B. Brooks, Bankruptcy Judge
Elizabeth E. Brown, Bankruptcy Judge
Joseph G. Rosania, Jr., Bankruptcy Judge
Howard R. Tallman, Bankruptcy Judge
Michael E. Hegarty, Magistrate Judge
Kristen L. Mix, Magistrate Judge
Craig B. Shaffer, Magistrate Judge
Kathleen M. Tafoya, Magistrate Judge
Nina Y. Wang, Magistrate Judge
Michael J. Watanabe, Magistrate Judge
David L. West, Magistrate Judge
Laird T. Milburn, Magistrate Judge (Part-time)

CONNECTICUT

Janet C. Hall, Chief Judge
Victor A. Bolden, District Judge
Robert Neil Chatigny, District Judge
Vanessa L. Bryant, District Judge
Stefan R. Underhill, District Judge
Jeffrey Alker Meyer, District Judge
Michael P. Shea, District Judge
Janet Bond Arterton, Senior Judge
Ellen B. Burns, Senior Judge
Alfred Vincent Covello, Senior Judge
Warren W. Eginton, Senior Judge
Dominic J. Squatrito, Senior Judge
Alvin W. Thompson, Senior Judge
Julie Ann Manning, Chief Bankruptcy Judge
Albert S. Dabrowski, Bankruptcy Judge
Alan H. W. Shiff, Bankruptcy Judge
Holly B. Fitzsimmons, Magistrate Judge
William I. Garfinkel, Magistrate Judge
Joan G. Margolis, Magistrate Judge
Donna F. Martinez, Magistrate Judge
Thomas P. Smith, Magistrate Judge

DELAWARE

Leonard P. Stark, Chief Judge
Sue Lewis Robinson, District Judge
Richard G. Andrews, District Judge
Gregory M. Sleet, Senior Judge
Brendan L. Shannon, Chief Bankruptcy Judge
Kevin J. Carey, Bankruptcy Judge
Mary F. Walrath, Bankruptcy Judge
Kevin Gross, Bankruptcy Judge
Laurie Selber Silverstein, Bankruptcy Judge
Christopher S. Sontchi, Bankruptcy Judge
Mary Pat Thynge, Chief Magistrate Judge
Christopher J. Burke, Magistrate Judge
Sherry R. Fallon, Magistrate Judge

DISTRICT OF COLUMBIA

Richard W. Roberts, Chief Judge
John D. Bates, District Judge
Rosemary M. Collyer, District Judge
Colleen Kollar-Kotelly, District Judge
Richard J. Leon, District Judge
Amit Priyavadan Mehta, District Judge
Randolph D. Moss, District Judge
Emmet G. Sullivan, District Judge
Reggie B. Walton, District Judge
James E. Boasberg, District Judge
Rudolph Contreras, District Judge
Beryl A. Howell, District Judge
Amy B. Jackson, District Judge
Tanya S. Chutkan, District Judge
Christopher R. Cooper, District Judge
Ketanji Brown Jackson, District Judge
Thomas F. Hogan, Senior Judge
Ellen Segal Huvelle, Senior Judge
Gladys Kessler, Senior Judge
Royce C. Lamberth, Senior Judge
Paul L. Friedman, Senior Judge
Henry H. Kennedy, Jr., Senior Judge
S. Martin Teel, Jr., Bankruptcy Judge
John M. Facciola, Magistrate Judge
G. Michael Harvey, Magistrate Judge
Alan Kay, Magistrate Judge
Deborah A. Robinson, Magistrate Judge

FLORIDA, MIDDLE

Steven D. Merryday, Chief Judge
Timothy J. Corrigan, District Judge
Virginia Hernandez Covington, District Judge
Marcia Morales Howard, District Judge
Elizabeth A. Kovachevich, District Judge
James D. Whittemore, District Judge
Charlene Edwards Honeywell, District Judge
Mary Stenson Scriven, District Judge
Paul G. Byron, District Judge
Roy B. Dalton, Jr., District Judge
Brian J. Davis, District Judge
Carlos Eduardo Mendoza, District Judge
Sheri P. Chappell, District Judge
John Antoon, II, Senior Judge
Susan Cawthon Bucklew, Senior Judge
William J. Castagna, Senior Judge
Annie C. Conway, Senior Judge
Patricia C. Fawsett, Senior Judge
William Terrell Hodges, Senior Judge
James S. Moody, Jr., Senior Judge
Harvey E. Schlesinger, Senior Judge
G. Kendall Sharp, Senior Judge
John E. Steele, Senior Judge
Henry Lee Adams, Jr., Senior Judge
Richard A. Lazzara, Senior Judge
Gregory A. Presnell, Senior Judge
Michael G. Williamson, Chief Bankruptcy Judge
Paul M. Glenn, Bankruptcy Judge
Caryl E. Delano, Bankruptcy Judge
Jerry A. Funk, Bankruptcy Judge
Karen S. Jenneman, Bankruptcy Judge
K. Rodney May, Bankruptcy Judge
Catherine McEwen, Bankruptcy Judge

FLORIDA, MIDDLE-*(Cont'd)*

Cynthia C. Jackson, Bankruptcy Judge
Elizabeth A. Jenkins, Magistrate Judge
Gregory J. Kelly, Magistrate Judge
James R. Klindt, Magistrate Judge
Thomas McCoun, III, Magistrate Judge
Mac R. McCoy, Magistrate Judge
Mark A. Pizzo, Magistrate Judge
Monte C. Richardson, Magistrate Judge
Karla R. Spaulding, Magistrate Judge
Thomas G. Wilson, Magistrate Judge
Philip R. Lammens, Magistrate Judge
Anthony Porcelli, Magistrate Judge
Thomas B. Smith, Magistrate Judge
Joel B. Toomey, Magistrate Judge
David A. Baker, Magistrate Judge
Patricia D. Barksdale, Magistrate Judge
Carol Mirando, Magistrate Judge

FLORIDA, NORTHERN

M. Casey Rodgers, Chief Judge
Robert L. Hinkle, District Judge
Richard Smoak, Jr., District Judge
Roger Vinson, District Judge
Mark E. Walker, District Judge
Lacey A. Collier, Senior Judge
Maurice M. Paul, Senior Judge
William H. Stafford, Jr., Senior Judge
Stephan P. Mickle, Senior Judge
Karen K. Specie, Bankruptcy Judge
Larry A. Bodiford, Magistrate Judge (Part-time)
Elizabeth M. Timothy, Magistrate Judge
Gary R. Jones, Magistrate Judge
Charles J. Kahn, Jr., Magistrate Judge
Charles A. Stampelos, Magistrate Judge

FLORIDA, SOUTHERN

K. Michael Moore, Chief Judge
Cecilia M. Altonaga, District Judge
James I. Cohn, District Judge
Marcia G. Cooke, District Judge
William P. Dimitrouleas, District Judge
Joan A. Lenard, District Judge
Kenneth A. Marra, District Judge
Jose E. Martinez, District Judge
Donald M. Middlebrooks, District Judge
Federico A. Moreno, District Judge
Ursula Ungaro, District Judge
William J. Zloch, District Judge
Robin L. Rosenberg, District Judge
Robert N. Scola, Jr., District Judge
Kathleen M. Williams, District Judge
Beth Bloom, District Judge
Darrin P. Gayles, District Judge
Jose A. Gonzalez, Jr., Senior Judge
Donald L. Graham, Senior Judge
William M. Hoeveler, Senior Judge
James Lawrence King, Senior Judge
Kenneth L. Ryskamp, Senior Judge
Patricia A. Seitz, Senior Judge
Alan S. Gold, Senior Judge
Paul C. Huck, Senior Judge
Daniel T. K. Hurley, Senior Judge
Paul G. Hyman, Jr., Chief Bankruptcy Judge
A. Jay Cristol, Bankruptcy Judge
Laurel Myerson Isicoff, Bankruptcy Judge
Erik P. Kimball, Bankruptcy Judge
Robert A. Mark, Bankruptcy Judge
John K. Olson, Bankruptcy Judge

FLORIDA, SOUTHERN-*(Cont'd)*

Raymond B. Ray, Bankruptcy Judge

Barry S. Seltzer, Chief Magistrate Judge

Alicia O. Valle, Magistrate Judge

Ted E. Bandstra, Magistrate Judge

Barry L. Garber, Magistrate Judge

James M. Hopkins, Magistrate Judge

Frank J. Lynch, Magistrate Judge

Chris M. McAliley, Magistrate Judge

John J. O'Sullivan, Magistrate Judge

Andrea Miles Simonton, Magistrate Judge

Lurana Snow, Magistrate Judge

Edwin G. Torres, Magistrate Judge

William C. Turnoff, Magistrate Judge

Patrick A. White, Magistrate Judge

Robert Dube, Magistrate Judge

Dave Lee Brannon, Magistrate Judge

Jonathan Goodman, Magistrate Judge

William D. Matthewman, Magistrate Judge

Alicia M. Otazo-Reyes, Magistrate Judge

Peter R. Palermo, Magistrate Judge

GEORGIA, MIDDLE

Clay D. Land, Chief Judge
Leslie Joyce Abrams, District Judge
C. Ashley Royal, District Judge
Marc Thomas Treadwell, District Judge
Hugh Lawson, Senior Judge
Willie Louis Sands, Senior Judge
John T. Laney, III, Chief Bankruptcy Judge
James P. Smith, Bankruptcy Judge
G. Mallon Faircloth, Magistrate Judge
Richard L. Hodge, Magistrate Judge
M. Stephen Hyles, Magistrate Judge
Thomas Q. Langstaff, Magistrate Judge
Charles H. Weigle, Magistrate Judge

GEORGIA, NORTHERN

Thomas W. Thrash, Jr., Chief Judge
Timothy C. Batten, Sr., District Judge
Mark H. Cohen, District Judge
William S. Duffey, Jr., District Judge
Leigh Martin May, District Judge
Harold L. Murphy, District Judge
Eleanor L. Ross, District Judge
Richard W. Story, District Judge
Steve C. Jones, District Judge
Amy Totenberg, District Judge
Willis B. Hunt, Jr., Senior Judge
William C. O'Kelley, Senior Judge
Charles A. Pannell, Jr., Senior Judge
Marvin H. Shoob, Senior Judge
Robert L. Vining, Jr., Senior Judge
Clarence Cooper, Senior Judge
Orinda D. Evans, Senior Judge
Joyce Bihary, Chief Bankruptcy Judge
Paul M. Baisier, Bankruptcy Judge
Paul W. Bonapfel, Bankruptcy Judge
Mary Grace Diehl, Bankruptcy Judge
W. Homer Drake, Jr., Bankruptcy Judge
C. Ray Mullins, Bankruptcy Judge
Barbara Ellis-Monro, Bankruptcy Judge
Wendy L. Hagenau, Bankruptcy Judge
James R. Sacca, Bankruptcy Judge
Gerrilyn G. Brill, Chief Magistrate Judge
Justin S. Anand, Magistrate Judge
Alan Baverman, Magistrate Judge
Susan S. Cole, Magistrate Judge
Walter E. Johnson, Magistrate Judge
Janet F. King, Magistrate Judge
J. Clay Fuller, Magistrate Judge
Russell G. Vineyard, Magistrate Judge
Linda T. Walker, Magistrate Judge

GEORGIA, SOUTHERN

Lisa Godbey Wood, Chief Judge
William T. Moore, Jr., District Judge
James Randal Hall, District Judge
Dudley H. Bowen, Jr., Senior Judge
Susan D. Barrett, Chief Bankruptcy Judge
Edward J. Coleman, III, Bankruptcy Judge
John S. Dalis, Bankruptcy Judge
R. Stan Baker, Magistrate Judge
G. R. Smith, Magistrate Judge

GUAM, DISTRICT COURT OF

Frances Marie Tydingco-Gatewood, Chief Judge
Joaquin V.E. Manibusan, Jr., Magistrate Judge

HAWAII

J. Michael Seabright, Chief Judge
David A. Ezra, Senior Judge
Derrick Kahala Watson, District Judge
Leslie E. Kobayashi, District Judge
Alan Cooke Kay, Senior Judge
Susan Oki Mollway, Senior Judge
Helen W. Gillmor, Senior Judge
Robert J. Faris, Bankruptcy Judge
Lloyd King, Bankruptcy Judge
Kevin S. Chang, Magistrate Judge
David Faucher, Magistrate Judge (Part-time)
Barry M. Kurren, Magistrate Judge
Richard L. Puglisi, Magistrate Judge

IDAHO

B. Lynn Winmill, Chief Judge
Edward J. Lodge, Senior Judge
Terry Myers, Chief Bankruptcy Judge
Jim D. Pappas, Bankruptcy Judge
Candy W. Dale, Chief Magistrate Judge
Larry M. Boyle, Magistrate Judge
Ronald E. Bush, Magistrate Judge
Mikel H. Williams, Magistrate Judge

ILLINOIS, CENTRAL

James E. Shadid, Chief Judge
Sara L. Darrow, District Judge
Sue Myerscough, District Judge
Colin S. Bruce, District Judge
Joe B. McDade, Senior Judge
Michael M. Mihm, Senior Judge
Harold Albert Baker, Senior Judge
Richard Mills, Senior Judge
Thomas L. Perkins, Chief Bankruptcy Judge
William V. Altenberger, Bankruptcy Judge
David Bernthal, Magistrate Judge
Byron G. Cudmore, Magistrate Judge
Charles H. Evans, Magistrate Judge
Jonathan E. Hawley, Magistrate Judge
Thomas P. Schanzle-Haskins, Magistrate Judge

ILLINOIS, NORTHERN

Ruben Castillo, Chief Judge
Jorge Luis Alonso, District Judge
John Robert Blakey, District Judge
John W. Darrah, District Judge
Samuel Der-Yeghiayan, District Judge
Robert M. Dow, Jr., District Judge
Thomas M. Durkin, District Judge
Frederick J. Kapala, District Judge
Virginia M. Kendall, District Judge
Matthew F. Kennelly, District Judge
Charles R. Norgle, Sr., District Judge
Rebecca R. Pallmeyer, District Judge
Amy J. St. Eve, District Judge
James B. Zagel, District Judge
Edmond E. Chang, District Judge
Sharon Johnson Coleman, District Judge
Gary Scott Feinerman, District Judge
John Z. Lee, District Judge
John J. Tharp, Jr., District Judge
Sara Lee Ellis, District Judge
Manish S. Shah, District Judge
Andrea R. Wood, District Judge
Ronald A. Guzman, Senior Judge
Joan H. Lefkow, Senior Judge
Marvin E. Aspen, Senior Judge
Suzanne B. Conlon, Senior Judge
John F. Grady, Senior Judge
William T. Hart, Senior Judge
Charles P. Kocoras, Senior Judge
Harry D. Leinenweber, Senior Judge
George W. Lindberg, Senior Judge
George M. Marovich, Senior Judge
Paul E. Plunkett, Senior Judge
Philip G. Reinhard, Senior Judge
Milton I. Shadur, Senior Judge
Elaine E. Bucklo, Senior Judge

ILLINOIS, NORTHERN-*(Cont'd)*

Robert W. Gettleman, Senior Judge
Joan B. Gottschall, Senior Judge
Bruce W. Black, Chief Bankruptcy Judge
Carol A. Doyle, Bankruptcy Judge
Jacqueline P. Cox, Bankruptcy Judge
A. Benjamin Goldgar, Bankruptcy Judge
Pamela S. Hollis, Bankruptcy Judge
Thomas M. Lynch, Bankruptcy Judge
Janet S. Baer, Bankruptcy Judge
Timothy A. Barnes, Bankruptcy Judge
Donald R. Cassling, Bankruptcy Judge
Jack B. Schmetterer, Bankruptcy Judge
Deborah Lee Thorne, Bankruptcy Judge
Geraldine Soat Brown, Magistrate Judge
Jeffrey N. Cole, Magistrate Judge
Susan E. Cox, Magistrate Judge
Iain D. Johnston, Magistrate Judge
Sidney I. Schenkier, Magistrate Judge
Michael T. Mason, Magistrate Judge
Maria G. Valdez, Magistrate Judge
Sheila M. Finnegan, Magistrate Judge
Jeffrey T. Gilbert, Magistrate Judge
Young B. Kim, Magistrate Judge
Daniel Martin, Magistrate Judge
Mary M. Rowland, Magistrate Judge

ILLINOIS, SOUTHERN

David R. Herndon, Chief Judge
Michael J. Reagan, District Judge
Nancy J. Rosenstengel, District Judge
Staci Michelle Yandle, District Judge
Kenneth J. Meyers, Chief Bankruptcy Judge
Laura K. Grandy, Bankruptcy Judge
Philip M. Frazier, Magistrate Judge
Clifford J. Proud, Magistrate Judge
Donald Wilkerson, Magistrate Judge
Stephen C. Williams, Magistrate Judge

INDIANA, NORTHERN

Philip P. Simon, Chief Judge
Theresa L. Springmann, District Judge
Joseph S. Van Bokkelen, District Judge
Jon E. DeGuillo, District Judge
William C. Lee, Senior Judge
Rudolfo (Rudy) Lozano, Senior Judge
Robert L. Miller, Jr., Senior Judge
James T. Moody, Senior Judge
Robert E. Grant, Chief Bankruptcy Judge
J. Philip Klingeberger, Bankruptcy Judge
Russell Kent Lindquist, Bankruptcy Judge
Harry C. Dees, Jr., Bankruptcy Judge
Paul R. Cherry, Magistrate Judge
Roger B. Cosbey, Magistrate Judge
Christopher A. Nuechterlein, Magistrate Judge
John E. Martin, Magistrate Judge

INDIANA, SOUTHERN

Richard L. Young, Chief Judge
William T. Lawrence, District Judge
Tanya W. Pratt, District Judge
Jane E. Magnus-Stinson, District Judge
Sarah Evans Barker, Senior Judge
Larry J. McKinney, Senior Judge
James M. Carr, Bankruptcy Judge
Jeffrey J. Graham, Bankruptcy Judge
Basil H. Lorch, III, Bankruptcy Judge
Anthony J. Metz, III, Bankruptcy Judge
Frank J. Otte, Bankruptcy Judge
Robyn L. Moberly, Bankruptcy Judge
Tim A. Baker, Magistrate Judge
Matthew P. Brookman, Magistrate Judge
William G. Hussmann, Jr., Magistrate Judge
Mark Dinsmore, Magistrate Judge
Denise K. LaRue, Magistrate Judge
Debra McVicker Lynch, Magistrate Judge
Craig M. McKee, Magistrate Judge (Part-time)
Van T. Willis, Magistrate Judge (Part-time)

IOWA, NORTHERN

Linda R. Reade, Chief Judge
Leonard T. Strand, District Judge
Mark W. Bennett, Senior Judge
Edward J. McManus, Senior Judge
Thad J. Collins, Chief Bankruptcy Judge
Jon S. Scoles, Magistrate Judge

IOWA, SOUTHERN

John A. Jarvey, Chief Judge
Rebecca Goodgame Ebinger, District Judge
Stephanie Marie Rose, District Judge
James E. Gritzner, Senior Judge
Ronald E. Longstaff, Senior Judge
Harold D. Vietor, Senior Judge
Charles R. Wolle, Senior Judge
Robert W. Pratt, Senior Judge
Anita L. Shodeen, Chief Bankruptcy Judge
Lee M. Jackwig, Bankruptcy Judge
Thomas J. Shields, Magistrate Judge
Celeste F. Bremer, Magistrate Judge
Stephen B. Jackson, Jr., Magistrate Judge
Ross A. Walters, Magistrate Judge
Helen C. Adams, Magistrate Judge

KANSAS

J. Thomas Marten, Chief Judge
Carlos Murguia, District Judge
Julie A. Robinson, District Judge
Eric F. Melgren, District Judge
Daniel D. Crabtree, District Judge
Kathryn Hoefer Vratil, Senior Judge
Monti L. Belot, III, Senior Judge
Sam A. Crow, Senior Judge
Richard D. Rogers, Senior Judge
John Watson Lungstrum, Senior Judge
Robert E. Nugent, Chief Bankruptcy Judge
Robert D. Berger, Bankruptcy Judge
Janice M. Karlin, Bankruptcy Judge
Dale L. Somers, Bankruptcy Judge
James P. O'Hara, Chief Magistrate Judge
Gwynne E. Birzer, Magistrate Judge
Donald W. Bostwick, Magistrate Judge
Gerald L. Rushfelt, Magistrate Judge (Part-time)
Keith G. Sebelius, Magistrate Judge
Kenneth G. Gale, Magistrate Judge
Teresa J. James, Magistrate Judge
David J. Waxse, Magistrate Judge

KENTUCKY, EASTERN

Karen K. Caldwell, Chief Judge
David L. Bunning, District Judge
Danny C. Reeves, District Judge
Amul R. Thapar, District Judge
Gregory F. Van Tatenhove, District Judge
William O. Bertelsman, Senior Judge
Joseph M. Hood, Senior Judge
Henry Rupert Wilhoit, Jr., Senior Judge
Tracey Wise, Chief Bankruptcy Judge
Gregory R. Schaaf, Bankruptcy Judge
Joe Lee, Bankruptcy Judge
Edward B. Atkins, Magistrate Judge
Robert E. Wier, Magistrate Judge
Hanly A. Ingram, Magistrate Judge
Candace J. Smith, Magistrate Judge
J. Gregory Wehrman, Magistrate Judge

KENTUCKY, WESTERN

Joseph H. McKinley, Jr., Chief Judge
David W. Hale, District Judge
Thomas B. Russell, District Judge
Charles R. Simpson, III, Senior Judge
Greg N. Stivers, District Judge
Joan A. Lloyd, Chief Bankruptcy Judge
Thomas Fulton, Bankruptcy Judge
Alan C. Stout, Bankruptcy Judge
E. Robert Goebel, Magistrate Judge
W. David King, Magistrate Judge
James D. Moyer, Magistrate Judge
Dave Whalin, Magistrate Judge
H. Brent Brennenstuhl, Magistrate Judge
Lanny King, Magistrate Judge

LOUISIANA, EASTERN

Sarah S. Vance, Chief Judge
Helen Ginger Berrigan, District Judge
Lance M. Africk, District Judge
Carl Joseph Barbier, District Judge
Kurt D. Engelhardt, District Judge
Eldon E. Fallon, District Judge
Martin L. C. Feldman, District Judge
Susie Morgan, District Judge
Jane M. Triche-Milazzo, District Judge
Jay C. Zainey, District Judge
Nannette J. Brown, District Judge
Peter Hill Beer, Senior Judge
Stanwood Richardson Duval, Jr., Senior Judge
Ivan L.R. Lemelle, Senior Judge
Mary Ann Vial Lemmon, Senior Judge
Elizabeth W. Magner, Chief Bankruptcy Judge
Jerry A. Brown, Bankruptcy Judge
Joseph C. Wilkinson, Jr., Chief Magistrate Judge
Daniel E. Knowles, III, Magistrate Judge
Karen Wells Roby, Magistrate Judge
Sally A. Shushan, Magistrate Judge
Michael B. North, Magistrate Judge

LOUISIANA, MIDDLE

Brian Anthony Jackson, Chief Judge
John W. deGravelles, District Judge
Shelly D. Dick, District Judge
James J. Brady, Senior Judge
Douglas D. Dodd, Chief Bankruptcy Judge
Stephen C. Riedlinger, Magistrate Judge
Richard L. Bourgeois, Jr., Magistrate Judge

LOUISIANA, WESTERN

Dee D. Drell, Cheif Judge
Robert G. James, District Judge
Rebecca F. Doherty, District Judge
S. Maurice Hicks, Jr., District Judge
Patricia H. Minaldi, District Judge
Elizabeth Erny Foote, District Judge
Tom Stagg, Senior Judge
James T. Trimble, Jr., Senior Judge
Donald E. Walter, Senior Judge
Tucker Lee Melancon, Senior Judge
Robert R. Summerhays, Chief Bankruptcy Judge
John W. Kolwe, Bankruptcy Judge
Jeffrey P. Norman, Bankruptcy Judge
Karen L. Hayes, Magistrate Judge
C. Michael Hill, Magistrate Judge
Mark L. Hornsby, Magistrate Judge
Kathleen Kay, Magistrate Judge
James D. Kirk, Magistrate Judge
Patrick J. Hanna, Magistrate Judge
Carol B. Whitehurst, Magistrate Judge

MAINE

Nancy Torresen, Chief Judge
John A. Woodcock, Jr., District Judge
Jon D. Levy, District Judge
George Z. Singal, Senior Judge
D. Brock Hornby, Senior Judge
Gene Carter, Senior Judge
Peter Cary, Chief Bankruptcy Judge
Louis H. Kornreich, Bankruptcy Judge
John H. Rich, III, Magistrate Judge
John C. Nivison, Magistrate Judge

MARYLAND

Catherine Curtis Blake, Chief Judge
Richard D. Bennett, District Judge
William D. Quarles, District Judge
James K. Bredar, District Judge
Paul W. Grimm, District Judge
Ellen Lipton Hollander, District Judge
George L. Russell, III, District Judge
Theodore D. Chuang, District Judge
Paul W. Grimm, District Judge
George J. Hazel, District Judge
Deborah K. Chasanow, Senior Judge
Marvin Joseph Garbis, Senior Judge
William M. Nickerson, Senior Judge
Frederic N. Smalkin, Senior Judge
Peter J. Messitte, Senior Judge
J. Frederick Motz, Senior Judge
Roger W. Titus, Senior Judge
Duncan W. Keir, Chief Bankruptcy Judge
Nancy V. Alquist, Bankruptcy Judge
Thomas J. Catliota, Bankruptcy Judge
E. Stephen Derby, Bankruptcy Judge
Robert A. Gordon, Bankruptcy Judge
Wendelin I. Lipp, Bankruptcy Judge
Paul Mannes, Bankruptcy Judge
James F. Schneider, Bankruptcy Judge
David E. Rice, Bankruptcy Judge
William G. Connelly, Magistrate Judge
J. Mark Coulson, Magistrate Judge
Charles B. Day, Magistrate Judge
Thomas M. DiGirolamo, Magistrate Judge
Beth P. Gesner, Magistrate Judge
Jillyn K. Schulze, Magistrate Judge
Stephanie A. Gallagher, Magistrate Judge
C. Bruce Anderson, Magistrate Judge (Part-time)
Timothy J. Sullivan, Magistrate Judge

MASSACHUSETTS

Patti B. Saris, Chief Judge
Allison Dale Burroughs, District Judge
Nathaniel M. Gorton, District Judge
George A. O'Toole, Jr., District Judge
F. Dennis Saylor, IV, District Judge
Richard G. Stearns, District Judge
William G. Young, District Judge
Denise J. Casper, District Judge
Timothy S. Hillman, District Judge
Mark G. Mastroianni, District Judge
Indira Talwani, District Judge
Leo T. Sorokin, District Judge
Mark L. Wolf, Senior Judge
Joseph L. Tauro, Senior Judge
Douglas P. Woodlock, Senior Judge
Rya W. Zobel, Senior Judge
Edward F. Harrington, Senior Judge
Michael A. Ponsor, Senior Judge
Frank J. Bailey, Chief Bankruptcy Judge
Henry Jack Boroff, Bankruptcy Judge
Joan N. Feeney, Bankruptcy Judge
Melvin S. Hoffman, Bankruptcy Judge
Christopher J. Panos, Bankruptcy Judge
Marianne B. Bowler, Magistrate Judge
Donald L. Cabell, Magistrate Judge
Robert B. Collings, Magistrate Judge
Judith G. Dein, Magistrate Judge
Jennifer C. Boal, Magistrate Judge
David H. Hennessy, Magistrate Judge
Mary Page Kelley, Magistrate Judge
Kenneth P. Neiman, Magistrate Judge

MICHIGAN, EASTERN

Gerald E. Rosen, Chief Judge
Paul D. Borman, District Judge
Robert H. Cleland, District Judge
Sean F. Cox, District Judge
Denise Page Hood, District Judge
David M. Lawson, District Judge
Thomas L. Ludington, District Judge
Stephen J. Murphy, III, District Judge
John Corbett O'Meara, District Judge
Victoria A. Roberts, District Judge
Gershwin A. Drain, District Judge
Mark A. Goldsmith, District Judge
Terrence G. Berg, District Judge
Matthew Frederick Leitman, District Judge
Judith Ellen Levy, District Judge
Laurie J. Michelson, District Judge
Linda Vivienne Parker, District Judge
Marianne O. Battani, Senior Judge
Nancy G. Edmunds, Senior Judge
Bernard A. Friedman, Senior Judge
George C. Steeh, III, Senior Judge
Arthur J. Tarnow, Senior Judge
Avern Cohn, Senior Judge
Julian A. Cook, Jr., Senior Judge
Patrick J. Duggan, Senior Judge
Paul V. Gadola, Senior Judge
Anna Diggs Taylor, Senior Judge
Phillip J. Shefferly, Chief Bankruptcy Judge
Marci B. McIvor, Bankruptcy Judge
Daniel S. Opperman, Bankruptcy Judge
Thomas J. Tucker, Bankruptcy Judge
Walter Shapero, Bankruptcy Judge
Charles E. Binder, Magistrate Judge
Stephanie Dawkins Davis, Magistrate Judge

MICHIGAN, EASTERN-*(Cont'd)*

Michael J. Hluchaniuk, Magistrate Judge
Paul J. Komives, Magistrate Judge
Mona K. Majzoub, Magistrate Judge
R. Steven Whalen, Magistrate Judge
David R. Grand, Magistrate Judge
Patricia T. Morris, Magistrate Judge
Mark A. Randon, Magistrate Judge
Elizabeth A. Stafford, Magistrate Judge

MICHIGAN, WESTERN

Robert J. Jonker, Chief Judge
Robert Holmes Bell, District Judge
Paul L. Maloney, District Judge
Janet T. Neff, District Judge
Gordon J. Quist, Senior Judge
Scott W. Dales, Chief Bankruptcy Judge
John T. Gregg, Bankruptcy Judge
Ellen S. Carmody, Magistrate Judge
Timothy P. Greeley, Magistrate Judge
Phillip J. Greene, Magistrate Judge
Raymond S. Kent, Magistrate Judge

MINNESOTA

John R. Tunheim, Chief Judge
Joan N. Ericksen, District Judge
Donovan W. Frank, District Judge
Ann D. Montgomery, District Judge
Patrick J. Schiltz, District Judge
Susan Richard Nelson, District Judge
Wilhelmina Marie Wright, District Judge
Donald D. Alsop, Senior Judge
Michael J. Davis, Senior Judge
David S. Doty, Senior Judge
Richard House Kyle, Senior Judge
Paul A. Magnuson, Senior Judge
Gregory F. Kishel, Chief Bankruptcy Judge
Katherine Constantine, Bankruptcy Judge
Robert J. Kressel, Bankruptcy Judge
Micheal E. Ridgway, Bankruptcy Judge
Kathleen H. Sanberg, Bankruptcy Judge
Hildy Bowbeer, Magistrate Judge
Jon T. Huseby, Magistrate Judge
Jeffrey J. Keyes, Magistrate Judge
Janie S. Mayeron, Magistrate Judge
Franklin L. Noel, Magistrate Judge
Leo I. Brisbois, Magistrate Judge
Tony N. Leung, Magistrate Judge
Steven Rau, Magistrate Judge
Becky R. Thorson, Magistrate Judge

MISSISSIPPI, NORTHERN

Sharion Aycock, Chief Judge
Debra M. Brown, District Judge
Michael P. Mills, District Judge
Neal Brooks Biggers, Jr., Senior Judge
Glen H. Davidson, Senior Judge
Jason D. Woodward, Chief Bankruptcy Judge
S. Allan Alexander, Magistrate Judge
David A. Sanders, Magistrate Judge
Jane M. Virden, Magistrate Judge

MISSISSIPPI, SOUTHERN

Louis Guirola, Jr., Chief Judge
Henry T. Wingate, District Judge
Daniel P. Jordan, III, District Judge
Halil Suleyman Ozerden, District Judge
Keith Starrett, District Judge
Carlton W. Reeves, District Judge
William H. Barbour, Jr., Senior Judge
David C. Bramlette, III, Senior Judge
Walter J. Gex, III, Senior Judge
Tom Stewart Lee, Senior Judge
Neil P. Olack, Chief Bankruptcy Judge
Edward Ellington, Bankruptcy Judge
Katharine M. Samson, Bankruptcy Judge
John M. Roper, Sr., Magistrate Judge
Linda R. Anderson, Magistrate Judge
John C. Gargiulo, Magistrate Judge
Michael T. Parker, Magistrate Judge
Robert H. Walker, Magistrate Judge
F. Keith Ball, Magistrate Judge

MISSOURI, EASTERN

Catherine D. Perry, Chief Judge
Carol E. Jackson, District Judge
Henry E. Autrey, District Judge
Stephen N. Limbaugh, Jr., District Judge
Rodney W. Sippel, District Judge
Audrey G. Fleissig, District Judge
John A. Ross, District Judge
Ronnie L. White, District Judge
E. Richard Webber, Jr., Senior Judge
Edward L. Filippine, Senior Judge
Jean C. Hamilton, Senior Judge
Charles A. Shaw, Senior Judge
Kathy Surratt-States, Chief Bankruptcy Judge
David P. McDonald, Bankruptcy Judge
Charles E. Rendlen, Bankruptcy Judge
Barry S. Schermer, Bankruptcy Judge
Terry I. Adelman, Magistrate Judge
Thomas C. Mummert, III, Magistrate Judge
David D. Noce, Magistrate Judge
Nannette A. Baker, Magistrate Judge
Noelle C. Collins, Magistrate Judge
Abbie S. Crites-Leoni, Magistrate Judge
Shirley P. Mensah, Magistrate Judge

MISSOURI, WESTERN

David G. Kays, Chief Judge
Stephen R. Bough, District Judge
Roseanne A. Ketchmark, District Judge
Mary E. Phillips, District Judge
Brian C. Wimes, District Judge
M. Douglas Harpool, District Judge
Gary A. Fenner, Senior Judge
Fernando J. Gaitan, Jr., Senior Judge
Ortrie D. Smith, Senior Judge
Howard F. Sachs, Senior Judge
Dean Whipple, Senior Judge
Nanette Kay Laughrey, Senior Judge
Dennis R. Dow, Chief Bankruptcy Judge
Arthur Federman, Bankruptcy Judge
Cynthia A. Norton, Bankruptcy Judge
James C. England, Chief Magistrate Judge
Sarah Hays, Magistrate Judge
Robert E. Larsen, Magistrate Judge
John T. Maughmer, Magistrate Judge
Matt J. Whitworth, Magistrate Judge
David P. Rush, Magistrate Judge

MONTANA

Dana L. Christensen, Chief Judge
Brian Morris, District Judge
Susan P. Watters, District Judge
Sam E. Haddon, Senior Judge
Jack D. Shanstrom, Senior Judge
Charles C. Lovell, Senior Judge
Donald W. Molloy, Senior Judge
Ralph B. Kirscher, Bankruptcy Judge
John L. Peterson, Bankruptcy Judge
John T. Johnston, Magistrate Judge
Jeremiah C. Lynch, Magistrate Judge
Carolyn S. Ostby, Magistrate Judge
Gerard M. Schuster, Magistrate Judge (Part-time)

U.S. DISTRICT COURTS

NEBRASKA

Laurie Smith Camp, Chief Judge
John M. Gerrard, District Judge
Joseph F. Bataillon, Senior Judge
Richard G. Kopf, Senior Judge
Lyle E. Strom, Senior Judge
Thomas L. Saladino, Chief Bankruptcy Judge
F. A. Gossett, Magistrate Judge
Thomas D. Thalken, Magistrate Judge
Cheryl R. Zwart, Magistrate Judge

NEVADA

Gloria Navarro, Chief Judge
Robert C. Jones, District Judge
Miranda Du, District Judge
James C. Mahan, District Judge
Richard F. Boulware II, District Judge
Jennifer A. Dorsey, District Judge
Andrew P. Gordon, District Judge
Larry R. Hicks, Senior Judge
Kent J. Dawson, Senior Judge
Roger L. Hunt, Senior Judge
Lloyd D. George, Senior Judge
Howard D. McKibben, Senior Judge
Bruce T. Beesley, Chief Bankruptcy Judge
Laurel E. Davis, Bankruptcy Judge
August B. Landis, Bankruptcy Judge
Mike K. Nakagawa, Bankruptcy Judge
Linda B. Riegle, Bankruptcy Judge
Gregg W. Zive, Bankruptcy Judge
William G. Cobb, Magistrate Judge
Valerie P. Cooke, Magistrate Judge
Vincent C. Ferenbach, Magistrate Judge
George W. Foley, Magistrate Judge
Carl W. Hoffman, Jr., Magistrate Judge
Robert Jake Johnston, Magistrate Judge
Nancy J. Koppe, Magistrate Judge
Peggy A. Leen, Magistrate Judge
Robert A. McQuaid, Jr., Magistrate Judge
Marion C. Ruffing, Magistrate Judge (Part-time)

NEW HAMPSHIRE

Joseph N. LaPlante, Chief Judge
Paul J. Barbadoro, District Judge
Landya B. McCafferty, District Judge
Steven J. McAuliffe, Senior Judge
Joseph A. DiClerico, Jr., Senior Judge
Bruce A. Harwood, Bankruptcy Judge
Andrea K. Johnstone, Magistrate Judge

NEW JERSEY

Jerome B. Simandle, Chief Judge
Renee Marie Bumb, District Judge
Madeline Cox Arleo, District Judge
Noel L. Hillman, District Judge
Robert B. Kugler, District Judge
Jose L. Linares, District Judge
Peter G. Sheridan, District Judge
Susan D. Wigenton, District Judge
Freda L. Wolfson, District Judge
Claire C. Cecchi, District Judge
Kevin McNulty, District Judge
Esther Salas, District Judge
Michael A. Shipp, District Judge
John Michael Vazquez, District Judge
Stanley R. Chesler, Senior Judge
William J. Martini, Senior Judge
Joseph H. Rodriguez, Senior Judge
Anne E. Thompson, Senior Judge
William H. Walls, Senior Judge
Mary L. Cooper, Senior Judge
Katharine S. Hayden, Senior Judge
Judith H. Wizmur, Chief Bankruptcy Judge
Andrew B. Altenburg, Jr., Bankruptcy Judge
Kathryn C. Ferguson, Bankruptcy Judge
Rosemary Gambardella, Bankruptcy Judge
Michael B. Kaplan, Bankruptcy Judge
Stacey L. Meisel, Bankruptcy Judge
Vincent F. Papalia, Bankruptcy Judge
Jerrold N. Poslusny, Bankruptcy Judge
John K. Sherwood, Bankruptcy Judge
Christine M. Gravelle, Bankruptcy Judge
Tonianne J. Bongiovanni, Magistrate Judge

NEW JERSEY-*(Cont'd)*

Ann Marie Donio, Magistrate Judge
Mark Falk, Magistrate Judge
Joel Schneider, Magistrate Judge
Douglas E. Arpert, Magistrate Judge
James B. Clark, III, Magistrate Judge
Joseph A. Dickson, Magistrate Judge
Lois H. Goodman, Magistrate Judge
Michael A. Hammer, Magistrate Judge
Steven C. Mannion, Magistrate Judge
Cathy L. Waldor, Magistrate Judge
Leda Dunn Wettre, Magistrate Judge
Karen M. Williams, Magistrate Judge

NEW MEXICO

M. Christine Armijo, Chief Judge
Martha A. Vazquez, District Judge
Robert C. Brack, District Judge
James O. Browning, District Judge
Judith C. Herrera, District Judge
William P. Johnson, District Judge
Kenneth John Gonzales, District Judge
Bruce D. Black, Senior Judge
Curtis LeRoy Hansen, Senior Judge
James A. Parker, Senior Judge
Robert H. Jacobvitz, Chief Bankruptcy Judge
David T. Thuma, Bankruptcy Judge
Karen Ballard Molzen, Chief Magistrate Judge
Joel M. Carson, III, Magistrate Judge
Laura Fashing, Magistrate Judge
Joe H. Galvan, Magistrate Judge
Carmen E. Garza, Magistrate Judge
Kirtan Khalsa, Magistrate Judge
William P. Lynch, Magistrate Judge
Lourdes A. Martinez, Magistrate Judge
Kea W. Riggs, Magistrate Judge (Part-time)
Don J. Svet, Magistrate Judge
Alan C. Torgerson, Magistrate Judge
Gregory B. Wormuth, Magistrate Judge
Stephan M. Vidmar, Magistrate Judge
B. Paul Briones, Magistrate Judge (Part-time)
Steven C. Yarbrough, Magistrate Judge

NEW YORK, EASTERN

Carol Bagley Amon, Chief Judge
Joan M. Azrack, District Judge
Joseph F. Bianco, District Judge
Pamela Ki Mai Chen, District Judge
Brian M. Cogan, District Judge
Ann Donnelly, District Judge
John Gleeson, District Judge
LaShann M. DeArcy Hall, District Judge
Dora L. Irizarry, District Judge
Kiyo A. Matsumoto, District Judge
Roslynn R. Mauskopf, District Judge
Allyne R. Ross, District Judge
Eric N. Vitaliano, District Judge
Margo K. Brodie, District Judge
William F. Kuntz, II, District Judge
Raymond J. Dearie, Senior Judge
Joanna Seybert, Senior Judge
Frederic Block, Senior Judge
Sandra J. Feuerstein, Senior Judge
I. Leo Glasser, Senior Judge
Nicholas G. Garaufis, Senior Judge
Nina Gershon, Senior Judge
Denis R. Hurley, Senior Judge
Sterling Johnson, Jr., Senior Judge
Edward R. Korman, Senior Judge
Thomas C. Platt, Jr., Senior Judge
Arthur D. Spatt, Senior Judge
Sandra L. Townes, Senior Judge
Jack B. Weinstein, Senior Judge
Leonard D. Wexler, Senior Judge
Carla E. Craig, Chief Bankruptcy Judge
Robert E. Grossman, Bankruptcy Judge
Louis A. Scarcella, Bankruptcy Judge
Elizabeth S. Stong, Bankruptcy Judge
Alan S. Trust, Bankruptcy Judge
Nancy Hershey Lord, Bankruptcy Judge

NEW YORK, EASTERN-*(Cont'd)*

Steven M. Gold, Chief Magistrate Judge

Lois S. Bloom, Magistrate Judge

Marilyn D. Go, Magistrate Judge

Peggy Kuo, Magistrate Judge

Robert Levy, Magistrate Judge

Arlene Rosario Lindsay, Magistrate Judge

Stephen I. Locke, Magistrate Judge

Roanne L. Mann, Magistrate Judge

James Orenstein, Magistrate Judge

Viktor V. Pohorelsky, Magistrate Judge

Cheryl L. Pollak, Magistrate Judge

Ramon E. Reyes, Magistrate Judge

Anne Y. Shields, Magistrate Judge

A. Kathleen Tomlinson, Magistrate Judge

Gary R. Brown, Magistrate Judge

E. Thomas Boyle, Magistrate Judge

Vera M. Scanlon, Magistrate Judge

NEW YORK, NORTHERN

Glenn T. Suddaby, Chief Judge
David N. Hurd, District Judge
Brenda K. Sannes, District Judge
Gary L. Sharpe, District Judge
Mae A. D'Agostino, District Judge
Lawrence E. Kahn, Senior Judge
Thomas J. McAvoy, Senior Judge
Norman A. Mordue, Senior Judge
Frederick J. Scullin, Jr., Senior Judge
Robert E. Littlefield, Jr., Chief Bankruptcy Judge
Margaret Cangilos-Ruiz, Bankruptcy Judge
Diane Davis, Bankruptcy Judge
Gary L. Favro, Magistrate Judge
David E. Peebles, Magistrate Judge
Daniel J. Stewart, Magistrate Judge
Andrew T. Baxter, Magistrate Judge
Therese Wiley Dancks, Magistrate Judge
Christian F. Hummel, Magistrate Judge

NEW YORK, SOUTHERN

Loretta A. Preska, Chief Judge
P. Kevin Castel, District Judge
Cathy Seibel, District Judge
George B. Daniels, District Judge
Paul G. Gardephe, District Judge
Kenneth M. Karas, District Judge
John G. Koeltl, District Judge
Colleen McMahon, District Judge
William H. Pauley, III, District Judge
Richard Sullivan, District Judge
Laura Taylor Swain, District Judge
Ronnie Abrams, District Judge
Vincent L. Briccetti, District Judge
Andrew L. Carter, Jr., District Judge
Paul A. Engelmayer, District Judge
Katherine B. Forrest, District Judge
Jesse Furman, District Judge
Alison J. Nathan, District Judge
J. Paul Oetken, District Judge
Edgardo Ramos, District Judge
Vernon S. Broderick, District Judge
Valerie E. Caproni, District Judge
Katherine Polk Failla, District Judge
Nelson Stephen Roman, District Judge
Lorna G. Schofield, District Judge
Analisa Torres, District Judge
Gregory Howard Woods, District Judge
Kimba M. Wood, Senior Judge
Deborah A. Batts, Senior Judge
Richard M. Berman, Senior Judge
Naomi Reice Buchwald, Senior Judge
Miriam Goldman Cedarbaum, Senior Judge
Denise L. Cote, Senior Judge
Paul A. Crotty, Senior Judge

NEW YORK, SOUTHERN-*(Cont'd)*

Kevin Thomas Duffy, Senior Judge
Thomas P. Griesa, Senior Judge
Alvin K. Hellerstein, Senior Judge
Jed S. Rakoff, Senior Judge
Shira A. Scheindlin, Senior Judge
Sidney H. Stein, Senior Judge
Charles S. Haight, Jr., Senior Judge
Lewis A. Kaplan, Senior Judge
John F. Keenan, Senior Judge
Victor Marrero, Senior Judge
Lawrence M. McKenna, Senior Judge
Richard Owen, Senior Judge
Leonard B. Sand, Senior Judge
Louis L. Stanton, Senior Judge
Robert W. Sweet, Senior Judge
Cecelia G. Morris, Chief Bankruptcy Judge
Stuart M. Bernstein, Bankruptcy Judge
Robert D. Drain, Bankruptcy Judge
James L. Garrity, Jr., Bankruptcy Judge
Robert E. Gerber, Bankruptcy Judge
Martin Glenn, Bankruptcy Judge
Shelley C. Chapman, Bankruptcy Judge
Sean H. Lane, Bankruptcy Judge
Michael E. Wiles, Bankruptcy Judge
Frank Maas, Chief Magistrate Judge
Michael H. Dolinger, Magistrate Judge
Ronald L. Ellis, Magistrate Judge
Kevin N. Fox, Magistrate Judge
James C. Francis, IV, Magistrate Judge
Debra Freeman, Magistrate Judge
Martin R. Goldberg, Magistrate Judge (Part-time)
Andrew J. Peck, Magistrate Judge
Henry Pitman, Magistrate Judge

NEW YORK, SOUTHERN-*(Cont'd)*

Lisa Margaret Smith, Magistrate Judge
James L. Cott, Magistrate Judge
Paul E. Davison, Magistrate Judge
Gabriel W. Gorenstein, Magistrate Judge
Judith C. McCarthy, Magistrate Judge
Sarah Netburn, Magistrate Judge

NEW YORK, WESTERN

Frank P. Geraci, Jr., Chief Judge
Lawrence Joseph Vilardo, District Judge
Elizabeth A. Wolford, District Judge
Richard J. Arcara, Senior Judge
John T. Curtin, Senior Judge
David G. Larimer, Senior Judge
Charles J. Siragusa, Senior Judge
William M. Skretny, Senior Judge
Michael A. Telesca, Senior Judge
Carl L. Bucki, Chief Bankruptcy Judge
Michael J. Kaplan, Bankruptcy Judge
Paul R. Warren, Bankruptcy Judge
Jonathan W. Feldman, Magistrate Judge
Leslie G. Foschio, Magistrate Judge
Jeremiah J. McCarthy, Magistrate Judge
Marian W. Payson, Magistrate Judge
H. Kenneth Schroeder, Jr., Magistrate Judge
Hugh B. Scott, Magistrate Judge

NORTH CAROLINA, EASTERN

James C. Dever, III, Chief Judge
Louise W. Flanagan, District Judge
Terrence W. Boyle, District Judge
W. Earl Britt, Senior Judge
James C. Fox, Senior Judge
Malcolm J. Howard, Senior Judge
Stephani W. Humrickhouse, Bankruptcy Judge
J. Rich Leonard, Bankruptcy Judge
David M. Warren, Bankruptcy Judge
James E. Gates, Magistrate Judge
Robert B. Jones, Jr., Magistrate Judge
Robert T. Numbers, II, Magistrate Judge
William A. Webb, Magistrate Judge
Kimberly A. Swank, Magistrate Judge (Part-time)

NORTH CAROLINA, MIDDLE

William L. Osteen, Jr., Chief Judge
Loretta Copeland Biggs, District Judge
James A. Beaty, Jr., Senior Judge
Thomas D. Schroeder, District Judge
Catherine C. Eagles, District Judge
Norwood Carlton Tilley, Jr., Senior Judge
William L. Stocks, Chief Bankruptcy Judge
Catharine Carruthers, Bankruptcy Judge
Lena M. James, Bankruptcy Judge
Benjamin A. Kahn, Bankruptcy Judge
Wallace W. Dixon, Magistrate Judge
Lawrence P. Auld, Magistrate Judge
Joi Elizabeth Peake, Magistrate Judge
Joe L. Webster, Magistrate Judge

NORTH CAROLINA, WESTERN

Frank D. Whitney, Chief Judge
Robert J. Conrad, Jr., District Judge
Martin K. Reidinger, District Judge
Richard Lesley Voorhees, District Judge
Max O. Cogburn, Jr., District Judge
Graham C. Mullen, Senior Judge
Laura Turner Beyer, Chief Bankruptcy Judge
J. Craig Whitley, Bankruptcy Judge
George R. Hodges, Bankruptcy Judge
Marvin R. Wooten, Bankruptcy Judge
Dennis L. Howell, Magistrate Judge
David C. Keesler, Magistrate Judge
David S. Cayer, Magistrate Judge

NORTH DAKOTA

Ralph R. Erickson, Chief Judge
Daniel L. Hovland, District Judge
Patrick A. Conmy, Senior Judge
Shon Kaelberer Hastings, Bankruptcy Judge
Karen K. Klein, Magistrate Judge
Charles S. Miller, Jr., Magistrate Judge
Alice R. Senechal, Magistrate Judge (Part-time)

OHIO, NORTHERN

Solomon Oliver, Jr., Chief Judge
John R. Adams, District Judge
Christopher A. Boyko, District Judge
Patricia Anne Gaughan, District Judge
James S. Gwin, District Judge
Sara E. Lioi, District Judge
Donald C. Nugent, District Judge
Dan A. Polster, District Judge
Jack Zouhary, District Judge
Jeffrey J. Helmick, District Judge
Benita Y. Pearson, District Judge
David D. Dowd, Jr., Senior Judge
David A. Katz, Senior Judge
Peter Constantine Economus, Senior Judge
James Gray Carr, Senior Judge
Pat E. Morgenstern-Clarren, Chief Bankruptcy Judge
Arthur I. Harris, Bankruptcy Judge
Russ Kendig, Bankruptcy Judge
Alan M. Koschik, Bankruptcy Judge
Mary Ann Whipple, Bankruptcy Judge
Kay Woods, Bankruptcy Judge
John P. Gustafson, Bankruptcy Judge
Jessica E. Price Smith, Bankruptcy Judge
William H. Baughman, Magistrate Judge
George J. Limbert, Magistrate Judge
Kenneth S. McHargh, Magistrate Judge
Jack B. Streepy, Magistrate Judge
Nancy A. Vecchiarelli, Magistrate Judge
Gregory A. White, Magistrate Judge
Kathleen B. Burke, Magistrate Judge
James R. Knepp, II, Magistrate Judge

OHIO, SOUTHERN

Edmund A. Sargus, Jr., Chief Judge
Michael R. Barrett, District Judge
Susan J. Dlott, District Judge
Gregory L. Frost, District Judge
Algenon L. Marbley, District Judge
Thomas M. Rose, District Judge
Michael H. Watson, District Judge
Timothy S. Black, District Judge
James L. Graham, Senior Judge
Walter H. Rice, Senior Judge
George C. Smith, Senior Judge
Herman J. Weber, Senior Judge
Sandra S. Beckwith, Senior Judge
Jeffery P. Hopkins, Chief Bankruptcy Judge
Charles M. Caldwell, Bankruptcy Judge
John E. Hoffman, Jr., Bankruptcy Judge
Guy R. Humphrey, Bankruptcy Judge
Burton Perlman, Bankruptcy Judge
C. Kathryn Preston, Bankruptcy Judge
Lawrence S. Walter, Bankruptcy Judge
Beth A. Buchanan, Bankruptcy Judge
Mark R. Abel, Magistrate Judge
Terence P. Kemp, Magistrate Judge
Norah M. King, Magistrate Judge
Sharon L. Ovington, Magistrate Judge
Stephanie K. Bowman, Magistrate Judge
Karen L. Litkovitz, Magistrate Judge
Michael R. Merz, Magistrate Judge
Michael J. Newman, Magistrate Judge
Elizabeth A. Preston Deavers, Magistrate Judge

OKLAHOMA, NORTHERN

Gregory K. Frizzell, Chief Judge
Claire V. Eagan, District Judge
John E. Dowdell, District Judge
Terence C. Kern, Senior Judge
Terrence L. Michael, Chief Bankruptcy Judge
Dana L. Rasure, Bankruptcy Judge
Paul J. Cleary, Magistrate Judge
Sam A. Joyner, Magistrate Judge
F. H. McCarthy, Magistrate Judge
Terrance L. Wilson, Magistrate Judge

OKLAHOMA, EASTERN

James H. Payne, Chief Judge
Ronald A. White, District Judge
Frank H. Seay, Senior Judge
Tom R. Cornish, Chief Bankruptcy Judge
Steven P. Shreder, Magistrate Judge
Kimberly E. West, Magistrate Judge

OKLAHOMA, WESTERN

Vicki Miles-LaGrange, Chief Judge
Timothy D. DeGiusti, District Judge
Joe L. Heaton, District Judge
Robin J. Cauthron, Senior Judge
Stephen Friot, Senior Judge
Tim Leonard, Senior Judge
David L. Russell, Senior Judge
Lee R. West, Senior Judge
Sarah A. Hall, Chief Bankruptcy Judge
Niles L. Jackson, Bankruptcy Judge
Janice D. Lloyd, Bankruptcy Judge
Shon T. Erwin, Magistrate Judge
Gary M. Purcell, Magistrate Judge
Ronald L. Howland, Magistrate Judge (Recalled)
Bernard M. Jones, Magistrate Judge
Charles B. Goodwin, Magistrate Judge
Suzanne Mitchell, Magistrate Judge

OREGON

Ann L. Aiken, Chief Judge
Anna J. Brown, District Judge
Michael W. Mosman, District Judge
Marco A. Hernandez, District Judge
Michael H. Simon, District Judge
Michael J. McShane, District Judge
Owen M. Panner, Senior Judge
James A. Redden, Senior Judge
Malcolm F. Marsh, Senior Judge
Ancer Lee Haggerty, Senior Judge
Robert E. Jones, Senior Judge
Garr M. King, Senior Judge
Trish M. Brown, Chief Bankruptcy Judge
Frank R. Alley, III, Bankruptcy Judge
Randall L. Dunn, Bankruptcy Judge
Peter C. McKittrick, Bankruptcy Judge
Elizabeth L. Perris, Bankruptcy Judge
Thomas M. Renn, Bankruptcy Judge
John V. Acosta, Magistrate Judge
Stacie F. Beckerman, Magistrate Judge
Mark D. Clarke, Magistrate Judge
Thomas M. Coffin, Magistrate Judge
John Jelderks, Magistrate Judge
Paul J. Papak, Magistrate Judge
Janice M. Stewart, Magistrate Judge
Patricia Sullivan, Magistrate Judge (Part-time)

PENNSYLVANIA, EASTERN

Petrese Brown Tucker, Chief Judge
Wendy Beetlestone, District Judge
Legrome D. Davis, District Judge
Paul S. Diamond, District Judge
James Knoll Gardner, District Judge
Mitchell S. Goldberg, District Judge
C. Darnell Jones, II, District Judge
Mark A. Kearney, District Judge
Joseph F. Leeson, Jr., District Judge
Gerald J. Pappert, District Judge
Gene E. K. Pratter, District Judge
Cynthia M. Rufe, District Judge
Juan R. Sanchez, District Judge
Timothy J. Savage, District Judge
Joel H. Slomsky, District Judge
Lawrence F. Stengel, District Judge
Nitza I. Quiñones Alejandro, District Judge
Gerald A. McHugh, Jr., District Judge
Jeffrey L. Schmehl, District Judge
Edward G. Smith, District Judge
Stewart Dalzell, Senior Judge
J. Curtis Joyner, Senior Judge
Harvey Bartle, III, Senior Judge
Michael M. Baylson, Senior Judge
Anita B. Brody, Senior Judge
Mary A. McLaughlin, Senior Judge
Eduardo C. Robreno, Senior Judge
Berle M. Schiller, Senior Judge
Richard B. Surrick, Senior Judge
Ronald L. Buckwalter, Senior Judge
Jan E. DuBois, Senior Judge
Robert F. Kelly, Senior Judge
Edmund V. Ludwig, Senior Judge
Thomas N. O'Neill, Jr., Senior Judge

PENNSYLVANIA, EASTERN-*(Cont'd)*

John R. Padova, Senior Judge
Norma L. Shapiro, Senior Judge
Donald W. VanArtsdalen, Senior Judge
Eric L. Frank, Chief Bankruptcy Judge
Ashely M. Chan, Bankruptcy Judge
Stephen Raslavich, Bankruptcy Judge
Richard E. Fehling, Bankruptcy Judge
Jean K. FitzSimon, Bankruptcy Judge
Magdeline D. Coleman, Bankruptcy Judge
Linda K. Caracappa, Chief Magistrate Judge
M. Faith Angell, Magistrate Judge
Jacob P. Hart, Magistrate Judge
Marilyn Heffley, Magistrate Judge
Elizabeth T. Hey, Magistrate Judge
Richard A. Lloret, Magistrate Judge
Henry S. Perkin, Magistrate Judge
Timothy R. Rice, Magistrate Judge
Thomas J. Rueter, Magistrate Judge
Lynne A. Sitarski, Magistrate Judge
David R. Strawbridge, Magistrate Judge
Carol Moore Wells, Magistrate Judge

PENNSYLVANIA, MIDDLE

Christopher C. Conner, Chief Judge
Yvette Kane, District Judge
John E. Jones, III, District Judge
Robert D. Mariani, District Judge
Malachy E. Mannion, District Judge
Matthew W. Brann, District Judge
A. Richard Caputo, Senior Judge
James M. Munley, Senior Judge
William W. Caldwell, Senior Judge
Richard Paul Conaboy, Senior Judge
Edwin M. Kosik, Senior Judge
William J. Nealon, Senior Judge
Sylvia H. Rambo, Senior Judge
Mary D. France, Chief Bankruptcy Judge
Robert N. Opel, II, Bankruptcy Judge
John J. Thomas, Bankruptcy Judge
William L. Arbuckle, Magistrate Judge
Martin C. Carlson, Magistrate Judge
Karolina Mehalchick, Magistrate Judge
Joseph F. Saporito, Jr., Magistrate Judge
Susan E. Schwab, Magistrate Judge

PENNSYLVANIA, WESTERN

Joy Flowers Conti, Chief Judge
David Cercone, District Judge
Nora Barry Fischer, District Judge
Kim R. Gibson, District Judge
Arthur J. Schwab, District Judge
Cathy Bissoon, District Judge
Mark R. Hornak, District Judge
Terrence F. McVerry, Senior Judge
Alan N. Bloch, Senior Judge
Maurice B. Cohill, Jr., Senior Judge
Gustave Diamond, Senior Judge
Donetta W. Ambrose, Senior Judge
Jeffery A. Deller, Chief Bankruptcy Judge
Thomas P. Agresti, Bankruptcy Judge
Carlota M. Bohm, Bankruptcy Judge
Gregory L. Taddonio, Bankruptcy Judge
Susan Paradise Baxter, Magistrate Judge (Part-time)
Lisa Pupo Lenihan, Magistrate Judge
Robert C. Mitchell, Magistrate Judge
Keith Alan M. Pesto, Magistrate Judge (Part-time)
Cynthia R. Eddy, Magistrate Judge
Maureen P. Kelly, Magistrate Judge

PUERTO RICO

Aida M. Delgado-Colon, Chief Judge
Jose Antonio Fuste, District Judge
Francisco A. Besosa, District Judge
Carmen C. Cerezo, District Judge
Jay A. Garcia Gregory, District Judge
Gustavo A. Gelpi, Jr., District Judge
Pedro A. Delgado Hernandez, District Judge
Raymond L. Acosta, Senior Judge
Salvador E. Casellas, Senior Judge
Juan M. Perez-Gimenez, Senior Judge
Daniel R. Dominguez, Senior Judge
Enrique S. Lamoutte, Chief Bankruptcy Judge
Brian K. Tester, Bankruptcy Judge
Mildred Caban, Bankruptcy Judge
Edward A. Godoy, Bankruptcy Judge
Marcos E. Lopez-Gonzalez, Magistrate Judge
Bruce J. McGiverin, Magistrate Judge
Camille L. Velez-Rive, Magistrate Judge
Silvia Carreno-Coll, Magistrate Judge

RHODE ISLAND

William E. Smith, Chief Judge
John J. McConnell, Jr., District Judge
Ronald R. Lagueux, Senior Judge
Mary M. Lisi, Senior Judge
Diane Finkle, Chief Bankruptcy Judge
Lincoln D. Almond, Magistrate Judge
Jacob Hagopian, Magistrate Judge
Robert Lovegreen, Magistrate Judge
David L. Martin, Magistrate Judge
Patricia A. Sullivan, Magistrate Judge

SOUTH CAROLINA

Terry L. Wooten, Chief Judge
David C. Norton, District Judge
R. Bryan Harwell, District Judge
Timothy M. Cain, District Judge
J. Michelle Childs, District Judge
Richard M. Gergel, District Judge
Mary Geiger Lewis, District Judge
Bruce Howe Hendricks, District Judge
Joseph F. Anderson, Jr., Senior Judge
Margaret B. Seymour, Senior Judge
Cameron McGowan Currie, Senior Judge
Henry M. Herlong, Jr., Senior Judge
Solomon Blatt, Jr., Senior Judge
C. Weston Houck, Senior Judge
Patrick Michael Duffy, Senior Judge
G. Ross Anderson, Jr., Senior Judge
David R. Duncan, Chief Bankruptcy Judge
John E. Waites, Bankruptcy Judge
Helen E. Burris, Bankruptcy Judge
Bristow Marchant, Magistrate Judge
Thomas E. Rogers, III, Magistrate Judge
Jacquelyn D. Austin, Magistrate Judge
Paige J. Gossett, Magistrate Judge
Shiva V. Hodges, Magistrate Judge
Kevin F. McDonald, Magistrate Judge
Kaymani D. West, Magistrate Judge

SOUTH DAKOTA

Jeffrey L. Viken, Chief Judge
Roberto A. Lange, District Judge
Karen E. Schreier, District Judge
Richard H. Battey, Senior Judge
John B. Jones, Senior Judge
Charles B. Kornmann, Senior Judge
Lawrence L. Piersol, Senior Judge
Charles L. Nail, Jr., Bankruptcy Judge
Veronica L. Duffy, Magistrate Judge (Part-time)
Mark A. Moreno, Magistrate Judge (Part-time)
William D. Gerdes, Magistrate Judge (Part-time)
Daneta L. Wollmann, Magistrate Judge

TENNESSEE, EASTERN

Thomas A. Varlan, Chief Judge
J. Ronnie Greer, District Judge
Harry S. Mattice, Jr., District Judge
Travis R. McDonough, District Judge
Pamela L. Reeves, District Judge
Curtis L. Collier, Senior Judge
Thomas W. Phillips, Senior Judge
R. Allan Edgar, Senior Judge
R. Leon Jordan, Senior Judge
Marcia Phillips Parsons, Chief Bankruptcy Judge
Suzanne H. Bauknight, Bankruptcy Judge
John C. Cook, Bankruptcy Judge
Shelley D. Rucker, Bankruptcy Judge
Dennis H. Inman, Chief Magistrate Judge
H. Bruce Guyton, Magistrate Judge
Susan K. Lee, Magistrate Judge
C. Clifford Shirley, Magistrate Judge
Christopher H. Steger, Magistrate Judge

TENNESSEE, MIDDLE

Kevin H. Sharp, Chief Judge
Todd J. Campbell, District Judge
Aleta A. Trauger, District Judge
William J. Haynes, Jr., Senior Judge
Thomas A. Higgins, Senior Judge
John T. Nixon, Senior Judge
Marian F. Harrison, Bankruptcy Judge
Keith M. Lundin, Bankruptcy Judge
Randal S. Mashburn, Bankruptcy Judge
Joe B. Brown, Magistrate Judge
John S. Bryant, Magistrate Judge
Barbara D. Holmes, Magistrate Judge
E. Clifton Knowles, Magistrate Judge

TENNESSEE, WESTERN

J. Daniel Breen, Chief Judge

Stanley Thomas Anderson, District Judge

John T. Fowlkes, District Judge

Sheryl H. Lipman, District Judge

Samuel H. Mays, Jr., Senior Judge

Jon P. McCalla, Senior Judge

James D. Todd, Senior Judge

David S. Kennedy, Bankruptcy Judge

Paulette J. Delk, Bankruptcy Judge

George W. Emerson, Bankruptcy Judge

Jennie D. Latta, Bankruptcy Judge

James Croom, Bankruptcy Judge

Tu M. Pham, Magistrate Judge

Diane K. Vescovo, Magistrate Judge

Edward G. Bryant, Magistrate Judge

Charmiane G. Claxton, Magistrate Judge

TEXAS, EASTERN

Ron Clark, Chief Judge
Marcia A. Crone, District Judge
J. Rodney Gilstrap, District Judge
Amos L. Mazzant, District Judge
Robert William Schroeder, District Judge
Thad Heartfield, Senior Judge
Richard A. Schell, Senior Judge
Michael H. Schneider, Sr., Senior Judge
Brenda T. Rhoades, Chief Bankruptcy Judge
Bill G. Parker, Bankruptcy Judge
Don D. Bush, Magistrate Judge
Caroline M. Craven, Magistrate Judge
Keith F. Giblin, Magistrate Judge
John D. Love, Magistrate Judge
Zachary J. Hawthorn, Magistrate Judge
Roy S. Payne, Magistrate Judge
Nicole Mitchell, Magistrate Judge

TEXAS, NORTHERN

Jorge Antonio Solis, Chief Judge
Jane J. Boyle, District Judge
Sidney A. Fitzwater, District Judge
David C. Godbey, District Judge
Ed Kinkeade, District Judge
Sam A. Lindsay, District Judge
Barbara M.G. Lynn, District Judge
John H. McBryde, District Judge
Reed C. O'Connor, District Judge
Sam R. Cummings, Senior Judge
A. Joe Fish, Senior Judge
Robert B. Maloney, Senior Judge
Terry R. Means, Senior Judge
Mary Lou Robinson, Senior Judge
Barbara J. Houser, Chief Bankruptcy Judge
Harlin D. Hale, Bankruptcy Judge
Stacey G. Jernigan, Bankruptcy Judge
Robert L. Jones, Bankruptcy Judge
Mark X. Mullin, Bankruptcy Judge
Russell F. Nelms, Bankruptcy Judge
Clinton E. Averitte, Magistrate Judge
Nancy M. Koenig, Magistrate Judge
Irma C. Ramirez, Magistrate Judge
Robert K. Roach, Magistrate Judge (Part-time)
Paul D. Stickney, Magistrate Judge
Jeffrey L. Cureton, Magistrate Judge
E. Scott Frost, Magistrate Judge
Renee Harris Toliver, Magistrate Judge
David L. Horan, Magistrate Judge

TEXAS, SOUTHERN

Ricardo H. Hinojosa, Chief Judge
Micaela Alvarez, District Judge
Alfred H. Bennett, District Judge
Randy Crane, District Judge
Keith P. Ellison, District Judge
Vanessa D. Gilmore, District Judge
Andrew S. Hanen, District Judge
George C. Hanks, Jr., District Judge
Melinda Furche Harmon, District Judge
Lynn N. Hughes, District Judge
Sim Lake, District Judge
Gray H. Miller, District Judge
Lee Hyman Rosenthal, District Judge
Marina Garcia Marmolejo, District Judge
Nelva Gonzales Ramos, District Judge
Jose Rolando Olvera, District Judge
Diana Saldana, District Judge
Nancy Friedman Atlas, Senior Judge
Kenneth M. Hoyt, Senior Judge
John D. Rainey, Senior Judge
Hilda G. Tagle, Senior Judge
David Hittner, Senior Judge
Ewing Werlein, Jr., Senior Judge
Hayden W. Head, Jr., Senior Judge
Janis Graham Jack, Senior Judge
George P. Kazen, Senior Judge
David R. Jones, Chief Bankruptcy Judge
Jeffrey E. T. Bohm, Bankruptcy Judge
Karen K. Brown, Bankruptcy Judge
Letitia Z. Paul, Bankruptcy Judge
Eduardo V. Rodriguez, Bankruptcy Judge
Marvin P. Isgur, Bankruptcy Judge
B. Janice Ellington, Magistrate Judge
John R. Froeschner, Magistrate Judge

TEXAS, SOUTHERN-*(Cont'd)*

Nancy K. Johnson, Magistrate Judge
Maryrose Milloy, Magistrate Judge
Peter E. Ormsby, Magistrate Judge
Dorina Ramos, Magistrate Judge
Stephen Wm. Smith, Magistrate Judge
Frances H. Stacy, Magistrate Judge
Guillermo R. Garcia, Magistrate Judge
J. Scott Hacker, Magistrate Judge
Ronald G. Morgan, Magistrate Judge
Diana Song Quiroga, Magistrate Judge
Jason B. Libby, Magistrate Judge
Ignacio Torteya, III, Magistrate Judge

TEXAS, WESTERN

Orlando Luis Garcia, Chief Judge
Walter S. Smith, Jr., District Judge
Kathleen Cardone, District Judge
Philip R. Martinez, District Judge
Frank Montalvo, District Judge
Robert Lee Pitman, District Judge
Xavier Rodriguez, District Judge
Sam Sparks, District Judge
Lee Yeakel, District Judge
David C. Guaderrama, District Judge
Alia Moses, District Judge
Fred Biery, Senior Judge
Robert A. Junell, Senior Judge
James R. Nowlin, Senior Judge
David Briones, Senior Judge
Ronald B. King, Chief Bankruptcy Judge
Craig A. Gargotta, Bankruptcy Judge
H. Christopher Mott, Bankruptcy Judge
Tony M. Davis, Bankruptcy Judge
Andrew W. Austin, Magistrate Judge
Robert F. Castaneda, Magistrate Judge
Victor R. Garcia, Magistrate Judge
Jeffrey C. Manske, Magistrate Judge
Pamela A. Mathy, Magistrate Judge
John W. Primomo, Magistrate Judge
Henry J. Bemporad, Magistrate Judge
W. David Counts, III, Magistrate Judge
David B. Fannin, Magistrate Judge
Mark P. Lane, Magistrate Judge
Leon Schydlower, Magistrate Judge
Miguel A. Torres, Magistrate Judge
Collis White, Magistrate Judge
Anne T. Berton, Magistrate Judge

UTAH

David Nuffer, Chief Judge
Jill N. Parrish, District Judge
Clark Waddoups, District Judge
Robert J. Shelby, District Judge
Dee Vance Benson, Senior Judge
Bruce Sterling Jenkins, Senior Judge
David Sam, Senior Judge
Tena Campbell, Senior Judge
Dale A. Kimball, Senior Judge
Ted Stewart, Senior Judge
William Thurman, Chief Bankruptcy Judge
Judith A. Boulden, Bankruptcy Judge
Joel T. Marker, Bankruptcy Judge
Russell Kimball Mosier, Bankruptcy Judge
Clark Allred, Magistrate Judge (Part-time)
Robert T. Braithwaite, Magistrate Judge
Paul M. Warner, Magistrate Judge
Brooke C. Wells, Magistrate Judge
Evelyn J. Furse, Magistrate Judge
Dustin B. Pead, Magistrate Judge

VERMONT

Christina Reiss, Chief Judge
Geoffrey W. Crawford, District Judge
J. Garvan Murtha, Senior Judge
William K. Sessions, III, Senior Judge
Colleen A. Brown, Bankruptcy Judge
John M. Conroy, Magistrate Judge

VIRGIN ISLANDS

Wilma A. Lewis, Chief Judge
Curtis V. Gomez, District Judge
Raymond L. Finch, District Judge
Geoffrey W. Barnard, Magistrate Judge
George W. Cannon, Jr., Magistrate Judge
Ruth Miller, Magistrate Judge

VIRGINIA, EASTERN

Rebecca Beach Smith, Chief Judge
Leonie M. Brinkema, District Judge
Mark S. Davis, District Judge
Henry E. Hudson, District Judge
Raymond A. Jackson, District Judge
Gerald Bruce Lee, District Judge
Liam O'Grady, District Judge
Arenda L. Wright Allen, District Judge
John A. Gibney, Jr., District Judge
Anthony J. Trenga, District Judge
M. Hannah Lauck, District Judge
James R. Spencer, Senior Judge
James C. Cacheris, Senior Judge
Robert G. Doumar, Senior Judge
T. S. Ellis, III, Senior Judge
Claude M. Hilton, Senior Judge
Henry Coke Morgan, Jr., Senior Judge
Robert E. Payne, Senior Judge
Douglas O. Tice, Jr., Chief Bankruptcy Judge
Kevin R. Huennekens, Bankruptcy Judge
Robert Mayer, Bankruptcy Judge
Frank J. Santoro, Bankruptcy Judge
Stephen C. St. John, Bankruptcy Judge
Brian F. Kenney, Bankruptcy Judge
Keith L. Phillips, Bankruptcy Judge
John F. Anderson, Magistrate Judge
Theresa C. Buchanan, Magistrate Judge
Ivan D. Davis, Magistrate Judge
Robert J. Krask, Magistrate Judge
David J. Novak, Magistrate Judge
Lawrence R. Leonard, Magistrate Judge
Douglas E. Miller, Magistrate Judge
Michael S. Nachmanoff, Magistrate Judge
Roderick C. Young, Magistrate Judge

VIRGINIA, WESTERN

Glen E. Conrad, Chief Judge

Elizabeth K. Dillon, District Judge

James P. Jones, District Judge

Michael T. Urbanski, District Judge

Norman K. Moon, Senior Judge

Jackson L. Kiser, Senior Judge

William F. Stone, Jr., Bankruptcy Judge

Rebecca Buehler Connelly, Bankruptcy Judge

Paul M. Black, Bankruptcy Judge

Pamela Meade Sargent, Magistrate Judge

James G. Welsh, Magistrate Judge

Robert S. Ballou, Magistrate Judge

Joel C. Hoppe, Magistrate Judge

WASHINGTON, EASTERN

Rosanna Malouf Peterson, Chief Judge
Thomas O. Rice, District Judge
Stanley A. Bastian, District Judge
Salvador Mendoza, Jr., District Judge
Lonny R. Suko, Senior Judge
William Fremming Nielsen, Senior Judge
Justin L. Quackenbush, Senior Judge
Edward F. Shea, Senior Judge
Fred Van Sickle, Senior Judge
Robert H. Whaley, Senior Judge
Frederick P. Corbit, Chief Bankruptcy Judge
Frank L. Kurtz, Bankruptcy Judge
John A. Rossmeissl, Bankruptcy Judge
James P. Hutton, Magistrate Judge
John T. Rodgers, Magistrate Judge

WASHINGTON, WESTERN

Marsha J. Pechman, Chief Judge
Robert S. Lasnik, District Judge
Ronald B. Leighton, District Judge
Ricardo S. Martinez, District Judge
James L. Robart, District Judge
Richard A. Jones, District Judge
Benjamin H. Settle, District Judge
Walter T. McGovern, Senior Judge
Carolyn R. Dimmick, Senior Judge
Robert J. Bryan, Senior Judge
Thomas S. Zilly, Senior Judge
John C. Coughenour, Senior Judge
Barbara J. Rothstein, Senior Judge
Brian D. Lynch, Chief Bankruptcy Judge
Christopher M. Alston, Bankruptcy Judge
Marc L. Barreca, Bankruptcy Judge
Timothy W. Dore, Bankruptcy Judge
Paul Snyder, Bankruptcy Judge
Dean R. Brett, Magistrate Judge (Part-time)
David W. Christel, Magistrate Judge (Part-time)
J. Richard Creatura, Magistrate Judge
James P. Donohue, Magistrate Judge
Karen L. Strombom, Magistrate Judge
Mary Alice Theiler, Magistrate Judge
Brian A. Tsuchida, Magistrate Judge
Ira J. Uhrig, Magistrate Judge (Part-time)

WEST VIRGINIA, NORTHERN

John P. Bailey, Chief Judge
Irene M. Keeley, District Judge
Gina M. Groh, District Judge
Frederick P. Stamp, Jr., Senior Judge
Patrick M. Flatley, Chief Bankruptcy Judge
Michael J. Aloi, Magistrate Judge
John S. Kaull, Magistrate Judge
James E. Seibert, Magistrate Judge
Robert W. Trumble, Magistrate Judge

WEST VIRGINIA, SOUTHERN

Robert C. Chambers, Chief Judge
John Thomas Copenhaver, Jr., District Judge
Joseph R. Goodwin, District Judge
Thomas E. Johnston, District Judge
David A. Faber, Senior Judge
Irene Cornelia Berger, District Judge
Frank W. Volk, Chief Bankruptcy Judge
Dwane L. Tinsley, Magistrate Judge
R. Clarke VanDervort, Magistrate Judge
Cheryl A. Eifert, Magistrate Judge

WISCONSIN, EASTERN

William C. Griesbach, Chief Judge
Rudolph T. Randa, District Judge
Lynn S. Adelman, District Judge
J. P. Stadtmueller, District Judge
Charles N. Clevert, Jr., Senior Judge
Pamela Pepper, District Judge
Margaret Dee McGarity, Bankruptcy Judge
Susan V. Kelley, Bankruptcy Judge
James E. Shapiro, Bankruptcy Judge
William Duffin, Magistrate Judge
William E. Callahan, Jr., Magistrate Judge
Patricia J. Gorence, Magistrate Judge
James Sickel, Magistrate Judge (Part-time)
Nancy Joseph, Magistrate Judge

WISCONSIN, WESTERN

William M. Conley, Chief Judge
James D. Peterson, District Judge
Barbara B. Crabb, Senior Judge
Catherine J. Furay, Chief Bankruptcy Judge
Robert D. Martin, Bankruptcy Judge
Stephen L. Crocker, Magistrate Judge
Peter A. Oppeneer, Magistrate Judge

WYOMING

Nancy D. Freudenthal, Chief Judge
Alan B. Johnson, District Judge
Scott W. Skavdahl, District Judge
Kelly H. Rankin, Chief Magistrate Judge
Robert W. Connor, Jr., Magistrate Judge (Part-time)
Richard D. Gist, Magistrate Judge (Part-time)
James K. Lubing, Magistrate Judge
Karen L. Marty, Magistrate Judge (Part-time)
Teresa M. McKee, Magistrate Judge (Part-time)

I. THE STATE BENCHES

U.S. Department of Justice
Office of Justice Programs
Bureau of Justice Statistics

━━━━━ **SPECIAL REPORT** ━━━━━

NOVEMBER 2013   NCJ 242850

State Court Organization, 2011

Ron Malega, Ph.D., and Thomas H. Cohen, J.D., Ph.D., *former BJS Statisticians*

From 1980 to 2011, the number of state trial court judges increased 11%, from 24,784 to 27,570 (figure 1). During the same period, the U.S. population increased 37%, and arrests in the U.S. increased 19%. Because of these increases, the ratio of judges per 100,000 U.S. residents declined 23%, from 13.2 in 1980 to 10.2 in 2011. In this report, judge refers to any judicial officer granted authority to preside over court proceedings.

Data for this report were drawn from the Bureau of Justice Statistics' (BJS) State Court Organization (SCO) report series. The SCO reports provide state-level data on court types, jurisdictional levels of state courts, the number of judges and support staff, funding sources, judicial education standards, and procedures for selecting judges. BJS previously released four comprehensive reports on state court organization covering survey years 1980, 1987, 1993, 1998, and 2004. The most recent SCO data collection explored the organizational structure and operations of state courts in all 50 states and the District of Columbia during 2011.

FIGURE 1
Number of state trial court judges and rate per 100,000 U.S. residents, 1980–2011

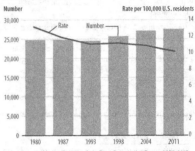

Source: Bureau of Justice Statistics, State Court Organization Survey, 1980, 1987, 1993, 1998, 2004, and 2011.

HIGHLIGHTS

- The organizational structure of the nation's trial and appellate courts changed modestly from 1980 to 2011.

- Six states added intermediate appellate courts between 1980 and 1998: Minnesota, Mississippi, Nebraska, North Dakota, Utah, and Virginia.

- From 1980 to 2011, the number of states with more than three types of limited jurisdiction trial courts declined from 31 to 21.

- The number of states with one or no limited jurisdiction trial courts increased from 14 in 1980 to 21 in 2011.

- From 1980 to 2011, the number of state appellate court judges increased 69%, and the number of state trial judges increased 11%.

- All judges in general jurisdiction trial courts had some legal qualification in 2011, compared to 59% of judges in limited jurisdiction trial courts.

- In 2011, 52% of appellate court judges were appointed to their initial terms, while 75% of trial court judges were elected to their initial terms.

- In 2011, two-thirds of state administrative court offices had full responsibility for judicial education and court technical assistance.

- All general jurisdiction trial courts juries were required to reach unanimous verdicts for felony or misdemeanor cases in 2011, compared to 47% for civil cases.

BJS

Jurisdictional level of state courts

States organize their court systems differently (figure 2). In general, each state uses some or all of the following four jurisdictional levels to organize its court system:

- **Limited jurisdiction courts (LJCs)**—also called inferior courts or lower courts, have jurisdiction on a restricted range of cases, primarily lesser criminal and civil matters, including misdemeanors, small claims, traffic, parking, and civil infractions. They can also handle the preliminary stages of felony cases in some states.

- **General jurisdiction courts (GJCs)**—often called major trial courts, have primary jurisdiction on all issues not delegated to lower courts, most often hearing serious criminal or civil cases. Cases are also designated to GJCs based on the severity of the punishment or allegation or on the dollar value of the case.

- **Intermediate appellate courts (IACs)**—hear appeals on cases or matters decided in GJCs and LJCs. IACs may also hear appeals from administrative agencies. Depending on the state, IACs represent the first—and often only—appeal because they exercise both mandatory and discretionary review of the cases they hear.

- **Courts of last resort (COLRs)**—also called state supreme courts, have final authority over all appeals filed in state courts. Most states have one COLR, but Oklahoma and Texas both have separate courts for civil and criminal appeals. Depending on the state, a COLR may have either a mandatory or discretionary docket for cases it will hear.

California has a unified court system consisting of one type of GJC (i.e., superior court) and a two-tier system of appeals courts (i.e., court of appeals and supreme court). California's court system does not use LJCs. In comparison, Georgia has a more fragmented court structure consisting of seven different types of LJCs (i.e., civil, state, juvenile, county recorders, magistrate, probate, and municipal), one type of GJC (i.e., superior court), and a two-tier system of appeals courts (i.e., court of appeals and supreme court). Such variations in state court structure are often reflected in court funding sources. Many LJCs are funded and operated at the local level (e.g., county), while GJCs are likely to be managed and funded at the state level.

FIGURE 2
Different structures of trial and appellate state court organization in California and Georgia, 2011

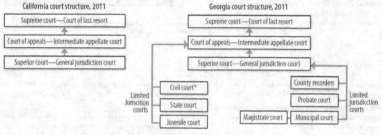

*Civil court serves two counties in Georgia (Bibb and Richmond).
Source: Bureau of Justice Statistics, State Court Organization Survey, 2011.

State court organization changed gradually from 1980 to 2011

Six states—Minnesota, Mississippi, Nebraska, North Dakota, Utah, and Virginia—added intermediate appellate courts (IACs) between 1980 and 1998. No states established IACs after 1998. In 2011, forty states had two-tier systems of intermediate and final review consisting of IACs and courts of last resort (COLRs) (table 1). While most states used one COLR and one IAC, some states used multiple COLRs or IACs. For example, Oklahoma and Texas used two COLRs and one IAC. Alabama, Indiana, New York, Pennsylvania, and Tennessee used two IACs. Eleven states relied exclusively on COLRs for final review: Delaware,

the District of Columbia, Maine, Montana, Nevada, New Hampshire, Rhode Island, South Dakota, Vermont, West Virginia, and Wyoming.

In 2011, 46 states used general jurisdiction courts (GJCs) and limited jurisdiction courts (LJCs). Over the past three decades, states have decreased their use of LJCs. Thirty-one states had three types of LJCs in 1980, compared to 21 states in 2011. The number of states with one or no LJCs increased from 14 to 21 during the same period. California, Illinois, Iowa, Minnesota, and the District of Columbia operated without LJCs in 2011. See map 1 and map 2 for the appellate and trial court structures for 2011.

TABLE 1
Appellate and trial court structure for 50 states and the District of Columbia, 1980, 1987, 1993, 1998, 2004, and 2011

Appellate and trial court structure	Number of states					
	1980	1987	1993	1998	2004	2011
Appellate court structure[a]						
1 COLR and 0 IACs	17	13	12	11	11	11
1 COLR and 1 IAC	28	31	32	33	33	33
1 COLR and multiple IACs	4	5	5	5	5	5
Multiple COLRs and 1 IAC	2	2	2	2	2	2
Trial court structure[b]						
GJC and 0 LJCs	3	4	4	4	5	5
GJC and 1 LJC	11	13	12	14	14	16
GJC and 2 LJCs	6	9	9	8	10	9
GJC and 3 or more LJCs	31	25	26	25	22	21

Notes: Table includes 50 states and the District of Columbia. North Dakota established a temporary IAC in 1987, which will continue until 2016.
[a]Includes intermediate appellate courts (IACs) and courts of last resort (COLRs).
[b]Includes general jurisdiction courts (GJCs) and limited jurisdiction courts (LJCs). States can have more than one GJC type; however, this table only tracks the number of LJCs.
Source: Bureau of Justice Statistics, State Court Organization Survey, 1980, 1987, 1993, 1998, 2004, and 2011.

MAP 1
Structure of appellate courts for 50 states and the District of Columbia, 2011

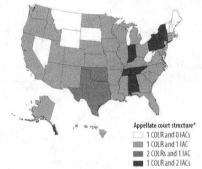

Appellate court structure*
- 1 COLR and 0 IACs
- 1 COLR and 1 IAC
- 2 COLRs and 1 IAC
- 1 COLR and 2 IACs

Note: Between 1987 and 2011, three states added an intermediate appellate court (IAC): Nebraska, Mississippi, and North Dakota. North Dakota established a temporary IAC in 1987, which will continue until 2016.
*Includes intermediate appellate courts (IACs) and courts of last resort (COLRs).
Source: Bureau of Justice Statistics, State Court Organization Survey, 2011.

MAP 2
Number of limited jurisdiction court types for 50 states and the District of Columbia, 2011

- 0
- 1
- 2
- 3 or more

Source: Bureau of Justice Statistics, State Court Organization Survey, 2011.

The unification of trial courts in some states reduced the percentage of judges serving in LJCs

The movement towards unification in some state courts has reduced the number of LJC judges. The percentage of trial court judges serving in LJCs, compared to GJCs, declined by 12 percentage points from 1980 to 2011 (table 2). In addition, the number of GJC judges increased 57% from 1980 to 2011, while the number of LJC judges declined 6% (table 3). These trends were primarily a result of California's court unification during the 1990s, which eliminated all LJCs and reclassified those judges to GJCs.

The distribution of appellate court judges between IACs and COLRs also changed from 1980 to 2011. During the past three decades, the number of IAC judges increased by about 400 judges, while the number of COLR judges remained stable. Much of growth in IAC judges can be attributed to the six states that established IACs between 1980 and 1998. The number of judges serving in state COLRs is often mandated by state constitutions; therefore, the number of COLR judges remained relatively stable during the same period, decreasing by two judges (1%).

TABLE 2
Jurisdictional levels of appellate and trial court judges for 50 states and the District of Columbia, 1980, 1987, 1993, 1998, 2004, and 2011

Year		Appellate court judges			Trial court judges	
			Percent serving in—			Percent serving in—
	Number	Courts of last resort	Intermediate appellate courts	Number	General jurisdiction	Limited jurisdiction
1980	933	37%	63%	24,784	27%	73%
1987	1,119	31	69	24,830	32	68
1993	1,209	29	71	24,565	35	65
1998	1,274	27	73	25,758	36	64
2004	1,316	27	73	27,160	38	62
2011	1,336	26	74	27,570	39	61

Note: Includes trial and appellate courts located in all 50 states and the District of Columbia. Totals include South Dakota's general jurisdiction courts but exclude limited jurisdiction courts, which were missing data for 1980, 1987, 1993, and 1998.
Source: Bureau of Justice Statistics, State Court Organization Survey, 1980, 1987, 1993, 1998, 2004, and 2011.

TABLE 3
Number of state trial and appellate court judges in 50 states and the District of Columbia, by court type, 1980, 1987, 1993, 1998, 2004, and 2011

Court types	Number of judges						Percent change	
	1980	1987	1993	1998	2004	2011	1980–2011	2004–2011
Total courts of last resort (COLRs) judges	348	347	349	349	349	346	-1%	-1%
Total intermediate appellate courts (IACs) judges[a]	585	772	860	925	967	990	69%	2%
Total trial court judges[b]	24,784	24,830	24,565	25,758	27,160	27,570	11%	2%
General jurisdiction	6,788	7,859	8,580	9,189	10,370	10,650	57	3
Limited jurisdiction	17,996	16,971	15,985	16,569	16,790	16,920	-6	1
Average number of trial judges per 100,000 persons	13.2	11.9	11.1	11.2	10.9	10.2	-23	-6

Note: Judicial staffing figures include courts from all 50 states and the District of Columbia unless otherwise noted. Increase in the number of general jurisdiction judges partly reflects the unification of California's courts and the reclassification of their judges from limited to general jurisdiction in 1998. The number of states with IACs increased from 34 in 1980 to 40 in 2011.
[a]Six states added IACs from 1980 to 2011.
[b]Includes South Dakota's general jurisdiction courts but excludes limited jurisdiction courts, which were missing judicial numbers for 1980, 1987, 1993, and 1998.
Source: Bureau of Justice Statistics, State Court Organization Survey, 1980, 1987, 1993, 1998, 2004, and 2011.

Three-quarters of all trial court judges needed some legal qualifications to serve as judge

The legal qualifications necessary to serve as a judge for a GJC compared to an LJC vary by state. In 2011, all GJC trial judges needed some type of legal qualification to serve as a judge (table 4). In comparison, 59% of LJC trial judges were required to obtain some type legal qualification to serve as a judge.[1] Possessing a law degree was the most commonly required legal qualification to serve as a judge. Sitting GJC judges were nearly 3 times more likely than LJC judges to need a law degree. GJC judges were about 2 times more likely than LJC judges to need state bar membership or have had an active legal practice.

Trial court judges were more likely than appellate court judges to be elected into the first term

In 2011, 52% of appellate court judges were appointed for their initial terms by judicial nominating committees, governors, legislators, or other methods (table 5). Of the appellate judges who were required to be elected to their initial terms, 59% ran in partisan elections. Eighty-one percent of all appellate court judges were required to run in some type of election to retain their positions. The majority of appellate judges (52%) that ran for office did so in retention elections rather than partisan or nonpartisan elections.[2] Only 3% of appellate court judges served life terms in 2011.

Among trial court judges, 75% were required to be elected to their initial terms. Of those trial court judges who ran in an election, 45% ran in partisan elections. For subsequent terms, 90% of all trial court judges were required to run in an election to retain their positions. Among trial court judges required to run in an election for subsequent terms, 48% ran in nonpartisan elections. Only 1% of trial court judges served life terms in 2011.

[1] Examples of legal qualifications less than a law degree include taking a judicial education course prior to office or passing a legal certification exam other than the state bar.
[2] In a retention election, a judge runs unopposed and is removed from office if a majority of votes are cast against retention. In a partisan election, a judge is listed with party affiliation, while in a nonpartisan election, the judge is listed on the ballot with no party affiliation.

TABLE 4
Legal qualifications to serve as trial court judge for 50 states and the District of Columbia, by trial courts of general and limited jurisdiction, 2011

Trial court judges	Number of judges	Any legal requirement	Law degree	State bar membership	Attorney license	Active legal practice	Prior service as state judge	Learned in law
All judges	27,544	75%	47%	38%	27%	12%	6%	2%
Judges serving in courts of—								
General jurisdiction	10,650	100%	79%	56%	33%	17%	15%	1%
Limited jurisdiction	16,894	59	27	26	23	9	--	2

Note: Detail may not sum to total because states could impose multiple requirements on trial court judges. Legal qualifications for appellate court judges are not shown. Data on legal qualifications to serve as trial court judges are available for 97% of all trial courts, 100% of general jurisdiction trial courts, and 95% of limited jurisdiction trial courts.
-- Less than 0.5%.
Source: Bureau of Justice Statistics, State Court Organization Survey, 2011.

TABLE 5
Selection of appellate and general jurisdiction trial court judges for initial and subsequent judicial terms for 50 states and the District of Columbia, 2011

			Methods of appellate court judicial selection and retention				
				Judicial election			Tenure to age
	Number of judges	Appointment[a]	Any election	Partisan	Nonpartisan	Retention	70 or older
Initial terms							
Appellate	1,336	52%	48%	29%	20%	~	~
Trial[b]	10,650	25	75	34	42	~	~
Subsequent terms							
Appellate	1,336	15%	81%	20%	20%	42%	3%
Trial[b]	10,650	9	90	20	43	27	1

Note: Data for the selection of appellate and general jurisdiction trial court judges for initial and subsequent terms are available for 50 states and the District of Columbia. Data on the selection methods for limited jurisdiction court judges are not shown because these are often determined at the local level.
~Not applicable.
[a] A variety of parties can exercise control over the judicial appointment process in state courts, including judicial nominating committees, governors, legislators, and the courts. The U.S. President appoints judges in the District of Columbia. All are included in the appointment category.
[b] The selection methods were not uniform within the jurisdictions of trial courts in Arizona, Kansas, Indiana, and Missouri. For these states, the data reflect the selection method used for judges presiding in courts in counties with the largest populations.
Source: Bureau of Justice Statistics, State Court Organization Survey, 2011.

Varied routes to judgeship

How judges come to the bench varies from state to state and may even vary within a state by type of court (e.g., trial compared to appellate court). States most often use one or more of the following methods to select judges:

- Appointment: Depending on the state, judges may be appointed by the governor, legislature, or a COLR chief justice. Some states use nominating committees, which provide the appointing body with a limited number of candidates from which to choose a judge (map 3).

- Partisan election: Judges may run in a contested election in which candidates must declare their political party affiliation (map 4).

- Nonpartisan election: Judges may run in a contested election but do not declare their political party affiliation.

- Retention election: Sitting judges may retain their office through an uncontested retention election at the end of each term. Judges maintain their bench if the majority votes that they should be retained in office.

MAP 3
Establishment of judicial nominating commissions for 50 states and the District of Columbia, 1940–2011

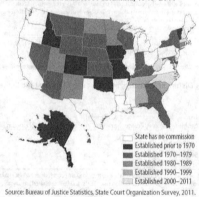

State has no commission
Established prior to 1970
Established 1970–1979
Established 1980–1989
Established 1990–1999
Established 2000–2011

Source: Bureau of Justice Statistics, State Court Organization Survey, 2011.

MAP 4
Method for selection of general jurisdiction judges for an initial term, 2011

Appointment
Partisan election
Nonpartisan election

Source: Bureau of Justice Statistics, State Court Organization Survey, 2011.

Fewer states used partisan elections to fill appellate and general jurisdiction trial court judgeships

Twelve states used partisan elections to fill appellate court judgeships for their initial terms in 1987, compared to 8 states in 2011 (table 6). Four states at the appellate court level moved away from using partisan elections. Tennessee changed from partisan election to appointment by the governor, while Arkansas, Mississippi, and North Carolina changed to nonpartisan elections.

Several states also moved away from using partisan elections to retain appellate court judges. In 1987, 10 states used partisan elections for the retention of appellate court judges, compared to 5 states in 2011. Arkansas, Mississippi, and North Carolina changed from partisan elections to nonpartisan elections for retention terms. New Mexico and Tennessee changed from partisan to uncontested retention elections.

Fourteen states used partisan elections to fill initial terms of GJC trial judges in 1987, compared to 11 states in 2011. Arkansas, North Carolina, and Mississippi all changed to nonpartisan elections to fill the initial terms of GJC judges.

The number of states using a partisan election for the retention of GJC judges declined by 4 states from 1987 to 2011. Arkansas, Mississippi, and North Carolina changed from partisan elections to nonpartisan elections for retention terms, while New Mexico changed from partisan to uncontested retention elections.

On average, judges serving in COLRs had the longest terms

The length of judicial term varies by state, type of court, and method of selection. Excluding states where judges served life terms, judges serving in COLRs had the longest average length of judicial term (8 years) (table 7). The average term for appellate and trial court judges was 7 years. Judges serving in COLRs had the largest range in judicial term (12 years), while judges serving in IACs had the least variation (9 years).

TABLE 6
Methods of judicial selection in state appellate and trial courts of general jurisdiction for 50 states and the District of Columbia, 1987 and 2011

| | Number of state courts | | | |
| | Appellate | | Trial[a] | |
Judicial selection methods	1987	2011	1987	2011
Initial terms				
Appointment[b]	27	29	22	22
Partisan election	12	8	14	11
Nonpartisan election	12	14	15	18
Retention terms				
Appointment[b]	10	10	9	9
Partisan election	10	5	12	8
Nonpartisan election	12	14	16	19
Retention election	16	19	11	12
Tenure to age 70 or older	3	3	3	3

Note: Includes 50 states and the District of Columbia.
[a]Includes only trial courts of general jurisdiction, as the selection processes in limited jurisdiction courts are often locally determined.
[b]A variety of parties can exercise control over the judicial appointment process in state courts, including judicial nominating committees, governors, legislators, and the courts. The U.S. President appoints judges in the District of Columbia. All are included in the appointment category.
Source: Bureau of Justice Statistics, State Court Organization Survey, 1987 and 2011.

TABLE 7
Length of judicial terms for 47 states and the District of Columbia in state appellate and trial courts of general jurisdiction, by retention methods, 2011

| Court types and judicial retention method | Number of states | Length of judicial terms | | |
		Average	Shortest	Longest
Courts of last resort				
All states	48	8 yrs.	3 yrs.	15 yrs.
Appointment	10	10	6	15
Partisan election	5	8	6	12
Nonpartisan election	14	7	6	10
Retention election	19	8	3	12
Intermediate appellate courts*				
All states	39	7 yrs.	3 yrs.	12 yrs.
Appointment	6	7	5	10
Partisan election	4	7	6	10
Nonpartisan election	12	7	6	8
Retention election	17	8	3	12
General jurisdiction courts				
All states	48	7 yrs.	4 yrs.	15 yrs.
Appointment	9	9	6	15
Partisan election	8	7	4	11
Nonpartisan election	19	6	4	15
Retention election	12	6	4	10

Note: Excludes Massachusetts, New Hampshire, and Rhode Island, where judges serve life terms. Data on the judicial term lengths for limited jurisdiction courts are not shown because these are often determined at the local level.
*Excludes states that do not have intermediate appellate courts.
Source: Bureau of Justice Statistics, State Court Organization Survey, 2011.

Salaries for trial court judges were most often funded by the state

Funding sources for GJCs and LJCs varied by type of expenditure. At least 50% of trial courts received their primary funding for the salaries of court administrators, research attorneys, court reporters, and judges from state funding sources (table 8). In comparison, expenditure items that were funded mostly at the county level included court security (57%), building property expenses (64%), pretrial services (61%), and Americans with Disabilities Act compliance (56%). While the majority of court expenditures were funded through the state, county, or a combination, 12% of state courts' primary funding for court-ordered treatment expenditures came from other sources, such as federal funds or local fees.

TABLE 8
Trial court funding sources for selected expenditure items for 50 states and the District of Columbia, 2011

Expenditure item	Total	State[a]	County[a]	Both state and county[a]	Other[b]
Court record for appeal					
Criminal	100%	42%	50%	4%	4%
Civil	100%	37	54	1	8
Equipment expenditures					
Information technology equipment	100%	41%	30%	27%	2%
Other capital equipment	100%	33	53	12	2
Expenses					
Travel expenses	100%	50%	31%	17%	2%
General operating expenses	100%	41	47	10	2
Court security expenses	100%	27	57	15	2
Building property expenses	100%	26	64	9	1
Language interpreters					
Sign language interpreters	100%	45%	40%	13%	2%
Foreign language interpreters	100%	41	37	20	2
Other items/services					
Child support enforcement	100%	46%	24%	23%	7%
Court-appointed child advocates	100%	43	25	28	4
Guardianship	100%	40	43	11	6
Indigent defense	100%	39	40	20	2
Court-ordered treatment	100%	30	27	31	12
Pretrial services	100%	30	61	9	1
Americans with Disabilities Act compliance	100%	28	56	15	2
Salaries					
Judicial salaries	100%	58%	28%	13%	2%
Court reporter salaries	100%	57	31	6	6
Research attorney salaries	100%	56	35	6	2
Court administrator salaries	100%	50	40	8	2
Juvenile probation officer salaries	100%	41	26	31	1
Court clerk salaries	100%	41	51	5	3
Other court personnel salaries	100%	41	46	11	2
Adult probation officer salaries	100%	36	49	14	1

Note: Includes funding and expenditure items for general and limited jurisdiction trial courts combined. Funding source issues were unknown for 3% to 10% of the trial court types per expenditure item.
[a]Includes supplemental funding from federal sources or local fees.
[b]Includes funding from only federal sources or local fees.
Source: Bureau of Justice Statistics, State Court Organization Survey, 2011.

Two-thirds of state administrative offices of the courts had full responsibility for providing technical assistance and judicial education

In every state, a central office is responsible for the administrative functions of the state's trial court system. Administrative offices of the courts (AOCs) provide a wide range of services to support state courts. Of the 48 states and the District of Columbia reporting information, all state AOCs reported having at least some responsibility for providing research planning (table 9). Forty-eight state AOCs reported having at least some responsibility for providing information technology, state court statistics, serving as the liaison to legislature, and providing technical assistance. Thirty-three state AOCs had full responsibility for providing the courts with technical assistance and judicial education, and eleven state AOCs provided some type adult probation services to the courts (map 5).

MAP 5
Administrative offices of the courts (AOCs) with at least some responsibilities for juvenile and adult probation, 2011

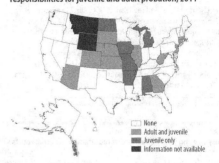

- ☐ None
- Adult and juvenile
- Juvenile only
- Information not available

Source: Bureau of Justice Statistics, State Court Organization Survey, 2011.

TABLE 9
Responsibilities and functions of administrative offices of the courts (AOCs) for 48 states and the District of Columbia, 2011

Responsibility	Any	Full	Partial	None
		Number of state AOCs with responsibility		
Research planning	49	27	22	0
Technical assistance	48	33	15	1
Liaison to legislature	48	27	21	1
State court statistics	48	25	23	1
Information technology	48	24	24	1
Public information	47	21	26	2
Budget preparation	46	20	26	3
Accounting	46	17	29	3
Judicial education	45	33	12	4
Human resources	45	15	30	4
Court records management	45	9	36	4
Court equipment purchases	44	15	29	5
Court records data processing	41	14	27	8
Court performance measurement	40	17	23	9
Financial audits	38	14	24	11
Emergency facility management	38	8	30	11
Security facilities management	38	7	31	11
Court facilities management	38	6	32	11
Legal representation/general counsel	31	16	15	18
Alternative dispute resolution	31	11	20	18
Legal research	29	8	21	20
Collecting financial legal obligations	29	5	24	20
Supplemental judge assignments	28	13	15	21
Law libraries	27	14	13	22
Sitting judge assignments	18	7	11	31
Foster care review	18	4	14	31
Juvenile probation	17	6	11	32
Judicial performance evaluation	16	8	8	33
Ombudsman	14	3	11	35
Adult probation	11	4	7	38

Note: Includes AOCs operating in 48 states and the District of Columbia. Montana and Wyoming did not provide information on AOC responsibilities and functions at the state level.
Source: Bureau of Justice Statistics, State Court Organization Survey, 2011.

Jury size and verdict requirements varied by court jurisdiction and case type

For GJCs, all states and the District of Columbia required a 12-person jury when trying felony cases (table 10). Fifteen states required such courts to have a 6-person jury when hearing misdemeanor cases. All states and the District of Columbia required juries in GJCs to reach a unanimous verdict for felony and misdemeanor trials.[3] For civil cases, 23 states and the District of Columbia required juries in GJCs to reach a unanimous verdict.

Twenty-five states allowed LJCs to try misdemeanor cases. All 25 states except Delaware, Ohio, and Texas used 6-person juries. In Oklahoma, the LJC judge decided if the jury needed to reach a unanimous verdict in misdemeanor cases. Twenty-seven states allowed LJCs to try civil cases. All 27 states, except Delaware, North Carolina, Ohio, and Texas, used 6-person juries. Eleven states required a unanimous verdict, while judges in Oklahoma decided if the jury needed to reach a unanimous verdict in civil cases.

[3]Kentucky's GJC does not have authority to adjudicate misdemeanor jury trials.

TABLE 10

Jury size and unanimous verdict requirements for trial courts in 50 states and the District of Columbia, 2011

Court jurisdiction and case types	Number of states	Percent of states requiring jury sizes of—			Percent with unanimous verdict requirements
		12 persons[a]	6 persons[b]	Other[c]	
General jurisdiction					
Felonies	51	100%	0%	0%	100%
Misdemeanor[d]	50	64	30	6	100
Civil	51	65	26	10	47
Limited jurisdiction					
Misdemeanor	25	4%	88%	8%	96%
Civil	27	7	85	7	41

Note: Some general and limited jurisdiction courts do not have jurisdiction over jury trials involving certain case types. For these reasons, not all 50 states will report jury trial requirements for their limited jurisdiction courts. Only those courts of limited and general jurisdiction that have authority over civil and misdemeanor cases are shown.
[a]Includes states that allow parties, with court consent, to stipulate to jury sizes below the 12-person requirement.
[b]Includes states that allow parties, with court consent, to stipulate to jury sizes below the 6-person requirement.
[c]Includes other jury sizes, such as 4- or 8-person juries.
[d]Kentucky's court of general jurisdiction does not have authority to adjudicate misdemeanors using jury trials.
Source: Bureau of Justice Statistics, State Court Organization Survey, 2011.

Methodology

Data for the 1980, 1987, 1993, 1998, 2004, and 2011 State Court Organization (SCO) reports were collected by the National Center for State Courts (NCSC) with funding provided by the Bureau of Justice Statistics (BJS). Data collections prior to 2011 were mail surveys to state court administrators in all 50 states, the District of Columbia, Puerto Rico, and U.S. territories. The 2011 SCO collected information from this same set of state court administrators, but the 2011 collection was primarily web-based with paper surveys made available for respondents that preferred or needed a traditional response mode. All SCO data collections obtained court information at the state and jurisdictional levels, depending on the type of information collected. A survey aimed at state court administrators was designed to collect information on court organization, administration, and operation. Separate surveys designed to collect descriptive information (e.g., budget and staffing) were sent to appellate courts and trial courts. While respondents provided most of the information to complete the survey, staff at NCSC also compiled information on specific laws, legal procedures, and legal practices that applied statewide.

Data for this report were drawn from the five previously released SCO reports and the 2011 web-based interactive application tool. BJS summarized select data from the SCO 2011 Interactive Application (accessed in February 2012) to produce the narrative, tables, maps, and figures found within the report. This report also used select standardized SCO data from 1980 to 2011, created by BJS staff, to analyze trends in state court organization over three decades. The topics presented in this report reflect many of the themes common to the SCO data collections and highlight some of the long-standing issues relevant to state court systems. This report presents information for all 50 states and the District of Columbia. It excludes information on Puerto Rico and the U.S. territories.

For more information, see *State Court Organization, 1980*, NCJ 76711, BJS website, May 1982; *State Court Organization, 1993*, NCJ 148346, BJS website, January 1995; *State Court Organization, 1998*, NCJ 178932, BJS website, June 2000; and *State Court Organization, 2004*, NCJ 212351, BJS website, August 2006. For analysis of trends, see *State Court Organization, 1987–2004*, NCJ 217996, BJS website, October 2007. Data for the individual 1998 and 2004 State Court Organization reports may be downloaded through the Inter-University Consortium for Political and Social Science Research (ICPSR) website at http://www.icpsr.umich.edu/icpsrweb/landing.jsp. The 2011 within-year data set and the standardized trend data sets for 1980 through 2011 used in this report are available for download through the ICPSR website.

APPENDIX TABLE 1
Number of appellate court judges in 50 states and the District of Columbia, 2011

State	Appellate court name	Number of judges
Alabama		
SC	Supreme Court	9
IA	Court of Civil Appeals	5
IA	Court of Criminal Appeals	5
Alaska		
SC	Supreme Court	5
IA	Court of Appeals	3
Arizona		
SC	Supreme Court	5
IA	Court of Appeals	22
Arkansas		
SC	Supreme Court	7
IA	Court of Appeals	12
California		
SC	Supreme Court	7
IA	Courts of Appeal	104
Colorado		
SC	Supreme Court	7
IA	Court of Appeals	22
Connecticut		
SC	Supreme Court	7
IA	Appellate Court	9
Delaware		
SC	Supreme Court	5
District of Columbia		
SC	Court of Appeals	9
Florida		
SC	Supreme Court	7
IA	District Courts of Appeal	61
Georgia		
SC	Supreme Court	7
IA	Court of Appeals	12
Hawaii		
SC	Supreme Court	5
IA	Intermediate Court of Appeals	6
Idaho		
SC	Supreme Court	5
IA	Court of Appeals	4
Illinois		
SC	Supreme Court	7
IA	Appellate Court	54
Indiana		
SC	Supreme Court	5
IA	Court of Appeals	15
IA	Tax Court	1
Iowa		
SC	Supreme Court	7
IA	Court of Appeals	9
Kansas		
SC	Supreme Court	7
IA	Court of Appeals	13
Kentucky		
SC	Supreme Court	7
IA	Court of Appeals	14
Louisiana		
SC	Supreme Court	7
IA	Courts of Appeal	60

APPENDIX TABLE 1 (continued)
Number of appellate court judges in 50 states and the District of Columbia, 2011

State	Appellate court name	Number of judges
Maine		
SC	Supreme Judicial Court	7
Maryland		
SC	Court of Appeals	7
IA	Court of Special Appeals[a]	12
Massachusetts		
SC	Supreme Judicial Court	7
IA	Appeals Court	28
Michigan		
SC	Supreme Court	7
IA	Court of Appeals	26
Minnesota		
SC	Supreme Court	7
IA	Court of Appeals	19
Mississippi		
SC	Supreme Court	9
IA	Court of Appeals	10
Missouri		
SC	Supreme Court	7
IA	Court of Appeals	32
Montana		
SC	Supreme Court	7
Nebraska		
SC	Supreme Court	7
IA	Court of Appeals	6
Nevada		
SC	Supreme Court	7
New Hampshire		
SC	Supreme Court	5
New Jersey		
SC	Supreme Court	6
IA	Appellate Division of Superior Court	34
New Mexico		
SC	Supreme Court	5
IA	Court of Appeals	10
New York		
SC	Court of Appeals	7
IA	Appellate Division of Supreme Court	58
IA	Appellate Terms of Supreme Court	15
North Carolina		
SC	Supreme Court	7
IA	Court of Appeals	15
North Dakota		
SC	Supreme Court	5
IA	Temporary Court of Appeals	3
Ohio		
SC	Supreme Court	7
IA	Courts of Appeals	70
Oklahoma		
SC	Supreme Court	9
SC	Court of Criminal Appeals	5
IA	Court of Civil Appeals	10

APPENDIX TABLE 1 (continued)
Number of appellate court judges in 50 states and the District of Columbia, 2011

State	Appellate court name	Number of judges
Oregon		
SC	Supreme Court	7
IA	Court of Appeals	10
Pennsylvania		
SC	Supreme Court	7
IA	Superior Court[b]	23
IA	Commonwealth Court	9
Rhode Island		
SC	Supreme Court	5
South Carolina		
SC	Supreme Court	5
IA	Court of Appeals[c]	9
South Dakota		
SC	Supreme Court	5
Tennessee		
SC	Supreme Court	5
IA	Court of Appeals	12
IA	Court of Criminal Appeals	12
Texas		
SC	Supreme Court	9
SC	Court of Criminal Appeals	9
IA	Courts of Appeals	80
Utah		
SC	Supreme Court	5
IA	Court of Appeals	7
Vermont		
SC	Supreme Court	5
Virginia		
SC	Supreme Court[d]	5
IA	Court of Appeals	11
Washington		
SC	Supreme Court	9
IA	Court of Appeals	22
West Virginia		
SC	Supreme Court of Appeals	5
Wisconsin		
SC	Supreme Court	7
IA	Court of Appeals	16
Wyoming		
SC	Supreme Court	5

Note: Includes appellate court judges for all 50 states and the District of Columbia for 2011. SC is a state court of last resort, and IA is a state intermediate appellate court.

[a]In 2011, the Maryland court of special appeals had 13 authorized judicial positions and 1 vacancy.

[b]The Pennsylvania superior court had 15 authorized judicial positions and 8 additional senior judges appointed to assist.

[c]The South Carolina court of appeals had 9 authorized judicial positions and 1 retired judge appointed to assist.

[d]In 2011, the Virginia supreme court had 7 authorized judicial positions with 2 vacancies.

Source: Bureau of Justice Statistics, State Court Organization Survey, 2011.

APPENDIX TABLE 2
Number of trial court judges in 50 states and the District of Columbia, 2011

State	Trial court name	Number of judges
Alabama		
GJ[b]	Circuit	144
LJ[b]	District	106
LJ	Municipal	315
LJ	Probate	68
Alaska		
GJ	Superior	38
LJ	District	22
Arizona[c]		
GJ	Superior	174
GJ	Tax[a]	1
LJ	Justice of the Peace	87
LJ	Municipal	154
Arkansas		
GJ	Circuit	121
LJ	District	115
LJ	City	70
California		
GJ	Superior	1,588
Colorado		
GJ	District	160
GJ	Denver Probate	1
GJ	Denver Juvenile	3
GJ	Water	0
LJ	County	103
LJ	Municipal	250
Connecticut		
GJ	Superior	180
LJ	Probate	54
Delaware		
GJ	Superior	19
GJ	Court of Chancery	5
LJ	Justice of the Peace	61
LJ	Family	15
LJ	Court of Common Pleas	9
LJ	Alderman's	6
District of Columbia		
GJ	Superior	62
Florida		
GJ	Circuit	599
LJ	County	322
Georgia		
GJ	Superior	205
LJ	Juvenile	125
LJ	Civil	5
LJ	State	122
LJ	Probate	174
LJ	Magistrate	488
LJ	County Recorder's	23
LJ	Municipal	350
Hawaii		
GJ	Circuit	33
LJ	District	36
Idaho		
GJ	District	42
LJ	Magistrate's Division	84

APPENDIX TABLE 2 (continued)
Number of trial court judges in 50 states and the District of Columbia, 2011

State	Trial court name	Number of judges
Illinois		
GJ	Circuit	917
Indiana		
GJ	Superior	225
GJ	Circuit	91
GJ	Probate	1
LJ	City	48
LJ	Town	27
LJ	Small Claims of Marion County	9
Iowa		
GJ	District	335
Kansas		
GJ	District	234
LJ	Municipal	255
Kentucky		
GJ	Circuit	94
GJ	Family	51
LJ	District	116
Louisiana		
GJ	District	217
GJ	Juvenile & Family	18
LJ	Justice of the Peace	385
LJ	Mayor's	255
LJ	City & Parish	73
Maine		
GJ	Superior	17
GJ	District	36
LJ	Probate	16
Maryland		
GJ	Circuit	146
LJ	District	109
LJ	Orphan's	66
Massachusetts		
GJ	Superior Court Department	80
LJ	District Court Department	147
LJ	Probate & Family Court Department	48
LJ	Juvenile Court Department	36
LJ	Housing Court Department	9
LJ	Boston Municipal Court Department	30
LJ	Land Court Department	6
Michigan		
GJ	Circuit	219
GJ	Claims	7
LJ	District	258
LJ	Probate	103
LJ	Municipal	4
Minnesota		
GJ	District	280
Mississippi		
GJ	Circuit	53
LJ	Chancery	49
LJ	County	30
LJ	Municipal	226
LJ	Justice	197

APPENDIX TABLE 2 (continued)
Number of trial court judges in 50 states and the District of Columbia, 2011

State	Trial court name	Number of judges
Missouri		
GJ	Circuit	331
LJ	Municipal	313
Montana		
GJ	District	46
GJ	Workers' Compensation	1
GJ	Water	5
LJ	Justice's Court	65
LJ	Municipal	9
LJ	City	88
Nebraska		
GJ	District	55
LJ	Separate Juvenile	11
LJ	County	58
LJ	Workers' Compensation	7
Nevada		
GJ	District	72
LJ	Justice	65
LJ	Municipal	22
New Hampshire[b]		
GJ	Superior	22
LJ	District	59
LJ	Probate	10
LJ	Family Division	0
New Jersey		
GJ	Superior	368
LJ	Tax	6
LJ	Municipal	334
New Mexico		
GJ	District	75
LJ	Magistrate	62
LJ	Metropolitan Ct. of Bernalillo County	16
LJ	Municipal	85
LJ	Probate	33
New York		
GJ	Supreme	263
GJ	County	126
LJ	Court of Claims	85
LJ	Surrogates'	31
LJ	Family	126
LJ	District	47
LJ	City	163
LJ	Civil Court of the City of NY	120
LJ	Criminal Court of the City of NY	106
LJ	Town & Village Justice	2,200
North Carolina		
GJ	Superior	112
LJ	District	270
North Dakota		
GJ	District	44
LJ	Municipal	94
Ohio[e]		
GJ	Court of Common Pleas	384
LJ	Municipal	200
LJ	County	46
LJ	Court of Claims	2
LJ	Mayor's	322[c]

APPENDIX TABLE 2 (continued)
Number of trial court judges in 50 states and the District of Columbia, 2011

State	Trial court name	Number of judges
Oklahoma		
GJ	District	241
LJ	Municipal Court Not of Record	352
LJ	Municipal Criminal Court of Record	2
LJ	Workers' Compensation	10
LJ	Tax Review	3
Oregon[d]		
GJ	Circuit	173
GJ	Tax	1
LJ	County	7[d]
LJ	Justice	30[d]
LJ	Municipal	225[d]
Pennsylvania		
GJ	Court of Common Pleas	449
LJ	Philadelphia Municipal	25
LJ	Magisterial District Judge	544
LJ	Philadelphia Traffic	7
Rhode Island[e,f]		
GJ	Superior	26
LJ	Workers' Compensation	10[e]
LJ	District	15
LJ	Family	18
LJ	Probate	39[f]
LJ	Municipal	29[f]
LJ	Traffic Tribunal	8
South Carolina		
GJ	Circuit	46
LJ	Family	52
LJ	Magistrate	310
LJ	Probate	46
LJ	Municipal	308
South Dakota		
GJ	Circuit	41
LJ	Magistrate	13
Tennessee		
GJ	Circuit	83
GJ	Chancery	34
GJ	Criminal	33
GJ	Probate	2
LJ	Juvenile	17
LJ	Municipal	170
LJ	General Sessions	154
Texas		
GJ	District	456
LJ	Constitutional County	254
LJ	County Courts at Law	233
LJ	Statutory Probate	18
LJ	Justice of the Peace	819
LJ	Municipal	1,531
Utah		
GJ	District	71
LJ	Justice	104
LJ	Juvenile	29

APPENDIX TABLE 2 (continued)
Number of trial court judges in 50 states and the District of Columbia, 2011

State	Trial court name	Number of judges
Vermont		
GJ	Superior	32
LJ	Judicial Bureau	18
Virginia		
GJ	Circuit	142
LJ	District	230
Washington		
GJ	Superior	179
LJ	District	109
LJ	Municipal	98
West Virginia		
GJ	Circuit	70
LJ	Magistrate	158
LJ	Municipal	122
LJ	Family	45
Wisconsin		
GJ	Circuit	249
LJ	Municipal	254
Wyoming		
GJ	District	22
LJ	Circuit	24
LJ	Municipal	81

Note: Includes trial court judges for all 50 states and the District of Columbia for 2011. GJ is a state general jurisdiction court and LJ is a state limited jurisdiction court.

[a]The Arizona tax court was excluded from analysis.

[b]The New Hampshire circuit court was made up of the three listed divisions.

[c]The Ohio mayor's courts consisted of 322 mayors and magistrates who were excluded from analysis.

[d]Information obtained via http://www.courtstatistics.org/Other-Pages/State_Court_Structure_Charts/Oregon.aspx.

[e]The Rhode Island worker's compensation courts consisted of 10 judges who were excluded from analysis.

[f]Information obtained via http://www.courtstatistics.org/Other-Pages/State_Court_Structure_Charts/Rhode-Island.aspx.

Source: Bureau of Justice Statistics, State Court Organization Survey, 2011.

The Bureau of Justice Statistics, located in the Office of Justice Programs, U.S. Department of Justice, collects, analyses, and disseminates statistical information on crime, criminal offenders, victims of crime, and the operation of justice systems at all levels of government. William J. Sabol is acting director.

This report was written by Ron Malega, Ph.D., and Thomas H. Cohen, J.D., Ph.D., former BJS Statisticians. Tara Martin provided verification.

Vanessa Curto and Jill Thomas edited the report, and Tina Dorsey produced the report.

November 2013, NCJ 242850

Survey of Judicial Salaries

Published January 2016, Vol. 40 No. 2
Data and Rankings as of July 1, 2015

SURVEY OF
Judicial Salaries

Ohio Judges Receive Long-Awaited Raise

On September 29, 2015, judges in Ohio received the first of four pay increases proposed to be phased in over the next three years. Each bump will be 5 percent. It is the first movement in compensation for Ohio judges since 2007. Before the 2015 boost, Ohio ranked 47th in the nation in pay for its general-jurisdiction, trial-court judges.

"I am grateful to Governor John Kasich, Senate President Keith Faber, and Speaker Cliff Rosenberger for working together to adjust judicial salaries to reflect the important work that judges do," Supreme Court of Ohio Chief Justice Maureen O'Connor said. Michigan continues to hold the mark as the state that has gone the longest without a judicial pay increase. In 2011 and 2013 commissions recommended increases for Michigan judges; however, such suggestions have not yet gained legislative approval.

The table on the left list states where judges have waited the longest for a pay increase. All states on the list except Kansas have salary commissions that provide recommendations to the legislature. More information on *How States Set Their Salaries* can be found here. The map below shows the 22 states that have received salary increases between January and July, 2015.

General-Jurisdiction Judges:
States without Recent Salary Increases

	Current Salary	Last Increase	Years Since Last Increase
Michigan	$139,919	2002	13
New Jersey	$165,000	2008	7
Nevada	$160,000	2008	7
Arizona	$145,000	2008	7
Alabama	$134,943	2008	7
Kansas	$120,037	2008	7
Kentucky	$124,620	2009	6

States Receiving Salary Increases as of July 2015

Judicial Salaries at a Glance

The average annual percent change for the four judicial positions, and the state court administrators analyzed by the *Survey*, is 1.61% for increases from January 1, 2015 through July 1, 2015. As indicated in the table below, this increase remains below the pre-recession (2003-2007) average increase of 3.24%. With the nation's economic recovery still tepid, the rebound in annual increases from the low seen during the 2010-2011 period of the recession will be slow and variable.

				Average Annual % Change			
				Pre-Recession	Recession	Recession	Recovery
	Mean	Median	Range	2003-2007	2008-2009	2010-2011	2012-2015
Chief, Highest Court	$171,306	$167,210	$133,174 to $241,978	3.19%	1.58%	0.67%	2.08%
Associate Justice, Court of Last Resort	$165,922	$166,159	$129,625 to $230,750	3.21%	1.88%	0.64%	2.11%
Judge, Intermediate Appellate Courts	$159,559	$159,484	$124,616 to $216,330	3.20%	1.60%	0.36%	2.09%
Judge, General-Jurisdiction Trial Courts	$149,392	$146,803	$118,385 to $201,100	3.30%	1.91%	0.58%	2.16%
State Court Administrators	$147,658	$139,059	$92,960 to $245,640	3.30%	1.38%	0.89%	1.98%
			Average	3.24%	1.67%	0.63%	2.09%

* "Survey of Judicial Salaries," Vol. 40, no. 2 (as of July 1, 2015). This survey was prepared by the Knowledge and Information Services (KIS) Office of the National Center for State Courts. Reprinted with permission.

Salaries and Rankings for Appellate and General-Jurisdiction Judges - Listed Alphabetically by State Name

The table below lists the salaries and rankings for associate justices of the courts of last resort, associate judges of intermediate appellate courts, and judges of general-jurisdiction trial courts (actual salaries and cost-of-living-adjusted salaries) as of July 1, 2015. Where possible, the salary figures are actual salaries. In jurisdictions where some judges receive supplements, the figures are the most representative available—either the base salary, the midpoint of a range between the lowest and highest supplemented salaries, or the median. Salaries are ranked from highest to lowest, with the highest salary for each position having a rank of "1." The lowest salary has a rank of "51" except for intermediate appellate courts, which exist in only 40 states. The mean, median, and salary range for each of the positions are also shown.

	Highest Court		Intermediate Appellate Court		General-Jurisdiction Trial Court				
								Adjusted for Cost of Living	
	Salary	Rank	Salary	Rank	Salary	Rank	Adjustment Factor	Adjusted Salary	Adjusted Rank
Alabama	$180,005	13	$178,878	6	$134,943	37	95.72	$140,964	19
Alaska	$200,172	6	$189,108	5	$165,088	5	131.37	$140,890	20
Arizona	$155,000	34	$150,000	29	$145,000	29	106.20	$136,537	28
Arkansas	$166,500	25	$161,500	16	$160,000	14	94.63	$169,073	4
California	$230,750	1	$216,330	1	$188,041	4	134.67	$140,389	21
Colorado	$173,024	16	$166,170	13	$159,320	18	108.66	$146,619	13
Connecticut	$185,610	10	$174,323	10	$167,634	10	133.42	$125,646	37
Delaware	$192,360	8			$180,733	6	106.39	$169,865	3
District of Columbia	$213,300	4			$201,100	1	139.94	$143,702	16
Florida	$162,200	32	$154,140	25	$146,080	28	104.58	$139,683	23
Georgia	$167,210	24	$166,186	12	$186,252	18	103.28	$151,262	6
Hawaii	$214,524	3	$198,624	3	$193,248	2	133.41	$144,851	15
Idaho	$135,000	48	$130,000	39	$124,000	46	101.24	$122,485	41
Illinois	$220,873	2	$207,682	2	$190,758	3	112.15	$170,066	2
Indiana	$165,078	27	$160,468	20	$137,062	35	99.09	$138,326	26
Iowa	$170,544	19	$154,556	24	$143,897	30	100.23	$143,565	17
Kansas	$135,905	45	$131,518	36	$120,037	50	101.84	$117,870	45
Kentucky	$135,504	47	$130,044	38	$124,820	44	95.48	$130,513	34
Louisiana	$164,590	30	$154,059	26	$148,108	25	100.31	$147,651	11
Maine	$129,825	51			$121,472	48	122.01	$99,557	51
Maryland	$176,433	14	$163,643	17	$154,433	20	113.46	$136,118	29
Massachusetts	$175,984	15	$165,087	14	$159,694	15	134.43	$118,791	44
Michigan	$164,610	29	$151,441	28	$139,919	32	100.57	$139,123	24
Minnesota	$162,530	31	$153,240	27	$143,851	31	103.56	$138,873	25
Mississippi	$142,320	39	$134,883	32	$128,042	40	93.66	$136,709	27
Missouri	$170,292	20	$155,709	23	$146,803	26	100.67	$145,828	14
Montana	$136,127	43			$128,131	42	103.91	$121,390	43
Nebraska	$166,159	26	$157,851	22	$153,587	21	101.98	$150,707	7
Nevada	$170,000	21	$165,000	15	$160,000	13	106.28	$150,544	8
New Hampshire	$195,907	33			$146,236	27	125.42	$115,600	46
New Jersey	$195,482	11	$175,534	9	$165,000	11	121.43	$135,881	30
New Mexico	$131,174	50	$124,616	40	$118,365	51	103.62	$114,244	47
New York	$192,500	7	$177,900	7	$174,000	8	152.68	$113,960	48
North Carolina	$139,696	41	$134,109	33	$125,875	41	102.11	$124,253	39
North Dakota	$152,436	35			$139,879	34	109.13	$138,439	31
Ohio	$141,600	40	$132,000	35	$121,350	49	98.48	$123,222	39
Oklahoma	$137,655	42	$130,410	37	$131,535	38	98.03	$134,482	33
Oregon	$135,688	46	$132,820	34	$124,468	45	114.32	$108,880	50
Pennsylvania	$203,409	5	$191,926	4	$176,572	7	114.83	$153,769	5
Rhode Island	$172,422	18			$155,235	19	127.64	$121,619	42
South Carolina	$144,111	38	$140,508	30	$136,905	36	101.31	$135,132	32
South Dakota	$131,713	49			$123,024	47	100.15	$122,845	40
Tennessee	$182,508	12	$176,436	8	$170,362	9	96.33	$176,845	1
Texas	$168,000	23	$158,800	21	$149,000	24	101.51	$146,764	12
Utah	$168,150	22	$160,500	19	$157,650	22	103.44	$147,770	10
Vermont	$147,095	37			$139,837	33	123.72	$113,031	49
Virginia	$188,949	9	$173,127	11	$162,670	12	109.02	$149,404	9
Washington	$172,531	17	$164,238	16	$155,363	17	111.92	$139,715	22
West Virginia	$136,000	44	$139,059	31	$128,000	43	98.02	$128,543	36
Wisconsin	$147,403	36			$131,187	39	101.64	$128,666	35
Wyoming	$165,000	28			$150,000	23	106.37	$141,012	18
Mean	$165,922		$159,484		$148,392				
Median	$166,159		$159,559		$146,803				
Range	$129,825 to $230,750		$124,616 to $216,330		$118,385 to $201,100				

Using the C2ER Cost-of-Living Index. The Council for Community and Economic Research—C2ER—is the most widely accepted U.S. source for cost-of-living indices, with nearly 400 reporting jurisdictions across America. The cost-of-living indices used in this report were developed by C2ER using a robust, multivariable model, which incorporates the costs of goods and services within a reporting jurisdiction along with seven additional variables to greatly improve predicted, statewide average C2ER factors. The seven variables are community population, population density, income, growth rate, utility rates, efficiency of the government sector, and location of the region. More detailed information can be found at www.c2er.org.

STATE JUDICIAL SALARIES

Salaries and Rankings for Appellate and General-Jurisdiction Judges - Listed in Order of State Rank

The table below lists the salaries and rankings for associate justices of the courts of last resort, associate judges of intermediate appellate courts, and judges of general-jurisdiction trial courts (actual salaries and cost-of-living-adjusted salaries) as of July 1, 2015. Where possible, the salary figures are actual salaries. In jurisdictions where some judges receive supplements, the figures are the most representative available—either the base salary, the midpoint of a range between the lowest and highest supplemented salaries, or the median. Salaries are ranked from highest to lowest, with the highest salary for each position having a rank of "1." The lowest salary has a rank of "51" except for intermediate appellate courts, which exist in only 40 states. The mean, median, and salary range for each of the positions are also shown.

Highest Court		Intermediate Appellate Court		General-Jurisdiction Trial Court			
				Salary		Adjusted for Cost of Living	
California	$230,750	California	$216,330	District of Columbia	$201,100	Tennessee	$176,845
Illinois	$220,873	Illinois	$207,882	Hawaii	$193,248	Illinois	$170,096
Hawaii	$214,524	Hawaii	$198,524	Illinois	$190,755	Arkansas	$169,073
District of Columbia	$213,300	Pennsylvania	$191,926	California	$189,041	Delaware	$159,885
Pennsylvania	$203,409	Alaska	$189,108	Alaska	$185,088	Pennsylvania	$153,769
Alaska	$200,172	Alabama	$178,675	Delaware	$180,733	Georgia	$151,292
New York	$192,500	New York	$177,900	Pennsylvania	$176,572	Nebraska	$150,707
Delaware	$192,360	Tennessee	$176,436	New York	$174,000	Nevada	$150,544
Virginia	$188,949	New Jersey	$175,534	Tennessee	$170,352	Virginia	$149,404
Connecticut	$186,510	Connecticut	$174,323	Connecticut	$167,634	Utah	$147,770
New Jersey	$185,482	Virginia	$173,177	New Jersey	$165,000	Louisiana	$147,851
Tennessee	$182,508	Georgia	$166,166	Virginia	$162,878	Texas	$146,784
Alabama	$180,005	Colorado	$166,170	Nevada	$160,000	Colorado	$146,619
Maryland	$176,433	Massachusetts	$165,087	Arkansas	$160,000	Missouri	$145,828
Massachusetts	$175,984	Nevada	$165,000	Massachusetts	$159,694	Hawaii	$144,851
Colorado	$173,024	Washington	$164,238	Colorado	$159,320	District of Columbia	$143,702
Washington	$172,531	Maryland	$163,633	Washington	$156,363	Iowa	$143,565
Rhode Island	$172,422	Arkansas	$161,500	Georgia	$156,252	Wyoming	$141,012
Iowa	$170,544	Utah	$160,500	Rhode Island	$155,235	Alabama	$140,964
Missouri	$170,292	Indiana	$160,468	Maryland	$154,433	Alaska	$140,880
Nevada	$170,000	Texas	$158,500	Nebraska	$153,697	California	$140,369
Utah	$168,150	Nebraska	$157,851	Utah	$152,850	Washington	$139,715
Texas	$168,000	Missouri	$155,709	Wyoming	$150,000	Florida	$139,583
Georgia	$167,210	Iowa	$154,556	Texas	$149,000	Michigan	$139,123
Arkansas	$166,500	Florida	$154,140	Louisiana	$148,108	Minnesota	$138,873
Nebraska	$166,159	Louisiana	$154,059	Missouri	$146,803	Indiana	$138,326
Indiana	$165,078	Minnesota	$153,240	New Hampshire	$146,236	Mississippi	$136,709
Wyoming	$165,000	Michigan	$151,441	Florida	$146,080	Arizona	$136,637
Michigan	$164,610	Arizona	$150,000	Arizona	$145,060	Maryland	$136,118
Louisiana	$164,590	South Carolina	$140,508	Iowa	$143,897	New Jersey	$135,691
Minnesota	$162,630	Wisconsin	$139,059	Minnesota	$143,851	North Dakota	$135,439
Florida	$162,200	Mississippi	$134,883	Michigan	$139,919	South Carolina	$135,132
New Hampshire	$155,907	North Carolina	$134,109	Vermont	$139,837	Oklahoma	$134,482
Arizona	$155,000	Oregon	$132,820	North Dakota	$139,679	Kentucky	$130,513
North Dakota	$152,436	Ohio	$132,000	Indiana	$137,062	Wisconsin	$128,686
Wisconsin	$147,403	Kansas	$131,518	South Carolina	$136,905	West Virginia	$128,543
Vermont	$147,095	Oklahoma	$130,410	Alabama	$134,943	Connecticut	$125,646
South Carolina	$144,111	Kentucky	$130,044	Oklahoma	$131,835	North Carolina	$124,253
Mississippi	$142,320	Idaho	$130,000	Wisconsin	$131,157	Ohio	$123,222
Ohio	$141,600	New Mexico	$124,616	Mississippi	$128,042	South Dakota	$122,845
North Carolina	$139,886			North Carolina	$126,875	Idaho	$122,485
Oklahoma	$137,655			Montana	$126,131	Rhode Island	$121,619
Montana	$136,177			West Virginia	$126,000	Montana	$121,390
West Virginia	$136,000			Kentucky	$124,620	Massachusetts	$118,791
Kansas	$135,905			Oregon	$124,468	Kansas	$117,870
Oregon	$135,688			Idaho	$124,000	New Hampshire	$116,600
Kentucky	$135,504			South Dakota	$123,024	New Mexico	$114,244
Idaho	$135,000			Maine	$121,472	New York	$113,960
South Dakota	$131,713			Ohio	$121,350	Vermont	$113,031
New Mexico	$131,174			Kansas	$120,037	Oregon	$106,880
Maine	$129,625			New Mexico	$115,385	Maine	$99,557

Mean	$185,922		$159,484		$149,392		
Median	$186,159		$159,559		$146,803		
Range	$129,625 to $230,750		$124,616 to $216,330		$118,385 to $201,100		

Information in this Survey is collected from designated representatives in each state. The National Center for State Courts has protocols in place to help ensure the accuracy of the data that are collected, analyzed, and ultimately reported.

Chief Justices of the States

CONFERENCE OF CHIEF JUSTICES

July 2016

PRESIDENT: Honorable David Gilbertson
Chief Justice of South Dakota

PRESIDENT-ELECT: Honorable John D. Minton, Jr.
Chief Justice of Kentucky

ALABAMA
Honorable Roy S. Moore
Chief Justice
Supreme Court of Alabama
300 Dexter Avenue
Montgomery, AL 36104-3741
(334) 229-0599 FAX (334) 229-0535

ALASKA
Honorable Craig Stowers
Chief Justice
Alaska Supreme Court
303 K Street, 5th Floor
Anchorage, AK 99501
(907) 264-0624 FAX (907) 264-0782

AMERICAN SAMOA
Honorable F. Michael Kruse
Chief Justice
The High Court of American Samoa
Courthouse, P.O. Box 309
Pago Pago, AS 96799
(684) 633-1410 FAX (684) 633-1318

ARIZONA
Honorable Scott Bales
Chief Justice
Supreme Court of Arizona
1501 W. Washington Street
Phoenix, AZ 85007
(602) 452-3534 FAX (602) 452-3906

ARKANSAS
Honorable Howard W. Brill
Chief Justice
Supreme Court of Arkansas
Justice Building, 625 Marshall Street
Little Rock, AR 72201
(501) 682-6873 FAX (501) 683-4006

CALIFORNIA
Honorable Tani G. Cantil-Sakauye
Chief Justice
Supreme Court of California
350 McAllister Street
San Francisco, CA 94102
(415) 865-7060 FAX (415) 865-7181

COLORADO
Honorable Nancy E. Rice
Chief Justice
Supreme Court of Colorado
2 East 14th Avenue
Denver, CO 80203
(720) 625-5460 FAX (720) 625-5465

CONNECTICUT
Honorable Chase T. Rogers
Chief Justice
Supreme Court of Connecticut
Connecticut Judicial Branch
Supreme Court Bldg., 231 Capitol Avenue
Hartford, CT 06106
(860) 757-2120 FAX (860) 757-2214

1

* Reprinted with permission from the Conference of Chief Justices. These directory listings reflect information available in July 1, 2016.

STATE SUPREME COURT JUSTICES

DELAWARE
Honorable Leo E. Strine, Jr.
Chief Justice
Supreme Court of Delaware
The Renaissance Centre
405 N. King Street, Suite 505
Wilmington, DE 19801
(302) 651-3902 FAX (302) 651-3919

DISTRICT OF COLUMBIA
Honorable Eric T. Washington
Chief Judge
District of Columbia Court of Appeals
Historic Courthouse/Judiciary Square
430 E Street, NW, Suite 319
Washington, DC 20001
(202) 879-2770 FAX (202) 824-8580

FLORIDA
Honorable Jorge Labarga
Chief Justice
Supreme Court of Florida
500 South Duval Street
Tallahassee, FL 32399-1925
(850) 413-8371 FAX (850) 487-4696

GEORGIA
Honorable Hugh P. Thompson
Chief Justice
Supreme Court of Georgia
State Judicial Building
40 Capitol Square, SW
Atlanta, GA 30334
(404) 656-3472 FAX (404) 651-8642

GUAM
Honorable Robert J. Torres, Jr.
Chief Justice
Supreme Court of Guam
Judiciary of Guam Building, Suite 300
120 West O'Brien Drive
Hagåtña, GU 96910-5174
(671) 475-3300 FAX (671) 475-3337

HAWAII
Honorable Mark E. Recktenwald
Chief Justice
Supreme Court of Hawaii
417 South King Street
Honolulu, HI 96813
(808) 539-4700 FAX (808) 539-4703

IDAHO
Honorable Jim Jones
Chief Justice
Idaho Supreme Court
451 W. State Street (83702)
P.O. Box 83720
Boise, Idaho 83720-0101
(208) 947-7575 FAX (208) 334-4701

ILLINOIS
Honorable Rita B. Garman
Chief Justice
Supreme Court of Illinois
3607 North Vermilion Street
Suite 1
Danville, IL 61832
(217) 431-8928 FAX (217) 431-8945

INDIANA
Honorable Loretta Rush
Chief Justice
Indiana Supreme Court
200 W. Washington Street
Room 324
Indianapolis, IN 46204
(317) 232-2548 FAX (317) 233-8691

IOWA
Honorable Mark S. Cady
Chief Justice
Supreme Court of Iowa
Judicial Branch Building
1111 East Court Avenue
Des Moines, IA 50319
(515) 281-3952 FAX (515) 281-3043

2

I-25

KANSAS
Honorable Lawton R. Nuss
Chief Justice
Supreme Court of Kansas
Kansas Judicial Center
301 West 10th Avenue
Topeka, KS 66612-1507
(785) 296-5322 FAX (785) 291-3274

KENTUCKY
Honorable John D. Minton, Jr.
Chief Justice
Supreme Court of Kentucky
State Capitol, Room 231
700 Capitol Avenue
Frankfort, KY 40601
(502) 564-4162 FAX (502) 564-1933

LOUISIANA
Honorable Bernette Joshua Johnson
Chief Justice
Supreme Court of Louisiana
Supreme Court Building
400 Royal Street
New Orleans, LA 70130-8102
(504) 310-2350 FAX (504) 310-2359

MAINE
Honorable Leigh I. Saufley
Chief Justice
Supreme Judicial Court of Maine
205 Newbury Street, Room 139
Portland, Maine 04101-4125
(207) 822-4286 FAX (207) 822-4202

MARYLAND
Honorable Mary Ellen Barbera
Chief Judge
Court of Appeals of Maryland
Judicial Center
50 Maryland Avenue
Rockville, MD 20850
(240) 777-9320 FAX (240) 777-9327

MASSACHUSETTS
Honorable Ralph D. Gants
Chief Justice
Massachusetts Supreme Judicial Court
John Adams Courthouse
One Pemberton Square
Boston, MA 02108-1735
(617) 557-1139 FAX (617) 557-1091

MICHIGAN
Honorable Robert P. Young, Jr.
Chief Justice
Supreme Court of Michigan
3034 West Grand Boulevard, Suite 8-500
Detroit, MI 48202
(313) 972-3250 FAX (313) 875-9329

MINNESOTA
Honorable Lorie Skjerven Gildea
Chief Justice
Supreme Court of Minnesota
424 Minnesota Judicial Center
25 Rev. Dr. Martin Luther King, Jr., Blvd.
St. Paul, MN 55155
(651) 296-3380 FAX (651) 282-5115

MISSISSIPPI
Honorable William L. Waller, Jr.
Chief Justice
Supreme Court of Mississippi
450 High Street (Zip Code 39201)
Post Office Box 117
Jackson, MS 39205-0117
(601) 359-2139 FAX (601) 359-2443

3

STATE SUPREME COURT JUSTICES

MISSOURI
Honorable Patricia Breckenridge
Chief Justice
Supreme Court of Missouri
207 West High Street (Zip Code 65101)
P.O. Box 150
Jefferson City, MO 65102
(573) 751-9652 FAX (573) 751-7359

MONTANA
Honorable Mike McGrath
Chief Justice
Supreme Court of Montana
215 North Sanders (Zip Code 59601)
P.O. Box 203001
Helena, MT 59620-3001
(406) 444-5490 FAX (406) 444-3274

NEBRASKA
Honorable Michael G. Heavican
Chief Justice
Supreme Court of Nebraska
2214 State Capitol
1445 K Street (68509)
P. O. Box 98910
Lincoln, NE 68509
(402) 471-3738 FAX (402) 471-0297

NEVADA
Honorable Ron D. Parraguirre
Chief Justice
Supreme Court of Nevada
201 South Carson Street
Carson City, NV 89701
(775) 684-1510 FAX (775) 684-1513

NEW HAMPSHIRE
Honorable Linda Stewart Dalianis
Chief Justice
Supreme Court of New Hampshire
One Charles Doe Drive
Concord, NH 03301
(603) 271-3751 FAX (603) 513-5475

NEW JERSEY
Honorable Stuart Rabner
Chief Justice
Supreme Court of New Jersey
Richard J. Hughes Justice Complex
25 Market Street
P.O. Box 023
Trenton, NJ 08625-0023
(609) 292-2448 FAX (609) 984-6988

NEW MEXICO
Honorable Charles W. Daniels
Chief Justice
Supreme Court of New Mexico
237 Don Gaspar Avenue (Zip code 87501)
P.O. Box 848
Santa Fe, NM 87504-0848
505 827-4889 FAX 505 827-4837

NEW YORK
Honorable Janet DiFiore
Chief Judge
New York State Unified Court System
Court of Appeals Chambers
230 Park Avenue, Suite 826
New York, NY 10169
(518) 455-7741 FAX (518) 455-7896

NORTH CAROLINA
Honorable Mark D. Martin
Chief Justice
Supreme Court of North Carolina
2 East Morgan Street (27601)
P.O. Box 1841
Raleigh, NC 27602-1841
(919) 831-5712 FAX (919) 831-5730

4

NORTH DAKOTA
Honorable Gerald W. VandeWalle
Chief Justice
Supreme Court of North Dakota
State Capitol Building
600 East Blvd. Ave., Dept 180
Bismarck, ND 58505-0530
(701) 328-4211 FAX (701) 328-4480

NORTHERN MARIANA ISLANDS
Honorable Alexandro C. Castro
Chief Justice
Supreme Court of the Commonwealth
 of the Northern Mariana Islands
P.O. Box 502165
Saipan, MP 96950
Physical Address:
Commonwealth Supreme Court
1st Floor, Guma Hustisia/Iimwal Aweewe/House of
Justice Building
Beach Road, Susupe
Saipan, MP 96950
(670) 236-9709/9800 FAX (670) 236-9702

OHIO
Honorable Maureen O'Connor
Chief Justice
Supreme Court of Ohio
65 South Front Street
Columbus, OH 43215-3431
(614) 387-9000 FAX (614) 387-9069

OKLAHOMA
Honorable John F. Reif
Chief Justice
Supreme Court of Oklahoma
Oklahoma Judicial Center
2100 North Lincoln Boulevard, Suite 1
Oklahoma City, OK 73105-4907
(405) 556-9336 FAX (405) 556-9122

OKLAHOMA
Honorable Clancy Smith
Presiding Judge
Oklahoma Court of Criminal Appeals
Oklahoma Judicial Center
2100 N. Lincoln Boulevard, Suite 2
Oklahoma City, OK 73105-4907
(405) 556-9605 FAX (405) 556-9400

OREGON
Honorable Thomas A. Balmer
Chief Justice
Supreme Court of Oregon
Supreme Court Building
1163 State Street
Salem, OR 97301
(503) 986-5717 FAX (503) 986-5730

PENNSYLVANIA
Honorable Thomas G. Saylor
Chief Justice
Supreme Court of Pennsylvania
200 North 3rd Street, 16th Floor
Harrisburg, PA 17101
(717) 772-1599 FAX (717) 772-1605

PUERTO RICO
Honorable Maite D. Oronoz Rodríguez
Chief Justice
Supreme Court of Puerto Rico
Ponce de León Avenue
P. O. Box 9022392
San Juan, PR 00902-2392
(787) 724-3535 FAX (787) 725-4910

RHODE ISLAND
Honorable Paul A. Suttell
Chief Justice
Supreme Court of Rhode Island
Licht Judicial Complex
250 Benefit Street
Providence, RI 02903
(401) 222-3266 FAX (401) 222-1059

5

STATE SUPREME COURT JUSTICES

SOUTH CAROLINA
Honorable Costa M. Pleicones
Chief Justice
Supreme Court of South Carolina
P.O. Box 11330
Columbia, SC 29211
(803) 734-1438 FAX (803) 734-0427

SOUTH DAKOTA
Honorable David Gilbertson
Chief Justice
Supreme Court of South Dakota
500 East Capitol Avenue
Pierre, SD 57501-5070
(605) 773-6254 FAX (605) 773-6128

TENNESSEE
Honorable Sharon G. Lee
Chief Justice
Tennessee Supreme Court
505 Main Street, Suite 200 (zip 37902)
Post Office Box 444
Knoxville, TN 37901-0444
(865) 594-6707 FAX (865) 594-6561

TEXAS
Honorable Nathan L. Hecht
Chief Justice
Supreme Court of Texas
201 W. 14th Street, Room 104 (Zip Code 78701)
P.O. Box 12248
Austin, TX 78711
(512) 463-1348 FAX: (512) 463-1365

Honorable Sharon F. Keller
Presiding Judge
Court of Criminal Appeals of Texas
201 W. Fourteenth Street (Zip Code 78701)
P.O. Box 12308, Capitol Station
Austin, TX 78711
(512) 463-1590 FAX (512) 463-7061

UTAH
Honorable Matthew B. Durrant
Chief Justice
Supreme Court of Utah
Scott Matheson Courthouse
450 South State Street
P.O. Box 140210
Salt Lake City, UT 84114-0210
(801) 238-7937 FAX (801) 238-7980

VERMONT
Honorable Paul L. Reiber
Chief Justice
Supreme Court of Vermont
109 State Street
Montpelier, VT 05609-0801
(802) 828-3278 FAX (802) 828-0536

VIRGINIA
Honorable Donald W. Lemons
Chief Justice
Supreme Court of Virginia
P.O. Box 385
Nellysford, VA 22958
(434) 361-0325 FAX (434) 361-0328

VIRGIN ISLANDS
Honorable Rhys S. Hodge
Chief Justice
Supreme Court of the Virgin Islands
8174 Crown Bay (00802)
P.O. Box 590
St. Thomas, VI 00804-0590
(340) 693-4142 FAX (340) 774-2258

WASHINGTON
Honorable Barbara A. Madsen
Chief Justice
Supreme Court of Washington
Temple of Justice
415 12th Avenue, SW (98504)
 P.O. Box 40929
Olympia, WA 98504-0929
(360) 357-2037 FAX (360) 357-2085

WEST VIRGINIA
Honorable Menis E. Ketchum, II
Chief Justice
West Virginia Supreme Court of Appeals
Building 1, Room E-307 State Capitol
Charleston, WV 25305
(304) 340-2318 FAX (304) 558-4308

WISCONSIN
Honorable Patience D. Roggensack
Chief Justice
Supreme Court of Wisconsin
16 East State Capitol (Zip Code 53702)
P.O. Box 1688
Madison, WI 53701-1688
(608) 266-1888 FAX (608) 261-8275

WYOMING
Honorable E. James Burke
Chief Justice
Supreme Court of Wyoming
Supreme Court Bldg., 2301 Capitol Avenue
Cheyenne, WY 82002
(307) 777-7557 FAX (307) 777-3503

7

CONFERENCE OF STATE COURT ADMINISTRATORS

May 1, 2016

PRESIDENT: Patricia W. Griffin
State Court Administrator,Delaware

PRESIDENT-ELECT: Gerald A. Marroney
State Court Administrator, Colorado

VICE PRESIDENT: Arthur W. Pepin
Director, New Mexico

ALABAMA

Mr. Rich Hobson
Administrative Director of Courts
300 Dexter Avenue
Montgomery, Alabama 36104-3741
(334) 954-5080 FAX (334) 954-2105

ALASKA

Ms. Christine Johnson
Administrative Director of the Courts
Alaska Court System
303 K Street
Anchorage, Alaska 99501
(907) 264-0547 FAX (907) 264-0881

AMERICAN SAMOA

Mr. Enele Seumanutafa
Acting Administrator
High Court of American Samoa
P.O. Box 309
Pago Pago, American Samoa 96799
011 (684) 633-1150
FAX 011 (684) 633-1318

ARIZONA

Mr. David K. Byers
Administrative Director of the Courts
Arizona Supreme Court
1501 W. Washington St., Suite 411
Phoenix, Arizona 85007
(602) 452-3301 FAX (602) 452-3484

ARKANSAS

Mr. James D. Gingerich
Director, Admin. Office of the Courts
Supreme Court of Arkansas
Justice Building
625 Marshall Street
Little Rock, Arkansas 72201
(501) 682-9400 FAX (501) 682-9410

CALIFORNIA

Mr. Martin Hoshino
Administrative Director
Judicial Council of California
455 Golden Gate Avenue, 5th Floor
San Francisco, California 94102
(415) 865-4235 FAX (415) 865-4244

---

* Reprinted with permission from the Conference of State Court Administrators.
The directory listings reflect information available on May 23, 2016.

COLORADO

Hon. Gerald A. Marroney
State Court Administrator
Colorado Judicial Department
1300 Broadway, Suite 1200
Denver, CO 80203
(720) 625-5801 FAX (720) 6255837

CONNECTICUT

Honorable Patrick L. Carroll III
Chief Court Administrator
Supreme Court of Connecticut
231 Capitol Avenue
Hartford, Connecticut 06106
(860) 757-2100 FAX (860) 757-2130

DELAWARE

Hon. Patricia W. Griffin
State Court Administrator
Administrative Office of the Courts
1 South Race Street
Georgetown, DE 19947
(302) 856-5406 FAX (302) 856-5408

DISTRICT OF COLUMBIA

Ms. Anne B. Wicks
Executive Officer
Courts of the District of Columbia
500 Indiana Avenue, N.W., Room 6680
Washington, D.C. 20001
(202) 879-1700 FAX (202) 879-4829

FLORIDA

Ms. Patricia Jameson
State Courts Administrator
Office of the State Courts
   Administrator
Supreme Court Building
500 South Duval Street
Tallahassee, Florida 32399-1900
(850) 922-5081 FAX (850) 488-0156

GEORGIA

Ms. Cynthia H. Clanton
Director/General Counsel
Administrative Office of the Courts
244 Washington St., SW, Suite 300
Atlanta, GA 30334
(404) 656-6692 FAX (770) 342-4778

GUAM

Mr. Joshua T. Tenorio
Administrator of the Courts
Judiciary of Guam
Guam Judicial Center
120 West O'Brien Drive
Hagatna, Guam 96910
(671) 475-3344/3278 FAX (671) 477-3184

HAWAII

Mr. Rodney A. Maile
Administrative Director of the Courts
The Judiciary, State of Hawaii
417 South King Street, Room 206A
Honolulu, Hawaii 96813
(808) 539-4900 FAX (808) 539-4855

IDAHO

Hon. Linda Copple Trout
Interim Administrative Director of the Courts
Supreme Court Building
451 West State Street
P.O. Box 83720
Boise, Idaho 83720-0101
(208) 334-2246 FAX (208) 947-7590

ILLINOIS

Mr. Michael Tardy
Director, Administrative Office of
the Illinois Courts
222 North LaSalle Street, 13th Floor
Chicago, Illinois 60601
(312) 793-1340 FAX (312) 793-0331

INDIANA

Ms. Lilia G. Judson
Executive Director
Division of State Court Administration
Indiana Supreme Court
30 South Meridian Street, Suite 500
Indianapolis, Indiana 46204-3568
(317) 232-2542 FAX (317) 233-6586

IOWA

Mr. David K. Boyd
State Court Administrator
Iowa Judicial Branch Building
1111 East Court Avenue
Des Moines, Iowa 50319
(515) 281-5241 FAX (515) 242-0014

KANSAS

Ms. Nancy Dixon
Judicial Administrator
Kansas Judicial Center
301 S. W. 10th Street
Topeka, Kansas 66612
(785) 296-4873 FAX (785) 296-7076

KENTUCKY

Ms. Laurie Dudgeon
Administrative Director
Administrative Office of the Courts
100 Millcreek Park
Frankfort, Kentucky 40601
(502) 573-2350 FAX (502) 573-0177

LOUISIANA

Ms. Sandra A. Vujnovich
Judicial Administrator
Supreme Court of Louisiana
400 Royal Street, Suite 1190
New Orleans, Louisiana 70130
(504) 310-2605 FAX (504) 310-2606

MAINE

Mr. James T. Glessner
State Court Administrator
Administrative Office of the Courts
P.O. Box 4820
Portland, Maine 04112-4820
(207) 822-0710 FAX (207) 822-0781

MARYLAND

Ms. Pamela Q. Harris
State Court Administrator
Administrative Office of the Courts
580 Taylor Avenue
Annapolis, Maryland 21401
(410) 260-1295 FAX (410) 974-2066

MASSACHUSETTS

Mr. Harry Spence
Court Administrator
Massachusetts Trial Court
One Pemberton Square
Boston, Massachusetts 02108
(617) 878-0212 FAX (617) 788-6199

MICHIGAN

Mr. Milton Mack, Jr.
State Court Administrator
State Court Administrative Office
925 W. Ottawa Street
Lansing, Michigan 48915
(517) 373-0128 FAX (517) 373-9831

MINNESOTA

Mr. Jeff Shorba
State Court Administrator
Minnesota Judicial Branch
135 Minnesota Judicial Center
25 Rev. Dr. Martin Luther King, Jr.,
   Blvd.
St. Paul, Minnesota 55155
(651) 296-2474 FAX (651) 215-6004

MISSISSIPPI

Mr. Kevin Lackey
Director, Administrative Office of the Courts
Supreme Court of Mississippi
P.O. Box 117
Jackson, MS 39205
(601) 576-4636 FAX (601) 576-4639

MISSOURI

Ms. Kathy S. Lloyd
State Courts Administrator
Supreme Court of Missouri
2112 Industrial Drive
P.O. Box 104480
Jefferson City, MO 65110
(573) 751-4377 FAX (573) 522-6152

MONTANA

Ms. Beth McLaughlin
State Court Administrator
Montana Supreme Court
P.O. Box 203005
Helena, MT 59620-3005
(406) 841-2950 FAX (406) 841-2955

NEBRASKA

Mr. Corey R. Steel
State Court Administrator
Nebraska Supreme Court
State Capitol Building
P.O. Box 98910
Lincoln, Nebraska 68509-8910
(402) 471-3730 FAX

NEVADA

Ms. Robin Sweet
State Court Administrator
Administrative Office of the Courts
Supreme Court Building
201 S. Carson Street, Suite 250
Carson City, NV 89701-4702
(775) 684-1717 FAX (775) 684-1733

NEW HAMPSHIRE

Mr. Christopher Keating
Director, Administrative Office of the Courts
Two Charles Doe Drive
Concord, New Hampshire 03301
(603) 271-9903 FAX (603) 513-5454

NEW JERSEY

Honorable Glenn A. Grant
Acting Administrative Director of the
    Courts
25 Market Street, 7th Floor
P.O. Box 037 RJH Justice Complex
Trenton, New Jersey 08625-0037
(609) 984-0275 FAX (609) 984-6968

NEW MEXICO

Mr. Arthur W. Pepin
Director
Administrative Office of the Courts
237 Don Gaspar, Room 25
Santa Fe, New Mexico 87501-2178
(505) 827-4800 FAX (505) 827-4824

NEW YORK

Hon. Lawrence K. Marks
Chief Administrative Judge
Office of Court Administration
25 Beaver Street, 11th Floor
New York, NY 10004
(212) 428-2884 FAX (212) 428-2190

NORTH CAROLINA

Hon. Marion R. Warren
Director, Administrative Office of the
    Courts
North Carolina Judicial Center
901 Corporate Center Drive
P.O. Box 2448
Raleigh, NC 27602
(919) 890-1391 FAX (919) 890-1915

NORTH DAKOTA

Ms. Sally Holewa
State Court Administrator
Supreme Court of North Dakota
State Capitol Bldg., 1st Floor, Judicial
    Wing
600 East Boulevard Avenue, Dept.180
Bismarck, North Dakota 58505-0530
(701) 328-4216 FAX (701) 328-2092

NORTHERN MARIANA ISLANDS

Ms. Sonia A. Camacho
Acting Director of Courts
Supreme Court of the Northern
    Mariana Islands
Guma ustisia, First Floor
Susupe, P.O. Box 502165
Saipan, MP 96950
(670) 236-9807 FAX (670) 236-9702

OHIO

Mr. Michael L. Buenger
Administrative Director
Supreme Court of Ohio
65 South Front Street
Columbus, Ohio 43215-3431
(614) 387-9500 FAX (614) 387-9509

OKLAHOMA

Ms. Jari Askins
Administrative Director of the Courts
Supreme Court of Oklahoma
2100 North Lincoln Blvd., Suite 3
Oklahoma City, Oklahoma 73105
(405) 556-9800 FAX (405) 556-9126

OREGON

Ms. Kingsley W. Click
State Court Administrator
Office of the State Court Administrator
Supreme Court Building

1163 State Street
Salem, Oregon 97301-2563
(503) 986-5500
FAX (503) 986-5503

PENNSYLVANIA

Mr. Thomas B. Darr
Court Administrator of Pennsylvania
Administrative Office of PA Courts
Pennsylvania Judicial Center
601 Commonwealth Avenue
P.O. Box 61260
Harrisburg, PA 17106-1260
(717) 231-3326 FAX (717) 231-3327

PUERTO RICO

Hon. Isabel Llompart Zeno
Administrative Director of the Courts
Office of Court Administration
P.O. Box 190917, Hato Rey Station
6 Vela Street, Stop 35–1/2
San Juan, Puerto Rico 00919-0917
(787) 641-6623 FAX (787) 766-9831

RHODE ISLAND

Mr. J. Joseph Baxter
State Court Administrator
Supreme Court of Rhode Island
Licht Judicial Complex, Suite 705
250 Benefit Street
Providence, Rhode Island 02903
(401) 222-3263 FAX (401) 222-5131

SOUTH CAROLINA

Ms. Rosalyn W. Frierson
Director
South Carolina Court Administration
1015 Sumter St., Suite 200
Columbia, South Carolina 29201
(803) 734-1800 FAX (803) 734-1355

SOUTH DAKOTA

Mr. Gregory L. Sattizahn
State Court Administrator
Unified Judicial System
500 East Capitol Avenue
Pierre, South Dakota 57501-5070
(605) 773-3474 FAX (605) 773-8437

TENNESSEE

Ms. Deborah Taylor Tate
Administrative Director
Administrative Office of the Courts
511 Union Street
Nashville City Center, Suite 600
Nashville, Tennessee 37219
(615) 741-2687 FAX (615) 741-6285

TEXAS

Mr. David W. Slayton
Administrative Director
Office of Court Administration
Tom C. Clark State Courts Building
205 West 14th Street, Suite 600 (78701)
P.O. Box 12066
Austin, Texas 78711-2066
(512) 463-1626 FAX (512) 463-1648

UTAH

Mr. Daniel Becker
State Court Administrator
450 South State
P.O. Box 140241
Salt Lake City, Utah 84114--0241
(801) 578-3806 FAX (801) 578-3843

VERMONT

Ms. Patricia Gabel
State Court Administrator
Vermont Judiciary
109 State Street
Montpelier, Vermont 05609-0701
(802) 828-3278 FAX (802) 828-3457

VIRGINIA

Mr. Karl R. Hade
Executive Secretary
Supreme Court of Virginia
100 North Ninth Street, Third Floor
Richmond, Virginia 23219-2334
(804) 786-6455
FAX (804) 786-4542

VIRGIN ISLANDS

Ms. Regina Petersen
Administrative Director
Supreme Court of the Virgin Islands
P.O. Box 590, Charlotte Amalie
St. Thomas, VI 00804
(340) 774-2237
FAX (340) 693-4109

WASHINGTON

Ms. Callie Dietz
State Court Administrator
Administrative Office of the Courts
415 12th Avenue, SW (98504)
P.O. Box 41170
Olympia, Washington 98504-1170
(360) 357-2120
FAX (360) 357-2127

WEST VIRGINIA

Mr. Steven D. Canterbury
Administrative Director
West Virginia Supreme Court of
  Appeals
Administrative Office
Room E-100, State Capitol Building
Charleston, West Virginia 25305-0832
(304) 558-0145
FAX (304) 558-1212

STATE SUPREME COURT JUSTICES

WISCONSIN

Mr. J. Denis Moran
Interim Director of State Courts
Supreme Court of Wisconsin
16 East State Capitol
P.O. Box 1688
Madison, Wisconsin 53701-1688
(608) 266-6828 FAX (608) 267-0980

WYOMING

Ms. Lily Sharpe
State Court Administrator
Supreme Court of Wyoming
Supreme Court Building
2301 Capital Avenue
Cheyenne, Wyoming 82002
(307) 777-7581 FAX (307) 777-3447

J. FEDERAL LITIGATION STATISTICS

Judicial Caseload Indicators
12-Month Periods Ending June 30, 2006, 2011, 2014, and 2015

Judicial Caseload	2006	2011	2014	2015	Percent Change Since 2006	Since 2011	Since 2014
U.S. Courts of Appeals [1]							
Cases Filed	68,313	55,353	55,260	53,032	-22.4	-4.2	-4.0
Cases Terminated	67,772	58,146	55,803	53,934	-20.4	-7.2	-3.3
Cases Pending	57,996	44,051	41,945 [2]	41,043	-29.2	-6.8	-2.2
U.S. District Courts							
Civil							
Cases Filed	244,343	289,630	298,713	280,037	14.6	-3.3	-6.3
Cases Terminated	264,734	301,773	260,352	273,562	3.3	-9.3	5.1
Cases Pending	245,667	275,068	334,261 [2]	340,736	38.7	23.9	1.9
Criminal (Includes Transfers)							
Defendants Filed	89,956	102,605	84,017	79,154	-12.0	-22.9	-5.8
Defendant Terminations	88,771	99,779	89,281	81,372	-8.3	-18.4	-8.9
Defendants Pending	100,544	112,715	102,539	98,535	-2.0	-12.6	-3.9
U.S. Bankruptcy Courts							
Cases Filed	1,484,570	1,529,560	1,000,083	879,736	-40.7	-42.5	-12.0
Cases Terminated	1,821,396	1,486,950	1,124,534	1,024,504	-43.8	-31.1	-8.9
Cases Pending	1,423,342	1,704,548	1,461,132 [2]	1,316,342	-7.5	-22.8	-9.9
Post-Conviction Supervision							
Persons Under Supervision	113,697	129,319	132,597	133,428	17.4	3.2	0.6
Pretrial Services							
Total Cases Activated	99,508	113,120	103,640	95,538	-4.0	-15.5	-7.8
Pretrial Services Cases Activated	97,800	112,181	102,949	94,757	-3.1	-15.5	-8.0
Pretrial Diversion Cases Activated	1,708	939	691	781	-54.3	-16.8	13.0
Total Released on Supervision	33,816	30,265	26,197	24,429	-27.8	-19.3	-6.7
Pretrial Supervision	32,112	28,903	25,183	23,368	-27.2	-19.2	-7.2
Diversion Supervision	1,704	1,362	1,014	1,061	-37.7	-22.1	4.6

[1] Excludes the U.S. Court of Appeals for the Federal Circuit.
[2] Revised.

[*] Administrative Office of the United States Courts. Statistical Tables for the Federal Judiciary June 30, 2015. Washington, D.C: 2016.

Table B.
U.S. Courts of Appeals—Cases Commenced, Terminated, and Pending
During the 12-Month Periods Ending June 30, 2014 and 2015

Circuit	Commenced			Terminated			Pending		
	2014	2015	Percent Change [1]	2014	2015	Percent Change [1]	2014 [2]	2015	Percent Change [1]
Total	55,260	53,032	-4.0	55,803	53,934	-3.3	41,945	41,043	-2.2
DC	930	1,117	20.1	996	1,144	14.9	1,416	1,389	-1.9
1st	1,456	1,470	1.0	1,426	1,512	6.0	1,375	1,333	-3.1
2nd	4,879	4,753	-2.6	5,091	4,870	-4.3	3,631	3,514	-3.2
3rd	4,088	3,425	-16.2	3,765	3,363	-10.7	2,671	2,733	2.3
4th	4,826	4,646	-3.7	4,908	4,720	-3.8	2,306	2,232	-3.2
5th	7,923	7,423	-6.3	7,940	7,347	-7.5	4,710	4,786	1.6
6th	4,737	4,518	-4.6	5,175	4,858	-6.1	3,514	3,174	-9.7
7th	3,032	2,841	-6.3	3,079	2,881	-6.4	1,854	1,814	-2.2
8th	3,018	2,833	-6.1	2,829	3,018	6.7	1,723	1,538	-10.7
9th	12,238	11,973	-2.2	12,353	12,231	-1.0	14,018	13,760	-1.8
10th	1,971	1,893	-4.0	2,134	1,921	-10.0	1,178	1,150	-2.4
11th	6,162	6,140	-0.4	6,107	6,069	-0.6	3,549	3,620	2.0

NOTE: This table does not include data for the U.S. Court of Appeals for the Federal Circuit. Beginning in March 2014, data include miscellaneous cases not included previously.
[1] Percent change not computed when fewer than 10 cases reported for the previous period.
[2] Revised.

Table B-1.
U.S. Courts of Appeals—Cases Commenced, Terminated, and Pending, by Circuit and Nature of Proceeding, During the 12-Month Period Ending June 30, 2015

Circuit and Nature of Proceeding	Pending July 1, 2014 [1]	Commenced			Terminated									Pending Jun. 30, 2015
		Total	Original	Reopened	Total	On Procedural Grounds				On the Merits				
						Total	By Consoli-dation	By Judge	By Staff	Total	By Consoli-dation	After Oral Argu-ment	After Sub-mission on Briefs	
Total	41,945	53,032	51,476	1,556	53,934	18,956	146	5,046	13,764	34,978	2,572	6,544	25,862	41,043
Criminal	9,771	10,902	10,786	116	10,986	2,423	2	638	1,783	8,563	863	1,675	6,025	9,687
U.S. Prisoner Petitions	2,484	4,650	4,501	149	4,936	1,629	1	394	1,234	3,307	78	123	3,106	2,198
Other U.S. Civil	2,220	2,821	2,744	77	2,615	936	12	243	681	1,679	123	575	981	2,426
Private Prisoner Petitions	5,736	9,678	9,388	290	9,783	3,525	-	1,109	2,416	6,258	169	532	5,557	5,631
Other Private Civil	10,505	12,183	11,760	423	12,080	5,134	96	1,288	3,750	6,946	777	2,864	3,305	10,608
Bankruptcy	771	864	833	31	845	311	7	105	199	534	104	212	218	790
Administrative Appeals	8,891	7,301	6,884	417	7,425	4,168	28	1,111	3,029	3,257	375	522	2,360	8,767
Original Proceedings	1,567	4,633	4,580	53	5,264	830	-	158	672	4,434	83	41	4,310	936
DC	1,416	1,117	1,113	4	1,144	408	19	113	276	736	259	248	229	1,389
DC Criminal	150	65	65	-	76	28	-	2	26	48	6	27	15	139
U.S. Prisoner Petitions	68	90	89	1	77	32	-	12	20	45	3	12	30	81
Other U.S. Civil	207	249	247	2	214	60	-	13	47	154	20	72	62	242
Private Prisoner Petitions	4	8	8	-	5	3	-	1	2	2	-	-	2	7
Other Private Civil	176	156	155	1	163	55	1	17	37	108	21	52	35	169
Bankruptcy	5	7	7	-	7	-	-	-	-	7	1	1	5	5
Administrative Appeals	737	459	459	-	486	170	18	28	124	316	205	76	35	710
Original Proceedings	69	83	83	-	116	60	-	40	20	56	3	8	45	36
1st	1,375	1,470	1,461	9	1,512	546	6	165	375	966	69	267	630	1,333
Criminal	606	486	483	3	514	138	1	20	117	376	32	101	243	578
U.S. Prisoner Petitions	104	93	91	2	109	29	1	11	18	80	1	5	74	88
Other U.S. Civil	51	81	81	-	63	23	1	3	19	40	-	11	29	69
Private Prisoner Petitions	74	106	105	1	90	36	-	16	20	54	5	14	35	90
Other Private Civil	337	439	439	-	452	221	4	63	154	231	23	119	89	324
Bankruptcy	22	26	26	-	27	12	-	5	7	15	3	8	4	21
Administrative Appeals	146	152	149	3	157	71	-	35	36	86	4	8	74	141
Original Proceedings	35	87	87	-	100	16	-	12	4	84	1	1	82	22

Table B-1. (June 30, 2015—Continued)

Circuit and Nature of Proceeding	Pending July 1, 2014[1]	Commenced			Terminated												Pending Jun. 30, 2015
		Total	Original	Reopened	Total	On Procedural Grounds					On the Merits						
						Total	By Consolidation	By Judge	By Staff	Total	By Consolidation	After Oral Argument	After Submission on Briefs					
2nd	3,631	4,753	4,506	247	4,870	1,968	14	574	1,380	2,902	297	820	1,785	3,514
Criminal	782	728	701	27	670	133	-	18	115	537	83	185	269	840
U.S. Prisoner Petitions	98	340	317	23	361	209	1	16	193	152	6	6	140	77
Other U.S. Civil	152	253	247	6	256	91	1	7	83	165	18	62	85	149
Private Prisoner Petitions	261	528	500	28	548	206	-	46	160	342	12	37	293	241
Other Private Civil	1,127	1,678	1,578	100	1,635	728	11	176	541	907	107	430	370	1,170
Bankruptcy	100	66	61	5	123	29	-	9	20	94	42	37	15	43
Administrative Appeals	993	872	816	56	960	509	2	289	218	451	27	59	365	905
Original Proceedings	118	288	286	2	317	63	-	13	50	254	2	4	248	89
3rd	2,671	3,425	3,373	52	3,363	1,153	3	284	866	2,210	83	229	1,898	2,733
Criminal	431	468	466	2	505	111	-	20	91	394	17	45	332	394
U.S. Prisoner Petitions	207	387	381	6	367	90	-	23	67	277	10	10	257	227
Other U.S. Civil	88	152	148	4	142	48	-	20	28	94	2	23	69	98
Private Prisoner Petitions	373	641	635	6	576	207	-	69	138	369	5	25	339	438
Other Private Civil	1,227	1,032	1,016	16	1,004	487	3	99	385	517	37	101	379	1,255
Bankruptcy	43	64	63	1	51	19	-	4	15	32	1	11	20	56
Administrative Appeals	186	296	289	7	274	112	-	47	85	162	2	12	148	208
Original Proceedings	116	385	375	10	444	79	-	2	77	365	9	2	354	57
4th	2,306	4,646	4,602	44	4,720	1,133	7	283	843	3,587	189	303	3,095	2,232
Criminal	839	1,065	1,063	2	1,180	164	-	43	121	1,016	72	86	858	724
U.S. Prisoner Petitions	359	740	731	9	773	150	-	30	120	623	6	13	604	326
Other U.S. Civil	89	229	227	2	201	48	-	12	36	153	6	20	127	117
Private Prisoner Petitions	301	978	967	11	955	344	-	90	254	611	10	12	589	324
Other Private Civil	444	833	820	13	808	268	6	68	194	540	51	135	354	469
Bankruptcy	30	51	49	2	53	17	1	4	12	36	3	7	26	28
Administrative Appeals	135	284	282	2	239	93	-	31	62	146	5	28	113	180
Original Proceedings	109	466	463	3	511	49	-	5	44	462	36	2	424	64

Table B-1. (June 30, 2015—Continued)

Circuit and Nature of Proceeding	Pending July 1, 2014	Commenced			Terminated									Pending Jun. 30, 2015
		Total	Original	Reopened	Total	On Procedural Grounds				On the Merits				
						Total	By Consoli-dation	By Judge	By Staff	Total	By Consoli-dation	After Oral Argu-ment	After Sub-mission on Briefs	
5th	**4,710**	**7,423**	**7,145**	**278**	**7,347**	**2,690**	**12**	**781**	**1,897**	**4,657**	**612**	**787**	**3,258**	**4,786**
Criminal	2,011	2,522	2,487	35	2,460	547	-	172	375	1,913	260	214	1,439	2,073
U.S. Prisoner Petitions	330	695	652	43	676	402	-	104	298	274	22	14	238	349
Other U.S. Civil	118	241	225	16	242	107	1	36	70	135	23	59	53	117
Private Prisoner Petitions	774	1,430	1,368	62	1,341	621	-	155	466	720	84	44	592	863
Other Private Civil	971	1,281	1,202	79	1,363	532	9	152	371	831	191	381	259	889
Bankruptcy	54	77	73	4	80	24	-	9	15	56	11	35	10	51
Administrative Appeals	249	480	466	14	412	249	2	148	99	163	14	31	118	317
Original Proceedings	203	697	672	25	773	208	-	5	203	565	7	9	549	127
6th	**3,514**	**4,518**	**4,459**	**59**	**4,858**	**1,343**	**18**	**379**	**946**	**3,515**	**188**	**568**	**2,759**	**3,174**
Criminal	867	1,021	1,011	10	1,024	223	-	55	168	801	75	126	600	864
U.S. Prisoner Petitions	247	329	324	5	390	85	-	31	54	305	4	7	294	186
Other U.S. Civil	168	188	184	4	212	65	1	18	46	147	5	35	107	144
Private Prisoner Petitions	716	1,032	1,011	21	1,042	320	-	122	198	722	15	63	644	706
Other Private Civil	884	1,082	1,070	12	1,148	405	14	95	296	743	60	304	379	818
Bankruptcy	53	30	29	1	59	29	1	11	17	30	2	15	13	24
Administrative Appeals	237	313	312	1	314	107	2	38	67	207	16	18	173	236
Original Proceedings	342	523	518	5	669	109	-	9	100	560	11	-	549	196
7th	**1,854**	**2,841**	**2,796**	**45**	**2,881**	**1,107**	**11**	**215**	**881**	**1,774**	**158**	**617**	**999**	**1,814**
Criminal	453	498	496	2	553	150	-	28	122	403	43	199	161	398
U.S. Prisoner Petitions	139	315	300	15	327	121	-	22	99	206	13	9	184	127
Other U.S. Civil	132	173	172	1	185	71	3	25	43	114	16	60	38	120
Private Prisoner Petitions	293	619	597	22	606	325	-	40	285	281	5	38	238	306
Other Private Civil	661	810	807	3	797	353	7	62	284	444	54	245	145	674
Bankruptcy	29	46	46	-	37	10	-	2	8	27	4	15	8	38
Administrative Appeals	121	171	170	1	159	55	1	19	35	104	22	50	32	133
Original Proceedings	26	209	208	1	217	22	-	17	5	195	1	1	193	18

Table B-1. (June 30, 2015—Continued)

| Circuit and Nature of Proceeding | Pending July 1, 2014 [1] | Commenced | | | Terminated | | | | | | | | | Pending Jun. 30, 2015 |
| | | Total | Original | Reopened | Total | On Procedural Grounds | | | | On the Merits | | | | |
						Total	By Consoli-dation	By Judge	By Staff	Total	By Consoli-dation	After Oral Argu-ment	After Sub-mission on Briefs	
8th	**1,723**	**2,833**	**2,809**	**24**	**3,018**	**585**	**6**	**250**	**329**	**2,433**	**123**	**441**	**1,869**	**1,538**
Criminal	451	759	758	1	736	104	-	37	67	632	47	107	478	474
U.S. Prisoner Petitions	145	320	316	4	361	65	-	42	23	296	4	8	284	104
Other U.S. Civil	110	145	140	5	156	43	-	15	28	113	3	36	74	99
Private Prisoner Petitions	265	576	566	10	640	172	-	101	71	468	6	29	433	201
Other Private Civil	483	557	553	4	605	129	6	45	78	476	50	229	197	435
Bankruptcy	31	29	29	-	34	6	-	-	6	28	2	12	14	26
Administrative Appeals	120	146	146	-	131	57	-	9	48	74	6	19	49	135
Original Proceedings	118	301	301	-	355	9	-	1	8	346	5	1	340	64
9th	**14,018**	**11,973**	**11,482**	**491**	**12,231**	**5,165**	**31**	**1,047**	**4,087**	**7,066**	**327**	**1,492**	**5,247**	**13,760**
Criminal	1,732	1,513	1,495	18	1,556	394	1	75	319	1,162	118	359	685	1,689
U.S. Prisoner Petitions	308	441	434	7	496	120	1	44	75	376	3	24	349	253
Other U.S. Civil	839	715	701	14	547	230	4	49	177	317	16	131	170	1,007
Private Prisoner Petitions	1,914	2,283	2,212	71	2,452	686	22	285	401	1,766	15	219	1,532	1,745
Other Private Civil	2,939	2,238	2,176	62	2,124	1,047	22	175	850	1,077	93	512	472	3,053
Bankruptcy	309	262	249	13	243	115	3	33	79	128	19	46	63	328
Administrative Appeals	5,688	3,664	3,361	303	3,839	2,517	1	383	2,133	1,322	63	188	1,071	5,513
Original Proceedings	289	857	854	3	974	56	-	3	53	918	-	13	905	172
10th	**1,178**	**1,893**	**1,881**	**12**	**1,921**	**581**	**10**	**183**	**388**	**1,340**	**36**	**352**	**952**	**1,150**
Criminal	296	405	405	-	419	83	-	42	41	336	11	127	198	282
U.S. Prisoner Petitions	83	199	196	3	209	60	-	22	38	149	-	4	145	73
Other U.S. Civil	110	141	140	1	138	28	1	4	23	110	5	30	75	113
Private Prisoner Petitions	148	304	303	1	323	126	1	57	69	197	-	13	184	129
Other Private Civil	405	582	578	4	544	214	7	35	172	330	13	150	167	443
Bankruptcy	21	18	17	1	23	5	-	-	5	18	2	11	5	16
Administrative Appeals	96	121	120	1	132	40	2	13	25	92	5	17	70	85
Original Proceedings	19	123	122	1	133	25	-	10	15	108	-	-	108	9

Table B-1. (June 30, 2015—Continued)

Circuit and Nature of Proceeding	Pending July 1, 2014 ¹	Commenced			Terminated										Pending Jun. 30, 2015
		Total	Original	Reopened	Total	On Procedural Grounds				On the Merits				
						Total	By Consoli-dation	By Judge	By Staff	Total	By Consoli-dation	After Oral Argu-ment	After Sub-mission on Briefs	
11th	**3,549**	**6,140**	**5,849**	**291**	**6,069**	**2,277**	**9**	**772**	**1,496**	**3,792**	**231**	**420**	**3,141**	**3,620**
Criminal	1,153	1,372	1,356	16	1,293	348	1	126	221	945	99	99	747	1,232
U.S. Prisoner Petitions	396	701	670	31	790	266	-	37	229	524	6	11	507	307
Other U.S. Civil	156	254	232	22	259	122	-	41	81	137	9	36	92	151
Private Prisoner Petitions	613	1,173	1,116	57	1,205	479	-	127	352	726	12	38	676	581
Other Private Civil	851	1,495	1,366	129	1,437	695	6	301	388	742	77	206	459	909
Bankruptcy	74	188	184	4	108	45	2	28	15	63	14	14	35	154
Administrative Appeals	183	343	314	29	322	188	-	71	117	134	6	16	112	204
Original Proceedings	123	614	611	3	655	134	-	41	93	521	8	-	513	82

NOTE: This table does not include data for the U.S. Court of Appeals for the Federal Circuit. Beginning in March 2014, data include miscellaneous cases not included previously.
¹ Revised.

J-7

Table C.
U.S. District Courts—Civil Cases Commenced, Terminated, and Pending
During the 12-Month Periods Ending June 30, 2014 and 2015

Circuit	Filings			Terminations			Pending		
	2014	2015	Percent Change[1]	2014	2015	Percent Change[1]	2014[2]	2015	Percent Change[1]
TOTAL	298,713	280,037	-6.3	260,352	273,562	5.1	334,261	340,736	1.9
DC	2,221	2,191	-1.4	2,087	2,175	4.2	2,422	2,438	0.7
1ST	7,714	8,160	5.8	6,852	6,560	-4.3	9,458	11,058	16.9
ME	498	540	8.4	428	569	32.9	423	394	-6.9
MA	5,007	5,260	5.1	2,868	3,084	7.5	5,624	7,800	38.7
NH	515	526	2.1	555	537	-3.2	475	464	-2.3
RI	733	541	-26.2	1,930	1,388	-28.1	1,627	780	-52.1
PR	961	1,293	34.5	1,071	982	-8.3	1,309	1,620	23.8
2ND	24,005	25,040	4.3	22,279	24,943	12.0	30,763	30,860	0.3
CT	2,023	2,138	5.7	1,983	2,100	5.9	2,411	2,449	1.6
NY,N	1,808	1,893	4.7	1,896	1,903	0.4	2,056	2,046	-0.5
NY,E	7,944	7,498	-5.6	6,437	7,426	15.4	9,754	9,826	0.7
NY,S	10,138	11,223	10.7	9,898	11,451	15.7	13,801	13,573	-1.7
NY,W	1,819	1,990	9.4	1,783	1,794	0.6	2,463	2,659	8.0
VT	273	298	9.2	282	269	-4.6	278	307	10.4
3RD	27,330	25,954	-5.0	27,304	28,497	4.4	25,589	23,046	-9.9
DE	1,883	1,433	-23.9	2,066	2,008	-2.8	2,518	1,943	-22.8
NJ	8,902	9,608	7.9	8,192	8,771	7.1	8,231	9,068	10.2
PA,E	11,012	9,473	-14.0	10,952	12,170	11.1	9,855	7,158	-27.4
PA,M	2,658	2,614	-1.7	3,066	2,614	-14.7	2,597	2,597	0.0
PA,W	2,661	2,591	-2.6	2,758	2,701	-2.1	1,953	1,843	-5.6
VI	214	235	9.8	270	233	-13.7	435	437	0.5
4TH	55,746	38,985	-30.1	19,245	28,709	49.2	78,701	88,977	13.1
MD	4,213	3,935	-6.6	3,892	4,079	4.8	3,362	3,218	-4.3
NC,E	1,967	1,961	-0.3	2,075	2,129	2.6	2,085	1,917	-8.1
NC,M	1,186	1,065	-10.2	1,437	1,283	-10.7	1,455	1,237	-15.0
NC,W	1,203	1,087	-9.6	1,352	1,233	-8.8	1,121	975	-13.0
SC	4,516	4,881	8.1	3,541	3,548	0.2	4,275	5,608	31.2
VA,E	3,421	3,498	2.3	3,308	3,270	-1.1	2,177	2,405	10.5
VA,W	1,192	1,183	-0.8	1,203	1,208	0.4	767	742	-3.3
WV,N	682	676	-0.9	653	752	15.2	644	568	-11.8
WV,S	37,366	20,699	-44.6	1,784	11,207	528.2	62,815	72,307	15.1

Page 1 of 3

Table C. (June 30, 2015—Continued)

Circuit	Filings			Terminations			Pending		
	2014	2015	Percent Change [1]	2014	2015	Percent Change [1]	2014 [2]	2015	Percent Change [1]
5TH	**30,353**	**30,330**	**-0.1**	**27,970**	**27,055**	**-3.3**	**36,661**	**39,936**	**8.9**
LA,E	3,122	3,466	11.0	4,281	3,203	-25.2	6,078	6,341	4.3
LA,M	862	854	-0.9	823	887	7.8	927	894	-3.6
LA,W	3,011	3,392	12.7	1,871	1,927	3.0	5,623	7,088	26.1
MS,N	790	697	-11.8	866	853	-1.5	723	567	-21.6
MS,S	1,891	1,701	-10.0	1,944	1,815	-6.6	1,850	1,736	-6.2
TX,N	6,845	6,420	-6.2	4,871	4,847	-0.5	9,873	11,446	15.9
TX,E	4,224	4,509	6.7	3,961	4,319	9.0	4,153	4,343	4.6
TX,S	6,118	6,035	-1.4	5,811	6,050	4.1	5,087	5,072	-0.3
TX,W	3,490	3,256	-6.7	3,542	3,154	-11.0	2,347	2,449	4.3
6TH	**22,322**	**25,144**	**12.6**	**21,557**	**24,176**	**12.1**	**29,743**	**30,711**	**3.3**
KY,E	1,556	1,219	-21.7	1,452	1,397	-3.8	1,412	1,234	-12.6
KY,W	1,667	1,716	2.9	1,236	1,287	4.1	2,026	2,455	21.2
MI,E	5,174	4,908	-5.1	5,496	4,895	-10.9	5,354	5,367	0.2
MI,W	1,709	1,593	-6.8	1,656	1,647	-0.5	1,561	1,507	-3.5
OH,N	4,024	5,025	24.9	3,166	7,194	127.2	11,362	9,193	-19.1
OH,S	2,765	5,969	115.9	2,738	2,782	1.6	2,757	5,944	115.6
TN,E	1,499	1,340	-10.6	1,648	1,486	-9.8	1,843	1,697	-7.9
TN,M	2,586	2,018	-22.0	2,725	2,143	-21.4	1,782	1,657	-7.0
TN,W	1,342	1,356	1.0	1,440	1,345	-6.6	1,646	1,657	0.7
7TH	**23,851**	**21,875**	**-8.3**	**21,184**	**29,077**	**37.3**	**33,293**	**26,091**	**-21.6**
IL,N	10,038	11,844	18.0	9,419	10,279	9.1	10,760	12,325	14.5
IL,C	1,463	1,386	-5.3	1,316	1,340	1.8	1,607	1,653	2.9
IL,S	3,522	1,500	-57.4	3,541	9,786	176.4	12,509	4,223	-66.2
IN,N	3,433	1,690	-50.8	1,717	2,242	30.6	3,967	3,415	-13.9
IN,S	2,913	2,868	-1.5	2,816	2,966	5.3	2,479	2,381	-4.0
WI,E	1,541	1,709	10.9	1,436	1,573	9.5	1,202	1,338	11.3
WI,W	941	878	-6.7	939	891	-5.1	769	756	-1.7
8TH	**15,117**	**15,495**	**2.5**	**18,343**	**14,582**	**-20.5**	**14,846**	**15,759**	**6.1**
AR,E	1,850	1,888	2.1	4,825	2,035	-57.8	1,619	1,472	-9.1
AR,W	1,153	1,047	-9.2	1,169	1,128	-3.5	1,172	1,091	-6.9
IA,N	525	609	16.0	586	593	1.2	387	403	4.1
IA,S	654	643	-1.7	683	693	1.5	561	511	-8.9
MN	4,468	5,440	21.8	4,618	4,129	-10.6	4,027	5,338	32.6
MO,E	2,900	2,258	-22.1	2,705	2,331	-13.8	3,759	3,686	-1.9
MO,W	2,337	2,279	-2.5	2,460	2,428	-1.3	1,944	1,795	-7.7
NE	638	642	0.6	639	643	0.6	579	578	-0.2
ND	285	306	7.4	328	251	-23.5	409	464	13.4
SD	307	383	24.8	330	351	6.4	389	421	8.2

Table C. (June 30, 2015—Continued)

Circuit	Filings			Terminations			Pending		
	2014	2015	Percent Change[1]	2014	2015	Percent Change[1]	2014[2]	2015	Percent Change[1]
9TH	**48,455**	**42,888**	**-11.5**	**48,938**	**43,692**	**-10.7**	**38,564**	**37,760**	**-2.1**
AK	315	300	-4.8	299	317	6.0	336	319	-5.1
AZ	7,448	3,660	-50.9	7,278	3,954	-45.7	3,230	2,936	-9.1
CA,N	6,021	5,678	-5.7	6,551	5,914	-9.7	5,462	5,226	-4.3
CA,E	4,972	4,784	-3.8	4,883	4,830	-1.1	5,697	5,651	-0.8
CA,C	14,597	14,320	-1.9	14,670	14,816	1.0	10,344	9,848	-4.8
CA,S	3,542	3,174	-10.4	3,280	2,926	-10.8	3,183	3,431	7.8
HI	722	585	-19.0	771	611	-20.8	556	530	-4.7
ID	536	555	3.5	552	570	3.3	692	677	-2.2
MT	811	580	-28.5	778	625	-19.7	573	528	-7.9
NV	2,921	3,026	3.6	2,894	2,849	-1.6	3,304	3,481	5.4
OR	2,296	2,255	-1.8	2,381	2,265	-4.9	2,198	2,188	-0.5
WA,E	820	785	-4.3	1,018	782	-23.2	685	688	0.4
WA,W	3,400	3,123	-8.1	3,503	3,187	-9.0	2,195	2,131	-2.9
GUAM	20	38	90.0	37	28	-24.3	51	61	19.6
NMI	34	25	-26.5	43	18	-58.1	58	65	12.1
10TH	**10,598**	**12,604**	**18.9**	**10,518**	**11,717**	**11.4**	**9,537**	**10,424**	**9.3**
CO	3,629	3,084	-15.0	3,461	3,263	-5.7	2,564	2,385	-7.0
KS	1,435	4,175	190.9	1,547	2,940	90.0	1,332	2,567	92.7
NM	1,269	1,155	-9.0	1,167	1,252	7.3	1,347	1,250	-7.2
OK,N	831	802	-3.5	782	810	3.6	797	789	-1.0
OK,E	540	559	3.5	566	559	-1.2	565	565	0.0
OK,W	1,431	1,507	5.3	1,354	1,438	6.2	1,155	1,224	6.0
UT	1,176	1,085	-7.7	1,343	1,191	-11.3	1,541	1,435	-6.9
WY	287	237	-17.4	298	264	-11.4	236	209	-11.4
11TH	**31,001**	**31,371**	**1.2**	**34,075**	**32,379**	**-5.0**	**24,684**	**23,676**	**-4.1**
AL,N	2,480	2,379	-4.1	5,725	2,500	-56.3	2,703	2,582	-4.5
AL,M	1,165	1,110	-4.7	1,096	1,292	17.9	1,236	1,054	-14.7
AL,S	632	657	4.0	744	603	-19.0	490	544	11.0
FL,N	1,806	1,959	8.5	1,923	1,919	-0.2	1,540	1,580	2.6
FL,M	8,481	8,499	0.2	8,730	9,148	4.8	7,466	6,817	-8.7
FL,S	8,746	8,994	2.8	8,427	9,399	11.5	5,053	4,648	-8.0
GA,N	5,116	5,353	4.6	5,123	5,047	-1.5	3,887	4,193	7.9
GA,M	1,497	1,297	-13.4	1,304	1,402	7.5	1,460	1,355	-7.2
GA,S	1,078	1,123	4.2	1,003	1,069	6.6	849	903	6.4

[1] Percent change not computed when fewer than 10 cases reported for the previous period.
[2] Revised.

Table C-1.
U.S. District Courts—Civil Cases Commenced, Terminated, and Pending
During the 12-Month Period Ending June 30, 2015

Circuit and District	Total Civil Cases				U.S. Civil Cases				Private Civil Cases			
	Pending Jun. 30, 2014 [1]	Commenced	Terminated	Pending Jun. 30, 2015	Pending Jun. 30, 2014 [1]	Commenced	Terminated	Pending Jun. 30, 2015	Pending Jun. 30, 2014 [1]	Commenced	Terminated	Pending Jun. 30, 2015
TOTAL	334,261	280,037	273,562	340,736	46,284	41,833	45,458	42,659	287,977	238,204	228,104	298,077
DC	2,422	2,191	2,175	2,438	1,248	1,057	1,021	1,284	1,174	1,134	1,154	1,154
1ST	9,458	8,160	6,560	11,058	1,411	1,179	1,260	1,330	8,047	6,981	5,300	9,728
ME	423	540	569	394	153	162	194	121	270	378	375	273
MA	5,624	5,260	3,084	7,800	685	493	541	637	4,939	4,767	2,543	7,163
NH	475	526	537	464	149	147	173	123	326	379	364	341
RI	1,627	541	1,388	780	101	104	108	97	1,526	437	1,280	683
PR	1,309	1,293	982	1,620	323	273	244	352	986	1,020	738	1,268
2ND	30,763	25,040	24,943	30,860	4,115	3,869	3,556	4,428	26,648	21,171	21,387	26,432
CT	2,411	2,138	2,100	2,449	453	386	366	473	1,958	1,752	1,734	1,976
NY,N	2,056	1,893	1,903	2,046	576	560	487	649	1,480	1,333	1,416	1,397
NY,E	9,754	7,498	7,426	9,826	1,068	916	919	1,065	8,686	6,582	6,507	8,761
NY,S	13,801	11,223	11,451	13,573	1,151	1,046	1,036	1,161	12,650	10,177	10,415	12,412
NY,W	2,463	1,990	1,794	2,659	762	838	631	969	1,701	1,152	1,163	1,690
VT	278	298	269	307	105	123	117	111	173	175	152	196
3RD	25,589	25,954	28,497	23,046	3,021	3,401	3,591	2,831	22,568	22,553	24,906	20,215
DE	2,518	1,433	2,008	1,943	137	69	81	125	2,381	1,364	1,927	1,818
NJ	8,231	9,608	8,771	9,068	917	1,032	1,047	902	7,314	8,576	7,724	8,166
PA,E	9,855	9,473	12,170	7,158	662	859	843	678	9,193	8,614	11,327	6,480
PA,M	2,597	2,614	2,614	2,597	769	864	948	685	1,828	1,750	1,666	1,912
PA,W	1,953	2,591	2,701	1,843	476	533	645	364	1,477	2,058	2,056	1,479
VI	435	235	233	437	60	44	27	77	375	191	206	360
4TH	78,701	38,985	28,709	88,977	5,509	3,883	4,537	4,855	73,192	35,102	24,172	84,122
MD	3,362	3,935	4,079	3,218	755	766	806	715	2,607	3,169	3,273	2,503
NC,E	2,085	1,961	2,129	1,917	992	836	1,001	827	1,093	1,125	1,128	1,090
NC,M	1,455	1,065	1,283	1,237	830	284	440	674	625	781	843	563
NC,W	1,121	1,087	1,233	975	404	311	383	332	717	776	850	643
SC	4,275	4,881	3,548	5,608	889	557	709	737	3,386	4,324	2,839	4,871
VA,E	2,177	3,498	3,270	2,405	473	441	489	425	1,704	3,057	2,781	1,980
VA,W	767	1,183	1,208	742	298	267	326	239	469	916	882	503
WV,N	644	676	752	568	131	181	166	146	513	495	586	422
WV,S	62,815	20,699	11,207	72,307	737	240	217	760	62,078	20,459	10,990	71,547

Page 1 of 3

J-11

Table C-1. (June 30, 2015—Continued)

Circuit and District	Total Civil Cases				U.S. Civil Cases				Private Civil Cases			
	Pending Jun. 30, 2014	Commenced	Terminated	Pending Jun. 30, 2015	Pending Jun. 30, 2014	Commenced	Terminated	Pending Jun. 30, 2015	Pending Jun. 30, 2014	Commenced	Terminated	Pending Jun. 30, 2015
5TH	**36,661**	**30,330**	**27,055**	**39,936**	**3,886**	**3,484**	**3,871**	**3,499**	**32,775**	**26,846**	**23,184**	**36,437**
LA.E	6,078	3,466	3,203	6,341	252	194	279	167	5,826	3,272	2,924	6,174
LA.M	927	854	887	894	100	75	94	81	827	779	793	813
LA.W	5,623	3,392	1,927	7,088	355	316	360	311	5,268	3,076	1,567	6,777
MS.N	723	697	853	567	122	107	147	82	601	590	706	485
MS.S	1,850	1,701	1,815	1,736	244	158	217	185	1,606	1,543	1,598	1,551
TX.N	9,873	6,420	4,847	11,446	588	843	805	626	9,285	5,577	4,042	10,820
TX.E	4,153	4,509	4,319	4,343	679	394	469	604	3,474	4,115	3,850	3,739
TX.S	5,087	6,035	6,060	5,072	949	818	860	907	4,138	5,217	5,190	4,165
TX.W	2,347	3,256	3,154	2,449	597	579	640	536	1,750	2,677	2,514	1,913
6TH	**29,743**	**25,144**	**24,176**	**30,711**	**5,031**	**3,872**	**4,301**	**4,602**	**24,712**	**21,272**	**19,875**	**26,109**
KY.E	1,412	1,219	1,397	1,234	597	434	571	460	815	785	826	774
KY.W	2,026	1,716	1,287	2,455	192	208	188	212	1,834	1,508	1,099	2,243
MI.E	5,354	4,908	4,895	5,367	1,119	862	1,006	975	4,235	4,046	3,889	4,392
MI.W	1,561	1,593	1,647	1,507	341	382	359	364	1,220	1,211	1,288	1,143
OH.N	11,362	5,025	7,194	9,193	655	592	707	540	10,707	4,433	6,487	8,653
OH.S	2,757	5,969	2,782	5,944	706	650	716	640	2,051	5,319	2,066	5,304
TN.E	1,843	1,340	1,486	1,697	539	263	266	536	1,304	1,077	1,220	1,161
TN.M	1,782	2,018	2,143	1,657	401	225	224	402	1,381	1,793	1,919	1,255
TN.W	1,646	1,356	1,345	1,657	481	256	264	473	1,165	1,100	1,081	1,184
7TH	**33,293**	**21,875**	**29,077**	**26,091**	**3,202**	**2,930**	**3,217**	**2,915**	**30,091**	**18,945**	**25,860**	**23,176**
IL.N	10,760	11,844	10,279	12,325	1,303	1,014	1,177	1,140	9,457	10,830	9,102	11,185
IL.C	1,607	1,386	1,340	1,653	262	247	212	297	1,345	1,139	1,128	1,356
IL.S	12,509	1,500	9,786	4,223	269	236	277	228	12,240	1,264	9,509	3,995
IN.N	3,967	1,690	2,242	3,415	387	341	347	381	3,580	1,349	1,895	3,034
IN.S	2,479	2,868	2,966	2,381	550	552	640	462	1,929	2,316	2,326	1,919
WI.E	1,202	1,709	1,573	1,338	224	312	300	236	978	1,397	1,273	1,102
WI.W	769	878	891	756	207	228	264	171	562	650	627	585
8TH	**14,846**	**15,495**	**14,582**	**15,759**	**3,386**	**3,039**	**3,526**	**2,899**	**11,460**	**12,456**	**11,056**	**12,860**
AR.E	1,619	1,888	2,035	1,472	431	397	500	328	1,188	1,491	1,535	1,144
AR.W	1,172	1,047	1,128	1,091	553	439	521	471	619	608	607	620
IA.N	387	609	593	403	173	235	236	172	214	374	357	231
IA.S	561	643	693	511	174	168	192	150	387	475	501	361
MN	4,027	5,440	4,129	5,338	303	303	320	286	3,724	5,137	3,809	5,052
MO.E	3,759	2,258	2,331	3,686	538	383	506	415	3,221	1,875	1,825	3,271
MO.W	1,944	2,279	2,428	1,795	951	869	1,014	806	993	1,410	1,414	989
NE	579	642	643	578	109	90	118	81	470	552	525	497
ND	409	306	251	464	45	60	40	65	364	246	211	399
SD	389	383	351	421	109	95	79	125	280	288	272	296

Table C-1. (June 30, 2015—Continued)

Circuit and District	Total Civil Cases				U.S. Civil Cases				Private Civil Cases			
	Pending Jun. 30, 2014 ¹	Commenced	Terminated	Pending Jun. 30, 2015	Pending Jun. 30, 2014 ¹	Commenced	Terminated	Pending Jun. 30, 2015	Pending Jun. 30, 2014 ¹	Commenced	Terminated	Pending Jun. 30, 2015
9TH	38,564	42,888	43,692	37,760	7,684	7,869	8,749	6,804	30,880	35,019	34,943	30,956
AK	336	300	317	319	129	113	110	132	207	187	207	187
AZ	3,230	3,660	3,954	2,936	819	830	1,002	647	2,411	2,830	2,952	2,289
CA,N	5,462	5,678	5,914	5,226	546	516	595	467	4,916	5,162	5,319	4,759
CA,E	5,697	4,784	4,830	5,661	960	763	796	927	4,737	4,021	4,034	4,724
CA,C	10,344	14,320	14,816	9,848	2,091	2,482	2,792	1,781	8,253	11,838	12,024	8,067
CA,S	3,183	3,174	2,926	3,431	389	406	398	397	2,794	2,768	2,528	3,034
HI	556	585	611	530	80	92	99	73	476	493	512	457
ID	692	555	570	677	152	82	108	126	540	473	462	551
MT	573	580	625	528	156	151	174	133	417	429	451	395
NV	3,304	3,026	2,849	3,481	451	255	316	390	2,853	2,771	2,533	3,091
OR	2,198	2,255	2,265	2,188	782	704	743	743	1,416	1,551	1,522	1,445
WA,E	685	785	782	688	342	425	412	355	343	360	370	333
WA,W	2,195	3,123	3,187	2,131	756	1,034	1,193	597	1,439	2,089	1,994	1,534
GUAM	51	38	28	61	20	13	7	26	31	25	21	35
NMI	58	25	18	65	11	3	4	10	47	22	14	55
10TH	9,537	12,604	11,717	10,424	2,484	2,231	2,358	2,357	7,053	10,373	9,359	8,067
CO	2,564	3,084	3,263	2,385	482	437	453	466	2,082	2,647	2,810	1,919
KS	1,332	4,175	2,940	2,567	402	428	454	376	930	3,747	2,486	2,191
NM	1,347	1,155	1,252	1,250	355	329	332	352	992	826	920	898
OK,N	797	802	810	789	282	284	285	281	515	518	525	508
OK,E	565	559	559	565	338	270	288	320	227	289	271	245
OK,W	1,155	1,507	1,438	1,224	291	272	299	264	864	1,235	1,139	960
UT	1,541	1,085	1,191	1,435	299	168	202	265	1,242	917	989	1,170
WY	236	237	264	209	35	43	45	33	201	194	219	176
11TH	24,684	31,371	32,379	23,676	5,307	5,019	5,471	4,855	19,377	26,352	26,908	18,821
AL,N	2,703	2,379	2,500	2,582	692	543	613	622	2,011	1,836	1,887	1,960
AL,M	1,236	1,110	1,292	1,054	203	154	171	186	1,033	956	1,121	868
AL,S	490	657	603	544	139	153	135	157	351	504	468	387
FL,N	1,540	1,959	1,919	1,580	375	296	336	335	1,165	1,663	1,583	1,245
FL,M	7,466	8,499	9,148	6,817	1,874	1,732	1,817	1,789	5,592	6,767	7,331	5,028
FL,S	5,053	8,994	9,399	4,648	890	952	1,146	696	4,163	8,042	8,253	3,952
GA,N	3,887	5,353	5,047	4,193	660	700	714	646	3,227	4,653	4,333	3,547
GA,M	1,460	1,297	1,402	1,355	259	231	294	196	1,201	1,066	1,108	1,159
GA,S	849	1,123	1,069	903	215	258	245	228	634	865	824	675

¹ Revised.

J-13

Table D. Defendants
U.S. District Courts—Criminal Defendants Commenced, Terminated, and Pending (Including Transfers) During the 12-Month Periods Ending June 30, 2014 and 2015

Circuit and District	Filings			Terminations			Pending [2]		
	2014	2015	Percent Change [1]	2014	2015	Percent Change [1]	2014	2015	Percent Change [1]
Total	84,017	79,154	-5.8	89,281	81,372	-8.9	102,539	98,535	-3.9
DC	415	237	-42.9	441	323	-26.8	960	861	-10.3
1st	3,021	2,291	-24.2	2,829	2,751	-2.8	3,496	3,034	-13.2
ME	208	213	2.4	231	204	-11.7	212	216	1.9
MA	423	463	9.5	478	538	12.6	726	646	-11.0
NH	170	201	18.2	167	197	18.0	132	145	9.8
RI	192	113	-41.1	191	158	-17.3	158	120	-24.1
PR	2,028	1,301	-35.8	1,762	1,654	-6.1	2,268	1,907	-15.9
2nd	3,800	3,349	-11.9	4,735	4,206	-11.2	11,550	10,577	-8.4
CT	355	285	-19.7	431	368	-14.6	680	589	-13.4
NY,N	513	381	-25.7	660	526	-20.3	926	771	-16.7
NY,E	827	748	-9.6	1,041	885	-15.0	3,159	2,908	-7.9
NY,S	1,415	1,213	-14.3	1,753	1,701	-3.0	5,317	4,842	-8.9
NY,W	462	530	14.7	618	529	-14.4	1,183	1,185	0.2
VT	228	192	-15.8	232	197	-15.1	285	282	-1.1
3rd	2,877	2,692	-6.4	3,055	2,888	-5.5	5,284	5,070	-4.0
DE	115	60	-47.8	127	106	-16.5	222	176	-20.7
NJ	902	807	-10.5	977	898	-8.1	1,148	1,075	-6.4
PA,E	722	743	2.9	902	782	-13.3	1,502	1,465	-2.5
PA,M	472	429	-9.1	454	473	4.2	810	739	-8.8
PA,W	542	577	6.5	518	556	7.3	762	784	2.9
VI	124	76	-38.7	77	73	-5.2	840	831	-1.1
4th	8,485	8,475	-0.1	8,961	7,956	-11.2	14,009	13,329	-4.9
MD	1,595	1,592	-0.2	1,591	1,408	-11.5	4,913	5,057	2.9
NC,E	1,226	1,251	2.0	1,400	1,097	-21.6	2,922	3,108	6.4
NC,M	523	599	14.5	566	562	-0.7	514	526	2.3
NC,W	556	581	4.5	729	720	-1.2	868	726	-16.4
SC	860	858	-0.2	972	836	-14.0	1,027	1,052	2.4
VA,E	2,467	2,487	0.8	2,500	2,143	-14.3	2,516	1,719	-31.7
VA,W	439	368	-16.2	462	415	-10.2	601	532	-11.5
WV,N	472	448	-5.1	389	440	13.1	365	374	2.5
WV,S	347	291	-16.1	352	335	-4.8	283	235	-17.0

Table D. Defendants (June 30, 2015—Continued)

Circuit and District	Filings 2014	Filings 2015	Percent Change[1]	Terminations 2014	Terminations 2015	Percent Change[1]	Pending[2] 2014	Pending[2] 2015	Percent Change[1]
5th	**17,967**	**17,314**	**-3.6**	**18,529**	**17,186**	**-7.2**	**16,646**	**16,627**	**-0.1**
LA,E	415	548	32.0	348	477	37.1	475	546	14.9
LA,M	162	222	37.0	196	174	-11.2	266	311	16.9
LA,W	262	281	7.3	360	286	-20.6	306	293	-4.2
MS,N	150	204	36.0	246	203	-17.5	239	246	2.9
MS,S	416	336	-19.2	354	353	-0.3	362	325	-10.2
TX,N	1,572	1,556	-1.0	1,397	1,500	7.4	1,773	1,790	1.0
TX,E	1,053	785	-25.5	936	1,095	17.0	1,855	1,473	-20.6
TX,S	6,618	6,479	-2.1	7,151	6,238	-12.8	6,868	7,146	4.0
TX,W	7,319	6,903	-5.7	7,541	6,860	-9.0	4,502	4,497	-0.1
6th	**5,527**	**5,204**	**-5.8**	**6,124**	**5,417**	**-11.5**	**7,093**	**6,769**	**-4.6**
KY,E	636	451	-29.1	635	644	1.4	816	621	-23.9
KY,W	517	442	-14.5	610	454	-25.6	904	852	-5.8
MI,E	1,016	951	-6.4	1,098	943	-14.1	1,441	1,400	-2.8
MI,W	424	335	-21.0	408	433	6.1	310	207	-33.2
OH,N	754	685	-9.2	852	733	-14.0	648	586	-9.6
OH,S	704	703	-0.1	719	654	-9.0	709	759	7.1
TN,E	768	826	7.6	871	746	-14.4	794	868	9.3
TN,M	212	245	15.6	318	267	-16.0	486	466	-4.1
TN,W	496	566	14.1	613	543	-11.4	985	1,010	2.5
7th	**2,875**	**2,569**	**-10.6**	**3,349**	**2,714**	**-19.0**	**4,264**	**4,104**	**-3.8**
IL,N	740	729	-1.5	967	749	-22.5	1,816	1,791	-1.4
IL,C	370	280	-24.3	494	412	-16.6	432	303	-29.9
IL,S	451	361	-20.0	434	388	-10.6	404	380	-5.9
IN,N	330	291	-11.8	480	324	-32.5	471	438	-7.0
IN,S	429	368	-14.2	435	404	-7.1	497	445	-10.5
WI,E	407	401	-1.5	382	303	-20.7	421	516	22.6
WI,W	148	139	-6.1	157	134	-14.6	223	231	3.6
8th	**5,149**	**5,372**	**4.3**	**5,308**	**5,007**	**-5.7**	**5,596**	**5,933**	**6.0**
AR,E	402	496	23.4	436	404	-7.3	614	708	15.3
AR,W	322	287	-10.9	366	351	-4.1	384	317	-17.4
IA,N	380	386	1.6	385	367	-4.7	231	248	7.4
IA,S	315	336	6.7	348	326	-6.3	297	302	1.7
MN	370	588	58.9	312	339	8.7	400	647	61.8
MO,E	745	803	7.8	792	639	-19.3	652	815	25.0
MO,W	908	910	0.2	864	971	12.4	1,405	1,353	-3.7
NE	689	580	-15.8	714	643	-9.9	618	556	-10.0
ND	430	447	4.0	379	442	16.6	491	477	-2.9
SD	588	539	-8.3	712	525	-26.3	504	510	1.2

Table D. Defendants (June 30, 2015—Continued)

Circuit and District	Filings			Terminations			Pending [2]		
	2014	2015	Percent Change [1]	2014	2015	Percent Change [1]	2014	2015	Percent Change [1]
9th	**18,835**	**16,698**	**-11.3**	**20,096**	**17,678**	**-12.0**	**17,842**	**16,751**	**-6.1**
AK	197	217	10.2	209	191	-8.6	237	265	11.8
AZ	7,053	6,421	-9.0	7,281	6,437	-11.6	2,558	2,518	-1.6
CA,N	866	736	-15.0	838	731	-12.8	1,319	1,323	0.3
CA,E	750	713	-4.9	1,016	934	-8.1	2,749	2,536	-7.7
CA,C	1,526	1,127	-26.1	1,523	1,263	-17.1	3,136	2,854	-9.0
CA,S	4,552	4,070	-10.6	4,988	4,122	-17.4	2,741	2,585	-5.7
HI	325	214	-34.2	410	343	-16.3	569	449	-21.1
ID	274	328	19.7	331	322	-2.7	322	328	1.9
MT	451	387	-14.2	407	421	3.4	380	347	-8.7
NV	566	506	-10.6	616	573	-7.0	1,154	1,070	-7.3
OR	704	545	-22.6	710	673	-5.2	759	644	-15.2
WA,E	498	369	-25.9	512	487	-4.9	499	410	-17.8
WA,W	969	946	-2.4	1,113	1,045	-6.1	1,264	1,286	1.7
GUAM	74	102	37.8	114	119	4.4	120	103	-14.2
NMI	30	17	-43.3	28	17	-39.3	35	33	-5.7
10th	**7,708**	**7,901**	**2.5**	**7,865**	**7,851**	**-0.2**	**6,957**	**6,995**	**0.5**
CO	563	577	2.5	630	500	-20.6	1,220	1,275	4.5
KS	788	776	-1.5	816	792	-2.9	1,356	1,350	-0.4
NM	4,273	4,481	4.9	4,258	4,583	7.6	1,757	1,641	-6.6
OK,N	262	290	10.7	290	221	-23.8	170	234	37.6
OK,E	97	96	-1.0	103	114	10.7	99	82	-17.2
OK,W	555	573	3.2	542	506	-6.6	948	1,015	7.1
UT	805	755	-6.2	866	837	-3.3	762	696	-8.7
WY	365	353	-3.3	360	298	-17.2	645	702	8.8
11th	**7,358**	**7,052**	**-4.2**	**7,989**	**7,395**	**-7.4**	**8,842**	**8,485**	**-4.0**
AL,N	473	412	-12.9	577	367	-36.4	502	547	9.0
AL,M	239	223	-6.7	258	217	-15.9	386	385	-0.3
AL,S	415	350	-15.7	424	382	-9.9	406	379	-6.7
FL,N	390	410	5.1	471	393	-16.6	585	599	2.4
FL,M	1,452	1,456	0.3	1,579	1,405	-11.0	1,705	1,813	6.3
FL,S	2,319	2,395	3.3	2,404	2,377	-1.1	1,998	1,959	-2.0
GA,N	760	673	-11.4	693	771	11.3	1,488	1,373	-7.7
GA,M	570	589	3.3	665	534	-19.7	552	611	10.7
GA,S	740	544	-26.5	918	949	3.4	1,220	819	-32.9

NOTE: This table includes defendants in all cases filed as felonies or Class A misdemeanors, but includes only those defendants in cases filed as petty offenses that were assigned to district judges rather than magistrate judges.

[1] Percent change not computed when fewer than 10 defendants reported for the previous period.

[2] Pending totals exclude defendants who had been fugitives more than 12 months before the end of the period indicated.

Table D-1.
U.S. District Courts—Criminal Defendants Commenced, Terminated, and Pending (Including Transfers), During the 12-Month Period Ending June 30, 2015

| Circuit and District | Not Terminated as of June 30, 2014[1] | | | | Commenced | | | | | | | |
| | Total | Felony | Class A Misdemeanor | Petty Offense | Total Commenced | Original Proceedings | | | | | |
						Total	Felony	Class A Misdemeanor	Petty Offense	Reopens[2]	Transfers
TOTAL	102,539	86,806	14,831	902	79,154	78,592	69,741	8,688	163	331	231
DC	960	941	19	-	237	235	228	7	-	-	2
1ST	3,496	3,480	15	1	2,291	2,259	2,209	30	20	21	11
ME	212	208	4	-	213	212	208	4	-	1	7
MA	726	724	2	-	463	455	448	7	-	1	7
NH	132	132	-	-	201	200	195	5	-	-	1
RI	158	157	1	-	113	112	107	5	-	1	1
PR	2,268	2,259	8	1	1,301	1,280	1,251	9	20	18	3
2ND	11,550	10,872	638	40	3,349	3,316	3,199	116	1	12	21
CT	680	655	24	1	285	284	281	3	-	-	1
NY,N	926	783	141	2	381	378	308	70	-	-	3
NY,E	3,159	3,072	84	3	748	736	729	7	-	10	2
NY,S	5,317	4,963	320	34	1,213	1,200	1,180	20	-	-	13
NY,W	1,183	1,118	65	-	530	528	512	15	1	-	2
VT	285	281	4	-	192	190	189	1	-	2	-
3RD	5,284	5,049	192	43	2,692	2,658	2,461	194	3	20	14
DE	222	193	28	1	60	60	59	-	-	-	-
NJ	1,148	1,043	104	1	807	799	641	158	1	7	1
PA,E	1,502	1,474	21	7	743	733	720	12	1	7	7
PA,M	810	784	22	4	429	425	413	11	1	3	1
PA,W	762	758	4	-	577	565	555	10	-	7	5
VI	840	797	13	30	76	76	73	2	1	-	-
4TH	14,009	6,710	6,771	528	8,475	8,408	5,275	3,030	103	46	21
MD	4,913	1,276	3,595	42	1,592	1,581	743	836	2	9	2
NC,E	2,922	671	1,903	348	1,251	1,239	590	555	94	5	7
NC,M	514	507	3	4	599	596	591	5	-	-	7
NC,W	868	823	36	9	581	573	562	11	13	7	3
SC	1,027	1,002	18	7	858	840	831	9	6	5	1
VA,E	2,516	1,221	1,190	105	2,487	2,479	927	1,546	-	5	3
VA,W	601	566	22	13	368	366	334	32	1	5	-
WV,N	365	361	4	-	448	444	425	18	-	4	-
WV,S	283	283	-	-	291	290	272	18	-	1	-

Table D-1. (June 30, 2015—Continued)

Circuit and District	Terminated							Not Terminated as of June 30, 2015 [1]			
	Total Terminated	Original Proceedings				Reopens [2]	Transfers	Total	Felony	Class A Misdemeanor	Petty Offense
		Total	Felony	Class A Misdemeanor	Petty Offense						
TOTAL	81,372	80,936	71,362	8,275	1,299	243	193	98,535	82,944	14,717	874
DC	323	322	311	11	-	1	-	861	838	23	-
1ST	2,751	2,733	2,682	32	19	13	5	3,034	3,018	14	2
ME	204	200	194	6	-	3	1	216	214	2	-
MA	538	536	529	7	-	1	1	646	644	2	-
NH	197	197	195	2	-	-	-	145	142	3	-
RI	158	156	154	2	-	2	2	120	116	4	-
PR	1,654	1,644	1,610	15	19	9	1	1,907	1,902	3	2
2ND	4,206	4,187	3,979	168	40	12	7	10,577	9,964	574	39
CT	368	366	348	18	-	1	-	589	578	10	1
NY.N	526	526	429	63	34	1	-	771	665	104	2
NY.E	885	877	862	14	1	5	3	2,908	2,823	83	2
NY.S	1,701	1,696	1,650	43	3	4	1	4,842	4,496	312	34
NY.W	529	526	498	27	1	1	2	1,185	1,125	60	-
VT	197	196	192	3	1	1	-	282	277	5	-
3RD	2,888	2,852	2,657	192	3	20	16	5,070	4,827	198	45
DE	106	102	101	1	-	-	4	176	147	28	1
NJ	898	889	726	163	-	6	3	1,075	973	101	1
PA.E	782	773	761	11	1	4	5	1,465	1,434	23	8
PA.M	473	471	458	13	-	2	-	739	713	21	5
PA.W	556	544	541	3	-	8	4	784	773	11	-
VI	73	73	70	1	2	-	-	831	787	14	30
4TH	7,956	7,909	5,312	1,993	604	23	24	13,329	6,025	6,835	469
MD	1,408	1,400	807	448	145	5	3	5,057	1,152	3,862	43
NC.E	1,097	1,093	531	363	199	3	1	3,108	722	2,024	362
NC.M	562	561	555	6	-	-	1	526	519	3	4
NC.W	720	715	675	40	-	2	3	726	701	14	11
SC	836	826	812	13	1	8	2	1,052	1,022	23	7
VA.E	2,143	2,137	810	1,070	257	1	5	1,719	825	864	30
VA.W	415	414	399	14	-	1	1	532	478	42	12
WV.N	440	435	412	22	1	4	1	374	372	2	-
WV.S	335	328	311	17	-	-	7	235	234	1	-

Table D-1. (June 30, 2015—Continued)

Circuit and District	Not Terminated as of June 30, 2014 [1]				Total Commenced	Commenced — Original Proceedings				Reopens [2]	Transfers
	Total	Felony	Class A Misdemeanor	Petty Offense		Total	Felony	Class A Misdemeanor	Petty Offense		
5TH	**16,646**	**15,755**	**819**	**72**	**17,314**	**17,239**	**16,522**	**709**	**8**	**48**	**27**
LA,E	475	471	4	-	548	547	489	58	-	-	1
LA,M	266	234	28	4	222	221	219	2	-	-	1
LA,W	306	251	52	3	281	275	238	37	-	3	3
MS,N	239	226	8	5	204	204	199	5	-	-	-
MS,S	362	338	7	17	336	333	313	17	3	2	1
TX,N	1,773	1,710	43	20	1,556	1,546	1,521	24	1	2	8
TX,E	1,855	1,831	23	1	785	784	777	7	-	-	1
TX,S	6,868	6,735	120	13	6,479	6,444	6,425	17	2	26	9
TX,W	4,502	3,959	534	9	6,903	6,885	6,341	542	2	15	3
6TH	**7,093**	**6,372**	**694**	**27**	**5,204**	**5,153**	**4,846**	**299**	**8**	**17**	**34**
KY,E	816	801	10	5	451	451	447	1	3	-	-
KY,W	904	422	471	11	442	438	261	177	-	1	3
MI,E	1,441	1,421	16	4	951	931	909	20	2	7	13
MI,W	310	303	7	-	335	334	325	9	-	-	1
OH,N	648	643	4	1	685	684	673	11	-	1	-
OH,S	709	620	87	2	703	690	636	52	2	3	10
TN,E	794	788	5	1	826	819	815	4	-	3	4
TN,M	486	485	1	-	245	242	239	3	-	1	2
TN,W	985	889	93	3	566	564	541	22	1	1	1
7TH	**4,264**	**4,200**	**60**	**4**	**2,569**	**2,532**	**2,462**	**69**	**1**	**27**	**10**
IL,N	1,816	1,797	19	-	729	723	709	14	-	2	4
IL,C	432	410	21	1	280	279	244	35	-	1	-
IL,S	404	399	3	2	361	358	355	3	-	2	1
IN,N	471	466	5	-	291	291	287	4	-	-	-
IN,S	497	494	2	1	368	364	362	1	1	2	2
WI,E	421	416	5	-	401	381	373	8	-	17	3
WI,W	223	218	5	-	139	136	132	4	-	3	-
8TH	**5,596**	**5,495**	**90**	**11**	**5,372**	**5,347**	**5,194**	**151**	**2**	**9**	**16**
AR,E	614	608	6	-	496	492	469	23	-	-	4
AR,W	384	364	20	-	287	282	245	37	-	2	3
IA,N	231	229	2	-	386	385	384	1	-	-	1
IA,S	297	297	-	-	336	334	333	1	-	2	-
MN	400	397	3	-	588	588	586	2	-	-	-
MO,E	652	616	36	-	803	802	751	50	1	-	1
MO,W	1,405	1,402	3	-	910	903	886	17	-	2	5
NE	618	608	8	2	580	577	572	5	-	2	1
ND	491	488	3	-	447	446	439	7	-	-	1
SD	504	486	9	9	539	538	529	8	1	1	-

Table D-1. (June 30, 2015—Continued)

Circuit and District	Total Terminated	Terminated — Original Proceedings				Reopens [2]	Transfers [2]	Not Terminated as of June 30, 2015 [1]			
		Total	Felony	Class A Misdemeanor	Petty Offense			Total	Felony	Class A Misdemeanor	Petty Offense
5TH	**17,186**	**17,142**	**16,292**	**721**	**129**	**28**	**16**	**16,527**	**15,664**	**881**	**82**
LA,E	477	473	419	53	1	1	3	546	535	11	-
LA,M	174	174	170	4	-	-	-	311	278	29	4
LA,W	286	278	237	38	3	8	-	293	254	36	3
MS,N	203	202	198	4	-	1	2	246	232	9	5
MS,S	353	350	330	17	3	1	3	325	301	7	17
TX,N	1,500	1,493	1,453	30	10	4	3	1,790	1,730	42	18
TX,E	1,095	1,094	1,079	12	3	-	1	1,473	1,451	22	-
TX,S	6,238	6,229	6,210	19	-	6	1	7,146	7,002	123	21
TX,W	6,860	6,849	6,196	544	109	7	4	4,497	3,881	602	14
6TH	**5,417**	**5,385**	**5,026**	**333**	**26**	**14**	**18**	**6,769**	**6,072**	**670**	**27**
KY,E	644	641	632	4	5	1	2	621	611	7	3
KY,W	454	448	257	186	5	1	6	852	394	447	11
MI,E	943	935	911	20	4	7	6	1,400	1,378	20	2
MI,W	433	428	405	23	-	1	4	207	204	3	-
OH,N	733	731	721	10	-	1	2	586	581	4	1
OH,S	654	652	581	59	12	2	2	759	670	84	5
TN,E	746	744	739	5	-	2	2	868	862	5	1
TN,M	267	264	256	8	-	3	-	466	465	1	-
TN,W	543	542	524	18	-	-	1	1,010	907	99	4
7TH	**2,714**	**2,698**	**2,616**	**80**	**2**	**8**	**8**	**4,104**	**4,042**	**60**	**2**
IL,N	749	747	729	18	-	8	-	1,791	1,774	17	-
IL,C	412	409	365	43	1	-	3	303	286	17	-
IL,S	388	388	386	2	1	-	-	380	372	6	2
IN,N	324	323	320	3	-	-	1	438	432	6	-
IN,S	404	399	394	4	1	2	3	445	445	-	-
WI,E	303	299	294	5	-	4	-	516	507	9	-
WI,W	134	133	128	5	-	1	-	231	226	5	-
8TH	**5,007**	**4,979**	**4,733**	**231**	**15**	**7**	**21**	**5,933**	**5,818**	**103**	**12**
AR,E	404	400	383	17	-	1	4	708	692	16	-
AR,W	351	346	311	35	-	1	4	317	294	23	-
IA,N	367	365	361	4	-	-	2	248	248	-	-
IA,S	326	322	316	6	-	2	2	302	301	1	-
MN	339	336	333	3	-	-	3	647	643	4	-
MO,E	639	637	576	59	2	-	2	815	783	32	-
MO,W	971	969	953	16	-	-	2	1,342	1,342	11	-
NE	643	640	623	17	-	1	2	556	547	7	2
ND	442	442	410	27	5	-	-	477	475	2	-
SD	525	522	467	47	8	1	2	510	493	7	10

Table D-1. (June 30, 2015—Continued)

Circuit and District	Not Terminated as of June 30, 2014 [1]				Commenced						
					Total Commenced	Original Proceedings				Reopens [2]	Transfers
	Total	Felony	Class A Misdemeanor	Petty Offense		Total	Felony	Class A Misdemeanor	Petty Offense		
9TH	**17,842**	**15,931**	**1,793**	**118**	**16,698**	**16,564**	**13,777**	**2,775**	**12**	**92**	**42**
AK	237	207	24	6	217	214	195	19	12	1	2
AZ	2,558	2,528	16	14	6,421	6,376	4,419	1,957	-	39	6
CA,N	1,319	1,177	142	-	736	730	675	55	-	1	5
CA,E	2,749	2,213	524	12	713	696	619	76	1	9	8
CA,C	3,136	2,904	168	64	1,127	1,101	1,036	61	4	20	6
CA,S	2,741	2,693	46	2	4,070	4,062	4,035	25	2	6	2
HI	569	449	117	3	214	208	179	29	1	5	1
ID	322	303	18	1	328	324	319	4	-	1	3
MT	380	362	16	2	387	384	378	6	1	2	1
NV	1,154	1,137	14	3	506	502	490	11	1	4	-
OR	759	741	15	3	545	538	509	26	3	2	5
WA,E	499	489	7	3	369	367	367	-	-	1	1
WA,W	1,264	584	675	5	946	943	461	482	-	1	2
GUAM	120	109	11	-	102	102	78	24	-	-	-
NMI	35	35	-	-	17	17	17	-	-	-	-
10TH	**6,957**	**4,821**	**2,105**	**31**	**7,901**	**7,870**	**7,217**	**648**	**5**	**21**	**10**
CO	1,220	724	492	4	577	576	538	36	2	1	3
KS	1,356	818	534	4	776	768	634	134	-	5	3
NM	1,757	1,715	42	-	4,481	4,476	4,431	45	-	2	3
OK,N	170	167	2	1	290	289	282	6	1	1	-
OK,E	99	97	2	-	96	92	91	1	-	4	1
OK,W	948	342	605	1	573	570	334	236	-	2	1
UT	762	562	199	1	755	748	649	99	-	6	1
WY	645	396	229	20	353	351	258	91	2	-	2
11TH	**8,842**	**7,180**	**1,635**	**27**	**7,052**	**7,011**	**6,351**	**660**	**5**	**18**	**23**
AL,N	502	439	62	1	412	407	354	53	-	1	4
AL,M	386	323	62	1	223	222	206	16	-	1	1
AL,S	406	399	6	1	350	350	340	10	-	-	-
FL,N	585	332	250	3	410	405	286	119	-	5	-
FL,M	1,705	1,672	26	7	1,456	1,447	1,427	20	-	3	6
FL,S	1,998	1,986	12	-	2,395	2,385	2,380	5	-	2	8
GA,N	1,488	1,142	336	10	673	668	652	16	-	2	2
GA,M	552	370	180	2	589	587	418	169	-	1	3
GA,S	1,220	517	701	2	544	540	288	252	-	4	-

Table D-1. (June 30, 2015—Continued)

Circuit and District	Total Terminated	Terminated — Original Proceedings				Reopens[2]	Transfers	Not Terminated as of June 30, 2015[1]			
		Total	Felony	Class A Misdemeanor	Petty Offense			Total	Felony	Class A Misdemeanor	Petty Offense
9TH	**17,678**	**17,571**	**14,195**	**2,948**	**428**	**81**	**26**	**16,751**	**14,805**	**1,811**	**135**
AK	191	183	167	14	2	1	7	265	231	28	6
AZ	6,437	6,403	4,278	2,047	78	33	1	2,518	2,467	31	20
CA,N	731	729	645	82	2	2	1	1,323	1,198	125	13
CA,E	934	928	880	46	2	4	2	2,536	1,960	563	13
CA,C	1,263	1,247	1,184	63	-	15	1	2,854	2,605	179	70
CA,S	4,122	4,110	3,848	59	203	10	2	2,585	2,543	38	4
HI	343	342	296	38	8	1	-	449	334	112	3
ID	322	320	299	12	8	-	2	328	312	15	1
MT	421	413	402	8	3	6	2	347	329	17	1
NV	573	570	557	13	-	3	-	1,070	1,051	15	4
OR	673	667	631	31	5	2	4	644	622	18	4
WA,E	487	485	470	9	6	1	1	410	402	4	4
WA,W	1,045	1,040	431	499	110	2	3	1,286	624	657	5
GUAM	119	117	90	27	-	1	1	103	94	9	-
NMI	17	17	17	-	-	-	-	33	33	-	-
10TH	**7,851**	**7,810**	**7,132**	**660**	**18**	**26**	**15**	**6,995**	**4,824**	**2,137**	**34**
CO	500	498	462	35	1	1	1	1,275	770	500	5
KS	792	779	704	73	2	8	5	1,350	754	592	4
NM	4,583	4,579	4,518	51	10	4	1	1,641	1,593	48	-
OK,N	221	219	210	9	-	1	1	234	230	2	2
OK,E	114	112	109	3	-	2	-	82	82	-	-
OK,W	506	498	285	213	-	4	4	1,015	385	630	-
UT	837	829	625	202	2	6	2	696	573	122	1
WY	298	296	219	74	3	-	2	702	437	243	22
11TH	**7,395**	**7,348**	**6,427**	**906**	**15**	**10**	**37**	**8,485**	**7,047**	**1,411**	**27**
AL,N	367	361	315	46	-	2	4	547	475	71	1
AL,M	217	217	206	11	-	-	-	385	316	68	1
AL,S	382	380	369	10	1	1	-	379	373	6	-
FL,N	393	385	264	121	-	2	6	599	349	246	4
FL,M	1,405	1,393	1,355	28	10	1	11	1,813	1,780	26	7
FL,S	2,377	2,367	2,358	9	-	1	9	1,959	1,947	12	-
GA,N	771	767	744	21	2	1	3	1,373	1,027	336	10
GA,M	534	533	341	190	2	1	2	611	446	163	2
GA,S	949	945	475	470	-	2	1	819	334	483	2

NOTE: This table includes defendants in all cases filed as felonies or Class A misdemeanors, but includes only those defendants in cases filed as petty offenses that were assigned to district judges rather than magistrate judges.

[1] Excludes defendants who had been fugitives more than 12 months before the end of the period indicated.

[2] Includes appeals from magistrate judges, reopens, remands, and retrials after mistrial.

Table F-8.
U.S. Bankruptcy Courts—Adversary Proceedings Commenced, Terminated, and Pending Under the Bankruptcy Code During the 12-Month Periods Ending June 30, 2014 and 2015

Circuit and District	Filings			Terminations			Pending		
	2014	2015	Percent Change[1]	2014	2015	Percent Change[1]	2014[2]	2015	Percent Change[1]
TOTAL	**38,451**	**35,036**	**-8.9**	**46,484**	**36,891**	**-20.6**	**50,161**	**48,310**	**-3.7**
DC	53	30	-43.4	68	42	-38.2	86	74	-14.0
1ST	**1,090**	**922**	**-15.4**	**1,434**	**1,024**	**-28.6**	**1,661**	**1,559**	**-6.1**
ME	94	62	-34.0	110	53	-51.8	40	49	22.5
MA	539	401	-25.6	704	475	-32.5	1,012	938	-7.3
NH	116	106	-8.6	173	129	-25.4	119	96	-19.3
RI	50	38	-24.0	78	49	-37.2	44	33	-25.0
PR	291	315	8.2	369	318	-13.8	446	443	-0.7
2ND	**2,748**	**1,828**	**-33.5**	**4,120**	**3,047**	**-26.0**	**11,756**	**10,538**	**-10.4**
CT	229	168	-26.6	287	258	-10.1	412	323	-21.6
NY,N	105	103	-1.9	117	123	5.1	5,256	5,236	-0.4
NY,E	628	639	1.8	951	727	-23.6	820	732	-10.7
NY,S	1,655	726	-56.1	2,594	1,663	-35.9	4,963	4,026	-18.9
NY,W	113	160	41.6	147	258	75.5	283	185	-34.6
VT	18	32	77.8	24	18	-25.0	22	36	63.6
3RD	**4,410**	**4,481**	**1.6**	**5,611**	**3,993**	**-28.8**	**5,153**	**5,641**	**9.5**
DE	1,787	1,568	-12.3	2,467	1,302	-47.2	2,478	2,744	10.7
NJ	1,198	1,650	37.7	1,376	1,375	-0.1	1,436	1,711	19.2
PA,E	613	644	5.1	664	639	-3.8	397	402	1.3
PA,M	292	238	-18.5	419	244	-41.8	376	370	-1.6
PA,W	515	380	-26.2	660	425	-35.6	393	348	-11.5
VI	5	1	-	25	8	-68.0	73	66	-9.6
4TH	**3,024**	**2,923**	**-3.3**	**3,323**	**2,781**	**-16.3**	**2,343**	**2,485**	**6.1**
MD	845	831	-1.7	831	892	7.3	688	627	-8.9
NC,E	238	264	10.9	251	249	-0.8	203	218	7.4
NC,M	231	171	-26.0	252	164	-34.9	119	126	5.9
NC,W	361	365	1.1	383	381	-0.5	261	245	-6.1
SC	150	215	43.3	203	152	-25.1	69	132	91.3
VA,E	783	784	0.1	997	631	-36.7	613	766	25.0
VA,W	211	157	-25.6	240	151	-37.1	89	95	6.7
WV,N	57	43	-24.6	89	47	-47.2	53	49	-7.5
WV,S	148	93	-37.2	77	114	48.1	248	227	-8.5

Table F-8. (June 30, 2015—Continued)

Circuit and District	Filings			Terminations			Pending		
	2014	2015	Percent Change [1]	2014	2015	Percent Change [1]	2014 [2]	2015	Percent Change [1]
5TH	**1,995**	**1,732**	**-13.2**	**2,296**	**1,830**	**-20.3**	**2,233**	**2,135**	**-4.4**
LA,E	90	84	-6.7	136	45	-66.9	62	101	62.9
LA,M	57	116	103.5	70	83	18.6	44	77	75.0
LA,W	97	86	-11.3	125	104	-16.8	151	133	-11.9
MS,N	111	103	-7.2	173	135	-22.0	206	174	-15.5
MS,S	191	159	-16.8	166	200	20.5	212	171	-19.3
TX,N	476	328	-31.1	578	371	-35.8	372	329	-11.6
TX,E	148	154	4.1	208	155	-25.5	159	158	-0.6
TX,S	529	411	-22.3	394	449	14.0	794	756	-4.8
TX,W	296	291	-1.7	446	288	-35.4	233	236	1.3
6TH	**5,417**	**5,117**	**-5.5**	**6,077**	**5,159**	**-15.1**	**4,092**	**4,049**	**-1.1**
KY,E	142	218	53.5	148	139	-6.1	102	181	77.5
KY,W	189	204	7.9	194	201	3.6	105	108	2.9
MI,E	1,863	1,748	-6.2	1,965	1,759	-10.5	794	783	-1.4
MI,W	339	326	-3.8	427	325	-23.9	214	215	0.5
OH,N	769	611	-20.5	944	669	-29.1	1,172	1,115	-4.9
OH,S	727	530	-27.1	918	632	-31.2	644	542	-15.8
TN,E	208	243	16.8	318	196	-38.4	169	216	27.8
TN,M	492	654	32.9	485	596	22.9	394	452	14.7
TN,W	688	583	-15.3	678	642	-5.3	498	437	-12.2
7TH	**3,444**	**3,139**	**-8.9**	**4,187**	**3,171**	**-24.3**	**2,267**	**2,235**	**-1.4**
IL,N	1,144	1,005	-12.2	1,587	988	-37.7	800	817	2.1
IL,C	190	200	5.3	185	198	7.0	139	141	1.4
IL,S	193	206	6.7	242	211	-12.8	51	46	-9.8
IN,N	487	475	-2.5	538	506	-5.9	299	268	-10.4
IN,S	417	406	-2.6	524	404	-22.9	451	453	0.4
WI,E	804	671	-16.5	880	704	-20.0	425	392	-7.8
WI,W	209	176	-15.8	231	160	-30.7	102	118	15.7
8TH	**1,818**	**1,726**	**-5.1**	**2,238**	**1,747**	**-21.9**	**1,177**	**1,156**	**-1.8**
AR,E	139	127	-8.6	171	123	-28.1	118	122	3.4
AR,W	115	146	27.0	142	100	-29.6	93	139	49.5
IA,N	70	79	12.9	141	99	-29.8	80	60	-25.0
IA,S	87	60	-31.0	83	68	-18.1	65	57	-12.3
MN	554	496	-10.5	688	525	-23.7	358	329	-8.1
MO,E	317	364	14.8	363	366	0.8	153	151	-1.3
MO,W	330	273	-17.3	337	279	-17.2	179	173	-3.4
NE	127	122	-3.9	217	132	-39.2	87	77	-11.5
ND	23	23	0	31	15	-51.6	17	25	47.1
SD	56	36	-35.7	65	40	-38.5	27	23	-14.8

Table F-8. (June 30, 2015—Continued)

Circuit and District	Filings			Terminations			Pending		
	2014	2015	Percent Change[1]	2014	2015	Percent Change[1]	2014[2]	2015	Percent Change[1]
9TH	**7,402**	**6,195**	**-16.3**	**8,740**	**6,798**	**-22.2**	**7,690**	**7,088**	**-7.8**
AK	18	21	16.7	17	22	29.4	16	15	-6.3
AZ	1,185	1,101	-7.1	1,413	1,107	-21.7	1,160	1,154	-0.5
CA,N	716	601	-16.1	951	740	-22.2	753	615	-18.3
CA,E	544	495	-9.0	640	596	-6.9	775	674	-13.0
CA,C	2,418	1,968	-18.6	2,963	2,026	-31.6	2,655	2,598	-2.1
CA,S	273	223	-18.3	333	308	-7.5	391	306	-21.7
HI	89	60	-32.6	84	75	-10.7	94	79	-16.0
ID	162	263	62.3	169	141	-16.6	128	250	95.3
MT	53	46	-13.2	41	61	48.8	68	53	-22.1
NV	312	263	-15.7	325	283	-12.9	487	467	-4.1
OR	559	479	-14.3	527	502	-4.7	212	188	-11.3
WA,E	131	56	-57.3	138	137	-0.7	188	107	-43.1
WA,W	936	617	-34.1	1,135	798	-29.7	746	565	-24.3
GUAM	5	2	-	4	2	-	4	4	-
NMI	1	0	-	0	0	-	13	13	0.0
10TH	**2,024**	**1,762**	**-12.9**	**2,377**	**2,002**	**-15.8**	**2,610**	**2,370**	**-9.2**
CO	779	572	-26.6	880	700	-20.5	698	570	-18.3
KS	342	351	2.6	442	390	-11.8	886	847	-4.4
NM	123	121	-1.6	185	179	-3.2	220	162	-26.4
OK,N	70	70	0.0	77	73	-5.2	51	48	-5.9
OK,E	24	19	-20.8	25	23	-8.0	17	13	-23.5
OK,W	119	305	156.3	123	160	30.1	145	290	100.0
UT	517	291	-43.7	592	427	-27.9	550	414	-24.7
WY	50	33	-34.0	53	50	-5.7	43	26	-39.5
11TH	**5,026**	**5,181**	**3.1**	**6,013**	**5,297**	**-11.9**	**9,093**	**8,980**	**-1.2**
AL,N	354	582	64.4	417	570	36.7	384	398	3.6
AL,M	267	266	-0.4	290	249	-14.1	171	188	9.9
AL,S	125	199	59.2	107	140	30.8	91	150	64.8
FL,N	83	64	-22.9	100	59	-41.0	72	77	6.9
FL,M	1,947	1,858	-4.6	2,463	2,018	-18.1	2,782	2,623	-5.7
FL,S	1,069	872	-18.4	1,231	992	-19.4	981	861	-12.2
GA,N	714	917	28.4	917	834	-9.1	4,315	4,398	1.9
GA,M	276	198	-28.3	263	217	-17.5	137	118	-13.9
GA,S	191	225	17.8	225	218	-3.1	160	167	4.4

[1] Percent change not computed when fewer than 10 cases reported for the previous period.
[2] Revised.

PART III

GOVERNMENT DEPARTMENTS AND AGENCIES

K. FEDERAL GOVERNMENT
U.S. Executive Branch

THE PRESIDENT OF THE UNITED STATES
The White House
1600 Pennsylvania Avenue, NW
Washington, DC 20500
(202) 456-1414
www.whitehouse.gov/president/

THE CABINET
The White House
1600 Pennsylvania Avenue, NW
Washington, DC 20500

EXECUTIVE OFFICE OF THE PRESIDENT
The White House
1600 Pennsylvania Avenue, NW
Washington, DC 20500

THE WHITE HOUSE OFFICE
1600 Pennsylvania Avenue, NW
Washington, DC 20500
(202) 456-1414
(202) 456-2461 FAX
www.whitehouse.gov

OFFICE OF MANAGEMENT AND BUDGET
New Executive Office Building
Washington, DC 20503
(202) 395-3080
www.whitehouse.gov/omb

COUNCIL OF ECONOMIC ADVISERS
Seventeenth and Pennsylvania Avenue, NW
Washington, DC 20502
(202) 395-5084
www.whitehouse.gov/cea

---

* Adapted from the 2015 Edition (July) U.S. Government Manual.

NATIONAL SECURITY COUNCIL
Eisenhower Executive Office Building
Washington, DC 20504
(202) 456-1414
www.whitehouse.gov/nsc

OFFICE OF THE UNITED STATES TRADE REPRESENTATIVE
600 Seventeenth Street NW
Washington, DC 20508
(202) 395-3230
www.ustr.gov

COUNCIL ON ENVIRONMENTAL QUALITY
722 Jackson Place NW
Washington, DC 20503
(202) 456-6224 or (202) 395-5750
(202) 456-2710 FAX
www.whitehouse.gov/administration/eop/ceq

OFFICE OF SCIENCE AND TECHNOLOGY POLICY
Eisenhower Executive Office Building
1650 Pennsylvania Avenue, NW
Washington, DC 20502
202-456-4444
202-456-6021 FAX
www.ostp.gov

OFFICE OF ADMINISTRATION
Eisenhower Executive Office Building
1650 Pennsylvania Avenue NW
Washington, DC 20503
(202) 456-2861
www.whitehouse.gov/oa

OFFICE OF NATIONAL DRUG CONTROL POLICY
Executive Office of the President
Washington, DC 20503
(202) 395-6700
(202) 395-6708 FAX
www.ondcp.gov

OFFICE OF THE VICE PRESIDENT OF THE UNITED STATES
Eisenhower Executive Office Building
Washington, DC 20501
(202) 456-7549
www.whitehouse.gov/vicepresident/

OFFICE OF POLICY DEVELOPMENT
Domestic Policy Council
Room 469
Eisenhower Executive Office Building
Washington, DC 20502
(202) 456-5594
www.whitehouse.gov/administration/eop/dpc
National Economic council
Room 235
Eisenhower Executive Office Building
Washington, DC 20502
(202) 456-2800
www.whitehouse.gov/administration/eop/nec

Executive Departments

DEPARTMENT OF AGRICULTURE
1400 Independence Avenue SW
Washington, DC 20250
202-720-4623
www.usda.gov

Farm Service Agency (FSA)
Office of External Affairs
Farm Service Agency
Department of Agriculture, Stop 0506
1400 Independence Avenue SW
Washington, DC 20250
202-720-7807
http://www.fsa.usda.gov/index

Information Division
Foreign Agricultural Service
Department of Agriculture, Stop 1004
1400 Independence Avenue SW
Washington, DC 20250
202-720-7115
Fax, 202-720-1727

Public Affairs Division
Foreign Agricultural Service, Stop 1004
1400 Independence Avenue SW
Department of Agriculture
Washington, DC 20250-1004
202-720-7115
Fax, 202-720-1727
http://www.fas.usda.gov

Office of the Administrator
Risk Management Agency
Department of Agriculture, Stop 0801
1400 Independence Avenue SW
Washington, DC 20250
202-690-2803
http://www.rma.usda.gov

Office of Public Information
Center for Nutrition Policy and Promotion, Suite 200
1120 20th Street NW
Washington, DC 20036-3406
202-418-2312
http://www.cnpp.usda.gov

Public Information Officer
Food and Nutrition Service
Department of Agriculture
3101 Park Center Drive
Alexandria, VA 22302
703-305-2286

Food Safety and Inspection Service (FSIS)
Assistant Administrator
Office of Public Affairs and Consumer Education
Department of Agriculture
1400 Independence Avenue SW
Washington, DC 20250
202-720-3884
http://www.fsis.usda.gov

Public Affairs Staff
Agricultural Marketing Service
Department of Agriculture, Room 2532
South Agriculture Building, Stop 0273
1400 Independence Ave, SW
Washington, DC 20250
202-720-8998
http://www.ams.usda.gov

Animal and Plant Health Inspection Service (APHIS)
Legislative and Public Affairs
Animal and Plant Health Inspection Service
Department of Agriculture
1400 Independence Avenue SW
Washington, DC 20250
202-799-7030
https://www.aphis.usda.gov/wps/portal/aphis/home

Grain Inspection, Packers, and Stockyards Administration
Department of Agriculture
1400 Independence Avenue SW

Washington, DC 20250
202-720-0219
http://www.gipsa.usda.gov

Forest Service (FS)
1400 Independence Ave., SW
Washington, D.C. 20250
800-832-1355
http://www.fs.fed.us/research/research-topics

Natural Resources Conservation Service (NRCS)
Public Affairs Division
1400 Independence Ave., SW, Room 6121-S
Washington, DC 20250
202-720-3210
Fax: 202-720-1564
http://www.nrcs.usda.gov/wps/portal/nrcs/site/national/home

Agricultural Research Service (ARS)
Department of Agriculture
1400 Independence Avenue SW
Washington, DC 20250
202-720-3656
Fax, 202-720-5427

Communications Staff
The National Institute of Food and Agriculture
Department of Agriculture
1400 Independence Avenue SW
Washington, DC 20250-2207
202-720-4651
Fax, 202-690-0289
http://nifa.usda.gov

Economic Research Service
Information Services Division
Department of Agriculture
1400 Independence Avenue SW
Washington, DC 20250
202-694-5100
Fax, 202-245-4781
http://www.ers.usda.gov

Customer Service Center
National Agricultural Statistics Service
Department of Agriculture
1400 Independence Avenue SW
Washington, DC 20250-2000
202-720-3878
http://www.nass.usda.gov

Rural Development Legislative and Public Affairs Staff
Department of Agriculture, Stop 0705
1400 Independence Avenue SW
Washington, DC 20250-0320
800-670-6553

Office of the Inspector General
U.S. Department of Agriculture
P.O. Box 23399
Washington, DC 20026
800-424-9121 or 202-690-1622
TDD, 202-690-1202
Fax, 202-690-2474

Office of Public Liaison
Office of Communications
U.S. Department of Agriculture
1400 Independence Avenue SW
Washington, DC 20250
202-720-2798

Office of Communications
Department of Agriculture
1400 Independence Avenue SW
Washington, DC 20250
202-720-4623

DEPARTMENT OF COMMERCE
Fourteenth Street and Constitution Avenue NW
Washington, DC 20230
202-482-2000
www.doc.gov

Office of Public Affairs
Department of Commerce
Fourteenth Street and Constitution Avenue NW, Room 5040

Washington, DC 20230
202-482-3263
http://www.doc.gov

Inspector General
Complaint Intake Unit
Mail Stop 7886
1401 Constitution Avenue, NW
Washington, DC 20230
202-482-2495 or 800-424-5197
TTD, 202-482-5923 or 856-860-6950
Fax, 855-569-9235
http://www.oig.doc.gov

Bureau of Industry and Security
Office of Public Affairs, Room 3895
Fourteenth Street and Constitution Avenue NW
Washington, DC 20230
202-482-2721
http://www.bis.doc.gov

Economic Development Administration
Department of Commerce
Washington, DC 20230
202-482-5081
Fax, 202-273-4781
http://www.eda.gov

Economics and Statistics Administration
Department of Commerce
Washington, DC 20230
202-482-6607
ESAwebmaster@doc.gov
http://www.esa.gov

Public Information Office
Bureau of Economic Analysis
Department of Commerce
Washington, DC 20230
202-606-9900
Fax, 202-606-5310

Public Information Office
Bureau of the Census
Department of Commerce
Washington, DC 20233
301-763-3030
Fax, 301-763-3762

International Trade Administration
Department of Commerce
Washington, DC 20230
202-482-3917
http://www.trade.gov

Office of the National Director
Minority Business Development Agency
Department of Commerce
Washington, DC 20230
202-482-2332
http://www.mbda.gov

Office of Communications and External Affairs
National Oceanic and Atmospheric Administration, Room 6013
Fourteenth Street and Constitution Avenue NW
Washington, DC 20230
202-482-6090
Fax, 202-482-3154
http://www.noaa.gov

National Environmental Satellite, Data, and Information Service
1335 East-West Highway
Silver Spring, MD 20910-3283
301-713-3578
Fax, 301-713-1249
http://www.nesdis.noaa.gov/about_nesdis.html

National Marine Fisheries Service
1315 East-West Highway
Silver Spring, MD 20910
301-713-2239
Fax, 301-713-1940
http://www.nmfs.noaa.gov

National Ocean Service
Room 13231, SSMC 4
1305 East-West Highway
Silver Spring, MD 20910
301-713-3074
Fax, 301-713-4307
http://www.nos.noaa.gov

National Weather Service–Executive Affairs
1325 East-West Highway
Silver Spring, MD 20910-3283
301-713-0675
Fax, 301-713-0049
http://www.weather.gov

Office of Marine and Aviation Operations
Suite 500
8403 Colesville Rd.
Silver Spring, MD 20910
301-713-7600
Fax, 301-713-1541
http://www.omao.noaa.gov/about.html

Office of Oceanic and Atmospheric Research
Room 11458
1315 East-West Highway
Silver Spring, MD 20910
301-713-2458
Fax, 301-713-0163
http://www.oar.noaa.gov

National Telecommunications and Information Administration
Department of Commerce
Washington, DC 20230
202-482-1551
http://www.ntia.doc.gov

National Institute of Standards and Technology
100 Bureau Drive, Mail Stop 1070
Gaithersburg, MD 20899-1070
301-975-6478 (NIST)
Fax, 301-926-1630
inquiries@nist.gov
http://www.nist.gov

National Technical Information Service
5301 Shawnee Road
Alexandria, VA 22312
703-605-6000 or 800-553-6847
http://www.ntis.gov

United States Patent and Trademark Office
600 Dulany Street
Alexandria, VA 22314
571-272-8700
http://www.uspto.gov

Office of the Chief Communications Officer
United States Patent and Trademark Office
600 Dulany Street
Alexandria, VA 22314
571-272-8400
http://www.uspto.gov

Commissioner for Patents
Office of Petitions
Alexandria, VA 22314
571-272-3282

DEPARTMENT OF DEFENSE
Office of the Secretary
The Pentagon
Washington, DC 20301-1155
703-545-6700
http://www.defense.gov

Director, Small Business Program
Office of the Secretary of Defense
1155 Defense Pentagon
Washington, DC 20301-3061
703- 545-0542
http://business.defense.gov/ForBusiness.aspx

Executive Services and Communications Directorate
Washington Headquarters Services
1155 Defense Pentagon
Washington, DC 20301-1155
703-571-1001
http://www.dtic.mil/whs/directives

Director, Directorate for Public Inquiry and Analysis
Office of the Assistant Secretary of Defense for Public Affairs
1400 Defense Pentagon
Washington, DC 20301-1400
703- 697-9312
http://www.defense.gov/Contact

Department of the Air Force
1690 Air Force Pentagon
Washington, DC 20330-1670
703-697-6061
http://www.af.mil

Office of the Director of Public Affairs
Department of the Air Force
1690 Air Force Pentagon
Washington, DC 20330-1670
703-697-6061
http://www.af.mil

Department of the Army
The Pentagon
Washington, DC 20310
703-695-6518
http://www.army.mil

U.S. Army Public Affairs
Community Relations Division
Office of the Chief of Public Affairs
1500 Army Pentagon
Washington, DC 20310-1500
http://www.army.mil/info/institution/publicAffairs

U.S. Army Forces Command
FORSCOM Public Affairs Office
910-570-7200
http://www.forscom.army.mil

U.S. Army Training and Doctrine Command
TRADOC Public Affairs Office
757-501-5876
http://www.tradoc.army.mil

U.S. Army Materiel Command
AMC Public Affairs Office
256-450-7978
http://www.army.mil/amc

U.S. Army Pacific
USARPAC Public Affairs
808-438-9761
http://www.usarpac.army.mil

U.S. Army Europe
USAREUR Public Affairs Office
011-49-0611-705-3045 or 3058
http://www.eur.army.mil

U.S. Army Central
USARCENT Public Affairs Office
803-885-8879 or 8266
http://www.arcent.army.mil

U.S. Army North
USARNORTH Public Affairs Office
210-221-0015
http://www.arnorth.army.mil

U.S. Army South
ARSOUTH Public Affairs Office
210-216-2497
http://www.arsouth.army.mil

U.S. Army Africa / Southern European Task Force
USARAF / SETAF Public Affairs Office
011-39-0444-71-7618
http://www.usaraf.army.mil

U.S. Army Special Operations Command
USASOC Public Affairs Office
910-432-6005
http://www.soc.mil

U.S. Army Military Surface Deployment and Distribution Command
SDDC Public Affairs Office
618-220-6284
http://www.sddc.army.mil

U.S. Army Space and Missile Defense Command/Army Strategic
Command
SMDC Public Affairs Office
256-955-3887
*http://www.army.mil/info/organization/unitsandcommands/command
structure/smdc*

Superintendent
Arlington National Cemetery
Arlington, VA 22211
703-614-0615
http://www.arlingtoncemetery.mil

Army National Guard
1411 Jefferson Davis Highway
Arlington, VA 22202-3231
703-627-7273
http://www.arng.army.mil

U.S. Army Cadet Command, Recruiting, Retention and Operations
Directorate
ATCC-OP
55 Patch Road
Fort Monroe, VA 23651
757-788-3770
http://www.goarmy.com/rotc/find-schools.html

U.S. Army Human Resources Command
1600 Spearhead Division Avenue
Fort Knox, KY 40122
888-276-9472
https://www.hrc.army.mil

U.S. Army Recruiting Command
1307 Third Avenue
Fort Knox, KY 40121-2726
502-626-0722 or 866-684-1571

Deputy Assistant Secretary of the Army–Procurement, Office of the
Assistant Secretary of the Army–Acquisition, Logistics and Technology
103 Army Pentagon
Washington, DC 20310-0103
703-695-2488
http://www.micc.army.mil/contracting-offices.asp

National Audiovisual Center
National Technical Information Service
5301 Shawnee Road
Alexandria, VA 22312
800-553-6847
http://www.ntis.gov/Index.aspx

Army Judge Advocate Recruiting Office
9275 Gunston Road
Suite 4000
Fort Belvoir, VA 22060
866-276-9524
http://www.goarmy.com/jag

Commander
U.S. Army Research, Development and Engineering Command
Attn: AMSRD–PA
3071 Aberdeen Boulevard, Room 103
Aberdeen Proving Ground, MD 21005
410-306-4489 (Public Affairs) or 4549 (Media Relations)
http://www.army.mil/info/organization/unitsandcommands/command structure/rdecom

Office of Small Business Programs
Office of the Secretary of the Army
106 Army Pentagon, Room 3B514
Washington, DC 20310-0106
703-697-2868
Fax, 703-693-3898
http://www.micc.army.mil/small-business.asp

Director of Admissions
U.S. Military Academy
606 Thayer Road, Building 606
West Point, NY 10996
845-938-4041
http://www.usma.edu

Department of the Navy
The Pentagon
Washington, DC 20350
703-697-7391
http://www.navy.mil

Office of the Judge Advocate General
Department of the Navy
Washington Navy Yard, Suite 3000
1322 Patterson Avenue SE
Washington Navy Yard, DC 20374-5066
202-685-5190
http://www.navy.mil/local/jag/index.asp

Naval Criminal Investigative Service
27130 Telegraph Road
Quantico, VA 22134
877-579-3648
http://www.ncis.navy.mil

Public Affairs Office
Office of Naval Research
One Liberty Center
875 North Randolph Street
Arlington, VA 22203-1995
703-696-5031
http://www.onr.navy.mil

Commander
Naval Air Systems Command
47123 Buse Road, Building 2272, Suite 540
Patuxent River, MD 20670-1547
301-757-7825
http://www.navair.navy.mil

Public Affairs
Naval Network Warfare Command
112 Lake View Parkway
Suffolk, VA 23435
757-203-0205
http://www.public.navy.mil/fcc-c10f/nnwc/Pages/default.aspx

NETC Office of Public Affairs
250 Dallas Street
Pensacola, FL 32508-5220
850-452-4858
http://www.navy.mil/local/cnet/

Commander
Naval Facilities Engineering Command and Chief of Civil Engineers
Washington Navy Yard
1322 Patterson Avenue SE., Suite 1000
Washington, DC 20374-5065
202-685-1423
http://www.navy.mil/local/navfachq

Office of Public Affairs
Office of Naval Intelligence
Department of the Navy
4251 Suitland Road
Washington, DC 20395-5720
301-669-5670
http://www.oni.navy.mil

Bureau of Naval Personnel
Department of the Navy
Federal Office Building 2
Washington, DC 20370-5000
703-614-2000
http://www.navy.mil/cnp/index.asp

Bureau of Medicine and Surgery
Department of the Navy
2300 E Street NW
Washington, DC 20373-5300
202-762-3211
http://www.med.navy.mil

Commander
Naval Meteorology and Oceanography Command
1100 Balch Boulevard
Stennis Space Center, MS 39529-5005
228-688-4384
http://www.navmetoccom.navy.mil

Oceanographer of the Navy
U.S. Naval Observatory
3450 Massachusetts Avenue NW
Washington, DC 20392-1800
202-762-1026
http://www.usno.navy.mil/USNO

Office of Public Affairs
Naval Sea Systems Command
1333 Isaac Hull Avenue SE.
Washington Navy Yard, DC 20376-1010
202-781-4123
http://www.navsea.navy.mil

Commander
Space and Naval Warfare Systems Command
4301 Pacific Highway
San Diego, CA 92110-3127
619-524-3428
http://www.spawar.navy.mil

Director
Strategic Systems Programs
Department of the Navy
Nebraska Avenue Complex
287 Somers Court NW, Suite 10041
Washington, DC 20393-5446
202-764-1608
http://www.ssp.navy.mil

Commander
Naval Supply Systems Command
5450 Carlisle Pike
P.O. Box 2050
Mechanicsburg, PA 17055-0791
717-605-3565
http://www.navy.mil/local/navsup

Commander
Navy Warfare Development Command
686 Cushing Road
Sims Hall
Newport, RI 02841
401-841-2833
http://www.navy.mil/local/nwdc

Office of Naval Research–Public Affairs
One Liberty Center
875 N. Randolph Street
Arlington, VA 22203-1995

703-696-5031
osbp.info@navy.mil
http://smallbusiness.navy.mil

Office of Small Business Programs
720 Kennon Avenue SE., Building 36, Room 207
Washington Navy Yard, DC 20374-5015
202-685-6485
http://www.secnav.navy.mil/eie/Pages/Environment.aspx

Deputy Assistant Secretary–Environment
1000 Navy Pentagon, Room 4A674
Washington, DC 20350-1000
703-614-5493
http://www.navy.mil

Office of Information
Department of the Navy
1200 Navy Pentagon, Room 4B463
Washington, DC 20350-1200
703-695-0965
http://www.navyoutreach.org/newsite2

Office of Information
Department of the Navy
1200 Navy Pentagon
Washington, DC 20350-1200
703-697-7391 or 703-697-5342
http://www.navy.mil

Superintendent
U.S. Naval Observatory
3450 Massachusetts Avenue NW
Washington, DC 20392-5420
202-762-1438

United States Marine Corps
Commandant of the Marine Corps
Headquarters
U.S. Marine Corps, 2 Navy Annex (Pentagon 5D773)
Washington, DC 20380-1775
703-614-1034
http://www.usmc.mil

Commandant of the Marine Corps
Headquarters
U.S. Marine Corps (PHC), Room 5E774
The Pentagon
Washington, DC 20380-1775
703-614-4309
http://www.hqmc.marines.mil/cmc/Home.aspx

Director of Public Affairs
Headquarters
U.S. Marine Corps, 2 Navy Annex–Pentagon 5D773
Washington, DC 20380-1775
703-614-1492
http://www.marines.mil

United States Naval Academy
121 Blake Road
Annapolis, MD 21402-5018
410-293-1500
http://www.usna.edu

Defense Agencies

Defense Advanced Research Projects Agency
675 North Randolph Street
Arlington, VA 22203-2114
703-526-6630
http://www.darpa.mil

Defense Commissary Agency
1300 E Avenue
Fort Lee, VA 23801-1800
804-734-8720
http://www.commissaries.com

Defense Contract Audit Agency
8725 John J. Kingman Road, Suite 2135
Fort Belvoir, VA 22060-6219
703-767-3265
dcaaweb@dcaa.mil
http://www.dcaa.mil

Defense Contract Management Agency
3901 A Avenue
Fort Lee, VA 23801
703-428-1700
http://www.dcma.mil

Defense Finance and Accounting Service
4800 Mark Center Drive, Suite 08J25-01
Alexandria, VA 22350-3000
571-372-7883
http://www.dfas.mil

Defense Information Systems Agency
P.O. Box 549
Command Building
Fort Meade, MD 20755
301-225-6000
dia-pao@dia.mil
http://www.disa.mil

Defense Intelligence Agency
200 MacDill Boulevard
Washington DC 20340-5100
202-231-0800
dia-pao@dia.mil
http://www.dia.mil

Defense Legal Services Agency
The Pentagon
Washington, DC 20301-1600
703-695-3341
http://www.dod.mil/dodgc

Defense Logistics Agency
8725 John J. Kingman Road, Suite 2533
Fort Belvoir, VA 22060-6221
703-767-5264
http://www.dla.mil

Defense Security Cooperation Agency
201 Twelfth Street South, Suite 203
Arlington, VA 22202-5408
703-604-6605
info@dsca.mil
http://www.dsca.mil

Defense Security Service
27130 Telegraph Road
Quantico, VA 22134
703-617-2352
http://www.dss.mil

Defense Threat Reduction Agency
8725 John J. Kingman Road, MS 6201
Fort Belvoir, VA 22060-6201
703-767-7594
http://www.dtra.mil

Missile Defense Agency
5700 Eighteenth Street, Bldg 245
Fort Belvoir, VA 22060-5573
703-695-6420
mda.info@mda.mil
http://www.mda.mil

National Geospatial-Intelligence Agency
7500 Geoint Drive, MS N73-OCCAE
Springfield, Virginia 22150
571-557-7300
http://www.nga.mil

National Security Agency / Central Security Service
Fort Meade, MD 20755-6248
301-688-6524 or 301-688-6198
http://www.nsa.gov

Pentagon Force Protection Agency
9000 Defense Pentagon
Washington, DC 20301
703-697-1001
http://www.pfpa.mil

Joint Service Schools

Defense Acquisition University
9820 Belvoir Road
Fort Belvoir, VA 22060-5565
703-805-2764
http://www.dau.mil

Director
Operations Support Group
Defense Acquisition University
9820 Belvoir Road
Fort Belvoir, VA 22060-5565
800-845-7606
http://www.dau.mil

National Intelligence University
Defense Intelligence Analysis Center
Washington, DC 20340-5100
202-231-5466
http://www.ni-u.edu

Admissions Office
National Intelligence University
200 MacDill Blvd (MCA-2)
Washington, DC 20340-5100
202-231-5466 or 202-231-3319
http://www.ni-u.edu

National Defense University
300 Fifth Avenue, Building 62
Fort McNair, DC 20319-5066
202-685-2649
http://www.ndu.edu

College of International Security Affairs
260 Fifth Avenue, Building 64
Fort McNair, DC 20319-5066
202-685-3870
http://cisa.ndu.edu

Dwight D. Eisenhower School for National Security and Resource
Strategy
408 Fourth Avenue, Building 59
Fort McNair, DC 20319-5062
202-685-4333

Information Resources Management College
300 Fifth Avenue, Building 62
Fort McNair, DC 20319-5066
202-685-6300
http://icollege.ndu.edu

Joint Forces Staff College
7800 Hampton Boulevard
Norfolk, VA 23511-1702
757-443-6124
http://jfsc.ndu.edu

National War College
300 D Street SW, Building 61
Fort McNair, DC 20319-5078
202-685-3674 or 202-685-6461
http://nwc.ndu.edu

Uniformed Services University of the Health Sciences
4301 Jones Bridge Road
Bethesda, MD 20814-4799
301-295-3190
http://www.usuhs.mil

President
Uniformed Services University of the Health Sciences
4301 Jones Bridge Road
Bethesda, MD 20814-4799
301-295-3013
http://www.usuhs.mil

DEPARTMENT OF EDUCATION
400 Maryland Avenue SW
Washington, DC 20202
202-401-2000
TTY, 800-437-0833
http://www.ed.gov

Information Resources Center
Department of Education
Room 5E248 (FB–6)
400 Maryland Avenue SW
Washington, DC 20202
800-872-5327
http://www.ed.gov

Federal Aided Corporations

American Printing House for the Blind
P.O. Box 6085
Louisville, KY 40206
502-895-2405
http://www.aph.org

Gallaudet University
800 Florida Avenue NE.
Washington, DC 20002
202-651-5000
http://www.gallaudet.edu

Howard University
2400 Sixth Street NW
Washington, DC 20059
202-806-6100
http://www.howard.edu

National Technical Institute for the Deaf
Rochester Institute of Technology
52 Lomb Memorial Drive
Rochester, NY 14623
585-475-6317
http://www.ntid.rit.edu

DEPARTMENT OF ENERGY
1000 Independence Avenue SW
Washington, DC 20585
202-586-5000
http://www.energy.gov

Bonneville Power Administration
905 Eleventh Avenue NE.
Portland, OR 97232-4169
503-230-3000 or 800-282-3713
http://www.bpa.gov/Pages/home.aspx

Southeastern Power Administration
1166 Athens Tech Road
Elberton, GA 30635-4578
706-213-3800
http://www.energy.gov/sepa/southeastern-power-administration

Southwestern Power Administration
Suite 1600, Williams Center Tower One
One West Third Street
Tulsa, OK 74103-3532
918-595-6600
http://www.swpa.gov

Western Area Power Administration
12155 West Alameda Parkway
Lakewood, CO 80228-1213
720-962-7000
http://www.wapa.gov/Pages/western.aspx

Office of Public Affairs
Department of Energy
1000 Independence Avenue SW
Washington, DC 20585
202-586-4940
http://www.energy.gov/contact-us

Federal Energy Regulatory Commission
888 First Street NE.
Washington, DC 20426
202-502-8055
http://www.ferc.gov

DEPARTMENT OF HEALTH AND HUMAN SERVICES
200 Independence Avenue SW
Washington, DC 20201
202-690-6343
http://www.hhs.gov

Administration for Children and Families
370 L'Enfant Promenade SW
Washington, DC 20447
202-401-9200
http://www.acf.hhs.gov

Administration for Community Living
1 Massachusetts Avenue NW, Suite 5100
Washington, DC 20201
202-401-4634
TTY, 800-877-8339
http://www.acl.gov

Agency for Healthcare Research and Quality
540 Gaither Road
Rockville, MD 20850
301-427-1364
http://www.ahrq.gov

Agency for Toxic Substances and Disease Registry
MS E–61, 4770 Buford Highway NE.
Atlanta, GA 30341
770-488-0604
http://www.atsdr.cdc.gov

Centers for Disease Control and Prevention
1600 Clifton Road
Atlanta, GA 30333
800-232-4636
http://www.cdc.gov

Centers for Medicare and Medicaid Services
7500 Security Boulevard
Baltimore, MD 21244
410-786-3000
http://www.cms.gov

Food and Drug Administration
10903 New Hampshire Avenue
Silver Spring, MD 20993
888-463-6332
http://www.fda.gov

Health Resources and Services Administration
5600 Fishers Lane
Rockville, MD 20857
301-443-3376
http://www.hrsa.gov

Indian Health Service
801 Thompson Avenue
Rockville, MD 20852
301-443-2650
http://www.ihs.gov

National Institutes of Health
1 Center Drive
Bethesda, MD 20892
301-496-4000
http://www.nih.gov

Substance Abuse and Mental Health Services Administration
1 Choke Cherry Road
Rockville, MD 20857
240-276-2130
http://www.samhsa.gov

DEPARTMENT OF HOMELAND SECURITY
Washington, DC 20528
202-282-8000
http://www.dhs.gov

Office of Public Affairs
Department of Homeland Security
Washington, DC 20528
202-282-8010
http://www.dhs.gov/office-public-affairs

DEPARTMENT OF HOUSING AND URBAN DEVELOPMENT
451 Seventh Street SW
Washington, DC 20410
202-708-1422
http://www.hud.gov

Office of Public Affairs
Department of Housing and Urban Development
451 Seventh Street SW
Washington, DC 20410
202-708-0980
http://www.hud.gov

Office of Community Planning and Development
202-708-2690
http://portal.hud.gov/hudportal/HUD?src=/program_offices/comm_planning

Office of Fair Housing and Equal Opportunity
202-708-4252
http://portal.hud.gov/hudportal/HUD?src=/program_offices/fair_housing_equal_opp

Government National Mortgage Association--Ginnie Mae
202-708-0926
http://www.ginniemae.gov/pages/default.aspx

Office of Housing
202-708-3600
http://portal.hud.gov/hudportal/HUD?src=/program_offices/housing

Office of Lead Hazard Control and Healthy Homes
202-755-1785
http://portal.hud.gov/hudportal/HUD?src=/program_offices/healthy_homes

Office of Public and Indian Housing
202-708-0950
*http://portal.hud.gov/hudportal/HUD?src=/program_offices/public_indian_
housing/ih*

DEPARTMENT OF THE INTERIOR
1849 C Street NW
Washington, DC 20240
202-208-3100
http://www.doi.gov

Office of Acquisition and Property Management
1849 C Street NW, Rm. 4262
Washington, DC 20240
202-513-7554
https://www.doi.gov/businesses

Bureau of Indian Affairs
Department of the Interior
1849 C Street NW
Washington, DC 20240
202-208-3710
http://www.bia.gov

Bureau of Indian Education
Department of the Interior
1849 C Street NW
Washington, DC 20240
202-208-3710
http://www.bie.edu

Bureau of Land Management
Department of the Interior
1849 C Street NW
Washington, DC 20240
202-912-7415
http://www.blm.gov

Bureau of Ocean Energy Management
Department of the Interior
1849 C Street NW
Washington, DC 20240
202-208-6474
http://www.boem.gov

Bureau of Reclamation
Department of the Interior
1849 C Street NW
Washington, DC 20240
202-513-0575
http://www.usbr.gov

Bureau of Safety and Environmental Enforcement
Department of the Interior
1849 C Street NW
Washington, DC 20240
202-208-3985
http://www.bsee.gov

National Park Service
Department of the Interior
1849 C Street NW
Washington, DC 20240
202-208-6843
http://www.nps.gov

Office of Surface Mining Reclamation and Enforcement
Department of the Interior
1951 Constitution Avenue NW
Washington, DC 20240
202-208-2565
TDD, 202-208-2694
http://www.osmre.gov

United States Fish and Wildlife Service
Department of the Interior
1849 C Street NW
Washington, DC 20240
703-358-4545
http://www.fws.gov

United States Geological Survey
12201 Sunrise Valley Drive
Reston, VA 20192
703-648-4000
ASK@usgs.gov
http://www.usgs.gov

DEPARTMENT OF JUSTICE
950 Pennsylvania Avenue NW
Washington, DC 20530
202-514-2000
http://www.justice.gov

Director
Community Relations Service
Department of Justice
Suite 2000, 600 E Street NW
Washington, DC 20530
202-305-2935
http://www.justice.gov/crs/contact-office

Office of the Pardon Attorney
Department of Justice
Suite 5E–508, 145 N Street NE
Washington, DC 20530
202-616-6070
http://www.justice.gov/pardon

Executive Officer
Office of the Solicitor General
Room 5142, 950 Pennsylvania Avenue NW
RFK Justice Building (Main)
Washington, DC 20530-0001
http://www.justice.gov/osg

Executive Office for U.S. Attorneys
Department of Justice
Room 2261, 950 Pennsylvania Avenue NW
Washington, DC 20530
202-514-1020
http://www.justice.gov/usao/eousa

Executive Office for U.S. Trustees
Department of Justice
Suite 6150, 441 G Street NW
Washington, DC 20530
202-307-1391
http://www.justice.gov/ust

Office of the Assistant Attorney General
Antitrust Division
Department of Justice
950 Pennsylvania Avenue NW
Washington, DC 20530
202-514-2401
http://www.justice.gov/atr

Office of the Assistant Attorney General
Civil Division
Department of Justice
Tenth Street and Pennsylvania Avenue NW
Washington, DC 20530
202-514-3301
http://www.justice.gov/civil

Executive Officer
Civil Rights Division
Department of Justice
950 Pennsylvania Avenue NW
Washington, DC 20035
202-514-4224
http://www.justice.gov/crt

Office of the Assistant Attorney General
Criminal Division
Department of Justice
Tenth Street and Pennsylvania Avenue NW
Washington, DC 20530
202-514-2601
http://www.justice.gov/criminal

Office of the Assistant Attorney General
Environment and Natural Resources Division
Department of Justice
Tenth Street and Pennsylvania Avenue NW
Washington, DC 20530
202-514-2701
http://justice.gov/enrd

Office of the Assistant Attorney General
National Security Division
Department of Justice
Tenth Street and Pennsylvania Avenue NW
Washington, DC 20530
202-514-5600
http://www.justice.gov/nsd

Office of the Assistant Attorney General
Tax Division
Department of Justice
Tenth Street and Pennsylvania Avenue NW
Washington, DC 20530
202-514-2901
http://www.justice.gov/tax

Office of Public Affairs
Department of Justice
Tenth Street and Constitution Avenue NW
Washington, DC 20530
202-514-2007
TDD, 202-786-5731
http://www.justice.gov/contact-us

Bureaus

Bureau of Alcohol, Tobacco, Firearms and Explosives
99 New York Avenue NE
Washington, DC 20226
202-648-8500
http://www.atf.gov

Bureau of Prisons
320 First Street NW
Washington, DC 20534
202-307-3198
http://www.bop.gov

Drug Enforcement Administration
8701 Morrissette Drive
Springfield, VA 22152
202-307-1000
http://www.dea.gov/index.shtml

Federal Bureau of Investigation
935 Pennsylvania Avenue NW
Washington, DC 20535
202-324-3000
http://www.fbi.gov

International Criminal Police Organization (INTERPOL)–Washington
Department of Justice
Washington, DC 20530
202-616-9000 or 202-616-8400
http://www.justice.gov/interpol-washington

Office of Justice Programs
810 Seventh Street NW
Washington, DC 20531
202-307-0703
askojp@ojp.usdoj.gov
http://www.ojp.gov

United States Marshals Service
Department of Justice
Washington, DC 20530
202-307-9000
http://www.usmarshals.gov

Offices and Boards

Executive Office for Immigration Review
Falls Church, VA 22041
703-305-0289
http://www.usdoj.gov/eoir

Foreign Claims Settlement Commission of the United States
Suite 6002, 600 E Street NW
Washington, DC 20579
202-616-6975 or 202-616-6993
http://www.justice.gov/fcsc

Office of Community Oriented Policing Services
935 N. Street NE
Washington, DC 20530
202-514-2058
http://www.cops.usdoj.gov

Office on Violence Against Women
145 N Street NE., Suite 10W–121
Washington, DC 20530
202-307-6026
http://www.justice.gov/ovw

United States Parole Commission
90 K Street NE
Washington, DC 20530
202-346-7000
http://www.usdoj.gov/uspc

DEPARTMENT OF LABOR
200 Constitution Avenue NW
Washington, DC 20210
202-693-6000
http://www.dol.gov

Office of the Solicitor
Department of Labor
200 Constitution Avenue NW
Washington, DC 20210
202-693-5260
http://www.dol.gov/sol

Office of the Director
Office of Workers' Compensation Programs
Department of Labor
Room S-3524, 200 Constitution Avenue NW
Washington, DC 20210
202-343-5580
http://www.dol.gov/owcp

Office of Contracts Management
Suite N–4643, 200 Constitution Avenue, NW
Washington, DC 20210
202-693-3701
http://www.dol.gov

Office of Inspector General
Department of Labor
200 Constitution Avenue NW, Room S–5506
Washington, DC 20210
202-693-6999

800-347-3756
Fax, 202-693-7020
https://www.oig.dol.gov/hotline.htm

Office of Public Affairs
Department of Labor
Room S–1032, 200 Constitution Avenue NW
Washington, DC 20210
202-693-4650
http://www.dol.gov/dol/contact/media-contact-regional.htm

Bureau of International Labor Affairs
200 Constitution Avenue NW
Washington, DC 20210
202-693-4770
http://www.dol.gov/ilab

Bureau of Labor Statistics
2 Massachusetts Avenue NE
Washington, DC 20212
202-691-7800
800-877-8339 (TDD)
http://www.bls.gov

Employee Benefits Security Administration
Department of Labor
Washington, DC 20210
866-444-3272
http://www.dol.gov/ebsa

Employment and Training Administration
Department of Labor
Washington, DC 20520
877-872-5627
http://www.doleta.gov

Mine Safety and Health Administration
201 12th Street South, Suite 400
Arlington, Virginia 22202
202-693-9400
http://www.msha.gov

Occupational Safety and Health Administration
Department of Labor
Washington, DC 20210
800-321-6742
http://www.osha.gov

Veterans' Employment and Training Service
Department of Labor
Washington, DC 20210
866-487-2365
http://www.dol.gov/vets

Wage and Hour Division
Department of Labor
Washington, DC 20210
866-487-9243
http://www.dol.gov/whd

Women's Bureau
Department of Labor
Washington, DC 20210
202-693-6710
http://www.dol.gov/wb

DEPARTMENT OF STATE
2201 C Street NW
Washington, DC 20520
202-647-4000
http://www.state.gov

Bureau of Administration
703-875-7000
http://www.state.gov/m/a

Bureau of Arms Control, Verification and Compliance
202-647-6830
Fax, 202-647-1321
http://www.state.gov/t/avc

Bureau of Budget and Planning
202-647-8515
http://www.state.gov/s/d/rm

Bureau of the Comptroller and Global Financial Services
202-647-7490
http://www.state.gov/m/cgfs

Bureau of Conflict Stabilization Operations
202-663-0323
http://www.state.gov/j/cso

Bureau of Consular Affairs
http://travel.state.gov/content/travel/en.html

Bureau of Counterterrorism
Office of Public Affairs
202-647-1845
http://www.state.gov/j/ct

Bureau of Democracy, Human Rights, and Labor
202-647-1337
http://www.state.gov/j/drl

Bureau of Diplomatic Security Office of Public Affairs
571-345-2502
http://www.state.gov/m/ds

Bureau of Economic and Business Affairs
202-647-7971
Fax, 202-647-5713
http://www.state.gov/e/eb

Bureau of Educational and Cultural Affairs
202-632-6445
Fax, 202-632-2701
http://exchanges.state.gov

Bureau of Energy Resources
202-647-3423
http://www.state.gov/e/enr

Foreign Service Institute
703-302-6729
Fax, 703-302-7227
http://www.state.gov/m/fsi

Bureau of Information Resource Management
202-647-2977
http://www.state.gov/m/irm

Office of Inspector General
202-663-0340
http://www.oig.state.gov

Bureau of Intelligence and Research
202-647-1080
http://www.state.gov/s/inr

Bureau of International Information Programs
202-632-9942
Fax, 202-632-9901
http://www.state.gov/r/iip

Bureau of International Narcotics and Law Enforcement Affairs
202-647-2842
Fax, 202-736-4045
http://www.state.gov/j/inl

Bureau of International Organization Affairs
202-647-9600
Fax, 202-647-2175
http://www.state.gov/p/io

Bureau of International Security and Nonproliferation
202-647-9868
Fax, 202-736-4863
http://www.state.gov/t/isn

Office of the Legal Adviser
202-647-9598
Fax, 202-647-7096
http://www.state.gov/s/l

Bureau of Legislative Affairs
202-647-1714
http://www.state.gov/s/h

Office of Medical Services
202-663-1649
Fax, 202-663-1613
http://www.state.gov/m/med

Bureau of Oceans and International Environmental and Scientific Affairs
202-647-6961
Fax, 202-647-0217
http://www.state.gov/e/oes

Bureau of Overseas Buildings Operations
703-875-4131
Fax, 703-875-5043
http://overseasbuildings.state.gov

Bureau of Political-Military Affairs
202-647-9022
Fax, 202-736-4413
http://www.state.gov/t/pm

Bureau of Population, Refugees, and Migration
202-453-9339
Fax, 202-453-9394
http://www.state.gov/j/prm

Office of the Chief of Protocol
202-647-1735
Fax, 202-647-1560
http://www.state.gov/s/cpr

Bureau of Public Affairs
202-647-6575
http://www.state.gov/r/pa

Office of Acquisitions Management (A/LM/AQM)
Department of State
P.O. Box 9115
Arlington, VA 22219
703-516-1706
Fax, 703-875-6085
http://www.state.gov/m/a/c8020.htm

Office of Information Programs and Services
A/GIS/IPS/RL, Department of State, SA-2
Washington, DC 20522-8100
http://foia.state.gov/Search/Search.aspx

Office of Children's Issues
Bureau of Consular Affairs
Department of State
SA-29, 2201 C Street NW
Washington, DC 20520-4818
888-407-4747 or 202-501-4444 (international)
http://travel.state.gov/content/adoptionsabroad/en.html

Overseas Citizens Services
Bureau of Consular Affairs
Department of State
SA–29, 2201 C Street NW
Washington, DC 20520
http://travel.state.gov/content/passports/english/emergencies.html

Correspondence Branch
Passport Services
Room 510, 1111 Nineteenth Street NW
Washington, DC 20524
http://travel.state.gov/content/travel/english.html

Office of Public Communication
Public Information Service
Bureau of Public Affairs
Department of State
Washington, DC 20520
202-647-6575
http://www.state.gov/r/pa/pl/index.htm

DEPARTMENT OF TRANSPORTATION
1200 New Jersey Avenue SE
Washington, DC 20590
202-366-4000
http://www.dot.gov

Office of the Secretary
Human Resource Operations
1200 New Jersey Avenue SE., Room W75–340
Washington, DC 20590
202-366-9391
800-525-2878
https://www.transportation.gov/careers

DOT Inspector General
1200 New Jersey Avenue SE.
West Building–7th floor
Washington, DC 20590
202-366-1461
800-424-9071
https://www.oig.dot.gov/Hotline

Government Publishing Office and the National Technical Information
Service
5285 Port Royal Road
Springfield, VA 22151
http://www.gpo.gov/customers/p-i-sales.htm

Technical Library
Room 2200
1200 New Jersey Avenue SE
Washington, DC 20590
202-366-0745
library@dot.gov
http://ntl.bts.gov/about_ntl.html

Law Library
Room W12–300
1200 New Jersey Avenue SE
Washington, DC 20590
202-366-0746
library@dot.gov
http://ntl.bts.gov/about_ntl.html

Surface Transportation Board–Office of Public Assistance,
Governmental Affairs, and Compliance
395 E Street SW
Washington, DC 20423-0001
202-245-0238
http://www.stb.dot.gov/stb/about/overview.html

Surface Transportation Board–Office of the Secretary
395 E Street SW
Washington, DC 20423-0001
202-245-0232
http://www.stb.dot.gov/stb/about/overview.html

Department of Transportation–Office of Public Affairs
1200 New Jersey Avenue SE
Washington, DC 20590
202-366-5580
https://www.transportation.gov/briefingroom/administration-news

Federal Aviation Administration
800 Independence Avenue SW
Washington, DC 20591
202-366-4000
866-835-5322
http://www.faa.gov

Federal Highway Administration
1200 New Jersey Avenue SE
Washington, DC 20590
202-366-0650
http://www.fhwa.dot.gov

Federal Railroad Administration
1200 New Jersey Avenue, SE
West Building, Washington, DC 20590
202-493-6014
http://www.fra.dot.gov

National Highway Traffic Safety Administration
1200 New Jersey Avenue SE
Washington, DC 20590
202-366-9550
888-327-4236
http://www.nhtsa.gov

Federal Transit Administration
1200 New Jersey Avenue SE
Washington, DC 20590
202-366-4043
http://www.fta.dot.gov

Maritime Administration
1200 New Jersey Avenue SE
Washington, DC 20590
202-366-5807
800-996-2723
http://www.marad.dot.gov

Saint Lawrence Seaway Development Corporation
55 M Street, SE., Suite 930
Washington, DC 20003
202-366-0091
800-785-2779
202-366-7147
Mailing address:
1200 New Jersey Avenue, SE
Washington, DC 20590
Operations address:
180 Andrews Street, Massena, NY 13662
315-764-3200
315-764-3235
http://www.seaway.dot.gov

Pipeline and Hazardous Materials Safety Administration
1200 New Jersey Avenue SE
Washington, DC 20590
202-366-4433
http://www.phmsa.dot.gov

Federal Motor Carrier Safety Administration
1200 New Jersey Avenue SE
Washington, DC 20590
202-366-2519
http://www.fmcsa.dot.gov

Surface Transportation Board
395 E Street SW
Washington, DC 20423
202-245-0245
http://www.stb.dot.gov

DEPARTMENT OF THE TREASURY
1500 Pennsylvania Avenue NW
Washington, DC 20220
202-622-2000
http://www.treasury.gov

Senior Procurement Executive
1500 Pennsylvania Avenue NW, Suite 400–W
Washington, DC 20220

202-622-1039
https://www.treasury.gov/about/organizational-structure/offices/Pages/
Office-of-the-Procurement-Executive.aspx

Office of the Assistant Secretary for Management
Treasury Department
Washington, DC 20220
202-622-0410
https://www.treasury.gov/about/organizational-structure/offices/Pages/
Environment-and-Energy.aspx

Public Affairs and Public Liaison
Room 3430, Departmental Offices
Treasury Department
Washington, DC 20220
202-622-2920
https://www.treasury.gov/connect/Pages/contact-us.aspx

Office of Inspector General
1500 Pennsylvania Avenue NW
Washington, DC 20220
800-359-3898
http://www.treas.gov/inspector-general

Freedom of Information Act Request
Treasury OIG
Office of Counsel
Suite 510, 740 15th Street NW
Washington, DC 20220
https://www.treasury.gov/FOIA/Pages/reading_room.aspx

Treasury Library
Room 1428, Main Treasury Building
1500 Pennsylvania Avenue NW
Washington, DC 20220
202-622-0990
https://www.treasury.gov/FOIA/Pages/reading_room.aspx

Office of Small and Disadvantaged Business Utilization
1500 Pennsylvania Avenue NW
Mail Code 655, 15th Street, 6th Floor
Washington, DC 20220
202-622-0530
https://www.treasury.gov/resource-center/sb-programs/Small-
Disadvantaged-Business/Pages/Small-and-Disadvantaged-Business-
Utilization1.aspx

Assistant Secretary–Tax Policy
Departmental Offices
Treasury Department
Washington, DC 20220
202-622-0050
https://www.treasury.gov/resource-center/tax-policy/Pages/default.aspx

Treasury Inspector General for Tax Administration
P.O. Box 589
Ben Franklin Station
Washington, DC 20044-0589
800-366-4484
https://www.treasury.gov/tigta

Public Affairs Office
Department of the Treasury
1500 Pennsylvania Avenue NW
Washington, DC 20220
202-622-2960
https://www.treasury.gov/about/organizational-structure/offices/Pages/
Public-Affairs.aspx

Alcohol and Tobacco Tax and Trade Bureau
1310 G Street NW, Box 12
Washington, DC 20005
202-453-2000
http://www.ttb.gov

Office of the Comptroller of the Currency
400 7th Street SW
Washington, DC 20219
202-649-6800
http://www.occ.gov

Bureau of Engraving and Printing
Fourteenth and C Streets SW
Washington, DC 20228
202-874-4000
http://www.moneyfactory.com

Bureau of the Fiscal Service
401 Fourteenth Street SW
Washington, DC 20227
202-874-6950
http://www.fiscal.treasury.gov

Internal Revenue Service
1111 Constitution Avenue NW
Washington, DC 20224
202-622-5000
http://www.irs.gov

United States Mint
801 Ninth Street NW
Washington, DC 20220
202-354-7200
http://www.usmint.gov

DEPARTMENT OF VETERANS AFFAIRS
810 Vermont Avenue NW
Washington, DC 20420
202-461-4800
http://www.va.gov

Media Services Division (032B)
Department of Veterans Affairs
810 Vermont Avenue NW
Washington, DC 20420
202-461-5282
http://www.va.gov/OFCADMIN/FAQ/Media.asp

FOIA Service (005R1C)
810 Vermont Avenue NW
Washington, DC 20420
877-750-3642
Fax 202-273-0487
http://www.va.gov/oig/foia

VA Inspector General (53E)
P.O. Box 50410
Washington, DC 20091-0410
800-488-8244
vaoighotline@va.gov
http://www.va.gov/oig/default.asp

Office of Public and Intergovernmental Affairs
Department of Veterans Affairs
810 Vermont Avenue NW
Washington, DC 20420
202-273-6000
http://www.va.gov/opa

Independent Agencies and Government Corporations

Administrative Conference of the United States
1120 Twentieth Street NW
Suite 706 South
Washington, DC 20036
(202) 480-2080
(202) 386-7190 FAX
http://www.acus.gov

UNITED STATES AFRICAN DEVELOPMENT FOUNDATION
1400 I Street NW, Suite 1000
Washington, DC 20005
(202) 673-3916
(202) 673-3810 FAX
www.usdaf.gov

BROADCASTING BOARD OF GOVERNORS
330 Independence Avenue SW
Washington, DC 20237
(202) 203-4545
www.bbg.gov

CENTRAL INTELLIGENCE AGENCY
Washington, DC 20505
(703) 482-0623
www.cia.gov

COMMODITY FUTURES TRADING COMMISSION
1155 21st Street NW
Washington, DC 20581
(202) 418-5000
(202) 418-5521 FAX
www.cftc.gov

CONSUMER FINANCIAL PROTECTION BUREAU
1700 G Street NW., Washington, DC 20552
(202) 435-7000
www.consumerfinance.gov

---

* Adapted from the 2015 Edition (July) U.S. Government Manual.

CONSUMER PRODUCT SAFETY COMMISSION
4330 East-West Highway
Bethesda, MD 20814
(301) 504-7923
www.cpsc.gov

CORPORATION FOR NATIONAL AND COMMUNITY SERVICE
1201 New York Avenue NW
Washington, DC 20525
(202) 606-5000
www.nationalservice.org

DEFENSE NUCLEAR FACILITIES SAFETY BOARD
Suite 700
625 Indiana Avenue NW
Washington, DC 20004
(202) 694-7000
(202) 208-6518 FAX
www.dnfsb.gov

ENVIRONMENTAL PROTECTION AGENCY
1200 Pennsylvania Avenue NW
Washington, DC 20460-0001
(202) 272-0167
www.epa.gov

EQUAL EMPLOYMENT OPPORTUNITY COMMISSION
131 M Street NE
Washington, DC 20507
(202) 663-4900
(202) 663-4444 TTY
www.eeoc.gov

EXPORT-IMPORT BANK OF THE UNITED STATES
811 Vermont Avenue NW
Washington, DC 20571
(202) 565-3946 or (800) 565-3946
www.exim.gov

FARM CREDIT ADMINISTRATION
1501 Farm Credit Drive
McLean, VA 22102-5090
(703) 883-4000
(703) 734-5784 FAX
www.fca.gov

FEDERAL COMMUNICATIONS COMMISSION
445 Twelfth Street SW
Washington, DC 20554
(888) 225-5322
(888) 835-5322 TTY
www.fcc.gov

FEDERAL DEPOSIT INSURANCE CORPORATION
550 Seventeenth Street NW
Washington, DC 20429
(703) 562-2222
www.fdic.gov

FEDERAL ELECTION COMMISSION
999 E Street NW
Washington, DC 20463
(202) 694-1100; (800) 424-9530
www.fec.gov

FEDERAL HOUSING FINANCE AGENCY
400 7th Street SW,
Washington, DC 20024
(202) 649-3800
www.fhfa.gov

FEDERAL LABOR RELATIONS AUTHORITY
1400 K Street NW
Washington, DC 20005
(202) 218-7770
www.flra.gov

FEDERAL MARITIME COMMISSION
800 North Capitol Street NW
Washington, DC 20573-0001
(202) 523-5707
www.fmc.gov

FEDERAL MEDIATION AND CONCILIATION SERVICE
2100 K Street NW
Washington, DC 20427
(202) 606-8100
www.fmcs.gov

FEDERAL MINE SAFETY AND HEALTH REVIEW COMMISSION
Suite 520N
1331 Pennsylvania Avenue NW
Washington, D.C. 20004
(202) 434-9900
www.fmshrc.gov

FEDERAL RESERVE SYSTEM
Twentieth Street and Constitution Avenue NW
Washington, DC 20551
(202) 452-3000
www.federalreserve.gov

FEDERAL RETIREMENT THRIFT INVESTMENT BOARD
77 K Street NE
Washington, DC 20002
(202) 942-1600
(202) 942-1676 FAX
www.frtib.gov/Home.html

FEDERAL TRADE COMMISSION
600 Pennsylvania Avenue NW
Washington, DC 20580
(202) 326-2222
www.ftc.gov

GENERAL SERVICES ADMINISTRATION
1800 F Street NW
Washington, DC 20405
www.gsa.gov

> Federal Acquisition Service
> 2200 Crystal Drive, 11th Floor
> Arlington, VA 22202
> (703) 605-5400
> *www.gsa.gov/fas*

> Civilian Board of Contract Appeals
> Washington, DC 20405
> (202) 606-8800
> *www.cbca.gsa.gov/*

> Citizen Services and Innovative Technologies
> Federal Citizen Information Center's
> National Contact Center
> (800) 333–4636
> *http://www.gsa.gov/portal/category/101011*

Public Buildings Service
1800 F Street NW
Washington, DC 20405
(202) 501-1100
www.gsa.gov/pbs

Office of Governmentwide Policy
1800 F Street NW
Washington, DC 20405
(202) 501-8880
www.gsa.gov/portal/content/104550

Office of Real Property Disposal
Public Buildings Service
1800 F Street NW
Washington, DC 20405
(202) 501-0084
www.gsa.gov/portal/content/105035

Office of Communications and Marketing
General Services Administration
1800 F Street NW
Washington, DC 20405
(202) 501-1231
www.gsa.gov/portal/category/25728

INTER-AMERICAN FOUNDATION
1331 Pennsylvania Avenue NW
Suite 1200 North
Washington, DC 20004
(202) 360-4530
www.iaf.gov

MERIT SYSTEMS PROTECTION BOARD
Fifth Floor
1615 M Street NW
Washington, DC 20419
(202) 653-7200; (800) 209-8960
(202) 653-7130 FAX
www.mspb.gov

NATIONAL AERONAUTICS AND SPACE ADMINISTRATION
300 E Street SW
Washington, DC 20546
(202) 358-0000
www.nasa.gov

NATIONAL ARCHIVES AND RECORDS ADMINISTRATION
700 Pennsylvania Avenue NW
Washington, DC 20408-0001
(866) 272-6272
www.archives.gov

NATIONAL CAPITAL PLANNING COMMISSION
Suite 500
401 Ninth Street NW
Washington, DC 20004
(202) 482-7200
www.ncpc.gov

NATIONAL CREDIT UNION ADMINISTRATION
1775 Duke Street
Alexandria, VA 22314-3428
(703) 518-6300
www.ncua.gov

NATIONAL FOUNDATION ON THE ARTS AND THE HUMANITIES
National Endowment for the Arts
400 7th Street SW
Washington, DC 20506-0001
(202) 682-5400
(202) 682-5496 TDD
www.arts.gov

National Endowment for the Humanities
400 7th Street SW
Washington, DC 20506
(202) 606-8400 or (800) 634-1121
E-Mail: *info@neh.gov*
www.neh.gov

Institute of Museum and Library Services
9th Floor
1800 M Street NW
Washington, DC 20036

(202) 653-4657
E-mail: *imlsinfo@imls.gov*
www.imls.gov

NATIONAL LABOR RELATIONS BOARD
1099 Fourteenth Street NW
Washington, DC 20570
(202) 273-1000
(202) 273-4300 TDD
www.nlrb.gov

NATIONAL MEDIATION BOARD
Suite 250 East
1301 K Street NW
Washington, DC 20005
(202) 692-5000
www.nmb.gov

NATIONAL RAILROAD PASSENGER CORPORATION (AMTRAK)
60 Massachusetts Avenue NE
Washington, DC 20002
(202) 906-3000
www.amtrak.com

NATIONAL SCIENCE FOUNDATION
4201 Wilson Boulevard
Arlington, VA 22230
(703) 292-5111
(800) 281-8749 TDD
E-mail: *info@nsf.gov*
www.nsf.gov

NATIONAL TRANSPORTATION SAFETY BOARD
490 L'Enfant Plaza SW
Washington, DC 20594
(202) 314-6000
(202) 314-6110 FAX
www.ntsb.gov

NUCLEAR REGULATORY COMMISSION
Washington, DC 20555
(301) 415-7000
E-mail: *opa.resource@nrc.gov*
www.nrc.gov

OCCUPATIONAL SAFETY AND HEALTH REVIEW COMMISSION
1120 Twentieth Street NW
Washington, DC 20036-3457
(202) 606-5380
(202) 418-3017 FAX
www.oshrc.gov

OFFICE OF THE DIRECTOR OF NATIONAL INTELLIGENCE
Washington, DC 20511
(703) 733-8600
www.dni.gov

OFFICE OF GOVERNMENT ETHICS
Suite 500
1201 New York Avenue NW
Washington, DC 20005-3917
(202) 482-9300
(800) 877-8339 TDD
(202) 482-9237 FAX
www.oge.gov

OFFICE OF PERSONNEL MANAGEMENT
1900 E Street NW
Washington, DC 20415-0001
(202) 606-1800
(202) 606-2532 TTY
www.opm.gov

OFFICE OF SPECIAL COUNSEL
Suite 218
1730 M Street NW
Washington, DC 20036-4505
(202) 254-3600; (800) 872-9855
(202) 653-5151 FAX
www.osc.gov

OVERSEAS PRIVATE INVESTMENT CORPORATION
1100 New York Avenue NW
Washington, DC 20527
(202) 336-8400
(202) 336-7949 FAX
www.opic.gov

PEACE CORPS
1111 Twentieth Street NW
Washington, DC 20526
(202) 692-2000 or (855) 855-1961
(202) 692-2231 FAX
www.peacecorps.gov

PENSION BENEFIT GUARANTY CORPORATION
1200 K Street NW
Washington, DC 20005
(202) 326-4400; (800) 400-7242
www.pbgc.gov

POSTAL REGULATORY COMMISSION
901 New York Avenue NW, Suite 200
Washington, DC 20268-0001
(202) 789-6800
(202) 789-6861 FAX
www.prc.gov

RAILROAD RETIREMENT BOARD
844 North Rush Street
Chicago, IL 60611-2092
(312) 751-4777
(312) 751-7154 FAX
E-mail: *opa@rrb.gov*
www.rrb.gov

> Office of Legislative Affairs:
> Suite 500
> 1310 G Street NW
> Washington, DC 20005-3004
> (202) 272-7742
> (202) 272-7728 FAX
> E-Mail: *ola@rrb.gov*
> *www.rrb.gov/org/ogc/ola.asp*

SECURITIES AND EXCHANGE COMMISSION
100 F Street NE
Washington, DC 20549
(202) 551-7500
www.sec.gov

SELECTIVE SERVICE SYSTEM
National Headquarters
Arlington, VA 22209-2425
(703) 605-4100
www.sss.gov

SMALL BUSINESS ADMINISTRATION
409 Third Street SW
Washington, DC 20416
(202) 205-6600
(202) 205-7064 FAX
www.sba.gov

SOCIAL SECURITY ADMINISTRATION
6401 Security Boulevard
Baltimore, MD 21235
(410) 965-1234
www.socialsecurity.gov

TENNESSEE VALLEY AUTHORITY
400 West Summit Hill Drive
Knoxville, TN 37902
(865) 632-2101
Washington Office:
One Massachusetts Avenue NW
Washington, DC 20444-0001
(202) 898-2999
www.tva.gov

TRADE AND DEVELOPMENT AGENCY
Suite 1600
1000 Wilson Boulevard
Arlington, VA 22209-3901
(703) 875-4357
(703) 875-4009 FAX
www.ustda.gov

UNITED STATES AGENCY FOR INTERNATIONAL DEVELOPMENT
1300 Pennsylvania Avenue NW
Washington, DC 20523-0001
(202) 712-0000
www.usaid.gov

UNITED STATES COMMISSION ON CIVIL RIGHTS
1331 Pennsylvania Avenue NW, Suite 1150
Washington, DC 20425
(202) 376-8128; (202) 376-8116 TTY
www.usccr.gov

UNITED STATES INTERNATIONAL TRADE COMMISSION
500 E Street SW
Washington, DC 20436
(202) 205-2000
www.usitc.gov

UNITED STATES POSTAL SERVICE
475 L'Enfant Plaza SW
Washington, DC 20260-0010
(202) 268-2000
www.usps.gov

THE UNITED STATES GOVERNMENT MANUAL

Boards, Commissions, and Committees

Below is a list of Federal boards, commissions, councils, etc., not listed elsewhere in the Manual, which were established by congressional or Presidential action, whose functions are not strictly limited to the internal operations of a parent department or agency and which are authorized to publish documents in the Federal Register. While the editors have attempted to compile a complete and accurate listing, suggestions for improving coverage of this guide are welcome. Please address your comments to the Office of the Federal Register, National Archives and Records Administration, Washington, DC 20408. Phone, 202-741-6040. E-mail, fedreg.info@nara.gov. Internet, www.ofr.gov.

Federal advisory committees, as defined by the Federal Advisory Committee Act, as amended (5 U.S.C. app.), have not been included here. Information on Federal advisory committees may be obtained from the Committee Management Secretariat, General Services Administration, General Services Building (MC), Room G-230, Washington, DC 20405. Phone, 202-273-3556. Internet, www.gsa.gov/committeemanagement.

Administrative Committee of the Federal Register

Office of the Federal Register, National Archives and Records Administration, 8601 Adelphi Road, College Park, MD 20740-6001. Phone, 202-741-6000. E-mail, fedreg.info@nara.gov. Internet, www.ofr.gov.

Advisory Council on Historic Preservation

401 F. Street NW., Suite 308, Washington, DC 20001-2637. Phone, 202-517-0200. E-mail, achp@achp.gov. Internet, www.achp.gov.

American Battle Monuments Commission

2300 Clarendon Boulevard, Court House Plaza 2, Suite 500, Arlington, VA 22201. Phone, 703-696-6900. E-mail, info@abmc.gov. Internet, www.abmc.gov.

Appalachian Regional Commission

1666 Connecticut Avenue NW., Suite 700, Washington, DC 20009-1068. Phone, 202-884-7700. E-mail, info@arc.gov. Internet, www.arc.gov.

* Reprinted from the 2015 Edition (July) U.S. Government Manual.

Architectural and Transportation Barriers Compliance Board[1]

1331 F Street NW., Suite 1000, Washington, DC 20004-1111. Phone, 202-272-0080, toll free, 800-872-2253 or TTY, 202-272-0082, toll free, 800-993-2822. Fax, 202-272-0081. E-mail, info@access-board.gov. Internet, www.access-board.gov.

Arctic Research Commission

4350 North Fairfax Drive, Suite 510, Arlington, VA 22203. Phone, 703-525-0111. Fax, 703-525-0114. E-mail, info@arctic.gov. Internet, www.arctic.gov.

Arthritis and Musculoskeletal Interagency Coordinating Committee

1 AMS Circle, Bethesda, MD 20892-3675. Phone, 301-495-4484. Fax, 301-480-2814. E-mail, NIAMSinfo@mail.nih.gov. Internet, www.niams.nih.gov.

Barry M. Goldwater Scholarship and Excellence in Education Program

Phone, 319-688-4335. Internet, www.act.org/goldwater.

Chemical Safety and Hazard Investigation Board

2175 K Street NW., Suite 400, Washington, DC 20037-1809. Phone, 202-261-7600. Fax, 202-261-7650. Internet, www.csb.gov.

Citizens' Stamp Advisory Committee

United States Postal Service c/o Stamp Development, 475 L'Enfant Plaza SW., Room 3300, Washington, DC 20260-3501. Internet, http://about.usps.com/who-we-are/csac.

U.S. Commission of Fine Arts

National Building Museum, 401 F Street NW., Suite 312, Washington, DC 20001-2728. Phone, 202-504-2200. Fax, 202-504-2195. E-mail, cfastaff@cfa.gov. Internet, www.cfa.gov.

---

[1] Also known as the Access Board.

Committee on Foreign Investment in the United States

Department of the Treasury, 1500 Pennsylvania Avenue NW., Washington, DC 20220. Phone, 202-622-1860. E-mail, CFIUS@treasury.gov. Internet, http://www.treasury.gov/resource-center/international/Pages/Committee-on-Foreign-Investment-in-US.aspx

Committee for the Implementation of Textile Agreements

Office of Textiles and Apparel, U.S. Department of Commerce, Washington, DC 20230. Phone, 202-482-5078. Fax, 202-482-2331. E-mail, OTEXA@trade.gov. Internet, otexa.ita.doc.gov/cita.htm.

Committee for Purchase From People Who Are Blind or Severely Disabled

1401 S. Clark Street, Suite 10800, Arlington, VA 22202-3259. Phone, 703-603-7740. Fax, 703-608-0655. E-mail, info@abilityone.gov. Internet, www.abilityone.gov.

Coordinating Council on Juvenile Justice and Delinquency Prevention

Department of Justice, Office of Juvenile Justice and Delinquency Prevention, 810 7th Street NW., Washington, DC 20531. Phone, 202-616-7567. Fax, 202-307-2819. E-mail, ddunston@aeioonline.com. Internet, www.juvenilecouncil.gov.

Delaware River Basin Commission

25 State Police Drive, P.O. Box 7360, West Trenton, NJ 08628-0360. Phone, 609-883-9500. Fax, 609-883-9522. E-mail, clarke.rupert@drbc.state.nj.us. Internet, www.nj.gov/drbc.

Endangered Species Program

5275 Leesburg Pike, Falls Church, VA 22041. Phone, 703-358-2171. Internet, www.fws.gov/endangered.

Export Administration Operating Committee

Department of Commerce, Bureau of Industry and Security, 14th Street and Constitution Avenue, NW., Washington, DC 20230. Phone, 202-482-4811. Internet, www.bis.doc.gov/index.htm.

Federal Financial Institutions Examination Council

3501 Fairfax Drive, D8073a, Arlington, VA 22226. Phone, 703-516-5590. Internet, www.ffiec.gov.

Federal Financing Bank

Department of the Treasury, 1500 Pennsylvania Avenue NW., Washington, DC 20220. Phone, 202-622-2470. Fax, 202-622-0707. E-mail, ffb@do.treas.gov. Internet, www.treasury.gov/ffb.

Federal Interagency Committee on Education

Department of Education, 400 Maryland Avenue SW., Washington, DC 20202. Phone, 202-401-3673. Internet, ed.gov/about/bdscomm/list/com.html.

Federal Laboratory Consortium for Technology Transfer

Washington, DC Liaison Office. Phone, 240-444-1383. E-mail, gkjones.ctr@federallabs.org. Internet, www.federallabs.org.

Federal Library and Information Center Committee

Library of Congress, 101 Independence Avenue SE., Washington, DC 20540-4935. Phone, 202-707-4800. Internet, www.loc.gov/flicc/.

Harry S. Truman Scholarship Foundation

712 Jackson Place NW., Washington, DC 20006. Phone, 202-395-4831. Fax, 202-395-6995. E-mail, office@truman.gov. Internet, www.truman.gov.

Indian Arts and Crafts Board

U.S. Department of the Interior, Room MS 2528-MIB, 1849 C Street NW., Washington, DC 20240. Phone, 202-208-3773. E-mail, iacb@ios.doi.gov. Internet, www.iacb.doi.gov.

J. William Fulbright Foreign Scholarship Board

Department of State, Bureau of Educational and Cultural Affairs, 2200 C Street NW., Washington, DC 20522-0500. Phone, 202-203-7010. E-mail, fulbright@state.gov. Internet, fulbright.state.gov.

James Madison Memorial Fellowship Foundation

1613 Duke Street Alexandria, VA 22314. Phone, 571-858-4200. Internet, www.jamesmadison.com.

Japan-US Conference on Cultural and Educational Interchange (CULCON)

1201 15th Street NW., Suite 330, Washington, DC 20005. Phone, 202-653-9800. Fax, 202-653-9802. E-mail, culcon@jusfc.gov. Internet, culcon.jusfc.gov.

Joint Board for the Enrollment of Actuaries

Internal Revenue Service, SE: RPO, REFM, 1111 Constitution Avenue, NW, Park 4, Floor 4, Washington, DC 20224. Fax, 703-414-2225. E-mail, nhqjbea@irs.gov. Internet, www.irs.gov/taxpros/actuaries/index.html.

Marine Mammal Commission

4340 East-West Highway, Suite 700, Bethesda, MD 20814. Phone, 301-504-0087. Fax, 301-504-0099. E-mail, mmc@mmc.gov. Internet, www.mmc.gov.

Medicare Payment Advisory Commission

425 Eye St., N.W. Suite 701 Washington, DC 20001. Phone, 202-220-3700. Fax, 202-220-3759. Internet, www.medpac.gov.

Migratory Bird Conservation Commission

Secretary, Migration Bird Conservation Commission, Mail Code: ARLSQ-622, 4401 North Fairfax Drive, Arlington, VA 22203-1610. Phone, 703-358-1713. Fax, 703-358-2223. Email, realty@fws.gov. Internet, www.fws.gov/refuges/realty/mbcc.html.

Mississippi River Commission

Mississippi River Commission, 1400 Walnut Street, Vicksburg, MS 39180-0080. Phone, 601-634-5757. E-mail, cemvd-pa@usace.army.mil. Internet, www.mvd.usace.army.mil/

Morris K. and Stewart L. Udall Foundation

130 South Scott Avenue, Tucson, AZ 85701-1922. Phone, 520-901-8500. Fax, 520-670-5530. Internet, www.udall.gov.

National Council on Disability

1331 F Street NW., Suite 850, Washington, DC 20004. Phone, 202-272-2004. TTY, 202-272-2074. Fax, 202-272-2022. E-mail, ncd@ncd.gov. Internet, www.ncd.gov.

National Indian Gaming Commission

90 K Street NE., Suite 200, Washington, DC 20002. Phone, 202-632-7003. Fax, 202-632-7066. E-mail, contactus@nigc.gov. Internet, www.nigc.gov.

National Park Foundation

1201 Eye Street NW., Suite 550B, Washington, DC 20005. Phone, 202-354-6460. Fax, 202-371-2066. E-mail, ask-npf@nationalparks.org. Internet, www.nationalparks.org.

Northwest Power and Conservation Council

851 SW. Sixth Avenue, Suite 1100, Portland, OR 97204. Phone, 503-222-5161 or 800-452-5161. Fax, 503-820-2370. E-mail, info@nwcouncil.org. Internet, www.nwcouncil.org.

Office of Navajo and Hopi Indian Relocation

201 East Birch Avenue, Flagstaff, AZ 86001. Phone, 928-779-2721. TTY, 800-877-8339. Fax, 928-774-1977. E-mail, webmaster@onhir.gov. Internet, http://onhir.gov

Permanent Committee for the Oliver Wendell Holmes Devise

Library of Congress, Manuscript Division, 101 Independence Avenue SE., #102, Washington, DC 20540. Phone, 202-707-5383.

President's Intelligence Advisory Board

New Executive Office Building, Room 5020, Washington, DC 20502. Phone, 202-456-2352. Fax, 202-395-3403. Internet, www.whitehouse.gov/administration/eop/piab.

Presidio Trust

103 Montgomery Street, P.O. Box 29052, San Francisco, CA 94129-0052. Phone, 415-561-5300. TTY, 415-561-5301. Fax, 415-561-5315. E-mail, presidio@presidiotrust.gov. Internet, www.presidio.gov.

Social Security Advisory Board

400 Virginia Avenue SW., Suite 625, Washington, DC 20024. Phone, 202-475-7700. Fax, 202-475-7715. E-mail, ssab@ssab.gov. Internet, www.ssab.gov.

Susquehanna River Basin Commission

4423 North Front Street, Harrisburg, PA 17110. Phone, 717-238-0423. Fax, 717-238-2436. E-mail, srbc@srbc.net. Internet, www.srbc.net.

Trade Policy Staff Committee

Office of the United States Trade Representative, 600 17th Street NW.,Washington, DC 20508. Phone, 202-395-3475. Fax, 202-395-4549. Internet, www.ustr.gov.

United States Nuclear Waste Technical Review Board

2300 Clarendon Boulevard, Suite 1300, Arlington, VA 22201. Phone, 703-235-4473. Fax, 703-235-4495. Internet, www.nwtrb.gov.

Veterans Day National Committee

Department of Veterans Affairs, 810 Vermont Avenue NW., Mail Code 002C, Washington, DC 20420. Phone, 202-461-5386. E-mail, vetsday@va.gov. Internet, www1.va.gov/opa/vetsday.

White House Commission on Presidential Scholars

Department of Education, 400 Maryland Avenue SW., Washington, DC 20202-8173. Phone, 202-401-0961. Fax, 202-260-7464. E-mail, presidential.scholars@ed.gov. Internet, www.ed.gov/programs/psp/index.html.

(Last Revised: December 22, 2015)

Quasi-Official Agencies

LEGAL SERVICES CORPORATION
3333 K Street NW
Washington, DC 20007-3522
(202) 295-1500
(202) 337-6797 FAX
www.lsc.gov

SMITHSONIAN INSTITUTION
1000 Jefferson Drive SW
Washington, DC 20560
(202) 633-1000
www.si.edu

JOHN F. KENNEDY CENTER FOR THE PERFORMING ARTS
Washington, DC 20566
(202) 467-4600
www.kennedy-center.org

NATIONAL GALLERY OF ART
4th and Constitution Avenue NW
Washington, DC 20565
(202) 737-4215
www.nga.gov

WOODROW WILSON INTERNATIONAL CENTER FOR SCHOLARS
Scholar Administration Office
Woodrow Wilson Center
One Woodrow Wilson Plaza
1300 Pennsylvania Avenue NW
Washington, DC 20004-3027
(202) 691-4000
(202) 691-4001 FAX
www.wilsoncenter.org

STATE JUSTICE INSTITUTE
11951 Freedom Drive, Suite 1020
Reston, VA 20190
(571) 313-8843
www.sji.gov

* Adapted from the 2015 Edition (July) U.S. Government Manual.

UNITED STATES HOLOCAUST MEMORIAL MUSEUM
100 Raoul Wallenberg Place, SW
Washington, DC 20024-2126
(202)488-0400
(TTY)(202)488-0406
http://www.ushmm.org

UNITED STATES INSTITUTE OF PEACE
2031 Constitution Ave NW
Washington, DC 20037
(202) 457-1700
(202) 429-6063 FAX
www.usip.org

International Organizations

African Development Bank
Avenue Jean-Paul II
01 BP 1387
Abidjan 01
Côte d'Ivoire
+225 20 26 10 20
www.afdb.org
E-mail: *afdb@afdb.org*

Asian Development Bank
6 ADB Avenue
Mandaluyong City
1550 Metro Manila, Philippines
(632) 632-4444
(632) 636-2444 FAX
www.adb.org
E-mail: *information@adb.org*

ADB North American Representative Office
900 17th Street NW, Suite 900
Washington DC 20006
(202) 728-1500
(202) 728-1505 FAX

European Bank for Reconstruction and Development
One Exchange Square
London EC2A 2JN
United Kingdom
(+44) 20 7338 6000
www.ebrd.com

Inter-American Defense Board
2600 Sixteenth Street NW
Washington, DC 20441
(202) 939-6041
www.jid.org
E-mail: *protocol@jid.org*

Inter-American Development Bank
1300 New York Avenue NW
Washington, DC 20577

(202) 623-1000
FAX: (202) 623-3096
www.iadb.org

Inter-American Investment Corporation
1350 New York Avenue NW
Washington, DC 20577
(202) 623-3901
www.iic.int

World Bank Group
1818 H Street NW
Washington, DC 20433
(202) 473-1000
(202) 477-6391 FAX
www.worldbank.org

> International Centre for the Settlement of Investment Disputes
> 1818 H Street NW
> MSN J2-200
> Washington, DC 20433
> (202) 458-1534
> (202) 522-2615 FAX
> *http://icsid.worldbank.org/ICSID/*
>
> International Finance Corporation
> 2121 Pennsylvania Avenue NW
> Washington, DC 20433
> (202) 473-7711
> (202) 974-4384
> *www.ifc.org*

Multilateral Investment Guarantee Agency
1818 H Street NW
Washington, DC 20433
(202) 458-2538
(202) 522-0316
www.miga.org

International Monetary Fund
700 Nineteenth Street NW
Washington, DC 20431
(202) 623-7000
(202) 623-4661 FAX
www.imf.org

International Organization for Migration
Washington Office:
Suite 700
1752 N Street NW
Washington, DC 20036
(202) 862-1826
(202) 862-1879 FAX
E-mail: *IOMWashingtonRMF@iom.int*

Organization of American States
Seventeenth Street and Constitution Avenue NW
Washington, DC 20006
(202) 370-5000
(202) 458-3967
www.oas.org

United Nations
New York, NY 10017
(212) 963-1234
www.un.org
Washington, DC office:
U.N. Information Centre
Suite 400
1775 K Street NW
Washington, DC 20006
(202) 331-8670
(202) 331-9191 FAX
www.unicwash.org
E-mail: *unicdc@unicwas.org*

THE UNITED STATES GOVERNMENT MANUAL

Other International Organizations

Below is a list of other international organizations that do not have separate entries elsewhere in the *Manual*. The United States participates in these organizations in accordance with the provisions of treaties, other international agreements, congressional legislation, or executive arrangements. In some cases, no financial contribution is involved.

Various commissions, councils, or committees subsidiary to the organizations listed here are not named separately on this list. These include the international bodies for drugs and crime, which are subsidiary to the United Nations.

This listing is provided for reference purposes and should not be considered exhaustive. For more information on international organizations and United States participation in them, contact the State Department's Bureau of International Organization Affairs. Phone, 202-647-9600. Internet, http://go.usa.gov/UjzR.

I. Specialized Agencies of the United Nations and Related Organizations

Food and Agricultural Organization
International Atomic Energy Agency
International Civil Aviation Organization
International Fund for Agriculture Development
International Labor Organization
International Maritime Organization
International Telecommunication Union
United Nations Educational, Scientific and Cultural Organization (UNESCO)
Universal Postal Union
World Health Organization
World Intellectual Property Organization
World Meteorological Organization

II. Peacekeeping and Political Missions Administered by the United Nations Department of Peacekeeping Operations

Africa

African Union/United Nations Hybrid Operation in Darfur (UNAMID)
United Nations Multidimensional Integrated Stabilization Mission in Mali (MINUSMA)

---

* Reprinted from the 2015 Edition (July) of the U.S. Goverment Manual.

United Nations Interim Security Force for Abyei (UNISFA)
United Nations Mission for the Referendum in Western Sahara (MINURSO)
United Nations Mission in Liberia (UNMIL)
United Nations Mission in the Republic of South Sudan (UNMISS)
United Nations Operation in Côte d'Ivoire (UNOCI)
United Nations Organization Stabilization Mission in the Democratic Republic of the Congo (MONUSCO)
United Nations Multidimensional Integrated Stabilization Mission in the Central African Republic (MINUSCA)

Americas

United Nations Stabilization Mission in Haiti (MINUSTAH)

Middle East

United Nations Assistance Mission in Afghanistan (UNAMA)
United Nations Disengagement Observer Force (UNDOF)
United Nations Interim Force in Lebanon (UNIFIL)
United Nations Military Observer Group in India and Pakistan (UNMOGIP)
United Nations Truce Supervision Organization (UNTSO)

Europe

United Nations Interim Administration Mission in Kosovo (UNMIK)
United Nations Peacekeeping Force in Cyprus (UNFICYP)

III. Inter-American Organizations

Border Environment Cooperation Commission Caribbean Postal Union
Inter-American Center of Tax Administrators
Inter-American Children's Institute
Inter-American Commission of Human Rights
Inter-American Commission of Women
Inter-American Committee Against Terrorism
Inter-American Committee on Natural Disaster Reduction
Inter-American Council for Integral Development
Inter-American Drug Abuse Control Commission
Inter-American Institute for Cooperation in Agriculture
Inter-American Institute for Global Change Research
Inter-American Investment Corporation
Inter-American Telecommunications Commission
Inter-American Tropical Tuna Commission
Pan American Health Organization

Pan American Institute of Geography and History
Postal Union of the Americas, Spain and Portugal

IV. Regional Organizations

Antarctic Treaty System
Arctic Council
Asia-Pacific Economic Cooperation
Asia Pacific Energy Research Center
Colombo Plan for Cooperative Economic and Social Development in Asia and the Pacific
Commission for Environmental Cooperation
Commission for Labor Cooperation
International Commission for the Conservation of Atlantic Tunas
NATO Parliamentary Assembly
North Atlantic Treaty Organization
North Atlantic Salmon Conservation Organization
North Pacific Anadromous Fish Commission
North Pacific Coast Guard Forum
North Pacific Marine Science Organization
Northwest Atlantic Fisheries Organization
Secretariat of the Pacific Community
South Pacific Regional Environment Program
Western and Central Pacific Fisheries Commission

V. Other International Organizations

Bioversity International
Center for International Forestry Research (CIFOR)
Commission for the Conservation of Antarctic Marine Living Resources
Community of Democracies
Comprehensive Nuclear Test Ban Treaty Organization
Consultative Group on International Agricultural Research (CGIAR)
COSPAS-SARSAT (Search and Rescue Satellite System)
Global Biodiversity Information Facility
Global Environment Facility
Hague Conference on Private International Law)
Human Frontier Science Program
International Ocean Discovery Program
International Agency for Research on Cancer (IARC)
International Bureau for the Permanent Court of Arbitration
International Bureau of Weights and Measures
International Center for Agricultural Research in the Dry Areas
International Center for the Study of the Preservation and the Restoration of Cultural
    Property

International Coffee Organization
International Committee of the Red Cross (ICRC)
International Cotton Advisory Committee
International Council for the Exploration of the Seas
International Court of Justice
International Criminal Police Organization (INTERPOL)
International Customs Tariffs Bureau
International Development Law Organization
International Energy Agency
International Energy Forum
International Fertilizer Development Center
International Grains Council
International Hydrographic Organization
International Institute for Applied Systems Analysis
International Institute for the Unification of Private Law
International Mobile Satellite Organization
International Organization of Legal Metrology
International Organization of Supreme Audit Institutions
United Nations International Research and Training Institute for the Advancement of Women
International Science and Technology Center
International Seed Testing Association
International Telecommunications Satellite Organization
International Tropical Timber Organization
International Union of Credit and Investment Insurers (Berne Union)
International Whaling Commission
Iran-United States Claims Tribunal
Multinational Force and Observers
Nuclear Energy Agency (NEA)
Organization for Economic Cooperation and Development
Organization for the Prohibition of Chemical Weapons
Organization for Security and Cooperation in Europe
Preparatory Commission for the Comprehensive Nuclear Test-Ban Treaty
Regional Environmental Center for Central and Eastern Europe
Science and Technology Center in Ukraine
Standards and Trade Development Facility
Wassenaar Arrangement
World Association for Waterborne Transport Infrastructure
World Association of Investment Promotion Agencies
World Customs Organization
World Heritage Fund
World Organization for Animal Health
World Trade Organization (WTO)

VI. Special Voluntary Programs

Asian Vegetable Research and Development Center
Convention on International Trade in Endangered Species of Wild Fauna and Flora (CITES)
Global Fund to Fight HIV/AIDS, Tuberculosis, and Malaria
International Council for Science
International Crop Research Institute for Semi-Arid Tropics
International Federation of the Red Cross and Red Crescent Societies
International Food Policy Research Institute
International Fund for Agricultural Development
International Institute of Tropical Agriculture
Joint United Nations Program on HIV/AIDS (UNAIDS)
Korean Peninsula Energy Development Organization
Multilateral Fund for the Implementation of the Montreal Protocol
Ramsar Convention on Wetlands
United Nations Capital Development Fund
United Nations Children's Fund (UNICEF)
United Nations Conference on Trade and Development
United Nations Convention to Combat Desertification
United Nations Democracy Fund
United Nations Development Fund for Women (UNIFEM)
United Nations Development Program
United Nations Economic Commission for Europe
United Nations Environment Program
United Nations Framework Convention on Climate Change
United Nations Office of the High Commissioner for Human Rights
United Nations High Commissioner for Refugees Programs
United Nations Human Settlements Program (UN HABITAT)
United Nations International Strategy for Disaster Reduction
United Nations Population Fund (UNFPA)
United Nations Relief and Works Agency for Palestine Refugees (UNRWA)
United Nations Voluntary Fund for Technical Cooperation in the Field of Human Rights
United Nations Voluntary Fund for the Victims of Torture
United Nations World Food Program
World Agroforestry Center

(Last Revised: December 22, 2015)

THE UNITED STATES GOVERNMENT MANUAL

Selected Bilateral Organizations

Below is a list of bilateral organizations in which the United States participates with its two neighbors, Mexico and Canada. This listing is for reference purposes only and should not be considered exhaustive.

Border Environment Cooperation Commission

United States Section: P.O. Box 221648, El Paso, TX 79913. Phone, 877-277-1703. Fax, 915-975-8280. E-mail, becc@cocef.org. Internet, www.becc.org.

Mexican Section: Bulevar Tomas Fernadez 8069, Ciudad Juarez, Chihuahua, 32470. Phone, 011-52-656-688-4600. Fax, 011-52-656-625-6180. Internet, www.cocef.org.

Great Lakes Fishery Commission

2100 Commonwealth Boulevard, Suite 100, Ann Arbor, MI 48105. Telephone, 734-662-3209. Fax, 734-741-2010. Email, info@glfc.org. Internet, www.glfc.org.

International Boundary Commission, United States and Canada

United States Section: 2000 L Street NW., Suite 615, Washington, DC 20036. Phone, 202-736-9102. Fax, 202-632-2008. E-mail, hipsleyk@ibcusca.org. Internet, www.internationalboundarycommission.org.

Canadian Section: 575-615 Booth Street, Ottawa, Ontario K1A 0E9 Canada. Phone, *(613) 944-4515*. Fax, *(613) 992-1122*. E-mail, ibc-cfi@nrcan.gc.ca. Internet, www.internationalboundarycommission.org.

International Boundary and Water Commission, United States and Mexico

United States Section: Suite C-100, 4171 North Mesa Street, El Paso, TX 79902. Phone, 800-262-8857. Internet, www.ibwc.state.gov.

Mexican Section: Avenue Universidad 2180, Zona Chamizal, C.P. 32310, Ciudad Juarez, Chihuahua, 32310. Phone, 011-52-656-639-7951 or 011-52-656-613-7311. Fax, 011-52-656-613-9943. E-mail, cilamex@cila.gob.mx. Internet, www.sre.gob.mx/cila.

* Reprinted from the 2015 Edition (July) of the U.S. Goverment Manual.

SELECTED BILATERAL ORGANIZATIONS

International Joint Commission—United States and Canada

United States Section: 2000 L Street NW., Suite 615, Washington, DC 20440. Phone, 202-736-9009. Fax, 202-632-2007. E-mail: commission@washington.ijc.org. Internet, www.ijc.org.

Canadian Section: 234 Laurier Avenue West, 22d Floor, Ottawa, Ontario K1P 6K6. Phone, 613-995-2984. Fax, 613-993-5583. E-mail: commission@ottawa.ijc.org. Internet, www.ijc.org.

Great Lakes Regional Office: 100 Ouellette Avenue, 8th Floor, Windsor, Ontario N9A 6T3. Phone, 519-257-6700. Fax, 519-257-6740. E-mail: commission@windsor.ijc.org. Internet, www.ijc.org.

International Pacific Halibut Commission

2320 W. Commodore Way, Suite 300, Seattle, WA 98199-1287. Phone, 206-634-1838. Fax, 206-632-2983. Internet, www.iphc.int.

Joint Mexican-United States Defense Commission

United States Section: Room 2E773, The Pentagon, Washington, DC 20318. Phone, 703-695-8164.

Mexican Section: 6th Floor, 1911 Pennsylvania Avenue NW., Mexican Embassy, Washington, DC 20006. Phone, 202-728-1748.

Permanent Joint Board on Defense—United States and Canada

United States Section: Room 2E773, The Pentagon, Washington, DC 20318. Phone, 703-695-8164.

Canadian Section: Director of Western Hemisphere, 101 Colonel By Drive, Ottawa, ON K1A 0K2. Phone, 613-992-4423.

(Last Revised: December 22, 2015)

U.S. Attorneys Address List[†]

ALABAMA, Middle District
George L. Beck, United States Attorney[†]
131 Clayton Street, Montgomery 36104
Phone: (334) 223-7280
Fax: (334) 223-7560

ALABAMA, Northern District
Joyce White Vance, United States Attorney
1801 Fourth Avenue North, Birmingham 35203-2101
Phone: (205) 244-2001
Fax: (205) 244-2171
400 Meridian Street, Suite 304
Huntsville, AL 35801
Phone: (256) 534-8285
Fax: (256) 539-3270

ALABAMA, Southern District
Kenyen Ray Brown, United States Attorney
63 S. Royal Street, Suite 600, Mobile 36602
Phone: (251) 441-5845
Fax: (251) 441-5277

ALASKA
Karen L. Loeffler, United States Attorney
222 W. 7th Ave., #9, Rm. 253, Anchorage 99513-7567
Phone: (907) 271-5071
Fax: (907) 271-4054
101 12th Ave., Rm. 310, Fairbanks 99701
Phone: (907) 456-0245
Fax: (907) 456-0577
709 West 9th Street, Room 937, Juneau 99802
Phone: (907) 796-0400
Fax: (907) 796-0409

ARIZONA
John S. Leonardo, United States Attorney
Two Renaissance Square, 40 North Central Ave., Ste. 1200,
Phoenix 85004-4408

[†] Adapted from United States Attorney Listing, *www.justice.gov/usao/districts/*

Phone: (602) 514-7500
405 West Congress St., Ste. 4800
Tucson 85701-5040
Phone: (520) 620-7300
123 N. San Francisco Street, Suite 410
Flagstaff 86001
Phone: (928) 556-0833
7102 E. 30th Street, Suite 101
Yuma 85365
Phone: (928) 314-6410

ARKANSAS, EASTERN DISTRICT
Christopher R. Thyer, United States Attorney
425 West Captiol Avenue
Suite 500
Little Rock 72201
Post Office Box 1229, Little Rock 72203
Phone: (501) 340-2600
Fax: (501) 340-2728

ARKANSAS, Western District
Kenneth Elser, United States Attorney
414 Parker Avenue, Fort Smith 72901
Phone: (479) 783-5125

CALIFORNIA, Central District
Eileen M. Decker, United States Attorney
312 N. Spring St., Suite 1200 Los Angeles 90012
Phone: (213) 894-2400
Fax: (213) 894-0141

CALIFORNIA, Eastern District
Phillip A. Talbert, United States Attorney (Acting)
501 "I" Street, Suite 10-100, Sacramento 95814-2322
Phone: (916) 554-2700
Fax: (916) 554-2900
2500 Tulare Street, Suite 4401, Fresno 93721
Phone: (559) 497-4000
Fax: (559) 497-4099

CALIFORNIA, Northern District
Brian Stretch, United States Attorney
450 Golden Gate Ave., San Francisco 94102
Phone: (415) 436-7200
Fax: (415) 436-7234

TTY: (415) 436-7221
1301 Clay St., Oakland 94612
Phone: (510) 637-3680
Fax: (510) 637-3724
TTY: (510) 637-3678
150 Almaden Blvd., Suite 900, San Jose 95113
Phone: (408) 535-5061
Fax: (408) 535-5066
TTY: (408) 535-3690

CALIFORNIA, Southern District
Laura E. Duffy, United States Attorney
880 Front St., Room 6293, San Diego 92101-8893
Phone: (619) 557-5610
Toll free: (800) 544-1106
Fax: (619) 546-0720
TTY: (619) 557-3450
516 Industry Way, Suite C, Imperial 92251
Phone: (760) 370-0893
Fax: (760) 335-3975

COLORADO
Robert C. Troyer, United States Attorney (Acting)
1225 Seventeenth Street, Suite 700
Denver, CO 80202
Phone: (303) 454-0100
Fax: (303) 454-0400
103 Sheppard Drive, No. 215, Durango 81303
Phone: (970) 247-1514
Fax: (970) 247-8619
205 N. 4th Street, Suite 400
Phone: (970) 257-7113
Fax: (970) 248-3630

CONNECTICUT
Deirdre M. Daly, United States Attorney (Acting)
Connecticut Financial Center, 157 Church Street Floor 25, New Haven 06510
Phone: (203) 821-3700
Fax: (203) 773-5376
1000 Lafayette Blvd., 10th Floor Bridgeport 06604
Phone: (203) 696-3000
Fax: (203) 579-5575
450 Main St., Room 328 Hartford 06103
Phone: (860) 947-1101
Fax: (860) 760-7979

DELAWARE
Charles M. Oberly III, United States Attorney
Nemours Building, 1007 Orange Street, Suit 700, Wilmington 19801
Phone: (302) 573-6277
Fax: (302) 573-6220
Toll free: (888) 293-8162
TTY: (302) 573-6274

DISTRICT OF COLUMBIA
Channing D. Phillips, United States Attorney
Judiciary Center Building, 555 Fourth Street, NW, Washington, 20530
Phone: (202) 252-7566

FLORIDA, Middle District
A. Lee Bentley, III, United States Attorney (Acting)
400 North Tampa St., Suite 3200, Tampa 33602
Phone: (813) 274-6000
Fax: (813) 274-6358
2110 First St., Suite 3-137, Fort Myers 32902
Phone: (239) 461-2200
Fax: (239) 461-2219
300 N. Hogan St., Suite 700, Jacksonville 32202
Phone: (904) 301-6300
Fax: (904) 301-6310
35 SE 1st Avenue, Suite 300, Ocala 34471
Phone: (352) 547-3600
Fax: (352) 547-3623
400 W. Washington Street, Suite 3100, Orlando 32801
Phone: (407) 648-7500
Fax: (407) 648-7643

FLORIDA, Northern District
Christopher P. Canova, United States Attorney (Acting)
111 N. Adams Street, 4th Floor, Tallahassee 32301
Phone: (850) 942-8430
300 East University Avenue, Suite 310, Gainesville 32601
Phone: (352) 378-0996
1001 East Business Highway 98, 2d Floor, Panama City 32401
Phone: (850) 785-3495
21 E. Garden Street, Suite 400, Pensacola 32502
Phone: (850) 444-4000

FLORIDA, Southern District
Wifredo A. Ferrer, United States Attorney
99 N.E. 4th St., Miami 33132
Phone: (305) 961-9001
Fax: (305) 530-7679
500 East Broward Blvd., Fort Lauderdale 33394
Phone: (954) 356-7255
Fax: (954) 356-7336
101 South U.S.1, Suite 3100, Fort Pierce 34950
Phone: (772) 466-0899
Fax: (772) 466-1020
500 S. Australian Ave., Suite 400, West Palm Beach 33401
Phone: (561) 820-8711
Fax: (561) 820-8777
301 Simonton Street, Key West 33040
Phone: (305) 294-7070
Fax: (305) 292-1423

GEORGIA, Middle District
G.F. "Pete" Peterman III, United States Attorney (Acting)
P.O. Box 1702, Macon 31202-1702
Phone: (478) 752-3511
201 W. Broad Avenue, 2d Floor, Albany 31701
Phone: (229) 430-7754
Post Office Box 2568, Columbus 31902-2568
Phone: (706) 649-7700

GEORGIA, Northern District
John A. Horn, United States Attorney (Acting)
75 Spring Street S.W., Suite 600 Atlanta 30303-3309
Phone: (404) 581-6000
Fax: (404) 581-6181

GEORGIA, Southern District
Edward J. Tarver, United States Attorney
22 Barnard Street, Suite 300, Savannah 31401
Phone: (912) 652-4422
Fax: (912) 652-4388
600 James Brown Blvd., Suite 200, Augusta 30901
Phone: (706) 724-0517
Fax: (706) 724-7728

GUAM & NORTHERN MARIANA ISLANDS
Alicia A.G. Limtiaco, United States Attorney
Sirena Plaza, 108 Hernan Cortez, Suite 500, Hagatna 96910
Phone: (671) 472-7332
Fax: (671) 472-7334
Post Office Box 500377, Saipan, 96950-0377
Phone: (670) 236-2980
Fax: (670) 236-2985

HAWAII
Florence T. Nakakuni, United States Attorney
Rm. 6-100, 300 Ala Moana Blvd., Honolulu 96850
Phone: (808) 541-2850
TTD: (808) 541-1830

IDAHO
Wendy J. Olson, United States Attorney
Washington Group Plaza, 800 Park Blvd., Ste. 600, Boise 83712-9903
Phone: (208) 334-1211
Fax: (208) 334-9375
6450 N. Mineral Drive, Suite 210, Coeur d'Alene 83815
Phone: (208) 667-6568
Fax: (208) 667-0814
801 E. Sherman, Suite. 192, Pocatello 83201
Phone: (208) 478-4166
Fax: (208) 478-4175

ILLINOIS, Central District
James A. Lewis, United States Attorney
318 S. Sixth St., Springfield 62701
Phone: (217) 492-4450
Fax: (217) 492-4512
One Technology Plaza, 211 Fulton Street, Suite 400, Peoria 61602
Phone: (309) 671-7050
Fax: (309) 671-7259
211 19th St., 2d Floor, Rock Island 61201
Phone: (309) 793-7760
Fax: (309) 786-5663
201 S. Vine St., Suite 226, Urbana 61802
Phone: (217) 373-5875
Fax: (217) 373-5891

ILLINOIS, Northern District
Zachary T. Fardon, United States Attorney
219 S. Dearborn St., 5th Floor, Chicago 60604
Phone: (312) 353-5300
327 South Church Street, Room 3300, Rockford 61101
Phone: (815) 987-4444

ILLINOIS, Southern District
Donald S. Boyce, Jr., United States Attorney (Interim)
Nine Executive Dr., Fairview Heights 62208
Phone: (618) 628-3700
Fax: (618) 628-3730
TTY: (618) 628-3826
402 W. Main St., Suite 2A, Benton 62812
Phone: (618) 439-3808
Fax: (618) 439-2401
TTY: (618) 435-4037
750 Missouri Avenue, 3rd Floor, East St. Louis 62201
Telephone: (618) 482-9361
Fax Line: (618) 482-9302

INDIANA, Northern District
David A. Capp, United States Attorney
5400 Federal Plaza, Suite 1500, Hammond 46320
Phone: (219) 937-5500
Fax: (219) 852-2770
3128 Fed. Bldg., 1300 S. Harrison St., Fort Wayne 46802
Phone: (260) 422-2595
Fax: (260) 426-1616
204 S. Main St., Rm. MO-1, South Bend 46601
Phone: (574) 236-8287
Fax: (574) 236-8155

INDIANA, Southern District
Joshua Minkler, United States Attorney
10 West Market Street, Ste. 2100, Indianapolis 46204-3048
Phone: (317) 226-6333
Toll-free: (888) 368-5067
Fax: (317) 226-6125
TTY: (317) 226-5438
101 NW MLK Blvd, Ste. 250, Evansville 47708
Phone: (812) 465-6475
Fax: (812) 465-6444
TTY: (812) 465-6441

IOWA, Northern District
Kevin W. Techau, United States Attorney
111 7th Ave., SE, Box #1, Cedar Rapids 52401-4950
Phone: (319) 363-6333
Fax: (319) 363-1990
TTY: (319) 286-9258
600 4th Street, Suite 670, Sioux City 51101
Phone: (712) 255-6011
Fax: (712) 252-2034
TTY: (712) 258-4761

IOWA, Southern District
Kevin E. Vander Schel, United States Attorney
Suite 286, U.S. Cthse. Annex, 110 E. Court Ave., Des Moines 50309-2053
Phone: (515) 473-9300
Fax: (515) 473-9288
U.S. Courthouse, Suite 310
131 East 4th Street, Davenport 52801
Phone: (563) 449-5432
Fax: (563) 449-5433
P.O. Box 1887, Council Bluffs 51502
Main Phone: (712) 256-5009
Fax: (712) 256-5112

KANSAS
Thomas E. Beall, United States Attorney (Acting)
1200 Epic Center, 301 N. Main, Wichita 67202-4812
Phone: (316) 269-6481
Fax: (316) 269-6484
500 State Avenue, Ste. 360, Kansas City 66101
Phone: (913) 551-6730
Fax: (913) 551-6541
444 SE Quincy St., Suite 290, Topeka 66683
Phone: (785) 295-2850
Fax: (785) 295-2853

KENTUCKY, Eastern District
Kerry B. Harvey, United States Attorney
Suite 300, 260 West Vine St., Lexington 40507-1612
Phone: (859) 233-2661
TTY: (859) 233-2573
207 Grandview Drive, Suite 400, Ft. Mitchell 41017-2762
Phone: (859) 655-3200
TTY: (859) 655-9080

601 Meyers Baker Road, 2nd Floor, London 40741
Phone: (606) 864-5523
TTY: (606) 862-0258

KENTUCKY, Western District
John E. Kuhn, Jr., United States Attorney
717 W. Broadway, Louisville 40202
Phone: (502) 582-5911
Fax: (502) 582-5097
501 Broadway, Room 29, Paducah 42001
Phone: (270) 442-7104
Fax: (270) 444-6794

LOUISIANA, Eastern District
Kenneth A. Polite, United States Attorney
650 Poydras St., Suite 1600
New Orleans 70130
Phone: (504) 680-3000
Fax: (504) 589-4510

LOUISIANA, Middle District
Walt Green, United States Attorney
Russell B. Long Federal Bldg., 777 Florida St., Suite 208
Baton Rouge 70801
Phone: (225) 389-0443
Fax: (225) 389-0561
Fax-Civil: (225) 389-0685

LOUISIANA, Western District
Stephanie A. Finley, United States Attorney
300 Fannin St., Ste. 3201, Shreveport 71101-3068
Phone: (318) 676-3600
Fax: (318) 676-3641
800 Lafayette St., Ste. 2200, Lafayette 70501-6832
Phone: (337) 262-6618
Fax: (337) 262-6682
201 Jackson St., Rm. B-107, Monroe 71201
Phone: (318) 322-0766
Fax: (318) 325-2990
515 Murray St., Rm. 320, Alexandria 71301
Phone: (318) 473-7440
Fax: (318) 473-7439

MAINE
Thomas Edward Delahanty II, United States Attorney
100 Middle Street
East Tower Sixth Floor,
Portland 04101-4100
Phone: (207) 780-3257
Fax: (207) 780-3304
TTY: (207) 780-3060
202 Harlow Street, Room 111, Bangor 04401
Phone: (207) 945-0373
Fax: (207) 945-0319
TTY: (207) 945-0307

MARYLAND
Rod J. Rosenstein, United States Attorney
36 S. Charles St., 4th Floor, Baltimore 21201
Phone: (410) 209-4800
Fax: (410) 962-0122
6406 Ivy Lane, Suite 800, Greenbelt 20770
Phone: (301) 344-4433
Fax: (301) 344-4518

MASSACHUSETTS
Carmen Milagras Ortiz, United States Attorney
1 Courthouse Way, John Joseph Moakley Cthse, Suite 9200, Boston 02210
Phone: (617) 748-3100
TTY: (617) 748-3696
Fax: (617) 748-3974
U.S. Courthouse, 300 State St., Ste. 230, Springfield 01105
Phone: (413) 785-0235
Fax: (413) 785-0394
Donohue Federal Building, Room 206, 595 Main Street, Worcester 01608
Phone: (508) 368-0100
Fax: (508) 923-0742

MICHIGAN, Eastern District
Barbara L. McQuade, United States Attorney
Suite 2001, 211 W. Fort St., Detroit 48226
Phone: (313) 226-9100
TTD: (313) 226-9560
Fax: (313) 226-2311
101 First St., Suite 200, Bay City 48708
Phone: (989) 895-5712
TTD: (989) 895-2501

Fax: (989) 895-5790
210 Fed. Bldg., 600 Church St., Flint 48502
Phone: (810) 766-5177
TTD: (810) 766-5100
Fax: (810) 766-5427

MICHIGAN, Western District
Patrick A. Miles, Jr., United States Attorney
330 Ionia Avenue, S.W., Suite 501, Grand Rapids 49503
Phone: (616) 456-2404
Fax: (616) 456-2408
FirstMerit Bank, 2nd Floor, 1930 U.S. 41 W., Marquette 49855
Phone: (906) 226-2500
Fax: (906) 226-3700
315 W. Allegan, Rm. 252, Lansing 48933
Phone: (517) 377-1577
Fax: (517) 377-1698

MINNESOTA
Andrew M. Luger, United States Attorney
300 South 4th St., Suite 600, Minneapolis 55415
Phone: (612) 664-5600
316 North Robert St., Suite 404, St. Paul 55101
Phone: (651) 848-1950

MISSISSIPPI, Northern District
Felicia C. Adams, United States Attorney
900 Jefferson Avenue, Oxford 38655-3608
Phone: (662) 234-3351
Fax: (662) 234-4818

MISSISSIPPI, Southern District
Gregory K. Davis, United States Attorney
501 East Court St., Suite 4-430, Jackson 39201
Phone: (601) 965-4480
1575 20th Avenue, 2nd Floor, Gulfport 39501-2040
Phone: (228) 563-1560

MISSOURI, Eastern District
Richard G. Callahan, United States Attorney
Thomas F. Eagleton, U.S. Courthouse, 111 South 10th St, 20th Floor
St. Louis 63102
Phone: (314) 539-2200
Fax: (314) 539-2309

TDD: (314) 539-7690
Rush H. Limbaugh, Sr. U.S. Courthouse, 555 Independence Street,
Cape Girardeau 63703
Phone: (573) 334-3736
Fax: (573) 335-2393
TDD: (573) 332-1208

MISSOURI, Western District
Tammy Dickinson, United States Attorney
Charles E. Whittaker Courthouse, 400 E. 9th Street, Room 5510, Kansas City
    64106
Phone: (816) 426-3122
Toll free: 800-733-6558
Fax: (816) 426-4210
80 Lafayette St., Suite 2100, Jefferson City 65101
Phone: (573) 634-8214
Toll free: 800-836-3518
Fax: (573) 634-8723
901 St. Louis St., Ste. 500, Springfield 65806-2511
Phone: (417) 831-4406
Toll free: 800-347-4493
Fax: (417) 831-0078

MONTANA
Michael Cotter, United States Attorney
2601 Second Ave, N., Suite 3200, Billings 59101
Phone: (406) 657-6101
Toll free: (800) 291-6108
Fax: (406) 657-6989
119 1st Ave. N. #300, Great Falls 59401
Phone: (406) 761-7715
Toll free: (888) 326-2894
Fax: (406) 453-9973
Paul G. Hatfield Courthouse, 901 Front St., Suite 1100, Helena 59626
Phone: (406) 457-5120
Toll free: (866) 333-8835
Fax: (406) 457-5130
Post Office Box 8329, Missoula 59807
Phone: (406) 542-8851
Toll free: (866) 291-3836
Fax: (406) 542-1476

NEBRASKA
Deborah R. Gilg, United States Attorney
1620 Dodge Street, Ste. 1400, Omaha 68102-1506
Phone: (402) 661-3700
Toll free: (800) 889-9124
Fax: (402) 345-6958
487 Fed. Bldg., 100 Centennial Mall North, Lincoln 68508
Phone: (402) 437-5241
Toll free: (800) 889-9123
Fax: (402) 437-5390

NEVADA
Daniel G. Bogden, United States Attorney
333 Las Vegas Blvd., South, Suite 5000, Las Vegas 89101
Phone: (702) 388-6336
Toll free: (800) 593-8002
100 W. Liberty St., Ste. 600, Reno 89501
Phone: (775) 784-5438
Toll free: (800) 303-5545

NEW HAMPSHIRE
Emily Gray Rice, United States Attorney
55 Pleasant St., 4th Floor, Concord 03301-3904
Phone: (603) 225-1552
Fax: (603) 225-1470
TTY: (603) 226-7777

NEW JERSEY
Paul J. Fishman, United States Attorney
970 Broad St., Suite 700, Newark 07102
Phone: (973) 645-2700
TTY: (973) 645-6227
Fax: (973) 645-2702
Camden Fed. Bldg. & U.S. Courthouse, 401 Market Street, 4th Floor
Camden 08101
Phone: (856) 757-5026
Fax: (856) 968-4917
402 East State St., Rm. 430, Trenton 08608
Phone: (609) 989-2190
Fax: (609) 989-2275

NEW MEXICO
Damon P. Martinez, United States Attorney
Post Office Box 607, Albuquerque 87102
Phone: (505) 346-7274

Fax: (505) 346-7296
555 So. Telshor, Suite 300, Las Cruces 88011
Phone: (505) 522-2304
Fax: (505) 522-2391

NEW YORK, Eastern District
Robert L. Capers, United States Attorney
271 Cadman Plaza East, Brooklyn 11201
Phone: (718) 254-7000
Fax: (718) 254-7508
610 Federal Plaza, Central Islip 11722-4454
Phone: (631) 715-7900
Fax: (631) 715-7922

NEW YORK, Northern District
Richard S. Hartunian, United States Attorney
James Foley Bldg.
445 Broadway, Rm. 218, Albany 12207
Phone: (518) 431-0247
Fax: (518) 431-0249
Post Office Box 7198, 100 South Clinton St., Syracuse 13261-7198
Phone: (315) 448-0672
Fax: (315) 448-0689
304 Federal Bldg., 15 Henry St., Binghamton 13901
Phone: (607) 773-2887
Fax: (607) 773-2901
14 Durkee St., Ste. 340, Plattsburgh 12901
Phone: (518) 314-7800
Fax: (518) 314-7811

NEW YORK, Southern District
Preet Bharara, United States Attorney
One St. Andrews Plaza, New York 10007
Phone: (212) 637-2200
300 Quarropas St., White Plains, NY 10601
Phone: (914) 993-1900
86 Chambers Street, New York 10007
(212)637-2800

NEW YORK, Western District
William J. Hochul, Jr., United States Attorney
138 Delaware Ave., Buffalo 14202
Phone: (716) 843-5700
Fax: (716) 551-3052

100 State St., 620 Federal Bldg., Rochester 14614
Phone: (585) 263-6760
Fax: (585) 263-6226

NORTH CAROLINA, Eastern District
John Stuart Bruce, United States Attorney
310 New Bern Ave., Ste. 800, Terry Sanford Fed. Bldg., Raleigh 27601-1461
Phone: (919) 856-4530
Fax: (919) 856-4487

NORTH CAROLINA, Middle District
Ripley Rand, United States Attorney
101 South Edgeworth Street, 4th Floor, Greensboro 27401
Phone: (336) 333-5351
Fax: (336) 333-5438
251 North Main Street, Suite 726, Winston-Salem 27101
Phone: (336) 631-5268
Fax: (336) 631-5049

NORTH CAROLINA, Western District
Jill Westmoreland Rose, United States Attorney
227 West Trade Street, Suite 1650, Charlotte 28202
Phone: (704) 344-6222
Fax: (704) 344-6629
Rm. 233, U.S. Cthse., 100 Otis St., Asheville 28801
Phone: (828) 271-4661
Fax: (828) 271-4670

NORTH DAKOTA
Christopher C. Myers, United States Attorney (Acting)
655 First Ave. North, Suite 250
Fargo 58102-4932
Phone: (701) 297-7400
Fax: (701) 297-7405
William L. Guy Federal Building, 220 East Rosser Avenue, Room 372
Bismarck 58502
Phone: (701) 530-2420
Fax: (701) 530-2421

OHIO, Northern District
Carole S. Rendon, United States Attorney
801 W. Superior Ave., Suite 400, Cleveland 44113-1852
Phone: (216) 622-3600
Fax: (216) 522-3370
2 S. Main St., Akron 44308

Phone: (330) 375-5716
Fax: (330) 375-5492
Four Seagate, Ste. 308, Third Floor, Toledo 43604
Phone: (419) 259-6376
Fax: (419) 259-6360
City Centre One, 100 E. Federal Plaza, Suite 325, Youngstown, OH 44503
Phone: (330) 746-7974
Fax: (330) 746-0239

OHIO, Southern District
Benjamin C. Glassman, United States Attorney (Acting)
303 Marconi Blvd., Suite 200, Columbus 43215
Phone: (614) 469-5715
Fax: (614) 469-5653
Fed. Bldg., 200 W. 2nd St., #600, Dayton 45402
Phone: (937) 225-2910
Fax: (937) 225-2564
221 East 4th Street, Suite 400, Cincinnati 45202
Phone: (513) 684-3711
Fax: (513) 684-6385

OKLAHOMA, Eastern District
Mark F. Green, United States Attorney
520 Denison, Muskogee 74401
Phone: (918) 684-5100
Fax: (918) 684-5130

OKLAHOMA, Northern District
Danny C. Williams, Sr., United States Attorney
110 West 7th Street, Suite 300, Tulsa 74119
Phone: (918) 382-2700
Fax: (918) 560-7938

OKLAHOMA, Western District
Mark A. Yancey, United States Attorney (Acting)
210 W. Park Ave., Ste. 400, Oklahoma City 73102
Phone: (405) 553-8700
Fax: (405) 553-8888

OREGON
Billy J. Williams, United States Attorney
1000 S.W. 3rd Avenue, Suite 600, Portland 97204-2902
Phone: (503) 727-1000
405 E. 8th Avenue, Suite 2400, Eugene 97401-2708

Phone: (541) 465-6771
310 W. 6th St., Medford 97501
Phone: (541) 776-3564

PENNSYLVANIA, Eastern District
Zane D. Memeger, United States Attorney
615 Chestnut St., Ste. 1250, Philadelphia 19106
Phone: (215) 861-8200
Fax: (215) 861-8618
504 W. Hamilton St., #3701, Allentown 18101
Phone: (215) 861-8540
Fax: (610) 439-6059

PENNSYLVANIA, Middle District
Peter J. Smith, United States Attorney
Ste. 220, Fed. Bldg., 228 Walnut St., Harrisburg 17108-1754
Phone: (717) 221-4482
Fax: (717) 221-4493
235 N. Washington Ave., Suite 311, Scranton 18503
Phone: (570) 348-2800
Fax: (570) 348-2037
Herman T. Schneebeli Federal Building, 240 West Third Street, Suite 316,
Williamsport 17701
Phone: (570) 326-1935
Fax: (570) 326-7916

PENNSYLVANIA, Western District
David J. Hickton, United States Attorney
U.S. Post Office & Cthse, 700 Grant St., Ste 4000 Pittsburgh 15219
Phone: (412) 644-3500
Fax: (412) 644-4549
Federal Courthouse, Room A330, 17 South Park Row, Erie 16501-1158
Phone: (814) 452-2906
Fax: (814) 455-6951
Ste. 200, Penn Traffic Bldg., 319 Washington St., Johnstown 15901
Phone: (814) 533-4547
Fax: (814) 533-4545

PUERTO RICO
Rosa E. Rodriguez-Velez, United States Attorney
Torre Chardon, Ste. 1201, 350 Carlos Chardon Ave., San Juan 00918
Phone: (787) 766-5656
Toll free: (877) 872-5656
Fax: (787) 771-4043

RHODE ISLAND
Peter F. Neronha, United States Attorney
Fleet Center, 50 Kennedy Plaza, 8th Floor, Providence 02903
Phone: (401) 709-5000
Fax: (401) 709-5001

SOUTH CAROLINA
Beth Drake, United States Attorney (Acting)
Wells Fargo Bldg., 1441 Main St., Ste. 500, Columbia 29201
Phone: (803) 929-3000
Fax: (803) 254-2912
Liberty Center Bldg., 151 Meeting St., Suite 200, Charleston 29402
Phone: (843) 727-4381
Fax: (843) 727-4443
401 West Evans St, Room 222, Florence 29501
Phone: (843) 665-6688
Fax: (843) 678-8809
One Liberty Square Bldg, 55 Beattie Place, Suite 700, Greenville 29601
Phone: (864) 282-2100
Fax: (864) 233-3158

SOUTH DAKOTA
Randy Seiter, United States Attorney (Acting)
P.O. Box 2638, Sioux Falls 57101-2638
Phone: (605) 330-4400
Fax: (605) 330-4410
P.O. Box 7240, Pierre 57501
Phone: (605) 224-5402
Fax: (605) 224-8305
201 Federal Bldg., & U.S. Courthouse, 515 Ninth Street, Rapid City 57701
Phone: (605) 342-7822
Fax: (605) 342-1108
303 Post Office & U.S. Courthouse, Aberdeen 57401
Phone: (605) 226-7264
Fax: (605) 226-7266

TENNESSEE, Eastern District
Nancy S. Harr, United States Attorney (Acting)
800 Market Street, Ste. 211, Knoxville 37902
Phone: (865) 545-4167
Fax: (865) 545-4176
1110 Market St., Ste. 515, Chattanooga 37402
Phone: (423) 752-5140
Fax: (423) 752-5150

220 West Depot Street, Greenville 37743
Phone: (423) 639-6759
Fax: (423) 639-6451

TENNESSEE, Middle District
David Rivera, United States Attorney
110 Ninth Ave. South, Ste. A961, Nashville 37203-3870
Phone: (615) 736-5151
Fax: (615) 401-6626
817 S. Garden Street, Room 205, Columbia 37083
Phone: (931) 388-6030
Post Office & Courthouse, 9 East Broad Street, Cookeville 38503
Phone: (931) 528-2709

TENNESSEE, Western District
Edward L. Stanton III, United States Attorney
167 N. Main St., Suite 800, Memphis 38103-1898
Phone: (901) 544-4231
Fax: (901) 544-4230
109 South Highland, Ste. 300, Jackson 38301
Phone: (731) 422-6220
Fax: (731) 422-6668

TEXAS, Eastern District
John Malcolm Bales, United States Attorney
350 Magnolia Ave., Suite 150, Beaumont 77701-2237
Phone: (409) 839-2538
Fax: (409) 839-2550
Bank of America Bldg., 415 S. First Street, Lufkin 75901
Phone: (409) 839-2538
Fax: (936) 639-4033
One Grand Centre, 600 East Taylor Street, Suite 2000, Sherman 75090
Phone: (903) 868-9454
Fax: (903) 892-2792
110 N. College, Ste. 700, Tyler 75702
Phone: (903) 590-1400
Fax: (903) 590-1439
101 East Park Blvd., Ste. 500, Plano 75704
Phone: (972) 509-1201
Fax: (972) 509-1209
500 State Line Avenue N., Suite 402, Texarkana, 77501
Phone: (903) 590-1400
Fax: (903) 792-5164

TEXAS, Northern District
John R. Parker, United States Attorney
1100 Commerce St., 3rd Floor, Dallas 75242-1699
Phone: (214) 659-8600
Fax: (214) 659-8806
Amarillo Nat'l Plaza Two
500 S. Taylor St., Amarillo 79101-2446
Phone: (806) 324-2356
Fax: (806) 324-2399
801 Cherry St., Unit 4, Burnett Plaza, Ste. 1700, Ft. Worth 76102-6897
Phone: (817) 252-5200
Fax: (817) 252-5455
1205 Texas Ave., Ste. 700, U.S. Fed. Bldg., Lubbock 79401-4002
Phone: (806) 472-7351
Fax: (806) 472-7394

TEXAS, Southern District
Kenneth Magidson, United States Attorney
1000 Louisiana Street, Ste. 2300, Houston 77002
Phone: (713) 567-9000
Fax: (713) 718-3300
U.S. Courthouse, 600 East Harrison, Suite 201, Brownsville 78520
Phone: (956) 548-2554
Fax: (956) 548-2711
One Shoreline Plaza South Tower, 800 N. Shoreline Blvd., Suite 500, Corpus
  Christi 78401
Phone: (361) 888-3111
Fax: (361) 888-3200
11204 McPherson Rd., Suite 100A, Laredo 78042
Phone: (956) 723-6523
Fax: (956) 726-2266
Bentsen Tower, 1701 W. Highway 83, Suite 600, McAllen 78501
Phone: (956) 618-8010
Fax: (956) 618-8009

TEXAS, Western District
Richard L. Durbin, Jr., United States Attorney
601 N.W. Loop 410, Ste. 600, San Antonio 78216-5597
Phone: (210) 384-7100
Fax: (210) 384-7105
2500 N. Highway 118, Ste. A200, Alpine 79830
Phone: (432) 837-7332
Fax: (432) 837-7485
816 Congress Ave., Ste. #1000, Austin 78701

Phone: (512) 916-5858
Fax: (512) 916-5854
U.S. Cthse, 3rd Floor, Rm. A300, 111 East Broadway, Del Rio 78840
Phone: (830) 703-2025
Fax: (830) 703-2030
700 E. San Antonio St., Ste. 200, El Paso 79901
Phone: (915) 534-6884
Fax: (915) 534-6024
400 W. Illinois Street Ste. 1200, Midland 79702
Phone: (432) 686-4110
Fax: (432) 686-4131
410 S. Cedar, Rm. 255, U.S. Courthouse, Pecos 79772
Phone: (432) 445-4343
Fax: (432) 445-2225
800 Franklin, Suite 280, Waco 76701
Phone: (254) 750-1580
Fax: (254) 750-1599

UTAH
John W. Huber, United States Attorney
185 South State Street, Suite 300, Salt Lake City 84111
Phone: (801) 524-5682
Fax: (801) 524-6924
20 North Main Street, Suite 208, St. George 84770
Phone: (435) 634-4270
Fax: (435) 634-4272
Unstaffed Office:
350 S. Main St., Room 400, Salt Lake City 84101

VERMONT
Eric S. Miller, United States Attorney
P.O. Box 570, Burlington 05402
Phone: (802) 951-6725
Fax: (802) 951-6540
P.O. Box 10, Rutland 05702
Phone: (802) 773-0231
Fax: (802) 773-0214

VIRGIN ISLANDS
Ronald W. Sharpe, United States Attorney
Fed. Bldg., & U.S. Cthse., 5500 Veterans Drive, Rm. 260, St. Thomas 00802-6424
Phone: (340) 774-5757
Fax: (340) 776-3474

1108 King St., Ste. 201, Christiansted, St. Croix 00820-4951
Phone: (340) 773-3920
Fax: (340) 773-1407

VIRGINIA, Eastern District
Dana J. Boente, United States Attorney
2100 Jamieson Ave., Alexandria 22314
Phone: (703) 299-3700
Fax: (703) 299-2584
101 W. Main St., Ste. 8000, World Trade Center, Norfolk 23510
Phone: (757) 441-6331
Fax: (757) 441-6689
919 E. Main Street, Ste. 1900, Main Street Centre, Richmond 23219
Phone: (804) 819-5400
Fax: (804) 771-2316
Fountain Plaza Three, Suite 300, 721 Lakefront Commons, Newport News 23606
Phone: (757) 591-4000
Fax: (757) 591-0866

VIRGINIA, Western District
John P. Fishwick, Jr., United States Attorney
P.O. Box.1709, Roanoke 24008
Phone: (540) 857-2250
Fax: (540) 857-2614
180 W. Main Street, Abingdon 24210
Phone: (276) 628-4161
Fax: (276) 628-7399
255 West Main Street, Rm. 130, Charlottesville 22902
Phone: (434) 293-4283
Fax: (434) 293-4910
116 N. Main St., Rm. 130, Harrisonburg 22802
Phone: (540) 432-6636
Fax: (540) 433-9296

WASHINGTON, Eastern District
Michael Ormsby, United States Attorney
Post Office Box 1494, Spokane 99210-1494
Phone: (509) 353-2767
Fax: (509) 835-6397
402 E. Yakima Ave., Ste. 210, Yakima 98901
Phone: (509) 454-4425
Fax: (509) 249-3297

WASHINGTON, Western District
Annette L. Hayes, United States Attorney (Interim)
700 Stewart St., Suite 5220, Seattle 98101-1271
Phone: (206) 553-7970
Fax: (206) 553-0882
Ste. 700, 1201 Pacific Ave., Tacoma 98402
Phone: (253) 428-3800
Fax: (253) 428-3826

WEST VIRGINIA, Northern District
William J. Ihlenfeld II, United States Attorney
1125 Chapline St., Wheeling 26003-0011
Phone: (304) 234-0100
Fax: (304) 234-0110
Federal Center, 320 W. Pike St., Ste. 300, Clarksburg, 26301-2710
Phone: (304) 623-7030
Fax: (304) 623-7031
300 Third St., Ste. 300, Elkins 26241-0190
Phone: (304) 636-1739
Fax: (304) 636-1967
U.S. Cthse. & P.O. Bldg., 217 West King St., Ste. 400,
Martinsburg 25401-3286
Phone: (304) 262-0590
Fax: (304) 262-0591

WEST VIRGINIA, Southern District
Carol A. Casto, United States Attorney (Acting)
300 Virginia St., Ste. 4000, Charleston 25301
Phone: (304) 345-2200
Fax: (304) 347-5104
Sydney L. Christie Building, 845 Fifth Avenue, Room 209,
Box 1239, Huntington 25701
Phone: (304) 529-5799
Fax: (304) 529-5545
United States Courthouse and IRS Complex,
110 North Heber Street, Room 257,
Beckley 25801
Phone: (304) 253-6722
Fax: (304) 253-9206

WISCONSIN, Eastern District
Greg Haanstad, United States Attorney (Acting)
517 E. Wisconsin Ave., Rm. 530, Federal Bldg., Milwaukee 53202
Phone: (414) 297-1700

Fax: (414) 297-1738
TTY: (414) 297-1088
205 Doty St, Ste. 301, Green Bay 54301
Phone: (920) 884-1066
Fax: (920) 884-2997

WISCONSIN, Western District
John William Vaudreuil, United States Attorney
222 W. Washington Ave., Ste. 700, Madison 53703
Phone: (608) 264-5158
Fax: (608) 264-5172

WYOMING
Christopher A. Crofts, United States Attorney
Post Office Box 668, Cheyenne 82003-0668
Phone: (307) 772-2124
Fax: (307) 772-2123
Dick Cheney Federal Bldg., P.O. Box 22211, Casper 82602
Phone: (307) 261-5434
Fax: (307) 261-5471
P.O. Box 449, Lander 82520
Phone: (307) 332-8195
Fax: (307) 332-7104
P.O. Box 703, Yellowstone National Park, 82190-0703
Phone: (307) 690-7394
Fax: (307) 344-9266

Legislative Branch

The Senate
The Capitol, Washington, DC 20510
(202) 224-3121
www.senate.gov

The House of Representatives
The Capitol, Washington, DC 20515
(202) 225-3121
www.house.gov

---

* Adapted from the 2015 Edition (July) of the U.S. Government Manual.

LEGISLATIVE BRANCH

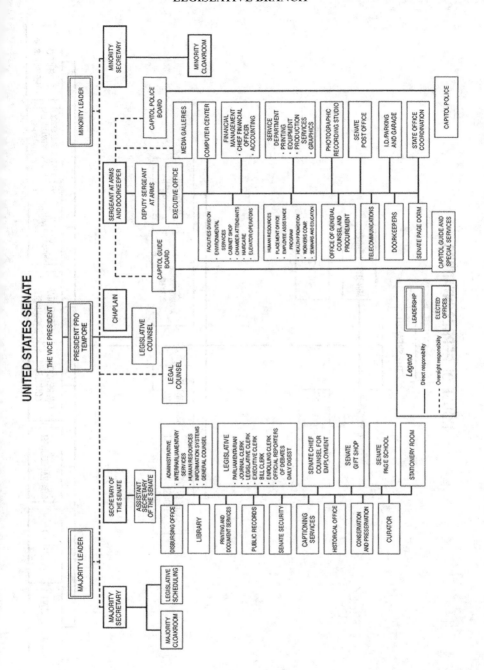

* Reprinted from the 2015 Edition (July) of the U.S. Government Manual.

K-103

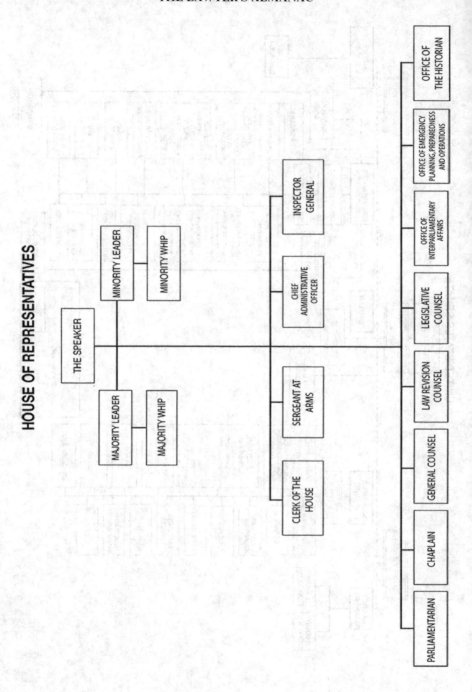

HOUSE OF REPRESENTATIVES

* Reprinted from the 2015 Edition (July) U.S. Government Manual at *www.gpo.gov*.

Standing Committees of the Senate

Senate Committee	Room*
Agriculture, Nutrition, and Forestry	SR328A
Appropriations	S128
Armed Services	SR228
Banking, Housing, and Urban Affairs	SD534
Budget	SD624
Commerce, Science, and Transportation	SD512
Energy and Natural Resources	SD304
Environment and Public Works	SD410
Finance	SD219
Foreign Relations	SD423
Health, Education, Labor, and Pensions	SD428
Homeland Security and Governmental Affairs	SD340
Judiciary	SD224
Rules and Administration	SR305
Small Business and Entrepreneurship	SR428A
Veterans' Affairs	SR412

*Room numbers preceded by S are in the Senate wing of the Capitol Building; those preceded by SD are in the Dirksen Office Building; and those preceded by SR are in the Russell Office Building.

* Reprinted from the 2015 Edition (July) U.S. Government Manual at *www.gpo.gov*.

Standing Committees of the House of Representatives

House Committee	Room*
Agriculture	1301
Appropriations	H307
Armed Services	2120
Budget	207
Education and the Workforce	2181
Energy and Commerce	2125
Ethics	1015
Financial Services	2129
Foreign Affairs	2170
Homeland Security	H2-176
House Administration	1309
House Administration (Franking Office)	1313
Judiciary	2138
Natural Resources	1324
Oversight and Government Reform	2157
Rules	H312
Rules (Minority)	1627
Science, Space, and Technology	2321
Small Business	2361
Transportation and Infrastructure	2165
Veterans' Affairs	335
Ways and Means	1102

* Room numbers with three digits are in the Cannon House Office Building, four digits beginning with 1 are in the Longworth House Office Building, and four digits beginning with 2 are in the Rayburn House Office Building. Room numbers preceded by H or HT are in the House wing of the Capitol Building."

* Reprinted from the 2015 Edition (July) U.S. Government Manual at *www.gpo.gov*.

House of Representatives

114th CONGRESS
UNITED STATES HOUSE OF REPRESENTATIVES
June 9, 2016

REPRESENTATIVES

Republicans in roman; Democrats in *italic*; Resident Commissioner and Delegates in **boldface**.
The names of Members who have died or resigned appear in bold brackets [ ].
Three-digit room numbers are in the Cannon House Office Building, four-digit room numbers beginning with 1 are in the Longworth House Office Building, and four-digit numbers beginning with 2 are in the Rayburn House Office Building.
Calls from outside the Capitol complex can be made by dialing (202) 22 plus the five-digit number listed in this directory.
Washington, DC 20515

Compiled by **KAREN L. HAAS, Clerk of the House**
http://clerk.house.gov

Name	Phone	Room	Name	Phone	Room
Abraham, Ralph Lee, 5th LA	58490	417	Buchanan, Vern, 16th FL	55015	2104
Adams, Alma S., 12th NC	51510	222	Buck, Ken, 4th CO	54676	416
Aderholt, Robert B., 4th AL	54876	235	Bucshon, Larry, 8th IN	54636	1005
Aguilar, Pete, 31st CA	53201	1223	Burgess, Michael C., 26th TX	57772	2336
Allen, Rick W., 12th GA	52823	513	*Bustos, Cheri, 17th IL*	55905	1009
Amash, Justin, 3d MI	53831	114	*Butterfield, G. K., 1st NC*	53101	2305
Amodei, Mark E., 2d NV	56155	332	Byrne, Bradley, 1st AL	54931	119
Ashford, Brad, 2d NE	54155	107	Calvert, Ken, 42d CA	51986	2205
Babin, Brian, 36th TX	51555	316	*Capps, Lois, 24th CA*	53601	2231
Barletta, Lou, 11th PA	56511	115	*Capuano, Michael E., 7th MA*	55111	1414
Barr, Andy, 6th KY	54706	1432	*Cárdenas, Tony, 29th CA*	56131	1510
Barton, Joe, 6th TX	52002	2107	*Carney, John C., Jr., At Large, DE*	54165	1406
Bass, Karen, 37th CA	57084	408	*Carson, André, 7th IN*	54011	2453
Beatty, Joyce, 3d OH	54324	133	Carter, Earl L. "Buddy", 1st GA	55831	432
Becerra, Xavier, 34th CA	56235	1226	Carter, John R., 31st TX	53864	2110
Benishek, Dan, 1st MI	54735	514	*Cartwright, Matt, 17th PA*	55546	1419
Bera, Ami, 7th CA	55716	1535	*Castor, Kathy, 14th FL*	53376	205
Beyer, Donald S., Jr., 8th VA	54376	431	*Castro, Joaquin, 20th TX*	53236	212
Bilirakis, Gus M., 12th FL	55755	2112	Chabot, Steve, 1st OH	52216	2371
Bishop, Mike, 8th MI	54872	428	Chaffetz, Jason, 3d UT	57751	2236
Bishop, Rob, 1st UT	50453	123	*Chu, Judy, 27th CA*	55464	2423
Bishop, Sanford D., Jr., 2d GA	53631	2407	*Cicilline, David N., 1st RI*	54911	2244
Black, Diane, 6th TN	54231	1131	*Clark, Katherine M., 5th MA*	52836	1721
Blackburn, Marsha, 7th TN	52811	2266	*Clarke, Yvette D., 9th NY*	56231	2351
Blum, Rod, 1st IA	52911	213	*Clawson, Curt, 19th FL*	52536	228
Blumenauer, Earl, 3d OR	54811	1111	*Clay, Wm. Lacy, 1st MO*	52406	2428
Bonamici, Suzanne, 1st OR	50855	439	*Cleaver, Emanuel, 5th MO*	54535	2335
Bordallo, Madeleine Z. (Delegate), GU	51188	2441	*Clyburn, James E., 6th SC*	53315	242
Bost, Mike, 12th IL	55661	1440	Coffman, Mike, 6th CO	57882	2443
Boustany, Charles W., Jr., 3d LA	52031	1431	*Cohen, Steve, 9th TN*	53265	2404
Boyle, Brendan F., 13th PA	56111	118	Cole, Tom, 4th OK	56165	2467
Brady, Kevin, 8th TX	54901	301	Collins, Chris, 27th NY	55265	1117
Brady, Robert A., 1st PA	54731	102	Collins, Doug, 9th GA	59893	1504
Brat, Dave, 7th VA	52815	330	Comstock, Barbara, 10th VA	55136	226
Bridenstine, Jim, 1st OK	52211	216	Conaway, K. Michael, 11th TX	53605	2430
Brooks, Mo, 5th AL	54801	1230	*Connolly, Gerald E., 11th VA*	51492	2238
Brooks, Susan W., 5th IN	52276	1505	*Conyers, John, Jr., 13th MI*	55126	2426
Brown, Corrine, 5th FL	50123	2111	Cook, Paul, 8th CA	55861	1222
Brownley, Julia, 26th CA	55811	1019	*Cooper, Jim, 5th TN*	54311	1536

REPRESENTATIVES

Name	Phone	Room	Name	Phone	Room
Costa, Jim, 16th CA	53341	1314	Forbes, J. Randy, 4th VA	56365	2135
Costello, Ryan A., 6th PA	54315	427	Fortenberry, Jeff, 1st NE	54806	1514
Courtney, Joe, 2d CT	52076	2348	*Foster, Bill*, 11th IL	53515	1224
Cramer, Kevin, At Large, ND	52611	1032	Foxx, Virginia, 5th NC	52071	2350
Crawford, Eric A. "Rick", 1st AR	54076	1711	*Frankel, Lois*, 22d FL	59890	1037
Crenshaw, Ander, 4th FL	52501	2161	Franks, Trent, 8th AZ	54576	2435
Crowley, Joseph, 14th NY	53965	1436	Frelinghuysen, Rodney P., 11th NJ	55034	2306
Cuellar, Henry, 28th TX	51640	2209	*Fudge, Marcia L.*, 11th OH	57032	2344
Culberson, John Abney, 7th TX	52571	2372	*Gabbard, Tulsi*, 2d HI	54906	1609
Cummings, Elijah E., 7th MD	54741	2230	*Gallego, Ruben*, 7th AZ	54065	1218
Curbelo, Carlos, 26th FL	52778	1429	*Garamendi, John*, 3d CA	51880	2438
Davidson, Warren, 8th OH	56205	1011	Garrett, Scott, 5th NJ	54465	2232
Davis, Danny K., 7th IL	55006	2159	Gibbs, Bob, 7th OH	56265	329
Davis, Rodney, 13th IL	52371	1740	Gibson, Christopher P., 19th NY	55614	1708
Davis, Susan A., 53d CA	52040	1214	Gohmert, Louie, 1st TX	55035	2243
DeFazio, Peter A., 4th OR	56416	2134	Goodlatte, Bob, 6th VA	55431	2309
DeGette, Diana, 1st CO	54431	2368	Gosar, Paul A., 4th AZ	52315	504
Delaney, John K., 6th MD	52721	1632	Gowdy, Trey, 4th SC	56030	1404
DeLauro, Rosa L., 3d CT	53661	2413	*Graham, Gwen*, 2d FL	55235	1213
DelBene, Suzan K., 1st WA	56311	318	Granger, Kay, 12th TX	55071	1026
Denham, Jeff, 10th CA	54540	1730	Graves, Garret, 6th LA	53901	204
Dent, Charles W., 15th PA	56411	2211	Graves, Sam, 6th MO	57041	1415
DeSantis, Ron, 6th FL	52706	308	Graves, Tom, 14th GA	55211	2442
DeSaulnier, Mark, 11th CA	52095	327	*Grayson, Alan*, 9th FL	59889	303
DesJarlais, Scott, 4th TN	56831	413	*Green, Al*, 9th TX	57508	2347
Deutch, Theodore E., 21st FL	53001	2447	*Green, Gene*, 29th TX	51688	2470
Diaz-Balart, Mario, 25th FL	54211	440	Griffith, H. Morgan, 9th VA	53861	1108
Dingell, Debbie, 12th MI	54071	116	*Grijalva, Raúl M.*, 3d AZ	52435	1511
Doggett, Lloyd, 35th TX	54865	2307	Grothman, Glenn, 6th WI	52476	501
Dold, Robert J., 10th IL	54835	221	Guinta, Frank C., 1st NH	55456	326
Donovan, Daniel M., Jr., 11th NY	53371	1725	Guthrie, Brett, 2d KY	53501	2434
Doyle, Michael F., 14th PA	52135	239	*Gutiérrez, Luis V.*, 4th IL	58203	2408
Duckworth, Tammy, 8th IL	53711	104	*Hahn, Janice*, 44th CA	58220	404
Duffy, Sean P., 7th WI	53365	1208	Hanna, Richard L., 22d NY	53665	319
Duncan, Jeff, 3d SC	55301	106	Hardy, Cresent, 4th NV	59894	430
Duncan, John J., Jr., 2d TN	55435	2207	Harper, Gregg, 3d MS	55031	307
Edwards, Donna F., 4th MD	58699	2445	Harris, Andy, 1st MD	55311	1533
Ellison, Keith, 5th MN	54755	2263	Hartzler, Vicky, 4th MO	52876	2235
Ellmers, Renee L., 2d NC	54531	1210	*Hastings, Alcee L.*, 20th FL	51313	2353
Emmer, Tom, 6th MN	52331	503	*Heck, Denny*, 10th WA	59740	425
Engel, Eliot L., 16th NY	52464	2462	Heck, Joseph J., 3d NV	53252	132
Eshoo, Anna G., 18th CA	58104	241	Hensarling, Jeb, 5th TX	53484	2228
Esty, Elizabeth H., 5th CT	54476	405	Herrera Beutler, Jaime, 3d WA	53536	1130
Farenthold, Blake, 27th TX	57742	1027	Hice, Jody B., 10th GA	54101	1516
Farr, Sam, 20th CA	52861	1126	Higgins, Brian, 26th NY	53306	2459
Fattah, Chaka, 2d PA	54001	2301	Hill, J. French, 2d AR	52506	1229
Fincher, Stephen Lee, 8th TN	54714	2452	Himes, James A., 4th CT	55541	1227
Fitzpatrick, Michael G., 8th PA	54276	2400	*Hinojosa, Rubén*, 15th TX	52531	2262
Fleischmann, Charles J. "Chuck", 3d TN	53271	230	Holding, George, 13th NC	53032	507
Fleming, John, 4th LA	52777	2182	*Honda, Michael M.*, 17th CA	52631	1713
Flores, Bill, 17th TX	56105	1030	*Hoyer, Steny H.*, 5th MD	54131	1705

REPRESENTATIVES

Name	Phone	Room	Name	Phone	Room
Hudson, Richard, 8th NC	53715	429	Lewis, John, 5th GA	53801	343
Huelskamp, Tim, 1st KS	52715	1110	Lieu, Ted, 33d CA	53976	415
Huffman, Jared, 2d CA	55161	1630	Lipinski, Daniel, 3d IL	55701	2346
Huizenga, Bill, 2d MI	54401	1217	LoBiondo, Frank A., 2d NJ	56572	2427
Hultgren, Randy, 14th IL	52976	2455	Loebsack, David, 2d IA	56576	1527
Hunter, Duncan, 50th CA	55672	2429	Lofgren, Zoe, 19th CA	53072	1401
Hurd, Will, 23d TX	54511	317	Long, Billy, 7th MO	56536	1541
Hurt, Robert, 5th VA	54711	125	Loudermilk, Barry, 11th GA	52931	238
Israel, Steve, 3d NY	53335	2457	Love, Mia B., 4th UT	53011	217
Issa, Darrell E., 49th CA	53906	2269	Lowenthal, Alan S., 47th CA	57924	108
Jackson Lee, Sheila, 18th TX	53816	2252	Lowey, Nita M., 17th NY	56506	2365
Jeffries, Hakeem S., 8th NY	55936	1607	Lucas, Frank D., 3d OK	55565	2405
Jenkins, Evan H., 3d WV	53452	502	Luetkemeyer, Blaine, 3d MO	52956	2440
Jenkins, Lynn, 2d KS	56601	1526	Luján, Ben Ray, 3d NM	56190	2446
Johnson, Bill, 6th OH	55705	1710	Lujan Grisham, Michelle, 1st NM	56316	214
Johnson, Eddie Bernice, 30th TX	58885	2468	Lummis, Cynthia M., At Large, WY	52311	2433
Johnson, Henry C. "Hank", Jr., 4th GA	51605	2240	Lynch, Stephen F., 8th MA	58273	2369
Johnson, Sam, 3d TX	54201	2304	MacArthur, Thomas, 3d NJ	54765	506
Jolly, David W., 13th FL	55961	1728	Maloney, Carolyn B., 12th NY	57944	2308
Jones, Walter B., 3d NC	53415	2333	Maloney, Sean Patrick, 18th NY	55441	1529
Jordan, Jim, 4th OH	52676	1524	Marchant, Kenny, 24th TX	56605	2313
Joyce, David P., 14th OH	55731	1124	Marino, Tom, 10th PA	53731	410
Kaptur, Marcy, 9th OH	54146	2186	Massie, Thomas, 4th KY	53465	314
Katko, John, 24th NY	53701	1123	Matsui, Doris O., 6th CA	57163	2311
Keating, William R., 9th MA	53111	315	McCarthy, Kevin, 23d CA	52915	2421
Kelly, Mike, 3d PA	55406	1519	McCaul, Michael T., 10th TX	52401	131
Kelly, Robin L., 2d IL	50773	1239	McClintock, Tom, 4th CA	52511	2331
Kelly, Trent, 1st MS	54306	1427	McCollum, Betty, 4th MN	56631	2256
Kennedy, Joseph P., III, 4th MA	55931	306	McDermott, Jim, 7th WA	53106	1035
Kildee, Daniel T., 5th MI	53611	227	McGovern, James P., 2d MA	56101	438
Kilmer, Derek, 6th WA	55916	1520	McHenry, Patrick T., 10th NC	52576	2334
Kind, Ron, 3d WI	55506	1502	McKinley, David B., 1st WV	54172	412
King, Peter T., 2d NY	57896	339	McMorris Rodgers, Cathy, 5th WA	52006	203
King, Steve, 4th IA	54426	2210	McNerney, Jerry, 9th CA	51947	2265
Kinzinger, Adam, 16th IL	53635	1221	McSally, Martha, 2d AZ	52542	1029
Kirkpatrick, Ann, 1st AZ	53361	201	Meadows, Mark, 11th NC	56401	1024
Kline, John, 2d MN	52271	2439	Meehan, Patrick, 7th PA	52011	434
Knight, Stephen, 25th CA	51956	1023	Meeks, Gregory W., 5th NY	53461	2234
Kuster, Ann M., 2d NH	55206	137	Meng, Grace, 6th NY	52601	1317
Labrador, Raúl R., 1st ID	56611	1523	Messer, Luke, 6th IN	53021	508
LaHood, Darin, 18th IL	56201	2464	Mica, John L., 7th FL	54035	2187
LaMalfa, Doug, 1st CA	53076	322	Miller, Candice S., 10th MI	52106	320
Lamborn, Doug, 5th CO	54422	2402	Miller, Jeff, 1st FL	54136	336
Lance, Leonard, 7th NJ	55361	2352	Moolenaar, John R., 4th MI	53561	117
Langevin, James R., 2d RI	52735	109	Mooney, Alexander X., 2d WV	52711	1232
Larsen, Rick, 2d WA	52605	2113	Moore, Gwen, 4th WI	54572	2245
Larson, John B., 1st CT	52265	1501	Moulton, Seth, 6th MA	58020	1408
Latta, Robert E., 5th OH	56405	2448	Mullin, Markwayne, 2d OK	52701	1113
Lawrence, Brenda L., 14th MI	55802	1237	Mulvaney, Mick, 5th SC	55501	2419
Lee, Barbara, 13th CA	52661	2267	Murphy, Patrick, 18th FL	53026	211
Levin, Sander M., 9th MI	54961	1236	Murphy, Tim, 18th PA	52301	2332

* Reprinted from the Congressional telephone directory at *www.clerk.house.gov.*

REPRESENTATIVES

Name	Phone	Room	Name	Phone	Room
Nadler, Jerrold, 10th NY	55635	2109	Rigell, E. Scott, 2d VA	54215	418
Napolitano, Grace F., 32d CA	55256	1610	Roby, Martha, 2d AL	52901	442
Neal, Richard E., 1st MA	55601	341	Roe, David P., 1st TN	56356	407
Neugebauer, Randy, 19th TX	54005	1424	Rogers, Harold, 5th KY	54601	2406
Newhouse, Dan, 4th WA	55816	1641	Rogers, Mike, 3d AL	53261	324
Noem, Kristi L., At Large, SD	52801	2422	Rohrabacher, Dana, 48th CA	52415	2300
Nolan, Richard M., 8th MN	56211	2366	Rokita, Todd, 4th IN	55037	1717
Norcross, Donald, 1st NJ	56501	1531	Rooney, Thomas J., 17th FL	55792	2160
Norton, Eleanor Holmes (Delegate), DC	58050	2136	Roskam, Peter J., 6th IL	54561	2246
Nugent, Richard B., 11th FL	51002	1727	Ros-Lehtinen, Ileana, 27th FL	53931	2206
Nunes, Devin, 22d CA	52523	1013	Ross, Dennis A., 15th FL	51252	229
Olson, Pete, 22d TX	55951	2133	Rothfus, Keith J., 12th PA	52065	1205
O'Rourke, Beto, 16th TX	54831	1330	Rouzer, David, 7th NC	52731	424
Palazzo, Steven M., 4th MS	55772	331	*Roybal-Allard, Lucille*, 40th CA	51766	2330
Pallone, Frank, Jr., 6th NJ	54671	237	Royce, Edward R., 39th CA	54111	2310
Palmer, Gary J., 6th AL	54921	206	*Ruiz, Raul*, 36th CA	55330	1319
Pascrell, Bill, Jr., 9th NJ	55751	2370	*Ruppersberger, C. A. Dutch*, 2d MD	53061	2416
Paulsen, Erik, 3d MN	52871	127	*Rush, Bobby L.*, 1st IL	54372	2188
Payne, Donald M., Jr., 10th NJ	53436	103	Russell, Steve, 5th OK	52132	128
Pearce, Stevan, 2d NM	52365	2432	Ryan, Paul D., 1st WI	53031	1233
Pelosi, Nancy, 12th CA	54965	233	*Ryan, Tim*, 13th OH	55261	1421
Perlmutter, Ed, 7th CO	52645	1410	**Sablan, Gregorio Kilili Camacho**		
Perry, Scott, 4th PA	55836	1207	(Delegate), MP	52646	423
Peters, Scott H., 52d CA	50508	1122	Salmon, Matt, 5th AZ	52635	2349
Peterson, Collin C., 7th MN	52165	2204	*Sánchez, Linda T.*, 38th CA	56676	2329
Pierluisi, Pedro R. (Resident			*Sanchez, Loretta*, 46th CA	52965	1211
Commissioner), PR	52615	2410	Sanford, Mark, 1st SC	53176	2201
Pingree, Chellie, 1st ME	56116	2162	*Sarbanes, John P.*, 3d MD	54016	2444
Pittenger, Robert, 9th NC	51976	224	Scalise, Steve, 1st LA	53015	2338
Pitts, Joseph R., 16th PA	52411	420	*Schakowsky, Janice D.*, 9th IL	52111	2367
Plaskett, Stacey E. (Delegate), VI	51790	509	*Schiff, Adam B.*, 28th CA	54176	2411
Pocan, Mark, 2d WI	52906	313	*Schrader, Kurt*, 5th OR	55711	2431
Poe, Ted, 2d TX	56565	2412	Schweikert, David, 6th AZ	52190	409
Poliquin, Bruce, 2d ME	56306	426	Scott, Austin, 8th GA	56531	2417
Polis, Jared, 2d CO	52161	1433	*Scott, David*, 13th GA	52939	225
Pompeo, Mike, 4th KS	56216	436	*Scott, Robert C. "Bobby"*, 3d VA	58351	1201
Posey, Bill, 8th FL	53671	120	Sensenbrenner, F. James, Jr., 5th WI	55101	2449
Price, David E., 4th NC	51784	2108	*Serrano, José E.*, 15th NY	54361	2227
Price, Tom, 6th GA	54501	100	Sessions, Pete, 32d TX	52231	2233
Quigley, Mike, 5th IL	54061	2458	*Sewell, Terri A.*, 7th AL	52665	1133
Radewagen, Aumua Amata Coleman			Sherman, Brad, 30th CA	55911	2242
(Delegate), AS	58577	1339	Shimkus, John, 15th IL	55271	2217
Rangel, Charles B., 13th NY	54365	2354	Shuster, Bill, 9th PA	52431	2268
Ratcliffe, John, 4th TX	56673	325	Simpson, Michael K., 2d ID	55531	2312
Reed, Tom, 23d NY	53161	2437	*Sinema, Kyrsten*, 9th AZ	59888	1530
Reichert, David G., 8th WA	57761	1127	*Sires, Albio*, 8th NJ	57919	2342
Renacci, James B., 16th OH	53876	328	*Slaughter, Louise McIntosh*, 25th NY	53615	2469
Ribble, Reid J., 8th WI	55665	1513	*Smith, Adam*, 9th WA	58901	2264
Rice, Kathleen M., 4th NY	55516	1508	Smith, Adrian, 3d NE	56435	2241
Rice, Tom, 7th SC	59895	223	Smith, Christopher H., 4th NJ	53765	2373
Richmond, Cedric L., 2d LA	56636	240	Smith, Jason, 8th MO	54404	1118

HOUSE OF REPRESENTATIVES

REPRESENTATIVES

Name	Phone	Room	Name	Phone	Room
Smith, Lamar, 21st TX	54236	2409	Walberg, Tim, 7th MI	56276	2436
Speier, Jackie, 14th CA	53531	2465	Walden, Greg, 2d OR	56730	2185
Stefanik, Elise M., 21st NY	54611	512	Walker, Mark, 6th NC	53065	312
Stewart, Chris, 2d UT	59730	323	Walorski, Jackie, 2d IN	53915	419
Stivers, Steve, 15th OH	52015	1022	Walters, Mimi, 45th CA	55611	236
Stutzman, Marlin A., 3d IN	54436	2418	Walz, Timothy J., 1st MN	52472	1034
Swalwell, Eric, 15th CA	55065	129	Wasserman Schultz, Debbie, 23d FL	57931	1114
Takai, Mark, 1st HI	52726	422	Waters, Maxine, 43d CA	52201	2221
Takano, Mark, 41st CA	52305	1507	Watson Coleman, Bonnie, 12th NJ	55801	126
Thompson, Bennie G., 2d MS	55876	2466	Weber, Randy K., Sr., 14th TX	52831	510
Thompson, Glenn, 5th PA	55121	124	Webster, Daniel, 10th FL	52176	1039
Thompson, Mike, 5th CA	53311	231	Welch, Peter, At Large, VT	54115	2303
Thornberry, Mac, 13th TX	53706	2208	Wenstrup, Brad R., 2d OH	53164	1318
Tiberi, Patrick J., 12th OH	55355	1203	Westerman, Bruce, 4th AR	53772	130
Tipton, Scott R., 3d CO	54761	218	Westmoreland, Lynn A., 3d GA	55901	2202
Titus, Dina, 1st NV	55965	401	Whitfield, Ed, 1st KY	53115	2184
Tonko, Paul, 20th NY	55076	2463	Williams, Roger, 25th TX	59896	1323
Torres, Norma J., 35th CA	56161	516	Wilson, Frederica S., 24th FL	54506	208
Trott, David A., 11th MI	58171	1722	Wilson, Joe, 2d SC	52452	2229
Tsongas, Niki, 3d MA	53411	1714	Wittman, Robert J., 1st VA	54261	2454
Turner, Michael R., 10th OH	56465	2239	Womack, Steve, 3d AR	54301	1119
Upton, Fred, 6th MI	53761	2183	Woodall, Rob, 7th GA	54272	1724
Valadao, David G., 21st CA	54695	1004	Yarmuth, John A., 3d KY	55401	403
Van Hollen, Chris, 8th MD	55341	1707	Yoder, Kevin, 3d KS	52865	215
Vargas, Juan, 51st CA	58045	1605	Yoho, Ted S., 3d FL	55744	511
Veasey, Marc A., 33d TX	59897	414	Young, David, 3d IA	55476	515
Vela, Filemon, 34th TX	59901	437	Young, Don, At Large, AK	55765	2314
Velázquez, Nydia M., 7th NY	52361	2302	Young, Todd C., 9th IN	55315	1007
Visclosky, Peter J., 1st IN	52461	2328	Zeldin, Lee M., 1st NY	53826	1517
Wagner, Ann, 2d MO	51621	435	Zinke, Ryan K., At Large, MT	53211	113

K-111

UNITED STATES SENATE

SENATORS

Republicans in roman; Democrats in *italic*; Independents in SMALL CAPS

Room numbers beginning with SD are in the Dirksen Senate Office Building, room numbers beginning with SH are in the Hart Senate Office Building, and room numbers beginning with SR are in the Russell Senate Office Building. Calls from outside the Capitol complex can be made by dialing (202) 22 plus the five-digit number listed in this directory.

Washington, DC 20510

Name	Phone	Room	Name	Phone	Room
Vice Pres. Biden, Joseph R., Jr.	42424		Grassley, Chuck (IA)	43744	SH-135
Alexander, Lamar (TN)	44944	SD-455	Hatch, Orrin G. (UT)	45251	SH-104
Ayotte, Kelly (NH)	43324	SR-144	*Heinrich, Martin* (NM)	45521	SH-303
Baldwin, Tammy (WI)	45653	SH-717	*Heitkamp, Heidi* (ND)	42043	SH-110
Barrasso, John (WY)	46441	SD-307	Heller, Dean (NV)	46244	SH-324
Bennet, Michael F. (CO)	45852	SR-261	*Hirono, Mazie K.* (HI)	46361	SH-330
Blumenthal, Richard (CT)	42823	SH-706	Hoeven, John (ND)	42551	SH-338
Blunt, Roy (MO)	45721	SR-260	Inhofe, James M. (OK)	44721	SR-205
Booker, Cory A. (NJ)	43224	SD-359	Isakson, Johnny (GA)	43643	SR-131
Boozman, John (AR)	44843	SH-141	Johnson, Ron (WI)	45323	SH-328
Boxer, Barbara (CA)	43553	SH-112	*Kaine, Tim* (VA)	44024	SR-231
Brown, Sherrod (OH)	42315	SH-713	KING, ANGUS S., Jr. (ME)	45344	SR-133
Burr, Richard (NC)	43154	SR-217	Kirk, Mark (IL)	42854	SH-524
Cantwell, Maria (WA)	43441	SH-511	*Klobuchar, Amy* (MN)	43244	SH-302
Capito, Shelley Moore (WV)	46472	SR-172	Lankford, James (OK)	45754	SH-316
Cardin, Benjamin L. (MD)	44524	SH-509	*Leahy, Patrick J.* (VT)	44242	SR-437
Carper, Thomas R. (DE)	42441	SH-513	Lee, Mike (UT)	45444	SR-361A
Casey, Robert P., Jr. (PA)	46324	SR-393	*Manchin, Joe, III* (WV)	43954	SH-306
Cassidy, Bill (LA)	45824	SH-703	*Markey, Edward J.* (MA)	42742	SD-255
Coats, Daniel (IN)	45623	SR-493	McCain, John (AZ)	42235	SR-218
Cochran, Thad (MS)	45054	SD-113	*McCaskill, Claire* (MO)	46154	SH-730
Collins, Susan M. (ME)	42523	SD-413	McConnell, Mitch (KY)	42541	SR-317
Coons, Christopher A. (DE)	45042	SR-127A	*Menendez, Robert* (NJ)	44744	SH-528
Corker, Bob (TN)	43344	SD-425	*Merkley, Jeff* (OR)	43753	SH-313
Cornyn, John (TX)	42934	SH-517	*Mikulski, Barbara A.* (MD)	44654	SH-503
Cotton, Tom (AR)	42353	SR-124	Moran, Jerry (KS)	46521	SD-521
Crapo, Mike (ID)	46142	SD-239	Murkowski, Lisa (AK)	46665	SH-709
Cruz, Ted (TX)	45922	SR-404	*Murphy, Christopher* (CT)	44041	SH-136
Daines, Steve (MT)	42651	SH-320	*Murray, Patty* (WA)	42621	SR-154
Donnelly, Joe (IN)	44814	SH-720	*Nelson, Bill* (FL)	45274	SH-716
Durbin, Richard J. (IL)	42152	SH-711	Paul, Rand (KY)	44343	SR-167
Enzi, Michael B. (WY)	43424	SR-379A	*Perdue, David* (GA)	43521	SR-383
Ernst, Joni (IA)	43254	SR-111	*Peters, Gary C.* (MI)	46221	SH-724
Feinstein, Dianne (CA)	43841	SH-331	Portman, Rob (OH)	43353	SR-448
Fischer, Deb (NE)	46551	SR-454	*Reed, Jack* (RI)	44642	SH-728
Flake, Jeff (AZ)	44521	SR-413	*Reid, Harry* (NV)	43542	SH-522
Franken, Al (MN)	45641	SH-309	Risch, James E. (ID)	42752	SR-483
Gardner, Cory (CO)	45941	SR-354	Roberts, Pat (KS)	44774	SH-109
Gillibrand, Kirsten E. (NY)	44451	SR-478	Rounds, Mike (SD)	45842	SH-502
Graham, Lindsey (SC)	45972	SR-290	Rubio, Marco (FL)	43041	SR-284

* Reprinted from the Congressional telephone directory at *www.clerk.house.gov.*

SENATE

SENATORS

Name	Phone	Room	Name	Phone	Room
SANDERS, BERNARD (VT)	45141	SD-332	Thune, John (SD)	42321	SD-511
Sasse, Ben (NE)	44224	SR-386A	Tillis, Thom (NC)	46342	SD-185
Schatz, Brian (HI)	43934	SH-722	Toomey, Patrick J. (PA)	44254	SR-248
Schumer, Charles E. (NY)	46542	SH-322	Udall, Tom (NM)	46621	SH-531
Scott, Tim (SC)	46121	SH-520	Vitter, David (LA)	44623	SH-516
Sessions, Jeff (AL)	44124	SR-326	Warner, Mark R. (VA)	42023	SR-475
Shaheen, Jeanne (NH)	42841	SH-506	Warren, Elizabeth (MA)	44543	SH-317
Shelby, Richard C. (AL)	45744	SR-304	Whitehouse, Sheldon (RI)	42921	SH-530
Stabenow, Debbie (MI)	44822	SH-731	Wicker, Roger F. (MS)	46253	SD-555
Sullivan, Dan (AK)	43004	SH-702	Wyden, Ron (OR)	45244	SD-221
Tester, Jon (MT)	42644	SH-311			

COMMITTEES

HOUSE COMMITTEES AND SUBCOMMITTEES

Three-digit room numbers are in the Cannon House Office Building or the Ford House Office Building, as indicated. Four-digit numbers beginning with 1 are in the Longworth House Office Building; with 2, the Rayburn House Office Building; and with 4, 5, or 6, the O'Neill Federal Office Building. Room numbers beginning with SB, ST, HB, and HT or with H or S, followed by three digits, are in the Capitol. Room numbers beginning with CVC, HVC, or SVC are in the Capitol Visitor Center. Calls from outside the Capitol complex can be made by dialing (202) 22 plus the five-digit extension listed in this directory.

STANDING COMMITTEES

	Phone	Room
Agriculture	52171	1301
Biotechnology, Horticulture, and Research	52171	1301
Commodity Exchanges, Energy, and Credit	52171	1301
Conservation and Forestry	52171	1301
General Farm Commodities and Risk Management	52171	1301
Livestock and Foreign Agriculture	52171	1301
Nutrition	52171	1301
Appropriations	52771	H305
Agriculture, Rural Development, Food and Drug Administration, and Related Agencies	52638	2362A
Commerce, Justice, Science, and Related Agencies	53351	H310
Defense	52847	H405
Energy and Water Development, and Related Agencies	53421	2362B
Financial Services and General Government (RHOB)	57245	B300
Homeland Security (RHOB)	55834	B307
Interior, Environment, and Related Agencies (RHOB)	53081	B308
Labor, Health and Human Services, Education, and Related Agencies	53508	2358B
Legislative Branch	67252	HT2
Military Construction, Veterans Affairs, and Related Agencies	53047	HVC227
State, Foreign Operations, and Related Programs	52041	HT2
Transportation, and Housing and Urban Development, and Related Agencies	52141	2358A
Armed Services	54151	2216
Emerging Threats and Capabilities	62843	2340
Military Personnel	57560	2340
Oversight and Investigations	65048	2119
Readiness	68979	2340
Seapower and Projection Forces	62211	2340
Strategic Forces	51967	2340
Tactical Air and Land Forces	54440	2340
Budget (CHOB)	67270	207
Education and the Workforce	54527	2176
Early Childhood, Elementary, and Secondary Education	54527	2176
Health, Employment, Labor, and Pensions	54527	2176
Higher Education and Workforce Training	54527	2176
Workforce Protections	54527	2176
Energy and Commerce	52927	2125
Commerce, Manufacturing, and Trade	52927	2125
Communications and Technology	52927	2125
Energy and Power	52927	2125
Environment and the Economy	52927	2125
Health	52927	2125

* Reprinted from the Congressional telephone directory at *www.clerk.house.gov*

COMMITTEES

	Phone	Room
Oversight and Investigations	52927	2125
Select Investigative Panel of the Committee on Energy and Commerce	52927	2125
Ethics	57103	1015
Financial Services	57502	2129
Capital Markets and Government Sponsored Enterprises	57502	2129
Financial Institutions and Consumer Credit	57502	2129
Housing and Insurance	57502	2129
Monetary Policy and Trade	57502	2129
Oversight and Investigations	57502	2129
Foreign Affairs	55021	2170
Africa, Global Health, Global Human Rights, and International Organizations	67812	5210
Asia and the Pacific	67825	5190
Europe, Eurasia, and Emerging Threats	66434	5210
Terrorism, Nonproliferation, and Trade	61500	5100
The Middle East and North Africa	53345	5210
The Western Hemisphere	69980	5100
Homeland Security (FHOB)	68417	176
Border and Maritime Security (FHOB)	68417	176
Counterterrorism and Intelligence (FHOB)	68417	176
Cybersecurity, Infrastructure Protection, and Security Technologies (FHOB)	68417	176
Emergency Preparedness, Response, and Communications (FHOB)	68417	176
Oversight and Management Efficiency (FHOB)	68417	176
Transportation Security (FHOB)	68417	176
House Administration	58281	1309
Commission on Congressional Mailing Standards:		
Majority	60647	1216
Minority	59337	1307
Judiciary	53951	2138
Courts, Intellectual Property, and the Internet	55741	6310
Crime, Terrorism, Homeland Security, and Investigations	55727	6340
Immigration and Border Security	53926	6320
Regulatory Reform, Commercial, and Antitrust Law	67680	6240
The Constitution and Civil Justice (FHOB)	52825	362
Publications	50408	2138
Natural Resources	52761	1324
Energy and Mineral Resources	59297	1333
Federal Lands	67736	1332
Indian, Insular and Alaska Native Affairs	69725	4450
Oversight and Investigations	57107	4170
Water, Power and Oceans	58331	4120
Oversight and Government Reform	55074	2157
Government Operations	55074	2157
Health Care, Benefits and Administrative Rules	55074	2157
Information Technology	55074	2157
National Security	55074	2157
The Interior	55074	2157
Transportation and Public Assets	55074	2157
Rules	59191	H312
Legislative and Budget Process	59191	H312
Rules and Organization of the House	59191	H312
Minority	59091	1627

COMMITTEES

	Phone	Room
Science, Space, and Technology	56371	2321
Energy	56371	2319
Environment	56371	2319
Oversight	56371	2321
Research and Technology	56371	4220
Space	56371	4220
Small Business	55821	2361
Agriculture, Energy and Trade	55821	2361
Contracting and Workforce	55821	2361
Economic Growth, Tax and Capital Access	55821	2361
Health and Technology	55821	2361
Investigations, Oversight and Regulations	55821	2361
Transportation and Infrastructure	59446	2251
Aviation	63220	2251
Coast Guard and Maritime Transportation (FHOB)	63552	507
Economic Development, Public Buildings, and Emergency Management (FHOB)	53014	586
Highways and Transit	56715	2251
Railroads, Pipelines, and Hazardous Materials (RHOB)	60727	B329
Water Resources and Environment (FHOB)	54360	585
Veterans' Affairs (CHOB)	53527	335
Disability Assistance and Memorial Affairs (CHOB)	59164	337
Economic Opportunity (CHOB)	65491	335
Health (CHOB)	59154	338
Oversight and Investigations (CHOB)	53569	337A
Ways and Means	53625	1102
Health	53943	1104
Human Resources	51025	1129
Oversight (RHOB)	59263	B317
Social Security (RHOB)	59263	B317
Tax Policy	55522	1136
Trade	56649	1103

SELECT COMMITTEES

	Phone	Room
Permanent Select Committee on Intelligence	54121	HVC304
Central Intelligence Agency	54121	HVC304
Department of Defense Intelligence and Overhead Architecture	54121	HVC304
Emerging Threats	54121	HVC304
National Security Agency and Cybersecurity	54121	HVC304
Select Committee on the Events Surrounding the 2012 Terrorist Attack in Benghazi	67100	1036

SENATE COMMITTEES

Room numbers beginning with SR are in the Russell Senate Office Building, room numbers beginning with SD are in the Dirksen Senate Office Building, and room numbers beginning with SH are in the Hart Senate Office Building. Room numbers beginning with SB, ST, HB, and HT or with H or S, followed by three digits, are in the Capitol.

STANDING COMMITTEES

	Phone	Room
Agriculture, Nutrition and Forestry	42035	SR-328A
Appropriations	47257	S-128
Armed Services	43871	SR-228
Banking, Housing and Urban Affairs	47391	SD-534
Budget	40642	SD-624
Commerce, Science, and Transportation	41251	SD-512
Energy and Natural Resources	44971	SD-304
Environment and Public Works	46176	SD-410
Finance	44515	SD-219
Foreign Relations	44651	SD-423
Health, Education, Labor, and Pensions	45375	SD-428
Homeland Security and Governmental Affairs	44751	SD-340
Indian Affairs	42251	SH-838
Judiciary	45225	SD-224
Rules and Administration	46352	SR-305
Small Business and Entrepreneurship	45175	SR-428A
Veterans' Affairs	49126	SR-412

SPECIAL AND SELECT COMMITTEES

	Phone	Room
Aging	45364	SD-G31
Ethics	42981	SH-220
Intelligence	41700	SH-211

JOINT COMMITTEES

	Phone	Room
Economic	45171	SD-G01
Library	46352	SR-305
Printing	58281	1309
Taxation		
FHOB	53621	502
DSOB	45561	SD-G18

LIAISON OFFICES

	Phone	Room
Air Force (Virginia: 703-695-7364) (RHOB)	56656	B322
Army (RHOB)	53853	B325
Coast Guard (RHOB)	54775	B320
Marine Corps (RHOB)	57124	B324
Navy (RHOB)	57126	B324
Office of Personnel Management (RHOB)	54955	B332
Social Security (RHOB)	53133	G3, Lobby1
State Department (RHOB)	64644	B330
Veterans Affairs (RHOB)	52280	B328

Congressional Agencies

ARCHITECT OF THE CAPITOL
U.S. Capitol Building
Washington, DC 20515
(202) 228-1793
www.aoc.gov

UNITED STATES BOTANIC GARDEN
Office of the Executive Director
245 First Street SW
Washington, DC 20024
(202) 226-8333
www.usbg.gov

Conservatory
100 Maryland Avenue SW
Washington, DC 20001
(202) 226-8333

Production Facility
4700 Shepherd Parkway SW
Washington, DC 20032
(202) 226-4780

GOVERNMENT ACCOUNTABILITY OFFICE
441 G Street NW
Washington, DC 20548
(202) 512-3000
www.gao.gov

Office of Public Affairs
441 G Street NW
Washington, DC 20548
(202) 512-4800
www.gao.gov

GOVERNMENT PUBLISHING OFFICE
732 North Capitol Street NW
Washington, DC 20401
(202) 512-1800
www.gpo.gov

* Adapted from the 2015 Edition (July) U.S. Government Manual.

Office of Congressional Relations
Government Publishing Office
732 North Capitol Street NW
Washington, DC 20401
(202) 512-1991
(202) 512-1293 FAX
www.gpo.gov/congressional

Public Relations
Government Printing Office
732 North Capitol Street NW
Washington, DC 20401
(202) 512-1957
(202) 512-1998 FAX
www.gpo.gov/newsroom-media

Customer Services
Government Publishing Office
Washington, DC 20401
(202) 512-0526
www.gpo.gov/procurement/index.html

LIBRARY OF CONGRESS
101 Independence Avenue SE
Washington, DC 20540
(202) 707-5000
www.loc.gov

Office of the Director for Preservation
Library of Congress
Washington, DC 20540-4500
(202) 707-1840

National Library Service for the Blind and Physically Handicapped
Library of Congress
1291 Taylor Street NW
Washington, DC 20542-4960
(202) 707-5100

Copyright Office
Library of Congress
101 Independence Avenue SE
Washington, DC 20559-6000
(202) 707-3000
www.loc.gov/copyright

Reference Referral Service
Library of Congress
101 Independence Avenue SE
Washington, DC 20540-4720
(202) 707-5522
(202) 707-1389 FAX
www.loc.gov/rr/askalib/

Science, Technology and Business Division
Library of Congress
Science Reference Section
101 Independence Avenue SE
Washington, DC 20540-4750
(202) 707-5639
www.loc.gov/rr/scitech

Federal Research Division
Marketing Office
Library of Congress
Washington, DC 20540-4840
(202) 707-9133
(202) 707-3920 FAX

Public Affairs Office
Library of Congress
101 Independence Avenue SE
Washington, DC 20540-8610
(202) 707-2905
(202) 707-9199 FAX
www.loc.gov
E-mail: *pao@loc.gov*

Congressional Research Service
101 Independence Avenue SE
Washington, DC 20540
(202) 707-5000
http://www.loc.gov/crsinfo

CONGRESSIONAL BUDGET OFFICE
Second and D Streets SW
Washington, DC 20515
(202) 226-2600
www.cbo.gov

L. STATE GOVERNMENTS

The Attorneys General of the States and Other Jurisdictions

ALABAMA	Honorable Luther Strange Attorney General of Alabama Office of the Attorney General 501 Washington Avenue, P.O.Box 300152 Montgomery, AL 36130 *www.ago.state.al.us*	(334) 242-7300
ALASKA	Honorable Jahna Lindemuth Attorney General of Alaska Office of the Attorney General 1031 W. 4th Avenue Suite 200 Anchorage, AK 99501-1994 *www.law.state.ak.us/*	(907) 269-5602
AMERICAN SAMOA	Honorable Talauega Eleasalo V. Ale Attorney General of American Samoa Office of the Attorney General American Samoa Gov't, Exec. Office Bldg., Utulei, Territory of American Samoa Pago Pago, AS 96799 *http://americansamoa.gov/index.php/2012-04-25-19-44-32/2012-04-25-19-52-04/departments/legal-affairs*	(684) 633-4163
ARIZONA	Honorable Mark Brnovich Attorney General of Arizona Office of the Attorney General 1275 West Washington Street Phoenix, AZ 85007 *www.azag.gov/*	(602) 542-4266
ARKANSAS	Honorable Leslie Rutledge Attorney General of Arkansas Office of the Attorney General 200 Tower Building 323 Center Street Little Rock, AR 72201-2610 *www.ag.arkansas.gov/*	(800) 482-8982

---

* Reprinted with permission from the National Association of Attorneys General.

CALIFORNIA	Honorable Kamala Harris Attorney General of California Office of the Attorney General 1300 I Street, Suite 1740 Sacramento, CA 95814 *http://ag.ca.gov*	(916) 445-9555
COLORADO	Honorable Cynthia Coffman Attorney General of Colorado Office of the Attorney General 1300 Broadway, 10th floor Denver, CO 80203 *www.coloradoattorneygeneral.gov*	(720) 508-6000
CONNECTICUT	Honorable George Jepsen Attorney General of Connecticut Office of the Attorney General 55 Elm Street Hartford, CT 06106 *www.ct.gov/ag/*	(860) 808-5318
DELAWARE	Honorable Matthew Denn Attorney General of Delaware Office of the Attorney General Carvel State Office Building 820 North French Street Wilmington, DE 19801 *http://attorneygeneral.delaware.gov/*	(302) 577-8338
DISTRICT OF COLUMBIA	Honorable Carl A. Racine 441 4th Street, NW, Suite 1100S Washington, DC 20001 *http://oag.dc.gov*	(202) 727-3400
FLORIDA	Honorable Pam Bondi Attorney General of Florida Office of the Attorney General The Capitol PL 01 Tallahassee, FL 32399-1050 *http://myfloridalegal.com*	(850) 414-3300

GEORGIA	Honorable Sam Olens Attorney General of Georgia Office of the Attorney General 40 Capitol Square, S.W. Atlanta, GA 30334-1300 *http://law.ga.gov*	(404) 656-3300
GUAM	Honorable Elizabeth Barrett-Anderson Attorney General of Guam Office of the Attorney General ITC Building. St. 706 590 S. Marine Corps Drive Tamuning, Guam 96913 *www.guamag.org*	(671) 475-3409
HAWAII	Honorable Douglas S. Chin Attorney General of Hawaii Office of the Attorney General 425 Queen Street Honolulu, HI 96813 *http://ag.hawaii.gov/*	(808) 586-1500
IDAHO	Honorable Lawrence Wasden Attorney General of Idaho Office of the Attorney General Statehouse Boise, ID 83720-1000 *www.ag.idaho.gov/*	(208) 334-2400
ILLINOIS	Honorable Lisa Madigan Attorney General of Illinois Office of the Attorney General James R. Thompson Center 100 West Randolph Street Chicago, IL 60601 *http://illinoisattorneygeneral.gov/*	(312) 814-3000
INDIANA	Honorable Greg Zoeller Attorney General of Indiana Office of the Attorney General Indiana Government Center South Fifth Floor 302 West Washington Street Indianapolis, IN 46204 *www.in.gov/attorneygeneral/*	(317) 232-6201

IOWA	Honorable Tom Miller Attorney General of Iowa Office of the Attorney General Hoover State Office Building 1305 East Walnut Des Moines, IA 50319 *www.IowaAttorneyGeneral.org*	(515) 281-5164
KANSAS	Honorable Derek Schmidt Attorney General of Kansas Office of the Attorney General 120 S.W. 10th Avenue, 2nd Floor Topeka, KS 66612-1597 *www.ag.ks.gov*	(785) 296-2215
KENTUCKY	Honorable Andy Beshear Attorney General of Kentucky Office of the Attorney General 700 Capitol Avenue, Capitol Building, Suite 118 Frankfort, KY 40601 *http://ag.ky.gov*	(502) 696-5300
LOUISIANA	Honorable Jeff Landry Attorney General of Louisiana Office of the Attorney General Post Office Box 94095 Baton Rouge, LA 70804-4095 *www.ag.state.la.us/*	(225) 326-6000
MAINE	Honorable Janet T. Mills Attorney General of Maine Office of the Attorney General State House Station Six Augusta, ME 04333 *www.maine.gov/agl*	(207) 626-8800
MARYLAND	Honorable Brian Frosh Attorney General of Maryland Office of the Attorney General 200 Saint Paul Place Baltimore, MD 21202-2202 *www.oag.state.md.us*	(410) 576-6300

MASSACHUSETTS	Honorable Maura Healey Attorney General of Massachusetts Office of the Attorney General One Ashburton Place Boston, MA 02108-1698 *www.mass.gov/ago*	(617) 727-2200
MICHIGAN	Honorable Bill Schuette Attorney General of Michigan Office of the Attorney General Post Office Box 30212 525 West Ottawa Street Lansing, MI 48909-0212 *www.michigan.gov/ag*	(517) 373-1110
MINNESOTA	Honorable Lori Swanson Attorney General of Minnesota Office of the Attorney General State Capitol, Suite 102 St. Paul, MN 55155 *www.ag.state.mn.us*	(651) 296-3353
MISSISSIPPI	Honorable Jim Hood Attorney General of Mississippi Office of the Attorney General Department of Justice Post Office Box 220 Jackson, MS 39205 *www.ago.state.ms.us/*	(601) 359-3680
MISSOURI	Honorable Chris Koster Attorney General of Missouri Office of the Attorney General Supreme Court Building 207 West High Street Jefferson City, MO 65101 *www.ago.mo.gov/*	(573) 751-3321
MONTANA	Honorable Tim Fox Attorney General of Montana Office of the Attorney General Justice Building 215 North Sanders Helena, MT 59620-1401 *www.doj.mt.gov*	(406) 444-2026

NEBRASKA	Honorable Doug Peterson Attorney General of Nebraska Office of the Attorney General State Capitol Post Office Box 98920 Lincoln, NE 68509-8920 *www.ago.ne.gov*	(402) 471-2682
NEVADA	Honorable Adam Paul Laxalt Attorney General of Nevada Office of the Attorney General Old Supreme Court Building 100 North Carson Street Carson City, NV 89701 *http://ag.state.nv.us/*	(775) 684-1100
NEW HAMPSHIRE	Honorable Joseph A. Foster Attorney General of New Hampshire Office of the Attorney General State House Annex, 33 Capitol Street Concord, NH 03301-6397 *www.doj.nh.gov/*	(603) 271-3658
NEW JERSEY	Honorable Christopher S. Porrino Attorney General of New Jersey Office of the Attorney General Richard J. Hughes Justice Complex 25 Market Street, P.O. Box 080 Trenton, NJ 08625 *www.state.nj.us/lps/*	(609) 292-8740
NEW MEXICO	Honorable Hector Balderas Attorney General of New Mexico Office of the Attorney General Post Office Drawer 1508 Santa Fe, NM 87504-1508 *www.nmag.gov/*	(505) 827-6000
NEW YORK	Honorable Eric Schneiderman Attorney General of New York Office of the Attorney General Department of Law—The Capitol 2nd Floor Albany, NY 12224 *www.ag.ny.gov/*	(518) 474-7330

NORTH CAROLINA	Honorable Roy Cooper Attorney General of North Carolina Office of the Attorney General Department of Justice Post Office Box 629 Raleigh, NC 27602-0629 *www.ncdoj.gov/*	(919) 716-6400
NORTH DAKOTA	Honorable Wayne Stenehjem Attorney General of North Dakota Office of the Attorney General State Capitol 600 East Boulevard Avenue Bismarck, ND 58505-0040 *www.ag.state.nd.us*	(701) 328-2210
N. MARIANA ISLANDS	Honorable Edward Manibusan Office of the Attorney General Administration Building, P.O. Box 10007 Saipan, MP 95960 *www.oagcnmi.net*	(670) 664-2341
OHIO	Honorable Mike Dewine Attorney General of Ohio Office of the Attorney General State Office Tower 30 East Broad Street Columbus, OH 43266-0410 *www.ohioattorneygeneral.gov*	(614) 466-4320
OKLAHOMA	Honorable Scott Pruitt Attorney General of Oklahoma Office of the Attorney General 313 NE 21st Street Oklahoma City, OK 73105 *www.oag.state.ok.us*	(405) 521-3921
OREGON	Honorable Ellen F. Rosenblum Attorney General of Oregon Office of the Attorney General Justice Building 1162 Court Street NE Salem, OR 97301 *www.doj.state.or.us*	(503) 378-6002

PENNSYLVANIA Honorable Kathleen Kane   (717) 787-3391
Attorney General of Pennsylvania
Office of the Attorney General
1600 Strawberry Square
Harrisburg, PA 17120
www.attorneygeneral.gov

PUERTO RICO Honorable Cesar R. Miranda-Rodriguez   (787) 721-2900
Attorney General of Puerto Rico
Office of the Attorney General
GPO Box 902192
San Juan, PR 00902-0192
www.justicia.gobierno.pr

RHODE   Honorable Peter Kilmartin   (401) 274-4400
ISLAND   Attorney General of Rhode Island
Office of the Attorney General
150 South Main Street
Providence, RI 02903
www.riag.ri.gov

SOUTH   Honorable Alan Wilson   (803) 734-3970
CAROLINA   Attorney General of South Carolina
Office of the Attorney General
Rembert C. Dennis Office Building
Post Office Box 11549
Columbia, SC 29211-1549
www.scattorneygeneral.org

SOUTH   Honorable Marty J. Jackley   (605) 773-3215
DAKOTA   Attorney General of South Dakota
Office of the Attorney General
1302 East Highway 14, Suite 1
Pierre, SD 57501-8501
http://atg.sd.gov/

TENNESSEE   Honorable Herbert H. Slatery III   (615) 741-3491
Attorney General of Tennessee
Office of the Attorney General
425 5th Avenue North
Nashville, TN 37243
www.tn.gov/attorneygeneral

TEXAS	Honorable Ken Paxton Attorney General of Texas Office of the Attorney General Capitol Station Post Office Box 12548 Austin, TX 78711-2548 *www.texasattorneygeneral.gov*	(512) 463-2100
UTAH	Honorable Sean Reyes Attorney General of Utah Office of the Attorney General State Capitol, Room 236 Salt Lake City, UT 84114-0810 *http://www.attorneygeneral.utah.gov*	(801) 538-9600
VERMONT	Honorable William H. Sorrell Attorney General of Vermont Office of the Attorney General 109 State Street Montpelier, VT 05609-1001 *http://www.atg.state.vt.us/*	(802) 828-3173
VIRGIN ISLANDS	Honorable Claude E. Walker Attorney General of the Virgin Islands Office of the Attorney General Department of Justice G.E.R.S. Building 34-38 Kronprinsdens Gade St. Thomas, VI 00802	(340) 774-5666
VIRGINIA	Honorable Mark Herring Attorney General of Virginia Office of the Attorney General 202 North Ninth Street Richmond, VA 23219 *www.oag.state.va.us*	(804) 786-2071
WASHINGTON	Honorable Bob Ferguson Attorney General of Washington Office of the Attorney General 1125 Washington Street SE P.O. Box 40100 Olympia, WA 98504-0100 *www.atg.wa.gov/*	(360) 753-6200

WEST VIRGINIA	Honorable Patrick Morrisey Attorney General of West Virginia Office of the Attorney General State Capitol 1900 Kanawha Boulevard East Charleston, WV 25305 *www.wvago.gov/*	(304) 558-2021
WISCONSIN	Honorable Brad Schimel Attorney General of Wisconsin Office of the Attorney General State Capitol Suite 114 East Post Office Box 7857 Madison, WI 53707-7857 *www.doj.state.wi.us*	(608) 266-1221
WYOMING	Honorable Peter K. Michael Attorney General of Wyoming Office of the Attorney General State Capitol Building Cheyenne, WY 82002 *http://attorneygeneral.state.wy.us*	(307) 777-7841

State Insurance Commissioners

ALABAMA - AL

JIM L. RIDLING Commissioner *Executive Committee* *(Chair, Southeast Zone)*	Alabama Department of Insurance PO Box 303351 Montgomery, Alabama 36130-3351 **Street Address** 201 Monroe Street, Suite 502 Montgomery, Alabama 36104	Main 334-269-3550 Fax 334-241-4192 Toll Free *In-State Only* 800-433-3966

ALASKA - AK

LORI K. WING-HEIER Director *(Western Zone)*	**Primary Address** State of Alaska Dept. of Commerce, Community & Economic Development Division of Insurance 550 West 7th Avenue, Suite 1560 Anchorage, Alaska 99501-3567 **Juneau Mailing Address** PO Box 110805 Juneau, Alaska 99811-0805 **Juneau Street Address** 333 Willoughby, 9th Floor Juneau, Alaska 99801	Main 907-269-7900 Fax 907-269-7910 Toll Free *In-State Only* 800-467-8725 **Juneau** Main 907-465-2515 Fax 907-465-3422

AMERICAN SAMOA - AS

TAU FATI TANUVASA Insurance Commissioner *(Western Zone)*	Office of the Governor American Samoa Government A P Lutali Executive Office Building Pago Pago, American Samoa 96799	Main 684-633-4116 Fax 684-633-2269

ARIZONA - AZ

LESLIE R. HESS Interim Director *(Western Zone)*	Arizona Department of Insurance 2910 North 44th Street, Suite 210 Phoenix, Arizona 85018-7269	Main 602-364-3100 Fax 602-364-3470

ARKANSAS - AR

ALLEN W. KERR Commissioner *(Southeast Zone)*	Arkansas Insurance Department 1200 West Third Street Little Rock, Arkansas 72201-1904	Main 501-371-2600 Fax 501-371-2618 Toll Free 800-282-9134

* Reprinted with permission from the National Association of Insurance Commissioners, www.naic.org.

CALIFORNIA - CA

| DAVE JONES
Commissioner

Executive Committee
(Chair, Western Zone) | California Department of Insurance
300 Capitol Mall, Suite 1700
Sacramento, California 95814

San Francisco Office
45 Fremont Street, 23rd Floor
San Francisco, California 94105

Los Angeles Office
300 South Spring Street, South Tower
Los Angeles, California 90013 | Main 916-492-3500
Fax   916-445-5280

San Francisco
Main 415-538-4010
Fax   415-904-5889

Los Angeles
Main 213-346-6464
Fax   213-897-9051

Consumer Hotline
  Out-of-state
    213-897-8921
  In State
    800-927-4357 |

COLORADO - CO

| MARGUERITE SALAZAR
Commissioner

(Western Zone) | Colorado Dept. of Regulatory Agencies
Division of Insurance
1560 Broadway, Suite 850
Denver, Colorado 80202 | Main 303-894-7499
Fax   303-894-7455

Toll Free
    800-930-3745 |

CONNECTICUT - CT

| KATHARINE L. WADE
Commissioner

Executive Committee
(Vice President, Northeast Zone) | Connecticut Insurance Department
PO Box 816
Hartford, Connecticut 06142-0816

Street Address
153 Market Street, 7th Floor
Hartford, CT 06103 | Main 860-297-3800
Fax   860-566-7410

Toll Free
    800-203-3447 |

DELAWARE - DE

| KAREN WELDIN STEWART
Commissioner

(Northeast Zone) | Delaware Department of Insurance
841 Silver Lake Boulevard
Dover, Delaware 19904 | Main 302-674-7300
Fax   302-739-5280

Toll Free
    800-282-8611 |

INSURANCE COMMISSIONERS

DISTRICT OF COLUMBIA - DC

STEPHEN C. TAYLOR Commissioner *(Northeast Zone)*	Government of the District of Columbia Department of Insurance, Securities, and Banking 810 First Street, N. E., Suite 701 Washington, DC 20002	Main 202-727-8000 Fax 202-535-1196

FLORIDA - FL

DAVID ALTMAIER Commissioner *(Southeast Zone)*	Office of Insurance Regulation The Larson Building 200 E. Gaines Street, Rm 101A Tallahassee, Florida 32399-0305	Main 850-413-5914 Fax 850-488-3334 Toll Free *In State Only* 877-693-5236 Helpline *Out-of-State* 850-413-3089
JEFF ATWATER Chief Financial Officer	Department of Financial Services J. Edwin Larson Building 200 E. Gaines Street Tallahassee, Florida 32399-0301	Main 850-413-2850 Fax 850-413-2950

GEORGIA - GA

RALPH T. HUDGENS Commissioner *(Southeast Zone)*	Office of Insurance and Safety Fire Commissioner Two Martin Luther King, Jr. Dr. West Tower, Suite 704 Atlanta, Georgia 30334	Main 404-656-2070 Fax 404-657-8542 Toll Free 800-656-2298

GUAM - GU

ARTEMIO B. ILAGAN Banking and Insurance Commissioner *(Western Zone)*	Department of Revenue & Taxation Regulatory Division PO Box 23607 GMF Barrigada, Guam 96921 **Street Address** 1240 Army Drive Barrigada, Guam 96913	Main 671-635-1817 Fax 671-633-2643

HAWAII - HI

| GORDON I. ITO
Commissioner

(Western Zone) | Department of Commerce and Consumer
Affairs (DCCA)
Insurance Division
PO Box 3614
Honolulu, Hawaii 96811-3614

Street Address
King Kalakaua Building
335 Merchant Street, Room 213
Honolulu, Hawaii 96813 | Main 808-586-2790
Fax 808-586-2806 |

IDAHO - ID

| DEAN CAMERON
Director

(Western Zone) | Idaho Department of Insurance
PO Box 83720
Boise, Idaho 83720-0043

Street Address
700 West State Street, 3rd Floor
Boise, Idaho 83720-0043 | Main 208-334-4250
Fax 208-334-4398

Toll Free *In-State Only*
800-721-3272 |

ILLINOIS - IL

| ANNE MELISSA DOWLING
Acting Director

(Midwest Zone) | Illinois Department of Insurance
320 W. Washington Street
Springfield, Illinois 62767-0001

122 S. Michigan Avenue, 19th Floor
Chicago, Illinois 60603 | Main 217-782-4515
Fax 217-782-5020

Main 312-814-2420
Fax 312-814-5416 |

INDIANA - IN

| STEPHEN W. ROBERTSON
Commissioner

(Midwest Zone) | Indiana Department of Insurance
311 W. Washington Street
Suite 103
Indianapolis, Indiana 46204 | Main 317-232-2385
Fax 317-232-5251 |

INSURANCE COMMISSIONERS

IOWA - IA

NICK GERHART Commissioner *Executive Committee* *(Vice Chair, Midwest Zone)*	Iowa Insurance Division Two Ruan Center 601 Locust, 4th Floor Des Moines, Iowa 50309-3438	Main 515-281-5705 Fax 515-281-3059 Toll Free *In State Only* 877-955-1212

KANSAS - KS

KEN SELZER Commissioner *(Midwest Zone)*	Kansas Insurance Department 420 SW 9th Street Topeka, Kansas 66612-1678	Main 785-296-3071 Fax 785-296-7805 Toll Free 800-432-2484

KENTUCKY - KY

BRIAN MAYNARD Commissioner *(Southeast Zone)*	Kentucky Department of Insurance PO Box 517 Frankfort, Kentucky 40602-0517 **Street Address** 215 West Main Street Frankfort, Kentucky 40601	Main 502-564-3630 Fax 502-564-1453 Toll Free *In State Only* 800-595-6053

LOUISIANA - LA

JAMES J. DONELON Commissioner *Executive Committee* *Past President* *(Vice Chair, Southeast Zone)*	Louisiana Department of Insurance PO Box 94214 Baton Rouge, Louisiana 70804-9214 **Street Address** 1702 N 3rd Street Baton Rouge, Louisiana 70802	Main 225-342-5900 Fax 225-342-8622 Toll Free 800-259-5300 800-259-5301

MAINE - ME

ERIC A. CIOPPA **Superintendent** **NAIC Secretary-Treasurer** *Executive Committee* *(Northeast Zone)*	Department of Professional & Financial Regulation Maine Bureau of Insurance 34 State House Station Augusta, Maine 04333-0034 **Street Address** 76 Northern Avenue Gardiner, Maine 04345	Main 207-624-8475 Fax 207-624-8599 Toll Free 800-300-5000

MARYLAND - MD

AL REDMER JR. Commissioner *Executive Committee* *(Chair, Northeast Zone)*	Maryland Insurance Administration 200 St. Paul Place Suite 2700 Baltimore, Maryland 21202-2272	Main 410-468-2090 Fax 410-468-2020 Toll Free 800-492-6116

MASSACHUSETTS - MA

DANIEL R. JUDSON Commissioner *(Northeast Zone)*	Office of Consumer Affairs and Business Regulation (OCABR) Massachusetts Division of Insurance 1000 Washington Street, 8th Floor Boston, Massachusetts 02118-6200	Main 617-521-7794 Fax 617-753-6830

MICHIGAN - MI

PATRICK M. MCPHARLIN Director *(Midwest Zone)*	Dept. of Insurance & Financial Services PO Box 30220 Lansing, Michigan 48909-7720 **Street Address** Mason Building, 8th Floor 530 W. Allegan Street Lansing, Michigan 48933	Main 517-284-8800 Fax 517-284-8844 Toll Free 877-999-6442

MINNESOTA - MN

MIKE ROTHMAN Commissioner *(Midwest Zone)*	Minnesota Department of Commerce 85 7th Place East, Suite 500 St. Paul, Minnesota 55101	Main 651-539-1500 Fax 651-539-1547

INSURANCE COMMISSIONERS

MISSISSIPPI - MS

MIKE CHANEY Commissioner *Executive Committee (Secretary, Southeast Zone)*	Mississippi Insurance Department PO Box 79 Jackson, Mississippi 39205-0079 **Street Address** 1001 Woolfolk State Office Building 501 N. West Street Jackson, Mississippi 39201	Main 601-359-3569 Fax 601-359-2474 Toll Free 800-562-2957

MISSOURI - MO

JOHN M. HUFF **Director** **NAIC President** *Executive Committee (Midwest Zone)*	Missouri Department of Insurance, Financial Institutions and Professional Registration (DIFP) PO Box 690 Jefferson City, Missouri 65102-0690 **Street Address** 301 West High Street, Room 530 Jefferson City, Missouri 65101	Main 573-751-4126 Fax 573-751-1165 Toll Free 800-726-7390

MONTANA - MT

MONICA J. LINDEEN **Commissioner of** **Securities and Insurance,** **Montana State Auditor** **NAIC Most Recent President** *Executive Committee (Western Zone)*	Montana Office of the Commissioner of Securities and Insurance, Montana State Auditor 840 Helena Avenue Helena, Montana 59601	Main 406-444-2040 Fax 406-444-3497 Toll Free 800-332-6148

NEBRASKA - NE

BRUCE R. RAMGE Director *Executive Committee (Chair, Midwest Zone)*	Nebraska Department of Insurance PO Box 82089 Lincoln, NE 68501-2089 **Street Address** 941 O Street, Suite 400 Lincoln, Nebraska 68508	Main 402-471-2201 Fax 402-471-4610 Toll Free 877-564-7323

NEVADA - NV

BARBARA RICHARDSON Commissioner	Nevada Dept. of Business & Industry Division of Insurance 1818 East College Pkwy, Suite 103 Carson City, Nevada 89706	Main 775-687-0700 Fax 775-687-0787 Toll Free 888-872-3234
(Western Zone)	**Las Vegas Office** 2501 E. Sahara Avenue, Suite 302 Las Vegas, Nevada 89104	Main 702-486-4009 Fax 702-486-4007

NEW HAMPSHIRE - NH

ROGER A. SEVIGNY Commissioner *Executive Committee* *Past President* *(Secretary, Northeast Zone)*	New Hampshire Insurance Department 21 South Fruit Street, Suite 14 Concord, New Hampshire 03301	Main 603-271-2261 Fax 603-271-1406 Toll Free 800-852-3416

NEW JERSEY - NJ

RICHARD J. BADOLATO Acting Commissioner *(Northeast Zone)*	State of New Jersey Department of Banking and Insurance 20 West State Street PO Box 325 Trenton, New Jersey 08625-0325	Main 609-292-7272 Fax 609-984-5273 Toll Free 800-446-SHOP

NEW MEXICO - NM

JOHN G. FRANCHINI Superintendent *(Western Zone)*	Office of Superintendent of Insurance PO Box 1689 Santa Fe, New Mexico 87504-1689 **Street Address** P.E.R.A. Building 1120 Paseo De Peralta Santa Fe, New Mexico 87501	Main 505-827-4601 Fax 505-827-4734 Toll Free 855-427-5674

NEW YORK - NY

MARIA T. VULLO Acting Superintendent *(Northeast Zone)*	New York State Dept. of Financial Services One State Street New York, New York 10004-1511	Main 212-709-3500 Fax 212-709-3520

INSURANCE COMMISSIONERS

NORTH CAROLINA - NC

WAYNE GOODWIN Commissioner *(Southeast Zone)*	North Carolina Department of Insurance 1201 Mail Service Center Raleigh, North Carolina 27699-1201 **Street Address** Dobbs Building 430 N. Salisbury Street Raleigh, North Carolina 27603-5926	Main 919-807-6000 Fax 919-733-6495 Toll Free 800-662-7777 800-546-5664

NORTH DAKOTA - ND

ADAM HAMM Commissioner *Past President* *(Midwest Zone)*	North Dakota Insurance Department State Capitol, Fifth Floor 600 E. Boulevard Avenue Bismarck, North Dakota 58505-0320	Main 701-328-2440 Fax 701-328-4880 Toll Free 800-247-0560

NORTHERN MARIANA ISLANDS - MP

MARK O. RABAULIMAN Secretary of Commerce *(Western Zone)*	Commonwealth of the N Mariana Islands Department of Commerce Office of the Insurance Commissioner Caller Box 10007 CK Saipan, MP 96950	Main 670-664-3077 Fax 670-664-3067

OHIO - OH

MARY TAYLOR Lt. Governor/Director *(Midwest Zone)*	Ohio Department of Insurance 50 West Town Street Third Floor, Suite 300 Columbus, OH 43215	Main 614-644-2658 Fax 614-644-3743 Toll Free 800-686-1526

OKLAHOMA - OK

JOHN D. DOAK Commissioner *Executive Committee* *(Secretary, Midwest Zone)*	**Oklahoma City Office** Five Corporate Plaza 3625 NW 56th Street, Suite 100 Oklahoma City, OK 73112 **Tulsa Office** Oklahoma Insurance Department 7645 E. 63rd St., Suite 102 Tulsa, OK 74133	Main 405-521-2828 Fax 405-521-6635 Toll Free 800-522-0071 Main 918-295-3700 Fax 918-994-7916

OREGON - OR

LAURA N. CALI Insurance Commissioner/Chief Actuary *Executive Committee* *(Vice Chair, Western Zone)*	Oregon Dept. of Consumer & Bus Srvcs Division of Financial Regulation PO Box 14480 Salem, Oregon 97309-0405 **Street Address** 350 Winter Street NE Salem, Oregon 97301-3883	Main 503-947-7980 Fax 503-378-4351 Toll Free 888-877-4894

PENNSYLVANIA - PA

TERESA D. MILLER Commissioner *(Northeast Zone)*	Pennsylvania Insurance Department 1326 Strawberry Square Harrisburg, Pennsylvania 17120	Main 717-787-7000 Fax 717-772-1969 Toll Free *In State Only* 877-881-6388

PUERTO RICO - PR

ÁNGELA WEYNE Commissioner of Insurance *(Southeast Zone)*	Office of the Commissioner of Insurance B5 Calle Tabonuco Suite 216 PMB356 Guaynabo, Puerto Rico 00968-3029	Main 787-304-8686 Fax 787-273-6365

RHODE ISLAND - RI

ELIZABETH KELLEHER DWYER Superintendent *(Northeast Zone)*	State of Rhode Island Department of Business Regulation Division of Insurance 1511 Pontiac Avenue, Building 69-2 Cranston, Rhode Island 02920	Main 401-462-9520 Fax 401-462-9602

SOUTH CAROLINA - SC

RAYMOND G. FARMER Director *(Southeast Zone)*	South Carolina Department of Insurance PO Box 100105 Columbia, South Carolina 29202-3105 **Street Address** Capitol Center 1201 Main Street, Suite 1000 Columbia, South Carolina 29201	Main 803-737-6160 Fax 803-737-6205

INSURANCE COMMISSIONERS

SOUTH DAKOTA - SD

LARRY DEITER Director *(Midwest Zone)*	South Dakota Dept. of Labor & Regulation Division of Insurance South Dakota Division of Insurance 124 South Euclid Avenue, 2nd Floor Pierre, SD 57501	Main 605-773-3563 Fax 605-773-5369

TENNESSEE - TN

JULIE MIX MCPEAK **Commissioner** **NAIC Vice President** *Executive Committee* *(Southeast Zone)*	Tennessee Department of Commerce & Insurance (TDCI) Davy Crockett Tower Twelfth Floor 500 James Robertson Parkway Nashville, Tennessee 37243-0565	Main 615-741-6007 Fax 615-532-6934 Toll Free 800-342-4029

TEXAS - TX

DAVID MATTAX Commissioner *Executive Committee* *(Secretary, Western Zone)*	Texas Department of Insurance PO Box 149104 Austin, Texas 78714-9104 **Street Address** 333 Guadalupe Street Austin, Texas 78701	Main 512- 676-6000 Fax 512-490-1045 Toll Free 800-578-4677

UTAH - UT

TODD E. KISER Commissioner *(Western Zone)*	Utah Insurance Department 3110 State Office Building Salt Lake City, Utah 84114-6901	Main 801-538-3800 Fax 801-538-3829 Toll Free 800-439-3805

U.S. VIRGIN ISLANDS - VI

OSBERT POTTER Lt. Governor/Commissioner *(Southeast Zone)*	Office of the Lieutenant Governor Division of Banking & Insurance 1131 King Street, 3rd Floor, Suite 101 Christiansted, St. Croix, VI 00820	Main 340-773-6459 Fax 340-719-3801
	St. Thomas Office 5049 Kongens Gade St. Thomas, Virgin Islands 00802	Main 340-774-7166 Fax 340-774-9458

VERMONT - VT

SUSAN L. DONEGAN Commissioner *(Northeast Zone)*	Department of Financial Regulation 89 Main Street Montpelier, Vermont 05620-3101	Main 802-828-3301 Fax 802-828-3306 Toll Free 800-964-1784

VIRGINIA - VA

JACQUELINE K.
CUNNINGHAM
Commissioner
 	
(Southeast Zone)
	Virginia State Corporation Commission
	Bureau of Insurance
	PO Box 1157
	Richmond, Virginia 23218
	
	Street Address
	1300 East Main Street
	Richmond, Virginia 23219
		Main 804-371-9741
		Fax 804-371-9873
		
		Toll Free
		    800-552-7945
		Ombudsman/Consumer
		Services *Out of State*
		    877-310-6560

WASHINGTON - WA

MIKE KREIDLER Commissioner *(Western Zone)*	Washington State Office of the Insurance Commissioner PO Box 40256 Olympia, Washington 98504-0256 **Street Address** 5000 Capitol Boulevard, SE Tumwater, Washington 98501	Main 360-725-7000 Fax 360-586-3535 Toll Free 800-562-6900

INSURANCE COMMISSIONERS

WEST VIRGINIA - WV

MICHAEL D. RILEY Commissioner *(Southeast Zone)*	West Virginia Offices of the Insurance Commissioner PO Box 50540 Charleston, West Virginia 25305-0540 NEW! **Street Address** 900 Pennsylvania Avenue, Charleston, WV 25302	Main 304-558-3354 Fax 304-558-0412 Toll Free 888-879-9842

WISCONSIN - WI

TED NICKEL **Commissioner** **NAIC President-Elect** *Executive Committee* *(Midwest Zone)*	State of Wisconsin Office of the Commissioner of Insurance PO Box 7873 Madison, Wisconsin 53707-7873 **Street Address** 125 South Webster Street GEF III – Second Floor Madison, Wisconsin 53703-3474	Main 608-266-3585 Fax 608-266-9935 Toll Free 800-236-8517

WYOMING - WY

TOM GLAUSE Commissioner *(Western Zone)*	Wyoming Insurance Department 106 East 6th Avenue Cheyenne, Wyoming 82002-0440	Main 307-777-7401 Fax 307-777-2446 Toll Free 800-438-5768

NAIC OFFICES:

Central Office
1100 Walnut Street, Suite 1500
Kansas City, Missouri
64106-2197
Main   816-842-3600
Fax   816-783-8175

Executive Office
Hall of States Building
444 North Capitol Street NW,
Suite 700
Washington, DC 20001
Main   202-471-3990
Fax   816-460-7493

Capital Markets and
Investment Analysis Office
One New York Plaza
Suite 4210
New York, NY 10004
Main   212-398-9000
Fax   212-382-4207

W:\EXEC\CMSRS\Membership List.docx

State Mental Health Departments

Alabama
Department of Mental Health
100 North Union Street
Montgomery, AL 36130-1410
Phone: 334-242-3454 or 800-367-0955
   (AL only)
FAX: 334-242-0725
http://www.mh.alabama.gov

Alaska
Department of Health and Social
   Services
Division of Behavioral Health
P.O. Box 110620
350 Main Street, Suite 214
Juneau, AK 99811
Phone: 907-465-3370
Fax: 907-465-2668
http://dhss.alaska.gov/dbh/Pages/default
   .aspx

Arizona
Department of Health Services
150 N. 18th Avenue, 2d Floor
Phoenix, AZ 85007
Phone: 602-542-1025
Fax: 602-542-0883
Toll Free: 1-800-867-5808
http://www.azdhs.gov/bhs/index.htm

Arkansas
Department of Human Services
Division of Behavioral Health Services
305 S. Palm Street
Little Rock, AR 72205
Phone: 501-686-9164
TDD: 501-686-9176
Fax: 501-686-9182
http://humanservices.arkansas.gov/dbhs/
   Pages/default.aspx

California
Department of Health Care Services
Mental Health Services Division
1501 Capitol Avenue, MS 4000
P.O. Box 997413
Sacramento, CA 95899-7413
Phone: 916-322-7445
http://www.dhcs.ca.gov/services/Pages/
   MentalHealthPrograms-Svcs.aspx

Colorado
Department of Human Services
Office of Behavioral Health
3824 W. Princeton Circle
Denver, CO 80236-3111
Phone: 303-866-7400
Fax: 303-866-7481
http://www.colorado.gov/cs/Satellite/
   CDHS-BehavioralHealth/CBON/
   1251578892077

Connecticut
Department of Mental Health and
   Addiction Services
410 Capitol Avenue
P.O. Box 341431
Hartford, CT 06134
Phone: 860-418-7000
http://www.ct.gov/dmhas/site/default.asp

Delaware
Health and Social Services
Division of Substance Abuse and
   Mental Health
1901 N . DuPont Highway
New Castle, DE 19720
Phone: 302-255-9040
Fax: 302-255-4429
http://www.dhss.delaware.gov/dhss/dsamh/

Florida

Department of Children and Families
Substance Abuse and Mental Health
Department
1317 Winewood Blvd.
Building 1, Room 202
Tallahassee, FL 32399-0700
Phone: 850-487-1111
Fax: 850-922-2993
http://www.myflfamilies.com/service-programs/mental-health

Georgia

Department of Behavioral Health and
Developmental Disabilities
Two Peachtree Street, N.W.
24th Floor
Atlanta, GA 30303
Phone: 404-657-2252
http://dbhdd.georgia.gov

Hawaii

Department of Health
Behavioral Health Services
Administration
Phone: 808-586-4686
http://health.hawaii.gov/about/links-to-doh-program-information/behavioral-health-services-administration/

Idaho

Department of Health and Welfare
Mental Health Services
Phone: 208-334-0800
http://healthandwelfare.idaho.gov/Medical/MentalHealth/tabid/103/Default.aspx

Illinois

Department of Human Services
Division of Mental Health
901 Southwind Dr.
Springfield, IL 62703
Phone: 217-786-6058
http://www.dhs.state.il.us

Indiana

Family and Social Services
Administration
Division of Mental Health and
Addiction
Phone: 800-901-1133
http://www.in.gov/fssa/dmha/index.htm

Iowa

Iowa Department of Human Services
Mental Health and Disability Services
1305 E. Walnut Street
5th Floor SE
Des Moines, IA 50319
515-281-7277
http://dhs.iowa.gov/mhds/mental-health

Kansas

Kansas Department of Health and
Environment
Bureau of Community Health Systems
1000 SW Jackson, Suite 340
Topeka, Kansas 66612-1365
Phone: 785-296-1200
http://www.kdheks.gov/olrh/RH_Mental Health.htm

Kentucky
Kentucky Cabinet for Health and
  Family Services
Department for Behavioral Health,
  Developmental and Intellectual
  Disabilities
275 E. Main Street 4WF
Frankfort, KY 40621
Phone: 502-564-4527
TTY: 502-564-5777
FAX: 502-564-5478
dbhdid.ky.gov/kdbhdid/

Louisiana
Mental Health Advocacy Service
1450 Poydras Street
Suite 1105
New Orleans, LA 70112
Phone: 504-568-8904
http://wwwcfprd.doa.louisiana.gov/
  laservices/publicpages/Service
  Detail.cfm?service_id=2848

Maine
Department of Health and Human
  Services
Office of Substance Abuse and Mental
  Health Services
41 Anthony Avenue
State House Station #11
Augusta, ME 04333-0011
Phone: 207-287-2595
TTY: Maine relay 711
Fax: 207-287-4334
http://www.maine.gov/dhhs/samhs/

Maryland
Department of Health and Mental
  Hygiene
201 West Preston Street
Baltimore, MD 21201
Phone: 410-767-6500 or 877-463-3464
http://dhmh.maryland.gov

Massachusetts
Office of Health and Human Services
Department of Mental Health
25 Staniford Sreet
Boston, MA 02114
Phone: 617-626-8000
http://www.mass.gov/

Michigan
Michigan Mental Health Commission
P.O. Box 30013
Lansing, MI 48909
Phone: 517-335-7858
http://www.michigan.gov/mentalhealth/

Minnesota
Department of Human Services
Mental Health Division
P.O. Box 64981, St. Paul, MN 55164
Phone: 651-431-2225
Fax: 651-431-7418
http://mn.gov/dhs/people-we-serve/adults/
  health-care/mental-health/

Mississippi
Department of Mental Health
1101 Robert E. Lee Building
239 N. Lamar Street
Jackson, MS 39201
Phone: 601-359-1288
FAX: 601-359-6295
TDD: 601-359-6230
http://www.dmh.state.ms.us

Missouri
Department of Mental Health
1706 E. Elm Street
P.O. Box 687
Jefferson City, MO 65101
Phone: 573-751-4122 or 800-364-9687
FAX: 573-751-8224
http://dmh.mo.gov

Montana
Department of Public Health and
  Human Services
Addictive and Mental Disorders
  Division
100 N. Park, Suite 300
P.O. Box 202905
Helena, MT 59620-2905
Phone: 406-444-3964
FAX: 406-444-4435
http://www.dphhs.mt.gov/amdd

Nebraska
Department of Health and Human
  Services
Division of Behavioral Health
301 Centennial Mall South
Lincoln, NE 68509
Phone: 402-471-3121
http://dhhs.ne.gov/behavioral_health

Nevada
Department of Health and Human
  Services
Division of Public and Behavioral
  Health
4126 Technology Way
Carson City, NV 89706
Phone: 775-684-4200
FAX: 775-684-4211
http://www.health.nv.gov

New Hampshire
Department of Health and Human
  Services
Bureau of Behavioral Health
129 Pleasant Street
Concord, NH 03301-3852
Phone: 603-271-5007
FAX: 603-271-5058
http://www.dhhs.nh.gov/dcbcs/bbh

New Jersey
Department of Human Services
Division of Mental Health and
  Addiction Services
Capital Place One
P.O. Box 700
Trenton, NJ 08625
Phone: 800-382-6717
*http://www.state.nj.us/humanservices/
  dmhs/home/index.html*

New Mexico
Department of Health
Behavioral Health Institute
3695 Hot Springs Boulevard
Las Vegas, NM 87701
Phone: 505-454-2100 or 800-446-5970
http://archive.nmbhi.org

New York
Office of Mental Health
44 Holland Avenue
Albany, NY 12229
Phone: 800-597-8481
http://www.omh.ny.gov/index.html

North Carolina
Department of Health and Human
  Services
Division of Mental Health,
  Developmental Disabilities, and
  Substance Abuse Services
Bath Building, MSC#3001
306 N. Wilmington Street
Raleigh, NC 27601
Phone: 919-733-7011
FAX: 919-508-0951
http://www.ncdhhs.gov/mhddsas/index.htm

North Dakota

Department of Human Services
Division of Mental Health and
  Substance Abuse Services
1237 W. Divide Avenue, Suite 1C
Bismarck, ND 58501-1208
Phone: 701-328-8920 or 800-755-2719
  (ND only)
FAX: 701-328-8969
http://www.nd.gov/humanservices/
  services/mentalhealth/index.html

Ohio

Department of Mental Health and
  Addiction Services
The James A. Rhodes State Office
  Tower
30 East Broad Street, 8th Floor
Columbus, OH 43215-3430
Phone: 614-466-2596 or 877-275-6364
TTY: 614-752-9696
http://mha.ohio.gov

Oklahoma

Department of Mental Health and
  Substance Abuse Services
1200 NE 13th Street
Oklahoma City, OK 73117
Phone: 405-522-3908 or 800-522-9054
TDD: 405-522-3851
FAX: 405-522-3650
http://ok.gov/odmhsas/

Oregon

Addictions and Mental Health Services
500 Summer Street NE
Salem, OR 97301-1079
Phone: 503-945-5763
TTY: 800-375-2863
http://www.oregon.gov/oha/amh/Pages/
  index.aspx

Pennsylvania

Department of Human Services
Office of Mental Health and Substance
  Abuse Services
P.O Box 2675
Harrisburg, PA 17105-2675
Phone: 717-787-6443
http://www.dhs.pa.gov

Rhode Island

Department of Behavioral Healthcare,
  Developmental Disabilities and
  Hospitals
Mental Health Services
14 Harrington Road
Cranston, RI 02920
Phone: 401-462-3291
FAX: 401-462-3204
http://www.bhddh.ri.gov

South Carolina

Department of Mental Health
2414 Bull Street
Columbia, SC 29202
Phone: 803-898-8581
http://www.state.sc.us/dmh/

South Dakota

Department of Social Services
Behavioral Health Services
811 E. 10th Dept. 9
Sioux Falls, SD 57103
Phone: 605-367-5236
http://dss.sd.gov/behavioralhealthservices/

Tennessee

Department of Mental Health and
  Substance Abuse Services
Andrew Jackson Building
500 Dearderick Street, 6th Floor
Nashville, TN 37243
Phone: 615-532-6500
http://www.tn.gov/mental/

Texas
Department of State Health Services
Mental Health and Substance Abuse
   Division
P.O. Box 149347
Mail Code 2053
Austin, TX 78714
Phone: 866-378-8440 option 3
FAX: 512-419-2063
https://www.dshs.state.tx.us/mhsa/

Utah
Department of Human Services
Division of Substance Abuse and
   Mental Health
195 North 1950 West
West Salt Lake City, UT 84116
Phone: 801-538-3939
FAX: 801-538-9892
http://www.hsmh.state.ut.us/#

Vermont
Department of Mental Health
Redstone Building
280 State Drive
NOB 2 North
Waterbury, VT 05671-2010
Phone: 802-241-0090
Fax: 802-241-0100
http://mentalhealth.vermont.gov

Virginia
Department of Behavioral Health and
   Developmental Services
1220 Bank Street
Richmond, VA 23219
Phone: 804-786-3921
TDD: 804-371-8977
FAX: 804-371-6638
http://www.dbhds.virginia.gov

Washington
Department of Social and Health
   Services
Division of Behavioral Health and
   Recovery
P.O. Box 45330
Olympia, WA 98504-5330
Phone: 360-725-3700
http://www.dshs.wa.gov/dbhr

West Virginia
Department of Health and Human
   Services
Bureau for Behavioral Health and
   Health Facilities
Room 350
350 Capitol Street
Charleston, WV 25301
Phone: 304-356-4811
FAX: 304-558-1008
*http://www.dhhr.wv.gov/bhhf/Pages/
   default.aspx*

Wisconsin
Department of Health Services
Division of Care and Treatment
   Services
1 West Wilson Street
Madison, WI 53707
Phone: 608-266-2717
TTY: 888-701-1251
*http://www.dhs.wisconsin.gov/aboutdhs/
   DMHSAS/index.htm*

Wyoming
Department of Health
Behavioral Health Division
6101 Yellowstone Road, Suite 220
Cheyenne, WY 82002
Phone: 307-777-6494 or 800-535-4006
FAX: 307-777-5849
http://health.wyo.gov/mhsa/index.html

State Securities Commissioners

Alabama
Securities Commission
401 Adams Avenue
Suite 280
P.O. Box 304700
Montgomery, AL 36130-4700
(334) 242-2984
(800) 222-1253
(334) 242-0240 (Fax)

Joseph P. Borg
Director

Alaska
Dept. of Commerce, Community
and Economic Development
Division of Banking and Securities
P.O. Box 110807
Juneau, AK 99811-0807
(907) 465-2521
(907) 465-2549 (Fax)

Kevin Anselm
Director

Arizona
Corporation Commission
Securities Division
1300 West Washington Street
Third Floor
Phoenix, AZ 85007
(602) 542-4242
(602) 388-1335 (Fax)

Matthew J. Neubert
Director

Arkansas
Securities Department
Heritage West Building
201 East Markham, Room 300
Little Rock, AR 72201-1692
(501) 324-9260
(501) 324-9268 (Fax)

Edmond Waters
Securities Commissioner

Montana
Commissioner of Securities & Insurance
Montana State Auditor's Office
Securities Department
840 Helena Avenue
Helena, MT 59601
(406) 444-2040
(406) 444-5558 (Fax)

Lynne Egan
Deputy Securities Commissioner

Nebraska
Nebraska Department of Banking & Finance
Bureau of Securities
1526 K Street, Suite 300
Lincoln, NE 68508
(402) 471-3445

Claire McHenry
Deputy Director – Securities Bureau

Nevada
Secretary of State
Securities Division
555 East Washington Avenue
Suite 5200
Las Vegas, NV 89101
(702) 486-2440
(702) 486-2452 (Fax)

Diana Foley
Securities Administrator

New Hampshire
Bureau of Securities Regulation
Department of State
107 North Main Street, # 204
Concord, NH 03301-4989
(603) 271-1463
(603) 271-7933 (Fax)

Barry Glennon
Director of Securities Regulation

SECURITIES COMMISSIONERS

California
Department of Business Oversight
1515 K Street
Suite 200
Sacramento, CA 95814-4052
(866) 275-2677
(916) 322-1559 (Fax)

Jan Lynn Owen
Commissioner of the Department of Business
Oversight

Colorado
Division of Securities
1560 Broadway
Suite 900
Denver, CO 80202
(303) 894-2320
(303) 861-2126 (Fax)

Gerald Rome
Securities Commissioner

Connecticut
Department of Banking
260 Constitution Plaza
Hartford, CT 06103-1800
(860) 240-8230
(860) 240-8295 (Fax)

Cynthia Antanaitis
Assistant Director of Securities

Delaware
Delaware Department of Justice
Investor Protection Unit
Carvel State Office Building
820 North French Street, 5th Fl.
Wilmington, DE 19801
(302) 577-8424
(302) 577-6987 (Fax)

Gregory Strong
Investor Protection Director

District of Columbia
Department of Insurance, Securities and
Banking
Securities Bureau
810 First Street, NE
Suite 701 Washington, DC 20002
(202) 442-7800
(202) 354-1092 (Fax)

New Jersey
Office of the New Jersey Attorney General
Bureau of Securities
153 Halsey Street
6th Floor
Newark, NJ 07102
(973) 504-3600
(973) 504-3601 (Fax)

Laura Posner
Bureau Chief

New Mexico
Regulation & Licensing Department
Securities Division
2550 Cerrillos Road
Santa Fe, NM 87505
(505) 476-4580
(505) 984-0617 (Fax)

Alexis Lotero
Director of Securities

New York
Office of the Attorney General
Investor Protection Bureau
120 Broadway
23rd Floor
New York, NY 10271
(212) 416-8222
(212) 416-8816 (Fax)

Vacant
Bureau Chief

North Carolina
Department of the Secretary of State
Securities Division
2 South Salisbury Street
Raleigh, NC 27601
(919) 733-3924
(919) 807-2183 (Fax)

Kevin Harrington
Deputy Securities Administrator

North Dakota
Securities Commission
600 East Boulevard
State Capitol, 5th Floor
Bismarck, ND 58505-0510
(701) 328-2910
(701) 328-2946 (Fax)

Theodore A. Miles
Associate Commissioner, Securities

Florida
Office of Financial Regulation
200 East Gaines Street
Tallahassee, FL 32399-0372
(850) 410-9500
(850) 410-9748 (Fax)

Gregory C. Luers
Director, Division of Securities

Georgia
Office of Secretary of State
Securities Division
2 Martin Luther King, Jr., Drive, SE
Suite 313, West Tower
Atlanta, Georgia 30334
(404) 654-6023

Noula Zaharis
Securities Division Director

Hawaii
Department of Commerce & Consumer
Affairs
Division of Business Regulation
335 Merchant Street
Room 203
Honolulu, HI 96813
(808) 586-2744
(808) 586-2733 (Fax)

Ty Nohara
Commissioner of Securities

Idaho
Department of Finance
800 Park Boulevard
Suite 200
Boise, ID 83712
(208) 332-8004
(208) 332-8099 (Fax)

Karen Tyler
Commissioner

Ohio
Division of Securities
77 South High Street, 22nd Floor
Columbus, OH 43215-6131
(614) 644-7381
(614) 466-3316 (Fax)

Andrea Seidt
Commissioner

Oklahoma
Securities Commissioner
Oklahoma Department of Securities
204 N Robinson, Ste. 400
Oklahoma City OK 73102-7001
(405) 280-7700
(405) 280-7742 (Fax)

Irving Faught
Administrator

Oregon
Department of Consumer and Business Services
Division of Financial Regulation
350 Winter Street, NE
Room 410
Salem, OR 97301-3881
(503) 378-4140
(503) 947-7862 (Fax)

Laura Cali
Division Administrator

Pennsylvania
Pennsylvania Department of
Banking and Securities
17 North 2nd Street, Suite 1300
Harrisburg, PA 17101-2290
(717) 787-2665
(717) 783-5125 (Fax)

SECURITIES COMMISSIONERS

Jim Burns
Securities Bureau Chief

Robin Wiessmann
Commissioner (Vice Chair) and Secretary of Banking and
Securities

Illinois
Office of the Secretary of State
Securities Department
69 West Washington Street, Suite 1220
Chicago, IL 60602
(312) 793-3384
(312) 793-1202 (Fax)

Puerto Rico
Commissioner of Financial Institutions
PO Box 11855
San Juan, PR 00910-3855
(787) 723-3131
(787) 723-4225 (Fax)

Tanya Solov
Director of Securities

Damaris Mendoza-Roman
Securities Administrator

Indiana
Office of the Secretary of State
Securities Division
302 West Washington, Room E-111
Indianapolis, IN 46204
(317) 232-6681
(317) 233-3675 (Fax)

Rhode Island
Department of Business Regulation
1511 Pontiac Avenue
John O. Pastore Complex Bldg. 69-1
Cranston, RI 02920-4407
(401) 462-9527
(401) 462-9645 (Fax)

Alex Glass
Securities Commissioner

Maria D'Alessandro
Deputy Director Securities, Commercial Licensing and Gaming
and Athletics Divisions

Iowa
Insurance Division
Securities Bureau
601 Locust – 4th floor
Des Moines, IA 50309
(515) 281-5705
(515) 281-3059 (Fax)

South Carolina
Office of the Attorney General
Securities Division
Rembert C. Dennis Office Building, Suite 501
1000 Assembly Street
PO Box 11549
Columbia, SC 29211-1549
(803) 734-9916
(803) 734-3677 (Fax)

Rosanne Mead
Securities Administrator

T. Stephen Lynch
Deputy Securities Commissioner

Kansas
Office of the Securities Commissioner
109 SW 9th Street
Suite 600
Topeka, KS 66612
(785) 296-3307
(785) 296-6872 (Fax)

South Dakota
Division of Securities
124 South Euclid Avenue
Suite 104
Pierre, SD 57501-3185
(605) 773-4823
(605) 773-5953 (Fax)

Joshua Ney
Securities Commissioner

Michael Youngberg
Director

Kentucky
Department of Financial Institutions
1025 Capital Center Drive
Suite 200
Frankfort, KY 40601
(502) 573-3390
(800) 223-2579
(502) 573-2182 (Fax)

Shonita Bossier
Director, Div. of Securities

Louisiana
Securities Commission
Office of Financial Institutions
8660 United Plaza Blvd.
Second Floor
Baton Rouge, LA 70809-7024
(225) 925-4512

Len Riviere
Deputy Commissioner of Securities

Maine
Dept. of Professional & Financial Regulation
Office of Securities
121 State House Station
Augusta, ME 04333-0121
(207) 624-8551
(207) 624-8590 (Fax)

Judith M. Shaw
Securities Administrator

Maryland
Office of the Attorney General
Division of Securities
200 Saint Paul Place
Baltimore, MD 21202-2020
(410) 576-6360
(410) 576-6532 (Fax)

Melanie Senter Lubin
Securities Commissioner

Massachusetts
Securities Division
One Ashburton Place, Room 1701
Boston, MA 02108
(617) 727-3548
(617) 248-0177 (Fax)

Bryan Lantagne
Director

Tennessee
Department of Commerce & Insurance
Securities Division
Davy Crockett Tower, Suite 680
500 James Robertson Parkway
Nashville, TN 37243-0575
(615) 741-2947
(615) 532-8375 (Fax)

Frank Borger-Gilligan
Assistant Commissioner for Securities

Texas
State Securities Board
208 East 10th Street
5th Floor, PO Box 13167
Austin, TX 78701
(512) 305-8300
(512) 305-8310 (Fax)

John Morgan
Securities Commissioner

U.S. Virgin Islands
Division of Banking and Insurance
18 Kongens Gade
Saint Thomas, VI 00802
(340) 774-7166

Deverita Sturdivant
Chief of Securities Regulation

Utah
Department of Commerce
Division of Securities
160 East 300 South
2nd FloorPO Box 146760
Salt Lake City, UT 84114-6760
(801) 530-6600
(801) 530-6980 (Fax)

Keith Woodwell
Director

Vermont
Department of Financial Regulation
89 Main Street, 3rd Floor
Montpelier, VT 05620-3101
(802) 828-3420
(802) 828-2896 (Fax)

Michael Pieciak
Commissioner

SECURITIES COMMISSIONERS

Michigan
Department of Licensing and Regulatory Affairs
Corporations, Securities and Commercial Licensing Bureau
2501 Woodlake Circle, Okemos, MI 48864
PO Box 30018
Lansing, MI 48909
517-241-6470

Julia Dale
Acting Bureau Director

Minnesota
Department of Commerce
85 East 7th Place
Suite 500
Saint Paul, MN 55101
(651)539-1638
(651) 296-4328 (Fax)

Mike Rothman
Commissioner

Mississippi
Office of the Secretary of State
Securities Division
125 S. Congress Street, PO Box 136
Jackson, MS 39201
(601) 359-1334
(601) 359-9070 (Fax)

Cheryn Netz
Asst. Secretary of State

Missouri
Office of the Secretary of State
Securities Division
600 West Main Street
Jefferson City, MO 65101
(573) 751-4136
(573) 526-3124 (Fax)

Andrew Hartnett
Securities Commissioner

Virginia
State Corporation Commission
Division of Securities & Retail Franchising
1300 East Main Street
9th FloorPO Box 1197
Richmond, VA 23218
(804) 371-9051
(804) 371-9911 (Fax)

Ronald W. Thomas
Director

Washington
Department of Financial Institutions
Securities Division
150 Israel Rd, SWPO Box 9033
Tumwater, WA 98507-9033
(360) 902-8760
(360) 902-0524 (Fax)

William Beatty
Director of Securities

West Virginia
Office of the State Auditor
Securities Division
Building 1
Room W-100
Charleston, WV 25305-0230
(304) 558-2257
(304) 558-4211 (Fax)

Lisa Hopkins
Senior Deputy Commissioner of Securities

Wisconsin
Department of Financial Institutions
Division of Securities
201 W. Washington Avenue
Suite 300PO Box 1768
Madison, WI 53701-1768
(608) 266-1064
(608) 264-7979 (Fax)

Leslie Van Buskirk
Administrator

Wyoming
Secretary of State
Compliance Division
2020 Carey Avenue, Suite 700
Cheyenne, WY 82002
(307) 777-7370
(307) 777-7640 (Fax)

Kelly Janes
Division Director

Canada

Alberta
Securities Commission
Suite 600, 250 – 5th Street S.W.
Calgary, AB T2P 0R4
Canada
(403) 297-4233
(403) 297-6156 (Fax)

David Linder
Executive Director

British Columbia
Securities Commission
P.O. Box 10142, Pacific Centre
701 West Georgia Street
Vancouver, BC V7Y 1L2
Canada
(604) 899-6500
(604) 899-6506 (Fax)

Brenda Leong
Chair

Manitoba
Securities Commission
500-400 St. Mary Avenue
Winnipeg, MB R3C 4K5
Canada
(204) 945-2548
(204) 945-0330 (Fax)

Donald G. Murray
Chair

New Brunswick
Financial and Consumer Services
Commission
85 Charlotte Street, Suite 300
Saint John, NB E2L 2J2
Canada
(506) 643-7691
(506) 658-3059 (Fax)

Kevin Hoyt
Executive Director

Nunavut
Department of Justice
Legal Registries Division
P.O. Box 1000 – Station 570
1st Floor, Brown Building
Iqaluit, NU X0A 0H0
Canada
(867) 975-6598
(867) 975-6594 (Fax)

Jeff Mason
Director

Ontario
Securities Commission
20 Queen Street West, Suite 1900
Box 55
Toronto, ON M5H 3S8
Canada
(416) 593-8314
(416) 593-8122 (Fax)

Kelly Gorman
Deputy Director of Enforcement

Prince Edward Island
Department of Environment, Labour and Justice
95 Rochford Street
4th Floor, Shaw Building
Charlottetown, PE C1A 7N8
Canada
(902) 368-4550
(902) 368-5283 (Fax)

Steven Dowling
Superintendent of Securities

Québec
Autorité des Marchés Financiers
800 Square Victoria, 22nd Floor
C.P. 246, tour de la Bourse
Montreal, PQ H4Z 1G3
Canada
(514) 395-0337
(514) 873-3090 (Fax)

Jean Lorrain
Director, International Affairs
Regulation Directorate

SECURITIES COMMISSIONERS

Newfoundland & Labrador
Financial Services Regulation Division
PO Box 8700
St. John's, NL A1B 4J6
Canada
(709)-729-4189
(709)-729-6187 (Fax)

John O'Brien
Superintendent of Securities

Northwest Territories
Office of Superintendent of Securities
Department of Justice
1st Floor Stuart M. Hodgson Building
5009 – 49th Street
PO Box 1320
Yellowknife, NT X1A 2L9
Canada
(867) 873-7490
(867) 873-0243 (Fax)

Tom Hall
Superintendent of Securities

Nova ScotiaSecurities Commission
5251 Duke Street
Suite 400, Duke TowerPO Box 458
Halifax, NS B3J 2P8
Canada
(902) 424-7768
(902) 424-4625 (Fax)

Paul E. Radford
Chair

Mexico
Comisión Nacional Bancaria y de Valores
Av. Insurgentes Sur 1971, Torre Sur
Piso 11
Plaza Inn, Col. Guadalupe Inn, C.P. 01020
Mexico
011 52 55 1454-6020

Jose Loyola
Director General of International Affairs

Saskatchewan
Financial and Consumer Affairs Authority
601 – 1919 Saskatchewan Drive
Regina, SK S4P 4H2
Canada
(306) 787-5879
(306) 787-5899 (Fax)

Dean Murrison
Director

Yukon
Department of Community Services
Corporate Affairs C-6
P.O. Box 2703
Whitehorse, YT Y1A 2C6
Canada
(867) 667-5314
(867) 393-6251 (Fax)

Frederik Pretorius
Superintendent of Securities

Where to Write for Vital Records
(Updated November 2015)

Introduction

As part of its mission to provide access to data and information relating to the health of the Nation, the National Center for Health Statistics produces a number of publications containing reference and statistical materials. The purpose of this publication is solely to provide information about individual vital records maintained only on file in State or local vital statistics offices.

An official certificate of every birth, death, marriage, and divorce should be on file in the locality where the event occurred. The Federal Government does not maintain files or indexes of these records. These records are filed permanently either in a State vital statistics office or in a city, county, or other local office.

To obtain a certified copy of any of the certificates, write or go to the vital statistics office in the State or area where the event occurred. Addresses and fees are given for each event in the State or area concerned.

To ensure that you receive an accurate record for your request and that your request is filled expeditiously, please follow the steps outlined below for the information in which you are interested:

- Write to the appropriate office to have your request filled.
- Under the appropriate office, information has been included for birth and death records concerning whether the State will accept checks or money orders and to whom they should be made payable. This same information would apply when marriage and divorce records are available from the State office. However, it is impossible for us to list fees and addresses for all county offices where marriage and divorce records may be obtained.
- For all certified copies requested, make check or money order payable for the correct amount for the number of copies you want to obtain. Cash is not recommended because the office cannot refund cash lost in transit.
- Because all fees are subject to change, a telephone number has been included in the information for each State for use in verifying the current fee.
- States have provided their home page address for obtaining current information.
- Type or print all names and addresses in the letter.
- Give the following facts when writing for birth or death records:

1. Full name of person whose record is being requested.
2. Sex.
3. Parents' names, including maiden name of mother.
4. Month, day, and year of birth or death.

5. Place of birth or death (city or town, county, and State; and name of hospital, if known).
6. Purpose for which copy is needed.
7. Relationship to person whose record is being requested.

- Give the following facts when writing for marriage records:

1. Full names of bride and groom.
2. Month, day, and year of marriage.
3. Place of marriage (city or town, county, and State).
4. Purpose for which copy is needed.
5. Relationship to persons whose record is being requested.

- Give the following facts when writing for divorce records:

1. Full names of husband and wife.
2. Date of divorce or annulment.
3. Place of divorce or annulment.
4. Type of final decree.
5. Purpose for which copy is needed.
6. Relationship to persons whose record is being requested.

* Source: U.S. Department of Health and Human Services, National Center for Health Statistics, Hyattsville, MD. (*http://www.cdc.gov/nchs*)

BIRTH, DEATH, MARRIAGE, AND DIVORCE RECORDS

Alabama

Place of event	Cost of copy	Address	Remarks
Birth or Death	$15.00	Alabama Center for Health Statistics Alabama Department of Public Health P.O. Box 5625 Montgomery, AL 36103-5625	State office has records since January 1908. Additional copies of the same record ordered at the same time are $6.00 each. Personal check or money order should be made payable to **State Board of Health**. To verify current fees, the telephone number is (334) 206-5418. This is a recorded message. Information on how to obtain certified copies is also available via the Internet at http://adph.org/vitalrecords. A signature of the applicant is required.
Marriage	$15.00	Same as Birth or Death	State office has records since August 1936. Additional copies ordered at the same time are $6.00 each. Personal check or money order should be made payable to **State Board of Health**. To verify current fees, the telephone number is (334) 206-5418. This is a recorded message. Information on how to obtain certified copies is also available via the Internet at http://adph.org/vitalrecords. A signature of the applicant is required.
	Varies	See remarks	For marriages prior to August 1936, contact Probate Court in county where license was issued.
Divorce	$15.00	Same as Birth or Death	State office has records since January 1950. Additional copies ordered at the same time are $6.00 each. Personal check or money order should be made payable to **State Board of Health**. To verify current fees, the telephone number is (334) 206-5418. This is a recorded message. Information on how to obtain certified copies is also available via the Internet at http://adph.org/vitalrecords. A signature of the applicant is required.
	Varies	See remarks	For divorces prior to 1950, contact Clerk of Circuit Court in county where divorce was granted.

Alaska

Place of event	Cost of copy	Address	Remarks
Birth or Death	$30.00	Department of Health and Social Services Bureau of Vital Statistics P.O. Box 110675 Juneau, AK 99811-0675	State office has records since the 1890's; however, many events before 1930 were never registered with the Bureau. Personal check or money order should be made payable to **Bureau of Vital Statistics**. Additional copies of the same record ordered at the same time are $25.00. To verify current fees, the telephone number is (907) 465-3391. This will be a recorded message. Information on how to obtain certified copies is also available via the Internet at http://dhss.alaska.gov/dph/VitalStats. **ALL REQUESTS MUST INCLUDE A COPY OF A PICTURE ID OF THE APPLICANT.** Enlarge the copy and lighten it as much as possible to be sure that it is clear and readable when sent to the Bureau. A signature under the copied ID is also required.
Heirloom Birth	$55.00	Same as Birth or Death	Two different certificates by Alaskan artists are available. Friends and relatives may order gift certificates for persons entitled to order the record. The heirloom certificates as well as instructions and order forms may be viewed via the Internet at http://dhss.alaska.gov/dph/VitalStats. Additional copies of the same certificate ordered at the same time are $50.00.
Marriage	$30.00	Same as Birth or Death	State office has records since the 1890's; however, many events before 1930 were never registered with the Bureau. Additional copies of the same record ordered at the same time are $25.00.
Heirloom Marriage	$65.00	Same as Birth or Death	Three different heirloom marriage certificates are available. Friends and relatives may order gift certificates for persons entitled to order the record. The heirloom certificates as well as instructions and order forms may be viewed via the Internet at http://dhss.alaska.gov/dph/VitalStats. Additional copies of the same certificate ordered at the same time are $60.00.
Divorce	$25.00	Same as Birth or Death	State office has records since 1950. Additional copies of the same record ordered at the same time are $25.00.
	Varies	See remarks	Clerk of Superior Court in judicial district where divorce was granted. Juneau and Ketchikan (First District), Nome (Second District), Anchorage (Third District), Fairbanks (Fourth District).

American Samoa

Place of event	Cost of copy	Address	Remarks
Birth or Death	$5.00	American Samoa Government	Registrar has birth records since 1890 and death
Amendments	$7.00	Department of Homeland	records since 1900. Money order should be made
		Security	payable to the **Office of Vital Statistics/ASG.**
		Office of Vital Statistics	Personal checks are not accepted. To verify current
		P.O. Box 6894	fees, the telephone numbers are: (684) 633-
		Pago Pago, AS 96799	1405/1406. For Health Information Office, Health
			and Vital Statistics call (684) 633-4606/2262.
			Personal identification is required for verification
			and a notarized letter before record will be sent.
Marriage	$5.00	Same as Birth or Death	
Marriage License	$20.00		
Divorce	$5.00	High Court of American Samoa	
		American Samoa Government	
		Pago Pago, AS 96799	

Arizona

Place of event	Cost of copy	Address	Remarks
Birth	Varies	Office of Vital Records	State office has records since July 1909 and
Death	Varies	Arizona Department of	abstracts of records filed in counties before then.
		Health Services	
		P.O. Box 6018	Some county offices in Arizona are able to provide
		Phoenix, AZ 85005	certified copies of birth and death certificates. Please go to http://www.azdhs.gov for a listing of county offices.
			The State Office of Vital Records does not accept personal checks. A money order or cashier's check should be made payable to **Office of Vital Records**. To verify current fees, the telephone number is (602) 364-1300. This is a recorded message. Information on how to obtain certified copies is also available via the Internet at http://www/azdhs.gov.
			Applicants must submit a copy of picture identification or have their request notarized and need to include a self-addressed stamped envelope.
Marriage	Varies	See remarks	Clerk of Superior Court in county where license was issued.
Divorce	Varies	See remarks	Clerk of Superior Court in county where divorce was granted.

BIRTH, DEATH, MARRIAGE, AND DIVORCE RECORDS

Arkansas

Place of event	Cost of copy	Address	Remarks
Birth Death	$12.00 $10.00	Arkansas Dept. of Health Vital Records Section Slot 44 4815 West Markham St. Little Rock, AR 72205	State office has records since February 1914 and some original Little Rock and Fort Smith records from 1881. Additional copies of the same birth record, when requested at the same time, are $10.00 each. Additional copies of the same death record, when requested at the same time, are $8.00 each. Personal check or money order should be made payable to **Arkansas Department of Health**. To verify current fees, the telephone number is (501) 661-2336. This is a recorded message. Information on how to obtain certified copies is also available via the Internet at http://www.healthyarkansas.com. A photo ID of the person requesting the record is required with each application.
Marriage	$10.00	Same as Birth or Death	Coupons since 1917. Additional copies of the same marriage record, when requested at the same time, are $10.00 each.
Marriage (County)	Varies	Same as Birth or Death	Full certified copy may be obtained from County Clerk in county where license was issued. A certified copy of a marriage coupon may be obtained from the state.
Divorce	$10.00	Same as Birth or Death	State office has coupons since 1923. Additional copies of the same marriage record, when requested at the same time, are $10.00 each.
	Varies	See remarks	Full certified copy may be obtained from Circuit or Chancery Clerk in county where divorce was granted. A certified copy of a divorce coupon may be obtained from the state.

California

Place of event	Cost of copy	Address	Remarks
Birth	$25.00	CA Department of Public Health - Vital Records MS: 5103 P.O. Box 997410 Sacramento, CA 95899-7410	The State office has records since July 1905. For earlier records, contact the County Recorder in the county where the event occurred.
			A personal check or money order should be made payable to **CDPH Vital Records**. Please do not send cash. To verify current fees, the telephone number is (916) 445-2684. This is a recorded message with an option to talk to a customer service representative. Information on how to obtain certified copies is also available via the California Department of Public Health website at: http://www.cdph.ca.gov
			In order to obtain a Certified Copy you MUST complete the sworn statement included with the birth certificate application form, sign the statement under penalty of perjury, and your sworn statement must be notarized. If your request indicates that you want a Certified Copy but does not include a notarized statement sworn under penalty of perjury, the request will be rejected as incomplete and returned to you without being processed. If you request a Certified **Informational** Copy of the record, a notarized sworn statement is not required. Please refer to the CDPH website for further information about Informational copies. **Effective November 1, 2013, CDPH-Vital Records is no longer embossing certified copies of records.**
Death	$21.00	CA Department of Public Health - Vital Records MS: 5103 P.O. Box 997410 Sacramento, CA 95899-7411	The State office has records since July 1905. For earlier records, contact the County Recorder in the county where the event occurred.
			A personal check or money order should be made payable to **CDPH Vital Records**. Please do not send cash. To verify current fees, the telephone number is (916) 445-2684. This is a recorded message with an option to talk to a customer service representative. Information on how to obtain certified copies is also available via the California Department of Public Health website at: http://www.cdph.ca.gov
			In order to obtain a Certified Copy you MUST complete the sworn statement included with the death certificate application form, sign the statement under penalty of perjury, and your sworn

BIRTH, DEATH, MARRIAGE, AND DIVORCE RECORDS

statement must be notarized. If your request indicates that you want a Certified Copy but does not include a notarized statement sworn under penalty of perjury, the request will be rejected as incomplete and returned to you without being processed. If you request a Certified **Informational** Copy of the record, a notarized sworn statement is not required. Please refer to the CDPH website for further information about Informational copies. **Effective November 1, 2013, CDPH-Vital Records is no longer embossing certified copies of records.**

Marriage (State)	$15.00	CA Department of Public Health - Vital Records MS: 5103 P.O. Box 997410 Sacramento, CA 95899-7412	State office only has indexes for public marriage certificates that occurred from 1949-1986 and 1998-1999. For all other years, contact the County Recorder in the county where the event occurred; for confidential marriages, contact the County Clerk where the marriage license was issued. A personal check or money order should be made payable to **CDPH Vital Records.** Please do not send cash. To verify current fees, the telephone number is (916) 445-2684. This will be a recorded message, with an option to talk to a customer service representative. Information on how to obtain a marriage certificate, as well as information about current processing times, is available via the California Department of Public Health website at: http://www.cdph.ca.gov.

In order to obtain a Certified Copy, you MUST complete the sworn statement included with the marriage certificate application form, sign the statement under penalty of perjury, and your sworn statement must be notarized. If your request indicated that you want a Certified Copy but does not include a notarized statement sworn under penalty of perjury, the request will be rejected as incomplete and returned to you without processed. If you request a Certified **Informational** Copy of the record, a notarized sworn statement is not required. Please refer to the CDPH website for further information about Informational Copies. **Effective November 1, 2013, CDPH-Vital Records is no longer embossing certified copies of records.**

Marriage (County)	Various	See Remarks	Contact the County Recorder (for public marriages) or County Clerk (for confidential marriages) in the county where the license was issued. Contact information is available via the California Department of Public Health website at: http://www.cdph.ca.gov.

| Divorce (State) Certificates of Record only | $14.00 | CA Department of Public Health - Vital Records MS: 5103 P.O. Box 997410 Sacramento, CA 95899-7413 | A Certificate of Record includes only the names of the parties to the divorce, the filing date, the county where the divorce was filed, and the court case number – It is not a certified copy of the divorce decree and does not indicate whether the divorce was ever finalized in court. The California Department of Public Health-Vital Records only has information for divorces that were filed with the court between 1962 and June, 1984, and the processing times may exceed six months. For all other years or for a copy of the decree, contact the Superior Court in the county where the event occurred. A personal check or money order should be made payable to **CDPH Vital Records**. Please do not send cash. To verify current fees, the telephone number is (916) 445-2684. This will be a recorded message. Information on how to obtain a divorce record, as well as current processing times, is available via the California Department of Public Health website at: http://www.cdph.ca.gov **Effective November 1, 2013, CDPH-Vital Records is no longer embossing certified copies of records.** |
| Divorce -Decrees (County) | Varies | See remarks | Contact the Clerk of Superior Court in county where the divorce was granted. Contact information is available via the California Department of Public Health website at: http://www.cdph.ca.gov |

Canal Zone

Place of event	Cost of copy	Address	Remarks
Birth or Death	$30.00	Vital Records Section Passport Services U.S. Department of State 1111 19th Street NW Suite 510 Washington, DC 20522-1705	Records available from May 1904 to September 1979. Additional copies of the same record requested at the same time are $20.00 each. Personal check or money order must be signed, dated and made payable to **U.S. Department of State**. Remittance must be payable in U.S. dollars through a U.S. Bank. No credit cards or cash accepted. Telephone or facsimile requests are not accepted. To verify current fees, the telephone number is (202) 955-0307. A signed and notarized written request must be submitted along with a copy of the requester's valid photo identification.
Marriage	$30.00	Same as Birth or Death	Records available from May 1904 to September 1979.

Colorado	Cost of copy	Address	Remarks
Place of event			
Birth	$17.75	Vital Records Section	State office has birth records since 1910 and death
Death	$20.00	CO Department of Public Health and Environment 4300 Cherry Creek Drive South HSVRD-VS-A1 Denver, CO 80246-1530	records since 1900. Additional copies of the same birth record ordered at the same time are $10.00 each. Additional copies of the same death record ordered at the same time are $13.00 each.

Personal check or money order should be made payable to **Vital Records Section**. To verify current fees, the telephone number is (303) 692-2200. This is a recorded message. Information on how to obtain certified copies is also available via the Internet at http:www.cdphe.state.co.us/certs/index.html.

A request for a birth or death record must be accompanied by a photo copy of the requestor's identification before processing.

	Cost of copy	Address	Remarks
Marriage	See remarks	Same as Birth or Death	Certified copies are not available from State Health Department. Fee for verification is $17.00.
	Varies	See remarks	Copies available from County Clerk in county where license was issued.

	Cost of copy	Address	Remarks

Connecticut

Place of event

State issued:			Requests for certified copies of birth should be submitted to the vital records office in the city/town where the person was born, or where the mother lived at the time of the birth. Requests for certified copies of birth and death certificates may also be submitted to the State Vital Records Office.
Birth	$30.00	CT Dept. of Public Health 410 Capitol Ave, MS #11 VRS Hartford, CT 06134	
Death	$20.00	Same as Birth	
Marriage	$20.00	Same as Birth	
Civil Union	$20.00	Same as Birth	A copy of a valid, government issued photographic identification such as a driver's license must be submitted with any request for a birth certificate.
City/Town issued:			
Birth	$20.00	See remarks	If a photo ID is not available, photocopies of two alternative forms of identification may be accepted.
Death	$20.00	See remarks	
Marriage	$20.00	See remarks	For additional details about ordering vital records from CT, please refer to the CT Department of Public Health (DPH) website at
Civil Union	$20.00	See remarks	http://www.ct.gov/dph "Vital Records" or contact a Customer Service Representative at (860) 509-7897 between 12:00 and 4:00 pm EST.

Payment for requests sent to the town of the vital event must be in the form of a check or money order made payable to the respective town or city. Requests sent to the State Vital Records Office require a postal money order made payable to the **Treasurer, State of Connecticut**.

Refer to the CT DPH website above for town contact information via a link to a listing of the CT Town Clerk and Registrar Directory.

Requests for certified copies of a marriage or civil union certificate may be submitted to the city/town where the marriage or civil union ceremony took place, to the town in which either of the parties resided at the time of the marriage or civil union, or to the State Vital Records Office.

Dissolution of Marriage or Civil Union	See remarks	Applicant must contact the Clerk of Superior Court where the dissolution of marriage/civil union was granted. The State Office of Vital Records does not have dissolution decrees and cannot issue certified copies.

Delaware

Place of event	Cost of copy	Address	Remarks
Birth	$25.00	Office of Vital Statistics Division of Public Health 417 Federal Street Dover, DE 19901	State office has birth records from 1942 – present. For previous years, write to Archives Hall of Records, Dover, DE 19901. Photo identification is REQUIRED for all transactions. If submitting by mail, a copy of ID IS REQUIRED. Personal check or money order should be made payable to **Office of Vital Statistics**. To verify current fees, the telephone number is (302) 744-4549. Information on how to obtain certified copies is also available via the Internet at http://www.dhss.delaware.gov/dhss/dph/ss/vitalstats.html.
Death	$25.00	Office of Vital Statistics Division of Public Health 417 Federal Street Dover, DE 19901	State office has death records from 1974 – present. For previous years, write to Archives Hall of Records, Dover, DE 19901. A photo identification is REQUIRED for all transactions. If submitting by mail, a copy of ID IS REQUIRED. Personal check or money order should be made payable to **Office of Vital Statistics**. To verify current fees, the telephone number is (302) 744-4549. Information on how to obtain certified copies is also available via the Internet at http://www.dhss.delaware.gov/dhss/dph/ss/vitalstats.html
Marriage	$25.00	Same as Birth or Death	Records since 1974.
Divorce (state)	$25.00	Same as Birth or Death	Records since 1935. Inquiries will be forwarded to appropriate office. Certified copies are not available from State Office..
Divorce (County)		See remarks	Prothonotary in county where divorce was granted up to 1975. For divorces granted after 1975, the parties concerned should contact Family Court in county where divorce was granted. Certified copies are not available from the State office.

District of Columbia

Place of event	Cost of copy	Address	Remarks
Birth	$23.00	Vital Records Division	Office has birth and death records since August
Death	$18.00	899 North Capitol Street, NE	1874.
		First Floor	
		Washington, DC 20002	Personal check or money order should be made payable **to DC Treasurer**. A copy of government issued picture identification must accompany each request. To verify current fees and obtain general information, the telephone number (202) 671-5000. This is a recorded message. Information on how to obtain certified copies is also available via the Internet at http://www.dchealth.dc.gov.
Marriage	$10.00	DC Superior Court	Marriage information telephone number:
		500 Indiana Avenue, NW	202-879-4840.
		Room 4485	
		Washington, DC 20001	
Divorce	$6.50	DC Superior Court	Records since September 16, 1956.
		500 Indiana Avenue, NW	Divorce information telephone number:
		Room 4335	202-879-1261.
		Washington, DC 20001	
Divorce	Varies	Clerk, U.S. District Court	Records before September 16, 1956.
		for the District of Columbia	
		Washington, DC 20001	

Florida

Place of event	Cost of copy	Address	Remarks
Birth	$9.00	Department of Health	State office has some birth records dating back to
Death	$5.00	Bureau of Vital Statistics	April 1865. The majority of records date from
		P.O. Box 210	January 1917. (If the exact date is unknown, the
		1217 Pearl Street (Zip 32202)	fee is $9.00 (births) or $5.00 (deaths) for the first
		Jacksonville, FL 32231-0042	year searched and $2.00 for each additional year
			up to a maximum of $50.00. Fee includes one
			certification of record if found or statement stating
			record not on file.) Additional copies are $4.00
			each when requested at the same time.

Personal check or money order should be made payable to **Bureau of Vital Statistics**. To verify current fees, please visit our website at http://www.floridavitalstatisticsonline.com or call our telephone number (904) 359-6900. This is a recorded message.

All letters or applications for birth and death must include the signature and relationship/eligibility stated, and a copy of a valid **PICTURE ID** (Driver's License, Passport, Military ID, or State Identification card) of the applicant.

If requesting cause of death, you must also include a copy of a valid **PICTURE ID** (Driver's License, Passport, Military ID, or State Identification card) of the applicant.

Birth records and cause-of-death information in Florida are confidential by law. Please visit our website for information on eligibility.

A self-addressed stamped envelope is appreciated.

Marriage	$5.00	Same as Birth or Death	Records since June 6, 1927. (If the exact date is unknown, the fee is $5.00 for the first year searched and $2.00 for each additional year up to a maximum of $50.00. Fee includes one copy of record if found or certified statement stating record not on file.) Additional copies are $4.00 each when requested at the same time.
Divorce	$5.00	Same as Birth or Death	

BIRTH, DEATH, MARRIAGE, AND DIVORCE RECORDS

Georgia

Place of event	Cost of copy	Address	Remarks
Birth or Death	$25.00	State Office of Vital Records 2600 Skyland Drive, NE Atlanta, GA 30319-3640 *Some records may be obtained at the 159 County Offices.	Date since records have been on file. 1919 to present
			Additional copies of the same record ordered at the same time are $5.00.
			A personal check or money order should be made payable to **George Office of Vital Records**. To verify current fees, the telephone number is (404) 679-4702. This is a recorded message. Information on how to obtain certified copies is also available via the Internet at www.dph.georgia.gov/vitalrecords
			The requestor must provide a copy of a valid government-issued photo ID and signature of applicant.
			*Some counties may have older birth, death, marriage, or divorce records in their files. The county files only contain records of vital events that occurred in that county.
Marriage	$10.00	Same as Birth or Death	Date since records have been on file are June 1952-August 1996.
			All other years contact the Probate Judge in the county where the license was issued.
			Information on how to obtain certified copies is also available via the Internet at www.dph.georgia.gov/vitalrecords
			*Some counties may have older birth, death, marriage, or divorce records in their files. The county files only contain records of vital events that occurred in that county.
Divorce (State)	$10.00	Same as Birth or Death	Date since records have been on file are 1952 to present.
			Information on how to obtain certified copies is also available via the Internet at www.dph.georgia.gov/vitalrecords *Some counties may have older birth, death, marriage, or divorce records in their files. The county files only contain records of vital events that occurred in that county.

Guam

Place of event	Cost of copy	Address	Remarks
Birth or Death	$5.00	Office of Vital Statistics P.O. Box 2816 Hagatna, Guam 96932	Office has records since October 26, 1901. Money order should be made payable to **Treasurer of Guam**. Personal checks are not accepted. To verify current fees, the telephone number is 671-735-7292.
Marriage	$10.00	Same as Birth or Death	
Divorce	Varies	Clerk, Superior Court of Guam Guam Judicial Center 120 West O'Brian Drive Hagatna, Guam 96910	

Hawaii

Place of event	Cost of copy	Address	Remarks
Birth or Death	$10.00	State Department of Health Office of Health Status Monitoring Issuance/Vital Statistics Section P.O. Box 3378 Honolulu, HI 96801	State office has some records as early as 1853. Additional copies ordered at the same time are $4.00 each. Cashiers check, certified check, or money order should be made payable to **State Department of Health.** Personal checks are not accepted. To verify current fees, the telephone number is (808) 586-4533. This is a recorded message. Information on how to obtain certified copies is also available via the Internet at http://health.hawaii.gov/vitalrecords/.
Marriage	$10.00	Same as Birth or Death	
Divorce	$10.00	Same as Birth or Death	Records since July 1951-December 2002. From January 2003, divorce records are available only through the county circuit court.
	Varies	See remarks	Circuit Court in county where divorce was granted.

Idaho

Place of event	Cost of copy	Address	Remarks
Birth Death	$16.00 Computer generated $21.00 Photo Static copy and $16 for additional Photo Static copies	Vital Records Unit Bureau of Vital Records and Health Statistics P.O. Box 83720 Boise, ID 83720-0036	The state office has records since July 1911. Also, some birth records before 1911. For records from 1907 to 1911, write to the County Recorder in the county where the event occurred. Birth records at the state office are legally confidential for 100 years and death records are legally confidential for 50 years. Personal check or money order should be made payable to **Idaho Vital Records**. To verify current fees, the telephone number is (208) 334-5988. This is a recorded message. Information on how to obtain certified copies is also available via the Internet at Idaho Vital Records website: http://www.healthandwelfare.idaho.gov/Health/Vit alRecordsandHealthStatistics/Birth,Death,Marriag e,Divorcecertificates/tabid/82/Default.aspx. Applicants must provide a government-issued photo identification with a signature. If this is not available, the applicant must provide a copy of two forms of identification with one having a signature.
Marriage	$16.00 Computer generated $21.00 Photo Static copy and $16 for additional Photo Static copies	Same as Birth or Death	The state office has records since May 1947. Earlier records are with the County Recorder in the county where the license was issued. Records at the state office are legally confidential for 50 years. Personal check or money order should be made payable to **Idaho Vital Records**. To verify current fees, the telephone number is (208) 334-5988. This is a recorded message. Information on how to obtain certified copies is also available via the Internet at Idaho Vital Records website: http://www.healthandwelfare.idaho.gov/Health/Vit alRecordsandHealthStatistics/Birth,Death,Marriag e,Divorcecertificates/tabid/82/Default.aspx. Applicants must provide a government issued photo identification with a signature. If this is not available, the applicant must provide a copy of two other forms of identification with one having a signature
	Varies	See remarks	County Recorder in county where license was issued.

IDAHO

Place of event	Address		Remarks
Divorce	$16.00 Computer generated	Same as Birth or Death	The state office has records since May 1947. Only a Certificate of Divorce is available from 1950 to present. Records prior to May 1947 are with the Clerk of the Court in the county where the divorce was granted. Records at the state office are legally confidential for 50 years.
	$21.00 Photo Static copy and $16 for additional Photo Static copies		Personal check or money order should be made payable to **Idaho Vital Records**. To verify current fees, the telephone number is (208) 334-5988. This is a recorded message. Information on how to obtain certified copies is also available via the Internet at Idaho Vital Records website: http://www.healthandwelfare.idaho.gov/Health/Vit alRecordsandHealthStatistics/Birth,Death,Marriag e,Divorcecertificates/tabid/82/Default.aspx.
			Applicants must provide a clear and readable copy of both sides of their current driver's license or other current government issued identification with signature. If this is not available, the applicant must either provide a clear and readable copy of both sides of two other forms of current identification with a signature or have their request notarized
	Varies	See remarks	A full certified copy of the divorce decree is available from the Clerk of the Court in the county where the divorce was granted.

Illinois

Place of event	Cost of copy	Address	Remarks
Birth	$15.00 certified copy $10.00 certification	Division of Vital Records Illinois Department of Public Health 925 E Ridgely Avenue Springfield, IL 62702	State office has records since January 1916. For earlier records and for copies of State records since January 1916, write to County Clerk in county where event occurred (county fees vary). The fee for a search of the State files is $10.00. If the record is found, one certification is issued at no additional charge. Additional certifications of the same record ordered at the same time are $2.00 each. The fee for all full certified copy is $15.00. Additional certified copies of the same record ordered at the same time are $2.00 each.

Money orders, certified checks, or personal checks should be made payable to **Illinois Department of Public Health**. To verify current fees, the telephone number is (217) 782-6553. This is a recorded message. Information on how to obtain certified copies is also available via the Internet at http://www.dph.illinois.gov/. |
| Death | $19.00 certified copy $10.00 genealogical copy | | State office has records since January 1916. For earlier records and for copies of State records since January 1916, write to County Clerk in county where event occurred (county fees vary). Genealogical (uncertified) copies are available from the state for death records 20 years or older for $10.00. Additional genealogical copies of the same record ordered at the same time are $2.00 each. The fee for a full certified copy of $19.00. Additional certified copies of the same record ordered at the same time are $4.00 each.

Money orders, certified checks, or personal checks should be made payable to **Illinois Department of Public Health**. To verify current fees, the telephone number is (217) 782-6553. This is a recorded message. Information on how to obtain certified copies is also available via the Internet at http://www.dph.illinois.gov/. |
| Marriage/Civil Union | $5.00 | Same as Birth or Death | Marriage Index since January 1962. Civil Union Index since January 2012. Selected items may be verified (fee $5.00). Certified copies are NOT available from State office.

For certified copies, write to the County Clerk in county where license was issued. Information on how to obtain certified copies is also available via the Internet at http://www.dph.illinois.gov/. |

Dissolution on Marriage/Civil Union	$5.00	Same as Birth or Death	Dissolution of Marriage Index since January 1962. Selected items may be verified (fee $5.00). Certified copies are NOT available from State office.

For certified copies, write to the Clerk of Circuit Court in county where divorce was granted. Information on how to obtain certified copies is also available via the Internet at http://www.dph.illinois.gov/.

Indiana

Place of event	Cost of copy	Address	Remarks
Birth	$10.00	Vital Records	State office birth records begin in October 1907
Death	$8.00	Indiana State Department of Health P.O. Box 7125 Indianapolis, IN 46206-7125	and death records since January 1900. Additional copies of the same birth or death record ordered at the same time are $4.00 each. For earlier records, write to Health Officer in city or county where event occurred.
			Personal check or money order should be made payable to **Indiana State Department of Health**. To verify current fees, the telephone number is (317) 233-2700. Information on how to obtain certified copies is also available via the Internet at http://www.in.gov/isdh/index.htm.
			Applicant must provide a photocopy of a valid identification with picture and signature along with the application. Proof of relationship may be required.
Marriage (State)	$8.00	Same as Birth or Death	State office retain index for marriages since 1958. Certified copies of Record of Marriage are available from the state. However, certified copies of Marriage Certificates are only available from county Clerk of Circuit Court or Clerk of Superior Court in the county where event occurred.
	Varies	See remarks	Clerk of Circuit Court or Clerk of Superior Court in county where license was issued.
Divorce	Varies	See remarks	County Clerk in county where divorce was granted.

Iowa

Place of event	Cost of copy	Address	Remarks
Birth or Death	$15.00	Iowa Department of Public Health Bureau of Vital Records Lucas Office Building 1st Floor 321 East 12th Street Des Moines, IA 50319-0075	State office has records since July 1880. Personal check or money order should be made payable to **Iowa Department of Public Health**. To verify current fees, the telephone number is (515) 281-4944. This is a recorded message. Information on how to obtain certified copies is also available via the Internet at http://www.idph.state.ia.us/. Applicants for all records must provide a photo identification when applying in person. Written applications must include a clear photo copy of a current government issued ID and applicant's notarized signature.
Marriage	$15.00	Same as Birth or Death	State office has records since July 1880.
Divorce	See remarks	Same as Birth or Death	Brief statistical record only since 1960. Inquiries will be forwarded to appropriate office. Certified copies are not available from State Health Department.
	$6.00	See remarks	Clerk of District Court in county where divorce was granted.

Kansas

Place of event	Cost of copy	Address	Remarks
Birth	$15.00	Office of Vital Statistics	State office has records since July 1911. For
Death	$15.00	Curtis State Office Building	earlier records, write to County Clerk in county
		1000 SW Jackson Street	where event occurred. Additional copies of the
		Suite 120	same record ordered at the same time are $15.00
		Topeka, Kansas 66612-2221	each.

Personal check or money order should be made payable to **Vital Statistics**. To verify current fees, the telephone number is (785) 296-1400. This is a recorded message with the option to speak with a Customer Service Representative. Information on how to obtain certified copies is also available via the Internet at http://www.kdheks.gov/vital.

The applicant **MUST** include a copy of a photo ID and a handwritten signature with the request.

Place of event	Cost of copy	Address	Remarks
Marriage	$15.00	Same as Birth or Death	State office has records since May 1913. Additional copies of the same record ordered at the same time are $7.00 each.
	Varies	See remarks	Write to: District Judge in county where license was issued.
Divorce	$15.00	Same as Birth or Death	State office has records since July 1951. Additional copies of the same record ordered at the same time are $7.00 each.
	Varies	See remarks	Write to: Clerk of District Court in county where divorce was granted.

Kentucky

Place of event	Cost of copy	Address	Remarks
Birth	$10.00	Office of Vital Statistics	State office has records since January 1911.
Death	$6.00	Department for Public Health	
		Cabinet for Health and Family	Personal check or money order should be made
		Services	payable to **Kentucky State Treasurer**. To verify
		275 East Main Street 1E-A	current fees, the telephone number is (502) 564-
		Frankfort, KY 40621-0001	4212. Information on how to obtain certified
			copies is also available via the Internet at
			http://chfs.ky.gov/dph/vital/.
Stillbirth	$6.00	Same as Birth or Death	State office has records since January 1911.
			Personal check or money order should be made
			payable to **Kentucky State Treasurer**. To verify
			current fees, the telephone number is (502) 564-
			4212. Information on how to obtain certified
			copies is also available via the Internet at
			http://chfs.ky.gov/dph/vital/.
Marriage	$6.00	Same as Birth and Death	Records since June 1958.
	Varies	See remarks	Clerk of County Court in county where license was issued.
Divorce	$6.00	Same as Birth or Death	Records since June 1958.
	Varies	See remarks	Clerk of Circuit Court in county where decree was issued.

Louisiana

Place of event	Cost of copy	Address	Remarks
Birth (long form) Birth (short form)	$15.00 $9.00 (A $0.50 charge must be added to each mail order) Fees for mail-in services are payable by check or money order. Checks and money orders should be made payable to "Louisiana Vital Records". A copy of a valid photo ID for the applicant is required.	Vital Records Registry PO Box 60630 New Orleans, Louisiana 70160 Main Number: (504) 593-5100	Birth records are strictly confidential, and are maintained by the Center of Vital Records and Statistics for 100 years. Birth records older than 100 years are maintained by the Louisiana State Archives (PO Box 94125, Baton Rouge, LA 70804). For more information on who may obtain a birth record, how to submit a request, special requirements, and other information regarding birth records, please visit the Louisiana Center of State Registrar and Vital Records Website http://vitalrecords.dhh.la.gov.
Death	$7.00 A $0.50 state charge must be added to each mail-in order. Fees for mail-in services are payable by check or money order. Checks and money orders should be made payable to "Louisiana Vital Records". A copy of a valid photo ID for the applicant is required.	Vital Records Registry PO Box 60630 New Orleans, Louisiana 70160 Main Number: (504) 593-5100	Death records are strictly confidential and are maintained by the Center of Vital Records and Statistics for 50 years. Death records older than 50 years are retained at the Louisiana State Archives (PO Box 94125, Baton Rouge, LA 70804). For more information on who may obtain a death records, how to submit a request, special requirements, and additional information regarding death records, please visit the Louisiana Center of State Registrar and Vital Records Website http://vitalrecords.dhh.la.gov.
Marriage Licenses Purchased in Orleans Parish Only	$5.00 A $0.50 state charge must be added to each mail-in order.	Vital Records Registry PO Box 60630 New Orleans, Louisiana 70160 Main Number: (504) 593-5100	The Louisiana Vital Records Registry only maintains marriage records for marriage licenses that were purchased in Orleans Parish. If a marriage license was purchased in a different parish, the marriage records can be obtained by the Clerk of Court in that parish.

Fees for mail-in services are payable by check or money order. Checks and money orders should be made payable to "Louisiana Vital Records".

A copy of a valid photo ID for the applicant is required.

Orleans Parish Marriage records are maintained for 50 years. Marriage records older than 50 years are retained at the Louisiana State Archives (PO Box 94125, Baton Rouge, LA 70804).

For more information on Orleans Parish marriage records, how to submit a request, special requirements, and any additional information regarding marriage records, please visit the Louisiana Center of State Registrar and Vital Records Website http://vitalrecords.dhh.la.gov.

Divorce	Varies	See remarks	Contact the Clerk of Court in the parish where the divorce was granted.

Maine

Place of event	Cost of copy	Address	Remarks
Birth or Death	Certified $15.00 Non-Certified $10.00	Maine Center for Disease Control and Prevention 11 State House Station 220 Capitol Street Augusta, Maine 04333-0011	State office physically houses records since 1923. Records for 1892-1922 housed at the Maine State Archives. For earlier records, write to the municipality where the event occurred. Additional copies of same record ordered at same time are $6.00 each.

To purchase a record, the request must include proof of identification (valid photo IDs such as a driver's license, passport, or other government-issued photo identification) and proof of lineage, if applicable.

Personal check or money order should be made payable to **Treasurer, State of Maine**. To verify current fees, the telephone number is (207) 287-3181, or toll-free at 1-888-664-9491. This will be a recorded message. Information on how to obtain certified copies is also available via the Internet at http://www.state.me.us. |
Marriage	$15.00	Same as Birth or Death	Same as Birth or Death.
Divorce	$15.00	Same as Birth or Death	Same as Birth or Death.
Divorce	Varies	See remarks	Clerk of District Court in judicial division where divorce was granted.

Maryland

Place of event	Cost of copy	Address	Remarks
Birth	$24.00	Division of Vital Records Department of Health and Mental Hygiene 6550 Reisterstown Road P.O. Box 68760 Baltimore, MD 21215-0036	State office has records since August 1898. Records for city of Baltimore are available from January 1875. The cost for the Commemorative Birth Certificate is $50.00. For genealogical studies and older records, you must apply through the Maryland State Archives, 350 Rowe Blvd., Annapolis, MD 21401, (410) 260-6400. Personal check or money order should be made payable to **Division of Vital Records**. To verify current fees, the telephone number is (410) 764-3038. This will be a recorded message. Information on how to obtain certified copies is also available via the Internet at http://www.vsa.state.md.us.
Death	$24 for first copy, $12.00 for additional copy **ordered at the same time.**	Division of Vital Records Department of Health and Mental Hygiene 6550 Reisterstown Road P.O. Box 68760 Baltimore, MD 21215-0036	State office has records since 1969. For Genealogical studies and older records, you must apply through the Maryland State Archives, 350 Rowe Blvd., Annapolis, MD 21401, (410) 260-6400. Personal check or money order should be made payable to **Division of Vital Records**. To verify current fees, the telephone number is (410) 764-3038. This will be a recorded message. Information on how to obtain certified copies is also available via the Internet at http://www.vsa.state.md.us.
Marriage (State, county)	$12.00	Same as Birth or Death	Records since January 1990. Clerk of Circuit Court in county where license was issued or Clerk of Court of Common Pleas of Baltimore City (for licenses issued in City of Baltimore).
Divorce (State, county)	12.00	Same as Birth or Death	Records since January 1992. Certified divorce decrees may be obtained through the Clerk of Circuit Court in the city/county where the divorce was granted. Some items may be verified.

Massachusetts

Place of event	Cost of copy	Address	Remarks
Birth or Death	$20.00 (In person) $32.00 (Mail request) $3.00 (State Archives)	Registry of Vital Records and Statistics 150 Mount Vernon Street 1st Floor Dorchester, MA 02125-3105	State office has no records previous to 1921. For earlier records, write to The Massachusetts Archives at Columbia Point, 220 Morrissey Boulevard, Boston, MA 02125 (617) 727-2816.

Personal check or money order should be made payable to **Commonwealth of Massachusetts**. To verify current fees, the telephone number is (617) 740-2600. This is a recorded message.

Information on how to obtain certified copies is also available via the Massachusetts Department of Public Health, Registry of Vital Records and Statistics website at: http://www.mass.gov/dph.rvrs. |
Marriage	$20.00 (In person) $32.00 (Mail request) $3.00 (State Archives)	Same as Birth or Death	Records since 1916.
Divorce	No Fee	Same as Birth or Death	Index only since 1952. Inquirer will be directed where to send request. Certified copies are not available from State office.
Divorce (county)	Varies	See remarks	Registrar of Probate Court in county where divorce was granted.

BIRTH, DEATH, MARRIAGE, AND DIVORCE RECORDS

Michigan

Place of event	Cost of copy	Address	Remarks
Birth or Affidavit of Parentage	$34.00 Rush fee additional $12.00	Vital Records Request P.O. Box 30721 Lansing, MI 48909	State office has records of births that occurred and were filed with the state since 1867. Some of the records (especially pre-1906 births) were not filed with the state. Affidavit of Parentage records are on file in Central Paternity Registry since June 1, 1997 and can be ordered from the State Office and can be ordered from the State Office. Records prior to that date would have to be obtained from the court where they were filed.
Search for Vital Record for: Certified Copy Administrative Use Copy Statistical Use Copy Official No Find Statement	New Fee $34.00 Rush Fee $12.00 Add. Copies $16.00 Add. Years $12.00		
Authenticated Copies of Vital Record	New Fee $42.00 Rush Fee $25.00 Add. Copies $26.00		Personal check or money order should be made payable to **State of Michigan**. Fees are $34.00 for the search and first certified copy of any birth, or Affidavit of Parentage record. Exception is Senior Citizen age 65+ ($14.00) requesting their own birth record. Additional copies of any record ordered at the same time are $16.00 each. To request an application call the recorded message at (517) 335-8656 to leave your name and mailing address with type of application needed. To speak to a customer service representative call 517- 335-8666 and press option #4. Information on how to obtain certified copies is also available via the website at http://www.michigan.gov/mdch/0,4612,7-132-4645---,00.html.
Verification of Events	New Fee $18.00 Add. Copies $12.00		
Establishment of Vital Record Delayed Birth Delayed Death Delayed Stillbirth Delayed Foreign Born Adoption	New Fee $50.00 Add. Copies $16.00		
Veteran's Use Adoption Agency Senior Citizen	No Fee No Fee New Fee $14.00 Rush Fee $12.00 Add. Copies $16.00 Add. Years $12.00		
Creation of New Record/Correction Adoption Legal Name Change of Minor Acknowledgement of Paternity Sex Change Order of Filiation Replace Court Ordered Adoption Minor error before birth Amend Birth or Death Record Legal Name Change of Adult	New Fee $50.00 Rush Fee $25.00 Add. Copies $16.00		Michigan birth records and Affidavit of Parentage records are restricted documents and are available only to eligible individuals. A photocopy of an eligible individual's current photo identification (state driver's license, state personal ID card, or passport, etc.) is required to be sent in, along with the signed application and appropriate fee. Copies of records may also be obtained from the County Clerk in county where event occurred. Fees vary from county to county. City of Detroit Vital Records office was closed effective 12/13/13 and all records transferred to Wayne County. You may obtain Detroit records from the State Office or the Wayne County Office.
Application for Documentation	New Fee $12.00 Rush Fee $12.00		

Death	$34.00 Rush fee additional $12.00	Vital Records Request P.O. Box 30721 Lansing, MI 48909	State office has records of deaths that occurred and were filed with the state since 1867. Some of the records (especially pre-1897 deaths) were not filed with the state. Death records are not restricted so anyone can order. Please check or money order should be made payable to **State of Michigan.** Fees $34.00 for the search and first certified copy of any death record. Additional copies of any record ordered at the same time are $16.00 each. To request an application the telephone number is (517) 335-8656. This will be a recorded message. To speak to a customer service representative the telephone number is 517-335-8666 and press option #4. Information on how to obtain certified copies is also available via the http://www.michigan.gov/mdch/0,4612,7-132-4645---,00.html.
Marriage (State)	$34.00 Rush fee additional $12.00	Same as Birth or Death	Records since 1867. Some marriages (especially pre-1926) were not filed with the state. Marriage records are not restricted so anyone can order. To request an application the telephone number is (517) 335-8656. This will be a recorded message. To speak to a customer service representative the telephone number is 517- 335-8666 and press option #4. Information on how to obtain certified copies is also available via the http://www.michigan.gov/mdch/0,4612,7-132-4645---,00.html.
Marriage (County)	Varies	See remarks	County Clerk in county where license was issued.
Divorce (State)	$34.00 Rush fee additional $12.00	Same as Birth or Death	Records since 1897. Some divorces (especially pre-1924) were not filed with the state. Divorce records are not restricted so anyone can order. The state office will only have the record of

divorce. Judgment must be obtained from the court that finalized.

To request an application the telephone number is (517) 335-8656. This will be a recorded message. To speak to a customer service representative the telephone number is 517 -335-8666 and press option #4. Information how to obtain certified copies is also available via the http://www.michigan.gov/mdch/0,4612,7-132-4645---,00.html.

| Divorce (County) | Varies | See remarks | County Clerk in county where divorce was granted. |

Minnesota

Place of event	Cost of copy	Address	Remarks
Birth	$26.00	Minnesota Department of Health	Office of the State Registrar has birth records on
Death	$13.00	Central Cashiering –	file from January 1900 to current. Copies of birth
		Vital Records	records can be obtained from any Local Registrar.
		P.O. Box 64499	Additional copies of the birth record when ordered
		St. Paul, MN 55164	at the same time are $19.00.

Death records on file from January 1908 to current. Copies of earlier records may be obtained from Local Registrar in county where event occurred.

Personal check or money order should be made payable to **Minnesota Department of Health**. To verify current fees, the telephone number is (651) 201-5970. This is a recorded message. Information on how to obtain certified copies is also available via the Internet at https://www.moms.mn.gov.

Any questions in regards to obtaining a certified copy, the telephone number are (651) 201-5980. An application and credit card information and also be faxed to (651) 201-5980.

Marriage	See remarks		Marriage records are not recorded at the state level.
	$9.00	See remarks	Local Registrar in county where license was issued. Additional copies of the marriage record when ordered at the same time are $2.00 each.
Divorce	See remarks		Divorce records are not recorded at the state level.
	$10.00	See remarks	Court Administrator in county where divorce was granted.

Mississippi

Place of event	Cost of copy	Address	Remarks
Birth and Death	$15..00	Mississippi Vital Records State Department of Health P.O. Box 1700 Jackson, MS 39215-1700	State office has records since November 1, 1912. Additional copies of same record ordered at the same time are $5.00 each. Personal check, bank or postal money order or bank cashier's check are accepted and should be made payable to **Mississippi State Department of Health.**
			A copy of a valid photo ID for the applicant is required.
			To verify current fees, the telephone number is (601) 576-7981. A recorded message may be reached on (601) 576-7450. Information on how to obtain certified copies is also available via the Internet at http://www.msdh.state.ms.us.
Marriage	$15.00	Same as Birth or Death	Statistical records only from January 1, 1926 to July 1, 1938, and since January 1942.
			Additional copies of the same record ordered at the same time are $5.00.
Marriage (County)	Varies	See remarks	Circuit Clerk in county where license was issued.
Divorce	See remarks	Same as Birth or Death	Records since January 1926. Certified copies are not available from State office. Index search only available at $15.00 for each 5-year increment. Book and page number for county record provided.
Divorce	Varies	See remarks	Chancery Clerk in county where divorce was granted.

Missouri

Place of event	Cost of copy	Address	Remarks
Birth	$15.00	Missouri Department of Health and Senior Services Bureau of Vital Records 930 Wildwood P.O. Box 570 Jefferson City, MO 65102-0570	State office has records since January 1910. Certified copies of most Missouri birth and death records are also available from local county health department or the Recorder of Deeds in St. Louis City. For details, please contact these offices directly. If event occurred in St. Louis (City), St. Louis County, or Kansas City before 1910, write to the city or county Health Department. Copies of these records are $15.00 each. Personal check or money order should be made payable to **Missouri Department of Health and Senior Services**. Please include a legal size self-addressed stamped envelope. To verify current fees on birth and death records, the telephone number is (573) 751-6387. Information on how to obtain certified copies is also available via the Internet at http://www.dhss.mo.gov. A valid photo ID is required for walk-in applicants. A signature is required. Notarized requests are required for mail-in orders.
Death	$13.00	Missouri Department of Health and Senior Services Bureau of Vital Records 930 Wildwood P.O. Box 570 Jefferson City, MO 65102-0570	State office has records since January 1910. Certified copies of most Missouri birth and death records are also available from local county health department or the Recorder of Deeds in St. Louis City. For details, please contact these offices directly. If event occurred in St. Louis (City), St. Louis County, or Kansas City before 1910, write to the city or county Health Department. Copies of these records are $13.00 each. Additional copies of the same death record ordered at the same time are $10.00 each. Personal check or money order should be made payable to **Missouri Department of Health and Senior Services**. Please include a legal size self-addressed stamped envelope. To verify current fees on birth and death records, the telephone number is (573) 751-6387. Information on how to obtain certified copies is also available via the Internet at http://www.dhss.mo.gov. A valid photo ID is required for walk-in applicants. A signature is required. Notarized requests are required for mail-in orders.

Marriage (County) $15.00   See remarks

Reports of marriage records are on file from July 1948 to the present. Recorder of Deeds in county where license was issued.

Certified copies of Missouri marriage records are also available from the county recorder of deeds where the marriage license was obtained. For details, please contact these offices directly. Certified copies of reports of divorce records are $15.00 each.

Personal check or money order should be made payable to **Missouri Department of Health and Senior Services**. Please include a self-addressed stamped envelope. To verify current fees on marriage records, the telephone number is (573) 751-6387. Information on how to obtain certified copies is also available via the Missouri Department of Health and Senior Services, Vital Records website.

A valid photo ID is required for walk-in applicants. A signature is required. Notarized requests are required for mail-in orders

Divorce (County) $15.00   See remarks

Reports of divorce records are on file from July 1948 to the present.

Certified copies of Missouri divorce records are also available from the county circuit clerk where the divorce was granted. For details, please contact these offices directly. Certified copies of reports of divorce records are $15.00 each.

Personal check or money order should be made payable to **Missouri Department of Health and Senior Services**. Please include a self-addressed stamped envelope. To verify current fees on divorce records, the telephone number is (573) 751-6387. Information on how to obtain certified copies is also available via the Missouri Department of Health and Senior Services, Vital Records website.

A valid photo ID is required for walk-in applicants. A signature is required. Notarized requests are required for mail-in orders

Montana

Place of event	Cost of copy	Address	Remarks
Birth or Death	$12.00	Office of Vital Statistics MT Dept of Public Health and Human Services 111 N Sanders, Rm. 6 P.O. Box 4210 Helena, MT 59604	State office has records since late 1907. Additional copies of the same record requested at the same time are $5.00. Applicants **MUST** provide a clear and readable copy of both sides of their current driver's license or other current government issued identification with signature. If this is not available, the applicant must either provide a clear and readable copy of two other forms of current identification with one having a signature or have their request notarized. Personal check or money order should be made payable to **Montana Vital Records**. To verify current fees, the telephone number is 1-(406) 444-2685. Information on how to obtain certified copies is also available via the Internet at http://www.dphhs.mt.gov.
Marriage	See remarks	Same as Birth or Death	Indexes to locate marriage license since July 1943. Certified copies are not available from State Office. Fee for search and verification of essential facts of marriage is $10.00. Apply to Clerk of District Court were marriage license was purchased if known.
	Varies	See remarks	Clerk of District Court in county where marriage license was purchased.
Divorce	See remarks	Same as Birth or Death	Indexes to locate divorce decrees since July 1943. Certified copies are not available from State Office. Fee for search and verification of essential facts of divorce is $10.00. Apply to Clerk of District Court where divorce was granted if known.
	Varies	See remarks	Clerk of District Court in county where divorce was granted.

Nebraska

Place of event	Cost of copy	Address	Remarks
Birth	$17.00	Nebraska Vital Records P.O. Box 95065 Lincoln, NE 68509-5065	State office has records since late 1904. If birth or death occurred before then, write the State office for information.
			Personal check or money order should be made payable to **Nebraska Vital Records**. To verify current fees, the telephone number is (402) 471-
Death	$16.00		2871. This is a recorded message. Information on how to obtain certified copies is also available via the Internet at http://dhhs.ne.gov/publichealth/Pages/public_healt h_index.aspx.
			All requests must include a photocopy of the requestor's valid government issued photo identification, i.e., valid driver's license, valid State ID card, valid passport or visa.
Marriage (State)	$16.00	Nebraska Vital Records P.O. Box 95065 Lincoln, NE 68509-5065	Records since late 1909. Personal check or money order should be made payable to **Nebraska Vital Records**. To verify current fees, the telephone number is (402) 471-2871. This is a recorded message. Information on how to obtain certified copies is also available via the Internet at http://dhhs.ne.gov/publichealth/Pages/public_healt h_index.aspx
			All requests must include a photocopy of the requestor's valid government issued photo identification, i.e., valid driver's license, valid State ID card, valid passport or visa.
Marriage (County)	Varies	See remarks	County Court in county where license was issued.
Divorce (State)	$16.00	Nebraska Vital Records P.O. Box 95065 Lincoln, NE 68509-5065	Records since late 1909. Personal check or money order should be made payable to **Nebraska Vital Records**. To verify current fees, the telephone number is (402) 471-2871. This is a recorded message. Information on how to obtain certified copies is also available via the Internet at http://dhhs.ne.gov/publichealth/Pages/public_healt h_index.aspx
			All requests must include a photocopy of the requestor's valid government issued photo identification, i.e., valid driver's license, valid State ID card, valid passport or visa.
Divorce (County)	Varies	See remarks	Clerk of District Court in county where divorce was granted.

Nevada

Place of event	Cost of copy	Address	Remarks
Birth or Death	$20.00	Office of Vital Records 4150 Technology Way Suite 104 Carson City, NV 89706	State office has records since July 1911. For earlier records, write to County Recorder in county where event occurred.
			Personal check or money order should be made payable to **Office of Vital Records**. To verify current fees, the telephone number is (775) 684-4242. This is a recorded message. Information on how to obtain certified copies is also available via the Internet at Nevada State Health Division website: http://dpbh.nv.gov/Programs/BirthDeath/Birth_and_Death_Vital_Records_-_Home/
			The applicant **MUST** include a copy of a photo ID with the request.
Marriage	See remarks	Same as Birth or Death	Indexes since January 1968 through September 2005 with a $10.00 search fee to locate information of the record.
	Varies	See remarks	County Recorder in county where license was issued.
Divorce	See remarks	Same as Birth or Death	Indexes since January 1968 through September 2005 with a $10.00 search fee to locate information of the record.
	Varies	See remarks	County Clerk in county where divorce was granted.

New Hampshire

Place of event	Cost of copy	Address	Remarks
Birth	$15.00	Division of Vital Records Administration Archives Building 71 South Fruit Street Concord, NH 03301-2410	State office has records since 1631. Copies of records may be obtained from State office or from City or Town Clerk in place where birth occurred. Recent records (birth since 1982) may be obtained from ANY City or Town running the Vital Records Automated software called NHVRIN.
			Additional copies ordered at the same time are $10.00 each.
			Applicant must submit a written request and a photo ID with signature of the requestor or notarized assignment of access from registrant authorizing non-direct or tangibly related individual access and a self-addressed stamped envelope.
			Personal check or money should be made payable to **Treasurer, State of New Hampshire**. For further information, the telephone number is (603) 271-4651. Information on how to obtain certified copies is also available via the Internet at http://www.sos.nh.gov/vitalrecords.
Death	$15.00	Division of Vital Records Administration Archives Building 71 South Fruit Street Concord, NH 03301-2410	State office has records since 1654. Copies of records may be obtained from State office or from City or Town Clerk in place where death occurred. Recent records (death since 1990) may be obtained from ANY City or Town running the Vital Records Automated software called NHVRIN.
			Additional copies ordered at the same time are $10.00 each.
			Applicant must submit a written request and a photo ID with signature of the requestor or notarized assignment of access from registrant authorizing non-direct or tangibly related individual access and a self-addressed stamped envelope.
			Personal check or money should be made payable to **Treasurer, State of New Hampshire**. For further information, the telephone number is (603) 271-4651. Information on how to obtain certified copies is also available via the Internet at http://www.sos.nh.gov/vitalrecords.

Marriage	$15.00	Division of Vital Records Administration Archives Building 71 South Fruit Street Concord, NH 03301-2410	State office has records since 1652. Copies of records may be obtained from State office or from City or Town Clerk in place where the marriage license was issued. Recent records (marriage since 1989) may be obtained from ANY City or Town running the Vital Records Automated software called NHVRIN.

Additional copies ordered at the same time are $10.00 each.

Applicant must submit a written request and a photo ID with signature of the requestor or notarized assignment of access from registrant authorizing non-direct or tangibly related individual access and a self-addressed stamped envelope.

Personal check or money should be made payable to **Treasurer, State of New Hampshire**. For further information, the telephone number is (603) 271-4651. Information on how to obtain certified copies is also available via the Internet at http://www.sos.nh.gov/vitalrecords.

Divorce	$15.00	Division of Vital Records Administration Archives Building 71 South Fruit Street Concord, NH 03301-2410	Copies of records may be obtained from State office or Clerk of Superior/Family Division Court in the county where divorce was granted. Recent records (divorce since 1990) may be obtained from ANY City or Town running the Vital Records Automated software called NHVRIN.

Additional copies ordered at the same time are $10.00 each.

Applicant must submit a written request and a photo ID with signature of the requestor or notarized assignment of access from registrant authorizing non-direct or tangibly related individual access and a self-addressed stamped envelope.

Personal check or money should be made payable to **Treasurer, State of New Hampshire**. For further information, the telephone number is (603) 271-4651. Information on how to obtain certified copies is also available via the Internet at http://www.sos.nh.gov/vitalrecords.

New Jersey

Place of event	Cost of copy	Address	Remarks
Birth	$25.00 Additional copies of the same record ordered at the same time are $2.00 each.	Office of Vital Statistics & Registry NJ Department of Health P.O. Box 370 Trenton, NJ 08625-0370 Please visit www.state.nj.us/health/vital. For the most up to date information regarding ordering options and information or call toll-free at 1-866-649-8726.	The State Office of Vital Statistics and Registry maintains records from 1915 to present. For older records, please see information for the State Archives. All requests must include a copy of the requestor's valid identification, payment of the appropriate fee and proof of relationship to the individual listed on the vital record. A State or local Registrar may issue a certified copy of a vital record only to persons who establish themselves as the subject of the vital record, the subject's parent, legal guardian or legal representative, spouse, child, grandchild or sibling, if of legal age, to a State or Federal agency for official purposes, pursuant to court order or under other emergent circumstances as determined by the Commissioner. All other applicants will be issued a Certification that state the document is not for identification or legal purposes.
Genealogical Birth, Marriage, or Death	$10.00-$15.00	Office of Vital Statistics & Registry NJ Department of Health P.O. Box 370 Trenton, NJ 08625-0370	The New Jersey State Archives holds original birth, marriage, and death records from the period May 1, 1848 to December 31, 1914. The New Jersey State Archives also holds microfilm copies of: birth records 1848-1914; marriage records 1848-1914; and death records 1848-1914. These materials are available for in-person use only. Personal check or money order should be made payable to **New Jersey General Treasury**. The general information telephone number is (609) 292-6260. Website: www.archives.nj.gov
Death	$25.00 Additional copies of the same record ordered at the same time are $2.00 each.	Office of Vital Statistics & Registry NJ Department of Health P.O. Box 370 Trenton, NJ 08625-0370 Please visit www.state.nj.us/health/vital. For the most up to date information regarding ordering options and information or call toll-free at 1-866-649-8726.	The State Office of Vital Statistics and Registry maintains records from 1915 to present. For older records, please see information for the State Archives. All requests must include a copy of the requestor's valid identification, payment of the appropriate fee and proof of relationship to the individual listed on the vital record.

A State or local Registrar may issue a certified copy of a vital record only to persons who establish themselves as the subject of the vital record, the subject's parent, legal guardian or legal representative, spouse, child, grandchild or sibling, if of legal age, to a State or Federal agency for official purposes, pursuant to court order or under other emergent circumstances as determined by the Commissioner. All other applicants will be issued a Certification that state the document is not for identification or legal purposes.

| Marriage, Civil Union or Domestic Partnership (State) | $25.00 Additional copies of the same record ordered at the same time are $2.00 each. | Office of Vital Statistics & Registry NJ Department of Health P.O. Box 370 Trenton, NJ 08625-0370

Please visit www.state.nj.us/health/vital. For the most up to date information regarding ordering options and information or call toll-free at 1-866-649-8726. | The State Office of Vital Statistics and Registry maintains records from 1915 to present. For older records, please see information for the State Archives.

All requests must include a copy of the requestor's valid identification, payment of the appropriate fee and proof of relationship to the individual listed on the vital record.

A State or local Registrar may issue a certified copy of a vital record only to persons who establish themselves as the subject of the vital record, the subject's parent, legal guardian or legal representative, spouse, child, grandchild or sibling, if of legal age, to a State or Federal agency for official purposes, pursuant to court order or under other emergent circumstances as determined by the Commissioner. All other applicants will be issued a Certification that state the document is not for identification or legal purposes. |
| Divorce | $10.00 | Clerk of the Superior Court Superior Court of NJ Public Information Center 171 Jersey Street P.O. Box 967 Trenton, NJ 08625-0967 | The fee is for a certified Blue Seal copy. Make check payable to **Clerk of the Superior Court**. |

New Mexico

Place of event	Cost of copy	Address	Remarks
Birth	$10.00	NM Vital Records	State office has records since 1920 and delayed
Death	$5.00	P.O. Box 25767	records since 1880.
		Albuquerque, NM 87125	
			Personal check or money order should be made payable to **NM Vital Records**. To verify current fees, the telephone number is 1-866-534-0051. This is a recorded message. Information on how to obtain certified copies is also available via the Internet at http://www.VitalRecordsNM.org
Marriage	Varies	See remarks	County Clerk in county where license was issued.
Divorce	Varies	See remarks	Clerk of Court where divorce was granted.

New York
(except New York City)

Place of event	Cost of copy	Address	Remarks
Birth or Death	$30.00	Certification Unit Vital Records Section 2nd Floor 800 North Pearl Street Menands, NY 12204	State office has records since 1880. For records before 1914 in Albany, Buffalo, and Yonkers, or before 1880 in any other city, write to Registrar of Vital Statistics in city where event occurred. For the rest of the State, except New York City, write to State office. Personal check or money order should be made payable to **New York State Department of Health**. Payment of mail order copies submitted from foreign countries must be made by a check drawn on a United States bank or by an international money order. To verify current fees, the telephone number is 1-855-322-1022. This is a recorded message. Information on how to obtain certified copies is also available via the Internet at http://www.health.state.ny.us. For all types of State and local issued copies, the applicant is required to provide government issued photo identification.
Marriage	$30.00	Same as Birth or Death	Records from 1881 to present.
	$10.00	See remarks	For records from 1880-1907 and licenses issued in the cities of Albany, Buffalo, or Yonkers, apply to Albany: City Clerk, City Hall, Albany, NY 12207; Buffalo: City Clerk, City Hall, Buffalo, NY 14202; Yonkers: Registrar of Vital Statistics, Health Center Building, Yonkers, NY 10701.
Divorce	$30.00	Same as Birth or Death	Records since January 1963.
	Varies	See remarks	County Clerk in county where divorce was granted.

New York City

Place of event	Cost of copy	Address	Remarks
Birth or Death	$15.00	NYC Health Department Office of Vital Records 125 Worth St., CN4, Rm. 133 New York, NY 10013	The Office has birth and death records for people who were born and/or died in the five boroughs of New York City: Brooklyn, the Bronx, Manhattan, Queens, or Staten Island. Birth records issued before 1910 and death records issued before 1949 must be ordered through the Municipal Archives. For more information please visit http://www.nyc.gov/html/doh/html/services/vr.shtml or write to Department of Records and Information Services, 31 Chambers Street, New York, NY 10007. Additional information on ordering and correcting NYC birth and death records can be found by visiting http://www.nyc.gov/vitalrecords or calling 311(or 212-639-9675 outside New York City).
Marriage Manhattan Borough	$15.00	Office of the City Clerk 141 Worth Street New York, NY 10013	Marriage Record Requests in Person: Marriage records from 1996 to present can be obtained in person from any office of the New York City Clerk. Marriage records from 1930 to 1955 can be obtained solely in the Manhattan Office. For additional information go to http://nycmarriagebureau.com/MarriageBureau/index.htm?RecordRoom.htm. Additional copies of the same record ordered at the same time are $10.00 each.
Bronx Borough	$15.00	Office of the City Clerk Supreme Court Building 851 Grand Concourse Room B131 Bronx, NY 10451	
Brooklyn Borough	$15.00	Office of the City Clerk Brooklyn Municipal Building 210 Joralemon Street, Room 205 Brooklyn, NY 11201	Marriage Record Requests by Mail: To obtain a Marriage Record by mail, please call the main office at (212) 669-8090 to request a form or to download the Marriage Record mail request form go to http://nycmarriagebureau.com/MarriageBureau/MailRequestForm.htm

New York City

Place of event	Cost of copy	Address	Remarks
Queens Borough	$15.00	Office of the City Clerk Borough Hall Building 120-55 Queens Boulevard Ground Floor, Room X001 Kew Gardens, NY 11424	Please mail all Marriage Record Requests to the following address: Office of the City Clerk Municipal Building 1 Centre Street, Room 252 South New York, New York 10007
Staten Island Borough (no longer called Richmond)	$15.00	Office of the City Clerk Borough Hall Building 10 Richmond Terrace Room 311 Staten Island, NY 10301	
Divorce			Go to the New York State page on this website at http://www.cdc/gov/nchs/howto/w2w/newyork.htm.

North Carolina

Place of event	Cost of copy	Address	Remarks
Birth or Death	Cost of first copy: $24.00 Cost of each additional copy: $15.00	NC Vital Records 1903 Mail Service Center Raleigh, NC 27699-1903	The State office has birth records beginning with October 1913. Business or certified check or money order should be made payable to **NC Vital Records**. To verify current fees and access additional information on how to obtain copies of vital records, the telephone number is (919) 733-3000 or visit the North Carolina Vital Records website. A copy of a valid photo ID and a signed application is required for all certificate requests. See NC Vital Records' certificate application for a list of acceptable IDs. The Register of Deeds in the county where the birth or death occurred can also provide copies of birth certificates upon request.
Marriage	Cost of first copy: $24.00 Cost of each additional copy: $15.00	NC Vital Records 1903 Mail Service Center Raleigh, NC 27699-1903	The State Office has marriage records beginning with 1962. Business or certified check or money order should be made payable to **NC Vital Records**. To verify current fees and access additional information on how to obtain copies of vital records, the telephone number is (919) 733-3000 or visit the North Carolina Vital Records website. A copy of a valid photo ID and a signed application is required for all certificate requests. See NC Vital Records' certificate application for a list of acceptable IDs. The Register of Deeds in the county where the marriage license was obtained can also provide copies of marriage certificates upon request, including records prior to 1962.
Divorce	Cost of first copy: $24.00 Cost of each additional copy: $15.00	NC Vital Records 1903 Mail Service Center Raleigh, NC 27699-1903	The State Office has divorce records beginning with 1958. Business or certified check or money order should be made payable to **NC Vital Records**. To verify current fees and access additional information on how to obtain copies of vital records, the telephone number is (919) 733-3000 or visit the North Carolina Vital Records website. A copy of a valid photo ID and a signed application is required for all certificate requests. See NC Vital Records' certificate application for a list of acceptable IDs.

The Clerk of Court in the county where the divorce occurred can also provide copies of divorce certificates, including those prior to 1958.

North Dakota

Place of event	Cost of copy	Address	Remarks
Birth Death	$7.00 $5.00	ND Dept. of Health Division of Vital Records 600 East Boulevard Avenue Dept. 301 Bismarck, ND 58505-0200	State office has some birth records since 1870 and some death records since July 1893. Birth years from 1870 to 1920 are incomplete. Death years from 1894 to 1920 are incomplete. Additional copies of birth records are $4.00 each and death records are $2.00 each. Copies are generally processed in 5-7 working days after request is received. Personal check or money order should be made payable to **ND Department of Health**. To verify current fees, the telephone number is (701) 328-2360. This is an automated attendant with a recorded message. Information on how to obtain certified copies is also available via the Internet at http://www.ndhealth.gov/vital/birth.htm. The applicant must submit a photocopy of a government issued ID with their request.
Marriage	Varies	The following link provides county contact information regarding certified copies of marriage records: http://www.ndhealth.gov/vital/marriage.htm	As of January 1, 2008, the ND Department of Health no longer issues certified copies of marriage records.
Divorce	Varies	The following link provides county contact information regarding certified copies of marriage records: http://www.ndhealth.gov/vital/divorce.htm	Certified copies are not available from the ND Department of Health.

Northern Mariana Islands

Place of event	Cost of copy	Address	Remarks
Birth Death	$20.00 $15.00	Commonwealth Healthcare Corporation Vital Statistics Office P.O. Box 500409 Saipan, MP 96950	Office has records for birth and death since 1946. Records from 1946 to 1950 are incomplete. Money order or bank cashiers check should be made payable to **Commonwealth Healthcare Corporation**. To verify current fees, call (670) 236-8717 or (670) 236-8702. E-mail address is info@vs-cnmi.org.
Marriage	$10.00	Commonwealth Recorder Superior Court Vital Records Section P.O. Box 307 Saipan, MP 96950	Money order or bank cashiers check should be made payable to **Commonwealth Healthcare Corporation**. To verify current fees, call (670) 236-9830 or fax (670) 236-9831.
Divorce	$0.50 per page for Divorce Decree plus $2.50 for certification	Commonwealth Recorder Superior Court Vital Records Section P.O. Box 307 Saipan, MP 96950	Office has records for divorce since 1960.

Ohio

Place of event	Cost of copy	Address	Remarks
Birth or Death	$21.50	Vital Statistics Ohio Department of Health P.O. Box 15098 Columbus, OH 43215-0098	State office has birth records since December 20, 1908 and death records since January 1, 1954. For earlier birth and death records, write to the Probate Court in the county where the event occurred. Death records that occurred December 20, 1908–December 31, 1954, can be obtained from the Ohio Historical Society, Archives Library Division, 1982 Velma Avenue, Columbus, OH 43211-2497. A searchable index to records from 1913 to 1944 is also available via the Internet at http://www.odh.ohio.gov/vs. Personal check or money order should be made payable to **Treasury, State of Ohio**. To verify current fees, the telephone number is (614) 466-2531. This is a recorded message. Information on how to obtain certified copies is also available via the Internet at http://www.odh.ohio.gov/vs
Marriage	See remarks	Same as Birth or Death	Copies of marriage records are not available from the State Health Department. For certified copies of marriage records, please write to the Probate Court in the in the county where the event occurred. Information on how to obtain certified copies is also available via the Internet at http://www.odh.ohio.gov/vitalstatistics/vitalmisc/mrgdiv.aspx.
	Varies	See remarks	
Divorce	See remarks	Same as Birth or Death	Certified copies are not available from the State Health Department. For certified copies of divorces, please write to Clerk of Court of where the divorce was granted divorce was granted .
	Varies	See remarks	Information on how to obtain certified copies is also available via the Internet at

Oklahoma

Place of event	Cost of copy	Address	Remarks
Birth or Death	$15.00	Vital Records Service State Department of Health 1000 Northeast 10th Street Oklahoma City, OK 73117	State office has records since October 1908. Personal check or money order should be made payable to **OSDH**. To verify current fees, the telephone number is (405) 271-4040. This will be a recorded message. Information on how to obtain certified copies, eligibility requirements, and a list of acceptable IDs are also available via the Internet at http://vr.health.ok.gov/. A copy of a current legal photo ID from the applicant is required, as well as a completed application and appropriate fees. Commemorative heirloom certificates are also available: cost $35.oo and includes one (1) certified copy. Detailed description of the heirloom certificate is available at http://vr.health.ok.gov/.
Marriage	Varies	See remarks	Clerk of Court in county where license was issued.
Divorce	Varies	See remarks	Clerk of Court in county where divorce was granted.

BIRTH, DEATH, MARRIAGE, AND DIVORCE RECORDS

Oregon

Place of event	Cost of copy	Address	Remarks
Birth or Death	$20.00	Oregon Vital Records P.O. Box 14050 Portland, OR 97293-0050	State vital records office has birth and death records starting from 1903. Oregon State Archives has birth records for the City of Portland from 1864 to 1902 and statewide delayed birth records from 1845 to 1902; City of Portland death records from 1862 to 1902 and statewide death records from 1903 to 1955. Additional copies of the same record ordered at the same time are $15.00 each. Personal check or money order should be made payable to **OHA/Vital Records**. To verify current fees, the telephone number is (971) 673-1190. This is a recorded message. Information on how to obtain certified copies is also available via the Internet at http://healthoregon.org/chs.
		Oregon State Archives 800 Summer Street, NE Salem, OR 97310	The telephone number for the Oregon State Archives is (503) 373-0701 and the fax number is (503) 373-0953. Information on how to obtain copies is also available via the internet at http://arcweb.sos.state.or.us/reference.html
Heirloom Birth	$45.00	Same as Birth or Death	Presentation-style calligraphy certificate suitable for framing.
Marriage	$20.00	Same as Birth or Death	State vital records office has marriage records starting from 1911. Oregon State Archives has some county records from the 1800s and statewide records for 1906-1910.
	Varies	See remarks	County Clerk in county where license was issued. County Clerks also have some records before 1906. Some older county records have been transferred to the Oregon State Archives, 800 Summer Street NE, Salem, OR 97310
Divorce	$20.00	Same as Birth or Death	State vital records office has divorce records starting from 1925.
(Certificates Only)	Varies	See remarks	County Circuit Court Clerk in county where divorce was granted. County Clerks also have some records before 1925.

Pennsylvania

Place of event	Cost of copy	Address	Remarks
Birth	$20.00	Division of Vital Records ATTN: Birth Unit 101 South Mercer Street Room 401 P.O. Box 1528 New Castle, PA 16103	State office has records since January 1906. All requests must be submitted on an application form, which requires the signature of the individual requesting the certificate and a legible copy of his/her valid government issued photo ID that verifies name and mailing address of the individual requesting the certificate. Application forms, eligibility requirements, fees, and additional information, including how to apply online with a credit card for an additional fee are available via the Pennsylvania Department of Health, Vital Records website:
Death	$9.00	Division of Vital Records ATTN: Death Unit 101 South Mercer Street Room 401 P.O. Box 1528 New Castle, PA 16103	http://www.health.state.pa.us/vitalrecords. The telephone number is (724) 656-3100. Personal check or money order should be made payable to **Vital Records**. Pennsylvania birth or deaths certificates prior to 1906 can be accessed through the courthouse in the county were the person was born or died. A list of court houses is available via the Internet at http://www.health.state.pa.us/vitalrecords.
Marriage	Varies		Make application to the Marriage License Clerks, County Court House, in county where license was issued. A list of court houses is available via the Internet at http://www.pacourts.us/courts/courts-of-common-pleas/individual-county-courts
Divorce	Varies		Make application to the Prothonotary, Court House, in county seat of county where divorce was granted. A list of court houses is available via the Internet at http://www.pacourts.us/courts/courts-of-common-pleas/individual-county-courts

BIRTH, DEATH, MARRIAGE, AND DIVORCE RECORDS

Puerto Rico

Place of event	Cost of copy	Address	Remarks
Birth or Death	$5.00	$4.00 each additional copy requested on the same application. Registrants over 60 years of age and Veterans of the United States Armed Forces can obtain copies of their birth records free of charge. Maximum three (3) copies per registrant per year. Beneficiaries of a Veteran of the United States Armed Forces can obtain copies of their death records free of charge (widow or children under 21 years of age). All mail in applications must be sent to: Department of Health Demographic Registry P.O. Box 11854 Fernández Juncos Station San Juan, PR 00910	The Central Office of the Demographic Registry has records pertaining to all citizens born or deceased as of June 22, 1931. Copies of earlier records may be obtained by writing to the Local Registrar's Office in the municipality where the event occurred. Payment method via money orders, which should be made payable to the **Secretary of Treasury**. Neither cash, personal nor bank checks are accepted. To verify the current fees, the telephone number is 787-765-2929 Ext. 6131. All applications must be accompanied by a legible photocopy of a valid form of identification (driver's license, Passport, or a government emitted ID). Veterans must submit a copy of their DD214 or Veterans Affairs Identification card to receive benefits. Applicants must considered to be an *interested party* established by law, which are: the proper registrant, mother/father, children over 18 years of age, legal custodian, legal representatives or heirs if existent.
		If using an Express Service (FedEx, UPS, DHL, USPS Express or Priority Mail, applications must be sent to the following PHYSICAL ADDRESS: Department of Health Demographic Registry 414 Barbosa Avenue Lincoln Building San Juan, PR 00925	Additional copies ordered at the same time by the same person are $4.00 each. Information on how to obtain certified copies is also available via the Internet at http://www.prfaa.com/services.asp?id=44 Money order should be made payable to **Secretary of the Treasury**. Personal checks are not accepted. To verify current fees, the telephone number is (787) 767-9120.
Marriage	$5.00	Same as Birth or Death	Same as Birth or Death All applications must be accompanied by a photocopy of a recent, valid IDENTIFICATION OF APPLICANT.
Divorce	$2.00	Same as Birth or Death	The Central Office of the Demographic Registry has records pertaining to divorces registered as of 1941. Divorce certifications are NOT actual divorce decrees but an abstract of the information provided on the final court resolution, submitted to our agency for official use only. **Availability varies**; not all divorce decrees are submitted to the

Demographic Registry. In the case where a divorce decree does not appear registered in our agency, a negative certification of divorce will be issued for the same cost. Payment method via money orders, which should be made payable to the **Secretary of Treasury**. Neither cash, personal nor bank checks are accepted. To verify the current fees, the telephone number is 787-765-2929 Ext. 6131. All applicants must be accompanied by a legible photocopy of a valid form of identification (driver's license, Passport, or a government emitted ID).

See remarks

Superior Court where divorce was granted.

BIRTH, DEATH, MARRIAGE, AND DIVORCE RECORDS

Rhode Island

Place of event	Cost of copy	Address	Remarks
Birth or Death	$20.00	RI Department of Health Office of Vital Records Room 101 3 Capitol Hill Providence, RI 02908-5097	State office keeps birth and marriage/civil union records for 100 years and keeps death records for 50 years. In general, copies can be obtained from the State office, the city/town clerk where the event occurred or the city of residence at the time of the occurrence. Additional copies of the same record ordered at the same time are $15.00 each. Information for city/town addresses are available via the Internet at: http://www.health.ri.gov/chic/vital/clerks.php. For earlier records, write to the city/town clerk where the event occurred or to the Rhode Island State Archives, 337 Westminster Street, Providence, RI 02903. Personal check or money order should be made payable to **Rhode Island General Treasurer**. To verify current fees after office hours, the telephone number is (401) 222-2811. To verify current fees and general information during office hours, please call the Health Hot Line at (401) 222-5960. Information on how to obtain certified copies is also available via the Internet at http://www.health.ri.gov. All requests must be accompanied by a photocopy of the applicant's valid government-issued picture identification, e.g., driver's license. In lieu of a valid government-issued picture identification, two pieces of mail are accepted showing the correct name and address of the individual requesting the record.
Pre-Adoption Non-Certified Birth	$20.00	Same as Birth or Death	In June, 2011 the State of Rhode Island passed a law allowing adult adoptees born in Rhode Island access to a non-certified copy of their unaltered, original birth certificate. If you are an adoptee who was born in Rhode Island and you are age 25 or older, you can request a non-certified copy of your original, pre-adoption birth record from the State Office of Vital Records. According to state law, we can only release your record to you, the adoptee. Relatives cannot request copies of your record on your behalf. Please visit the web-site at www.health.ri.gov under Adult Adoptees for

L-97

further information on applications, ID requirements and access.

Personal check or money order should be made payable to **General Treasurer, State of Rhode Island.**

All requests must be accompanied by a photocopy of the applicant's valid government-issued picture identification, e.g., driver's license. In lieu of valid government-issued picture identification, two pieces of mail are accepted showing the correct name and address of the individual requesting the record.

Marriage/Civil Union	$20.00	Same as Birth or Death
Divorce	$3.00	Clerk of Family Court 1 Dorrance Plaza Providence, RI 02903

BIRTH, DEATH, MARRIAGE, AND DIVORCE RECORDS

South Carolina

Place of event	Cost of copy	Address	Remarks
Birth or Death	$12.00	Office of Vital Records SCDHEC 2600 Bull Street Columbia, SC 29201	State office has records since January 1915. Additional copies of the same birth records ordered at the same time of certification are $3.00 each. Acceptable method of payment is a money order or cashiers check made payable to **SCDHEC-Vital Records**. To verify current fees, the telephone number is (803) 898-3630. Information on how to obtain certified copies is also available via the Internet at http://www.scdhec.net/vr. Anyone requesting a vital record must submit a photocopy of their valid picture identification.
Marriage	$12.00	Same as Birth or Death	State office has records since January 1915. Additional copies of the same birth records ordered at the same time of certification are $3.00 each. Anyone requesting a vital record must submit a photocopy of their valid picture identification.
Marriage (County)	$12.00	See County Offices on website link in Remarks	Records prior to July 1950 and after December 2010, contact Probate Judge in county where license was issued. Anyone requesting a vital record must submit a photocopy of their valid picture identification.
Divorce	$12.00	Same as Birth or Death	Records since July 1962.
Divorce (County)	$12.00	See County Offices on website link in Remarks	Records since December 2010 contact Clerk of Court in county where petition was filed. Anyone requesting a vital record must submit a photocopy of their valid picture identification.

South
Dakota

Place of event	Cost of copy	Address	Remarks
Birth or Death	$15.00	Vital Records State Department of Health 207 E Missouri Ave, Ste 1-A Pierre, SD 57501	State office has records filed after July 1905. Anyone requesting a vital record must submit a photocopy of their identification. Personal check or money order should be made payable to **South Dakota Department of Health**. To verify current fees, the telephone number is (605) 773-4961. Information on how to obtain certified copies is also available via the Internet at http://vitalrecords.sd.gov. Mail-in applicants must send in a clear copy of a government- issued photo ID OR have their signature notarized.
Marriage	$15.00	Same as Birth or Death	Records since July 1905. Marriages can also be obtained from the County Register of Deeds where the marriage occurred.
Divorce	$15.00	Same as Birth or Death	Records since July 1905. Divorces can also be obtained from the Clerk of Courts in the county where the divorce was granted.

Tennessee

Place of event	Cost of copy	Address	Remarks
Birth (long form) Birth (short form) Death	$15.00 $8.00 $7.00	Tennessee Vital Records Central Services Building 421 5th Avenue, North Nashville, TN 37243	State office has birth records for entire State since January 1914, for Nashville since June 1881, for Knoxville since July 1881, and for Chattanooga since January 1882. Birth enumeration records by school district are available for July 1908 through June 1912. Birth records more than 100 years old are maintained by Tennessee Library and Archives, Archives Division, Nashville, Tennessee 37243-0312. Additional copies of the same birth, marriage, or divorce record requested at the same time are $5.00 each. If the birth has been amended by adding the father with a Voluntary Acknowledgement Of Paternity (VAOP), a certified copy of the VAOP may be ordered if a $15 long form birth certificate is ordered at the same time. The cost of the certified VAOP is an additional $5.00. Vital Records office keeps death records for 50 years; older records are maintained by Tennessee Library and Archives, Archives Division, Nashville, Tennessee 37243-0312. Personal check or money order should be made payable to **Tennessee Vital Records**. To verify current fees, the telephone number is (615) 741-1763. Information on how to obtain certified copies is also available via the Internet at http://health.state.tn.us/vr/. A photocopy of a valid government-issued form of identification which includes the requestor's signature, usually a driver's license, must accompany the request.
Marriage	$15.00	Same as Birth or Death	Vital Records Office keeps marriage records for 50 years. Older records are maintained by Tennessee Library and Archives, Archives Division, Nashville, TN 37243-0312.
	Varies	See remarks	County Clerk in county where license was issued.
Divorce	$15.00	Same as Birth or Death	Vital Records Office keeps divorce records for 50 years. Older records are maintained by Tennessee Library and Archives, Archives Division, Nashville, TN 37243-0312.
	Varies	See remarks	Clerk of Court in county where divorce was granted.

Texas

Place of event	Cost of copy	Address	Remarks
Birth	$22.00	Texas Vital Records	State office has birth and death records since 1903. Additional copies of the birth record ordered at same time are $22.00 each. Additional copies of the death record ordered at the same time are $3.00 each.
Death	$20.00	Department of State Health Services P.O. Box 12040 Austin, TX 78711-2040	

Request for certified copies of birth and death certificates can be made via the internet, with a credit card, through Texas.gov. An Expedited Application for Birth and Death Record (see Form VS142.21.pdf) can also be completed and sent by an overnight service or by USPS Express Mail, with a check or money order, to the address on the application. Most Texas.gov and Expedited mail requests will be processed within 10 to 15 business days.

Mail-in requests must be made by personal check or money order made payable to **DSHS**. To verify current fees, the telephone number is (512) 776-7111. This is a recorded message. Information on how to obtain certified copies is also available via the Internet at http://www.dshs.state.tx.us/vs.

Marriage (State)	See remarks		Records since January 1966. Certified copies are not available from State office. Fee for search and verification of essential facts of marriage is $20.00 each.

Request for marriage verification can be made via the internet, with a credit card, through Texas.gov.

Marriage verification requests may also be sent via mail and paid with a check or money order by completing the Mail Application for Marriage and Divorce Verification (http://www.dshs.state.tx.us/vs/reqproc/forms.shtm #birthdeath). Personal checks or money orders should be made payable to **DSHS.**

Marriage (County)	Varies	See remarks	County Clerk in county where license was issued. Texas County contact information can be found at the Texas Department of State Health Services website.

BIRTH, DEATH, MARRIAGE, AND DIVORCE RECORDS

Texas

Place of event	Cost of copy	Address	Remarks
Divorce (State)	See remarks		Records since January 1968. Certified copies are not available from State office. Fee for search and verification of essential facts of divorce is $20.00 each.

Request for divorce verification can be made via the internet, with a credit card, through Texas.gov.

Divorce verification requests may also be sent via mail and paid with a check or money order by completing the Mail Application for Marriage and Divorce Verification (http://www.dshs.state.tx.us/vs/reqproc/forms.shtm #birthdeath). Personal checks or money orders should be made payable to **DSHS.** |
| Divorce (County) | Varies | See remarks | Clerk of District Court in county where divorce was granted. Texas District Clerk contact information can be found at http://localoffices.texasvsu.org. |

Utah

Place of event	Cost of copy	Address	Remarks
Birth	$20.00	Office of Vital Records and Statistics Utah Department of Health 288 North 1460 West P.O. Box 141012 Salt Lake City, UT 84114-1012	State office has records since 1905. Identification is now required for the purchase of a Utah Birth Certificate. Mailed request must include an enlarged and easily identifiable photocopy of the back and front of your identification. If no proofs are enclosed, your application will be returned. For a list of acceptable identification see our website at http://www.health.utah.gov/vitalrecords.

Additional copies, when requested at the same time, are $8.00 each.

Personal check or money order should be made payable to **Vital Records**. To verify current fees, the telephone number is (801) 538-6105. This is a recorded message. Information on how to obtain certified copies is also available via the Internet at http://www.health.utah.gov/vitalrecords. |
| Death | $18.00 | Office of Vital Records and Statistics Utah Department of Health 288 North 1460 West P.O. Box 141012 Salt Lake City, UT 84114-1012 | State office has records since 1905. Identification is now required for the purchase of a Utah Death Certificate. Mailed request must include an enlarged and easily identifiable photocopy of the back and front of your identification. If no proofs are enclosed, your application will be returned. For a list of acceptable identification see our website at http://www.health.utah.gov/vitalrecords.

Additional copies, when requested at the same time, are $8.00 each.

Personal check or money order should be made payable to **Vital Records**. To verify current fees, the telephone number is (801) 538-6105. This is a recorded message. Information on how to obtain certified copies is also available via the Internet at http://www.health.utah.gov/vitalrecords. |
| Marriage | $18.00 | Same as Birth or Death | State office has records since 1978. Only short form certified copies are available.

Additional copies, when requested at the same time, are $8.00 each. |
| | Varies | See remarks | County Clerk in county where license was issued. |
| Divorce | $18.00 | Same as Birth or Death | State office has records since 1978. Only short form certified copies are available. Additional copies, when requested at the same time, are $8.00 each. |

BIRTH, DEATH, MARRIAGE, AND DIVORCE RECORDS

| Varies | See remarks | County Clerk in county where divorce was granted. |

Vermont

Place of event	Cost of copy	Address	Remarks
Birth or Death	$10.00	Department of Health Vital Records Section P. O. Box 70 108 Cherry Street Burlington, VT 05402-0070	State office has records for the most recent five years. Personal check or money order should be made payable to **Vermont Department of Health**. To verify current fees, the telephone number is (802) 863-7275. This is a recorded message. Information on how to obtain certified copies is also available via the Internet at the Vermont State Archives and Records Administration website: https://www.sec.state.vt.us/archives-records/vital-records.aspx.
Birth, Death, Marriage or Divorce	$10.00	VT State Archives and Records Administration Office of the Secretary 1078 US Route 2, Middlesex Montpelier, VT 05633-7701	Records more than five years old (as early as 1909). Personal check or money order should be made payable to **Vermont Secretary of State**. To verify current fees, the telephone number is (802) 828-3286. Information on how to obtain certified copies is also available via the Internet at the Vermont State Archives and Records Administration website: https://www.sec.state.vt.us/archives-records/vital-records.aspx .
Birth or Death	$10.00	See remarks	Town or City Clerk of town/city where birth or death occurred.
Marriage	$10.00	Same as Birth or Death	State office has records for the most recent 5 years.
	$10.00	See remarks	Town or City Clerk in town/city where license was issued.
Divorce	$10.00	Same as Birth or Death	State office has records for the most recent 5 years.
	$10.00	See remarks	Family court in county where divorce was granted.

BIRTH, DEATH, MARRIAGE, AND DIVORCE RECORDS

Virginia

Place of event	Cost of copy	Address	Remarks
Birth or Death	$12.00	Division of Vital Records P.O. Box 1000 Richmond, VA 23218-1000	State office has records from January 1853 to December 1896 and since June 14, 1912. Personal check or money order should be made payable to **State Health Department**. To verify current fees, the telephone number is (804) 662-6200. This is a recorded message. Information on how to obtain certified copies is also available via the Internet at http://www.vdh.virginia.gov/. Anyone requesting a vital record must submit a photocopy of their identification.
Marriage	$12.00	Same as Birth or Death	Records since January 1853.
	Varies	See remarks	Clerk of Court in county or city where license was issued.
Divorce	$12.00	Same as Birth or Death	Records since January 1918.
	Varies	See remarks	Clerk of Court in county or city where divorce was granted.

Virgin Islands

Place of event	Cost of copy	Address	Remarks
Birth or Death St. Croix	$15.00 (Mail request)	Department of Health Vital Statistics Charles Harwood Memorial Hospital	Registrar has birth and death records on file since 1840.
	$12.00 (In person)	St. Croix, VI 00820	
St. Thomas and St. John	$15.00 (Mail request)	Department of Health Vital Statistics Knud Hansen Complex	Registrar has birth records on file since July 1906 and death records since January 1906.
	$12.00 (In person)	St. Thomas, VI 00802	Money order for birth and death records should be made payable to **Department of Health**. Personal checks are not accepted. To verify current fees, the telephone number is (340) 774-9000 ext. 4685 or 4686.
Marriage	See remarks	Bureau of Vital Records and Statistical Services Virgin Islands Department of Health Charlotte Amalie St. Thomas, VI 00801	Certified copies are not available. Inquiries will be forwarded to the appropriate office.
St. Croix	$2.00	Chief Deputy Clerk Family Division Territorial Court of the Virgin Islands P.O. Box 929 Christiansted St. Croix, VI 00820	
St. Thomas and St. John	$2.00	Clerk of the Territorial Court of the Virgin Islands Family Division P.O. Box 70 Charlotte Amalie St. Thomas, VI 00801	
Divorce	See remarks	Same as Marriage	Certified copies are not available. Inquiries will be forwarded to appropriate office.
St. Croix	$5.00	Same as Marriage	Money order for marriage and divorce records should be made payable to Territorial Court of the Virgin Islands. Personal checks are not accepted.
St. Thomas and St. John	$5.00	Same as Marriage	

Washington

Place of event	Cost of copy	Address	Remarks
Birth or Death	$20.00	Department of Health Center for Health Statistics P.O. Box 47814 Olympia, WA 98504-7814	Must have exact information for births. State office has birth records since July 1907 to present. For King, Pierce, and Spokane counties copies may also be obtained from county health departments. County Auditor of county of birth has registered births prior to July 1907. State office has death records from July 1, 1907 to 2 months before present date. Personal check or money order should be made payable to **Department of Health**. To verify current fees, the telephone number is (360) 236-4300. Information on how to obtain certified copies is also available via the Internet at Washington State Department of Health website: http://www.doh.wa.gov/LicensesPermitsandCertificates/BirthDeathMarriageandDivorce
Heirloom Birth			
Marriage	$40.00	Same as Birth or Death	State office has records since January 1968.
	$20.00		Information on how to obtain certified copies is also available via the Internet at Washington State Department of Health website: http://www.doh.wa.gov/LicensesPermitsandCertificates/BirthDeathMarriageandDivorce
	Varies	See remarks	County Auditor in county where license was issued.
Divorce	$20.00	Same as Birth or Death	State office has records since January 1968. Information on how to obtain certified copies is also available via the Internet at Washington State Department of Health website: http://www.doh.wa.gov/LicensesPermitsandCertificates/BirthDeathMarriageandDivorce
	Varies	See remarks	County Clerk in county where divorce was granted.

West Virginia

Place of event	Cost of copy	Address	Remarks
Birth or Death	$12.00	Vital Registration Office Room 165 350 Capitol Street Charleston, WV 25301-3701	State office was established in 1917. Earlier records may be on file at the state office as "delayed certificates" if they were placed on file after 1917 and were not already on file in a county clerk's office. Both offices may need to be queried but it is recommended that for births before 1917 that county office be queried first. Personal check or money order should be made payable to **Vital Registration**. To verify current fees, the telephone number is (304) 558-2931. Information on how to obtain certified copies is also available via the Internet at http://www.dhhr.wv.gov/Pages/default.aspx
Marriage	$12.00	Same as Birth or Death	Marriage indexes from 1921 forward. Certified copies available from 1964 forward. Before 1964, see county below.
Marriage (County)	Varies	See remarks	County Clerk in county where license was issued.
Divorce	See remarks	Same as Birth or Death	Indexes only since 1968. Certified copies are not available from state office. See county below.
Divorce (County)	Varies	See remarks	Certified copies of divorce orders may be obtained from the Clerk of the Circuit Court in the county where the divorce was granted.

Wisconsin

Place of event	Cost of copy	Address	Remarks
Birth or Death	$20.00	WI Vital Records Office 1 West Wilson Street P.O. Box 309 Madison, WI 53701-0309 **Customer Service:** 608-266-1373	State Office has scattered records earlier than 1857. Records before October 1, 1907, are very incomplete. Additional copies of the same record ordered at the same time are $3.00 each. Customers should use a state birth or death certificate application form to apply. A copy of a valid photo ID and a signature is required of the applicant. Personal check or money order should be made payable to **State of Wisconsin Vital Records**. A stamped, self-addressed business size (#10) envelope should be included with the request. Information on how to obtain certified copies including application forms is available via the Internet at Wisconsin Vital Records Services website http://www.dhs.wi.gov/vitalrecords.
Marriage	$20.00	WI Vital Records Office 1 West Wilson Street P.O. Box 309 Madison, WI 53701-0309 **Customer Service:** 608-266-1373	State Office has scattered records earlier than 1857. Records before October 1, 1907, are very incomplete. Additional copies of the same record ordered at the same time are $3.00 each. Customers should use a state marriage certificate application form to apply. A copy of a valid photo ID and a signature is required of the applicant. Personal check or money order should be made payable to **State of Wisconsin Vital Records**. A stamped, self-addressed business size (#10) envelope should be included with the request. Information on how to obtain certified copies including application forms are available via the internet at the Wisconsin Vital Records Services website http://www.dhs.wi.gov/vitalrecords.
Divorce	$20.00	WI Vital Records Office 1 West Wilson Street P.O. Box 309 Madison, WI 53701-0309 **Customer Service:** 608-266-1373	Divorce certificates are not available before October 1, 1907. Additional copies of the same record ordered at the same time are $3.00 each. Customers should use a state divorce certificate application form to apply. A copy of a valid photo ID and a signature is required of the applicant. Personal check or money order should be made payable to **State of Wisconsin Vital Records**. A stamped, self-addressed business size (#10) envelope should be included with the request. Information on how to obtain certified copies including application forms are available via the internet at the Wisconsin Vital Records Services website http://www.dhs.wi.gov/vitalrecords.

Wyoming

Place of event	Cost of copy	Address	Remarks
Birth	$13.00	Vital Statistics Services	State office has birth records since 1909.
Death	$10.00	Hathaway Building	
		Cheyenne, WY 82002	After 100 years birth records are available through WY State Archives. WY Vital Records Office is covered entity under the Health Insurance Portability and Accountability Act of 1996 (HIPAA)
			Death records more than 50 years old should be obtained from the Wyoming State Archives at (307) 777-7826 or WyArchive@state.wy.us.
			Personal check or money order should be made payable to **Vital Records Services**. A personal check is accepted only if personalized with the name of current address of individual signing the request. To verify current fees, the telephone number is (307) 777-7591. Information on how to obtain certified copies is also available via the Internet at http://www.health.wyo.gov.
			A legible photocopy of a current state issued ID or passport is required which bears the signature of the applicant. ID with no expiration date is not accepted unless recently issued and additional proof of identification may be requested.
Marriage	$13.00	Same as Birth or Death	Marriage records more than 50 years old should be obtained from the Wyoming State Archives at (307) 777-7826 or WyArchive@state.wy.us.
	Varies	See remarks	County Clerk in county where license was issued.
Divorce	$13.00	Same as Birth or Death	Divorce records more than 50 years old should be obtained from the Wyoming State Archives at (307) 777-7826 or WyArchive@state.wy.us.
	Varies	See remarks	Clerk of District Court where divorce took place.

BIRTH, DEATH, MARRIAGE, AND DIVORCE RECORDS

Foreign, high-seas, or Panama Canal Zone births and deaths and certificates of citizenship

Birth records of persons born in foreign countries who are U.S. citizens at birth

The birth of a child abroad to U.S. citizen parent(s) should be reported to the nearest U.S. Consulate or Embassy as soon after the birth as possible. A $100.00 fee is charged for reporting the birth at a U.S. embassy or consulate abroad. See Department of State link for more information:

http://travel.state.gov/law/family_issues/birth/birth_593.html

The application must be supported by evidence to establish the child's U.S. citizenship. Usually, the following documents are needed:
1.   The child's foreign birth certificate;
2.   Evidence of the U.S. citizenship of the parent(s) such as a certified copy of a birth certificate, U.S. passport, or Certificate of Naturalization or Citizenship;
3.   Evidence of the parents' marriage, if applicable; and
4.   Affidavit of the physical presence of the parent(s) in the United States.

Each document should be certified as a true copy of the original by the registrar of the office that issued the document. Other documents may be needed in some cases. Contact the nearest U.S. Embassy or Consulate for details on what evidence is needed.

When the application is approved, a Consular Report of Birth Abroad of a Citizen of the United States of America (Form FS-240) is given to the applicant. This document, known as the Consular Report of Birth, has the same value as proof of citizenship as the Certificate of Citizenship issued by the Immigration and Naturalization Service.

A Consular Report of Birth can be prepared only at a U.S. Embassy or Consulate overseas and only if the person who is the subject of the report is under 18 years of age when the application is made. A person residing abroad who is now 18 years of age or over, and whose claim to U.S. citizenship has never been documented, should contact the nearest U.S. Embassy or Consulate for assistance in registering as a U.S. citizen.

The Department began issuing a new consular Report of Birth on January 3, 2011. You may request multiple copies of this document at any time. As of December 31, 2010 the Certificate of Report of Birth Abroad (DS-1350) is no longer issued. All previously issued FS-240 and DS-1350 documents are still valid for proof of identity, citizenship and other legal purposes.

The Consular Report of Birth documents are issued only to the subject of the Consular Report of Birth, the subject's parents (if subject is under age 18) or legal guardian. Effective September 1, 2003 all requests must be notarized and include a copy of the requester's valid photo identification.

To request a replacement FS-240, write to:
Department of State
Passport Vital Records Section
44132 Mercure Cir.
PO Box 1213
Sterling, VA 20166-1213

Please include the following items:
1.   The full name of the child at birth (and any adoptive name);
2.   The date and place of birth;
3.   The names of the parents;
4.   The serial number of the FS-240 (if the FS-240 was issued after November 1, 1990);
5.   Any available passport information;
6.   The signature of the requestor and the requestor's relationship to the subject; If subject is 18 years of

older, they must provide a written statement authorizing a third party to act on their behalf.
7. A check or money order for $50.00 for the FS-240, made payable to the U.S.
8. Department of State. Do Not Send Cash and

To obtain an amended Consular Report of Birth in a new name, send a written request and fees as noted above, the original (or replacement) Consular Report of Birth, or if not available, a notarized affidavit about its whereabouts. Also, send a certified copy of the court order or final adoption decree which identifies the child and shows the change of name with the request. If the name has been changed informally, submit public records and affidavits that show the change of name.

To obtain a Consular Report of Birth in a new name, send a written request and fees as noted above, the original (or replacement) Consular Report of Birth, or if not available, a notarized affidavit about its whereabouts. Also, send a certified copy of the court order or final adoption decree which identifies the child and shows the change of name with the request. If the name has been changed informally, submit public records and affidavits that show the change of name.

See Department of State link for more information regarding the above mentioned:
http://travel.state.gov/law/family_issues/birth/birth_593.html

Birth records of alien children adopted by U.S. citizens

Birth certifications for alien children adopted by U.S. citizens and lawfully admitted to the United States may be obtained from the Immigration and Naturalization Service (INS) if the birth information is on file. (Address can be found in a telephone directory.) To obtain the birth data, it is necessary to provide the Immigration Office with proof of adoption or legitimation.

Certificate of citizenship

Persons who were born abroad and later naturalized as U.S. citizens or who were born in a foreign country to a U.S. citizen (parent or parents) may apply for a Certificate of Citizenship pursuant to the provisions of Section 341 of the Immigration and Nationality Act. Application can be made for this document in the United States at the nearest office of the Bureau of Citizenship and Immigration Services in the Department of Homeland Security. Upon approval, a Certification of Citizenship will be issued for the person if proof of citizenship is submitted and the person is within the United States. The decision whether to apply for a Certificate of Citizenship is optional; its possession is not mandatory because a valid U.S. passport or a Form FS-240 has the same evidentiary status.

Death and marriage records of U.S. citizens that occurred in a foreign country

The death of a U.S. citizen in a foreign country may be reported to the nearest U.S. consular office. If reported, and a copy of the local death certificate and evidence of U.S. citizenship are presented, the consul prepares the official Report of the Death of an American Citizen Abroad' (Form OF-180). A copy of the Report of Death is then filed permanently in the U.S. Department of State (see exceptions below).

To obtain a copy of a report filed in 1975 or after, write to:
Department of State
Passport Vital Records Section
44132 Mercure Cir.
PO Box 1213
Sterling, VA 20166-1213

The fee for a copy is $50.00 per document. Please submit a notarized request to include a picture ID. Fee may be subject to change.

See http://travel.state.gov/content/passports/english/abroad/events-and-records/death/CRDA-copy.html to Request a Copy of a Consular Report of Death Abroad (CRDA)

BIRTH, DEATH, MARRIAGE, AND DIVORCE RECORDS

Reports of Death filed before 1975 are maintained by the National Archives and Records Service, Diplomatic Records Branch, Washington, DC 20408. Requests for such records should be sent directly to that office.

Reports of deaths of persons serving in the Armed Forces of the United States (Army, Navy, Marines, Air Force, or Coast Guard) or civilian employees of the Department of Defense are not maintained by the U.S. Department of State. In these cases, requests for copies of records should be sent to the National Personnel Records Center (Military Personnel Records), 9700 Page Ave., St. Louis, Missouri 63132-5100.

To obtain a copy of a Certificate of Witness to Marriage (FS-87) you may write to the address above, the fee is $50.00 per document. As of November 9, 1989 a Consular Officer no longer serves as a witness to marriages performed abroad. Persons married abroad after 1989 may contact the embassy or consulate of the country where the marriage was performed for a certified copy. Foreign marriage documents are not maintained by the Department.

Records of birth and death occurring on vessels or aircraft on the high seas

When a birth or death occurs on the high seas, whether in an aircraft or on a vessel, the record is usually filed at the next port of call.

1.   If the vessel or aircraft docked or landed at a foreign port, requests for copies of the record may be made to the U.S. Department of State, Washington, DC 20036.

2.   If the first port of entry was in the United States, write to the registration authority in the city where the vessel or aircraft docked or landed in the United States.

3.   If the vessel was of U.S. registry, contact the local authorities at the port of entry and/or search the vessel logs at the U.S. Coast Guard Facility at the vessel's final port of call for that voyage.

Records maintained by foreign Countries

Most, but not all, foreign countries record births and deaths. It is not possible to list in this publication all foreign vital records offices, the charges they make for copies of records, or the information they may require to locate a record. However, most foreign countries will provide certifications of births and deaths occurring within their boundaries.

Persons who need a copy of a foreign birth or death record should contact the Embassy or the nearest Consulate in the U.S. of the country in which the death occurred. Addresses and telephone numbers for these offices are listed in the U.S. Department of State Publication 7846, Foreign Consular Offices in the United States, which is available in many local libraries. Copies of this publication may also be purchased from the U.S. Government Printing Office, Washington, DC 20402.

If the Embassy or Consulate is unable to provide assistance, U.S. citizens may obtain assistance by writing to the Office of Overseas Citizens Services, U.S. Department of State, Washington, DC 20520-4818. Aliens residing in the United States may be able to obtain assistance through the Embassy or Consulate of their country of nationality.

Records of birth, death, or marriage in the Panama Canal Zone for U.S. citizens and foreign nationals

From 1904 until 1979, the Canal Zone Government registered all civil acts of birth, death, and marriage in the Canal Zone for U.S. citizens and foreign nationals. Since 1979, the Panama Canal Commission has issued certified copies of these documents in response to requests from the public. On December 31, 1999, the Panama Canal Commission ceased to exist. On December 1, 1999, those records were transferred to Passport Services in the U.S. Department of State, which will provide the certification service just as it does for similar records issued by U.S. Embassies and Consulates abroad.

To request copies of Canal Zone Birth and Death Records, write to:
Department of State
Passport Vital Records Section
44132 Mercure Cir.
PO Box 1213
Sterling, VA 20166-1213

To request copies of Canal Zone Marriage Records, write to:
Civilian Records (NWCTC)
Textual Archives Services Division
8601 Adelphi Road
National Archives
College Park, MD 20740-6001

Please include the following items for birth, death, or marriage:

1. The full name of subject at the time of event;

2. Month, day and year of event;

3. Place of event (city and country);

4. Parents' names, date and place of birth, and nationality for birth record;

5. Any available U.S. passport information;

6. Signature of the requestor, parent or guardian, or legal representative;

7. Requestor address and telephone number;

8. A check or money order for $50.00 for each copy made payable to U.S. Department of State. Remittance must be payable in U.S. dollars through a U.S. bank. Do not send cash.

PART IV
COMMONLY USED ABBREVIATIONS

M. COMMONLY USED ABBREVIATIONS AND ACRONYMS

THE UNITED STATES GOVERNMENT MANUAL

Commonly Used Agency Acronyms

ABMC	AMERICAN BATTLE MONUMENTS COMMISSION
ACF	ADMINISTRATION OF CHILDREN AND FAMILIES
ACFR	ADMINISTRATIVE COMMITTEE OF THE FEDERAL REGISTER
ADF	AFRICAN DEVELOPMENT FOUNDATION
AFRH	ARMED FORCES RETIREMENT HOME
AHRQ	AGENCY FOR HEALTHCARE RESEARCH AND QUALITY
AMS	AGRICULTURAL MARKETING SERVICE
AMTRAK	NATIONAL RAILROAD PASSENGER CORPORATION
AOA	ADMINISTRATION ON AGING
APHIS	ANIMAL AND PLANT HEALTH INSPECTION SERVICE
APPAL	APPALACHIAN STATES LOW LEVEL RADIOACTIVE WASTE COMMISSION
ARCTIC	ARCTIC RESEARCH COMMISSION
ARS	AGRICULTURAL RESEARCH SERVICE
ARTS	NATIONAL FOUNDATION ON THE ARTS AND THE HUMANITIES
ATBCB	ARCHITECTURAL AND TRANSPORTATION BARRIERS COMPLIANCE BOARD
ATF	ALCOHOL, TOBACCO, FIREARMS, AND EXPLOSIVES BUREAU
ATSDR	AGENCY FOR TOXIC SUBSTANCES AND DISEASE REGISTRY
BBG	BROADCASTING BOARD OF GOVERNORS
BEA	BUREAU OF ECONOMIC ANALYSIS
BGSEEF	BARRY M. GOLDWATER SCHOLARSHIP AND EXCELLENCE IN EDUCATION FOUNDATION
BIA	BUREAU OF INDIAN AFFAIRS
BIS	BUREAU OF INDUSTRY AND SECURITY
BLM	BUREAU OF LAND MANAGEMENT
BLS	BUREAU OF LABOR STATISTICS
BOP	FEDERAL PRISONS BUREAU
BOR	BUREAU OF RECLAMATION
BPA	BONNEVILLE POWER ADMINISTRATION
BPD	BUREAU OF PUBLIC DEBT
CBO	CONGRESSIONAL BUDGET OFFICE
CCC	COMMODITY CREDIT CORPORATION
CCJJDP	COORDINATING COUNCIL ON JUVENILE JUSTICE AND DELINQUENCY PREVENTION
CDC	CENTERS FOR DISEASE CONTROL AND PREVENTION
CDFI	COMMUNITY DEVELOPMENT FINANCIAL INSTITUTIONS FUND
CEQ	COUNCIL ON ENVIRONMENTAL QUALITY

* Reprinted from the 2015 Edition (July) of the U.S. Government Manual at *www.gpo.gov*.

CFTC	COMMODITY FUTURES TRADING COMMISSION
CFPB	CONSUMER FINANCIAL PROTECTION BUREAU
CIA	CENTRAL INTELLIGENCE AGENCY
CITA	COMMITTEE FOR THE IMPLEMENTATION OF TEXTILE AGREEMENTS
CMS	CENTERS FOR MEDICARE & MEDICAID SERVICES
CNCS	CORPORATION FOR NATIONAL AND COMMUNITY SERVICE
COE	CORPS OF ENGINEERS
COFA	COMMISSION OF FINE ARTS
COLC	COPYRIGHT OFFICE, LIBRARY OF CONGRESS
COPS	COMMUNITY ORIENTED POLICING SERVICES
CORP	CORPORATION FOR NATIONAL AND COMMUNITY SERVICE
CPPBSD	COMMITTEE FOR PURCHASE FROM PEOPLE WHO ARE BLIND OR SEVERELY DISABLED
CPSC	CONSUMER PRODUCT SAFETY COMMISSION
CRB	COPYRIGHT ROYALTY BOARD, LIBRARY OF CONGRESS
CRC	CIVIL RIGHTS COMMISSION
CSB	CHEMICAL SAFETY AND HAZARD INVESTIGATION BOARD
CSEO	CHILD SUPPORT ENFORCEMENT OFFICE
CSOSA	COURT SERVICES AND OFFENDER SUPERVISION AGENCY FOR THE DISTRICT OF COLUMBIA
CSREES	COOPERATIVE STATE RESEARCH, EDUCATION, AND EXTENSION SERVICE
DARPA	DEFENSE ADVANCED RESEARCH PROJECTS AGENCY
DARS	DEFENSE ACQUISITION REGULATIONS SYSTEM
DC	DENALI COMMISSION
DCAA	DEFENSE CONTRACT AUDIT AGENCY
DEA	DRUG ENFORCEMENT ADMINISTRATION
DEPO	DISABILITY EMPLOYMENT POLICY OFFICE
DFAS	DEFENSE FINANCE AND ACCOUNTING SERVICES
DHS	DEPARTMENT OF HOMELAND SECURITY
DIA	DEFENSE INTELLIGENCE AGENCY
DISA	DEFENSE INFORMATION SYSTEMS AGENCY
DLA	DEFENSE LOGISTICS AGENCY
DNFSB	DEFENSE NUCLEAR FACILITIES SAFETY BOARD
DOC	DEPARTMENT OF COMMERCE
DOD	DEPARTMENT OF DEFENSE
DOE	DEPARTMENT OF ENERGY
DOI	DEPARTMENT OF THE INTERIOR
DOJ	DEPARTMENT OF JUSTICE
DOL	DEPARTMENT OF LABOR
DOS	DEPARTMENT OF STATE
DOT	DEPARTMENT OF TRANSPORTATION
DRBC	DELAWARE RIVER BASIN COMMISSION

DSCA	DEFENSE SECURITY COOPERATION AGENCY
DSS	DEFENSE SECURITY SERVICE
DTRA	DEFENSE THREAT REDUCTION AGENCY
EAB	BUREAU OF ECONOMIC ANALYSIS
EAC	ELECTION ASSISTANCE COMMISSION
EBSA	EMPLOYEE BENEFITS SECURITY ADMINISTRATION
ECAB	EMPLOYEES' COMPENSATION APPEALS BOARD
ECSA	ECONOMICS AND STATISTICS ADMINISTRATION
ED	DEPARTMENT OF EDUCATION
EDA	ECONOMIC DEVELOPMENT ADMINISTRATION
EEOC	EQUAL EMPLOYMENT OPPORTUNITY COMMISSION
EERE	ENERGY EFFICIENCY AND RENEWABLE ENERGY OFFICE
EIA	ENERGY INFORMATION ADMINISTRATION
EIB	EXPORT IMPORT BANK OF THE UNITED STATES
EOA	ENERGY OFFICE, AGRICULTURE DEPARTMENT
EOIR	EXECUTIVE OFFICE FOR IMMIGRATION REVIEW
EOP	EXECUTIVE OFFICE OF THE PRESIDENT
EPA	ENVIRONMENTAL PROTECTION AGENCY
ERS	ECONOMIC RESEARCH SERVICE
ESA	EMPLOYMENT STANDARDS ADMINISTRATION
ETA	EMPLOYMENT AND TRAINING ADMINISTRATION
FAA	FEDERAL AVIATION ADMINISTRATION
FAR	FEDERAL ACQUISITION REGULATION
FAS	FOREIGN AGRICULTURAL SERVICE
FASAB	FEDERAL ACCOUNTING STANDARDS ADVISORY BOARD
FBI	FEDERAL BUREAU OF INVESTIGATION
FCA	FARM CREDIT ADMINISTRATION
FCC	FEDERAL COMMUNICATIONS COMMISSION
FCIC	FEDERAL CROP INSURANCE CORPORATION
FCSIC	FARM CREDIT SYSTEM INSURANCE CORPORATION
FDA	FOOD AND DRUG ADMINISTRATION
FDIC	FEDERAL DEPOSIT INSURANCE CORPORATION
FEC	FEDERAL ELECTION COMMISSION
FEMA	FEDERAL EMERGENCY MANAGEMENT AGENCY
FERC	FEDERAL ENERGY REGULATORY COMMISSION
FFIEC	FEDERAL FINANCIAL INSTITUTIONS EXAMINATION COUNCIL
FHEO	FAIR HOUSING AND EQUAL OPPORTUNITY
FHFA	FEDERAL HOUSING FINANCE AGENCY
FHFB	FEDERAL HOUSING FINANCE BOARD
FHWA	FEDERAL HIGHWAY ADMINISTRATION
FINCEN	FINANCIAL CRIMES ENFORCEMENT NETWORK
FINCIC	FINANCIAL CRISIS INQUIRY COMMISSION

FISCAL	FISCAL SERVICE
FLETC	FEDERAL LAW ENFORCEMENT TRAINING CENTER
FLRA	FEDERAL LABOR RELATIONS AUTHORITY
FMC	FEDERAL MARITIME COMMISSION
FMCS	FEDERAL MEDIATION AND CONCILIATION SERVICE
FMCSA	FEDERAL MOTOR CARRIER SAFETY ADMINISTRATION
FNS	FOOD AND NUTRITION SERVICE
FPPO	FEDERAL PROCUREMENT POLICY OFFICE
FR	OFFICE OF THE FEDERAL REGISTER
FRA	FEDERAL RAILROAD ADMINISTRATION
FRS	FEDERAL RESERVE SYSTEM
FRTIB	FEDERAL RETIREMENT THRIFT INVESTMENT BOARD
FS	FOREST SERVICE
FSA	FARM SERVICE AGENCY
FSIS	FOOD SAFETY AND INSPECTION SERVICE
FTA	FEDERAL TRANSIT ADMINISTRATION
FTC	FEDERAL TRADE COMMISSION
FTZB	FOREIGN TRADE ZONES BOARD
FWS	FISH AND WILDLIFE SERVICE
GAO	GOVERNMENT ACCOUNTABILITY OFFICE
GEO	GOVERNMENT ETHICS OFFICE
GIPSA	GRAIN INSPECTION, PACKERS AND STOCKYARDS ADMINISTRATION
GPO	GOVERNMENT PRINTING OFFICE
GSA	GENERAL SERVICES ADMINISTRATION
HHS	DEPARTMENT OF HEALTH AND HUMAN SERVICES
HHSIG	INSPECTOR GENERAL OFFICE, HEALTH AND HUMAN SERVICES DEPARTMENT
HOPE	BOARD OF DIRECTORS OF THE HOPE FOR HOMEOWNERS PROGRAM
HPAC	HISTORIC PRESERVATION, ADVISORY COUNCIL
HRSA	HEALTH RESOURCES AND SERVICES ADMINISTRATION
HST	HARRY S. TRUMAN SCHOLARSHIP FOUNDATION
HUD	DEPARTMENT OF HOUSING AND URBAN DEVELOPMENT
IAF	INTER AMERICAN FOUNDATION
ICEB	IMMIGRATION AND CUSTOMS ENFORCEMENT BUREAU
IHS	INDIAN HEALTH SERVICE
IIO	INTERNATIONAL INVESTMENT OFFICE
IRS	INTERNAL REVENUE SERVICE
ISOO	INFORMATION SECURITY OVERSIGHT OFFICE
ITA	INTERNATIONAL TRADE ADMINISTRATION
ITC	INTERNATIONAL TRADE COMMISSION
JBEA	JOINT BOARD FOR ENROLLMENT OF ACTUARIES
LMSO	LABOR MANAGEMENT STANDARDS OFFICE

LOC	LIBRARY OF CONGRESS
LSC	LEGAL SERVICES CORPORATION
MARAD	MARITIME ADMINISTRATION
MBDA	MINORITY BUSINESS DEVELOPMENT AGENCY
MCC	MILLENNIUM CHALLENGE CORPORATION
MDA	MISSILE DEFENSE AGENCY
MISS	MISSISSIPPI RIVER COMMISSION
MKU	MORRIS K. UDALL SCHOLARSHIP AND EXCELLENCE IN NATIONAL ENVIRONMENTAL POLICY FOUNDATION
MMC	MARINE MAMMALCOMMISSION
MMS	MINERALS MANAGEMENT SERVICE
MSHA	MINE SAFETY AND HEALTH ADMINISTRATION
MSHFRC	FEDERAL MINE SAFETY AND HEALTH REVIEW COMMISSION
MSPB	MERIT SYSTEMS PROTECTION BOARD
NARA	NATIONAL ARCHIVES AND RECORDS ADMINISTRATION
NASA	NATIONAL AERONAUTICS AND SPACE ADMINISTRATION
NASS	NATIONAL AGRICULTURAL STATISTICS SERVICE
NCA	NATIONAL CEMETERY ADMINISTRATION
NCD	NATIONAL COUNCIL ON DISABILITY
NCLIS	NATIONAL COMMISSION ON LIBRARIES AND INFORMATION SCIENCE
NCPPCC	NATIONAL CRIME PREVENTION AND PRIVACY COMPACT COUNCIL
NCS	NATIONAL COMMUNICATIONS SYSTEM
NCUA	NATIONAL CREDIT UNION ADMINISTRATION
NEC	NATIONAL ECONOMIC COUNCIL
NEIGHBOR	NEIGHBORHOOD REINVESTMENT CORPORATION
NHTSA	NATIONAL HIGHWAY TRAFFIC SAFETY ADMINISTRATION
NIFA	NATIONAL INSTITUTE OF FOOD AND AGRICULTURE
NIGC	NATIONAL INDIAN GAMING COMMISSION
NIH	NATIONAL INSTITUTES OF HEALTH
NIL	NATIONAL INSTITUTE FOR LITERACY
NIST	NATIONAL INSTITUTE OF STANDARDS AND TECHNOLOGY
NLRB	NATIONAL LABOR RELATIONS BOARD
NMB	NATIONAL MEDIATION BOARD
NNSA	NATIONAL NUCLEAR SECURITY ADMINISTRATION
NOAA	NATIONAL OCEANIC AND ATMOSPHERIC ADMINISTRATION
NPREC	NATIONAL PRISON RAPE ELIMINATION COMMISSION
NPS	NATIONAL PARK SERVICE
NRC	NUCLEAR REGULATORY COMMISSION
NRCS	NATURAL RESOURCES CONSERVATION SERVICE
NSA	NATIONAL SECURITY AGENCY/CENTRAL SECURITY SERVICE
NSF	NATIONAL SCIENCE FOUNDATION
NTIA	NATIONAL TELECOMMUNICATIONS AND INFORMATION

	ADMINISTRATION
NTSB	NATIONAL TRANSPORTATION SAFETY BOARD
NWTRB	NUCLEAR WASTE TECHNICAL REVIEW BOARD
OCC	COMPTROLLER OF THE CURRENCY
ODNI	OFFICE OF THE DIRECTOR OF NATIONAL INTELLIGENCE
OEPNU	OFFICE OF ENERGY POLICY AND NEW USES
OFAC	OFFICE OF FOREIGN ASSETS CONTROL
OFCCP	OFFICE OF FEDERAL CONTRACT COMPLIANCE PROGRAMS
OFHEO	FEDERAL HOUSING ENTERPRISE OVERSIGHT OFFICE
OFPP	OFFICE OF FEDERAL PROCUREMENT POLICY
OJJDP	JUVENILE JUSTICE AND DELINQUENCY PREVENTION OFFICE
OJP	JUSTICE PROGRAMS OFFICE
OMB	OFFICE OF MANAGEMENT AND BUDGET
ONDCP	OFFICE OF NATIONAL DRUG CONTROL POLICY
ONHIR	OFFICE OF NAVAJO AND HOPI INDIAN RELOCATION
OPIC	OVERSEAS PRIVATE INVESTMENT CORPORATION
OPM	OFFICE OF PERSONNEL MANAGEMENT
OPPM	OFFICE OF PROCUREMENT AND POLICY MANAGEMENT
OSC	OFFICE OF SPECIAL COUNSEL
OSHA	OCCUPATIONAL SAFETY AND HEALTH ADMINISTRATION
OSHRC	OCCUPATIONAL SAFETY AND HEALTH REVIEW COMMISSION
OSM	OFFICE OF SURFACE MINING RECLAMATION AND ENFORCEMENT
OSTP	OFFICE OF SCIENCE AND TECHNOLOGY POLICY
OTS	OFFICE OF THRIFT SUPERVISION
PACIFIC	PACIFIC NORTHWEST ELECTRIC POWER AND CONSERVATION PLANNING COUNCIL
PBGC	PENSION BENEFIT GUARANTY CORPORATION
PC	PEACE CORPS
PHMSA	PIPELINE AND HAZARDOUS MATERIALS SAFETY ADMINISTRATION
PHS	PUBLIC HEALTH SERVICE
PRC	POSTAL REGULATORY COMMISSION
PRES	PRESIDENTIAL DOCUMENTS
PT	PRESIDIO TRUST
PTO	PATENT AND TRADEMARK OFFICE
RATB	RECOVERY ACCOUNTABILITY AND TRANSPARENCY BOARD
RBS	RURAL BUSINESS COOPERATIVE SERVICE
RHS	RURAL HOUSING SERVICE
RISC	REGULATORY INFORMATION SERVICE CENTER
RITA	RESEARCH AND INNOVATIVE TECHNOLOGY ADMINISTRATION
RMA	RISK MANAGEMENT AGENCY
RRB	RAILROAD RETIREMENT BOARD
RTB	RURAL TELEPHONE BANK

ABBREVIATIONS AND ACRONYMS

RUS	RURAL UTILITIES SERVICE
SAMHSA	SUBSTANCE ABUSE AND MENTAL HEALTH SERVICES ADMINISTRATION
SBA	SMALL BUSINESS ADMINISTRATION
SEC	SECURITIES AND EXCHANGE COMMISSION
SIGIR	SPECIAL INSPECTOR GENERAL FOR IRAQ RECONSTRUCTION
SJI	STATE JUSTICE INSTITUTE
SLSDC	SAINT LAWRENCE SEAWAY DEVELOPMENT CORPORATION
SRBC	SUSQUEHANNA RIVER BASIN COMMISSION
SSA	SOCIAL SECURITY ADMINISTRATION
SSS	SELECTIVE SERVICE SYSTEM
STB	SURFACE TRANSPORTATION BOARD
SWPA	SOUTHWESTERN POWER ADMINISTRATION
TA	TECHNOLOGY ADMINISTRATION
TREAS	DEPARTMENT OF THE TREASURY
TSA	TRANSPORTATION SECURITY ADMINISTRATION
TTB	ALCOHOL AND TOBACCO TAX AND TRADE BUREAU
TVA	TENNESSEE VALLEY AUTHORITY
URMCC	UTAH RECLAMATION MITIGATION AND CONSERVATION COMMISSION
USA	ARMY DEPARTMENT
USAF	AIR FORCE DEPARTMENT
USAID	UNITED STATES AGENCY FOR INTERNATIONAL DEVELOPMENT
USBC	BUREAU OF THE CENSUS
USCBP	CUSTOMS AND BORDER PROTECTION BUREAU
USCC	U.S. CHINA ECONOMIC AND SECURITY REVIEW COMMISSION
USCERT	UNITED STATES COMPUTER EMERGENCY READINESS TEAM
USCG	COAST GUARD
USCIS	U.S. CITIZENSHIP AND IMMIGRATION SERVICES
USDA	DEPARTMENT OF AGRICULTURE
USEIB	EXPORT IMPORT BANK
USGS	U.S. GEOLOGICAL SERVICE
USHMM	UNITED STATES HOLOCAUST MEMORIAL MUSEUM
USIP	UNITED STATES INSTITUTE OF PEACE
USJC	JUDICIAL CONFERENCE OF THE UNITED STATES
USMINT	UNITED STATES MINT
USN	NAVY DEPARTMENT
USPC	PAROLE COMMISSION
USPS	POSTAL SERVICE
USSC	UNITED STATES SENTENCING COMMISSION
USSS	SECRET SERVICE
USTR	OFFICE OF UNITED STATES TRADE REPRESENTATIVE
USUHS	UNIFORMED SERVICES UNIVERSITY OF THE HEALTH SCIENCES
VA	DEPARTMENT OF VETERANS AFFAIRS

VCNP	VALLES CALDERA TRUST
VETS	VETERANS EMPLOYMENT AND TRAINING SERVICE
WAPA	WESTERN AREA POWER ADMINISTRATION
WCPO	WORKERS COMPENSATION PROGRAMS OFFICE
WHD	WAGE AND HOUR DIVISION

(Last Revised: September 22, 2014)

N. ABBREVIATIONS OF STATE AND FEDERAL COURTS

The listed state courts include each state's court of last resort, any intermediate appellate court, and trial courts of general jurisdiction. Courts are listed hierarchically, with the highest court in the state appearing first.

A. State Courts

Court	Abbrev.
Alabama Supreme Court	Ala.
Alabama Court of Civil Appeals	Ala. Civ. App.
Alabama Court of Criminal Appeals	Ala. Crim. App.
Alabama Circuit Court	Ala. Cir.
Alaska Supreme Court	Alaska
Alaska Court of Appeals	Alaska App.
Alaska Superior Court	Alaska Super.
Arizona Supreme Court	Ariz.
Arizona Court of Appeals	Ariz. App.
Arizona Superior Court	Ariz. Super.
Arkansas Supreme Court	Ark.
Arkansas Court of Appeals	Ark. App.
Arkansas Circuit Court	Ark. Cir.
Arkansas Chancery Court	Ark. Ch.
California Supreme Court	Cal.
California Court of Appeal	Cal. App.
California Superior Court	Cal. Super.
Colorado Supreme Court	Colo.
Colorado Court of Appeals	Colo. App.
Colorado District Court	Colo. Dist.
Connecticut Supreme Court	Conn.
Connecticut Appellate Court	Conn. App.
Connecticut Superior Court	Conn. Super.
Connecticut Circuit Court	Conn. Cir.

* Reprinted from the ALWD Citation Manual: A Professional System of Citation, Third Edition. © 2006 Association of Legal Writing Directors. Reprinted by permission of Aspen Publishers, New York, N.Y. 10011.

Court	Abbrev.
Delaware Supreme Court	Del.
Delaware Superior Court	Del. Super.
Delaware Court of Chancery	Del. Ch.
Delaware Family Court	Del. Fam.
District of Columbia Court of Appeals	D.C. App.
District of Columbia Superior Court	D.C. Super.
Florida Supreme Court	Fla.
Florida District Court of Appeal	Fla. Dist. App.
Florida Circuit Court	Fla. Cir.
Georgia Supreme Court	Ga.
Georgia Court of Appeals	Ga. App.
Georgia Superior Court	Ga. Super.
Hawaii Supreme Court	Haw.
Hawaii Intermediate Court of Appeals	Haw. App.
Hawaii Circuit Court	Haw. Cir.
Idaho Supreme Court	Idaho
Idaho Court of Appeals	Idaho App.
Idaho District Court	Idaho Dist.
Illinois Supreme Court	Ill.
Illinois Appellate Court	Ill. App.
Illinois Circuit Court	Ill. Cir.
Indiana Supreme Court	Ind.
Indiana Court of Appeals	Ind. App.
Indiana Superior Court	Ind. Super.
Iowa Supreme Court	Iowa
Iowa Court of Appeals	Iowa App.
Iowa District Court	Iowa Dist.
Kansas Supreme Court	Kan.
Kansas Court of Appeals	Kan. App.
Kansas District Court	Kan. Dist.

COURT ABBREVIATIONS

Court	Abbrev.
Kentucky Supreme Court	Ky.
Kentucky Court of Appeals	Ky. App.
Kentucky Circuit Court	Ky. Cir.
Louisiana Supreme Court	La.
Louisiana Court of Appeal	La. App.
Louisiana District Court	La. Dist.
Maine Supreme Judicial Court	Me.
Maine Superior Court	Me. Super.
Maryland Court of Appeals	Md.
Maryland Court of Special Appeals	Md. Spec. App.
Maryland Circuit Court	Md. Cir.
Massachusetts Supreme Judicial Court	Mass.
Massachusetts Appeals Court	Mass. App.
Trial Court of the Commonwealth	Mass. Cmmw.
Michigan Supreme Court	Mich.
Michigan Court of Appeals	Mich. App.
Michigan Circuit Court	Mich. Cir.
Minnesota Supreme Court	Minn.
Minnesota Court of Appeals	Minn. App.
Minnesota District Court	Minn. Dist.
Mississippi Supreme Court	Miss.
Court of Appeals of the State of Mississippi	Miss. App.
Mississippi Circuit Court	Miss. Cir.
Mississippi Chancery Court	Miss. Ch.
Missouri Supreme Court	Mo.
Missouri Court of Appeals	Mo. App.
Missouri Circuit Court	Mo. Cir.
Montana Supreme Court	Mont.
Montana District Court	Mont. Dist.
Nebraska Supreme Court	Neb.
Nebraska Court of Appeals	Neb. App.
Nebraska District Court	Neb. Dist.
Nevada Supreme Court	Nev.
Nevada District Court	Nev. Dist.
New Hampshire Supreme Court	N.H.
New Hampshire Superior Court	N.H. Super.
New Jersey Supreme Court	N.J.
New Jersey Superior Court, Appellate Division	N.J. Super. App. Div.
New Mexico Supreme Court	N.M.
New Mexico Court of Appeals	N.M. App.
New Mexico District Court	N.M. Dist.
New York Court of Appeals	N.Y.
New York Supreme Court, Appellate Division	N.Y. App. Div.
New York Supreme Court	N.Y. Sup.
North Carolina Supreme Court	N.C.
North Carolina Court of Appeals	N.C. App.
North Carolina Superior Court	N.C. Super.

Court	Abbrev.
North Dakota Supreme Court	N.D.
North Dakota Court of Appeals	N.D. App.

(Note: The North Dakota Court of Appeals was a temporary court, effective July 1, 1987 through January 1, 2000.)

North Dakota District Court	N.D. Dist.
Ohio Supreme Court	Ohio
Ohio Court of Appeals	Ohio App.
Ohio Court of Common Pleas	Ohio Com. Pleas
Oklahoma Supreme Court	Okla.
Oklahoma Court of Criminal Appeals	Okla. Crim. App.
Oklahoma Court of Appeals	Okla. App.
Oklahoma District Court	Okla. Dist.
Oregon Supreme Court	Or.
Oregon Court of Appeals	Or. App.
Oregon Circuit Court	Or. Cir.
Pennsylvania Supreme Court	Pa.
Pennsylvania Superior Court	Pa. Super.
Pennsylvania Commonwealth Court	Pa. Cmmw.
Rhode Island Supreme Court	R.I.
Rhode Island Superior Court	R.I. Super.
South Carolina Supreme Court	S.C.
South Carolina Court of Appeals	S.C. App.
South Carolina Circuit Court	S.C. Cir.
South Dakota Supreme Court	S.D.
South Dakota Circuit Court	S.D. Cir.
Tennessee Supreme Court	Tenn.
Tennessee Court of Appeals	Tenn. App.
Tennessee Court of Criminal Appeals	Tenn. Crim. App.
Tennessee Circuit Court	Tenn. Cir.
Tennessee Criminal Court	Tenn. Crim.
Tennessee Chancery Court	Tenn. Ch.
Texas Supreme Court	Tex.
Texas Court of Criminal Appeals	Tex. Crim. App.
Texas Court of Appeals	Tex. App.
Texas District Court	Tex. Dist.
Texas Criminal District Court	Tex. Crim. Dist.
Utah Supreme Court	Utah
Utah Court of Appeals	Utah App.
Utah District Court	Utah Dist.
Vermont Supreme Court	Vt.
Vermont Superior Court	Vt. Super.
Vermont District Court	Vt. Dist.
Virginia Supreme Court	Va.
Virginia Court of Appeals	Va. App.
Virginia Circuit Court	Va. Cir.
Washington Supreme Court	Wash.
Washington Court of Appeals	Wash. App.

Court	Abbrev.
Washington Superior Court	Wash. Super.
West Virginia Supreme Court	W. Va.
West Virginia Circuit Court	W. Va. Cir.
Wisconsin Supreme Court	Wis.
Wisconsin Court of Appeals	Wis. App.
Wisconsin Circuit Court	Wis. Cir.
Wyoming Supreme Court	Wyo.
Wyoming District Court	Wyo. Dist.

B. Federal Courts

Court	Abbrev.
United States Supreme Court	U.S.

United States Courts of Appeals

Court	Abbrev.
First Circuit	1st Cir.
Second Circuit	2d Cir.
Third Circuit	3d Cir.
Fourth Circuit	4th Cir.
Fifth Circuit	5th Cir.
Sixth Circuit	6th Cir.
Seventh Circuit	7th Cir.
Eighth Circuit	8th Cir.
Ninth Circuit	9th Cir.
Tenth Circuit	10th Cir.
Eleventh Circuit	11th Cir.
D.C. Circuit	D.C. Cir.
Federal Circuit	Fed. Cir.

United States District Courts

Court	Abbrev.
Middle District of Alabama	M.D. Ala.
Northern District of Alabama	N.D. Ala.
Southern District of Alabama	S.D. Ala.
District of Alaska	D. Alaska
District of Arizona	D. Ariz.
Eastern District of Arkansas	E.D. Ark.
Western District of Arkansas	W.D. Ark.
Central District of California	C.D. Cal.
Eastern District of California	E.D. Cal.
Northern District of California	N.D. Cal.
Southern District of California	S.D. Cal.
District of the Canal Zone	D.C.Z.

(*Note:* The D.C.Z. ceased to exist on March 31, 1982.)

Court	Abbrev.
District of Colorado	D. Colo.
District of Connecticut	D. Conn.
District of Delaware	D. Del.

Court	Abbrev.
District of D.C.	D.D.C.
Middle District of Florida	M.D. Fla.
Northern District of Florida	N.D. Fla.
Southern District of Florida	S.D. Fla.
Middle District of Georgia	M.D. Ga.
Northern District of Georgia	N.D. Ga.
Southern District of Georgia	S.D. Ga.
District of Guam	D. Guam
District of Hawaii	D. Haw.
District of Idaho	D. Idaho
Central District of Illinois	C.D. Ill.
Northern District of Illinois	N.D. Ill.
Southern District of Illinois	S.D. Ill.
Northern District of Indiana	N.D. Ind.
Southern District of Indiana	S.D. Ind.
Northern District of Iowa	N.D. Iowa
Southern District of Iowa	S.D. Iowa
District of Kansas	D. Kan.
Eastern District of Kentucky	E.D. Ky.
Western District of Kentucky	W.D. Ky.
Eastern District of Louisiana	E.D. La.
Middle District of Louisiana	M.D. La.
Western District of Louisiana	W.D. La.
District of Maine	D. Me.
District of Maryland	D. Md.
District of Massachusetts	D. Mass.
Eastern District of Michigan	E.D. Mich.
Western District of Michigan	W.D. Mich.
District of Minnesota	D. Minn.
Northern District of Mississippi	N.D. Miss.
Southern District of Mississippi	S.D. Miss.
Eastern District of Missouri	E.D. Mo.
Western District of Missouri	W.D. Mo.
District of Montana	D. Mont.
District of Nebraska	D. Neb.
District of Nevada	D. Nev.
District of New Hampshire	D.N.H.
District of New Jersey	D.N.J.
District of New Mexico	D.N.M.
Eastern District of New York	E.D.N.Y.
Northern District of New York	N.D.N.Y.
Southern District of New York	S.D.N.Y.
Western District of New York	W.D.N.Y.
Eastern District of North Carolina	E.D.N.C.
Middle District of North Carolina	M.D.N.C.
Western District of North Carolina	W.D.N.C.
District of North Dakota	D.N.D.
District of the Northern Mariana Islands	D.N. Mar. I.
Northern District of Ohio	N.D. Ohio
Southern District of Ohio	S.D. Ohio
Eastern District of Oklahoma	E.D. Okla.
Northern District of Oklahoma	N.D. Okla.

COURT ABBREVIATIONS

Court	Abbrev.
Western District of Oklahoma	W.D. Okla.
District of Oregon	D. Or.
Eastern District of Pennsylvania	E.D. Pa.
Middle District of Pennsylvania	M.D. Pa.
Western District of Pennsylvania	W.D. Pa.
District of Puerto Rico	D.P.R.
District of Rhode Island	D.R.I.
District of South Carolina	D.S.C.
District of South Dakota	D.S.D.
Eastern District of Tennessee	E.D. Tenn.
Middle District of Tennessee	M.D. Tenn.
Western District of Tennessee	W.D. Tenn.
Eastern District of Texas	E.D. Tex.
Northern District of Texas	N.D. Tex.
Southern District of Texas	S.D. Tex.
Western District of Texas	W.D. Tex.
District of Utah	D. Utah
District of Vermont	D. Vt.
Eastern District of Virginia	E.D. Va.
Western District of Virginia	W.D. Va.
District of the Virgin Islands	D.V.I.
Eastern District of Washington	E.D. Wash.
Western District of Washington	W.D. Wash.
Northern District of West Virginia	N.D.W. Va.
Southern District of West Virginia	S.D.W. Va.
Eastern District of Wisconsin	E.D. Wis.
Western District of Wisconsin	W.D. Wis.
District of Wyoming	D. Wyo.

Military Courts

Court	Abbrev.
United States Court of Appeals for the Armed Forces	Armed Forces App.

Court	Abbrev.
United States Court of Veterans Appeals	Vet. App.
United States Air Force Court of Criminal Appeals	A.F. Crim. App.
United States Army Court of Criminal Appeals	Army Crim. App.
United States Coast Guard Court of Criminal Appeals	Coast Guard Crim. App.
United States Navy-Marine Corps Court of Criminal Appeals	Navy-Marine Crim. App.

Bankruptcy Courts

Each United States District Court has a corresponding bankruptcy court. To cite a bankruptcy court, add Bankr. to the district court abbreviation.

Examples:
Bankr. N.D. Ala.
Bankr. D. Mass.

Other Federal Courts

Court	Abbrev.
Court of Federal Claims	Fed. Cl.
Court of Customs and Patent Appeals	Cust. & Pat. App.
Court of Claims	Ct. Cl.
Claims Court	Cl. Ct.
Court of International Trade	Ct. Intl. Trade
Tax Court	Tax